# Handbook of Research on Digital Crime, Cyberspace Security, and Information Assurance

Maria Manuela Cruz–Cunha
*Polytechnic Institute of Cávado and Ave, Portugal*

Irene Maria Portela
*Polytechnic Institute of Cávado and Ave, Portugal*

A volume in the Advances in Digital Crime,
Forensics, and Cyber Terrorism (ADCFCT) Book
Series

Information Science
**REFERENCE**
An Imprint of IGI Global

| | |
|---|---|
| Managing Director: | Lindsay Johnston |
| Production Editor: | Christina Henning |
| Development Editor: | Erin O'Dea |
| Acquisitions Editor: | Kayla Wolfe |
| Typesetter: | Thomas Creedon |
| Cover Design: | Jason Mull |

Published in the United States of America by
Information Science Reference (an imprint of IGI Global)
701 E. Chocolate Avenue
Hershey PA, USA 17033
Tel: 717-533-8845
Fax: 717-533-8661
E-mail: cust@igi-global.com
Web site: http://www.igi-global.com

Library of Congress Cataloging-in-Publication Data

Handbook of research on digital crime, cyberspace security, and information assurance / Maria Manuela Cruz-Cunha and Irene Portela, editors.
     pages cm
    ISBN 978-1-4666-6324-4 (hardcover) -- ISBN 978-1-4666-6325-1 (ebook) -- ISBN 978-1-4666-6327-5 (print & perpetual access) 1. Computer crimes. 2. Computer security. 3. Computer networks--Security measures. 4. Data protection. 5. Information technology. I. Cruz-Cunha, Maria Manuela, 1964- II. Portela, Irene Maria, 1965-
    HV6773.H375 2014
    005.8--dc23
                                        2014017272

This book is published in the IGI Global book series Advances in Digital Crime, Forensics, and Cyber Terrorism (ADCF-CT) (ISSN: 2327-0381; eISSN: 2327-0373)

British Cataloguing in Publication Data
A Cataloguing in Publication record for this book is available from the British Library.

For electronic access to this publication, please contact: eresources@igi-global.com.

# Advances in Digital Crime, Forensics, and Cyber Terrorism (ADCFCT) Book Series

ISSN: 2327-0381
EISSN: 2327-0373

## MISSION

The digital revolution has allowed for greater global connectivity and has improved the way we share and present information. With this new ease of communication and access also come many new challenges and threats as cyber crime and digital perpetrators are constantly developing new ways to attack systems and gain access to private information.

The **Advances in Digital Crime, Forensics, and Cyber Terrorism (ADCFCT) Book Series** seeks to publish the latest research in diverse fields pertaining to crime, warfare, terrorism and forensics in the digital sphere. By advancing research available in these fields, the **ADCFCT** aims to present researchers, academicians, and students with the most current available knowledge and assist security and law enforcement professionals with a better understanding of the current tools, applications, and methodologies being implemented and discussed in the field.

## COVERAGE

- Hacking
- Information Warfare
- Telecommunications Fraud
- Cyber Warfare
- Digital Crime
- Data Protection
- Cyber Terrorism
- Malware
- Database Forensics
- Identity Theft

IGI Global is currently accepting manuscripts for publication within this series. To submit a proposal for a volume in this series, please contact our Acquisition Editors at Acquisitions@igi-global.com or visit: http://www.igi-global.com/publish/.

# Titles in this Series

*For a list of additional titles in this series, please visit: www.igi-global.com*

*The Psychology of Cyber Crime Concepts and Principles*
Gráinne Kirwan (Dun Laoghaire Institute of Art, Design and Technology, Ireland) and Andrew Power (Dun Laoghaire Institute of Art, Design and Technology, Ireland)
Information Science Reference • copyright 2012 • 372pp • H/C (ISBN: 9781613503508) • US $195.00 (our price)

*Cyber Crime and the Victimization of Women Laws, Rights and Regulations*
Debarati Halder (Centre for Cyber Victim Counselling (CCVC), India) and K. Jaishankar (Manonmaniam Sundaranar University, India)
Information Science Reference • copyright 2012 • 264pp • H/C (ISBN: 9781609608309) • US $195.00 (our price)

*Digital Forensics for the Health Sciences Applications in Practice and Research*
Andriani Daskalaki (Max Planck Institute for Molecular Genetics, Germany)
Medical Information Science Reference • copyright 2011 • 418pp • H/C (ISBN: 9781609604837) • US $245.00 (our price)

*Cyber Security, Cyber Crime and Cyber Forensics Applications and Perspectives*
Raghu Santanam (Arizona State University, USA) M. Sethumadhavan (Amrita University, India) and Mohit Virendra (Brocade Communications Systems, USA)
Information Science Reference • copyright 2011 • 296pp • H/C (ISBN: 9781609601232) • US $180.00 (our price)

*Handbook of Research on Computational Forensics, Digital Crime, and Investigation Methods and Solutions*
Chang-Tsun Li (University of Warwick, UK)
Information Science Reference • copyright 2010 • 620pp • H/C (ISBN: 9781605668369) • US $295.00 (our price)

*Homeland Security Preparedness and Information Systems Strategies for Managing Public Policy*
Christopher G. Reddick (University of Texas at San Antonio, USA )
Information Science Reference • copyright 2010 • 274pp • H/C (ISBN: 9781605668345) • US $180.00 (our price)

www.igi-global.com

701 E. Chocolate Ave., Hershey, PA 17033
Order online at www.igi-global.com or call 717-533-8845 x100
To place a standing order for titles released in this series, contact: cust@igi-global.com
Mon-Fri 8:00 am - 5:00 pm (est) or fax 24 hours a day 717-533-8661

# List of Contributors

# Table of Contents

### Section 1
### Cybercrimes Examples, Risks, and Threats

## Section 2
## Cyber Security Approaches and Developments

## Section 3
## Legal Aspects and ICT Law

## Section 4
## Case Studies

# Detailed Table of Contents

### Section 1
### Cybercrimes Examples, Risks, and Threats

    *Ana Kovacevic, University of Belgrade, Serbia*
    *Dragana Nikolic, University of Belgrade, Serbia*

We are facing the expansion of cyber incidents, and they are becoming more severe. This results in the necessity to improve security, especially in the vulnerable field of critical infrastructure. One of the problems in the security of critical infrastructures is the level of awareness related to the effect of cyberattacks. The threat to critical infrastructure is real, so it is necessary to be aware of it and anticipate, predict, and prepare against a cyber attack. The main reason for the escalation of cyberattacks in the field of Critical Infrastructure (CI) may be that most control systems used for CI do not utilise propriety protocols and software anymore; they instead utilise standard solutions. As a result, critical infrastructure systems are more than ever before becoming vulnerable and exposed to cyber threats. It is important to get an insight into what attack types occur, as this may help direct cyber security efforts. In this chapter, the authors present vulnerabilities of SCADA systems against cyber attack, analyse and classify existing cyber attacks, and give future directions to achieve better security of SCADA systems.

    *Slawomir Grzonkowski, Symantec, Ireland*
    *Laurentiu Vasiliu, Peracton Ltd., Ireland*
    *Adamantios Koumpis, National University of Ireland Galway, Ireland*

The shift towards cyberspace created a very wide range of opportunities for various criminal activities, in both the real and the virtual world, such as identity theft, fraud, organized crime, and seriously organized crime, on an unprecedented scale. In this chapter, the authors propose a combination of integration activities for the best tools that help identify threats and security gaps for business and industrial users, for new analytical tools proposed to check if existing security features of the used networked structures are adequate and up-to-date and up-to-speed to address potential threat scenarios.

*Teresa Sofia Pereira Dias de Castro, University of Minho, Portugal*
*António José Osório, University of Minho, Portugal*

The Internet imprints a great complexity to new and old risks as threats become more available in children's lives. Criminals have greater access to the victims and Internet crimes are favoured by ambiguities in the law. This chapter presents preliminary data from an on-going doctoral investigation about the upsetting phenomenon of violence perpetrated by, with, and among school-aged children using online services and devices. To better understand the subjectivity, delicacy, and complexity of matters and meanings that participants bring to their online experiences, the authors follow a qualitative approach, based on a structured and interpretive analysis. They work with a group of children aged between 6 and 15 years old. With this chapter, the authors intend to contribute to a greater understanding and reflection about this complex problem and its impact in order to increase awareness about how children behave online and in what way it may influence their well-being.

*Vanessa N. Cooper, Kennesaw State University, USA*
*Hossain Shahriar, Kennesaw State University, USA*
*Hisham M. Haddad, Kennesaw State University, USA*

As mobile applications are being developed at a faster pace, the security aspect of user information is being neglected. A compromised smartphone can inflict severe damage to both users and the cellular service provider. Malware on a smartphone can make the phone partially or fully unusable, cause unwanted billing, steal private information, or infect every name in a user's phonebook. A solid understanding of the characteristics of malware is the beginning step to prevent much of the unwanted consequences. This chapter is intended to provide an overview of security threats posed by Android malware. In particular, the authors focus on the characteristics commonly found in malware applications and understand the code level features that allow us to detect the malicious signatures. The authors also discuss some common defense techniques to mitigate the impact of malware applications.

*Avelina Alonso de Escamilla, CEU San Pablo University, Spain*

This chapter aims mainly to carry out a study of a new type of harassment named stalking. After the study of its contents through the opinions of the most recognized specialist on it, the chapter defines the crime based on the expert's opinion. A study of comparative law is done, and this study focuses on the different ways stalking happens. This chapter offers a critical study of the inclusion of stalking as a felony in the criminal amendment Organic Criminal Law 10/1995 of 23 November, Criminal Law Code. To finish, this chapter proposes some improvements to that regulation and focuses on the new realities that bring about cyber stalking.

In the 21st century, thus far, we have seen a growing dependence on and usage of the Internet and communications technology. This has been especially true for youth who spend much of their time communicating in cyber space. This allows for developing and maintaining relationships. At the same time, an ugly and dangerous phenomenon called cyber bullying has reared its head. In this chapter, the authors discuss various aspects of this phenomenon, including, but not limited to, incidence rates, comparison to traditional bullying, risk factors for being involved either as a bully or a victim, how it affects its victims, relevant legal aspects, and most importantly, how to defend against it. The discussion of coping strategies is especially detailed and provide suggestions for schools, parents, bystanders, victims, and broader society.

This chapter studies the establishment of DNA databases and their relevance at two levels. On the one hand, as a basis for criminal investigation, they contribute to the protection of the public against potentially criminal behavior. In our societies, mass violence is not a sporadic occurrence and knowledge. When DNA databases allow for preventive action, they may be synonymous with safety. On the other hand, DNA databases pose deeper problems, such as a felon's data are still personal data and as such need to be protected. Any violation of this right is against the law. Therefore, a society that wants to be lawfully protected must first protect. The study is focused on Spanish and Portuguese statutes enforced in 2007 and 2008, respectively, as well as on doctrine and jurisprudence produced in both countries and intended to strengthen cyberspace security and to guarantee access to information.

Given the multifaceted problems and complexities of information security, the manner in which top management teams make investment and management decisions regarding security technologies, policy initiatives, and employee education could have a significant impact on the likelihood of information security breaches in organizations. In the context of information security management, it is not clear from management literature regarding how the characteristics of the top management team are associated with the possibility of information security breaches. The results demonstrate that the average length and heterogeneity of tenure could increase the possibility of breaches. However, age heterogeneity and the size of the top management team are negatively related to such a possibility. In addition, the findings suggest a nonlinear association between average age and tenure and the possibility of security breaches. The authors conclude the chapter with theoretical and practical implications on the organizational and managerial aspects of information security management.

Clickjacking attacks are an emerging threat on the Web. The attacks allure users to click on objects transparently placed in malicious Web pages. The resultant actions of the click operations may cause unwanted operations in the legitimate websites without the knowledge of users. Recent reports suggest that victims can be tricked to click on a wide range of websites such as social network (Facebook, Twitter), shopping (Amazon), and online banking. One reported incident on clickjacking attack enabled the webcam and microphone of a victim without his/her knowledge. To combat against clickjacking attacks, application developers need to understand how clickjacking attacks occur along with existing solutions available to defend the attacks. This chapter shows a number of basic and advanced clickjacking attacks. The authors then show a number of detection techniques available at the client, server, and proxy levels.

This chapter is about the use of large-scale databases that has increased considerably in the last two years. It is a powerful tool to predict future situations that may affect society. The use of an environmental scanner to fight cybercrime—as an organized crime—is the project for using this technique of large-scale databases to try to guarantee the security against the risk of new, developing forms of criminal activities. On the other hand, the use of large-scale databases utilizes a great amount of personal data to try to predict where and how organized crime or new forms of criminality will develop. This means that we have to evaluate the interests of security of society and the privacy of the person, and we have to find the way to balance both in a democratic society. There are important ethical issues to be considered in the employment of this new and unregulated instrument.

## Section 2
## Cyber Security Approaches and Developments

Workflow management systems are used to run day-to-day applications in numerous domains, often including exchange and processing of sensitive data. Their native "leakage-proneness," being the consequence of their distributed and collaborative nature, calls for sophisticated mechanisms able to guarantee proper enforcement of the necessary privacy protection measures. Motivated by the principles of Privacy by Design and its potential for workflow environments, this chapter investigates the associated issues, challenges, and requirements. With the legal and regulatory provisions regarding privacy in information systems as a baseline, the chapter elaborates on the challenges and derived requirements in the context of workflow environments, taking into account the particular needs and implications of the latter. Further, it highlights important aspects that need to be considered regarding, on the one hand, the incorporation of privacy-enhancing features in the workflow models themselves and, on the other, the evaluation of the latter against privacy provisions.

## Chapter 12

In a bid to discover, uncover, and stamp out digital crime while ensuring information security and assurance, there is a need to investigate the crime once it has taken place. This will help trace the criminals and also secure an organization against future attacks. Forensic readiness entails that an organization be at alert in terms of digital evidence collection and storage – that is, collecting and storing such evidence constantly in a forensically sound manner, not just when the need for such evidence arises. In the event litigation arises or is anticipated, digital evidence may need to be reviewed by the opposing parties prior to court proceedings to assess quality of the evidence; this is eDiscovery. This chapter explores eDiscovery and forensic readiness. Digital evidence for eDiscovery needs to be forensically sound and provided in a timely and efficient manner - forensic readiness helps to ensure this. This chapter seeks to establish how forensic readiness is relevant to the eDiscovery process.

## Chapter 13

The growth of the Internet has changed our lives significantly. Not so long ago, computers used to be viewed as luxury items to have at home. People used to rely mainly on televisions and newspapers as the primary sources of news. Today, the Internet has become an essential service to depend on for many industries, such as news agencies, airports, and even utility companies. This was the beginning of a new-trillion-dollar industry: the Internet industry. However, the Internet was designed to be an open, academic tool, never to be secure. As a result, cybercrimes, cyber warfare, and other cyber illegal activities have spread to become a significant portion of Internet traffic. Cybercrimes often challenge law enforcement. It is difficult to know the exact location where an attack originated, and there are no cyber borders between nations. As a result, fighting cybercrimes requires international cooperation. The purpose of this chapter is to shed some light on motives of cybercrimes, technologies used by hackers, and solutions that can be adopted by individuals, organizations, and governments. This chapter also presents the United States (USA) and international perspectives on cybercrimes and privacy laws. In summary, individuals, organizations, and nations have roles to play in achieving security and reducing cyber risks.

## Chapter 14

At young ages there is an increase in reports of intimidation, harassment, intrusion, fear, and violence experienced through Information Technologies (IT). Hacking, spamming, identity theft, child pornography, cyber bullying, and cyber stalking are just few examples of cyber-crimes. This chapter aims to contribute, from a psychological and design perspective, to an integrative viewpoint about this complex field of cyber-crime. In this chapter, the most common types of cyber-crimes, epidemiological data, and the profiles of cyber victims and aggressors' are approached. The studies that identify the factors contributing to IT misuse and to growing online vulnerability, principally in adolescents, are also discussed. Likewise, the central explanatory theories for the online victimization and the risk factors for victimization and perpetration online are addressed. Finally, some cyber-crime prevention strategies are anticipated, in particular among young people, seeking to provide clues to the consolidation of recent policies, namely at the digital design level.

Yoan Chabot, University of Bourgogne, France & University College Dublin, Ireland
Aurélie Bertaux, University of Bourgogne, France
Tahar Kechadi, University College Dublin, Ireland
Christophe Nicolle, University of Bourgogne, France

Event reconstruction is one of the most important steps in digital forensic investigations. It allows investigators to have a clear view of the events that have occurred over a time period. Event reconstruction is a complex task that requires exploration of a large amount of events due to the pervasiveness of new technologies. Any evidence produced at the end of the investigative process must also meet the requirements of the courts, such as reproducibility, verifiability, validation, etc. After defining the most important concepts of event reconstruction, the authors present a survey of the challenges of this field and solutions proposed so far.

Robert Layton, Federation University, Australia
Paul A. Watters, Massey University, New Zealand

We are now in an era of cyberconflict, where nation states, in addition to private entities and individual actors, are attacking each other through Internet-based mechanisms. This incorporates cyberespionage, cybercrime, and malware attacks, with the end goal being intellectual property, state secrets, identity information, and monetary gain. Methods of deterring cybercrime ultimately require effective attribution; otherwise, the threat of consequences for malicious online behaviour will be diminished. This chapter reviews the state of the art in attribution in cyberspace, arguing that due to increases in the technical capability of the most recent advances in cyberconflict, models of attribution using network traceback and explicit identifiers (i.e. direct models) are insufficient build trustworthy models. The main cause of this is the ability of adversaries to obfuscate information and anonymise their attacks from direct attribution. Indirect models, in which models of attacks are built based on feature types and not explicit features, are more difficult to obfuscate and can lead to more reliable methods. There are some issues to overcome with indirect models, such as the complexity of models and the variations in effectiveness, which present an interesting and active field of research.

## Chapter 17

*Rajashekhar C. Biradar, Reva Institute of Technology and Management, India*
*Raja Jitendra Nayaka, Reva Institute of Technology and Management, India*

The performance of Next Generation Networks (NGN) in terms of security, speed, synchronization, latency, and throughput with variable synchronous or asynchronous packet sizes has not been sufficiently addressed in novel crypto systems. Traditional crypto systems such as block and stream ciphers have been studied and implemented for various networks such as wire line and wireless systems. Since NGN comprises of wire line and wireless networks with variable packet-based communication carrying various traffic like multimedia, video, audio, multi conferencing, and a large amount of data transfers at higher speeds. The modern crypto systems suffer with various challenges such as algorithm implementation, variable packet sizes, communication, latency, throughput, key size, key management, and speed. In this chapter, the authors discuss some of the important issues and challenges faced by modern crypto systems in Next Generation Networks (NGN) such as algorithm implementation, speed, throughput and latency in communication, point-to-multipoint, broadcast and key size, remote key management, and communication speed.

## Chapter 18

*Ana Kovacevic, University of Belgrade, Serbia*
*Dragana Nikolic, University of Belgrade, Serbia*

The Internet has become an inevitable form of communication, which enables connections with colleagues, friends, or people with similar interests, regardless of physical barriers. However, there is also a dark side to the Internet, since an alarming number of adolescents admit they have been victims or bystanders of cyberbullying. In order to make the Internet a safer environment, it is necessary to develop novel methods and software capable of preventing and managing cyberbullying. This chapter reviews existing research in dealing with this phenomenon and discusses current and potential applications of text mining techniques for the detection of cyberbullying.

## Chapter 19

*Anil Saini, Malaviya National Institute of Technology, India*
*Manoj Singh Gaur, Malaviya National Institute of Technology, India*
*Vijay Laxmi, Malaviya National Institute of Technology, India*

Browser attacks over the years have stormed the Internet world with so many malicious activities. They provide unauthorized access and damage or disrupt user information within or outside the browser. This chapter focuses on the complete attack actions adopted by an attacker while crafting an attack on Web browser. The knowledge gained from the attacker's actions can be framed into a suitable taxonomy, which can then be used as a framework for examining the browser attack footprints, vulnerability in browser design, and helps one to understand the characteristics and nature of an attacker. This chapter presents a browser attack taxonomy that helps in combating new browser attacks and improving browser security. Keywords: Vulnerability, Browser Attack, Browser Security, Attack Taxonomy, Privilege Escalation Code Injection, Web Application Attacks

This chapter addresses some concerns and highlights some of the major problems affecting cyberspace. This chapter focuses on defensive attitudes and concerns pertaining to the cybersecurity issues. Section 1, "Facing Cyberspace Security," opens the area of threats and the need of defensive attitudes. Section 2, "Remembering Internet Issues," deals with known Internet problems in what concerns cybersecurity as a generic term. In –Section 3, "Defensive Cybersecurity," the focus is on the need to add more defensive features to security policies. Section 4, "In Search of Better Solutions," emphasizes the need to invest continuously in scientific research and the creation of more sophisticated processes in order to prevent new forms of attack and mitigate negative results.

This chapter treats computer networks as a cyber warfighting domain in which the maintenance of situational awareness is impaired by increasing traffic volumes and the lack of immediate sensory perception. Sonification (the use of non-speech audio for communicating information) is proposed as a viable means of monitoring a network in real time and a research agenda employing the sonification of a network's self-organized criticality within a context-aware affective computing scenario is given. The chapter views a computer network as a cyber battlespace with a particular operations spectrum and dynamics. Increasing network traffic volumes are interfering with the ability to present real-time intelligence about a network and so suggestions are made for how the context of a network might be used to help construct intelligent information infrastructures. Such a system would use affective computing principles to sonify emergent properties (such as self-organized criticality) of network traffic and behaviour to provide effective real-time situational awareness.

This chapter examines the threats in cyber security. It identifies the risk of cyber attacks and argues the inability to defend against those threats in a cyber security program. The introduction provides a brief history of cyber security and how the information highway arrived at this point in cyber security. The first analysis examines the threats in cyber security in personal, private, and government computer systems. The second analysis examines the approaches to attacking those systems. The third analysis examines threats against private companies and government agencies. The final analysis examines major threats to cyber security.

Cyberspace, like the territories grounded in the physical world, is an environment subject to border control and surveillance for various purposes: governmental, economic, security, among others. As in the physical sphere, governance can serve to enforce rules to avoid abuses and to allow users and institutions to build effective relationships, transparent and harmonious. The purpose of this chapter is to discuss the Civil Rights Framework for the Internet in Brazil ("Marco Civil da Internet"), a project created in 2009 that aims to establish rights and obligations for the operation of the network in this Latin American nation. Before that, however, it is critical to address the issue of control and surveillance on the Internet, revealing their motivations, goals, and work tools.

The chapter covers the international law due diligence principle as applied to the prevention of transboundary cyberthreats. The analysis is based on the work of the International Law Commission referring to state responsibility and international liability as applicable to the challenge of international cybersecurity. The first attempts of this application by European international organizations are discussed. This is done in the light of the current political challenge of engaging all states in the discussion on the appropriate standard of cyberthreats prevention. Reaching to the no harm principle of international law, the author argues that all states need to take all necessary measures in order to prevent significant transboundary damage originated by online activities of individuals within their jurisdiction, power, or control. Should they fail to show due diligence they may be held internationally responsible for an omission contrary to their obligation of preventing harm to other states, foreigners, or shared resources.

Since the government began tackling the problems of cybercrime, many laws have been enacted. A lack of a comprehensive definition and taxonomy of cybercrime makes it difficult to accurately identify report and monitor cybercrime trends. There is not just a lack of international agreement on what cybercrime is; there are different laws in every state within the United States, reflecting the inconsistency of dealing with cybercrime. There is also concern that many times lawyers and information technology professions are unable to understand each other well. The deficiency of cyber laws is an obvious problem and development of effective laws is emerging as an important issue to deal with cybercrime. This research uses the routine activity theory to develop a unified framework by including the motivation of the offender to use a computer as a tool/target, suitability of the target, and the presence (or absence) of guardian. It could help states that want to update their existing laws and cover areas that were previously uncovered.

The Internet of Things (IoT), a metaphor for smart, functional Cyberphysical Environments (CPE), is finding some usefulness in various sectors including healthcare, security, transportation, and the Smart Home (SH). Within the IoT, objects potentially operate autonomously to provide specified services and complete assigned tasks. However, the introduction of new technologies and/or the novel application of existing ones usually herald the discovery of unfamiliar security vulnerabilities, which lead to exploits and sometimes to security breaches. There is existing research that identifies IoT-related security concerns and breaches. This chapter discusses existing Digital Forensics (DF) models and methodologies for their applicability (or not) within the IoT domain using the SH as a case in point. The chapter also makes the argument for smart forensics, the use of a smart autonomous system (tagged the Forensics Edge Management System [FEMS]) to provide forensic services within the self-managed CPE of the SH.

"Sticks and Stones" is a well-known adage that means that whatever nasty things people say, they will not physically harm one. This is not often the case, as bullying, especially via the Internet, can be quite harmful. There are few anti-bullying laws emanating from the European Union, which is a trading block of 28 member states that have pooled their sovereignty in order to have common laws and practices to boost trade and peace. However, the common legal rules that exist in the EU have implications for those who run websites, including relating to cyber-bullying. These people, known as systems operators, or sysops, can be limited in the powers they have and rules they make through "sysop prerogative." Sysop prerogative means that a systems operator can do anything which has been permitted or not taken away by statute, or which they have not given away by contract. This chapter reviews how the different legal systems in Europe impact on sysops and change the way in which sysop prerogative can be exercised. This includes not just from the EU legal structure, but equally the European Convention on Human Rights (ECHR), which also has implications for sysops in the way they conduct their activities.

# Chapter 28

This chapter seeks to explore the role media content ratings play in the age of "Internet trolling" and other electronic media issues like "sexting." Using ANOVA to validate a four-factor approach to media ratings based on maturity, the chapter finds the ability of a person to withstand various media content, measured in "knol," which is the brain's capacity to process information, can be used to calculate media ratings. The study concludes it is feasible to have brain-computer interfaces for PCs and kiosks to test the maturity of vulnerable persons and recommend to parents/guardians or cinema managers whether or not to allow someone access to the content they wish to consume. This could mean that computer software could be programmed to automatically censor content that person is likely to be distressed or grossly offended by. Public policy issues relating to these supply-side interventions are discussed.

**Section 4**
**Case Studies**

**Chapter 29**

*José Manuel Fernández Marín, University of Almería, Spain*
*Juan Álvaro Muñoz Naranjo, University of Almería, Spain*
*Leocadio González Casado, University of Almería, Spain*

This chapter presents a review and a case of study of honeypots and honeynets. First, some of the most important and widely used honeypots in the current market are selected for comparative analysis, evaluating their interaction capacity with an attacker. Second, a self-contained honeynet architecture is implemented with virtual machines. An intrusion test is performed against the honeynet to observe the quality and quantity of the information collected during the attack. The final goal of this analysis is to assess the capacity of monitoring and threat detection of the honeynets and honeypots.

**Chapter 30**

*Vítor João Pereira Domingues Martinho, Polytechnic Institute of Viseu, Portugal*

The main objective of this chapter is to analyze the crimes related to the new information technologies in the European Union using the data provided by the European Commission and the spatial econometrics approaches. The data were analyzed with several tests, namely the Moran´s I, to verify the existence of global (for all countries of the European Union) and local spatial autocorrelation. The presence of spatial autocorrelation in the data means that the variable analyzed in a determined country is auto correlated with the same variable in the neighboring countries. The data analysis was complemented with some cross-section estimations, considering namely the Lagrange Multiplier tests, to examine the spatial lag and the spatial error autocorrelation. The spatial autocorrelation is a statistical infraction, so the consideration of these subjects prevents result bias and on the other hand allows some conclusions important to help in the definition of adjusted policies.

**Chapter 31**

*Calin Ciufudean, Stefan cel Mare University, Romania*

Cyber Security Model of Artificial Social System Man-Machine takes advantage of an important chapter of artificial intelligence, discrete event systems applied for modelling and simulation of control, logistic supply, chart positioning, and optimum trajectory planning of artificial social systems. "An artificial social system is a set of restrictions on agents` behaviours in a multi-agent environment. Its role is to allow agents to coexist in a shared environment and pursue their respective goals in the presence of other agents" (Moses & Tennenholtz, n.d.). Despite conventional approaches, Cyber Security Model of Artificial Social System Man-Machine is not guided by rigid control algorithms but by flexible, event-adaptable ones that makes them more lively and available. All these allow a new design of artificial social systems dotted with intelligence, autonomous decision-making capabilities, and self-diagnosing properties. Heuristics techniques, data mining planning activities, scheduling algorithms, automatic data identification, processing, and control represent as many trumps for these new systems analyzing formalism. The authors challenge these frameworks to model and simulate the interaction of man-machine in order to have a better look at the human, social, and organizational privacy and information protection.

*Clare Doherty, National University of Ireland Galway, Ireland*
*Michael Lang, National University of Ireland Galway, Ireland*
*James Deane, Cora Systems, Ireland*
*Regina Connor, Allied Irish Bank, Ireland*

This chapter explores how six constructs—control, trust, perceived risk, risk propensity, perceived legal protection, and privacy disposition—affect information disclosure on the Social Networking Site (SNS) Facebook. Building upon previous related work, an extended causal model of disclosure behaviour is proposed. The hypothesised relationships in this model were tested using survey data collected from 278 social networking site users in Ireland. The results of the analysis provide strong support for the proposed model.

# Preface

## ABOUT THE SUBJECT

In the digital age, ICT raises new concerns that are not accounted for within the existing data protection/privacy legal framework, so some action is necessary to ensure that individual rights are protected. After providing an overview of ICT as a new development that creates opportunities but also risks, this book discusses the need to integrate, at a practical level, data protection, privacy, and security from the very inception of new information and communication technologies.

Digital crime is prevailing in all sectors of activity in our dynamic world and assuming a threatening dimension to people, society, and organizations. The combat to this form of crime is increasing awareness towards fast developments in the area of computer science forensics, investigation methods, technologies, and tools, and appealing to the global information security and assurance and ICT Law fields and its applications.

## ORGANIZATION OF THE BOOK

This handbook of research collects the most recent discoveries in cyber-crimes approaches, developments, practical examples, and case studies, together with the counterpart of cyberspace security developments, personal and global privacy, information assurance, protection, and ICT Law in all the embraced dimensions. The book is intended to support a professional audience of investigators, practitioners of computer forensics, security, experts in ICT law, and also an academic audience (teachers, researchers, and students, mainly of post-graduate studies).

This collection of 32 chapters is written by a group of 62 authors that includes many internationally renowned and experienced authors in the field and a set of younger authors, showing a promising potential for research and development. At the same time, the book integrates contributions from academe, research institutions, and industry, representing a good and comprehensive representation of the state-of-the-art approaches and developments that address several dimensions of this fast evolutionary thematic.

A very important and enriching characteristic of this handbook of research is that it includes contributions from the five continents. Contributions came from Australia, Belgium, Brazil, France, Greece, India, Ireland, Israel, New Zeeland, Nigeria, Poland, Portugal, Romania, Serbia, Spain, Taiwan, the United Kingdom, and the USA.

The *Handbook of Research on Digital Crime, Cyberspace Security, and Information Assurance* integrates 32 chapters organized in four sections, which are briefly introduced below.

With 10 chapters, Section 1, "Cybercrimes Examples, Risks, and Threats" presents a compilation of examples and reviews of digital crime, threats, risks, techniques, and challenges.

We are facing the expansion of cyber incidents, and they are becoming more severe. This results in the necessity to improve security, especially in the vulnerable field of critical infrastructure. One of the problems in the security of critical infrastructures is the level of awareness related to the effect of cyberattacks. The threat to critical infrastructure is real, so it is necessary to be aware of it and anticipate, predict, and prepare against a cyber attack. The main reason for the escalation of cyberattacks in the field of Critical Infrastructure (CI) may be that most control systems used for CI do not utilise propriety protocols and software anymore; they instead utilise standard solutions. As a result, critical infrastructure systems are more than ever before becoming vulnerable and exposed to cyber threats. It is important to get an insight into what attack types occur, as this may help direct cyber security efforts. In the 1st chapter, "Cyber Attacks on Critical Infrastructure: Review and Challenges," Kovacevic and Nikolic defend that the threat to critical infrastructure is real, so it is necessary to be aware of it, and anticipate, predict, and be prepared against a cyber-attacks.

The shift towards cyberspace created a very wide range of opportunities for various criminal activities, in both the real and the virtual world, such as identity theft, fraud, organized crime, and seriously organized crime, on an unprecedented scale. In "Raptor: Early Recognition and Elimination of Network Attacks," Grzonkowski, Vasiliu, and Koumpis propose a combination of integration activities for the best tools that help identify threats and security gaps for business and industrial users, for new analytical tools proposed to check if existing security features of the used networked structures are adequate and up-to-date and up-to-speed to address potential threat scenarios.

The Internet imprints a great complexity to new and old risks as threats become more available in children's lives. Criminals have greater access to the victims and Internet crimes are favoured by ambiguities in the law. The 3rd chapter, "Online Violence: Listening to Children's Online Experiences," by Castro and Osório, presents preliminary data from an on-going doctoral investigation about the upsetting phenomenon of violence perpetrated by, with, and among school-aged children using online services and devices. To better understand the subjectivity, delicacy, and complexity of matters and meanings that participants bring to their online experiences, the authors follow a qualitative approach, based on a structured and interpretive analysis. With this chapter, the authors intend to contribute to a greater understanding and reflection about this complex problem and its impact in order to increase awareness about how children behave online and in what way it may influence their well-being.

As mobile applications are being developed at a faster pace, the security aspect of user information is being neglected. A compromised smartphone can inflict severe damage to both users and the cellular service provider. Malware on a smartphone can make the phone partially or fully unusable, cause unwanted billing, steal private information, or infect every name in a user's phonebook. A solid understanding of the characteristics of malware is the beginning step to prevent much of the unwanted consequences. The 4th chapter, "Development and Mitigation of Android Malware," an overview of security threats posed by Android malware. In particular, the authors focus on the characteristics commonly found in malware applications and understand the code level features that allow us to detect the malicious signatures. The authors also discuss some common defense techniques to mitigate the impact of malware applications.

In "Answering the New Realities of Stalking," Avelina Escamilla presents the study of a new way of harassment named stalking. After the study of its contents through the opinions of the most recognized specialist on it, the chapter defines the crime based on the expert's opinion. A study of comparative law is done, and this study focuses on the different ways stalking happens. This chapter offers a critical study of the inclusion of stalking as a felony in the criminal amendment Organic Criminal Law 10/1995 of 23 November, Criminal Law Code. To finish, this chapter proposes some improvements to that regulation and focuses on the new realities that bring about cyber stalking.

In the 21st century, thus far, we have seen a growing dependence on and usage of the Internet and communications technology. This has been especially true for youth who spend much of their time communicating in cyber space. This allows for developing and maintaining relationships. At the same time, an ugly and dangerous phenomenon called cyber bullying has reared its head. In this 6th chapter, "Cyberbullying: Keeping our Children Safe in the 21st Century," Iris and Sukenik discuss various aspects of this phenomenon, including, but not limited to, incidence rates, comparison to traditional bullying, risk factors for being involved either as a bully or a victim, how it affects its victims, relevant legal aspects, and most importantly, how to defend against it. The discussion of coping strategies is especially detailed and provide suggestions for schools, parents, bystanders, victims, and broader society.

"DNA Databases for Criminal Investigation," by Henrique Curado, presents the establishment of DNA databases and their relevance at two levels. On the one hand, as a basis for criminal investigation, they contribute to the protection of the public against potentially criminal behavior. In our societies, mass violence is not a sporadic occurrence and knowledge. When DNA databases allow for preventive action, they may be synonymous with safety. On the other hand, DNA databases pose deeper problems, such as a felon's data are still personal data and as such need to be protected. Any violation of this right is against the law. Therefore, a society that wants to be lawfully protected must first protect. The study is focused on Spanish and Portuguese statutes enforced in 2007 and 2008, respectively, as well as on doctrine and jurisprudence produced in both countries and intended to strengthen cyberspace security and to guarantee access to information.

Given the multifaceted problems and complexities of information security, the manner in which top management teams make investment and management decisions regarding security technologies, policy initiatives, and employee education could have a significant impact on the likelihood of information security breaches in organizations. In the context of information security management, it is not clear from management literature regarding how the characteristics of the top management team are associated with the possibility of information security breaches. In the 8th chapter, "Composition of the Top Management Team and Information Security Breaches," Hsu and Wang demonstrate that the average length and heterogeneity of tenure could increase the possibility of breaches. However, age heterogeneity and the size of the top management team are negatively related to such a possibility. In addition, the findings suggest a nonlinear association between average age and tenure and the possibility of security breaches. The authors conclude the chapter with theoretical and practical implications on the organizational and managerial aspects of information security management.

Clickjacking attacks are an emerging threat on the Web. The attacks allure users to click on objects transparently placed in malicious Web pages. The resultant actions of the click operations may cause unwanted operations in the legitimate websites without the knowledge of users. Recent reports suggest that victims can be tricked to click on a wide range of websites such as social network (Facebook, Twitter), shopping (Amazon), and online banking. One reported incident on clickjacking attack enabled the webcam and microphone of a victim without his/her knowledge. To combat against clickjacking attacks, application developers need to understand how clickjacking attacks occur along with existing solutions available to defend the attacks. In Chapter 9, "Hijacking of Clicks: Attacks and Mitigation Techniques," Shahriar and Devendran show a number of detection techniques available at the client, server, and proxy levels.

The use of Internet by organized crime groups to commit their crimes is increasing and sometimes there is no other effective way to fight it other than by exploring the Internet, as discussed by Valls-Prieto in Chapter 10, "Fighting Cybercrime and Protecting Privacy: DDoS, Spy Software, and Online Attacks." The use of an environmental scanner to fight cybercrime—as an organized crime—is the project for using this technique of large-scale databases to try to guarantee the security against the risk of new, developing forms of criminal activities. On the other hand, the use of large-scale databases utilizes a great amount of personal data to try to predict where and how organized crime or new forms of criminality will develop. This means that we have to evaluate the interests of security of society and the privacy of the person, and we have to find the way to balance both in a democratic society. As these tools are not limited to one national state, but affect the whole world, the author discusses the European regulation on the use of large-scale databases and the limits needed to protect privacy rights. On 31 July 2013, in reaction to the use of these instruments by NSA, a group of institutions linked to privacy on the Internet created a project with the rights that should be guaranteed when processing this type of investigation as a way of controlling their use by the state. There are important ethical issues to be considered in the employment of this new and unregulated instrument; the third part of the chapter deals with the multiple possibilities of massive data.

Section 2, "Cyber Security Approaches and Developments," presents a collection of 12 chapters addressing the latest techniques, technologies, and contributions to prevent digital crime and its associated consequences.

Workflow management systems are used to run day-to-day applications in numerous domains, often including exchange and processing of sensitive data. Their native "leakage-proneness," being the consequence of their distributed and collaborative nature, calls for sophisticated mechanisms able to guarantee proper enforcement of the necessary privacy protection measures. Motivated by the principles of Privacy by Design and its potential for workflow environments, in "Privacy Compliance Requirements in Workflow Environments," Koukovini et al. investigate the associated issues, challenges, and requirements. With the legal and regulatory provisions regarding privacy in information systems as a baseline, the chapter elaborates on the challenges and derived requirements in the context of workflow environments, taking into account the particular needs and implications of the latter. Further, it highlights important aspects that need to be considered regarding, on the one hand, the incorporation of privacy-enhancing features in the workflow models themselves and, on the other, the evaluation of the latter against privacy provisions.

In a bid to discover, uncover, and stamp out digital crime while ensuring information security and assurance, there is a need to investigate the crime once it has taken place. This will help trace the criminals and also secure an organization against future attacks. Forensic readiness entails that an organization be at alert in terms of digital evidence collection and storage – that is, collecting and storing such evidence constantly in a forensically sound manner, not just when the need for such evidence arises. In the event litigation arises or is anticipated, digital evidence may need to be reviewed by the opposing parties prior to court proceedings to assess quality of the evidence; this is eDiscovery. Digital evidence for eDiscovery needs to be forensically sound and provided in a timely and efficient manner, and forensic readiness helps to ensure this. In "Forensic Readiness and eDiscovery," Sauda Sule seeks to establish how forensic readiness is relevant to the eDiscovery process.

The Internet has become an essential service to depend on for many industries, such as news agencies, airports, and even utility companies. This was the beginning of a new-trillion-dollar industry: the Internet industry. However, the Internet was designed to be an open, academic tool, never to be secure. As a result, cybercrimes, cyber warfare, and other cyber illegal activities have spread to become a significant portion of Internet traffic. Cybercrimes often challenge law enforcement. It is difficult to know the exact location where an attack originated, and there are no cyber borders between nations. As a result, fighting cybercrimes requires international cooperation. The purpose of this chapter, "Cybercrimes Technologies and Approaches," is to shed some light on motives of cybercrimes, technologies used by hackers, and solutions that can be adopted by individuals, organizations, and governments. This chapter also presents the United States (USA) and international perspectives on cybercrimes and privacy laws. In summary, individuals, organizations, and nations have roles to play in achieving security and reducing cyber risks.

At young ages there is an increase in reports of intimidation, harassment, intrusion, fear, and violence experienced through Information Technologies (IT). Hacking, spamming, identity theft, child pornography, cyber bullying, and cyber stalking are just few examples of cyber-crimes. Chapter 14, "Cyber-Crimes against Adolescents: Bridges between a Psychological and a Design Approach," by Pereira, Matos, and Sampaio, aims to contribute, from a psychological and design perspective, to an integrative viewpoint about this complex field of cyber-crime. The most common types of cyber-crimes, epidemiological data, and the profiles of cyber victims and aggressors' are approached. The studies that identify the factors contributing to IT misuse and to growing online vulnerability, principally in adolescents, are discussed. Likewise, the central explanatory theories for the online victimization and the risk factors for victimization and perpetration online are addressed. Finally, some cyber-crime prevention strategies are anticipated, in particular among young people, seeking to provide clues to the consolidation of recent policies, namely at the digital design level.

# Chapter 15

Event reconstruction is one of the most important steps in digital forensic investigations. It allows investigators to have a clear view of the events that have occurred over a time period. Event reconstruction is a complex task that requires exploration of a large amount of events due to the pervasiveness of new technologies. Any evidence produced at the end of the investigative process must also meet the requirements of the courts, such as reproducibility, verifiability, validation, etc. After defining the most important concepts of event reconstruction, Chabot, Bertaux, Kechadi, and Nicolle present a survey of the challenges of this field and solutions proposed so far, in their chapter, "Event Reconstruction: A State of the Art."

We are now in an era of cyberconflict, where nation states, in addition to private entities and individual actors, are attacking each other through Internet-based mechanisms. This incorporates cyberespionage, cybercrime, and malware attacks, with the end goal being intellectual property, state secrets, identity information, and monetary gain. Methods of deterring cybercrime ultimately require effective attribution; otherwise, the threat of consequences for malicious online behaviour will be diminished. The 16th chapter, "Indirect Attribution in Cyberspace," by Layton and Watters, reviews the state of the art in attribution in cyberspace, arguing that due to increases in the technical capability of the most recent advances in cyberconflict, models of attribution using network traceback and explicit identifiers (i.e. direct models) are insufficient build trustworthy models. The main cause of this is the ability of adversaries to obfuscate information and anonymise their attacks from direct attribution. Indirect models, in which models of attacks are built based on feature types and not explicit features, are more difficult to obfuscate and can lead to more reliable methods. There are some issues to overcome with indirect models, such as the complexity of models and the variations in effectiveness, which present an interesting and active field of research.

# Chapter 17

The performance of Next Generation Networks (NGN) in terms of security, speed, synchronization, latency, and throughput with variable synchronous or asynchronous packet sizes has not been sufficiently addressed in novel crypto systems. Traditional crypto systems such as block and stream ciphers have been studied and implemented for various networks such as wire line and wireless systems. Since NGN comprises of wire line and wireless networks with variable packet-based communication carrying various traffic like multimedia, video, audio, multi conferencing, and a large amount of data transfers at higher speeds, the modern crypto systems suffer with various challenges such as algorithm implementation, variable packet sizes, communication, latency, throughput, key size, key management, and speed. In

"Modern Crypto Systems in Next Generation Networks: Issues and Challenges," Biradar and Nayaka discuss some of the important issues and challenges faced by modern crypto systems in Next Generation Networks (NGN) such as algorithm implementation, speed, throughput and latency in communication, point-to-multipoint, broadcast and key size, remote key management, and communication speed.

The Internet has become an inevitable form of communication, which enables connections with colleagues, friends, or people with similar interests, regardless of physical barriers. However, there is also a dark side to the Internet, since an alarming number of adolescents admit they have been victims or bystanders of cyberbullying. In order to make the Internet a safer environment, it is necessary to develop novel methods and software capable of preventing and managing cyberbullying. In Chapter 18, "Automatic Detection of Cyberbullying to make Internet a Safer Environment," Kovacevic and Nikolic review existing research in dealing with this phenomenon and discusses current and potential applications of text mining techniques for the detection of cyberbullying.

# Chapter 19

Browser attacks over the years have stormed the Internet world with so many malicious activities. They provide unauthorized access and damage or disrupt user information within or outside the browser. This chapter focuses on the complete attack actions adopted by an attacker while crafting an attack on Web browser. The knowledge gained from the attacker's actions can be framed into a suitable taxonomy, which can then be used as a framework for examining the browser attack footprints, vulnerability in browser design, and helps one to understand the characteristics and nature of an attacker. Saini, Gaur, and Laxmi present "A Taxonomy of Browser Attacks" that helps in combating new browser attacks, and improving browser security.

This chapter addresses some concerns and highlights some of the major problems affecting cyberspace. In "Defending Information Networks in Cyberspace: Some Notes on Security Needs," Alberto Carneiro focuses on defensive attitudes and concerns pertaining to the cybersecurity issues. Section 1, "Facing Cyberspace Security," opens the area of threats and the need of defensive attitudes. Section 2, "Remembering Internet Issues," deals with known Internet problems in what concerns cybersecurity as a generic term. In –Section 3, "Defensive Cybersecurity," the focus is on the need to add more defensive features to security policies. Section 4, "In Search of Better Solutions," emphasizes the need to invest continuously in scientific research and the creation of more sophisticated processes in order to prevent new forms of attack and mitigate negative results.

Chapter 21, "Network Situational Awareness: Sonification and Visualization in the Cyber Battlespace," by Fairfax, Laing, and Vickers, treats computer networks as a cyber warfighting domain in which the maintenance of situational awareness is impaired by increasing traffic volumes and the lack of immediate sensory perception. Sonification (the use of non-speech audio for communicating information) is proposed as a viable means of monitoring a network in real time and a research agenda employing the sonification of a network's self-organized criticality within a context-aware affective computing scenario is given. The chapter views a computer network as a cyber battlespace with a particular operations spectrum and dynamics. Increasing network traffic volumes are interfering with the ability to present real-time intelligence about a network and so suggestions are made for how the context of a network might be used to help construct intelligent information infrastructures. Such a system would use affective computing principles to sonify emergent properties (such as self-organized criticality) of network traffic and behaviour to provide effective real-time situational awareness.

The research presented by Raisinghani and Jarret in "Can Total Quality Management Exist in Cyber Security: Is it Present? Are we Safe?" examines the threats in cyber security. It identifies the risk of cyber attacks and argues the inability to defend against those threats in a cyber security program. The introduction provides a brief history of cyber security and how the information highway arrived at this point in cyber security. The first analysis examines the threats in cyber security in personal, private, and government computer systems. The second analysis examines the approaches to attacking those systems. The third analysis examines threats against private companies and government agencies. The final analysis examines major threats to cyber security.

Section 3, "Legal Aspects and ICT Law," discusses several aspects of cyberspace regulation and cybercrime combat.

Cyberspace, like the territories grounded in the physical world, is an environment subject to border control and surveillance for various purposes: governmental, economic, security, among others. As in the physical sphere, governance can serve to enforce rules to avoid abuses and to allow users and institutions to build effective relationships, transparent and harmonious. The purpose of Chapter 23, "The Gatekeepers of Cyberspace: Surveillance, Control, and Internet Regulation in Brazil," by Elisianne Soares, is to discuss the Civil Rights Framework for the Internet in Brazil ("Marco Civil da Internet"), a project created in 2009 that aims to establish rights and obligations for the operation of the network in this Latin American nation.

Chapter 24, "Surveillance, Privacy, and Due Diligence in Cybersecurity: An International Law Perspective," by Joanna Kulesza, covers the international law due diligence principle as applied to the prevention of transboundary cyberthreats. The analysis is based on the work of the International Law Commission referring to state responsibility and international liability as applicable to the challenge of international cybersecurity. The first attempts of this application done by European international organizations are discussed. This is done in the light of the current political challenge of engaging all states in the discussion on the appropriate standard of cyberthreats prevention. Reaching to the no harm principle of international law, the author argues that all states need to take all necessary measures in order to prevent significant transboundary damage originated by online activities of individuals within their jurisdiction, power, or control. Should they fail to show due diligence they may be held internationally responsible for an omission contrary to their obligation of preventing harm to other states, foreigners, or shared resources.

Since the government began tackling the problems of cybercrime, many laws have been enacted. A lack of a comprehensive definition and taxonomy of cybercrime makes it difficult to accurately identify report and monitor cybercrime trends. There is not just a lack of international agreement on what cybercrime is; there are different laws in every state within the United States, reflecting the inconsistency of dealing with cybercrime. There is also concern that many times lawyers and information technology professions are unable to understand each other well. The deficiency of cyber laws is an obvious problem and development of effective laws is emerging as an important issue to deal with cybercrime. The research presented by Glasser and Taneja in "A Routine Activity Theory-Based Framework for Combating Cybercrime" uses the routine activity theory to develop a unified framework by including the motivation of the offender to use a computer as a tool/target, suitability of the target, and the presence (or absence) of guardian. It could help states that want to update their existing laws and cover areas that were previously uncovered.

The Internet of Things (IoT), a metaphor for smart, functional Cyberphysical Environments (CPE), is finding some usefulness in various sectors including healthcare, security, transportation, and the Smart Home (SH). Within the IoT, objects potentially operate autonomously to provide specified services and complete assigned tasks. However, the introduction of new technologies and/or the novel application of existing ones usually herald the discovery of unfamiliar security vulnerabilities, which lead to exploits and sometimes to security breaches. There is existing research that identifies IoT-related security concerns and breaches. Edewede Oriwoh discusses existing Digital Forensics (DF) models and methodologies for their applicability (or not) within the IoT domain using the SH as a case in point, in his chapter, "Internet of Things: The Argument for Smart Forensics." The chapter also makes the argument for smart forensics, the use of a smart autonomous system (tagged the Forensics Edge Management System [FEMS]) to provide forensic services within the self-managed CPE of the SH.

"Sticks and Stones" is a well-known adage that means that whatever nasty things people say, they will not physically harm one. This is not often the case, as bullying, especially via the Internet, can be quite harmful. There are few anti-bullying laws emanating from the European Union, which is a trading block of 28 member states that have pooled their sovereignty in order to have common laws and practices to boost trade and peace. However, the common legal rules that exist in the EU have implications for those who run websites, including relating to cyber-bullying. These people, known as systems operators, or sysops, can be limited in the powers they have and rules they make through "sysop prerogative." Sysop prerogative means that a systems operator can do anything which has been permitted or not taken away by statute, or which they have not given away by contract. Chapter 28, "Sticks and Stones will break my Euros: The Role of EU Law in Dealing with Cyber-Bullying through Sysop-Prerogative," by Jonathan Bishop, reviews how the different legal systems in Europe impact on sysops and change the way in which sysop prerogative can be exercised. This includes not just from the EU legal structure, but equally the European Convention on Human Rights (ECHR), which also has implications for sysops in the way they conduct their activities.

In "Trolling is not just an Art. It is a Science: The Role of Automated Affective Content Screening in Regulating Digital Media and Reducing Risk Trauma," Jonathan Bishop seeks to explore the role media content ratings play in the age of "Internet trolling" and other electronic media issues like "sexting." Using ANOVA to validate a four-factor approach to media ratings based on maturity, the chapter finds the ability of a person to withstand various media content, measured in "knol," which is the brain's capacity to process information, can be used to calculate media ratings. The study concludes it is feasible to have brain-computer interfaces for PCs and kiosks to test the maturity of vulnerable persons and recommend to parents/guardians or cinema managers whether or not to allow someone access to the content they wish to consume. This could mean that computer software could be programmed to automatically censor content that person is likely to be distressed or grossly offended by. Public policy issues relating to these supply-side interventions are discussed.

The last section of this handbook of research, Section 4, "Case Studies," offers four analysis and discussions on threats and attempts to privacy, security, and integrity.

The 29th chapter, "Honeypots and Honeynets: Analysis and Case Study," by Marín, Naranjo, and Casado, presents a review and a case of study of honeypots and honeynets. First, some of the most important and widely used honeypots in the current market are selected for comparative analysis, evaluating their interaction capacity with an attacker. Second, a self-contained honeynet architecture is implemented with virtual machines. An intrusion test is performed against the honeynet to observe the quality and quantity of the information collected during the attack. The final goal of this analysis is to assess the capacity of monitoring and threat detection of the honeynets and honeypots.

The main objective of the study presented in Chapter 30, "Analysis of the Cybercrime with Spatial Econometrics in the European Union Countries," by Vítor Martinho is to analyze the crimes related to the new information technologies in the European Union using the data provided by the European Commission and the spatial econometrics approaches. The data were analyzed with several tests, namely the Moran´s I, to verify the existence of global (for all countries of the European Union) and local spatial autocorrelation. The presence of spatial autocorrelation in the data means that the variable analyzed in a determined country is auto correlated with the same variable in the neighboring countries. The data analysis was complemented with some cross-section estimations, considering namely the Lagrange Multiplier tests, to examine the spatial lag and the spatial error autocorrelation. The spatial autocorrelation is a statistical infraction, so the consideration of these subjects prevents result bias and on the other hand allows some conclusions important to help in the definition of adjusted policies.

Cyber Security Model of Artificial Social System Man-Machine takes advantage of an important chapter of artificial intelligence, discrete event systems applied for modelling and simulation of control, logistic supply, chart positioning, and optimum trajectory planning of artificial social systems. Despite conventional approaches, Cyber Security Model of Artificial Social System Man-Machine is not guided by rigid control algorithms but by flexible, event-adaptable ones that makes them more lively and available. All these allow a new design of artificial social systems dotted with intelligence, autonomous decision-making capabilities, and self-diagnosing properties. Heuristics techniques, data mining planning activities, scheduling algorithms, automatic data identification, processing, and control represent as many trumps for these new systems analyzing formalism. In "Cyber Security Model of Artificial Social System Man Machine," Calin Ciufudean challenges these frameworks to model and simulate the interaction of man-machine in order to have a better look at the human, social, and organizational privacy and information protection.

The last chapter, "Information Disclosure on Social Networking Sites: An Exploratory Survey of Factors Impacting User Behaviour on Facebook," by Doherty, Lang, Deane, and Connor, explores how six constructs—control, trust, perceived risk, risk propensity, perceived legal protection, and privacy disposition—affect information disclosure on the Social Networking Site (SNS) Facebook. Building upon previous related work, an extended causal model of disclosure behaviour is proposed. The hypothesised relationships in this model were tested using survey data collected from 278 social networking site users in Ireland. The results of the analysis provide strong support for the proposed model.

## EXPECTATIONS

The book provides researchers, scholars, and professionals with some of the most advanced research, developments, discussions, and case studies on digital crime and digital threats from one side, and security, privacy, information assurance, law and regulation, and human aspects on the other. It was compiled and edited to be a tool for academics (teachers, researchers, and students of several graduate and postgraduate courses), professionals of law, information technology, psychology, and policymakers.

We strongly hope it meets your expectations!

*Maria Manuela Cruz-Cunha*
*Polytechnic Institute of Cávado and Ave, Portugal*

*Irene Maria Portela*
*Polytechnic Institute of Cávado and Ave, Portugal*

# Acknowledgment

Editing a book is a quite hard but compensating and enriching task, as it involves a set of different activities like contacts with authors and reviewers, discussion and exchange of ideas and experiences, process management, organization and integration of contents, etc., with the permanent objective of creating a book that meets the readers' expectations. And this task cannot be accomplished without a great help and support from many sources. As editors we would like to acknowledge the help, support, and belief from all who made possible this creation.

First of all, the edition of this book would not have been possible without the continuing professional support of the team of professionals at IGI Global. We are grateful to Jan Travers, Director of Intellectual Property and Contracts, for the opportunity. A very very special mention of gratitude is due to the Editorial Assistants Brett Snyder and Erin O'Dea, for their professional support and friendly words of advice, encouragement, and prompt guidance.

Special thanks go also to all the staff at IGI Global, whose contributions were invaluable throughout the process of production and making this book available all over the world.

We are grateful to all the authors for their insights and excellent contributions to this book. Also, we are grateful to most of the authors who simultaneously served as referees for chapters written by other authors, for their insights, valuable contributions, prompt collaboration, and constructive comments. Thank you all, authors and reviewers, you made this book! The communication and exchange of views within this truly global group of recognized individualities from the scientific domain and from the industry was an enriching and exciting experience!

We are also grateful to all who acceded to contribute to this book, some of them with high quality chapter proposals, but unfortunately, due to several constraints could not have seen their work published.

Thank you.

*Maria Manuela Cruz-Cunha*
*Polytechnic Institute of Cávado and Ave, Portugal*

*Irene Maria Portela*
*Polytechnic Institute of Cávado and Ave, Portugal*

# Section 1
# Cybercrimes Examples, Risks, and Threats

# Chapter 1
# Cyber Attacks on Critical Infrastructure:
## Review and Challenges

**Ana Kovacevic**
*University of Belgrade, Serbia*

**Dragana Nikolic**
*University of Belgrade, Serbia*

## ABSTRACT

*We are facing the expansion of cyber incidents, and they are becoming more severe. This results in the necessity to improve security, especially in the vulnerable field of critical infrastructure. One of the problems in the security of critical infrastructures is the level of awareness related to the effect of cyberattacks. The threat to critical infrastructure is real, so it is necessary to be aware of it and anticipate, predict, and prepare against a cyber attack. The main reason for the escalation of cyberattacks in the field of Critical Infrastructure (CI) may be that most control systems used for CI do not utilise propriety protocols and software anymore; they instead utilise standard solutions. As a result, critical infrastructure systems are more than ever before becoming vulnerable and exposed to cyber threats. It is important to get an insight into what attack types occur, as this may help direct cyber security efforts. In this chapter, the authors present vulnerabilities of SCADA systems against cyber attack, analyse and classify existing cyber attacks, and give future directions to achieve better security of SCADA systems.*

## INTRODUCTION

In recent years cyberspace has been expanded significantly and evolved into a large, dynamic, and tangled web of computing devices. This situation has also influenced critical infrastructure systems. Besides positive effects of technological expansion, there are also drawbacks. Critical infrastructure is the backbone of everyday lives in modern society, and thus a proper functioning of it is essential. For a long time most critical infrastructure systems have been considered immune to cyberattacks because of their reliance on proprietary networks and hardware. However, recent experiences and cyber attacks indicate that this is unsustainable – the move to open standards and web technologies is making critical infrastructure systems more vulnerable.

DOI: 10.4018/978-1-4666-6324-4.ch001

Unintentional or malevolent actions taken in cyberspace have consequences on critical infrastructures in the physical world. After a few sporadic attacks it became clear that attacks in cyberspace are not limited to government activities for intelligence purposes, but any part of critical infrastructure may be subject to attacks, from the banking system and utilities to the transport or supply of essential goods and commodities. The modes of these attacks on critical infrastructure are diverse and include direct or anonymous access to protected networks via the Internet and Supervisory Control and Data Acquisition (SCADA), or breach of the employees who do not follow security procedures leading to malware propagation inside the firewall. The problem with analyzing cyber attacks in the field of critical infrastructure is that some cyber attacks remain unnoticed; and also some organizations are extremely unwilling to report incidents, because they are viewed as potential embarrassments. Furthermore, the appearance of new complex malware, such as Stuxnet, with unpredictable features, is creating new dimensions in cyber security. One of the most pernicious problems with cyberspace is that the fight is so unbalanced that it takes huge resources to protect critical infrastructure, but just one infected computer drive to launch an attack. Therefore, cyber defence has become one of the most important issues in national defence strategies. This paper presents an overview of the cyber attacks on critical infrastructure.

The remainder of this paper is organized as follows: Section 2 presents Critical Infrastructure. Section 3 presents SCADA systems that are used for Critical Infrastructure and vulnerabilities of SCADA systems against cyber attacks. Section 4 analyzes and classifies cyber attacks on SCADA systems for critical infrastructure. Section 5 discusses future directions to achieve better security of Critical infrastructure sectors using SCADA systems. Section 6 provides the concluding remarks.

## CRITICAL INFRASTRUCTURE

There is a slight difference between countries concerning their definition of critical infrastructure (CI) sectors. CIs are defined as those systems, assets, or part thereof which are essential for the maintenance of vital societal functions, security and economic security, and the disruption or destruction of which would have a significant impact on the state/nation as a result of the failure to maintain those functions (European Commission, 2008). The US approach is more comprehensive and inclusive, and it has been particularly evolving since the attacks of September 11, 2001. The U.S. Patriot Act defined CIs as "systems and assets, whether physical or virtual, so vital to the U.S. that the incapacity or destruction of such systems and assets would have a debilitating impact on security, national economic security, national public health or safety, or any combination of those matters" (USA- PA, 2001). *Homeland Security Act* of 2002 (P.L. 107-296, Sec. 2(4)) established the Department of Homeland Security (DHS) and also formally introduced the concept of "key resources" (Congress U.S., 2002). "Key resources" are defined as "publicly or privately controlled resources essential to the minimal operations of the economy and government" (Sec. 2(9)). Without articulating exactly what they are, the act views key resources as distinct from critical infrastructure, albeit worthy of the same protection.

The most conventional list of critical infrastructure sectors includes: agriculture and food, water, public health and safety, emergency services, government, defense industrial base, information and telecommunications, energy, transportation, banking and finance, industry/manufacturing, postal and shipping.

Each of these sectors has its own infrastructures such as highways, electric power generation and distribution, etc. In any of these, a critical infrastructure system is a great public investment. A minor disruption in the functioning of these systems may degrade the system's performance and incur big economic losses. The identification and designation of state's critical infrastructures is established by prioritizing particular infrastructure sectors, and specific assets within those sectors, on the basis of national importance.

Critical infrastructure (CI) sectors are not isolated islands; there are interdependencies among them. For example, if the energy sector is attacked, this will have consequences on other sectors as well, as illustrated in Figure 1. Dependencies and interdependencies among sectors of critical infrastructures must be taken into account in protective programs because the impact of the disruption of one sector can propagate to other sectors.

In order to improve CI protection, it is necessary to monitor incidents in each of the infrastructure sectors, maintain a database of vulnerabilities and integrate the database with threat analyses. Such measures are introduced in countries with extensive infrastructures, such as the US, where the federal government is required to interact with each critical infrastructure and support their implementation. It is very important to record and analyze attacks on critical infrastructure, as well as their consequences, in order to be better prepared for any further attacks.

## SCADA SYSTEMS FOR CRITICAL INFRASTRUCTURES

The first control networks were simple point-to-point networks connecting a monitoring or command device to a remote sensor or actuator, while nowadays they have evolved into complex networks that support communication between a central control unit and multiple remote units on a common communication bus (Igure et al., 2006). Supervisory Control and Data Acquisition systems (SCADA) are often used for critical

infrastructures, e.g. electric power distribution, oil and natural gas distribution, water and waste-water treatment, transportation systems, etc. SCADA systems perform basically two main tasks: centralized monitoring of the system and control of it. Data is collected, stored and interpreted in terms of different set points that have been set by human operators. When the system detects any unusual action, it sends commands or alert human operator. Systems may consist of thousand of assets capable of measuring and/or controlling the process. The nodes on these networks are usually special-purpose embedded computing devices such as sensors, actuators and Programmable Logic Controllers (PLCs) (Igure et al., 2006). Typical SCADA system is composed of the following components (GAO, 2004):

- Human-machine interface (HMI) responsible for data presentation to a human operator for monitoring and controlling the process.
- Remote terminal units (RTUs) are microprocessor-controlled electronic devices that interface the sensors to SCADA by transmitting telemetry data.
- The supervisory system is responsible for data acquisition and for control activities on the process.
- Programmable logic controllers (PLCs) are the final actuators used as field devices.
- Communication infrastructure connecting the supervisory system to the remote terminal units.
- Various process and analytical instrumentation.

In the plant, sensors are monitored and controlled over the SCADA network by either PC or a Programmable Logic Controller (PLC). Usually, there is a dedicated control centre to screen the entire plant, mainly located in a separate physical part of the factory and it has advanced computa-

*Figure 1. Cascading consequence example (adapted from Rinaldi et al., 2001)*

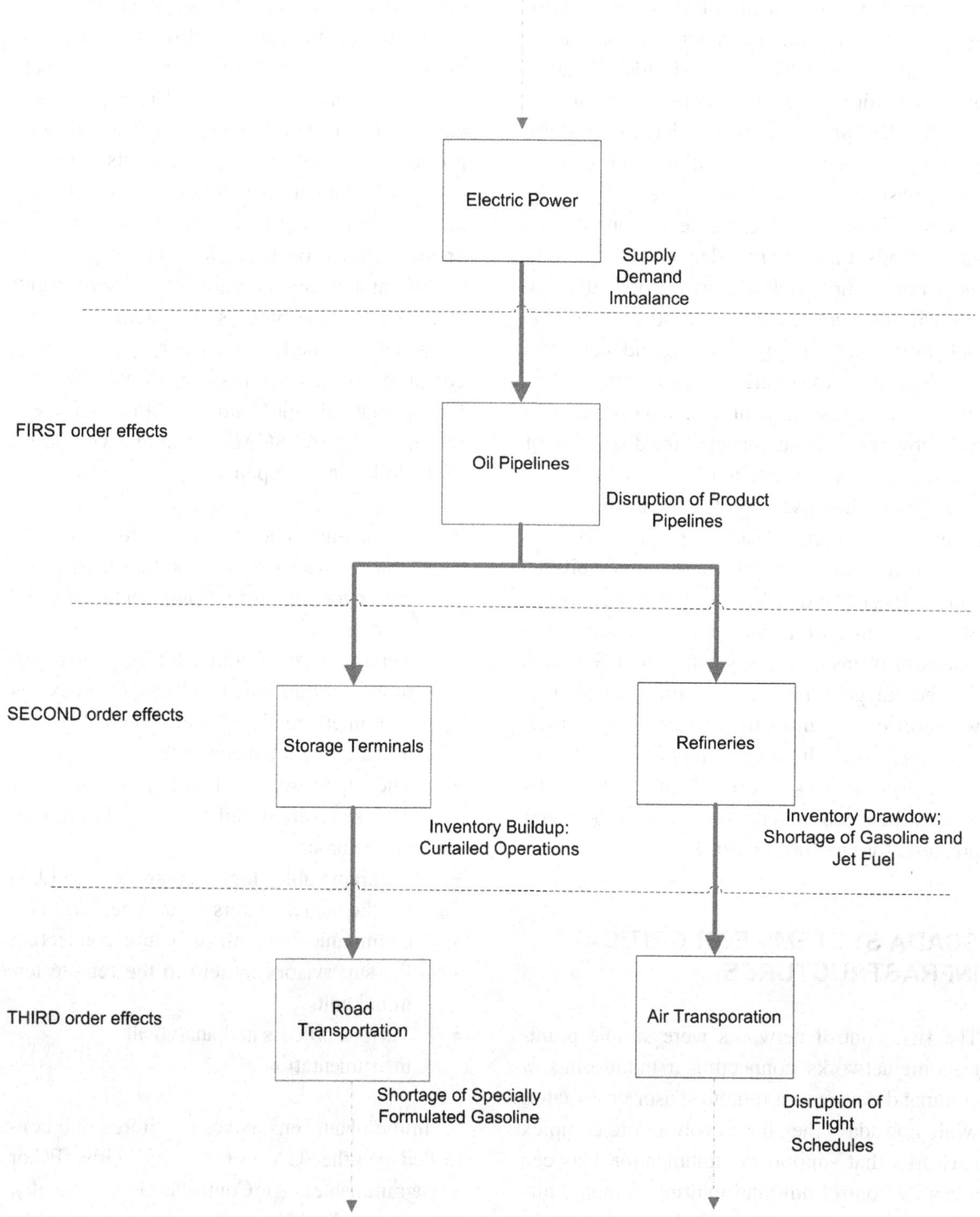

tion and communication facilities (Igure et al., 2006). The attacker has several entry points to compromise the system.

SCADA networks are usually connected to an outside corporate network and/or Internet through specialized gateways (providing the interface between IP-based network and filed bus protocol-based SCADA networks on the factory floor).

In recent years SCADA systems are increasingly becoming targets of cyber attacks. Today, many of the current SCADA networks are also connected to a company's corporate networks and the Internet. Although improved connectivity is essential for reducing costs and efficiency, it also causes SCADA networks to become more vulnerable because of the security problems of the Internet. Specifically, the sophistication of new malware attacking SCADA systems, as Stuxnet, shows difficulties in preventing and detecting this attack when they are based only on IT system information.

SCADA systems have many similarities with IT systems, but they also have some specific requirements where the usual security solutions are not applicable to SCADA systems, e.g. because of time requirements, they have a higher demand on availability and are often more difficult to upgrade.

## SCADA Systems and Administrative IT Systems

Although SCADA systems have specific operational requirements, they are nowadays very similar to administrative IT systems. During the last decade, when SCADA systems were using standard protocols and hardware/software as in administrative IT systems, differences between SCADA systems and IT systems were reduced. Also, the connectivity between SCADA systems and other systems increased (Stouffer et al., 2007). The result of this is that SCADA systems have become more similar to administrative IT systems in regard to their vulnerabilities.

Generally, the main aim of IT security is to obtain:

- Confidentiality (protect information from disclosure).
- Integrity (protect information form unauthorized change).
- Availability (it is possible to use the data and/or resources of the system when it is requested).

Confidentiality, Integrity and Availability is usually referred to as CIA. The requirements of IT security are prioritized as CIA (Confidentiality, Integrity, Availability), while in SCADA systems they might instead be prioritized as AIC (Stouffer et al., 2007). The reason for this is that SCADA systems work with actual physical processes and the loss of availability may have a real serious impact on physical processes (such as human life, environment, damage of equipment etc.), while the typical IT system has no interaction with physical processes.

The example of an attack on confidentiality may be sniffing the data transmitted across the network. Since many of SCADA protocols do not use cryptography, sniffing communication on the network is possible if the attacker succeeds in intruding into the network. The example of an attack on integrity of SCADA systems is when the attacker changes control signals to cause a device malfunction, which might ultimately affect the availability of the network.

SCADA systems are time-critical and delay is not allowed, while the throughput may not be as high; the situation is opposite in a typical IT system. In SCADA system the operator may respond to the event immediately, so it is important that security measures do not slow down these processes (e.g. using passwords for executing critical commands). Real-time availability provides a stricter operational environment than most traditional IT systems.

System software patching and frequent updates can not be easily performed for SCADA systems e.g. upgrading a system may require months of previous planning to put a system offline, while system patches and other changes need to be thoroughly tested before they can be applied. It is economically difficult to justify suspending the operation of an industrial computer on a regular basis to install new security patches (Cardenas et al., 2011). Sometimes there are problems with security patches, such as violating certification or causing accidents to control systems. Usually, vendors of SCADA system do not permit the installation of a third party application, e.g. anti-virus softer, or it may lead to the loss of support on the system.

Some conditions are less demanding to SCADA systems than to administrative IT systems, e.g. server changes rarely, fixed topology, stable user population, regular communication patterns, and a limited number of protocols. Accordingly, implementing network intrusion detection systems, anomaly detection, and white listing may be easier than in traditional enterprise systems (Cheung et al., 2007). A major distinction of SCADA systems with respect to other IT systems is the interaction of SCADA systems with the physical world (Cardenas et al., 2011).

## Vulnerabilities of SCADA Systems

Critical infrastructure relies on SCADA systems, so vulnerabilities affecting SCADA systems may be a threat to critical infrastructure e.g. disruption of critical services.

At the onset of using SCADA systems, the goal was to achieve good performance, and network security was hardly a concern, as the dominant concern was for physical security. Until recently these networks were isolated, so that an attacker could not access them. But today there is a high demand for interconnectivity between SCADA systems and corporate networks. There are multiple access points to SCADA systems and physi-

cal isolation does not guarantee network security. Therefore, the concern for the security of SCADA networks is rising.

With the evolution of SCADA systems, propriety standards for SCADA communication were moved to open international standards and now it is easy for an attacker to gain in-depth knowledge about the functioning of SCADA networks (Igure et al., 2006). A factor for the decreasing security of SCADA networks is the use of COTS (short for commercial off-the-shelf) hardware and software to develop devices for operating in the SCADA network. COTS-based design saves cost and reduces design time, but it also raises concerns about the overall security of the end product. Using COTS equipment has led to the development of a number of SCADA protocols that can operate on traditional Ethernet networks and the TCP/IP stack (Igure et al., 2006).

Besides direct financial consequences of a cyber incident on critical infrastructure, there are also other negative impacts. Some of them may be easily quantifiable financially, but other consequences are not so explicit (e.g. reputation, impact on health, safety, environment, even human life etc.). These attacks may also be politically motivated or state-sponsored, which is a great concern for governments and enterprises that are involved in the critical infrastructure sector. Accordingly, the security of SCADA networks is becoming more and more important to the whole society.

Frei (2013) stated in his report that vulnerabilities in SCADA systems have almost doubled from 72 in 2011 to 124 in 2012. These 124 vulnerabilities in SCADA systems affect the products of 49 vendors.

The vulnerability analysis proposed by the Department of Homeland Security's Industrial Control Systems Cyber Emergency Response Team (ICS-CERT) and carried out for the fiscal year 2012 shows that 171 unique vulnerabilities affecting ICS products were tracked. ICS-CERT coordinated the vulnerabilities with 55 different vendors. The total number of different vulnerabilities increased from fiscal 2011 to fiscal 2012. The most vulnerable sector in 2012 was energy (41% of reported events), followed by water with 15% (ICS-CERT, 2013).

## Cyber Attacks on Critical Infrastructure

Cyber-attacks are a progression of physical attacks: they are cheaper, less risky for the attacker, not constrained by distance, easier for replication and coordination.

Cyber-attacks on SCADA systems may generally be classified as:

- **NON-Targeted Attacks:** Incidents caused by the same attacks that any computer connected to the Internet may suffer (e.g. the Slammer worm infecting the Davis Davis-Besse nuclear power plant).
- **Targeted Attacks:** Attacks tailored to damage the physical system under control of the attacked SCADA system (e.g. Attack on Maroochy Water System, Stuxnet, etc).

Targeted attacks are especially dangerous for critical infrastructure because they are tailored to affect a specific organization, usually within the critical infrastructure sector where a huge impact of disruption can be expected.

Attacks against SCADA systems escalate constantly. To get a more accurate picture of the attacks on SCADA systems, British Columbia Institute of Technology in Canada created a database of SCADA security incidents: the BCIT Industrial Security Incident Database (ISID). It is interesting that prior to 2000 most incidents (70%) were either due to accidents or disgruntled insiders acting maliciously. Between 2001 and 2004 almost 70% of the incidents were attacks from outside SCADA systems (Byres & Lowe, 2004). Hardly had the number of internal attacks lowered when the number of external attacks rose so much as to generate these figures.

Firstly, data for ISID are collected from publicly known incidents and from private reporting by member companies that wish to access database. In the second step incidents are investigated and rated according to reliability. According to traditional business crime reporting, less than one in ten of the actual incidents is collected, since most organisations are not willing to report security incidents because of the negative impact they may have (Byres & Eng, 2004). Hiding attacks is especially the case with cyber incidents.

Turk (2005) in his report presented 120 cyber security incidents involving control systems and concluded that the majority of incidents came from the Internet by malicious codes, and there were also a large number of incidents which were direct acts of sabotage. There is a problem with reporting cyber attacks because of the potential financial repercussions for a company. Also, there is another problem with available information about cyber incidents i.e. the lack of availability of detailed data. Just 30% of contributors provide a financial measure of the impact of the cyber attack; it shows that almost half of those incidents have sizeable financial losses (Turk, 2005). Incidents show loss of the ability to view and/or control the process or system, causing an increased resilience of emergency and safety systems (41% reported loss of production, while 29% reported a loss of ability to view or control the plant). Also, he concluded that there is a lack of awareness about cyber attacks, i.e. there is indication that only 13% of the users of PLC configured and used the Web service, while the others left the Web servers in the PLCs active with default passwords deployed (Turk, 2005).

Industrial Security Incident Database, which provides a comprehensive search engine for SCADA incidents, is presented by Hentea (2008).

In this database, incidents are categorized according to their severity, consequences, entry point, etc. He concluded that attacks are getting more frequent and becoming more externally than internally oriented.

In the next section we analyze and classify several Critical Infrastructure attacks.

## Classification of Attacks on Critical Infrastructure

For the purposes of this paper we have used the modified taxonomy proposed by Kjarelnad (2006) and classified CI attacks according to that taxonomy. Kjarelnad (2006) categorized cyber attacks based on four categories: Method of operation, Impact, Source and Target. Kjaerland uses these facets to compare commercial versus government incidents, focusing on the motive of attacker and where attacks originated, highlighting cyber-criminals and victims.

We used Method and Impact of operation as in Kjarelnad taxonomy (or Miller&Rowe, 2012) and instead of Source and Target facets, we include new categories Perpetrators and Critical Infrastructure Sectors, to have better picture of motives of attacks, and specific Critical Infrastructure Sector, as shown in Table 1.

Methods of operation used by a perpetrator to carry out an attack include the following (Kjaerland, 2006; Simmons et al., 2009; Miller&Rowe, 2012):

- **Misuse of Resources:** Unauthorized use of IT resources.
- **User Compromise:** Attacker gaining unauthorized use of user privileges on a host, as a user compromise.
- **Root Compromise:** A perpetrator gains unauthorized administrator privileges on a host.
- **Web Compromise:** Using website vulnerabilities to attack further.
- **Social Engineering:** gaining unauthorized access to privileged information through human interaction and targeting people's minds rather than their computers.
- Malicious code installed on a system can allow an adversary to gain full control of the compromised system leading to the exposure of sensitive information or remote control:
  - **Virus:** A piece of code that will attach itself through some form of infected files, which will self-replicate upon execution of program.
  - **Trojan:** A program that seems benign to the user but that allows unauthorized backdoor access to a compromised system.
  - **Worm:** A self-replicated program.
  - **Spyware:** A program that is covertly installed and infects its target by collecting information from a computing system without the owner's consent.

*Table 1. Proposed taxonomy*

| Method of Operation (MO) | Impact | Perpetrators | Critical Infrastructure Sector |
|---|---|---|---|
| Misuse of Resources<br>User Compromise<br>Root Compromise<br>Web Compromise<br>Social Engineering<br>Malicious code (Virus, Trojan, Worm, Spyware, Arbitrary code execution)<br>Denial of Service<br>Others | Disrupt<br>Distort<br>Destruct<br>Disclosure<br>Death<br>Unknown | Hackers<br>Terrorists<br>Disgruntled employees/inside attacks<br>Hobbyists/Script kiddies<br>Hacktivists<br>Unknown | Agriculture and food<br>Water<br>Public health and safety<br>Emergency services, Government<br>Defense industrial base<br>Information and telecommunications<br>Energy<br>Transportation<br>Banking and finance<br>Industry/manufacturing<br>Postal and shipping. |

- **Arbitrary Code Execution:** Involves a malicious entity that gains control through some vulnerability injecting its own code to perform any operation for which the overall application has permission (Douligeris, & Mitrokotsa, 2004).
- **Denial of Service:** An attack in which victim is denied access to a particular resource or service.
- Others (e.g. unintentional accidents).

Impact represents the effect of an attack and include the following (Kjaerland, 2006; Miller&Rowe, 2012):

- **Disrupt:** The least invasive nature of an attack; denying legitimate user's access to data; e.g. Denial of Service attack.
- **Distort:** Data modification.
- **Destruct:** Deletion of a file, removal of information from the victim. Destruct would be seen as the most invasive and malicious, and may include Distort or Disrupt.
- **Disclosure:** Illegitimate access to or disclosure of sensitive, confidential information (data) that may lead to further compromise; ex. Download of a password file.
- **Death:** Loss of human life.
- **Unknown:** Insufficient information to classify.

Classification of Critical Infrastructure's perpetrators:

- **Hackers**
  - **State Hackers:** May be hackers hired by governments to join specialised task forces. Stuxnet was first publicly documented attack on SCADA systems which is considered to have been made by state hackers (Nicholas et al, 2012).

  - **Non-State Hackers/Organized Crime:** Organized crime is motivated by money and the idea of blackmailing a company to avoid an attack on SCADA system may be the way to achieve it. Organised criminals are likely to have access to funds, meaning that they can hire skilled hackers or buy tools to attack a SCADA system from the underground economy. Numerous SCADA-based automated attack tools have been created in the form of Metasploit add-ons (Goodin, 2008).
- Terrorists are among the most worrying groups. There are suggestions that terrorists are interested in attacks on critical infrastructure, although they still have not acquired sufficient skills (Blau, 2004).
- Disgruntled employees/inside attacks are the most common internal perpetrators. Insider attackers usually have authorized access to network and in that way they bypass the typical "castle wall" security that an external offender must past; insider attackers may insert an infected USB device into a machine to compromise it (Nicholas et al, 2012).
- **Hobbyists/Script Kiddies** (Nicholas et al, 2012).
  - Hobbyists look for a thrill or challenge. It may seem that their intention is harmless, but sometimes it may be destructive to critical infrastructure. Hobbyists usually do not have enough money or adequate motivation to purchase zero-day exploits or similar products, which may be found on the underground market.
  - Script kiddies are usually defined as low-life hackers who use free easy-to-configure tools that mostly irritate other PC users. Script kiddies should

be stopped by general security prac-
tises, e.g. patch management, policy
enforcement, AV software, intrusion
detection systems and firewalls.
- Hacktivists or activist hackers are based on
political reasoning, and they may make attacks on SCADA systems.
- Unknown (e.g. Security/vulnerability
incident).

Attacks are represented in chronological order
and a brief description is given for each attack.

## Attacks on Critical Infrastructure

For each attack on critical infrastructure a short
description is given, followed by a classification
using the previously mentioned taxonomy.

### Siberian Pipeline Explosion (1982)

This is the first well-known cyber security incident
on critical infrastructure. The attacker planted a
Trojan in the SCADA system that controls the
Siberian Pipeline. A consequence of this was
an explosion equivalent to 3 kilotons of TNT
(Daniela, 2011).

- **Method of Operation:** Installed malware:
Trojan.
- **Impact:** Distort.
- **Critical Infrastructure Sector:** Energy.
- **Perpetrator:** Unknown.

### Chevron Emergency Alert System (1992)

A former Chevron employee disabled its emergency alert systems in 22 states in the USA
(Denning, 2000). This was not discovered until
an emergency that needed alerting happened.

- **Method of Operation:** Misuse of resources, User Compromise.
- **Impact:** Disrupt.

- **Critical Infrastructure Sector:**
Emergency services.
- **Perpetrator:** Disgruntled employ.

### Salt River Project (1994)

An attacker gained access to the network of the
Salt River Project and installed a back door. Data
vulnerable during the intrusions included water
and power monitoring and delivery, financial, and
customer and personal information. The hacker
altered/taken login and password files, computer
system log files and administrator's privileges
(Turk, 2005).

- **Method of Operation:** Installed malware:
Trojan, Root Compromise.
- **Impact:** Disclosure.
- **Critical Infrastructure Sector:** Water.
- **Perpetrator:** Hacker.

### Worcester, MA Airport (1997)

A hacker penetrated and disabled the telephone
company computer of Worcester Airport in Massachusetts in 1997 (Denning, 2000). Telephone
services to the Federal Aviation Administration
control tower, the airport fire department, airport
security, the weather service and various private
airfreight companies were cut off for six hours. The
consequences were financial losses and threatened
public health and public safety.

- **Method of Operation:** Root Compromise,
Denial of Service
- **Impact:** Disrupt
- **Critical Infrastructure Sector:**
Communications, Transportation
- **Perpetrator:** Hacker

### Gazprom (1999)

Hackers broke into a gas company in Russia, Gaz-
prom. The hackers used Trojans to gain control
of the central switchboard, which controlled gas
flow in pipelines (Denning, 2000).

- **Method of Operation:** User Compromise, Installed malware.
- **Impact:** Disrupt.
- **Critical Infrastructure Sector:** Energy.
- **Perpetrator:** Hackers.

## *Bellingham, Gas Pipeline (1999)*

The gas pipeline in Bellingham (WA) was exacerbated by a control system not being able to perform the control and monitoring functions. One of the key causes of the accident was performing database development work on the SCADA system while the system was being used to operate the pipeline. Although this is not technically an attack, the loss of human life in this incident shows the danger of any type of failure in a critical infrastructure system (Turk, 2005).

- **Method of Operation:** Misuse of Resources.
- **Impact:** Disrupt, Death.
- **Critical Infrastructure Sector:** Energy.
- **Perpetrator:** Employee.

## *Maroochy Water System (2000)*

In Maroochy Shire, Queensland (Australia) a disgruntled employee wreaked havoc by causing millions of litters of raw sewage to spill out into local parks and rivers (Smith, 2001). He gained access by installing company software on his laptop and infiltrating the company's network at least 46 times to take control of the waste management system. (He was sentenced to two years in prison)

- **Method of Operation:** User Compromise, Misuse of Resources.
- **Impact:** Disrupt.
- **Critical Infrastructure Sector:** Water.
- **Perpetrator:** Disgruntled employee.

## *Davis-Besse Nuclear Power Plant (2003)*

Ohio Davis-Besse Nuclear Power Plant was infected by a worm (Slammer) through network by a contractor of the company. The worm then managed to crash the power plant's display panel and monitoring system for 5 hours (Poulsen, 2003). Luckily, at that time the plant was not in use (it had been shut down months before), but the employees using the corporate network segment faced a performance issue. In 2003 the Slammer worm managed to infect 90% of its 75000 victims on the Internet in 10 minutes.

- **Method of Operation:** Installed malware.
- **Impact:** Disrupt.
- **Critical Infrastructure Sector:** Energy.
- **Perpetrator:** Unknown.

## *CSX Corporation (2003)*

In 2003, a computer virus named Sobig shut down train signaling systems in the CSX Corporation in Florida (Niland, 2003). The consequences of this attack were that trains were delayed, but luckily there were no major incidents caused by the Sobig virus.

- **Method of Operation:** Installed malware.
- **Impact:** Disrupt.
- **Critical Infrastructure Sector:** Transportation.
- **Perpetrator:** Unknown.

## *Browns Ferry Nuclear Plant (2006)*

Browns Ferry Nuclear plant in Alabama (U.S.) was manually shut down because of the failure of a number of recirculation pumps (Nuclear Regulatory Commission, 2007). The failure had occurred due to an overload of network traffic. It is assumed that the overload of network traffic was caused by a DOS attack, and maid system unresponsive.

- **Method of Operation:** Denial of Service.
- **Impact:** Disrupt.
- **Critical Infrastructure Sector:** Energy.
- **Perpetrator:** State hackers.

### Tehama Colusa Canal Authority (2007)

A former electrical supervisor installed unauthorised software on SCADA systems at Tehama Colusa Canal Authority. The disgruntled employee is reported to have installed it on the day he was dismissed, having worked for the company for 17 years. There were no publicly available technical analyses of whether any damage had been caused. However, he was charged with installing unauthorised software and computer damage, and got 10 years in prison and a $250,000 fine (Goodin, 2007).

- **Method of Operation:** Misuse of Resources.
- **Impact:** Unknown.
- **Critical Infrastructure Sector:** Water.
- **Perpetrator:** Disgruntled employee.

### US Electric Power Grid (2009)

Chinese and Russian spies penetrated the US electrical power grid, leaving potentially disruptive software (Gorman, 2009). It is assumed that the main idea was to map US critical infrastructure using network mapping tools. The US Government has not given any technical details, but other countries have responded, e.g. UK minister Lord West has stated that the UK asked Russian and Chinese governments to cease their probing against UK critical infrastructure (BBC News, 2009).

- **Method of Operation:** Installed malware.
- **Impact:** Disclosure.
- **Critical Infrastructure Sector:** Energy.
- **Perpetrator:** State hackers.

### Hospital Dallas, USA (2009)

A hospital security guide (Jessie William McGraw, aka GhostExodus) took advantage of his position to install malware on hospital machines and also control the heating, ventilation and air conditioning (HVAC) system (Walsh, 2009). McGraw boasted about his hacking activities on forums and downloaded videos and pictures, which led to his conviction.

- **Method of Operation:** Distributed Denial of Service.
- **Impact:** Disrupt.
- **Critical Infrastructure Sector:** Public Health.
- **Perpetrator:** Hobbyists.

### Stuxnet

Stuxnet is considered to be the first malware that attacked critical infrastructures of foreign governments. This was the idea used in the attack on the nuclear plant in Natanz, in order to interfere with the Iranian nuclear program.

Stuxnet is one of the most expensive and most complicated malicious programs ever. It is assumed that creating the code took several years (Zetter, 2010). Stuxnet is highly-sophisticated malware that has characteristics of a worm, virus and Trojan, extremely hard to detect because it uses zero-day vulnerabilities. There is evidence that Stuxnet kept evolving since its initial deployment, since attackers upgraded the infections with encryption and exploits, apparently adapting to conditions they found on the way to their target (Cardenas et al., 2011). The ultimate goal of Stuxnet is to sabotage that facility by reprogramming controllers to operate, most likely out of their specified boundaries, and without the operator of the PLC ever realizing it (Falliere et al., 2010). In addition, victims attempting to detect modifications to their embedded controllers would not see any rogue code as Stuxnet hides its modifications with sophisticated PLC rootkits, and validates its drivers with trusted certificates (Cardenas et al., 2011)

Stuxnet is targeted malware, designed to propagate itself as widely as possible, and to attack automatically once it comes into contact with the target system. It may infect only SCADA configuration and particularly attacks devices which are connected to Siemens S7-300.

It is assumed that the engineer brought Stuxnet to an isolated network through a USB stick. The idea was to achieve propagation by LAN, while propagation through removable drives was used to reach PCs not connected to other networks. This proves that being isolated from the Internet or other networks is not a complete defense. The malware that targeted Iran's uranium-enrichment program, particularly centrifuges at the Natanz plant, contained a set of codes. In Symantec they reported that in August 2010, 60% of infected computers were in Iran (Symantec, 2010). Subsequent to infecting the Siemens software in the facility's supervisory control and data-access control systems, the malware took over the control systems of frequency converters. After monitoring motor frequency, Stuxnet only attacks systems that spin between 807Hz and 1,210Hz. It changes the speed of the centrifuge motor by sporadically speeding up the machines to 1,410Hz, then slowing them back down to 2Hz. Finally, it restores the machines to a frequency of 1,064Hz, the normal operating speed. Such a change in frequency imposes severe stress on the machinery and causes higher crash rates. Reportedly, the working capacity of centrifuges in Natanz was reduced by 30% over the previous year because of Stuxnet's effects (Melman, 2010).

- **Method of Operation:** Installed malware, Root Compromise.
- **Impact:** Disrupt, Distort.
- **Critical Infrastructure:** Energy.
- **Perpetrator:** State hackers.

## Night Dragon

In 2011, five global energy and oil firms were targeted by a combination of attacks including social engineering, Trojans and Windows-based exploits. The attack was named "Night Dragon" and has been ongoing for two years and there is an assumption that they have been of Chinese origin. The corporate network segments belonging to companies that operate SCADA infrastructure were attacked, but no SCADA systems were directly attacked (Nicholson et al, 2012).

- **Method of Operation:** Social Engineering, User Compromise, Root Compromise.
- **Impact:** Disclosure.
- **Critical Infrastructure:** Energy.
- **Perpetrator:** State hackers.

## Duqu

Duqu is malware similar to Stuxnet, containing part of codes almost identical to Stuxnet. It is assumed to be designed to conduct reconnaissance of an unknown industrial control system (Zetter, 2011).

- **Method of Operation:** Installed malware.
- **Impact:** Disclosure.
- **Critical Infrastructure:** Energy.
- **Perpetrator:** State hackers.

## Flame

Flame has been appearing in the Middle East and North Africa for at least two years. It is assumed that this malware is sponsored by the same group which sponsored Stuxnet. There is indication that it is primarily designed to spy on the users of infected computers and steal data and open a back door to infected systems to allow the attacker to add new functionality It was discovered that the Iranian National Oil Co. had been hit with malware which were stealing and deleting information from the systems (Miller&Rowe, 2012).

- **Method of Operation:** Installed malware.
- **Impact:** Disclosure, Destruct.
- **Critical Infrastructure:** Energy.
- **Perpetrator:** State hackers.

## Analysis of Incidents

Figure 2 shows number of attacks according to impact they made based on previously identified findings.

*Figure 2. Method of operations*

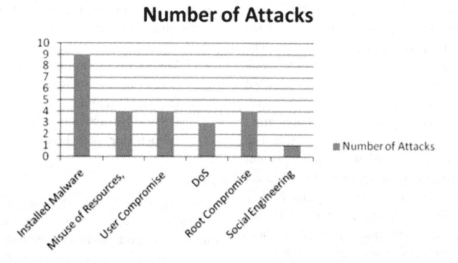

While this is 17 publicly known incidents on Critical Infrastructure, we are aware that attacked companies are not willing to publicly acknowledge attacks and results are provided with the best available knowledge.

The impact of these attacks is shown in the Figure 3. The majority of the attacks (10) caused disruption of operations, others lead to disclosure of data (5), distortion of data (2), and in one case data were destructed. There was also one death recorded, while the impact of one attack remained unknown.

## FUTURE DIRECTIONS

In order to improve analysis of SCADA systems and discover their vulnerabilities that are present, a test-bed method is developed. SCADA security testbed is used to model real system and analyse the effects of attacks on them. The method enables detection of vulnerabilities within SCADA protocols in order to find out how easy it is to bypass security measures in such protocols (Luders, 2005; Chunlei et al., 2010; Giani et al.,2008;) or perform an attack on the SCADA network (Oman&Phillips, 2007, Beresford, 2011; Udassin, 2008; Queiroz et al,, *2009*).

The general conclusion is that SCADA protocols and components are very vulnerable, and that it is very important to find an immediate solution to these vulnerabilities. Because of a similarity in technology between enterprise IT systems and Industrial Control Systems, many of the security practices used for IT systems apply to ICS and can be used to efficiently secure these systems with minimal additional costs.

Until recently, most of the efforts for protecting SCADA systems have focused on safety and reliability, not on intentional actions or systematic failures. After some attacks, there has been a growing concern for protecting control systems against malicious cyber attacks (Turk, 2005, Igure et al., 2006, US-CERT, 2008; GAO, 2007; Byres&Low, 2004; Cardenas et al., 2011). There are initiatives for improving security of control systems, and several sectors of critical infrastructure are developing programs for securing their infrastructure (NERC-CIP, 2008; Stouffer et al., 2006; INL, 2008; NIST 800-82).

It is important that future standards address shortcomings of current problems in SCADA systems architecture, administrative policies and platform security mechanisms, where both vendors and end users conform standards (Nicholson et al., 2012).

*Figure 3. Impact of attack*

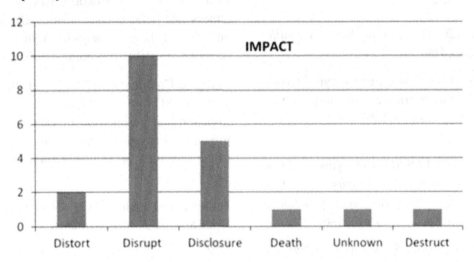

Cardenas et al. (2011) believe that to understand interactions of the control system with the physical world, it is necessary to develop a general and systematic framework for securing control systems in three fundamental new areas:

- Better understanding of the consequences of an attack for risk assessment.
- Design of a new attack-detection algorithm
- Design of new attack-resilient algorithms and architectures: need to design and operate control systems to survive an intentional cyber assault with no loss of critical functions.

## CONCLUSION

Cyber attacks on critical infrastructure have become everyday reality and it is necessary to respond and provide adequate protection.

The risk to the critical infrastructure that uses SCADA systems is exposed to high risk that system may be damaged or compromised.

The particular attention has to be given to protection of the SCADA systems, since they are at the centre of many critical infrastructure sectors' functions. Failures of SCADA systems can be safety-critical; they may cause irreparable harm to physical systems being controlled in national critical infrastructures, such as electric power distribution, oil and natural gas distribution, water and waste-matter treatment and transportation systems, etc. Interruption in the SCADA systems may have significant consequences on public health, safety and economic losses.

Because new malware is becoming more and more sophisticated, there is a significant problem of detecting attacks on critical infrastructure, based only on IT system information. Therefore, the growing concern for the whole society is to protect critical infrastructure against malicious attacks and improve the security of critical infrastructure. There is a strong commitment of governments to invest in cyber security. On the other hand, the lack of investments in the security of control systems that are privately owned creates the optimal conditions for the attackers.

## ACKNOWLEDGMENT

This work was financially supported by the Ministry of Education, Science, and Technology Development of the Republic of Serbia under projects 47017 and TR37012.

## REFERENCES

Beresford, D. (2011). *Exploiting Siemens simatic S7 PLCs*. Black Hat.

Blau, J. (2004). The battle against cyber terror. *Computer World*. Retrieved from http://www.computerworld.com/s/article/97953/The_battle_against_cyberterror

Byres, E., & Eng, P. (2004). The myths and facts behind cyber security risks for industrial control systems the BCIT industrial security incident database (ISID). *Security*, *116*(6), 1–6.

Cárdenas, A. A., Amin, S., & Lin, Z.-S. (2011). Attacks against process control systems: Risk assessment, detection, and response categories and subject descriptors. *Security*, 355-366. Retrieved from http://portal.acm.org/citation.cfm?id=1966959

Cheung, S., Dutertre, B., Fong, M., Lindqvist, U., Skinner, K., & Valdes, A. (2007, January). Using model-based intrusion detection for SCADA networks. In *Proceedings of the SCADA Security Scientific Symposium* (pp. 1-12). SCADA.

Chunlei, W., Lan, F., & Yiqi, D. (2010, March). A simulation environment for SCADA security analysis and assessment. In *Proceedings of Measuring Technology and Mechatronics Automation (ICMTMA),* (Vol. 1, pp. 342-347). IEEE.

Congress, . (2002). Homeland security act of 2002. *Public Law*, 107.

Daniela, T. (2011, June). Communication security in SCADA pipeline monitoring systems. In *Proceedings of Roedunet International Conference (RoEduNet),* (pp. 1-5). IEEE.

Denning, D. E. (2000). Cyberterrorism: The logic bomb versus the truck bomb - Centre for world dialogue. *Global Dialogue*, 2, 4.

Douligeris, C., & Mitrokotsa, A. (2004). DDoS attacks and defense mechanisms: classification and state-of-the-art. *Computer Networks*, *44*(5), 643–666. doi:10.1016/j.comnet.2003.10.003

European Commission. (2008). Council directive 2008/114/EC of 8 December 2008 on the identification and designation of European critical infrastructures and the assessment of the need to improve their protection. *Official Journal L*, *345*(23), 12.

Falliere, N., Murchu, L. O., & Chien, E. (2011). *W32: Stuxnet dossier*. Symantec Corp., Security Response.

Frei, S. (2013). Vulnerability threat trends, NSS labs. Retrieved from https://www.nsslabs.com/reports/vulnerability-threat-trends

GAO. (2004). United State government accountability office report: GAO-04-354. Retrived from http://www.gao.gov/new.items/d04354.pdf

GAO. (2007). *Critical infrastructure protection: Multiple efforts to secure control systems are under way, but challenges remain* (Technical Report GAO-07-1036). Report to Congressional Requesters.

Giani, A., Karsai, G., Roosta, T., Shah, A., Sinopoli, B., & Wiley, J. (2008). A testbed for secure and robust SCADA systems. *SIGBED Review*, *5*(2), 1. doi:10.1145/1399583.1399587

Goodin, D. (2007). Electrical supe charged with damaging California canal system. *The Register*. Retrieved from http://www.theregister.co.uk/2007/11/30/canal_system_hack/

Goodin, D. (2008). Gas refineries at defcon 1 as scada exploit goes wild. The Register. Retrieved from http://www.theregister.co.uk/2008/09/08/scada_exploit_released/

Gorman, S. (2009). Electricity grid in U.S. penetrated by spies. *The Wall Street Journal*. Retrieved from: http://online.wsj.com/article/SB123914805204099085.html

Hentea, M. (2008). Improving security for SCADA control systems. *Interdisciplinary Journal of Information, Knowledge, and Management, 3*(12), 4.

ICS-CERT. (2013). ICS-CERT Monthly Monitor Oct-Dec 2012. Retrieved from http://ics-cert.us-cert.gov/monitors/ICS-MM201210

Igure, V., Laughter, S., & Williams, R. (2006). Security issues in SCADA networks. *Computers & Security, 25*(7), 498–506. doi:10.1016/j.cose.2006.03.001

INL. (2008). *Idaho national laboratory*. National SCADA Test Bed Program. Retrieved from http://www.inl.gov/scada

Kjaerland, M. (2006). A taxonomy and comparison of computer security incidents from the commercial and government sectors. *Computers & Security, 25*(7), 522–538. doi:10.1016/j.cose.2006.08.004

Lüders, S. (2005). *Control systems under attack?* (No. CERN-OPEN-2005-025). Academic Press.

Melman, M. (2010). Computer virus in Iran actually targeted larger nuclear facility, 28 September 2010. Retrieved from http://www.haaretz.com/print-edition/news/computer-virus-in-iran-actually-targeted-larger-nuclear-facility-1.316052

Miller, B., & Rowe, D. (2012, October). A survey SCADA of and critical infrastructure incidents. In *Proceedings of the 1st Annual conference on Research in information technology* (pp. 51-56). ACM.

NERC-CIP. (2008). *Critical infrastructure protection*. North American Electric Reliability Corporation. Retrieved from http://www.nerc.com/cip.html

BBC News. (2009). *UK has cyber attack capability*. Retrieved from http://news.bbc.co.uk/1/hi/uk_politics/8118729.stm

Nicholson, A., Webber, S., Dyer, S., Patel, T., & Janicke, H. (2012). SCADA security in the light of cyber-warfare. *Computers & Security, 31*(4), 418–436. doi:10.1016/j.cose.2012.02.009

Niland, M. (2003) Computer virus brings down train signals. *InformationWeek*. Retrieved from http://www.informationweek.com/news/security/vulnerabilities/showArticle.jhtml?articleID1/413100807

Nuclear Regulatory Commission. (2007). *NRC information notice: 2007e15: effects of ethernet-based, non-safety related controls on the safe and continued operation of nuclear power stations*. Retrieved from http://www.nrc.gov/reading-rm/doc-collections/gen-comm/info-notices/2007/in200715.pdf

Oman, P., & Phillips, M. (2007). *Intrusion detection and event monitoring in SCADA networks*. Springer. doi:10.1007/978-0-387-75462-8_12

Poulsen, K. (2003). Slammer worm crashed Ohio nuke plant net. *The Register*. Retrieved from http://www.theregister.co.uk/2003/08/20/slammer_worm_crashed_ohio_nuke/

Queiroz, C., Mahmood, A., Hu, J., Tari, Z., & Yu, X. (2009, October). Building a SCADA security testbed. In *Proceedings of Network and System Security*, (pp. 357-364). IEEE.

Rinaldi, S. M., Peerenboom, J. P., & Kelly, T. K. (2001). Identifying, understanding, and analyzing critical infrastructure interdependencies. *Control Systems IEEE*. Retrieved from http://ieeexplore.ieee.org/lpdocs/epic03/wrapper.htm?arnumber=969131

Simmons, C., Shiva, S., Dasgupta, D., & Wu, Q. (2009). *AVOIDIT: A cyber attack taxonomy* (Technical Report CS-09-003). University of Memphis.

Smith, T. (2001). Hacker jailed for revenge sewage attacks. *The Register*. Retrieved from http://www.theregister.co.uk/2001/10/31/hacker_jailed_for_revenge_sewage/

Stouffer, K., Falco, J., & Scarfone, K. (2007). *Guide to industrial control systems (ICS) security special publication 800-82 second public draft.* National Institute of Standards and Technology.

Symantec. (2010). *Symantec intelligence quarterly report: October - December, 2010, targeted attacks on critical infrastructures.* Author.

Turk, R. (2005) *Cyber incidents involving control systems* (Technical Report INL/EXT-05-00671). Idaho National Laboratory.

Udassin, E. (2008). Control system attack vectors and examples: Field site and corporate network. In *Proc. S4 SCADA security conference.* SCADA.

US-CERT. (2008). *Control systems security program.* Retrieved from http://www.us-cert.gov/control_systems/index.html

USA-PA. (2001). *U.S.A. Patriot Act, 2001.* Retrieved from http://www.epic.org/privacy/terrorism/hr3162.html

Walsh, S. (2009). *Dallas security guard facing charges for installing malware on hospital computers.* Retrieved from http://www.technologytell.com/gadgets/48623/dallas-security-guard-facing-charges-for-installing-malware-on-hospital-com/

Zetter, K. (2010). Blockbuster worm aimed for infrastructure, but no proof Iran nukes were target. Wired. Retrieved from http://www.wired.com/threatlevel/2010/09/stuxnet/

Zetter, K. (2011). *How digital detectives deciphered stuxnet, the most menacing malware in history.* Retrieved from http://www.wired.com/threatlevel/2011/07/how-digital-detectives-decipheredstuxnet/all/1

Zhu, B., & Sastry, S. (2010, April). SCADA-specific intrusion detection/prevention systems: A survey and taxonomy. In *Proceedings of the 1st Workshop on Secure Control Systems (SCS).* SCS.

## KEY TERMS AND DEFINITIONS

**Critical Infrastructure:** Is the backbone of everyday lives in modern society. Critical infrastructures are defined as those systems, assets, or part thereof which are essential for the maintenance of vital societal functions, security and economic security, and the disruption or destruction of which would have a significant impact on the state/nation as a result of the failure to maintain those functions (European Commission, 2008).

**Cyber Attacks:** Cyber attacks use malicious code to alter computer code, logic or data, resulting in disruptive consequences that can compromise data and lead to cybercrimes, such as information and identity theft.

**Information Security:** Is designed to protect the confidentiality, integrity and availability of computer system data from those with malicious intentions.

**Malware:** Short for malicious software, is software designed specifically to damage or gain access without the knowledge of the owner.

**SCADA Security Testbed:** Is used to model real system and analyse the effects of attacks on them. The method enables detection of vulnerabilities within SCADA protocols in order to find out how easy it is to bypass security measures in such protocols or perform an attack on the SCADA network.

**Stuxnet:** Is considered to be the first malware that attacked critical infrastructures of foreign governments.

**Supervisory Control and Data Acquisition Systems (SCADA):** Refers to industrial control systems (ICS) that are employed to control and keep track of data. It is often used for critical infrastructures, e.g. electric power distribution, oil and natural gas distribution, water and waste-water treatment, transportation systems, etc. SCADA is a computer system used to gather and analyze real-time data.

# Chapter 2
# Raptor:
## Early Recognition and Elimination of Network Attacks

**Slawomir Grzonkowski**
*Symantec, Ireland*

**Laurentiu Vasiliu**
*Peracton Ltd., Ireland*

**Adamantios Koumpis**
*National University of Ireland Galway, Ireland*

## ABSTRACT

*The shift towards cyberspace created a very wide range of opportunities for various criminal activities, in both the real and the virtual world, such as identity theft, fraud, organized crime, and seriously organized crime, on an unprecedented scale. In this chapter, the authors propose a combination of integration activities for the best tools that help identify threats and security gaps for business and industrial users, for new analytical tools proposed to check if existing security features of the used networked structures are adequate and up-to-date and up-to-speed to address potential threat scenarios.*

## INTRODUCTION

The shift towards cyberspace created a very wide range of opportunities for various criminal activities, in both real and virtual world, such as identity theft, fraud, organized crime or seriously organized crime on an unprecedented scale. These activities are now easier than ever before and are much more efficient with the possibility of accessing the global scale from locations that are often beyond victim's jurisdictions. This is in particular critical for private and public organi-sations, as well as government agencies that are being exposed to new and pervasive threats that are hard to identify and contain. In the same time at every second, massive volumes of real time new data are being created worldwide. In order to process such data efficiently in an attempt to identify vulnerabilities and threats, robust analytics platforms capable of handling such volumes and complexities are required.

In this respect, this chapter presents a combination of integration activities for:

DOI: 10.4018/978-1-4666-6324-4.ch002

- Best of breed tools that helps identify threats and subsequently the relevant security gaps for business and industrial users that connect to new networks and thus exposing their systems to potential new entry points for cyber-attacks.
- New and innovative analytical tools proposed to check if existing security features of the networked structures used are adequate, up-to-date and up-to-speed to address potential threat scenarios.

The chapter concludes by testing and validating the chosen approach, developing conclusions and recommendations for best practice guidelines and policy actions to better protect European critical information infrastructure in five pilot case studies for

1. E-Government,
2. SMEs,
3. Financial industry,
4. Telecommunications, and
5. Power utility and energy providers.

It also introduces a standardized five level warning system proposal for detecting, managing and eliminating threats. This five level warning system proposal could be suitable for commercial exploitation to both EU and USA customers and aims to comply with the EU initiative on Critical Information Infrastructures Protection.

The proposed RAPTOR system architecture targets as end users IT financial/business networks, private, hybrid, public and government clouds, national electricity grids, industrial power facilities, financial organisations, telecom providers and strategic defence networks objectives.

The analytic tools covered are aimed to execute security checks in any network environment and able to go beyond computers line, down to PLCs (Programmable Logic Controllers) that are used for automation of electro-mechanical processes as well as critical mission servers used in Finance and eGoverment.

This may constitute a clear differentiation from other existing approaches and products currently offered in the market, and will help determine a much wider range of vulnerabilities and not only infect and disable the first line of computers but infect and disable a second line of servers and computers for industrial control with the ultimate goal to hamper and defect core applications in eGovernment, Finance and Power Industry.

RAPTOR tools are designed to scan the targeted networks within eGov/Finance/PowerGrid/Telecom organisations, will extract required data, process it, rank threats/vulnerabilities and then produce warnings, alerts and recommendations. RAPTOR aims to integrate best of breed tools that will help industrial users identify the relevant security features in case of linking their activities to new networks and thus exposing their systems to potential new entry points for cyber-attacks while also checking if existing security features of the already deployed networked structures are adequate, up-to-date and up-to-speed to address potential threat scenarios. As such, we employ the MAARS platform of Peracton Ltd. Ireland (www.peracton.com), where various data management approaches, analytics tools and methods can address the requirements of various threats, crimes, cyber-crimes, serious organized crimes and terrorism.

More specifically, the MAARS (Multi Attribute Analysis Ranking System) platform is a smart analytics recommendation and back-testing platform that allows ranking any entity that can be described by any number of attributes. This is done in a stable and consistent manner, based on any individual search criteria. The power of MAARS allows complex, high volume calculations to determine which results best suit a particular search profile with a simple click of a button and convenience of repeating this evaluation as often as they want. Further, results can be back-tested inside MAARS using historic data. MAARS has been matured and validated within Finance Industry, where it ranks any type of equities for any type of investment profile. However, the MAARS engine can be easily re-used to rank threats based on risk profiles desired by the user. As MAARS is domain independent, there is no need for development work, only just integration and some required adaptations. The delivery channel of RAPTOR is via the cloud.

## BACKGROUND AND CHALLENGES AHEAD

The last two decades (1992-2012) have been remarkable in the transition of our lives from the purely physical world to the cyberspace. Unfortunately this process did not only make our lives always easier. This shift towards cyberspace also created a very wide range of opportunities for various criminal activities, in both real and virtual world, such as identity theft, fraud, organized crime or seriously organized crime on an unprecedented scale. These activities are now easier than ever before and are much more efficient with the possibility of accessing the global scale from locations that are often beyond victim's jurisdictions. This is in particular critical for private and public organisations, as well as government agencies that are being exposed to new and pervasive threats that hard to identify and contain. A recent study conducted by EMC predicts a 44 fold growth of data from 2009 to 2020. We envisage that such a rapid growth of available and deployable data will create new opportunities, which could be exploited to address new security challenges and problems. Since more and more information sources and data system become available and online (every second, massive volumes of real time data are being created worldwide), it will open exponentially various entry points for exploiting valuable information. In order to process efficient such data to identify crime, robust analytics platforms capable of handling such volumes and complexities are required. In the same time, exploitable vulnerabilities sometimes originate from a handful of mostly known sources (e.g., memory safety); they remain there because of deficits in tools, languages and hardware that could address and prevent vulnerabilities at the design, implementation and execution stages. Often, making a small change in one of these stages can greatly ease the task in another..

Looking at United States, the Pentagon is expected to "dramatically increase its cyber-security staff to counter threats against US government computer networks" according to media reports (BBC, 2013). "The US Cyber Command, established three years ago, is expected to grow as much as fivefold over the next few years and this planned expansion comes amid a series of successful attacks, including a virus that wiped data from 30,000 computers at a Saudi oil firm. Cyber Command currently has 900 staff members, both military and civilian. Though the expansion comes at a time when the US military is balancing decreased budgets and a shift towards Asia and the Pacific, according to reports, the plan calls for creating three types of forces under the Cyber Command:

- Protecting computer systems that involve electrical grids and other kinds of infrastructure,
- Offensive operations overseas, as well as
- Protection of the defence department's internal systems."

It should be noted that RAPTOR is specifically addressing all three of the above areas while looking to go beyond their reach within European context. Further several of the RAPTOR service functionalities which are foreseen to be offered according to our approach are driven in the United States by the US Department of Defense (DoD) (www.defence.gov). This is not new as US DoD exhibits a long record of proactiveness also in matters related to both Internet uptake and adoption as well as Internet governance and control. More specifically, it is worth to mention the following entities all of which are controlled by DoD:

- USCYBERCOM coordinates and conducts activities related to operations and the defence of specified DoD information networks as well as full-spectrum military cyberspace operations in order to enable actions in all domains.
- NETCOM maintains and defends the Network Enterprise to enable information superiority and ensure the operating and generating forces freedom of access to the network in all phases of operations.
- The 1st Information Operations Command provides support to Army commands for planning and execution of Information Operations - also known as IO.
- The U.S. Intelligence and Security Command (INSCOM) conducts intelligence, security and information operations for military commanders and national decision makers.

However, it is important to mention that an essential element that distinguishes the nature of RAPTOR to the above activities of US DoD is that RAPTOR is solely for civic use and protection of information and data integrity, i.e. there is clearly no element of a dual technology within its encompassing technologies and, in this respect, it fully respects European and all EU member countries legislation on privacy of data and information. As such, it is aimed to be uptaken by public and private services of non-military purpose and can offer superb capabilities that may help all three types of addressed and potential users namely (1) public organisations, (2) private enterprises and (3) individuals to increase their levels of protection for all types of their networked information infrastructures.

Also, it is not by chance that another US organisation – DARPA (www.darpa.mil) - takes also a multipronged approach to securing military's cloud, according to which the core of the DoD plans to reduce its 1,500 data centers by means of implementing a secure, "coherent and consistent architecture across thousands of computing environments" (Roulo 2013). Interestingly the DARPA DSO (Defence Sciences Offices) states that on fundamental mathematics the objectives are "DSO's fundamental mathematics focus area includes the development of new theoretical mathematics with high potential for future applications. Current program themes include topological and geometric methods, extracting knowledge from data, [...].(DAPRA, 2013). Within RAPTOR, extracting knowledge of data via advanced mathematical algorithms (MAARS) is one of the targeted objectives.

US DOD has been addressing security on several fronts, one of which is its Mission-oriented Resilient Clouds (MRC) initiative, announced in 2011 (MRC, 2013), that aimed to develop resilient cloud services that would continue to operate and support military objectives despite being hit by a cyberattack. Another initiative launched one year earlier (2010) was CRASH (: Clean-Slate Design of Resilient, Adaptive, Secure Hosts) that aimed to pursue innovative research into the design of new computer systems that would be highly resistant to cyber-attack, while also exhibit the capability to adapt after a successful attack to continue rendering useful services, learn from previous attacks how to guard against and cope with future attacks, and can repair themselves after attacks have succeeded.

DARPA has issued several grants to develop solutions, including one to the Massachusetts Institute of Technology and a second to Johns Hopkins University, Purdue University and the University of Virginia. MRC system design and development will run through the end of 2014, with integration and testing ending by 2015.The program indicates a shift in the way DOD is approaching cloud security, Bryan Ward, cloud computing practice director at Serco, a military technical services provider, said in a Defense Systems report in 2011 (Edwards, 2011). Most traditional tools focus on the physical infrastructure. DARPA aims to explore several means to developing MRC, including providing redundant hosts, correlating attack information from across the ensemble, and providing for diversity across the network. In essence, it's taking the cloud's networking capabilities and turning it into a security tool. Each node would monitor its own applications as well as others, MRC program manager Howard Shrobe said in an AOL Defense report (Kenyon, 2013). One method is to have multiple nodes compute an answer, with any node deviating from the consensus answer considered suspect, he said. Shrobe described the model as similar to a public health system's immunization program, with reports of possible attacks collected and analyzed for trends and patterns such as an "epidemic" of a particular type of system failure, according to the article. At that point MRC's diagnostic and self-repair capabilities would kick in, isolating the problem to prevent multi-stage attacks and then automatically patching the vulnerability.

A second security method being studied is resource allocation to ensure maximum mission effectiveness. There may be several possible ways to achieve a mission's goal, each requiring a unique set of resources. By developing a trust model, the DOD can measure the probability of a corruption to those resources, causing the mission to fail, Shrobe said. To this, MRC is intended to be a companion program to the Clean-slate design of Resilient, Adaptive, Secure Hosts (CRASH, 2013) effort that focuses on limiting the vulnerabilities within each host.

A third approach the DOD is using to ensure secure network systems is taking it one step at a time, with multiple pilot cloud programs. "We're moving at a very deliberate pace," Carey stated as reported in (Roulo, 2013). "We have lots of [pilot programs] going on to evaluate these kinds of things and to make sure we understand . . . the pros, cons and risks of moving into the cloud space."

One research and development initiative in the DOD budget request for Fiscal Year 2013 is a cloud solution to support information sharing and to bridge the performance capability gaps in the Pacific Command. A second is for using cloud services to facilitate command and control operations, reported Safegov, a forum for IT providers and industry experts trusted and responsible cloud computing solutions for the public sector (Anderson, 2012).

## MAIN FOCUS OF THE CHAPTER

Therefore, RAPTOR proposes a combination of integration activities for:

- Best of breed tools that helps identify threats and subsequently the relevant security gaps for business and industrial users that connect to new networks and thus exposing their systems to potential new entry points for cyber-attack.
- New and innovative analytical tools that will be tested in order to check if existing security features of the used networked structures are adequate, up-to-date and up-to-speed to address potential threat scenarios.

Our approach concludes by testing and validating the chosen platform, developing conclusions and recommendations for best practice guidelines and policy actions to better protect European critical information infrastructure legacy systems in the form of a standardized five level warning system for detecting, managing and eliminating threats. This five level warning system which we call DETCON shown in the Figure below shall be the subject of commercial exploitation to both EU and USA customers and will comply with the EU initiative on Critical Information Infrastructures Protection. A further outcome that the consortium shall seek to leverage and offer on a commercial basis is the creation of a mechanism for the EU-wide certification concerning networked infrastructure security.

*Figure 1. DEtect Threat CONdition (DETCON) levels*

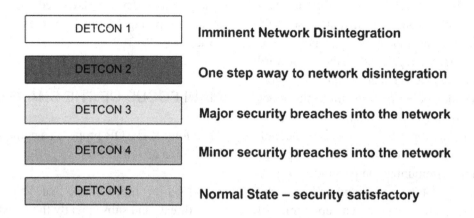

The high level platform and the taken approach as in Figure 2, are made of mature and state-of—the-art technologies (as MAARS/ONAR/SmartCloud etc) where various data management approach, analytics tools and methods can address the requirements of various threats, crimes, cyber-crimes, serious organized crimes and terrorism.

Figure 2 shows at high level how MAARS, ONAR and SmartCloud integrate in order to achieve a consolidated and innovative analytical tool. Within RAPTOR context, ONAR and SMARTcloud will provide the required cloud and deployment support and functionality for all case studies (e-Gov, Power Grid, Finance and Telecom). All inputs received from case studies will be processed and formatted so the data can be further analysed and classified into Threats / CyberThreats / Crime and Classified Threats. Within these categories, data will be further processed by MAARS so the top threats/medium/low level threats are determined and signalled in shape of reports to the stakeholders. Indicators are going to be reported as well as warnings and alerts. Finally countermeasures will be generated so the end user can start looking into solutions to overcome the threats and vulnerabilities discovered within their systems.

The RAPTOR platform is designed for end users IT financial/business networks, private, hybrid, public and government clouds, national electricity grids, industrial power facilities and strategic defence networks objectives.

This is in order to determine a much wider range of vulnerabilities such as STUXNET, DUQU and FLAME and variations of them that can penetrate networks and not only infect and disable the first line of computers but infect and disable a second line of servers and computers for industrial control with the ultimate goal to hamper and defect core applications in eGovernment, Finance and Power Industry as presented in Figure 2.

The core contributions are but are not limited to:

- End of day data/real time information harvesting and processing – tool.
- Advanced Data Analytics – tool.
- Stream processing-prototype.
- Threat Visualization-prototype.
- Threats ranking on multiple sources and back-testing-tool.
- Real time reporting and warning-too and methodology.
- Joint solutions commercialization.
- PR and marketing buzz.

*Figure 2. MAARS/ONAR/SmartCloud integration*

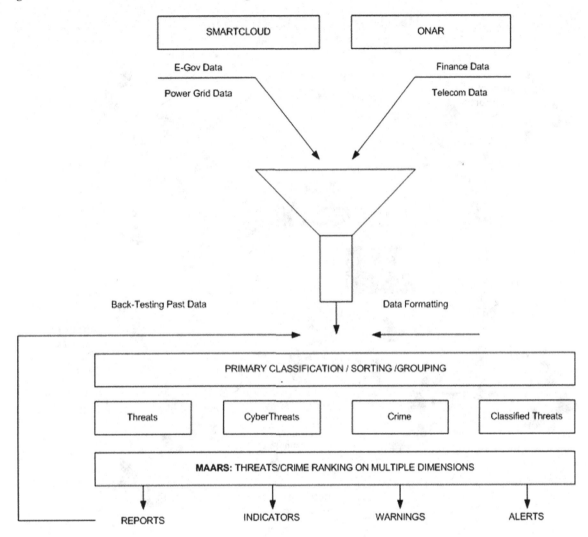

## FUTURE RESEARCH DIRECTIONS

In this section we discuss two basic scenarios which are followed by two explorations for pilot introduction of RAPTOR. More specifically:

### Scenario 1: Defence Supply Chain

Today business networks are a complex environment, made up of a hybrid set of applications services running many different implementation models. The defence supply chain adds an extra complexity, due to the use of private networks as well as the Internet.

The example in the diagram has a combination of business applications run on an internal network, business applications run on an IaaS platform and a set of SaaS applications (SalesForce.Com, Office365, LinkedIn, Twitter...). In addition there are both local users, and remote users – some will run BYOD technology.

You could potential add to this supply chain connectivity over private networks (not on the diagram) – a collaborative working environment supply chain partners. In the defence supply chain, this is quite common, and will likely increase in the UK Government with the advent of PSN and G-Cloud.

*Figure 3. Representation of 3 circle levels of penetration possible for hackers*

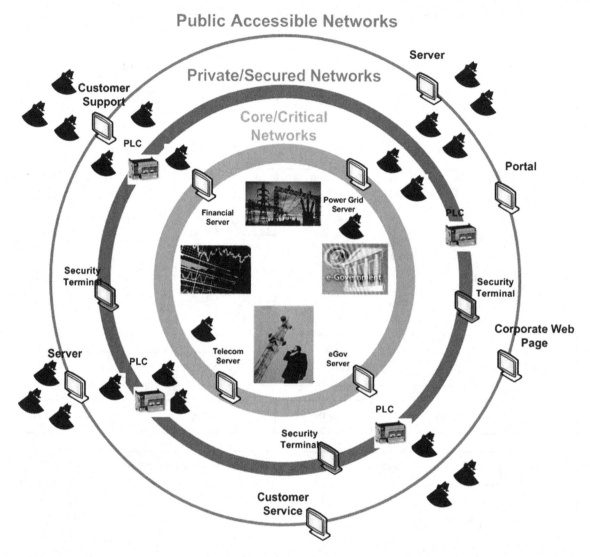

Mapping such an organisation in its own right is a complex scenario, monitoring the threats is even more complex. In some cases security information is available (e.g, internal network status), but for others the data is scarce (Saas). There are market developments to change this, lead by the cloud security alliance.

There are also other data feed of threat information that are likely to be available that can feed the model, for example from WARPS (Warning, Advice and Reporting Points) and information exchanges (IXs).

This scenario shall focus on how to obtain:

- Useful threat and risk information for the open cloud services, and feed them into the model.
- How to integrate feeds for WARPs and IXs.
- How to factor in private network connectivity.

*Figure 4. Raptor targeting vulnerabilities and attacks in a network*

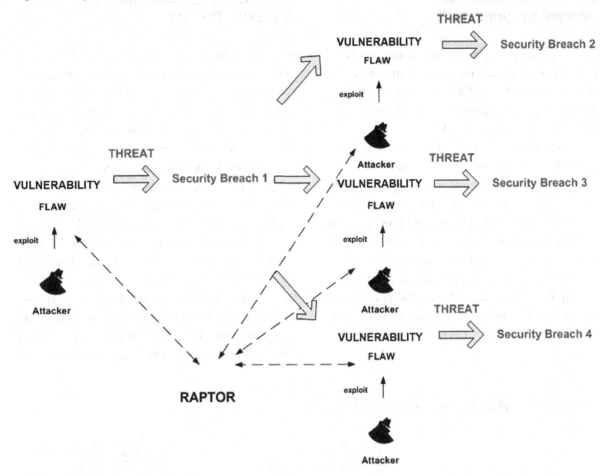

*Figure 5. Defence supply chain scenario pattern*

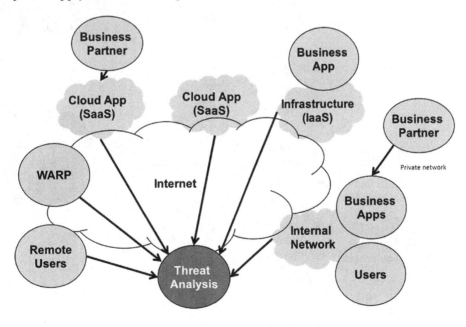

## Scenario 2: Industrial Control Systems (ICS)

Industrial Control Systems are becoming increasingly network connected – this brings with it a significant number of threats and vulnerabilities that need to be managed. The figure below identifies a few of these potential issues.

In some environments the arrows indicate network connections, in other cases these are air-gaps, and others specialist security equipment such as data-diodes to enforce one way data flows.

The scenario will demonstrate how the various threat assessment tools can be used in such networks to detect potential attacks and assess residual risk. A key challenge will be how to share the required data between these networks, without compromising the security of the networks – an area RAPTOR Partner DATERA are experts in.

## RAPTOR in E-Government Security Threats

Greece is facing nowadays various challenges. The government debt crisis, political instability, high unemployment rates and the need to control the illegal immigration flows, pose without doubt great security concerns to Greece. Nevertheless, there is also another national threat that is rapid, asymmetric, complicated and involves cyberspace. Cyber threats are a growing menace, spreading to all industry sectors that rely on Information and Communication Technology (ICT) systems.

Vasilis is a civil servant working for the Ministry of Transport in Athens, Greece. He is Head of a Unit dealing with the immatriculation of imported vehicles in Greece and the provision of the necessary documents for any exported vehicles. He works together with 75 colleagues in the central headquarters and supervises also the work of 32

*Figure 6. Industrial Control System scenario pattern*

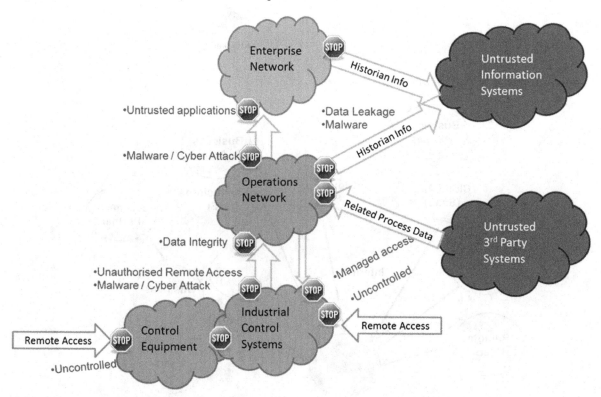

other employees who are distributed all over the country working either from Regional Authorities or from local branch offices of the Ministry of Transport called Divisions of Transport.

They manage on a daily basis about 3000 processes – many of them are in the processing pipeline for several weeks and only 6% is dealt and completed within one working day. The difficulty is that a great extent of what they do depends on metadata ignorant processes or (to a lesser degree) on scattered or closed metadata. It is only in the last years that effort has been given to open metadata at least to humans. This has as a result the increase of the complexity in the processing from their side and the difficulty to fully automate vehicle immatriculation processes.

Their department has been target of several attempts to get unauthorised access to data and, as expected, change records. Most of these attempts were performed by professional cybercrimers working on contract by criminal organisations who are dealing with the illegal import and export of vehicles to and from Greece. It has been estimated that only for 2009 (last year for which full records have been kept) about 1,2 billion Euros have been traded in this business, using Greece as a hub for moving vehicles (new or second hand) to other countries. In this respect securing of their digital assets as a critical infrastructure has emerged as a need and as a priority for this particular domain of the public sector.

Though they had been actively involved in the establishment of a 'Task Force on Digital Security' with the name DART (Digital Awareness & Responses to Threats), aiming to prevent and address risks associated with the new technologies and electronic communications, they recognise the need for an infrastructure that would allow them to continuously provide an independent risk and security audit multi-purpose platform that will analyze ICT systems threats in a remote manner, while also determine threats and risks, analyze results and perform advanced security analytics over the retrieved data.

Within this e-Government case study we aim to demonstrate the capabilities as well as the potential limitations or weaknesses of the RAPTOR platform regarding the resilience and assurance of a selected portfolio of e-government applications, services and procedures in Greece and for the aforementioned area, and to report relevant experiences from a set of real-world cases.

Of particular concern are the following three contexts which are of immediate utility to the specific case of the Ministry of Transport but also for a plethora of similar cases in the public sector: (1) Transition towards cloud-based solutions, (2) Migration of data repositories from local level to the cloud, and (3) offering mobile e-work solutions for public sector employees working off their office e.g. in case of telework or when being in a mission.

As security architecture is commonly though mistakenly developed separately from the Enterprise Architecture of an organisation, and tending to be used as an input and constraint on the latter, the requirements that will be captured for the profiling of the e-Gov pilot will be based on four dimensions: (1) Business needs of the particular public authority, (2) Regulations that govern the particular public authority, (3) Legal needs as these are specified by the ruling (national and European) legislation, and (4) practices and procedures with their Partners (i.e. other e-Gov authorities supervising or administering the one under consideration, citizens or businesses, any other 3rd parties, etc.).

Vulnerability assessment and penetration tests as well as behavior analysis will take place at at the particular organisation resource levels as well as for the individual user, while both role-based and policy-based access control are foreseen. Some hypothetical cases that should be subject of RAPTOR identification so that Vasilis and his colleagues will be assisted in their duties are the following:

- An insider uses privileged access to steal data: this is the case of an authorized user glean for use by any criminal organisation from within Greece or abroad that is interested to buy this information. According to this case, unexpected patterns of system use – or, same well also expected ones should be examined and studied to identify potential or real threats.

- **Malicious Software:** this is the case of an attacker delivering software updates that surreptitiously enable a back door in critical information systems. This case may not be subject of an instantaneous but span over a period of months same as with the Athens Affair in July 2005 where attackers uploaded components of software to Ericsson phone switches that, when complete, gave them backdoor access which was used to tap the cell phones of 100 officials and diplomats. While the perpetrators were never identified it was revealed that the Ericsson software was actually developed in Greece.

- **Hardware Backdoors:** Here we consider the case of the supply chain of network equipment that is subverted to allow the installation of remote command and control capability.

- **Insider Abuse:** This case is much closer to the routine faced in several organisations. According to it, an insider uses his knowledge of IT operations to subvert them to his own purposes.

For all the above mentioned types and many others which are not mentioned or even not identified yet, RAPTOR has to provide information similar to the defense readiness condition (DEFCON) that is a well-known alert posture used by the United States Armed Forces. The aim is that for each of the five different DETCON scale levels below, Vasilis should be capable of following a corresponding procedure that will aim to the elimination of the lowering of the risk e.g. that from DETCON 4 (blue) the condition of a particular system, service or organisational component in the Ministry of Transport will go down to DETCON 5 (green).

The interest from the Ministry of Transport point of view is to use the RAPTOR platform in order to guide and inform decisions for the change of the DETCON level from one to another – not always incrementally but also decrementally in case a threat has been eliminated or reduced.

To the best of our knowledge it is the first time that such a system will be introduced for a non-military context of use and in a country that after the Athens Affair (http://spectrum.ieee.org/telecom/security/the-athens-affair) has faced numerous cases of similar – though smaller scale – security breaches.

## RAPTOR for the World of SMEs: Detecting and Neutralising Threats for SMEs

SMEs are a favorite recipient of interest from the governments and the Commission – they are amongst others regarded as being at the forefront of the shift in the way jobs are created and economic value is added. Traditionally, and while such small, self-starting, service-driven companies would have been described as small- and medium-sized enterprises, or SMEs, but thanks to the Internet, the emergence of new business platforms and the increased openness of the global economy, these companies can enter markets with a minimum of bureaucracy and overhead. Add to that their unparalleled ability to respond promptly to changing market developments, and the lack of the institutional inertia and legacy relationships plaguing larger organizations, and one can see their transformative capabilities and their paradigm-changing potential.

Furthermore, today's technology makes it possible for small companies to gain the reach and traction of big companies at very low cost. Nothing has empowered and enabled small- antd medium-sized companies more than technology. However, nothing comes without the necessary cost:

- Security is usually very basic or even worse it is non-existent;
- They do not have money to upgrade it;
- They do not have money/time/mindset to hire specialists to audit their systems from the security point of view;
- They hire the cheapest cloud to host their website/systems as they don't have money to go for professional solutions directly;
- They have lack of in-house IT specialists - they tend to hack their own IT set-ups;
- Because they do all by themselves, many security features are left on default, that is a 'blessing' for hackers, malware etc.;
- Usually they have little back-up or none for the critical systems;
- Even in case they are aware of a loophole and the need to fix some things, they postpone security to address sales/clients/systems set-ups etc.

Hence many SMEs bet on the luck and on the fact that they are too small and no one will attack them. We take the case of Manuel, a Portuguese importer of iron railings for balconies from China, who also purchases various goods from several import companies in Atnwerpes, Belgium. Manuel employs four people in his business: his nephew, his cousin, his brother-in-law and his daughter. All five of them have only limited knowledge of computer use so in no case would someone consider them as power users. In case their Website crashes down, it may stay so for long till someone might see the problem. The IT operation of his business relies on external partners who are visiting him after a request. Manuel cares only about keeping his cots at the lowest level. For him security is not an issue at all. As long as your doorlock is safe, the rest is not making any sense.

With the proliferation of service architectures and more recently cloud computing, Manuel saw an once-in-a-lifetime opportunity for reducing severely his operational and maintenance costs: The cloud seems to him as to several other millions of people out there as a technology many SMEs should adopt because of the benefits of flexibility, pay-for-use and reduced hardware investment. Questions over its security might remain at a theoretical level only.

According to the Verizon Breach Report 2011 "It appeared that there were more data breaches in 2010, but the compromised data decreased due to the size of the compromised company's databases. This shows willingness in the cybercriminal underground to go after the smaller, easier targets that provide them with a smaller yet steady stream of compromised data" (Verizon, 2011).

It is for this reason that the Information Systems Security Association (ISSA-UK) creates a new security standard for small businesses, namely ISSA5173. Manuel's business is different from large organisations, not in security threats which are the same, but more in the way they operate and cope with them. SMEs don't need paper and labour-intensive controls that big companies like. So RAPTOR could provide them with the necessary tools and insight over the threats, so that with low costs they could also improve dramatically their security set-up.

Table 1 is a list of routine operations that Manuel does and how these shall be improved with the introduction of RAPTOR seamlessly to his daily routine.

## CONCLUSION

RAPTOR is soliciting the uptake and adoption of a highly innovative technology that is the result of a several years and multi-million Euros research carried out by the Coordinator in the area of security and resilience of large scale networked computing systems including both cloud computing

*Table 1. Improvements expected with the introduction of RAPTOR*

| Routine Operation | Currently (without RAPTOR): | After (with RAPTOR – What Does RAPTOR for This?) |
|---|---|---|
| Coping with potential insider attacks | Verizon's Intrusion Response Team investigated 500 intrusions in 4 years and could attribute 18% of the breaches to corrupt insiders. Of that 18%, about half arose from the IT staff itself… | RAPTOR oversees behaviour and seeks for anomalous or suspicious patterns |
| Lack of contingency | Manuel prides himself on being "nimble" and "responsive" though he achieves that speed by abandoning standardization, mature processes, and contingency planning. | RAPTOR automates the process by offering bedsides the collection and processing of the raw data also automated preparation of Business Continuity Plans, Disaster Recovery Plans, Intrusion Response Policy, as well as an up-to-date backup system from which you can actually restore, or off-site storage. Certainly if Manuel had the necessary budget for it, he would hire an expert to help him develop sound information assurance methodologies. However, and as he does not have much money to work with, he relies on RAPTOR's performance. |
| Poor configuration leading to compromise | Inexperienced or underfunded SMEs often install routers, switches, and other networking gear without involving anyone who understands the security ramifications of each device. Manuel's nephew, an amateur networking guy being just happy to get everything uccessfully sending data traffic back and forth. It doesn't occur to him that he should change the manufacturer's default username and password login credentials... | RAPTOR perform an automated vulnerability audit scan. As Manuel is unable to hire consultants, he probably can afford RAPTOR to make a one-time-per-day or per-week, automated scan of his entire corporate network… |
| Reckless use of hotel networks, kiosks and public Wi-Fi hot spots | Each time Manuel or any of his colleagues are off office working from hotel networks which are notoriously lousy with viruses, worms, spyware, and malware, and are often run with poor security practices overall, their company IT suffers. Public kiosks make also a convenient place for an attacker to leave a keylogger, just to see what falls into his net. Laptops that don't have up-to-date personal firewall software, anti-virus, and anti-spyware can get compromised on the road. Traditional defences can be rendered useless when the user literally carries the laptop around the gateway firewall, and connects from inside the corporate trusted zone. | RAPTOR sets and enforces a policy forbidding employees from turning off defences… |

infrastructures and large-scale distributed systems running on an ensemble of interconnected hosts acting in concert. Technology development has been financed and leveraged by both national and European agencies over a span of the last years and the deployment that we intend to conduct as part of the RAPTOR platform aspires to enable revolutionary advances in context-aware adaptive and resilient networked computing systems.

Networked information infrastructures both in the public and the private sector of the economies today act as vulnerability amplifiers, magnifying the reach and effect of any host vulnerability and allowing attacks to propagate rapidly within an enclave. Even in networks that are not directly connected to the public internet, any vector of attack is amplified hugely.

RAPTOR addresses a well identified need in the market that is propelled by three related driving forces:

1. The economics of large scale computation infrastructure (e.g. data-centers),

2. The ability to provide fungible computation on demand, and
3. The ability to centralize vast collections of data for common analytics.

Typically, there is a high degree of implicit trust between the computational nodes within a networked information infrastructure, which allows malware to propagate rapidly once it is within the enclave. Cloud computing infrastructures, in particular, tightly integrate large numbers of hosts using high speed interconnection fabrics that can serve to propagate attacks even more rapidly than conventional networked systems. Today's hosts, of course, are highly vulnerable, but even if the hosts within a cloud are reasonably secure, any residual vulnerability in the hosts will be amplified dramatically.

RAPTOR does not only address host vulnerabilities but also pursues clean-slate approaches to the design of networked computations and cloud-computing infrastructures.

The technologies we employ take a clean-slate approach to limiting the vulnerabilities within each host. More specifically, we seek to turn this around and use the network as a vulnerability damper and a source of resiliency for all different types of public and private networked information infrastructures. The goal is to provide resilient support to them through adaptation. Loss of individual hosts and tasks within the ensemble is allowable as long as effectiveness is preserved.

## DISCLAIMER

Work reported in this chapter has been conducted while Dr Slawomir Grzonkowski was working for DERI at the National University of Ireland, Galway, Ireland. Hence, the views expressed in this chapter are those of the authors and do not necessarily reflect those of the organisations they have been affiliated with in the past or are affiliated at the time of publication.

## REFERENCES

Anderson, J. (2012). *The department of defense needs an enterprise-wide approach to cloud.* Retrieved from http://safegov.org/2012/5/17/the-department-of-defense-needs-an-enterprise-wide-approach-to-cloud

BBC News US & Canada. (2013). *US cyber command in 'fivefold' staff expansion.* Retrieved from http://www.bbc.co.uk/news/world-us-canada-21235256

CRASH. (2013). *Clean-slate design of resilient, adaptive, secure hosts (CRASH) program.* Retrieved from http://www.darpa.mil/Our_Work/I2O/Programs/Clean-slate_design_of_Resilient_Adaptive_Secure_Hosts_(CRASH).aspx

DARPA. (2013). *Defense science office.* Retrieved from http://www.darpa.mil/Our_Work/DSO/Focus_Areas/Mathematics.aspx

Edwards, J. (2011). *DARPA to help shield cloud networks from cyberattack: Mission-oriented resilient clouds program would boost security and reliability.* Retrieved from http://defensesystems.com/articles/2011/08/08/tech-watch-darpa-cloud-security.aspx

Kenyon, H. (2013). *Cloud of iron: DARPA hardens cloud computing against cyber attack.* Retrieved from http://breakingdefense.com/2013/01/10/cloud-of-iron-darpa-hardens-cloud-computing-against-cyber-attac/

MRC. (2013). *Mission-oriented resilient clouds initiative.* Retrieved from http://www.darpa.mil/Our_Work/I2O/Programs/Mission-oriented_Resilient_Clouds_(MRC).aspx

Roulo, C. (2013). *DOD information technology evolves toward cloud computing.* Retrieved from http://www.defense.gov/news/newsarticle.aspx?id=118999

Verizon. (2013). *2011 data breach investigations report*. Retrieved from http://www.verizonenterprise.com/resources/reports/rp_data-breach-investigations-report-2011_en_xg.pdf

## KEY TERMS AND DEFINITIONS

**Analytical Tools:** IT-supported methods and practices used to quantify or estimate qualitative aspects of a decision-making process.

**Critical Information Infrastructure Legacy Systems:** Any type of corporate or organisational system e.g. ERPs, business software, accounting, billing or reservation systems that are considered as mission-critical for the owner.

**Cyberattacks:** Any centrally coordinated or loosely/unplanned malicious actions aiming to reduce an organisation's capabilities and operational capacities to protect its own information infrastructures (both hardware and software as well as data).

**Cyberthreats:** All potential sources of threats that may theoretically or practically cause problems to an organisation's functioning.

**Detection of Vulnerabilities:** Identification of all types of possible or potential threats or loopholes to an organisation's or a system's infrastructure. These may also include hypothetical ones which may appear if certain conditions are satisfied.

**Security for Networked Infrastructures:** The entire spectrum of professional methods, practices and business processes used to support key aspects of an organisation's secure operation.

# Chapter 3
# Online Violence:
## Listening to Children's Online Experiences

**Teresa Sofia Pereira Dias de Castro**
*University of Minho, Portugal*

**António José Osório**
*University of Minho, Portugal*

## ABSTRACT

*The Internet imprints a great complexity to new and old risks as threats become more available in children's lives. Criminals have greater access to the victims and Internet crimes are favoured by ambiguities in the law. This chapter presents preliminary data from an on-going doctoral investigation about the upsetting phenomenon of violence perpetrated by, with, and among school-aged children using online services and devices. To better understand the subjectivity, delicacy, and complexity of matters and meanings that participants bring to their online experiences, the authors follow a qualitative approach, based on a structured and interpretive analysis. They work with a group of children aged between 6 and 15 years old. With this chapter, the authors intend to contribute to a greater understanding and reflection about this complex problem and its impact in order to increase awareness about how children behave online and in what way it may influence their well-being.*

## INTRODUCTION

This chapter presents preliminary data from an on-going doctoral investigation about the worrying and emergent phenomenon of violence perpetrated by, with and among school-aged children, using online services and devices. For this text we selected and will briefly describe some online experiences from children's point of view.

In Portuguese context, the General Attorney (http://cibercrime.pgr.pt/) advocates the need to

broaden the knowledge and raise awareness of the phenomenon once it exploits the vulnerabilities of young people and expose them to new forms of practicing old criminal activities (such as grooming, harmful content, pornography, sexual exploitation, sexual abuse) and also new kinds of criminal activity. Therefore, the General Attorney launched an Action Plan on Crimes against Children on the Internet to deal more effectively with the criminal phenomena, which involves using the information and communication technologies to

DOI: 10.4018/978-1-4666-6324-4.ch003

victimize children. Reiterating the previous UNICEF's global agenda for children's rights in the digital age pinpoints that "[r]esearch is needed to discover which risk factors operate in particular cultural or national contexts and what protective factors exist in children's environments that can be strengthened" (Livingstone & Bulger, 2013, p. 23).

By 'online violence' we mean the use of online digital services and devices to participate in activities that may result in child's own physical, psychological, emotional harm or in causing harm to other people. In the end, with this doctoral research we aim to understand: i) the current online threats that are perceived by children as risks; ii) which typified risky behaviours online are not recognised as risks (and why) by children; iii) how children engage and deal with online negative and risky online experiences.

This text is organized in six sections including this "Introduction". The second section presents a short review of the state of the art on the discussion surrounding how risk is present in children's online lives; the difference between risk and harm; and online violence as an emergent and worrying health problem. The third section describes our methodological approach. The fourth section presents a preliminary, descriptive and interpretive analysis of data collected. In the fifth section we make some brief and final remarks about the provisional findings. Finally, in the sixth section we pinpoint some future research directions.

## WHEN RISK LIVES IN THE CHILD'S POCKET

In a world saturated with attractive possibilities enabled by the online digital technologies, and where time is money, we don't get all that surprised when we find parents using digital devices to entertain their children, while they keep on distracted or worried with their busy lives. We often observe this picture, in gatherings with couples, in restaurants or malls. Though imagined, designed

and built by adults, technologies, that favour the interaction and communication between people, won the attention of children and young people through the last decades, taking a central role in their daily life (Huesmann, 2007).

Interesting is that society seems to accept that these digital devices babysit children but then get all surprised and suspicious when young people choose the computer instead of having fun outdoors, or when they use the online devices to: i) talk with strangers; ii) learn about sex; iii) involve in sexual experiments; iv) engage in self-harm practices or unhealthy eating behaviours[1]; or v) harass others. The so-called 'digital natives' or 'net generation' are growing in a wired rapidly changing, complex and ambiguous world and their digital trends reinforce the generation gap between adults and children. Therefore, despite entitling themselves experts in digital matters (Ponte & Cardoso, 2008), we are not all that sure they are using the online digital opportunities wisely. But, certainly they are using them differently.

Quite often we hear or read about national and international tragic news that urge us to reflect on how adults and children behave online. There are cases where parents themselves contribute for an unwanted precocious and unauthorized digital footprint that may endanger children, when they innocently publish online pictures of their sons and daughters, contributing for the possibility of an unauthorized distribution and misuse. And, sometimes, children may get themselves or others in real trouble because they i) lack maturity; ii) lack life experience; iii) lack internet literacy; iv) like to push boundaries; v) challenge their limits; vi) don't think about the consequences; vii) need to fit in and be accepted and respected by their peers.

Thereby, as online digital technologies evolve and become more sophisticated, interactive and mobile, a greater amount of exposure to risk in the network is favoured: i) the Internet is faster and cheaper enabling people to share and distribute larger files (pictures, video and audio); ii) children arc creative and actively producing, distributing and consuming contents online; iii) an increasing number of users and contents (King, Walpole, & Lamon, 2007) are available and accessible on the web; iv) children are accessing the Internet at increasingly younger ages; v) mobile technologies and Internet services are promoting higher levels of online exposure (Donnerstein, 2012) to new and renewed dangers; vi) the actual technological environment hinders parental supervision and monitoring (adults take time to catch up with young people's online trends; they are not aware of the risks; they have low media literacy; they lack of time and/or resources; they experience difficulties in monitoring situations when children use more than one device, or use them privately).

Researching children, young people and how they use online digital technologies implies to consider some facts. First of all, computers, smartphones or tablets have a huge influence in youngsters' daily lives and their interpersonal interactions, social connections, self-expression, and school achievements. Secondly, the way technology is changing and going mobile promotes a more ubiquitous, more portable, unmonitored and private use of online services and devices. Thirdly, children and youth use the Internet to expand their social circle, and associated to this we have to consider that they will not talk only with real world friends, they will meet new friends and acquaintances online, and also push boundaries and take risks. Lastly, we also have to remember that no longer makes sense distinguish between offline and online world, they are merged (Unicef, 2011), so Internet is the real world with real (good and bad) people (Whitby, 2011). Thereby, online digital technologies (devices, platforms and services) are not only altering and producing new routines in a wired and connected society, they are also shifting the role and status of childhood in contemporary western societies, challenging principles and rights previously regarded as obvious and guaranteed.

Revisiting the information and communication technologies in a diachronic perspective, we realize that to each and every new technology, society responded with resistance, scepticism, anxiety and moral panic, afterwards people got informed and familiarised with them, included them in their daily routines, and after a while did not realize life without them. Though imagined, designed and built by adults, technologies, that favour the interaction and communication between people, won the attention of children and young people through the last decades, taking a central role in their daily life (Huesmann, 2007). According to Giedd (2012), the way young people learn, play and interact has changed more over the last 15 years than in the previous 570, since Gutenberg. Buijzen and Valkenburg (2003) concluded that from the age of 10 children are increasingly interested in developing relationships, creating a greater concern with intimacy and personal identity.

Also the transition from the 'street culture' to the 'bedroom culture' (Bovill & Livingstone, 2001) combined with the spread of mobile and digital devices *per capita* contributed to the fading of family time that old media once promoted. Reiterating these facts, the EU KIDS ONLINE survey data reveals that Portuguese children are the ones who have more personal laptops and access to the Internet from the bedroom (Ponte, 2012). In this scenario, not only youngsters' access to the Internet becomes more autonomous and private far away from the surveillance of parents (Jorge, 2012), but also children's experiences of risk become a more isolated and secret experience.

This brings new concerns, fears and anxieties to parents, caregivers, teachers, educators, and society. While the worries of adults in the past were focused on the insecurity of the streets and bad companies, with a child being victim of a crime or having access to drugs, nowadays we have to add those that became more sophisticated or arise with Internet, such as unwanted contacts with strangers, harmful contents and threats caused by others (Ponte, 2012). According to Livingstone and Haddon (2009), sexual predators are among the most feared risks.

The Internet imprints a great complexity to new and old risks, as dangers become more available and accessible to children and young people. Not only criminals have greater access to the victims (anyone, anytime, anyplace), but also the Internet crimes are favoured by ambiguities of law in matters of geographical space. Internet child protection became more difficult and compromised since, even at home, children are not totally safe and protected from threats and harm. Against this backdrop, protecting children from online threats and dangers is an increasingly complex task for parents, caregivers, teachers, educators and society.

## Risk and Harm

The definition of risk is not a *stricto sensu* definition as it may vary across countries and cultures, or even among adults and children. For instance, while adults regard meeting people online as a risk, children and young people often see it as an opportunity to expand their social circle (Livingstone & Haddon, 2009).

About this matter the EU KIDS ONLINE project makes a significant contribution by making the distinction between risk and harm and classifying the possible online risks that one can encounter using the online digital technologies (four categories of online risks: aggressive, sexual, values and commercial). According to evidence gathered by this European project, more use is related with more exposure to positive and negative online experiences. And for that matter, reducing risk would also reduce opportunities.

Reiterating this, the exposure to risk is an opportunity to learn to cope and build resilience[2] (Ringrose, Gill, Livingstone, & Harvey, 2012) and reduce harm (Duerager & Livingstone, 2012). Reduce risk-taking and increase protective measures would open up space for additionally

increasing vulnerability (Ringrose et al., 2012). Children can only learn how to be resilient if we reduce the damage without reducing the risks and opportunities (Ringrose et al., 2012). Risky behaviours when using the online digital technologies can be considered harmful when they have negative social, academic, physical, emotional, psychological, and health impacts in the young user. And with regard to children, many people see as intolerable any chance of risk. But excessive protection actions may also increase the vulnerability of children when dealing with risks on the Internet, denying them opportunities to develop important skills to help them identify, avoid and protect themselves from those risks (Byron, 2008). To get to the nub of the problem, according to Lüders, Brandtzæg and Dunkels (2009), we have to: i) focus on the causes; ii) understand what triggers risky behaviours (for the victim and the aggressor); iii) identify the triggers, motivations and interests of children and young people on the Internet. Keeping risky behaviours online does not necessarily imply harmful and distressing outcomes for children.

On the other hand, sometimes children and young people put themselves at risk on the Internet driven by i) risk-taking behaviour, ii) the search for new experiences and emotions, iii) the desire to move away from parental influence and get peer influence (Giedd, 2012). Resilient users are more experienced, empowered and skilled consumers, more capable of evaluating and think critically about their behaviour online and how to deal with possible threats (Jorge, 2012) because they are exposed to different life experiences.

According to EU KIDS ONLINE, there are four categories of online risks (aggressive, sexual, values, commercial) where children can: i) receive passively unwanted and risky content (e.g. violence, pornography, racism, hate, marketing); ii) be targeted and participate in stranger initiated activity (e.g. harassment, stalking, grooming, meeting strangers, sexual predators, ideological persuasion, misuse or personal information); or

*Table 1. EU KIDS ONLINE Classification of online risks (Livingstone, Haddon, Görzig & Ólafsson, 2011)*

| | Content<br>Child as Receiver<br>(of Mass Productions) | Contact<br>Child as Participant<br>(Adult-Initiated Activity) | Conduct<br>Child as Actor<br>(Perpetrator/Victim) |
|---|---|---|---|
| Aggressive | Violent/gory content. | Harassment, stalking. | Bullying, hostile peer activity. |
| Sexual | Pornographic content. | 'Grooming', sexual abuse on meeting strangers. | Sexual harassment, 'sexting'. |
| Values | Racist/hateful content. | Ideological persuasion. | Potentially harmful user-generated content. |
| Commercial | Embedded marketing. | Personal data misuse. | Gambling, copyright infringement. |

iii) have an active role as perpetrators in risky activities (e.g. bullying, hostile to peers, sexual harassment, sexting, produce harmful content, gambling, infringe copyright).

We can not totally agree with Huesmann (2007) when the author argues that electronic media did not introduce new global psychological threats to children and young people. However, we agree and support Huesmann when he says that these tools hinder the protection of children and young people against the digital threats to the extent that many more are exposed to hazards that only some might have experienced before (2007).

In the online digital context, attacks may occur and young people can be criminals or victims in new places that break the boundaries of family, community, neighbourhood, which to some extent protected the youngsters in the past against bad companies and bad neighbourhoods. Nowadays, adults have to worry about dangers brought into the house and up to the intimacy of the bedroom. Online digital technologies simplified the entry of outsiders (ill-formed people, aggressors, stalkers, predators and criminals) in the intimacy and privacy of children (even when they are at home with parents around) (Muir, 2005).

Confronted with this challenge, our wiser response should not be to panic and keep children 'indoors', because the virtual 'streets' are dangerous. The virtual venues also provide wonderful and enriched experiences that help children and young people to become savvy, resilient and responsible users. The recognition of threats in cyberspace is an important first step in building a plan for action based on constructive solutions based in productive learning experiences (Berson, Berson & Ferron, 2002).

Thus, taking into account that the online experiences may influence the emotional well-being and safety (Berson, 2000) of children and young people and their families (Huesmann, 2007; Kane & Portin, 2008), we have to i) understand the dangers of these virtual 'streets', 'neighbourhoods' and 'friends', ii) help children and young people understand how risky behaviours can endanger themselves and why they should avoid them, iii) stimulate children and young people to think critically and take informed decisions; iv) promote children and young people to behave respectfully when online; v) be actively involved in children's internet use.

## Online Violence: An Emerging Health Problem

Aggression has always occurred in children's interactions. With the advent of online digital technologies violence migrated to the digital environment, and gained exquisite contours that, in many cases, offer more protection to the offender than to the victim.

Online violence is a novel (Mura, Topcu, Erdur-Baker, & Diamantini, 2011) social phenomenon (Ringrose et al., 2012), but several years ago experts warn for the likelihood that this is a growing and concerning public health problem (Agatston, Kowalski, & Limber, 2007; Finkelhor, Mitchell, & Wolack, 2000; Kane & Portin, 2008; Ybarra, 2004) that rapidly evolves according the technological advancements (Mura et al., 2011), the sophistication of devices (Pessoa, Matos, Amado, & Jäger, 2011), affecting children "across different age groups regardless of their cultural background" (Mura et al., 2011, p. 3805).

On the one hand, few doubt that digital technologies have brought very positive and beneficial online opportunities for children and young people in education, communication, socialization, information and entertainment. However, we cannot ignore or downplay the darker side of online services and devices and how they influence children's and young people's social development and interactions, as well as their physical and emotional development and well-being.

Having a greater number of children and young people online inevitably raises the risk of children using digital technologies for less healthy purposes, acting as offenders, aggressors, stalkers, predators and/or as victims (Hinduja & Patchin, 2011). The literature suggests that although the prevalence rate of electronic aggression is relatively low, the number of teenage victims has been growing (David-Ferdon & Hertz, 2007; David-Ferdon & Hertz, 2009; Hertz & David-Ferdon, 2008, 2011).

Consequently, this is an issue that increasingly concerns parents, caregivers, children, educators, and society in general. The violence that occurs among children and young people with the support of online digital technologies at a "click of a button" (Ackers, 2012, p. 155) is a vast new area of research, still sparsely documented (David-Ferdon & Hertz, 2007; Gross, 2004; Kowalski & Limber, 2007; Law, Shapka, Hymel, Olson, & Waterhouse, 2012; Wolak, Mitchell, & Finkelhor, 2007; Worthen, 2007; Ybarra, 2004; Ybarra & Mitchell, 2004). Research studies show a diversity of concepts and definitions (Wolak et al., 2007)

around the phenomena of violence mediated by online digital technologies that hinder the immense work of the researcher. Because this is a relatively recent phenomenon, many researchers still resort to literature that exists on traditional bullying and/or school violence (Ybarra & Mitchell, 2004), as well as studies about television.

However, others advocate that, despite being a recent phenomenon, it has its own characteristics, which we must identify in light of its specificity. Different media have different impacts on children and youth. Digital technologies appeal to online disinhibition (Donnerstein, 2012) and a richer interaction than media previously studied, bringing profound changes with regard to the impact of potential risks (Donnerstein, 2012) as well as for mental development, psychological and relational children and youth (Byron, 2008).

Clearly, online digital technologies bring new and complex challenges to adults about children's online social behaving, connections and interactions. And though most of teens online social interactions are pleasurable, experts suggest that a significant minority of young people engage in negative interactions, either as aggressor, victim, or both (Werner, Bumpus, & Rock, 2010).

Away from adult supervision young people do and say things they would not normally do or say in face-to-face context (Muir, 2005). The possibility of anonymity seems to promote aggressive and inappropriate behaviours (Postmes & Spears, 1998; Postmes, Spears, & Lea, 1998). Probably many of these conflicts result from misunderstandings, since many of the non-verbal signals - look, breathing patterns, body posture, touch, smell, and voice fluctuations - are excluded from a large part of the interactions conveyed by online digital technologies. The absence of non-verbal signals, according to some authors, can be a facilitator for the occurrence of online aggression (Byron, 2008; Kowalski & Limber, 2007). Since the aggressor does not witness the suffering, it looks like he doesn't feel empathy for the sufferer.

The truth is that through online digital technologies each can show their best and worst. The Internet offers many temptations that test children's and young people's empathy, and ethical and moral code. Children are venturous creative and active participants on the Internet. However, that same agency may leave them vulnerable online, at risk of becoming aggressors (Berson, 2000) and/or the victims. Favoured by a relative degree of anonymity online, the offenders use these tools with a certain freedom to harass the victims (Muir, 2005) and expose children and young people to risk and harm.

We have covered the number of aspects showing the relevance and the need to deeply research complex and challenging issues that arise from new online phenomena, which require clear understanding for children, adults and society.

## SOME CONSIDERATIONS ABOUT THE METHODOLOGY

We will briefly describe the methodology, the fieldwork and the participants involved in the research.

Considering children and young people as social creators capable to reflect about their own experiences, we planned and combined different techniques, strategies and dynamics in order to: i) observe everyday online experiences; ii) recreate everyday online experiences; iii) promote the debate and stimulate critical thinking and self-awareness; iv) disclose online (in)experiences; v) reflect on emotions and behaviours; vi) stimulate empathy; vii) promote healthy and safe online behaviours. In weekly meetings with each group, it was our aim to respect the specificities of each group and create a secure and reliable environment where everyone can openly express their opinions and share their digital experiences.

Research with children and about children represents a complex challenge for the researcher because there's always the adult and the children's

interpretation of meanings and values (Soares, 2006). The difficulty of seeing through the children's lens sometimes poses difficulties to the researcher and this is the reason why so many studies often neglect children's point of view (Livingstone & Bober, 2003). This is a research with a 'child-centred' (Livingstone & Bober, 2003) approach, meaning that we recognise children's and young people's expertise, perceptions and experience, as active creators of their social contexts willing to help us understand the social phenomenon we are studying (France, Bendelow, & Williams, 2000). Our methodological design combines strategies and techniques to gather and organize field information that privilege the voice, and the point of view of children.

There's a real generational, cultural and social gap between the researcher and the children involved in this study, well noticed in the rites and slang used and Internet habits and behaviours. Aware of this gap and aiming to bond and build trusty relationships, we favour a humble, honest and transparent environment since day one in order to stimulate the sharing. Without tricks or half-truths we explained to children our role and work as a researcher as well as i) what we want from them; ii) how data will be used; iii) what is the purpose of an informed consent and how it protects their rights of confidentiality and privacy; and iv) what happens to the recordings made during the activities.

Throughout the sessions we realized that children's timing is different from the researcher's timing. So, it is important to struggle against data anxiety, and make activities embracing and enjoyable moments for everyone. When working with children, despite how well prepared the activities are, sometimes there are unpredictable events that request an alternative plan; or delicate circumstances and issues that emerge and one must be flexible, creative, non-judgemental nor condescending to deal with challenging opinions or unexpected behaviours.

*Table 2. Number and age of the participants enrolled in the research, distributed per group*

| Group 1: 'Escolhas' - Braga | | | Group 2: 'Escolhas' - Porto | | | Group 3: Leisure and activity centre - Braga | | | Group 4: Leisure and activity centre - Braga | | |
|---|---|---|---|---|---|---|---|---|---|---|---|
| Ages | Boys | Girls | Ages | Boys | Girls | Ages | Boys | Girls | Ages | Boys | Girls |
| 6-10 | 1 | 8 | 10-15 | 3 | 6 | 10-13 | 3 | 10 | 10-12 | 1 | 8 |
| Total: 9 | | | Total: 9 | | | Total: 13 | | | Total: 9 | | |
| Total of participants | | | 40 | | | | | | | | |

*Table 3. Testimonials*

| Classifying and Grouping Data by Themes | Extract (Our Translation) and Participant Identification |
|---|---|
| Meeting strangers online<br>*We've noticed that among children, online stranger dangers are internalised.*<br>*They internalised strangers' advances on the Internet (if adults) as potential paedophiles, rapists or kidnappers. According to them, strangers are usually much older than them, and male.*<br>*Interestingly, two girls report, that they have experienced receiving requests (to chat, friendship request) from a female stranger.*<br>*They externalise those internalised messages (possibly instilled by parents) by lying about personal information, deleting, blocking or reporting the threatening contact.*<br>*The risk here is that these are mechanical and empty answers that can produce positive short-term and preventive results. But little or no contribute is expected in a long-term digital citizenship itinerary.* | *Example 1:*<br>"I was there [on Facebook] and a guy sends me the thing [friendship request]. It seemed to me I had seen his picture, so I accepted. After all, he was a man in his late forties but seemed a child when talking to me, and so he asked: 'Who are you?' And he started talking to me. When I went to see his pictures, he was pot-bellied, had no teeth, and he was talking with a child... 'What school do you attend?', 'How old are you?'. I eliminated him."<br>(I., 12 yo, G, G2)<br>*Example 2:*<br>"Many kidnappings happen because of that, because they think they are meeting one person, and it's another person after all."<br>(I., 12 yo, G, G2)<br>*Example 3:*<br>[about contacts from strangers] "(…) adults pretending to be children (....) who want to do harm to children."<br>(I., 11 yo, G, G4)<br>*Example 4:*<br>"It happened to me. A girl impersonating a boy. (...) I deleted her immediately."<br>(T., 13 yo, G, G2)<br>*Example 5:*<br>*[a dialogue with the girls]*<br>*I: "(...) there's this woman who is always sending friend requests to S. [on the Facebook]"*<br>*S: (...) She has nude photos... on the bed... showing her panties and ass.(...) She looks like a hooker."*<br>(I., 12 yo, G, G2) and (S., 11 yo, G, G2)<br>*Example 6:*<br>"To friends I know I tell the truth (...) when they [strangers] ask 'what school are you in?' I always answer the wrong school (...) the wrong age (...) never give out my real information."<br>(T., 13 yo, G, G2) |

*continued on the following page*

## Implementing the Research in the Field

We submitted a research proposal to the Portuguese nationwide government program 'Escolhas' [3]('Choices' http://www.programaescolhas.pt/) with a description of the research goals and the activities to carry out with the children. We attended some meetings with the national and local coordinators, and in 2013 we got the research proposal approval. In September we visited the host institutions (one in Porto and one in Braga) and attended to meetings with local representatives in order to get to know the professionals and prepare the fieldwork.

A second research proposal was also submitted to several school parents associations in Braga. One school parents association expressed interest in the research and after a meeting with the director we began working in the fieldwork few days later, in an activity centre, inside the school.

We are currently (2013-2014) collecting data in the field and working with 4 groups of 39 children (Braga and Porto). Summarizing, two groups of children come from institutions of the 'Escolhas' ('Choices') program, and two other groups attend the leisure and activity centre managed by a parents association in Braga. As mentioned before, the children involved in the research are aged between 6 and 15.

*Table 3. Continued*

| Classifying and Grouping Data by Themes | Extract (Our Translation) and Participant Identification |
|---|---|
| Pornographic contents<br>*Sometimes children search for pornographic contents out of curiosity or for fun, but there are also cases in which this type of content pop-up as advertisements in websites that children visit or sometimes they appear out of the blue in seemingly innocuous virtual games. Other times they pop up the subject to test us and see adult's reaction.*<br>*They react to the subject with expressions like 'How disgusting' or laughs and a lot of excitement and curiosity and, sometimes, they even place us their doubts and questions*<br>*It is important to note that the participants that come from median/high household income reveal a greater ignorance, innocence and inexperience about the subject.*<br>*On the other hand, the participants that come from low household income (in particular, group 2, 'Escolhas' - Porto), although they belong to the same age group, they prove to be more sexually savvy (e.g., information, and how they speak about it, the use of bad words and pornographic language).*<br>*In any way this 'expertise' is suitable or appropriate to their age.*<br>*In the meetings they give us implied information that helps us draw a bigger picture.*<br>*Getting the pieces of the puzzle together, we would venture to say that this expertise is the result of a close contact with abusive experiences. In the meetings they confide us with abusive (sexual and domestic violence) stories involving people that also live in the neighbourhood.*<br>*During our stay, the director of the association, shared with us cases of abuse, violence, crime, and neglect involving also the families of the participants (e.g. domestic violence, negligence, suicide attempt, drug use and trafficking).* | *Example 1:*<br>"[someone] told me to write 'xxx' and I did it, but I didn't know what it was, I was younger, so I wrote 'xxx' and it appeared to me and I did not know what it was." (A., 10 yo, G, G3)<br>"How did you feel when you saw that?" [Researcher]<br>"GOOoooooooooD" (H. 11, yo, B, G3)<br>"I dunno, I was paralyzed, nor knew what it was" (A., 10 yo, G, G3)<br>[Laughs]<br>"I never saw it!" (H., 11yo, B, G3)<br>[Laughs]<br>*Example 2:*<br>"Once we were playing a game called Akinator, who guessed what we were thinking." (A.,10 yo, G, G3)<br>"What was the name of the game?" [Researcher]<br>"Akinator.... uh uh... he knows what you're thinking. A-KI-NA-TOR. And we think a TV character, or a singer or whatever and he guesses... and he makes us questions and guess, and then, once I was loading the luck and in the end he asked me this: a celebrity, man, known as porn actor [laughs] then I just put on the internet: I want to see the picture! Then, I clicked in images and he appeared all naked! [Laughs] but he had those tape covering it [the genitals]... not to see. [Laughs]" (A.,10 yo, G, G3)<br>*Example 2:*<br>[Extract taken from field notes]<br>After one of the sessions, before we left, J. (10 yo, G, G1) asked us 'what is xxx?'<br>We replied: 'is a letter, which in this case is repeated three times.'<br>J. insists: 'what happens if I write xxx on the Internet?'.<br>We retorted: 'why would you write that?'.<br>J. and F. (10 yo, G, G1) looked at each other.<br>Then, I. (10 yo, G, G1) says: 'I'm gonna write it to see what pops up'.<br>J. adds: 'my uncle wrote xxx in my cousin's tablet'<br>We asked: 'and then, what happened?'<br>J replied: 'I don't know, because the Internet was down, and that's why I wanted to know.'<br>It was evident that the three girls were accomplices in the situation.<br>I. wrote in the browser 'xxx'. A pre-visualization of a pornographic video appeared and I. says: 'how disgusting' and she closes the browser. The three laughed about it.<br>(J., 10 yo, G, G1); (F., 10 yo, G, G1); (I., 10 yo, G, G1) |
| Sexting<br>*In one meeting the participants had to examine and discuss about given situations. The activity was entitled 'what would you do?' The given situation was: 'A boy sends you a text asking you to send him a sexy picture of you'. What would you do?*<br>*The oldest girls dominated the conversation, reporting someone else's experience. The stories were told in the third person about bad experiences that happened with close friends or classmates.*<br>*During adolescence there's a growing interest for sex.*<br>*And with the help of online digital technologies, the way young people express themselves sexually, relate romantically, or exploit sexuality reached a new level.* | *Example 1:*<br>[A girl talks about a sexting episode that happened with a close friend]<br>"He asked her to send a photo of her in bra and panties, and she stood like that [she did the pose for us] on my bed. I asked her: 'Are you sure you want me to take this picture?' (...) And I took the photo. [then, she asked her friend] 'Is this Okay?' (...) [the friend answered]: 'It does not favour my tits'.<br>[The girl finally sends the picture to the boy mobile phone...]<br>[T. reports what happens next between her girl friend and the boy] [Boy]'I wanted a picture of you, dressed, not in bra and panties. You are perverse!'<br>[Girl] 'Please erase the pictures.'<br>[The boy sends another message and T. opens it] 'Uhhh. Disgusting! It was his 'thing' [the boy's sexual organ]. He was lying in the bed and his 'thing' was standing up, and he took the picture! [Her friend asked the boy]: 'Why is this standing up?'<br>[The boy answered]: 'I saw your picture and got excited!'"<br>(T., 13 yo, G, G2)<br>*Example 2:*<br>"Boys ask them [girls to send them pictures], they show them, they take their pictures, then it's all over the Internet. (...) And the suckers let and show to them. Yeah... why don't they say 'oh, show me your dick' and then, they would take their picture, just like that. But they [boys] do not show them!..."<br>(I., 12 yo, G, G2) |

*continued on the following page*

*Table 3. Continued*

| Classifying and Grouping Data by Themes | Extract (Our Translation) and Participant Identification |
|---|---|
| Being rude online<br>*Children and young people who are rude or leave rude comments on the*<br>*Internet is a risk often mentioned in the sessions.*<br>*When we asked them if that makes them feel sad, some girls answered 'yes',*<br>*other girls and boys said 'no'.*<br>*But what seems most disturbing for them, is not so much the critics or the*<br>*rudeness, but the fact that those comments are visible for everyone.*<br>*Some mentioned that some young people use Internet to be rude undercover,*<br>*for instance on Ask platform.*<br>*On this subject, it is noteworthy that the boys peremptory respond with a big*<br>*'no', while, in turn, the girls were divided between 'yes' and 'no'. We are led*<br>*to believe that these responses are linked to gender-related issues.*<br>*Consistent with their social roles, the boys did not reveal any trace of*<br>*vulnerability in their short, quick and assertive replies, while the girls more*<br>*easily disclose their feelings talk about what hurts them.* | *Example 1:*<br>"Some make fun of friends on Facebook and this is paltry."<br>(I., 12, G, G2)<br>*Example 2:*<br>"When boys post comments saying that we are ugly and all (...), sometimes I<br>get sad" (C., 12 yo, G, G2)<br>"Because everybody sees it..." (I., 12 yo, G, G2)<br>"And... ashamed. It's not that it offends me, is more because others can see."<br>(C., 12 yo, G, G2)<br>*Example 3:*<br>"When I'm in Habbo, I say 'hello' and people move away from me. Nobody<br>talks to me. They [boys and girls] move away from me. (...) But then, they<br>have no problems in coming to our house and destroy our stuff."<br>(I., 12 yo, G, G2)<br>*Example 4:*<br>[About Ask] "It's cool. I have. But there are people who go there, get their<br>status anonymous and call us ugly names... names that I won't repeat here."<br>(T., 11 yo, G, G4) |

*continued on the following page*

As Table 2 shows the participants are mostly girls, aged 10 to 13. The children from groups 1 and 2 come from families with low socio-economic incomes with at least one of the two parents unemployed and living on a reintegration subsidy. Children in Group 1 are mostly gipsy (8 in 9), which allowed us to have a stimulating insight at how ethnicity discloses cultural specificities in the use of Internet (this topic is only of interest for the reader to consider when reading the data. It will not be detailed because this is not the focus of the present text).

We present Table 2 with the number, age, region and institutional provenance of the participants enrolled in the research. The children from 'Escolhas' ('Choices') groups have a more random participation, which sometimes poses some difficulties to carry out some activities.

The activities are a work in progress, designed to combine work and play (Anderson, 2001) and adapted to the group singularities. In the first meetings we use ice-breaking activities to help the children get more relaxed and engaged. Each session lasts between 60 to 240 minutes. We choose to combine different approaches, materials, techniques and procedures like games, puzzles, role-playings, drawings or discussions about a topic, short films, or pictures to involve children in activities and sustain the enthusiasm of the volunteer participants (Anderson, 2001).

In order to protect children's rights to confidentiality and preservation of identity, we designed an informed consent to get parents and children agreement to be part of the investigation and to record the sessions (video and audio). The form includes the title of the investigation, an explanation and the objectives of the research, and also researcher's contacts. The informed consent is distributed to all the children and young people after an informal presentation. They were also informed that sessions are not mandatory and participants can freely express their consent or refusal to take part in the activities.

The sessions are documented on audio and field notes and sometimes video and photography. At the end of each session, a report is made with notes about the activities, fieldwork concerns, difficulties, interactions and considerations. The data are gathered in computer files organized by group and date.

We believe we have accomplished our research goals, achieved a privileged involvement of the children and consequently, gather valuable insight of their online experiences. To better understand the subjectivity, the delicacy and complexity of matters and meanings that participants bring to their online experiences, we followed a qualitative approach, based on structured and interpretive analysis.

*Table 3. Continued*

| Classifying and Grouping Data by Themes | Extract (Our Translation) and Participant Identification |
|---|---|
| 'StarDoll': just a game?<br>*StarDoll is a virtual game played by girls and boys. In the game users can choose a female or male character, dress the doll, buy clothes and participate in interactive activities with other players (games, clubs, chatrooms). One of the girls (T., 11 yo, G, G4) at the end of a session explained more about StarDoll.*<br>*The topic arose previously, when we asked children to complete the sentence: 'When I'm on the Internet I do not like when...'*<br>*In her turn, a girl answered: 'I do not like when I'm at parties and people ask my address'.*<br>*A little surprised and confused with her answer, we asked her to explain us what she meant.*<br>*The girls explained to us that StarDoll is an online game that can also be played through Facebook, but according to them it's 'not so cool'.*<br>*T. speaks about the game like an 'expert', because she plays it for 'quite a while'. I asked her how long was that. She replied that it was 'more or less for one year'.*<br>*The other girls, B. (10 yo, G, G4), I. (10 yo, G, G4) L. (10 yo, G, G4), and T. play StarDoll.*<br>*In the game they customize, dress and buy clothes for their doll(s). They have more than one doll.*<br>*In the game one can also go shopping and attend to 'parties'. The 'parties' are places one can go and meet and talk with others gamers (known and unknown others).*<br>*They can read about what people talk about at the 'parties' because of the dialogue balloons.*<br>*At the parties T. has been asked to give her address and age. She lies and gives another address and age. She says, 'I'm 13'. Another girl says that she replies that she is 15.*<br>*T. has several dolls. One has her name. She says that when someone asks her name she says the truth, because 'they do not know if it's my real name, or not'. And she continues: 'I have 3 dolls', one I called her 'Evilllllllll, with 8 l's'.*<br>*She uses the Evilllllllll doll - with 'ugly hair'- to mistreat people at the parties, because 'it's funny'. 'I call someone ugly, but I do not know if the person is ugly or not, it's just for fun'.*<br>*She has several dolls because 'when someone mistreats you, you can block and report the person'. And this is the reason why she and the other girls have 'fake' dolls, because if someone reports them, they are banned from the game. It's their scheme for behaving badly without running the risk of getting their favourite dolls banned from the game.*<br>*T. continues: 'when I see someone mistreating another doll, I stay quiet at a corner'. We didn't understand, and asked her 'why'. Two of the girls replied that acting like that they were protecting themselves from being banned.*<br>*T. and I. often play the game and go to 'parties' together. They enjoy mistreating each other at the parties, just for 'fun'.*<br>*I. told us that at the parties sometimes people also ask her address. B. adds that she doesn't answer to that kind of questions. But, according to I. that sometimes that is 'not enough, because some people don't give up easily'. When this happens, T. and I. leave the game.*<br>*They also explained that some people offer them gifts in exchange for accepting their friend request. They explained that in these cases, they accept the request in order to get the gift (the gift is an item of the game, clothes, etc...).*<br>*StarDoll raises questions to which we have no clear answers yet. It is a children's game or it can be a door to potential persecution and abusive activities?*<br>*Does the game promote body dissatisfaction and disruptive eating behaviours among young girls and boys? What are the real benefits of the game?*<br>*Although played by boys and girls, StarDoll is a 'girls game'. This is a social game with no educational value. The game is all about choosing and building the doll body and appearance, dressing up the doll, and give in to a materialist and consumerism appeal (shops, stardollars, fashion, real-life brands).*<br>*Members can create clubs and there are clubs about several topics: e.g. strikes, free things, fashion designers, top models, style, celebrities, brands, animals, love)*<br>*This game seems ease some risks like being harassed by strangers (chat rooms, and the free gifts in exchange of friendship), bad language (chat rooms), scams (the girls often report that 'someone' enters their account, and rob their money and their stuff), virus, and Trojan horses (fake StarDoll pages).* | *Example 1:*<br>"But I like to create a mess, I create dolls to go [to StarDoll] only to create a mess [smiling]. They all get the... the... annoyed and so on... and it's funny. I say that they are ugly, that they are horrible. I say: 'hi beautiful'. They think I'm complimenting, then I say 'you're ugly as hell' [noise] (...) I have a doll called 'evilllllllll'. And people say: 'Oh, you're ugly and so on' [noise] (she explains me that she made the doll ugly, so people would come to mess with her) (...) then people say: 'You're Evil? I do not fear you' [laughs]."<br>(T., 11 yo, G, G4)<br>"I create [an account on] ask to win 5 gold coins in StarDoll."<br>(T., 11 yo, G, G4) |

*continued on the following page*

## PRELIMINARY DATA ANALYSIS

Although they lack life experience, children seem to see themselves as aware and empowered to deal with the challenges and dangers that lurk in the Internet. However, it is necessary to understand the universe in which they move, play, learn, and connect, through their own eyes, voices and experiences, to better ascertain these assumptions.

The data collection is still an on-going process. We have selected some testimonials of the participants and grouped them into themes. We discuss the data along with the examples. We also have to warn that this is still raw data that has not yet been analysed within a larger picture. After each extract, we placed between brackets information about the research participant's identification, (name, age, gender[4], group).

*Table 3. Continued*

| Classifying and Grouping Data by Themes | Extract (Our Translation) and Participant Identification |
|---|---|
| A walk on the wild [web]site<br>*As children become more comfortable around us they tell us stories about their online experiences and discoveries.*<br>*In one of the groups a participant (F., 15 yo, B, G2) told me that he once has done online violence. With a netbook, he hacked a Facebook account to get revenge on a bully that bothered him at school, when we was 12 years old. The boy did not like F., because of a girl, and so he threatened and humiliated him. Since he 'knows much about computers', he masterminded a vengeance over the Internet, 'because [that way] nobody catches me'*<br>*With software he hacked the bully Facebook. He wiped IP's, formatted the computer and put it in private mode, and then he sent insulting messages to the bully's friends from the bully's Facebook account.*<br>*Although at the time, revenge seemed the best way, presently he doesn't think the same way. According to him, he now understands that revenge hurts oneself and the others.*<br>*However, he states that the bully stopped harassing him.*<br>*In another group, a girl (T., 11 yo, G, G4) confided us that she found out about a very bad thing regarding Facebook.*<br>*One time, she was on You Tube and found a video on 'how to hack a Facebook account' and told us all about her experience.*<br>*Used as a one-time solution or regarded as the only solution, revenge/ retaliation is often mentioned as the only way out for their problems.*<br>*According to them, no one respects a whiner, and most the times, because he only gets in deeper trouble.*<br>*Others, on the other hand, agree that vengeance is the worst way out, because it creates a snowball effect.* | *Example 1:*<br>'To get back at him, I used Facebook, a social network, I revenged myself on him. I used Internet hackers to get back at him. I used his password and, then, called his friends names (...) and his friends were all furious with him (...)<br>Well, now that I'm more grown up, I know that I should not have done that. But yeah, it was good, he regretted, because he felt [the same] on his skin (...) so, I did a good deed.<br>On the Internet there is this website, you can go there if you want, facebook/ hacking.br (...) put the mail and (...) it shows the password down. You pay €2 per phone and you get the code (...) Revenge is very powerful.<br>*Example 2:*<br>'Imagine I know the e-mail you use on Facebook. That's no problem, right? But if I get your Facebook email and click some stuff there... in your personal settings appears something down there that has your password written. From there we can go to everyone's Facebook if we know the person's email. I got to try. I was on YouTube listening to a Rihanna's song, the new one, some time ago. And appeared to me some videos like 'how to hack Facebook'. I loaded and see some of the videos, because I'm a bit nosy. I saw it and then tried. I put my email and as I had not entered the password, I was trying to find it. I did what the man said and got into my email, my Facebook.'<br>(T., 11 yo, G, G4)<br>*[In the next session she asked my permission to use my laptop and showed me the video on You Tube.]* |

## PROVISIONAL FINDINGS

The provisional data discussed so far reveals that children's online experiences are not a black and white reality. Their speech reveals that they are bombarded with information and lectures about Internet security and what adults instil in them. During the stay in the field we got the feeling that the young participants knew all the politically correct answers, but they weren't always able of analyse and evaluate about given situations.

There's a false sense of security on children's judgement regarding their online choices. It's like they memorised the alphabet, but, not always, are they capable of building words, and sentences. Adults tend to trust in recipes, but handbooks don't teach much about how to create empathy, resilience, respect, responsibility, and feelings… Recipes don't help children to deal with a low self-esteem or frustration.

Sometimes what they say does not match what they do. For instance, they claim it's wrong to talk with strangers, but they do not bother to learn more about or adjust the privacy settings on their social networking site profile, disregarding that their pictures can fall into paedophile rings, or stay forever in the network.

During the sessions we have noticed that the threats of most concern to them are: identity theft, misuse of personal information, cyberbullying, pornography, and the possibility of someone hurting them (kidnapping, rapping).

Regarding issues involving sexual content, there's obviously a wider and easier access to products or the production of sexual content, and a distorted image of sex (unromantic, twisted, primitive and empty of affection).

Misbehaving online can either be upsetting or fun. It is upsetting for the victim (especially when it is anonymous as in ask.fm), but according to some it can be just for fun when is a practical joke (e.g. StarDoll).

In one case, an offline victim became an online aggressor to get revenged from a bully that used bothered him at school. The anonymity encourages the offender who manages to undertake his vengeance plan without being discovered.

As threats and "methods of antisocial online behaviour" (Paul, Smith, & Blumberg, 2012, p. 128) become more difficult to control or prevent, it is increasingly important to study this growing problem that gets into the house and up to the intimacy of the bedroom, challenging children's rights and adult's job regarding children's safety. For the reasons listed above, and because risks cannot be ignored, we are led to believe that despite being more informed, children are vulnerable to get involved in cybercriminal activities.

## FUTURE RESEARCH DIRECTIONS

The speed with which Internet and technology evolves and involves society reconfiguring habits and behaviours, requires more research to deepen these and other issues and, in particular, to build knowledge on how children move in this complex, kaleidoscopic, networked and wired environment. This is a field we intend to continue to explore deeply in order to fully understand the issues at stake and to get the authentic young people's point of view on their personal online experiences.

Since this is still an on-going investigation, at the end we intend to contribute for a greater understanding and reflection about this complex problem and its impact in order to increase awareness about how children behave online and in what way it may influence their well-being, in order to contribute to the discussion of policies, guidelines and strategies to ensure proactive and balanced preventive measures. In order to take action and protect children from being threatened online, adults need to i) get acquainted with online risks; ii) and children's online friends ii) learn about how youth online world works; iii) as it becomes more difficult to monitor what children do online, adults need to be prepared to lose control and instead get involved and communicate with children; iv) set boundaries and rules.

## ACKNOWLEDGMENT

This doctoral investigation is financed by POPH – QREN – Type 4.1 – Advanced Training, European Social Fund and Portuguese national funding from the Ministry of Education and Science, through FCT – Fundação para a Ciência e a Tecnologia, under a research grant with the reference SFRH/BD/68288/2010.

## REFERENCES

Ackers, M. J. (2012). Cyberbullying: through the eyes of children and young people. *Educational Psychology in Practice*, 28(2), 141–157. doi:10.1080/02667363.2012.665356

Agatston, P.W., Kowalski, R., & Limber, S. (2007). Students' Perspectives on Cyber Bullying. *The Journal of Adolescent Health*, 41(6), S59–S60. doi:10.1016/j.jadohealth.2007.09.003 PMID:18047946

Anderson, P. (2001). Children as researchers - The effects of participation rights on research methodology. In P. Christensen, & A. James (Eds.), *Research with children - Perspectives and practices* (pp. 241–275). London: Routledge Falmer.

Berson, M. (2000). The Computer can't see you blush. *Kappa Delta Pi Record*, 158–162. doi:10.1080/00228958.2000.10518777

Bovill, M., & Livingstone, S. (2001). *Bedroom culture and the privatization of media use*. Retrieved from http://eprints.lse.ac.uk/archive/00000672

Byron, T. (2008). *Safer Children in a Digital World - The Report of the Byron Review*. Byron Review – Children and New Technology.

David-Ferdon, C., & Hertz, M. F. (2007). Electronic media, violence, and adolescents: an emerging public health problem. *The Journal of Adolescent Health*, 41(6Suppl 1), S1–S5. doi:10.1016/j.jadohealth.2007.08.020 PMID:18047940

David-Ferdon, C., & Hertz, M. F. (2009). *Electronic media and youth violence: A CDC issue brief for researchers*. Atlanta, GA: Centers for Disease Control.

Donnerstein, E. (2012). Internet bullying. *Pediatric Clinics of North America, 59*(3), 623-633, viii. doi: 10.1016/j.pcl.2012.03.019

Duerager, A., & Livingstone, S. (2012). How can parents support children's internet safety? EU Kids Online.

Finkelhor, D., Mitchell, K., & Wolack, J. (2000). *Online Victimization: A Report on the Nation's Youth*. National Center for Missing & Exploited Children.

France, A., Bendelow, G., & Williams, S. (2000). A 'risky' bussiness: researching the health beliefs of children and young people. In A. Lewis & G. Lindsay (Eds.), Researching Children's Perspectives (pp. 150-162). Open University Press.

Giedd, J. N. (2012). The Digital Revolution and Adolescent Brain Evolution. *The Journal of Adolescent Health, 51*, 101–105. doi:10.1016/j.jadohealth.2012.06.002 PMID:22824439

Gross, E. F. (2004). Adolescent Internet use: What we expect, what teens report. *Journal of Applied Developmental Psychology, 25*(6), 633–649. doi:10.1016/j.appdev.2004.09.005

Haenens, L. d., Vandoninck, S., & Donoso, V. (2013). How to cope and build online resilience? EU Kids Online.

Hertz, M. F., & David-Ferdon, C. (2008). *Electronic Media and Youth Violence: A CDC Issue Brief for Educators and Caregivers*. Atlanta, GA: Centers for Disease Control.

Hertz, M. F., & David-Ferdon, C. (2011). Online aggression: a reflection of in-person victimization or a unique phenomenon? *The Journal of Adolescent Health, 48*(2), 119–120. doi:10.1016/j.jadohealth.2010.11.255 PMID:21257108

Hinduja, S., & Patchin, J. W. (2011). High-tech cruelty. *Educational Leadership, 68*(5), 48-52.

Huesmann, L.R. (2007). The Impact of Electronic Media Violence: Scientific Theory and Research. *The Journal of Adolescent Health, 41*(6), S6–S13. doi:10.1016/j.jadohealth.2007.09.005 PMID:18047947

Jorge, A. (2012). Em risco na internet? Resultados do inquérito EU KIDS ONLINE. In C. Ponte, A. Jorge, J. A. Simões, & D. S. Cardoso (Eds.), *Crianças e Internet em Portugal - Acessos, usos, riscos, mediações: resultados do inquérito europeu EU KIDS ONLINE* (pp. 93–104). MinervaCoimbra.

Kane, J., & Portin, P. (2008). *Violência e tecnologia. Bélgica: Comissão Europeia*. DG Justiça, Liberdade e Segurança. Programa Daphne.

King, J.E., Walpole, C., & Lamon, K. (2007). Surf and Turf Wars Online—Growing Implications of Internet Gang Violence. *The Journal of Adolescent Health, 41*(6), S66–S68. doi:10.1016/j.jadohealth.2007.09.001 PMID:18047950

Kowalski, R.M., & Limber, S. (2007). Electronic Bullying Among Middle School Students. *The Journal of Adolescent Health, 41*(6), S22–S30. doi:10.1016/j.jadohealth.2007.08.017 PMID:18047942

Law, D. M., Shapka, J. D., Hymel, S., Olson, B. F., & Waterhouse, T. (2012). The changing face of bullying: An empirical comparison between traditional and internet bullying and victimization. *Computers in Human Behavior, 28*(1), 226–232. doi:10.1016/j.chb.2011.09.004

Livingstone, & Bober, M. (2003). *UK children go online: Listening to young people's experiences*. Retrieved from http://eprints.lse.ac.uk/archive/0000388

Livingstone, & Bulger, M. (2013). *A global agenda for children's rights in the digital age - Recommendations for developing UNICEF's Research Strategy*. Unicef.

Lüders, M. H., Brandtzæg, P. B., & Dunkels, E. (2009). Risky contacts. In S. Livingstone, & L. Haddon (Eds.), *Kids Online: Opportunities and risks for children* (pp. 123–134). The Policy Press.

Muir, D. (2005). *Violence against Children in Cyberspace. ECPAT International*. End Child Prostitution, Child Pornography and Trafficking of Children for Sexual Purposes.

Mura, G., Topcu, C., Erdur-Baker, O., & Diamantini, D. (2011). An international study of cyber bullying perception and diffusion among adolescents. *Procedia - Social and Behavioral Sciences, 15*, 3805-3809. doi:10.1016/j.sbspro.2011.04.377

Paul, S., Smith, P. K., & Blumberg, H. H. (2012). Comparing student perceptions of coping strategies and school interventions in managing bullying and cyberbullying incidents. *Pastoral Care in Education, 30*(2), 127–146. doi:10.1080/02643944.2012.679957

Pessoa, T., Matos, A., Amado, J., & Jäger, T. (2011). Cyberbullying – do diagnóstico de necessidades à construção de um manual de formação. *SIPS - Pedagogía Social: Revista Interuniversitária*, 57-70.

Postmes, T., & Spears, R. (1998). Deindividuation and anti-normative behavior: A meta-analysis. *Psychological Bulletin, 123*, 238–259. doi:10.1037/0033-2909.123.3.238

Postmes, T., Spears, R., & Lea, M. (1998). Breaching or building social boundaries? SIDE-effects of computer-mediated communication. *Communication Research, 25*, 689–715. doi:10.1177/009365098025006006

Ringrose, J., Gill, R., Livingstone, S., & Harvey, L. (2012). *A qualitative study of children, young people and 'sexting'*. NSPCC.

Soares, N. F. (2006). A Investigação Participativa no Grupo Social da Infância: Currículo sem Fronteiras. *Currículo sem Fronteiras, 6*, 25-40.

UNICEF. (2011). *Child Safety online: Global challenges and strategies*. UNICEF.

Valkenburg, P. M., & Buijzen, M. (2003). Children, computer games, and the Internet. *Netherlands Journal of Social Sciences, 39*(1), 24–34.

Werner, N. E., Bumpus, M. F., & Rock, D. (2010). Involvement in internet aggression during early adolescence. *Journal of Youth and Adolescence, 39*(6), 607–619. doi:10.1007/s10964-009-9419-7 PMID:20422350

Whitby, P. (2011). *Is your child safe online? A parents guide to the internet, Facebook, mobile phones & other new media*. White Ladder.

Wolak, J., Mitchell, K., & Finkelhor, D. (2007). Does Online Harassment Constitute Bullying? An Exploration of Online Harassment by Known Peers and Online-Only Contacts. *The Journal of Adolescent Health, 41*(6), S51–S58. doi:10.1016/j.jadohealth.2007.08.019 PMID:18047945

Worthen, M. R. (2007). Education Policy Implications from the Expert Panel on Electronic Media and Youth Violence. *The Journal of Adolescent Health, 41*(6), S61–S63. doi:10.1016/j.jadohealth.2007.09.009 PMID:18047948

Ybarra, M. L. (2004). Youth engaging in online harassment: associations with caregiver?child relationships, Internet use, and personal characteristics*1. *Journal of Adolescence, 27*(3), 319–336. doi:10.1016/j.adolescence.2004.03.007 PMID:15159091

Ybarra, M. L., & Mitchell, K. (2004). Online aggressor/targets, aggressors, and targets: a comparison of associated youth characteristics. *Journal of Child Psychology and Psychiatry, and Allied Disciplines, 45*(7), 1308–1316. doi:10.1111/j.1469-7610.2004.00328.x PMID:15335350

## KEY TERMS AND DEFINITIONS

**Child-Centred Research:** A research model approach based in children's voice and point of view about topics that concern their best interest.

**Children:** A person younger than the age of majority (as it is defined by the United Nations Convention on the Rights of the Child).

**Facebook:** A popular online social networking service.

**Online Experiences:** How children behave and interact on the Internet alone or with others.

**Online Risks:** Online experiences that can harm of threats children's safety and well-being.

**Online Violence:** The use of online digital devices or services to engage in activities that result in physical, psychological, emotional self-harm or cause harm to another person.

**Sexting:** Sending, distributing or receiving sexual and/or erotic texts, images or videos.

## ENDNOTES

[1]  You can read more about this issue in the articles: (a) Castro, T., & Osório, A. (2013). 'I love my bones!' - Self-harm and dangerous eating youth behaviours in Portuguese written blogs. Young Consumers: Insight and Ideas for Responsible Marketers, Vol.14 Iss: 4, pp. 321-330. (b) Castro, T., & Osório, A. (2012). Online violence: not beautiful enough… not thin enough; anorectic testimonials in the web. PsychNology Journal, 10(3), 169 – 186, disponível em Error! Hyperlink reference not valid. (c) Castro, T., & Osório, A. (2013) 'Fat and Happy? I'd Rather Die!' Online Violence Involving Children: Pro-Anorexia Communities and Dangerous Eating Behaviours on the Web, Skins, Visual Culture and Youth, Inter-Disciplinary Press, Oxford, UK, ISBN: 978-1-84888-255-3, pp. 101-111.

[2]  "Resilience is the ability to deal with negative experiences online or offline. Resilient children are able to tackle adverse situations in a problem-focused way, and to transfer negative emotions into positive (or neutral) feelings. Risk and resilience go hand in hand, as resilience can only develop through exposure to risks or stressful events. Consequently, as children learn how to adequately cope with (online) adversities, they develop (online) resilience." (Haenens, Vandoninck, & Donoso, 2013, p. 2)

[3]  This Portuguese nationwide government program promotes the social inclusion of children and youth that live in contexts of socioeconomic vulnerability.

[4]  G for 'girl' and B for 'boy'.

# Chapter 4
# Development and Mitigation of Android Malware

**Vanessa N. Cooper**
*Kennesaw State University, USA*

**Hossain Shahriar**
*Kennesaw State University, USA*

**Hisham M. Haddad**
*Kennesaw State University, USA*

## ABSTRACT

*As mobile applications are being developed at a faster pace, the security aspect of user information is being neglected. A compromised smartphone can inflict severe damage to both users and the cellular service provider. Malware on a smartphone can make the phone partially or fully unusable, cause unwanted billing, steal private information, or infect every name in a user's phonebook. A solid understanding of the characteristics of malware is the beginning step to prevent much of the unwanted consequences. This chapter is intended to provide an overview of security threats posed by Android malware. In particular, the authors focus on the characteristics commonly found in malware applications and understand the code level features that allow us to detect the malicious signatures. The authors also discuss some common defense techniques to mitigate the impact of malware applications.*

## INTRODUCTION

Android is an open source operating system for mobile devices. Statistics indicate that Android is having the fastest growth in the market share of the operating systems in the United States. Android has become the leading smartphone Operating System (OS) in the world with staggering sales figure of 60 million phones in the third quarter of 2011, 50% market share (Aaron, 2011). A recent study shows

that more than 50% of mobile devices running Android OS have unpatched vulnerabilities, opening them up to malicious applications (malware) and attacks. A compromised smartphone can inflict severe damage to both users and the cellular service provider. Malware applications on Android can make the phone partially or fully unusable, cause unwanted billing, steal private information, or infect every name in a user's phonebook (Reza & Mazumder, 2012).

DOI: 10.4018/978-1-4666-6324-4.ch004

Recently, a malware affected more than 100,000 Android devices in China (known as *MMarketPay*). This malware is a hidden application that appeared to be legitimate and is designed to purchase applications and contents without the consent of the device users (victims). As a result, victims saw a staggering amount of bills (Baldwin, 2012). The incident prompted Google to introduce stricter rules for applications on Android such as naming of applications and banning applications that disclose personal information without user permission. An Android SMS malware firm was fined £50,000 by the UK premium phone services regulator (*"PhonePay Plus", 2013*). The company, *SMSBill*, produced a malicious Facebook link that led to the downloading of malware in Android phones (Baldwin et al. 2012).

Possible attack vectors into smart phones include Cellular networks, Internet connections (via Wi-Fi, GPRS/EDGE or 3G network), USB and other peripherals (Shabtai, Fledel, & Elovici, 2010). Given all these possible outcomes, it is important to study malicious Android applications and their characteristics. A solid understanding of the characteristics of malware is the beginning step to prevent much of the unwanted consequences. This chapter is intended to provide an overview of security threats posed by Android malware. In particular, we focus on the characteristics commonly found in malware applications and understand the code level features that allow us to detect the malicious signatures. We also discuss some common defense techniques to mitigate the impact of malware applications.

The chapter is organized as follows. Section 2 discusses an overview of Android OS structure as well as common security features offered. We also discuss the three types of applications that affect the security and privacy of users in general: grayware, spyware, and malware. Section 3 discusses code level examples showing malicious activities as well as some signatures that can be used to identify them. Section 4 discusses selected defense techniques to mitigate malware activities. Finally, Section 5 concludes the chapter.

## BACKGROUND

In this section, we first provide an overview of the Android OS including its features and programming guidelines in Section 2.1. Section 2.2 highlights the architecture of the Android Operating Systems (OS) as well as brief discussion on security and privacy features. Section 2.3 highlights different types of malware that we consider in our discussion.

## Overview of Android

Android is an open source operating system based on the Linux first launched in 2007 and intended for mobile phones (Rehm, 2012). Between the two major variants of smartphone (Android and iOS), Android is the most popular one. As of October 2013, the latest version of Android OS is 4.4 (commonly known as KitKat, API level 19). Being developed and supported by Google, all Android devices allow users to synchronize access to storage and communication services provided by Google. For example, users can login to Google Gmail to check email and access contact list, calendar, and other free applications automatically. The default desktop of Android has five screens that can be switched by tapping. A user can move any icon to any place on the desktop by tapping and hovering. Android devices allow users to download and install new applications for legitimate purposes that may include game, business, communication, photography, and services. The common place to find applications is Google Play Store ("Google Play", 2013).

The Android Developer manual recommends some common practices for programmers for developing applications ("Android Design", 2013). These include the guidelines for developing applications that are visually appealing to users. A developer can reuse standard theme that control visual properties of the elements for user interface of an application such as color, height, padding, and font size. Recommended guidelines for color and illumination of icons are provided to represent different state of an icon (e.g., a gray colored icon means static, illuminated icon means "pressed", 50% illumination means "focused", 30% of illumination means "disable"). Developers can choose different color styles and text font sizes. The guide recommends using *textColorPrimaryInverse* and *textColorSecondaryInverse* for light themes. Also to maintain consistency of look and feel in the same UI, it is recommended to use scale-independent pixels (sp) wherever possible.

Legitimate applications support well-known gestures to allow users interacting with applications based on the screen objects. Table 1 shows the core gesture set that is supported in Android. Unlike desktop or laptop computers, activities and operations can be performed on Android devices based on touching (also known as tapping). Note that a "tap" is a brief touch followed by the release of touch on a certain entity of Android screen. Usually, "tap" is considered as a single event for smartphone device and applicable for a visible icon. Most legitimate applications are developed in a way so that useful operations are performed based on user-initiated gestures. However, most malware are not developed to operate based on user-initiated gestures. Nevertheless, some legitimate applications may not need gestures to perform operations (*e.g.*, an application that is intended to clear cache data periodically upon installation).

## Android Architecture and Security Features

The Android OS framework has a number of layers to facilitate the execution of applications (Shabtai et al. 2010). Table 2 shows an overview of the OS framework ("Android Design", 2013). The bottom layer has the Linux kernel. On top of the kernel, a set of native libraries (C/C++) and the Android virtual machine (Dalvik, which is the Android-specific implementation of the Java virtual machine) reside. The Dalvik VM relies on the underlying Linux kernel to handle low-level functionalities such as process and memory management. The Dalvik VM executes .dex files (Dalvik executable), which can be created by transforming Java classes using the SDK tools ("Memory Management in Android", 2010).

The next layer is the Application Framework encompassing the Java core libraries, which rely on the native libraries. The topmost layer contains the Java-based applications that are created using the Application Framework layer. Java Applications communicate with the Android Framework through a variety of key applications, such as Messaging, Gallery, and the Camera (Shabtai et al. 2010).

Android has a number of built-in security mechanisms to protect the data and memory that belong to processes or applications running in

*Table 1. A list of gesture type supported in Android ("Android Design", 2013)*

| Type | Description | Action |
|---|---|---|
| Touch (tap) | Triggers the default functionality for a given item. | Press, lift |
| Long press | Enters data selection mode. Allows a user to select one or more items in a view and act upon the data using a contextual action bar. | Press, wait, lift |
| Swipe | Scrolls overflowing content, or navigates between views in the same hierarchy. | Press, move, lift |
| Drag | Rearranges data within a view, or moves data into a container (e.g. folders on Home Screen). | Long press, move, lift |
| Double touch | Zooms into content. Also used as a secondary gesture for text selection. | Two touches in quick succession |
| Pinch open | Zooms into content. | 2-finger press, move outwards, lift |
| Pinch close | Zooms out of content. | 2-finger press, move inwards, lift |

*Table 2. Architectural overview of Android OS ("Android Design", 2013)*

| Applications | | | | |
|---|---|---|---|---|
| Home | Contacts | Phone | Browser | |
| **Application Framework** | | | | |
| Activity Manager | Window Manager | Content Providers | | View System |
| Package Manager | Telephony Manager | Resource Manager | Location Manager | Notification Manager |
| **Libraries** | | | **Android Runtime** | |
| Surface Manager | Media Framework | SQLite | Core Libraries | |
| OpenGL I ES | FreeType | WebKit | Dalvik Virtual Machine | |
| SGL | SSL | libc | | |
| **Linux Kernel** | | | | |
| Display Driver | Camera Driver | Flash Memory Driver | | Binder (IPC) Driver |
| Keypad Driver | WiFi Driver | Power Management | | Audio Drivers |

the device ("Security Tips", 2013). We discuss some core security features below that include *sandbox, permission-based access control, secure Inter Process Communication (IPC), safe memory management*, and *data encryption*.

- **Sandbox:** Android prevents one application to access data and memory contents from another application. Each application is run in a sandbox (each process has their own copy of virtual machine). As a result, an application cannot access the data and code of another application.
- **Permission-Based Access Control:** User-granted permissions for each application are the basis to grant or restrict access to system features and user data. During installation of an application, the permissions required to operate different peripherals are declared and a user is prompted whether or not he/she intends to grant/deny the permission. If a user does not grant the permission, the application is not installed.
- **Secure IPC:** An application cannot directly access other applications memory space (containing data). Thus, the Inter Process Communication (IPC) mechanism plays a key feature in accessing data from one ap-

plication to another application. A developer can benefit from IPC by implementing the following three steps ("Android IDL Example with Code Description – IPC", 2013):

- ○ **Implement Android Interface Definition Language (AIDL) Interface:** An AIDL interface defines a list of services available to other applications from the provider.
- ○ **Implementation of Remote Service:** Remote services hold the data that needs to be shared among other applications. Remote services can include methods so that other applications can access data by invoking the methods. Intents are messages that components can send and receive. It is a universal mechanism of passing data between processes. With the help of intents one can start services or activities, invoke broadcast receivers, and so on.
- ○ **Expose the Remote Service to Other Local Clients:** The data/method we need to share with other applications needs to be exposed so that other applications can access and

share data from the remote service. Binders are the entity that allows activities and services obtain a reference to another service. Binders allow sending messages to services and directly invoking methods that belong to the services.

- **Safe Memory Management**: Each Android application runs in a separate process within its own Dalvik instance. Dalvik is a register-based virtual machine optimized to ensure that a device can run multiple instances efficiently. Dalvik is responsible for memory and process management during run time and can stop and kill processes as necessary. Memory management related vulnerabilities such as buffer overflow, memory leak, and uninitialized pointer usage are eliminated by incorporating some of the well-known technologies like Address Space Layout Randomization (to prevent code injection attack), NX (non-executable stack due to buffer overflow), and ProPolice (return address space corruption prevention).

- **Data Encryption**: Android allows users to encrypt their data and other profile information. It is possible to encrypt accounts, downloaded applications, media file, and settings. An encrypted device can be decrypted based on a user chosen password (during each time the device is powered on). The encryption process is costly both in terms of processing power (device needs to be plugged with power) and time (can take more than an hour) (Brinkmann, 2012).

## Type of Malware

Malware or "malicious software" is implemented with malicious intention. Malware is often installed without the victim's knowledge (i.e., a victim usually overlooks the list of permissions needed to run the malware and voluntarily grants the permission without understanding the effect of malicious actions). Under the broad definition of malware several categories are well-known including virus (a malicious program that can copy itself in an infected computer), worms (similar to virus, except having the ability of propagation in new machines), and Trojan horses (a program that installs a backdoor in an infected computer to communicate with hacker-controlled computer) ("What is Malware?", 2013). However, in this chapter, we classify applications as malware that are capable of performing specific operations in Android platform (see Table 3). These may include the changing of the desktop setting by installing wallpaper without user knowledge (m1), accessing device and personal profile information and sending it over the Internet to unwanted third parties (m2), launching phone calls and sending messages to premium numbers (m3), asking for ransom by locking the desktop and suggesting to pay for unlocking (m4), and hacking social network accounts (m5).

Note that some of the malware applications are labeled as spyware. Spywares are the programs developed to monitor and log activities performed on a computer (e.g., Keylogger). Spyware not only collects sensitive personal information (e.g., websites visited, typed password), but also steals information, and in the worst case can send them to others for long-term damage ("Difference between Adware and Spyware", 2005).

We are also aware of another specific application type known as "Adware" which displays advertisements and marketing contents automatically after the installation. Advertisements are displayed in a small section of the interface or as a pop-up window. It is used for legitimate reason such as generating revenues for companies who intend to sell products. An example of adware is the popular e-mail program, Eudora. It can be purchased in sponsored mode, when Eudora displays an advertisement window containing toolbar links. We do not consider adware as malicious.

*Table 3. A list of malicious actions performed by Android malware (Felt, Finifter, Chin, Hanna, & Wagner, 2011)*

| Malware Type | Example Action | Required Permissions |
|---|---|---|
| Changing Wallpaper (m1) | Novelty and amusement by change the default wallpaper without user's permission. | SET_WALLPAPER<br>BIND_WALLPAPER |
| Accessing User Credentials (m2) | Secretly accessing contact information from Android device and send the information over the internet or text message. | USE_CREDENTIALS<br>READ_PROFILE<br>MANAGE_ACCOUNTS |
| SMS Message and Premium Rate Calls (m3) | Bills victim by arbitrarily initiating phone calls to premium numbers or sending text messages to premium numbers. | READ_SMS<br>WRITE_SMS<br>SEND_SMS |
| Phone Ransom (m4) | Locking a client's phone by changing default setting on password or other profile information and demand to pay an amount by visiting a location for tapping or specific website to unlock it. | WRITE_SETTINGS |
| Hacking Social Networks (m5) | Secretly accessing and updating user profile information. | READ_SOCIAL_STREAM<br>WRITE_SOCIAL_STREAM |

## TAXONOMY OF ANDROID MALWARE

In this section, we show code level examples that can represent the five types of malware shown in Table 3. We discuss the key part of Java code and the list of permissions that appear in AndroidManifest.xml file for the reader's convenience. It is important to note that both sections of code, Java code and permissions, are necessary to perform the listed malware actions. All java source files and interactive user views (activities) must be listed. This is a requirement of all mobile applications. In mostly all malicious actions, a user is first required to agree to the allowable permissions when downloading the mobile application. Therefore, it is very important for a user to remain vigilant about requested permissions in mobile applications.

### Changing Wallpaper

In Figure 1, one may examine the source code responsible for executing the malicious action of changing the wallpaper without the user's specification. In this case, the required permission is 'SET_WALLPAPER", shown in Figure 2. Without this line of code, the malicious code would be ineffective. During development, most permis-

sions are automatically added when a developer uses certain Android classes directly linked to that permission. However, the system is not able to fully determine if the developer is attempting to use the permission in a malicious way.

### Accessing User Credentials

In Figure 3, we show how easily a malicious mobile application can access and retrieve user account information. The GET_ACCOUNTS permission, shown in Figure 4, is the only required permission for retrieving user accounts. However, if a developer wanted to make changes to the user account information, they would be required to list permissions for editing the user account.

### SMS Message and Premium Rate Call

SMS message sending is one of the most popular types of malicious activities. As shown in Figure 5, only one permission is required to send an SMS message. However, sending an SMS message is also a motivating case because there are two ways to send a message. The first option is shown in Figure 6, and it outlines a hidden attempt to send

*Figure 1. Required source code to change wallpaper ("Set Wallpaper using WallpaperManager", 2011)*

```
//Retrieve instance of the application
WallpaperManager myWallpaperManager =
    WallpaperManager.getInstance(getApplicationContext());

//R.drawable.five presents a stored image
myWallpaperManager.setResource(R.drawable.five);
```

*Figure 2. Required permission for changing wallpaper ("Set Wallpaper using WallpaperManager", 2011)*

```
<uses-permission
    android:name="android.permission.SET)_WALLPAPER" />
```

an SMS message. This line of code can easily be included in any method or loop without the user's knowledge. Since the action is hidden and does not require user input, it can be flagged as suspicious or malicious activity. Figure 7 shows how to send an SMS message that will often display an activity screen in which the user will interact.

In Figure 8, we review how easily a mobile application can Code for initiating phone call. In this case, the dialer is never shown to the user and a hard-coded premium number is called without the user's knowledge. This can be incredibly expensive for the user, especially if the mobile application is left running overnight while the user is away from the device. In order to perform this action, a malicious developer would include the permission, listed in Figure 9, into the AndroidManifest.xml file.

## Phone Ransom

In Figure 10, we examine a code snippet on how to change the sound settings on the mobile device. A malicious application can access the AudioManager and set the ringer volume to zero. As a result, a victim will not be altered or notified for related activities such as incoming phone call or SMS messages. Figure 11 shows the required permissions to edit phone settings and save them accordingly.

Another common malicious action is to lock the screen of a mobile device as shown Figure 12 This action is commonly referred to as ransom. Here, the *KeyguardManager* is accessed which further accesses the *KeyguardLock* for enabling or disabling the default lock. One objective of malware is to disable the lock for the purpose of ransom. A message is later displayed prompting the user to pay a fee in order to unlock the device and continue unharmed. However, this is often just a ploy in order to retrieve funds from a very desperate person. Figure 13 outlines the required permissions to perform this action.

## Hacking Social Networks

Malicious activities have escalated even higher with Android's added ability to synch mobile application with social networks in API Level 15. Now, a user can update their statuses on Facebook, Twitter, and a plethora of other social networks directly from their mobile device. With this added implementation, there are many more security threats such as susceptibility to malicious attacks. In Figure 14, we examine how a malicious mobile application can easily gain access to a user account and send fraudulent status updates to the user profile. Figure 15 outlines the required permissions for accessing and updating a user profile on a social network, as shown in Figure

*Figure 3. Required source code to access user account information ("How to get the Android device's Primary Email Address", 2010)*

```
//Retrieve the constant, email address, of class
Pattern emailPattern = Patterns.EMAIL_ADDRESS;

// Functionality is availabile for API level 8+
Account[] accounts = AccountManager.get(context).getAccounts();

//Retrieve account name for email account
for (Account account : accounts) {
        if (emailPattern.matcher(account.name).matches()) {
                String possibleEmail = account.name;
        }
}
```

*Figure 4. Required permissions for retrieving user account information ("How to get the Android device's Primary Email Address", 2010)*

```
<uses-permission
        android:name="android.permission.GET_ACCOUNTS" />
```

*Figure 5. Required permission to send SMS message ("Send SMS in Android", 2013)*

```
<uses-permission
        android:name="android.permission.SEND_SMS"/>
```

*Figure 6. Hidden method to send SMS message ("Send SMS in Android", 2013)*

```
//Retrieve the default SMS engine
SmsManager sms = SmsManager.getDefault();

//Send a text message using hard-coded or desired text
sms.sendTextMessage(phoneNumber, null, message, null, null);
```

*Figure 7. Visible method to send SMS message ("Send SMS in Android", 2013)*

```
//Send a text message using text from user's screen
startActivity(new Intent(Intent.ACTION_VIEW, Uri.parse("sms:"
+ phoneNumber)));
```

*Figure 8. Initiating a phone call without using phone dialer ("How to make a phone pall in Android and come back to my when activity call is done", 2011)*

```
//Initiate a phone call using desired phone number
Intent callIntent = new Intent(Intent.ACTION_CALL, Uri.parse(number));
startActivity(callIntent);
```

*Figure 9. Required permission to make phone call without phone dialer ("How to make a phone pall in Android and come back to my when activity call is done", 2011)*

```
<uses-permission
        android:name="android.permission.CALL_PHONE"/>

<uses-permission
        android:name="android.permission.CALL_PRIVILEGED"/>
```

*Figure 10. Silence the sound settings on an android device ("How to make android phone silent in java", 2012)*

```
//Access system settings for the audio
AudioManager audio = (AudioManager)getSystemService(Context.AUDIO_SERVICE);

//Change Ringer to Silent
audio.setRingerMode(0);
```

*Figure 11. Required permission to change phone's audio settings ("How to make android phone silent in java", 2012)*

```
<uses-permission
        android:name="android.permission.WRITE_SETTINGS "/>

<uses-permission
        android:name="android.permission.WRITE_SECURE_SETTINGS"/>
```

*Figure 12. Lock an Android device and disable keyguard ("Lock and Android phone", 2012)*

```
//Access system settings for the keyguard
KeyguardManager mgr =  (KeyguardManager)getSystemService(Activity.KEYGUARD_SERVICE);

// Lock the device
KeyguardLock lock = mgr.newKeyguardLock(KEYGUARD_SERVICE);
lock.reenableKeyguard();
```

*Figure 13. Required permissions to disable keyguard ("Lock and Android phone", 2012)*

```
<uses-permission
        android:name="android.permission.DISABLE_KEYGUARD "/>
```

14. After gaining access to the user profile, a malicious activity can then gather the user's interests, friend's list, and a multitude of other details. Since individuals also tend to post birthday pictures, pet names, and other private information, there are also vulnerable for identity theft.

## CLASSIFICATION OF DETECTION TECHNIQUES

Many techniques have been proposed in the literature to enhance the security of Android platforms and deployed applications. These techniques include sandboxing, machine learning, model-

*Figure 14. Code snippet demonstrating how to modify social network account ("Get Social Updates of your contact list using Ice cream sandwich", 2012)*

```
//Create content to post on user account
ContentValues values = new ContentValues();
values.put(StreamItems.RAW_CONTACT_ID, rawContactId);
values.put(StreamItems.TEXT, "Lunch at 3.00 PM");
values.put(StreamItems.TIMESTAMP, timestamp);
values.put(StreamItems.COMMENTS, "Family and Friends");

//Specify where content will be posted
Uri.Builder builder = StreamItems.CONTENT_URI.buildUpon();
builder.appendQueryParameter(RawContacts.ACCOUNT_NAME, accountName);
builder.appendQueryParameter(RawContacts.ACCOUNT_TYPE, accountType);

//Send request to post content
Uri streamItemUri = getContentResolver().insert(builder.build(), values);
long streamItemId = ContentUris.parseId(streamItemUri);
```

*Figure 15. Required Permissions to modify social network account ("Get Social Updates of your contact list using Ice cream sandwich", 2012)*

```
<uses-permission
        android:name="android.permission.READ_SOCIAL_STREAM "/>

<uses-permission
        android:name="android.permission.WRITE_SOCIAL_STREAM"/>
```

based testing, fuzz testing, and static analysis (or decompiling), and secure software architecture. In this section we highlight the following techniques: Sandboxing system for Android application (Blasing, Batyuk, Schmidt, Camtepe, & Albayrak, 2012), Applying machine learning to extract static features of Android applications (Shabtai et al. 2010), Decompiler-based static analysis (Enck, Octeau, McDaniel, & Chaudhuri, 2011), and Secure software architecture for Android applications (Reza et al. 2012)

## Sandboxing

A sandbox (Blasing et al. 2010) provides a realistic execution environment, but in an isolated manner. As a result, the effect of a potential malicious application does not affect the outside environment. It is useful not only for signature identification, but also for disinfecting a malware. The sandbox has two steps: *static* and *dynamic* analysis.

An Android application is shipped as a compressed (apk extension) installation file. In the static analysis, the sandbox decompresses installation files and disassembles executable files to identify malicious code fragments. When decompressed, the content is saved into three main parts: *AndroidManifest.xml* (an XML file having the meta-information of the application including its description and security permissions), *classes.dex* (a file having the Java bytecode that can be interpreted by Dalvik Virtual Machine), and *res* (a special folder having files that define the layout, language, and so on).

The manifest file contains the main "launchable activity" information. The byte code (from *classes.dex*) of the application is converted into human readable format having a folder hierarchy containing files with parsable pseudo-code. The code is then scanned for suspicious patterns. A list of static code patterns that are commonly considered as Android malware (Blasing et al. 2010) are below:

1. Usage of the Java Native Interface.
2. Usage of *getRuntime*.
3. Usage of Java reflection.
4. Usage of services and IPC provision.
5. Usage of android permissions.

The dynamic analysis phase of the sandbox system is intended to monitor system and library calls with arguments. In general, system calls are function invocations made from user space into the kernel to request services or resources from the operating system (Hyatt, 2013). A loadable kernel module (LKM) is implemented and placed in the Android emulator environment. The modified kernel keeps logging the function calls invoked by applications and their arguments for later analysis. This gives a low-level system call sequence responsible for malicious activities.

## Advantages

The sandbox reduces the generation of signatures based on system level call tracing. It has been shown that on average it takes 48 days to come up with the signatures of a new malware, which leaves the window of damaging opportunity by malware wide (Oberheide, Cooke, & Jahanian, 2008).

## Disadvantages

As the lowest level of system calls are intercepted and logged, implementation of a loadable kernel module (LKM) is daunting and error prone task. Special attention is needed as emulator tends are very unstable if low-level changes are performed.

## Machine Learning

Shabtai *et al.* (2010) apply the machine learning technique to differentiate the characteristic of applications between two categories: tools and games. They extracted features from the byte-code (dex files) and XML (permission). The learned features were used to identify the general type of the application, which can be used as an indicator for potential malicious activities.

Machine Learning algorithms originated as heuristic-based detection methods (Shabtai et al. 2010) that could easily evaluate software in search of malware. Since machine learning is automated, malicious features are predetermined and normally classified by their distinct code patterns. In addition, machine learning can process static code and determine its malicious capability. Static analysis uses significantly less time and resources. More importantly, it does not require the mobile application to be executed as in dynamic analysis (Shabtai et al. 2010).

The machine learning process has two phases: training and testing. First, a classification model is derived from a group of predetermined vectors and labels that represents the learning algorithm. This model is referred to as the training set. For accuracy and inclusion, the training set should include a wide variety of malicious applications. However, it's equally important that learning algorithm is able to properly identify the varying code patterns the malicious mobile applications. Then, a testing set of APKs is parsed according to its identifier, or its obvious malicious features. Each of the malicious actions exist within a representative vector and can be used to predict the origin of the malicious activity. If a malicious feature is flagged in the testing phase, the learning algorithm is able to determine which class files are affected.

Lastly, there are three main problems with the extraction of malicious features: misleading the learning algorithm with inaccurate features, overfitting or crowding with the amount of features to be evaluated, and creating a model complexity which exceeds the power of the learning algorithm (Shabtai et al. 2010). For accuracy and efficiency, filters are used to prevent the occurrence of the three difficulties above. These filters are responsible for ranking and scoring the features and determining which features are selected for the classification model.

Shabtai *et al.* (2010) evaluate three feature selection measures to determine which feature have a higher possibly of triggering a malicious attack. The feature selection measures are as follows: Chi-Square, Fisher Score, and Information Gain. In Table 4, those measures are used to determine the accuracy of the filter per each number of selected features. In the table, the data reflects a bias towards having a higher number of "top" features. In Table 5, the best configurations are shown for the same feature selection measures.

## Advantages

The approach is automated and can enable the static detection of malware applications. This proves to be extremely beneficial in cases where executing a possibly malicious application would cause harm to the evaluator's machine.

## Disadvantages

Depending on the type of classification algorithms, performance will vary. Also, the accuracy of training is important. A good initial dataset representing all types of applications are needed. If an application fits into overlapping category (e.g., a game application need to send information over the internet to store score of a user online which may be of similar to an application intended for browsing on the web), then machine learning is prone to false positive warning for benign application.

## Decompiler-Based Static Analysis

Enck et al. (2011) analyzed a large set of android applications collected from market to identify a set of dataflow, structure, and semantic patterns. The dataflow patterns identify whether any sensitive data information piece should not be sent to outside

*Table 4. Mean accuracy per measure and the number of selected features (Shabtai et al. 2010)*

| | Number of Features | ChiSquare | FisherScore | InfoGain |
|---|---|---|---|---|
| Accuracy | 50 | 0.839 | 0.847 | 0.856 |
| | 100 | 0.861 | 0.868 | 0.871 |
| | 200 | 0.877 | 0.879 | 0.880 |
| | 300 | 0.881 | 0.882 | 0.882 |
| | 500 | 0.888 | 0.885 | 0.890 |
| | 800 | 0.891 | 0.884 | 0.890 |
| FPR | 50 | 0.336 | 0.349 | 0.308 |
| | 100 | 0.303 | 0.293 | 0.288 |
| | 200 | 0.283 | 0.270 | 0.279 |
| | 300 | 0.283 | 0.268 | 0.269 |
| | 500 | 0.283 | 0.269 | 0.279 |
| | 800 | 0.254 | 0.261 | 0.260 |

*Table 5. Best configurations for mean accuracy in feature selection (Shabtai et al. 2010)*

| Configuration | Accuracy | FPR | AUC |
|---|---|---|---|
| Boosted BN ChiSquare 800 | 0.922 | 0.190 | 0.945 |
| Boosted BN InfoGain 800 | 0.918 | 0.172 | 0.945 |

(*e.g.*, IMEI, IMSI, ICC-ID). The structural analysis logs any API usage for retrieving sensitive information such as device ID or telephone manager. The semantic analysis performs the arguments of parameter method calls. For example, when a text message is being sent, it is checked if it is being used either to a constant or a dynamic number. The earlier might represent a malicious application activity. Their observation from seemingly benign applications can be considered as features to develop signatures.

The *ded decompiler* (Enck et al. 2011) method can recover the original application source code. This source code is then scanned and analyzed to uncover possible security threats. Enck et al. (2011) did not find malware in their study, the *ded decompiler* did uncover misuse of phone metadata. The key focus here is to address the greater potential of threats due to the fluidity of the mobile application market. Also, because mobile applications are being developed at a faster pace, most companies sacrifice the security aspect. More importantly, Enck et al. (2011) uncovered the misuse of mobile user information that can be used for a multitude of malicious activities. It is also very important to evaluate the development background and run-time environment compilation of an Android application, such as the application structure, register architecture, and the instruction set.

The analysis of the application source code revealed the following findings (Enck et al. 2011):

1.  "Phone identifiers are frequently leaked through plaintext requests.
2.  "Phone identifiers are used as device fingerprints.
3.  "Phone identifiers, specifically the IMEI, are used to track individual users.
4.  "The IMEI is tied to personally identifiable information (PII).
5.  "Not all phone identifier use leads to ex-filtration.
6.  "Phone identifiers are sent to advertisement and analytics servers.
7.  "The granularity of location reporting may not always be obvious to the user.
8.  "Location information is sent to advertisement servers.
9.  "Applications do not appear to be using fixed phone number services.
10.  "Applications do not appear to be misusing voice services.
11.  "Applications do not appear to be misusing video recording.
12.  "Applications do not appear to be misusing audio recording.
13.  "A small number of applications include code that uses the Socket class directly.
14.  "There was no evidence of malicious behavior by applications using Socket directly.
15.  "Applications do not appear to be harvesting information about installed applications.
16.  "Ad and analytics library use of phone identifiers and location is sometimes configurable.
17.  "Analytics library reporting frequency is often configurable.
18.  "Ad and analytics libraries probe for permissions.
19.  "Some developer toolkits replicate dangerous functionality.
20.  "Some developer toolkits probe for permissions.
21.  "Popular brands sometimes commission developers that include dangerous functionality.
22.  "Private information is written to Android's general logging interface.
23.  "Applications broadcast private information in IPC accessible to all applications.
24.  "Few applications are vulnerable to forging attacks to dynamic broadcast receivers.
25.  "Some applications define intent addresses based on IPC input.
26.  "Few applications unsafely delegate actions.
27.  "Applications frequently do not perform null checks on IPC input."

Though the findings above are not malware, they illustrate how easily a mobile application can be infiltrated due to poor coding practices or suspicious activity. These findings are very useful in determining potential risks and allow developers to close possible loopholes beforehand.

## Advantages

There are a wide variety of possible threats identified by this method and could be used to set a new standard of proper coding practices.

## Disadvantages

It is very difficult to uncover malicious applications using this method because many poorly written mobile applications could be flagged as false positives.

## Secure Software Architecture

Reza *et al.* (2012) analyze five operating systems: Android (Linux), Blackberry, iPhone (Mac OS X), Symbian, and Windows Mobile. In their analysis, the authors identify security issues and propose possible solutions to mitigate security breaches. Though the number of mobile users has surpassed the number of desktop users, the security of the mobile devices has yet to catch up. Because of this, mobile users are susceptible to many malicious and phishing threats.

The current architecture of Android does not accurately identify malicious applications according the analysis of the executable (Android APKs). In addition, new Android releases add another layer of complexity to the problem by preventing consistency for security features. Most subsequent releases can be significantly different from the former release. In addition, developers are often given more control over the mobile application with each release; this provides ample time and opportunity to malicious developers to determine how to infiltrate the operating system.

Reza *et al.* (2012) propose a solution to those security threats by starting at the root of the problem: the mobile operating system. There is a booming industry for many desktop-based operating systems, and there may be an added benefit for the mobile industry if they follow that lead. In Table 2, we illustrated the current architecture of the Android OS. Reza *et al.* (2012) propose a new architecture that ensures device efficiency (speed) and application security (reliability). Their architecture utilizes Android's built-in SQLite in order to integrate database functionality into the mobile applications.

## Advantages

The Android operating system shows the most promise (Reza et al. 2012) because of its ease of portability and the openness of the platform. Security issues can easily be incorporated into the Android operating system.

## Disadvantages

The Android operating system can currently be penetrated through APIs and method calls by the use of Android permissions. Though the permissions aspect works greats for Android application, it could also be counterproductive for maintaining overall security for the Android device.

## CONCLUSION

This chapter provides an overview of security threats posed by Android malware. We discuss the overall structure of the Android OS and how its security features attempt to prevent malware attacks. We also discuss the details of Android's privacy features and overall architecture. We discuss three different types of malware (grayware, spyware, and malware) and how they affect Android security. In particular, we focus on the characteristics commonly found in malware applications and understand the code level features that allow us to detect the malicious signatures. In addition, our examination of the code level demonstrates the likelihood of an Android application's malicious activities by those specific method signatures.

We also discuss some common defense techniques to mitigate the impact of malware applications. Those defense techniques are as follows: sandboxing, machine learning algorithms, decompiler-based static analysis, and secure software architecture for Android applications. A secure Android operating system and better coding practices will greatly reduce the possibilities of Android malware. These defense techniques enhance the security of the Android platform and deployed applications. We discuss both the advantages and disadvantages of each of these techniques.

# REFERENCES

Aaron, D. B. (2011, November 17). Google android passes 50% of Smartphone Sales. *Bloomberg Businessweek*. Retrieved August 21, 2013, from http://www.businessweek.com/news/2011-11-17/google2android-passes-50-of-smartphone-sales-gartner-says.html

*Android Design. (2013)*. Retrieved August 21, 2013, from http://developer.android.com/design/index.html

*Android IDL Example with Code Description – IPC*. (2013, July 20). Retrieved August 21, 2013, from http://techblogon.com/android-aidl-example-with-code-description-ipc

Baldwin, C. (2012, September 17). Android devices vulnerable to security breaches. *ComputerWeekly.com*. Retrieved August 21, 2013, from http://www.computerweekly.com/news/2240163351/Android-devices-vulnerable-to-security-breaches

Blasing, T., Batyuk, L., Schmidt, A., Camtepe, S., & Albayrak, S. (2010). An Android Application Sandbox System for Suspicious Software Detection. In *Proceedings of the Proceedings of the 5th International Conference on IEEE Malicious and Unwanted Software*, (pp. 55-62). IEEE.

Brinkmann, M. (2012, October 13). *Encrypt all data in Android phone*. Retrieved August 21, 2013, from http://www.ghacks.net/2012/10/13/encrypt-all-data-on-your-android-phone

*Difference between Adware and Spyware*. (2005, July 17). Retrieved August 21, 2013, from http://www.techiwarehouse.com/engine/41cc4355/Difference%20Between%20Adware%20&%20Spyware

Enck, W., Octeau, D., McDaniel, P., & Chaudhuri, S. (2011). A study of android application security. In *Proceedings of the 20th USENIX Conference on Security* (SEC 2011). USENIX Association.

Felt, A. P., Finifter, M., Chin, E., Hanna, S., & Wagner, D. (2011. A survey of mobile malware in the wild. In *Proceedings of the 1st ACM workshop on Security and privacy in smartphones and mobile devices* (SPSM 2011). ACM.

*Get Social Updates of your contact list using Ice cream sandwich*. (2012). Retrieved August 21, 2013, from http://creativeandroidapps.blogspot.com/2012/07/get-social-updates-of-your-contact-list.html

Google Play. (2013). *Google play store*. Retrieved August 21, 2013, from https://play.google.com/store?hl=en

*How to get the Android device's Primary Email Address*. (2010). Retrieved August 21, 2013, from http://stackoverflow.com/questions/2112965/how-to-get-the-android-devices-primary-e-mail-address

*How to make a phone pall in Android and come back to my when activity call is done.* (2011). Retrieved August 21, 2013, from http://stackoverflow.com/questions/1556987/how-to-make-a-phone-call-in-android-and-come-back-to-my-activity-when-the-call-i

*How to make android phone silent in java.* (2012). Retrieved August 21, 2013, from://stackoverflow.com/questions/10360815/how-to-make-android-phone-silent-in-java

Hyatt, E. C. (2013). *Custom Android Phone.* Retrieved August 21, 2013, from http://sites.google.com/site/edwardcraighyatt/projects/custom-android-phone

*Lock and Android phone.* (2012). Retrieved August 21, 2013, from http://stackoverflow.com/questions/4793339/lock-an-android-phone

*Memory Management in Android.* (2010, July 5). Retrieved August 21, 2013, from http://mobworld.wordpress.com/2010/07/05/memory-management-in-android/

Oberheide, J., Cooke, E., & Jahanian, F. (2008). Cloudav: N version antivirus in the network cloud. In *Proceedings of the 17th USENIX Security Symposium* (Security'08). San Jose, CA: USENIX.

PhonePay Plus. (2013). *Phonepayplus.org.uk.* Retrieved August 21, 2013, from http://www.phonepayplus.org.uk

Rehm, L. (2012, October 25). *A Guide to Android OS.* Retrieved August 21, 2013, from http://connect.dpreview.com/post/8437301608/guide-to-android-os

Reza, H., & Mazumder, N. (2012). A secure software architecture for mobile computing. In *Proceedings of the 9th International Conference on Information Technology- New Generations* (ITNG 2012). Las Vegas, NVL ITNG.

*Security Tips.* (2013). Retrieved August 21, 2013, from http://developer.android.com/training/articles/security-tips.html

*Send S. M. S. in Android.* (2013). Retrieved August 21, 2013, from http://stackoverflow.com/questions/4967448/send-sms-in-android

*Set Wallpaper using WallpaperManager.* (2011, March 28). Retrieved August 21, 2013, from http://android-er.blogspot.com/2011/03/set-wallpaper-using-wallpapermanager.html

Shabtai, A., Fledel, Y., & Elovici, Y. (2010). Automated static code analysis for classifying android applications using machine learning. In *Proceedings of the 2010 International Conference on Computational Intelligence and Security* (CIS 2010) (pp. 329-333). CIS.

Shabtai, A., Fledel, Y., Kanonov, U., Elovici, Y., Dolev, S., & Glezer, C. (2010, March). Google Android: A Comprehensive Security Assessment. *IEEE Security & Privacy*, 35-44.

*What is Malware?* (2013). Retrieved August 21, 2013, from http://www.microsoft.com/security/resources/malware-whatis.aspx

## KEY TERMS AND DEFINITIONS

**Android OS:** Linux-based operating system for mobile devices.

**Dynamic Analysis:** Analysis of software in real time by program execution.

**Machine Learning:** Study and analysis of system data to teach computers to learn.

**Malware:** Software that implemented with a malicious intent.

**Sandbox:** Detection technique that allows separately monitoring programs.

**Secure Software Architecture:** Implementing a well-designed program with security in mind.

**Static Analysis:** Analysis of software while executing a program.

# Chapter 5
# Answering the New Realities of Stalking

**Avelina Alonso de Escamilla**
*CEU San Pablo University, Spain*

## ABSTRACT

*This chapter aims mainly to carry out a study of a new type of harassment named stalking. After the study of its contents through the opinions of the most recognized specialist on it, the chapter defines the crime based on the expert's opinion. A study of comparative law is done, and this study focuses on the different ways stalking happens. This chapter offers a critical study of the inclusion of stalking as a felony in the criminal amendment Organic Criminal Law 10/1995 of 23 November, Criminal Law Code. To finish, this chapter proposes some improvements to that regulation and focuses on the new realities that bring about cyber stalking.*

## INTRODUCTION

The term stalking, first introduced by the Anglo-Saxon law tradition, can be explained as an intentional and malicious behavior of obsessive following, spying or harassment towards a certain individual. It therefore forms a pattern of behavior, a sort of abnormal harassment strategy, which is directed during a long interval of time towards a specific person (MELOY/GOTHARD, 1995, pp.259). It must therefore consist in more than a single act of persecution, and these repeated acts must be unwanted by the victim. It can have, among others, the following forms: following, enclosing, prowling, approaching, communicating, repetitive phoning, sending mail, ordering an object or service for the victim, breaking into the victim's house or properties, making false accusations, menacing or assaulting the victim.

As it can be seen from the aforementioned list, these different behaviors vary widely in seriousness: whereas some constitute felonies, others are legally irrelevant, and might even count with social approval. Furthermore we cannot fail to mention the new forms of stalking which the Internet has allowed to appear, such as sending e-mails on a constant basis, sending threatening messages on social networks such as Facebook or Twitter, posting defaming comments on the personal or professional webpages of the victim, hacking the victim's email account, etc. A lot of these actions can be carried out anonymously or even through a fake identity, which makes it much harder to identify the culprit. This harassment can occur even if the victim has never seen the stalker and has no way of figuring out who it could possibly be.

DOI: 10.4018/978-1-4666-6324-4.ch005

The literature has not reached a consensus when it comes to determining what must be taken into account in order to charge this behavior. Some authors consider that the defining factor is the number of attacks suffered by the victim (i.e. 10 times during 4 weeks or twice a week during a 6 month interval), irrespective of the seriousness of the behavior itself (PATHE/MULLEN, 1997, pp.12). On the other hand, other authors believe that a consensus must be reached regarding which out of all these acts are legally relevant for the legal classification of this felony (KAMPHUIS/ EMMELKAMP, 2000, pp.207).

The regulation of stalking emerged in the United States of America, where it was defined as a repetitive behavior directed towards a specific individual, who must see such behavior as intrusive and frightening. This kind of definition is similar to the methodology employed in the DSM IV (Diagnostic and Statistical Manual of Disorders, 4th Edition), insofar as it requires a series of criteria to be met (WESTRUP, 1998, pp. 279).

To summarize, among the factors of stalking are the following: a series of act that form a pattern of behavior, which are clearly unwanted by the victim, and that cause him or her uneasiness, fear, shame or discomfort, and which hamper the victim from leading a normal life and/or cause her anxiety or some other psychological harm. It is precisely this idea of unceasing persecution that is interesting for criminal law. In some systems of comparative law this behavior has been characterized as a kind of domestic violence, but since harassment occurs in many different forms, some of which are unrelated to the victim's home place, this definition is clearly insufficient.

Stalkers do not necessarily have clinical features in common, so it is difficult to make a psychological profile about their personality. Sometimes they truly believe the victim wants to be with them, sometimes they suffer a romantic obsession which makes them want to be with the victim above anything else. Frequently the stalker follows a person with whom they were previously romantically involved, refusing to acknowledge that relationship is over. And these are just a few among many of the motivations that stalkers use to justify their behavior. Sometimes the victim will minimize such as a behavior due to feelings of guilt or fear or because they believe it will be short-lived.

## THE MANIFESTATION OF STALKING BEHAVIOR AND ITS DEMARCATION FROM OTHER CRIMES

In most of the European legal systems in which *stalking* have been introduced, it has been placed among the felonies against the freedom to act. This is the case in the Netherlands, Austria, Germany or Italy. This freedom to act is understood in a broad way and spans throughout the whole process of volition: the freedom to form a will, the freedom to decide upon a will, and the freedom to carry out a will (or freedom to act strictly speaking (VILLACAMPA, 2010, pp. 41).

Even though stalking attacks this freedom to act, we will see that the current definition of felonies such as duress or threats is not enough to include this predatory form of harassment among its typical manifestations, something that was already proposed in the Project's Statement of Purpose.

To begin with the felony of threats, this crime is usually defined as an attack against the freedom to form a will, and hence some forms of stalking can be subsumed under it. After all such harassment will force the victim to change his or her behavior, and this clearly affects his or her will. However, this crime requires a verbal expression, an announcement of a serious harm that depends on the victim's will, and there are various forms of stalking that do not occur in this way. When a stalker wants to establish a relationship with the victim, or continue a relationship that is over, his or her behavior might appear as intimidating and persecutory, but not necessarily threatening.

Other problems appear when one attempts to subsume stalking under the felony of duress, as has been frequently done by the jurisprudence. In order to do so, one has to interpret the law in such a way that the violence it typically requires is not only understood as brute force (*vis fisica),* but also as intimidation (*vis psiquica)* or even as force against property. Such an interpretation trespasses the limits imposed by the principle of legitimacy. Furthermore, even though duress is an attack against the freedom to carry out a will, stalking can go much further and be an attack against the freedom to form a will and the freedom to decide upon a will. Therefore not all the forms of stalking can be subsumed under the duress felony.

We could also attempt to include *stalking* among the crimes against moral integrity or of degrading treatment, since it is a form of harassment and resembles other types of harassment such as mobbing or bullying. In order to do so, we must distinguish between moral and psychological harassment. The former seeks to humiliate the victim, whereas the later does not seek to cause feelings of humiliation, but rather worry, fear, insecurity or discomfort. Stalking appears to have more in common with this second kind of harassment. Nevertheless, if we observe some of the typical behaviors of this crime, we will see that considering it as a form of mobbing is problematic, since it assimilates it to the sort of harassment that occurs among coworkers.

The crime of domestic violence, which is also placed among the crimes against the freedom to act, consists in treating a person in a degrading way, harming his moral integrity, understood as his or her right to act according to his or her will, ideas, thoughts or feelings (ALONSO DE ESCAMILLA, 2013, pp.164). A lot of the behavior associated with *stalking* can produce in the victim similar feelings. Nevertheless other behaviors that produce feelings of fear or discomfort or anxiety, which are also typical of *stalking*, would be excluded from its legal characterization. There is the additional issue that the Criminal Code requires a relation-ship of kinship to exist for domestic violence to take place, and as we know stalking can occur in the absence of such a link.

With regards to the crime of sexual harassment, it is also too limited to subsume all forms of stalking, since it is defined as a special felony, it requires a labor or academic relationship to be in place, and it consists in demanding sexual favors. There are forms of sexual harassment that can be included as forms of cyberstalking, like childgrooming, but the later is defined as a crime when the victim is under thirteen (or under sixteen according to the draft of the next amendment of the Organic Criminal Law 10/1995 November 23th, Criminal Law Code).

Therefore, it appears that in our Criminal Code there is no precept that can include all the behavior associated with the behavior we are analyzing, even though there are felonies under which some forms of stalking can be subsumed. Thus we are lead into the question of whether a new crime should be defined in the Criminal Code for stalking, and if we answer in the affirmative, what the content of that crime should be.

## STALKING IN COMPARATIVE LAW

### Stalking in Anglo-Saxon Countries

#### United States of America

The criminalization of stalking first occurred in the USA during the nineties, only after several high-profile cases, which gained national attention as the murder of singer John Lennon at the beginning of the eighties or actress Rebecca Schaeffer at the end of that decade. The murder of four women by their husbands at Orange County or the harassments or stalking to other actress as Jodie Foster or Theresa Saldana or the singer Madonna, cause a great impact on the American society.

Up to then, only some of the states of the Union had got laws that regulate harassment or assault, but were not suitable to protect victims of harassment. This situation and the high-profile cases related before, determine that the state of California enacted the first stalking state law of the United States. In a few months, thirty states followed that decision and in 1993 the nineteen remaining states did the same, so nowadays all fifty states that integrate the Confederation plus the District of Columbia have passed laws criminalizing stalking.

As respective laws consider stalking in a different way, even denominating it such as stalking, criminal harassment or criminal menace (DE LA CUESTA /MAYORDOMO, 2011, pp.27) in 1992 the United States Congress commissioned the National Institute of Justice to elaborate the Model stalking Code who served as a pattern for the different states. That Code has been lately revisited to be adapted to new realities of stalking, over all those that become facts of cyber stalking. In 1996 stalking become a federal crime and was included in the United States Code (Interstate Stalking Punishment and prevention Act).

## Canada

Harassment is a crime in Canada, where was introduced into its legislation in 1993. Afterwards in 1997 it was published A Handbook for Police and Crown Prosecutor in Criminal Harassment, guide that incorporates a lot of patterns and conclusions and recommendations.

## United Kingdom

The Stalking Law came into force in 1997 for England and Wales and brought in two crimes, stalking strictly speaking and other that take place when a person fears another with some kind of violence for twice. As we see, this law combines the rule of fear with the frequency of the acts. In addition, Common Law allows prosecute stalkers although they have not yet assault their victims, if they have caused psychological harm.

In Scotland, the Protection from Harassment Act considers harassment as a civil offence and allows the victim to ask for a forbidding approach. Its violation becomes a crime.

As we can see, before becoming a federal crime in the United States, stalking had spread out to Canada and Australia and after to United Kingdom and New Zealand.

## Stalking in Continental European Countries

Despite that stalking comes from Common Law legal tradition countries, it influence has reached some European countries as Ireland, Germany, Austria, The Netherlands, Denmark, Belgium or Italy, country in which has been penalize recently (2009).

## Germany

Stalking is regulate in the German Criminal Code, paragraph 238 that includes several behaviours as searching for closeness, getting in touch, ordering goods or services on behalf of the victim, threaten with injuries on life, integrity wealth or freedom of the victim or close relatives or put at risk life or integrity of the victim or close relatives. As we can appreciate, these behaviours are impossible to bring back to a unique pattern. Some are even socially suitable but they are committed without the wish of the victim. In all cases these behaviours have to produce a deep disruption on the victim.

## Austria

Stalking is regulated in the Austrian Criminal Code, paragraph 107 that considers stalking as a crime that needs the disagreement of the victim. The Code establishes behaviours such as searching for closeness, getting in touch, ordering goods or services on behalf of the victim. As we can appreciate, very similar to conducts regulate in the German Criminal Code.

## Italy

Italy first pay attention to this behaviour through the National Stalking Observatory, created in 2002 and the National Stalking Centre, created in 2006. After the research held in those institutions, a specific crime of stalking was introduced in the Italian Criminal Code, article 612bis. It contents includes a behaviour of threatening or disturbing or bothering a person repeatedly that causes a permanent and deep state of anxiety or fear that makes her/him change patterns of conduct (VIL-LACAMPA, 2009, pp.20).

## Spain

As to Spain, there is a proposal of modifying the Criminal Code to include stalking as a crime in article 172ter. This proposal follows the intention of the previous amendment of the Criminal Code that included sort of harassment as mobbing, bullying, blockbusting or child grooming. Most of the problems that arise from that regulation appear again with the punishment of stalking. The proposal comes from a legal willingness but with not a single empiric study of stalking which may made easier the draft of the article.

## SPECIAL MENTION TO SPANISH REGULATION

In the Statement or Purpose of the next criminal amendment that is held by the draft of Organic Criminal Law 10/1995 November 23rd, Criminal Law Code, gives the following reasons to include stalking as a crime.

*Stalking is criminalized as a felony against freedom, to answer to those behaviours of unquestionable importance that in most cases can not be described as compulsion or threat. These are all those cases in which without suggest the intention of causing harm or evil (compulsion) or the use of violence to restrict the freedom of the victim (threat), repeatedly conducts by means of diminishing freedom or security of victim by prosecuting or constant vigilance, repeated phone calls or others continuous harrying.*

Article 172ter of the next amendment that is held by the draft, includes the criminalization of stalking as a felony. It includes a sort of behaviours as follows:

- Supervise or harass or searching for closeness.
- Getting in touch or attempting to through any way of communication or third party.
- Ordering goods or services by wrongful use of his/her data.
- Make an attempt on his/her freedom or private property or freedom or private property of close relatives.
- Any other analogous behaviour.

These conducts may be aggravated in some cases. Those are situations in which the stalker takes particular advantage of the vulnerability of the victim. The vulnerability may depend on the age, illness or special situation of the victim or in any previous relationship between the stalker and the victim.

Law allows punishing stalking and other crimes that may commit the stalker while stalking as robbery or sexual assault and gives the judge the opportunity to add to prison a security measure as supervised release.

In most of the European Criminal Codes, in which stalking has become a felony, the location where that crime has been included is between crimes against freedom to act, understood in a broad sense: freedom to form a will, freedom to decide upon a will and freedom to carry out a will. As to Spain, stalking is included into crimes against freedom, as well.

Until this legal initiative, there was in our Criminal Law a lapse concerning those generic stalking behaviours in spite of the insufficient regulation of this conducts.

Concerning it regulation, some considerations may be done:

- Stalking is regulated as a crime that can be committed by any person.
- It requires bad break of everyday routine, through the fulfilment of any of the behaviours that include article 172ter.
- Our proposal prefers European model of incrimination, avoiding to refer to a number of conducts as Anglo-Saxon model does and defining the behaviours itself even at the expense of not including all the situations that may be examples of stalking.

The text that includes the proposal was positively reported by the General Prosecution Service that defends the text as the Statement of Purpose and with very similar arguments.

In a very analogous way the General Council of the Judiciary enhanced the criminalization of stalking mentioning the previous trajectory in Anglo-Saxon countries and in those European countries where stalking is already a crime.

Finally the Advisory Council to the Government pronounced about article 172ter criticising the inclusion of the expression "any other analogous behaviour" as it may go against article 25 Spanish Constitution that establish principle of legitimate.

## Some Controversial Questions

Article 172bis of the next amendment that is held by the draft, includes the criminalization of stalking as a felony. It includes some controversial questions as follows.

First of all, harassment or stalking may be committed through specific ways. But the article does not give all the situations as a *numerus clausus* clause. And it is followed by the expression "any other analogue behaviour", open clause that may go against article 25 Spanish Constitution that established principle of legitimate. That objection

was made by the Advisory Council to the Government and as well by some specialised doctrine, (MUÑOZ CONDE, 2011, pp.23).

The doctrine mostly agree to propose to include into the article the expression "in an illegal way", jus to lay out of stalking behaviours, those which are the result of those prosecutions that may take place in the case of a criminal investigation as well as in the case of investigating some piece of new that is the result of the right to be informed (ex: journalists), (VILLACAMPA, 2013, pp.603).

Spanish proposal of stalking as a crime follows German Criminal Code and requires a concrete result which is a bad break of everyday routine, but nothing else is told about the meaning of that expression. So justice will have to explain through precedents the contents of that common saying.

The article 172ter of the next amendments that is held by the draft, includes as stalking the following behaviours: supervise or harass or searching for closeness. But those misconducts are not of the same meaning. While supervise or harass may have many similarities and are the most common ways of harassment, searching for closeness is a previous state to stalking so that is to say is not yet a felony.

Even though also article 172ter includes getting in touch and trying to get in touch as similar conducts, they are not the same. The first means that you have already get in touch while the last indicates you are still trying to. So you can not punish both with the same penalty as our proposal happens to do.

Spanish proposal of stalking as a crime includes making an attempt on victim freedom or private property or freedom or private property of close relatives. A suggestion of including as well a reference to attempt to life or integrity is also needed, as life and integrity are as important as freedom to be protected by Criminal Law.

Furthermore of these considerations, one more must be done. Battle against stalking must be done not only through Criminal Law but using as well protection mechanisms that offers Civil Law.

Those are civil protection orders or temporary restraining orders. These have been developed in the United States of America where they are in use successfully and they are included in the legislation of the fifty states plus the District of Columbia. They can be ordered by the civil judge without a previous civil or criminal procedure as they can be decided in an independent way or process that includes forbidding approach or contact with the victim or close relatives, (DE LA CUESTA /MAYORDOMO, 2011,pp.47).

According to the proposal, there will be more punishment if stalking is done over a victim with a previous relationship with the stalker. Even though cases in which the stalker take particular advantage of the vulnerability of the victim are not going to deserve that much sentence. That does not make much sense and in both cases the sentence would be the same. And what is more, it might be added the circumstance of committing stalking in presence of minors as a collective of actors have already demanded in court in the state of California while they have to support incessant attacks against their children who are indirect victims of stalking against their parents, (12). That regulation would satisfy the obligation with the partner member states of European Union after the signature of the Agreement of European Council to prevent and fight domestic violence against women signed in Istanbul in may, 11th 2011.

The article stipulates that the victim has to report stalking to the police so they can prosecute the crime and that he/she can forgive the stalker without precluding the intervention of the Public Prosecutor under the authority conferred upon him by the law in cases of stalking over minors.

The article 172ter gives the judge the possibility of according a kind of supervised release which starts when the liberty deprivation sentence is finished and the offender is released. The meaning of this institution is analogous to the United States federal system of supervised release in that it is imposed by a judge during sentencing and it is to be fulfilled after a custodial sentence so it

goes further than the penalty itself. That is why most of the Spanish doctrine has criticised this security measure, (NUÑEZ FERNANDEZ, 2011, pp.921). It contents includes several obligations such as being always available or to attend citations or restraining orders that suits the specific criminological profile ok the delinquent. Those obligations may apply all together or separately or vary during it length. The proposal established a period of five years that may be extended for equal periods of five years. So it becomes as an unlimited security measure, something unknown in our Criminal Law.

As to Spain, this security measure introduced in Spanish Criminal Code in the last amendment on 2010 was reserved to major crimes as terrorism, murder or sexual assault and was applied to those delinquents that were not receptive to rehabilitation through penalty. But none of these arguments may be applied to stalkers as Spain has not yet empiric studies about stalkers and it criminological profile, (ALONSO DE ESCAMILLA/NUÑEZ FERNANDEZ, 2010, pp.72). So we had better to think about giving up this security measure for stalkers.

After all these considerations we have to conclude that the content of article 172ter that includes stalking as a crime in Spanish Criminal Code, has serious defects that may be solved before publishing. That would be much better than to amend the law after it entry into force. Amending and amending Criminal Code has a very bad impression on society which is the final concern of it.

## STALKING IN THE INTERNET: CYBERSTALKING AND NEW REALITIES

As a consequence of the new technologies eruption and due to the huge growth of Internet in the past ten years, it is thought to be necessary to limit and regulate the information which is being thrown to the internet. This fast growth makes controlling cybernetic stalking really difficult. Cyberstalking can be considered as an abusive behavior or repetitive harassment without the victims consent, using any tools that Internet provides us, as can be email, chat, texts, WhatsApp, social networks like Facebook or Twitter, web pages, etc.

This new way of stalking has specific characteristics that are determined by the media they are done in which are the following:

- Being anonymous, a quality that Internet gives us is a pretext for stalkers to use more direct and violent language towards the victim than in real life.
- The stalker, thanks to that anonymity, enjoys being in a power. That power can be used against people they already know or against others who they met at a chat as in any other social network.
- The stalker has many resources to get information about the victim through their Internet presence and profiles, which may include personal and private details which are the main aim of the stalker.
- The worrying circumstance is that it is the Internet that provides this advantage to stalkers. As an example, sending messages online of any type (insulting, menacing and of variable, systematic or massive rhythm (mail bombing) can be done by signing for a free email or altered so it seems they were sent by the victim, putting them in a difficult situation, concerning the burden of proof.
- The stalker has easy access to pictures posted by the victim in any of their social network sites or chats. Another option is posting offensive information concerning the victim or sending SMS from the site, which can not be tracked easily.

All this circumstances put the stalker in a power situation over the victim, who is now defenseless.

To relieve somehow this defenseless situation, this can adopt some protection measures, like choosing an e-mail account as aseptic as possible, in which it is not possible to distinguish the gender of the person (since women shape the most numerous group of victims of cyberstalking), to restrict to the maximum the privacy in your profile of any chats or social network pages, deleting any personal or private information. Victims may not include in the e-mail any head-board information as the name or the address. Being important also, to save any evidence from that bullying and never building a relationship with the stalker by replying consistently, so it can not be misleading.

In consequence, the irruption and the progressive increase of new technologies have modified the way in which harassment can occur, which before required contact and now can be avoided deliberately. That is to say, the above mentioned personal contact will be able or not to take place. The stalker and his victim will meet or will not but it is necessary to understand that it is not necessary anymore to demand physical proximity between the stalker and the victim to satisfy the definition of harassment. The contact takes place now in another way that is equally intimidating for the victim who often can not perform everyday tasks such as answering their phones, reading their mail or using their computers without fear of unwanted contact from the person who is stalking them. New forms of technological stalking can be done from a distance by the new widely available monitoring technology as GPS, spycam or spyware programs which are going to let the stalker locate the victim wherever she/he is. The findings of research in all these areas will surely provide crucial clues to drafters of stalking legislation, especially on those countries in which stalking is not yet a specific crime.

In this respect, a lot of problems will arise when legislating on these new realities, like the limits that have to be imposed to each law in order for it not to become unconstitutional as consequence of its excessive generality or its vagueness or imprecision.

The challenge is to enact laws that address stalking perpetrated by all the currently known technologies, as well as through future technologies not yet developed or available to stalkers.

## CONCLUSION

After the accomplishment of the present study, it is necessary to highlight the following conclusions:

- It is possible to define stalking as a series of concatenated acts that turn into a patterned conduct towards a specific person, which make the victim have feelings of dread, clear discomfort, uneasiness, shame or worry and wreaks havoc on a victim´s life, deriving in clinical diagnosis of anxiety or another psychological hurt.

- The incrimination of the stalking comes from the United States of America, where it takes place in the 90s. In the same decade it is regulated also as a crime in Canada, United Kingdom, Australia and New Zealand. In the continental Europe it is regulated as well in Germany, Austria, Belgium, Denmark, Holland, Ireland and Italy and very soon it will be a crime in Spain. Until to this legal initiative, there was in the Spanish Criminal Law a lapse related to those generic harassment behaviors in spite of the insufficient regulation of this conducts. In spite of the above mentioned legislative initiative, the article that regulates the incrimination of stalking, suffers from serious technical faults that should be corrected before his incorporation to the Criminal Code. The inclusion of a new felony into the Criminal Code has to

respond to empirical studies done with the sufficient thought and the necessary rigor that should justify such decision. So once it forms a part of the Criminal Code it can be permanently, since the constant reforms of criminal laws and changes just reduces credibility in front of society which is it final concern.

- In most of the juridical European classifications in which the stalking has got into, the location chosen by the legislator has been in the crimes against freedom of act understood in a board sense: freedom to form a will, freedom to decide upon a will and freedom to carry out a will.

- Battle against stalking must be done, not only through the Criminal law, but also from other area as the Civil Law, across the protection orders, which would allow a better defense for the victims of harassment, as it is already happening in other countries as in United States of America, where the civil protection orders or temporary restraining orders are in use successfully.

- The irruption of the new technologies, the advance and generalization and the enormous growth of Internet during the last decade have turned the cybernetic harassment into a global problem of difficult control, since it uses the tools that the Internet provides as e-mail, SMS, WhatsApp, Facebook or Twitter, arising many problems when legislating about these new realities. Those regulations will have to challenge the constitutionality of stalking laws, in order not to become overbroad or vague or imprecise.

- Internet places the stalker in a position of proportional force over the victim suffering from ciberstalking, for what the current challenge consists of enacting laws that give response to the new realities of stalking that happen due to new technologies that already exist, as well as across those appearing in the future.

# REFERENCES

Alonso de Escamilla, A., & Nuñez Fernandez, J. (2010). Fundamentos de derecho penal. Colección Praxis, Ed. Universitas.

Alonso de Escamilla, A. (2013). Torturas y otros delitos contra la integridad moral. In *Delitos y faltas* (2nd ed.). Ed. Colex.

de la Cuesta Arzamendi, J.L., & Mayordomo Rodrigo, V. (2011). Acoso y derecho penal. *Cuadernos del Instituto Vasco de Criminología*, (25).

InDret2009*La introducción del delito de "atti persecutori" en el Código penal italiano*. InDret. Available on line in http://www.indret.com

Kamphuis, J.H., & Emmelkamp, P.M.G. (2000). Stalking-A contemporary challenger for forensic and clinical psychiatry. *The British Journal of Psychiatry*, 176.

Meloy, R., & Gothard, S. (1995). Demographic and clinical comparison of obsessional followers and offenders with mental disorders. *The American Journal of Psychiatry*, *152*, 2.

Muñoz Conde, F. (2011). Diversas modalidades de acoso punible en el Código Penal. In T. lo Blanch (Ed.), El acoso: Tratamiento penal y procesal. Academic Press.

Nuñez Fernandez, J. (2011). Las medidas de seguridad y reinserción social in Curso de Derecho penal. Parte General. Ed. Dykinson.

Pathe, M., & Mullen, P.E. (1997). The impact o f stalkers in their victims. *The British Journal of Psychiatry*, 174.

ReCrim2010*La respuesta jurídico-penal frente al stalking en España: presente y future*. ReCrim. Available on line in http://www.uv.es/recrim

Villacampa Estiarte, C. (2013). Delito de acecho/ stalking: Art. 172 ter in Estudio crítico sobre el Anteproyecto de reforma penal de 2012. Ed. Tirant lo Blanch Reformas.

Westrup, D. (1998). Applying functional analysis to stalking. In The psychology of stalking: Clinical and forensic perspectives. New York: Academic Press.

## KEY TERMS AND DEFINITIONS:

**Abuse:** Physical or sexual maltreatment of a person, injury.

**Bullying:** A person who hurts or persecutes or intimidates weaker people.

**Chat:** Online conversation.

**Compulsion:** The act of compelling or the state of being compelled.

**Cyberstalking:** Abusive behaviour or repetitive harassment without the victims consent, using any tools that the Internet provides us as can be email, chat, texts, whatsapp, social networks like facebook or twitter, web pages, etc.

**Harassment:** To trouble or torment or confuse by continuant persistent attacks or questions.

**Maltreatment:** To treat badly, cruelly or inconsiderate.

**Mobbing:** Many European languages use *mobbing* in the sense of bullying or harassment, unlike the original meaning of English.

**Persecution:** To oppress, harass or maltreat or to bother persistently.

**Social Network:** The exchange of information or services among individuals, groups or institutions using facebook or twitter.

**Stalking:** To pursue persistently and sometimes attack a person with whom one is obsessed.

**Threat:** A declaration of the intention to inflict harm, pain or misery.

# Chapter 6
# Cyberbullying:
## Keeping Our Children Safe in the 21st Century

**Iris Reychav**
*Ariel University, Israel*

**Shraga Sukenik**
*Ariel University, Israel*

## ABSTRACT

*In the 21st century, thus far, we have seen a growing dependence on and usage of the Internet and communications technology. This has been especially true for youth who spend much of their time communicating in cyber space. This allows for developing and maintaining relationships. At the same time, an ugly and dangerous phenomenon called cyber bullying has reared its head. In this chapter, the authors discuss various aspects of this phenomenon, including, but not limited to, incidence rates, comparison to traditional bullying, risk factors for being involved either as a bully or a victim, how it affects its victims, relevant legal aspects, and most importantly, how to defend against it. The discussion of coping strategies is especially detailed and provide suggestions for schools, parents, bystanders, victims, and broader society.*

## INTRODUCTION

In recent years we have seen many wonders that can be accomplished through information and communications technology. Young people have especially benefited from these advances, accruing many advantages from the Internet and mobile phones such as access to educational information, resources and collaborative learning networks, the development and maintenance of relationships and friendships with their peers, and an outlet for creativity, to name a few (Kowalski, Limber, & Agatston, 2012). However, there have also been risks and dangers that have accompanied the expansion of the 'virtual' world. Cyberbullying is one of the online risks youth face, and the one they are most likely to encounter (Livingstone, Haddon, Gorzig, & Olafsson, 2011).

Cyberbullying is defined as actions that use information and communication technologies to

DOI: 10.4018/978-1-4666-6324-4.ch006

support deliberate, repeated, and hostile behavior by an individual or group, that is intended to harm another or others (Dilmac, 2009). These crimes have been shown to have serious consequences for their victims. For example, victims will isolate themselves socially, display more anger and depression, and in some cases will be driven to suicide, as was the case with Phoebe Prince (ABC News, 2010), Megan Meier (New York Times, 2007), and several others. Cyberbullying has become a major concern to modern society (Martin & Rice, 2011). One way this is reflected is that the general awareness and media attention have grown in the last decade (Dooley, Pyżalski, & Cross, 2009; Patchin & Hinduja, 2011). One needs to address the problem of cyber bullying broadly and systematically, involving peers, teachers, school administrators, mental health professionals, law enforcement, parents, and of course the victim (Mishna et al, 2010). We will address each of these parties and their respective roles in cyber bullying prevention (see Figure 1).

We will present a "multi-pronged defense" in which all members and groups in society can play a part in preventing cyber bullying (e.g. schools, law enforcement agencies, bystanders).

Before one can discuss ways of preventing cyber bullying we first have to understand the phenomenon better. This includes defining the relevant terms and how it differs from traditional bullying, its prevalence, risk factors for being a bully or victim, the negative effects on the cyber victim, and the like. To this end, this chapter will include definitions and typology of cyber bullying, rate of incidence, possible motives for the perpetrators, risk factors for both bully and victim, negative effects on cyber victims, the similarities and differences to traditional bullying, the legal aspects involved in combating and prosecuting cyber bullying, and most importantly, strategies for preventing and coping with cyber bullying.

## BACKGROUND

Many definitions of cyber bullying have been used, which is problematic in terms of conceptualization and challenges our ability to compare studies in this field. The definition which appears to have a great degree of adherence, and will be adopted in this chapter as well, is that of Dilmac (2009) *"an individual or a group willfully using information and communication involving electronic technologies to facilitate deliberate and repeated harassment or threat to another individual or group by sending or posting cruel text and/or graphics using technological means"*. Cassidy, Faucher, & Jackson's (2013) quote a popular definition (Smith, Mahdavi, Carvalho, Fisher, Russell, & Tippett, 2008) that adds the element of a victim who cannot easily defend him or herself.

A cyber bully can either act alone or get others to assist. Assisting a cyber bully is an act called "cyber bullying by proxy". According to Anderson (2010) cyber bullying refers specifically to situations in which both parties are children. Once an adult becomes involved, it is known as cyber harassment or cyber stalking. Cyberbullying by proxy may involve adults and that makes it all the more dangerous.

Someone can engage in direct or indirect cyber bullying. Direct cyber bullying occurs where the cyber bully directs the electronic communications directly at the victim while direct cyber bullying occurs privately between the bully and the victim. Indirect cyber bullying occurs when the bully posts the bullying message, video, etc. on a public platform in cyber space (e.g. Facebook, a blog, MySpace, etc.) (Brenner & Rehberg, 2009).

Cyber bullies will use methods such as cyber stalking, and cyber harassment to achieve their aims.

Cyberstalking uses the Internet, email or other electronic communications to stalk, generally referring to a pattern of threatening or malicious

*Figure 1. Coping strategies*

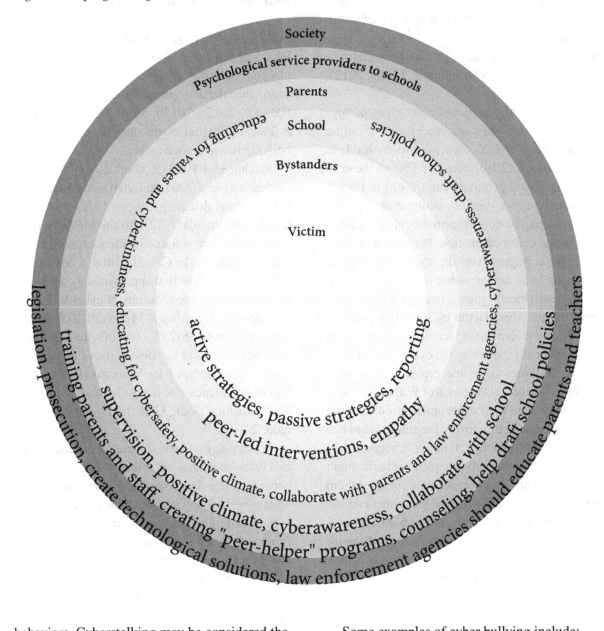

behaviors. Cyberstalking may be considered the most dangerous and potentially harmful of the types of Internet harassment.

Cyberharassment differs from cyber stalking in that it generally does not involve a credible threat. Cyberharassment usually pertains to threatening or harassing email messages, instant messages, blog entries or websites dedicated solely to tormenting an individual. (National Conference of State Legislatures, 2012)

Some examples of cyber bullying include:

- Sending an abusive or threatening email or text message;
- Posting derogatory comments, pictures or videos about an individual online;
- Emailing a computer virus or pornography to someone;
- Signing someone up for online junk mail;

- Stealing another person's password and pretending to be that person in a chat room; and
- Building fake online profiles on social networking sites. (Trevathan & Myers, 2012).

Willard (2007) proposed eight types of "cyber bullying activities and other forms of online social cruelty" (p. 5). Pieschl, Porsch, Kahl, & Klockenbusch (2013) consider five of these to be cyber bullying: harassment (insults or threats against the cyber -victim), denigration (spreading damaging rumors to harm the cyber -victim's reputation), impersonation (assuming a fake identity to impersonate the cyber -victim and behaving in an embarrassing or damaging way), outing and trickery (gaining and then violating the trust of the cyber -victim by spreading publicly private and embarrassing secrets), and exclusion (systematically excluding the cyber -victim from online activities or online groups). They have excluded the other categories of Willard's (2007) taxonomy from their conceptualization of cyber bullying because they involve arguments between equally powerful peers ("flaming"), because they view them as being sub-categories of harassment ("cyber threats"), or because they consider them more closely related to sexual harassment on the Internet than to cyber bullying ("cyber stalking"). It is perhaps not surprising that there are different incidence rates of cyber bullying as it's not agreed upon what cyber bullying includes.

## MAIN FOCUS

Firstly, we will demonstrate the seriousness of cyber bullying in that it is commonplace, has serious, even life-threatening consequences, and is hard to catch the perpetrators. Once the need to deal with this threat is understood clearly, we will detail coping strategies for all the relevant parties.

## Incidence of Cyberbullying

Some researchers (e.g. Kowalski et al., 2012; Rivers & Noret, 2010) write that the incidence of cyber bullying has grown in the eight to ten years since the emergence of the problem. Others (Olweus, 2012a, 2012b; Smith, 2012a; Hinduja & Patchin, 2012a) claim that the rate of cyber bullying has remained stable.

Patchin and Hinduja conducted a series of studies between 2004 and 2010, and found incidence rates that ranged from 18.8% to 40.6% (Patchin & Hinduja, 2012). In other studies which they reviewed most found incidence rates greater than 20%. Studies by Cassidy, Brown, & Jackson (2009, 2012b) show that approximately one third of students have been victims of cyber bullying. According to Trevathan & Myers (2012) statistics suggest that between 25% - 40% of school children have been exposed to some form of cyber bullying. Some studies have reported significantly higher prevelance rates (e.g. Juvonen & Gross, 2008; Mishna, Cook, Gadalla, Daciuk, & Solomon, 2010).

We can suggest a few sources for the discrepancies between studies other than the disagreement between researchers mentioned above regarding what cyber bullying includes. One possible source is the wording of the questionnaire participants filled out. When students were explicitly asked about "bullying" and "being bullied" online (and had the terms defined) rather than being asked to respond to involvement in specific behaviors, they reported lower rates of bullying involvement (Mishna et al., 2010).

A related explanation is that the participants need to understand the constructs being studies. To this end the measurement instruments need to capture the full extent of the construct. For example, not all teens will be aware that exclusion constitutes cyber bullying. As such, a study's detected prevalence rates may overestimate or underestimate the actual incidence of cyber bullying (Pieschl et al. 2013).

A third explanation for the varied statistical data may be as a result of the studies being conducted in different countries. As Beckman, Hagquist, & Hellström (2013) note "The estimated prevalence rates for cyber bullying, as for traditional bullying, vary between countries."

## Compare and Contrast Cyberbullying and Traditional Bullying

The same adolescents are frequently involved in both conventional bullying and cyber bullying (Dempsey, Sulkowski, Dempsey, & Storch, 2011). In Germany, Katzer and colleagues (Katzer, Fetchenhauer, & Belschak, 2009) found a correlation of .55 between victims of conventional bullying and victims of cyber bullying and a correlation of .59 between perpetrators of conventional bullying and perpetrators of cyber bullying, indicating a significant overlap between conventional bullying and cyber bullying. This overlap would suggest that the core behavior of bullying may be more significant than the medium through which it is carried out (Dooley et al., 2009). Other similarities between traditional bullying and cyber bullying include: they both may cause considerable distress to the victims; they both often result in part from a lack of supervision; and incidents usually start at school and have an impact on the school day (Hinduja & Patchin, 2012a; Kowalski et al., 2012; Olweus, 2012a).

However, researchers have increasingly found differences between traditional face-to-face bullying and cyber bullying. For instance, the fact that the victim and perpetrator are communicating in cyber space means that the perpetrator is unable to see the victim's immediate reaction (Smith, 2012b). Some argue that this allows for disinhibition and deindividuation (Patchin & Hinduja, 2011; von Marées & Petermann, 2012). Being cut off from the emotional impact of one's behavior may create a disconnect that blunts the empathetic response elicited by seeing the pain one causes. On the other hand, it may be that the inability to see the victim's reaction or to demonstrate one's

power in front of others may make cyber bullying less appealing for those bullies who enjoy this type of feedback (Smith & Slonje, 2010). Others, however, suggest that some bullies enjoy the anticipation of seeing the reaction or the impact of the cyber bullying at a later time (Nathan, 2009).

Another distinction between face-to-face bullying and cyber bullying, is the possibility of anonymity in online communications. While anonymous messages may be perceived as more threatening and more fear- and anxiety-inducing, cyber bullying by known and/or trusted persons can also be very damaging (Dooley et al., 2009; Nocentini, Calmaestra, Schultze-Krumboltz, Scheithauer, Ortega, & Menesini, 2010). Some investigators point out that anonymity may embolden certain individuals who might never engage in face-to-face bullying (Dooley et al., 2009; Kowalski et al., 2012).

As opposed to traditional bullying, which is conducted face to face, it is a matter of debate among researchers whether most victims of cyber bullying know their tormentor. Mishna et al. (2010) are of the opinion that the perpetrator is more often than not someone the victim knows. Even more surprising, is that Mishna et al's study found that students were often cyber bullied by someone they considered a friend. Anderson & Sturm (2007), Hinduja & Patchin (2007), and Raskauskas & Stotlz (2007) line up on the other side of the argument, and claim that most victims of cyber bullying do not know the one bullying them.

The issue of power differential (the bully being physically or psychologically stronger or more popular than the victim) is considered a classical aspect of traditional bullying. However, in cyber bullying, the power differential can take different forms and may not be as crucial to defining the acts (Menesini, 2012; Smith, 2012b). As Grigg (2010) points out, no research has shown that cyber bullies have superior technological skills. This lack of power differential means that cyber victims are much more comfortable retaliating and capable of doing so. Thus, in cyber bullying it is more likely that the victim will also engage in bullying than in traditional bullying (Kowalski & Limber, 2007; Werner, Bumpus, & Rock, 2010). As the online retaliatory interactions continue, it is likely to draw in friends and bystanders from both sides, who might also begin to engage in aggressive online behavior, further blurring the role distinctions between bully and victim. Another example of role-blurring would be if a person decides to share or post something that was initiated by somebody else. That person may have crossed over from being a bystander to being a bully (Law, Shapka, Hymel, Olson, & Waterhouse, 2012).

There is also some empirical evidence to support the notion that cyber bullying is not merely bullying in cyber space but a unique phenomenon. The correlations between conventional bullying and cyber bullying are generally only of moderate effect size. This indicates that there are a significant number of adolescents who are only involved in cyber bullying, but not in conventional bullying (Pieschl et al., 2013). Factor analyses demonstrate that acts of cyber aggression load on a unique factor compared with other acts of adolescent aggression (Dempsey et al., 2011). Additionally, there are cyber-specific risk factors for cyber bullying that are not relevant for conventional bullying, such as being more technologically savvy, and using the Internet and electronic communication tools more frequently (Pieschl et al., 2013).

Other distinctions between cyber bullying and traditional bullying include: the greater challenges in policing of the online behaviors, 24/7 accessibility of the victim, the potential repetition of the harmful behavior without further involvement of the original perpetrator (the belittling information stays online for all to see and to make fun of the victim), and the larger audience (Cassidy et al., 2013; Slonje & Smith, 2008). On the other hand, nasty text messages or emails can be simply deleted and future messages blocked; and there is no actual physical hurt (Slonje & Smith, 2008).

Regarding age, most self-report studies of being bullied in traditional ways find a decrease with age after 11 years through to 18 (Smith, Madsen & Moody, 1999). On the other hand, the opportunity for cyber bullying may increase with age as older pupils more often will have mobile phones or access to the Internet. Ybarra and Mitchell (2004) found that older students (15+ years) were more often Internet aggressors than younger students (10–14 years). Smith, Mahdavi, Carvalho, & Tippett (2006) found no age differences in the 11–16 year age range, but their sample was small. Another difference is while traditional bullying more often occurs on school premises, cyber bullying occurs more frequently outside school than at school (Smith et al., 2008).

## Negative Effects on Victim

In order to fully appreciate the severity of the problem we are discussing, one needs to be aware of the effects cyber bullying has on its victims. There have been many documented effects of cyber bullying on the mental health of victims, including feelings of sadness, hurt, anger, frustration, confusion, stress, distress, vulnerability, loneliness, depression, and low self-esteem. Other effects include feelings of helplessness, social anxiety, suicidal ideation, emotional problems, fear, and relationship problems (Kowalski et al., 2012; von Marées & Petermann, 2012). Some studies have also noted psychosomatic complaints such as headaches, abdominal pains, and sleeping difficulties (Marczak & Coyne, 2010; von Marées & Petermann, 2012).

There is also research linking cyber bullying victimization to maladaptive behaviors such as aggressive behavior, externalizing behaviors, deviant behaviors, more alcohol and drug use/abuse and smoking, and delinquency (shoplifting, property damage, physical assaults, weapons possession) (Marczak & Coyne, 2010; Patchin & Hinduja, 2012). However, it should be noted that it has not been determined whether these maladaptive behaviors are a result of being victimized or if victims are the ones more likely to be engaging in these behaviors in the first place.

Hinduja & Patchin (2010) found that youth who experienced traditional bullying or cyber bullying, as either an offender or a victim, had more suicidal thoughts and were more likely to attempt suicide than those who had not. They do, however, point out that a causal link between cyber bullying and suicide has not been proven (Patchin & Hinduja, 2012). Similarly, Klomeck, Sourander, Gould in their review (2010), while they cite several studies that proved correlation between suicide attempts and bullying or cyber bullying, they did not find evidence that cyber bullying causes suicide.

There are a number of ways in which cyber bullying can impact academic performance and school-related well-being, including: reduced concentration, school avoidance, isolation, lower academic achievement, negative perceptions of school climate, not feeling safe at school, higher risk for school problems, and a greater likelihood of carrying weapons to school (Hinduja & Patchin, 2007; Marczak & Coyne, 2010).

## Correlated Factors for Being Cyberbully or Victim

A broad range of risk factors for being a cyber bully or cyber victim are discussed in the literature. Some lend themselves to potentially being linked causally to cyber bullying, while others are merely correlated. In any case, some studies explicitly offer explanations as to why a person would wish to engage in cyber bullying.

According to Kowalski et al (2012), the reasons for cyber bullying include exerting control over others, getting pleasure from aggressive behaviors, gaining prestige among friends, acting out aggressive fantasies in a virtual environment, trying to take revenge for something else the victim does to them, desire to appear strict and cold blooded, and the low possibility of being arrested.

According to Stover (2006, p. 41), adolescents use social network sites such as Facebook, MySpace or Xanga "to build their social status

by cozying up to those who are higher up on the social ladder than they are themselves and trying to denigrate or exclude others." Teens find the attention or sympathy they could not find in their off-line daily life, by engaging in cyber bullying.

Smith et al's studies (2008) combined qualitative and quantitative aspects. They created focus groups of students and interviewed them regarding various aspects of cyber bullying such as why people engage in it and how it can be prevented. The focus group students provided some insights as to why some students might engage in cyber bullying. Some perceived the bully's motivation as due to a lack of confidence and desire for control: 'bullying on the computer is quite cowardly, because they can't face up to the person themselves'; 'there is less fear of getting caught'. Another theme was how the lack of face-to-face interaction in cyber bullying reduces empathy in bullies. Some students attributed the phenomenon to fun-seeking or boredom-relief.

Dracic (2009) echoes Smith et al.'s conclusions regarding the bully's lack of confidence and insecurity. As such, bullies seek external validation and total control of situations they find themselves in.

Dilmac & Aydoğan (2010) found that the dimensions camaraderie, respect, tolerance, pacifism, responsibility, and honesty (namely lack thereof) in part individually explained students' cyber bullying behavior. As such, they recommend that schools educate their students on these values, as a preventative measure.

There are other studies that demonstrate a range of risk factors and correlated factors with being engaged in cyber bullying, either as a perpetrator or as a victim. Dilmac (2009) demonstrated that soliciting sympathy, affection, and emotional support from others, positively predicted engagement in cyber bullying. Walrave and Heirman (2011) found out that past involvement in cyber bullying and engaging in online risk behavior increase the likelihood of victimization

Cyberbullying is also associated with hyperactive behavior, conduct problems, and less prosocial behavior among one's peer group (von Marées & Petermann, 2012). Cyberbullies show more aggression, a positive attitude towards aggression, less empathy, a less positive relationship with their parents, less perceived peer support, less commitment to school, more delinquency, and more smoking and drinking than non-cyber -bullies (Ang & Goh, 2010; Calvete, Orue, Estévez, Villardón, & Padilla, 2010). Cyberbullies are often themselves victims of traditional bullying (Patchin & Hinduja, 2012). Media violence exposure was a risk factor leading to both cyber bullying and cyber victimization (Fanti, Demetriou, & Hawa, 2012).

A study done by Sengupta & Chaudhuri (2011) found several factors which were significantly correlated with the likelihood of being cyber bullied. These included posting pictures online, chatting online, disclosing school information and instant messaging ID, and flirting online. An additional predictor was the location of the computer in the home. Using the Internet privately, away from parents' watchful eyes, is associated with a 60% higher likelihood of being cyber bullied. Simply having access to social networking sites is not a predictor of cyber -bullying. Wolak, Mitchell, & Finkelhor (2007) found that intensive use of the Internet is a risk factor for being a cyber -victim.

Regarding gender, two separate studies done on Turkish teens (Erdur-Baker, 2010; Şahin, Aydin, & Sari, 2012) showed that males were more likely to perpetrate or be the victims of cyber bullying than females. Their studies are in direct contrast with those of Mishna et al (2010) and Slonje & Smith (2008) who found no gender differences in the overall perpetration of cyber bullying. They are also opposed to Sengupta & Chaudhuri (2011) who found that females are more likely to be cyber bullied and to Ybarra & Mitchell (2004) who found no significant gender differences for Internet bullies or victims.

However, Mishna et al (2010) did find gender differences regarding the form of cyber bullying in which participants were involved. The nature of these differences is consistent with the well-documented gender differences evident in traditional bullying, whereby boys are more involved in direct or overt and physical forms of aggression and girls are more involved in indirect and relational forms (Cullerton-Sen & Crick, 2005).

According to Mishna et al's (2010) findings, in the online environment too, there is evidence that boys are more likely to be victims or perpetrators of direct bullying such as threatening and that girls are more likely to be victims or perpetrators of indirect bullying such as rumors or pretending to be someone else. Şahin et al.'s (2012) results differed from Mishna et al.'s (2010) perhaps unsurprisingly, as the Turkish teens were asked about cyber bullying without differentiating between types of bullying. A study from Spain (Calvete et al., 2010) reported that girls are more often cyber victims and boys are more often cyber bullies. In concurrence with them, in the US, Wang, Iannotti, & Nansel, (2009) reported girls as more likely to be cyber victims.

## Coping Strategies

One needs to address the problem of cyber bullying broadly and systematically, involving peers, teachers, school administrators, mental health professionals, law enforcement, parents, and of course the victim (Mishna et al, 2010). We will address each of these parties and their respective roles in cyber bullying prevention.

## For Victims

Some of the coping strategies suggested in the literature can be described as passive strategies — ignore the offensive content, avoid the website, limit any damage the perpetrator can cause. Limiting potential damage can be done by shutting down social networking accounts and restarting while being careful about friend selection, changing passwords and/or mobile phone number if they are known by the bully, and blocking the bully from accessing his/her social networking site profile (Tokunaga, 2010; Trevathan & Myers, 2012). However, Perren, Corcoran, Cowie, Dehue, Garcia, McGuckin, Sevcikova, Tsatsou, & Vollink (2012) did not find evidence that clearly supports the efficacy of such strategies.

Other approaches would fall under the category of active strategies: Confront the bully, tell them to stop, or threaten to tell on them (Tokunaga, 2010). In the studies reviewed by Perren et al. (2012), it was found that such approaches are more likely to lead to an escalation of the bullying rather than to deter the cyber bully. Despite this concern, some researchers do offer suggestions in this vein: Get the authorities to track down the number or Internet service provider; contact the Internet service provider; report abuse on message board; report the bully (if known) on an anonymous website; alert someone; keep a record; ask the bully to stop; and fight back (Monks, Robinson, & Worlidge, 2012; Smith & Slonje, 2010).

There are also suggested ways of using technology to counter cyber bullying such as implementing privacy settings, changing one's email address, refraining from visiting a particular site, and keeping evidence of cyber bullying (Kowalski et al., 2012; Tokunaga, 2010; Trevathan & Myers, 2012). Here too, Perren et al. (2012) suggest that there isn't conclusive evidence in support of such approaches.

Most cyber victims do not alert adults (Smith, 2012b; Yilmaz, 2011). This may be explained by the fear young people have of losing access to their technology if they tell adults, because they fear the cyber bully will retaliate further (Jackson, Cassidy, & Brown, 2009), or because they think that adults could not do anything to stop it even if they tried. Cross, Shaw, Hearn, Epstein, Monks, Lester, & Thomas (2009) found that of those cyber bullied students who told an adult, 46% said the situation got worse or did not improve after telling.

Other reasons cited by students for not reporting to adults include: They do not know who is doing it; if it is occurring outside school, it is not clear to them why they should tell school personnel;

they fear they will not be believed or they will be blamed for their own aggressive response to the cyber bullying; they are embarrassed; they fear the situation will be trivialized; they worry about being labeled 'a rat' (Smith 2012b; von Marées & Petermann, 2012).

On the other hand, victims often tell their friends (Cassidy et al., 2009; Smith, 2012b) and according to Perren et al. (2012), social support is probably the coping strategy with the best indicators of success. Interestingly enough, Fanti et al. (2012) found that family social support was a protective factor for both cyber bullies and their victims.

## Role of Students/Bystanders

It has been suggested that students should play a greater role in developing approaches for dealing with cyber bullying. Peer-led interventions have been found to be effective, especially when the peers receive extensive training (Agatston, Kowalski, & Limber, 2012; Menesini & Nocentini, 2012). Additionally, students may respond better to initiatives where they play a leading role, due to a pervasive belief that youth understand technology better than do adults. The Cyber-Friendly Schools Project in Australia is one example of a program that, as part of its mission statement, declares they will use students in planning and implementing anti-bullying programs (Cyber Friendly Schools Project, 2011).

The impact of empowerment also comes into play here. When we assist students in taking the lead on a problem such as cyber bullying and provide them with training to support that role, we are giving them skills and confidence, which in and of itself beneficial. Empowerment also extends to bystanders. Hinduja and Patchin (2012b) remind us that most youth do not cyber bully others; as such the non-bullies are the 'normative' group. This knowledge should be used in empowering bystanders to stand up to bullies and reject this behavior. Helping bystanders to know what to do and to feel capable of intervening can also help to reduce cyber bullying and its negative impacts on victims and schools (Cassidy et al., 2013).

## For Parents

It has been shown that students are more likely to confide in their parents than in school personnel when they are victims of cyber bullying (Cassidy, Brown, & Jackson, 2011); therefore, it is important that parents be prepared to respond in helpful ways if such a situation arises.

Recognition by parents and educators of the importance of Internet activity, particularly online communication, may facilitate disclosure of cyber bullying among children and youth who fear that online prohibitions may result from any discussion of cyber victimization or perpetration (Mishna et al, 2010). Parents need to provide an environment where their children feel free to talk openly about their experiences online to talk openly and often with children and listen to their concerns and try to understand the situation that concerns them. Parents should also monitor their kids for early signs of conduct disorder, which can be warning signs of them bullying others in the future (Dracic, 2009).

In addition to recognizing the centrality of cyber interactions in youth's socialization, adults need to differentiate technology use that is neutral or positive from technology use that is abusive or negative. A survey of parents from three schools in British Columbia, Canada, found that parents' knowledge of the newer social networking sites their children use was limited, as was their awareness of the extent of cyber bullying among their children (Cassidy, Brown, & Jackson, 2012a). Although 32% of these parents' children reported being victims of cyber bullying and 36% reported participating in cyber bullying, only 11% of parents reported that their child had been a victim and less than 1% a cyber bully. (Cassidy, et al., 2013).

What is especially effective, is when parents receive training alongside educators, and they are able to work collaboratively with school person-

nel and their children to find effective solutions (Dracic, 2009), since there is a strong interrelationship between negative interactions on the school grounds and cyber bullying on the home computer (Cassidy et al., 2012a).

Perren and colleagues (2012) found some evidence to suggest that monitoring online activity and restricting certain websites may help somewhat in preventing cyber bullying. Eastin, Greenberg, and Hofschire (2006) found that when the child has a computer in the bedroom, away from parental eyes, computer time increases, as does the opportunity to cyber bully. On the other hand, several studies have shown that parental supervision is sporadic at best, and therefore generally ineffective (Cassidy et al., 2012a; Davies, 2011). Liau, Khoo, and Ang (2008), found that even when parents sat with their child to review their online activities, inspected their child's web history, and used filters, risky online behavior wasn't reduced.

## For Schools

Overwhelmingly, researchers in the field stress the need to address cyber bullying through education on a number of different levels (Cassidy et al., 2012a, 2012b; Donlin, 2012; Jackson et al., 2009a; Marczak & Coyne, 2010; Patchin & Hinduja, 2011; Perren et al., 2012). Donlin (2012) suggests incorporating content that is correct, clear, and current into the curriculum. In two separate surveys of middle and high school students, the development of programs to teach about cyber bullying and its effects was among the top-three solutions to cyber bullying identified by participants (Cassidy et al., 2011). In a related study (Cassidy et al., 2012a), parents strongly recommended that school personnel develop lessons on cyber bullying and its effects and that students be given the opportunity to engage with the issues through open and frank discussion. Beyond merely teaching about cyber bullying, the curriculum should focus on empowering students in terms of technological skills, critical thinking skills, Internet etiquette, e-safety, assessing their own online risks, measures to protect themselves, their reputation, and their privacy online (Grigg, 2010; Marczak & Coyne, 2010; Perren et al., 2012). In fact, Yilmaz, (2011) found that, 'Most students do not know how to keep themselves safe in cyber space' (p. 651). Of those who did know particular strategies, only 15.4% said they had learned them at school (Yilmaz, 2011).

It also has been suggested that the focus of research and practice should shift to fostering cyber kindness instead of trying to stop cyber bullying (Cassidy et al., 2011, 2012a), that is positively oriented solutions rather than "anti" measures. School norms should be prosocial, promote helping, and encourage civility and courage in bystanders (Grigg, 2010). Additionally, the curriculum should include an emphasis on fostering empathy and positive self-esteem. Fostering positive self-esteem in students was found to be among top three best solutions to cyber bullying suggested by students in two separate surveys (Cassidy et al., 2011). Bystanders would also benefit from empathy education because, if they understand suffering, they are less likely to inflict it. Students must be given the opportunity to practice those empathetic responses so cyber bullying bystanders are not immobilized by fear in the moment (Davis & Nixon, 2012). Of course, any empathy and self-esteem curriculum needs to be reinforced through the informal curriculum of the school culture and practices, including being modeled by the adults in the schools, in order to be effective (Cassidy & Bates, 2005). Similarly, Dilmac & Aydoğan (2010) recommend educating students with the following values: camaraderie, respect, tolerance, pacifism, responsibility, and honesty. This is because students who lacked these values were found to be more likely to engage in cyber bullying.

Developing healthy behaviors and social skills also should be part of the overall curriculum. Patchin and Hinduja (2011) have demonstrated that cyber bullying may stem from strain, anger, and frustration when the would-be bullies are unable to cope with these feelings in a healthy way. As such, they recommend providing health education programming and emotional self management skills.

Students view most adults as unknowledgeable about cyber bullying and the online world in general, a perception validated by studies done with educators (Cassidy et al., 2009, 2012b). For this reason and for the ones mentioned above, students are unlikely to tell school personnel if they do not think that they can help them. Ideally, students should feel comfortable approaching adults in school to discuss problems (Agatston et al., 2012; Patchin & Hinduja, 2011). To further this goal, school personnel, like parents, should be educated on the technologies their kids use, the associated dangers like cyber bullying, and preventative measures they can take (Tangen & Campbell, 2010). Additionally, the school and the other adults in their lives should promote a positive and non-judgemental atmosphere (Hinduja & Patchin, 2012b). Youth are more inclined to report to adults who are open-minded, trustworthy, and who do not blame the victim (Agatston et al., 2012).

Administrators, psychological service providers, teachers, students, and parents must work together to devise a clear school policy against cyber bullying (Agatston et al., 2012; Cassidy et al., 2012a). Furthermore, existing policies and practices need to be updated and accompanied by monitoring and sanctioning of unacceptable behaviors. Schools should keep records of Internet use and make this practice known. In addition to the drafting of a policy, it is equally important to evaluate the impact of prevention activities derived from the policy and to review the policy regularly (Marczak & Coyne, 2010).

There is also some evidence to support general anti-bullying strategies as means of preventing and curtailing cyber bullying (Perren et al., 2012). This is perhaps not surprising given the considerable overlap between cyber and traditional bullying victimization and perpetration (Monks et al., 2012; Patchin & Hinduja, 2012; von Marées & Petermann, 2012). Fear-based and punitive programs are generally ineffective and possibly counterproductive, preventing children from seeking the help they need (MacKay, 2012). However, in a study done by Kraft and Wang (2009) students, no matter whether they were offenders, victims, or both, believed that not allowing bullies access to social networking sites and parents taking away their child the bully's computers and cell phones are among the three most effective strategies for preventing cyberbullying. These measures serve to deter the offender on a few levels. Firstly, teenagers today engage in cyber immersion. Cyber immersion means that the Internet serves as the primary way that they communicate for relationships, commerce, and recreation (Brown, Jackson, & Cassidy, 2006). By taking away access to Internet and technology teenagers would lose their primary means of communication and feel isolated. Additionally, teenagers view their cell phone and computer as prize possessions. Having these personal possessions taken away by their parents, even for a short period of time, would cause them to lose their social status within their peer group. The students studies believed that the social isolation together with the stigma of losing your technological devices would serve as an adequate deterrent (Kraft & Wang, 2009).

## Role of Psychological Service Providers to Schools

School personnel can assist efforts to counter cyber bullying in a number of ways: (1) helping draft effective policies (2) classroom guidance (e.g. teaching to recognize legal and personal consequences, improved problem-solving and anger management skills for students) (3) counseling victims and bullies (4) training parents, staff, and other care-takers (e.g. help them reduce the risk of cyber bullying through relational solutions or technological solutions), and making oneself available for consultation and (5) initiating and developing a peer helper program (Sabella, 2012).

## Role of the Wider Community

Cassidy et al. (2013) recommend viewing cyber bullying not as a child-problem or a school-problem, but rather as a community-problem. If everyone tries to help rather than expecting someone else to do it, then there will be a greater chance of addressing this problem successfully. Thaxter (2010) encourages schools and juvenile law enforcement agencies to cooperate. This can be done in the area of prevention through education. Thaxter, himself a juvenile police officer, goes into schools and addresses students and their parents. He defines what cyber bullying is and demonstrates that definition by describing both cases that he and other officers have addressed. He then focuses on the effect that cyber bullying has on the victims and on the school atmosphere, as well as the potential consequences that it has for the bully. He also discusses ways in which bystanders can intervene. He stresses the importance of reporting cyber bullying to adults and the mechanisms for doing this. The school-police collaboration is of course important in identifying perpetrators and bringing them to justice.

Legislation is also part of the solution on a societal level. By this we of course mean meaningful and relevant legislation, although this is sometimes overlooked. For example, most legislation is written to deal with cyber bullying on school grounds (Anderson, 2010), while in reality most of the cyber bullying happens outside of school (Smith et al., 2008).

In the United Sates all fifty states have laws against cyber harrasment and/or cyber stalking. Some legislate specifically against cyber crime, while others word laws against stalking and harrasment in such a way that they include these crimes being carried out electronically (Anderson,

2010). The law should be derived from, and help to further establish core social values. School personnel should increase their awareness of the legal context that applies to them (e.g. human rights law for harassment and discrimination; constitutional law for freedom of expression and privacy) in order to frame their responses in terms of policies and practices (Cassidy et al., 2013).

## TECHNOLOGICAL INTERVENTIONS

As we have seen, the suggested interventions, be it for victims, schools, parents, or potential cyber bullies, are focused on educating the various parties in the cyber bullying process. A notable exception to this trend is the research that took place in MIT in 2011 (Lieberman, Dinakar, & Jones, 2011). They were developing a technological intervention to combat cyber bullying. This had two facets to it: detecting possible cases of cyber bullying and designing intervention technologies for participants as well as network providers and moderators.

Most cyber bullying occurs around a small number of topics: race and ethnicity, sexuality and sexual identity, physical appearance, intelligence, and social acceptance and rejection (Dracic, 2009; Lieberman et al, 2011). If one can understand whether a message is about those topics, and whether its tone is positive or negative, one can identify many possible cyber bullying messages. Their proposed program doesn't directly accuse an individual of being a bully. The goal isn't to achieve 100 percent certainty in detecting cyber bullying, but to call out the possibility of its occurrence. If a pattern is repeated over time, seems to be escalating, or has a consistently negative tone, one's confidence in estimation might increase.

Since then, technology-oriented prevention tools have become quite common, with several programs, such as internet filters or kid-friendly web browsers being offered with this purpose in mind. These aren't meant to replace the education-oriented interventions mentioned, but rather to supplement them. These by-in-large block objectionable content and allow parents to track their child's online activity. These don't address, however, the issue of cyberbullying which uses the platform of social media. A step in this direction would be monitored email such as ZooBuh.com offers. ZooBuh.com allows parents to monitor their kids email activity, select a list of permitted contacts, filter out selected bad words, and to receive all emails and only send on to their kids those they approve. The option of the parents sifting through all the kid's emails, to our mind, is the only fool-proof option of the ones ZooBuh.com offers, but this requires a huge investment of time and effort on the part of the parent. Most parents won't have the time to read all their kids emails and even those who do are unlikely to maintain this level of involvement over long periods of time.

It is worth keeping in mind that many of these sites are geared to preteens and younger while the phenomenon of cyberbullying is most prevalent among teenagers.

What makes Lieberman et al.'s proposed program unique is the fact it deals with social media which is the primary platform for cyberbullying, not just email and blocking objectionable websites. Also, each participant in the cyberbullying process (the perpetrator, the victim, friends, family, teachers, and so on) gets an intervention specifically designed for their role. For example, when a possible cyber bullying message is detected, the program will provide a link to educational material appropriate to the user on his or her screen. For potential cyber bullies, the material could encourage empathy for the victim and warn of possible damage to the bully's social reputation. The intervention could encourage victims to seek emotional support, learn how others have dealt with similar situations, give suggestions for appropriate responses, and discourage them from retaliating. The material could induce friends to defend the victim rather than join in with the bully. The key is to offer advice that is personalized, specific, and actionable. The material can take many forms including written stories, video, or interactive narratives.

Other measures could subtly change the social network interface to encourage reflection, or to slow the spread of a potentially insulting message that has been sent. Instead of just a simple "Send" message, for example, the button could be changed to remind the user of the consequences: "Send to 247 people in your network." Likewise, an "Are you sure?" confirmation could be added to potentially problematic messages. Or delivery could be delayed overnight to give the sender a chance to rescind the message in the morning before it's actually delivered.

In summation, the adults who are meant to keep our youths' world safe, can and should be doing more. It starts with building awareness. What role does the Internet play in children's social lives? What are the hazards involved, especially in social networking sites? What technological measures can I, as a parent, teacher, or law enforcement officer, be taking to protect children against these dangers? No less important is creating a positive climate in the home or school which encourages the child to report any threats or suspicious doings he is involved in. Preventative measures aren't the only available option. There is much to be said for educating towards and modeling positive values. Once the adults teach and model behaviors of cyber kindness, empathy, and good social skills, children will internalize these healthy behaviors. Bullying loses its "effectiveness" when there is no supportive, or at least passive audience. .

## Legal Aspects

A zero tolerance policy of cyber bullying should be promoted in our society. Perpetrators should be prosecuted and penalized accordingly. Unfortunately, this is easier said than done. There are many technical obstacles to prosecution and proving that an individual has been a victim of cyber stalking (cyber bullying). These obstacles

include jurisdiction, account and user information, and anonymizing tools. Jurisdiction is difficult especially if the stalker is in a different city or state than the victim. Anonymity makes it difficult to identify the perpetrator, collect the necessary evidence, and track the bully to a physical location so that an arrest can be made. As with anything that needs to be proved, documentation is key. Any individual who feels that she/he is being stalked or otherwise bullied needs take appropriate precautions. All incidents must be documented and reported to the authorities. Often the Internet service providers or social networking sites are reluctant to reveal user information even for individuals who are suspected of cyber bullying.

Tools are constantly being developed and improved that allow the bully to send and receive information with no user information attached (Anderson, 2010). While the stalker leaves "electronic footprints" and there are detection capabilities that law enforcement agencies can take advantage of (Thaxter, 2010), the authorities are hampered because they follow the law regarding privacy (Anderson, 2010).

Brenner & Rehberg (2009) discuss at length another challenge facing those who want to prosecute cyber bullies. Whether prosecuting under stalking laws or harassment laws, the prosecution has to prove beyond a reasonable doubt the bully's intent to cause harm ("mens rea") and that his conduct did in fact cause the emotional distress that befell the victim ("causal nexus"). It may be easier for prosecutors to seek justice under statutes dealing with harassment, in which some statutes imply that simply annoying the victim, as opposed to substantial emotional distress, is sufficient grounds for prosecution. However, ever since the 1971 Supreme Court decision in *Coates v. Cincinnati*, in which they declared the term "annoy" too vague to legislate ("conduct that annoys some people does not annoy others"), other courts have followed suit. Therefore laws which attempt to ban annoying behavior (some legal definitions of harassment include the word annoy) are voided by the courts on the grounds of vagueness. It would therefore not be possible to prosecute a cyber bully for harassment on the grounds that they merely "annoyed" the victim. Also, a one-time occurrence is not enough to warrant prosecution as stalking and harassment statutes require repeated hostile or unsettling communications.

What makes a prosecutor's job somewhat easier is that it is sufficient to infer intent to harm. Generally, courts have upheld harassment statutes when they include some limiting conditions, such as a requirement that the conduct have "'no legitimate purpose'" or harm requirements that go beyond merely annoying or alarming the victims because that infers malicious even though it doesn't prove it conclusively. A prosecutor could probably prosecute a direct cyber bully for harassment if he or she could show that the cyber bully acted with the specific intent of inflicting the proscribed harm (e.g., harassment, annoyance, or alarm) and that the conduct at issue had no legitimate purpose.

In short, the stringent *mens rea* requirements for both crimes will make it at the very least difficult to bring such prosecutions when the conduct involved in the bullying was isolated or sporadic and the substance tended to be petty rather than malicious.

Indirect cyber bullying, has two additional issues unique to it, neither of which arises with direct cyber bullying: To what extent did the cyber bully intentionally direct the online communications at the victim? And to what extent did he/ she intend that the communications would be seen by others whose reactions were likely to have a negative impact on the victim? For instance, the defendant can claim that posting their comment was simply in order to communicate information to the public, rather than an intentionally harming the victim (Brenner & Rehberg, 2009)

In any case, if any gossip made public falls under the category of indirect cyber bullying, then either we can outlaw it and be inundated with law suits and violate the freedom of speech granted by the first amendment in the US Constitution to publish non-defamatory content and opinion. Alternatively, we can allow it and potentially turn every individual into a public figure who is exposed to his very own paparazzi without having to attain celebrity status.

Brenner and Rehberg also discuss the possibility of prosecuting indirect cyber bullying under defamation laws. Here too the prosecution has to prove malicious intent in publishing information to one or more persons that was false and had the capacity to expose the person it concerned to public hatred, contempt or ridicule.

Brenner and Rehberg, are fully aware of the existence of legal loopholes in relevant areas of law that benefit perpetrators of cyber bullying or cyber harassment. At the same time they feel that society cannot criminalize every instance in which people hurt each other's feelings. Firstly, hurting other people's feelings, intentionally or not, is an unpleasant but unavoidable aspect of life. Second of all, prosecuting these low-level cases would trivialize criminal law.

## Cyberbullying Laws

The Council of Europe created the "Convention on cyber crime," in November of 2001. Twelve years later, this Convention has been signed by 51 countries, 40 of whom ratified it as well, including countries that are not members of the Council of Europe (Canada, Japan, South Africa and the United States). This Convention is what's known as a Framework Convention because it is directly applicable, in that each country should implement it in their own legislation. In 2003 the Council of Europe created the "Additional Protocol to the Convention on cyber crime crime acts of racism and xenophobia committed through computer systems". The Additional Protocol was signed by many countries, but not the United States. The signatories agreed to criminalize dissemination of racist and xenophobic content through the computer system and xenophobic-racist threats and insults, and denial of the Holocaust and genocide (Dracic, 2009).

In the United States, the federal government has left punishment to the states (Anderson, 2010). The first state to have a law against cyber stalking was California in 1999. All fifty states have laws against cyber harrasment and or cyber stalking. Some legislate specifically against cyber crime and some use language in laws against stalking and harassment in such a way that they include these crimes being carried out electronically. The punishment for cyber stalking is similar to the punishment for physical stalking. This punishment can include imprisonment or fines or both (Anderson, 2010).

## FUTURE DIRECTIONS FOR RESEARCH

The topic of cyber bullying has been researched and written on extensively. Still, there are other aspects that should be explored in the future. Targeted analyses can yield important information. As we have indicated the incidence rates and the type of bullying engaged in may differ between genders. As such, studies should explore the effects of gender differences alongside the variables under examination and the interaction between them. Comparison on cross-national studies conducted by EUKidsOnline and by the World Health Organization suggest important variations in prevalence rates by country (Cassidy et al., 2013). It is worth exploring the possibility of other cultural differences in bullying behavior patterns and the coping strategies employed in each culture. The research should allow for parents and educators to tailor prevention messages and measures to the gender and culture of the child at risk.

There is a paucity of longitudinal research in the field of cyber bullying. Such studies would be useful in ascertaining the success of programs instituted to combat this phenomenon. Also, there is very little systematic assessment of these programs. Efforts should be made to scientifically reach conclusions regarding optimal strategies for coping with cyber bullying in the various populations (e.g. control groups, randomization, etc.). Only then can evidence-based recommendations be formulated and implemented in an ideal fashion (Perren et al., 2012).

## CONCLUSION

We've come a long way since 2007 when a St. Charles County Sheriff's Department spokesman, Lt. Craig McGuire, said that what was done against Megan Meier "might've been rude, it might've been immature, but it wasn't illegal." (New York Times, 2007). The awareness of the prevalence and severity of cyber bullying has led to it being outlawed throughout the United States and in tens of other countries as well. Now, in 2014, there are foundations, websites, and curriculum dedicated to combating this phenomenon. When bullying behaviors are ostracized at all levels we believe the incidence rates will drop considerably. If in some way our discussion of the issues and suggested resolutions has contributed to their efforts in keeping our children safe, we will be deeply gratified.

## REFERENCES

Agatston, P., Kowalski, R., & Limber, S. (2012). Youth views on cyber bullying. In J. W. Patchin, & S. Hinduja (Eds.), *Cyber bullying prevention and response: Expert perspectives* (pp. 57–71). New York, NY: Routledge.

Anderson, T., & Sturm, B. (2007, Winter). Cyber bullying from playground to computer. *Young Adult Library Services*, 24-27.

Anderson, W. L. (2010). Cyber stalking (cyber bullying)-proof and punishment. *Insights to a Changing World Journal, 4*, 18–23.

Ang, R. P., & Goh, D. H. (2010). Cyber bullying among adolescents: The role of affective and cognitive empathy, and gender. *Child Psychiatry and Human Development, 41*(4), 387–397. doi:10.1007/s10578-010-0176-3 PMID:20238160

Beckman, L., Hagquist, C., & Hellström, L. (2013). Discrepant gender patterns for cyber bullyiyng and traditional bullying – An analysis of Swedish adolescent data. *Computers in Human Behavior, 29*(5), 1896–1903. doi:10.1016/j.chb.2013.03.010

Bhat, C. S. (2008). Cyber bullying: Overview and strategies for school counsellors, guidance officers, and all school personnel. *Australian Journal of Guidance & Counselling, 18*(1), 53–66. doi:10.1375/ajgc.18.1.53

Brenner, S. W., & Rehberg, M. (2009). Kiddie crime-The utility of criminal law in controlling cyber bullying. *First Amend. L. Rev., 8*, 1.

Brown, K., Jackson, M., & Cassidy, W. (2006). Cyber-bullying: Developing Policy to direct responses that are equitable and effective in addressing this special form of bullying. *Canadian Journal of Educational Administration and Policy, 57*, 1–36.

Brunstein Klomek, A., Sourander, A., & Gould, M. (2010). The association of suicide and bullying in childhood to young adulthood: a review of cross-sectional and longitudinal research findings. *Canadian Journal of Psychiatry, 55*(5), 282–288. PMID:20482954

Calvete, E., Orue, I., Estévez, A., Villardón, L., & Padilla, P. (2010). cyber bullying in adolescents: Modalities and aggressors' profile. *Computers in Human Behavior, 26*(5), 1128–1135. doi:10.1016/j.chb.2010.03.017

Cassidy, W., & Bates, A. (2005). 'Drop-outs' and 'push-outs': Finding hope at a school that actualizes the ethic of care. *American Journal of Education, 112*, 66–102. doi:10.1086/444524

Cassidy, W., Brown, K., & Jackson, M. (2011). Moving from cyber -bullying to cyber -kindness: What do students, educators and parents say? In E. Dunkels, G.-M. Franberg, & C. Hallgren (Eds.), *Youth culture and net culture: Online social practices* (pp. 256–277). Hershey, NY: Information Science Reference.

Cassidy, W., Brown, K., & Jackson, M. (2012a). Making Kind Cool": Parents' Suggestions for Preventing Cyber Bullying and Fostering Cyber Kindness. *Journal of Educational Computing Research, 46*(4), 415–436. doi:10.2190/EC.46.4.f

Cassidy, W., Brown, K., & Jackson, M. (2012b). 'Under the radar': Educators and cyber bullying in schools. *School Psychology International, 33*, 520–532. doi:10.1177/0143034312445245

Cassidy, W., Faucher, C., & Jackson, M. (2013). cyber bullying among youth: A comprehensive review of current international research and its implications and application to policy and practice. *School Psychology International.* doi:10.1177/0143034313479697

Cassidy, W., Jackson, M., & Brown, K. (2009). Sticks and stones can break my bones, but how can pixels hurt me? Students' experiences with cyber -bullying. *School Psychology International, 30*(4), 383–402. doi:10.1177/0143034309106948

Cross, D., Shaw, T., Hearn, L., Epstein, M., Monks, H., Lester, L., & Thomas L. (2009). *Australian covert bullying prevalence study (ACBPS).* Available at http://www.deewr.gov.au/Schooling/NationalSafeSchools/Pages/research.aspx

Cullerton-Sen, C., & Crick, N. (2005). Understanding the effects of physical and relational victimization: The utility of multiple perspectives in predicting social-emotional adjustment. *School Psychology Review, 34*, 147–160.

Cyber Friendly Schools Project. (2011). *Year 9 curriculum*. Available at http://www.cyberfriendly.com.au/images/uploads/school_pdf/teacher-curriculum-cyber 9.pdf

Davies, C. (2011). Digitally strategic: How young people respond to parental views about the use of technology for learning in the home. *Journal of Computer Assisted Learning, 27*, 324–335. doi:10.1111/j.1365-2729.2011.00427.x

Davis, S., & Nixon, C. (2012). Empowering bystanders. In J. W. Patchin, & S. Hinduja (Eds.), *Cyber bullying prevention and response: Expert perspectives* (pp. 93–109). New York, NY: Routledge.

Dempsey, A. G., Sulkowski, M. L., Dempsey, J., & Storch, E. A. (2011). Has cyber technology produced a new group of peer aggressors? *Cyberpsychology, Behavior and Social Networking, 14*(5), 297–302. doi:10.1089/cyber.2010.0108

Dilmac, B. (2009). Psychological needs as a predictor of cyber bullying: A preliminary report on college students. *Educational Sciences: Theory and Practice, 9*(3), 1307–1325.

Dilmac, B., & Aydoğan, D. (2010). Values as a predictor of cyber -bullying among secondary school students. *International Journal of Human and Social Sciences, 5*(3), 185–188.

Donlin, M. (2012). You mean we gotta teach that, too? In J. W. Patchin, & S. Hinduja (Eds.), *cyber bullying prevention and response: Expert perspectives* (pp. 110–127). New York, NY: Routledge.

Dooley, J. J., Pyżalski, J., & Cross, D. (2009). Cyber bullying versus face-to-face bullying. *The Journal of Psychology, 217*(4), 182–188.

Dracic, S. (2009). Bullying and peer victimization. Rev. Materia SocioMédica, 21(4), 216-219.

Eastin, M. S., Greenberg, B. S., & Hofschire, L. (2006). Parenting the Internet. *The Journal of Communication, 56*(3), 486–504. doi:10.1111/j.1460-2466.2006.00297.x

Erdur-Baker, Ö. (2010). Cyberbullying and its correlation to traditional bullying, gender and frequent and risky usage of Internet-mediated communication tools. *New Media & Society, 12*(1), 109–125. doi:10.1177/1461444809341260

Fanti, K. A., Demetriou, A. G., & Hawa, V. V. (2012). A longitudinal study of cyber bullying: Examining risk and protective factors. *European Journal of Developmental Psychology, 9*(2), 168–181. doi:10.1080/17405629.2011.643169

Grigg, D. W. (2010). Cyber-aggression: Definition and concept of cyber bullying. *Australian Journal of Guidance & Counselling, 20*, 143–156. doi:10.1375/ajgc.20.2.143

Hinduja, S., & Patchin, J. W. (2007). Offline consequences of online victimization. *Journal of School Violence, 6*(3), 89–112. doi:10.1300/J202v06n03_06

Hinduja, S., & Patchin, J. W. (2010). Bullying, cyber bullying, and suicide. *Archives of Suicide Research, 14*(3), 206–221. doi:10.1080/13811118.2010.494133 PMID:20658375

Hinduja, S., & Patchin, J. W. (2012a). cyber bullying: Neither an epidemic nor a rarity. *European Journal of Developmental Psychology, 9*, 539–543. doi:10.1080/17405629.2012.706448

Hinduja, S., & Patchin, J. W. (2012b). *School climate 2.0: Preventing cyber bullying and sexting one classroom at a time*. Thousand Oaks, CA: Corwin.

Jackson, M., Cassidy, W., & Brown, K. (2009). Out of the mouth of babes: Students' voice their opinions on cyber -bullying. *Long Island Education Review, 8*(2), 24–30.

Juvonen, J., & Gross, E. F. (2008). Extending the school grounds? Bullying experiences in cyber space. *The Journal of School Health, 78*(9), 496–505. doi:10.1111/j.1746-1561.2008.00335.x PMID:18786042

Katzer, C., Fetchenhauer, D., & Belschak, F. (2009). cyber bullying: Who are the victims? A comparison of victimization in Internet chatrooms and victimization in school. *Journal of Media Psychology, 21*(1), 25–36. doi:10.1027/1864-1105.21.1.25

Kowalski, R. M., Limber, S. P., & Agatston, P. W. (2012). Cyber bullying: Bullying in the digital age (2nd ed.). Malden, MA: Wiley-Blackwell.

Kraft, E. M., & Wang, J. (2009). Effectiveness of cyber bullying prevention strategies: A study on students' perspectives. *International Journal of Cyber Criminology, 3*(2).

Li, Q. (2006). Cyber bullying in schools a research of gender differences. *School Psychology International, 27*(2), 157–170. doi:10.1177/0143034306064547

Liau, A., Khoo, A., & Ang, P. (2008). Parental awareness and monitoring of adolescent Internet use. *Current Psychology (New Brunswick, N.J.), 27*, 217–233. doi:10.1007/s12144-008-9038-6

Lieberman, H., Dinakar, K., & Jones, B. (2011). Let's gang up on cyber bullying. *Computer, 44*(9), 93–96. doi:10.1109/MC.2011.286

Livingstone, S., Haddon, L., Gorzig, A., & Olafsson, K. (2011). *EU kids online final report.* Available at http://www2.lse.ac.uk/media@lse/research/EUKidsOnline/EU20Kids20II20(2009-11)/EUKidsOnlineIIReports/Final%20report.pdf

MacKay, W. (2012). *Respectful and responsible relationships: There's no app for that (the report of the nova scotia task force on bullying and cyber bullying).* Nova Scotia Task Force on Bullying and Cyber Bullying.

Marczak, M., & Coyne, I. (2010). Cyber bullying at school: Good practice and legal aspects in the United Kingdom. *Australian Journal of Guidance & Counselling, 20*(2), 182–193. doi:10.1375/ajgc.20.2.182

Martin, N., & Rice, J. (2011). Cybercrime: Understanding and addressing the concerns of stakeholders. *Computers & Security, 30*(8), 803–814. doi:10.1016/j.cose.2011.07.003

Menesini, E. (2012). Cyber bullying: The right value of the phenomenon. Comments on the paper 'cyber bullying: An overrated phenomenon?'. *European Journal of Developmental Psychology, 9*, 544–552. doi:10.1080/17405629.2012.706449

Menesini, E., & Nocentini, A. (2012). Peer education intervention: Face-to-face versus online. In A. Costabile, & B. A. Spears (Eds.), *The impact of technology on relationships in educational settings* (pp. 139–150). New York, NY: Routledge.

Mishna, F., Cook, C., Gadalla, T., Daciuk, J., & Solomon, S. (2010). Cyber bullying behaviors among middle and high school students. *The American Journal of Orthopsychiatry, 80*(3), 362–374. doi:10.1111/j.1939-0025.2010.01040.x PMID:20636942

Monks, C. P., Robinson, S., & Worlidge, P. (2012). The emergence of cyber bullying: A survey of primary school pupil's perceptions and experiences. *School Psychology International, 33*, 477–491. doi:10.1177/0143034312445242

Nathan, E. (2009). *Reputational orientations and aggression: Extending reputation enhancement theory to upper primary school aged bullies.* (Doctoral thesis). The University of Western Australia, Perth, Australia. Retrieved from https://repository. uwa.edu.au/R/-?func¼dbin-jump-ull&object_id¼12681&local_base¼GEN01-INS01

National Conference of State Legislatures. (2012). *State cyberstalking and cyberharassment laws.* Available at http://www.ncsl.org/IssuesResearch/TelecommunicationsInformationTechnolgy/CyberstalkingLaws/tabid/13495/Default.aspx

New York Times. (2007). *A hoax turned fatal draws anger but no charges.* Available at http://www.nytimes.com/2007/11/28/us/28hoax.html?ref=meganmeier&_r=0

ABC News. (2010). *Immigrant teen taunted by cyberbullies hangs herself.* Available at http://abcnews.go.com/Health/cyber bullying-factor-suicidemassachusetts-teen-irishimmigrant/story?id=9660938

Nocentini, A., Calmaestra, J., Schultze-Krumboltz, A., Scheithauer, H., Ortega, R., & Menesini, E. (2010). cyber bullying: Labels, behaviours and definition in three European countries. *Australian Journal of Guidance & Counselling, 20,* 129–142. doi:10.1375/ajgc.20.2.129

Olweus, D. (2012a). Cyber bullying: An overrated phenomenon? *European Journal of Developmental Psychology, 9,* 520–538. doi:10.1080/17405629.2012.682358

Olweus, D. (2012b). Comments on cyber bullying article: A rejoinder. *European Journal of Developmental Psychology, 9,* 559–568. doi:10.1080/17405629.2012.705086

Patchin, J. W., & Hinduja, S. (2011). Traditional and non-traditional bullying among youth: A test of General Strain Theory. *Youth & Society, 43,* 727–751. doi:10.1177/0044118X10366951

Patchin, J. W., & Hinduja, S. (2012). Cyber bullying: An update and synthesis of the research. In J. W. Patchin, & S. Hinduja (Eds.), Cyber bullying prevention and response: Expert perspectives (pp. 13–35). New York, NY: Routledge.

Perren, S., Corcoran, L., Cowie, H., Dehue, F., Garcia, D., Mc Guckin, C., Sevcikova, A., Tsatsou, P., & Vollink, T. (2012). *Coping with cyber bullying: A systematic literature review.* Final Report of the COST IS 0801 Working Group 5 (published online).

Pieschl, S., Porsch, T., Kahl, T., & Klockenbusch, R. (2013). Relevant dimensions of cyber bullying — Results from two experimental studies. *Journal of Applied Developmental Psychology.* doi:10.1016/j.appdev.2013.04.002

Raskauskas, J., & Stotlz, A. (2007). Involvement in traditional and electronic bullying among adolescents. *Developmental Psychology, 43,* 564–575. doi:10.1037/0012-1649.43.3.564 PMID:17484571

Rivers, I., & Noret, N. (2010). 'I h8 u': Findings from a five-year study of text and email bullying. *British Educational Research Journal, 36,* 643–671. doi:10.1080/01411920903071918

Sabella, R. (2012). How school counselors can help. In J. W. Patchin, & S. Hinduja (Eds.), *cyber bullying prevention and response: Expert perspectives* (pp. 72–92). New York, NY: Routledge.

Sahin, M., Aydin, B., & Sari, S. V. (2012). Cyber Bullying Cyber Victimization and Psychological Symptoms: A Study in Adolescent. *Cukurova University Faculty of Education Journal, 41*(1), 53–59.

Sengupta, A., & Chaudhuri, A. (2011). Are social networking sites a source of online harassment for teens? Evidence from survey data. *Children and Youth Services Review, 33,* 284–290. doi:10.1016/j.childyouth.2010.09.011

Slonje, R., & Smith, P. K. (2008). cyber bullying: Another main type of bullying. *Scandinavian Journal of Psychology, 49*(2), 147–154. doi:10.1111/j.1467-9450.2007.00611.x PMID:18352984

Smith, P. K. (2012a). cyber bullying: Challenges and opportunities for a research program— a response to Olweus (2012). *European Journal of Developmental Psychology, 9,* 553–558. doi:10.1080/17405629.2012.689821

Smith, P. K. (2012b). Cyber bullying and cyber aggression. In S. R. Jimerson, A. B. Nickerson, M. J. Mayer, & M. J. Furlong (Eds.), Handbook of school violence and school safety: International research and practice (2nd ed.) (pp. 93–103). New York, NY: Routledge.

Smith, P. K., Madsen, K. C., & Moody, J. C. (1999). What causes the age decline in reports of being bullied at school? Towards a developmental analysis of risks of being bullied. *Educational Research, 41*(3), 267–285. doi:10.1080/0013188990410303

Smith, P. K., Mahdavi, J., Carvalho, M., Fisher, S., Russell, S., & Tippett, N. (2008). cyber bullying: Its nature and impact in secondary school pupils. *Journal of Child Psychology and Psychiatry, and Allied Disciplines, 49*(4), 376–385. doi:10.1111/j.1469-7610.2007.01846.x PMID:18363945

Smith, P. K., Mahdavi, J., Carvalho, M., & Tippett, N. (2006). *An investigation into cyber bullying, its forms, awareness and impact, and the relationship between age and gender in cyber bullying.* Research Brief No. RBX03-06. London: DfES.

Smith, P. K., & Slonje, R. (2010). Cyber bullying: The nature and extent of a new kind of bullying, in and out of school. In S. R. Jimerson, S. M. Swearer, & D. L. Espelage (Eds.), Handbook of bullying in schools: An international perspective (pp. 249–262). New York, NY: Routledge.

Stover, D. (2006). Treating cyber bullying as a school violence issue. *Education Digest, 72*(4), 40–42.

Tangen, D., & Campbell, M. (2010). cyber bullying prevention: One primary school's approach. *Australian Journal of Guidance & Counselling, 20,* 225–234. doi:10.1375/ajgc.20.2.225

Tokunaga, R. S. (2010). Following you home from school: A critical review and synthesis of research on cyber bullying victimization. *Computers in Human Behavior, 26,* 277–287. doi:10.1016/j.chb.2009.11.014

Trevathan, J., & Myers, T. (2012). Anti-social networking? *World Academy of Science. Engineering and Technology, 72,* 127–135.

von Marées, N., & Petermann, F. (2012). cyber bullying: An increasing challenge for schools. *School Psychology International, 33*(5), 467–476. doi:10.1177/0143034312445241

Walrave, M., & Heirman, W. (2011). cyber bullying: Predicting victimization and perpetration. *Children & Society, 25*(1), 59–72. doi:10.1111/j.1099-0860.2009.00260.x

Wang, J., Iannotti, R. J., & Nansel, T. R. (2009). School bullying among adolescents in the United States: Physical, verbal, relational, and cyber. *The Journal of Adolescent Health, 45*(4), 368–375. doi:10.1016/j.jadohealth.2009.03.021 PMID:19766941

Willard, N. (2007). *Educator's guide to cyber bullying and cyber threats 2007.* Available at http://www.cyberbully.org/cyber bully/docs/cbcteducator

Wolak, J., Mitchell, K. J., & Finkelhor, D. (2007). Does online harassment constitute bullying? An exploration of online harassment by known peers and online-only contacts. *The Journal of Adolescent Health, 41,* S51–S58. doi:10.1016/j.jadohealth.2007.08.019 PMID:18047945

Ybarra, M. L., & Mitchell, K. J. (2004). Online aggressor/targets, aggressors, and targets: a comparison of associated youth characteristics. *Journal of Child Psychology and Psychiatry, and Allied Disciplines, 45*(7), 1308–1316. doi:10.1111/j.1469-7610.2004.00328.x PMID:15335350

Yilmaz, H. (2011). Cyber bullying in Turkish middle schools: An exploratory study. *School Psychology International, 32,* 645–654. doi:10.1177/0143034311410262

## KEY TERMS AND DEFINITIONS

**Bully:** An aggressive person who intentionally harasses weaker or less popular people.

**Cyber:** Having to do with electronic communications.

**Harassment:** Disturbing repeatedly.

**Internet:** An immensely large computer network which links computers worldwide.

**Prevention:** Active avoidance.

**Social Networking Sites:** Websites that serve as platforms for people to develop and maintain relationships.

**Victim:** A person who suffers injurious action.

# Chapter 7
# DNA Databases for Criminal Investigation

**Henrique Curado**
*ESTSP-IPP, Portugal*

## ABSTRACT

*This chapter studies the establishment of DNA databases and their relevance at two levels. On the one hand, as a basis for criminal investigation, they contribute to the protection of the public against potentially criminal behavior. In our societies, mass violence is not a sporadic occurrence and knowledge. When DNA databases allow for preventive action, they may be synonymous with safety. On the other hand, DNA databases pose deeper problems, such as a felon's data are still personal data and as such need to be protected. Any violation of this right is against the law. Therefore, a society that wants to be lawfully protected must first protect. The study is focused on Spanish and Portuguese statutes enforced in 2007 and 2008, respectively, as well as on doctrine and jurisprudence produced in both countries and intended to strengthen cyberspace security and to guarantee access to information.*

## INTRODUCTION

Any attempt to conceptually map the theories and thoughts of different authors produces a network of notions whose intersections inevitably refer to the issue of human dignity. Such a mapping leads to questions about four main topics. Firstly, the reason why DNA databases have been created despite all the controversy around them. Secondly, the scope and range of the law. Thirdly, the analysis of their repercussions, that is to say, the problems posed by the collection of personal data, which constitutes a sensitive matter and makes us vulnerable before the society and diverse stakeholders. Lastly, the issues concerning information security.

It must be pointed out that the analysis of all these aspects also reveals a fundamental concern with the human person, particularly the protection of the personality. For this reason, this paper has been structured in subchapters dealing with the first three aspects mentioned above. Information security, which, as we will see, is at the core of the matter, will be approached in future research work. An introductory subchapter intends to contextualize these aspects and articulate them with the central issue of human dignity.

When its related concepts are analyzed - needs, repercussions, legal aspects and security, they all eventually lead to the main concern of human dignity, particularly the protection of the

DOI: 10.4018/978-1-4666-6324-4.ch007

personality. It is necessary then to understand the significance of personal data collection and storage in databases of which citizens do not know when, how or to what purposes they are accessed by third parties. In fact, "knowledge management has not generated a consensus basis, leading to questions related to privacy and its compatibility with public interest" (Curado *et al.,* 2011, p. 32).

In addition, it is important to understand the reason why DNA databases have been created; in other words, why humankind needs databases containing information about a few members of the community. The answer is twofold. Collectively, people need to keep society safe. As recent events of mass violence have shown, profiling potential criminals may lead to higher levels of security. Individually, for personal or humanitarian reasons, people may choose to register their DNA profiles in order to determine kinship or to be used in catastrophe situations (CNECV, 2007, p. 3), not forgetting regenerative medicine, which must be ruled according to the values of fairness and solidarity (Nunes, 2013, p. 121-3), particularly equal and fair access (Nunes (Relat.), 2006, p. 14). The creation of databases, however, is not a problem in itself, since privacy is not seized by society, but results from individual availability, as "the right to privacy may be considered available, only requiring the consent of the person holding that right" (Greco & Braga, 2012, p. 163).

In order to understand the scope and range of the law, the legislation in force in both Spain and Portugal has to be analyzed. On the one hand, the specific regulations on DNA profiles and databases may be found in the Spanish Organic Law 10/2007, dated 8 October, dealing with police DNA databases, as well as in the Portuguese Law 5/2008, dated 12 February, which approved the creation of a DNA database for purposes of civil and criminal identification. On the other hand, information protection is regulated in Spain by Organic Law 15/1999, dated 13 December, for the Protection of Personal Data, and in Portugal by Law 67/98 for the Protection of Personal Data,

dated 26 October. Before the enforcement of these statutes, both the Spanish (Guridi, 2008, p. 5) and Portuguese (Court's ruling No. 0546541, 2006) legal frameworks already allowed for certain latitude in the interpretation of fundamental rights.

Another aspect to be considered is that DNA databases have legal repercussions at two levels, regarding the methods of sample collection and the possible invasion of privacy. In fact, if a person does not consent to the collection of his/her DNA, samples may be taken against the person's will (Kappler, 2008, p. 76-92), which may lead to a possible invasion of privacy. Also, DNA sampling makes us vulnerable when obtained by "would-be employers", as it "may exclude individuals from the labor market and even deprive them of a decent life if found out to have a genetic predisposition to develop certain diseases" (Doneda, 2000).

It has become clear by now that this paper tries to find a point of balance between two apparently conflicting interests, such as the protection of privacy and the creation of databases of DNA profiles for criminal investigation. Therefore, the next subchapter contextualizes the issues of privacy and the need for DNA databases. On the subchapter *torn between two types of fear* the third issue will be discussed with the study of Spanish and Portuguese frameworks and their consequences, as well as of the well-founded fears felt before the above-mentioned regulations were enforced. On the same subchapter we will study the repercussions of DNA databases. Our fourth question shows us some limitations. So we ask: are we facing an imperfect method?

## CONTEXT AND BACKGROUND

Though resulting from a comprehensive social debate, the creation of a DNA database is mainly a political decision, based on the belief in its many advantages for society. Other, ethical and philosophical, aspects, while not completely neglected, do not receive too much attention (Machado,

2011), particularly those related to individuals, the unavoidable exposure of their lives and the surrender of their rights. Thus, the establishment of DNA databases has traditionally entailed two possibilities, or better, two realities (on the one hand, the loss of privacy and its legal frame, and, on the other, general belief in its social benefits), which demand a solution to balance these two apparently conflicting interests.

Two opposing sides take part in this debate. Though not openly against it, authors like Machado (2005) and Costa (2001) warn us about the dangers of the loss of privacy and the delusion that DNA databases may solve cases. In contrast, political discourse, based on national security claims appealing to the collective consciousness, as well as on philosophical and juridical grounds, argues that humans are naturally sociable beings who must not be self-centered in their own individual rights (Doneda, 2000; Ascensão, 2008). According to Nunes (2013, p. 110), "it is somewhat consensual that [DNA databases] are ethically and socially acceptable", particularly "in order to fight crime, and, assuming that the severity of the offense has been taken into account, the common good is important enough to justify some reduction in the citizen's basic rights, such as the right to individual privacy". In this regard, Greco & Braga (2012, p. 159) claim that the right to privacy is a variable right.

It is important then to pin down these two apparently contradictory concepts of individual and public interests, as privacy is an individual right, whereas DNA databases are a collective need.

## Privacy, Points of Departure and Arrival, and Limitations

In addition to all the technical aspects related to biology and the forensic sciences, as well as to security issues and political options for the sake of the common good, any discussion on the uses of DNA databases for criminal investigation must begin and end with the ethical value of privacy as

inherent to human dignity. It is a point of departure because the individual personality draws a limiting line, and a point of arrival, as men and women are both individual and social beings, defining their own limits as a response to the necessary social coexistence. As a precaution, "the main tendency has been to consider genetic information [...] as pertaining to the sphere of human dignity, regardless of the means used to obtain that information" (Nunes, 2013, p. 112). Although political discourse does not completely neglect this axiom, it usually "dismisses the risks of eroding individual rights" (Machado, 2011: 162)[2]. But what is privacy then?

As a juridical notion, it is an individual right. As pointed out by Garfinkel (2001, p. 5) "privacy is fundamentally about the power of the individual", mainly because it gained juridical force by being considered inherent to human dignity. Therefore, privacy "includes a person's intimacy, private life and honor". As a consequence, "individuals are entitled to decide whether their personal information is kept under their sole control, as they have the right to choose who, when, where and how their personal information may be revealed" (Fortes & Spinetti, 2004, p. 1328). "The right to privacy is like a room locked from the inside. Any attempt to break in shall be taken as a breach, an unjustified violation deserving punishment" (Greco & Braga, 2012, p. 157).

In accordance with this definition of privacy, the creation and use of DNA and other databases collide with individual fundamental rights. In particular, mandatory data collection against a person's will usually (though not always) goes against physical integrity as well as the protection of personal data. This conflict is a permanent concern of the current juridical systems in Spain and Portugal, as seen in the statutes analyzed below, as they make specific reference to the protection of personal data[3].

A more comprehensive discussion is necessary, however. In fact, the loss of privacy, or the lack of protection of individual rights, goes way beyond the scope of this paper, as the private sphere is constantly threatened by technology at different levels: "video cameras observe personal moments; computers store personal facts; and communications networks make personal information widely available throughout the world" (Garfinkel, 2001, p. 5). To this list we may add the supervision of workers' emails carried out by a number of state and private organizations. More relevantly to our study, however, clinical records may be stored for the sake of an alleged public interest or the common good. In this case, instead of the potential danger for society (as in the use of DNA databases for criminal investigation), what matters is the study of personal data for the sake of the common good, and information that used to be confidential may now be accessed in order to conduct research in the field of medicine (CNPD, 2007b).

Therefore, as in the latter situation, conflict may be resolved due to a specific factor, such as the fact that public access to sensitive material might be advantageous for the entire society, though the identities of the persons involved must be protected. Even so, personal data are subject to special protection, as stressed by the Spanish Agency for Data Protection (AEPD, 2011) when referring to Art. 7 - *Specially protected data* - of Organic Law for the Protection of Personal Data (Ley Orgánica 15/1999), as well as by Art. 7 - *Processing sensitive data* - of the Portuguese law (Lei Nº 67/98).

These situations show that technical tools must make a rapid assessment and not wait for a juridical answer to become effective. As the law is usually incomplete and does not cover the whole range of possible events, the relationship between law and actual facts is reversed. Thus, it is not the law that determines actual behavior, but facts that require new legislation, "mainly because new technologies provide the tools to solve some problems, while generating new ones" (Costa, 2001, p. 171). But the answers provided by the law have the human person as their ultimate concern. It is always the human being, but not always from the same

viewpoint. In fact, "the very right to privacy is not an absolute notion, but varies depending on personal, cultural and social standards" (Greco & Braga, 2012, p. 159). Besides, the concept of privacy has evolved through time, therefore "today, defining privacy as *the right to be left alone* is equal to utterly ignoring its growing importance" (Doneda, 2000). Indeed, given that people are social beings and that societies are in constant change, individual rights must not be understood as individualistic rights, but as social rights, including the ideas of coexistence and sociability. Otherwise, individual rights could be reduced to mere egotism "contradicting what should be its foundation, that is, the defense of the human person. Coexistence and sociability are parts of the human nature. The protection of individual rights cannot be stronger than this essential feature of human personality" (Ascensão, 1995)[4].

Even when identifying elements are stored in different databases, with no risk of jeopardizing fundamental rights, that is not the case, either in Spain or in Portugal, when genetic data are stored together with the person's identity, and some reduction of individual rights will be observed. In fact, "privacy and intimacy, freedom, physical integrity, and the right to health and dignity are in opposition to the right of effective protection and the need to preserve society and the proper administration of justice" (Sesé, 2007, p. 7). We agree with Garfinkel that privacy must be understood in the context of today's society and technological advances, calling for everyone's concern: "today's war on privacy is intimately related to the dramatic advances in technology we've seen in recent years" (Garfinkel, 2001, p. 5).

In Spain and Portugal, the juridical boundaries of individual privacy have already been established. But before going through the Spanish and Portuguese legislation, it is necessary to analyze the need for DNA databases determining those boundaries.

## The Need for Databases and the Faith in Their Social Benefits

Trying to understand the reason why DNA databases have been created despite all the controversy around them, we find that they have several purposes beside that of criminal investigation, but all of them are based on the idea of their advantages for the entire society. However, in view of their "exponential growth in recent years" and of their diverse uses, "their ethical and juridical implications are increasingly questionable" (Nunes, 2013, p. 115), especially when, regardless of their potentially harmful or beneficial effects, privacy and human dignity are at stake.

Their advantages, more than their risks, are usually emphasized, leading to deeper concern by those upholding the protection of privacy. And the truth is that this conflict cannot be solved by dismissing the risks of DNA databases in favor of the rhetoric of public safety and the fight against crime (Machado, 2011, p. 156). Though transnational crime has grown due to globalization and to the free movement of goods and people across European borders after the Schengen Agreement, the rights of the individual must not be neglected. That is the common standard for DNA analysis in the member-states, which define their own methods. Thus, Recommendation 10 of the Council of Europe "advised member-states to standardize methods for DNA analysis, at both national and international levels" (Guridi, 2008, p. 12). This standardization is far from consensual. Costa (2001, p. 174) points out that "instead of reducing uncertainty, this technique has contributed, especially in England and the United States, to a heated debate about the 'universality' of science", underlining "its vulnerability and contingency brought about by local and particular differences". Therefore, it is important to understand the nature and purposes of DNA databases.

## DNA PROFILE DATABASES

*Although some special technology may be used to protect personal information and autonomy, the overwhelming tendency of advanced technology is to do the reverse (Garfinkel, 2001, p. 5).*

For the definition of the concept of DNA database and of others needed in this respect, we follow the second section of the Portuguese law (Lei No 5/2008), as it provides a set of definitions on which the legal text is based. A DNA profile database is then "a structure made up of files containing DNA profiles as well as personal data, to be used exclusively for identification purposes".

With the sole purpose of making positive identifications in civil or criminal processes, DNA databases combine diverse concepts demanding a closer look: personal data, DNA profiles, personal data files and DNA profile files. In accordance with the same law, a "DNA profile is the result of a sample analysis through techniques validated and recommended by the international scientific community", and "personal data are all the information of any kind and in any format, including audio and image, of an identified or identifiable person" (Lei No 5/2008, art. 2).

Now, if a DNA database is "a structure made up of files containing DNA profiles as well as personal data, to be used exclusively for identification purposes", it may include the person's "full name, date and place of birth, current known address, personal identification number (ID, work permit, passport or any other), parents' names, marital status, gender, ethnicity, height and the presence of physical malformations".

Also, if the person may be identified or identifiable, this means that, according to the law, (s)he "may be identified, directly or indirectly, through an identification number or through one or more specific elements characterizing his/her physical, physiological, psychic, economic, cultural or social identity". Such is the origin of the fear caused by DNA databases as sources of information accessible according to predefined criteria. That is the reason why the possibility to access files with personal information is an offense to human dignity (to privacy). So, we ask why DNA databases have been created.

## DNA Databases and Their Advantages

The need for DNA databases is closely related to the confidence in their juridical benefits. Together with fingerprints, DNA profiles are believed to reveal people's biological singularity, which may be used for unequivocal identification (Costa, *et al.,* 2002, p. 206). As Neto (2003, p. 27) remarks: "they are presented as powerful, indispensable tools to turn criminal investigations into mathematical, error-free processes". But what is the point of such evidence? How relevant is it to know whether some personal information belongs to one particular person and not to any other?

DNA databases are currently used in three types of legal investigation: "the identification of crime suspects and victims, of accident and disaster casualties, and for parental testing" (Machado, *et al.,* 2008, p. 123). As to whether or not these uses are important enough to significantly reduce the individual's private sphere, there are two opposing tendencies. Contrary to the supporters of the databases, those who stand for individual rights are adamant against DNA profiling. In both fields, however, human dignity is at the forefront of the debate.

Back to the three-tiered application of databases, it must be pointed out that the approach of this paper - their use in criminal investigation - is motivated by their growing relevance in extremely violent crimes. These cases are also the stronghold of social sustainability. Three examples of mass violence in the last decade will suffice to make any reader acknowledge the need for public safety: 9/11 in the United States, March 11 2004 in Spain, and the 2011 Breivik case in Norway

constitute clear evidence of how much society needs not only to protect itself from violence but to prevent it. The recent Sandy Hook Elementary School shooting on 14 December 2012 was another example, especially when we learnt about the shooter's home arsenal.

Within this context, the bases for the Spanish and Portuguese legal texts are very revealing. In the Spanish Parliament, the debates that resulted in the Organic Law 10/2007, dated 8 October, regulating police databases made up of DNA profiles, "showed the importance of DNA databases in criminal investigation conducted by forensic laboratories, not only for solving crimes committed by unknown perpetrators, but for the identification of missing persons" (Sesé, 2007, p. 2). In Portugal, during the debate leading to the approval of Law 5/2008, dated 12 February, regulating the creation of a DNA profile database for civil and criminal identification purposes, former Minister Alberto Costa claimed that "the credibility of courthouses and of criminal investigation institutions will be strengthened by the use of highly precise and reliable technical means: identification through genetic profiles" (2007, quoted by Machado, 2011, p. 157).

The rigorous methods of forensic sciences, together with the near certainty that evidence produced by forensic experts may lead to potential criminals, give a sense of security and gain public support for the collection and identification of samples. The need to know beforehand and prevent criminal behavior has great social interest. That is why public interest has been stronger than those subjective rights upholding human dignity, such as the rights to privacy, physical integrity and against self-incrimination, as enshrined in the Constitution. "When analyzing conflicting interests [...] it is important to find out whether individual rights may be eroded if the right to privacy collides with national security and individual safety, to conclude that privacy may have to give in" (Curado et al., 2012, p. 32).

In order to reconcile these two sides (the loss of privacy and the general belief in the overall benefits of DNA databases), a multidisciplinary approach must build the legal framework of each state on solid theoretical principles, allied to common standards. Though the fear of privacy loss is an important aspect, it must be remembered that before the bill resulting in the creation of DNA databases, DNA profiles were already stored as described below.

## TORN BETWEEN TWO TYPES OF FEAR

We believe that the perfect balance between the wish to protect privacy and the need to collect, access and exchange personal data for criminal investigation (in particular to fight and prevent violent crimes), requires the citizen's trust. This is only possible through safer storage of sensitive data, especially when most of them can be found in digital databases and unlawful access may lead to interference with private life through the retrieval of a large amount of personal information. Trust is then essential to make these two types of fear compatible, and requires an increase in cyberspace security. As Garfinkel (2001) remarks, "in many ways, the story of technology's attack on privacy is really the story of how institutions and the people who run them use technology to gain control over the human spirit, for good and ill".

The debate over DNA databases shows two opposing tendencies, one more restrictive than the other. Both place human dignity at the forefront, but fear is the dividing line - fear of the violation of privacy and fear of predictable violence. When confronted with an act of mass terrorism, or even with an isolated event of extreme violence (like the murders committed by a serial killer), it is inevitable to think that society could have done more to protect itself but did not.

Apart from the analyses of Spanish and Portuguese legislation as juridical tools for the creation of DNA databases, it must be added that in both countries the debate is still ongoing and includes the views of legal scientists, biologists and information scientists.

## Specific Legislation Regarding DNA Databases

Within the Spanish and Portuguese legislation and jurisprudence, the use of DNA databases has legal implications at two main levels: the first concerns those samples obtained without the person's consent, whereas the second refers to the loss of privacy when samples are taken. Jurisprudence in both countries was rather flexible in what concerned the taking of samples, even when against a suspect's will, as shown by two verdicts pronounced before the approval of the Spanish and Portugal bills.

## Spanish Organic Law 10/2007, Dated 8 October

In Spain, the creation of a police database containing genetic profiles went beyond the provisions contained in the Criminal Procedure Code, especially in what concerns the use of DNA databases in criminal investigation. According to Sesé (2007), this law allows for the concentration of data up to then scattered through "DNA files belonging to state security agencies" and to other organizations unrelated to law enforcement.

As important as data concentration is the possibility, included in the third additional provision, to obtain biological samples. During the investigation of serious offences, especially those threatening a person's life, freedom, indemnity, sexual freedom, physical integrity or property through the use of force, violence or intimidation, as well as of organized crime, criminal investigative forces may collect samples and fluids from the suspect, detainee or accused without their consent, as well as from the crime scene, as long as they have a warrant issued by a competent judicial authority, in compliance with the Criminal Procedure Code (Ley Orgánica N° 10/2007).

Two conclusions may be drawn. First, before the bill was passed regulating the creation of DNA databases, the existing files were dispersed, which was a source of even more uncertainty and insecurity. Consequently, Organic Law 10/2007 does not jeopardize privacy, as that danger already existed. On the contrary, the law limited and contained the problem. Second, and equally important, collecting samples without the person's consent is now regulated by law. Those who consider it a violation of privacy, particularly as it is a nonconsensual physical intervention in conflict with the right against self-incrimination, must not forget that in actual practice Spanish criminal investigation, though not completely confirmed by case-law, already used those methods. Although the Spanish Constitutional Court had already established guidelines by distinguishing between body searches and physical interventions (Court's ruling 207/1996), and acknowledging the person's right to refuse physical intervention through a writ of amparo, "law enforcement bodies, in the course of an investigation, may obtain biological samples from any persons without their consent and require authorization from a judge to conduct forensic examinations on those samples" (Sesé, 2007, p. 5). Nonetheless, constitutional case-law did not rule out the possibility of collecting samples without the person's consent, as pointed out by Moreno (2010): "although constitutional jurisprudence has never claimed that a person's uncooperative attitude should be met with physical coercion, it has never excluded that possibility either". In short, in reality Spanish criminal investigation before Law 10/2007 already obtained biological samples without people's consent. It also incorporated them into dispersed databases. Those procedures, however, cannot be interpreted as *contra legem*, as the law for the protection of personal data (Ley Orgánica

15/1999) favored that reading, as "consent shall not be necessary when personal data are collected to carry out the tasks within the competence of the public administration". Law 10/2007 made the matter more transparent by giving police forces more power, but the truth is that art. 22 of Organic Law 15/1999 already authorized law enforcement and security agencies to collect and process biological samples. And although those data were specifically protected by art. 7 of the same law, samples could be taken "whenever it was absolutely necessary to pursue the ends of a specific investigation" (Sesé, 2007, p. 7).

## Portuguese Law 5/2008, Dated 12 February

In Portugal, the creation of DNA databases for criminal investigation was made possible in 2008. At first glance, the legal text seems to focus on civil identification as its main objective, as observed in the first paragraph of art.1. The second paragraph, however, extends the scope of the law, as databases "shall also be used for criminal investigation". In addition, art.4 underlines that they have those two purposes (Lei N° 5/2008).

In what concerns the ambit of this paper, this law does not result in a reduction of fundamental rights, at least when compared to what had been the use in Portugal till then. Investigators usually took biological samples against the person's will, and this practice had been acknowledged by case-law. Machado (2011, p. 158-9) records the following statement from a police expert and attorney: "The police secretly use those things [databases] already [...], the purpose of this one [a DNA database] is to regulate something that already exists, though not in the right place, that is, in forensic institutions; right now they are found in police laboratories". Even though this is just one testimony, case-law shows that police did take samples without the person's will and stored those samples at least until the end of the trial.

Two years before the law was enforced, the Porto Court of Appeals had ruled as "valid the evidence obtained through an analysis of the defendant's saliva, taken against his will in the course of the investigation, as authorized by the public prosecutor" (Court's ruling No. 0546541, 2006). The decision was based on the need to reduce fundamental rights for the sake of public interest.

Another ruling (Coimbra Court of Appeals, No. 3261/01) admitted the reduction of fundamental rights within the constitutional limits defined by arts. 18 and 25. Although the latter article includes physical integrity and self-determination as inviolable rights, these are not absolute concepts. In compliance with art. 18, restrictions to rights and liberties are constitutionally possible if limited to those strictly necessary to safeguard other constitutionally protected rights or interests. Restrictions shall be considered illegitimate "when they affect the essential core of subjective rights, in detriment of the (minimum) values representing the idea of human dignity and making up the foundation and the essence of each constitutional provision in this matter…".

As we read in the Court's ruling Nº 0546541 (2006) "this is the reason why the Portuguese legal system considers a number of situations in which the rights to physical integrity and to physical self-determination give way before dominant social interests" and it doesn't matter if it is "in the field of public health, national defense, justice or other areas." That judgment alerts us that these interventions occur in different physical domains "like mandatory vaccination, X-rays, compulsory treatment of certain diseases, the ban on doping for athletes […] and psychiatric expert examinations" (*Ibidem*, 2006).

As already mentioned, Portuguese case-law was more willing than Spanish jurisprudence to admit the nonconsensual reduction of fundamental rights (Kappler, 2008, p. 76-92). A very different situation arises from the storage of a person's samples together with their personal informa-tion. Before Law 5/2008 for the creation of DNA databases, the only legal text concerned with this matter was the Law for the Protection of Personal Data (Lei No 67/98, 1998).

The Portuguese Data Protection Commission took a position about the draft law establishing "the guidelines for the creation and maintenance of a DNA database for civil identification and criminal investigation" (CNPD, 2007a). This position restated previous opinions of the Commission about the protection of personal data. The list of principles (par. III) is based on the human dignity and the protection of privacy of "actual people, real men and women, not an ideal or an abstraction". Among a number of principles (precaution, prevention, transparency, finality, technical competence, confidentiality and control), two stand out: autonomy and informed consent, which have always been present in the Commission's interpretation of the law for the protection of personal data. Autonomy has always been highlighted, as people have the right to make their life plans regardless of a state database that knows everything about them. Informed consent has usually been necessary unless for procedures within the law or when a CNPD is produced, in compliance with par. 2 of art. 7 (Lei No 67/98, 1998).

Thus, before Law 5/2008 was enforced, samples were in fact collected, with or without the person's consent, as well as stored and examined by the police. The new law, however, not only defined what was understood by each term, but specified under what conditions samples should be taken – art. 11 states that "the collection of samples shall be conducted by means of noninvasive methods, respecting human dignity and personal physical and moral integrity, such as a mouth mucosal swab or a similar method".

As a result, the new law regulating DNA databases cannot be said to be more lenient than the previous practices of criminal investigation. On the contrary, art. 26 introduced a more protective disposition, regarding the elimination of data.

# REPERCUSSIONS OF DNA IDENTIFICATION: AN IMPERFECT METHOD?

Now we try understand how when and why the establishment of a database of DNA is a threat to privacy. Indeed, in spite of the advantages of DNA-based evidence, the doctrine has pointed out limitations at several levels, including severe deficiencies from ethical, scientific and legal viewpoints, which makes us wonder whether this is not in fact an imperfect method.

A summary of the promises and risks of genetics at the service of justice (Machado et al., 2008, p. 144-65) shows an "eminently ideological" debate, though "some aspects also reveal technical and scientific discrepancies". Following Deryck Beyleveld, Machado's work illustrates the claims of enthusiasts and pessimists regarding controversial issues to which there is no straightforward answer. The relevance of this lack of consensus is related to the intended use of DNA databases for criminal investigation – it would be legitimate to ask whether justice can be fair, that is, equal, when there is a discrepancy regarding the extent to which DNA profiles may be considered. For some, "a conviction based on a DNA profile providing the suspect's identification is ultimately acceptable", whereas for others, the pessimists, "it is utterly unacceptable to convict someone on the basis of DNA identification" (ibidem, p. 146). If the issue cannot be resolved within a single country, let alone the European space, and judges are free to accept DNA-based evidence or not, equity is out of the question.

Among other relevant questions, Costa (2001, p. 173-6) points out the procedures followed by experts, particularly as it is impossible to have "a single, global forensic science, in which standardized techniques" are compatible with non-standardized law due to local factors. Any attempt to have a single common procedure for the chain of custody (the essential, controlled mechanism for the preservation and integrity of the evidence, from the collection of material evidence at the crime scene, to its use in the course of a trial) in different legal systems is pointless, as every legal system has its own local contingencies.

We have already mentioned the vulnerability of privacy depending on the type of data collected. However, it is worth underlining that any juridical solution must respect human dignity and ethical principles, not only at the time of writing a bill but at the time of implementing a law. A case in point is the "myth of the infallibility" of technology (Machado et al., 2008, p. 150-1), leading judges to overrate a piece of evidence due to their scientific ignorance (Costa, 2001, p. 185). Other examples include the disagreement about the need for certified laboratories, the conviction that it is (im)possible to make an entire case rest on DNA-based evidence, and, again, the need for consent (or not) in order to collect biological samples.

If it is true that forensic biology can be a very reliable tool for criminal investigation, it is no less true that the "CSI effect"[5] has led some people to have unrealistic expectations, as reality "is not up to the high-tech idealization that we watch on TV" (Machado et al., 2008, p. 130).

Simple procedural aspects, like access by the defense to DNA test results, are also relevant, but different from one legal system to the next (Costa, 2001, p. 185). This is related to the chain of custody, because a piece of evidence may play a crucial role; that is why "it is so important for the defense to know who collected, analyzed and interpreted it (ibidem, p. 176). But its importance goes deeper than that. It is essential for the defense to know whether they can have access to DNA test results, otherwise they are forced to trust the chain of custody, the evidence gathered and the tests conducted.

Within the ambit of biological sciences, particularly molecular genetics, which made DNA profiling possible, the weakness of scientific evidence is still an ongoing debate. A simple example is provided by DNA paternity tests – whereas negative results are conclusive, positive results are not, which means that a match between the alleged father and child does not prove that they are in fact father and child. Indeed, the test can find a match with a sibling, a parent or any other relative of the alleged father. Therefore a positive DNA result paves the way to further testing, as has always been the case of blood type matching. The situation is made worse due to judges' difficulty to make probability judgments, as pointed out by Costa (*ibidem*, p. 184-5), in addition to the fact that probability judgments are not used in criminal trials. These two factors make DNA-based evidence even weaker. The question of paternity will provide a good example to better understand this point.

In order to understand a paternity investigation, it is worth reminding that DNA patterns are inherited from both parents in the same proportion. So, a paternity investigation to establish whether the alleged father is in fact the father needs to find out if he shares the alleged son's patterns. In order to do that, the son's DNA patterns must be first compared to those of the mother and only later with those of the alleged father, as those DNA patterns that do not match the mother's are no doubt inherited from the father. In this way, if the alleged father's DNA does not match the son's, paternity is ruled out. But if both share the same genetic patterns (those that the son did not inherit from his mother), it is necessary to determine the likelihood ratio of that man being in fact the father. This is done using the Hummel Table, an important aid for the judges' work (FMUP, 2004, p. 32).

If Spanish and Portuguese judges do not follow a probabilistic criteria to assess DNA-based evidence, the social benefits of this type of evidence become highly questionable. To make matters worse, judges do not determine the likelihood ratio and admit or reject a piece of evidence without questioning it, "blindly accepting the conclusions of forensic science" (Costa, 2001). The procedural dangers of this attitude are self-evident, as "public deconstruction of forensic evidence is never carried out".

Other technological deficiencies must not be dismissed, like the need for correct procedures to guarantee the safety of sensitive information. Issues like the controlled access and sharing of information are extremely relevant (between the Spanish state and regional security and law enforcement bodies, for example), such as the storage of information in one or more secure computers, the type of database and of information recorded, etc.

The fragilities of the law due to juridical reasons can be found at several levels. As Guridi (2008) points out regarding the Spanish law, two of these negative aspects are "para-judicial processes and the maintenance of data for excessive periods of time".

## Limits to Privacy: Before or After the Law?

Though an inherent right, a person's privacy is not self-centered, as man is a social being. Thus, the law about DNA databases does not go beyond previous regulations in what concerns the reduction of individual rights. The tension between privacy and public interest is not new, and the possibility of searching people for evidence had been common practice in Spain and Portugal before those bills were passed in 2007 and 2008. Therefore, privacy was a limited right, not only in Spain and Portugal, but in other countries as well.

Commenting on the convenience of creating a single DNA database in Spain, Guridi (2008, p. 2) pointed out that "separate state security and law enforcement institutions (the Police and the Civil Guard) had databases where they recorded genetic profiles obtained in the course of criminal investigations, although those databases had been created due to administrative decisions".

Even though the fear of privacy loss is an important factor, it must be borne in mind that DNA profiles were recorded before the approval of the laws regulating the creation of DNA databases. Besides, in both countries case-law admitted the collection of samples against a suspect's will, as observed in Spanish and Portuguese court rulings before the dates of the laws under analysis.

## SOLUTIONS AND RECOMMENDATIONS

The subject under study is an analysis of the dichotomy between privacy and public interest. Although the concept of freedom demands maximum protection of privacy, life in society requires some degree of compromise in what concerns individual liberties, through the collection and exchange of personal data. It is a simple dichotomy after all – although personal data are necessary mainly for the sake of public safety, those personal data and the respective physical interventions for civil identification and crime investigation are protected by the Constitution.

In spite of the ideal of a unified Europe, the states making up the EU have many different legal and juridical characteristics, much unlike federated states like the USA. Those differences can also be seen in their histories and cultures, their standards of living, their demographics and crime rates. That is the reason why European directives are transposed so differently in countries like England and Portugal.

EU member-states are expected to lay down their own laws in accordance to their local characteristics, without losing sight of the much wider European reality. The border-free space defined by the Schengen Agreement must not let us forget that evolution brings about responsibility and therefore restrictions as a counterpart of rights, especially the free movement of people and goods. At the same time, people are at the core of the debate, or, as has already been said, at the point of departure and arrival. DNA databases may be necessary and a reduction of privacy inevitable. But if the rules were clear and effective, risks could be lessened. Just as the collective interest may justify some privacy loss, human dignity

requires a commitment to the rigorous compliance with the law at all levels: type of data, consent and storage time. And those who do not respect the law must be punished.

A balanced solution requires security and information systems to be more reliable and trustworthy, as is the case of the civil and criminal registries. Today, DNA databases are a "public figure", as the information society has made us acquainted with concepts like "database", "data communication", "file", which we associate with computers and network communications. In other words, the possibility of sharing tons of information in a couple of seconds makes us feel even more vulnerable and helpless. The problem, however, does not lie in technology but in what people choose to do with it. In fact, "technology by itself doesn't violate our privacy or anything else: it's the people using this technology and the policies carried out that create violations" (Garfinkel, 2001).

As argued by Muñoz (1996, p. 258), the Human Genome Project (HGP) has ethical, social and legal repercussions. DNA databases, heralded as the most accurate tool to solve criminal cases, raise the same questions requiring close attention. But "a purely sociological, political or scientific reflection is not enough to suggest reasonable alternatives when conflict arises. An ethical and interdisciplinary debate" must be carried out by every state and their agents "in the field of praxis [...] where a wide range of options can be found, some of them compatible with the interests of the majority, others restrictive of fundamental rights" (*ibidem*: 258). Otherwise, any solution will lead to new problems.

## FUTURE RESEARCH DIRECTIONS

The wide scope of this subject, as it revolves around human dignity, leaves many unanswered questions – some are prior to the entire debate, others are caused by it. In a first stage, all the ethical issues related to dignity and privacy should be studied. In other words, it would be necessary to establish if life in society, which requires security provided by the state, may erode privacy and if so, up to what extent. Should anyone lose their privacy for the sake of a social value like security? The answer is ethical. As emphasized by Muñoz, "the ethical consequences of HGP are related to the possible conflicts arising from its medical, social and political uses" (*ibidem, p.* 258).

Finally, the security of information must be questioned, as that is the key to a satisfactory balance. If information security were tighter, the problem would certainly be less acute. In fact, there are databases containing information about all of us, from public institutions like schools and hospitals, to private organizations and numberless information networks. And if we do not object, that is for two reasons – first, because we usually provide that information willingly, as in the case of digital networks; second, and closely connected with the first one, because we trust. Similarly, DNA databases, no matter if the information in them has been provided willingly or not, are sustainable on the base of trust at several levels: trust in the security of the storage, of access, and in the compliance with legal storage periods. The last two aspects demand compliance with the law. The first one requires trust in the technical mechanisms used. Storage, for instance, whether in computer or paper files, is as aspect frequently analyzed exclusively by computer specialists, when in fact it would require the participation of multidisciplinary teams.

## CONCLUSION

No matter how great our fears, DNA databases are not going away. They are essential in societies that have decided to open their borders. We, as social beings, have come to the conclusion that there should be no frontiers to the free movement of people and goods, and now we have to live up to the challenge. Although not a universal right, the mere possibility of allowing people and goods within a certain juridical space to circulate freely makes us all more vulnerable. The combination of these liberties means that any device may be sent to any destination and that anyone who wants to commit a crime may get there when the time comes. After weighing up the two types of fear, reality shows that "when collective or individual damage is produced, the most adequate protection of privacy is no longer isolation and secrecy, but a more comprehensive approach to how the circulation of personal information should be controlled" (Doneda, 2000, p. 7).

Neither privacy will ever be absolute nor security complete. But we have to find a balance leading to an agreement between the private sphere of privacy and the public sphere of security. That entails a multidisciplinary reflection, both theoretical and practical – if privacy cannot guarantee complete safety, only practical experience of the problems arising from possible solutions will lead us to a better analysis and a more accurate definition of the potentials of any system (Muñoz, 1996, p. 258).

The reduction of privacy is a consequence of previous human decisions, and a duty derived from them. It is also the acknowledgment of mankind's social nature. We agree with Ascensão (2008) that are necessary mandatory "precautions [...] to avoid the disclosure of personal information [...] but that does not mean that privacy may become the Right of Individual Selfishness, or the right to save the powerful from criminal investigation." Ascensão work illustrates that "every individual right must be justified by an ethical imperative":

Privacy exists so that each person may, in full conscience, fulfill his/her personal development. If people are deprived of that goal, becoming a fortress of free will and, as is so often today, oblivious of any type of social solidarity and of their duties towards their community, privacy turns into an empty formula of facile and futile justification. Only a substantial notion of the human person can let us find balance between two extremes and guide us through the interpretation of the law (*Ibidem*, 2008)[6].

Although the debate is far from closed, the solution, or breakeven point, depends on the certainty that there is effective control of the use made by others of our personal information. Only then can public trust in its widest sense be gained – not only in the technical aspects of a security system (centralized information with or without remote access, clearance levels; access controls, data elimination), but also in law enforcement and the judicial system. In other words, trust must be placed in the entire legal system, from the advances in forensic sciences to the new technologies that make them possible, and in all those involved in the administration of justice. Only then can "the definition of privacy go through a radical transformation, from 'the right to be left alone' to the right to control the use made by third parties of the information concerning the individual" (Doneda, 2000, p. 7).

## REFERENCES

Acórdão Nº 0546541. (2006). *Tribunal da Relação do Porto* (p. 7). Retrieved from http://www.dgsi.pt/jtrp.nsf/c3fb530030ea1c61802568d9005cd5bb/c4d2a9d88f8d235780257172003d20f2

AEPD. (2011). *El derecho fundamental a la protección de datos - Guía para el Ciudadano*. Madri: Agencia Española de Protección de Datos. Retrieved from https://www.agpd.es/portalwebAGPD/CanalDelCiudadano/guias_recomendaciones/index-ides-idphp.php

Ascensão, J. O. (1995). Teoria geral do direito civil. (Associação de Estudantes, Ed.) (Faculdade., p. 121). Lisboa: Faculdade de Direito.

CNECV. C. N. de É. para as C. da V. (2007). *Parecer nº 52/CNECV/07*. Lisboa. Retrieved from http://www.cnecv.pt/admin/files/data/docs/1273054082_Parecer_052_CNECV_2007_BasesdadosADN.pdf

CNPD. (2007a). *Parecer Nº 18/2007D*. Retrieved from http://www.cnpd.pt/bin/decisoes/par/40_18_2007.pdf

CNPD. C. N. de P. de D. (2007b). *Deliberação Nº 227/2007* (p. 15). Retrieved from http://www.estsp.ipp.pt/fileManager/editor/Documentos_Publicos/Comissao de Etica/Acervo C.E./Privacidade_e_Confidencialidade_dos_Dados_Pessoais/7.pdf

Costa, S. (2001, October). *A Justica em Laboratorio*. Retrieved from http://www.ces.uc.pt/publicacoes/rccs/artigos/60/SusanaCosta-AJusticaemLaboratorio.pdf

Costa, S., Machado, H., & Nunes, J. A. (2002). *O ADN e a justiça : A biologia forense e o direito como mediadores entre a ciência e os cidadãos*. Publicações Dom Quixote. Retrieved from http://repositorium.sdum.uminho.pt/handle/1822/5320

Curado, H., & Gomes, P. V. (2011). Os Sistemas de Inteligência num Contexto de Homeland Defence e a Tutela da Privacidade Parte I, 32–37.

Curado, H., & Gomes, P. V. (2012). Os Sistemas de Inteligência num Contexto de Homeland Defence e a Tutela da Privacidade Parte II.

Doneda, D. C. M. (2000). *Considerações iniciais sobre os bancos de dados informatizados e o direito à privacidade*. Retrieved from http://www.estig.ipbeja.pt/~ac_direito/Consideracoes.pdf

FMUP. F. de M. da U. do P. (2004). *Noções gerais sobre outras ciências forenses* (Medicina legal). Retrieved from http://medicina.med.up.pt/legal/NocoesGeraisCF.pdf

Fortes, P. A. de C., & Spinetti, S. R. (2004). O agente comunitário de saúde e a privacidade das informações dos usuários. *Cadernos de Saúde Pública*, 1328–1333. Rio de Janeiro. Retrieved from http://www.scielo.br/pdf/csp/v20n5/27.pdf

Garfinkel, S. (2001). In D. Russel (Ed.), *Database Nation: The Death of Privacy in the 21st Century*. O'Reilly Media, Inc.

Greco, R., & Braga, R. R. P. (2012, January 23). Da principiologia penal ao direito à intimidade como garantia constitucional. *Direito E Desenvolvimento*. Retrieved from http://unipe.br/periodicos/index.php/direitoedesenvolvimento/article/view/119

Guridi, E. (2008). La LO 10/2007, de 8 de octubre, reguladora de la base de datos policial sobre identificadores obtenidos a partir del ADN. *DIARIO LA LEY, Nº 6901*(Año XXIX, Ref. D-78, Editorial LA LEY 6603/2008). Retrieved from http://www.larioja.org/upload/documents/679894_DLL_N_6901-2008.La_LO_102007_reguladora.pdf

Kappler, S. Á. de N. (2008). La prueba de ADN en el proceso penal. (S. L. Comares, Ed.). Granada.

*Lei Nº 5/2008*. (2008). Assembleia da República Portuguesa.

*Lei Nº 67/98*. (1998). Assembleia da República Portuguesa.

Machado, H. (2011). Construtores da bio(in)segurança na base de dados de perfis de ADN. *Etnográfica (on Line)*. Centro de Estudos de Antropologia Social (CEAS). Retrieved from http://www.scielo.gpeari.mctes.pt/scielo.php?script=sci_arttext&pid=S0873-65612011000100008&lng=pt&nrm=iso&tlng=pt

Machado, H., Silva, S., & Santos, F. (2008). Justiça tecnológica: Promessas e desafios. (E. Ecopy, Ed.) (DS/CICS., p. 176). Porto: Ecopy.

Muñoz, M. M. (1996). *El debate sobre las implicaciones científicas, éticas, sociales y legales del Proyecto Genoma Humano. Aportaciones epistemológicas*. Universidad de Granada.

Neto, J. B. de A. (2003). *Banco de dados genéticos para fins criminais: considerações iniciais*. Porto Alegre. Retrieved from http://www3.pucrs.br/pucrs/files/uni/poa/direito/graduacao/tcc/tcc2/trabalhos2008_2/joao_beccon.pdf

Nunes, R. (2013). GeneÉtica. (Almedina, Ed.). Coimbra.

Nunes (Relat.), R. (2006). *Estudo Nº E/07/APB06 sobre a perspectiva ética das bases de dados genéticos* (Vol. 1997, pp. 1–18). Porto: APB - Associação Portuguesa de Bioética. doi:ESTUDO N.º E/07/APB/06

Orgánica, L. (1999). *15/1999. Cortes Generales de España*. Madrid: España.

Orgánica, L. (2007). *10/2007. Cortes Generales de España*. Madrid: España.

Sesé, M. O. (2007). *La nueva ley del ADN en España*. Retrieved from http://librosgratis.net/book/espana-material-de-derecho-procesal-civil-basado-en-la-ley-de-enjuiciamiento-civil_79459.html

## ADDITIONAL READING

Atienza, J. C. (2002). La Protección de los derechos fundamentales en la Unión Europea. (I. I. de S. J. de Oñati, Ed.) (Dykinson., p. 685). Madrid.

Burley (Ed.), J. (1999). *The genetic revolution and human rights : the Oxford Amnesty lectures 1998*. Oxford: Oxford University Press.

Caro, J. S., & Abellán, F. (2002). *Telemedicina y protección de datos sanitarios: Aspectos legales y éticos*. Granada: Comares.

Casabona, C. M. R. C. (1996). *Del gen al derecho*. Bogotá: Universidad Externado de Colombia, Centro de Estudios sobre Genética y Derecho.

Casabona, C. M. R. C. (2003). *Genética y derecho: II* (L. Print, Ed.). Madrid: Consejo General del Poder Judicial.

Casabona (Ed.), C. M. R. (2002). *Bases de Datos de Perfiles de ADN y Criminalidad (p. 239)*. Granada: Comares, Editorial SL.

del Valle, J. P. (2004). *Genética y derecho (Cuadernos.)*. Madrid: Consejo General del Poder Judicial, Centro de Documentación Judicial.

Delgado, L. R. (2004). *Derechos fundamentales y protección de datos*. Madrid: Dykinson.

Delgado, L. R. (2005). El derecho fundamental a la intimidad. (Dykinson, Ed.) (2a ed., p. 468). Madrid: Dykinson.

Di Maio, V. J. M., & Dana, S. E. (2003). *Manual de patología forense*. Madrid: Díaz de Santos.

Domínguez, A. G. (2004). Tratamiento de datos personales y derechos fundamentales. (Dykinson, Ed.). Madrid: Universidad Carlos III de Madrid. Instituto de Derechos Humanos Bartolomé de las Casas.

Drummond, V. (2004). *Internet, privacidad y datos personales*. Madrid: Reus.

Llompart, J. B., & Miralles (Editores), Á. A. (2004). *Biotecnología, dignidad y derecho: Bases para un diálogo* (p. 250). Eunsa. Ediciones Universidad de Navarra, S.A.

Martín, M. A. R. (2004). *Protección penal de la intimidad personal e informática (Justicia P.)*. Barcelona: Atelier Justicia Penal.

Miranda, C. M. G. (1997). *Perspectiva ética y jurídica del proyecto del genoma humano. Coruña: Universidade da Coruña*. Servicio de Publicacóns.

Morán (Coord.), N. M., Casabona, C. M. R., Cid, B. de C., Ayllón, J., Beriaín, I. de M., Estéfani, R. J. de, … Azofra, M. J. (2003). *Biotecnología, derecho y dignidad humana* (p. 413). Editorial Comares.

Ortúzar (coord.), I. F. B. (2002). *Genética humana en el tercer milenio : aspectos éticos y jurídicos*. Madrid: Akal Ediciones.

Portilla (director), F. J. M. (2002). *La protección de los derechos fundamentales en la Unión Europea*. Madrid: Civitas.

Ramos, F. M. J., Gómez-Pallete, J. Z., Suárez, F. R., Serrano, N. P., Casanova, N. M., López, A. S.-C., & Linares, J. C. (2002). La Protección de Datos Personales en el Ámbito Sanitario. (Aranzadi, Ed.) (Legalia.). Navarra.

Sánchez, N. de M. (2004). *Tratamiento de datos personales en el ámbito sanitario : intimidad "versus" interés público*. Valencia: Tirant lo Blanch.

Sanz (Ed.), P. L. (2004). *La implantación de los derechos del paciente*. (U. de Navarra, Ed.) (Eunsa.). Barañáin (Navarra).

Soleto Muñoz, H. (2009). *La identificación del imputado : rueda, fotos, ADN, de los métodos basados en la percepción a la prueba científica*. Valencia: Tirant lo Blanch.

Vidal, J. M. (2003). *Protección penal de la intimidad frente a las nuevas tecnologías* (E. P. de Derecho, Ed.). Valencia.

Williams, R., & Johnson, P. (2008). *Genetic policing: the use of DNA in criminal investigations*. Devon: Willan.

Williams, R., Johnson, P., & Martin, P. (2004). *Genetic Information & Crime Investigation*. Durham: Wellcome T.

## KEY TERMS AND DEFINITIONS

**Database of DNA Profiles:** A structured group consisting of DNA profiles and personal data files with exclusive identification purposes.

**DNA Marker:** A specific region of the genome that typically contains different information on different individuals, which according to scientific knowledge does not allow obtaining health information or specific hereditary characteristics, in short non-coding DNA.

**DNA Profile:** The result of an analysis of the sample using a DNA marker obtained by the scientifically validated techniques and internationally recommended.

**File of DNA Profiles:** A structured set of DNA profiles, accessible according to specific criteria.

**Human Dignity:** Also known as the dignity of the human person is an intrinsic quality of each person who determines the right to a life with minimum conditions of existence and respect of the community and the state. So, as a personal value, is also an important social value, to define the rights and duties of citizens.

**Identifiable Natural Person:** Means any person who can be identified, directly or indirectly, in particular by reference to an identification number or to one or more factors specific to his physical, physiological, mental, economic, cultural or social identity.

**Information Security (of Databases of DNA Profiles):** Security assurances, guaranteed to the database of DNA profiles, to prevent the query, modification, deletion, the addition, destruction or disclosure of information that are not consented by law.

**Informed Consent:** A manifestation of free will and informed in writing under which the holder accepts that their personal data are processed.

**Personal Data Filing System:** Means any structured set of personal data which are accessible according to specific criteria, whether centralized, decentralized or dispersed on a functional or geographical basis.

**Personal Data:** Means all information of any kind and on whatever medium, including sound and video, on a identified or identifiable natural person, which includes the full name, date of birth, place of birth, current known residence the personal identification number (number of identity card, residence card, passport or other analog), affiliation, marital status, sex, ethnicity, height, and the existence of physical deformities.

**Privacy:** As a legal concept is a personnel right inherent to human dignity. Includes intimacy, private life, honor people. Consequently individuals have the right to decide which personal information is kept under his sole control, as they have the right to communicate to whom, when, where and under what conditions personal information should be disclosed.

## ENDNOTES

[1]  School of Allied Health Sciences – Polytechnic Institute of Porto (Escola Superior de Tecnologia da Saúde do Porto – Instituto Politécnico do Porto).

[2]  Particularly significant is the title of Machado's work: Construtores da bio(in)segurança na base de dados de perfis de ADN, that is, Builders of bio (in) security in the database of DNA profiles..

[3]  Information protection is regulated in Spain by Organic Law 15/1999, dated 13 December, for the Protection of Personal Data (LOPD), and in Portugal by Law 67/98 for the Protection of Personal Data (LPDP), dated 26 October.

[4]  My translation.

[5]  Due to the well-known American TV series, *Crime Scene Investigation*.

[6]  My translation.

# Chapter 8
# Composition of the Top Management Team and Information Security Breaches

**Carol Hsu**
*National Taiwan University, Taiwan*

**Tawei Wang**
*University of Hawaii – Manoa, USA*

## ABSTRACT

*Given the multifaceted problems and complexities of information security, the manner in which top management teams make investment and management decisions regarding security technologies, policy initiatives, and employee education could have a significant impact on the likelihood of information security breaches in organizations. In the context of information security management, it is not clear from management literature regarding how the characteristics of the top management team are associated with the possibility of information security breaches. The results demonstrate that the average length and heterogeneity of tenure could increase the possibility of breaches. However, age heterogeneity and the size of the top management team are negatively related to such a possibility. In addition, the findings suggest a nonlinear association between average age and tenure and the possibility of security breaches. The authors conclude the chapter with theoretical and practical implications on the organizational and managerial aspects of information security management.*

## INTRODUCTION

In recent years, the growing number of information security incidents (e.g., TJ Maxx, Sony, and Target), together with the pressure of regulatory compliance (e.g., the Sarbanes–Oxley Act, SOX) has focused managerial attention on the issue of effective information security management in organizations (Johnson & Goetz, 2007). The purpose of information security management is to develop and maintain a sound policy for the protection of an organization's information technology (IT) and non-IT information assets. To achieve this objective, managers need to implement an information security program whose scope encompasses physical, operational, and human resource management. Numerous studies stressed the significance of top management support in the implementation of an information security program in an organization (Kankanhalli, Teo, & Wei, 2003; Straub & Nance,

DOI: 10.4018/978-1-4666-6324-4.ch008

1990) and highlighted how managerial perceptions and an understanding of information security issues influence the implementation process of information security programs (Hsu, 2009; Hu, Hart, & Cooke, 2007). In particular, the research on information security shows that an information security program requires top management to be involved in, and take responsibility for, defining the parameters of risk management to preserve organizational assets, and that such a process requires a degree of collective managerial effort.

With a focus on the composition of the top management team, we draw on the literature on organizational demography to investigate the characteristics of the organizational decision-making team in relation to the likelihood of information security breaches in organizations. The stream of organizational demography literature has shown that the heterogeneity (i.e., diversity) of the top management team can lead, directly or indirectly, to different organizational outcomes, such as financial performance (e.g., Kilduff, Angelmar, & Mehra, 2000), innovation levels (e.g., Bantel & Jackson, 1989), and competitive advantage (e.g., Hambrick, Cho, & Chen, 1996). We argue that the composition of the top management team is an issue that deserves the attention of information security researchers. For instance, one needs to know the extent to which the likelihood of information security breaches is associated with the diversity of top management skills, the manner in which the team's demography influences the organization's appetite for risk, and how such an appetite is reflected in attitudes toward security management. Our empirical research explores some of these issues. However, insightful and empirical analyses on the potential relation between the composition of the top management team and the likelihood of information security breaches in organizations are lacking. Building on the above arguments, we contend that the efficacy of decision making and information sharing among different senior managers could have an impact on the implementation and success of an

organization's initiatives concerning information security management, which would in turn be reflected in the likelihood of information security breaches in such organizations.

To address our research question, we collect the sample from 1992 to 2008 based on S&P 1500 firms. Our results indicate that the average tenure, defined as the number of years the executives has served in the firm, and the heterogeneity of tenure are positively associated with the possibility of information security breaches. Differently, age heterogeneity and the size of the top management team are negatively related to such a possibility. In addition, our findings suggest a nonlinear association between average age and tenure and the possibility of security breaches. Our findings generally support the arguments regarding the influence of top management on information security breaches in prior literature (Hsu, 2009; Hu et al., 2007; Kankanhalli et al., 2003) and provide empirical evidence that the diversity of top management can influence the efficacy of information security management.

The remainder of the paper is organized as follows. In the next section, we review the literature on information security management with a focus on studies dealing with top management behavior. We then introduce our proposed hypotheses. Next, we present the research methodology and discuss the findings from our empirical analysis. In the last section, we conclude with the implications of the present study and suggest avenues for future research.

## LITERATURE REVIEW AND STATEMENT OF HYPOTHESES

From the practical viewpoint, a number of practitioner-oriented reports have highlighted the imperative role of management in information security management. For example, 2012 Deloitte Global Financial Services Industry Security Study shows that most organizations now have documentation and approval process for information security strategy as well as the requirement of security reporting to the senior and executive management. Respondents from KPMG Luxembourg IT security survey 2012-2013 indicated that organizations are increasingly having a dedication of Information Security Officer (ISO) n charge of adequate IT security governance structure. Within the academic literature, there is also a growing attention of information security management from an organization's perspective such as the development and adoption of security policies and standards (Backhouse, Hsu, & Silva, 2006; Hsu, 2009; Siponen & Iivari, 2006), the economics of information security investment (Gordon & Loeb, 2002; Gordon & Loeb, 2006) and the risk management implementation process and its effectiveness (Dhillon & Backhouse, 1996; Straub, 1990; Straub & Nance, 1990; Straub & Welke, 1998). Whereas the majority of studies have managerial implications, comparatively few consider management as the unit of analysis in this area of research. Thus, we only discuss the studies that place a strong emphasis on managerial decision-making and actions in relation to information security management. The first influential study on this subject is the empirical investigation conducted by Straub and his colleagues (Straub, 1990; Straub & Nance, 1990; Straub & Welke, 1998), who found that insufficient knowledge and awareness hinders managers' ability to identify, evaluate, and manage security risks. Through comparative qualitative studies, they demonstrated that security awareness programs are effective mechanisms for modifying managerial perceptions and, thus, improving the quality of decision making during the risk management process. In other studies on information security effectiveness, (Kankanhalli et al., 2003) and Kotulic and Clark (2004) stressed the importance of top management support for programs to manage information security in organizations. Hu et al. (2007) found a significant effect of external regulatory pressure on senior managers in the rollout of information security reforms in

organizations. In another study on implementing a certification program for information security in a financial institution, Hsu (2009) showed how coercive pressure and competitive mimicry strongly influences management's perception and interpretation of security certification strategy during the implementation process. Farahmand, Navathe, Sharp, and Enslow (2005) pointed out the security challenges that management faces in the context of electronic commerce and proposed a risk management approach to address these possible threats. The previously noted studies highlight the strategic importance of management decisions and support in the development and the implementation of information security management programs in organizations.

Another relevant body of research focused on the economic effects of information security breaches on corporations. Campbell, Gordon, Loeb, and Zhou (2003) found a significantly negative stock market reaction to information security breach announcements in the media of publicly traded U.S. corporations. In particular, their results showed that the negative market reaction is significant for confidentiality type breaches. Similarly, Cavusoglu, Mishra, and Raghunathan (2004) also indicated that news articles about Internet security breaches are negatively associated with the market value of the breached firms. Furthermore, they argued that the loss of market value was larger than the estimated financial costs reported in the CSI-FBI survey. Nonetheless, research by Hovav and D'Arcy (2003, 2004) found that denial of service attack (DOS) and virus attack do not have a significant negative impact on a firm's business value. Recently, a study by Gordon, Loeb, and Sohail (2010) examined the impact of voluntary disclosures regarding information security on the market value of the firm, and found that the market values information security related disclosures in annual reports. Wang, Kannan, and Rees (2013) showed that the market may not be able to fully understand the textual contents of the disclosures while Wang, Rees, and Kannan (2013) suggested that there exists a possible short-term profitable opportunity around the breach announcement day. Overall, the above studies highlight the possible impact of information security breaches on a firm's market value.

In summary, the first body of literature emphasized the importance of managerial decisions and actions in the design, implementation, and success of information security programs in organizations. The second body of research examined the external relation between information security breaches and their effect on the market. Both areas of study implicitly addressed the importance of management in reducing security risk and information security breaches. However, in the current literature on information security management, a dearth of empirical analysis exists on how the diversity of a top management team influences the decision-making process and, thereby, the subsequent likelihood of an organization's information security breaches. Thus, we argue that this research gap needs to be addressed because a more in-depth understanding of the management decision process on information security could have both theoretical and practical implication.

With this research objective, we develop our hypotheses by drawing on the organizational literature, which extensively analyzes the relation between the characteristics of top management teams and firm performance. In this stream of literature, different theoretical lenses have been proposed, including the psychological characteristics of executives (Finkelstein & Hambrick, 1990), the social network approach (e.g., Collins & Clark, 2003)), and top management demography (e.g., Kilduff et al., 2000). This study found that the demographic approach (e.g., Pfeffer, 1983) provides an interesting theoretical perspective for investigating top management heterogeneity, for the following reasons.

Smith et al. (1994, p. 412) defined demography as "the aggregated external characteristics of the team, such as heterogeneity, tenure, and size".

How is this approach relevant to our research objectives? As previously noted, an enterprise-wide implementation of an information security management program requires a collective understanding and efforts of the top management team. Demographical literature highlights how demographic dynamics can influence the quality and effectiveness of team decisions and communications. In other words, we argue that the characteristics of the top management team can contribute to how it identifies issues, formulates strategies, and evaluates solutions associated with various aspects of information security management, such as the design of security policy and the level of investment in information security. The decision taken will have a significant impact on the likelihood of information security breaches.

In accordance with the previous definition, we propose a number of hypotheses on the relation between the characteristics of top management and the likelihood of information security breaches. Namely, to be consistent with the studies on organizational demography, we develop our hypotheses in terms of 1) average age and organizational tenure and 2) heterogeneity of age and organizational tenure, as detailed below.

The impacts of age and tenure on managerial decisions have been widely discussed in the literature. The arguments for the age of the top management team are based on the cognitive ability in information processing and the attitude toward risk. Researchers have found that, as people mature, they become less flexible, more reluctant to change, and more risk averse (Carlson & Karlsson, 1970; Vroom & Pahl, 1971; Wiersema & Bantel, 1992). The argument for organizational tenure is that, with shared organizational experience and socialization, members tend to view the world in a similar fashion and are able to communicate effectively. In other words, increasing group tenure contributes to the stability of group development and a reduction in group conflict during the decision-making process. Stevens,

Beyer, and Trice (1978) noted that longer tenure is positively related to senior executives' commitment to the status quo.

In the context of information security management, the average age and tenure of top management is relevant in determining the effectiveness of information security initiatives within the organization. For example, using a model of managerial perceptions on system risk, Straub and Welke (1998) pointed out that the awareness and knowledge of local system risk is important in effectively planning and implementing security programs. Furthermore, they pointed out that managers need to receive ongoing feedback within the organizational structure to be able to institute an information security program. From the perspective of organizational demography, we posit that older members of a top management team or members with a longer organizational tenure tend to have more knowledge of organizational and local environment risks because of their experience. They are also more likely to develop a better understanding of organization-specific security management issues and to commit to a long-term improvement program. Furthermore, the commoditization of IT means that contemporary organizations should increasingly emphasize "vulnerabilities, not opportunities" (Carr, 2003, p. 11). We speculate that older managers and those with long organizational tenure are more likely to be more sensitive to risk and committed to ensure the protection of organizational assets. Therefore, we propose the following hypotheses:

**Hypothesis 1a.** The average age of the top management team is negatively associated with the likelihood of information security breaches.

**Hypothesis 1b.** The average tenure of the top management team is negatively associated with the likelihood of information security breaches.

The relation between the heterogeneity of the management team and firm performance has been widely examined in the management literature. The fundamental thought is that the organization's members must coordinate and organize various activities to maintain its survival in a competitive environment. Team heterogeneity provides the group with the benefits of diverse viewpoints and wider cognitive resources, which stimulate discussion. This phenomenon is evident in the studies on the relation between management team diversity and innovation (Bantel & Jackson, 1989). However, team diversity also has its drawbacks. A group with a high degree of heterogeneity has members with different beliefs, values, and perspectives. This structure undermines the group's ability to reach a consensus and is more likely to result in internal conflicts (e.g., Pfeffer, 1983; Wiersema & Bantel, 1992). That is, the diversity of a group requires the management of multiple interpretations and disagreements among its members. Consequently, according to (Smith et al., 1994, p. 415), "the increased bureaucracy necessary to monitor and control heterogeneous teams will adversely affect the organization's performance," as documented in other empirical studies (Ancona & Caldwell, 1992).

In the context of information security management, we consider that the heterogeneity of age and organizational tenure of the top management team have different implications for the management of information security risks in organizations. First, we contend that age diversity is beneficial in managing an information security program. A sound security program requires the support of both technical and managerial solutions. In our view, designing a security solution includes developing the capability to deal with the growth in computer- and Internet-related crimes. In view of the changing nature of attacks and security vulnerabilities, Bagchi and Udo (2003) considered security breaches as a form of innovation. Following the argument put forward by Bantel and Jackson (1989), younger managers tend to have access to more recent education, enabling them to acquire knowledge about innovative technologies and know-how. Thus, younger managers are arguably expected to possess a better understanding of technical security problems and solutions than older managers because they more likely have better knowledge of the trends in, and the emergence of, new technologies. Nevertheless, while younger managers are able to assist with the identification of new security problems, our previous argument emphasized the point that older managers are able to contribute their organizational knowledge during the problem solving stage because doing so requires the input of organization-specific knowledge to implement appropriate managerial actions. Therefore, we argue that heterogeneity in age could balance the technical and managerial requirements in instituting security program in organizations.

**Hypothesis 2a.** The heterogeneity of the age of the top management team members is negatively associated with the likelihood of information security breaches.

With regard to the heterogeneity of organizational tenure, organizational researchers focused more on its impact on the quality and the effectiveness of group interactions and discussion during the decision-making process (Hambrick et al., 1996; Smith et al., 1994). Tenure heterogeneity refers to the extent to which a top management team shares similar functional and organizational experiences. Some studies showed that executives from different functional areas view organizational problems differently (e.g., Lawrence, 1997; Waller, Huber, & Glick, 1995). Michel and Hambrick (1992) explained that tenure homogeneity, in other words, members with a similar organizational background, "contributes to the development of common schemata among team members and increases cohesion by providing a common premise for decision making" (p.18). Smith et al. (1994) further argued that an increase in team heterogeneity entails that an organization implement more monitoring and control mechanisms. In turn, this implementation will increase the administrative burden for the CEO and adversely influence firm performance.

In the context of information security management, tenure heterogeneity could have a negative impact on the effectiveness of information security management for the following reasons. First, heterogeneity of the top management team could affect the team's efficacy of coordination and communication because the executives' backgrounds and perceptions are likely to be diverse. That is, the greater the heterogeneity, the more difficult it is for senior executives to reach consensus on recognizing security problems, developing potential responses, selecting solutions, and implementing decisions. Second, given the reliance on technologies and the emergence of different security risks, modern organizations need to build their capacity to manage risk and preserve the confidentiality, integrity, and availability of information. The swiftness of the responses to security threats is also potentially important to ensure the continuity of the organizations in a competitive environment. Team heterogeneity leads to more bureaucratic controls. Consequently, it can adversely affect an organization's responsiveness to environmental changes (Smith et al., 1994). An organization that is slow to respond to a security problem suffers greater financial and reputational loss, and incurs a higher cost in correcting the problem. Therefore, we propose the following hypothesis:

**Hypothesis 2b.** The heterogeneity of the tenure of the top management team's members is positively associated with the likelihood of information security breaches.

## DATA COLLECTION AND EMPIRICAL MODELS

### Sample

Our initial sample consisted of the *S&P 1500* firms from the *ExecuComp* database in the period between 1992 and 2008.[1] From the *ExecuComp* database, we gathered the size of the top management team and the age/tenure of the executives for each firm. We then used the *Factiva* database and the *CNet* as well as the *ZDNet* websites to search for news articles regarding information security breaches from 1992 to 2008 in the following major media outlets: the *Wall Street Journal*, *USA Today*, the *Washington Post*, and the *New York Times*. We also use the list provided by DataLossDB at http://datalossdb.org/ to ensure that we did not exclude any major breaches. The search terms used were: (1) security breach, (2) hacker, (3) cyber attack, (4) virus or worm, (5) computer break-in, (6) computer attack, (7) computer security, (8) network intrusion, (9) data theft, (10) identity theft, (11) phishing, (12) cyber fraud, and (13) denial of service. These search terms and the media outlets are similar to those used in prior studies (e.g., Campbell et al., 2003; Garg, Curtis, & Halper, 2003; Wang, Rees, & Kannan, 2013; Wang et al., 2013). Campbell et al. (2003) argued that public media and the press have shown their interests in a broad spectrum of firms and corporate information security breaches. Furthermore, in the finance and organizational literature, researchers also use fraudulent events reported in the public media as a proxy when analyzing the relation between management or board composition and the likelihood of financial fraud in organizations (Beasley, 1996; Uzun, Szewczyk, & Varma, 2004). Therefore, we consider news articles from the public media as providing a good source of information for this exploratory research.

The news articles regarding information security breaches were used to compile a list of firms affected by security breaches. If a firm in our sample was included in the list, the variable *Breach* was coded as 1, and 0 otherwise (see Table 1 for the definitions of the variables).

We further control for a firm's corporate governance mechanisms as corporate governance mechanisms may affect the likelihood of information security incidents. We include the following governance measures in our model: (1) the percentage of independent directors on its board (*IBSize*), (2) whether an earnings restatement announcement was made in a year (*Restate*), (3) audit fees (*Fee*), and (4) institutional ownership (*INSTOWN*). We also control for the following variables in our model. First, we control for the size and the age of the firm at the beginning of the year (*CSize*, in millions, logarithm of the total assets at the beginning of the year; *CAge*, in years). Second, we control for firms in the IT industry, which are firms with 4-digit SIC codes 3570, 3571, 3572, 3575, 3576, 3577, 3670, 3672, 3674, 3677, 3678, 3679, 3690, 3695, 7370, 7372, 7373, and 7374. Third, we control for the market-to-book ratio of the firm (*MB*), which equals the market value of the firm divided by the book value of common stockholders' equity at the beginning of the year.

The resulting sample size was 16,979 firms from 63 industries. The industry distribution is given in Table 2. As shown in Table 2, our sample does not concentrate in any specific industry and our industry distribution is indistinguishable from the Compustat universe (the *p*-value for the Kolmogorov-Smirnov test is almost 1.00).

### Measures and Research Models

To test our hypotheses, we consider the average age/tenure and the heterogeneity of age/tenure as the demographic characteristics of the top management team. Specifically, we consider the average age/tenure and the heterogeneity of age/tenure of the executives in each firm. The average age/tenure for the executives for each firm-year is then calculated (*avgAge* in years and *avgTenure* in days). To measure the heterogeneity of age/tenure,

*Table 1. Variable definitions*

| Variable | Definition | Data Source |
|---|---|---|
| Breach | A dummy variable indicating whether a firm has information security breaches. The variable equals 1 if the firm has an information security breach announcement(s), 0 otherwise. | news articles from: the Wall Street Journal, USA Today, the Washington Post, and the New York Times. |
| CIO | A dummy variable indicating whether a firm has a CIO position, which equals 1 if the firm has a CIO position, 0 otherwise. | ExecuComp |
| CSize | Firm size, which equals the logarithm of the total assets at the beginning of the year. | Compustat |
| Cage | Firm age, which equals the logarithm of the age of the firm at the beginning of the year. | Compustat |
| MB | Market-to-book ratio, which equals the market value of the firm divided by the book value of common stockholders' equity at the beginning of the year. | Compustat |
| Ind | An indicating variable for industries that equals 1 if the firm is in one of the following IT industries (two-digit SIC code): 3570, 3571, 3572, 3575, 3576, 3577, 3670, 3672, 3674, 3677, 3678, 3679, 3690, 3695, 7370, 7372, 7373, 7374, 0 otherwise. | Compustat |
| ExeSize | Size of the top management team, which is the number of executives at the beginning of the year. | ExecuComp |
| avgAge | Average age of the top management team for each firm at the beginning of the year. | ExecuComp |
| avgTenure | Average tenure of the top management team for each firm at the beginning of the year. | ExecuComp |
| CVAge | Heterogeneity of age, which is the coefficient of variation of age (the standard deviation divided by the mean of age) at the beginning of the year. | ExecuComp |
| CVTenure | Heterogeneity of tenure, which is the coefficient of variation of tenure (the standard deviation divided by the mean of tenure) at the beginning of the year. | ExecuComp |
| IBSize | The percentage of independent directors on the board of the firm for a year. | RiskMetrics |
| InstOwn | The percentage of outstanding shares held by institutions of the firm in a year. | ThomsonReuters |
| Restate | An dummy variable indicating whether a firm announces a restatement, which equals 1 if the firm announces a restatement in a year, 0 otherwise. | Audit Analytics |
| Fee | Audit fee, which is the logarithm of audit fee for a year. | Audit Analytics |

we use the "coefficient of variation," which has been widely used to measure diversity in prior literature (e.g., Williams & O'Reilly, 1998). The coefficient of variation is derived by dividing the standard deviation by the mean of age/tenure for each firm-year (Bedeian & Mossholder, 2000).

Table 3 presents the descriptive statistics, which show that the median (Q2) and the mean of the size of the top management team (*ExeSize*) are about six executives. The average age (*avgAge*)

in our sample is about 48, on average, and the average tenure (*avgTenure*) is about 4 years. In terms of heterogeneity, on average, the standard deviation is 4.3 times the average age (*CVAge*) and 0.66 for tenure (*CVTenure*). The quartiles demonstrate that, in our sample, most of the firms do not have the CIO position and do not have financial restatements. We also considered the potential multicollinearity issues by investigating

*Table 2. Industry breakdown and comparison with compustat universe*

| 2-Digit SIC Code | % in Our Sample | % in Compustat | 2-Digit SIC Code | % in Our Sample | % in Compustat |
|---|---|---|---|---|---|
| # 10 | 0.82% | 2.81% | #47 | 0.46% | 0.35% |
| #12 | 0.16% | 0.23% | # 48 | 3.00% | 3.34% |
| # 13 | 3.13% | 5.00% | # 49 | 5.34% | 2.62% |
| #14 | 0.16% | 0.29% | # 50 | 1.94% | 2.17% |
| # 15 | 0.56% | 0.54% | # 51 | 1.15% | 1.31% |
| #16 | 0.30% | 0.25% | # 52 | 0.30% | 0.22% |
| #17 | 0.16% | 0.27% | # 53 | 1.05% | 0.61% |
| # 20 | 2.14% | 2.11% | #54 | 0.63% | 0.63% |
| # 21 | 0.16% | 0.10% | # 55 | 0.43% | 0.29% |
| #22 | 0.63% | 0.63% | #56 | 1.52% | 0.55% |
| # 23 | 0.86% | 0.91% | # 57 | 0.59% | 0.45% |
| # 24 | 0.49% | 0.50% | # 58 | 1.55% | 1.27% |
| #25 | 0.40% | 0.42% | # 59 | 1.78% | 1.56% |
| #26 | 1.38% | 0.81% | # 60 | 6.99% | 6.66% |
| # 27 | 1.32% | 1.20% | # 61 | 0.92% | 1.72% |
| # 28 | 6.23% | 5.23% | # 62 | 1.71% | 1.07% |
| # 29 | 0.86% | 0.49% | # 63 | 4.05% | 1.73% |
| # 30 | 0.82% | 1.00% | # 64 | 0.46% | 0.39% |
| #31 | 0.26% | 0.20% | #65 | 0.13% | 1.51% |
| # 32 | 0.56% | 0.62% | # 67 | 2.83% | 9.70% |
| # 33 | 1.75% | 1.16% | # 70 | 0.30% | 0.52% |
| # 34 | 1.09% | 1.41% | # 72 | 0.30% | 0.26% |
| # 35 | 5.74% | 4.54% | # 73 | 9.92% | 9.41% |
| # 36 | 6.76% | 5.27% | # 75 | 0.16% | 0.22% |
| # 37 | 2.34% | 1.63% | # 78 | 0.40% | 0.80% |
| # 38 | 4.88% | 4.23% | # 79 | 0.92% | 0.99% |
| #39 | 0.82% | 0.98% | # 80 | 2.08% | 1.51% |
| # 40 | 0.33% | 0.21% | #82 | 0.40% | 0.29% |
| #41 | 0.13% | 0.07% | #83 | 0.10% | 0.12% |
| # 42 | 0.63% | 0.62% | # 87 | 1.38% | 1.52% |
| # 44 | 0.26% | 0.41% | #99 | 0.36% | 1.25% |
| # 45 | 0.69% | 0.63% | | | |

the variance inflation factor (VIF) values in the analyses below and our results remain similar.

Based on the above description, we use the following main equations to test the hypotheses. The dependent variable is *Breach*. The variables in the equations were previously defined, where $\beta$s denotes the coefficients and $\varepsilon$s is the residual term. We use the logistic regression model to estimate the coefficients with robust standard errors. The results are similar to those when controlling for serial correlation as suggested by Petersen (2009).

*Table 3. Descriptive statistics*

| Variables | N | Mean | Std. Dev. | Quartiles | | |
|---|---|---|---|---|---|---|
| | | | | Q1 | Q2 | Q3 |
| Breach | 192,012 | 0.00 | 0.054 | 0.00 | 0.00 | 0.00 |
| CIO | 192,012 | 0.01 | 0.093 | 0.00 | 0.00 | 0.00 |
| CSize | 190,217 | 3.18 | 0.797 | 2.61 | 3.12 | 3.69 |
| CAge | 189,393 | 1.22 | 0.396 | 0.95 | 1.26 | 1.57 |
| MB | 77,640 | 2.11 | 156.757 | 1.33 | 2.58 | 4.97 |
| Ind | 192,012 | 0.13 | 0.333 | 0.00 | 0.00 | 0.00 |
| ExeSize | 191,959 | 6.18 | 1.444 | 5.00 | 6.00 | 7.00 |
| avgAge | 192,012 | 47.52 | 29.713 | 48.00 | 52.60 | 56.80 |
| avgTenure | 192,012 | 3.70 | 8.464 | 0.00 | 0.00 | 2.00 |
| CVAge | 192,012 | 4.30 | 13.544 | 0.00 | 3.54 | 6.96 |
| CVTenure | 192,012 | 0.66 | 2.803 | 0.00 | 0.00 | 0.00 |
| IBSize | 57,254 | 1.41 | 2.248 | 0.56 | 0.70 | 0.83 |
| InstOwn | 72,119 | 0.76 | 0.231 | 0.62 | 0.78 | 0.91 |
| Restate | 77,852 | 0.15 | 0.354 | 0.00 | 0.00 | 0.00 |
| Fee | 77,852 | 6.16 | 0.517 | 5.81 | 6.14 | 6.50 |

$$Breach = \beta_0 + \beta_1 CIO + \beta_2 CSize + \beta_3 CAge$$
$$+\beta_4 MB + \beta_5 Ind + \beta_6 ExeSize + \beta_7 avgAge$$
$$+\beta_8 avgTenure + \beta_9 IBSize + \beta_{10} InstOwn$$
$$+\beta_{11} restate + \beta_{12} Fee + \Sigma Year + \varepsilon_1$$

$$(1)$$

$$Breach = \beta_0 + \beta_1 CIO + \beta_2 CSize + \beta_3 CAge$$
$$+\beta_4 MB + \beta_5 Ind + \beta_6 ExeSize + \beta_7 CVAge$$
$$+\beta_8 CVTenure + \beta_9 IBSize + \beta_{10} InstOwn$$
$$+\beta_{11} restate + \beta_{12} Fee + \Sigma Year + \varepsilon_2$$

$$(2)$$

$$Breach = \beta_0 + \beta_1 CIO + \beta_2 CSize + \beta_3 CAge$$
$$+\beta_4 MB + \beta_5 Ind + \beta_6 ExeSize + \beta_7 avgAge$$
$$+\beta_8 avgTenure + \beta_9 CVAge + \beta_{10} CVTenure$$
$$+\beta_{11} IBSize + \beta_{12} InstOwn + \beta_{13} restate$$
$$+\beta_{14} Fee + \Sigma Year + \varepsilon_3$$

$$(3)$$

# EMPIRICAL RESULTS

## Main Results

The results for Equation (1), (2), and (3) are presented in Table 4. For each equation, the full model and the models after eliminating the variables that raise multicollinearity concerns (VIF values larger than 10) are considered. The results show that the relation between average age and the likelihood of information security breaches is consistently insignificant based on Equation (1) and Equation (3). A surprising finding is that the results for Equation (1) and Equation (3) demonstrate that the average tenure is consistently and positively associated with the possibility of breaches. This result contradicts our hypothesis that long average group tenure leads to an increase in group knowledge about organizational risk and commitment in instituting an information security program. The organization dynamics literature shows a possible alternative explanation. In particular, although the literature acknowledges that long average group tenure contributes to group stability and improves organizational specific knowledge, other studies challenge the value of team longevity and argue that longer organizational tenure is more likely to increase the resistance of top management to initiate strategic changes and, thus, has a negative effect on firm performance (Wiersema & Bantel, 1992). Managers with longer tenure are less likely to accept challenges and are relatively more conservative. Studies also indicate that team longevity can hinder group members' information processing capabilities because they tend to be more comfortable when relying on their past experiences instead of new stimuli (e.g., Michel & Hambrick, 1992). These studies might offer an explanation for why the average tenure of top management team can be positively associated with information security breaches. We reason that the organizational aspects of information security management are relatively new compared with other items on the management agenda. This new perspective might compel senior executives to learn new techniques and embark on strategic changes to institutionalize information security practices in organizations. Thus, undergoing strategic changes in information security management are arguably easier when the top management team has a relatively short organizational tenure because they are open and willing to accept new challenges and implement organizational changes.

Although we find explanations for this result from the existing literature, we further explore whether there exists a non-linear association between average age/tenure and the possibility of security breaches. The results are also presented in Table 4. In particular, we consider the square term for average age and the square term for average tenure. Our findings demonstrate that, when adding a square term of average age, this term is significant positive (0.002, $p < 0.10$) but the coefficient of *avgAge* remains insignificant. This result suggests a U-shaped relation between average age and the likelihood of security breaches.

That is, when the average age is greater than a certain age, the conservative attitude starts to outweigh the knowledge as well as experience. In contrast, for average tenure, the square term is significantly negative (-0.001, $p < 0.10$) and *avgTenure* is still significantly positive (0.046, $p < 0.05$). The result reflects an inverse U-shaped relation between average tenure and the possibility of information security events. In particular, when the average tenure increases over a certain point, the stability of the top management team becomes more important than the conflicts in the context of information security management.

With regard to the heterogeneity of age and organizational tenure, the empirical results from Equations (2) and (3) suggest that the heterogeneity of age is negatively related to the possibility of information security breaches but that the heterogeneity of tenure is positively associated with the possibility of security breaches, consistent with Hypothesis 2a and Hypothesis 2b. The results of age heterogeneity are interesting when comparing with the insignificance results of *avgAge*. This result may imply that the diversity in the top management team is more relevant in the context of information security management. As previously noted, a successful information security program requires decision makers to have updated knowledge about the variety of technological developments and emerging attacks, and an ingenious understanding of organizational practices. These findings show that a team with diversity in age may result in an overall increase in both its technical and managerial capabilities when determining the appropriate management tools to use in mitigating information security risks. The empirical results also provide evidence that heterogeneity makes communication among team members and shared behavior more difficult. In the information security context, the lack of effective coordination among team members could affect the team's ability to respond to the uncertainties associated with security risks and increase the likelihood of information security

Table 4. Empirical results

| | Equation (1) | | | | | Equation (2) | | | Equation (3) | | |
|---|---|---|---|---|---|---|---|---|---|---|---|
| Intercept | -4.697 (-1.05) | -11.130*** (-26.70) | -11.470*** (-11.72) | -11.040*** (-7.68) | -10.391*** (-22.72) | -10.342*** (-22.63) | -10.200*** (-8.82) | -11.170*** (-26.59) | -10.302*** (-22.51) | -10.821*** (-10.46) | -9.632*** (-6.42) |
| CIO | 0.721 (1.37) | 0.759 (1.43) | 0.733 (1.39) | 0.965* (1.87) | 0.729 (1.37) | 0.748 (1.38) | 0.961* (1.85) | 0.767 (1.45) | 0.789 (1.46) | 0.747 (1.38) | 0.992* (1.91) |
| CSize | 1.835*** (19.86) | 1.818*** (20.80) | 1.822*** (19.63) | 1.239*** (9.06) | 1.858*** (21.36) | 1.848*** (20.69) | 1.272*** (9.13) | 1.830*** (20.81) | 1.835*** (20.41) | 1.833*** (19.33) | 1.292*** (9.16) |
| Cage | | | | -0.624*** (-2.97) | | | -0.663*** (-3.25) | | | | -0.727*** (-3.58) |
| MB | -0.001** (-2.08) | -0.001** (-2.13) | -0.001** (-2.00) | -0.001** (-2.13) | -0.001** (-2.11) | -0.002*** (-3.19) | -0.002*** (-3.11) | -0.001** (-2.37) | -0.002*** (-3.34) | -0.002*** (-3.13) | -0.002*** (-3.26) |
| Ind | 0.662*** (3.36) | 0.684*** (3.70) | 0.681*** (3.52) | 0.302 (1.41) | 0.643*** (3.49) | 0.530*** (2.80) | 0.182 (0.89) | 0.679*** (3.67) | 0.552*** (2.91) | 0.555*** (2.82) | 0.207 (0.96) |
| Exesize | | | | -0.140*** (-3.28) | -0.146*** (-3.34) | | -0.124*** (-2.67) | | | | -0.140*** (-3.12) |
| avgAge$^2$ | 0.002* (1.69) | | | | | | | | | | |
| avgAge | -0.242 (-1.55) | | | -0.004 (-0.19) | 0.007 (0.38) | | | | | 0.010 (0.54) | -0.002 (-0.13) |
| avgTenure$^2$ | | | -0.001* (-1.81) | | | | | | | | |
| avgTenure | | 0.012** (2.21) | 0.046** (2.38) | 0.014*** (2.64) | | | | | 0.016*** (2.68) | | 0.018*** (3.15) |
| CVAge | | | | | | -0.118*** (-4.82) | -0.108*** (-4.29) | | -0.125*** (-5.02) | -0.118*** (-4.81) | -0.116*** (-4.51) |
| CVTenure | | | | | | 0.120*** (4.16) | 0.128*** (4.41) | | 0.112*** (3.86) | 0.120 (4.16) | 0.122*** (4.12) |
| IBSize | 0.002 (0.06) | 0.004 (0.12) | 0.001 (0.04) | -0.010 (-0.34) | 0.002 (0.05) | -0.019 (-0.52) | -0.032 (-0.99) | 0.001 (0.04) | -0.015 (-0.42) | -0.018 (-0.48) | -0.027 (-0.88) |
| InstOwn | | | | -2.259*** (-5.86) | | | -2.345*** (-6.09) | | | | -2.348*** (-5.95) |
| Restate | -0.658*** (-2.63) | -0.621** (-2.56) | -0.632*** (-2.59) | -0.516** (-2.15) | -0.592** (-2.48) | -0.605** (-2.55) | -0.513** (-2.16) | -0.629*** (-2.60) | -0.604** (-2.53) | -0.614*** (-2.56) | -0.506** (-2.11) |
| Fee | | | | 0.911*** (4.32) | | | 0.866*** (3.92) | | | | 0.813*** (3.76) |
| Year Effect | Included | Included | Included | Included | Included | Included | Included | Included | Included | Included | Included |
| Model χ² | 658.26 | 625.42 | 639.02 | 779.28 | 647.80 | 674.43 | 859.18 | 618.73 | 661.61 | 674.69 | 852.26 |
| Pseudo R² | 0.26 | 0.26 | 0.26 | 0.28 | 0.26 | 0.27 | 0.29 | 0.26 | 0.28 | 0.27 | 0.29 |
| N | 25,916 | 25,916 | 25,916 | 24,962 | 25,916 | 25,916 | 24,962 | 25,916 | 25,916 | 25,916 | 24,962 |

* significant at 10%, ** significant at 5%, *** significant at 1%, z statistics are in parenthesis and are estimated using Huber-White standard errors. Note that the results are similar when using clustered standard errors by firm as suggested by Petersen (2009).

breaches. Furthermore, the results highlight a noteworthy point about the difference in effects between age and heterogeneity of organizational tenure. The findings support the hypothesis that, in contrast to age heterogeneity, organizational tenure heterogeneity is positively associated with the likelihood of information security breaches. To some extent, the opposing results are consistent with the argument about the importance in balancing technical and organizational know-how to maintain the success of the information security program in organizations. In this particular context, the value of age diversity in facilitating access to greater resources in new technical know-how might be said to outweigh the dampening effects of group conflicts and strains generally associated with team heterogeneity.

In addition to age and organizational tenure, we also explore the possible implication of top management size. The results suggest that the size of the top management team is negatively associated with the possibility of security breaches. Team size is another demographic variable common in the studies of top management teams and firm performance (Smith et al., 1994; Wiersema & Bantel, 1992). The literature on group dynamics research indicates that an increase in the number of group members could have a negative impact on group performance. However, a larger group collectively pools together greater resources and opinions that may contribute to innovative thinking and creativity, and may improve group performance. Nevertheless, difficulties in coordination and communication may arise as the group grows. Our findings demonstrate that, as the team becomes larger, viewing organizational problems differently becomes easier for executives (Lawrence, 1997; Waller et al., 1995). In the context of information security and the rapid changes in technology, a larger top management team permits the team to assess risks more easily from a variety of viewpoints. A larger team is also able to cultivate and discover the full breadth of its creativity and knowledge to more effectively cap-

ture and respond to the dynamics of ever-changing threats. Such advantages can offset the potential problems of large team conflict and inefficiency.

## Additional Analyses

The following additional analyses further validate our results and provide additional insights. First, we estimate our model using conditional fixed effect logistic models to consider potentially unobserved firm effects. The results are presented in Table 5, which shows that our main results remain consistent with those reported in the previous section.

Furthermore, we consider the possible interaction effects of average and heterogeneity of age, and how tenure (both average and heterogeneity) moderates the association between industry and the possibility of security breaches. We believe that tenure can affect such a relation because a top manager with longer tenure not only tends to be more knowledgeable about both organizational and environmental risks based on experience in that position, but also is more conservative. The heterogeneity of tenure can also affect the decision and communication processes. These characteristics may change a firm's attitude to-

*Table 5. Conditional fixed effect logistic models*

|  | Model (1) | Model (2) | Model (3) |
|---|---|---|---|
| avgAge | 0.044 | | |
|  | (1.43) | | |
| avgTenure | | -0.102*** | |
|  | | (-5.47) | |
| CVAge | | | 0.058* |
|  | | | (1.75) |
| CVTenure | | | -0.060** |
|  | | | (-2.10) |
| Control Variables | Included | Included | Included |
| Model χ² | 228.84 | 273.91 | 235.52 |
| N | 1,772 | 1,772 | 1,772 |

* significant at 10%, ** significant at 5%, *** significant at 1%, z statistics are in parenthesis

ward information security management, which in turn affects the risks inherent in the industry. The results, presented in Table 6, show that, first, although average age is still insignificant, it can reduce the effect of heterogeneity on the possibility of security breaches. Second, although the interaction of average tenure and industry is not significant, the interaction between the heterogeneity of tenure and industry is significant. Therefore, the heterogeneity of tenure can increase the possibility of security breaches inherent in the industry. However, because adding this interaction term changes the significance level of the industry, the results need to be interpreted with caution.

## IMPLICATIONS

Our exploratory results have several theoretical and practical implications in the field of information security management. From a theoretical perspective, our findings generally support the arguments presented on the influence of top management in the information security literature (Hsu, 2009; Hu et al., 2007; Kankanhalli et al., 2003). However, these studies placed more emphasis on the value of top management in developing and implementing security initiatives, which can have a strong effect on user behavior by increasing employee awareness or reducing potentially negative behavior. The researchers in these studies failed to be specific about the composition of top management and whether they referred to the CEO, CIO or to a team collectively composed of senior executives from various departments. In comparison, the unique contribution of this research is that it examines the influence of top management from a team's perspective and provides empirical evidence that the diversity of top management can influence the efficacy of information security management. Our findings show that demographic characteristics, such as age and tenure, can influence the roll-out of information security programs in an organization, as does the size of the management team.

In addition, age and tenure have a non-linear association with the effectiveness of information security management. These results add value to the existing research by extending the argument beyond the simple need for top management support and by pointing to the dynamics of top management characteristics in the context of information security management. The results may also offer some valuable insights into the optimal number of management team members required for making decisions regarding information security strategy and investment. In view of the archival nature of the data used, these results may encourage other case study-based research on the actual decision-making process of top management teams. Further empirical studies may enable an in-depth understanding of the team dynamics and processes involved with implementing information security management in organizations.

Furthermore, we believe that our work contributes to the emerging research on the organizational aspects of information security management by illustrating how organizational theories could be applied to analyze the managerial problem in this area. Although we adopt organizational theories, such as the neo-institutional theory and the theory of sense-making, we also draw scholarly attention to the value of group dynamic literature in understanding the managerial implications of information security management. Here, we highlighted the theoretical importance and relevance of management heterogeneity in IS security research. The opportunity exists for further research on top management team demography and various aspects of information security management, such as the willingness to take risks, information security investment, and the speed at which a firm responds when implementing its decisions. Moreover, other relevant organizational theories, such as the social network approach and group dynamics theory, could be applied to deepen our understanding of the relation between the composition of the top management team and information security breaches in organizations.

*Table 6. Results for moderating effects*

| | Model (1) | Model (2) | Model (3) | Model (4) |
|---|---|---|---|---|
| Intercept | -10.720*** | -9.217*** | -11.120*** | -10.280*** |
| | (-10.68) | (-6.44) | (-26.67) | (-22.38) |
| CIO | 0.723 | 0.743 | 0.756 | 0.756 |
| | (1.34) | (1.37) | (1.43) | (1.40) |
| CSize | 1.827*** | 1.820*** | 1.819*** | 1.838*** |
| | (19.22) | (19.07) | (20.83) | (20.42) |
| MB | -0.002*** | -0.002*** | -0.001** | -0.002*** |
| | (-3.01) | (-2.92) | (-2.11) | (-2.99) |
| Ind | 0.634*** | 0.626*** | 0.668*** | 0.497 |
| | (3.23) | (3.16) | (3.44) | (1.50) |
| avgAge | 0.008 | -0.017 | | |
| | (0.46) | (-0.68) | | |
| avgTenure | | | 0.012** | |
| | | | (2.05) | |
| CVAge | -0.122*** | -0.534** | | -0.117*** |
| | (-4.93) | (-2.19) | | (-4.43) |
| CVTenure | | | | 0.068*** |
| | | | | (2.71) |
| avgAge*CVAge | | 0.007* | | |
| | | (1.72) | | |
| Ind*avgTenure | | | 0.006 | |
| | | | (0.27) | |
| Ind*CVAge | | | | -0.012 |
| | | | | (-0.19) |
| Ind*CVTenure | | | | 0.087* |
| | | | | (1.80) |
| IBSize | -0.015 | -0.016 | 0.004 | -0.020 |
| | (-0.40) | (-0.44) | (0.10) | (-0.55) |
| Restate | -0.649*** | -0.651*** | -0.622** | -0.593** |
| | (-2.68) | (-2.67) | (-2.57) | (-2.48) |
| Year Effect | Included | Included | Included | Included |
| Model $\chi^2$ | 680.67 | 949.84 | 624.52 | 785.31 |
| Pseudo $R^2$ | 0.27 | 0.27 | 0.26 | 0.27 |
| N | 25,916 | 25,916 | 25,916 | 25,916 |

* significant at 10%, ** significant at 5%, *** significant at 1%, z statistics are in parenthesis and are estimated using Huber-White standard errors. Note that the results are similar when using clustered standard errors by firm as suggested by Petersen (2009).

Practically, our work calls for managerial consideration of the composition of the top management team and its effect on information security management. For instance, the empirical results show that for start-up companies, having someone who is younger on the top management team to provide updated technological knowledge may be important, as such knowledge is crucial to the management of information security risks. Moreover, we argue that although age diversity and a large team size are beneficial for obtaining a variety of technical and managerial know-how, a highly heterogeneous team requires a CIO or chief information security officer (CISO) with strong interpersonal skills to mitigate the conflicts and strains of internal coordination. Therefore, when considering candidates for the position of CIO or CISO, the selection committee must consider the quality of the candidates' interpersonal skills. Our findings also suggest that the existing CISO needs to pay attention to the effect of the diversity of top management on the organization's information security program and must stress the importance of communication at the senior management level. This practical contribution is valuable because much of the focus has centered on the management of an end-user awareness program. In addition, the literature review showed a highly significant negative market reaction to information security breaches. Therefore, investors or shareholders of companies are interested in understanding the relation between the composition of the management and the possibility of information security breaches. The findings from this study provide useful insights for investors regarding management characteristics and their effect on the likelihood of information breaches in organizations.

To summarize, this empirical study explores an under-researched area, namely, the relation between a company's top management team and information security management. The exploratory results support the value of applying organizational demography theories to understand information security management. In particular, by focusing on the top management team, we hope that this study stimulate further research into the characteristics and attitudes of the top management team and how they affect the management of information security programs in an organization.

## CONCLUSION

The research objective of this study is to explore the relation between the composition of an organization's top management team and information security breaches. Analysis of previous studies indicated that, although scholars emphasized the importance of top management's involvement in information security management and the significance of information security breaches on a firm's market value, comparatively little research was conducted on the effect of the demographic characteristics of the top management team. To address this issue, this study draws on the organizational demographic literature to develop and test empirically various hypotheses on the relation between the characteristics of top management teams and the likelihood of information security breaches within an organization.

## REFERENCES

Ancona, D. G., & Caldwell, D. F. (1992). Demography and design: predictors of new product team performance. *Organization Science*, *3*(3), 321–341. doi:10.1287/orsc.3.3.321

Backhouse, J., &, & Dhillon, G. (1996). Structures of Responsibility and Security of Information Systems. *European Journal of Information Systems*, *5*, 2–9. doi:10.1057/ejis.1996.7

Backhouse, J., Hsu, C., & Silva, L. (2006). Circuits of Power in Creating De Jure Standards: Shaping an International Information Systems Security Standard. *Management Information Systems Quarterly*, *30*(Special issue), 413–438.

Bagchi, K., & Udo, G. (2003). An analysis of the growth of computer and internet security breaches. *Communications of the Association for Information Systems*, *12*, 684–700.

Bantel, K. A., & Jackson, S. E. (1989). Top management and innovations in banking: Does the composition of the top team make a difference? *Strategic Management Journal*, *10*, 107–124. doi:10.1002/smj.4250100709

Beasley, M. S. (1996). An empirical analysis of the relation between the board of director composition and financial statement fraud. *Accounting Review*, *71*(4), 443–465.

Bedeian, A. G., & Mossholder, K. W. (2000). On the use of the coefficient of variation as a measure of diversity. *Organizational Research Methods*, *3*(3), 285–297. doi:10.1177/109442810033005

Campbell, K., Gordon, L. A., Loeb, M. P., & Zhou, L. (2003). The economic cost of publicly announced information security breaches: empirical evidence from the stock market. *Journal of Computer Security*, *11*, 431–448.

Carlsson, R., & Karlsson, K. (1970). Age, cohorts, and the generation of generations. *American Sociological Review*, *35*, 710–718. doi:10.2307/2093946

Carr, N. (2003). Does IT matter? *Harvard Business Review*, *81*(5), 5–12.

Cavusoglu, H., Mishra, B., & Raghunathan, S. (2004). A model for evaluating IT security investments. *Communications of the ACM*, *47*(7), 87–92. doi:10.1145/1005817.1005828

Collins, C. J., & Clark, K. D. (2003). Strategic human resource practices, top management team social networks, and firm performance: The role of human resource practices in creating organizational competitive advantage. *Academy of Management Journal*, *46*(6), 740–751. doi:10.2307/30040665

Farahmand, F., Navathe, S. B., Sharp, G. P., & Enslow, P. H. (2005). A Management Perspective on Risk of Security Threats to Information Systems. *Information Technology Management*, *6*(2-3), 203–225. doi:10.1007/s10799-005-5880-5

Finkelstein, S., & Hambrick, D. C. (1990). Top-management-team tenure and organizational outcomes: The moderating role of managerial discretion. *Administrative Science Quarterly*, *35*, 484–503. doi:10.2307/2393314

Garg, A., Curtis, J., & Halper, H. (2003). Quantifying the financial impact of IT security breaches. *Information Management & Computer Security*, *11*(2), 74–83. doi:10.1108/09685220310468646

Gordon, L., & Loeb, M. (2002). The economics of information security investment. *ACM Transactions on Information and System Security*, *5*(4), 438–457. doi:10.1145/581271.581274

Gordon, L., & Loeb, M. (2006). Budgeting process for information security expenditures. *Communications of the ACM*, *49*(1), 121–125. doi:10.1145/1107458.1107465

Gordon, L., Loeb, M. P., & Sohail, T. (2010). Market value of voluntary disclosures concerning information security. *Management Information Systems Quarterly*, *34*(3), 567–594.

Hambrick, D. C., Cho, T. S., & Chen, M.-J. (1996). The Influence of Top Management Team Heterogeneity on Firms' Competitive Moves. *Administrative Science Quarterly*, *41*, 659–684. doi:10.2307/2393871

Hovav, A., & D'Arcy, J. (2003). The impact of denial-of-service attack announcements on the market value of firms. *Risk Management & Insurance Review*, *6*(2), 97–121. doi:10.1046/J.1098-1616.2003.026.x

Hovav, A., & D'Arcy, J. (2004). The impact of virus attack announcements on the market value of firms. *Information Systems Security*, *13*(3), 32–40. doi:10.1201/1086/44530.13.3.20040701/83067.5

Hsu, C. (2009). Frame misalignment: interpreting the implementation of information systems certification in an organization. *European Journal of Information Systems*, *18*(2), 140–150. doi:10.1057/ejis.2009.7

Hu, Q., Hart, P., & Cooke, D. (2007). The role of external and internal influences on information systems security - a neo-institutional perspective. *The Journal of Strategic Information Systems, 16*(2), 153–172. doi:10.1016/j.jsis.2007.05.004

Johnson, M. E., & Goetz, E. (2007). Embedding information security into the organization. *IEEE Security and Privacy, May/June*, 16-24.

Kankanhalli, A., Teo, H. H., & Wei, K. K. (2003). An integrative study of information systems security effectiveness. *International Journal of Information Management, 23*(2), 139–154. doi:10.1016/S0268-4012(02)00105-6

Kilduff, M., Angelmar, R., & Mehra, A. (2000). Top management-team diversity and firm performance: examining the role of cognitions. *Organization Science, 11*(1), 21–34. doi:10.1287/orsc.11.1.21.12569

Kotulic, A. G., & Clark, J. G. (2004). Why there aren't more information security research studies. *Information & Management, 41*(5), 597–607. doi:10.1016/j.im.2003.08.001

Lawrence, B. S. (1997). The Black Box of Organizational Demography. *Organization Science, 8*(1), 1–22. doi:10.1287/orsc.8.1.1

Michel, J., & Hambrick, D. (1992). Diversificatio posture and top management team characteristics. *Academy of Management Journal, 35*, 9–37. doi:10.2307/256471

Petersen, M. A. (2008). Estimating standard errors in finance panel data sets: Comparing approaches. *Review of Financial Studies, 22*(1), 435–480. doi:10.1093/rfs/hhn053

Pfeffer, J. (1983). *Organizational Demography*. Greenwich: JAI Press.

Siponen, M., & Iivari, J. (2006). Six design theories for IS security policies and guidelines. *Journal of the Association for Information Systems, 7*(7), 445–472.

Smith, K. G., Smith, K. A., Sims, H. P. Jr, O'Bannon, D. P., Scully, J. A., & Olian, J. D. (1994). Top management team demography and process: The role of social integration and communication. *Administrative Science Quarterly, 39*(3), 412–438. doi:10.2307/2393297

Stevens, J. M., Beyer, J. M., & Trice, H. M. (1978). Assessing personal, role, and organizational predictors of managerial commitment. *Academy of Management Journal, 21*(3), 380–396. doi:10.2307/255721 PMID:10246524

Straub, D. W. (1990). Effective IS security: An empirical study. *Information Systems Research, 1*(3), 255–276. doi:10.1287/isre.1.3.255

Straub, D. W., & Nance, W. (1990). Discovering and discipline computer abuse in organizations: A field study. *Management Information Systems Quarterly, 14*(1), 45–60. doi:10.2307/249307

Straub, D. W., & Welke, R. J. (1998). Coping with systems risk: Security planning models for management decision making. *Management Information Systems Quarterly, 22*(4), 441–469. doi:10.2307/249551

Uzun, H., Szewczyk, S. H., & Varma, R. (2004). Board composition and corporate fraud. *Financial Analysts Journal, 60*(3), 33–43. doi:10.2469/faj.v60.n3.2619

Vroom, V., & Pahl, B. (1971). Relationship between age and risk-taking among managers. *The Journal of Applied Psychology, 55*, 399–405. doi:10.1037/h0031776

Waller, M. J., Huber, G. P., & Glick, W. H. (1995). Functional Background as a determinnant of executives' selective perception. *Academy of Management Journal, 38*, 943–974. doi:10.2307/256616

Wang, T., Kannan, K. N., & Rees, J. (2013). The association between the disclosure and the realization of information security risk factors. *Information Systems Research, 24*(2), 201–218. doi:10.1287/isre.1120.0437

Wang, T., Rees, J., & Kannan, K. (2013). The Textual Contents of Media Reports of Information Security Breaches and Profitable Short-Term Investment Opportunities. *Journal of Organizational Computing and Electronic Commerce*, *23*(3), 200–223. doi:10.1080/10919392.2013.807712

Wiersema, M. F., & Bantel, K. A. (1992). Top management team demography and corporate strategic change. *Academy of Management Journal*, *35*(1), 91–121. doi:10.2307/256474

Williams, K. Y., & O'Reilly, C. A. (1998). *Demography and diversity in organizations*. Greenwich: JAI Press.

## KEY TERMS AND DEFINITIONS

**Age:** Age of the top management team.

**Breach Announcement:** Media articles about information security breaches.

**Demography:** Structure about the composition of the top management team.

**Information Security:** The protection of information and information systems from unauthorized access, use, disruption, or modification, in order to provide confidentiality, integrity, and availability.

**Tenure:** The number of year the top management team works for the firm.

**Top Management Team:** The c-suite executives of a firm.

**Top Management Team Heterogeneity:** The diversity of the composition of the top management team.

## ENDNOTES

[1] Our sample size was relatively small as we limited our sample (1) to be U.S. firms and in the period from 1992 to 2008, (2) to be publicly traded firms, and (3) with executive information from *ExecuComp*, which we consider a limitation of the study.

# Chapter 9
# Hijacking of Clicks:
## Attacks and Mitigation Techniques

**Hossain Shahriar**
*Kennesaw State University, USA*

**VamsheeKrishna Devendran**
*Kennesaw State University, USA*

## ABSTRACT

*Clickjacking attacks are an emerging threat on the Web. The attacks allure users to click on objects transparently placed in malicious Web pages. The resultant actions of the click operations may cause unwanted operations in the legitimate websites without the knowledge of users. Recent reports suggest that victims can be tricked to click on a wide range of websites such as social network (Facebook, Twitter), shopping (Amazon), and online banking. One reported incident on clickjacking attack enabled the webcam and microphone of a victim without his/her knowledge. To combat against clickjacking attacks, application developers need to understand how clickjacking attacks occur along with existing solutions available to defend the attacks. This chapter shows a number of basic and advanced clickjacking attacks. The authors then show a number of detection techniques available at the client, server, and proxy levels.*

## INTRODUCTION

Hijacking of Click (also known as Clickjacking) attacks steal clickable actions from victims and direct clicks towards legitimate websites without the knowledge of the victims (Clickjacking-OWASP 2014). When multiple applications or websites (or OS principals in general) share a common graphical display, they are subject to clickjacking (Aharonovsky 2008) attacks. To perform a clickjacking attack, an attacker first designs a malicious web page containing an iframe which may load a legitimate web page. The iframe opacity level is set very low to make it barely visible by a victim. The malicious web page allures the victim to click on visible GUI element (overlapping the invisible legitimate webpages loaded in an iframe). If a victim clicks on the visible GUI element supplied by an attacker, it results in an action on the legitimate web page and may cause unwanted actions.

Some common incidents due to the hijacking of clicks include posting unwanted messages in Twitter without the knowledge of victims, sharing

DOI: 10.4018/978-1-4666-6324-4.ch009

dubious links as well as liking other users on the Facebook, and making individual profile public (Balduzzi, M., Egele, M., Kirda, E., Balzarotti, D., & Kruegel 2010). Clickjacking attacks are being used to generate revenues for large scale botnet operators (Hachman 2014). To address and mitigate the loss due to hijacking of clicks, one key step is to understand the basic and advanced attack types as well as the capability of the state-of-the art mitigation techniques.

In this chapter, we provide a detailed overview of techniques to hijacking the clicks while users visit malicious webpages. We discuss advanced attack techniques that are built on top of existing defense mechanisms applicable at the server and client-sides. We also explore well-known anti-clickjacking solutions applicable at the client, server, and proxy sides. The chapter will enable practitioners to understand the working principle of existing defense techniques and select appropriate techniques based on their needs.

The chapter is organized as follows. Section 2 discusses three common variants of clickjacking attacks. Section 3 discusses the framebusting technique, a common defense against clickjacking attacks followed by a number of advanced attack techniques. Section 4 describes some client-side defense techniques, whereas Section 5 highlights some server-side defense techniques. Section 6 shows an example of proxy-level approach for detecting clickjacking attacks. Finally Section 7 concludes the chapter.

## BASIC CLICKJACKING ATTACK TECHNIQUE

A clickjacking attacker has all the capabilities of a web attacker. He/she owns a domain name and controls the contents served from web servers, and can make a victim visit a malicious website, thereby rendering attacker's supplied content in the victim's browser. When a victim visits the attacker's page, the page hides a sensitive UI ele-

ment visually or temporally, and lures a user to perform actions (*e.g.*, clicking on element) which may be out of context and without the knowledge of a user where it is actually being clicked.

To date, there are two kinds of widespread clickjacking attacks in the wild: *Tweetbomb* and *Likejacking* (Kharif 2012). In both attacks, an attacker tricks victims to click on Twitter's Tweet or Facebook's Like button using hiding techniques, causing a link to the attacker's site to be reposted to the victim's friends and thus propagating the link virally. These attacks increase traffic to the attacker's site and harvest a large number of friends or followers.

We classify clickjacking attacks into three types based on how users are forced or allured to click on objects out of context (Huang, Moshchuk, Wang, Schechter & Jackson, 2012): (i) target display manipulation, (ii) modification of pointer location, and (iii) modification of timer event. We discuss the three techniques with examples below:

## Target Display Manipulation

Here, a user believes that he fully sees and recognizes the target element before clicking an object. An HTML element is rendered in an invisible frame where the element if clicked may perform a legitimate action. However, an attacker places another webpage on top of the invisible iframe so that a victim does not understand that the click is effective for the invisible GUI element. We show an example of target display manipulation attacks by loading Facebook "Like" GUI element and hiding it in an iframe of a web page controlled by an attacker. The hiding of the GUI element is being done by making the iframe invisible based on Cascading Style Sheet (CSS) styling features. Figure 1(a) shows the HTML code while Figure 1(b) shows the display result.

In Figure 1(a), a *div* tag named *icontainer* has a lower CSS *z-index* with an opacity level of zero. The *div* includes iframe (*fbframe*) that loads a clickable object "Like" from Facebook for an

*Figure 1. (a) Code for clickjacking attack using an iframe; (b) display of malicious page hiding iframe*

```
<html>
  <body>
    <h1> CLICK HERE TO WIN AN IPAD</h1>
      <div style="overflow: hidden; width: 10px; height: 12px; position:
          absolute; filter:alpha(opacity=0);" id="icontainer">
        <iframe src="http://www.facebook.com/plugins/like.php?href=https://www.facebook.com/
pages/xyz&amp;layout=standard&amp;show_faces=false&amp;width=450&amp;action=like
&amp;font=tahoma&amp;colorscheme=light&amp;height=80"; overflow:hidden; width:50px;
height:23px; allowTransparency="true"  id="fbframe" >
        </iframe>
      </div>
  </body>
</html>
```

(a)

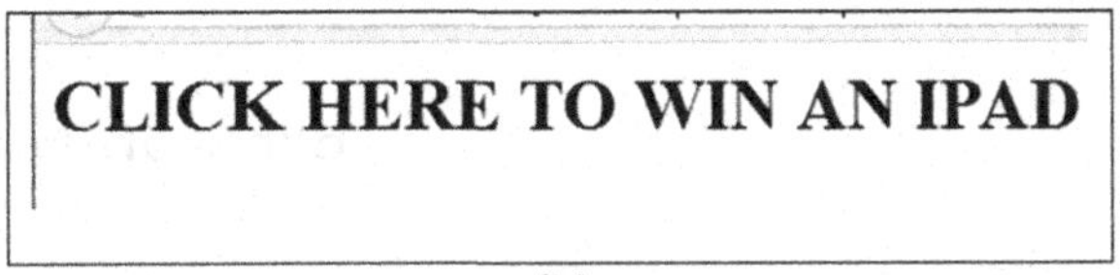

**CLICK HERE TO WIN AN IPAD**

(b)

individual's profile (*xyz*). The URL represents a clickable "Like" action element which can be embedded in any web page and if the element is clicked then the profile of *xyz* is being liked by the person who clicked it. Since the visibility of the *div* is zero, the loaded iframe will not be visible to the victim. To lure the victim to click on the element, the attacker places a lucrative message (*CLICK HERE TO WIN AN IPAD*) in the iframe (Figure 1(b)). Thus, making the victim think that clicking on the message will take him/her to another web page. However, clicking the link will initiate a "Like" action on Facebook for profile *xyz* without the victim's knowledge.

## Modification of Pointer Location

In this technique, a victim believes that the location where he clicks with mouse pointer is the place for triggering an input event. An attacker displays a fake cursor to mislead the target of clickable object. Using the CSS cursor property, an attacker can easily hide the default cursor and programmatically draw a fake cursor elsewhere (Huang and Jackson 2011). As a result, when a victim clicks on an object, action will be triggered for another object not intended by him. This technique is also known as cursor jacking. An alternative approach is to set a custom mouse icon to a deceptive image that has a close look and feel of a genuine cursor icon, except the co-ordinates are shifted by several pixels off the original position. We show an example HTML code for cursorjacking in Figure 2(a) and the corresponding display in a browser in Figure 2(b) (adapted from Cursor Jacking Again 2012).

In Figure 2(a), the HTML code deceives a user by using a custom cursor image (cursor), where the pointer was displayed with an offset in the method *onmove*. In the example, the original cursor is hidden by setting the property *cursor:none*. A new cursor is drawn based on the new image (*cursor.png*). The drawn cursors's left position is shifted 600 pixel right to the original cursor (invisible). As a result, when a user clicks on an element, he/she is clicking an object located 600 pixel right. There are two elements: a button (located at 630px left) and a hyperlink (located

*Figure 2. (a) HTML code for cursor jacking in a browser; (b) display of the alert dialog after clicking the hyperlink*

```
<html>
  <body style="cursor:none;height: 1000px;">
  <img style="position: absolute;z-index:1000;" id= "cursor" src="cursor.png" />
  <button id=fake style="font-size: 150%;position:absolute;top:100px;left:630px;"
      onclick= "alert('button was clicked'); >Button </button>
  <div style="position:absolute;top:100px;left:30px;">
      <a href="#" onclick="alert('hyperlink was clicked');">click on hyperlink</a>
  </div>
  <script>
   var  oNode = document.getElementById('cursor');
   var onmove = function (e) {
     var nMoveX =  e.clientX, nMoveY =  e.clientY;
     oNode.style.left = (nMoveX + 600)+"px";  oNode.style.top = nMoveY + "px";
   }; document.body.addEventListener('mousemove', onmove, true);
   </script> </body>
</html>
```

(a)

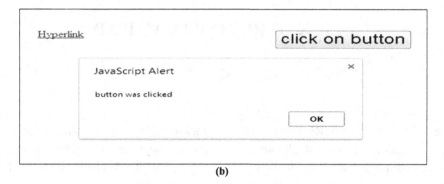

(b)

at 30px). When a user clicks on the hyperlink, the button action is activated (located at 630px). As a result, the *onclick* method for the button is invoked instead of the hyperlink. Figure 2(b) shows the effect of clicking on the hyperlink. The displayed alert dialog indicates that the click was on the button. In the same manner, it is possible to place a Facebook "Like" element object on button location to fool a user and place it in an invisible frame to hijack click.

## Modification of Timer Event

In this attack, victims believe that they have sufficient time to understand clickable objects and respond accordingly. In other words, UI elements are manipulated after victims decide to click on objects. Humans typically require a few hundred milliseconds to react to visual changes [5], and

attackers can take advantage of our slow reaction to launch timing attacks. The target elements can be moved in milliseconds whereas it might take some time for the user to perform a click. The attacker can also change the position of target clicks after the first click by changing the CSS properties.

## FRAMEBUSTING PROTECTION AND ADVANCED CLICKJACKING ATTACKS

One common approach to prevent clickjacking attacks is employ framebusting code (Rydstedt, Bursztein, Boneh, & Jackson 2010). It is a special piece of JavaScript code that needs to be present at the beginning of each web page that needs protection. Specifically, if a webpage needs to be prevented from being loaded in an *iframe*, then the code snippet shown in Figure 3 can enforce that it is rendered at the top page. The code checks if a loaded web page is at the top window or not. If the current page is not in the top window, then it is loaded on the top window, thereby stopping the page loading in the *iframe*.

However, it is possible to circumvent framebusting code-based clickjacking defense technique. We now discuss six advanced attack techniques that we gather from Clickjacking Defense Cheat Sheet 2014.

## Multiple iFrame ($a_1$)

In this attack, the target web page is loaded in an inner *iframe* and an outer *iframe* contains the inner iframe. We show a code snippet in Figure 4 for multiple iframe-based clickjacking attack. The left hand side of the figure (*Page2.html*) is having an *iframe* which is loading *Page1.html*. Inside Page1.html, there is another iframe (inner) that is loading the like button of Facebook applications (similar to the example shown in Figure 1(a)). If Facebook has framebusting code, then it will throw an error while attempting to find the *top.location* (*Page2.html*) from Page1.html. It becomes a violation of browser security policy which prohibits a web page to access the *top.location* from a nested iframe.

## Event Handler Overriding ($a_2$)

While loading a legitimate web page in an iframe, a user can manually cancel the navigation. An attacker can mount a clickjacking attack under this circumstance by registering an *onBeforeUnload* handler method at the top of his malicious web page. This handler is invoked when a page is about to be unloaded. The newly defined method can return a simple message to warn a victim of leaving the legitimate website. If a user chooses not to close that page, the action results in loading the target page in the iframe. Figure 5 shows sample code for the *onBeforeUnload* event handler overriding with a customized message "Do you want to leave http://www.xyz.com?". Note that a legitimate website (http://www.xyz.com) is being loaded in an iframe after overriding the method (Clickjacking Defense Cheat Sheet, 2014).

## No-Content Response ($a_3$)

The event handler-based clickjacking attack requires user interaction. An alternative approach to avoid user interaction is to repeatedly submit navigation requests to a website and receiving HTTP response of 204 (no-content) from the legitimate website. Receiving a no-content flushes the request and cancels the original request forcing

*Figure 3. JavaScript code for frame busting*

```
if (top.location != self.locaton) {
    parent.location = self.location;
}
```

*Figure 4. Advanced clickjacking attack with multiple iframes*

| Page2.html (Outer iframe) | Page1.html (Inner iframe has the target URL) |
|---|---|
| <iframe src="Page1.html"> | <iframe src="http://www.facebook.com?..action=like&amp;..."> |

*Figure 5. Example code for event handler overriding*

```
<script>
    window.onbeforeunload = function(){
        return "Do you want to leave http://www.xyz.com?"; }
</script>
<iframe src="http://www.xyz.com">
```

*Table 1. Example of clobbering-based clickjacking attack*

| Location | Code |
|---|---|
| Legitimate web page (http://www.xyz.com) | if(top.location != self.location){ <br> top.location = self.location; <br> } |
| Attacker web page | \<script\> var location = "foo"; \</script\> <br> \<iframe src="http://www.xyz.com"\> \</iframe\> |

the original URL to load in an iframe (Clickjacking Defense Cheat Sheet, 2014).

## Reflective XSS Filtering *(a₄)*

Browsers have built-in reflective cross-site scripting (XSS) filters that can match known attack signatures containing suspected JavaScript code snippet in request URLs. If JavaScript code is found, then the browser disables all inline JavaScript code received in the response page. Thus, framebusting code present in a web page will not run at all. As an example, an attacker may load the victim's web page as follows: *<iframe src=*"http:// www.xyz.com/?v=<script>if">*. The built-in XSS filter in a browser finds the matching XSS attack signature *<script>if*. The browser disables the entire inline frame busting code present in the response page. This technique has been found to be effective for Internet Explorer (IE) 8 and Chrome browsers (Clickjacking Defense Cheat Sheet, 2014).

## Clobbering of Object *(a₅)*

Some versions of browsers (IE 7 and Safari 4.0.4) consider specific built-in objects (relevant to frame busting code such as *top, self,* and *location*) as

mutable attributes. So, these objects can be redefined or overridden in web page. An attacker can redefine the related attributes that are used for framebusting code such as top, self, and location. This will result in circumventing frame busting techniques. Table 1 shows two code snippets present in a legitimate website (the first row) and an attacker controlled web page (the second row).

In the attacker's web page, the object *location* is defined to an arbitrary value *foo* in an attempt to nullify the effect of frame busting code present in the legitimate web page. Since the victim website (http://www.xyz.com) is rendered in an iframe, the browser does not allow the access of a locally defined variable present on the top page from an iframe. This results in a security violation by trying to read a local variable. Thus, the framebusting code in the legitimate web page will not run.

## Restricting JavaScript *(a₆)*

JavaScript can be disabled inside an iframe. So, the victim's web page being loaded in the iframe cannot execute framebusting code to prevent clickjacking attack. We show two examples of restricting JavaScript code in Figure 6 for IE 8 and Chrome browsers.

*Figure 6. Examples of JavaScript code execution restriction*

```
(IE 8):
<iframe src="http://www.xyz.com" security="restricted"> </iframe>
(Chrome):
<iframe src="http://www. xyz.com" sandbox> </iframe>
```

*Figure 7. An example of HTML5 sandbox attribute*

```
<iframe sandbox="allow-scripts allow-forms" src=http://www.xyz.com/foo.html
   style = "height:80px">
</iframe>
```

## Double-Clicking-Based Clickjacking (a₇)

Google deploys X-Frame-Options on their OAuth approval pages. Although the attacker can no longer embed the approval page in an IFRAME, it is possible to load the approval page in a *pop-under window* (Sclafani, 2009). A pop-under window is a basically a popup window that is hidden behind the main browser window right after it was opened. Since modern browsers block popup windows unless triggered by user-initiated clicks, this attack requires multiple clicks to bypass popup blockers. It is possible to read data from the user's Google contacts, and read the user's GMail messages (Sclafani, 2009). The attack has been shown to be working on for the major browsers (IE, Chrome, Firefox, Opera).

## HTML5 Sandbox (a₈)

In some web browsers (Chrome, Webkit), it is possible to use HTML5 sandbox attribute to allow scripts and forms, but forbid top navigation (*no allow-top-navigation*) (Kantor, 2011 and Suto, 2008). Thus, an iframe can use JavaScript code. However, the script code may not access or change *top.location*. An example of sandboxing is shown in Figure 7.

## CLICKJACKING ATTACK DETECTION AT THE CLIENT-SIDE

Although the same-origin policy is supposed to protect distrusting web sites from interfering with one another, it fails to stop any of the clickjacking attacks we described above. As a result, several anti-clickjacking defenses have been proposed that can be deployed at the browsers.

## User Confirmation (Huang, Moshchuk, Wang, Schechter, & Jackson, 2012)

A solution for preventing clickjacking at the client-side is to generate a confirmation dialog for end users to understand a possible out-of-context click. Facebook currently deploys this approach for the Like button, asking for confirmation whenever requests come from blacklisted domains. Unfortunately, this approach degrades user experience, especially on single-click buttons.

## UI Randomization (Huang, Moshchuk, Wang, Schechter, & Jackson, 2012)

Another technique is to protect a target element by randomizing the UI (GUI element) layout of a legitimate web page. As a result, an attacker would fail to correctly locate the position of the target element.

## Blocking of Mouse Click (Huang, Moshchuk, Wang, Schechter, & Jackson, 2012)

Instead of completely disallowing framing, an alternative is to allow rendering transparent frames, but block mouse clicks if the browser detects that the clicked cross-origin frame is not fully visible. Adobe has added such protection to Flash Player's webcam access dialog in response to webcam clickjacking attacks. However, this defense only protects the dialog and is not available for other web content.

## ClickIDS (Balduzzi, Egele, Kirda, Balzarotti, & Kruegel, 2010)

ClickIDS is a Firefox extension. It compares the bitmap of the clicked object on a given web page to the bitmap of that object rendered in isolation (*i.e.*, without transparency inherited from a malicious parent element). It alerts users when the clicked element overlaps with other clickable elements. Unfortunately, ClickIDS cannot detect attacks based on partial overlays or cropping, and it shows false positive warning.

## GuardedID (Brenner, 2009)

It has an added feature of Clickjacking warning. It makes potential elements under clickjacking visible to the end user. It does not interfere with operation of legitimate iframes, frames, AJAX, or script code. The GuardedID can prevent the browser from storing the keystrokes.

## NoScript (NoScript, 2014)

The NoScript is a Firefox browser extension that can allow the execution of JavaScript code from user specified web sites. It protects against click-jacking attack in the browser. NoScript complies with framebusting code based on Frame Break Emulation. Thus, if a framed page contains a "frame busting" script, it automatically replaces the framed page as the topmost document independent of the setting of the browser to enable or disabling of JavaScript code.

## CLICKJACKING ATTACK DETECTION AT THE SERVER-SIDE

## HTTP Header (MDN, 2014)

From the server side, the X-Frame-Options HTTP response header (Suto, 2008) can be used to indicate whether a page can be rendered in an iframe or not. The header can have three possible values: deny (prevents any domain from framing the content of a URL), same-origin (only allows framing of pages from the current website), and allow-from (a set of whitelisted domains that can frame a given URL). However, this technique requires sending HTTP header from each of the pages that need protection against clickjacking attacks. Another difficulty is the lack of support at the browser side to understand the header and act appropriately (e.g., older versions of IE and Firefox will ignore the header).

## HEAD Element (Clickjacking Defense Cheat Sheet, 2014)

A workaround for dealing with lack of browser support for HTTP header-based solution is to apply a special HTML HEAD element containing a special style id with no display for a framed page. The page is displayed only if it is located as the top window. We show sample code snippet in Figure 8. Here, we define a style object named clk1 which has no display information. The JavaScript code is a modification of the traditional frame busting code where the framed page is loaded on the top window (else part of the code).

If the web page is loaded without any frame, then the defined style object is removed from the page and the original display is restored (i.e., if part of the code). However, this prevention technique can be easily thwarted based on reflective XSS filtering, clobbering of object, restricting JavaScript zone, event handler overriding, and multiple iframe usage.

## CLICKJACKING ATTACK DETECTION AT THE PROXY

Defense technique to mitigate clickjacking attack can be applied between the client and server sides which we denote the proxy level. Below we discuss the sole work named ProClick (Shahriar, Devendran, & Haddad, 2013) from the literature.

## ProClick

It is a proxy-based technique that can intercept and analyze requests (issued from browsers) and response pages (received from remote web servers) to check the attack symptoms early. Figure 9 shows the flow of operations for ProClick which has four stages: request analysis, sending request to website, response page analysis, and sending response to the browser. We briefly discuss the request analysis and response page analysis below.

### Request Analysis of ProClick

In this stage, a list of known reflected XSS attack payloads are matched with the URL parameter and values. For example, an attack signature can be of partial script tag containing framebusting code in part.

*Figure 8. Clickjacking defense using HEAD element*

```
<style id="clk1"> body{display:none;} </style>
<script type="text/javascript">
  if (self == top) {
     var antiClickjack = document.getElementById("clk1");
     antiClickjack.parentNode.removeChild(antiClickjack);
  } else {
     top.location = self.location;
  }
</script>
```

*Figure 9. ProClick-based clickjacking testing*

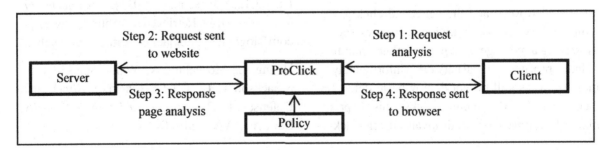

The more matching of framebusting code tokens is present in the parameter values of a URL, the more likely the request contains clickjacking attack payloads. A threshold value can be applied to detect the attack.

## Response Page Analysis of ProClick

When a response page is received, ProClick performs a number of checks to identify the symptoms of a clickjacking attack in the response page.

The number of iframe can be counted and also the presence of frame busting code is detected for the URLs present in iframes. If the number of iframe is zero, the response page is considered as benign. If the number of iframe is one or more, then the opacity parameter value is checked against a threshold level of visibility to consider a page having clickjacking attack payload or not.

The inline JavaScript code present in the response page can be checked to detect the presence of mouse event handlers related to clickjacking attacks (e.g., *mousemove*, *mousedown*, *mouseup*, *onclick*, *doubleclick*). Clobbering of objects related to frame busting code is checked (e.g., redefining variables such as *self*, *top*, *location*, *parent*, and *document*). The iframe tag attribute is checked form HTML 5 sandboxing or restricted JavaScript code zone for detecting suspected clickjacking attacks.

## CONCLUSION

Clickjacking attacks are a threat for most users on the web who may accidentally click on an object not intended for it and the generated click gets redirected to perform malicious activities such as sending a message or liking an unknown individual's profile on social network. Unfortunately, most websites still do not deploy basic defense mechanism for clickjacking attacks. This chapter highlights some basic and advanced clickjack-ing attack techniques. It also discusses defense mechanism against clickjacking for client, server, and proxy levels.

## REFERENCES

Aharonovsky, G. (2008). *Malicious camera spying using ClickJacking*. Retrieved from http://blog.guya.net/2008/10/07/malicious-camera-spying-using-clickjacking, 2008

Balduzzi, M., Egele, M., Kirda, E., Balzarotti, D., & Kruegel, C. (2010). A solution for the automated detection of clickjacking attacks. In *Proceedings of the 5th ACM Symposium on Information, Computer and Communications Security* (pp. 135-144). Beijing, China: ACM.

Brenner, M. (2009). *Clickjacking and GuardedID*. Retrieved from http://ha.ckers.org/blog/20090204/clickjacking-and-guardedid

Clickjacking. (2012). *Clicjakcing*. Retrieved from https://www.owasp.org/index.php/Clickjacking

*Clickjacking Defense Cheat Sheet*. (2014). Retrieved from https://www.owasp.org/index.php/Clickjacking_Defense_Cheat_Sheet

*Cursor Jacking Again*. (2012). Retrieved from http://blog.kotowicz.net/2012/01/cursorjacking-again.html

Hachman, M. (2014). *Chameleon Clickjacking Botnet Stealing $6 Million a Month*. Retrieved from http://slashdot.org/topic/datacenter/chameleon-clickjacking-botnet-stealing-6-million-a-month/

Huang, L., & Jackson, C. (2011). *Clickjacking attacks unresolved*. Retrieved from http://mayscript.com/blog/david/clickjacking-attacks-unresolved

Huang, L., Moshchuk, A., Wang, Schechter, S., & Jackson, C. (2012). Clickjacking: Attacks and Defenses. In *Proceedings of USENIX Security*. Bellevue, WA: USENIX.

Kantor, I. (2011). *The Clickjacking Attack*. Retrieved from http://javascript.info/tutorial/clickjacking

Kharif, O. (2012). *'Likejacking': Spammers Hit Social Media*. Retrieved from http://www.businessweek.com/articles/2012-05-24/likejacking-spammers-hit-social-media

MDN. (2014). *X-Frame-Options*. Retrieved from https://developer.mozilla.org/en-US/docs/HTTP/X-Frame-Options

Noscript. (2014). *Noscript Firefox Extension*. Retrieved from http://noscript.net

Rydstedt, G., Bursztein, E., Boneh, D., & Jackson, C. (2010). Busting frame busting: A study of clickjacking vulnerabilities at popular sites. In *Proceedings of the Web 2.0 Security and Privacy*. Oakland, CA: Academic Press.

Sclafani, S. (2009). *Clickjacking & OAuth*. Retrieved from http://stephensclafani.com/2009/05/04/clickjacking-oauth

Shahriar, H., Devendran, V., & Haddad, H. (2013). ProClick: A Framework for Testing Clickjacking Attacks in Web Applications. In *Proceedings of 6th ACM/SIGSAC International Conference on Security of Information and Networks*, (pp. 144-151). Aksaray, Turkey: ACM.

Suto, L. (2008). *Clickjacking Details*. Retrieved from http://ha.ckers.org/blog/20081007/clickjacking-details

## KEY TERMS AND DEFINITIONS

**ClickIDS:** An automated tool to prevent clickjacking attacks within browsers.

**Clickjacking:** Stealing of clickable actions on web page through overlay frame.

**Cursorjacking:** Similar to pointer jacking.

**Framebsting:** Javascript code to stop web page rendering within iframe.

**Noscript:** A browser extension tool to prevent JavaScript code execution.

**Pointer Jacking:** Stealing of actions based on mouse pointer-based clicks.

**Web Security:** A set of procedure and practices to protect web servers and end users.

# Chapter 10

# Fighting Cybercrime and Protecting Privacy:
## DDoS, Spy Software, and Online Attacks

**Javier Valls-Prieto**
*University of Granada, Spain*

## ABSTRACT

*This chapter is about the use of large-scale databases that has increased considerably in the last two years. It is a powerful tool to predict future situations that may affect society. The use of an environmental scanner to fight cybercrime—as an organized crime—is the project for using this technique of large-scale databases to try to guarantee the security against the risk of new, developing forms of criminal activities. On the other hand, the use of large-scale databases utilizes a great amount of personal data to try to predict where and how organized crime or new forms of criminality will develop. This means that we have to evaluate the interests of security of society and the privacy of the person, and we have to find the way to balance both in a democratic society. There are important ethical issues to be considered in the employment of this new and unregulated instrument.*

## INTRODUCTION

Cybercrime, as a part of organized crime, is considered one of the most serious potential risks in twenty-first century society. Crimes such as cyber espionage, system attacks, child pornography, on-line fraud and extortion are a reality and may become worse. The World Economic Forum takes cyber attacks as having the most impact and the most considerable risk in the global area (WEF, 2013). And this risk is not only for private users but for governments and societies throughout the world. The problem found in cybercrime is that criminals can hide just waiting to attack, and moreover addition victims do not want to report the case in order not to amplify the issue. Many problems arise when considering how to fight this kind of criminality. One of them is the invisibility of the act. It remains confined to the net and only the perpetrator and the victim know about it. If the victim does not report anything to the police it is impossible to know that it has happened. But where the victim is a public institution the risks are so high for society that they cannot be allowed

DOI: 10.4018/978-1-4666-6324-4.ch010

to happen. Therefore, prevention is the only way to fight them. And that is exactly the idea behind the use of the Environmental Scanning. The use of robots to detect cybercrime is an effective tool because they work in the same environment, have the possibility of finding evidence and can predict future attacks.

To achieve these goals robots need to use large-scale databases with large quantities of personal information. But this poses a serious risk in using them in the fight against organized crime, and in particular, because of the conflict between the use of personal data and respect for human rights. Online criminal investigations are needed in the twenty-first century. As we have seen with the NSA investigations, the development of these robots is already a reality. A world with these cyber risks cannot be a democracy and a world without privacy, which also affects the right of freedom of speech, cannot be a democracy. Both are indispensable to live in a democratic society.

How to balance both is exactly the question that this paper seeks to solve. As it is a global problem both the EU legislation and projects on the protection of privacy and control of state investigations are going to be analysed. To this end, we are going to see from a criminological point of view how botnets work and how the European Union Law on the processing of personal data could control the use of big data on criminal investigations.

## HOW THE BOTNETS WORK AND DESCRIPTION OF A FEW CYBERCRIME TYPES

Cybercrime has become an important topic for the police and security services. As has been pointed out by Clough the "rapid technological development continues, and will continue, to present new challenges" (Clough, 2012) and crime is not apart of these changes. According to Moore cybercrime covers plenty of crimes as intellectual property theft, child pornography, financial fraud, online harassment, identity theft, etc. (Moore, 2011) but some of them are only an online action with no a big difference to the offline world. That is why we are going to focus our work on the cybercrimes that all the process is online and has nearly nothing to do with the offline crime.

The three kinds of crimes that we are going to study (denying system attack, spy software and infrastructure online attacks) have points in common. Basically, the three of them involve the introduction of a malware in a computer that could be either the final-computer or a third part computer, from where the attack comes out but controlled by the botmaster.

Trying to explain the modus operandi is really complicated because it changes according to regions, groups of criminals and technology. Anyway, it is possible to identify some common points.

As we have said, these kinds of cyber attacks have to control computers to produce the result. The criminals use a botnet. 'Botnets' (a term derived from the words 'robot' and 'network') consist of a network of interconnected, remote-controlled computers generally infected with malicious software that turn the infected systems into so-called 'bots', 'robots', or 'zombies'. The legitimate owners of such systems may often be unaware of the fact of infection. Zombies within the botnet connect to computers controlled by perpetrators (known as 'command and control servers' or C&Cs), or to other zombies in order to receive instructions, download additional software, and transmit back information harvested from the infected system (UNODC, Comprehensive Study on Cybercrime, 2013).

Once the botnet is in the computer the hackers can control it. The classical way was to use the IRC chat system, but recently more sophisticated structures are being used (by working on TCP, UDP and ICMP protocols) (INFOSEC Institute, 2013). The first generation botnet was based on Command & Control Server (C&C) but it was quite easy to control by just shutting off the

C&C. The second generation of botnets is based on peer-to-peer (P2P) to avoid this defence by a decentralized network. These new strategy third generation botnets are characterized by their economical motivation and design sophistication (Sood A. K., Enbody R. J. & Bansal R., 2013).

The malware is distributed in incredibly different ways. A classical one is through the web site where the victim downloads a file and without his knowledge there is an installation of the file that is normally quite small (Sood A. K., Enbody R. J. & Bansal R., 2013). This little file, normally no bigger that some hundred Kbs, sends and collects information from the infected computer (zombie). The zombie can be asleep for a long time till the botmaster sends the order to activate it.

That situation happens due to certain factors. One of them is that the users, private or small businesses, do not have the money to install a good secure system to protect their computers. Moreover, they do not have the time or the computer knowledge to have their machines patched (Eriksen-Jensen, M., 2013). That is the reason where the security companies put all their effort, but the mother language also plays a big role. So the lack of English language skills in China means that that population is not able to use IT security products developed in English. The result is that, in that country, 80% of computers connected with the Internet are controlled by botnets (Kshetri, N., 2013a). These characteristics of the zombie computer owner do not mean that the final victim has to be in that country.

## Perpetrators

The profile of this kind of criminality has changed in the last decade. It is impossible to be more wrong than to think that the perpetrator is a teenage geek doing it for fun. The new cybercrime scene has more to be with organised crime than with the romantic idea of a David against Goliath. Nearly 80% of the digital crime may now originate in some form of organised crime (BAE SYSTEMS Detica, 2012). Although not all cybercrime has

connections with criminal groups we have to admit that criminal groups have found a good environment on the Internet.

The perpetrators have IT skills. They are good at mathematics, physics and computer science. They live in countries where the educational level is good and there is a tradition of mathematics (Kshetri, N., 2013b). But because of the poor economy they do not have a similar economic level. This difference makes it really attractive for them to work for cybercriminals, so they have a profit goal (Kshetri, N., 2013a, 2013b).

One interesting point, that Kshetri remarks on in his studies, is that they also have a non-profit making ideal that make their acts more justifiable. In the case of China the perpetrators consider their actions as a nationalist act against the attacks from Taiwan and USA to protect the motherland's honour (Kshetri, N., 2013a) Cybercrimes in the Former Soviet Union and Central and Eastern Europe: current status and key drivers Cybercrimes in the Former Soviet Union and Central and Eastern Europe: current status and key drivers (Kshetri, N., 2013b). But something similar happens in the post-communist countries. In these cases the perpetrators consider their crimes rather as a fair action to give something to society, and the idea is to use his knowledge to contribute to improve the society. The people in these countries have a great tradition of mathematical, physics and computer sciences skills and use it for a point of honour to give something back to the society that has given them this knowledge (Kshetri, N., 2013b).

## Victims

The profile of the victims of the attack is also important, in particular, the one who is infected and those who are used to produce the attack. As this kind of cyber attack can be done from everywhere we have to realise that any lack in security can have serious consequences. One really grave mistake is not to take the measures needed to ensure real security. Eriksen-Jensen comments that private users and small businesses do not have the time or the money to update their systems. Some of them also believe that just patching the most important programs is enough (Eriksen-Jensen, M., 2013). Without doubt that reality results in a lack of security that enables the hackers to produce the attack, as does the victims' lack of English so that they fail to understand most of the technical solutions that can be found on the web (Kshetri, N., 2013a).

The end victims of these cyber attacks are basically States and big corporations. The former are linked to real situations of cyber warfare as has happened recently between China and USA (NYTIMES, 2013). In this case the perpetrators have a political goal and sometimes they act with the consent of the authorities. The latter have a profit motive. The idea is to blackmail big companies such as banks online or big Internet product sellers to earn money. The hackers know that in those cases the victims are reluctant to inform the relevant authorities that they have been attacked as to do so would show the vulnerabilities of the system and create mistrust in the consumers.

Against that kind of crime we don't have other choice as to fight it on the Internet and using the new techniques on surveillance in the Internet and the use of large amount of data.

## EUROPEAN LAW ON THE PROCESSING OF PERSONAL DATA ON THE DETECTION OR PROSECUTION OF CRIMINAL OFFENCES

The current centrepiece of European Union law on the processing of personal data is Directive 95/46/EC. The scope of this norm is not security and State activities in areas of criminal law (Article 3.2), but it is useful for the definitions that it contains and its influence on the development of all European regulation on personal data use, either commercial or for security use.

Thus, concepts like "personal data", "processing of data", "personal data filing system" or "the data subject's consent" remained exactly the same in the Council Framework Decision 2008/977/JHA on the protection of personal data processed in the framework of police and judicial cooperation in criminal matters. For our work the Directive defines personal data as "any information relating to an identified or identifiable natural person ('data subject'); an identifiable person is one who can be identified, directly or indirectly, in particular by reference to an identification number or to one or more factors specific to his physical, physiological, mental, economic, cultural or social identity". For example, the monies paid in a company (Joined Cases C-465/00, C-138/01, C-139/01, *Österreichischer Rundfunk and others*), name and address (Case C-553/07, *Rijkeboer*) the IP of the computer (Case C-461/10, *Bonnier and others*) have been considered personal data by the EUCJ.

In *Rijkeboer* case, the Court made a distinction between basic data and other data, which "concerns information on recipients or categories for recipient to whom those basic data are disclosed and on the content thereof and thus relates to the processing of the basic data". Only the first ones are considered personal data. In *Huber* case, data such as name, given name, date and place of birth, nationality, marital status, sex, record of his entries into and exists from the country, residence status, particulars of passports, record of his previous statements as to domicile and the different reference numbers by the administrative authorities are considered personal data (Case C-524/06, *Huber*).

Another concepts have been developed in the scope of criminal matters and some of them stay on the proposal for a Directive on the protection of individuals with regard to the processing of personal data by competent authorities for the purposes of prevention, investigation, detection or prosecution of criminal offences or the execution of criminal penalties, and the free movement of such data from 2012 (new definitions are those of "personal data breach", "genetic data" and "biometric data", "competent authorities" and of a "child"). This is the case of processor and recipient where 'processor' describes some examples of the bodies concerned ('processor' shall mean a natural or legal person, public authority, agency or any other body which processes personal data on behalf of the controller) and 'recipient' gives several examples but, at the same time, there is an exclusion so as not to interrupt criminal investigation ('recipient' shall mean a natural or legal person, public authority, agency or any other body to whom data are disclosed, whether a third party or not; however, authorities which may receive data in the framework of a particular inquiry shall not be regarded as recipients). Of course the Framework Decision has its own concepts that are valuable for the effective use of the data in future investigations. So, as the idea is to use those data in criminal investigation, there is necessarily a concept of who can use them: the competent authorities. These are described as agencies or bodies established by legal acts adopted by the Council pursuant to Title VI of the Treaty on European Union, as well as police, customs, judicial and other competent authorities of the Member States that are authorised by national law to process personal data. This is an important step and a guarantee for the citizen who knows that the use of these data will always be the responsibility of a legal person, which will be controlled by the law.

The other three new concepts in the Framework Decision relate to the management of the data. When working with data, particularly in criminal matters, it may be necessary to control some of the personal information; therefore, it may be essential to block some important information or to make it anonymous (Case C-524/06, *Huber*) in an investigation ('blocking' means the marking of stored personal data with the aim of limiting their processing in future and 'to make anonymous' means to modify personal data in such a way that details of personal or material circumstances can no longer or only with disproportionate invest-

ment of time, cost and labour be attributed to an identified or identifiable natural person.), as well as leaving some information open for other future investigation ('referencing' means the marking of stored personal data without the aim of limiting their processing in future)(Mayer-Schonberger, V. and Cukier, K, 2013).

It is different with the principles that have to be followed to collect that information. For the propose of security and criminal investigation the Framework Decision states that data collection may be done by the competent authorities and for specified, explicit and legitimate purposes. In the case of the fight against organized crime and, in particular cybercrime, this point is completely in agreement with the regulation. More problematic is the requirement of not processing the data excessively, as a great deal of data is required for the investigator and for an early warning (Article 3.1). That is exactly the point that the European legislator has thought of, and the next point of Article 3 enables that problem to be solved. The future processing of that data in other cases or situations is permitted if it is not incompatible with the purposes for which the data were collected (Case C-73/07, *Stakunnan Markkinapörssi Oy*), and the competent authorities are authorised to process such data for such other purpose in accordance with the applicable legal provisions and where processing is necessary and proportionate to that other purpose (Case C-524/06, *Huber*). As the scanner is designed for a general goal, the fight against organized crime, every specific investigation, e.g. denying system attacks, may be included within the provision for future use of the data because this kind of investigation needs the data from past cases to be stored, thus the fight against criminal acts is a specific use of them and has a legitimate propose. So the three points in our case follow exactly the system set out in the Framework Decision.

The Directive is a good foundation on which to develop the rights of the data subject. These rights are included on the Proposal from 2012 for a Directive on the protection of individuals with regard to the processing of personal data by competent authorities for the purposes of prevention, investigation, detection or prosecution of criminal offences or the execution of criminal penalties, and the free movement of such data. Taking into account that it was drafted in 1995 and how technology has improved since then, these rights continue to play an important role.

Article 12 of the Directive gives the right of access to personal information. Basically, it stipulates that the data subject can obtain from the controller confirmation as to whether or not data relating to him/her are being processed and information at least as to the purposes of the processing, the categories of data concerned, and the recipients or categories of recipients to whom the data are disclosed; s/he shall obtain the rectification, erasure or blocking of data the processing of which does not comply with the provisions of the Directive, in particular because of the incomplete or inaccurate nature of the data; and, finally, the notification, by the controller, to third parties to whom the data have been disclosed of any rectification, erasure or blocking carried out.

The European institutions have considered that is impossible to exercise that right on those terms when considering the processing of data in security and police investigations. That is the reason why this right to know and to modify the personal information is limited. So the data subject can only get confirmation from the controller or from the national supervisory authority as to whether or not data relating to him/her have been transmitted or made available and information on the recipients or categories of recipients to whom the data have been disclosed and communication of the data undergoing processing or a confirmation from the national supervisory authority that all necessary verifications have taken place (C-553-07, *Rijkeboer*). Probably it would be more interesting to have a European supervisory authority as the protection of privacy since it a overstate issue, as in USA (MacSíthigh, D., 2013).

But there are five situations in which the Member States can restrict the access to this information: to avoid obstructing official or legal inquiries, investigations or procedures; to avoid prejudicing the prevention, detection, investigation and prosecution of criminal offences or for the execution of criminal penalties; to protect public security; to protect national security and to protect the data subject or the rights and freedoms of others. In these cases, where there is a negative answer to the request, the data subject has to receive a written notification and s/he can appeal to the competent national supervisory authority, a judicial authority or to a court (Article 17 of the Council Framework Decision 2008/977/JHA). These situations are similar to those in Article 13 of the Directive. In that norm there is a general specification on security and criminal matters that can involve all those in the 2008 norm. So basically, the exceptions for this research are the same.

One important new right is that contained in Article 18 of the Framework Decision for rectification, erasure and blocking. Citizens have the right to expect the controller to fulfil its duties concerning the rectification, erasure or blocking of personal data, which arise from the Framework Decision. If the controller denies rectification, erasure or blocking, the refusal must be communicated in writing to the data subject who must be informed of the possibilities provided for in national law for lodging a complaint or seeking judicial remedy.

In the case where the data subject's rights are infringed (as a result of an unlawful processing operation or of any act incompatible with the national provisions adopted) he/she has the right to receive compensation. The terms of this right are similar as those set out in Article 23 of the Directive but this time there is a range of rights and not only the possibility of liability. This is, again, a good example of the influence of the Directive on the Framework Decision.

## ETHICAL ISSUES

We have already seen the legal aspects and the reaction of the community to protect peoples' rights. But ethical problems also arise when using this kind of completely legal technology.

The first such problem is that the use of these technologies can only justify attacking the right of the privacy when the objective of the investigation is to fight dangerous crimes. And that will be that cases where the State's or the community's democratic institution are at high risk, and that kind of crime cannot be fought in other ways.

Another problem is how to manage the data and in particular personal data. Here, we do not need to focus on the specific criminal but on the early warning of the commission of a crime. The data should be processed as anonymous data. In any case if the data is used in a criminal investigation it should remain anonymous to allow for the possibility of return the data to the original owner. Recently, the UK Court of Appeal decision in R (Catt) v Association of Chief Police Officers and Others [2013] EWCA Civ 192 affirms that there is a legitimate aim in the storing and retention of information on the Police Database when the goal is the prevention of disorder and crime, and safeguarding the rights and freedoms of others (Oswall, M., 2013). So its use can be accepted to protect the rights of others.

Should the scanner take information from minors? In general this should be avoided. As scanning collects much information to see where crime tends to be committed and minors' crimes are a small part of organized crime it is possible to do this work without these data. Minors have to have a high level of protection for their privacy because they are at a special age where their personality is not fully formed and, in their case, the protection of their privacy is very important for their future.

As the scanner is going to work with information from open sources, people who give this information voluntarily to the social media, such

as online forums, blogging platforms, social networking sites and any other interactive websites or applications (Whitcroft, O., 2013) are allowing other people to access it. This raises at least two ethical problems: firstly, the time for which the data are being used, (indefinite retention) and, secondly, that data protection law no longer applies to information that has been published (Article 29 Working Party Opinion 03/2013 (WP203) on the purpose limitation principle in the Data Protection Directive).

The processing of large-scale databases over a long period gives a complete idea of the personality, political ideas, religions feelings and everything linked to an individual's personality and it is a serious risk to democracy and freedom of speech.

The opinion of the Working Party about Open Data dealt with the private sector, and said nothing about public investigation but did comment on Open Data government projects. Here, the Working Party recommended an anonymised form for the use of such data or if this is not possible, to encourage public sector data controllers to undertake a compatibility assessment of further use (Treacy, B. & Bapat, A., 2013).

One open question is whether personal data that the State already has may be used or not (McDonagh, M., 2002). We could consider this data as an open source resource, but we must not forget that the consent of the person limits what the information can be used for. Also, it is really interesting to consider if third parties could request governments to provide personal data due to a transparency principle. In *Tietosoujacaltuutettu vs Stakunnan Markkinapörssi Oy and Satamedia Oy* case, C-73/07, Satamedia Oy published tax information of certain people, since in Finland that type of records are deemed to be public information. The Court considered that the creation of this list was processing of personal data. With in the frame of criminal investigations, it would be unethical to let this type of private information become public, since it can be both ruin the public reputation of the subject before the actual accusations are proven, and because it can interfere with the criminal investigation line.

## CONCLUSION

The use of Internet as a communications system or crime environment is a factor in organized crime. So Internet will inevitably be used in criminal investigation in this century. The development of large-scale data processing gives State institutions an important tool with which to fight this kind of criminality. But this has another side relating to human rights, particularly the right to privacy.

In any case, the use of big data has its restrictions. Big data techniques are good enough for non-casual correlations that normally cannot be used as evidence on a Court (Mayer-Schonberger, V. and Cukier, K, 2013). Therefore, the use of big data has to be limited to strategic investigations, since it cannot really be used in an operational way.

As we have seen in this paper, the use of large-scale data by the State is not questioned. The only remaining matter is how it will be done. Of course, its use by the State has no legitimation when there is not only a failure to protect human rights but they are infringed. Nevertheless, there has always been a thin line concerning privacy vulnerability for the greater good, but the risk nowadays is bigger than before with the developed of the previously explained techniques. Thus, the law has to change to regulate its use (Mayer-Schonberger, V. and Cukier, K, 2013). This is the challenge that the supranational regulation must face. A challenge the European Union is willing to take.

The EU regulations give enough guarantees to ensure the correct use by the police of these kinds of robots to get good results in the fight against international crime. The figure of an independent supervisor is basic to control these investigations to ensure that the privacy of users is adequately protected. But other problems remain.

As this kind of investigation is linked to more than one country and as the open source information systems are on Internet, where there are no national borders, it is necessary to think in terms of international regulations, international human rights protection systems and, probably, of an international jurisdiction to solve the problems that this kind of fight will pose.

Although the EU regulation and the privacy protection project have taken a big step on the regulation of this kind of technical facility there are many ethical issues, as we have seen. These are related not only to personal data but how they are used. One good example is children's rights to privacy. As mentioned above, children's data are not important in this kind of criminality because there are other ways to obtain the information needed to fight it, particularly when children are the perpetrators. But what about when they are the victims, as in child pornography? Should it be used when it is the only way to protect children's rights? How should children's data be used in those cases? In this particular situation the supervisory authority's work is vital to adapt this tool to the particular case.

## REFERENCES

*BAE Systems Detica*. (2012). Retrieved from http://www.baesystemsdetica.com/uploads/resources/ORGANISED_CRIME_IN_THE_DIGITAL_AGE_EXECUTIVE_SUMMARY_FINAL_MARCH_2012.pdf

*INFOSEC Institute*. (2013). Retrieved from http://resources.infosecinstitute.com/botnets-and-cybercrime-introduction/

Clough, J. (2012). *Principeles of cybercrime*. Academic Press.

Eriksen-Jensen, M. (2013). Holding back the tidal wave of cybercrime. *Computer Fraud & Security*, (3), 10–16

Kshetri, N. (2013a). Cybercrime and cyber-security issues associated with China: some economic and institutional considerations. *Electronic Commerce Research, 13*(1), 41–69. doi:10.1007/s10660-013-9105-4

Kshetri, N. (2013b). Cybercrimes in the Former Soviet Union and Central and Eastern Europe: current status and key drivers. *Crime, Law, and Social Change, 60*(1), 39–65. doi:10.1007/s10611-013-9431-4

McDonagh, M. (2002). E-Government in Australia: the Challenge to privacy of Personal Information. *Int. J Law Info Tech, 10*(3), 327–343. doi:10.1093/ijlit/10.3.327

Mac Sithigh, D. (2013). App law within: Rights and regulation in the smartphone age. *Int. J Law Info Tech, 21*(2), 154–186. doi:10.1093/ijlit/eat002

Mayer-Schonberger, V., & Cukier, K. (2013). *Big data: A revolution that will transform how we live, work, and think*. Academic Press.

Moore, R. (2011). *Cybercrime: Investigating high-technology computer crime*. Academic Press.

*NY Times*. (2013). Retrieved from http://www.nytimes.com/2013/02/25/world/asia/us-confronts-cyber-cold-war-with-china.html?pagewanted=all

Oswall, M. (2013). Joining the dots – Intelligence and proportionality. *PDP, 13*(6).

Sood, A. K., Enbody, R. J., & Bansal, R. (2013). Dissecting SpyEye: Understanding the design of third generation botners. *Computer Networks, 57*, 436–450. doi:10.1016/j.comnet.2012.06.021

Treacy, B., & Bapat, A. (2013). Purpose limitation – Clarity at last?. *PDP, 13*(11).

UNODC. (2013). *Comprehensive study on cybercrime*. UNODC.

WEF. (2013). *Global risk 2013*. WEF.

Whitcroft, O. (2013). Social media – Challenges in control of information. *PDP, 13*(7).

Working Party Opinion 03/2013 (WP203) on the purpose limitation principle in the Data Protection Directive (95/46/EC)

## KEY TERMS AND DEFINITIONS

**Bootnets:** A network of interconnected, remote-controlled computers generally infected with malicious software that turn the infected systems into so-called 'bots', 'robots', or 'zombies'.

**Cybercrime:** Crime committed using a computer or a network, where a computer may or may not have played an instrumental part in the commission of the crime.

**Data Subject:** Means an identified natural person or a natural person who can be identified, directly or indirectly, by means reasonably likely to be used by the controller or by any other natural or legal person, in particular by reference to an identification number, location data, online identifier or to one or more factors specific to the physical, physiological, genetic, mental, economic, cultural or social identity of that person.

**DDoS:** An attempt to make a machine or network resource unavailable to its intended users.

**Personal Data:** Means any information relating to a data subject.

**Privacy Right:** Fundamental human right recognized in the UN Declaration of Human Rights, the International Covenant on Civil and Political Rights. Privacy underpins human dignity and other key values such as freedom of association and freedom of speech.

**Spy Software:** Any software that can send or record information from a computer without the consent of the owner of this information.

## APPENDIX

## European Case Law

- Cases C-465/00, C-138/01, C-139/01, *Österrreichischer Rundfunk and others*
- Case C-461/10, *Bonnier and others*
- Case C-553/07, *Rijkeboer*
- Case C-524/06, *Huber*
- Case C-73/07, *Stakunnan Markkinapörssi Oy*

# Section 2
# Cyber Security Approaches and Developments

# Chapter 11
# Privacy Compliance Requirements in Workflow Environments

**Maria N. Koukovini**
*National Technical University of Athens, Greece*

**Nikolaos L. Dellas**
*SingularLogic S.A., Greece*

**Eugenia I. Papagiannakopoulou**
*National Technical University of Athens, Greece*

**Dimitra I. Kaklamani**
*National Technical University of Athens, Greece*

**Georgios V. Lioudakis**
*National Technical University of Athens, Greece*

**Iakovos S. Venieris**
*National Technical University of Athens, Greece*

## ABSTRACT

*Workflow management systems are used to run day-to-day applications in numerous domains, often including exchange and processing of sensitive data. Their native "leakage-proneness," being the consequence of their distributed and collaborative nature, calls for sophisticated mechanisms able to guarantee proper enforcement of the necessary privacy protection measures. Motivated by the principles of Privacy by Design and its potential for workflow environments, this chapter investigates the associated issues, challenges, and requirements. With the legal and regulatory provisions regarding privacy in information systems as a baseline, the chapter elaborates on the challenges and derived requirements in the context of workflow environments, taking into account the particular needs and implications of the latter. Further, it highlights important aspects that need to be considered regarding, on the one hand, the incorporation of privacy-enhancing features in the workflow models themselves and, on the other, the evaluation of the latter against privacy provisions.*

## INTRODUCTION

Workflows, that is, well-defined sequences of tasks coordinated in order to achieve a variety of business, scientific and engineering goals, have emerged as a prominent technology in current distributed and dynamic environments, fuelled also by the proliferation of Service Oriented Architectures (SOA) (Papazoglou & van den Heuvel, 2007) and their loose-coupling nature.

DOI: 10.4018/978-1-4666-6324-4.ch011

However, workflow systems are in many cases characterised by serious privacy implications due to their nature, which natively relies to a large extent on access to and exchange of data. Besides, they are often based on and foster collaboration within heterogeneous environments and among many stakeholders, something that significantly complicates the direct and effective use of already existing solutions to privacy protection. Indeed, in such systems, balancing the competing goals of collaboration and security aspects in general is a difficult, multidimensional problem: on the one hand, establishing useful connections among people, tools, and information is a prerequisite, while, on the other, the availability, confidentiality, and integrity of these same elements must also be ensured. The key challenge arising in such context is that the various activities must no longer be considered only "in isolation" but also with respect to operational and data flows, resulting in a holistic view across the corresponding procedures; in other words, required mechanisms (e.g., access control) must be effectively enforced regarding not only individual actions but also large-scale interrelations thereof at the workflow level.

At the same time, the privacy domain is increasingly becoming a legislated area. Data protection laws have been enacted worldwide in order to regulate personal information collection, processing and dissemination (Solove, 2006; Portela & Cruz-Cunha, 2010; Greenleaf, in press). The legal and regulatory framework naturally impacts workflow systems, since business processes implemented as workflows should comply with the associated requirements.

In light of the above, this chapter investigates the issues, challenges and specific requirements related with privacy compliance in workflow environments. In this direction, after some background on workflow technologies is provided, the core legal and regulatory requirements are highlighted in order for the associated challenges for workflow systems to be identified. Thereupon, the main limitations of current technologies with respect to these challenges are outlined. Finally, the fulfilment of the underlying requirements is investigated from a dual perspective: first, the need for the inclusion, at the workflow model level, of structures able to support the in-design specification of privacy policies, leading to targeted privacy configurations enforceable at run-time, and, second, the basic compliance patterns that need to be considered, in order to enable the automatic verification of workflow models against privacy provisions and their automatic transformation in the case of detected violations.

## BACKGROUND

In general terms, a workflow is a collection of tasks, i.e., well-specified steps to be completed by available resources towards performing a more complex operational procedure, along with their various interrelations, that denote the order in which tasks are executed and process the information exchanged among them, if any. A workflow is typically abstracted as a directed graph $<T, E>$, with the set of tasks $T$ constituting its vertices and its edges $E$ representing inter-task relations and associated parameters.

Emanating from the first office automation systems, when variants of Petri Nets (Petri, 1962) have been used in order to model related procedures, workflows originally had a purely business orientation and have in the meantime evolved to what is being referred to today as business workflow or, more broadly speaking, Business Process Management (BPM) technology. Indeed, the Workflow Management Coalition (WfMC) defined a workflow as the "*computerized facilitation or automation of a business process, in whole or part*" during which "*documents, information or tasks are passed between participants according to a defined set of rules to achieve, or contribute to, an overall business goal*" (WfMC, 1995). However, it later became apparent that the workflow paradigm could also benefit the sciences domain and their complex and data-intensive operations. This has led to the emergence of a new family of workflows referred to as scientific; in general terms, a scientific workflow is "*a formal description of a process for accomplishing a scientific objective, usually expressed in terms of tasks and their dependencies*" (Ludäscher et al., 2009a).

Business and scientific workflows present similarities but also differences, stemming from the purposes they serve; said differences concern mainly two aspects: their execution paradigm and the type and degree of human intervention (Ludäscher et al., 2009b). Business workflows focus on control flow, i.e., causal dependencies and sequence of tasks, and foresee the involvement of human users, while data flow plays a secondary role. On the contrary, scientific workflows are largely automated and focus on data flow; execution is driven by data dependencies among tasks.

Business workflows constitute a well-established area, supported by various tools and languages; among them, Business Process Modeling Notation (BPMN) (OMG, 2011) is the de facto modelling standard, whereas Yet Another Workflow Language (YAWL) (van der Aalst & ter Hofstede, 2005; Russell & ter Hofstede, 2009) is a particularly noteworthy approach coming from academia. On the other hand, scientific workflow management is a relatively recent field, and standardisation has not been yet achieved; targeting different domains, including, e.g., natural sciences, bioinformatics, medicine, environmental sciences, astronomy and engineering, with heterogeneous requirements, corresponding systems (e.g., Ludäscher et al., 2006; Churches et al., 2006) are characterised by a miscellany of architectural and operational patterns. However, despite their diversity, common denominator of all scientific workflow systems is their clear data flow orientation and the corresponding semantics and computation models they employ.

Regardless its type, a workflow can be seen from different perspectives, the most important being the *control perspective*, reflecting control dependencies among tasks, the *data perspective*, dealing with data tasks produce and require, and the *resource perspective*, concerned with the allocation of tasks to resources (Jablonski & Bussler, 1996). Workflow perspectives are ultimately reflected by the so-called *workflow patterns*, providing a collection of generic, recurrent constructs (patterns) that are often met in workflows and business processes, along with their description in a language-independent manner. In this context, control-flow patterns (van der Aalst et al., 2003; Russell et al., 2006) describe fundamental modelling features for managing the flow of control among tasks, such as branching, synchronization, concurrency and termination. Data patterns (Russell et al., 2005b) deal with the definition and management of data in terms of visibility, interaction, transfer and data-based routing, whereas resource patterns (Russell et al., 2005a) are concerned with the distribution of work to the available resources.

## LEGAL REQUIREMENTS AND CHALLENGES

Privacy is recognized as a fundamental human right by the Universal Declaration of Human Rights of the United Nations (1948), as well as the Charter of Fundamental Rights of the European Union (European Parliament, Council & Commission, 2000). It is protected by relevant legislation in all the democratic countries throughout the world (cf., e.g., Greenleaf, in press). A significant milestone in the privacy literature has been the codification of the fundamental privacy principles by the Organization for Economic Co-operation and Development (1980), as this codification lays out the basis for the protection of privacy. The OECD principles are reflected in the European Directive 95/46/EC (European Parliament and Council, 1995), "*on the protection of individuals with regard to the processing of personal data and on the free movement of such data*". The Directive 95/46/EC enforces a high standard of data protection and constitutes the most influential piece of privacy legislation worldwide, that seems to pull a general framework and has been characterized as an "engine of a global regime" (Birnhack, 2008), affecting many countries outside Europe in enacting similar laws.

Under Article 2, the Directive 95/46/EC defines personal data as "*any information relating to an identified or identifiable natural person ('data subject'); an identifiable person is one who can be identified, directly or indirectly, in particular by reference to an identification number or to one or more factors specific to his physical, physiological, mental, economic, cultural or social identity*". This definition stresses the explicit reference to indirect identification data, implying any information that may lead to the identification of the data subject through association with other available information (thus indirectly), that may be held by any third party.

The Directive 95/46 EC is further particularized and complemented by a number of other Directives, as well as various Decisions, Recommendations, and Opinions of the Article 29 Data Protection Working Party, among others, with some being domain-specific. Interestingly, many associated legal documents specifically concern domains in which operational procedures are often automated based on the workflow paradigm. For example and with reference to the electronic communication sector, the Directive 2002/58/EC (European Parliament and Council, 2002) imposes explicit obligations and sets specific limits on the processing of users' personal data by network and service providers in order to protect the privacy of the users of communications services and networks, whereas the Directive 2006/24/EC (European Parliament and Council, 2006) deals with data retention issues, mandating the preemptive storage of communications' context data and putting associated restrictions. Other examples include the healthcare domain (U.S. Congress, 1996; Article 29 Data Protection Working Party, 2007) and electronic governance (Article 29 Data Protection Working Party, 2003; Palanisamy & Mukerji, 2012).

## Summary of Legal and Regulatory Requirements

From the analysis of the legal and regulatory framework, certain requirements can be derived that should characterise workflow environments. The following overview has been based on the European framework since, as aforementioned, it affects many jurisdictions worldwide; nevertheless, it is stressed that similar requirements are derived by the jurisdictions of other countries.

### Lawfulness of the Data Processing

Each request for personal data should be evaluated regarding its lawfulness and with respect to applicable laws and regulations. The lawfulness of a given data processing activity should be evaluated against the type of collected information and the purposes for which it was collected, taking into account not only the legislation ruling on privacy and data security, but more generally of all applicable laws and regulations. It follows that the workflow management system should be configurable with a set of data types and purposes deemed to be lawful and, for these specified and pre-identified data types and purposes, the processing of the personal data should be allowed. Any request that is not specifically determined to be lawful according to the set of lawful purposes must be denied. If the request is concerned with a certain kind of activity on the basis of the specific purpose, the application of other mandatory legal requirements should be enforced by the workflow. For example, the use of data in anonymous or identifiable form would be permitted or not permitted depending upon the specific function to be carried out.

### Purposes for Which Data Are Processed

The purpose of workflow execution and, consequently, of any data collection and processing taking place therein, should be identified. That is, a workflow should function so that any collection and processing of personal data is carried out for specified, explicit and legitimate purposes. Further, the controller should act transparently; this means that the controller should specify and make explicit to the data subjects the reasons why the personal data are used. To this end, if needed, the workflow should include communication with data subjects, in order to make them explicit the purposes for which their personal data are being gathered and processed.

## Necessity, Adequacy, and Proportionality of the Data Processed

A workflow should operate according to the "proportionality principle", meaning that personal data may be gathered and processed only to the extent that they are adequate, relevant and not excessive. Therefore, the type and amount of personal data that may be processed within a workflow task should be determined and specified in detail. For example, if a task is aimed at producing statistical figures, the data may be processed in anonymous form and there is no need of using information that may identify the data subjects. Further, processing activities may be performed only on data that are functional and necessary to the specific purpose that is sought by the workflow; therefore, the workflow should provide for automatically deleting or making anonymous any data that are redundant or no longer needed.

## Quality of the Data Processed

It should be ensured that the data processed are correct, exact and updated. Inaccurate data must be deleted or rectified; outdated data must be deleted or updated.

## Identifiable Data

The specification of a workflow should minimise to the extent possible the use of identifiable and personal data, and allow their use only when this is a prerequisite to the specific task that is to be performed. When a given task may be achieved without personal identification data, anonymous data should be used, whereas the identification of the data subject should only be allowed under specific circumstances, e.g., in case of mandatory data retention obligations under the Directive 2006/24/EC (European Parliament and Council, 2006).

## Coordination with Competent Data Protection Authority

A workflow should comply with the notification requirement and the provisions regarding authorisations of the competent Data Protection Authorities, as ruled under applicable data protection legislation. In this context, a workflow should provide for communication with the Authorities, in order to notify them that a certain data processing activity, which is subject to notification and/or authorisation requirements, is being performed. Verification of compliance with notification and/or authorisation requirements may also be considered within the negotiation process with the entities asking access to the personal data.

## Enforcement of Privacy Rights by the Data Subject

The data subject should enabled to exercise the rights acknowledged by applicable data protection legislation in relation to intervention in the data processing (for example the right to access data, to ask for data rectification, erasure, blocking, the right to object the data processing, etc.).

## Consent and Withdrawal of Consent

During the execution of a workflow, it should be guaranteed that, when requested by applicable data protection legislation, the data subject's consent to the data processing will be obtained and that data processing is performed according to the preferences expressed by the data subject.

Further, withdrawal of consent and objection to data processing by the data subject should be handled appropriately.

## Data Security and Confidentiality

A workflow should provide for the application of appropriate security measures, in order to guarantee the confidentiality, integrity, and availability of the data processed. Moreover, it should provide that any kind of interception, surveillance, monitoring, recording and storage of information is performed only with the data subject's consent or when allowed or mandated by the applicable legislation.

## Special Categories of Data

During the execution of a workflow, it should be guaranteed that processing of special categories of data (such as traffic and other communication data, sensitive and judicial data) is performed in compliance with the specific requirements that the applicable data protection legislation sets forth for said categories of data, and taking into consideration any limitations applying to the purposes for which said special categories of personal data may be processed.

## Access Limitation

In the context of workflow execution, it should be made sure that the appropriate access level to data is granted to the different actors participating in the workflow. The access level should be granted based on a variety of parameters, including, for instance, each individual user's role, as well as the types of data to be accessed. Further, when necessary, a workflow should provide for logging of all access to data, for accountability reasons.

## Data Retention and Storage

Personal data should be kept in identifiable form only for the time that is strictly necessary for carrying out the associated activity. Personal data that are redundant or no longer needed should be deleted or anonymised. Further, there should be compliance with the requirements set by applicable data retention regulations (e.g., European Parliament and Council, 2006). This implies that specific data that are subject to retention should be stored for the time periods specified under the applicable regulatory framework. Compliance with data retention law requirements may additionally imply the application of specific security requirements prior to data storage and relevant access.

## Sharing of Data with Third Parties

When the execution of a workflow involves the participation of multiple organisations and, in this context, personal data are shared, data processing across the participating entities should comply with the underlying fair data practices. This is in particular important in cases where data are transferred to third countries, possibly with essentially different legislation regarding personal data collection and processing; compliance with the specific provisions ruling on transfer of data should be provided. For instance, consider the Safe Harbour Principles regulating data transfer between the European Union and the USA (European Commission, 2000).

## Flexibility and Adaptability of Legal Compliance Provisions

The domain of privacy protection has been characterised as a "regulatory jungle" (Pletscher, 2005). Given the complexity of the legal environment in which a distributed workflow involving heterogeneous organisations operates, the different legal requirements across different jurisdictions, and the law changing from time to time, flexibility and adaptability of workflow models is deemed necessary.

## Challenges for Workflow Systems

The elaboration of privacy principles and requirements has been the subject of various studies and extensive research (e.g., Solove, 2006; Lioudakis et al., 2010; Portela & Cruz-Cunha, 2010; Gutwirth et al., 2013). Rethought from the point of view of workflow environments, the corresponding principles converge to the following challenges:

- **Purpose:** The "purpose principle" is essential for privacy awareness, being a core part of data collection and processing lawfulness (European Parliament and Council, 1995); a workflow should comply with and provide for purpose specification and binding, and all actions should take place accordingly.
- **Access Rights Enforcement:** Any privacy violation certainly includes illicit access to personal data, resulting in the emergence of the field referred to as privacy-aware access control (Antonakopoulou et al., 2012). In workflows, access and usage control policies should be embedded in the models; this implies comprehensive task specification, as well as holistic, workflow-wide control.
- **Privacy-Aware Information Flow:** Beyond access and usage control, a workflow model should provide for "tracking" the data paths for possible flaws related to privacy, while information flows among computational units, stakeholders, even administrative domains.
- **Unlinkability:** A workflow might involve multiple data collection and retrieval points, fostering the danger of explicit or implicit data linkability; therefore, link-

ability should be controlled at the workflow model level, in terms of identification and prevention.

- **Context-Awareness:** It has become apparent that effective security and privacy policies largely depend on contextual parameters (Cuppens & Cuppens-Boulahia, 2008). A workflow should be self-adaptive with respect to underlying conditions, as well as the occurrence of events affecting its behaviour.
- **Separation of Duty and Binding of Duty (SoD/BoD):** They hold an important position among workflow authorisation requirements (Botha & Eloff, 2001), serving, among others, conflicts avoidance; effective enforcement may also be preventive for data linkability.
- **Data Subject Participation:** The role of the data subject is strongly entrenched, in the context of "self-determination"; this includes transparency and access rights, whereas a workflow should provide for information, consent, and privacy preferences elicitation.
- **Accountability:** Of particular importance in security and privacy, accountability in workflows implies, for instance, the incorporation of the appropriate means (especially in terms of tasks) for activities logging.
- **Semantics:** Vertical to all the above is the need for precise semantics of the underlying concepts; data, actors, actions, context, purposes, among others, should be semantically defined, fostering transparency, accountability and effectiveness in terms of privacy.

The future of privacy protection is manifested by the term *privacy by design* (Cavoukian, 2012), describing the concept whereby privacy compliance is designed *into* systems, inline with the requirement of Directive 95/46/EC for *"appropriate technical and organizational measures be taken, both at the time of the design of the processing system and at the time of the processing itself*". In fact, privacy by design is explicitly included in European Commission's proposal for the "General Data Protection Regulation" (European Commission, 2012).

Therefore, not only workflows and workflow management systems have to address the aforedescribed challenges, but they should also provide for their *by design* realisation. In this context, two broad needs are identified: first, the need for high expressiveness of workflow models, in order to be able to capture the associated provisions and incorporate comprehensive privacy policies in their design, and, second, the need for appropriate mechanisms for the evaluation of workflow models as far as their compliance is concerned. This implies workflow technologies that elaborate on all workflow perspectives outlined in the "Background" Section, as well as the identification of compliance aspects, being the structural requirements a workflow has to meet.

## LIMITATIONS OF CURRENT SYSTEMS

Current systems fail to address the above presented challenges at an adequate level. As far as modelling capabilities are concerned, BPMN supports quite a few control patterns, explicitly models access to and flow of data and possesses basic resource capturing capabilities. Still, it does not allow for fine-grained data modelling, nor does it provide for sophisticated resource assignment schemes or complex resource allocation constraints, like Separation of Duties. YAWL supports most control flow patterns and is remarkably powerful in capturing resourcing requirements; nevertheless, it lacks constructs explicitly capturing data elements and dependencies. Finally, scientific workflows do not even address the issue of assigning tasks to different resources, let alone associated authori-

sation considerations, due to the fact that, after their initiation, their execution proceeds mostly automatically. Moreover, even data modelling suffers from certain limitations, such as the lack of means for the detailed specification of the exchanged information itself.

From another viewpoint, a number of approaches have appeared in the literature aiming at ensuring that security and privacy are enforced during workflow execution. RBAC-WS-BPEL (Bertino, Crampton & Paci, 2006) specifies an extension to WS-BPEL, in order to implement role-based access control in workflows, while Ayed, Cuppens-Boulahia & Cuppens (2009) have introduced extensions to the OrBAC model (Cuppens & Cuppens-Boulahia, 2008), so that it can handle access and flow control in both intra- and inter-organisational workflow environments. In these solutions, however, security policies are eventually enforced at run-time and not during workflow formation. In some works (e.g., Wolter & Schaad, 2007; Wolter, Schaad & Meinel, 2008), the formal modelling of authorisation constraints as part of the workflow model specification is proposed, while approaches like the one by Wolter et al. (2009) go one step further by transforming, in a model-driven fashion, security goals modelled in the context of process models into concrete security implementations. Still, such work considers requirements specification to be under the control of the designer as part of the modelling procedure and not as an automated functionality performed on generated models, guided by a trusted knowledge base.

The latter can be achieved through either compliance-aware design or compliance checking mechanisms. In the former, requirements are automatically enforced in the design phase of new business processes (Goedertier & Vanthienen, 2006; Lu, Sadiq & Governatori, 2007). Conversely, compliance checking takes place in a post-design step, thus separating the modelling phase of a process model from the checking phase. Respective approaches, like the ones proposed by Governatori et al. (2009), Leyla et al. (2010), Awad, Weidlich & Weske (2011), are mostly based on formal methods, in order to ascertain the fulfilment of diverse requirements, while another field of related work deals with measuring the compliance degree of a given process model (Lu, Sadiq & Governatori, 2008). The above, albeit important and influential, are rather general-purpose frameworks, hence not always able to support particular needs related to privacy. In this direction, some interesting works that have recently appeared are the ones by Short & Kaluvuri (2011), Witt et al. (2012) and Alhaqbani et al. (2013), that emphasise on important facets of privacy awareness and propose solid solutions. Nevertheless, the workflow definition tools they are based on do not provide for adequate expressiveness regarding all privacy-related aspects, and, therefore, important factors are not considered in detail; finally, they do not address the issue of transforming workflow models towards privacy-compliant executable specifications.

## MODELLING REQUIREMENTS

The requirements outlined above result in the need for high expressiveness in all aspects of workflow modelling. At the level of a single task, proper enforcement of access rights implies effectively controlling the *operation* that *actor(s)* undertaking its execution perform on *asset(s)*, the latter being the object(s) on which the functionality of the task, reflected by its operation, is performed. In this sense, a task modelling approach should be able to capture these concepts, providing for the definition of valid {actor, operation, asset} structures. Furthermore, given that a workflow constitutes a hierarchical structure and tasks may be decomposed to elementary units and, inversely, compose higher level functional blocks scaling up to the level of the workflow, validity is fostered at all levels; thus, the human individual(s) intended to initiate the execution of the workflow must also be considered, as actors that act upon the workflow as a whole.

Similarly, in order to comprehensively express information flow, a number of factors must be incorporated. In particular, the detailed description of communicated data is necessary, since they denote the nature of information being accessed by the various tasks. Besides, distinct modelling of incoming data, independent from assets, is an additional step in achieving fine-grained control: though they may also constitute assets of the tasks receiving them, it might be the case that they serve only as input, without being affected by the corresponding tasks. On the other hand, the mere reading and consultation of a data item is considered processing activity, even if there is no storing or other manipulation of said information, and consequently should be controlled. What is more, the explicit modelling of inputs and assets serves to control data linkability, provided that also tasks are properly annotated, in order to denote the way they handle multiple incoming information or other sources thereof.

Going a step further, in order to achieve adequate expressiveness levels for fulfilling privacy requirements, additional concepts need to be captured and complement the basic features of tasks and information flow. To begin with, all elements described above have to be enriched with *attributes*, inline with attributed-based access and usage control models (e.g., Yuan & Tong, 2005). In fact, a comprehensive model cannot neglect the various attributes of data being processed and exchanged, actors, and operations, fostering fine-grained specification of the underlying concepts. Among them, an important characteristic of exchanged information is *data state*, i.e., the effect that preceding tasks have had on it, as opposed to its inherent properties. This is particularly useful for determining, e.g., if a data item has been anonymised by the time a task accesses it; indeed, anonymisation is critical for the level of data identifiability, thus affecting the restrictions applying to the corresponding data processing.

Data states and other attributes provide for the definition of constraints on the elements comprising a workflow that can be leveraged for enabling conditional behaviour of the latter. Nevertheless, these are not the only parameters that should be possible to be used in that respect; notable conditional behaviour enablers are also context and other external properties, the purpose underlying each action, as well as intra-workflow relations and dependencies. Along this line, a comprehensive workflow modelling approach should take contextual parameters into account. This concerns the application of respective constraints on tasks, in terms of conditional execution (e.g., alternative execution variants), and flow, enforcing conditional flow "routing", i.e., alternative control and data paths. Especially regarding flow, there are other external properties that must be able to be defined, as well, e.g., concerning secure communication means, like transmission of information over a trusted VPN connection.

With regard to the purpose principle, which constitutes a fundamental requirement for privacy awareness, the system must be able to identify the data processing purpose and ensure its lawfulness. One of the inherent implications workflows introduce is that data processing itself is not straightforward to determine, as it refers to both the processing performed by each individual task and the overall processing that data have been subject to along processing paths or after the execution of an entire workflow. In this direction, a well-elaborated approach is necessary, in order to introduce purpose-awareness at all abstraction levels of a workflow; therefore, purpose has to be associated with practically all participating entities (actors, operations, data, etc.) and be considered within the constraints that are referred to as *intra-workflow dependencies*. We use the latter term to describe interrelations among workflow elements that enable the definition of associations between them. These can be of various kinds; some representative examples are: the execution of a task, along with the associated parameters, are dependent on the purpose and/or the workflow initiator; the actor of a task should be the same as the actor of another; an actor that has accessed

a data item should not be granted with access to another; a task should not process two specific data items at the same time, etc.

Further, given that workflows favour collaboration and data exchange among many stakeholders, involving in some cases a number of different Controllers and Processors, even different jurisdictional domains, relevant information must also be explicitly mirrored in a workflow specification, associated with respective workflow tasks. Moreover, the appropriate means must be made available, that will assure the active role of certain entities, as are data subjects and competent data protection authorities; in that respect, transparency and configurability of the workflow system as to data subject preferences and applicable privacy provisions is necessary.

## ASPECTS OF COMPLIANCE EVALUATION

Apart from the comprehensive definition of workflow models, a holistic approach towards privacy compliance must involve sophisticated means for the evaluation of a workflow specification against a number of *compliance aspects*. Their main aim must be, on the one hand, to control access to and flow of information and prevent illegitimate activity, e.g., unlawful retention, while, on the other, to determine whether critical tasks are properly included and, if not, impose their execution, referring, for example, to information to, intervention of or consent by data subjects, notification to authorities, data storage or erasure, etc.

In the following sections, the main compliance aspects each workflow model must be evaluated against are elaborated upon. In brief, task and flow validity concern factors pertaining to the execution of individual tasks and direct associations among them, respectively. Furthermore, and borrowing some terminology from Awad, Weidlich & Weske (2011), before-, after-, parallel- and global-scope presence refer to the need for certain tasks to participate in the workflow; regarding each of them, a further distinction is made between requirements concerning mere sequential ordering of tasks, based on fundamental temporal relations as formalised by Allen's interval algebra (Allen, 1984), and those focusing on data processing interrelations. Finally, forbiddance refers to indirectly related tasks or flows that are not allowed to coexist in the same executing instance of the workflow. It is noted that, though not explicitly mentioned in each different case, all these aspects must additionally consider the purpose(s) served by the workflow, as well as the initiator(s) intended to trigger its execution; further, they all may on occasion be subject to various constraints, as are external conditions, the presence of certain tasks in the workflow (constituting, for instance, prerequisites for the enforcement of the corresponding requirements), or the way some of them are to be executed (e.g., particular actors defined).

## Task Validity

Each individual task must be privacy-compliant as an autonomous executable unit. This implies that the corresponding operation must be performed by an authorised actor, that may refer to any entity "capable of doing work" (Russel et al., 2005), human or non human (e.g., software), departments, organisations, etc., while it must affect associated assets, data or other, in a legitimate manner. Furthermore, each task, as overall defined, is considered to serve certain purposes, at least one of which must be compatible with the purpose served by the workflow as a whole, as well as with the purposes served by all other workflow tasks. For instance, in a workflow running in a hospital for the purpose of "providing medical treatment", an "EHR" (asset) may be "retrieved" (operation) only by an individual holding the role "Doctor" (actor); in addition, and as an example of constraints for defining intra-workflow dependencies mentioned above, it may be required that said doctor must

be the same person as the actor of the task "treat patient", leading to the specification of a BoD constraint between the two tasks.

## Flow Validity

The major factor that renders privacy implications harder to tackle in the context of workflows is the flow of information among computational units, stakeholders, even administrative domains. Considering also that, as aforementioned, even read access to data legally constitutes a form of data processing, it is necessary that for every two tasks connected through a direct control or data flow relation (edge), the information exchange between them, but also mere task succession, is legitimate. This specifically concerns the types of information communicated, if any, properties that may characterise them or some particular state that they might or might not be in. If such requirements are not fulfilled, it is often the case that appropriate tasks must be inserted into the path, in order to perform the necessary data transformations that will render the information flow compatible with the corresponding access provisions. Finally, it must also be ensured that properties related to low-level data transfer mechanisms, e.g., communication means or protocols, adequately provide for data security and confidentiality.

## Before-Scope Presence

With a particular workflow task as reference, there may be the requirement that other tasks have preceded in the course of workflow execution. This may take a number of forms, depending on the exact data processing relations or temporal restrictions it implies.

To begin with, a reference task $T_A$ may *require input* from task $T_B$. This basically dictates that $T_B$ must have already completed its execution and subsequently provided (some of) its output to $T_A$; therefore, in terms of workflow graph topology,

$T_B$ must belong to all possible alternative paths that may lead to $T_A$ at run time, while there must also be an edge connecting the two tasks and carrying the desired input (in terms of data types, attributes, etc.). Input requirement may appear in three variations, namely *simple, path-binding* and *direct-binding*. A simple input requirement indicates only the needed type of input and the task it must come from ($T_B$), not placing any restrictions as to the way $T_B$ is connected to the rest of the workflow, and can be satisfied by any topology ensuring said connection, e.g., Figure 1: a, b, c, e, f. Path-binding implies that $T_B$ must belong or

be connected (in terms of input relations) to an existing incoming path, even if it is not part of it, as in Figure 1: b, c, f. For example, $T_A$ may need to additionally receive as input a hash calculated on the data it receives, in order to validate their integrity. In a stricter version, direct-binding poses the additional constraint that $T_B$ must be performed on some input directly provided to $T_A$ or, in general, be related to a task directly providing some input to $T_A$ (Figure 1: f).

Another type of requirement concerning preceding data associations is the one of *data origin*, implying that the input to $T_A$ must have

*Figure 1. Indicative topological patterns satisfying before scope presence*

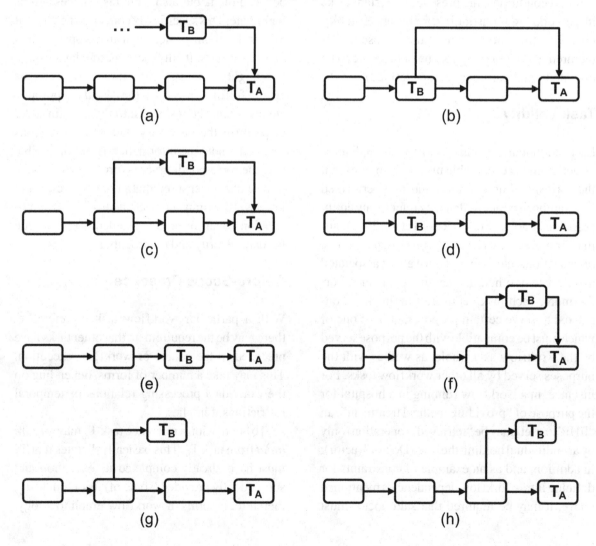

been generated or at least undergone some (pre-) processing by $T_B$ (Figure 1: b, d, e). Slightly different, *complementary pre-processing* by $T_B$ may be required, whereby the data fed as input to $T_A$, or data that appear in an incoming data path, must be subject to processing by $T_B$ at some point before $T_A$ is executed; such a requirement is fulfilled by all patterns of Figure 1. In contrast with data origin, though, data do not necessarily have to pass *through* $T_B$, which may as well dangle from the corresponding incoming flow, as shown in Figure 1: c, f, g, h. Complementary pre-processing is *path-binding* per se, implying that $T_B$ must have "affected" all relevant data in all corresponding incoming paths, no matter at which point exactly. For instance, before mitigating an incident that may result in personal data leakage, all corresponding alerts must have been previously stored for offline analysis. Somewhat stricter, *direct-binding* refers to the need to process accordingly the data during the final step, i.e., as currently provided to $T_A$ by another directly preceding task (e.g., in order to ensure that the last updated version of the data is considered), like in Figure 1: e, f, h.

Finally, a *data state requirement* implies that data provided as input to a task $T_A$ must before have been subject to processing by $T_B$ affecting their state. This resembles a data origin requirement, with the main difference being that special caution must be taken so that this state is not reversed in the meantime. As an example, consider the case where $T_A$ is only allowed to be executed on pseudonymised data; in such an occasion, not only must task $T_B$ performing pseudonymisation be located in all paths delivering said data to $T_A$, but there must also be no task between $T_B$ and $T_A$ reversing pseudonymisation.

On the other hand, from the perspective of execution sequence of tasks, $T_B$ may be necessary to have executed *immediately before* $T_A$. In other words, before $T_A$ starts its execution, $T_B$ must have just completed, i.e., it must be the last thing to have been executed before $T_A$ (Figure 1: f). For instance, immediately before processing

some data, it may need to be checked whether the respective consent by the data subject exists and has not expired. Relaxing the above requirement, the *complementary execution* of $T_B$ *before* $T_A$ just dictates that the latter must be preceded by the execution of $T_B$. This does not imply that it must be immediately preceded by $T_B$, but only that $T_B$ must have occurred at least once in any case. In its *simple* form, it suffices that $T_B$ has already started, and is satisfied by all patterns in Figure 1; if defined as *blocking*, $T_B$ must additionally have already completed its execution (Figure 1: a, b, c, d, e, f).

## After-Scope Presence

In the same direction, certain tasks may be needed to be executed after a reference task $T_A$. When *direct post-processing* by $T_B$ on some data is required, the latter must be the task immediately following $T_A$ along the corresponding data path, so that the (part of the) output of $T_A$ that is of interest undergoes the specified modification before being further accessed and/or processed by any successive workflow task (Figure 2: b). This is the case of, e.g., the requirement that all output of a given task must be encrypted before being accessed by all following workflow tasks. On the other hand, *complementary direct post-processing* implies extra processing, in the sense that $T_A$ is required to directly communicate (some of) its output to $T_B$, in addition to any data associations it already participates in (Figure 2: b, c, d). For example, right after the execution of a task, it may be mandated that some associated data are immediately deleted. Apart from this *simple* form, this requirement may also appear as *combinative* with respect to following workflow tasks, meaning that the latter must take the output of $T_B$ into account, in order for the workflow to proceed (Figure 2: b, d). Finally, according to a *complementary post-processing* requirement, constituting the least strict among data-oriented after-scope requirements, $T_B$ must be executed on some data produced/output by $T_A$ at some point along each alternative outgoing data path. In this case, direct proximity is not mandatory, as long as $T_B$ processes the correct data, irrespective of the tasks that have in the meantime been executed (satisfied by all patterns in Figure 2).

Regarding sequential ordering of tasks, $T_B$ may be required to be executed *immediately after* $T_A$ has completed (Figure 2: b, c, d). Indicatively, it may be necessary that when an incident has occurred, the Privacy Officer must immediately be notified thereof. Such a requirement may in some cases appear as *blocking*, in the sense that $T_B$ must also complete in order for the workflow to proceed (Figure 2: b, d). Besides the above, the necessity of the *complementary execution* of $T_B$ *after* $T_A$ regardless of its proximity may also arise. In such case, there are no temporal concerns other than $T_B$ commencing after $T_A$ has completed (all patterns in Figure 2).

## Parallel-Scope Presence

A separate category of requirements concerns parallelism in task execution. From the viewpoint of execution order, *complementary parallel execution* refers to the case that $T_A$ and $T_B$ must start at the same time, i.e., after the completion of the immediately preceding task(s), the execution token must simultaneously pass to both of them (Figure 3: a, b). Such a requirement being additionally characterised as *blocking*, means that both $T_A$ and $T_B$ must have completed before the workflow proceeds (Figure 3: b). When the emphasis is on information flow, though, parallelism may acquire different semantics, disregarding strict temporal constraints like the above. In that respect, *complementary parallel processing* requires that $T_A$ and $T_B$ must be executed based on the same or associated input, i.e., their input must originate from or be related to the same preceding task (Figure 3: a, b). For instance, when some data are communicated to a task undertaking their

*Figure 2. Indicative topological patterns satisfying after-scope presence*

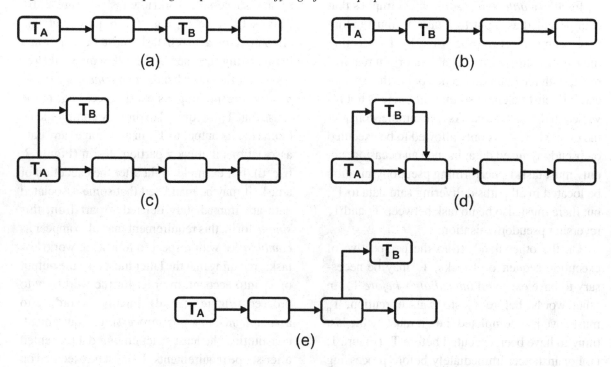

deletion, it may be required that, in parallel, all their copies are also deleted. In a stricter version, complementary parallel processing may appear as *combinative*, indicating that following tasks must be executed based jointly on the outputs of $T_A$ and $T_B$ (Figure 3: b).

## Global-Scope Presence

A task might be required to be executed in a given workflow, regardless of its position or relative ordering with respect to the rest of workflow tasks. From the perspective of mere task sequence, such a requirement, being referred to as *task existence*, may or may not stem from the presence of a reference task; it may, for instance, depend solely on the purpose and/or initiator linked to the workflow as a whole. In any case, it suffices that the required task appears at least once in every executable instance of the workflow graph. However, in a more restrictive sense, the existence of a task may be required to be present along a specific data path, so as to ensure that corresponding data undergo some particular processing during their lifetime in the workflow, with no interest on the exact stage that this happens.

## Forbiddance

Besides the requirements mandating the presence of certain tasks within the flow, others may forbid the execution of tasks or associations among them. At the level of individual tasks and direct flow relations, forbiddance is covered by the requirements for task and flow validity, respectively, described above. Extending forbiddance at larger scale, i.e., indirect flow relations, two tasks may be considered as mutually exclusive in a specific or any relative position within the same workflow. In terms of plain sequential ordering, the execution of a reference task $T_A$ might prohibit the execution of $T_B$ at any point before, after, in parallel or anywhere in the workflow, e.g., Figure 4: a, b, c. For example, in the direction of preventing data linkability, it may be prohibited that in an order processing workflow the same person handles both the preparation of an order and corresponding customer billing, in order to prevent any employee from knowing who has bought what (SoD). With a focus on the flow of data among processing activities, a forbiddance may be localised along the path that the data of interest traverse, implying that $T_A$ and $T_B$ must not access or affect the same data.

Finally, it may also be the case that the forbiddance does not concern the tasks themselves but rather the flows that connect them. As a simple example, depicted in Figure 4: d, it may be required that, given the data flow between $T_B$ and $T_A$ resulting in $T_A$ acquiring read access to an information item $II_1$, another task $T_C$ must not provide another information item $II_2$ to $T_A$; notably, $T_C$ itself may be allowed, or even the exact same flow between $T_C$ and $T_A$ might be absolutely acceptable, if it were not for the flow between $T_B$ and $T_A$ already present.

*Figure 3. Indicative topological patterns satisfying parallel-scope presence*

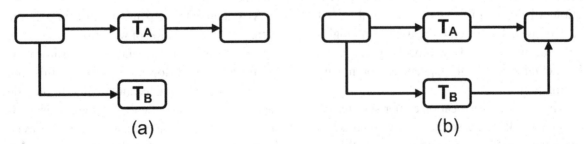

(a)                              (b)

*Figure 4. Indicative topological patterns related to forbiddance requirements*

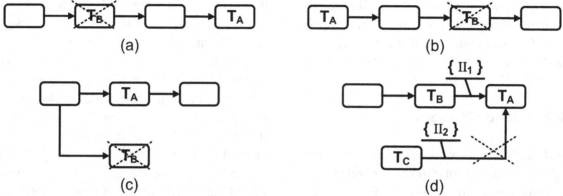

## FUTURE RESEARCH DIRECTIONS

Although it will soon be a regulatory requirement, *Privacy by Design* is still far from being adequately realised in contemporary information systems, especially the ones characterised by a significant degree of distribution in terms of control, as are workflows. From the analysis, it is derived that a framework able to address respective challenges must possess two core features: a comprehensive workflow modelling mechanism able to capture the privacy aspects *in* the workflow specification, and a procedure for the automatic privacy-aware verification and transformation of workflows, resulting in compliant specifications. These two aspects comprise the main prospective research directions.

Future workflow modelling research should focus on broadening coverage of workflow patterns, towards providing adequate support for data and resource perspectives. In this context, current models should be appropriately extended, and enriched with suitable structures for the specification of behavioural policies as integral part of the activities. To this end, the use of ontologies as the means for workflow models specification (Koukovini et al., 2014) appears as a promising starting point.

Privacy-aware verification comprises a recent research field; while some mature approaches have emerged (Short & Kaluvuri, 2011; Witt et al., 2012; Alhaqbani et al., 2013), there is much work to be done especially in the direction of compliance-oriented transformation. In that respect, the use of sophisticated privacy-aware policy models (e.g., Papagiannakopoulou et al., 2013) has to be considered, whereas, towards enhancing flexibility, devising the appropriate mechanisms for dynamic workflow adaptation according to privacy provisions at run-time represents another interesting research direction.

## CONCLUSION

"The machine is the problem: the solution is in the machine" (Poullet, 2006); along this line, this chapter, starting with a brief analysis of the legal and regulatory provisions regarding privacy in information systems, has investigated the special requirements and needs related to privacy that workflows present, stressing the value of making privacy awareness an integral part of workflow systems.

A fundamental step in this direction is the expressive specification of workflows, so that all aspects of importance to data protection are incorporated at the workflow model level. To this end, a workflow modelling technology has to provide the means for the specification of the corresponding, sometimes complex, associations between the elements comprising the workflow, while enabling the comprehensive semantic definition of underlying concepts. Further, automated methods are needed for the verification of any workflow model against privacy provisions, so that its lawful execution can be guaranteed. In that respect, the chapter has also presented basic compliance aspects to be considered, from the viewpoint of individual tasks but also their (direct or indirect) interrelations; these aspects refer to valid task and flow specifications, including positive (presence) and negative (forbiddance) requirements, while covering a wide range of flow topology patterns.

## ACKNOWLEDGMENT

The research of M. N. Koukovini is co-financed by the European Union (European Social Fund – ESF) and Greek national funds through the Operational Program "Education and Lifelong Learning" of the National Strategic Reference Framework (NSRF) – Research Funding Program: Heracleitus II: Investing in knowledge society through the European Social Fund.

## REFERENCES

Alhaqbani, B., Adams, M., Fidge, C. J., & ter Hofstede, A. H. M. (2013). Privacy-Aware Workflow Management. In M. Glykas (Ed.), *Business Process Management: Theory and Applications* (pp. 111–128). Berlin, Germany: Springer. doi:10.1007/978-3-642-28409-0_5

Allen, J. F. (1984). Towards a general theory of action and time. *Artificial Intelligence*, *23*(2), 123–154. doi:10.1016/0004-3702(84)90008-0

Antonakopoulou, A., Lioudakis, G. V., Gogoulos, F., Kaklamani, D. I., & Venieris, I. S. (2012). Leveraging Access Control for Privacy Protection: A Survey. In G. Yee (Ed.), *Privacy protection measures and technologies in business organizations: aspects and standards* (pp. 65–94). Hershey, PA: IGI Global.

Article 29 Data Protection Working Party. (2003). *Working Document on E-Government*. Retrieved November 30, 2013, from http://ec.europa.eu/justice/policies/privacy/docs/wpdocs/2003/e-government_en.pdf

Article 29 Data Protection Working Party. (2007). *Working Document on the processing of personal data relating to health in electronic health records (EHR)*. Retrieved November 30, 2013, from http://ec.europa.eu/justice/policies/privacy/docs/wpdocs/2007/wp131_en.pdf

Awad, A., Weidlich, M., & Weske, M. (2011). Visually Specifying Compliance Rules and Explaining their Violations for Business Processes. *Journal of Visual Languages and Computing*, *22*(1), 30–55. doi:10.1016/j.jvlc.2010.11.002

Ayed, A., Cuppens-Boulahia, N., & Cuppens, F. (2009). Deploying security policy in intra and inter workflow management systems. In *Proceedings of the 2009 International Conference on Availability, Reliability and Security (ARES 2009)* (pp. 58–65). Washington, DC: IEEE Computer Society.

Bertino, E., Crampton, J., & Paci, F. (2006). Access Control and Authorization Constraints for WS-BPEL. In *Proceedings of the 2006 International Conference on Web Services (ICWS 2006)* (pp. 275–284). Washington, DC: IEEE Computer Society.

Birnhack, M. D. (2008). The EU Data Protection Directive: An engine of a global regime. *Computer Law & Security Report*, *24*(6), 508–520. doi:10.1016/j.clsr.2008.09.001

Botha, R. A., & Eloff, J. H. P. (2001). Separation of duties for access control enforcement in workflow environments. *IBM Systems Journal*, *40*(3), 666–682. doi:10.1147/sj.403.0666

Cavoukian, A. (2012). Privacy by Design: Origins, Meaning, and Prospects for Assuring Privacy and Trust in the Information Era. In G. Yee (Ed.), *Privacy Protection Measures and Technologies in Business Organizations: Aspects and Standards* (pp. 170–208). New York: IGI Global Pubs.

Churches, D., Gombas, G., Harrison, A., Maassen, J., Robinson, C., & Shields, M. et al. (2006). Programming scientific and distributed workflow with Triana services. *Concurrency and Computation*, 18(10), 1021–1037. doi:10.1002/cpe.992

Cuppens, F., & Cuppens-Boulahia, N. (2008). Modeling contextual security policies. [Berlin, Germany: Springer.]. *International Journal of Information Security*, 7(4), 285–305. doi:10.1007/s10207-007-0051-9

European Commission. (2000). Commission Decision of 26 July 2000 pursuant to Directive 95/46/EC of the European Parliament and of the Council on the adequacy of the protection provided by the safe harbour privacy principles and related frequently asked questions issued by the US Department of Commerce. *Official Journal of the European Communities, L 215*, 7–47.

European Commission. (2012). *Proposal for a Regulation of the European Parliament and of the Council on the protection of individuals with regard to the processing of personal data and on the free movement of such data (General Data Protection Regulation)*. Retrieved November 30, 2013, from http://eur-lex.europa.eu/LexUriServ/LexUriServ.do?uri=COM:2012:0011:FIN:EN:PDF

European Parliament, Council, & Commission. (2000). Charter of Fundamental Rights of the European Union. *Official Journal of the European Communities, C 364*, 1–22.

European Parliament and Council. (1995). Directive 95/46/EC of the European Parliament and of the Council on the protection of individuals with regard to the processing of personal data and on the free movement of such data. *Official Journal of the European Communities, L 281*, 31–50.

European Parliament and Council. (2002). Directive 2002/58/EC of the European Parliament and of the Council concerning the processing of personal data and the protection of privacy in the electronic communications sector (Directive on privacy and electronic communications). *Official Journal of the European Communities, L 201*, 37–47.

European Parliament and Council. (2006). Directive 2006/24/EC of the European Parliament and of the Council of 15 March 2006 on the retention of data generated or processed in connection with the provision of publicly available electronic communications services or of public communications networks and amending Directive 2002/58/EC. *Official Journal of the European Communities, L 105*, 54–63.

Goedertier, S., & Vanthienen, J. (2006). Designing Compliant Business Processes with Obligations and Permissions. In J. Eder, & S. Dustdar (Eds.), *Business Process Management Workshops, LNCS 4103* (pp. 5–14). Berlin, Germany: Springer. doi:10.1007/11837862_2

Governatori, G., Hoffmann, J., Sadiq, S. W., & Weber, I. (2009). Detecting Regulatory Compliance for Business Process Models through Semantic Annotations. In D. Ardagna, M. Mecella, & J. Yang (Eds.), *Business Process Management Workshops 2008, LNBIP 17* (pp. 5–17). Berlin, Germany: Springer. doi:10.1007/978-3-642-00328-8_2

Greenleaf, G. (in press). Sheherezade and the 101 Data Privacy Laws: Origins, Significance and Global Trajectories. *Journal of Law & Information Science*.

Gutwirth, S., Leenes, R., De Hert, P., & Poullet, Y. (Eds.). (2013). *European Data Protection: Coming of Age*. Berlin, Germany: Springer. doi:10.1007/978-94-007-5170-5

Jablonski, S., & Bussler, C. (1996). *Workflow management — modeling concepts, architecture and implementation*. London, UK: International Thomson Computer Press.

Koukovini, M. N., Papagiannakopoulou, E. I., Lioudakis, G. V., Dellas, N. L., Kaklamani, D. I., & Venieris, I. S. (2014). An ontology-based approach towards comprehensive workflow modelling. *IET Software*.

Leyla, N., Mashiyat, A. S., Wang, H., & MacCaull, W. (2010). Towards workflow verification. In H. A. Müller, A. G. Ryman, & A. W. Kark (Eds.), *Proceedings of the 2010 Conference of the Center for Advanced Studies on Collaborative Research (CASCON 2010)* (pp. 253–267). Riverton, NJ: IBM.

Lioudakis, G. V., Gaudino, F., Boschi, E., Bianchi, G., Kaklamani, D. I., & Venieris, I. S. (2010). Legislation-Aware Privacy Protection in Passive Network Monitoring. In I. M. Portela, & M. M. Cruz-Cunha (Eds.), *Information Communication Technology Law, Protection and Access Rights: Global Approaches and Issues* (pp. 363–383). New York: IGI Global Pubs. doi:10.4018/978-1-61520-975-0.ch022

Lu, R., Sadiq, S., & Governatori, G. (2007). Modeling of Task-Based Authorization Constraints in BPMN. In A. H. M. ter Hofstede, B. Benatallah, & H.-Y. Paik (Eds.), *Business Process Management Workshops, LNCS 4928* (pp. 120–131). Berlin, Germany: Springer.

Lu, R., Sadiq, S., & Governatori, G. (2008). Measurement of Compliance Distance in Business Processes. *Information Systems Management, 25*(4), 344–355. doi:10.1080/10580530802384613

Ludäscher, B., Altintas, I., Berkley, C., Higgins, D., Jaeger, E., & Jones, M. et al. (2006). Scientific workflow management and the Kepler system. *Concurrency and Computation, 18*(10), 1039–1065. doi:10.1002/cpe.994

Ludäscher, B., Altintas, I., Bowers, S., Cummings, J., Critchlow, T., & Deelman, E. et al. (2009a). Scientific Process Automation and Workflow Management. In A. Shoshani, & D. Rotem (Eds.), *Scientific Data Management: Challenges, Technologies and Deployment* (pp. 467–508). Chapman & Hall/CRC. doi:10.1201/9781420069815-c13

Ludäscher, B., Weske, M., McPhillips, T., & Bowers, S. (2009b). Scientific Workflows: Business as Usual? In U. Dayal, J. Eder, J. Koehler, & H. Reijers (Eds.), *Business Process Management, LNCS 5701* (pp. 31–47). Berlin, Germany: Springer. doi:10.1007/978-3-642-03848-8_4

Object Management Group (OMG). (2011). *Business Process Modeling Notation (BPMN) Version 2.0*. Retrieved November 30, 2013, from http://www.omg.org/spec/BPMN/2.0/

Palanisamy, R., & Mukerji, B. (2012). Security and Privacy Issues in E-Government. In M. A. Shareef, N. Archer, & S. Dutta (Eds.), *E-Government Service Maturity and Development: Cultural, Organizational and Technological Perspectives* (pp. 236–248). New York: IGI Global Pubs.

Papagiannakopoulou, E. I., Koukovini, M. N., Lioudakis, G. V., Garcia-Alfaro, J., Kaklamani, D. I., & Venieris, I. S. et al. (2013). A Privacy-Aware Access Control Model for Distributed Network Monitoring. *Computers & Electrical Engineering, 39*(7), 2263–2281. doi:10.1016/j.compeleceng.2012.08.003

Papazoglou, M. P., & van den Heuvel, W.-J. (2007). Service Oriented Architectures: Approaches, Technologies and Research Issues. *The VLDB Journal, 16*(3), 389–415. doi:10.1007/s00778-007-0044-3

Petri, C. A. (1962). *Kommunikation mit Automaten.* (Ph. D. Thesis). University of Bonn, Bonn, Germany.

Pletscher, T. (2005). *Companies and the Regulatory Jungle.* Paper presented at the 27th International Conference of Data Protection and Privacy Commissioners. Monteux, Switzerland.

Portela, I. M., & Cruz-Cunha, M. M. (Eds.). (2010). *Information Communication Technology Law, Protection and Access Rights: Global Approaches and Issues.* New York: IGI Global Pubs. doi:10.4018/978-1-61520-975-0

Poullet, Y. (2006). The Directive 95/46/EC: Ten Years After. *Computer Law & Security Report, 22*(3), 206–217. doi:10.1016/j.clsr.2006.03.004

Russell, N., & ter Hofstede, A. H. M. (2009). newYAWL: towards workflow 2.0. In L. K. Jensen, & W. M. P. van der Aalst (Eds.), Transactions on Petri Nets and Other Models of Concurrency II, (LNCS) (vol. 5460, pp. 79–97). Berlin, Germany: Springer.

Russell, N., ter Hofstede, A. H. M., Edmond, D., & van der Aalst, W. M. P. (2005a). Workflow data patterns: identification, representation and tool support. In L. Delcambre, C. Kop, H. C. Mayr, J. Mylopoulos, & O. Pastor (Eds.), *Proceedings of the 24th International Conference on Conceptual Modeling (ER 2005),* (LNCS) (vol. 3716, pp. 353–368). Berlin, Germany: Springer.

Russell, N., ter Hofstede, A. H. M., van der Aalst, W. M. P., & Edmond, D. (2005b). Workflow resource patterns: identification, representation and tool support. In O. Pastor, & J. Falcão e Cunha (Eds.), *Proceedings of the 17th International Conference on Advanced Information Systems Engineering (CAiSE 2005),* (LNCS) (vol. 3520, pp. 216–232). Berlin, Germany: Springer.

Russell, N., ter Hofstede, A. H. M., van der Aalst, W. M. P., & Mulyar, N. (2006). *Workflow Control-Flow Patterns: A Revised View.* Technical Report BPM-06-22. BPM Center.

Short, S., & Kaluvuri, S. P. (2011). A Data-Centric Approach for Privacy-Aware Business Process Enablement. In M. van Sinderen & P. Johnson (Eds.), *Proceedings of the 3rd International IFIP Working Conference on Enterprise Interoperability (IWIT 2011), LNBIP 76* (pp. 191–203). Berlin, Germany: Springer.

Solove, D. J. (2006). A Brief History of Information Privacy Law. In C. Wolf (Ed.), *Proskauer on Privacy: A Guide to Privacy and Data Security Law in the Information Age* (pp. 1–46). New York: Practising Law Institute.

United Nations. (1948). *Universal Declaration of Human Rights.* Retrieved November 30, 2013, from http://www.ohchr.org/EN/UDHR/Documents/60UDHR/bookleten.pdf

U.S. Congress. (1996). Health Insurance Portability and Accountability Act. *Public Law,* 104–191.

van der Aalst, W. M. P., & ter Hofstede, A. H. M. (2005). YAWL: yet another workflow language. *Information Systems, 30*(4), 245–275. doi:10.1016/j.is.2004.02.002

van der Aalst, W. M. P., ter Hofstede, A. H. M., Kiepuszewski, B., & Barros, A. P. (2003). Workflow Patterns. *Distributed and Parallel Databases, 14*(1), 5–51. doi:10.1023/A:1022883727209

Witt, S., Feja, S., Speck, A., & Prietz, C. (2012). Integrated privacy modeling and validation for business process models, In *EDBT/ICDT Workshops (EDBT-ICDT '12)* (pp. 196–205). New York, NY, USA: ACM.

Wolter, C., Menzel, M., Schaad, A., Miseldine, P., & Meinel, C. (2009). Model-driven business process security requirement specification. *Journal of Systems Architecture*, *55*(4), 211–223. doi:10.1016/j.sysarc.2008.10.002

Wolter, C., & Schaad, A. (2007). Modeling of Task-Based Authorization Constraints in BPMN. In G. Alonso, P. Dadam, & M. Rosemann (Eds.), *Business Process Management, LNCS 4714* (pp. 64–79). Berlin, Germany: Springer. doi:10.1007/978-3-540-75183-0_5

Wolter, C., Schaad, A., & Meinel, C. (2008). Task-Based Entailment Constraints for Basic Workflow Patterns. In I. Ray, & N. Li (Eds.), *Proceedings of the 13th ACM Symposium on Access Control Models (SACMAT 2008)* (pp. 51–60). New York, NY: ACM.

Workflow Management Coalition (WfMC). (1995). *The Workflow Reference Model — Issue 1.1*. Retrieved November 30, 2013, from http://www.wfmc.org/reference-model.html

Yuan, E., & Tong, J. (2005). Attributed Based Access Control (ABAC) for Web Services. In *Proceedings of IEEE International Conference on Web Services (ICWS '05)* (pp. 561–569). Washington, DC: IEEE Computer Society.

## KEY TERMS AND DEFINITIONS

**Binding of Duty (BoD):** The requirement that an entity performing an action is bound to perform another action.

**Personal Data:** Any information relating to an identified or identifiable natural person.

**Privacy:** The claim of individuals, groups, or institutions to determine for themselves when, how, and to what extent information about them is communicated to others.

**Privacy-Aware Access Control:** The access control discipline devised for the protection of personal data.

**Privacy by Design:** The concept whereby privacy compliance is designed into systems.

**Separation of Duty (SoD):** The situation where two actions are mutually exclusive to be performed by the same entity.

**Workflow:** A well-defined sequence of tasks coordinated in order to achieve a business, scientific or engineering goal.

**Workflow Model:** The conceptual representation of the structure of a workflow in terms of tasks, as well as control and data dependencies among tasks.

**Workflow Patterns:** Abstractions of recurrent interaction forms that arise in workflow modeling.

**Workflow Perspectives:** The different aspects from which a workflow can be viewed and that affect its execution.

# Chapter 12
# Forensic Readiness and eDiscovery

**Dauda Sule**
*Audit Associates Ltd, Nigeria*

## ABSTRACT

*In a bid to discover, uncover, and stamp out digital crime while ensuring information security and assurance, there is a need to investigate the crime once it has taken place. This will help trace the criminals and also secure an organization against future attacks. Forensic readiness entails that an organization be at alert in terms of digital evidence collection and storage – that is, collecting and storing such evidence constantly in a forensically sound manner, not just when the need for such evidence arises. In the event litigation arises or is anticipated, digital evidence may need to be reviewed by the opposing parties prior to court proceedings to assess quality of the evidence; this is eDiscovery. This chapter explores eDiscovery and forensic readiness. Digital evidence for eDiscovery needs to be forensically sound and provided in a timely and efficient manner - forensic readiness helps to ensure this. This chapter seeks to establish how forensic readiness is relevant to the eDiscovery process.*

## INTRODUCTION

In this digital age, issues pertaining to information security and assurance abound; and with increased technological advancements, criminals are also improving on their skills and causing more and more havoc. Digital forensic investigations are one way of ensuring information assurance and security; in that it can lead to discovering how a digital crime was committed and possibly tracing and apprehending the perpetrators. Knowing how a digital crime was committed can also assist an organization strengthen its defenses as it reveals weaknesses and lapses in the organization's information security and assurance measures. Forensic readiness requires that an organization

be on its toes as regards gathering, storing and analyzing digital data in a forensically sound manner – such data has the potential of serving as digital evidence in the event of an incident or litigation. Such digital evidence can be used by an organization to trace how an incident happened, defend itself or indict a party, also to show regulatory compliance and best practices. With forensic readiness, investigations can be carried out faster and more efficiently with minimal disruption to normal operations, and it also reduces the cost of such evidence gathering. Electronic evidence is constantly gathered and stored until something occurs whereby it would be required to serve as evidence or used for backup and recovery – it is like saving for a rainy day. Therefore in the event of an

DOI: 10.4018/978-1-4666-6324-4.ch012

incident that requires investigation, the evidence only has to be presented, as it is already collected and stored in a forensically sound manner. This helps make evidence presentation and investigation much faster and allows for business continuity with minimal disruption to normal operations, which would have arisen if investigators had to gather the evidence after-the-fact. It also helps ensure that an attacker does not cover his tracks after an attack as evidence is collected before, during and after the breach – collecting evidence after the breach could afford an attacker time to wipe out his tracks before evidence gathering and investigations begin.

eDiscovery on the other hand comes up when there is litigation or litigation is anticipated, requiring opposing parties in litigation to possibly review each others' digital evidence to assess its quality prior to court proceedings. eDiscovery may also be viewed as the sum total of the processes involved in a digital investigation including evidence gathering and analysis. Seigle-Morris (2013) considered the whole point of eDiscovery to be reduction of data volume that requires review into a manageable and easily reviewable form, extracting only that which is relevant to the case at hand. eDiscovery can be a very delicate issue, its rules and guidelines have to be safeguarded by both parties in litigation. The digital evidence has to be forensically sound, timely, relevant, and in the format required by the requesting party; failure to meet up with the rules and guidelines can result in severe consequences for the erring party. In the case of *AMD vs. Intel (2005)*, Intel failed to provide digital evidence as requested by AMD in good time, resulting in heavy costs to Intel at the end of the day.

From the point of view of eDiscovery being litigation requirements for digital evidence review prior to court proceedings and the view that eDiscovery is the process of digital investigations, there is the need to have digital evidence collected in a forensically sound manner and for it to be provided in a timely and efficient manner. In order to achieve this, it would be best to collect

and store such evidence constantly, not only when the need for it arises – that is forensic readiness. Forensic readiness ensures constant collection of digital evidence in a forensically sound manner making the eDiscovery process much easier and efficient. Forensic readiness goes a long way in ensuring that an organization is adequately prepared for eDiscovery.

## BACKGROUND

The field of digital forensics is still an emerging one – there are not really any firmly established principles for it yet, although there are guidelines available. Digital forensics is an important aspect of information security especially in this digital age, it is used to investigate and establish proof of crimes committed using IT resources and platforms. Every activity carried out using IT systems and platforms leaves a digital footprint and tends to be stored in the form of Electronically Stored Information (ESI). A review of ESI can reveal a lot about what had occurred on the system and/ or platform.

Sule (2013) defined digital forensics as the use of computer and information systems knowledge, coupled with legal knowledge to analyze in a way that is legally acceptable digital evidence acquired, processed and stored in a legally acceptable manner. This definition takes into cognizance that digital forensics is where technology and the law meet. There is an emphasis on legal acceptability of evidence as it is usually the case that digital evidence will end up being used for civil or criminal court proceedings, bearing in mind that legal acceptability varies from country to country, and jurisdiction to jurisdiction. The most important thing is to ensure that the evidence is collected, stored and analyzed in a forensically sound manner to provide reasonable assurance that the evidence was not tampered with or damaged and also not giving room for anyone to claim such. Others have a more open definition of digital forensics without much emphasis on legal acceptability, as digital evidence may be collected and analyzed without any need for going to court; for example it could be used for internal consumption in an organization or for learning and experimentation or even just for fun by individuals. Kassner (2011) got a definition of digital forensics from Eric Huber simply as the collection, examination and reporting of digital evidence. It depends on how one looks at it, it is possible to carry out digital investigations without it resulting in either a civil or criminal court case, that would still be considered digital forensics; however, due care still has to be taken to ensure that the evidence is collected in a legally acceptable manner as the evidence still has potential of being used in legal proceedings.

The term "forensically sound" means that digital evidence should be collected, analyzed, handled and stored in such a way that it is not contaminated or corrupted, leading to doubts about its authenticity. One important way of assuring forensic soundness of digital evidence is the chain of custody. The chain of custody (also known as continuity of evidence in some jurisdictions) documents everything that happened to the digital evidence from point of acquisition to presentation in court - it records everything including who handled the evidence and when, and how and where it was stored, etc. This gives reasonable assurance that the evidence was collected and handled in a forensically sound manner. It is part of best practices not to analyze digital evidence directly from a system, rather a bit stream image of the disk is taken which copies everything on the system as it is including sectors and clusters; this allows for analysis without damaging the actual digital evidence which is very volatile.

A lot of digital evidence is generated during normal day-to-day operations of an organization which can potentially serve as evidence when the need arises; they can also be used as backup, and for disaster recovery and business continuity as well as for document retention policies. Some of this digital evidence might have no apparent use until there is an incident or litigation, and at such

time if it was not previously collected, it may not be easily available, or it may not be available at all. Another issue is that one cannot predict when any digital evidence will be required, whether for internal use, legal or regulatory requirements, and so on. To avoid such pitfalls, a forensic readiness policy being in place in an organization goes a long way in ameliorating such problems. Forensic readiness was defined by Rowlingson (2004) as the ability of an organization to maximize its potential use of digital evidence while minimizing the cost of investigation. Digital evidence use is maximized by ensuring it is constantly collected and stored in a forensically sound manner; hence when the need for it arises it is readily available. The cost of investigations is greatly reduced as evidence was collected before, during and after an incident requiring it, hence no need to employ and pay extra fees to investigators. Cost is also reduced in terms of minimal disruption of normal operations as a result of investigations which could have adverse effects on the organization's productivity. The National Archives (2011) quoted the CESG, Good Practice Guide No. 18, Forensic Readiness as defining forensic readiness to be:

*The achievement of an appropriate level of capability by an organization in order for it to be able to collect, preserve, protect and analyze digital evidence so that this evidence can be effectively used in any legal matters, in disciplinary matters, in an employment tribunal or court of law (p. 8).*

This definition sheds some more light as to what the digital evidence could be used for; which is not only legal matters, but internal issues as well, like disciplinary issues, insurance claims and so on.

Discovery in legal terms refers to the process in which parties in a legal dispute review relevant documents that would serve as evidence which is in their opponent's possession; the review usually takes place before full court proceedings to enable the parties assess the quality of evidence the opposing team has which may result in a withdrawal of the case or an out of court settlement – whichever the party considers most favorable, especially in terms of cost. eDiscovery came into being as a result of technological advancements that led to virtually all organizational activities being carried out on one form of digital device or platform or the other. Hence, eDiscovery came about: being discovery of digital evidence from ESI. Volonino and Redpath (2010), and Sommer (2012) adopted this view of eDiscovery being an electronic version of traditional discovery which was paper based – that is to say digital evidence required for review before full court proceedings begin. Rouse (2010), however, defined eDiscovery as the process of seeking, locating, securing and searching for electronic data with the intent of using it as evidence in a civil or criminal case. This view was supported by Burns (2013) with a very similar definition. Hughes (2013) considered the previous view of eDiscovery being in the pre-trial phase as outdated, and that today, eDiscovery refers to the investigative process. This view of Rouse, Burns and Hughes defines eDiscovery to be very similar to our first view of digital forensics – that is collection, analysis and storage of digital evidence in a forensically sound manner for a legal case. The apparently conflicting views of eDiscovery, however, do not affect the discourse of this chapter; forensic readiness is important for eDiscovery either way. The first view would consider forensic readiness as a supportive measure, while the second view would consider it to be part of the eDiscovery process. Either way forensic readiness is an important measure for smooth, efficient and effective eDiscovery.

## FORENSIC READINESS AND THE EDISCOVERY PROCESS

The Electronic Discovery Reference Model (EDRM) is a nine step model developed in 2005 to create best practices and guidelines for eDiscovery, and serve as a standard for going through the process while adhering to the United Sates' Federal Rules of Civil Procedure (FRCP) (LWG Consulting, 2009). The origin of eDiscovery can be traced to the FRCP amendment which took place in 2006 which codified the need for ESI in legal proceedings (Childress, 2012), although precedent was set in 2002 in the case of *Zubulake vs. UBS Warburg*. The Electronic Discovery Reference Model is depicted in Figure 1.

The EDRM has the following stages as depicted in Figure 1:

1. Information Management.
2. Identification.
3. Preservation.
4. Collection.
5. Processing.
6. Review.
7. Analysis.
8. Production.
9. Presentation.

## Information Management

Information management is simply the way an organization organizes and governs data and information. Good policies are the bedrock of proper information management. For eDiscovery, sound information management is key to ensuring that ESI is readily available in a forensically sound manner whenever required. Good information policies that cover incident response, document retention, disaster recovery and business continuity aid eDiscovery when the need for it arises; a forensic readiness policy compliments all the aforementioned and helps to ensure smooth, easy and efficient discovery.

Having a proper forensic readiness policy on ground enables an organization to produce forensically sound ESI in a timely manner whenever the need arises. Important data and information which are constantly generated in the course of normal business are collected and stored in a forensically sound manner, such that if there is an incident or

*Figure 1. The electronic discovery reference model (EDRM) (© 2009, EDRM.net. Used with permission under Creative Commons Attribution)*

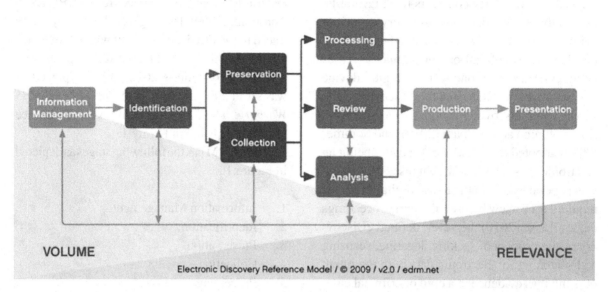

litigation or whatever calls for digital evidence, like eDiscovery, digital evidence is readily available with minimal disruption to business operations.

In the case of *AMD vs. Intel (2005)*, Intel's poor information management policy meant they could not provide email evidence requested by AMD in a timely manner as they had poor document retention and failed to properly communicate litigation hold to IT and end users; eventually they had to settle AMD out of court to the tune of over billion US dollars five years later (Shankland and Skillings, 2009; White, 2013). eDiscovery laws like the United States' Federal rules of Civil Procedure (FRCP) require that digital evidence be presented in a timely manner when requested, in a forensically sound manner and in the format requested by the requesting party, failure of which could result in dire consequences (as was seen in the AMD case).

## Identification

Once litigation is reasonably anticipated, digital evidence relevant to the case at hand has to be identified. For eDiscovery, it is important to identify which ESI are relevant in order to avoid

having unnecessary ESI being collected in addition to the relevant one, which would make it difficult to sort causing delays. There is also need to identify which ESI are privileged (confidential data and information that a party in litigation would not want shared with the other party, like critical business plans), so that it can be removed before sharing. A good forensic readiness policy would have collected ESI properly organized such that at any point, like when eDiscovery arises, it can be easily identified and sorted without having to go through all the stored ESI. Identification also helps to determine on which data litigation hold will be required; hence efforts can be made to protect and preserve such evidence. In the case of *Chura vs. Delmer Gardens of Lenexa, Inc. (2012)*, the defendant did not produce any of the digital evidence requested for by the plaintiff, this made the court assume either the defendant did not preserve digital evidence or did not respond to the opposing team by searching for relevant data; hence the defendant was ordered by the court to show evidence that ESI was preserved and searched for (K&L Gates, n.d.). Had the defendant been forensically ready, identifying and presenting the ESI would not have been a problem.

## Preservation

The duty to preserve ESI once identified as relevant for eDiscovery is the responsibility of the party that owns the ESI; and the party will be held liable for failure to do so. As such, it is expected as part of preservation that an organization communicate litigation hold to its IT department as well as end users of such digital evidence in order to preserve it - that is to protect it from being lost or modified (loosing forensic soundness). The IT department is meant to isolate such ESI to prevent it from being corrupted or lost, and if the ESI extends to the possession of end users beyond IT's reach, the end users are also informed not to work on that so as not to corrupt or destroy the digital evidence. A chain of custody is a very good proof of evidence preservation, and should be taken seriously. Forensic readiness ensures preservation of digital evidence, and being forensic ready can actually reduce or even eliminate the effects of litigation hold – as the ESI is properly collected, stored and preserved, there might be no need to communicate litigation hold to IT or end users, limiting disruption to normal business operations and minimizing cost. In the AMD case, lack of preservation of ESI was part of Intel's woes; they failed to properly communicate litigation hold and also had poor email retention policies leading to deletion of some email which were request for by AMD for discovery. The emails could have been preserved even without litigation hold if there was a good document retention policy or forensic readiness.

## Collection

Digital evidence is meant to be collected in a forensically sound manner. The collection of ESI could be in the form of manual copying of files, scanning documents, forwarding emails and the like; which is very volatile as the digital evidence could easily be damaged or lost (accidentally or on purpose) during collection. A more preferable

way of collecting digital evidence is bit-stream forensic imaging. Bit-stream images copy virtually everything on a drive including sectors and clusters; hence deleted items might be retrieved – for purposes of eDiscovery, however, this means privileged information and data may be included, therefore there is need to filter such out. Such filtering will be carried out during the review stage. Forensic readiness would go a long way in creating ease of collection as the ESI required would have been collected even prior to discovery. The problem that may arise is a variance in the format ESI was stored as part of forensic readiness and the format required for eDiscovery.

## Processing

Once digital data has been collected, it needs to be processed for sorting and arrangement, and removal of repeated and duplicated ESI. There may be need to convert ESI to a different format depending on what the party that requested for digital evidence requires and the court. Conversion may also be required if the format it is in is not available to the requesting party or the court (it could be in an outdated format or one more advanced than what they have). Forensic readiness is not directly relevant to the processing stage of EDRM since the requirements for the processing are not likely to be set or known prior to eDiscovery and litigation, forensic readiness only serves to make the processing easier as ESI is collected, sorted and stored making identification easier and conversion if need be.

## Review

Digital evidence is reviewed to ensure it meets required standards of a case (the other party's requested data and format as well as court requirements if any) and also to filter out privileged data and information. The ESI can be reviewed in native format or image-based review can be done. The native format review involves reviewing the ESI in its original format. Files are usually reviewed in read only format (although email tends to be converted to HTML format for native review) to minimize risk of corruption and damage. The image-based review involves review of files converted to image formats like PDF, TIFF, JPEG. The image conversion eliminates the risk of corruption and damage to the original file, however, it is only outputs that can be reviewed – where there is input data like formulae in a spreadsheet, it will not be available for the review.

The review stage is the most expensive stage in the eDiscovery process due to there being a lot of ESI and not all being relevant to the case at hand. Sorting and filtering to get relevant data can be a daunting task, hence there are tools and techniques that can be used for such sorting. One method of doing so is predictive coding. Predictive coding uses a combination of people, technology and workflow to get documents to sort out key documents, reducing the number of irrelevant and non-responsive documents from ESI that will go for manual review (Recommind, Inc., 2013 and Rouse, 2012). Predictive coding reduces the number of human reviewers required (cutting cost) by using mathematically precise technology that refines search based on set parameters by the reviewer.

Just like the previous stage (processing), forensic readiness does not have direct impact on the review stage. It only serves to make it faster and easier, more so if the ESI were stored in a format that can be easily reviewed.

## Analysis

Digital evidence is further analyzed to ensure compliance with legal requirements and the requirements of the requesting party for eDiscovery. Basically the same tools and techniques used in the review stage are used for analysis, like predictive coding. In reality, the analysis stage is not necessarily restricted to after review, it could be done simultaneously, and furthermore it oc-

curs constantly even before and after litigation. With respect to document retention policies, ESI need to be analyzed to determine what should be stored and archived, how to classify for storage and what should be discarded. It is imperative to discard some of the collected ESI in order to reduce cost of holding too much data which may not be useful. Filtering out what and what not to discard, and when to discard can be pretty tricky as ESI deemed as not important and irrelevant could later become required. Analysis forms part of forensic readiness as digital evidence that is to be stored has to be analyzed to determine whether it is worth storing and archiving.

## Production

According to EDRM LLC (2010), the aim of the production stage is to prepare and produce ESI in a format that is efficient and usable in order to minimize cost, risk and error while complying with agreed production specifications and timelines. The right to determine what format ESI is to be produced lies in the hands of the party that requests for ESI, including the timeframe for production. ESI could be produced in native format, image or paper printouts (paper printouts can be very cumbersome and expensive, and are not in high demand). Although the requesting party has the right to determine the production format, the opposing teams can meet and come to an agreement regarding eDiscovery (including production format), and in some instances the court may reject the format request if considered unreasonable. A clawback agreement can be used to retrieve produced ESI if privileged information was inadvertently disclosed. With forensic readiness, ESI would be stored in common formats like image and native, so once all prior stages have been done the evidence can be easily produced or converted to requested format where possible. Where the format is not as required by the requesting party, negotiations can still be made to convince the requesting party to accept the available format, and the court may also see it that way especially if required data and information can be retrieved from the available format.

## Presentation

Presentation of ESI in court of for settlement negotiations is the last step of the eDiscovery process. The presentation is meant to be convincing, persuasive and professional to prove or counter a claim. The evidence to be presented should be adequately backed up to avoid possible disappointment during presentation which can adversely affect a party's case. Failure to present would give the impression the presenting party is unserious or does not have anything to offer (if the party has a claim, it could be assumed to be unfounded; if defending, it could be assumed they are guilty and have no defense). Not presenting professionally or properly also has similar effects to not presenting at all, a poor unconvincing presentation is not going to be helpful to any party's case, and would gain annoyance of a judge. It is also recommended that the presentation be done such that it can be easily understood, should not be too technical as to lose comprehension of the judge and jury – it should be simplified as much as possible. Forensic readiness does not have a direct bearing on the presentation stage; presentation is done after all previous steps have been completed. A chain of custody would be very helpful in the presentation; this could be prepared right from the forensic readiness stage to show proper and sound handling of ESI.

## Issues, Controversies, Problems

Issues, problems and controversies tend to arise with new and emerging technology, digital forensics, whether in terms of forensic readiness or eDiscovery is not an exception. Some of the issues associated with eDiscovery and forensic readiness are highlighted in the following.

## What and What Not to Archive and for How Long

To be forensic ready, an organization needs to constantly collect and store ESI for a rainy day. The amount of ESI generated in an organization is very high and tends to increase exponentially with time. It is obvious that an organization cannot archive all the ESI it generates as this would be burdensome, especially in terms of cost. To avoid collecting and archiving unnecessary volume of ESI, the ESI has to be selectively reviewed before storing and archiving. This gives rise to the question: "what should be archived and what should be discarded?" what should be stored and archived is supposed to be ESI that is important and relevant, the opposite is discarded. The problem is how to determine such; and furthermore, ESI that was considered unimportant and irrelevant could subsequently become required when eDiscovery comes up.

## Privacy Concerns from Employees

Employees could feel their privacy is threatened by the constant collection of ESI they generate, as it implies they are being monitored. This gives a feeling of a "big brother" situation whereby employee privacy is non-existent. This can also have legal ramifications for an organization particularly in societies where there are strict privacy laws. Such laws may not tolerate aspects of a forensic readiness policy, they may be considered intrusive and in violation of employee privacy.

## Too Many IT Security Related Policies

Disaster recovery policies, business continuity policies, document retention policies, email policies; and now forensic readiness policy! There seems to be a teaming number of IT security policies (not to mention non-IT related policies) which appear cumbersome, and what's more they have many overlapping aspects. So why need another policy to add to already existing ones?

## Communication Gap between IT and Legal

There is an inherent communication problem between IT and Legal departments; each one has its own form of language for communication. Legal practitioners and IT professionals have different jargons they use in communicating; hence when eDiscovery comes up, there tends to be misunderstanding and possibly distrust. Legal might make requests to IT using language they consider being normal, but is strange to IT or misunderstood resulting in a wrong or incomplete response from IT. IT may understand Legal's request, but could get legal confused when communicating their response. Such lack of communication can also lead to distrust between the departments, Legal may think IT are trying to cover up something, suspecting them of being possibly guilty of some violation; while IT may assume Legal is trying to be chauvinistic by bossing them around.

## Foreign Discovery

What happens when ESI related to a case is generated or exists in a different country? What happens if such country does not have a good relationship with the country the eDiscovery is taking place? There are issues that arise when eDiscovery has to cut across international borders, differences in laws, different levels of development and politics. Problems can arise when an organization has part of ESI required for discovery in another country, could be as a result of having foreign offices, foreign customers and partners and outsourcing of some services to foreign countries. Countries that are not in good terms my find it difficult to cooperate on eDiscovery matters, they hardly cooperate on most matters.

## Laws and Guidelines Seem to Be US Based

Even in this chapter, most of the laws, case studies and guidelines discussed pertaining to digital forensics, eDiscovery and forensic readiness are US based. It is not very easy to get material on the subject matter that is not from either the US or UK. These countries have their own laws and culture based on their peculiarities, other countries cannot have these laws shoved down their throats. Other countries have their own peculiarities; moreover they are independent and have their integrity and sovereignty.

## Challenges from New Technology

Advancements in technology like mobile and cloud computing bring their own challenges to forensic readiness and eDiscovery. Location of ESI is widened with these technologies, and there is the problem of differentiating between what data belongs to the organization and which belongs to the individual, especially in the case of BYOD (Bring Your Own Device). Using personal devices for work makes it difficult for an organization to collect ESI, as the device is privately owned and does not belong to the organization, and it contains employee's personal data. Collecting such data can infringe on the employees' right to privacy. Mobile devices also tend to store data in the cloud, which might not be easily accessible to the organization, making data collection difficult. Using social networks for work also causes similar privacy issues. Forensically collecting ESI from mobile devices like smart phones and tablets are very costly, and that is not favorable to the organization.

## SOLUTIONS AND RECOMMENDATIONS

The following are recommendations and solutions for the above stated problems and issues.

## What and What Not to Archive and for How Long

Determining the relevance and importance of ESI depends on factors such as industry, nature of business and regulatory requirements. Some industries and businesses are more susceptible to litigation, and hence eDiscovery due to the sensitive nature of data that they processes – for example, banking and healthcare. Such organizations will store more ESI based on level of risk and possibility of litigation. In a bank for example, there will be more emphasis on collecting ESI from financial transactions on a customer's account than on an employee's performance records. Regulatory requirements also determine what to be archived, if laws and regulations require certain ESI must be collected and stored, then that has to be done.

The length of time to keep ESI in archives also depends on industry, nature of business and regulations. Higher risk data may be stored longer in industries highly prone to litigation like banking and healthcare. The higher the probability of ESI becoming subject of eDiscovery, the longer it is stored. Regulatory authorities may also require that certain data be stored for a minimum period of time. Data may also be stored longer if susceptible to more than one regulation; for example in the banking sector, data that is subject to both Payment Card Industry Security Standards (PCI DSS) and money laundering laws will be retained for the length of time of the regulation that requires a longer period of retention.

Good knowledge and proper planning are used to determine what data is relevant for storage and which should be discarded. Knowledge of industry, nature of business and regulatory requirements help an organization to identify which ESI is relevant and important for storage and which is not.

## Privacy Concerns from Employees

Employees have a right to defend their privacy, however, in the work place it is generally expected that personal issues and transactions are left at home. Although some employers allow their employees to carry out personal business in the work place and on the employer's platform, like general browsing and reading and sending personal email, that should be limited as it can affect concentration and productivity. Organizations need to have policies governing data collection, and should get their employees to sign acceptable usage agreements stating what and what not they should do in the workplace, and also educate them as to the type of monitoring and data collection that will take place and why. Employees agreeing to such terms do not have any cause for alarm, not only because they have agreed that ESI they generate will be collected and monitored, but because they have also been informed as to why such data collection is being carried out.

Any policy that an organization is developing and adopting has to work within the framework of laws and regulations; anything that goes against these should not form part of policies. The law usually takes into consideration security needs and requirements, and would not normally inhibit capturing of work-related ESI in some countries; some laws recognize the need for this and thus even form part of regulatory requirements.

## Too Many IT Security Related Policies

Different IT security policies exist and are necessary for proper and secure management of information and information systems for smooth and secure running of an organization, and also for its survival. These policies strengthen and secure the organization, and protect it against mishaps (whether natural, accidental, malicious or regulatory). Overlapping of certain aspects of the policies means that they augment one another in those aspects. Forensic readiness policies complement other policies like disaster recovery and business continuity, data retention and incident response, and also help ensure regulatory compliance. Some organizations could choose to merge similar and overlapping policies; for example, forensic readiness could be merged with data retention or incident response.

## Communication Gap between IT and Legal

The basic solution to the communication gap between IT and Legal is that each department should always remember that not everyone has the same background and discipline; hence not everyone understands a discipline or profession's jargons. Both departments when communicating with others should use simple terms that can be easily understood by everyone; not those specific to their discipline or profession. That said, since eDiscovery is now common place, the departments need to learn and comprehend more about each other – Legal should acquaint themselves with some IT knowledge particularly as it relates to eDiscovery; likewise IT need to learn legal requirements for IT and eDiscovery. As eDiscovery continues to develop and evolve, the communication gap is getting bridged; there are now courses offered in Universities and professional certifications covering digital forensics, IT law and the like, and there exist professionals and graduates of such courses who are familiar with digital forensics and eDiscovery. Such professionals do not have problems in terms of communication, and more and more are being employed by organizations.

## Foreign Discovery

eDiscovery across international borders can be problematic, especially if the country where ESI lies has very strict privacy laws (like within the European Union). An organization that knows it is going to have some ESI stored its country of domicile whether as a result of having foreign branches, outsourcing partners or customers and so on, should ensure it is well acquainted with the laws of such other countries in order to avoid complications when trying to be forensic ready or eDiscovery comes up. It should also get employees to sign service agreements that are compatible with the laws, and the same should go for outsourcing partners, customers and the like, they should have agreements that are compatible with laws of their host countries.

Where there are political differences and disagreements between countries, organizations should still take similar precautions as above, although it may be tougher in this case. Having international standards and agreements regarding cybersecurity and eDiscovery can also help bring some ease to the cross-border problem.

## Laws and Guidelines Seem to be US Based

Much of the laws, guidelines and legal precedent relating to digital forensics and eDiscovery are from the United States. Countries that do not have well-developed laws, guidelines and regulations pertaining to digital forensics and eDiscovery can use those of countries like the US, UK or any other country where such laws and regulations are more developed as precedent to develop their own laws and guidelines taking into consideration their own peculiarities. Doing so does not in any way compromise national sovereignty or integrity. The basis of digital forensics and eDiscovery laws, guidelines and procedures are generally the same irrespective of location or creed – that is to collect, review, analyze and store ESI in forensically sound manner.

## Challenges from New Technology

Issues pertaining to mobile computing, social networks, the cloud and new technology are best dealt with using good policies and agreements. For example, for an employee to use his or her personal device for work, he or she must sign an agreement as per acceptable use and the extent to which the employer has authority over the device. This gives the organization the right to access and retrieve work-related data from the personal device. The organization should also get the employees to agree that work-related usage of their personal device is logged and stored separately from other data such that when there is need to retrieve such ESI, the employees' right to privacy is not infringed. Network logging of work-related ESI form the personal device to the organization can go a long way to make it easier to capture and retrieve ESI without compromising employee privacy; it also helps to cut cost related with collecting ESI from mobile devices.

## FUTURE RESEARCH DIRECTIONS

Digital forensics and eDiscovery are still emerging and there are a lot of trends that are of interest for future research. There is a tendency to think digital forensics applies to only crimes committed on and through IT infrastructure, and digital crime, but in reality it also applies to non-digital crimes. Digital forensics can be used to trace criminals using mobile phone logs, GPS, and so on. Communication done through email, text messages, phone calls, chat and social media can be analyzed to trace and indict criminals; even items searched for on search engines and websites visited can help trace a criminal. Some topics for further research follow:

1.  **Presenting ESI for eDiscovery in Native Format:** There appears to be an increasing demand for ESI in native format for eDiscovery, whether by the opposing party or courts. This means measures have to be taken to protect such ESI from corruption. Privileged information also has to be protected, this could be by sorting and removing if possible or use of tools and techniques like redaction.

2.  **Big Data and Forensic Analysis:** The rise and rise of big data means eDiscovery and digital forensics become more stressful. Methods can be explored to see how to manage increasing ESI for purposes of retention and analysis in cost effective manner.

3.  **Predictive Coding – A Review:** The establishment of predictive coding as a means for filtering for data review and analysis needs further examination to see how it can become even more efficient. Predictive coding, for example, is best used for reviewing very large volumes of ESI, how can it be adapted for smaller volumes in a cost effective manner?

4.  **Professional eDiscovery Training and Certification:** A review of eDiscovery certifications and training to see how much value they can add to professionals and organizations. Do the certifications provide sufficient requirements for the eDiscovery process, how much are they in demand?

5.  **International Baseline for eDiscovery:** Having international basic standards and agreements regarding eDiscovery would be crucial in minimizing complications associated with cross-border eDiscovery. Measures can be explored to see the probability of developing such an international baseline.

## CONCLUSION

Evidence is necessary to trace, establish and indict. Digital forensics is a necessary tool in the fight against digital crime. It is used for investigations to establish how a breach happened, and to track and trace criminals. Knowing how a breach took place can aid in strengthening the security of an organization. With forensic readiness, digital forensic investigations are made easier and more cost effective as data is constantly collected and stored before, during and after an incident; hence significant evidence is collected. Waiting to collect digital evidence after an incident can result in loss of evidence. An attacker may wipeout his or her tracks, or evidence could be lost or corrupted due to its volatile nature, it could be overwritten or wiped out as a result of normal operations – moreover it is possible that a breach is not discovered until after a long period of time. eDiscovery has become more or less a staple in litigation, it requires analysis and provision of digital evidence in a timely, acceptable and forensically sound manner. Forensic readiness aids eDiscovery by ensuring digital evidence is available in a timely and efficient manner, saving a lot of cost in terms of investigations and also providing more reliable evidence in some cases. The evidence is more reliable because it is collected and stored, not in response to an incident which leaves room for potential loss, contamination or manipulation.

Forensic readiness helps provide information assurance and security, and helps in investigations and eDiscovery. Adopting a forensic readiness policy is important for organizations; it must not be a regulatory requirement before it is done. In the 1920's the judge in the TJ Hooper case declared that there are some precautions that essential to an industry that even their universal disregard does not excuse their being omitted (Tester, 2013). In those days having a receiver radio on a boat was not required; the TJ Hooper was a Tugboat with three barges which ran into a storm and sinking all the barges and cargo. Customers sued for losses, a testimony was made that the loss could have been avoided if the tugboat had a functional radio on board which would have been used to get information about the storm (Tester, 2013). It was this testimony that lead to the judge's declaration. This applies to the case of forensic readiness, since there is a means to avoid mishaps, it should be adopted whether a required practice or not.

eDiscovery can be used to detect digital crimes and their perpetrators. Litigation can be as a result of a claim of digital crime against a company, eDiscovery can help establish such a claim or exonerate the defendant. As time goes by, with more and more technological developments occurring digital forensics and eDiscovery will continue to evolve. New challenges are equally propping up with technological advancements, but good management and understanding of developments can mitigate any problems that arise.

## REFERENCES

Burns, A. E. (2013). Corporate e-discovery success starts with information governance. *eForensics Magazine, Database, 2*(8). Retrieved August 5, 2013 from http://eforensicsmag.com/ediscovery-compendium/

Childress, S. (2012). Electronic discovery: Where the law and technology collide. *E-Discovery – Legal Issues Guidebook*. Retrieved August 5, 2013 from http://eforensicsmag.com/e-discovery-legal-issues-guidebook-2/

LWG Consulting. (2009). *An introduction to the ediscovery process*. Retrieved November 6, 2013 from http://www.lwgconsulting.com/news/default.aspx?ArticleId=55

EDRM LLC. (2010). *Production guide*. Retrieved November 8, 2013 from http://www.edrm.net/resources/guides/edrm-framework-guides/production

Hughes, A. (2013). Ediscovery: Criminal process in a corporate world - How to ensure investigations do not fall short. *eForensics Magazine, 2*(8). Retrieved August 5, 2013 from http://eforensicsmag.com/ediscovery-compendium/

Kassner, M. (2011). Digital forensics: The science behind 'who done it'. *TechRepublic Blog*. Retrieved November 3, 2013 from http://www.techrepublic.com/blog/it-security/digital-forensics-the-science-behind-who-done-it/6660/

K&L Gates (n.d.). *Electronic discovery case database*. Retrieved November 10, 2013 from http://ediscovery.klgates.com/search.aspx

Recommind, Inc. (2013). *Predictive coding*. Retrieved November 11, 2013 from http://www.recommind.com/predictive-coding

Rouse, M. (2010). *Electronic discovery (e-discovery or discovery)*. Retrieved November 5, 2013 from http://searchfinancialsecurity.techtarget.com/definition/electronic-discovery

Rouse, M. (2012). *Predictive coding*. Retrieved November 11, 2013 from http://searchcompliance.techtarget.com/definition/predictive-coding

Rowlingson, R. (2004). A ten step process for forensic readiness. *International Journal of Digital Evidence, 2*(3). Retrieved February 16, 2013 from 3, http://www.utica.edu/academic/institutes/ecii/publications/articles/A0B13342-B4E0-1F6A-156F501C49CF5F51.pdf

Seigle-Morris, A. (2013). *Electronic disclosure (eDisclosure): Myths and reality*. Retrieved July 9, 2013 from http://www.portcullis-security.com/edisclosure-myths-and-reality

Shankland, S., & Skillings, J. (2009). *Intel to pay AMD $1.25 billion in antitrust settlement*. Retrieved November 8, 2013 from http://news.cnet.com/8301-1001_3-10396188-92.html

Sommer, P. (2012). Digital evidence, digital investigations and e-disclosure: A guide to forensic readiness for organisations, security advisers and lawyers (3rd ed.). Information Assurance and Advisory Council.

Sule, D. (2013). Digital forensics 101: Case study using FTK imager. *eForensics Magazine, 2*(2). Retrieved February 27, 2013 from http://eforensicsmag.com/forensics-analysis-with-ftk/

Tester, D. (2013). Is the TJ Hooper case relevant for today's information security environment? *ISACA Journal, 2*. Retrieved November 14, 2013 from m.isaca.org/Jounal/Past-Issues/2013/Volume-2/Pages/default.aspx

The National Archives. (2011). *Digital Continuity to Support Forensic Readiness*. Retrieved March 23, 2013 from http://www.utica.edu/academic/institutes/ecii/publications/articles/A0B13342-B4E0-1F6A-156F501C49CF5F51.pdf

Volonino, L., & Redpath, I. (2010). e-Discovery for dummies. Wiley Publishing, Inc.

White, B. (2013, March 12). *Lessons of AMD v. Intel* [Video file]. Retrieved from http://www.youtube.com/watch?v=jQ_9uLkw_Uo

## KEY TERMS AND DEFINITIONS

**Bit Stream Image:** A bit stream image of a disk drive is a clone copy of it. It copies virtually everything included in the drive, including sectors and clusters, which makes it possible to retrieve files that were deleted from the drive. Bit stream images are usually used when conducting digital forensic investigations in a bid to avoid tampering with digital evidence such that it is not lost or corrupted.

**Chain of Custody:** A chain of custody is a document that records all the processes digital evidence passed through from the point of collection to preservation as evidence in court or other proceedings. Details of how the evidence was collected, analyzed and stored are recorded, including who accessed it, when and why.

**Digital Forensics:** Digital forensics may also be referred to as cyber forensics or computer forensics. Digital forensics involves collection, retrieval, analysis, review and storage of digital evidence in a legally acceptable manner usually for civil or criminal investigations and proceedings or in-house investigations. There are different types of digital forensics like disk forensics, memory forensics, network forensics, mobile forensics, and so on.

**eDiscovery:** eDiscovery is the process whereby opposing parties in litigation review digital evidence in the other's possession to asses quality prior to full court proceedings. eDiscovery developed from discovery which involved review of evidence by litigating parties prior to court proceedings. eDiscovery may also be viewed as the sum total processes involved in a digital investigation from collection to analysis and review.

**ESI:** ESI stands for electronically stored information. This is data and information that is generated on IT media and devices, like PCs, mobile devices, the Internet, CCTV footage, and so on. ESI is constantly generated in the normal course of operations of an organization and also personal individual use.

**Forensic Readiness:** An organization habitually gathering and storing ESI in a forensically sound manner pre-empting an incident where the ESI could serve as potential evidence is forensic readiness. The main goal is to maximize the potential of such ESI while minimizing cost involved in investigation.

**Forensically Sound:** Digital evidence is said to be forensically sound if it was collected, analyzed, handled and stored in a manner that is acceptable by the law, and there is reasonable evidence to prove so. Forensic soundness gives reasonable assurance that digital evidence was not corrupted or destroyed during investigative processes whether on purpose or by accident.

**Litigation Hold:** Litigation hold is a preservation order requiring an organization to preserve all data that may serve as evidence relating to legal proceedings involving it. This is required to protect the evidence from corruption, damage and destruction. The litigation hold may be issued by an attorney or issued internally by the organization to employees. Preservation of data that has potential of becoming evidence in a legal case should begin once there is an anticipation of litigation.

**Predictive Coding:** Predictive coding is the use of IT tools and techniques, and workflow processes along with human input to filter out key documents for eDiscovery. This is used to reduce the quantity of non-responsive and irrelevant files contained in ESI that will be subjected to manual review.

# Chapter 13
# Cybercrimes Technologies and Approaches

**WeSam Musa**
*University of Maryland – University College, USA*

## ABSTRACT

*The growth of the Internet has changed our lives significantly. Not so long ago, computers used to be viewed as luxury items to have at home. People used to rely mainly on televisions and newspapers as the primary sources of news. Today, the Internet has become an essential service to depend on for many industries, such as news agencies, airports, and even utility companies. This was the beginning of a new-trillion-dollar industry: the Internet industry. However, the Internet was designed to be an open, academic tool, never to be secure. As a result, cybercrimes, cyber warfare, and other cyber illegal activities have spread to become a significant portion of Internet traffic. Cybercrimes often challenge law enforcement. It is difficult to know the exact location where an attack originated, and there are no cyber borders between nations. As a result, fighting cybercrimes requires international cooperation. The purpose of this chapter is to shed some light on motives of cybercrimes, technologies used by hackers, and solutions that can be adopted by individuals, organizations, and governments. This chapter also presents the United States (USA) and international perspectives on cybercrimes and privacy laws. In summary, individuals, organizations, and nations have roles to play in achieving security and reducing cyber risks.*

## INTRODUCTION

In the early 1980s, when the Advanced Research Projects Agency Network (ARPANET) developed the Transport Control Protocol/Internet Protocol (TCP/IP), the world became connected through the Internet. Nowadays, the Internet has a profound impact on society. Social interactions, economies, and fundamental life simply depend on cyberspace. The Internet, and more broadly cyberspace, has allowed social interaction worldwide. It has al-

lowed sharing of information and freedom of expression – such as what occurred during the Arab Spring. Social media services, such as Twitter and Facebook played an instrumental role in the Arab Spring movements. While the cyber world brings economical and social benefits, it is also vulnerable. The Internet was never designed to be secure. Identity theft, cybercrimes, cyber warfare, and others cyber illegal activities started surfacing due to lack of appropriate security controls. According to Symantec's annual security report, the

DOI: 10.4018/978-1-4666-6324-4.ch013

numbers of cyber-targeted-attacks are increasing. Cyber attacks target everyone including small companies, large companies, government agencies, executives, and even sales people (Symantec, 2012). The global economy is being affected by cybercrime activities.

Cybercriminals are using sophisticated methods to gain unauthorized access to information systems to steal sensitive data, Personality Identifiable Information (PII), or even classified materials. Some of the creative methods that attackers use to gain unauthorized access are backdoor programs, spear phishing attacks, and social engineering. Tini, Netcat, Wrappers, EXE maker, Pretator, Restorator, and Tetris are well-known backdoor tools that can be used by attackers to setup a backdoor that allows them to connect into the computer systems. Phishing is a technique that attackers use by sending email messages with false links claiming to be a legitimate site in an attempt to acquire users' personal information. Social engineering is a powerful human-based technique that bypasses all network countermeasures by relying on human weakness to gain unauthorized access to the network. The technique targets certain personal, such as helpdesk, or executives by creating an artificial situation by exerting pressure to release the needed information.

Countries may misuse cyberspace for spying on other nations. For example, U.S. National Security Agency (NSA) is being accused for spying on world leaders and listening to 100s of millions of phone conversations worldwide. Additionally, cybersecurity incidents could disrupt water resources, power plants, healthcare, or financial institutions. A study conducted by McGraw (2013) concluded that the U.S IT infrastructure is highly vulnerable to deliberate attacks with possibly disastrous effects. The current cybersecurity technical approaches for many nations do not provide adequate computer or network security. With no surprise, President Obama has declared that, "cyber threat is one of the most serious economic and national security challenges we

face as a nation" (Obama, 2012). Similarly, in 2013, in order to fight cybercrimes, the European Commission established the European Cybercrime Centre (EC3) at the European police headquarters in the Netherlands.

For the above stated reasons, governments across the world have started to collaborate by developing cybersecurity strategies. The European Union (EU) has created a cybersecurity strategy that consists of seven pillars. These pillars focus on using cyberspace to befit economically, socially, and even politically. Furthermore, the EU has put forward a framework to set the actions required to build a strong and effective countermeasures against cyber threats. In May 2013, the European Union Agency for Network and Information Security received a new authority, granting it the power to make bigger difference in protecting Europe's cyberspace. Furthermore, the U.S. has passed an executive order in 2013 to develop cybersecurity performance standards to reduce cyber risks to critical infrastructure. In addition, the United Nations Economic and Social Council (ECOSOC) has initiated an international treaty seeking to bring into line national criminal laws of cybercrimes, such as fraud, child pornography, and hate crimes.

The objective of this chapter is to provide an overview of the historical background, and trend of cybercrimes technologies and approaches. This chapter will also discuss relationship between the U.S. and global Internet operations in terms of international collaboration efforts to fight cybercrime activities. The chapter will also cover broader implications for relationships between civil liberties, innovation, and security.

## MOTIVES OF CYBERCRIMINALS

Cybercrime by definition is committing an illegal act using a computer or network device (Musa, 2013). Cyber warfare, cybercrime, cyber espionage, and cyber terrorism are all similar activities, and they do overlap. They all share and use telecommunications networks to conduct all sorts of activities with different motives of course. Motives vary from revenge, jokes, terrorism, political and military espionage, business espionage, hate, to personal gain or fame. Cybercrimes can be committed against a person, an organization, or even a government. Cybercrimes against people may include crimes, such as child pornography, sexual harassment, stealing personal credit cards, and even murder. For example, in 2012, a Facebook dispute ended with a man shot in San Bernadino, California.

Cybercrime is typically driven by money or profit (Hunton, 2012). While the activities are usually aimed to harvest the financial transactions and to perform fraudulent transactions, the potential harm to individuals can be catastrophic, especially children – they are the most vulnerable. According to the Internet World Stats website, there are over 2.5 billion Internet users worldwide. Children and teenagers are among the fastest groups of Internet users; representing about 40% of Internet users (Internet Users, 2012). At present, the Internet provides predators secrecy to target children for criminal activities. Offenders can target children through chat rooms, email, or even gaming websites. The possession of online child pornography is illegal in the EU, the U.S, and many other nations. For example, in Mexico, in May 2012, a resident was sentenced to 29 years in prison for possession and production of child pornography. On the contrary, many other countries still lack adequate cybercrime laws. As a result, child pornography has become a billion dollar industry.

Cyber warfare is one of the most destructive cyber-based activities. The aim of cyber warfare can be summarized in one word, destruction. Cyber warfare simply uses cyber mediums, such as Internet or telecommunication lines, as weapons to brutally destroy enemies' critical infrastructures, such as power plants, transportation system, water plants, etc. Cyber warfare may consist of acts, such

as espionage or sabotage. Cyber espionage is performed by exploiting vulnerabilities in computer systems to steal military, political, or industrial information of an adversary's networks. Cyber warfare is usually performed by a State. STUXNET virus represents a cyber-warfare activity, as it was aimed to destroy an infrastructure of an adversary (Clarke, 2010). Many believe that the U.S. helped Israel to initiate the attack, due to its level of sophistication.

Anonymous is a well-known cyber group that conducts cyber attacks with "revenge" motives. According to the Guardian magazine, Anonymous claims that it has over 9000 members and their aim is to cyber-fight for perceived injustices (Arthur, 2011). Recently, Anonymous has attacked visa.com, paypal.com, mastercard.com, and many other financial institutions in support of Wiki Leaks. The attack came after these institutions' decision to stop processing donation transfers to the Wiki Leaks group. In 2012, Time magazine categorized Anonymous as one of the 100 most influential people in the world.

## CYBER INCIDENT AND SPENDING TRENDS

In the 1990s, cyber attacks and identity theft started developing. Shortly after, organized attacks started to be performed more often. The low cost of cyber network tools required to engage in cybercriminal activities makes it extremely attractive. Absurdly, it costs neither much to buy a couple of computers nor to learn a few computer programs to get engaged in cybercriminal activities.

The protection of information systems is a constant challenge, and the cost of data breach is expensive and severe. Cybercrimes cost over 100 billion dollars annually worldwide (INSA, 2011). Companies spend millions of dollars to ensure that their information systems are protected from various types of cyber attacks. In Fiscal Year (FY) 2012, The U.S. federal government agencies reported total IT security spending of $14.6 billion (OMB, 2012). Figure 1 shows the spending trend for U.S. federal agencies from 2006 to 2012.

On the contrary, the number of attacks against U.S. federal networks increased nearly 20% in 2011 (OMB, 2011). In fact, a recent ArcSight study that was conducted in 2011 concluded that the median annualized cost of companies, as a result of cyber attacks ranges from $8.9 million in US, $6.0 million in Germany, $5.1 in Japan, to $3.2 million in the United Kingdom (UK) (ArcSight, 2011). Despite all of this spending, security breaches are still on the rise. Consequently, it appears that more spending doesn't necessary imply better security or less breaches. Figure 2 illustrates the total reported incidents from 2006 to 2012. According to the U.S. Computer Emergency Readiness

Team (CERT), the number of reported incidents increased from 5144 in 2006 to 46,043 incidents in 2012 (US-CERT, 2013).

## TYPES OF CYBERATTACKS

Risk is the probability of a system being exploited by a threat. Threat is any person or a tool that can take advantage of vulnerabilities. Information systems' vulnerabilities continue to rise due to many factors. Automation and sophistication of hacking tools are ones of the leading causes. Not surprising, 96% of attacks were not highly difficult to launch. In 2011, there were 403 million unique variations of malware verses 286 million in 2010 (Symantec, 2012). Moreover, hackers penetrate

*Figure 1. Total U.S. Federal Government spending in billions (data source: FISMA reports)*

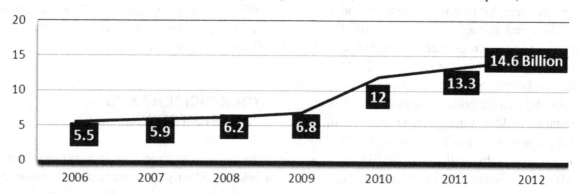

*Figure 2. Total incidents per year (data source: US-CERT)*

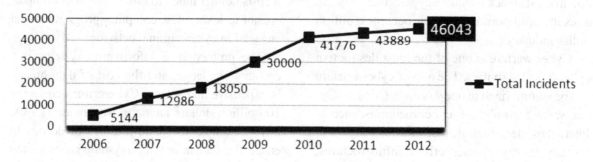

systems by using various types of attacks, such as Trojan horse attacks, denial of service, zero-day-attack, fast flux botnet, buffer overflow, spoofing, sniffing, Structured Query Language (SQL) injection, Domain Name Services (DNS) poisoning, and many others.

Trojans are malicious programs that pretend to be something desirable. A Trojan acts as a backdoor that allows an attacker to access a system without users' consent. Trojan horse attack is one of the most critical types of attack, as the Trojan's malicious content appears to be harmless. Trojans are created to steal personal information, credit cards, banking information, and can even use a compromised computer to conduct illegal cyber activities. There are many types of Trojans, such as remote access, proxy, FTP, ICMP backdoor, and reverse connecting Trojans. Trojans use both TCP and User Datagram Protocol (UDP) to transmit information. The transmission works in a client-server relationship, where the infected computer acts as the server and the attacker or command and control machine acts as the client. Many Trojans are known to use common high ports. For example, the GirlFriend Trojan is known to use TCP port 21544, and Online KeyLogger Trojan is known to use UDP port 49301.

Banking Trojans are reaching alarming levels of sophistication. Carberp, Citadel, SpyEye, and Zeus are the most widespread banking Trojans that hit the Internet. Most of banking Trojans are difficult to detect, as they operate in stealth mode. Trojans also act as binary generator, as each Trojan creates a new binary file, which makes it difficult for anti-virus programs to detect. For example, Sdra64.exe program uses process injection to inject code into winlogon.exe or explorer.exe to exit the running processes list. Additionally, Zeus has the ability to can make registry changes to hide its attributes. Zeus allows cybercriminal to search for personal credential, and then sends them to a command and control server in real-time. Zeus Trojan often generates DNS queries to attempt to find the command and control server using DNS

fast flux. Zeus can also allow an attacker to combine infected machines into groups to form a high performance botnet. Zeus has many variants. One variant uses encrypted communication. Thus, Zeus Decryptor tool can be used to decrypt the traffic.

SQL injection is a well-known form of code injection that is used to perform a denial of service attack. SQL injection attacks harm database servers by inserting SQL commands into input fields (Walker, 2012). Input validation can be used to mitigate sequel injection and remote file inclusion attacks. Validating input could also be used to reduce the chances of processing unexpected data by denying inclusion of special characters, such as "%" sign. On the other hand, buffer overflow occurs when data copied into the temporary buffers exceed the size of the buffer. Buffers are temporary blocks of memory used to store data. The extra copied data may overflow into enamoring buffers; as a result, it may overwrite existing data. There are several measures that can be taken to reduce or mitigate buffer overflow vulnerabilities. Some of these measures include, but not limited to, code auditing (automated and/ or manual), non-executable stack, safe functions, compiler techniques, continuous scanning, and training programmers/software developers to prevent using unsafe functions and group standards.

Advanced Persistent Threat (APT) is a set of stealthy and continuous hacking processes often orchestrated by human targeting a specific entity. APT usually targets organizations and or nations for business or political motives. APT processes require high degree of covertness over a long period of time. As the name implies, APT consists of three major processes, advanced, persistent, and threat. The advanced process signifies sophisticated techniques using malware to exploit vulnerabilities in systems. The persistent process suggests that an external command and control is continuously monitoring and extracting data off a specific target. The threat process indicates human involvement in orchestrating the attack. APTs often breach entities via Internet, infected media, external exploitation, or internal exploitation. Internet breach may take place by sending malicious payload via email attachments, peer-to-peer file sharing, or spear phishing. On the other hand, medial infection may consist of infected Universal Serial Bus (USB) memory sticks, infected memory card, or infected appliance. Furthermore, external exploitation may occur through rogue WiFi penetration, zero day attack, or smart phone bridging. Internal exploitation on the other hand can be encountered by a rogue employee, social engineering, or funded placement. One example of internal exploitation is insider attack. Approximately, 60% of network attacks occur inside the network. An inside attack is easy to initiate and not so easy to detect or prevent. A disgruntled employee who takes revenge of his/her company by compromising its sensitive data is considered an insider attack. Some competitors go even further by sending people to get interviewed for jobs posted by their competitors. Once they get hired, they start stealing sensitive data and eventually bring down the entire organization.

There are 100s of millions of malware variations, which make is extremely challenging to pro-

tect organizations from APT. While APT activities are stealthy and hard to detect, the command and control network traffic associated with APT can be detected at the network layer level. Deep log analyses and log correlation from various sources can be useful in detecting APT activities – it's all about the logs. Agents can be used to collect logs (TCP and UDP) directly from assets into a syslog server. Then a Security Information and Event Management (SIEM) tool can correlate and analyze logs. While it is challenging to separate noises from legitimate traffic, a good log correlation tool, such as logRhythm or ArcSight can be used to filter out the legitimate traffic, so security staff can focus on the noises.

As the name implies, in a denial of service attack, a hacker attempts to deny access to a particular service or Internet site by processing so many transactions more than the targeted computers can handle. Denial of service attack can also target a network to a point that nothing can get in or out of the network. Figure 3 explains the most reported attacks by US-CERT. Incident data reveal that malicious code continuous to be the most widely reported incident type across the

*Figure 3. Incidents per category 2010-2012 (data source: US-CERT)*

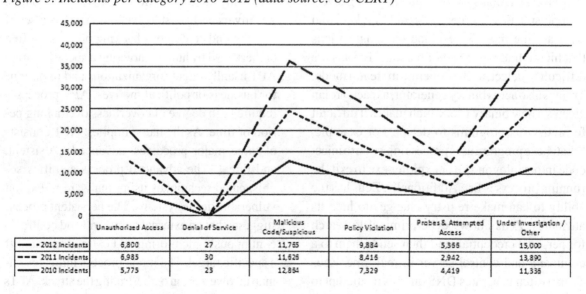

| | Unauthorized Access | Denial of Service | Malicious Code/Suspicious | Policy Violation | Probes & Attempted Access | Under Investigation / Other |
|---|---|---|---|---|---|---|
| ── ∙ 2012 Incidents | 6,800 | 27 | 11,765 | 9,884 | 5,355 | 15,000 |
| ─ ─ ─ 2011 Incidents | 6,985 | 30 | 11,626 | 8,416 | 2,942 | 13,890 |
| ── 2010 Incidents | 5,775 | 23 | 12,864 | 7,329 | 4,419 | 11,336 |

U.S. federal government. In 2011 malicious code accounted for 26% of total incidents reported by U.S. federal agencies.

Another reason for the continuous rise of cyber attacks is the weakness of information systems (Whitman, 2011). Whitman, a Computer Science professor at Kennesaw State University, believes that the recurring events of virus and warm attacks simply illustrate the weakness in current information systems; it suggests the need to provide better security for these systems (Whitman, 2011). Whitman stresses that the purpose of his book, *Principles of Information Security*, is to provide surveys and discipline of information security with a balanced of security management and technical components of security. Whitman argues that people and procedures have always been threats to the system, and they should not be overlooked (Whitman, 2011). Whitman goes further by explaining that a bottom-up approach can be used to the implementation of information security in organizations. He stresses that system administrators who work on a day-to-day basis on these systems, possess the in-depth knowledge that can and must be enhanced to develop and improve information security. Whitman encourages the top-down-approach by strong upper management support and dedicated funding for implementing security.

## INTERNATIONAL PRIVACY LAWS

Privacy laws deal with regulation of information and how to collect, store, and use data. Privacy laws can also target specific types of information, such as health, communications, and financial. Many nations, such as Canada, U.S., Brazil, Australia, India, and others, have well-established privacy laws in place.

In 1950, the Council of Europe adopted Article 8 on Human Rights. The purpose of the article is to protect the right to respect for private and family life. Additionally, the United Nations, in 1966, developed Article 17 on Civil and Political Rights. The aim of the article is to prohibit interference with individuals' privacy, family, and home correspondence.

In 1993, the New Zealand Privacy Act was created to establish standards related to collection, storage, and disclosure of personal information. In 1995, China enacted the Computer Processed Personal Information Protection Act. The aim of the act is to protect personal information managed by computers. In 1998, the U.K. enacted the Data Protection Act, which defines U.K. law on data processing. The legislation focuses on the protection of personal data. In India, Information Technology Act of 2000 was enacted to protect individuals' privacy. In 2011 India passed a new privacy law that applies to companies and consumers. In Canada, individuals' privacy is protected by the federal Personal Information Protection and Electronic Documents Act (PIPEDA). Finally, in Brazil, people are protected by the country's constitution. Article 5 of the constitution of Brazil clearly states that "the intimacy, private life, honor and image of the people are inviolable" (Brazil. Const. art. V).

Unfortunately, not all nations follow their privacy laws. Recently, the U.S. intelligence community admitted conducting surveillance on individuals and world leaders. People in Europe and U.S. were not aware of how much data was being collected or how much assistance U.S. companies were providing for the intelligence community. In response to such a privacy breach, in October 2013, the European Parliament voted to fortify Europe's data protection and privacy laws. The parliament is planning to enforce fines of up to 100 million euros on companies that break privacy laws. The parliament is also planning to impose strict rules on how data can be shared or transferred to non-EU countries.

## U.S. PRIVACY LAWS

Of the many laws that control data protection in the U.S., there are four major data security acts that promote data privacy and cyber protection. The four acts are the Privacy Act of 1974, the Children's Online Privacy Protection Act the Fair and Accurate Credit Transaction Act (COPPA), the Fair and Accurate Credit Transaction Act (FACTA), and the Health Insurance Portability and Accountability Act (HIPPA).

The Privacy Act was enacted in December 31, 1974. This law governs the collection, storage, use, and dissemination of Personally Identifiable Information (PII). The Privacy Act prohibits the disclosure of information without a written consent of the individual. There are 12 statutory exceptions. Some of these exceptions include disclosure for law enforcement purposes, congressional investigations, and for statistical purposes by the Census Bureau.

The U.S. enacted COPPA in 1998. The aim of the act is to protect the privacy of children under the age of 13. COPPA imposes an obligation on the operations of websites that are directed at children to publish privacy policies specifying whether personal information is being collected. If information is to be collected, the site operators must obtain parental consent. The U.S. Federal Trade Commission (FTC) has brought a number of actions against websites host providers for failure to comply with COPPA. UMG Recording, for example, was fined $400,000 for COPPA violations.

FACTA was passed by the U.S. Congress on November 22, 2003. The aim of the act is to help protect consumers' credit information from the risk of data and identity theft. The law contains seven major titles: identity theft prevention and credit history restoration, improvements in use of and consumer access to credit information, enhancing the accuracy of consumer report information, limiting the use and sharing of medical information in the financial system, financial literacy and education improvement, protecting

employee misconduct investigations, and relation to state laws . In response to FACTA, credit cards receipts do not list more than the last four digits of the card number. The act also grants individuals the right to request free credit report from the three credit reporting agencies (Equifax, Experian, and TransUnion).

HIPPA was enacted by President Bill Clinton in 1996. The aim of the act is to protect individuals' health information. The act has two major titles. Title I is health care access, portability, and renewability. The title regulates the group market rules, the availability, and span of group health plans. Title II is the preventing health care fraud and abuse – administrative simplification medical liability reform. The title defines policies and procedures for maintaining the privacy and security of individually identifiable health information.

## U.S. CYBERSECURITY STRATEGY

In the U.S., federal cybersecurity regulations are derived from the Congress and the White House. The aim of these regulations is to safeguard the nation as a whole, including infrastructures, and information systems. The purpose of the regulations is to force corporations and government agencies to protect their systems from cyber attacks. Cyber attacks may include code injection, phishing, social engineering, or backdoor Trojans. Cyber attacks are increasing and targeting everyone. Cybersecurity is essential to the economy, as it is vital to the operation of critical systems, such as power plants, hospitals, schools, and even financial institutions. As a result, cybersecurity regulations must exist.

While the U.S. is considered a top-spamming country, it also fosters many cybersecurity related laws – Electronic Communications Privacy Act (ECPA), National Infrastructure Protection Act (NIPA), Cyberspace Electronic Security Act (CESA), Patriot Act, Cyber Security Enhancement Act (CSEA), and Anti-Phishing Act are just a few. The U.S. has federal and state cybersecurity regulations in place. The Federal Information Security Act (FISMA) regulates federal agencies information systems. FISMA requires federal agencies to undergo security assessment to assure the security of the information systems. On the other hand, a state such as California passed the Notice of Security Breach Act. The act requires companies to disclose details of security incidents. This law, in a way, penalizes companies for not protecting their systems against cyber threats.

The U.S. congress has passed multiple bills that expand cybersecurity regulations. For example, the Consumer Data Security and Notification Act (CDSNA) requires disclosure of security breaches by financial institutions. Additionally, the Security Protect Yourself Against Cyber Trespass Act (SPYACT) requires companies to improve cybersecurity; the bill focuses on phishing and spyware. It makes it unlawful to modify settings, or install software without authorization.

In the spirit of enhancing the security and resiliency of the cyber and communications infrastructure of the U.S., the Senate introduced a bill in 2012, which may be cited as the Cybersecurity Act of 2012. Mr. Lieberman, Ms. Collins, Mr. Rockefeller, and Mrs. Feinstein introduced the bill, which consists of nine titles:

**Title I:** Protecting critical infrastructure;
**Title II:** Protecting government networks (FISMA Reform);
**Title III:** Clarifying and strengthening existing roles and authorities;
**Title IV:** Reduction, recruitment, and workforce development;
**Title V:** Research and development;
**Title VI:** Federal acquisition risk management strategy;
**Title VII:** Information sharing;
**Title VIII:** Public awareness reports; and
**Title IX:** International cooperation.

Unfortunately, the bill did not pass. In August 2012, in a 52 to 46 vote, the Senate did not enact the Cybersecurity Act of 2012. The bill failed to gain the 60 required votes, in order to move the bill up for a full vote. In response to the senate's vote on the bill, Senator Lieberman stated "this is one of those days when I fear for our country and I'm not proud of the U.S. Senate. We've got a crisis, and it's one that we all acknowledge. It's not just that there's a theoretical or speculative threat of cyber attack against our country - it's real" (Lieberman, 2012). The blockage of the bill does not necessarily mean the government will stop imposing security measures. The US President, for example, could issue a prudential directive to order federal agencies to establish certain cybersecurity measures. HSPD-23 for example was ordered in 2008. The directive requires government agencies to act as a single network enterprise with Trusted Internet Connection (TIC). It required agencies to deploy Intrusion Prevention Systems (IPS) and Intrusion Detection System (IDS) to detect and prevent malicious traffic within the federal enterprise.

In February 2013, President Obama issued an executive order on Improving Critical Infrastructure Cybersecurity. The Order requires the National Institute of Standards and Technology (NIST) to work with other agencies to develop a voluntary framework for reducing cyber risks to critical infrastructure (White House, 2013). In response, NIST started communicating with other agencies to develop the framework. The framework will consist of standards, guidelines, and best practices to encourage the protection of information systems supporting critical infrastructure operations. The intention of the framework is to create a scalable and cost-effective approach to help agencies to manage cybersecurity related risks, while protecting confidentiality, integrity, and availability of data (NIST, 2013).

## EU PRIVACY LAWS

In Europe, privacy laws are a highly mature legal specialty area. The European Convention on Human Rights (ECHR) is an international treaty to protect human rights in Europe. The treaty was drafted in 1950 and then came into force in 1953. Article 8 of this treaty concerns privacy. Article 8 provides the rights to respect for one's private, family life, and home. Furthermore, in 1980, the Organization for Economic Cooperation and Development (OECD), an international economic organization of 34 countries, issued seven principles to help governing personal data. The principles included notice, purpose, consent, security, disclosure, access, and accountability principles pertaining to processing, handling, and storing data. In addition to Article 8 of the ECHR and the seven principles of OECD, directive 1995/46/EC and 2002/58/EC are the two major legislative bodies that govern privacy and electronic communications security in EU.

Directive 95/46/EC is known as the data protection directive. The scope of the directive is to protect individuals with regard to collecting, processing, and storing personal data by automatic means. The directive consists of 34 articles. Article 6 of the directive ensures that the data controller is in compliance with data quality principles. Some of these principles include, but not limited to, fair processing of data, legitimate purpose for processing data, and accuracy of data. In addition, Article 10 and 11 of the directive requires that the data subject must include the identity of the controller, the purpose of processing the data. Article 12 specifically calls for the member States to guarantee that every data subject has the right to know to whom the data was disclosed, and the right to obtain the erasure or blocking of data that do not comply with the directive (European Commission, 1995).

E-privacy directive 2002/58/EC is the second major legal authority that regulates data projection in EU. Directive 2002/58/EC of the European Parliament was enacted on July 12, 2002. The directive is concerning the processing of personal data and the protection of privacy in the electronic communications sector. Electronic communications include, but not limited to, Internet transactions, email, automated calling machines, telefaxes, and SMS messages. The directive consists of 21 articles that discuss the data traffic, unsolicited communications, security, and confidentiality of the data. Article 13 specifically discusses unsolicited communications. The article requires the member States to take proper measures to guarantee that unsolicited communications not to be allowed without a permission of the concerned subscriber, free of charge. The directive makes it clear that equipment on the network is part of the private domain of the users requiring protection under the European Conventional of the protection of Human Rights and Fundamental Freedoms (European Commission, 2002). The directive also prohibits spyware or other unsolicited software to be installed without the users' knowledge. Furthermore, the directive grants users the right to refuse cookies or similar programs stored on computer.

## EU CYBERSECURITY STRATEGY

Understanding the increasing threat of cyber crimes and its profound impact on the economy, the European Commission has established a new cybersecurity strategy. According to the European Commission website, the new strategy, also known as Europe 2020 initiative, has a digital agenda that consists of seven pillars (Europe Commission 2020 initiative, 2013).

The first pillar is the digital single market. The aim of the digital single market pillar is to protect EU consumers in cyberspace, and to remove the obstacles that are hindering free flow of online services. The strategy of the pillar is geared toward enhancing the music download business and launching a single area for online payments. Some of the proposed action initiatives that are proposed to achieve the objective of the first pillar, include, but not limited to, simplifying pan-European licensing for online works, revision of the e-Signature directive, and protecting intellectual property rights online.

The second pillar applies to interoperability and standards. The goal of the pillar is to ensure that Europe IT devices, applications, services, and data repositories interact flawlessly (Europe Commission 2020 initiative, 2013). Some of the proposed actions initiatives to achieve this goal include creating a European interoperability framework, promoting standards-setting rules, and identifying and assessing means of requesting significant market to license information about products and services.

The third pillar is pertaining to trust and security. The goal of the pillar is to reduce the risks of malicious software and online fraud. Some of the proposed action solutions, include but not limited to, coordinated European responses to cyber attacks, reinforcing network and information security policy, establish a European cybercrime platform, creating a European Cybercrime Centre, strengthen the fight against cybercrime at the international level, supporting the report of illegal content online, awareness movements on online safety for children, and enforcing rules on personal data protection,

The fourth pillar concerns fast and ultra-fast Internet access. High definition televisions and videoconferences services require high-speed Internet. As a result, currently, Europe needs to have a download speed rate of 30 Mbps for its citizens and 100 Mbps by 2020 (Europe Commission 2020 initiative, 2013). Some of the proposed action solutions include developing national broadband plans, safeguarding the open Internet for consumers, reduction of the cost of deploying high-speed electronic communications network.

The fifth pillar is about enhancing digital literacy, skills and inclusion. 30% of Europeans have never used the Internet at all (Europe Commission 2020 initiative, 2013). The goal of this pillar is to enhance digital skills to people, in order to fully participate in society. Some of the items that the digital agenda is proposing to tackle include prioritizing digital literacy for European social fund, developing a framework to recognize Information and Communication Technology (ICT) skills, and to mainstream e-Learning in national policies.

The sixth pillar focuses on research and innovations. The objective of this pillar is to turn best research ideas into marketable products and services. Such an objective can be achieved by leveraging more private investment for ICT research and innovation, and by reinforcing coordination and merging of resources. Other strategies include developing new generation of web-based applications and services.

The seventh pillar focuses on enabling ICT benefits for EU society. ICT can be used to reduce energy consumption and transform health services. Some of the European Commission's proposed strategies to achieve the objective of the seventh pillar include partnership between the ICT sectors. Other initiatives include launching green paper on solid state lighting, and fostering EU-wide standards interoperability testing and certification of e-Health.

As a collective EU response to the increasing amount of cybercrimes, the European Commission decided to establish a European Cybercrime Centre (EC3) at Europol, which is the European law enforcement agency in The Hague, Netherlands. The objective of the center is to act as a focal point in Europe to fight cybercrime, contribute to the faster reactions in the event of online crimes, and to support international allies. The EC3 officially started its activities on January 1st, 2013. However, it is expected to be fully functional by 2015.

## CYBERSPACE CHALLENGES

There is a bridging now from the digital-world to the physical-world. Cyber attacks are capable of taking over industrial systems, such as STUXNET virus that attacked the Iranian nuclear power plant. Cyberspace has a target attribution problem; it is very difficult to know the exact location where the attack originated. For example, an attacker in China could lease a server in Europe to hack into a system in Russia, and then deliver an attack on a financial institution in the U.S. Due to lack of international cybersecurity policies, many governments and businesses are in a very difficult situation in pursuing legal actions against cybercriminals. Consequently, many nations that lack cybersecurity laws are considered cyber-sanctuary to hackers.

The sophistication and relatively cheap cost of hacking tools make cyberspace even more challenging. Cybercriminals constantly evolve their hacking techniques, and even minor changes enable them to escape automated detection. Hackers also share their intelligence as the speed of the Internet. They communicate and collaborate much more freely than law enforcement and security professionals do. Unlike law enforcement or federal agencies, hackers are not regulated. Furthermore, lack of web regulations, lack of skilled security analysts, and poor information security posture are among the leading factors that have led to the flourishing of cybercrimes. The following are some of the causes of poor security posture in many organizations (Musa, 2013):

1. Lack of continuous monitoring.
2. Lack of continuous specialized training.
3. Lack of funding to implement security projects.
4. Lack of cybersecurity awareness training.
5. Lack of knowledgeable assessors.
6. Lack of leadership and leadership support.
7. Lack of strategic planning.
8. Misconfiguration of network devices.
9. Vague security policies and procedures.

Other challenges involved in fighting cybercrime include lack of cybersecurity research and development, and insufficient collaboration between government and private sectors. Governments are encouraged to embrace and effectively fund cybersecurity research and development. Governments must place emphasis on enhancing coordination efforts and fostering cybersecurity initiatives between government and private sectors. Additionally, private sectors need to collaborate in joint initiatives. Some private sectors are hesitant to work collaboratively with other private sectors: they are afraid that their competitors may find a breach to gain competitive advantage. The truth is most competitors are in the same boat of vulnerability; they face the same threats. Working together will most likely enhance their resistance mechanisms against cybercrimes, in both collaborative development and also by peer review. A simple memorandum of agreement or privacy disclosure agreement can protect collaborators.

Jurisdiction is another cyberspace challenge that many nations are facing. Jurisdiction is usually determined based on the location where the offense was committed. In real court systems, judges work on cases that are within their jurisdiction. But in the cyber world, an attacker could be anywhere in the world far from the crime scene. Even if a cybercriminal is brought to trial, law enforcement on an international criminal is very complex in countries which do not have uniform or equivalent cybersecurity laws.

## CIVIL LIBERTY AND PRIVACY CONCERNS

Almost all types of communications, including Internet and mobile phones leave trails or digital footprint. Digital footprint provides data on visited web sites, searched links, what was typed, what was said, and even physical location. Some companies use such data in targeted marketing or social influence. Some digital footprint data may be available to the public by performing a simple Internet search, and other material may be inaccessible without access rights. Digital footprint data may deduce personal information, such as race, religion, political views, or intelligence. Therefore, data collected via digital footprint may impact personal privacy and civil liberty.

Digital footprint is controversial in that privacy is in competition. In the U.S., the recent update to the Cyber Intelligence Sharing and Protection Act (CISPA) is a great example. Recently, 34 civil liberties organizations have opposed the new amendments to CISPA. CISPA provides exception to privacy laws. CISPA information sharing allows companies to transfer sensitive data, including Internet data, emails, and others to other companies and government agencies, without prior authorization of the concerned individuals. Unexpectedly, the White House threatens to veto the controversial CISPA unless privacy and civil liberties protections are included to the updated act.

## TECHNICAL APPROACHES

Risks can be managed in four ways: they can be accepted, avoided, mitigated, or simply transferred. Risk acceptance indicates accepting the loss from the risk, when it occurs. On the other hand, risk avoidance signifies eliminating the risk by not performing the activity that could carry risk (Poolsappasit, 2010). An example would be not buying a program that handles electronic transactions on an unsecured port, such as port 80. Mitigating the risk would involve reducing the likelihood of the loss from occurring. Additionally, buying insurance on property signifies risk transfer.

There are numerous measures available to mitigate cyber risks. Risks can be mitigated by technical and non-technical approaches. Technical approaches may include access control measures, such as firewall, anti-virus software, content filtering proxy servers, white listing, intrusion detection and prevention systems, vulnerability assessment, disk encryption, and certification and accreditation to ensure that systems have the appropriate security controls in place. Port security and MAC

filtering can also be used to prevent rogue devises from connecting to the network. Also, there are several measures that can be taken to reduce or mitigate buffer overflow vulnerabilities, such as code auditing, non-executable stack, safe functions, and compiler techniques.

Layer two security best practices may include using dedicated Virtual Local Area Network (VLAN) identification for trunk ports, avoiding using VLAN1, setting ports to non-trunking, and disabling unused ports. In addition, Dynamic Host Configuration Protocol (DHCP) snooping and VLAN Access List (ACL) can be deployed to stop most DHCP attacks. Furthermore, layer three best practices may include ingress/egress filtering using Unicast Reverse Path Forwarding (RPF) or ACL as necessary. Routers need to be configured with ACL, role based sub-netting, and routing protocol authentication. Other best practices to defeat network attacks may include keeping security patches up to date, shutting down unused services and ports, using passphrases and change them periodically, avoiding unnecessary web page inputs, performing data backup regularly, and enabling full disk encryption. Minimizing administrators' privileges, applying application directory white listing, and implementing digital signature and two-factor authentication solutions are also highly recommended.

NIST suggests that real-time monitoring of security controls using automated tools will provide agencies with a dynamic outlook of the efficiency of security controls and the organization security position. NIST encourages agencies to adopt a hybrid continuous monitoring solution that consists of both manual processes and automated process that consist of vulnerability scanning, penetration testing, log monitoring, log analysis, and log correlation tools.

Some vulnerability assessment methods include network discovery, wireless scanning, password cracking, penetration testing, social engineering, and systems vulnerability scans. There are many vulnerability assessment tools currently available for no change, also known as open source. Some of these tools include, but not limited to, Wireshark, NMAP, OpenVAS, Air Crack, Nikto, WebSecurkity, SQLmap, and Nessus. Nessus is one of the most widely used vulnerability assessment tool. Many security experts consider Nessus as one of the most powerful vulnerability assessment tools (Gascon, Orfila & Blasco, 2011). Nessus is capable of performing verity of network scans, such as discovery, auditing, compliance, patch management, and vulnerability analysis scans.

Penetration testing is a very powerful form of vulnerability assessment that can be used to continuously monitor the network security posture and the network ability to resist attacks. Penetration testing is a security testing that mimics real-world attack. It is used as a method for circumventing the security features of a system (Bechtsoudis & Sklavos, 2012). In addition to the tools referenced above, Core impact pro and Metaspolit framework are considered by many security experts as the best two penetration testing tools.

One of the most powerful automated continuous monitoring tools is IPS. As the name implies, IPS detects and prevents intrusions. There are three major detection methods that most of the IPSs rely on: behavior, signature, and anomaly based detections (Gade & Kumar, 2012). The behavior-based monitoring method depends on the formation of a baseline. Once this baseline is established, the monitoring tool is able to detect activities that vary from that standard of normal. The signature-based monitoring method depends on a database of signatures of known malicious or unwanted activities. An advantage of the signature-based method is that it can rapidly and accurately distinguish any event from its database of signatures (Pao, Or & Cheung, 2013). The anomaly-based monitoring method depends on rules by detecting out of normal operation or invalid form of activity (Stanciu, 2013).

## NON-TECHNICAL APPROACHES

Security policies and awareness training are non-technical approaches that can be used as measures to reduce cyber risks. As indicated above, some of the causes of weak security posture include devices misconfiguration, lack of training, and lake of security awareness. Misconfiguration of network devices is a direct result of lack of training (Musa, 2013). A study conducted by Stout (2006) concluded that lack of security training is a factor of the increase of systems' vulnerabilities. Training and motivating employees to work together enables faster problem detection and resolution (Ahmad, Wasay, & Malik, 2012). On the contrary, not providing training is one of the root causes for employees being disgruntled (Raines, 2013). Dissatisfied employees are the greatest threat in an organization when it comes to data leaks. Raines (2013) suggests that employees' satisfaction or dissatisfaction will impact the organization's performance. Therefore, training can be utilized as a tool to mitigate cyber risks.

Developing international agreements between nations is a non-technical solution that can be utilized to minimize cyber risks. The Budapest Convention (also known as the convention of cybercrime) is one of the most powerful international agreements on fighting cybercrimes. The agreement was adopted by committee of Ministers of the Council of Europe (CMCE) in 2001. The agreement targets infringements of copyright, child pornography, hate crimes, and violations of network security. Additionally, EU established EC3, which is cross-border law enforcement against cybercrime. US Vice-President Joe Biden, speaking at the 2011 London Conference on Cyberspace, called EC3 "the best form of international agreement in this area".

In 1997, the Group of Eight (G8), eight great industrialized countries (US, UK, Russia, France, Italy, Japan, Germany, and Canada) released a "Minister's Communique" as a roadmap to fight cybercrime. The agreement mandates that law enforcement must be equipped with the latest technology, in order to properly fight cybercrimes. Furthermore, in 2002, Asia-Pacific Economic Cooperation (APEC) adopted cybersecurity strategy to fight cybercrimes. The strategy consists of six major areas: legal developments, information sharing, security and technical guidelines, public awareness, and training and education. In 2009, the Economic Community of West African States (ECOWAS) adopted a framework on fighting cybercrimes.

National Initiative for Cybersecurity Education (NICE) is a national public awareness program lead by the U.S. NIST to guide the American people to a higher level of Internet safety. The goal of the program is to raise awareness among the American public about the need to strengthen cybersecurity. The objective of the program is to persuade Americans to see Internet safety as a shared responsibility.

## FUTURE RESEARCH DIRECTIONS

Cybercriminals continue to target different industries and different users each new year that passes. Cybercriminals are continuously changing the way they target people. Cybercrimes simply gets more sophisticated every year. Many enterprise technologies, such as Bring Your Own Device (BYOD), cloud computing, social media, or mobile devices are transforming the face of information security. Some of the top cybercrime trends that are expected to evolve include, but not limited to, financial industries, human trafficking, and mobile transactions. There are billions of users that are currently using smartphones. People use smartphones to listen to music, conduct banking transactions, purchase clothing, and conduct business transactions. As people depend more on mobile devices, cybercriminals may refine their approaches to exploit mobile transactions.

## CONCLUSION

The Internet has become an essential service for support of many industries, such as academic institutes, news agencies, airports, and even utility companies. However, the Internet was designed to be an open, academic tool, never to be secure. As a result, cybercrimes, cyber warfare, and other cyber illegal activities have spread to become a significant portion of Internet traffic. The protection of information systems is a constant challenge, and the cost of each data breach is expensive, but also severe to trust and reputation: cybercrimes cost over $100 billion dollars annually worldwide. Companies spend millions of dollars to protect their assets; despite all of this spending, security breaches are still on the rise. Consequently, it appears that more spending doesn't necessary imply better security or fewer breaches. Factors that contribute to the rise of cybercrime include, but not limited to, lack of international regulations, lack of web security standards, insufficiency of user awareness, lack of collaboration between agencies, and extreme sophistication of hacking tools. While government agencies are regulated, hackers are not. Hackers communicate and collaborate much more freely than law enforcement agencies do.

Today, the Internet offers predators anonymity to target children for criminal activities. While the Internet can be a great knowledge source for children, children can be targeted by offenders through the relative anonymity and insecurity of social media websites, chat rooms, email, and even gaming websites. Many nations have many laws to protect children online; however, children's best online protection is parents. Parents must become computer literate, in order to get involved with their children's online activities. Parents are responsible for mentoring their children about the Internet safety. Parents are also liable for verifying the identity of the individuals interacting with their children. Furthermore, parents should use the parental-control features which are provided by many Internet service providers to control what children can see and browse on the Internet. Parents are highly encouraged to contact local authorities if they suspect that their children have been targeted by sex offenders.

Jurisdiction and target attribution are technical challenges involved in fighting cybercrime. It is difficult to know the exact location where an attack originated, and since cybercriminals can initiate attacks from anywhere in the world, it is challenging to determine who has jurisdiction on a court case. Simply, there are no cyber borders between nations. Making cyberspace reliable and secure is imperative for international economic growth and democracy. Therefore, fighting cybercrimes requires international collaboration; cybersecurity is inherently a global issue, and a global approach is now indispensable.

There are technical and non-technical approaches that can be utilized to mitigate cyber risks. Technical solutions may include white listing, firewall, intrusion prevention systems, and anti-virus services at the host level and gateway level. Trojans and other cyber threats can be detected and prevented by applying layering technologies, such as two-factor authentication, and transaction verification processes. IPS indicators and signatures may also be used to detect and block malware Trojans. Non-technical solutions may include national cybersecurity awareness programs for less-sophisticated users, enforceable policies and procedures on cybersecurity for corporations, and cybersecurity agreements between nations. The United Nations could play a vital role in fighting cybercrimes by fostering and enforcing international cybersecurity frameworks. Governments are encouraged to place primary emphasis on cybersecurity research and development, to harmonize cybersecurity efforts between public and private sectors, and to adopt uniform procedures for enforcement and prosecution. Public and private sectors simply need to collaborate aggressively in joint initiatives. In conclusion, cybercrime impacts public and private sectors together, and it will take society to work collaboratively, in order to make a significant impact against cybercrime. Individuals, organizations, and governments all have roles to play in achieving security and reducing cyber risks.

# REFERENCES

Ahmad, M., Wasay, E., & Malik, S. (2012). Impact of employee motivation on customer satisfaction: Study of airline industry in Pakistan. *Interdisciplinary Journal of Contemporary Research in Business, 4*(6), 531–539.

ArcSight. (2011). *Second annual cost of cybercrime study*. Retrieved from http://www.hpenterprisesecurity.com/collateral/report

Arthur, C. (2011, February 7). Anonymous attacks US security company. *The Guardian Magazine*. Retrieved from http://www.theguardian.com

Bechtsoudis, A., & Sklavos, N. (2012). Aiming at higher network security through extensive penetration tests. *IEEE Latin America Transactions, 10*(3), 1752–1756. doi:10.1109/TLA.2012.6222581

Brazil Constitution. (n.d.). *Article V*. Retrieved from http://english.tse.jus.br/arquivos/federal-constitution

Clarke, R. (2010). *Cyber war: The next threat to national security and what to do about it*. New York: Ecco.

European Commission. (1995). *Directive 95/46/EC of the European Parliament and of the Council on the protection of individuals with regard to the processing of personal data and on the free movement of such data*. Retrieved from http://ec.europa.eu/justice/policies/privacy/docs/95-46-ce/dir1995-46_part1_en.pdf

European Commission. (2002). *Directive 2002/58/EC of the European Parliament and of the Council of 12 July 2002 concerning the processing of personal data and the protection of privacy in the electronic communications sector.* Retrieved from http://eur-lex.europa.eu/LexUriServ/LexUriServ.do?uri=OJ:L:2002:201:0037:0037:EN:PDF

European Commission. (2013). *Europe 2020 initiative.* Retrieved from http://ec.europa.eu/digital-agenda/en

Gascon, H., Orfila, A., & Blasco, J. (2011). Analysis of update delays in signature-based network intrusion detection systems. *Computers & Security*, *30*(8), 613–624. doi:10.1016/j.cose.2011.08.010

Hunton, P. (2012). Data attack of the cybercriminal: Investigating the digital currency of cybercrime. *Computer Law & Security Report*, *28*(2), 201–207. doi:10.1016/j.clsr.2012.01.007

Intelligence and National Security Alliance (INSA). (2011). *Cyber Intelligence.* Retrieved from http://issuu.com/insalliance/docs/insa_cyber_intelligence/1

*Internet Users.* (2012). Retrieved from http://www.internetworldstats.com/stats.htm

Kumar, S., & Gade, R. (2012). Experimental evaluation of Cisco ASA-5510 intrusion prevention system against denial of service attacks. *Journal of Information Security*, *3*(2), 122–137. doi:10.4236/jis.2012.32015

Lieberman, J. (2012). Senator Lieberman's speech on cybersecurity act. *Washington Post.* Retrieved from http://www.washingtonpost.com/blogs/2chambers/post/cybersecurity-bill-fails-in-the-senate/2012/08/02/gJQABofxRX_blog.html

McGraw, G. (2013). Cyber war is inevitable (unless we build security in). *The Journal of Strategic Studies*, *36*(1), 109–119. doi:10.1080/01402390.2012.742013

Musa, W. (2013). *Improving cybersecurity audit processes in the U.S. government.* (Unpublished doctoral dissertation). National Graduate School, Falmouth, MA.

Obama, B. (2012). *President Obama's comments on cyber security.* Retrieved from http://www.whitehouse.gov/cybersecurity

Pao, D., Or, N., & Cheung, R. C. (2013). A memory-based NFA regular expression match engine for signature-based intrusion detection. *Computer Communications*, *36*(10-11), 1255–1267. doi:10.1016/j.comcom.2013.03.002

Poolsappasit, N. (2010). *Towards an efficient vulnerability analysis methodology for better security risk management* (Doctoral dissertation). Retrieved from ProQuest dissertations and theses database. (Document ID 3419113).

Privacy Act of 1974 § 102, 42 U.S.C. § 4332 (1974).

Raines, S. (2013). *Conflict management for managers: resolving workplace, client, and policy disputes.* San Francisco, CA: Jossey-Bass.

Stanciu, N. (2013). Technologies, methodologies and challenges in network intrusion detection and prevention systems. *Informatica Economica*, *17*(1), 144–156. doi:10.12948/issn14531305/17.1.2013.12

Stout, T. (2006). *Improving the decision making process for information security through a pre-implementation impact review of security countermeasures* (Doctoral dissertation). Retrieved from ProQuest dissertations and theses database (Document ID 3215299)

Symantec Corporation. (2012). *2012 Annual Security Report.* Retrieved from http://www.symantec.com/annualreport

United States Computer Emergency Readiness Team (US-CERT). (2013). *Malicious Code*. Retrieved from http://www.us-cert.gov/government-users/reporting-requirements

United States National Institute of Standards and Technology (NIST). (2013). *Cyber Framework*. Retrieved from http://www.nist.gov/itl/cyber-framework.cfm

United States Office of Management and Budget (OMB). (2011). *FY2011 Report to congress on implementation the federal information security management act of 2002*. Retrieved from http://www.whitehouse.gov/sites/default/files/omb/assets/egov_docs/fy11_fisma.pdf

United States Office of Management and Budget (OMB). (2012). *FY2011 Report to congress on implementation the federal information security management act of 2002*. Retrieved from http://www.whitehouse.gov/sites/default/files/omb/assets/egov_docs/fy12_fisma.pdf

Walker, M. (2012). *Certified Ethical Hacker: Exam guide: All-in-one*. New York: McGraw-Hill.

White House. (2013). *Executive order on improving critical infrastructure cybersecurity*. Retrieved from http://www.whitehouse.gov/the-press-office/2013/02/12/executive-order-improving-critical-infrastructure-cybersecurity

Whitman, M. (2011). *Principles of information security*. Boston, MA: Course Technology.

## KEY TERMS AND DEFINITIONS

**APT:** Advanced Persistent Threat (APT) is a set of stealthy and continuous hacking processes often orchestrated by human targeting a specific entity.

**Cybercrime:** Committing an illegal act using a computer or network device.

**Cyber Warfare:** Utilizes cyber mediums, such as Internet or telecommunication lines, as weapons to brutally destroy enemies' critical infrastructures, such as power plants.

**Digital Footprint:** A process that provides data on visited web sites, searched links, what was typed, what was said, and even physical location.

**IDS/IPS:** Intrusion Detection/Prevention System - Software or appliance that detects and prevents malicious traffic.

**Risk:** The probability of a vulnerability being exploited.

**Threat:** Entity presenting a danger to an asset.

**Trojan:** A malicious program that pretends to be something desirable. It hides its true identity.

# Chapter 14
# Cyber–Crimes against Adolescents:
## Bridges between a Psychological and a Design Approach

**Filipa da Silva Pereira**
*University of Minho, Portugal*

**Marlene Alexandra Veloso de Matos**
*University of Minho, Portugal*

**Álvaro Miguel do Céu Gramaxo Oliveira Sampaio**
*Polytechnic Institute of Cávado and Ave, Portugal*

## ABSTRACT

*At young ages there is an increase in reports of intimidation, harassment, intrusion, fear, and violence experienced through Information Technologies (IT). Hacking, spamming, identity theft, child pornography, cyber bullying, and cyber stalking are just few examples of cyber-crimes. This chapter aims to contribute, from a psychological and design perspective, to an integrative viewpoint about this complex field of cyber-crime. In this chapter, the most common types of cyber-crimes, epidemiological data, and the profiles of cyber victims and aggressors' are approached. The studies that identify the factors contributing to IT misuse and to growing online vulnerability, principally in adolescents, are also discussed. Likewise, the central explanatory theories for the online victimization and the risk factors for victimization and perpetration online are addressed. Finally, some cyber-crime prevention strategies are anticipated, in particular among young people, seeking to provide clues to the consolidation of recent policies, namely at the digital design level.*

## INTRODUCTION

During the last 15th years, the Internet and the other ITs have radically transformed the world, mainly in terms of communication and social interaction. In areas such as science, education, health, public administration, commerce and the development of the global net, the Internet offers an unmatched variety of benefits. Therefore, information technologies turn out to be a communication tool deep rooted in the quotidian of world population. This applies especially to youths who present high

DOI: 10.4018/978-1-4666-6324-4.ch014

indices of utilization and digital skills (Haddon, Livingstone & EU Kids Online network, 2012; Madden, Lenhart, Cortesi, Gasser, Duggan, Smith & Beaton, 2013). In this way, it is not surprising, as IT imposes as a mean of mass communication, the increase in reports of harm, intimidation, harassment and violence experienced through IT: experiences commonly known as cyber-crime (Dempsey, Sulkowsk, Dempsey & Storch, 2011).

Cyber-crime is a concept that integrates a set of activities related to the use of telecommunications networks for criminal purposes (Kraemer-Mbula, Tang & Rush, 2013) and it is described in the Portuguese law n° 109/2009 of 15th of September. It can comprises a diversity of (1) anti-social activities, such as those supported by computers (e.g., sending spam, malware) and (2) offenses aimed at a specific target (e.g., cyber stalking, cyber bullying) (Kim, Jeong, Kim & So, 2011). To accomplish cyber-crime activities, there are a variety of manipulation techniques (e.g., bribe, threat) and different ways through which Internet users can find themselves involved in risk behaviors (e.g., contact with strangers, the sharing of personal information) (Whittle, Hamilton-Giachritsis, Beech & Collings, 2013). However, the Portuguese penal code only contemplates as cyber-crime, anti-social activities supported by computer (material damages of technical content). In contrast to what happens in the United States, for example, cyber stalking or cyber bulling is not criminalized in the Portuguese law as a criminal offense, being only possible to criminalize individual actions that make up this form of persistent persecution and harassment (e.g., threats, identity theft and invasion of privacy).

The Internet turned into a space in which the more traditional crimes may take new forms and prosper in a totally immaterial environment (Clarke, 2004). The criminal activities that previously required the physical presence of his actors, in a place and specific time, are now possible independently of the physical location or time

(Reyns, 2013). Because of this, the mysticism that surrounds the cyberspace and the anonymous nature of Internet means that individuals with reduced likelihood to start a criminal act in the real context (e.g., children and adolescents) can easily began to have a high probability to do so in the online context (McGrath & Casey, 2002).

As acknowledged previously, with the diffusion of IT, there is a tendency for cyber-crime to increase, both in its frequency as in the sophistication of the acts and techniques to commit it. However, it is not possible to eradicate this side of the online world. Thus, the solution is to investigate those new forms of cyber aggression in order to understand, control and minimize potential forms of cybernetic victimization and their impact (physical, mental and social health loss) (Marinos et al., 2011).

Despite cyber-crime being looked at with a growing scientific interest, this has not been sufficiently reflected from the psychological approach, which may have an important role in understanding the key factors that allow an early identification of features and enables the prediction of the course and evolution of these behaviors.

Cyber-crime is substantially different from traditional crimes, since it benefits from the timelessness, the possibility of anonymity and the absence of a restricted space (Yar, 2005). There are several theories that have been developing explanations about cyber-crime, including the routine activity theory (Cohen & Felson, 1979), the general theory of crime (Gottfredson & Hirschi, 1990) and the social learning theory (Skinner & Fream, 1997).

After exploring the cyber victims and aggressors' profiles, we address the main contributions of the above-mentioned theories for the understanding of the data related to cyber aggressors and cyber victims. The recognition of the steps implicated on cyber-crime and the conditions that facilitate it, permits allows the development of preventive actions towards cyber-crime (Clarke, 2004).

This chapter is organized as follows: the first part describes the literature background about cyber-crime in general population, specifically against IT devices and against IT users. Part two analyzes cyber-crime against adolescents, discussing common cyber-crimes typologies and targets, and risk factors for cyber victimization in adolescence are also discussed. Subsequently, various issues and controversies are discussed (e.g., strengths and weaknesses) related to psychological and digital approaches to cyber-crime against adolescents. The role of the victim, the offender, the digital environment, and the importance of parental involvement in cyber-crime prevention are problematized. Finally, solutions and future directions to achieve enhanced security of adolescents are addressed.

## BACKGROUND

The Norton cyber-crime report (2011), carried out by Symantec-Norton, concludes that more than 2/3 of online adults (69%) were victims of cyber-crime throughout their lives, which is equivalent to more than a million victims per day and 14 victims per second. In 2012 the Norton Cyber-crime Report documented a worsening in cyber victimization to 18 victims per second. At the same time, during the year of 2010, cyber-crime grew 337% in Portugal and in Spain, which corresponds to nine million cyber-attacks (Kasperksy Lab, 2010). The most common targets are, according to the aforementioned study, men between 18 and 31 years, who access the Internet often via cell phone.

According to Bossler and Holt (2010), sending malicious software (e.g., spam, malware) is the most common type of cyber-crime. Their study shows that 37% of American college students (N=573) have experienced this type of victimization during the year of 2009. More specifically, 16.8% was a target of password theft; 9.8% experienced the improper access to their computer data and 4.4% was victim of credit card theft through electronic means. In relation to these forms of theft, invasion and misuse, spamming, phishing and hacking are the three most common ways to acquire sensitive data (e.g., usernames, passwords, banking information) towards financial gain and scams (e.g., obtain goods and services or sell information to other cyber aggressors) (Kraemer-Mbula et al., 2013). The number of spammers has grown exponentially and the new trend points to the growing use of social networking sites (e.g., Facebook, MySpace) for the diffusion of indiscriminate messages, inducing Internet users to access web pages with malware (e.g., virus, worms, Trojan horses, spyware) (Kraemer-Mbula et al., 2013). In turn, phishing is a sophisticated form of spam that appears many times through an email of an apparent reliable entity. Hacking happens when a non-authorized person breaks into a computer (Holt, 2007). This last strategy is generally known as cyber terrorism and is achieved through the application of specific tools that requires superior programming skills to the earlier mentioned forms of digital crime (Kraemer-Mbula et al., 2013).

Despite the existence of various anti-virus software, encryption and fraud detection, the ENISA Threat Landscape Report (Marinos, 2013) assumes that we are witnessing a growing proficiency, sophistication and effectiveness by cyber criminals that outweigh the protection and preventive mechanisms. In addition, the current literature has pointed to the combination of online methods (e.g., through Trojans, phishing, hacking) with offline methods (e.g., intercepting mail and bank documents, verification of the victims personal garbage) for accessing private information and for the execution of identity theft and other frauds, which may indicate more effectiveness and extent of the illegal practices committed (Kraemer-Mbula et al., 2013).

Considering its consequences, data from the Norton cyber-crime annual report (2012) indicate that the cost of cyber-crimes supported by computer has as principal aggressors and targets adults' population and it ascends to 110 billion dollars annually. It illustrates the vast business and economic impact of this emerging phenomenon. Besides adults, the "actors" can also be children and adolescents, especially when we talk about the forms of cyber-crime against the person and/ or their dignity (e.g., cyber stalking, cyber bullying and harassment) and it can result in important emotional and social implications at the individual level). The EU Kids Online network (2013) concluded that about 15 to 20% of online adolescents have reported significant levels of discomfort and threat regarding this form of cyber-crime experience. Because some adolescents achieve offline encounters with strangers and are targets of cyber bullying and/or cyber stalking, they are becoming more likely to experience a greater impact (Almeida, Delicado & Alves, 2008; Bocij, 2004; Haddon et al., 2012; Helsper, Kalmus, Hasebrink, Sagvari & Haan, 2013). Still, it is especially pertinent to point out that not all risk means negative experiences or damage to the adolescent: it depends on the individual and social factors such as self-confidence, acquired skills and mediation held, and prior experiences of victimization and / or perpetration in the cyberworld (Smahel, Helsper, Green, Kalmus, Blinka & Ólafsson, 2012; Vandoninck, d'Haenens & Roe, 2013).

In that context, online harassment (e.g., cyber stalking, cyber bullying) is a form of cyber-crime that involves sending threatening or sexual messages through email, instant messaging services or posts in online chats (Bocij, 2004; Fisher, Cullen & Turner, 2002) and it can lead victims to feel fear, emotional and psychological stress, equivalent to harassment and persecution experienced in the real world (Finn, 2004). In Bossler and Holt's study (2010), online harassment was the second most common form of victimization experienced by college students (18.8%). However, the complexity of the phenomenon and the different settings and samples taken in the study of online harassment are some of the obstacles to reliable comparison of the online harassment incidence and to understand the phenomenon. The fact that this crime occurs

in the virtual environment, guided by anonymity, innovation and versatility of the strategies of intrusion used, makes the understanding of online harassment and the study of the profiles of cyber victims more complex (Wolak, Mitchell & Finkelhor, 2007; Pratt, Holtfreter & Reisig, 2010).

After the explanation of the two bigger forms of cyber-crime and respective targets this chapter presents some contributions, which are focused on cyber-crime against people as an emerging topic of concern, especially among adolescents. The type of crime (against the person and their dignity), the population, the psychological and emotional damage, as well as the invisibility of this cyber-crime typology in the Portuguese penal code, justify the relevance of this approach focus. We also expect to contribute to the acknowledgement of the necessity to develop effective strategies at the preventive level.

## CYBER-CRIME AGAINST ADOLESCENTS

Adolescence is a phase that is characterized by the need for sexual and moral maturity as well as the construction of identity (Subrahmanyam, Greenfield & Tynes, 2004). The complexity involved in understanding oneself leads to an increased curiosity on specific topics (e.g., sexuality) and to the need of adolescents to extend their interpersonal relationships (e.g., make new friendships with peers or adults) and to explore multiple social and relational contexts. As a result, their social activity and exposure to different interpersonal relationships is greater (Subrahmanyam et al., 2004). In order to broaden these opportunities for socialization and development, adolescents have joined cyberspace (as a complement to the real world), specifically social networks.

Concerning the American reality, the study of Pew Internet & American Life (Madden et al., 2013) concludes that one in four adolescents, between the ages of 12-17 ($N$=802) are "cell-mostly" internet users; they mostly go online using their phone instead of using some other device such as a desktop or laptop computer. Ninety-five of these adolescents used the Internet during 2012, 78% had a cell phone, and almost half (47%) of them own smartphones (Madden et al., 2013). In Europe, studies with adolescents suggest similar results. The network EU Kids Online (2011) concluded that 93% (N=25142) of European adolescents (9-16 years) access the Internet at least once a week and 60% access all, or almost every day, and the average daily time spent online is 88 minutes. The study also documents that 59% of adolescents are registered in a social network and within those active users, 26% have the profile in public mode. The most popular networks are Facebook and Twitter, but new types of social networks continue to arise and some, like Instagram or Pinterest, begin to engage many members. In Portugal, for example, 54% of adolescents use the Internet daily and about half of the adolescents above 11 years old have reported signs of Internet overuse (the second highest value in European terms) (Smahel et al., 2012). Smahel et al. (2012) also revealed that Portugal is one of the countries where more adolescents access the Internet in their bedrooms (67% vs. 49% of the European average) and where fewer parents access the Internet (30%), noting that youth population is the one that masters the use of IT. Based on these data, it is evident the great vulnerability of adolescents towards victimization and perpetration of negative behaviors in the virtual environment (Bilic, 2013; Wolak, Mitchel & Finkelhor, 2006, 2007).

The Internet seems to be a virtual laboratory and a stage for a series of developments and transformations in the process of construction of adolescents' identity (Palfrey & Gasser, 2008). One of the reasons for this increasing membership and digital enhancement may be the fact that adolescents perceived too many restrictions in the real world (e.g., need for physical confrontation, geographical and temporal limitation) and/or feel rejected by the social and cultural patterns prevail-

ing in offline world (e.g., on the sexuality theme) (Palfrey & Gasser, 2008). Adolescents need to be constantly connected to their peers may also cause a greater adherence to IT and the establishment of an increasingly positive attitude about cyberspace. However, recent estimates on Internet usage habits suggest that adolescents are sharing an increasing amount of information at different public virtual environments (Madden et al., 2013). Based on these data, and bearing in mind that the virtual environment assigns a greater fragility to information disclosed (e.g., increases the potential for manipulation, falsification and misuse), it is understandable the greater vulnerability of these adolescents to the online victimization (Bilic, 2013; Wolak et al., 2006, 2007).

So, recent estimates on adolescence cyber-crime indicate that this is a growing and transversal problem (Marinos, 2013; Marinos et. al, 2011; Madden et al., 2013; Mitchell, Finkelhor, Jones & Wolak, 2010; Wolak et al., 2007) that may take different forms and involve several Internet resources (e.g., chat rooms, social networks, email) and mobile devices (e.g., image or text messages) (Child Exploitation and Online Protection Centre [CEOP], 2013; Haddon et al., 2012). However, there are still few studies on cyber-crime that answer the question of "how" and "why". Therefore the next section presents an analysis of predominant online risks among adolescents, seeking to answer the question: How do the conditions of access and use, as well as the cyber activities, constitute risk factors for adolescent cyber victimization?

## Common Cyber-Crimes Typology and Targets

About 5722 (N=25000) European adolescents (9-16 years) already experienced one or more online risks, being Portugal one of the European countries associated with a moderate use and an incidence rate of low-risk online (Helsper et al., 2013). According to the EU Kids Online project, the risk exposure to sexual explicit material (e.g., pornography) seems to be the most common European threat (4 out of 10 adolescents have already experienced it). These data are in accordance with the previous European and international literature (CEOP, 2013; Wolak, Mitchell & Finkelhor, 2004; Wolak et al., 2007; Marcum, 2008). In addition, the viewing of violent content (e.g., maltreatment of animals or people, real murders, torture) seems to be experienced in a proportion of 1 in every 3 adolescents. Being the target of cyber bullying and cyber stalking, for example, comes in the fourth place (in a proportion of 1 in every 5/6 online adolescents), followed by being a target of unwanted sexual comments, reported by 1 in every 10 adolescents in Germany, Ireland and Portugal. Finally, scheduling offline meetings with someone whose adolescent just met online (another adolescent or adult) seem to be one of the less common risks (1 in every 11 adolescents) (Helsper et al., 2013). This victimization sorting is also the ranking of the most reported concerns by online adolescents – biggest concern to the exposure to inappropriate content, while they are less worried about the possibility of offline meetings with someone unknown – which may go against the trend of many parents and digital prevention professionals (which typically care more about the risk of contact with strangers) (Livingstone, Kirwil, Ponte & Staksrud, 2013).

On the basis of these data, it is possible to conclude that, once online, children and adolescents have high probability to find potentially disturbing material and expose themselves to violent and/or sexual content. These data must be analyzed in the light of the literature and studies on multiple victimization in childhood and youth (e.g. Finkelhor, Ormrod & Turner, 2007), taking an intersectional approach (e.g. Berguer & Guidorz, 2009). Studies in this field indicate a significant percentage of children who experience multiple types of victimization and suggest the cumulative risk of the disadvantaged children and young people (Finkelhor et al., 2007). The

intersections of some disadvantage conditions (poverty, lower socioeconomic status, lower education) and socio-demographic characteristics (lower age, being a girl) may potentiate the risk of cumulative victimization in cyberspace. Girls, for example, are slightly more likely to use chat rooms and other communication platforms, being more easily targeted by unwanted messages and/or unpleasant questions (by strangers online) about their personal life. On the other hand, boys tend to play more online and show a greater tendency for the involvement in risk situations (e.g., hacking) and to the exposure to violent or pornographic content (Livingstone & Haddon, 2009; Helsper et al., 2013). Boys also seem to be more likely to achieve offline meetings with individuals who they only met over the Internet (Livingstone & Haddon, 2009). Similarly, it is important to highlight that, although older adolescents with a higher socioeconomic status can get access more often and longer to a greater number of IT, the experience of cyber-crime seems to be higher among younger adolescents with social disadvantages (Livingstone & Haddon, 2009). Such vulnerability is due to the fact that online victimization is related to the adolescents' digital literacy skills, which in turn also relate to the socio-economic level of the household and their respective countries' development (Livingstone & Haddon, 2009; Palfrey & Gasser, 2008). Older adolescents, who belong to more educated households and digitally more developed societies (e.g., United States) have greater probability to present digital literacy rates (e.g., possess greater knowledge and skills), which gives them a higher capacity of online risk management and of problem solving. These competencies are sustained by the formal (e.g., through schools) and informal (e.g., parenting) educational systems, which often teach safety skills to adolescents and emphasize their critical judgment. Instead, younger adolescents who belong to aggregates and to digitally less-developed countries tend to have lower literacy rates, lacking the number of teachers and guardians that are able to transmit the skills required for the use, management and prevention of the online risk (Palfrey & Gasser, 2008).

Once cyber-crime in adolescence is a complex and dynamic concept, encompassing a variety of ambiguous and controversial ways, it has not been easy to know the phenomenon of cyber-crime against adolescents as a whole neither to determine objective and static cyber victimization profiles (Marcum, 2008). Thus, it becomes necessary to develop more investigations in this area, as individuals and society give evidence of their digital development.

## Factor Risks for Cyber Victimization in Adolescence

Despite the rise of cyber-crime threats, the understanding and explanation of cyber-crime is still at an embryonic stage of development, since there are limited investigations available with research focus on the adolescent phase and/or that privilege sufficiently comprehensive methodological approaches (e.g., quantitative and qualitative, with victims and offenders) for the understanding of cyber-crime. However, some authors have examined some risk factors – at situational, at peers and at individual levels - that may explain the greater vulnerability of adolescents (Helsper et al., 2013; Mitchell, Finkelhor & Wolak, 2003, 2007; Wolak et al., 2004; Ybarra, Mitchell, Finkelhor, & Wolak, 2007). Through the analysis of these factors and the exploitation of their interaction, we intended to provide a better understanding of the complexity of the adolescent victimization in the online world, and to compete for the opportunity to act in a preventive and increasingly effective way.

## Cyber Lifestyles-Routines

Marcum (2008) examined how the online routine activities affect the probability of adolescents becoming online victims. According to this study, the sharing of personal information (e.g., name,

address and pictures) is one of the risk factors that best predict the online victimization of adolescents. These results were consistent with other empirical studies that concluded that adolescents who spend more time online, participating in a wide range of online activities (e.g., social networks, chat rooms, games) and discussing sexual matters with virtual contacts, are also the most likely to encounter a online hazard (Helsper et al., 2013; Mitchell et al., 2007; Wolak et al., 2007; Ybarra et al., 2007; Sengupta & Chaudhuri, 2011). Virtual environments frequented by adolescents also seem to predict an increased predisposition to this victimization. More specifically, adolescents between 9 and 16 years of age (N=9904) are commonly subjected to inappropriate content (e.g., violent, pornographic), mainly due to surfing in video sharing websites, such as Youtube (32%). The general sites (29%) and the social networking sites (13%) and online games (10%) also appear to provide a greater risk of exposure to inappropriate material (Livingstone et al., 2013). On the other hand, chat rooms and other communication platforms tend to be often associated with the experience of unwanted contact by unknown users (43%) and the risk of conducts related to interpersonal violence (27%) (e.g., cyber bullying, cyber stalking, sexting) (Livingstone et al, 2013). This is precisely the principle supported by the routine activities theory (Cohen & Felson, 1979): the achievement of certain routine activities and the frequency of certain virtual environments are factors that may explain the victim's exposure and, consequently, the greater vulnerability to cyber victimization (Eck & Clarke, 2003). Risk opportunities arise when a motivated offender intersects, in an unprotected environment (e.g., no filters, blocking the window, low parental mediation) with a vulnerable target (Cohen & Felson, 1979). The fact that Internet broke through adolescents' lifestyles increased the process of changing their daily routine activities the likelihood of adolescents intersects with a motivated cyber offender. The fact that digital literacy at certain ages, parents-children generations and households could still be very incipient and/or uneven increases the likelihood of online surfing under low protection. Consequently, criminal opportunities multiply in adolescent population. Although the cyber victim and offender may never have interacted in the same physical place, the integrity of these theories would be ensured by the offender-victim interaction within a virtual unprotected network. However, it is pertinent to note that adolescents' vulnerability to cyber victimization does not result only from the simple convergence of the vulnerable target, the motivated offender and of the unprotected environment. In fact there are no data that support the suggestion that only just adolescents spend long periods of time online, and share information about them. Nevertheless, the risks that adolescents face is substantial (Palfrey & Gasser, 2008). As a result, there is a need to explore additional risk factors associated with potentially deviant peers or friends and individual psychological characteristics.

## Deviant Behaviors and Association with Deviant Peers

The risky lifestyles, including the practice of crimes based on computer misuse (e.g. hacking), crimes against people (e.g., cyber stalking, cyber bullying) and the association to deviant cyber peers have been considered important risk factors for the increased experience of cyber-crime (Bossler, Holt & May, 2012). More specifically, the fact that adolescents had some friends who occasionally become involved in piracy crime or other illegal behaviors seem to increase the likelihood of these to also become involved in cyber-crime activities as an aggressor (Hollinger, 1997. Thus, there is a process of social learning and behaviors' imitation, as advocated by the social learning theory (Skinner & Fream, 1997). The prolonged coexistence with deviant peers leads to a constant exposure to criminal practices and to the possibility of transmission and learning criminal strategies. Access to cyber-crime software (e.g., hacking) is

also facilitated, by a kind of social reinforcement between these peers to commit cyber-crime. Such cyber-crime is often assumed as legitimate and necessary (Bossler & Holt, 2009, 2010). However, this contact with the criminal world could have two mainly consequences: 1) the proximity to motivated cyber aggressors, and 2) the reduction of individual protection of adolescent (increasing the vulnerability to be a potential target). In the same context, the practice of offline and/or online harassment against other peers or individuals can also increase the risk of the offender become a cyber-crime victim. Given a previous harassment experience, some victims may exhibit high levels of reactive aggression, being able to carry out retaliatory attacks, through IT, against their aggressor (Sontag, Cleman, Graber & Lyndon, 2011; Ybarra et al., 2007). We can witness, in this case, that the roles overlap between victim and aggressor. For this reason, although there are certain factors that may be more related to victimization or online perpetration, it is not correct to dichotomize the standardization of risk factors, since the fact that a person became a victim may also explain the practice of cyber-crime (Jennings, Piquero & Reingle, 2012).

## Socio-Psychological Characteristics

Livingstone et al. (2011) and Wolak et al. (2004) concluded that adolescents with psychological problems (e.g., depression, isolation), with relationship problems with parents and/or friends and belonging to minority groups (e.g., gay groups), are more likely to face the risk of contacts and grooming.

The personality traits, still incipient, and the socio-psychological characteristics also seem to influence the way adolescents interact with the online world (Olson, Daggs, Ellevold & Rogers, 2007). In particular, low self-confidence and self-esteem and poor social competence and problem solving, present a greater vulnerability for adolescents to be manipulated and to respond in accordance with the motivations of cyber aggressors, even developing strong emotional ties with their cyber aggressors (Livingstone & Helsper, 2007). These individual characteristics are advocated by the general theory of crime (Gottfredson & Hirschi, 1990). This theory conceptualizes crime as a result of low self-control, and there is a set of studies that corroborate this relationship (Buzzell, Foss & Middleton, 2006; Higgins, 2005; Higgins, Fell & Wilson, 2006; Higgins & Makin, 2004). Being adolescence a phase of development of the ability to control impulses, digital media can be a potentially dangerous tool.

In the online world, the metrics that matter to adolescents are how many "friends" they have on their social profile, how many comments they can attract to their Facebook wall and who is saying what and to whom, via the Internet (Palfrey & Gasser, 2008). This means that adolescents are focused on being accepted and on expanding their relations and competencies, regardless of the risk (e.g., sharing of private information). Accordingly, and regarding to the general theory of crime referred above, low self-control (characteristic of this age) leads to the adolescents tending to act impulsively (e.g., in order to achieve benefits and instant gratification), without reflecting sufficiently on potential risks and consequences of their actions (e.g., contact from strangers, legal punishment or retaliation attacks) (Bossler & Holt, 2010). Similarly, the low tolerance can lead to frustration among adolescents, with the complexity of many digital security devices (e.g., jammers of Windows, alarm systems), ending with the not regular update of these devices or even installing them at all (Schreck, 1999). The same is true, for example, in social networks, in which definitions of privacy and security are too complex and demanding for younger users. As a result, they surf the Internet unprotected, increasing their vulnerability to criminal victimization (Bossler & Holt, 2010; Forde & Kennedy, 1997).

Another individual characteristic of adolescents is the zeal for privacy. When they use IT and interact with content and virtual contacts, one of the normal procedures of adolescence is therefore to avoid any controls or parental supervision. However, the absence of monitoring and parental mediation is a risk factor that adds to the previously stated (Livingstone & Haddon, 2009; Marcum, 2008; Wolak et al., 2004).

As above mentioned, the type of online activities, the type of peers and the personal characteristics of adolescents' vulnerability are important components in order to understand the cyber victimization. Additionally, cyber-crime can be a "normal" and common experience in the daily life of adolescents, due to the growing need for adherence to new activities and exploration of new experiences of freedom, allowed by the virtual environment (Haddon, Livingstone, & EU Kids Online network, 2012). The investigation of risk factors based on lifestyles, peers, individual characteristics and routine activities of individuals is therefore crucial, and can provide important insights for designing situational prevention initiatives for the different types of cyber-crime against adolescents (Reyns, Henson & Fisher, 2011).

## ISSUES, CONTROVERSIES, PROBLEMS

According to the presented information, the online victimization seems to be due not only with psychological and developmental characteristics but also with to the preferences and choices of the activities that adolescents do while they are online.

However, this assumption should not be reflected as a problem of the victims (i.e., was the victim that exposed herself too much) (Clarke, 2004). In fact, some forms of cyber-crime can effectively take place even if the victim is provided with digital protection systems (e.g., antivirus, antispyware and firewall). That is why the principle of the routine activity theory is subject to empirical controversy. If, from one point of view, Choi (2008) argues that the use of digital protection decreases the probability of a computer be target by malware, on the other, Reyns et al. (2011) state that, in the case of cyber stalking, for example, this method is not fully effective in protecting targets against unwanted contacts and threats. The same is also corroborated by Marcum (2008). In addition, some young people, because they are digital natives or because they have superior knowledge of technology, can alter security settings and/or filter preferences that their parents, teachers or educators have defined for their safety (e.g. against pornography). At the level of exposure of adolescents to pornography and other inappropriate content, one must still point out that often these experiences happen because the adolescents are looking for them. Although parents, educators and professionals in the field can choose to believe otherwise, a set of studies has documented that about a third of American adolescents (10-17 years) who were exposed to pornography were in fact looking for it (e.g., Wolak et al., 2007). The same is also true in the real world. How many adolescents did the educators surprise while viewing, on their own initiative, a magazine or a porno video?

Exposure to risk during adolescence is therefore a common reality, necessary and inevitable, extensible to the virtual world and the real world. Often, adolescents do not perceive these risks as an adverse situation, but as an opportunity to promote a moral development experience, and sexual identity.

However, experiences in the virtual world can differ from experiences in the real world, because: 1) the immaterial nature of cyberspace, 2) to the reduced probability of mediators (e.g., parents and educators) between the adolescents and the experience, 3) to the increased diversity of information available. While in the physical world educators may feel safer about the kind of content

that adolescents have access, in cyberspace this awareness may be diminished. In addition, it is much easier to access disturbing information via the Internet, maximizing the chances of unwanted criminal victimization. The fact that cyberspace is a place where users can present themselves often in the form of an avatar (fictional character), or an anonymous user, leads to greater behavioral disinhibition, characterized by a greater sense of freedom, creativity, relaxation and sense of impunity (Blais, Craig, Pepler, & Connolly, 2008). Such characteristics may thus substantiate the greatest difficulty in reducing the online impulses and a greater propensity of adolescents, including female, to engage in socially objectionable activities (e.g., of cyber bullying, cyber stalking, identity theft), either as targets or as cyber aggressors (Finkelhor, Mitchell, & Wolak, 2000; Alexy, Burgess, Baker, & Smoyak, 2005; Curtis, 2012). Finally, we highlight that the impact of physical experiences can be confined and restricted to a time and a specific space, while the online victimization (e.g., cyber stalking, cyber bullying) tends to have uncontrollable proportions by the victim and being witnessed by dozens or thousands of users (e.g., colleagues, relatives, strangers). Take as an example the sharing of private information or victimization by cyber bullying: from the moment that the information and the insults are disseminated by IT, the adolescent has no control over its proportion, about who gains access to information and how it is being interpreted by others. In this way, the online environment can maximize the diffusion and impact of victimization, transforming the victim perception about these experiences.

Several studies have been documented the importance of parental involvement for the promotion of online safety of adolescents, for the critical use of ICT and for the crime prevention (Marinos, et al., 2011; Wolak et al., 2004; Whittle et al., 2013; Hertz & David-Ferdon, 2011; Livingstone & Haddon, 2009; Sengupta & Chaudhuri, 2011; Helweg-Larsen, Schütt & Larsen,

2012). The aim is not to implement a restrictive mediation or authoritarian posture, which limits access to information or freedom of exploration and expression of young people. On the contrary, it is intended to adopt a parental mediation that is fair and moderate (e.g., parents as a source of information and support before, during and after the online surfing) (Helpser et al., 2013, Marinos, et al., 2011). Teaching safety skills to adolescents, as well as instrumental tasks and/or information seems to be a crucial protective factor that helps adolescents to develop their digital and safety skills (Livingstone & Haddon, 2009). Teaching technological skills to professors and parents will be also necessary in order to overcome differences in the level of knowledge between themselves and the adolescents (Marinos, et al., 2011).

Regarding the difficulty in controlling impulses by adolescents while they are online, it is also important to reflect on that issue. Bossler e Holt (2010) in their study with university sample concludes that, while the low self-control has been associated with cyber-crime where the individual is the specific victim (e.g., cyber stalking, information theft); the same is not the case when individuals were victim of cyber-crime based on computer misuse (e.g., malware, identity theft). Consequently, the static vision that any cyber-crime (based on the specific target choice and on a random choice) is always a product of disadvantage and that people involved in cyber-crime present difficulties in terms of psycho-cognitive (e.g., low self-control), economics (e.g., membership of disadvantaged households) and/or social (e.g., isolation) skills, must be rejected (Clarke, 2004; Palfrey & Gasser, 2008). In contrast, this viewpoint can also be adopted when we are dealing with the scenario of perpetration (versus victimization) by an adolescent. Regarding an adolescent as a hacker or cyberbullying aggressor, for example, this cannot be also explained by adolescents' disadvantage but rather by the presence of sophisticated digital skills and higher social status among peers. The social learning theory approach strengthens this

last idea focused on perpetration behaviors. Certain types of cyber-crime perpetration result of learning procedures, pursuit techniques, specific and advanced computational programming and monitoring, being the adolescents also taught motive, means and specific rationalizations that legitimize the practice of cyber-crime (Fox, Nobles & Akers, 2011; Skinner & Fream, 1997). In some cases, adolescents are extremely capable of assessing the risks and the potential consequences of their actions in the online environment, acting informed, conscious and controlled.

Another perspective that should be abandoned is the idea that all cyber aggressors (adolescents or adults) begin their online browsing with the goal of finding criminal opportunities (Clarke, 2004). In fact, the existence of many available criminal opportunities can easily attract people in general to commit situational crimes, whether they had the motivation or not. Take as an example the number of available literature – through books, journals, and websites – which enables, either children or adolescents or adults, to have a fast learning about new forms of cyber-crime to those who occasionally had access to this type of information. In this field, we must also point out that some risks and criminal opportunities that adolescents are daily exposed do not result necessarily from the characteristics of the context, the peers or the individual. Sometimes these results are caused by the way the digital design itself is built and how the designers design the use of virtual resources. The design of social networks (which contains thousands of adolescent users), for example, contains specific fields that encourage the sharing of a large amount of personal information. However, these pages can hardly guarantee the total privacy of user identity, or even the stability of the information disclosed. Although sometimes adolescents create their virtual identities thinking in a private and secure environment, the truth is that, due to the need for conservation and users attraction, the digital design allows the contact with unknown users, as well as the location (fast and free) of the social profiles, from the search engines available on the Web. This enables the rise of improper access to personal information, the augmented exposure to crime and the decrease of the notion of privacy and security. Everything that could be "our" is attainable by thousands of users, inhabitants of this global village that is the Internet.

## SOLUTIONS AND RECOMMENDATIONS

Cyber-crime is common in modern society and in most cases committed by individuals who are socially integrated.

Towards digital protection of adolescents, we ought to invest more in the awareness of digital protection measures, complemented by a parental balanced mediation. Contrary to the notion of restriction, there is a need for a creative use, proactivity, consciousness and informed criticism of IT by the adolescents. In this way, the importance of initiatives of the academic community is reinforced (e.g., Social Adventure Project), such as telecommunications initiatives (e.g., New Project Genesis, index analysis of cyber-crime-Norton Cyber-crime Index), organizational (e.g., DADUS project, safer Internet Centre, SeguraNet project, MiudosSegurosNa.Net project) and the media, all of whom have developed important advances in online security and promotion of good practices of adolescents, without limiting their activities online.

Since the lower educational level and the lower socio-economic status are associated with higher levels of risk, it is recommended to investment in awareness and education to families, schools and less privileged neighborhoods, in order to increase competence in the use of the Internet and in the understanding of its risks. Schools present a leading role in digital education, as they may present resources greater than those of their parents, being therefore in a privileged position to educate

adolescents in an effectively and efficiently way (Livingstone & Haddon, 2009). These forms of awareness should be adapted as new risks arise (e.g., via cell phone or other platforms of content generated by users), addressing both cyber-crimes types (based on computer and crimes against people). The ultimate goal should be the infusion of this knowledge in the general population (especially among the most vulnerable group, but also among the others). In this way, it prevails the need to redesign the current pedagogical proposal remains, to ensure the inclusion of a couple of hours centered on digital education. These hours could be included in an existing discipline or a curriculum unit set up for this purpose. With regard to the curriculum, these should focus on the development of digital skills, critical thinking and decision-making of adolescents, as well as the ethical, legal and safe use of digital media. This is the approach advocated in the CyberSmart Australian program. Nevertheless, we must recall the importance of preparing the teacher through awareness-raising and specific training on the subject. In this way they will be able to bring knowledge to the classroom and effectively prepare students for the new model of society: the digital society.

Regarding the cyber-crime prevention against adolescents, it is recommended to redesign the interface basing it on the video-sharing sites, online games, social networks and chat rooms. Since technology evolution, the economy, politics and culture shape the processes of diffusion and use of Internet, these digital protection mechanisms should also be the constantly developed and evaluated. A multidisciplinary perspective (e.g., psychology, criminology, economics, demographics, design) during the construction, implementation and evaluation of the effectiveness of the prevention strategies used is also crucial (Clarke, 2004).

One important role is had by the designers. Designers use their knowledge to understand the needs of users and the technologies available, to develop new products, systems or services that satisfy the needs and desires of consumers (Press & Cooper, 2003). Crime is one factor that occurs within this process. In many cases the ineffectiveness of designers to anticipate the vulnerability of their creations to crime or the use of those creations to commit criminal acts means that individual victims and society in general have to deal with a legacy of opportunities for crime (Ekblom, 1997). Therefore, it seems that designers belong to the group of professionals who are better placed to address crime issues. Pease (2001) observes that designers are trained to anticipate several issues: the needs and desires of users, environmental impacts, ergonomic aspects, etc. As such they are the best placed to anticipate the criminal consequences of products and services and make easier to gain the technological race against crime. As such, design can be used as a tool to prevent crime, incorporating features in potential targets that transform the criminal event in a less attractive act for criminals and therefore breaking the criminal event. This could be done with a variety of mechanisms that need to be addressed during the design development phase (Ekblom & Tilley, 2000). Towards reducing criminal opportunities, Cornish and Clark (2003) have proposed 5 main techniques that are based on: (1) the increasing of the effort, (2) the increasing of the risk, (3) on reducing the rewards, and (4) reducing provocations and (5) on removing excuses. These main techniques present 25 sub techniques all focused on breaking the criminal event. These techniques have already been applied in the design field trough the Design Against Crime initiative (Design Council, 2002, 2003). Although this initiative had the focus on the real world, some studies had made particular correlations to the virtual environment (Wooton, Davey, Cooper & Press, 2003). One particular study by Wooton et al. (2003) had developed the crime life-cycle model to help and encourage designers to implement preventive measures in their creations. This model, that divides the criminal event in 10 phases, describes ways to address the crime, before, during and after the criminal event.

Additionally, in the context of cyber-crime, Verma et al. (2012) have proposed several techniques to prevent crime that is in line with the concept of preventing crime trough design. These techniques are centered in measures to reduce opportunities through the use of authentication technologies, adequate language and placing alerts. Nevertheless, digital design, far from security software development, can also, create intuitive and secure virtual environments, by developing clean and not dubious virtual spaces. Accordingly, the digital manipulation of criminal opportunities can certainly decrease the motivation for crime, the rewards and increase the likelihood of identifying the potential cyber aggressor (causing changes in the criminal behavior).

In sum, the criminal prevention must focus not only on individuals, but also on interaction routines, design interfaces and on the control structures and incentives that are applied on digital users.

## FUTURE RESEARCH DIRECTIONS

The subject of cyber-crime against adolescents has not yet been sufficiently explored in all its dimensions, although currently there is a growing body of national (e.g., Project Adventure, SeguraNet, DADUS Project, Internet Segura), European [e.g., EU Kids online network, Inform to Prevent Project (LEAD), ENISA, ClickCEOP button] and international studies (e.g., CyberSmart, Pew Internet & American Life Project) which focus their attention on IT use. More scientific studies are needed to estimate the extent and severity of this phenomenon in order to create specific structures to give appropriate answers to the needs of adolescents' victims of cyber-crime.

This domain, stresses the importance of participants selection be random and held in the community itself (versus clinical specimen or forensic), being also useful to opt for a decoded language and enhance the collection of data online, with adolescents. This investigator attitude will enable a better overall understanding of cyber-crime and provide a higher availability of teenagers to get involved in this kind of studies. In regard to ethical guidelines, it will be required to provide immediate answers aimed to the resources of the community, whenever an adolescent is in online risk.

Exploratory interviews with adolescents who are cyber aggressors and/or cyber victims are needed. Future investigations should focus on integrated and complementary methodologies (use of qualitative and quantitative design), as well as a constant dialogue between research and action. This will provide a greater insight into the motivations, the dynamics and the context of the occurrence of cyber-crime. An additional advantage would be the knowledge and understanding of existing problems in terms of digital design and difficulties and/or needs of victims when they are using the Internet. In addition, it becomes pertinent to investigate strategies that are more effective in responding to different types of online risk.

Based on this knowledge, the role of the primary sector (e.g., at the awareness campaigns level) may be more focused and efficient. Being Portugal one of the European countries in which the parental mediation is based on the application of restrictive measures on Internet access (Helsper et al., 2013), there is a need for further promotion of awareness-raising actions, among parents and educators: 1) a greater awareness for the potential that IT provide to education and psycho-social development of adolescents, and 2) improved skills for active parental mediation (e.g., through parental involvement).

We must reflect on the prevention of cyber-crime in general and on the online victimization in particular, since for example, there are currently more than 1 million Portuguese homes that already have mobile Internet access in which a few clicks stand between adolescents and adult content.

National initiatives such as the National Commission for Data Protection (e.g., through the Project DADUS, the creation of "Quiz na ótica

do utilizador" and the self-assessment questionnaire of identity theft), the APAV (e.g., through its online page aimed at the safety of young people) and of the SeguraNet (e.g., through their activities, awareness-raising, promotion of videos and games), for example, must be valued and expanded. It becomes therefore important to continue to invest in the construction and dissemination of electronic platforms to support the population, as well as in the construction of specific guidelines for the self-assessment of risk. These are the current best practices which allow testing the knowledge of the general population and the level of awareness on how to use the computer and Internet services.

## CONCLUSION

In recent decades society has seen profound changes in how to deal and conceptualize crime. Similarly to traditional crime, cyber-crime has brought with it a series of risks, insecurities and problems of social control, becoming a true test of social order and government policies, as well as a challenge for civil society, democracy and human rights (Garland, 2001). In this sense, this chapter is helpful to understand the social and psychological elements relevant to the domain of cyber-crime.

Empirical data indicates that cyber-crime can be a common experience in online adolescents' routine, due to the growing need to engage in new activities and explore new freedom experiences, allowed by the virtual environment (Haddon et al., 2012). Also, the economic and individual impact of this emerging phenomenon is being documented.

The type of online activities, the type of peers, and the personal characteristics of adolescents' vulnerability are components that can help understanding cyber victimization. However, it is important to remember that, despite some risk factors (e.g., online exposure, criminal association) and recommendations (e.g., information and awareness-raising) that were presented in this chapter are transversal to all age groups, socio-psychological characteristics that adolescents present make them a peculiar group. Adolescents are a risk group with needs (e.g., information, guidance) and specificities (e.g., developmental level) that are a priority at the intervention level. In this sense, further investigation of risk factors based on lifestyles, peer network, individual characteristics and an individual's routine activities is crucial, as it can provide important insights for designing situational prevention initiatives for the various types of cyber-crime against this specific and priority group: adolescents (Reyns, at al., 2011).

Nevertheless, the addressed controversies highlight that there is no single understanding for cyber-crime against adolescents. There is the increasingly need to conceptualize cyber-crime against adolescents as a product of interaction of the existing theoretical perspectives and of a multitude of intrinsic and extrinsic risk factors. This chapter advocates the necessity of field agents (e.g., psychologists, criminologists, digital designers) to conceptualize cyber-crime as a complex phenomenon that requires an integrative approach of different areas of knowledge.

As cyber-crime is transcultural, it also requires the effort of establishing more cyber-crime research partnerships between different countries, as well as a judicial and criminal recognition, in order to increase the success of the investigation and discourage the practice of this type of crime by its criminalization.

# REFERENCES

Alexy, E., Burgess, A., Baker, T., & Smoyak, S. (2005). Perceptions of cyberstalking among college students. *Brief Treatment and Crisis Intervention*, *5*(3), 279–289. doi:10.1093/brief-treatment/mhi020

Almeida, A. N., Delicado, A., & Alves, N. A. (2008). *Crianças e internet: Usos e representações, a família e a escola*. Unpublished doctoral dissertation, Instituto de Ciências Sociais da Universidade de Lisboa, Lisbon.

Berguer, M. T., & Guidorz, K. (2009). Intersectional approach. Chapel Hill, NC: The University of North Carolina Press.

Bilic, V. (2013). Violence among peers in the real and virtual world. *Paediatrics Today*, *9*(1), 78–90. doi:10.5457/p2005-114.65

Blais, J., Craig, W., Pepler, D., & Connolly, J. (2008). Adolescents online: The importance of internet activity choices to salient relationships. *Journal of Youth and Adolescence*, *37*(5), 522–536. doi:10.1007/s10964-007-9262-7

Bocij, P. (2004). *Cyberstalking: Harassment in the internet age and how to protect your family*. Westport, CT: Praeger.

Bossler, A. M., & Holt, T. J. (2009). On-line activities, guardianship, and malware infection: An examination of routine activities theory. *International Journal of Cyber Criminology*, *3*(1), 400–420.

Bossler, A. M., & Holt, T. J. (2010). The effect of self-control on victimization in the cyberworld. *Journal of Criminal Justice*, *38*(3), 227–236. doi:10.1016/j.jcrimjus.2010.03.001

Bossler, A. M., Holt, T. J., & May, D. C. (2012). Predicting online harassment victimization among a juvenile population. *Youth & Society*, *44*(4), 500–523. doi:10.1177/0044118X11407525

Buzzell, T., Foss, D., & Middleton, Z. (2006). Explaining use of online pornography: A test of self-control theory and opportunities for deviance. *Journal of Criminal Justice and Popular Culture*, *13*(2), 96–116.

Child Exploitation and Online Protection Centre (CEOP). (2013). Threat assessment of child sexual exploitation and abuse 2013. London, UK: Child Exploitation and Online Protection Centre.

Choi, K. C. (2008). Computer crime victimization and integrated theory: An empirical assessment. *International Journal of Cyber Criminology, 2*(1), 308–333. Retrieved September 1, 2010, from http://cyber.kic.re.kr/data/Kyungchoiijc-cjan2008.pdf

Clarke, R. V. (2004). Technology, criminology and crime science. *European Journal on Criminal Policy and Research, 10*(1), 55–63. doi:10.1023/B:CRIM.0000037557.42894.f7

Cohen, L. E., & Felson, M. (1979). Social change and crime rate trends: A routine activity approach. *American Sociological Review, 52*(August), 170–183.

Cornish, D. B., & Clarke, R. V. (2003). Opportunities precipitators and criminal dispositions: A reply to wortley's critique of situational crime prevention. In M. J. Smith, & D. B. Cornish (Eds.), *Theory and practice in situational crime prevention* (pp. 41–96). New York, USA: Criminal Justice Press.

Curtis, L. (2012). *Virtual vs. reality: An examination of the nature of stalking and cyberstalking.* (Unpublished doctoral dissertation). San Diego State University, San Diego, CA.

Dempsey, A., Sulkowsk, M., Dempsey, J., & Storch, E. (2011). Has cyber technology produced a new group of peer aggressors? *Cyberpshycology, Behavior, and Social Newtworking, 14*(5), 297–301. doi:10.1089/cyber.2010.0108 PMID:21162661

Design Council. (2002). *Evidence Pack. DAC case studies*. London, UK: Design Council.

Design Council. (2003). *Think thief: A designer's guide to designing out crime*. London, UK: Design Council.

Eck, J. E., & Clarke, R. V. (2003). Classifying common police problems: A routine activity approach. *Crime Prevention Studies, 16*, 7–39.

Ekblom, P. (1997). Gearing up against crime: A dynamic framework to help designers keep up with the adaptive criminal in a changing world. *International Journal of Risk. Security and Crime Prevention, 2*(4), 249–265.

Ekblom, P., & Tilley, N. (2000). Going equipped. *The British Journal of Criminology, 40*(3), 376–398. doi:10.1093/bjc/40.3.376

Finkelhor, D., Mitchell, K., & Wolak, J. (2000). *Online victimization: A report on the nation's youth (6-00-020)*. Alexandria, VA: National Center for Missing & Exploited Children. Retrieved May 10, 2011, from http://www.unh.edu/ccrc/pdf/jvq/CV38.pdf

Finkelhor, D., Ormrod, R. K., & Turner, H. A. (2007). Poly-victimization: A neglected component in child victimization. *Child Abuse & Neglect, 31*, 7–2. doi:10.1016/j.chiabu.2006.06.008 PMID:17224181

Finn, J. (2004). A survey of online harassment at a university campus. *Journal of Interpersonal Violence, 19*(4), 468–483. doi:10.1177/0886260503262083 PMID:15038885

Fisher, B. S., Cullen, F. T., & Turner, M. G. (2002). Being pursued: Stalking victimization in a national study of college woman. *Criminology & Public Policy, 1*(2), 257–308. doi:10.1111/j.1745-9133.2002.tb00091.x

Forde, L. W., & Kennedy, D. R. (1997). Risky lifestyles, routine activities, and the general theory of crime. *Justice Quarterly, 14*(2), 265–294. doi:10.1080/07418829700093331

Fox, K. A., Nobles, M. R., & Akers, R. L. (2011). Is stalking a learned phenomenon? An empirical test of social learning theory. *Journal of Criminal Justice*, *39*(1), 39–47. doi:10.1016/j.jcrimjus.2010.10.002

Garland, D. (2001). *The culture of control. Crime and social order in comtemporary society*. Chicago, IL: University of Chicago Press.

Gottfredson, M. R., & Hirschi, T. (1990). *A general theory of crime*. Standford, UK: Standford University Press.

Haddon, L., Livingstone, S., & EU Kids Online network. (2012). *EU Kids Online: National perspectives*. London, UK: EU Kids Online.

Helsper, E. J., Kalmus, V., Hasebrink, U., Sagvari, B., & Haan, J. (2013). *Country classification: Opportunities, risks, harm and parental mediation*. London, UK: EU Kids Online, London School of Economics & Political Science.

Helweg-Larsen, K., Schütt, N., & Larsen, H. B. (2012). Predictors and protective factors for adolescent internet victimization: Results from a 2008 nationwide Danish youth survey. *Acta Paediatrica (Oslo, Norway)*, *101*(5), 533–539. doi:10.1111/j.1651-2227.2011.02587.x PMID:22211947

Hertz, M. F., & David-Ferdon, C. (2011). Online aggression: A reflection of in-person victimization or a unique phenomenon? *The Journal of Adolescent Health*, *48*(2), 128–134. doi:10.1016/j.jadohealth.2010.11.255 PMID:21257110

Higgins, G. E. (2005). Can low self-control help with the understanding of the software piracy problem? *Deviant Behavior*, *26*(1), 1–24. doi:10.1080/01639620490497947

Higgins, G. E., Fell, B. D., & Wilson, A. L. (2006). Digital piracy: Assessing the contributions of an integrated self-control theory and social learning theory using structural equation modeling. *Criminal Justice Studies*, *19*(1), 3–22. doi:10.1080/14786010600615934

Higgins, G. E., & Makin, D. A. (2004). Self-control, deviant peers, and software piracy. *Psychological Reports*, *95*(3), 921–931. doi:10.2466/pr0.95.3.921-931 PMID:15666930

Hollinger, R. C. (1993). Crime by computer: Correlates of software piracy and unauthorized account access. *Security Journal*, *4*, 2–12.

Holt, T. J. (2007). Subcultural evolution? Examining the influence of on- and off-line experiences on deviant subcultures. *Deviant Behavior*, *28*(2), 171–198. doi:10.1080/01639620601131065

Jennings, W. G., Piquero, A. R., & Reingle, J. M. (2012). On the overlap between victimization and offending: A review of the literature. *Aggression and Violent Behavior*, *17*(1), 16–26. doi:10.1016/j.avb.2011.09.003

Kaspersky Lab. (2010). *Kaspersky security bulletin. Malware evolution 2010*. Retrieved October 21, 2013, from http://www.securelist.com/en/analysis/204792161/

Kim, W., Jeong, O.-R., Kim, C., & So, J. (2011). The dark side of the internet: Attacks, costs and responses. *Information Systems*, *36*(3), 675–705. doi:10.1016/j.is.2010.11.003

Kraemer-Mbula, E., Tang, P., & Rush, H. (2013). The cybercrime ecosystem: Online innovation in the shadows. *Technological Forecasting and Social Change*, *80*(3), 541–555. doi:10.1016/j.techfore.2012.07.002

Livingstone, S., & Haddon, L. (2009). *EU Kids Online: Final report*. London, UK: EU Kids Online, London School of Economics & Political Science. Retrieved August 10, 2012, from http://www.lse.ac.uk/media@lse/research/EUKidsOnline/EU%20Kids%20I%20(2006-9)/EU%20Kids%20Online%20I%20Reports/EUKidsOnlineFinalReport.pdf

Livingstone, S., & Helsper, E. J. (2007). Taking risks when communicating on the internet: The role of offline social–psychological factors in young people's vulnerability to online risks. *Information Communication and Society*, *10*(5), 619–644. doi:10.1080/13691180701657998

Livingstone, S., Kirwil, L., Ponte, C., & Staksrud, E. (2013). *In their own words: what bothers children online? with the EU Kids Online Network*. London, UK: EU Kids Online, London School of Economics & Political Science. Retrieved August 10, 2012, from http://www.lse.ac.uk/media@lse/research/EUKidsOnline/EU%20Kids%20III/Reports/Intheirownwords020213.pdf

Madden, M., Lenhart, A., Cortesi, S., Gasser, U., Duggan, M., Smith, A., & Beaton, M. (2013). *Teens, Social Media, and Privacy*. Washington, DC: Pew Research Center's Internet & American Life Project. Retrieved September 10, 2013, from http://www.pewinternet.org/Reports/2013/Teens-Social-Media-And-Privacy.aspx

Marcum, C. D. (2008). Identifying potencial factors of adolescent online victimization for high school seniors. *International Journal of Cyber Criminology*, *2*(2), 346–367.

Marinos, L. (2013). *ENISA Threat Landscape 2013. Overview of current and emerging cyberthreats*. Greece, Athens: European Union Agency for Network and Information Security. Retrieved January 30, 2014, from http://www.enisa.europa.eu/activities/risk-management/evolving-threat-environment/enisa-threat-landscape-2013-overview-of-current-and-emerging-cyber-threats

Marinos, L., et al. (2011). *Cyber-bullying and online grooming: Helping to protect against the risks. A scenario on data mining / profiling of data available on the Internet*. Greece, Athens: European Network and Information Security (ENISA). Retrieved January 30, 2014 from https://www.enisa.europa.eu/activities/risk-management/emerging-and-future-risk/deliverables/Cyber-Bullying%20and%20Online%20Grooming

McGrath, M., & Casey, E. (2002). Forensic psychiatry and the internet: Practical perspectives on sexual predators and obsessional harassers in cyberspace. *Journal of the American Academy of Psychiatry and the Law Online*, *30*(1), 81–94. PMID:11931372

Mitchell, K., Finkelhor, D., & Wolak, J. (2003). The exposure of youth to unwanted sexual material on the internet: A national survey of risk, impact and prevention. *Youth & Society*, *34*(3), 3300–3358. doi:10.1177/0044118X02250123

Mitchell, K., Finkelhor, D., & Wolak, J. (2007). Youth internet users at risk for the more serious online sexual solicitations. *American Journal of Preventive Medicine*, *32*(6), 532–537. doi:10.1016/j.amepre.2007.02.001 PMID:17533070

Mitchell, K. J., Finkelhor, D., Jones, L. M., & Wolak, J. (2010). Use of social networking sites in online sex crimes against minors: An examination of national incidence and means of utilization. *The Journal of Adolescent Health*, *47*(2), 183–190. doi:10.1016/j.jadohealth.2010.01.007 PMID:20638011

Olson, L. N., Daggs, J. L., Ellevold, B. L., & Rogers, T. K. (2007). Entrapping the innocent: Toward a theory of child sexual predators' luring communication. *Communication Theory*, *17*(3), 231–251. doi:10.1111/j.1468-2885.2007.00294.x

Palfrey, J., & Gasser, U. (2008). *Digital born. Understanding the first generation of digital natives*. New York, NY: Basic Books.

Pease, K. (2001). *Cracking crime through design*. London, UK: Design Council.

Pratt, T. C., Holtfreter, K., & Reisig, M. D. (2010). Routine online activity and internet fraud targeting: Extending the generality of routine activity theory. *Journal of Research in Crime and Delinquency*, *47*(3), 267–296. doi:10.1177/0022427810365903

Press, R., & Cooper, M. (2003). *The design experience*. Chichester, UK: John Wilet and Sons.

Reyns, B. W. (2013). Online routines and identity theft victimization: Futher expanding routine activity theory beyond direct-contact offenses. *Journal of Research in Crime and Delinquency, 50*(2), 216–238. doi:10.1177/0022427811425539

Reyns, B. W., Henson, B., & Fisher, B. S. (2011). Being pursued online: Apllying cyberlifestyle-routine activities theory to cyberstalking victimization. *Criminal Justice and Behavior, 38*(11), 1149–1169. doi:10.1177/0093854811421448

Schreck, C. J. (1999). Criminal victimization and self-control: An extension and test of a general theory of crime. *Justice Quarterly, 16*(3), 633–654. doi:10.1080/07418829900094291

Sengupta, A., & Chaudhuri, A. (2011). Are social networking sites a source of online harassment for teens? Evidence from survey data. *Children and Youth Services Review, 33*(2), 284–290. doi:10.1016/j.childyouth.2010.09.011

Skinner, W. F., & Fream, A. M. (1997). A social learning theory analysis of computer crime among college students. *Journal of Research in Crime and Delinquency, 34*(4), 495–518. doi:10.1177/0022427897034004005

Smahel, D., Helsper, E., Green, L., Kalmus, V., Blinka, L., & Ólafsson, K. (2012). *Excessive internet use among European children.* London, UK: EU Kids Online, London School of Economics & Political Science. Retrieved December 11, 2012, from http://www.lse.ac.uk/media@lse/research/EUKidsOnline/EU%20Kids%20III/Reports/ExcessiveUse.pdf

Sontag, L. M., Clemans, K. H., Graber, J. A., & Lyndon, S. (2011). Traditional and cyber aggressors and victims: A comparison of psychosocial characteristics. *Journal of Youth and Adolescence, 40*(4), 392–404. doi:10.1007/s10964-010-9575-9 PMID:20680425

Subrahmanyam, K., Greenfield, P. M., & Tynes, B. (2004). Constructing sexuality and identity in an internet teen chat room. *Journal of Applied Developmental Psychology, 25*(6), 651–666. doi:10.1016/j.appdev.2004.09.007

Symantec Corporation. (2011). *2011 Norton cybercrime report.* Retrieved October 15, 2013, from http://now-static.norton.com/now/en/pu/images/Promotions/2012/cybercrime/assets/downloads/en-us/NCR-DataSheet.pdf

Symantec Corporation. (2012). *2012 Norton cybercrime report.* Retrieved October 15, 2013, from http://now-static.norton.com/now/en/pu/images/Promotions/2012/cybercrimeReport/2012_Norton_Cybercrime_Report_Master_FINAL_050912.pdf

Vandoninck, S., d'Haenens, L., & Roe, K. (2013). Online risks: Coping strategies of less resilient children and teenagers across Europe. *Journal of Children and Media, 7*(1), 60–78. doi:10.1080/17482798.2012.739780

Verma, M., Hussain, S., & Kushwah, S. (2012). Cyber law: Approach to prevent cybercrime. *International Journal of Research in Engineering Science and Technology, 1*(3), 123–129.

Whittle, H., Hamilton-Giachritsis, C., Beech, A., & Collings, G. (2013). A review of online grooming: Characteristics and concerns. *Aggression and Violent Behavior, 18*(1), 62–70. doi:10.1016/j.avb.2012.09.003

Wolak, J., Mitchell, K., & Finkelhor, D. (2004). Internet-initiated sex crimes against minors: Implications for prevention based on findings from a national study. *The Journal of Adolescent Health, 35*, 11–20. doi:10.1016/j.jadohealth.2004.05.006 PMID:15488437

Wolak, J., Mitchell, K., & Finkelhor, D. (2006). *Online victimization of children: Five years later.* Washington, DC: National Center for Missing and Exploited Children.

Wolak, J., Mitchell, K., & Finkelhor, D. (2007). Unwanted and wanted exposure to online pornography in a national sample of youth internet users. *Pediatrics, 119,* 247–257. doi:10.1542/peds.2006-1891 PMID:17272613

Wootton, A. B., Davey, C., Cooper, R., & Press, M. (2003). *The crime lifecycle: Generating design against crime ideas.* Salford, UK: The University of Salford.

Yar, M. (2005). The novelty of "cyber-crime": An assessment in light of routine activity theory. *European Journal of Criminology, 2*(4), 407–427. doi:10.1177/147737080556056

Ybarra, M., Mitchell, K., Finkelhor, D., & Wolak, J. (2007). Internet prevention messages: Targeting the right online behaviors. *Archives of Pediatrics & Adolescent Medicine, 161*(2), 138–145. PMID:17283298

## KEY TERMS AND DEFINITIONS

**Adolescence:** Stage of human development that marks the transition between childhood and adulthood. According to the UN this phase extends between 15 and 24 years of age, while the World Health Organization defines adolescents as the individual who is between 10 and 20 years of age.

**Criminal Victimization:** To have been the target of some sort of crime that can cause discomfort and damage.

**Cyber Bullying:** A form of violence that involves the use of IT to commit repeated and intentional hostile behavior against a peer of the same context of the cyber victim.

**Cyber Stalking:** Default behavior implemented repeatedly and intentionally that is not desired by the target(s), with the use of IT. Some of the behaviors include routine and seemingly harmless actions (e.g., posting on Facebook, sending email), but also unambiguously intimidating actions (e.g., sending threatening messages, identity theft).

**Digital Design:** Focuses on the design of digitally mediated environments and experiences. It is centered in the development of digital platforms, web and mobile products.

**Harassment:** Unpleasant and unwanted behaviors that someone is repeatedly subject to, during a given period of time.

**Online Risk:** Likelihood of anyone being exposed to a danger or adverse situation, during navigation in the virtual world.

# Chapter 15
# Event Reconstruction:
## A State of the Art

**Yoan Chabot**
*University of Bourgogne, France & University College Dublin, Ireland*

**Tahar Kechadi**
*University College Dublin, Ireland*

**Aurélie Bertaux**
*University of Bourgogne, France*

**Christophe Nicolle**
*University of Bourgogne, France*

## ABSTRACT

*Event reconstruction is one of the most important steps in digital forensic investigations. It allows investigators to have a clear view of the events that have occurred over a time period. Event reconstruction is a complex task that requires exploration of a large amount of events due to the pervasiveness of new technologies. Any evidence produced at the end of the investigative process must also meet the requirements of the courts, such as reproducibility, verifiability, validation, etc. After defining the most important concepts of event reconstruction, the authors present a survey of the challenges of this field and solutions proposed so far.*

## INTRODUCTION

Cybercrime and digital forensics have become increasingly commonplace in today's world. Crimes committed with the aid of or against digital systems are being reported almost daily. Internet fraud, cyber-bullying, cyber-terrorism, systems intrusion perpetrated against both individuals and corporations are costing businesses and governments billions in lost revenue and security updates (Anderson, et al., 2012). Due to all these issues, digital forensics has become an important research area in the last few years. Digital forensics is defined by (Palmer, 2001) as a set of methods based on proven scientific theories which aim to

enable the reconstruction of past events related to an incident and the detection of criminal acts. To reach these objectives, each digital investigation is conducted according to a rigorous process (Palmer, 2001) starting with the identification of an incident and ending with the final decision of the court of justice. This process includes steps allowing to preserve the integrity of evidence, to seize sources of footprints from the crime scene, to examine these sources to find relevant information and finally to analyse this information to be able to make assumptions about the incident.

Several tools are available to help investigators during the first steps of this process. For example, EnCase or FTK can help investigative agents dur-

DOI: 10.4018/978-1-4666-6324-4.ch015

ing the collection and the examination of digital objects while preserving their integrity. However, these tools are limited regarding the analysis step, which allows to fully understand what happened during the incident. Collecting evidence and studying its properties is an important part of the investigative process. However, to extract acceptable evidence, it is also necessary to infer new knowledge such as the causes of the current state of the evidence (Carrier & Spafford, 2004). For example, a file illegally modified may be identified during the first steps of an investigation. Although the identification of such an object is interesting, only the analysis phase can help investigators to understand the causes of this modification. Among all the techniques used during the analysis phase, event reconstruction enables investigators to have a global overview of the events occurring before, during and after a given incident. The story produced as output of this process can answer many questions such as « What happened?" and "Why did these events took place?".

This chapter aims to present different aspects of the field of event reconstruction and outlines the various approaches proposed so far. After presenting several notions extensively used in this field (e.g. footprint, event, etc.), we reviewed challenges encountered during the conception of event reconstruction approaches. Then, the different approaches used to perform event reconstruction are introduced and assessed. For each of them, a description of the method used and a synthesis of strengths and limitations in relation to the challenges of the field are given. Finally, future directions for research are given.

## DEFINITIONS

*Event reconstruction* is "the process of identifying the underlying conditions and reconstructing the sequence of events that led to a security incident" (Jeyaraman & Atallah, 2006). There are several types of event reconstruction depending on the

nature of the incident. This chapter focuses on prosecutorial forensic analysis which is used to solve digital crime, and so, we explain the terminology we use.

First, the *crime scene* is a space where a crime or an incident takes place. (Carrier, Spafford, & others, 2003) defines a *physical crime scene* is defined as "a physical environment containing physical evidence related to an incident". The physical environment in which happen the incident is called the *primary physical crime scene*. Because of network connections for example, the crime scene can be extended to other places (e.g. if one of the protagonists has communicated with a remote party or download a file from a remote server, it can be necessary to seize the remote machines). The crime scene is not necessarily limited to a single building or environment and the subsequent scenes are called *secondary physical crime scene*. Then, a *digital crime scene* is defined as a component of a physical crime scene: "a virtual environment created by hardware and software and containing digital evidence related to an incident" (Carrier, Spafford, & others, 2003). A *physical crime scene* may contain several digital crime scene (a computer, a cell phone or other electronic device).

After the incident and the arrival of the officers in charge of the investigation, the crime scene becomes a protected space where the state of resources is preserved. After ensuring the protection of the crime scene, investigators start the *collection phase*. The purpose of this latter is to collect objects which carries footprints that can be relevant in respect to the objectives defined at the beginning of the investigation. The objects collected during an investigation carry digital footprints and may themselves contain many digital footprint sources (e.g. a computer may contain digital footprint sources such as Firefox logs, Apache logs, etc.). According to (Ribaux, 2013), a footprint (or a trace) is the sign of a past event. A footprint is the only available information to define the past events (e.g. a fingerprint indicates that an object was grasped by a person, information extracted from Firefox logs may indicate that the user has visited a given webpage, etc.). Footprints carry information about the events that have produced them and thus, they can be used by investigators to reconstruct the events that happened during an incident.

In a digital context, a footprint may be a piece of information about web activity, a document etc. There is a large number of footprints sources (Forensics Wiki, 2007) (Gudhjonsson, 2010):

- First, web browsing and emails can be used to get information about the user behaviour on the web. Each web browser stores in files or in databases a large number of potentially useful information for investigators. Regarding the web browser Mozilla Firefox for example, it is possible to obtain information about the webpages visited, the content entered into form fields, the bookmarks and downloads performed by a given user. Footprints extracted from web browsers allows to know the user's interests (based on query to search engines, bookmarks and visits, etc.), to identify potential accomplices (malicious file downloaded from a remote server, etc.). Contents and headers of emails are also a source of relevant information for an investigation.

- Social networks allow people to share information, location and other multimedia contents with private or business contacts. Information left by browsers, temporary files or data stored in the memory of mobile devices offering social applications may be useful for investigators to obtain information about user contacts as well as his activity (Al Mutawa, Baggili, & Marrington, 2012), e.g. sending date of a tweet on Twitter (Morrissey, 2010).

- Operating systems record a lot of information about events occurring on a machine.

In the Windows operating system for example, footprints can be collected from several locations:

- ○ Windows event log EVT and EVTX record information about various kind of events such as session login, start/stop service or software, error occurred during the execution of a program, installation of a new software, etc.

- ○ The registry is a database containing a large amount of data stored as keys. It stores information about system configuration, devices or software configuration.

- ○ Prefetch and superfetch folder are used to speed up the loading of applications which are used on a regular basis. For each software started, a file containing information about the software (loaded data, locations used, etc.) is created in the prefetch folder. These files are a potential source of information for the investigator because each of this file allows to see the name of the executable, the name of files used by this latter, the number of uses of the software and the date of the last launch.

- ○ The recycle bin and the restore points allow to discover deleted files which are potentially interesting for the investigation.

- Logs of software are also a rich source of information. For example, antivirus logs contain information about exploits and malicious software detected on the computer. Server logs such as Apache logs or Microsoft IIS logs can be used to get information about query sent to the server.

- Content of files allows to answer multiple purposes during an investigation. In addition, metadata associated to each file allows to know how and when a file was produced and who created it. For example, image metadata contains information about the user (location), the camera used, the date on which the image was taken, etc. XMP metadata used for PDF files allows to know the title, the author or the creation date of a document. Another example is the MAC times used by file systems. These allows to know when a file has been modified, accessed, created or last modified (in Linux).

When the extraction of footprints is completed, investigators need to convert them into events and build a timeline containing all the events related to the incident. This timeline allows investigators to have a global overview of the case and to know for example which machines was used, which applications were launched or which files were modified at a given time. An event is a single action occurring at a given time and for a certain duration. An event may be the drafting of a document, the reading of a webpage or a chat conversation with somebody. Each event carries temporal information allowing to know when the event occurred. This information takes the form of a time interval to define the beginning and the end of the event and implicitly, its duration. Besides the duration, the use of a time interval rather than an instant allows to represent the notion of uncertainty (Liebig, Cilia, & Buchmann, 1999). When the time at which the action occurs cannot be determined accurately, the use of an approximation by the use of an interval is an adequate solution.

## CHALLENGES

Event reconstruction has many issues which are directly related to the size of the data, digital forensics process complexity, and IT infrastructures challenges. While some of these challenges have been a focus of many researchers and develop-

ers for the last decade, the size of data volumes (Richard III & Roussev, 2006) and data heterogeneity are still very challenging. The first (large data sizes) introduced many challenges at every phase of the digital forensic process; from the data collection to the interpretation of the results. The evolution of new technologies (high increase of storage capacity, ubiquitous devices, etc.) leads to the necessity to handle very large volumes of data during an investigation. Thus, investigators are often confronted with the problem of cognitive overload during the interpretation of data. The second (data heterogeneity) is usually due to multiple footprint sources such as log files, information contained in file systems, etc. We can classify events heterogeneity into three categories:

- **Format:** The information encoding is not the same among sources due to the formatting or other issues. So, depending on the source, the footprint data may be different.
- **Temporal:** The use of sources from different machines may have timing problems (e.g., unsynchronised clocks, different time zones, etc.).
- **Semantic:** The same event can be interpreted or represented in different ways. For example, an event may appear in different forms in different sources.

In order to gather all the events found in footprint sources in a single timeline, a good handling of all these forms of heterogeneity is required. This leads to the development of an automated information processing approach that is able to extract knowledge from these heterogeneous sources. In addition, once extracted, this knowledge should be federated within the same model so as to facilitate their interpretation and future analysis.

In addition, all approaches have to satisfy some key requirements such as credibility, integrity, and reproducibility of the digital evidence (Baryamureeba & Tushabe, 2004). In recent years, the protagonists of digital forensics moved away from investigative techniques that are based on the investigators experience and intuition, to techniques based on proven theories. It is also necessary to provide clear explanation about the reasoning used to reach each conclusion of the investigation. These explanations allow to give support to the conclusions and enable the justice to fully understand and reproduce the reasoning process. In addition, one has to ensure that the tools used do not modify the data collected on the crime scene. Thus, it is necessary to develop tools that extract excellent quality of the evidence, while preserving the integrity of data.

## EVALUATION OF EXISTING APPROACHES

In this section, the most significant approaches to carry out event reconstruction are presented and discussed. For each of them, an overview of the architecture used and the functionalities proposed is given. We then study limits and strengths of each approach by focusing on a number of criterion.

### Classification of Approaches

Event reconstruction approaches can be classified depending on the sources used and the time at which the tool is used:

- Event reconstruction tool can be based on a unique source (e.g. timestamp from file system) or based on multiple sources (e.g. logs files, file system, operating system information) (inglot2012framework). In the first approach, the timeline does not fully represent what happened on the machine and therefore the investigators may miss important information. In the second approach (also called *super-timeline approach*), the timeline is more accurate than in the first approach but the produced timeline is large and therefore difficult to analyse.

- Tools can used *ex post evidence* or *ex ante logging* (Jeyaraman & Atallah, 2006). In the first case, the tool starts working after the incident happened and tries to identify and retrieve evidence to construct the timeline. In the second case, the tool starts working before the incident by recording all events occurring on the machine. When an incident occurs, the recorded information can be used to understand what happened.

In this study, we focus only on approaches which can cope with a large number of situations. Thus, we review only polyvalent approaches that are able to work without prior knowledge of the systems studied during the investigation (ex post evidence approach). In addition, we restrict this study to approaches able to fully complete the reconstruction of events (e.g. tools providing timeline visualization functionalities only are not taken into account).

### Criteria

Several criteria are assessed in this state of the art to evaluate the capacity of approaches to meet the needs of investigators and give solutions to challenges described above. First, the ability of approaches to solve problems related to information processing is assessed using the following criteria:

- The approach provides automated tools to extract the events from footprint sources and build the timeline associated.
- The approach is able to process multiple and various footprint sources and to federate information collected in a model in a coherent and structured way.
- Tools are proposed to assist investigators in the tasks of timeline analysis.

To study the capacity of the approaches to fulfil the justice requirements, we enrich our criteria with the following elements:

- A theoretical model is used to support the proposed approach and to explain the reasoning performed.
- The approach is able to cope with problems related to the preservation of the integrity of data used during the investigation.

## ECF: Event Correlation for Forensics Purposes

(Chen, Clark, De Vel, & Mohay, 2003) argue that it is possible to correlate the information contained in computers (log files, etc.) despite the heterogeneous nature of data. The ECF architecture proposed in this work is made of a storage element containing events extracted during an investigation in addition to tools able to settle and query this database. ECF is composed of events parsers, a database and a user interface. An overview of the ECF architecture is given in Figure 1.

In this proposal, a canonical representation of events is used to standardize the representation of events extracted from heterogeneous sources. The events are stored in a table that has eleven attributes including an identifier for the event, the date and time at which it occurs, information about the actor who caused the event (e.g. IP address), information about the object affected by the event (URL if the object is a webpage for example), the action represented by the event, the result of the event (success, failure, unknown) and information about the source used to identify the event. A second table is used to store specific information about events depending on the source from which they are extracted.

The system described offers four main functionalities:

- **Event Extraction:** This function allows to parse event sources, format events and populate the database. ECF proposes parsers to handle sources such as Apache logs, Windows 2000 logs or door logs.
- **Dynamic Queries:** This interface allows the investigator to query the database. Queries are built by assembling constraints on one or more fields of the event table using Boolean operators. For example, the investigator may look for events occurring between two dates or search for all events caused by a given person.
- **Custom Queries:** This interface allows to execute directly SQL queries. Therefore, this interface provides more flexibility to the user than dynamic queries.

*Figure 1. ECF architecture*

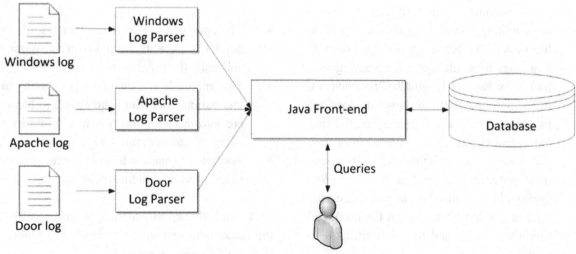

- **Hypotheses Testing:** This tool allows the user to create new events and test the validity of these assumptions.

The main contribution of this work is the introduction of an architecture able to gather events from heterogeneous sources into a single structure. The proposed system uses a set of automatic parsers and a canonical form to represent the events extracted during an investigation. This idea has been widely adopted in subsequent approaches. However, the main limitation of ECF is that it does not propose any functionality to assist the investigator during the analysis of the events. Thus, a large part of the investigation has to be carry out by investigators.

## Auto-ECF

(Abbott, Bell, Clark, De Vel, & Mohay, 2006) proposed Auto-ECF which is an evolution of the previous approach. Auto-ECF was designed to address several shortcomings of ECF. In this work, a new canonical form consisting in four required attributes is proposed to represent events:

- A unique identifier.
- The date and time at which the event occurred.
- The type of event (e.g. session login, file creation, etc.).
- The result of the event (success, failure or unknown).

Each event can also carry a number of additional attributes to allow the storage of more specific information. The main purpose of this approach is to provide automatic mechanisms to convert events extracted from heterogeneous sources to high-level events which are easier to understand for an investigator. To reach this objective, several concepts are introduced by the authors:

- Raw event: event contained in the event sources such as log files.
- Logical event: event stored in canonical form in the database.
- Simple event: logical event resulting from the conversion of a raw event.
- Composite event: logical event resulting from the aggregation of several logical events.

To convert the raw events in logical events and to construct composite events, Event Logical Patterns (LEP) are used. After extracting the events from sources, a dedicated algorithm is used to search for occurrences of the patterns (stored in a XML file) and to create new events associated to each pattern. This process is illustrated in *Figure 2*.

This approach allows to convert raw events into events that are more readable for humans. Even if this functionality is useful for investigators, it represents only a small part of the analysis and, thus, investigators have to carry out the rest of the analysis. For example, this approach does not allow to find relationships between events.

## FORE: Forensics of Rich Events

The FORE approach proposed by (Schatz, Mohay, & Clark, 2004) allows to carry out an investigation using heterogeneous sources of events. The aim of this work is to propose a solution to deal with the large amount of data to be processed during an investigation and the difficulties encountered by investigators to interpret these data. To serve this purpose, an ontology-centric architecture is introduce (*Figure 3*). The ontology is used to store events and is rooted by two classes which are the *Entity class* (representing objects of the world) and the *Event class* (representing the state changes of an object over time). The proposed ontology also includes temporal information on events in addition to causal relationships between events. It should be noted that all the expressiveness of

*Figure 2. Auto-ECF process*

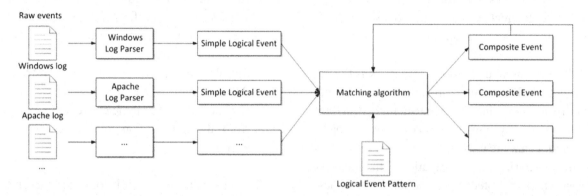

*Figure 3. FORE architecture*

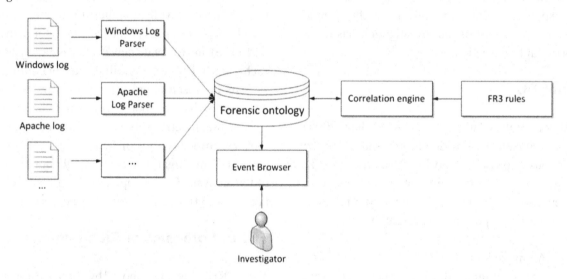

the ontological language used (OWL) is not used to described the ontology. Indeed, to model the knowledge on events, (Schatz, Mohay, & Clark, 2004) only uses a hierarchy of classes in addition to properties and individuals (no constraints on classes and properties).

The FORE architecture is composed of three parts which are *the extraction module*, *the ontology* and *the analysis tools*. In the extraction module, a set of parsers is used to extract knowledge from various sources such as Apache server logs, Windows 2000 logs, etc. The knowledge extracted is then used to populate the ontology with new instances of events. Each parser is dedicated to a specific type of source allowing to take into account the specificity of each source. Then, au-

tomated tools are proposed to process this knowledge. A correlation tool based on rules is used to identify causal relationships between events ("if event A is the cause of event B then event A has to occur to allow event B to occur"). To express rules, a rule language called FR3 was created. A rule expressed with the language FR3 is composed of *antecedents* and *consequences*. An inference engine is used to browse the knowledge base to find elements appearing in the antecedents of a rule. If all elements composing antecedents of a rule occur in the ontology, the rule is satisfied and elements appearing in the consequences of the rule are then added to the ontology. Finally, an interface is also provided to allow the user to visualize the knowledge contained in the ontology.

The use of an ontology is an efficient way to deal with heterogeneity of event sources. Regarding the analysis of the timeline, the proposed tool helps investigators by highlighting non-explicit relationships between events (causality). However, the use of a rule-based approach makes the use of this tool tedious and time-consuming (need to create and manage a large set of rules).

## Finite State Machine

(Gladyshev & Patel, 2004) argues that a formalization of the event reconstruction problem is needed to better structure the reconstruction process, facilitate its automation and ensure the completeness of the reconstruction. To address these problems, an approach based on finite state machine is proposed, where the behaviour of the system under investigation is represented using a state machine. Subsequently, some scenarios are removed using evidence collected by the investigator. Once the number of potential scenarios has been reduced, a backtracking algorithm is used from the final state (the state observed at the beginning of the investigation) to the initial state of the system. In this approach, the event reconstruction can be seen as a process finding the sequence of transitions that satisfies the constraints imposed by evidence.

One of the main strengths of this approach is to allow to conduct forensic investigations with the support of a theory widely recognized in the scientific community to explain the conclusions of the investigation. However, the finite state machine approach has several limitations. In particular, this approach cannot be used to conduct complex investigations. Indeed, the use of finite state machine to represent systems often results in combinatorial explosions. Thus, this approach seems inadequate for real forensic cases. For example, the investigation of a single computer may involve several processes such as web browsers, file system, instant messaging software, etc. Thus, the representation of such a system with a finite state machine seems not possible.

(James, Gladyshev, Abdullah, & Zhu, 2010) improves the previous approach. It highlights the main problem of the original approach: the exponential growth of the size of the state machine and therefore, the number of possible scenarios to examine during the backtracking phase. The solution carried by this paper is to convert the finite state machine into a deterministic finite state machine. However, even if this solution allows to reduce the size of the state machine, experiments show that the approach still not usable on real forensic cases.

## Zeitline

(Buchholz & Falk, 2005) introduces a timeline editor named Zeitline allowing the investigator to create scenarios from multiple sources of events. The proposed tool also provides functions to group and hierarchically organize events. To store events, the authors argue that a data structure able to withstanding the scalability is necessary to handle the knowledge used during an investigation. In addition, this data structure must allow to quickly sort and query knowledge. The authors chose to use a variant of balanced binary search tree. This approach distinguishes two types of events: *atomic events* which are extracted from event sources and *complex events* containing several atomic or complex events. Each of these types is implemented using a Java class inheriting from the class TimeEvent representing events. Whether they are complex or atomic, each event has a number of attributes including the date and time at which the event occurred, the name of the event, a description and a pointer to the "parent" event. In addition to these attributes, instances of AtomicEvent and ComplexEvent classes carry specific attributes such as the source of the event (for atomic event) and pointers to « children » for complex events.

In addition to the possibility to extract events from various sources, users can create their own extractors allowing them to easily extend the number of event sources supported by Zeitline. The tool also offers to investigators an interface allowing him to add new events to the timeline, to aggregate several events to build a complex event or to search for specific events using a query tool based on keywords. Finally, Zeitline is restricted by a number of rules that aim to prevent the alteration of evidence. These restrictions allow to take into account a part of the requirements of justice. To prevent the modification of evidence, a system of views is also used to avoid the removal of information contained in evidence. When the investigator deletes an event from the timeline, the event is removed from a view but still physically preserved. This special attention given to the preservation of the integrity of the information is one of the main contribution of this tool.

## A FRAMEWORK FOR POST-EVENT TIMELINE RECONSTRUCTION USING NEURAL NETWORKS

On the basis that most of the existing methods cannot efficiently handle large volumes of data, (Khan, Chatwin, & Young, 2007) introduces a new approach using a neural network to show the ability of machine learning techniques to quickly process large amounts of data. The use of machine learning techniques also allows to explicit the reasoning made to produce a conclusion which is one of the justice requirements. However, the authors indicate that this feature is not applicable to neural networks. Indeed, during the learning phase, some parameters used remain unknown.

The proposed approach uses traces left by user activities in the system to detect the activity of software. The proposed tool is composed of three parts:

- The parsers allowing to extract traces found in various types of sources (log files, registry, etc.).

- The preprocessor used to convert data extracted by parsers to make it usable by the neural network.
- The neural network used to identify launched applications using input data.

As admitted by the author, the performance of the proposed tool is low. In addition, the training of the neural network and the need to use the neural network several times to get a complete scenario make this tool very time-consuming.

## FACE: Forensics Automated Correlation Engine

(Case, Cristina, Marziale, Richard, & Roussev, 2008) points out that the consultation of data produced during an investigation is a tedious work. As the current forensic tools are limited to the extraction and presentation of information extracted from sources, there is an important need to develop tools able to assist investigators during the interpretation and the analysis of the data.

In this work, an approach called FACE is introduced to collect and analyse data (event correlation) from various sources. FACE is able to handle five different data sources which are memory dumps, network activities, disk images, log files and user configuration files. Once data is extracted, the correlation tool allows to discover logical relationships between events and between objects and events (e.g. a file). The output of the proposed tool is a report describing the activities of the user. This report is composed of activities linked by hyperlinks to facilitate the consultation of the timeline.

One of the main contributions of this approach is the introduction of a tool allowing to correlate events and thus, carry out a part of the analysis. The second contribution lies in the presentation of data. The proposed tool offers different views on events and objects in addition to hyperlinks to make the reading of the timeline easier and more intuitive for investigators.

## CFTL: Cyber-Forensic TimeLab

(Olsson & Boldt, 2009) discusses the need for a system to view and navigate into the data related to an investigation in an intuitive way to discover evidence. To reach this objective, the tool Cyber-Forensic TimeLab described in this work extracts timestamps found in a machine or a group of machines, builds the timeline and then provides a graphical view of all the events. The investigator can then browse the events and identify relevant information more easily.

The proposed tool is composed of two parts: a scanner and an event viewer. The scanner is used to extract timestamps from sources (file system, Windows or Unix logs, JPEG files) and store them in a XML file. Each evidence has three required attributes (name, type and identifier) and several optional attributes. Once timestamps are extracted, the event viewer reads the XML file, orders events and then displays them in a graphical timeline. The main added value of this approach is the improvement of the ergonomics of the interface between the timeline and the investigator.

## Log2Timeline

(Gudhjonsson, 2010) proposes a system allowing to construct automatically a super-timeline using a large number of sources. The author highlights several limitations of current event reconstruction approaches such as the limited number of sources used. This makes the truthfulness of the timeline vulnerable to anti-forensics techniques (e.g. alteration of timestamp). In addition, the quality of the timeline also suffers from the small number of sources. For example, some contextual events may not appear in the timeline. The proposed solution is to increase the number of event sources to enhance the quality of the timeline and to minimize the impact of anti-forensics techniques. The architecture presented in this work is composed of a module used to extract events and a module able to display the timeline produced or to serialize it in a CSV file. Each extracted event carries several attributes including a timestamp, a description of the event, an identifier and the type of the source used to determine the event. Log2timeline used a large number of sources: web browsers histories, log files of antivirus software, operating system logs, information extracted from the bin, etc.

One of the main limitation of this approach is the lack of functionalities to help the investigators during the analysis of the super-timeline. The use of a large number of sources lead to the creation of huge timeline which are very difficult to interpret by the investigator.

## AUTOMATED TIMELINE RECONSTRUCTION APPROACH

(Hargreaves & Patterson, 2012) proposes a system able to automatically reconstruct high-level events using large amount of low-level events extracted by log2timeline or Zeitline. The authors highlight that the amount of data and the number of events make the visualisation and the analysis of a timeline difficult, especially with the super-timeline approach. The aim of this work is to facilitate the reading of the timeline by introducing a mechanism allowing to create high-level events (which are easier to understand for investigator) from low-level events (events extracted from sources). This process can be compared to the production of a summary of the timeline. The authors also try to meet the needs of justice by storing traceability information during the process of summarization. For each high-level event, the investigator has therefore the possibility to know the low-level events used to create it.

The proposed solution implements a two-step process: the extraction of low-level events and the construction of high-level events. A system composed of parsers and bridges is used to carry out the low-level event extraction. Parsers are used to process the content of sources. Two types of sources are used: the file system and the information contained in the files themselves. Then, bridges convert the extracted data into the format used for low-level events. To represent events in memory, a standard format consisting of nine attributes is used (an identifier, a date of start and a date of end, the source used to identify the event, the information used to construct the event, the parser used for the extraction, the event type, objets related to the event and optionnal information).

One of the specificities of the proposed format compared to the format used in tools like Zeitline or log2timeline is the use of intervals to define dates. Indeed, the authors make the assumption that the dates may be inaccurate and thus, an interval is more suitable to represent them. Once the timeline containing low-level events is built, a process is used to produce high-level events. The timeline is browsed to search for specific patterns of one or several low-level events. When a pattern is found, the corresponding high-level event is added to the timeline. Each high-level event consists of fourteen attributes including information about the reasoning used to identify it (pattern used) and a description of the event. The summarization of the timeline is a useful functionality for investigators as it allows them to save time during the reading and the interpretation of the timeline. However, this functionality represents only a part of the analysis process.

## FUTURE RESEARCH DIRECTIONS

A large majority of the proposed approaches provide solutions to extract events which are spread across different types of sources and to build the associated timeline. However, the extraction of events from a large number of sources (approach super-timeline) lead to the creation of huge timelines which are very difficult to read and interpret for humans. Few solutions are provided to assist the investigator during this phase of the investigation. The solution provided in (Gladyshev & Patel, 2004) is able to identify relevant scenarios for a given incident but due to performance reasons and lack of automation, the approach is unusable for

real cases. Thus, there is a strong need to develop an approach providing a complete set of advanced techniques of timeline analysis:

- Processes to reduce the amount of data that investigators have to read by filtering data or summarize the timeline as proposed in (Abbott, Bell, Clark, De Vel, & Mohay, 2006) and (Hargreaves & Patterson, 2012).
- Operators to deduce new knowledge about events using the knowledge extracted from sources. In (Schatz, Mohay, & Clark, 2004) and (Case, Cristina, Marziale, Richard, & Roussev, 2008), correlation tools are proposed to identify implicit relationships between events for example.
- Tools able to highlight the most relevant information of a timeline to solve the case.

Regarding legal aspects, only few approaches are supported by formal theories. The use of the finite state machine theory allows (Gladyshev & Patel, 2004) and (James, Gladyshev, Abdullah, & Zhu, 2010) to provide an approach based on a proven theory. Regarding the preservation of the integrity of the information, the approach describes in (Buchholz & Falk, 2005) uses a set of restrictions to prevent the modification of evidence. Thus, future works should not only focus on the enhancement of analysis capabilities. The creation of sound theories is required to support tools to enable them to produce evidence that are admissible in a Court.

## CONCLUSION

In this chapter, we introduced the problem of event reconstruction which is a crucial step of a digital investigation. This phase allows investigators to understand what happened during an incident using footprints left on a crime scene. To ensure that investigators can successfully fulfill their mission in the time allocated by the court, efficient and accurate tools must be provided to them. Several approaches have been proposed to carry out the event reconstruction. A large part of them are able to construct a timeline by extracting events from heterogeneous sources. However, few of them provides tools able to facilitate the reading and the analysis of the timeline. There is currently a gap between the amount of data that tools can extract from a crime scene and the amout of information that an investigator can handle during the analysis of the timeline. So far, no tools are able to assist investigators during the whole investigative process (from the extraction of events to the analysis of the timeline) while meeting the constraints imposed by Justice.

# REFERENCES

Abbott, J., Bell, J., Clark, A., De Vel, O., & Mohay, G. (2006). Automated recognition of event scenarios for digital forensics. In *Proceedings of the 2006 ACM Symposium on Applied Computing*, (pp. 293-300). ACM.

Al Mutawa, N., Baggili, I., & Marrington, A. (2012). Forensic analysis of social networking applications on mobile devices. *Digital Investigation, 9*, S24–S33. doi:10.1016/j.diin.2012.05.007

Allen, J. (1983). Maintaining knowledge about temporal intervals. *Communications of the ACM, 26*(11), 832–843. doi:10.1145/182.358434

Anderson, R., Barton, C., Böhme, R., Clayton, R., van Eeten, M., Levi, M., . . . Savage, S. (2012). Measuring the cost of cybercrime. In *Proceedings of 11th Workshop on the Economics of Information Security*. Academic Press.

Baryamureeba, V., & Tushabe, F. (2004). The enhanced digital investigation process model. In *Proceedings of the Fourth Digital Forensic Research Workshop*. Academic Press.

Buchholz, F., & Falk, C. (2005). Design and implementation of Zeitline: Α forensic timeline editor. In *Proceedings of Digital Forensic Research Workshop*. Academic Press.

Carrier, B., & Spafford, E. et al. (2003). Getting physical with the digital investigation process. *International Journal of Digital Evidence, 2*(2), 1–20.

Carrier, B.D., & Spafford, E. (2004). Defining event reconstruction of digital crime scenes. *Journal of Forensic Sciences, 49*(6), 1291. doi:10.1520/JFS2004127 PMID:15568702

Case, A., Cristina, A., Marziale, L., Richard, G., & Roussev, V. (2008). FACE: Automated digital evidence discovery and correlation. *Digital Investigation, 5*, S65-S75.

Chandrawanshi, R., & Gupta, H. (2013). Implementation Of An Automated Server Timeline Analysis Tool For Web Forensics. *International Journal of Engineering, 2*(4).

Chen, K., Clark, A., De Vel, O., & Mohay, G. (2003, November). ECF-event correlation for forensics. In *Proceedings of First Australian Computer Network and Information Forensics Conference* (pp. 1-10). Perth, Australia: Edith Cowan University.

Cloppert, M. (2008). *Ex-tip: an extensible timeline analysis framework in perl*. Bethesda, MD: SANS Institute.

Forensics Wiki. (2007). *File formats*. Retrieved from http://www.forensicswiki.org/wiki/Category:File_Formats

Gladyshev, P., & Patel, A. (2004). Finite state machine approach to digital event reconstruction. *Digital Investigation, 1*(2), 130–149. doi:10.1016/j.diin.2004.03.001

Gudhjonsson, K. (2010). *Mastering the super timeline with log2timeline*. SANS Reading Room.

Hargreaves, C., & Patterson, J. (2012). An automated timeline reconstruction approach for digital forensic investigations. *Digital Investigation, 9,* S69–79. doi:10.1016/j.diin.2012.05.006

Inglot, B., Liu, L., & Antonopoulos, N. (2012). A Framework for Enhanced Timeline Analysis in Digital Forensics. In *Proceedings of Green Computing and Communications (GreenCom),* (pp. 253-256). IEEE.

Jeyaraman, S., & Atallah, M. (2006). An empirical study of automatic event reconstruction systems. *Digital Investigation, 3,* 108-115.

Khan, M., Chatwin, C., & Young, R. (2007). A framework for post-event timeline reconstruction using neural networks. *Digital Investigation, 4*(3), 146-157.

Liebig, C., Cilia, M., & Buchmann, A. (1999). Event composition in time-dependent distributed systems. In *Proceedings of the Fourth IECIS International Conference on Cooperative Information Systems* (pp. 70-78). Washington, DC: IEEE Computer Society.

Morrissey, S. (2010). *iOS forensic analysis: For iPhone, iPad, and iPod touch.* Apress.

Olsson, J., & Boldt, M. (2009, September). Computer forensic timeline visualization tool. *Digital Investigation, 6,* S78–87. doi:10.1016/j.diin.2009.06.008

Palmer, G. (2001). A road map for digital forensic research. In *Proceedings of First Digital Forensic Research Workshop,* (pp. 27-30). Academic Press.

Ribaux, O. (2013). *Science forensique.* Academic Press.

Richard, G., III, & Roussev, V. (2006). Digital forensics tools: the next generation. In Digital Crime and Forensic Science in Cyberspace (pp. 75-90). Idea Group Publishing.

Schatz, B., Mohay, G., & Clark, A. (2004). Rich event representation for computer forensics. In *Proceedings of the Fifth Asia-Pacific Industrial Engineering and Management Systems Conference (APIEMS 2004).* APIEMS.

## ADDITIONAL READING

Arasteh, A., Debbabi, M., Sakha, A., & Saleh, M. (2007). Analyzing multiple logs for forensic evidence. *digital investigation, 4,* 82--91.

Casey, E. (2002). Error, uncertainty, and loss in digital evidence. *International Journal of Digital Evidence, 1*(2), 1–45.

Cohen, M., Garfinkel, S., & Schatz, B. (2009). Extending the advanced forensic format to accommodate multiple data sources, logical evidence, arbitrary information and forensic workflow. *digital investigation, 6,* S57--S68.

Eiland, E. (2006). Time Line Analysis in Digital Forensics. *New México: sn.*

Garfinkel, S. (2010). Digital forensics research: The next 10 years. *Digital Investigation, 7,* S64–S73. doi:10.1016/j.diin.2010.05.009

Gladyshev, P., & PATEL, A. (2005). Finite state machine analysis of a blackmail investigation. *International Journal of Digital Evidence, 4*(1), 1–13.

Herrerias, J., & Gomez, R. (2007). A log correlation model to support the evidence search process in a forensic investigation. *Systematic Approaches to Digital Forensic Engineering, 2007. SADFE 2007. Second International Workshop on,* (pp. 31--42).

Jeyaraman, S. (2011). Practical automatic determination of causal relationships in software execution traces.

Marrington, A., Mohay, G., Clark, A., & Morarji, H. (2007). Event-based computer profiling for the forensic reconstruction of computer activity.

Schatz, B., Mohay, G., & Clark, A. (2004). Generalising event forensics across multiple domains. *2nd Australian Computer Networks Information and Forensics Conference* (pp. 136--144). Perth, Australia: School of Computer Networks Information and Forensics Conference, Edith Cowan University.

Schatz, B., Mohay, G., & Clark, A. (2006). A correlation method for establishing provenance of timestamps in digital evidence. *digital investigation, 3*, 98--107.

Sebastian, M., & Chandran, P. (2011). Towards designing a tool for event reconstruction using Gladyshev Approach. *Proceedings of the 2011 ACM Symposium on Applied Computing*, (pp. 193--194).

Undercoffer, J., Joshi, A., & Pinkston, J. (2003). *Modeling computer attacks: An ontology for intrusion detection* (pp. 113–135). RAID.

Undercoffer, J., Pinkston, J., Joshi, A., & Finin, T. (2004). A target-centric ontology for intrusion detection. *18th International Joint Conference on Artificial Intelligence*, (pp. 9--15).

## KEY TERMS AND DEFINITIONS

**Crime Scene:** The crime scene is a space where a crime or an incident takes place.

**Digital Forensics:** Use of computer science to help investigators to solve cybercriminal cases.

**Event:** An event is a single action occurring at a given time and for a certain duration. An event may be the drafting of a document, the reading of a webpage or a chat conversation with somebody.

**Event Reconstruction:** Process allowing to describe exhaustively an incident using information left on a crime scene.

**Evidence:** Entity used to affirm or refute an assertion.

**Footprint:** Trace of a past activity. In a digital context, a footprint may be a piece of information about web activity, a document or a file left in the bin.

**Legal Requirements:** To be admissible in a court, each evidence must meet several legal requirements such as reproducibility of the process used, credibility and integrity of data.

**Timeline:** Structure containing events chronologically ordered. A timeline allows investigators to have a global overview of the case and to know for example which machines was used, which applications were launched or which files have been modified at a given time.

# Chapter 16
# Indirect Attribution in Cyberspace

**Robert Layton**
*Federation University, Australia*

**Paul A. Watters**
*Massey University, New Zealand*

## ABSTRACT

*We are now in an era of cyberconflict, where nation states, in addition to private entities and individual actors, are attacking each other through Internet-based mechanisms. This incorporates cyberespionage, cybercrime, and malware attacks, with the end goal being intellectual property, state secrets, identity information, and monetary gain. Methods of deterring cybercrime ultimately require effective attribution; otherwise, the threat of consequences for malicious online behaviour will be diminished. This chapter reviews the state of the art in attribution in cyberspace, arguing that due to increases in the technical capability of the most recent advances in cyberconflict, models of attribution using network traceback and explicit identifiers (i.e. direct models) are insufficient build trustworthy models. The main cause of this is the ability of adversaries to obfuscate information and anonymise their attacks from direct attribution. Indirect models, in which models of attacks are built based on feature types and not explicit features, are more difficult to obfuscate and can lead to more reliable methods. There are some issues to overcome with indirect models, such as the complexity of models and the variations in effectiveness, which present an interesting and active field of research.*

## INTRODUCTION

In 2012, U.S. President Obama officially recognised that the Stuxnet virus, which targeted SCADA controllers operating Iranian nuclear facilities, was a state based attack that originated from the USA and Israel (Sanger, 2012). In that recognition, the world moved towards an era where state sponsored cyberconflict is no longer a conspiracy theory (or probable scenario of the world), but an accepted fact. Recent reports by industry and ex-government officials have pointed to other countries like China also being responsible for other attacks, with one allegation being the theft of confidential trading information that led to millions in losses in negotiation potential (Fowler & Cronau 2013). Both the US and China are organising a treaty on "cyber-arms" (Arimatsu, 2012), with a view to recognizing acceptable limits on this fifth domain of war (the first four being

DOI: 10.4018/978-1-4666-6324-4.ch016

land, sea, air and space). However a fundamental component to the enforcement and effectiveness of such a treaty is missing. Without the adequate attribution of cyberattacks, treaties are worth little at best and can be used for the deliberate misdirection of blame at worse (Watters et al. 2013).

In the rush to uptake technology as a core component of critical infrastructure, nations have now found that many of the systems they rely upon are open to potential attack. This includes water systems, intelligence networks and trading information. To protect this critical infrastructure, investment into defences against cyberattacks has increased dramatically over recent years. Governments across the world are increasing their capability and capacity in both defensive and offensive cyber-based programs. While offensive capabilities are increasing, deterrence of cyberattacks has not caught up, as Guitton (2013) notes: "if the adversary knows that the likeliness for a threat of retaliation is low due to the uncertainty of attribution, deterrence is unlikely to function" (p96).

Attribution can be absolute, in that it identifies an actor responsible for a given attack, or relative in that it can tell us that two attacks have the same origin. As noted by Sigholm and Bang (2013) of cyberattack attribution, "the process of attaining positive attribution is perceived as being ineffective" (p. 167). A number of reasons are cited for this, including a lack of access to data, but also the lack of a process that facilitates effective attribution in cyberattacks. In cases where data is available, Sigholm and Bang notes that "the inability to define adequate filters, to make sense of the collected data, and to understand what is important and not, that constitutes the main problem (of attribution of cyberattacks)" (p. 167).

In most recent cases where a cyberattack has been attributed, there has often been a critical mistake on the part of the attacker. In a recent Mandiant APT1 report, the attackers left their name within the attacking programs, linking their attacks to a long online history (Mandiant, 2013). Such mistakes cannot be relied upon, nor

expected to be uncovered in a timely fashion to determine if a country is breaking a treaty through a cyberattack.

Such mistakes, where they exist and the information can be trusted to be accurate, are highly effective pieces of evidence. One example is the use of an atypical and consistent misspelling by an author, which is one of the most effective forms of attribution for a written document (Juola, 2006). However such mistakes cannot be relied upon to exist. Therefore, they cannot form the basis of an effective attribution strategy that needs to be robust, trusted and timely to be used effectively. In addition, relying on commonly known features may open the risk of the attacker inserting deliberately misleading evidence to cause attribution to another actor. Modelling the vector of attack, content of the attack and other meta-data may not be as conclusive as a significant error on behalf of the attacker, but can be applied in more cases.

Cyberattacks, particularly at a state level, are generally technically capable, well resourced, and benefit from adding misdirection and complexity into their attacks. We argue that confidence in attribution can only come from indirect models, because direct features, such as the tracing of an attack through the network path it took, can be easily faked in complicated attacks. Indirect models aim to model intuitive and subconscious aspects to attacks which are more difficult to hide, as the user may not be aware of them. While sophistication is not a mutually exclusive condition of state-based attacks (Guitton & Korzak, 2013), this chapter focuses on such complex attacks.

It is often important to define exactly what is meant by a term, particularly when dealing with criminal behaviour, which often varies in terms of legality and definition in different contexts. For the purposes of this chapter, a computer or person is a *target* if there is some other actor wishing to attack them. We define the *victim* of an attack as someone who has been attacked, and the *attacker* as the person who initiated the attack. We also take the viewpoint as the defender of the victim or target, and therefore an *adversary* is someone who wishes to attack a computer system or target. This definition can be technical (i.e. entering the "attack command" into a computer, supervisory (i.e. the manager commanding the attack) or even political (i.e. creating an agency with a mandate to attack a certain target). In this chapter, we are mostly concerned with the notion of attribution against an intelligent, motivated and resourced attacker (simplified to *intelligent adversary*). Finally, we define a *cyberattack* as being an attack on a computer system or network that is performed over the internet. While there have been, and continue to be, instances of attacks on computer systems through physical access, we consider this a fundamentally different problem, i.e. physical security.

## DIRECT ATTRIBUTION

Many attribution methods that exist today work quite well, both in theory and in practice, but could not be relied upon against an intelligent adversary. For instance, marking based traceback schemes, which are identified later, work quite well if all routers in a network have not been tampered with. The stereotypical "script kiddie", who downloads and uses an attacking tool without properly understanding the attacks or techniques, may not be aware of such techniques of attribution. Traceback schemes may be able to attribute attacks from an unintelligent adversary who does nothing to cover their tracks, obfuscated evidence, or provide misleading evidence.

Wheeler and Larsen (2003) define attribution as "determining the identity or location of an attacker or an attacker's intermediary", and note that in public literature, this task is often referred to as "traceback" or "source tracking". In this report, they identified a number of techniques for network level attribution, which focuses quite heavily on the second part of their definition; "an attacker's intermediary". As we identify later, various authors have discussed the problems with this approach, most notably Clark and Landau (2010). The main concern is that an intermediate system can be, quite easily in relative terms, compromised to perform an attack on behalf of the attacker. This makes the direct tracing of an attack through the network, from the victim to the attacker, nearly impossible if performed with even a small amount of care to remove incriminating evidence on the intermediary system. Wheeler and Larsen (2003) do identify this problem as a limitation with these types of attribution techniques.

We use the term direct attribution to describe attribution techniques such as traceback and others aiming to directly attribute a piece of information from the victim's side the attack directly to the attacker. There are two major forms of this method. The first involves traceback techniques, such as monitoring the traffic flows on a network to determine where an attacking message originated. The second is the use of fixed identifiers, such as an email address or username, which directly links an attacker with an attack. Both of these techniques of direct attribution have been incredibly effective, and we wish to stress this is not an article dismissing them. The focus of this chapter is on attribution against an intelligent adversary, who may be both knowledgeable of these techniques and able to alter this evidence to either hide their own tracks, or to even frame another actor in their place.

This form of adversary is more capable in cyberattacks, and is a consequence of the use of a computer to perform the attack, which is able to alter any piece of data contained within an attack. For example, law enforcement often uses the mantra of "follow the money" when attributing crime, such as drug syndicates or trafficking (Sood & Enbody, 2013). The same is true of cybercrime, where money needs to be laundered, often using mules, and therefore some trail (however difficult to trace) of money can be followed (Aston et. al, 2009). In contrast, the actual attack that led to the cybercrime requires different thinking to attribute.

John and Sivakumar (2009) surveyed the field of traceback mechanisms for the purpose of identifying the attacker in a distributed denial of service attack (DDoS). They note that "most existing traceback techniques start from the upstream links until they determine which one is used to carry the attacker's traffic" (p. 242). In an ideal scenario we could repeat this until we find the originating source of the packets. However, routers often do not store enough state to be effective at this mechanism to adequately attribute packets, resulting in the requirement of improvement methods of attribution. Some of these, such as packet marking, require packets to be marked by routers as they pass through. Such a scheme relies on trusting the router's information, however a router's information logs can be deleted, or even altered to frame a different actor. This means that such information could not be relied upon in a real world attribution scenario against an intelligent adversary.

## MULTI-STAGE ATTACKS

Clark and Landau (2010) stated that "The Problem isn't Attribution; It's Multi-Stage Attacks" (p. 1). Their central thesis claims that while there have been, and continue to be, multiple calls for an improved Internet architecture to improve network level attribution, such as the requirement of attributable network packets; this will do little in practice to actually aid attribution. The real problem, as they establish, is that "multi-stage attacks" render network level forensics of limited value. In a multi-stage attack an intermediate device, or an arbitrary number of intermediate devices, is used to attack the victim.

Multi-stage attacks are relatively easy because, quite logically, if someone has the capability to attack an endpoint system, they most certainly can attack some intermediate computer to use for staging their attack. The ability to remove evidence trails from that intermediary is also relatively

straightforward, and therefore the ability to attribute an attack by stepping back through those intermediate systems is severely limited. This is the major problem prohibiting traceback from being generally useful against real world attacks from intelligent, motivated and skilled attackers.

In contrast to Clarke and Landau's (2010) argument against network forensics, other research suggests that we should not ignore network forensics so quickly. This is mostly due to the fact that a large majority of situations in which network forensics has value is not against intelligent adversaries and therefore such attribution can actually discover useful and reliable information (Pilli, Joshi & Niyogi, 2010). There is, and will continue to be, a significant use for network forensics and traceback schemes. One common example of this use is for quality of service on networks. There is also a role in attribution, on the assumption that the adversary is not technically capable (an assumption that would still hold true in a large number of criminal investigations).

While there are conflicting opinions on the ultimate usefulness of network forensics, this work aims to be forward thinking and focus on the problems inherent in attribution for intelligent adversaries. While network forensic techniques still have immense value in many scenarios, the relative ease of multi-stage attacks (relative, of course to the final attack) means that these forms of network level forensic methods are unlikely to be effective for cyberattack attribution against intelligent adversaries.

## CYBER-ATTRIBUTION

The attribution of cyberattacks is largely a manual process, whereby an expert analyst obtains a copy of the relevant data, then processes it to discover clues that would lead them to the attacker. In many ways, much of the obtained evidence is "circumstantial", rather than directly attributing the attack. The discovery of independent pieces of circumstantial data increases the reliability that could be given to the attribution, such as the discovery of character encoding and a misspelling common to a particular keyboard layout (such as the wrong symbol for the local currency). Independence, however, is hard to show, and an intelligent adversary may be sufficiently knowledgeable to be able to understand all the known cues of attribution, and modify their attack to not giving those cues out. For instance, the user agent string is a particular description of the web browser that is used by someone visiting a website. If unaltered, this gives information on the operating system version, browser, and even other information on the computer used by the website visitor. However, this piece of information is simply contained in the message and can be quite easily altered with freely available browser add-ons.

At the other end of the spectrum of properties under the control of the attacker, external factors, such as the speed of light, dictate how fast an attack can theoretically happen. This means that an attack that can respond to a new piece of data in less than *t* seconds, can be at most *ct* kilometres from the target (where *c* is the speed of light), however this exact form of information is often difficult to adequately model with large variations in network speeds and the use of intermediary computers (Sharma, Xu, Banerjee, & Lee, 2006).

In addition, the attacker must be sufficiently skilled to perform the attack, which removes a large segment of the population as potential attackers, especially if the attack exhibits traits that are not found in automated attack tools. In this section, we analyse the methods and problems of attribution, focusing on indirect methods of attribution. The central argument for attributing cybercrimes is that there are some aspects to an attack, either directly attributing data, attack patterns, behavioural information, etc., that are outside the control of the attacker to alter (either through ignorance or inability).

## Attribution from Industry

A number of reports have been released from organizations in the security industry. These reports detail a single incident, or range of linked incidents, and contain some details on how the organization analyses an attack. In particular, a number of recent reports have focused on attribution.

In 2013, security firm Mandiant released a report that quickly received worldwide press coverage. The report, titled "APT1 Exposing One of China's Cyber Espionage Units", was notable as one of the first overtly public accusations of a state based, and ongoing, cyberattack unit (Mandiant, 2013). Previous reports hinted at the possibility of state based attacks, while this report explicitly attributes an attack to a specific group with state based directives. Attribution in this report is a combination of number of pieces of evidence. Expert analysts from a number of countries have known about the APT1 group (under various names), which is identified in this report, since 2006. Their attacks are linked through the common use of customized malware, as well as attack strategies. What makes this report slightly different is the next step, in which the actual attackers are identified, as attribution on this scale is not publicly released for most attacks. The attribution was performed using a number of methods, including finding past posting history linking usernames (from the malware) to extra information posted online, and the identification of the likely building the attacks originate from by examination of government reports. This combination of technical attribution and open source intelligence gathering provides different confirmations of the same viewpoint, giving stronger confidence in the result. In many ways, this is a large amount of evidence that the report states provides a very strong likelihood that the attribution is accurate *and that the attacks are state-based*. While this is not the first instance of a state-based attribution of a cyberattack, it has been one of the more public announcements on such an attribution, gaining significant global media attention at the time.

FireEye (2013) released a report titled "Digital Bread Crumbs: Seven Clues to Identifying Who's Behind Advanced Cyber Attacks". This report outlines some of the strategies for attributing a cyberattack, either to a direct adversary or to a first language, as a proxy to country of origin. The report outlines seven features that can be used, which are:

1. **Keyboard Layout:** The layout of a keyboard determines which character is placed on a screen after a key is pressed. A simple example is the difference between US, which has a $ character, and British, which has a £ symbol instead. A more complex example is the use of special characters for creating words using Arabic keyboards, which still use the same "QWERTY" style keyboard commonplace around the world but with specific layouts for inputting Arabic letters. In some documents, such as text documents, Word documents, emails, or other programs, the keyboard layout of the author may be saved with the document.

2. **Malware Metadata:** When software is compiled, it is transformed from human readable source code into machine readable binary code through a program called a compiler. Compilers often have a large number of options and environment settings that are stored with the compiled program. This "metadata" can include folder names where source code is stored (such as E:/Code/my_program) or a date of compilation. In extreme cases, it can contain usernames of the person compiling the software.

3. **Embedded Fonts:** File formats such as the Portable Document Format (PDF) are designed to be readable, and look the same, on a large variety of computing systems. To allow for this, information on rendering

a document is stored with the document, including the fonts used. This process is referred to as *embedding*. In the same way that the keyboard layout can be used to determine attributions such as the first language of the user, so too can the embedded fonts.

4. **DNS Registration:** Domain Name Servers (DNS) map human readable names to IP addresses, in order for humans to easily navigate the Internet. For instance, remembering www.google.com is much easier than remembering 220.244.223.108, although the two are equivalent from a computer's point of view. DNS policy requires that every registration has a contactable person, with an actual address. There are large privacy concerns for this (especially for criminals), who can hire the services of other companies to register on behalf of them, hiding the true owner of the DNS registration. Still, information can be gathered from this registration, particularly if there is some overlapping data between different sites.

5. **Language:** All people use language in different ways, some more subtly different than others. However this is much more pronounced when people are speaking a second language, particularly a "learned" language rather than an extra language they grew up with. Common patterns are an increased rate of errors, no pronouns, missing determiners, referring to an object's gender explicitly or misusing common phrases. These errors are often regularly associated with a specific "first language" of the person speaking, and can therefore be used to establish the user's first language. As identified later, the field of authorship analysis aims to further improve these nuances to actually attribute a document to a specific author, rather than a demographic group.

6. **Remote Administration Tool (RAT) Configuration:** RATs are tools that attackers use to control a computer, once they have

exploited it. As with all computer users, attackers have tools they prefer to use and are more comfortable with. They may, for instance, use a particular piece of software for transferring files and another for taking screenshots of the victim's computer. The usage of these tools can be used to link attacks together.

7. **Behaviour:** As suggested earlier, attackers often like to use the same programs in the same ways. These behavioural patterns can be used to link attacks by the same author, and can also include commands used and timing of attacks (both the time of day and the time between commands).

The list from FireEye contains examples of both direct and indirect features for attribution. More direct examples include Keyboard layout and Embedded Fonts. If these values could be trusted or verified then the resulting attribution may be quite effective. However, they are alterable and configurable by the attacker, and therefore cannot be relied upon for robust attribution against an intelligent adversary. Implicit examples include language, and ultimately behaviour. These attributes are harder to formally define, harder to model and are less likely to be explicit in an attack. However, this also means they are more difficult to obfuscate and more reliable for attribution. High profile cyberattacks are difficult to create, and therefore it is unlikely that many variants are possible. This leads to a situation where experts must use some methodology they themselves have created, leading to an increased specialization in attack and therefore a stronger case for the use of indirect methods of attribution.

## Criminal Profiling

The profiling of criminal behaviours and characteristics of offenders responsible for certain crime types can often be used to identify suspects who may be responsible for committing a specific of-

fense (Rogers, 2003). This set of characteristics can be used to predict future criminal activity given a set of matches against the profiles, and in turn, can be used to inform situational crime prevention strategies (Preuß et al, 2007). For example, imagine that a retrospective study of all of the variables involved in bank robberies was undertaken; a number of common features might emerge from such an analysis, and the probabilities of each feature being present during a robbery could be determined. The presence of a gun, for example, might occur 89% of the time, but the covering of a face using a helmet could be present in 98% of cases. Thus, it is likely that carrying a gun near a bank, or wearing a helmet, could signal an imminent robbery; the bank could act to reduce the incidence of robberies through the use of policies (prohibiting guns being bought into the building and the removal of helmets) and use physical screening to enforce the policy. In the case that a robbery was not successfully prevented, then a geographic search of the local area could be undertaken using a database of known gun or motorbike registrations to see if a forensic match could be made between these items and video and image evidence captured during the offense.

In the cyber world, profiling is more restricted in some ways, but as yet, a relatively unexplored avenue. Stereotypes about "hackers" are abundant; they may be characterized as shy, awkward, highly intelligent, poor social skills etc. As Nachreiner (2013) points out, a key psychological variable is motivation – so whether the attacker is a hacktivist, cyber criminal or stat-sponsored attacker may provide useful clues about their approach to offending. A key question is how much evidence about behaviour can be derived from the artefacts observed from a cybercrime "scene", including data such as phishing emails, phishing websites, malicious object code etc. Surprisingly, these may well be a largely untapped source of data for creating profiles; a well-known characteristic of phishing emails, for example, is that they are written in broken English with numerous spelling errors (McCombie et al, 2008). Is it possible to analyse the textual content of phishing websites and messages and determine the first language of the author from the lexical characteristics and psycholinguistic features of their second language (Torney et al, 2012)? Having gathered about these characteristics for a sample representative of the population, could you then generate profiles with associated probabilities, and use these for screening (to prevent attacks) or identify likely attackers, based on their psycholinguistic profile? Further work is needed to determine the profiles associated with specific cybercrimes (e.g., in child exploitation; Prichard et al, 2011) and the characteristics which can be derived from lexical and other data, in relation to motivation, learning, personality, cognition and arousal.

## Models for Indirect Attribution

Indirect attribution is the process of attributing an attack to an attacker using statistical models of the behaviour of the attacker. It has been used for a very long time under a number of phrases (although not all are exactly synonymous), such as criminal profiling, behavioural analysis, and even just "attribution". We use the phrase "indirect attribution" as a term of distinction from direct methods.

There are a number of forms of attribution. For instance, an absolute attribution of an attack is the identification of an actor that is responsible (i.e. in a criminal sense) for an attack. In contrast, relative attribution can answer questions such as "did the same person perform these two attacks?" even if absolute attribution is not directly possible (Layton et. al, 2013a). Current methods for indirect attribution are more suited for relative attribution than absolute attribution. What relative attribution does allow is the collation of evidence and profiling of attacks. For instance, if attack A provides a small piece of evidence and attack B provides a separate piece of evidence, then knowing the same person performed both attacks gives us the ability to use both those parts of evidence. As an

example, attack A may leak the language of the attack (such as through keyboard layout) while attack B may leak the use of a customised version of a tool. This information could be used to triangulate future information on the attacker. Relative attribution is also useful when we have known information on a suspect. For instance, if we know that an actor wrote a particular document X, and can use relative attribution to show that whoever wrote document X wrote some other document Y, we then conclude that the actor wrote Y. It is important for the purposes of use in investigations that the confidence in such conclusions be known, which requires extensive training of appropriate methods (Watters et. al, 2012).

Recent work by Pfeffer et al. (2012) investigated attributing malware through the examination of the reuse of components in malware. This analysis led to the creation of MAAGI, Malware Analysis and Attribution using Genetic Information, which sees these reused components as being akin to the genetics of malware. Through this, we can analyse the genetic structure of malware, specifically how it relates to past pieces of malware and therefore how a sequence of variants of malware evolves over time. This assists in discovering the shared use of code, giving insight into the operations developing malware. In addition, malware was analysed using function linguistics to characterise the intent behind malware behaviour. Such linkages between malware give both information on the behaviour and provenance of the malware.

Parker (2011) examined the Stuxnet virus with intent on attributing the malware to its author. The Stuxnet virus was designed to cause problems with centrifuges used in the process of enriching uranium, ultimately targeting Iran's nuclear program. This analysis, presented at Blackhat Europe (before US President Obama officially recognised it as US state-based), examined the binary file and behaviour of Stuxnet in order to find evidence. The stated goals of the analysis were to provide actor deterrents, intelligence on adversaries and differentiating between actors. While absolute attribution is the "end goal" of attribution analysis, relative attribution is often considered to be effective enough for practical purposes, at least in developing counter-strategies and defences. Behavioural cues, such as attack methodology, are listed as sources for information, as well as the tools used within that methodology. This suggests that it is both the components of an attack and the sequence in which they are used that is important to attribution. The quality of the code, including normal software development aspects such as proper error handling, indicates the resourcefulness of the attackers. Poorly written code may be made in a hurry, with only one or two developers, little testing and no time allocated to improving the robustness of the code. Well established code, with custom libraries for handling common functions and proper error handling, are clues indicating well-resourced adversaries. Further, while the existence of zero day attacks may indicate an intelligence adversary, older attacks can often be reworked to bypass signature based detection mechanisms. This means that older vulnerabilities can still be used, if the patch that "addressed" the issue did not adequately fix the root cause. This reduces the technical complexity required to perform an attack.

Parker (2011) also discusses the likelihood of forging digital evidence, stating it requires knowledge of "what to forge" as well as noting that in some cases, forging evidence may be overly difficult to achieve and not worth the effort. Analysis of the Stuxnet virus shows a large number of functions, libraries and complex coding. This indicated a highly resourced adversary, including access to the centrifuges that were the target of the malware. The system for controlling the malware was deemed to be simplistic, indicating a lack of coding on that aspect of the malware. The attribution from Parker suggested that it was not a Western State attack, which ultimately was an incorrect conclusion. This incorrect conclusion has synergies with the argument of Guitton and Korzak (2013), who note that sophistication is not a prerequisite to state-based attacks.

## Authorship Analysis

When an attack consists of a written document, such as a phishing email, a field of study called authorship analysis can be applied to attribute these attacks. Authorship analysis is the process of identifying properties of an author from information contained within the documents they have written. The most commonly studied form of authorship analysis is authorship attribution, which is frequently performed as a supervised machine learning task. In this task, we have a set of documents for which we know the author, called the *training set*. We then have a set of documents for which we do not know the author, called the *test set*.

While the number and title of the major stages of a machine learning methodology vary from author to author, they are normally related to the following key steps:

1. **Data Pre-Processing:** In which the documents are processed to remove noisy information that does not correlate to authorship. For example, this can include normalising digits, i.e. converting all numbers to '0', as numbers are generally indicative of factual information and not normally controlled by the author.

2. **Document Representation:** Model training algorithms cannot normally accept raw text, and therefore documents need to be converted into a numerical format, such as a vector of values. One simple approach is to count the frequency of each word in the documents.

3. **Model Training:** The training set of documents is used to train some model, such as a support vector machine. The parameters of the model are usually set to maximise some optimization criteria.

4. **Prediction:** The trained model from the model training step is used to predict the author for each of the documents in the test

set. This is normally performed by finding the author that is statistically "most like" each test document, and therefore most likely to have authored it.

For the prediction phase, we often assume that the author of each of the test documents authored at least one document in the training set. This is known as the *closed set* problem. If we cannot make that assumption, this is an *open set* problem. In these cases, the prediction step can predict "none of the above" as the likely author of a test document, indicating that the model believes that none of the authors from the training set authored this particular document.

Authorship analysis has been applied to cybercrime attribution in a number of contexts. Zheng, Huang and Chen (2006) applied authorship analysis to cybercrime, such as spam, using stylistic features, structural features and content specific features for document representation. These features are extracted for each document (in both the training set and test set) to build a statistical model using three model building algorithms; C4.5, Neural networks and Support Vector Machines. Their results were between 70% and 98% for different datasets and model building combinations.

Layton, Watters and Dazeley (2012) applied authorship analysis methods to phishing websites to perform unsupervised authorship analysis. The key difference to the above procedure is the lack of a training set. In *unsupervised machine learning*, there is one set of documents, without any indication of who wrote any of them. A model must then be built that estimates the number of authors and the documents each author wrote. The most commonly used method for performing this process is called cluster analysis. One such example is the k-means algorithm, which finds k clusters, such that each item in a cluster is similar to each other, while being different to items in other clusters. The results from Layton, Watters and Dazeley (2012) of applying a more

complex technique to a set of phishing attacks agreed with expert opinion in over 95% of cases. The document representation methods here were also different from the previous work of Zheng, Huang and Chen (2006). Rather than having a set of static features, each document or author was profiled using the set of the $L$ most frequent character $n$-grams, where $L$ is a value often in the thousands and $n$ is usually between 3 and 6. A character $n$-gram is a sequence of n characters in a row in a document. For instance, for n=3 and the sentence "The cat in the hat", the first five character n-grams are (where spaces have been replaced by underscores):

- The.
- he_c.
- e_c.
- _ca.
- cat.

Models of this type are called "Local n-grams" (LNG) methods, and were first introduced by Kešelj et al (2003). LNG methods have been shown to outperform feature based approaches in many datasets (Luyckx & Daelemans, 2011).

One assumption that many authorship models make is that the authors are not attempting to hide their authorship style. Brennan, Afroz and Greenstadt (2012) examined this assumption, designing an experiment that encouraged authors to hide their authorship style. In the first experiment, authors were asked to provide normal samples of their writing. Then, they were asked to write a document and attempt to obfuscate their writing style (without giving any hints as to what to do). Finally, they were given an excerpt from a particular author and asked to imitate that author's writing. While Brennan, Afroz and Greenstadt (2012) were able to achieve accuracies of over 95% for the author's normal writings, they were unable to achieve much higher than chance rates for the obfuscation document. This was despite the fact that none of the candidate authors had any training in linguistics and were without any instruction on good ways to obfuscate. More concerning is that the imitation document was attributed to the author *being* imitated in 80% of cases. These results were replicated in more recent research.

## ISSUES, CONTROVERSIES, PROBLEMS

What are the limitations and problems of cyber-attribution, as applied in indirect models? There are a number of concerns about the effectiveness of indirect models of attribution. Some of these stem from similar concerns in the field of criminal profiling, while others are more directed at methods used in cyberattacks.

For cyberattacks, the distinction behind what is direct and what is indirect attribution actually contains little that *prohibits* an intelligent adversary from using such models to hide their tracks. For instance, an adversary wishing to hide their writing style could use a local n-gram based classifier as an oracle, asking it if the writing could be attributed to them or not. The intelligent adversary could then continually alter their writing until the model could no longer attribute it. The main advantage of indirect attribution in this sense is not that obfuscation is impossible, just that it is both significantly harder. Further, indirect models have the potential to grow in difficulty with advances in techniques, such as ensembles, in that no single model is relied upon to give a final answer, or computing power. This allows allowing larger forms of features to be incorporated, meaning that the adversary must use a significant amount of effort to hide their attack. In effect, the cost of obfuscation increases with the size of the indirect models.

Indirect attribution techniques also often require a significant amount of base knowledge and data about an attack in order to be effective. This may be more than an analyst could reasonably obtain about a single attack. This means

that information must be combined with other attacks, potentially leading to a loss of reliability if noisy data is included. The size of the data, and the resulting models, may also mean that such models are difficult for a human to understand or explain. This complexity may lead to a lack of trust in their conclusions. The same problem can be said of complex machine learning models like neural networks; despite using statistically sound models for evaluation many people still want to know "why did the computer make that decision?" (Baesens, Setiono, Mues, & Vanthienen, 2003). Giving a vector of weights and a decision function (the properties that define a neural network) is unlikely to adequately answer that question to either a layperson or to an application domain expert. Given the importance of attribution and the legal ramifications, finding solutions that can be explained is an important problem.

As a consequence of the above, it is also possible to misuse indirect models for attribution. For example, consider if an indirect attribution model was trained using a set of packed malware, where the original malware has been obfuscated using some other program, such that it looks different, but performs the same function (Alazab et. al, 2012). Such a model may be effective at attributing *the packing software used*, but is not effective at attributing the malware itself which appears as an obfuscated set of data. In order to perform attribution for the malware authors, the malware must be unpacked before training the indirect attribution model. In this sense, expert analysts are required in the process of building such models, and indirect attribution is not a replacement for their input into the process.

Finally, indirect models of attribution are effective at relative attribution, i.e. answering the question "did the same person perform these two attacks?". In contrast, direct models of attribution are more likely to achieve an answer to the question "who wrote this attack?". However, this does not mean that relative attribution is incapable of finding the actors. An indirect model can feed information into an intelligence gathering process, such as by finding that the actor that performed a given attack is the same person that wrote a blog article or who owns a specific social media (Layton et. al, 2013a). While this is relative attribution, metadata contained within the blog may be able to identify the actor themselves. A combination of indirect methods of attribution and open source intelligence has been used in past investigations to perform absolute attribution of attacks.

## FUTURE RESEARCH DIRECTIONS

There is significant scope for research into indirect methods of attribution. Major areas include improving OSINT[1] through linking information, the development of indirect methods of attribution for new forms of attacks and developing improved unsupervised methods of linking attacks with no prior knowledge. Major challenges include adversarial attacks on attribution methods; scalability to allow for web based searching and reducing the noise associated with a single attack.

The attribution of cyberattacks is currently performed using largely manual processes by an expert analyst. The reasons for this are many, but the main problems are (1) the lack of a consistent, reliable and robust framework for attribution, (2) a constant shift in the attack patterns, and (3) an ongoing evolution of technologies, both attacked and attacking. Understanding these problems and creating long-term solutions is essential for the development of tools to assist in the analysis of cyberattacks.

Unsupervised methods of attribution (Layton, Watters, & Dazeley, 2012, 2013b) are difficult to achieve. Firstly, there is no prior knowledge about the provenance (absolute or relative) of any of the attacks. Secondly, a single attack contains a significant amount of noise, which normally is reduced when multiple attacks from one attacker are analysed together. This noise can take the form of domain specific information, variance in net-

work traffic due, and unusual mistakes made by the attack (such as incorrectly setting a parameter in their attack). Finally, unsupervised methods are often more difficult to scale, as each attack needs to be considered individually, whereas information can be collated in supervised applications.

There is a strong need for tools to automate processing the large amount of data that comes from analysing cyberattacks (Alazab et al. 2010). In some cases, such as a distributed denial of service attack (DDoS), the volume of attacking data is incredibly large. In other attacks, such as an Advanced Persistent Threat (APT), the volume of attacking data is quite small, but hidden within the large amount of data that happens in even small corporate networks. This contrast of "analysing the avalanche" versus "find the needle in the haystack" approaches means that the knowledge needed to effectively analyse all forms of cyberattacks is quite extensive and rare to find in a single person or small team. The development of tools that incorporate expert knowledge into the analysis, rather than simply summarizing and visualizing data, is therefore an important future direction.

## CONCLUSION

In this chapter, the problem of attribution of cyberattacks against an intelligent, motivated and well-resourced adversary was considered. Many existing attribution schemes rely upon information that directly links an actor to an attack, referred to as *direct attribution*. One of the main concepts with computer systems is that almost any piece of information can be altered, meaning that system logs, routers, packet headers, malware metadata etc. cannot be relied upon.

In contrast, *indirect attribution* aims to attribute an actor to an attack by modeling the attack and environment using feature distributions that are not defined explicitly, often salient, difficult to obfuscate and become even more difficult in custom and complicated attack scenarios. This means that the problem of obfuscating attribution increases proportionally with the complexity of the attack for the attacker. This gives a robustness to the concept that it is more likely to remain trustworthy in more scenarios.

Indirect attribution techniques do have some disadvantages. They rely on a sufficient amount of data (where sufficient cannot be clearly defined), they are less accurate than *trustworthy* direct evidence, are difficult for a human to understand or explain, and finally, they must be clearly defined in order to perform adequate attribution. Overall, the field of indirect attribution has led to some interesting results so far, applicable to real world data and intelligent adversaries. In addition, there is a large amount of research that is being performed on the topic and a large scope for future research to be performed to investigate this important problem.

# REFERENCES

Alazab, M., Venkatraman, S., Watters, P., Alazab, M., & Alazab, A. (2012). Cybercrime: The case of obfuscated malware. In Global Security, Safety and Sustainability & e-Democracy (pp. 204–211). Springer.

Arimatsu, L. (2012). A treaty for governing cyber-weapons: Potential benefits and practical limitations. In *Proceedings of Cyber Conflict (CYCON)*, (pp. 1–19). CYCON.

Aston, M., McCombie, S., Reardon, B., & Watters, P. (2009). A preliminary profiling of internet money mules: An Australian perspective. In Proceedings of Ubiquitous, Autonomic and Trusted Computing, (pp. 482–487). UIC-ATC.

Baesens, B., Setiono, R., Mues, C., & Vanthienen, J. (2003). Using neural network rule extraction and decision tables for credit-risk evaluation. *Management Science*, 49(3), 312–329. doi:10.1287/mnsc.49.3.312.12739

Brennan, M., Afroz, S., & Greenstadt, R. (2012). Adversarial stylometry: Circumventing authorship recognition to preserve privacy and anonymity. [TISSEC]. *ACM Transactions on Information and System Security*, 15(3), 1. doi:10.1145/2382448.2382450

Clarke, R. V. G. (1997). *Situational crime prevention*. Criminal Justice Press.

Fowler, A., & Cronau, P. (2013, May 29). *HACKED! Four Corners*. Australian Broadcasting Corporation. Retrieved from http://www.abc.net.au/4corners/stories/2013/05/27/3766576.htm

Guitton, C. (2013). Modelling Attribution. In *Proceedings of the 12th European Conference on Information Warfare and Security* (Vol. 1, pp. 91–97). ACPI.

Guitton, C., & Korzak, E. (2013). The Sophistication Criterion for Attribution: Identifying the Perpetrators of Cyber-Attacks. *The RUSI Journal*, 158(4), 62–68. doi:10.1080/03071847.2013.826509

John, A., & Sivakumar, T. (2009). Ddos: Survey of traceback methods. *International Journal of Recent Trends in Engineering*, 1(2), 241–245.

Juola, P. (2006). Authorship attribution. *Foundations and Trends in Information Retrieval*, 1(3), 233–334.

Kešelj, V., Peng, F., Cercone, N., & Thomas, C. (2003). N-gram-based author profiles for authorship attribution. In *Proceedings of the Conference Pacific Association for Computational Linguistics, PACLING* (Vol. 3, pp. 255–264). PACLING.

Layton, R., Perez, C., Birregah, B., Watters, P., & Lemercier, M. (2013a). Indirect Information Linkage for OSINT through Authorship Analysis of Aliases. In *Trends and Applications in Knowledge Discovery and Data Mining* (pp. 36–46). Springer. doi:10.1007/978-3-642-40319-4_4

Layton, R., Watters, P., & Dazeley, R. (2012). Unsupervised authorship analysis of phishing webpages. In *Proceedings of 2012 International Symposium on Communications and Information Technologies (ISCIT)* (pp. 1104–1109). ISCIT. doi:10.1109/ISCIT.2012.6380857

Layton, R., Watters, P., & Dazeley, R. (2013b). Automated unsupervised authorship analysis using evidence accumulation clustering. *Natural Language Engineering*, *19*(01), 95–120. doi:10.1017/S1351324911000313

Luyckx, K., & Daelemans, W. (2011). The effect of author set size and data size in authorship attribution. *Literary and Linguistic Computing*, *26*(1), 35–55. doi:10.1093/llc/fqq013

McCombie, S., Watters, P. A., Ng, A., & Watson, B. (2008). Forensic Characteristics of Phishing-Petty Theft or Organized Crime? In Proceedings of WEBIST (pp. 149-157). WEBIST.

Nachreiner, C. (2013). *Profiling Modern Hackers: Hacktivists, Criminals, and Cyber Spies. Oh My!* Retrieved from http://watchguardsecuritycenter.com/2013/05/30/hacker-profiles/

Parker, T. (2011). *Stuxnet redux: Malware attribution & lessons learned.* Black Hat DC 2011. Retrieved from www. blackhat. com/html/bh-dc-11/bh-dc-11-archives. html# Parker

Pfeffer, A., Call, C., Chamberlain, J., Kellogg, L., Ouellette, J., Patten, T., et al. (2012, October). Malware analysis and attribution using genetic information. In *Proceedings of Malicious and Unwanted Software* (MALWARE), (pp. 39-45). IEEE.

Pilli, E. S., Joshi, R. C., & Niyogi, R. (2010). Network forensic frameworks: Survey and research challenges. *Digital Investigation*, *7*(1-2), 14–27. doi:10.1016/j.diin.2010.02.003

Preuß, J., Furnell, S. M., & Papadaki, M. (2007). Considering the potential of criminal profiling to combat hacking. *Journal in Computer Virology*, *3*(2), 135–141. doi:10.1007/s11416-007-0042-4

Prichard, J., Watters, P. A., & Spiranovic, C. (2011). Internet subcultures and pathways to the use of child pornography. *Computer Law & Security Report*, *27*(6), 585–600. doi:10.1016/j.clsr.2011.09.009

Rogers, M. (2003). The role of criminal profiling in the computer forensics process. *Computers & Security*, *22*(4), 292–298. doi:10.1016/S0167-4048(03)00405-X

Sanger, D. (2012, June 1). Obama order sped up wave of cyberattacks against Iran. *The New York Times*. Retrieved from http://www.nytimes.com/2012/06/01/world/middleeast/obama-ordered-wave-of-cyberattacks-against-iran.html

Sharma, P., Xu, Z., Banerjee, S., & Lee, S.-J. (2006). Estimating network proximity and latency. *ACM SIGCOMM Computer Communication Review*, *36*(3), 39–50. doi:10.1145/1140086.1140092

Sigholm, J., & Bang, M. (2013). Towards offensive cyber counterintelligence. In *Proceedings of the 2013 European Intelligence and Security Informatics Conference*, (pp. 166–171). Uppsala, Sweden: IEEE Computer Society.

Sood, A. K., & Enbody, R. J. (2013). Crimeware-as-a-service—A survey of commoditized crimeware in the underground market. *International Journal of Critical Infrastructure Protection*.

Torney, R., Vamplew, P., & And Yearwood, J. (2012). Using Psycholinguistic Features For Profiling First Language Of Authors. *Journal of the American Society for Information Science American Society for Information Science*, *63*, 1256–1269. doi:10.1002/asi.22627

Watters, P. A., McCombie, S., Layton, R., & Pieprzyk, J. (2012). Characterising and predicting cyber attacks using the Cyber Attacker Model Profile (CAMP). *Journal of Money Laundering Control, 15*(4), 430–441. doi:10.1108/13685201211266015

## ADDITIONAL READING

Alazab, M., Layton, R., Venkataraman, S., & Watters, P. (2010). Malware detection based on structural and behavioural features of api calls. In *Proceedings of International Cyber Resilience conference 2011*. http://ro.ecu.edu.au/icr/

Amuchi, F., Al-Nemrat, A., Alazab, M., & Layton, R. (2012). Identifying Cyber Predators through Forensic Authorship Analysis of Chat Logs. In *Cybercrime and Trustworthy Computing Workshop (CTC), 2012 Third* (pp. 28–37). doi:10.1109/CTC.2012.16

Burrows, S. (2010). *Source code authorship attribution*. RMIT University.

Chatzicharalampous, E., Frantzeskou, G., & Stamatatos, E. (2012). Author Identification in Imbalanced Sets of Source Code Samples. In *Tools with Artificial Intelligence (ICTAI), 2012 IEEE 24th International Conference on* (Vol. 1, pp. 790–797).

Chon, S., & Broadhurst, R. (2013). Online Data Theft and ZeuS Dropzones. *Available at SSRN 2338901*.

Chouchane, R., Stakhanova, N., Walenstein, A., & Lakhotia, A. (2013). Detecting machine-morphed malware variants via engine attribution. *Journal of Computer Virology and Hacking Techniques*, 1–21.

Du, H., & Yang, S. J. (2011). Discovering collaborative cyber attack patterns using social network analysis. In Social Computing, Behavioral-Cultural Modeling and Prediction (pp. 129–136). Springer.

Escalante, H. J., Montes-y-Gómez, M., & Solorio, T. (2011). A weighted profile intersection measure for profile-based authorship attribution. In *Advances in Artificial Intelligence* (pp. 232–243). Springer. doi:10.1007/978-3-642-25324-9_20

Escalante, H. J., Solorio, T., & Montes-y-Gómez, M. (2011). *Local Histograms of Character N-grams for Authorship Attribution* (pp. 288–298). ACL.

Frantzeskou, G., Stamatatos, E., & Gritzalis, S. (2007). Supporting the cybercrime investigation process: effective discrimination of source code authors based on byte-level information. In *E-business and Telecommunication Networks* (pp. 163–173). Springer. doi:10.1007/978-3-540-75993-5_14

Frantzeskou, G., Stamatatos, E., Gritzalis, S., & Chaski, C. E. (2007). Identifying authorship by byte-level n-grams: The source code author profile (SCAP) method. *Int. Journal of Digital Evidence, 6*.

Frantzeskou, G., Stamatatos, E., Gritzalis, S., & Katsikas, S. (2006). Effective identification of source code authors using byte-level information. In *Proceedings of the 28th international conference on Software engineering* (pp. 893–896).

Gelinas, R. R. (2010). *Cyberdeterrence and the problem of attribution*. Georgetown University.

Giffin, J., & Srivastava, A. (2011). Attribution of malicious behavior. In *Information Systems Security* (pp. 28–47). Springer.

Houvardas, J., & Stamatatos, E. (2006). N-gram feature selection for authorship identification. In *Artificial Intelligence: Methodology, Systems, and Applications* (pp. 77–86). Springer.

Kalutarage, H. K., Shaikh, S. A., Zhou, Q., & James, A. E. (2012). Sensing for suspicion at scale: A bayesian approach for cyber conflict attribution and reasoning. In *Cyber Conflict (CYCON), 2012 4th International Conference on* (pp. 1–19).

Kešelj, V., & Cercone, N. (2004). CNG method with weighted voting. In *P. Joula, Ad-hoc Authorship Attribution Competition. In Proceedings 2004 Joint International Conference of the Association for Literary and Linguistic Computing and the Association for Computers and the Humanities (ALLC/ACH 2004), Göteborg, Sweden.*

Layton, R., McCombie, S., & Watters, P. (2012). Authorship Attribution of IRC Messages Using Inverse Author Frequency. In *Cybercrime and Trustworthy Computing Workshop (CTC), 2012 Third* (pp. 7–13). doi:10.1109/CTC.2012.11

Layton, R., Watters, P., & Dazeley, R. (2010a). Automatically determining phishing campaigns using the USCAP methodology. In *eCrime Researchers Summit (eCrime), 2010* (pp. 1–8). doi:10.1109/ecrime.2010.5706698

Layton, R., Watters, P., & Dazeley, R. (2010b). Authorship Attribution for Twitter in 140 Characters or Less. In *Cybercrime and Trustworthy Computing Workshop (CTC), 2010 Second* (pp. 1–8). doi:10.1109/CTC.2010.17

Layton, R., Watters, P., & Dazeley, R. (2012). Recentred local profiles for authorship attribution. *Natural Language Engineering*, *18*(03), 293–312. doi:10.1017/S1351324911000180

Layton, R., Watters, P. A., & Dazeley, R. (2013). Automated unsupervised authorship analysis using evidence accumulation clustering. *Natural Language Engineering*, *19*(1), 95–120. doi:10.1017/S1351324911000313

McGee, S., Sabett, R. V., & Shah, A. (2013). Adequate Attribution: A Framework for Developing a National Policy for Private Sector Use of Active Defense. *Journal of Business & Technology Law*, *8*(1), 1.

Shahzad, R. M. K. (2013). *Classification of Potentially Unwanted Programs using supervised learning of n-grams*. Blekinge Institute of Technology.

Sigholm, J., & Bang, M. (2013). Towards Offensive Cyber Counterintelligence. In *Proceedings of the 2013 European Intelligence and Security Informatics Conference* (pp. 166–171). Uppsala, Sweden: IEEE Computer Society. doi:10.1109/EISIC.2013.37

Stamatatos, E. (2007). Author identification using imbalanced and limited training texts. In *Database and Expert Systems Applications, 2007. DEXA'07. 18th International Workshop on* (pp. 237–241).

Strouble, D. D., & Carroll, M. C. (2008). Law and Cyber War. In *Proceedings of the Southern Association for Information Systems Conference*. Richmond, VA, USA.

Watters, P. A., McCombie, S., Layton, R., & Pieprzyk, J. (2012). Characterising and predicting cyber attacks using the Cyber Attacker Model Profile (CAMP). *Journal of Money Laundering Control*, *15*(4), 430–441. doi:10.1108/13685201211266015

## KEY TERMS AND DEFINITIONS

**Authorship Analysis:** A field of study investigating attributing text documents using the contents.

**Cyberattack:** An attack over a computer network, usually over the internet.

**Cybercrime:** A crime, in the legal sense, using the internet or computer network.

**Cyberespionage:** An espionage activity, such as the collection of data, over the internet, usually involving one state based actor obtaining information against another state.

**Direct Attribution:** Linking an attack to the attacker using direct pieces of evidence.

**Indirect Attribution:** Linking an attack to the attacker using a model representing the attacker's style and behaviour.

**Intelligent Adversary:** An adversary that is knowledgeable about the processes, systems and techniques used to attack and identify the attacker.

It can be assumed that an intelligent adversary would take steps to mitigate such identification processes.

**Profiling:** Obtaining intelligence about an actor or attack.

## ENDNOTES

[1]   OSINT (Open Source INTelligence) is the collection of intelligence from publicly available sources.

# Chapter 17
# Modern Crypto Systems in Next Generation Networks:
## Issues and Challenges

**Rajashekhar C. Biradar**
*Reva Institute of Technology and Management, India*

**Raja Jitendra Nayaka**
*Reva Institute of Technology and Management, India*

## ABSTRACT

*The performance of Next Generation Networks (NGN) in terms of security, speed, synchronization, latency, and throughput with variable synchronous or asynchronous packet sizes has not been sufficiently addressed in novel crypto systems. Traditional crypto systems such as block and stream ciphers have been studied and implemented for various networks such as wire line and wireless systems. Since NGN comprises of wire line and wireless networks with variable packet-based communication carrying various traffic like multimedia, video, audio, multi conferencing, and a large amount of data transfers at higher speeds. The modern crypto systems suffer with various challenges such as algorithm implementation, variable packet sizes, communication, latency, throughput, key size, key management, and speed. In this chapter, the authors discuss some of the important issues and challenges faced by modern crypto systems in Next Generation Networks (NGN) such as algorithm implementation, speed, throughput and latency in communication, point-to-multipoint, broadcast and key size, remote key management, and communication speed.*

## INTRODUCTION

The rising requirement of larger amount of data, video, and cloud computing are driving tremendous demand for faster and more efficient networks is shown in Figure 1 depicts that an NGN includes a packet-based network that can be used for both IP telephony, video, data and support for

mobilility. Initially, the term NGN was used to refer to the transformation of the core network to IP (Internet Protocol).

NGNs must live up to the expectations of user and network service provider in terms of speed, trust and privacy. New crypto architectures require more sophisticated protection mechanisms to address various issues in modern applications.

DOI: 10.4018/978-1-4666-6324-4.ch017

*Figure 1. Number of internet users (billions) (Courtesy: Sogeti Labs)*

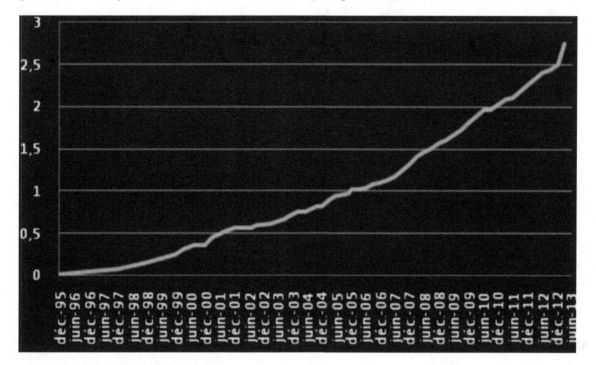

The NGN is characterized by the following parameters. (1) Variable packet-based transfer, (2) Support for a wide range of services, applications and mechanisms based on service building blocks such as real time, streaming, non-real time services, multi-media and video conferencing, (3) Broadband capabilities with end-to-end QoS (Quality of Service). (4) Interworking with legacy networks via open interfaces. (5) Generalized mobility issues. (6) Unrestricted access by users to different service providers. (6) Various identification schemes such as IP address for routing in IP networks and (7) converged services between fixed or mobile stations.

Next Generation Networks (NGNs) use high speed wireless devices with variable packet sizes that incorporate 2G/3G/LTE, Wi-Fi, Bluetooth, GPS, wireless sensor networks and other radios. It includes cellular communications, wire line or wireless broadband and other emerging applications as shown in Figure 2.

NGN network supports for a wide range of services, applications and network architectures based on service building and application. NGNs will carry not just traditional conversational services such as voice calls and data transfer but also transactional services like banking and online purchasing, streaming services like watching video-on-demand or IPTV (IP Television) and real-time interactive services such as video conferencing. NGNs must support the QoS demands of the application and it must provide adequate end-to-end bandwidth to consumers, typically several Gigabit NGN Interwork with legacy networks via standard interfaces. Existing telecommunication networks will be required for several years to support legacy services and Customer Premises Equipment (CPE) for consumers to facilitate a measured transition to NGN at interconnect points (Alptekin, 2013). NGNs typically adopt a backward compatibility model using traditional SS7 signaling and TDM at interconnect points. Mobility access to core network services becomes more generalized. It

*Figure 2. Next Generation Network architecture*

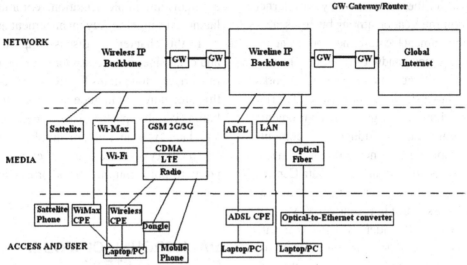

is necessary to manage mobility between service providers and access points into the service provider network. Unrestricted access by users to different service providers and legacy users, NGNs will increasingly allow services to be accessed from different access networks, including fixed line, traditional mobile and fixed wireless such as WiMax as shown in Figure 2.

Recent introduction of broadband services has enthused the customers to that extent that now there is a demand for wireless access for broadband. WiFi is the Standard that is enabling access to broadband internet on wireless environment in a short range and WiMax Standard is for mobile internet access for long range of 10 Km to 40 Km. The tremendous potential of WiMax standard in delivering wireless access for various services like data at high speed, GSM backhaul and enterprise services to the high-end corporate customers is expected to bring in a new communication revolution in the years to come. Wireless access networks based on WiMax compliant solutions provide an opportunity for operators to participate in the high growth opportunity that exist in emerging markets. Where the traditional wire line infrastructure is either non-existent or

only accessible to a small segment of the populations, WiMax-based access networks will enable local operators to cost-effectively reach millions of new potential customers and provide them with traditional voice and broadcast data services that. In recent year, there has been a spurt in the data traffic considerably. In fact, the data traffic in many countries has taken over the voice traffic. More countries are set to follow the trend. Internet had primarily played the catalytic role for the high growth of data traffic. Omnipresence of Internet and its cost effectiveness has been the driving force for the explosive growth of data based services. Wireless technologies are developing at a faster rate as WiFi and WiMax services are used in wireless LAN in access network. Wi-Fi as a technology has created lot of buzz as evidenced from the increasing number of hot-spots around the world. Besides providing enterprise solutions, the technology can be deployed by Internet service providers in innovative ways. This chapter provides implementation details of such initiative for Network Service Providers. While such services are in nascent stage, they have the potential to acquire significant importance for service providers and wireless broadband customers alike in near future.

NGN uses Carrier Ethernet. It is the use of high-bandwidth Ethernet technology for Internet access and communication among business, academic and government local area networks. Carrier Ethernet overcomes bandwidth bottlenecks that can occur when a large number of small networks are connected to a single larger network. Carrier Ethernet has minimal configuration requirements and can accommodate individual home computers as well as proprietary networks of all sizes. Carrier Ethernets are very useful in Data Centers since Data Centres are emerging as a core sector of IT business world in recent years. Most of the Internet Service Providers (ISPs) and private entrepreneurs concentrate more on these areas. Modern technology and business drives the corporate to integrate their applications in a central location so that the ways and needs of accessing, controlling and maintaining them becomes easy. The security issues of Data Centres become significant to safeguard sensitive information. Modern cryptosystems help in designing foolproof security for Data Centres.

The advances in computing and in the novel method of cryptanalysis have made it necessary to adopt novel and stronger algorithms with larger key sizes. Legacy algorithms are supported in current products to ensure backward compatibility and interoperability between different types of access device in NGN. However, some older algorithms and key sizes no longer provide adequate protection from modern threats and should be studied and replaced. The performance of NGNs in terms of security, speed, synchronization, latency and throughput with variable synchronous or asynchronous packet sizes need to be addressed. Traditional crypto systems such as block and stream ciphers have been studied and implemented for various wire line and wireless networks. NGN comprises of wire line and wireless networks, packet based communication carrying various traffic like multimedia, video, audio and large amount of data transfers at higher speed. The novel Crypto Systems have to secure sensitive

information addressing various challenges such as algorithm implementation, communication, latency, throughput, key management and speed.

In this chapter, we discuss important issues and challenges to be considered in the design of modern crypto systems for NGN. The challenges that are addressed include algorithm implementation, variable packet sizes, speed, throughput and latency, true random number generation, key memory size and remote key management, point- to-point, multipoint and broadcast secured communication.

## BACKGROUND OF MODERN CRYPTO SYSTEMS

Modern communication system uses electronic transmission of voice, video and text based information which is widely used today and it is expected to increase with time. Information age has seen the development of increasingly complex electronic systems, networks and devices that carry large amounts of sensitive data at higher speed. Modern information systems are now the target of sophisticated and malicious individuals and organizations intent on breaching confidentiality and disrupting the service. As a result of such on-going threats, there is a strong demand for securing vital electronic pathways and to offer both service providers and users a high level of confidence in systems integrity (Alptekin, 2013). In the modern communication networks, it is often desirable to protect the privacy of information in some manner. Probably, the most popular method to achieve privacy is through certain encryption mechanisms to safeguard important information and make it unreadable to anybody except the intended receiver.

Modern cryptosystems have seen an enormous growth in recent developments to overcome security violations in NGNs. The developments over earlier cryptosystems such as stream and block ciphers which involves various encryption mechanisms. Since the security features required to protect data are very difficult to design and implement, we need modern crypto systems to resolve such issues. They require considerable understanding of the underlying technical principles in order to be used effectively. In this section, we discuss some of the encryption mechanisms, crypt analysis and the role of crypto systems in NGNs.

Encryption is the process of converting the user data in a form such that it is impossible to compare with original data without the knowledge of keys used to encrypt it. Depending on the type of algorithm used for encryption, either symmetric or asymmetric keys are used. Symmetric key type algorithm, the data is encrypted and decrypted with the same key. However, in case of asymmetric type encryption algorithms, two types of keys are used; a public key to encrypt the data and the corresponding private key to decrypt it. The advantage of asymmetric key type of algorithms is that the key can be easily shared using the public key across a public network media and remote device uses this key to encrypt the data. Even if a hacker gets the public key, information cannot be decrypted since only the corresponding private key can decrypt the data. Some examples of symmetric encryption algorithms are DES, 3DES, AES, blowfish, Two fish, IDEA, CAST (Nidhi, 2002), IPSec, etc.

The IPSec standard provides a method to manage authentication and data protection between multiple crypto peers engaging in secure data transfer. IPSec uses symmetrical encryption algorithms for data protection. Symmetrical encryption algorithms are more efficient and easier to implement in hardware.

These algorithms need a secure method of key exchange to ensure data protection. This solution requires a standards-based way to secure data from eaves dropping and modification. IPsec provides such a method. IPsec provides a choice of transform sets so that a user can choose the strength of their data protection. IPsec also has several Hashed Message Authentication Codes from which to choose, each giving different levels of protection for attacks such as man-in-the-middle, packet replay and data integrity attacks. Authentication in IPSec is achieved by the addition of an Authentication Header (AH) which comes after the basic IP header and contains cryptographically secured hashes of the data and identification information. An orthogonal division of IPSec functionality is applied depending on whether the endpoint performing the IPSec encapsulation is the original source of the data or a gateway.

The modes used in IPSec are transport and tunnel modes. Transport mode in IPSec is used by a host that is generating the packets. In transport mode, the security headers are added before the transport layer (e.g TCP, UDP) headers, before the IP header is pretended to the packet. In other words, an AH added to the packet will cover the hashing of the TCP header and some fields of the end-to-end IP header, and an ESP (Encapsulating Security Protocol) header will cover the encryption of the TCP header and the data, but not the end-to-end IP header. Tunnel in IPSec mode is used when the end-to-end IP header is already attached to the packet, and one of the ends of the secure connection is only a gateway. In this mode, the AH and ESP headers are used to cover the entire packet including the end-to-end header, and a new IP header is repented to the packet that covers just the hop to the other end of the secure connection.

Modern cryptography is concerned with the rigorous analysis, communication and integration for various types of communication systems so as to withstand malicious attempts to crack the information over NGN. Since NGN has access to the communication channel at different interfaces, providing privacy remains a central goal. However, modern crypto encompasses many other security parameters such as guaranteeing integrity, algorithm strength and authenticity of communications. Modern crypto system emphasizes many aspects of the NGN such as high speed communication and several types of media, protocol and interfaces. In this section, we discuss some of the efforts to overcome above said security violations in NGNs.

Cryptanalysis methods are used for obtaining the meaningful information from encrypted information without access to the secret information. Cryptalysis involves knowing how the crypto system works and finding a secret key. Cryptanalysis is the practice of code breaking or cracking the code."Cryptanalysis" is also used to refer to any attempt to circumvent the security of other types of cryptographic algorithms and protocols. Even though, the goal has been the same, the methods and techniques of cryptanalysis have changed drastically through the history of cryptography, adapting to increasing cryptographic complexity, ranging from the pen-and-paper methods of the past, through machines like Bombes and Colossus computers in World War II, to the computer-based schemes of the present. The results of cryptanalysis have also changed and it is no longer possible to have unlimited success in code breaking, and there is a hierarchical classification of what constitutes an attack preventive action in NGN crypt attack are an important concern and crypto system design should resist more efficiently than traditional cryptanalysis.

Large size organisations are connected through NGN across the globe. There will be always threat of frequent cyber attacks. Cyber attacks are targeted at particular organizations, services and individuals to obtain private, technical and institutional information, and other intellectual assets (Matsui. 1993). Cyber attacks are socially or politically motivated attacks that are carried out primarily through the Internet. Attacks target the general public or national corporate organizations and are carried out through the spread of malicious programs, unauthorized web access, fake websites, and other means of stealing personal or institutional information from targets of attacks, causing far-reaching damage. NGN Crypto systems call

for multitier security. Multitier architecture of the application allow to design the network in a way that mirrors the grouping of the crypto components so that one can segment resources based on their exposure sensitivity and the likelihood that they can be compromised.

NGN Partitioned network architectures can be used to protect multitier applications accessible over the Web. In future, there will be a trend of crypto system design applications in an expandable and scalable manner (Elixmann, 2003; Akylidiz, 2006). These applications are often created by using modules that run on different servers and there are typically three distinct groups of servers: presentation, middleware, and data tiers. Crypto designer should begin by examining how the NGN architecture of such applications may influence the design the network security perimeter (Guseong-Dong, 2005). One way of deploying crypto system is that the designer has to examine the relationship between crypto devices in the network and other perimeter defense devices (Hamdan, 2010). When designing the network, we have to consider how other components of its perimeter, such as intrusion detection systems, routers, and VPNs, may impact security of the infrastructure.

## ISSUES AND CHALLENGES IN MODERN CRYPTOSYSTEMS

There are various issues and challenges faced by modern cryptosystems in NGN. The design and development of these cryptosystems involve many complexities in terms of design and implementation, processing overhead and maintenance. In this chapter, we have identified some of the issues and challenges in the design of modern cryptosystems. We have discussed important parameters to be considered in the implementation of modern crypto systems. It includes algorithm implementation, communication, variable packet sizes, speed, throughput and latency, true random number generation, key memory size and remote key management, point-to-point, multipoint and broadcast secure communication.

## Algorithm Implementation

NGN communications need data security for high speed data transfer with variable packet size, the need for reduced execution time and computation overhead associated with the execution of cryptographic algorithms increases. There are major benefits from parallel computing on multi core platforms. The advantage of such a system lies in its ability to handle large and extremely complex crypto computations. Parallelizing the computation of cryptographic algorithms on multi core computation platforms will be a promising approach to reduce the execution time and energy consumption of such algorithms. Software implementations of encryption algorithms have a limited throughput due to the inherent absence of parallelism. Parallelism can be achieved to some extent in software, but that generally requires multicore CPUs with high costs well beyond the application budget. A feasible alternative for modern crypto systems is the hardware implementation of ciphers using programmable logic devices like Field Programmable Gate Arrays (FPGAs) or hardwired ASICs. Usage of FPGA allows crypto designers to achieve high speed by using parallel architecture (Velentini, 2011). The flexibility and high speed capability of FPGAs make them a suitable platform for cryptographic applications (Chen Liu, 2012). FPGA based ciphers support the fundamental properties of a cryptographic system including data encryption and authentication.

Crypto SoC (System on Chip) is a single chip solution which will process the crypto application specific information as well as encrypt or decrypt user data will provide solution to NGN crypto system and has advantage over fault model attack (Cody, 2007). Hardwired ASIC crypto solution has got advantage of tamper proof and fault toler-

ant crypto systems. With increase in the number of cores on a single chip will increase the crypto computational speed and improve the energy consumption of the NGN Crypto system. Using techniques to increase the energy efficiency in multi core systems will reduce energy consumption, hardware space on board, lower operational costs and improve system reliability (Akylidiz, 2006). The emergence of multi-core systems provides the opportunity to revisit the realization of high speed crypto computing problems on more capable hardware.

## Communication

The next-generation network (NGN) enables the deployment of access independent services over converged fixed and mobile networks (Akylidiz, 2006). The NGN is packet based and uses IP to transport the various types of traffic like voice, video, data and signaling. Routers and firewalls are plagued by a constant stream of vulnerabilities and attacks. Most of modern communication uses variable length asynchronous data frame (i.e. Ethernet frame, SMS etc), standard blocks of data is the issues, padding may be added to have standard size block which in turn will contribute to low throughput of system. Novel algorithm should address variable length data blocks. Multi conference video communication systems will have crypto synchronization issues. Stream ciphers are suitable for synchronous point to point systems transmitting continuous stream and block cipher are suitable for asynchronous point to point, multipoint and broadcast packet based communication (Elixmann, 2003; Akylidiz, 2006). As NGN systems communicate data over point-to-point, point-to-multi point and broadcast or multicast mode with variable length of data blocks. The modern crypto system should address these issues.

NGN uses Ethernet IP based network as backbone network. It uses variable size of packet asynchronous communication at 10/100/1000Mb at user side and 10G/40G/100G on network side. Processing packet and applying encryption at this speed calls for high speed parallel architecture.

Mobile broadband is a high-speed wireless Internet connections and services designed to be used from arbitrary locations (Elixmann, 2003). Beside phones, Internet technologies are increasingly being incorporated into laptop computers and mobile handsets. Cellular networks normally provide broadband connections suitable for mobile access. The technologies in use today fall into two categories 3G (third generation cell networks) and 4G (fourth generation). Wireless communications such as GSM/CDMA / WiFi / WiMax /LTE based system calls for extra overhead bits in crypto solutions as shown in Figure 3.

## Variable Packet Length

Novel crypto solutions need for an encryption algorithm which deals with messages of varying packet sizes but at the same time preserves the property that the length of cipher text equals the length of the plaintext. This situation is very common in Internet applications where traffic consists of "packets" of varying sizes. If a block cipher is being used for encryption, then the blocks that need to be encrypted could be of varying lengths (Sarayar, 2005) and padding is required to make standard block size. Deferential packet sizes are also prevalent in wireless applications, this is due to the fact that the frames of data that are sent to each user may be different from user to user because of the difference in the so called path-loss of the users relative to the base station. Existing block ciphers operate on fixed input length block size (e.g. 64-bits for DES, 128-bit for AES) (Hamdan, 2010). Stream ciphers are suitable for point to point communication transmitting continuous synchronized stream of bits. Stream cipher is not attractive because it sacrifices data and key diffusion and it further requires synchrony between sender and receiver. Block ciphers standard block size adaptation in modern data communication

*Figure 3. Types of wire-line and wireless network*

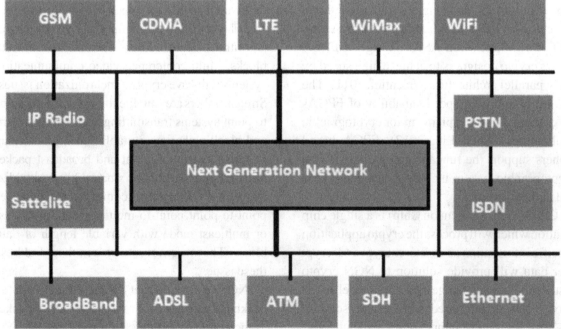

require dummy padding which in turn consumes unnecessary bandwidth (Schneier, 1993). NGN crypto system needs a variable input length algorithm that can operate on a deferent size input.

Variable packet size or Elastic Cipher crypto systems require hybrid algorithm which require combination of block and stream cipher with variable key management. The NGN solutions should combine the length preserving aspects of stream ciphers with the diffusion properties of block ciphers and should use well analyzed components or algorithms (GuseongDong, 2005; Sarayar, 2005).

## Speed

NGN supports time critical financial transactions, sensitive healthcare record storage, secure military communications and simply wireless voice or video connections. Today's NGN networking infrastructure is required to do more than ever in an environment of increasing threats.

NGN communication system transfers data at Gigabit and Terabit speed. Modern crypto system should address speed issues. Next generation network uses satellite, WiMax, LTE, STM-n etc. which uses speed from 2Mb to 1/10/40/100 Gigabit speed (Elixmann, 2003; Akylidiz, 2006). The modern crypto system should able to process data for encryption and decryption at this speed. The implementation of a cryptographic algorithm must achieve high processing rate to fully utilize the available network bandwidth. High speed encryptors have no impact on latency, ensuring the high quality of real time applications such as VoIP and video applications with smaller frame sizes. High availability of encryptors features support architectures with over 99% uptime. High speed encryptors provide the fastest network encryption available, operating at true line speed.

## Latency and Throughput

Performance crypto systems can be measured. Crypto performance metrics are Encryption latency time, Decryption latency Time and Throughput. encryption latency time is the time taken by encryption algorithm to produce a plaintext to cipher text and decryption time is the time that a decryption algorithm takes to produce a plaintext from a cipher text. The throughput of an encryption scheme define the speed of encryption and decryption . The throughput can be calculated as the total plaintext in Kilobytes to encrypted time.

Latency of crypto system depends on CPU process time. The CPU process time that a CPU is dedicated only to the particular process for calculations. More the CPU time used in the encryption process the higher is the CPU load. Memory Utilization is the memory access time also contributes to latency. Memory Utilization defines how much time memory is being accessed doing the encryption or decryption.

With rising speed of communication in NGN, the latency and throughput challenges become important factor in design of crypto system (Roukas, 1997). Software implementations of encryption algorithms have a limited throughput and latency due to the inherent absence of parallelism. However Parallelism can be achieved to some extent in software using multi-core CPUs at high costs. Modular algorithm architecture involving implementations pipelined blocks gives the best performance both in terms of latency and throughput for gigabit and terabit speed. Crypto systems should use a pipeline to increase the throughput, the latency should relate to the amount of pipelined data (GuseongDong, 2005). Among the various time space tradeoffs, modern crypto design should focus primarily on time performance. The time performance metrics are the key setup latency and the throughput. The key setup latency time and the throughput are associated with the key and the bulk-encryption efficiency respectively.

NGN crypto system should exploit the inherent parallelism of each cryptographic core and the low level hardware features of FPGAs to enhance the performance. Latency and throughput issues can be solved using FPGA based crypto designs (Chen Liu, 2012).

## True Random Number Generation (TRNG)

Since the random numbers are hard for an attacker to determine, we need to generate stronger true random numbers generation for the purpose. TRNG make a fundamental contribution to the security of key generation, key agreement protocols, identification, and authentication protocols. Stream ciphers use the output of a Pseudo Random Generator (PRG) to encrypt the information stream. Security strength of these stream cipher systems ultimately depend on the linear structure of PRG. There are few minimum necessary criteria for strength check for PRG such as long period, fat statistical distribution and high linear complexity, so that it should satisfy to resist the basic cryptanalytic attacks on such systems. The linear complexity of these generators is analysed and conditions that assure the highest possible linear complexity.

All TRNG outputs are run through various algorithms that mix and whiten the data to assure uniform statistical distribution, all TRNGs could be called PRNGs (Fischer, 2003; Epstin, 2003). However the crucial difference is that TRNG post-filter output is irreproducible where a pseudo random number generator will predictably generate identical streams of output given the same seed e TRNG produces output that is fully dependent on some unpredictable physical source that produces entropy. Hardware TRNG is different from a PRG that approximates the assumed behavior of a real hardware random number generator.

## Key Memory Size

In most of cryptographic algorithm, the key length and memory is an important security parameter, it plays important role in determining strength of algorithm. Keys are bunch of bits, such that any random sequence of bits of the right size is a possible key. Such keys are subject to brute force attacks. Encryption keys are used to protect valuable information. If the secrecy and integrity of the keys are damaged then the secrecy of the valuable information may be damaged and compromised. In NGN, we need to investigate different storage devices and design.

Large number storage of encryption keys will eventually reduce the attacks from intruders to decode keys. There are different concepts of cryptography related encryption keys and secure storage of encryption keys. Different kinds of storage devices like large capacity memory chips, USB and mini hard disk of capacity Gigabit to terabits storage size available in market and which help us in proposing a secure storage of encryption keys. Securing encryption keys is a challenging task in NGN.

The 32 and 64-bit key size should not be used for algorithm, since 32-bit keys offer no confidentiality and 64-bit offers only very poor protection. 128-bit, 256-bit and 1024 keys provide sufficient security against brute force key-search by the most reasonable adversaries, it should be noted that key size less than 128-bit bits would be practically breakable and one should consider attack models based on pre-computation and large amounts of available storage. As a simple rule of thumb, one may choose to double the key size to mitigate threats from such attacks. The National Institute of Standards and Technology (NIST) has disallowed the use of 1024-bit keys after 31 December 2013 because they are insecure. Due to rapid advances in computational power and cloud computing make it easy for cybercriminals to break 1024-bit keys.

## Remote Key Management

Managing cryptographic keys is a critical part of the information lifecycle. Keys are used to secure data-in-transit (e.g. to secure communication between systems). Cryptographic keys are also used for digital identities, enabling digital signatures and establishing trust in various ecosystems. Remote Key management can centrally manage and update them automatically. The Remote Key management provides a broad range of encryption key management functions including key generation, distribution, injection, deletion and tracking. It also securely and remotely distributes encryption keys over a secured IP network, thereby eliminating the costly and cumbersome manual process of having to physically input keys.

Keys generated can be securely and remotely transferred from one hardware system module to another without any security breach will reduce the risk of lost keys, high management costs and processes. NGN demands implementation of effective remote key management of cryptographic keys using dedicated hardware modules and centralized key management protocols (Velentini, 2011). Issues to be addressable in NGN applications are secure communication, identification, authentication, and secret sharing. More complicated NGN applications include systems for electronic commerce, certification, secure electronic mail, key recovery, and secure access.

Remote key management automatically changes encryption keys in the transit. Security administrators can define the frequency of key rotation based on internal security policies over the period. When a key change occurs, the new version of keys is created and the old version is moved to a historical database and available for cryptographic operations. Built in logging allows administrators to track all key retrieval, key management, and system activity. Reports can be sent automatically to central log management, alerting facilities.

## POINT-TO-POINT, MULTIPOINT, AND BROADCAST

In Point to Point packets are sent from user to user. The communication takes place between from a single host to another single host. There is one device transmitting a message destined for one receiver. Broadcast is when a single host is transmitting a message to all other host in a given IP address range. This broadcast could reach all hosts on the subnet or all hosts on all subnets. Broadcast packets have the host portion of the address set to all ones. IP Broadcasting is a suite of solutions providing IP based high definition video transport for broadcasters including video conferencing and cable TV transmission. With the needs of viewers becoming more sophisticated and expectations of real time reporting, high definition and 3D movies placing increasing demands on the network, the use of IP over traditional SDH and ATM networks has enabled a step change in broadcasting. Multi point or Multicast is a special protocol for use with IP. Multipoint enables a single device to communicate with a specific set of hosts, not defined by any standard IP address and mask combination. This communication resembles a conference call. Anyone from anywhere can join the conference, and everyone at the conference hears what the speaker has to say. The speaker's message is not broadcasted everywhere, but only to those in the conference call itself. A special set of addresses is used for multicast communication.

Multicast and broadcast applications require confidentiality and authenticity of the group members. Authentication is the primary requirement for most of the applications and many authentication schemes have been proposed for various applications . Common group key is used to provide confidentiality and authenticity among the group members. Rekeying is used to prevent backward and forward confidentiality. Backward confidentiality means new user must not read the past communication and forward confidentiality defines ex group member must not read the future communication. Re-keying is performed immediately whenever there is change in group membership either a single join or single leave known as immediate rekeying. Group key need to be updated whenever there is a change in the group membership which increases the communication.

NGNs Communicate in Point-to-point, Multipoint and Broadcast modes (Roukas, 1997). Typically data transfer use point to point, video stream uses multipoint and broadcast modes. Key massage exchange and usage in these modes are challenging. The multipoint option allows units to also secure fully meshed connections in a collision domain. The multipoint option secures the confidentiality of sensitive and high-value data, voice, and video by protecting broadcast and multicast connections (Elixmann, 2003; Roukas, 1997). The Gigabit and terabit models operating in this mode need for high-speed multipoint security over Wide Area Network (WAN) backbone infrastructures.

Key message exchange is in multipoint and broadcast is challenging and key management become complicated when density of users increase over the period. Remote Management keys in IPTV Broadcast across globe demands specialised high speed secured and reliable key management network. NGN encryption Crypto solutions must safeguard communication reliably and without loss of quality. The different area of application should reach from encryption of point-to-point connections to complex multipoint and broadcast networks. The crypto systems should optimal for the realization of network scenarios where the communication between distributed sites has be secured against passive and active attacks.

## SUMMARY

Next Generation Network comprises of wire line and wireless networks with variable packet sizes and speed ranging from 2Mb to 100 GB having different frame formats and protocols. These NGNs based communication carries vari-

ous traffic like multimedia, video, audio, multi conferencing and large amount of data transfers. Role of modern crypto systems is vital in securing information in NGN. In this book chapter, we have identified important issues and challenges to be considered in the design and development of novel crypto system solutions for NGNs. Important parameters to be considered in the implementation of modern cryptosystems includes algorithm implementation, communication, variable packet sizes, speed, throughput and latency, true random number generation, key memory size and remote key management, point-to-point, multipoint and broadcast secure communication.

## REFERENCES

Cody, B., Madigan, J., MacDonald, S., & Hsu, K. W. (2007). High speed SOC design for blowfish cryptographic algorithm. *Very Large Scale Integration*, 284-287.

Elixmann. (2003). *Next generation networks and challenges for future competition policy and regulation*. WIK-Diskussionsbeitrag: WIK Wissenschaftliches Institute for Kommunikations dienste GmbH

Epstein, M., Hars, L., Kransinski, R., Rosner, M., & Zheng, H. (2003). Design and Implementation of a true random number generator based on digital circuits artificats. *Springer Heidelberg*, *2779*, 152–165.

Fischer, V., & Drutarovsky, M. (2003). True Random Number Generator Embedded in Reconfigurable Hardware. *Springer Heidelberg*, *2523*, 415–430.

Guseong-Dong, Yuseong-Gu, & Daejeon. (2005). *High-performance variable-length packet scheduling algorithm for IP traffic*. CNR Lab. Dept. of EECS, KAIST.

Hamdan, O., Alanazi, B.B., Zaidan, A.A., Zaidan, H.A., Jalab, M., Shabbir, Y., & Al-Nabhani. (2010). New comparative study between DES, 3DES and AES within nine factors. *Journal of Computing, 2*(3).

Liu, C., Duarte, R., Granados, O., Tang, J., Liu, S., & Andrian, J. (2012). Critical path based hardware acceleration for cryptosystems. *Journal of Information Processing Systems, 8*(1), 133–144. doi:10.3745/JIPS.2012.8.1.133

Nidhi Singhal, J.P.S, & Raina. (2002). Comparative analysis of AES and RC4 algorithms for better utilization. *International Journal of Computer Trends and Technology, 11*, 177.

Patel, Ramzan, Ganapathy, & Sundaram. (2005). Efficient constructions of variable-input-length block ciphers. *LNCS, 3357*, 326–340.

Rouskas, G. N., & Baldine, I. (1997). Multicast Routing with End-to-End Delay and Delay Variation Constraints. *IEEE Journal on Selected Areas in Communications, 15*, 346–356. doi:10.1109/49.564133

Schneier. (1993). Description of a new variable-length key, 64-bit block cipher (blowfish). In *Proceedings of Fast Software Encryption, Cambridge Security Workshop*, (pp. 191-204). Academic Press.

Lan, F., Akylidiz, W.-Y., Lee, M. C., & Vuran, S. M. (2006). Next generation dynamic spectrum access cognitive radio wireless networks:Survey, . *Computer Networks, 50*, 2127–2159.

Valentini, G., & Lassonde, W. et al. (2011). An overview of energy efficiency techniques in cluster computing systems. *Cluster Computing*, 1–13.

## KEY TERMS AND DEFINITIONS

**Application Specific Integrated Circuits (ASIC):** Application Specific Integrated Circuits is a custom designed integrated chip.

**Code Division Multiple Access (CDMA):** Code Division Multiple Access employs spread-spectrum technology and a special coding scheme in which each transmitter is assigned a code to allow multiple users to be multiplexed over the same physical channel.

**Customer Premises Equipment (CPE):** Customer premises equipment used to extend broadband services over long distance on wire line and wireless media.

**Cryptography:** The discipline which embodies principles, means and methods for the transformation of data in order to hide its information content, prevent its undetected modification, prevent its unauthorized use or a combination thereof the study of transforming information in order to make it secure from unintended recipients.

**Field: Programmable Gate Array (FPGA):** Field Programmable Gate Array are programmable digital logic chips.

**Global Positioning System (GPS):** Global Positioning System is a space-based service that provides position, navigation, and timing information to users anywhere on Earth.

**Global System for Mobiles (GSM):** Global System for mobiles communication is digital cellular technology used for transmitting mobile voice and data services.

**Internet Protocol (IP):** Internet Protocol is the method or protocol by which data is sent from one computer to another on the Internet.

**Long Term Evolution (LTE):** Long Term Evolution is a wireless broadband technology designed to support mobile broadband Internet access via cell phones and handheld devices.

**Next Generation Networks (NGN):** Next Generation Networks is deployment of independent services over converged fixed and wireless mobile networks.

**National Institute of Standards and Technology (NIST):** The National Institute of Standards and Technology (NIST) organisation. It has been working with industry and the cryptographic community. The overall goal is to develop a Federal Information Processing Standard that specifies an encryption algorithm capable of protecting sensitive government information well into the next century.

**System-on-a-Chip (SoC):** System-on-a-chip technology is the packaging of all the necessary electronic circuits and parts for a system.

**Synchronous Transfer Mode (STM):** Synchronous Transfer mode is multiplexing technology used by telecommunication backbone networks to transfer packetized voice and data across long distances.

**Transmission Control Protocol (TCP):** The Transmission Control Protocol is a connection-oriented reliable protocol. It provides a reliable transport service between pairs of processes executing on End Systems using the network layer service provided by the IP protocol.

**User Datagram Protocol (UDP):** User Datagram Protocol is a simple OSI transport layer protocol for client or server network applications based on Internet Protocol. UDP is the main alternative to TCP. UDP is often used in videoconferencing applications or computer games specially tuned for real-time performance.

**Wi-Fi and Wi-Max:** Wireless technology which is used to provide internet access and multimedia services over the Air.

# Chapter 18
# Automatic Detection of Cyberbullying to Make Internet a Safer Environment

**Ana Kovacevic**
*University of Belgrade, Serbia*

**Dragana Nikolic**
*University of Belgrade, Serbia*

## ABSTRACT

*The Internet has become an inevitable form of communication, which enables connections with colleagues, friends, or people with similar interests, regardless of physical barriers. However, there is also a dark side to the Internet, since an alarming number of adolescents admit they have been victims or bystanders of cyberbullying. In order to make the Internet a safer environment, it is necessary to develop novel methods and software capable of preventing and managing cyberbullying. This chapter reviews existing research in dealing with this phenomenon and discusses current and potential applications of text mining techniques for the detection of cyberbullying.*

## INTRODUCTION

Cyberbullying has become an urgent problem during recent years, especially after several dramatic events, such as suicides. According to the definition of the National Crime Prevention Council, cyberbullying is the use of the Internet, cell phones or other technologies to send or post a text or images intended to hurt or embarrass another person (NCPC, 2006). Cyberbullying can be carried out through several technology platforms, such as chat rooms, emails, photo sharing websites, blogs, forums, social networking cites, cell phones, online games and voice mail.

Since cyberbullying has a major impact on society, especially on its sensitive part, such as teenagers in their formative years, it has become an intensive field of research. Although many researchers analyse the causes and consequences of cyberbullying, only a few of them suggest methods for its prevention. This article reviews the concepts of possible proposals on how the Internet may be made a safer environment, by using text mining techniques for detecting and tracking cyberbullying. If the problem of cyberbullying can be solved or minimized, social interaction will become safer for many users on the web, especially for those most vulnerable: teenagers. Therefore, focus on

DOI: 10.4018/978-1-4666-6324-4.ch018

prevention and intervention efforts is extremely important to ensure the safer usage of cyber space.

This article focuses on the utilisation of text mining techniques for the purpose of making the Internet a safer environment. An overview of the cyberbullying problem is presented in the following section. In the third section text mining techniques are explained briefly, and the forth section presents existing research efforts in cyberbullying detection by using the text mining techniques presented. The conclusion summarizes the specifics and efficiency of the proposed methods, and suggests possible paths for the future improvement of software which supports various technology platforms for communication.

## BACKGROUND

Bullying is not a new phenomenon, since it has existed since ancient times. However, it has acquired a novel dimension with the rise of a new environment – the Internet, and has developed a new form known as cyberbullying. Cyberbullying is a unique phenomenon associated with the use of electronic communication technologies, representing an instrument for threatening, embarrassing or socially excluding another person (Hinduja & Patchin, 2008). Bullying in the cyber environment is much crueller and more dangerous than "traditional" forms of bullying which take place in the real world. The reasons for that are primarily certain aspects of the web: persistence, the ability to search and copy, and invisible audiences (Boyd, 2007). Because of web persistence the victim is unable to hide anywhere, since the audience is not confined to the room, school yard or street, but a large online community.

Two basic characteristics of cyberspace are dominant for cyberbullying: anonymity in cyberspace and better control of social interaction in the cyber world (Dempsey, Sulkowski, Dempsey & Storch, 2011). Creating a new identity online is very easy, and can be done in a few minutes

without the true identity being checked. The anonymity of the bully is enabled through the Internet. Most (84%) cyber bullies know the identity of their victims, while only 30% of cyber victims can identify the perpetrators (Ybarra & Mitchell, 2004). Another peculiarity of cyberbullying is better control of social interaction in the cyber world. Abusers can choose when they want to harass their victim, how (through which medium), and whether they wish to bully in front of an audience.

In addition, along with greater control of social interactions and added anonymity, some pupils who have lower levels of aggression in the physical environment may behave aggressively in cyberspace (Dempsey et al., 2011). Cyberbullying detection is exacerbated by the fact that victims do not inform their parents or officers in schools because they fear that the use of their phone (at school) or ability to use the Internet (at home) (Agatston, Kowalski & Limber, 2007) may be denied to them (Williams & Guerra, 2007). Ybarra et al. (2007) found that 64% of pupils who were victims of cyberbullying (or were cyber bullied), reported that they were also "traditionally" bullied at school.

Dempsey et al. (2011) discovered that the majority of adolescents do not want to share the potential threats with adults, regardless of whether they are naive in relation to the risks in cyberspace or intentionally engaged in risky behaviour without supervision. Hence, it would be useful to inform parents about the features of new media and encourage them to supervise the way their child uses the Internet.

The main participants in the cyberbullying process are:

- The bullies,
- The victims,
- The observers, who may be:
  - Malicious, who encourage and support the bullying, or just watch, but do not intervene and help the victim,

○ Helpful, who seek to stop the abuse, provide support to the victim, or report to an adult.

In addition, it is necessary to encourage the observers to step up, and report incidents of bullying or help the victim. Wilard (2008) considered it a useful strategy to encourage viewers to become "good" observers who assist victims and stop abuse.

The types of cyberbullying that have been defined so far are as follows:

1. Flooding is the case when the bully monopolizes the media so that the victim cannot post a message (Maher, 2008).
2. Masquerade occurs when the bully logs on using another user's account to either bully a victim directly or damage the victim's reputation (Wilard, 2007).
3. Flaming, or bashing, involves two or more users attacking each other on a personal level (Wilard, 2007).
4. Trolling, also known as baiting, involves intentionally posting comments that disagree with other posts in an emotionally charged thread for the purpose of provoking a fight, even if the comments do not necessarily reflect the poster's actual opinion (Glossary, 2008).
5. Harassment most closely mirrors traditional bullying with the stereotypical bully-victim relationship. It usually involves repeatedly sending offensive messages to the victim over an extended period of time (Wilard, 2007).
6. Cyberstalking and cyber threats involve sending messages that include threats of harm, are intimidating or very offensive, or involve extortion (Wilard, 2007).
7. Denigration involves gossiping about someone online (Wilard, 2007).
8. Outing is similar to denigration, but requires the bully and the victim to have a close personal relationship, either online or in person. (Wilard, 2007).
9. Exclusion, or ignoring the victim in a chat room or conversation, was the most frequent type of cyberbullying reported among youth and teens (Patchin, & Hinduja, 2006).

## Cyberbullying Statistics

According to research conducted in the USA in 2003, most adolescents (97%) regularly use the Internet, while 50% of them use it daily (Dempsey et. al., 2011). Cyberbullying is growing as a social threat, especially for adolescents. But it also happens to their teachers (ATL, 2009), or generally in the workplace (Privitera, Campbell, 2009).

Preliminary studies of cyberbullying are fairly consistent in their results, while some oscillations are due to the way cyber abuse is defined and measured. Studies conducted by Wade et al., (2011) show that:

- 11-17% of participants in cyber space admitted that they had bullied someone (Li, 2006, 2007; Patchin & Hinduja, 2006; Ybarra & Mitchell, 2004).
- 19-29% of pupils have been the victims of cyberbullying (Beran & Li, 2005; Patchin & Hinduja, 2006; Ybarra & Mitchell, 2004).

## The Consequences of Cyberbullying

Cyberbullying, similar to traditional forms of bullying, has a deep negative impact on the victim, especially on those that are the most vulnerable, like pupils in their formative years (Dinakar et al., 2011). Besides the negative impact on the mental health of victims, which is more intense than in the case of "traditional" abuse, the consequences to bullies are identified as well (Blais, 2008).

According to the American Academy of Child and Adolescent Psychiatry, victims of cyberbullying usually suffer both emotionally and psychologically (AACAP, 2008). Most victims feel shame, embarrassment, anger, and depression and withdraw into themselves.

Ybarra et al., (2006) published their findings that 38% of the emotional pain that youth reported was the result of cyberbullying. Research shows that victims of cyberbullying have lower self-esteem, increased suicidal ideation, and numerous emotional problems; they are scared, frustrated, angry and depressed (Hinduja & Patchin, 2009).

## Previous Research

Most of the existing research in this field deals with the analysis of the causes and consequences of cyberbullying. Researchers in the social sciences are trying to analyse the causes of cyberbullying, and why it is especially widespread among children and youth (e.g. Li, 2007). Studies in psychiatry have analysed the short and long term effects of cyberbullying on its victims, and how parents, teachers and psychologists can deal with this problem, e.g. Smith et al., (2008). Such studies often include extensive surveys and interviews, provide an important indication of the scope of the problem, raise awareness and inform schools and parents.

IT studies are not that extensive and very little research has been conducted into technical solutions for cyberbullying detection. Research in the area of email spam detection is a similar real world application to detecting cyberbullying. Spamming on social media is a type of spam that prevents normal interactions among users. Usually, spam (especially comment and forum spam) violate current context, because they pertain to completely different issues and topics. It may be very annoying for users, and consequently is considered to be similar to cyberbullying. Recently, spam detection has come into the focus of extensive research (Michine et al., 2005; Kolari et al., 2006; Lin et al., 2008). The main difference between spamming and cyberbullying is that spamming is usually off-topic, and may have a potentially commercial purpose. Most of the methods used in spam detection on social media cannot be directly applied to cyberbullying detection because of the accessed features (e.g. links, and anchor text). The

use of support vector machines has proved to be an efficient technique for detecting email spam, similar to those most authors use for the detection of cyberbullying.

Only a few researchers proposed possible solutions for cyberbullying prevention that include using software systems beyond those based on key words (Yin et al., 2009; Dinakar et al., 2011; Bayzick et al., 2011, Sanchez & Kumar, 2011, Ptaszynski et al., 2010).

## TEXT MINING TECHNIQUES

Researchers in cyber security face increasing amounts of information and it is evident that more powerful tools are needed to handle this, and to keep pace with developments within their fields. The variety of tools needed spans from tools for search to those for knowledge discovery. Text mining is recognised as the technique with the potential to be applied for this range of requirements.

Although computers cannot fully understand a text, improvements in the processing of natural languages offers the hope that some parts of a text can be partially understood. Text mining refers to the process of the extraction of significant information and knowledge from unstructured text. Text mining was first mentioned by Feldman & Dagan's (1995), where the text mining indicated machine supported text analysis.

Text mining is the process of extracting hidden information from a large amount of text (Hearst, 1999). It is hard to find fuzzy and ambiguous relations in a textual document by using standard software. Text mining uncovers hidden information using methods that are on the one hand able to analyse numerous words and structures in natural language, and can cope with vagueness, uncertainty and often fuzziness within textual documents on the other (Hotho et al., 2005).

Text mining is an interdisciplinary field that encompasses many areas such as information retrieval, machine learning, statistics, and in its essence data mining (Hotho et al., 2005). Machine learning can detect the language patterns used by bullies, and on that basis develop rules that could facilitate the detection of cyber abuse.

Before using text mining algorithms for large collections of documents it is necessary to pre-process the analysed text. Most text mining approaches are based on the idea that a text in documents can be based on a set of words, i.e. a document is represented by the set of words of which it consists (bag-of-words representation). Applying the most commonly used vector representation, each word in the considered document is then assigned an importance value (an appropriate numerical value), even those with the smallest importance. The VSM (Vector Space Model, Salton et al., 1975) is based on this idea.

However, analysis is further complicated by the fact that the language used in online chat and social networking sites is jargon, often with syntax errors and the common use of emotions. There are "friendly insults", which are not considered cyberbullying, but a style of communication. Sarcasm makes it additionally difficult to detect bullying. Moreover, it is common for teenagers to exchange sarcastic comments without intending to hurt one another, and this should not be misinterpreted as cyberbullying.

Section 4 presents how cyberbullying may be detected by using text mining techniques, or more precisely classification. Text classification aims to assign pre-defined classes to textual documents. The basic idea is that the data mining classification task starts with a training set of documents (posts), that are labelled by class (or classes). The following task is to determine the classification model which is able to assign the correct class to a new document in the domain, or in the training process the model learns the logic of how to make a prediction. The next phase is testing, where separate data sets are required.

The test data set is sorted by means of the classification model and the estimated labels are compared with the true ones. The performance of the classification model is measured on the test data, which may be very useful because it provides

an unbiased estimate of its generalisation error, as well a comparison of the relative performance of different classifiers on the same domain. Some of the metrics are: accuracy, precision and recall, the F-score and kappa statistics.

The degree of accuracy is measured by the fraction of correctly classified documents in relation to the total number of documents. The problem lies in the fact that the target class often covers only a small percentage of the documents, and high accuracy is achieved when each document is assigned to the alternative class.

To avoid these effects different classification measures are often used. Precision and recall are most frequently used. Precision quantifies the fraction of retrieved documents that are relevant, while recall indicates which fraction of the relevant document is retrieved.

$$\text{Precision} = \frac{a}{c} \quad \text{Recall} = \frac{a}{b}$$

a.  Relevant documents retrieved.
b.  Relevant documents.
c.  Retrieved documents.

There is trade off between precision and recall. The precision is high only if documents of a high degree are assigned to the target class. However, relevant documents might be missed, and then a low recall is achieved. The F-score serves as a compromise of both (precision and recall) for measuring the overall performance of classifiers.

$$F = \frac{2}{\dfrac{1}{recall} + \dfrac{1}{precision}}$$

Some authors (such as Dinakara et al., 2011) also use kappa statistics (Cohen's kappa) which take into account chance agreement (Carletta, 1996).

# TEXT MINING FOR THE DETECTION OF CYBERBULLYING

Existing software for parental control, such as NetNanny (http://www.netnanny.com/) and IamBigBrother (http://www.iambigbrother.com), is capable of recording what is carried out on the Internet, forbidding some cites, and doing simple analysis based on key words, but cannot intelligently detect bullying in cyber space. Thus, there is a need for new software which could perform more comprehensive examination and provide users with a safer environment on the Internet. The following section explains how text mining techniques may be applied for these purposes.

There are several research teams that work on the detection of cyber abuse using text mining techniques (Yin et al., 2009; Dinakar et al., 2011; Bayzick et al., 2011; Sanchez &Kumar, 2011; Ptaszynski et al., 2010). Their research is related to applications in various technology platforms (e.g. social networking cites, chat rooms, forums), and some of their basic approaches and results are reviewed here.

## Detecting Cyberbullying in Messages

A research community gathered at the CAW 2.0 (Content Analysis for the Web 2.0) workshop (http://caw2.barcelonamedia.org/) to focus on specific tasks within the scope of text content mining. Data sets were collected from different sources to provide a corpus which would be used as an experimental compilation to conduct research

into three specific shared tasks: text normalization, opinion mining and misbehaviour detection.

Yin et al., (2009) conducted experiments on the three different data sets provided by CAW 2.0. The data sets were obtained from different sites/sources: Kongregate (http://www.kongregate.com/), Slashdot (http://www.slashdot.org/) and MySpace (http://www.myspace.com/), Table 1. The data from the Kongregate site included conversations from chartrooms for real-time communication between game players, while Slashdot and MySpace are more asynchronous discussion forums, where the users write longer messages and discussions last for days or weeks. MySpace is a popular social networking site where the registered users participate in discussions about several predefined topics. Anyone can start a new thread and participate freely in one created by another user. Depending on the forum topic, moderating may exist to eliminate certain types of content and certain users may even be banned. Slashdot is a forum for debating technology and its ramifications. Most users register and comment freely under their nicknames, although a considerable number participate anonymously (as "Anonymous Coward"). Moderation and meta-moderation mechanisms are employed to judge comments and enable readers to filter them by quality.

For cyberbullying detection Yin et al., (2009) applied the classification of positive and negative classes, depending on whether the message contains harassment in comments or not. Various methods were used to develop the attributes of entrance to the classifier, such as:

*Table 1. Summary of data set elements*

| | Website | Site URL | Main Characteristic of Data |
|---|---|---|---|
| 1. | Myspace | http://www.myspace.com/ | Forum discussions for registered users. |
| 2. | Slashdot | http://slashdot.org/ | Comments on news-posts related to technology and its ramifications. Most users registered, but anonymous participation is considerable. |
| 3. | Kongregate | http://www.kongregate.com/ | On-line games, real-time chats. |

- Standard text mining techniques based on term weights (in this case words), such as TF-IDF (term frequency - inverse document frequency), to extract indexed words and assign the appropriate value of each word.
  - Rule-based systems for the detection of feelings, e.g. posts that contained derogatory words and the word "YOU", may assume that an insult is directed at someone, and therefore can be regarded as an offensive post.
  - Analysing the context, comparing a given message with neighbouring messages, e.g. messages that are unusual or generated clusters of similar activities by other users, are likely to be cyberbullying.

After extracting the relevant characteristics, the authors developed a SVM (Support Vector Machine, Cortes & Vapnik, 1995) classifier to detect bullying. The level of bullying was very low: 42 out of 2892 posts in the Kongregate data set represented bullying, while in Slashdot the ratio was 60 out of 4302, and for MySpace 65 out of 1946.

The obtained results demonstrated that the use of the combined model, which in addition to text mining also included methods for adding context and the detection of feelings, improved the detection of cyberbullying. The F measure obtained is in the range between 0.298 and 0.442 (F= 0.298 for Slashdot, F=0.313 for MySpace, F=0.442 for Kongregate). Detailed results are shown in Table 2.

On the basis of the experimental results the authors conclude that it is possible to detect cyberbullying.

## Detection of Cyberbullying in Comments from Youtube Video Clips

Researchers at MIT (web.mit.edu) detected cyberbullying in comments from YouTube videos (Dinakar et al., 2011). The dataset was obtained by extracting comments via You Tube PHP API. The total number of comments was over 50,000. Video clips from controversial subjects are often a rich source of obscene comments.

Dinakar et al., (2011) assumed that for most children and youth, sensitive characteristics are usually one of the following: physical appearance, sexuality, race / culture and intelligence. These are features that people cannot change, and they are both personal and sensitive. The authors believe that negative comments that are profane, or topics that are personal and sensitive, are candidates for cyberbullying. They assumed that comment can be bullying if one of the above sensitive features are contained, with a negative tone.

The comments were pre-processed and manually categorised by assigning labels such as: sexuality, race & culture and intelligence. The authors carried out two experiments. The first was to train a binary classifier to reveal whether the feedback could be classified into sensitive issues or not, for each of the three sets. The second experiment was performed using a multi-classifier, which classifies instances from the set of sensitive topics.

The feature space considered in these experiments can be grouped into two divisions:

*Table 2. Performance of combined model*

|  | Kongregate | Slashdot | MySpace |
|---|---|---|---|
| Precision | 0.352 | 0.321 | 0.417 |
| Recall | 0.595 | 0.277 | 0.250 |
| F-measure | 0.442 | 0.298 | 0.313 |

- General characteristics common to all three labels, that consist of:
  - TF-IDF weight unigrams.
  - Words that denote a negative connotation (Ortony et al., 1987), or contain a list of words in English that denote affect, and use negative connotations.
  - Lists of profane words.
- Specific features: for the detection of each label:
  - The unigrams and bigrams depending on the topic.

The methods used in both of the above experiments are:

- Repeated Incremental Pruning to Produce Error Reduction (JRip) (Cohen & Singer, 1999).
- J48, a decision tree classifier based on the C4.5 method proposed by Ross Quinlan (Quinlan, 1993).
- SVM for classification.

Firstly, they analysed whether the comments belonged to sensitive issues such as sexuality, race/culture, intelligence or physical characteristics. Secondly, they determined the theme. Supervised learning methods were used in the experiment. The experiment showed that a binary classifier trained for individual labels achieved much better results than a multi-classifier trained for all labels.

The greatest accuracy is achieved for Rule based JRip (70.39%-80.20%) and Kappa for SVM (from 0.718-0.79) for 600 posts. The differences in the achieved accuracy depend on the data set. This result suggests that it is possible to detect cyber abuse employing text mining techniques.

## The BullyTracer Programme

The BullyTracer programme is designed to detect different types of cyber harassment in a chat on the Internet (Bayzick et al., 2011). A rule-based algorithm was used to detect cyberbullying. The data set used in the experiment was extracted from the MySpace website.

BullyTracer uses terms (words) from a selected dictionary, divided into three categories:

- Insulting words,
- Vulgar language and
- Pronouns for another person.

The authors selected these categories since they noticed that there is a significant correlation between the presence of these words and the occurrence of cyberbullying. In addition, it appears that if more than 50% of the text is written in capital letters, it may indicate cyberbullying.

The BullyTracer programme was used to examine the considered posts and search them for words from the above categories (e.g. insulting word or swearing). Posts that contained such wording were marked by the programme. Although BullyTracer achieved overall accuracy 58.63% (for 2,062 posts in 11 subsets), it is still in the development stage, and therefore cannot be implemented in software to track bullies. Nevertheless, BullyTracer is a useful tool for learning about language patterns used in cyberbullying, and can be applied as an initial testing algorithm for cyberbullying detection (Bayzick et al., 2011).

## Detection of Cyberbullying on Twitter

A framework for the detection of cyberbullying on Twitter was created by Sanchez & Kumar (2011). The data for the experiment were obtained by using Twitter's streaming API. The text used in messages (tweets, twitter messages) requires intensive pre-processing prior to classification, including the identification of syntax errors, emotions, and the use of slang. The idea was to classify the emotions (especially negative) contained in a message using sentiment analysis and opinion mining, and then to visualize the changes of message over time.

The messages were classified as negative or positive using the NaiveBayes algorithm, with respect to some frequently used words. The bag-of-words model was used in the classification. The aim of the authors was to identify the victims, followers and predators. After cyberbullying was identified, visualization was applied. By means of dynamic visualization cyberbullying was tracked down and illustrated over time. The authors concluded that although they encountered difficulties, it is possible to detect cyberbullying automatically. The achieved accuracy is 67.3% on 500 posts.

## Cyberbullying on Informal Web Sites

The problem of cyberbullying in Japanese society, particularly on unofficial scholars web sites, was analysed by Ptaszynski et al., (2010). In order to deal with cyberbullying problems, teachers and parents performed voluntary Online Patrol, with the objective to spot and delete those online entries deemed harmful to others. Since the number of existing cyberbullying cases is enormous and has a rapidly increasing tendency, it has become a problem to handle them manually. Therefore, the authors created an artificial Online Patrol agent, using the machine learning system for cyberbullying detection.

The machine learning method developed to handle cyberbullying activities consists of several stages:

- The creation of a lexicon comprising vulgar, slanderous and abusive words (in Japanese),
- A slanderous information detection module,
- Information ranking in accordance with the level of their harmfulness, and
- Visualization of the harmful information.

There are two general phases in the creation of the system: the training phase and the test phase. The training phase includes:

- Crawling the school Web sites,
- Manual detection of cyberbullying entries;
- Extraction of vulgar words and adding them to the lexicon;
- Estimation of word similarity in regard to the Leveishtein distance
- Training with SVM, to classify information as harmful or not harmful.

The test phase comprises:

- Crawling the school Web sites;
- Detecting cyberbullying entries with the SVM model;
- Part of speech analysis of the detected harmful entry;
- Estimating world similarity with the Levesthien distance;
- Marking and visualization of the key sentence.

Having classified a message as cyberbullying, it is also important to determine how harmful a certain entry is. Ptaszynski et al. (2010) adopted the approach whereby an entry is considered more harmful if the keywords that appear in it are more vulgar. Over 80% of vulgar words appear only once. The authors consider that this problem could be solved by increasing the number of training data, or applying a different method of rank setting. It is necessary to identify the means to automatically extract new vulgarities from the Internet in order to keep the lexicon up to date. For the classification of harmful or non-harmful data, the F-score is 88.2%, while precision is 79.9% and recall is 98.3% (for 966 posts).

For the purposes of comparative affect analysis the authors obtained additional Online Patrol data containing both cyberbullying activities and normal entries: 1,495 harmful and 1,504 non-harmful entries. The affect analysis was performed by means of the ML - Ask system (Ptaszynski et al., 2009). The database of emotive expressions is based on Nakamura's collection (Nakamura,

1993) and contains 2,100 classified, emotive expressions. Two features are determined: the emotiveness of an expression and the specific type of emotions. The basic assumption was that harmful data are considered less emotively emphasized than non-harmful, since cyberbullying is often based on irony or sarcasm, which is not highly emotive. Consequently, negative emotions were annotated most often on harmful data, and positive emotions on non-harmful data, which is both reasonable and predictable.

## Discussion

A summary of the evaluation of the aforementioned models is provided in Table 3. The results shown are quite dependent on the characteristics of the used data set, so a straightforward comparison of the final results is not feasible. Most researchers use SVM or the Naive Bayes algorithm for classification.

Although the obtained results do not demonstrate sufficient accuracy to be implemented in real world applications, they are promising, and improvements can be expected in the near future. For improvements to be made cooperation

between sociologists, psychologists and engineers is essential. Liberman et al., (2011) compare cyberbullying with spam at the beginning of the use of electronic mail, where spam threatened to disable access to and completely prevent the use of electronic mail. Thanks to the development of efficient algorithms for detecting spam, although spam today has not been completely eliminated, it has been sufficiently reduced so that the usage of electronic mail is not threatened.

## CONCLUSION AND FUTURE WORK

Cyberbullying is a real problem, and no software can be a substitute for teaching children or young adults how to have healthy relationships. However, cyberbullying is a problem that occurs on the Internet, and it is necessary to make the Internet a safer environment. One way would be to improve existing software, such as that for social networks (www.facebook.com, www.youtube.com). The basic idea would be to improve the software e.g. using text mining techniques, in order to detect cyberbullying. Following the identification of cyberbullying visualization may help to spot the

*Table 3. Summary of using classification algorithms in cyberbullying detection*

| Authors | Data Set | How the Dataset is Obtained | Algorithm Applied | Model Evaluation |
|---|---|---|---|---|
| Yin et al., 2009 | Kongregate Slashdot MySpace | Provided by CAW 2.0 | SVM | F= 0.298 for Slashdot (4,303 posts) F=0.313 for MySpace (1,946 posts) F=0.442 for Kongregate (4,802 posts) |
| Dinakar et al., 2011 | Comments from YouTube video | Extracting via YouTube ApI | JRip J48 SVM NaiveBayes | The geeatest accuracy is achieved for rule based JRip (70.39%-80.20% depending on the data set) and Kappa for SVM (from 0.718-0.79) for 600 posts. |
| Bayzick et al., 2011 | MySpace | - | Rule-based Algorithm | The overall accuracy is 58.63% (for 2,062 posts in 11 subsets) |
| Sanchez & Kumar, 2011 | Twitter (Short messages chatspeak) | Extracting via Twittter's streaming API | NaiveBayes | Accuracy 67.3% (on 500 posts) |
| Ptaszynski et al., 2010 | Informal web sites of Japanese secondary school | Existing data set from Online Patrol | SVM | Precision =0.799 Recall = 0.983 F-score = 0.882 (on 966 posts) |

bully (or bullies) more easily. After detecting an incident of cyberbullying appropriate action could be taken, such as preventing further abuse of the victim, slowing the spread of potentially offensive messages, providing additional educational materials to assist victims and alleviate the problem.

This paper presents pioneering efforts in reviewing measures to detect cyberbullying using software, with the help of text mining. Although currently a satisfactory level of accuracy that can be implemented in existing software (e.g., software for social networks) has not been reached, the results are promising, i.e. indicate that it is possible to detect cyberbullying using text mining techniques.

## ACKNOWLEDGMENT

This chapter is the result of research within the framework of the 47017 and TR37021 projects, which are financed by the Republic of Serbia Ministry of Education and Science.

## REFERENCES

AACAP. (2008). *Facts for families, the American Academy of Child Adolescent Psychiatry.* Retrieved December 5, 2011, from http://www.aacap.org/galleries/FactsFor-Families/80_bullying.pdf

Agatston, P.W., Kowalski, R., & Limber, S. (2007). Pupils' perspectives on cyberbullying. *The Journal of Adolescent Health, 41*(6), S59–S60. doi:10.1016/j.jadohealth.2007.09.003 PMID:18047946

*ATL.* (2009). Retrieved December 4, 2011, from http://www.atl.org.uk/Images/Joint%20ATL%20TSN%20cyberbullying%20survey%202009.pdf

Bayzick, J., Kontostathis, A., & Edwards, L. (2011). Detecting the Presence of Cyberbullying Using Computer Software. In *Proceedings of WebSci '11.* Retrieved December 4, 2011, from http://www.websci11.org/fileadmin/websci/Posters/63_paper.pdf

Beran, T. N., & Li, Q. (2005). Cyber-harassment: A study of a new method for an old behavior. *Journal of Educational Computing Research, 32*(3), 265–277. doi:10.2190/8YQM-B04H-PG4D-BLLH

Blais, J. (2008). *Chatting, befriending, and bullying. Adolescents' Internet experiences and associated psychosocial outcomes.* Queen's University.

Boyd, D. (2007). *Why Youth (Heart) Social Network Sites: The Role of Networked Publics in Teenage Social Life.* MIT Press.

Carletta, J. (1996). Assessing agreement on classification tasks: The kappa statistic. *Computational Linguistics, 22*(2), 249–254.

Cohen, W. W., & Singer, Y. (1999). A simple, fast, and effective rule learner. In *Proceedings of the Sixteenth National Conference on Artificial Intelligence.* Academic Press.

Cortes, C., & Vapnik, V. (1995). Support-vector networks. *Machine Learning, 20.* Retrieved December 23, 2011, from http://www.springerlink.com/content/k238jx04hm87j80g/

Dempsey, A., Sulkowski, M., Dempsey, J., & Storch, E. (2011). Has cyber technology produced a new group of peer aggressor. *Cyberpsychology, Behavior, and Social Networking, 14*(5), 297-302.

Dinakar, K., Reichart, R., & Lieberman, H. (2011). In International AAAI Conference on Weblogs and Social Media. *Artificial Intelligence,* 11-17.

Feldman, R., & Dagan, I. (1995). Knowledge discovery in texts. In *Proc. of the First Int. Conf. on Knowledge Discovery (KDD)*, (pp. 112–117). KDD.

Glossary. (2008). *Glossary of cyberbullying terms*. Retrieved November, 21, 2011, from http://www.adl.org/education/curriculum_connections/cyberbullying/glossary.pdf

Hearst, M. (1999). Untangling text data mining. In *Proc. of ACL'99 the 37th Annual Meeting of the Association for Computational Linguistics*, (pp. 3-10). ACL.

Hinduja, S., & Patchin, J. (2009). *Bullying beyond the schoolyard: Preventing and responding to cyberbullying*. Corwin Press.

Hinduja, S., & Patchin, J. W. (2008). Cyberbullying: An exploratory analysis of factors related to offending and victimization. *Deviant Behavior*, 29(2), 129–156. doi:10.1080/01639620701457816

Hotho, A., Nürnberger, A., & Paaß, G. (2005). A Brief Survey of Text Mining. *Forum American Bar Association*, 20(1), 19–62.

Kolari, P., Java, A., Finin, T., Oates, T., & Joshi, A. (2006). Detecting spam blogs: A machine learning approach. In *Proceedings of the 21st National Conference on Artificial Intelligence (AAAI)*. AAAI.

Li, Q. (2006). Cyberbullying in schools: A research of gender differences. *School Psychology International*, 27(2), 157–170. doi:10.1177/0143034306064547

Li, Q. (2007). New Bottle but Old Wine: A Research of Cyberbullying in Schools. *Computers in Human Behavior*, 23(4), 1777–1791. doi:10.1016/j.chb.2005.10.005

Lieberman, H., Dinakar, K., & Jones, B. (2011). Let's Gang Up on Cyberbullying. *Computer*, 44(9), 93–96. doi:10.1109/MC.2011.286

Lin, Y. R., Sundaram, H., Chi, Y., Tatemura, J., & Tseng, B. L. (2008). Detecting splogs via temporal dynamics using self-similarity analysis. *ACM Trans. Web*, 2(1), 1–35. doi:10.1145/1326561.1326565

Maher, D. (2008). Cyberbullying: An ethnographic case study of one Australian upper primary school class. *Youth Studies Australia*, 27(4), 50–57.

Mishne, G., Carmel, D., & Lempel, R. (2005). Blocking blog spam with language model disagreement. In *Proceedings of the First International Workshop on Adversarial Information Retrieval on the Web (AIRWeb)*. AIRWeb.

Nakamura, A. (1993). *Kanjo hyogen jiten* [Dictionary of Emotive Expressions]. Tokyo: Tokyodo Publishing. (in Japanese)

NCPC. (2006). *Cyberbullying*. Retrieved December 4, 2011, from http://www.ncpc.org/cyberbullying

Ortony, A., Clore, G., & Foss, M. (1987). The referential structure of the affective lexicon. *Cognitive Science*, 11(3), 341–364. doi:10.1207/s15516709cog1103_4

Patchin, J. W., & Hinduja, S. (2006). Bullies move beyond the schoolyard; a preliminary look at cyberbullying. *Youth Violence and Juvenile Justice*, 4(2), 148–169. doi:10.1177/1541204006286288

Privitera, C., & Campbell, M. (2009). Cyberbullying: The new face of workplace bullying? *Cyberpsychology & Behavior*, 12(4), 395–400. doi:10.1089/cpb.2009.0025 PMID:19594381

Ptaszynski, M., Dybala, P., Matsuba, T., Masui, F., Rzepka, R., & Araki, K. (2010). Machine learning and affect analysis against cyberbullying. In *Proceedings of the Linguistic And Cognitive Approaches To Dialog Agents Symposium*. De Montfort University.

Ptaszynski, M., Dybala, P., Rzepka, R., & Araki, K. (2009). Affecting corpora: Experiments with automatic affect annotation system - A case study of the 2channel forum. In *Proceedings of The Conference of the Pacific Association for Computational Linguistics 2009* (PACLING-09), (pp. 223-228). PACLING.

Quinlan, R. (1993). *C4.5: Programs for Machine Learning*. San Mateo, CA: Morgan Kaufmann Publishers.

Salton, G., Wong, A., & Yang, C. S. (1975). A vector space model for automatic indexing. *Communications of the ACM*, *18*(11), 613–620. doi:10.1145/361219.361220

Sanchez, H., Kumar, S. (2011). *Twitter Bullying Detection*. Retrieved December 34, 2011, from http://users.soe.ucsc.edu/~shreyask/ism245-rpt.pdf

Smith, P. K., Mahdavi, J., Carvalho, M., Fisher, S., Russell, S., & Tippett, N. (2008). Cyberbullying: its Nature and Impact in Secondary School Pupils. *Journal of Child Psychology and Psychiatry, and Allied Disciplines*, *49*(4), 376–385. doi:10.1111/j.1469-7610.2007.01846.x PMID:18363945

Wade, A., & Beran, T. (2011). Cyberbullying: The New Era of Bullying. *Canadian Journal of School Psychology*, *26*(1), 44–61. doi:10.1177/0829573510396318

Wilard, N. (2007). *Cyberbullying and Cyberthreats: Responding to the Challenge of Online Social Aggression, Threats, and Distress* (2nd ed.). Research Press.

Wilard, N. (2008). *Educator's Guide to Cyberbullying and Cyberthreats*. Retrieved December 24, 2011, from http://csriu.org/cyberbully/docs/cbcteducator.pdf

Williams, K. R., & Guerra, N. G. (2007). Prevalence and predictors of Internet bullying. *The Journal of Adolescent Health*, *41*(6), S14–S21. doi:10.1016/j.jadohealth.2007.08.018 PMID:18047941

Ybarra, M. L., D, P., Diener-west, M., Leaf, P. J. (2007). Examining the Overlap in Internet Harassment and School Bullying: Implications for School Intervention. *The Journal of Adolescent Health*, *41*(1), S42–50. doi:10.1016/j.jadohealth.2007.09.004 PMID:17577533

Ybarra, M. L., & Mitchell, K. J. (2004). Youth engaging in online harassment: associations with caregiver-child relationships, Internet use, and personal characteristics. *Journal of Adolescence*, *27*(3), 319–336. doi:10.1016/j.adolescence.2004.03.007 PMID:15159091

Ybarra, M. L., Mitchell, K. J., Wolak, J., & Finkelhor, D. (2006). Examining characteristics and associated distress related to Internet harassment: findings from the Second Youth Internet Safety Survey. *Pediatrics*, *118*(4), e1169–1177. doi:10.1542/peds.2006-0815 PMID:17015505

Yin, D., Xue, Z., Hong, L., Davison, B., Kontostathis, A., & Edwards, L. (2009). Detection of Harassment on Web 2.0. In *Proceedings of the 1st Content Analysis in Web 2.0 Workshop*. Madrid, Spain: CAW.

## KEY TERMS AND DEFINITIONS

**Cyberbullying:** Is a unique phenomenon associated with is the use of the Internet, cell phones or other technologies to send or post a text or images intended to hurt or embarrass another person.

**Precision and Recall:** Are most frequently used to measure the degree of accuracy of the proposed classification model. Precision quantifies the fraction of retrieved documents that are relevant, while recall indicates which fraction of the relevant document is retrieved. There is trade off between precision and recall.

**Social Networks:** A social structure made of nodes and links, where nodes usually represents individuals or organizations. Nodes are connected with links.

**Software for Parental Control:** Helps parents in supervising their children over the Internet, and is capable of recording what is carried out on the Internet, forbidding some cites, and doing simple analysis based on key words, but cannot intelligently detect bullying in cyber space.

**Spamming:** On social media is a type of spam that prevents normal interactions among users. Usually, spam (especially comment and forum spam) violate current context, because they pertain to completely different issues and topics. It may be very annoying for users.

**Text Classification:** Aims to assign pre-defined classes to textual documents. by building classification model which is able to assign the correct class to a new document in the domain, or in the training process the model learns the logic of how to make a prediction.

**Text Mining:** Refers to the process of the extraction of significant information and knowledge from unstructured text.

# Chapter 19
# A Taxonomy of Browser Attacks

**Anil Saini**
*Malaviya National Institute of Technology, India*

**Manoj Singh Gaur**
*Malaviya National Institute of Technology, India*

**Vijay Laxmi**
*Malaviya National Institute of Technology, India*

## ABSTRACT

*Browser attacks over the years have stormed the Internet world with so many malicious activities. They provide unauthorized access and damage or disrupt user information within or outside the browser. This chapter focuses on the complete attack actions adopted by an attacker while crafting an attack on Web browser. The knowledge gained from the attacker's actions can be framed into a suitable taxonomy, which can then be used as a framework for examining the browser attack footprints, vulnerability in browser design, and helps one to understand the characteristics and nature of an attacker. This chapter presents a browser attack taxonomy that helps in combating new browser attacks and improving browser security.*

## INTRODUCTION

A Web browser is an important component of every computer system as it provides the interface to the Internet world. The browser allows users to view and interact with content on the web pages. It provides users the interface to perform wide range of activities, such as, personal financial management, online shopping, social networking and professional business. Hence, the web browsers are becoming an increasingly adequate and important platform for millions of Internet users. With the rapid increase in the number of users, browsers are becoming the potential source of attacks. The appearance of various browser attacks executed on web browsers cause real challenges

to Internet user in protecting their information from an attacker. The browser attacks provide an unauthorized access, damage or disruption of the user information within or outside the browser. For example, suppose an attacker is able to inject malicious scripts that do not change the website's appearance, but silently redirect you to another web site controlled by an attacker without your notice. This redirected malicious web site may execute some malicious program to download a malicious file on your machine (Howes, 2004). The major goal of such attacks is to allow remote access of your machine to the attackers, and to capture personal information, often related to obtaining credit card, banking information and data used for identify theft.

DOI: 10.4018/978-1-4666-6324-4.ch019

Like other software, web browsers are vulnerable to attack and exploit if appropriate updates and security patches are not applied. Moreover, a fully patched web browser can still be vulnerable to attack or exploit if the browser plug-ins and add-ons are not fully patched. The plug-ins and add-ons are third party software used to enhance Browser functionality, but at the same time they are vulnerable to attacks. The vulnerabilities in Firefox extension system have been mentioned in the literature (Beaucamps, Reynaud & Loria-Nancy, 2008), where the risks associated with the Firefox extension have been explained. The plug-in and add-on softwares are not automatically patched with the Browser updates, instead they require some extra support from third party for updating their versions and patching vulnerabilities

Traditionally, browser-based attacks are commonly originated only from malicious web sites (Obied & Alhajj, 2009). However, the attackers have recently been introduced attacks which are beyond the malicious web sites. Over the years, the browser-based attacks are initiated different attack vectors apart from malicious web sites. The attacks may arises from trusted and legitimate web applications, since all web applications developers are not security experts and due to poor security coding the vulnerabilities occurs in these web applications. The attacker can exploit vulnerabilities present in trusted or legitimate web sites to deploy attacks. For instance, an attacker can take advantage of vulnerabilities within browser to run arbitrary code, which can steal user's sensitive information or install malware. Plug-in and extension vulnerabilities can also be exploited by an attacker to initiate browser-based attacks.

There are several questions, which could help to characterize an attacker: *Who is the attacker? What source an attacker used to enter into the system? What Vulnerabilities he exploited?* By answering these questions, we can get the clear picture of an attacker and what should be done next in order to protect the information. This chapter

will cover a concise survey of browser-based attacks and how these attacks are initiated by an attacker. In addition to that, the chapter focuses on the complete attack process, which helps to understand the characteristics, and the nature of an attacker. The actions taken by an attacker to execute Browser-based attack have been represented in the form of taxonomy using example attack scenario. The proposed taxonomy consists of an attacker side dimension, or vulnerability model, classifying how an attacker is launching an attack, and Browser side dimension, or security model, classifying how the Browser is trying to protect the attack. With the help of this taxonomy, we are able to analyze different weak points with an attacker can exploit, and at the same time what action the Browser will take to provide security against these attacks. Our taxonomy tries to provide the details of Browser attacks and vulnerabilities exploited in different Browser components. Thus, our taxonomy is different from other previously mentioned taxonomies discussed in Section 2 in two ways: First it will explain the vulnerabilities present at different Browser components, and second it will classify different attacks on those components. In addition to that, we also classify the security model which plays an important role in securing web Browsers. In nutshell, this chapter surveys Browser attacks caused due to vulnerabilities exits in different components, and discuss the security model adopted by Browser in order to provide protection against these attacks.

The rest of the chapter is organized as follows: The section two contains the background study of Browsers evolution, and taxonomies adopted in the field of security and attacks. In section 3, an overview of Browser attacks is presented, to better understand the Browser-based attacks, a taxonomy of attack is presented in section 4. Section 5 will discuss the adoption of proposed taxonomy in the field of Browser research, and future direction. Finally, we conclude in section 6.

## BACKGROUND

Early versions of Browser are implemented with monolithic architecture (Grosskurth & Godfrey, 2005) that combines the Browser components into single memory and process space. For Example, a Browser kernel and rendering engine runs into a single process space. If an attacker is able to exploit one of a Browser component, it can easily compromise the other Browser components because all components run in single process space. The vulnerabilities in this design cause an attacker to execute malicious code with full browser privileges. Older versions of popular Browsers, such as, *Internet Explorer 7, Firefox 3, and Safari 3.1* were executed in a single operating system protection domain. Since the inception of vulnerabilities (Silic & Delac, 2010) in web browsers design, the Browser research communities and developers have modified and extended the Browser architecture to minimize the Browser attacks. The OP web browser (Grier, Tang & King., 2008) runs multiple instances of a rendering engine, each in a separate protection domain isolated using different trust labels. The isolation namespace implemented in OP browser provides a protection domain to each web page. The Chromium Browser allocates the rendering engine into sandbox environment to provide isolation from browser kernel (Barth et al., 2008). The architecture allocates high-risk components, such as, the HTML parser, the JavaScript virtual machine, and the Document Object Model (DOM), to its sandboxed rendering engine. This feature helps to reduce the critical attacks on the Web Browser. Internet Explorer 8 Browser allocates separate process for tabs, each of which runs in protected mode. This architecture is designed to improve reliability, performance, and scalability (Zeigler, 2008).

Over the last three decades, the web has rapidly transitioned from a set of interconnected static documents into a platform for feature-rich dynamic and interactive web applications. Consequently, the web browsers have also evolved from mere user interfaces for remote documents into systems for running complex web applications. In other words, web browsers have become full-fledged operating systems for web-based programs (Reis & Adviser-Levy, 2009). But the advancement in the technology leads to various complicated and more sophisticated web-based attacks (Kruegel & Vigna, 2003) on Web Browsers. A code injection attack, such as Buffer Overflow, HTML injection, Cross Site Scripting, and SQL Injection (Hossain & Mohammad, 2012) are caused due to web application vulnerabilities. Social Engineering attacks (Chickowski, 2013), such as Cross-site request Forgery, Drive-by-Download, and Clickjacking attacks on web application are also considered serious threat to Browser users. Web application vulnerabilities have been addressed by researchers and developers for decades. Still, we observe different security breach (or vulnerability) reports through many publicly available databases such as the Open Source Vulnerability Database (OS-VDB, 2013) and Common Vulnerabilities and Exposures (CVE, 2013) A number of surveys report significant financial losses by individuals and organizations due to attacks exploiting vulnerabilities (Fossi et al., 2011).

The researcher in past has developed various different taxonomies in the field of network and computer security. The taxonomies aimed at classifying security threats or risks, such as computer and network attacks and vulnerabilities. Bishop et al. (1995) has made several important contributions to the field of security taxonomies. He presents taxonomy of UNIX vulnerabilities in which the underlying flaws of vulnerabilities are used to create a classification scheme. Howard et al. (1997) presents the taxonomy of computer and network attacks. The approach taken is broad and process-based, taking into account factors such as attacker motivation and objectives. Howard provides an incident taxonomy that classifies attacks by events, which is an attack directed at a specific target intended to result in a changed state. The event involves the action and the target. He highlights all steps that encompass an attack and how an attack develops. Simmons et al. (2009) has developed the taxonomy on cyber attacks to aid in identifying and defending against cyber attacks. A taxonomy called AVOIDIT (Attack Vector, Operational Impact, Defense, Information Impact, and Target) classifiers to characterize the nature of an attack, which are classification by attack vector, classification by attack target, classification by operational impact, classification by informational impact, and classification by defense. Hansman et al. (2005) has proposed the taxonomy with four unique dimensions that provide a holistic classification covering network and computer attacks. Their taxonomy provides assistance in improving computer and network security as well as consistency in language with attack description. Inspired from the above work on taxonomy, we attempt to create the novel taxonomy on Browser-based attacks that classifies and indentify different attack action taken by an attacker. But, the above mentioned taxonomies only deal with computer or network security, and attacks. Some of them discussed about only web–based attack deployed on the Browsers, but none given the deep explanation about internal details of attacks associated with core Browser components.

## UNDERSTANDING WEB BROWSER SECURITY

In order to better understand the security issues and challenges faced by the Internet community while using web browser, we first need to understand the Browser attacks on different Browser components. An attacker can execute several attacks on Web Browser in order to target user information. The major goal of an attacker is to find the vulnerability, either in Web program running onto Browser or

user itself (e.g. Social Engineering Attack). This section classifies various Browser-based attacks that an attacker can adopt.

## Web-Application Attacks

Web applications are the most common way to provide services, data and rich features to the Internet users. Unfortunately, with the increase in the number and complexity of these applications, there has also been an increase in the number and complexity of vulnerabilities. The web application attack arises from these vulnerabilities present in web pages. Since, all web application developers are not the security experts, which make them vulnerable, and easily targeted by attackers. The worst part is that the vast majority of websites, including those considered most business or financial critical, are riddled with web vulnerabilities. Web applications run in the browser, any security loop hole in browser will lead to exploiting vulnerability in web application. For example, an attacker who knows an unpatched security vulnerability in the victim Browser, and somehow is able to convince the victim browser to render malicious web content. This activity will allow an attacker to inject malicious script into the Browser page, this attack is known as Cross-site scripting attack or it downloads a malicious malware on victim machine, which is known as drive-by-download attack. The most common web application attacks include:

## Cross-Site Scripting Attack

Cross-Site Scripting (XSS) is a code injection attack (Athanasopoulos et al., 2009), which refers to a type of vulnerability that erroneously allows a malicious script from an attacker (untrusted) website to be executed in the context of another (trusted) site. XSS attack occurs when an attacker uses a web application to send malicious code, generally in the form of browser side script, to a different end user. The end user's browser will trust the web page, and execute the script without knowing that the script was injected by malicious user. Let's understand this attack with an example, suppose an attacker is able to find some input validation vulnerability (Scholte et al., 2012) in web application, it can then inject malicious script. When a victim user opens this web application, the browser will render the content and also execute the injected script code. At this point the browser "believes" the code belongs to the trusted website's context and will thus get full access to the site's data. This way the malicious script can steal user information, access any cookies, and session tokens of your browser. These scripts can even access the Brower Document Object Model (DOM) (Nicol, 2001) to modify the content of the HTML page.

## Cross-Site Request Forgery Attack

Cross-site request forgery (CSFR) vulnerability (Blatz, 2007) occurs when a malicious site can cause a victim browser to make a forged request to your server that causes a malicious activity on the server. The key to understanding CSRF attacks is to recognize that web originating servers typically don't verify that a request came from an authorized user. Instead they verify only that the request came from the browser of an authorized user, and hence the forged (malicious) request comes with the user's cookies (user authorization token) is executed on the server. This attack can be successfully crafted by an attacker using social engineering (like sending a link via email/chat), or by stealing user clicks. For example, using any social engineering trick, an attacker may force the user of a web application to execute or click the link which the attacker has forged. This can be done using hidden iframes (Sood & Enbody, 2011) or DIVs (Hickson & Hyatt, 2011), which a user never noticed. When user clicks on this forged link, the request will be send to server with authorized tokens which server trusts. A

successful CSRF exploit can compromise end user data and operation in case of normal user. If the targeted end user is the administrator account, this can compromise the entire web application.

## ClickJacking Attack

The prime objective of Clickjacking involves stealing of clicks from victim's user and directing towards the legitimate websites without victim's consent and knowledge. Clickjacking attack is an attack against web application users in which a malicious page is created by an attacker such that it tricks a victim into clicking on a page element of a different page that is only barely visible. With this technique, an attacker steal victim's click to target any authenticated web site such as social networking websites, Facebook (sharing malicious web pages links), and Twitter(posting unwanted messages), banking websites (initiate an online money transaction). The example attack scenario of Clickjacking attack is described in (Hansen et al., 2008), involves two different websites: A victim site *V*, and an attacker site *AT*. *V* is a normal legitimate website accessible to the victim and important for the attacker. Such sites include, for example, online-banking portals, auction sites, and web mail services. The goal of the attacker is to lure the victim into unsuspectingly clicking on elements of the target page on *V* site. The attacker can use Social Engineering tricks to solve this purpose. *AT*, on the other hand, is under control of the attacker. Commonly, this page is created in a way so that a transparent IFRAME containing *V* overlays the content of *AT*. Since the victim is not aware of the invisible IFRAME, by correctly aligning *V* over *AT*, an attacker can lure the victim into clicking elements in *V*, while she is under the impression of clicking element on *AT*. A successful Clickjacking attack, for example, might result in the victim deleting all messages from her web mail inbox, or generating artificial clicks on advertisement banners.

## Drive-by-Download

As noted in numerous papers (Cova et al., 2010) (Provos et al., 2007), drive-by-downloads have become common and an insidious form of threat that target specific vulnerabilities, often seen in web browsers and browser plug-ins. In drive-by-download, a victim is infected by a malicious web page or email attachment containing malicious code, typically written in JavaScript language. This commences series of attack vectors, such as exploiting vulnerabilities in the user agent (browser) or in the browser's plug-ins. If an attacker successfully crafts an attack, he can drop malware into the victim machine without the victim's knowledge. This technique usually involves posting exploit code to a legitimate website. This is done either by gaining access to the site through intrusion, SQL injection attack or by posting malicious code to a poorly secured Web form, like a comment field on a blog. In most cases, the exploit code itself is hosted on a different website and is exposed through the compromised webpage using a technique like a URL embedded in malicious script code or an inline frame, called an IFRAME for short. The work by Provos et al., (2007) has scanned billions of URLs to check maliciousness and discovered that approximately 3 million of URLs found malicious plunging drive-by-download attacks. The author also discovered that 1.3% of search results matching malicious URLs come out from Google searches.

## SQL Injection Attack

The SQL injection attack is common risks in the web applications, which let an attacker to compromise a database, which is an organized collection of data and supporting data structures. The data can include user names, passwords, text, etc. SQL Injection attacks take advantage of improperly coded applications to insert and execute attacker-specified commands, enabling access to critical data and resources. The primary cause of

SQL injection attack is insufficient validation of user input (OSWAP, 2009) (Scholte et al., 2012). In the case of SQL injection, an attacker provides malicious input that alters the intended meaning of a database query. Vulnerabilities are bugs (flaws) in applications (e.g., Web servers and Web browsers) that, if exploited, may cause the application to do things it should not.

## Extension Based Attacks

Modern web browsers support an architecture that lets third-party extensions to enhance the core functionality of the browser. Such extensions enhance the look and feel of the browser, and help render rich web content, such as multimedia. Although well-intentioned, extension developers are often not security experts and write vulnerable code that can introduce a security hole through which an attacker can penetrate a victim user's browser and steal the user's sensitive information. For instance, if an attacker is able to install malicious extension into victim browser, then it can access cross-domain network information, sensitive Browser APIs and user's file system. Ter et al., (2008) has examined security issues of functionality extension mechanisms supported by web browsers. The common extension-based attacks include:

## Man-in-the-Browser Attack

The MITB Trojan attack is the fastest growing critical threat effecting consumers and business banking customers. The attack has the ability to intercept and manipulate any web page information and web transaction which a user submits online in real time. With this attack, innocent organizations are being targeted, resulting in large data and financial losses. The major cause of MITB attack is malicious and vulnerable browser extensions. In past, the vulnerabilities have been observed in Browser APIs and Firefox extensions (Liverani & Freeman, 2008) (Ter et al., 2008). Unfortunately, various security methods, such as antivirus, strong authentication, and OS-patching are not effective against this attack. The MITB attack is carried out successfully on secured channel protected with security mechanisms like SSL/PKI, two or three factor authentication (Cheng & Liu, 2008). Thus, even a secured communication layer is not enough to provide effective solution against MITB attacks. For example, the primary target of MITB attack is Internet banking customers. An attacker applies a social engineering trick to lure victim user into installing malicious extension. This extension activates when user logged into banking website to capture all information from browser DOM, like, username and password, and sent this information to attacker. The attack can even modify transaction values (e.g. account number, amount etc) without user notice. The channel between user and banking website is encrypted and secured, but MITB attack captures information stored in Browser DOM, before it is send to the encrypted channel, and thus this attack is successful over encrypted channels.

## Code Injection and Privilege Escalation Attack

In browsers the extension scripts receive greater privileges than web application scripts. This allows an attacker to execute privilege escalation attacks (Provos et al., 2003) on victim using code injection attack. If an attacker is able to inject attack code from untrusted sources in the form of inputs and execute them, a browser has no way of preventing the code from causing malicious effects. For example, if a user installed an attacker's controlled vulnerable extension. An attacker can invoke various attack methods based on the vulnerability type of the extension. For instance, a new <input> node containing malicious event handler code can be appended to the DOM tree of the extension through the *node.innerHTML* property. When user invokes this input link the attacker code will be injected into victim page. Other methods might inject code through a dynamic code generation function such as *eval( )*. As browser extension code runs with much higher privileges, the malicious effects can be devastating. For example, it may even be possible to read cookies, get access to browser APIs, open a network connection to gain access to victim machine, and spawn OS process.

## Plug-in Based Attacks

The plug-in based attacks arises from the vulnerable plug-in installed in a Browser. The plug-in are installed as third party software to support additional feature in browser. A user can install Plug-in, whether for document reading, interactive content, Java run-time environment or ActiveX controls can be subjected to attack. The attackers look for vulnerabilities in plug-ins to carry out attacks like drive-by-download and Clickjacking attack. The attacker exploits vulnerabilities in JavaScript code running under Java run-time environment, one of the most susceptible languages to attack. For example, many attacks do spawn a pop-up message from Java asking for permission to execute a malicious Java file, but it's often too hard for users to tell which browser window created the pop-up. One accidental *allow* click is all it takes to start an attacker to control victim browser. Once the malicious Java applet is running, it takes only seconds for the malware payload to execute an attack. One more popular example of plug-in based attack called *Clickjacking attack* is discussed by author in (Hansen & Grossman, 2008).

## Architectural Based Attacks

The browser architecture consists of several sub-systems, such as, user interface, browser engine, rendering engine, networking, JavaScript interpreter, XML parser, display backend and data persistence subsystem (Grosskurth &

Godfrey, 2005). At runtime, all components are instantiated and executed in the same protection domain. Consequently, a fault in any of them can compromise all the others. For example, if an attacker is able to craft a successful attack on the JavaScript interpreter, it can take advantage of the data persistence subsystem and access available information. The attacker might also exploit the core component vulnerabilities of web Browser. The authors have reported various architecture vulnerabilities in web browser, which are patched by Browsers. However, attackers have adopted different new ways to exploit the web browser. For instance, the vulnerability in rendering engine can be exploited, which allows an attacker to render a malicious page inside web browser through which an attacker can execute arbitrary malicious code with high privileges.

# TOWARDS A TAXONOMY OF BROWSER ATTACKS

The proposed taxonomy of browser-based attack characterizes the nature of an attack. It will describe the complete attack action steps taken by an attacker to execute Browser-based attack. The classification is based on attacker and Browser side sequence of actions. The attack starts with an attack vector, vulnerability exploitation, and finally reach target. The Browser security model will act as a barrier to stop attacker from attack. The classifications represent the attack actions performed by an attacker to produce a browser-based attack and Browser actions to stop attacker. The taxonomy in Figure 1 shows the classification chart, which depicts how an attacker enters into browser by adopting attack vectors, how it propagates by exploiting vulnerabilities at different levels of Browser, what area it targets. The

*Figure 1. Browser attack taxonomy*

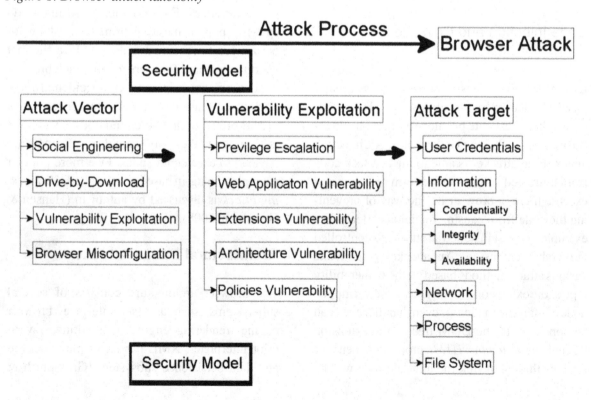

Security model would play its act if an attack is within its scope, otherwise the attack would successfully target the victim.

## Classification by Attack Vector

An attack process starts with an attack vector which an attacker uses as an entry point to the victim browser and reaches its target. An attack vector is defined as a path by which an attacker can gain access to a victim host. Attack vector classifies various entry points for the attackers. The most common trick adopted by an attacker is social engineering tricks in which an attacker lure a victim user to perform some task and gets infected. In this section, we list several attack vectors that are used to render various attacks. Our understanding of the attack vector motivates us to analyze weak points in the system which can be used by an attacker to route into the system.

## Social Engineering

Social engineering tricks are very popular and a successful attack vector adopted by attacker. An attacker employs these tricks to attract the victim user into downloading and rendering malicious website into browser, which result in the browser-based attack. Phishing scams (Youl, 2004) are the most serious attack in this category, which is responsible to steal the banking credential through fraudulent websites. Typically, a phished sends an e-mail, IM, comment, or text message that appears to come from a legitimate, big company, bank, school, or institution. When a victim user responds to these phishing links, the attacker enters into victim's browser. In addition to phishing, social engineering attacks can enter into your system in many different forms. For example, advertisement showing announcements of bogus lottery winnings, email spasm, email that masquerades as breaking news alerts, or greeting cards are also a form of social engineering. Social engineering attacks are also often used to trick users into infecting their own systems. For example, by disguising the malware

as a video codec or Flash update. An email is sent enticing the recipient to view a bogus video clip, when victim host visits this malicious URL or executes malicious email attachment, it tells users that they need to install a requisite plug-in, typically a flash player update to view videos files, which turns out to be a backdoor Trojan or keystroke logger.

## Drive-by-Download

As noted in numerous papers (Cova et al., 2010) (Provos et al., 2007), drive-by-downloads have become common and an insidious form of threat that target specific vulnerabilities, often seen in web browsers and browser plug-ins. In drive-by-download, a victim is infected by a malicious web page or email attachment containing malicious code, typically written in JavaScript language. This commences series of attack vectors, such as exploiting vulnerabilities in the user agent (browser) or in the browser's plug-ins. If an attacker successfully plots the attack, he can drop malware into the victim machine without the victim's knowledge. This technique usually involves posting exploit code to a legitimate website. This is done either by gaining access to the site through XSS, SQL injection attack or by posting malicious code to a poorly secured Web form, like a comment field on a blog. The drive-by-download technique is a very effective attack vector, since it is easy for an attacker to play tricks with users using social engineering techniques, such as flashing fancy ads and pop-ups windows. According to previous statistics on drive-by-download attacks, vulnerabilities in browsers are widespread (Vulnerabilities, 2001) and about 45% of Internet users use an outdated browser (Frei et al., 2008).

## Vulnerability Exploitation

Another method often used by attacker to attack victim host browser is by exploiting vulnerabilities. In this attack vector, an attacker can adopt any vulnerable path to attack and at the same time take complete control over the compromised system. Since, there exists a potentially large stack of vulnerabilities (Bandhakavi et al., 2010) (Frei et al., 2008) originated from Browser components and web applications rendered by browser. In addition to that, the other source of browser vulnerabilities comes from its plug-ins and extensions (Holzammer, 2008). A fully patched updated browser can be exploited if it has plug-in vulnerabilities. For example, if an attacker knows the vulnerability in Firefox add-on, it can execute or inject malicious code into a web page. Also, web application vulnerabilities can be exploited by attackers to execute XSS and CSFR attacks, for instance, if a program fails to validate the input sent to the program from a user. An attacker can exploit insufficient input validation vulnerability and inject arbitrary code, which commonly occurs within web applications. We discussed various security vulnerabilities in Section 4.2 through which, an attacker can enter in web browser to carry out attacks.

## Browser Misconfiguration

An attacker can use a configuration flaw within a web browser to gain access to a network or personal computer to cause a variety of attacks. Settings that are improperly configured, usually default settings, are an easy target for an attacker to exploit. The attacker can exploits a misconfigured browser that allows the execution of Java code. Thus, it is not necessary to enable, for example, the execution of JavaScript and Java code, as well as plug-ins like Flash, ActiveX, etc for all web sites. The use of cookies associated with previous visited sites, on the other hand, must also be taken into account. Normally the user always allows these configurations which might be helpful for attackers. The browser provides various security settings, but user mostly prefers to go with default settings that might end up in some attack. The US-CERT agency has given some security advice to user that a user can follow in order to provide security to Browser (Dormann & Rafail 2006).

## Classification by Browser Vulnerabilities

The taxonomy describes that how an attacker can exploit various vulnerabilities present in browser architecture. The current web browser model contains various design flaws, such as insufficient isolation of components and excessive privileges given to the browser extensions. Browser attacks can exploits the principle of isolation to run arbitrary code in the context of a running browser. The attacker gain excess privileges through the browser extensions to modify the browser components and corrupt the normal functioning of running components. The taxonomy presents the following exploitation points in Browser design, which can be used by an attacker.

## Exploiting Privilege Escalation Vulnerabilities

Privilege escalation vulnerabilities allow an attacker to execute malicious scripts with extra privileges space. This vulnerability is very common in Firefox Browser. The major source of this vulnerability is third party unsafe browser extensions and plug-ins. Since, the Firefox extensions execute with the full chrome privileges by invoking XPCOM interface (Turner & Oeschger, 2003). The XPCOM interface includes services such as file system access, process launching, network access, Browser components and APIs access. These interfaces allow browser extension to have full access to all the resources Firefox can access. In Firefox, JavaScript code of extensions receives higher privileges than JavaScript code of web applications.

The Figure 2 illustrates the permissions of the Firefox extension Javascript code. The JavaScript-based Extensions (JSEs) and Chrome JavaScript can access the browser and the system through XPCOM interface and no browser policy can limit the browser privileges. For example, the web applications are bound with same origin policy (SOP) (Zalewski, 2010) but extensions can

*Figure 2. Browser security model*

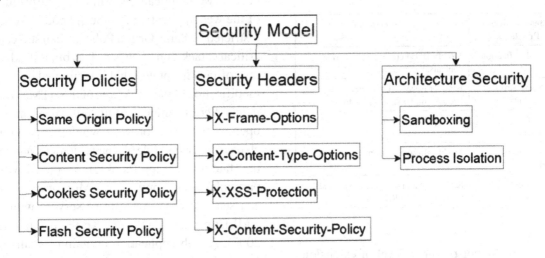

*Figure 3. Privileges level for JavaScript code in Firefox extension*

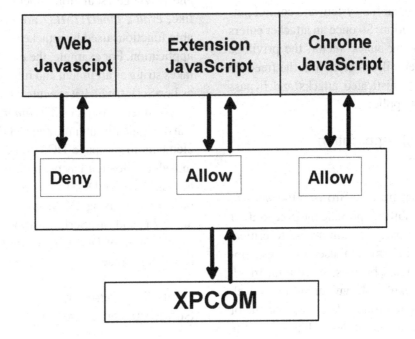

override the SOP and access cross domain components as well. Table 1 summarize the privileges of Firefox extension.

Thus, the privilege escalation vulnerabilities are caused due to bugs in unsafe extension and Firefox security model that handles the interaction between the privileged or trusted code and unprivileged or untrusted code. For example, the vulnerability reported in (Mlynski, 2013) allows

an attacker to open a chrome privileged web page through plug-in objects using SVG elements (Hickson & Hyatt, 2011) interaction, which allows an attacker to execute malicious code on the local system to craft an attack. The author in (Liverani & Freeman, 2009) also shown that how an attacker can inject malicious JavaScript code in an extension and this code with the privilege levels of the Browser extension. The attacker the

*Table 1. Privileges access of Firefox extension*

| Extension Script Privileges | Description |
|---|---|
| DOM Modification | Modify DOM content, Add new contents. |
| Accessing Browser Components | Browser password manager, cookies, file system, bookmarks, history etc. |
| Access OS Resources | Process, File system. |
| Modify Browser Interface | Modify Browser Chrome, User Interface. |
| Access Network | Send same and cross-domain request using XMLHttpRequest |

misuse this higher privilege level of extensions to craft powerful attacks, such as, creating OS process, access local file system and control network communication. So once an attacker enters into Browser using attack vector, the privilege escalation vulnerabilities gives him the freedom to craft more sophisticated attacks and bypass Browser security policies.

## Exploiting Web-Application Vulnerabilities

In spite of the secure Web Browser, the web application vulnerabilities provide the potential for an unauthorized party to gain access to critical and proprietary information, use resources inappropriately, interrupt business or commit fraud. An attacker can exploit the vulnerabilities in web applications to compromise Browser. The major web application vulnerabilities include, cross-site scripting, SQL injection, Buffer Overflow. The major cause of these vulnerabilities is inadequate validation of data coming from untrusted sources (e.g. user inputs). Tainted data may contain portions of HTML code (e.g. java-scripts) that could flow into the page under attack. Malicious scripts are meant to be eventually executed by web-browsers of legitimate users who access the pages under attack, for example to steal sensitive data. Javascript is the primary source of flaws that

occur in web applications. Although, the privilege of the web application JavaScript code has been restricted by Same Origin Policy, it can still cause critical attacks on browser. The biggest advantage of JavaScript was that it facilitated dynamic modification of the DOM tree of the HTML documents. Scripts embedded in web pages can also open or close new browser windows (pop-ups), change the visual style of a page element, and read the state information (cookie) associated with a particular web application. Moreover, scripts can send network requests to servers with the XMLHttpRequest API (Van Kesteren & Jackson, 2007). A web application containing malicious JavaScript functions can execute code injection and privilege escalation attacks. The functions, like, *eval(), innerHTML()* are common vulnerable functions used by attackers to exploit a web application. For example, the *eval()* function call takes string as argument and interprets that string as JavaScript, which it executes dynamically, lead to code injection attacks. The *innerHTM()* method can dynamically alter the page DOM and add new elements to the page DOM. A JavaScript code in web application has been given a privilege to access Browser DOM. The browser DOM can be exploited using DOM based XSS (Fogie et al., 2011) and JavaScript methods. The dynamic modification of DOM can be done using DOM-based XSS attacks.

## Exploiting Extension Script Vulnerabilities

Browser provides different privileges to the script-based web applications and script-based extensions. In this taxonomy, we discuss the web application scripting and Extension scripting vulnerabilities exploited by an attacker. The Browser extensions are developed using the JavaScript language. The JavaScript provides the rich set of functionality to the browser through extensions. The JavaScript code running in extensions allow to execute with full Browser privileges. A web browser enforces an access control mechanism known as the same origin policy only for the scripts embedded in web pages. However, browsers relax the same origin policy for JavaScript code of extensions. The extensions in Browser receive the high privileges, and hence the JavaScript code running in extensions gets unrestrained access to cross-origin web pages and internal components of the Browser. These extra privileges to Extension JavaScript code open vulnerable doors for attackers. For example, if an attacker is able to install vulnerable extension into Browser. It can launch far more devastating attacks that web-based attacks. Because, here an attacker has high privileges to execute the malicious code, which can access the local file system to upload malicious file, send or receive cross-domain network calls, and it can also hijack critical Browser APIs to steal information. The JavaScript functions can be used for code injection and privilege escalation attacks. The functions, like, *eval(), innerHTML() and wrappedJSObject()* are common vulnerable points used by attackers to exploit non-malicious extensions. For example, the *eval()* function call takes string as argument and interprets that string as JavaScript, which it executes dynamically, lead to code injection attacks. The *innerHTML()* method can dynamically alter the page DOM and add new elements to the page DOM. The Firefox automatically wraps the object to prevent malicious script from accessing the properties and methods of the document object. However, a developer can use *wrapperJSObject()* to bypass these restrictions to compromise the Firefox environment.

## Exploiting Architecture Vulnerabilities

In browser architecture, the malicious applications could be loaded and executed with full privileges and rights and results browser-based attacks. The modern applications require browser architecture to provide the compatibility support for all web technologies used to develop the web application and proper browser security to user. Although, the advancement of research on browser architecture has improved its architecture, but few popular modern browsers still use the original monolithic architecture design and are vulnerable to attacks. Monolithic browser architecture has many disadvantages that concern client code execution. Failure caused by one web application crashes down the entire browser instead of just the application that caused it. The vulnerabilities in browser architecture could lead to serious browser attacks, for example, an attacker could execute his arbitrary malicious code with full browser privileges and permissions, and cause damage on local machine. The attacker might know of an unpatched buffer overflow in the browser's HTML parser (Mitre, 2008), an integer overflow in the regular expression library (Mitre, 2006), or a buffer overflow in the bookmarks system (Mitre, 2007), it can execute any arbitrary malicious code in Browser.

## Exploiting Security Policies

The Same Origin Policy rules are not applied on the Browser Extensions. An attacker can exploit this weak point to execute malicious code into Browser. JavaScript code injection attacks can be successfully created because the Same Origin Policy failing to distinguish attack code from the benign JavaScript code of extensions or web applications. For example, Suppose a user visits an attacker's controlled website using a Browser with a vulnerable extension installed on it. An attacker might inject code through a dynamic code generation function such as *eval()*. The newly inserted code is executed with the same principal of the extension privileges. The attack code is able to execute as the Same Origin Policy assigns principals based on the origin of the executing code (extension), not the actual origin of the malicious code (attacker's website). Thus the Script Security Manager wrongly grants access to all the privileged APIs of the browser to the malicious code based on the incorrectly assigned principal, i.e., System. In this way, the malicious attack code runs with the principal of the benign extension code, gets all the privileges allowed for the System principal of the extension code, and utilizes the privileges to cause arbitrary damage. Another attack which can be possible by exploiting security policy is double framing Clickjacking attack. In this attack, an attacker has framed the target page in one frame which is nested in another one (a double frame), then try to access to *"parent.location"* becomes a security violation in all popular Browsers. This method works well until the target page is framed by a single page. However, if the attacker encloses the target web page in one frame which is nested in another one (a double frame), then trying to access to *"parent.location"* becomes a security violation in all popular browsers, due to the descendant frame navigation policy (Barth, 2007) (Barth, 2009). This security violation disables the counter-action navigation for preventing Clickjacking attack by blocking target site frame busting code. Thus, attacker can execute Clickjacking attack even if the victim is secured with frame busting protection code.

## Classification of Browser Security Model

A variety of security control techniques are placed in web browsers. The key to attack web browser, and applications is to find the vulnerabilities in the Browser security model or circumvent one of the policy or third-party add-on. Each security control attempts to be independent from the others, but if an attacker can inject a little JavaScript in the wrong place, all the security controls break down. This taxonomy provides an analysis of Browser-based attack, how it arises, and what challenges an attacker will face when an attack passes through Browser security model. The classification of various Browser security controls and policies are listed as follows:

## Security Policies

A web Browser has built in security policies in order to improve Browser security. These security policies will trigger if any security violation occur in a Browser. The following security policies have been implemented by majority of the Web Browsers.

### Same Origin Policy

Same Origin Policy is the most important built-in security concept in modern browsers. The principal intent for this mechanism is to forbid embedded scripts in a web page from accessing or interacting web pages from different origin, whilst completely preventing any interference between unrelated sites. The Same Origin Policy also prevents web application scripts from transforming the DOM tree, and sending network requests to servers other than an application's own origin. For example, if a document retrieved from http://mybrowser.com/chrome.html tries to access the DOM of a document retrieved from https://mybrowser.com/firefox.html, the same origin policy will denied the access because the origin of the first document, (http, mybrowser.com, 80), does not match the origin of the second document (https, mybrowser.com, 443). Thus, the web page document from one domain should match the *protocol://domain:port* of other domain. The prohibition on receiving information is intended to prevent malicious web sites from reading confidential information from other web sites, but also prevents web content from legitimately reading information offered by other web sites.

### Cookie Security Policy

Cookies are intended to store confidential information, such as authentication credentials, so the Browser has defined the security policies for cookies similar to those of the same domain policy. The cookies are controlled by Servers.

Servers can read cookies, write cookies, and set security controls on the cookies. The cookie security controls define the following parameters as the rules and guidelines:

*Domain and Path.* The cookie domain and path define the scope of the cookies, like same origin policy the domain is set for cookies but with little more restrictions. Here, the domain can be set to be one domain level higher. These attributes tell the browser that cookies should only be sent back to the server for the given domain and path. For example, if the HTTP request was to one.two.three.com, then one.two.three.com could set cookies for all of *.two.three.com, and one.two.three.com cannot set cookies for all of *.three.com. Apparently, no domain may set cookies for top level domains (TLDs) such as *.com. Similarly, say http://one.two.three.com/app/WebAppsetacookiewithpath/app; then the cookie would be sent to all requests to http://one.two.three.com/app/* only. The cookie would not be sent to http://one.two.three.com/index.html or http://one.two.three.com/app/pol/index.html.

*Expires.* The Expires directive tells the Browser when to delete the cookie. However, you can set a date in the Wdy, DD-Mon-YYYY HH:MM:SS GMT format to store the cookies on the user's computer and keep sending the cookie on every HTTP request until the expiry date. You can delete cookies immediately by setting the expires attribute to a past date.

*Secure.* If a cookie has this attribute set, the cookie communication limited to encrypted transmission, directing browsers to use cookies only over HTTPS connections. Note that both HTTP and HTTPS responses can set the secure attribute. Thus, an HTTP request/response can alter a secure cookie set over HTTPS. This is a big problem for some advanced man-in-the-middle attacks.

*HttpOnly.* The HttpOnly attribute directs browsers not to expose cookies through channels other than HTTP (and HTTPS) requests. If this attribute is set, browser will disallow the cookie to be read or written via non-HTTP methods such as call via JavaScript's document.cookie. This intended to prevent the attacker from stealing cookies and doing something bad.

## Flash Security Policy

Browser provides few restrictions on third-party Flash plugin. Flash's scripting language is called ActionScript. ActionScript allows the developer to create raw TCP socket connections to allow domains, for purposes such as crafting complete HTTP requests with spoofed headers. Flash does allow cross-domain communication, if a security policy on the other domain permits communication with the domain where the Flash application resides. The default security model for Flash is similar to that of the same origin policy. Namely, Flash can read responses from requests only from the same domain from which the Flash application have been originated. Flash also places some security around making HTTP requests, but you can make cross-domain GET requests via Flash's getURL function. Also, Flash does not allow Flash applications that are loaded over HTTP to read HTTPS responses.

## Security Headers

A web Browser supports several security HTTP headers in order to improve web application security. These security features can be used to modify the web browser behaviour and thus protect the user from browser based exploits. Let's understand the main Browser security headers and how they can improve the security of the website.

### X-Frame-Options

Microsoft has introduced in Internet Explorer 8 a specific defense header against Clickjacking attack. The X-Frame-Options HTTP response header is used to indicate whether or not a browser is allowed to render a page in a frame or iframe. Based on the header following values, the browser will take an action.

- **DENY:** Refuses any page to be rendered if loaded into a <frame> or <iframe> even from the same domain.
- **SAMEORIGIN:** Setting this option allows the browser to load page in an iframe only from the same origin.
- **ALLOW-FROM Origin:** Allows a page to be rendered in a frame on the specified origin.

### X-Content-Type-Options

This header protects Internet Explorer from "mime" based attacks. It will prevent IE from MIME-sniffing a response away from the declared Content-Type. Handling MIME-types correctly is important for any website, but especially for those serving user controlled content. When a resource is returned from a webserver, the response includes a *Content-Type* header to tell the browser what kind of resource was served.

### X-XSS-Protection

The XSS protection was also introduced in IE 8 as a security measure designed to thwart XSS (Cross Site Scripting) attacks. It turns on XSS filters which is by default is turned off. To turn on the XSS filter, set the header value to "1" whereas "0" value enforce the protection to be disabled. In short, IE tries to detect whether there has occurred an XSS attack, if so it will modify the page to block the attack and display a warning to the user.

### X-Content-Security-Policy/X-Content-Security-Policy-Report-Only

This header adds an extra layer of security that empowers to detect and mitigate certain types of attacks, including XSS and data injection attacks.

CSP disables execution of inline scripts in Web-Pages and lets you specify a whitelist of sources from where your WebPages are allowed to load scripts and other content. This feature effectively eliminates all stored and reflected XSS.

## Architecture Security

The architecture plays an important role in securing the user information from attacker. Since, all the web applications are designed and developed to be executed inside the Web Browser. The role of Browser is to render all kinds of web applications in it. The advancement of research on Browser architecture has improved its architecture by adding new features to it. The most importance feature added to modular browser is sandboxing and isolating environment.

### Sandboxed and Isolated Environment

The modern Web Browser architecture components run in a sandbox environment with restricted privileges. Browser critical component, such as, the rendering engine runs in a sandbox with restricted privileges and no direct access to the local file system or other OS level components. This sandbox restricts the rendering engine's process from issuing some system calls that could help the attacker reach the goals. For example, in Chrome architecture rendering engine runs in a sandbox and has no direct access to the local file system. When uploading a file, rendering engine uses browser kernel API for file upload. Apart from Sandbox environment, the web browser architecture provides isolation among web programs and modularizes their execution by assigning each web program or browser tab to the specific operating system process within the browser. The advantage of isolation is that if one program crashes, it does not effect the execution of other running programs.

## Classification by Attacker Target

The attack target(s) are classified at this step, an attacker can target the logical entities of browser, such as, user credentials, web page information, file system and running process, it can also target physical entity, such as, network protocols.

## Target Web Page Information

Attacker major goal is to extract the critical or sensitive information from web page which affects the confidentiality, availability and integrity of information. After deploying an attack on Browser, an attacker main goal is to capture personal information, often related to obtaining credit card, banking information and data used for identify theft. For example, a successful man-in-the-browser attack on Browser can steal confidential information, such as, user credentials from victim Browser. On injecting a malicious JavaScript code in Browser an attacker can execute a DoS attack, to attack on availability of information. An attacker can modify Browser DOM tree without user notification causing loss in information integrity.

## Target Cookies

The Cookies in Web Browser store critical information about the Browser session. An attacker can steal cookies to execute Session Hijacking attack. The session hijacking consists of the exploitation of the web session control mechanism. For instance, a user logs into a website, a session is created and cookies are stores on the client machine by the Web Server for that user. This session contains all this user's information being used by the server so the username and password is not needed at every page request. A Browser attacker can target these session cookies to hijack the authenticated user session, and then using this cookies information, it can communicate with server on user's behalf.

## Target Operating System Recourses

The Browser has the capability to access the operating system resources. An attacker can take advantage of these functionalities to target victim machine. The major targets of attacker are network, file-system and OS process. The Browser network communications can be exploited by the attackers. The attacker can plot attacks, like sending network requests to attacker server, jamming network with DoS attack. For example, a malicious extension can access to network APIs to transfer user data via networks. Extension based malicious scripts can send network requests to arbitrary web servers using XMLHttpRequest API. Using Browser attacks an attacker can target file system of victim machine. It can download some malware on victim machine that provides privilege access to an attacker. An attacker can access critical Browser files, such as, a bookmark files to read bookmarks, a password manager files to access the password storage of the Browser (Liverani, 2008). Another important resource, which an attacker might exploit is operating system processes. The attacker can misuse this higher privilege to launch such powerful attacks which can spawn arbitrary OS processes to remotely control the victim's computer (Liverani, 2008).

## Comparing Attack Taxonomies

In section 2, we have discussed previous taxonomies proposed in the field of security and attacks. Here, we are comparing taxonomies in more detail along with our proposed taxonomy. Table 2 shows the various attack taxonomies, and how these taxonomies are classified.

## EVALUATION OF TAXONOMY

We have evaluated our taxonomy of Browser attacks by applying our taxonomy on different attacks. The evaluation shows the attack to be

*Table 2. Comparison of attack taxonomies*

| Attack Taxonomies | Scope | Dimensions | Defense Model |
|---|---|---|---|
| Unix system and network vulnerability (bishop 1995) | Examine vulnerabilities in the UNIX operating system, its system and ancillary software, and classify the security-related problems. | Classification based on UNIX system flaws. | Defense model is defined to improve UNIX system security with minimal exploitable security flaws. |
| Taxonomy of computer and network attacks (Howard 1997) | Developing common language for computer security incidents. | Classification model consists of five stages: attackers, tools, access, results and objectives. | Defense model is not defined. |
| Web Attacks (Alvarez & Petrovic, 2003) | An attack life cycle is defined as its base, to make it structured and logical. | Multidimensional taxonomy based on a "Web attack life cycle." | The encoding of web attacks can be useful in IDS and Application level firewalls. |
| DDoS Attack and Defense Mechanisms (Mirkovic, Rejher 2004) | Structure the DDoS field and facilitate a global view of the problem and solution space. | Eight characteristics of an attack; three characteristics of defenses. | The metrics and benchmarks for DDoS defense evaluation is proposed. |
| Attacks (Hansman & Hunt 2005) | Develop a "pragmatic taxonomy that is useful to those dealing with attacks on a regular basis." | Classification based on four dimensions: Attack vector, Attack target, Vulnerability, Payload. | Briefly defined the defense dimension. |
| Attacks and Vulnerabilities(Igure & Williams 2008) | Survey of known vulnerabilities and attack taxonomies which can be used in security assessment process. | Classify Vulnerabilities and attacks based on their characteristics. | Defense model is not defined. |
| Web attacks (Lai 2008) | Classify the attack type with Vulnerability characteristic and efficiently response with actions and find the characteristic. | Classification focus on each http method and attacks associated with it. | Defense model is not defined. |
| Types of Cyber adversaries and attacks (Myers, Powers & Faisool 2009) | Taxonomies of cyber adversaries and methods of attack. | Classification based on Adversary Classes, in terms of increasing levels of skill, sophistication and Cyber Attacks. | Defense model is not defined. |
| Cyber attacks (Simmons & Charles 2009) | aid in identifying and defending against cyber attacks. | Classification based of four Dimensions: Attack Vector, Operational Impact, Defense, Information Impact, and Target. | Classification by defense is proposed to provide the network administrator with information of how to mitigate or remediate an attack. |
| Cyber crimes (Wales & Smith 2012) | Identifying and classifying patterns of cybercrimes. | Cybercrimes and users committing crimes | Facilitating information sharing, and improving security policies |
| Attack Tools (Hoque 2013) | taxonomy of attack tools in a consistent way for the benefit of network security researchers. | Classification is done on two dimensions: Attack and Defense tools. | Network defender tools are defined. |
| Browser Attacks (Proposed Taxonomy) | The major focus is to explore the complete attack actions adopted by an attacker while crafting attack on web Browser. The taxonomy shows the flow of attack. | Classification is done on Four Dimensions: Attack vector, Vulnerability exploiter, Attack target & Browser Security model. | We have defined the Browser security model which classifies the various security techniques that can be used to mitigate Browser attacks. |

executed and the various taxonomy dimensions, which are used to study or evaluate these attacks. Table 3 shows the evaluation of various Browser attacks using our taxonomy.

## Using the Taxonomy

In designing the above taxonomy, we selected those features of attack and defense mechanisms that, in our opinion, offer critical information regarding seriousness and type of threats, and effectiveness. We have identified the few themes in which we can apply our taxonomy:

- **Understanding Browser Attacks:** For security researchers, this taxonomy offer a comprehensive overview in understanding

attacks, which can be deployed or executed on Web Browsers. Experienced researchers can use and extend the proposed taxonomy to structure and organize their knowledge in the field of Browser security. This taxonomy would lead to identification of new direction in Browser attacks and vulnerabilities to understand the Web Browser threats.

- **Understanding Browser Attack Process:** The taxonomy is build to understand the step taken by an attacker and Browser while an attack is being executed on the Browser. For a Browser attack our taxonomy will state the entry point of attack, vulnerabilities that can be exploited and the target point. Besides that, our taxonomy will

*Table 3. Evaluation of browser attacks*

| Attacks | Attack Vector | Vulnerability Exploited | Attack Target | Mitigation Technique |
|---|---|---|---|---|
| XSS (Fogie 2011) | Vulnerability exploitation. | Web Application vulnerability. | Target web information (CIA). | Policies can be used such as Content security policy, X-XSS-Protection. |
| CSFR (Blatz 2007) | Social Engineering. | Web Application vulnerability. | Target User Credentials, and Confidentiality & integrity of web information. | Cookies can be used to identify forged request, content security policy can also be used. |
| Clickjacking (Hansen 2008) | Social Engineering. | Web Application vulnerability. | Target User Credentials, and Confidentiality & integrity of web information. | Content security policies, Same origin policy, X-Frame-Options can be used to defend this attack. |
| Malware Attack (Provos 2007) | Drive-by-Download & Social Engineering. | Web Application vulnerability. | Target web information (CIA), User Credentials, Network, File system & Process. | Sandboxing, Content security policy, & Same origin policy is used. |
| SQL Injection (OSWAP 2009) | Social Engineering & Vulnerability exploitation. | Web Application vulnerability. | Target User Credentials, and Confidentiality & integrity of web information. | Content security polices can be useful. |
| Man-in-the-Browser Attack (Guhring 2006) | Social Engineering & Vulnerability exploitation. | Privilege escalation & extension vulnerabilities, Bypassing policies. | Target web information (CIA), User Credentials. | Process isolation, sandboxing. |
| Extension-based attacks (Liverani 2008) | Social Engineering & Vulnerability exploitation. | Privilege escalation & extension vulnerabilities, Bypassing policies and some attack also exploits Architecture Vulnerability. | Target web information (CIA), User Credentials, Network, File system, Process & other OS components. | Process isolation, sandboxing. |

also state the mitigation technique, which a Browser may invoke to stop the attack.

- **Exploring New Attack Strategies:** In addition to known Browser attack that we have pointed in this chapter, the attack taxonomy is able to determine the attack process for novel attacks. For example, suppose an attacker invokes new attack on Browser, it must be adopt an attack vector. By knowing an attack vector, the taxonomy can state the other steps involved in the attack process.

- **Designing Attack Framework:** The taxonomy can be adopted to design a framework for Browser security. If our security model is mapped with every attack vector, it will able to defense the Browser attacks. The security model will help expose and identify common weaknesses of a class of Browser attacks. Using this security model one can design an experiment to test the weaknesses of Browser attacks and come out with a method to stop them.

- **Identifying Unexplored Research Areas:** Our taxonomy will help in exploring new research area in the field of Browser security. The security model can be made more secure, and is capable of securing Browser from novel Browser attacks.

## CONCLUSION AND FUTURE WORK

In this browser attack taxonomy, we have presented two different dimensions of attack classified on the basis of attacker's actions and Browser security model. The proposed taxonomy can be useful in finding the attack behavior along with other useful attack information. The attacker dimension classifies various attack steps, such as, actor vector to enter into Browser, vulnerability exploitation from different source, like architecture scripts, plug-ins and extensions. The complete attacker actions have been described in this dimension. The browser dimension classifies the Browser security model, which gives the approximation of current Browser security against attacks.

The taxonomy can be used towards future research direction for designing the Browser security. The taxonomy has raised various important points on Browser vulnerabilities that can be exploited by attackers. In order to locate strategies that are appropriate for securing Web Browser against attacker, the Browser developer has to address the vulnerabilities discussed in the taxonomy. We believe that the proposed taxonomy on browser attacks helps in understanding the Browser weakness, and Browser security model.

## REFERENCES

Alvarez, G., & Petrovic, S. (2003). A new taxonomy of web attacks suitable for efficient encoding. *Computers & Security*, *22*(5), 435–449. doi:10.1016/S0167-4048(03)00512-1

Athanasopoulos, E., Pappas, V., & Markatos, E. (2009). Code-Injection Attacks in Browsers Supporting Policies. In *Proceedings of the 2nd Workshop on Web 2.0 Security & Privacy (W2SP)*. W2SP.

Bandhakavi, S., King, S. T., Madhusudan, P., & Winslett, M. (2010, August). VEX: Vetting browser extensions for security vulnerabilities. In *Proceedings of USENIX Security Symposium* (Vol. 10, pp. 339-354). USENIX.

Barth, A. (2007). *Adopt "descendant" frame navigation policy to prevent frame hijacking.* Academic Press.

Barth, A., Jackson, C., & Mitchell, J. C. (2009). Securing frame communication in browsers. *Communications of the ACM*, *52*(6), 83–91. doi:10.1145/1516046.1516066

Barth, A., Jackson, C., Reis, C., & Team, T. G. C. (2008). *The security architecture of the Chromium browser*. Academic Press.

Beaucamps, P., Reynaud, D., & Loria-Nancy, F. (2008, June). Malicious firefox extensions. In Proceedings of Symp. Sur La Securite Des Technologies De L'Information Et Des Communications. Academic Press.

Bishop, M. (1995). *A taxonomy of unix system and network vulnerabilities* (Technical Report CSE-95-10). Department of Computer Science, University of California at Davis.

Blatz, J. (2007). *CSRF: Attack and Defense*. Academic Press.

Cheng, L., & Liu, H. (2008). Three-factor authentication mode of network payment. *Journal of Computer Applications, 7*, 58.

Chickowski, E. (2013). *10 Web-Based Attacks Targeting Your End Users, whitepaper, dark reading*. Retrieved from http://www.darkreading.com/applications/10-web-based-attacks-targeting-your-end/240159280

Cova, M., Kruegel, C., & Vigna, G. (2010, April). Detection and analysis of drive-by-download attacks and malicious JavaScript code. In *Proceedings of the 19th international conference on World Wide Web* (pp. 281-290). ACM.

CVE. (2013). *Common vulnerabilities and exposures*. Retrieved from http://cve.mitre.org

Dormann, W., & Rafail, J. (2006). *Securing your web browser*. CERT.

Fogie, S., Grossman, J., Hansen, R., Rager, A., & Petkov, P. D. (2011). *XSS Attacks: Cross Site Scripting Exploits and Defense*. Syngress.

Fossi, M., Egan, G., Haley, K., Johnson, E., Mack, T., Adams, T., ... & Wood, P. (2010). *Symantec internet security threat report trends for 2010*. Academic Press.

Frei, S., Duebendorfer, T., & Ollmann, G. (2008). *Understanding the Web browser threat: Examination of vulnerable online Web browser populations and the" insecurity iceberg*. ETH, Eidgenossische Technische Hochschule Zurich, Communication Systems Group.

Frei, S., Duebendorfer, T., Ollmann, G., & May, M. (2008). *Understanding the web browser threat. TIK*. ETH Zurich.

Grier, C., Tang, S., & King, S. T. (2008, May). Secure web browsing with the OP web browser. In *Proceedings of Security and Privacy, 2008*. IEEE.

Grosskurth, A., & Godfrey, M. W. (2005, September). A reference architecture for web browsers. In *Proceedings of Software Maintenance,* (pp. 661-664). IEEE.

Guhring, P. (2006). *Concepts against Man-in-the-Browser Attacks*. Academic Press.

Hansen, R., & Grossman, J. (2008). Clickjacking. *SecTheory: Internet Security*. Retrieved from http://www.sectheory.com/clickjacking.htm

Hansman, S., & Hunt, R. (2005). A taxonomy of network and computer attacks. *Computers & Security, 24*(1), 31–43. doi:10.1016/j.cose.2004.06.011

Hickson, I., & Hyatt, D. (2011). *Html5*. W3C Working Draft WD-html5-20110525, May.

Holzammer, A. (2008). *Security Issues about Web Browser Add-ons*. Seminar Internet Sicherheit, Technisc-he Universit at Berlin.

Hoque, N., Bhuyan, M. H., Baishya, R. C., Bhattacharyya, D. K., & Kalita, J. K. (2013). Network attacks: Taxonomy, tools and systems. *Journal of Network and Computer Applications*.

Hossain, S., & Mohammad, Z. (2012). Mitigating program security vulnerabilities: Approaches and challenges. *ACM Computing Surveys, 44*(3), 11:1–11:46.

Howard, J. D., & Longstaff, T. A. (1998). *A common language for computer security incidents* (Sandia Report: SAND98-8667). Sandia National Laboratories. Retrieved from http://www.cert.org/research/taxonomy_988667.pdf

Howes, E. L. (2004). *The Anatomy of a 'Drive-by-Download'*. Academic Press.

Igure, V., & Williams, R. (2008). Taxonomies of attacks and vulnerabilities in computer systems. *IEEE Communications Surveys & Tutorials, 10*(1), 6–19. doi:10.1109/COMST.2008.4483667

Kruegel, C., & Vigna, G. (2003, October). Anomaly detection of web-based attacks. In *Proceedings of the 10th ACM conference on Computer and communications security* (pp. 251-261). ACM.

Lai, J. Y., Wu, J. S., Chen, S. J., Wu, C. H., & Yang, C. H. (2008, August). Designing a taxonomy of web attacks. In *Proceedings of Convergence and Hybrid Information Technology*, (pp. 278-282). IEEE.

Liverani, R. S., & Freeman, N. (2009). *Abusing Firefox Extensions*. Defcon17.

Mavrommatis, N. P. P., & Monrose, M. A. R. F. (2008). All your iframes point to us. In *Proceedings of USENIX Security Symposium*. USENIX.

Mirkovic, J., & Reiher, P. (2004). A taxonomy of DDoS attack and DDoS defense mechanisms. *ACM SIGCOMM Computer Communication Review, 34*(2), 39–53. doi:10.1145/997150.997156

Mitre. (2006). *Exposures, C. V. MITRE Corporation. Mitre*. CVE-2006-7228.

Mitre. (2007). *Exposures, C. V. MITRE Corporation*. CVE-2007-3743.

Mitre. (2008). *Exposures, C. V. MITRE Corporation. Mitre*. CVE-2008-3360.

Mlynski, M. (2012). *Mozilla Foundation Security Advisory 2012*. Retrieved from http://www.mozilla.org/security/ann-ounce/2012/mfsa2012-60.html

Mlynski, M. (2013). *Mozilla Foundation Security Advisory 2013*. Retrieved from http://www.mozilla.org/security/ann-ounce/2013/mfsa2013-15.html

Myers, C., Powers, S., & Faissol, D. (2009). Taxonomies of cyber adversaries and attacks: A survey of incidents and approaches. Lawrence Livermore National Laboratory.

Nicol, G., Wood, L., Champion, M., & Byrne, S. (2001). *Document object model (DOM) level 3 core specification*. Academic Press.

Obied, A., & Alhajj, R. (2009). Fraudulent and malicious sites on the web. *Applied Intelligence, 30*(2), 112–120. doi:10.1007/s10489-007-0102-y

OSVDB. (2013). *Open source vulnerability database*. Retrieved from http://osvdb.org

OWASP. (2013). *Data Validation*. Retrieved from https://www.owasp.org/index.php/Data_Validation

Provos, N., Friedl, M., & Honeyman, P. (2003, August). Preventing privilege escalation. In *Proceedings of the 12th USENIX Security Symposium* (Vol. 12, pp. 231-242). USENIX.

Provos, N., McNamee, D., Mavrommatis, P., Wang, K., & Modadugu, N. (2007, April). The ghost in the browser analysis of web-based malware. In *Proceedings of the first conference on First Workshop on Hot Topics in Understanding Botnets* (pp. 4-4). Academic Press.

Reis, C., & Adviser-Levy, H. M. (2009). *Web browsers as operating systems: supporting robust and secure web programs*. University of Washington.

Scholte, T., Balzarotti, D., & Kirda, E. (2012). Quo vadis? a study of the evolution of input validation vulnerabilities in web applications. In *Financial Cryptography and Data Security* (pp. 284–298). Springer. doi:10.1007/978-3-642-27576-0_24

Silic, M., Krolo, J., & Delac, G. (2010, May). Security vulnerabilities in modern web browser architecture. In *Proceedings of the 33rd International Convention* (pp. 1240-1245). IEEE.

Simmons, C., Shiva, S., Dasgupta, D., & Wu, Q. (2009). *AVOIDIT: A cyber attack taxonomy* (Technical Report CS-09-003). University of Memphis.

Sood, A. K., & Enbody, R. J. (2011). Malvertising–exploiting web advertising. *Computer Fraud & Security*, (4), 11–16.

Ter Louw, M., Lim, J. S., & Venkatakrishnan, V. N. (2008). Enhancing web browser security against malware extensions. *Journal in Computer Virology*, *4*(3), 179–195. doi:10.1007/s11416-007-0078-5

Turner, D., & Oeschger, I. (2003). *Creating XPCOM Components*. Open Source.

Van Kesteren, A., & Jackson, D. (2007). *The xmlhttprequest object* (Working Draft WD-XMLHttpRequest-20070618). World Wide Web Consortium.

Vulnerabilities, C. (2001). *Exposures (CVE)*. Retrieved from http://cve.mitre.org/

Wales, N. S., & Smith, S. (2012). *Building a Taxonomy for Cybercrimes*. Academic Press.

Youl, T. (2004). *Phishing Scams: Understanding the latest trends*. The Confidence Group Pty Ltd.

Zalewski, M. (2010). *Browser security handbook*. Google Code.

Zeigler, A. (2008). IE8 and Loosely-Coupled IE (LCIE). *The Windows Internet Explorer Weblog (MSDN IEBlog), 11*.

## KEY TERMS AND DEFINITIONS

**Attack Taxonomy:** Classification of attacks scenarios.

**Browser Attack:** Offensive action against Browser.

**Browser Security:** Application of Internet security for securing Browsers.

**Code Injection:** Injecting malicious code in victim machine to gain access.

**Privilege Escalation:** Gaining elevated access to resources that are normally under protection.

**Vulnerability:** Security weakness in software.

**Web Application Attacks:** Malicious action against the Web Application.

# Chapter 20
# Defending Information Networks in Cyberspace:
## Some Notes on Security Needs

**Alberto Carneiro**
*Universidade Europeia, Portugal & Universidade Autónoma de Lisboa, Portugal*

## ABSTRACT

*This chapter addresses some concerns and highlights some of the major problems affecting cyberspace. This chapter focuses on defensive attitudes and concerns pertaining to the cybersecurity issues. Section 1, "Facing Cyberspace Security," opens the area of threats and the need of defensive attitudes. Section 2, "Remembering Internet Issues," deals with known Internet problems in what concerns cybersecurity as a generic term. In –Section 3, "Defensive Cybersecurity," the focus is on the need to add more defensive features to security policies. Section 4, "In Search of Better Solutions," emphasizes the need to invest continuously in scientific research and the creation of more sophisticated processes in order to prevent new forms of attack and mitigate negative results.*

## FACING CYBERSPACE SECURITY

Our presence in cyberspace is directly related to the security of the information that circulates here. For this reason, our thoughts have to concentrate on threats, potential risks arising from the absence of security, and on the need to maintain data, privacy and other assets, developing defensive attitudes and proactive behaviors.

### Cybersecurity: An Insecure World

Cybersecurity is a concept that arrived on the post-cold war agenda as a responsive reaction to a mixture of technological innovations and changing geopolitical conditions (Hansen & Nissenbaum, 2009; Carneiro, 2008). It can be faced as a distinct sector with a particular constellation of threats and entities. It is held that "network security" and "individual security" are significant technical and social areas, and their political importance arises from connections to other collective entities as "society," "nations", and "economy."

Shortly saying, it is essential to increase the levels of attention to cybersecurity. It is known that both organizations and individuals are poorly informed about cybersecurity and they are not sufficiently protected. In addition, attacks are becoming increasingly sophisticated (Kshetri, 2005; Saydjari, 2004) and may be made of denial of service, malevolence, and identity theft attacks in the lower layers of the network.

DOI: 10.4018/978-1-4666-6324-4.ch020

Everything happens as if cyberspace was a world even more insecure than the transactional world with which organizations are more accustomed to dealing with. In fact, the insecurity grows with the number of entities with which the organization connects. Additionally, when one opens a door to the outside world many presences can enter if we do not get proper care. This seems obvious, but many organizations are subject to undesirable presences within their networks because they did not take appropriate action according to a security policy.

The effectiveness of cybersecurity requires that national governments, private companies and non-governmental organizations can work together to understand the threats in cyberspace and to share information and resources that can mitigate them. Cyberspace is an environment where there are many connections that provide huge benefits for nations, organizations and individuals. However, this environment is also a space where there are criminals, terrorists and other actors whose intentions may affect the socio-economic values of the majority of its users. If most responsible entities fail to understand and mitigate these risks, national and economic security may be endangered.

A significant number of companies have been victims of cybercrime, including targeted attacks, industrial espionage and loss of confidentiality with regard to intellectual property. Companies can protect the confidentiality of their information by paying attention to three main areas: a) the protection of Information and Communication Technology (ICT) infrastructure; b) requiring identification, authentication and access control and c) ensure business continuity and risk management. Those situations lead to the conclusion that cyber threats are now much more important to business. Information security is an area often neglected and it seems that companies think that it can survive almost without investment. Perhaps many managers feel that the attacks of so-called "hackers" are things that only happen to other people and in science-fiction movies. Several criminal groups seem to have abandoned other activities with greater physical risk to engage in the cybercrime which is much more profitable. It is necessary to advocate for the urgent need to raise the level of cybersecurity in order to maintain competitiveness and sovereignty of each nation.

Global security in cyberspace must be based on the common will of the nations in order to use adequate skills that should be organized in order to defend themselves against common threats. Even though nation-states are the main actors of a global policy of the defense, private companies, political and military alliances and international organizations also play important roles in ensuring cybersecurity internationally.

Almost every day the dependence of many global organizations is increasing in what concerns their relationships with partners and markets they want to achieve. At a higher level, many countries and governments rely on computing infrastructure of cyberspace so that financial markets can function as well as the industries of transportation and power distribution networks. Regardless of their size, most companies want to safely use computer networks in real time, exploring technological innovations and their economic consequences. And yet it is essential to consider the national defense organisms and intelligence agencies that require different virtual networks to be able to act at distance, analyze data of varied nature in the name of internal security, military logistics and to create emergency response against contingencies. However, the efforts of the information security industry are almost always reactive, and in most cases the defensive position is not sufficiently favorable (Utin *et al.*, 2008). The growth of this dependence increases the likelihood of risks and increasingly differentiates the dangers to which organizations are subjected. Thus, the cyber infrastructure must be addressed and studied in conjunction with networks of organizations, of flows of materials, and information among nations.

The ability to provide a trusted environment for individuals and businesses to interact online is critical to innovation and growth (Carneiro, 2007). Digital transformation makes the protection and resilience of our common digital environment a critical element for the economic growth of firms and countries. The security of information systems is directly related to resistance to cyber risks, i.e., cyber resilience is an essential component of any business strategy or national strategy that wants to succeed and achieve good levels of sustainability.

The dependence of the global telecommunications and the Internet is increasing. Nations depend on a cyber infrastructure that enables the functioning of financial markets, transport networks and power grids, as well as government agencies that protect the health and safety of citizens. The great global multinational and local small businesses and startups also use the infrastructure online to facilitate economic and technological innovation. The organisms of national defense and intelligence depend on virtual networks to manage remote operations to analyze intelligence data and the implementation of internal security, military logistics and emergency services.

## Global Threats and Protective Measures

Threats and attacks are evolving quickly, so protective strategies and techniques must also evolve to counteract them. There are more intense threats that persist and show risks that come from enemies who are determined to cause serious damages that are very difficult to recover. These risks result from the architectures of networks and cybernetic nature of relationships among organizations. In fact, the technologies underlying the Internet are evolving causing a large positive potential, but also other vulnerabilities that disrupt the computer security of information systems and communication protocols (Carneiro, 2002). Security concerns should be targeted at counteracting the most significant threats and protecting the most strategic assets.

Many organizations continue to rely more and more on the Internet as a communication mechanism for promoting and delivering products and services. They should be aware that by moving to the Internet, they are also expanding their threat landscape from local or regional threats to global ones. Organizations need to obtain the latest data on threats, relate that to real-time insights into their dynamic ICT and business environments, determine what is relevant, make risk decisions, and take defensive action. By maximizing the use of available information, the organization can create and implement more precise protective strategies against evolving threats. This is why management has to be diligent to take the cautions needed to protect organizations and their customers from unwanted attacks.

In the world of electronic communication, commonly denominated by e-world, the crisis has got increasing attention by organizations' managers. It is a heavy challenge that is placed in the area of transactional relationships in the current context, where communication is mediated by computer networks. These trends and changes require organizations to rethink their communication strategies according to the following aspects:

- Achieving a better understanding of the characteristics of networks, integrated into the concept of cyberspace;
- Better understanding the consequences of communication through computer networks regarding the collection, processing and dissemination of information;
- Considering the possible presence of agents of threats and attacks on computer networks and their transformation into real risks, which require appropriate security policies.

It is well known that within 21st-century e-commerce, if an organization wants Internet access to a global array of customers and suppliers, then management has to invest in developing the intelligence capabilities to defend against global and advanced threats. Greater situational awareness is essential to detect and mitigate cyber attacks effectively.

Nowadays, organizations worldwide face a growing number of sophisticated cyber adversaries. Probably, many organizations do not know enough about the threats or their own security posture to defend themselves adequately against the rising tide of cyber attacks. Some of them cannot even see signs of an attack because they have not sufficiently analyzed data on the latest attack techniques.

The main threats in the field of international information security, such as the use of information technology and communication (ICT) as a tool of information for political and military purposes, the use of ICT for terrorism and cybercrime, including illegal access and virus dissemination, are already identified by United Nations itself (UNODC, 2012; UN, 1994). In addition, it is worth pointing out that the use of cyberspace for intervention in the internal affairs of member states, and to disturb the public order and coordinate antigovernment actions are also serious threats.

Measuring the effectiveness of technical security controls or technology devices/objects that are used in protecting the information systems is critical. Measurement can be based on the security performance for (1) network security controls such as firewall, Intrusion Detection Prevention System (IDPS), switch, wireless access point and network architecture; and (2) network services such as Hypertext Transfer Protocol Secure (HTTPS) and virtual private network (VPN) (Azuwa *et al.*, 2012). Another measure of the effectiveness of network security and organizational connections of individuals to cyberspace is the speed with which organizations react to these threats and even attacks. It is especially important to determine whether research can help to neutralize or prevent damages.

## REMEMBERING INTERNET ISSUES

Organizations and individuals have to deal with ongoing security problems when they are linked with internet sites and networks. Besides the problems of a technological nature, while surfing the internet users have relationships with other unknown users whose access to personal assets can bring many risks, since the loss of privacy to the destruction of files, massive attacks, and a complete failure of an information system, preventing communication activities with customers and sales activities of products and services.

It is well known that in computer networks that support commercial and other relations there are constant threats to the programs, operating systems, system databases and operation of networks. For each threat, best practices have been proposed, including the protection of infrastructure and information (Pfleeger & Pfleeger, 2006). The exchange of knowledge and experience about computer security is stimulated, especially with regard to the protection and sharing of information on critical assets of organizations; in fact, information sharing can lead to higher levels of security requirements (Gordon *et al.*, 2003)

A major problem is to distinguish between legitimate Internet users and a hacker who probes the back doors of computers in order to achieve an unauthorized entrance. Is it possible a balance between routine services and security needs in an international environment? How can we be sure of the identity and authentication of a strange entity during an internet session? In the current era of internet, security also means to have the possibility to block sessions from unknown computers, to require user authentication based on public key encryption certificates, to audit the use of files and directories, and to encrypt communications, preventing legitimate users from inadvertently activating viruses and trojans.

## Cyberspace: Dimensions and Risks

The dependence on the Internet grows and expands. Most countries depend on cyber infrastructure, which enable the functioning of financial markets, transport networks, business transactions and information dissemination. However, the cyberspace permits a diverse set of risks, information systems vulnerabilities become more obvious and serious, and there is the possibility of more attacks. For example, leaks of credit card information and hackers who vandalize websites for fun are possible events that could strike almost any business and personal assets. Enterprises' interests can be threatened by man-made accidents and also by malicious attacks by different actors, such as terrorists and organized criminals. The expansion of this space (cyberspace) increases different opportunities, but also causes the appearance of new threats and risks based on sophisticated methods.

Cyberspace can be defined as:

*Cyberspace includes the Internet plus lots of other networks of computers that are not supposed to be accessible from the Internet. Some of those private networks look just like the Internet, but they are, theoretically at least, separate. Other parts of cyberspace are transactional networks that do things like send data about money flows, stock market trades, and credit card transactions. Some networks are control systems that just allow machines to speak to other machines, like control panels talking to pumps, elevators, and generators (Clarke & Knake, 2010, p. 70).*

Which dimensions can we assign to cyberspace and what can we say about their implications? The term "cyberspace" must be understood as the environment where it is possible to communicate and intervene in virtual environment (virtual reality) and a complex set of computer networks, linked or not, throughout the whole planet, and even with the aid of satellites (Gotved, 2006; Wells & Chen, 2000). The notion of convergence will connect these two ideas related to cyberspace, because the networks will interconnect and permit the interaction in three-dimensional virtual worlds. Individuals and organizations move to a total interconnection of these two views of cyberspace, since networks are becoming more and more connected and at the same time, enabling the interaction of virtual worlds in various dimensions. Thus, cyberspace is a real entity, a vital part of a planetary cyberculture that becomes established in human minds. Cyberspace increases physical reality when it gives to our physical space in three dimensions a new electronic layer. Instead of being an enclosed space, away from the real world, cyberspace will be the implementation of an "augmented reality".

Now more than ever, knowing the risks that ICT systems could face, considering ICT security process key risk management — and increasing the security of an organization's information systems in response to these risks — are a critical stage. Risk management relates to some decisions of security policies and must be performed by processes, since these have a quantitative nature, which enables control and can be repeated, allowing changes for improvement (NIST, 2002). Without it, there would be a significant chance that resources, especially active assets, will not be deployed where and when most effective. The result could be that some risks were not addressed, leaving the organization more vulnerable.

Security managers can conduct a detailed risk assessment of the organization's ICT systems, using a formal structured process. This provides the greatest degree of assurance that all significant risks are identified and their implications considered. The advantage of this approach is that it provides a more detailed examination of the security risks of an organization's ICT system and offers a clear basis for the necessary expenses on the proposed controls.

The use of a formal, detailed risk analysis is often a legal requirement for some government organizations and businesses providing key services to them. It may also be the approach of choice for large organizations with ICT systems critical to their business objectives and with the resources available to perform this type of analysis. Management has to decide what constitutes an appropriate level of risk to accept. It is advisable to expend an amount of resources in reducing risks proportional to the potential costs to the organization should that risk occur.

Since cyberspace is a technology that is still evolving, vulnerabilities and cybersecurity issues create problems for Internet freedom, for network architectures, and for the economic potential of communications among the participants. Moreover, the security of information systems is directly related to resistance to cyber risks, that is, cyber resilience is an essential component of any national or business strategy that intends to succeed and achieve good levels of sustainability (Haimes, 2009). For these reasons, the architecture of networks and cyberspace itself must continue to be discussed and scientific research has to use new technologies to find the most effective protection mechanisms.

The new emerging technologies, such as cloud-based services, are still seen as another possible source of new risks to computer security. It is necessary that the different organizations, as well as governments in several countries, join efforts and establish the purpose of carrying out joint research, development, training and technology transfer, as well as, harness and leverage the capabilities of the members of each group. Thus, it will be possible to achieve significant progress in the implementation of strategic projects, in the strengthening of institutions and technological training programs.

## Secure Decisions and Cyber Threats

Some research has found a significant positive correlation between the effectiveness of acquisition decision making and organizational security attitudes, further suggesting that small improvements in acquisition decision making may result in substantial improvements in an organization's security posture (Goldman, 2012). These considerations evoke the need for creating a new approach based on building an organizational competency in cyber risk intelligence and fully leveraging data from internal and external sources. Increased security concerns, such as cyber-attacks and regulation, require organizations to proactively plan for and address security requirements.

In turbulent and high-velocity environments like those that exist in cyberspace, organizations are subjected to various tensions due to the need of quick decisions and the increased requirement for emergence and improvisation. The management of these critical tensions needs to be fused into the day-to-day fabric of management practices for decision support processes (Carlsson & Sawy, 2008). In the field of cyber security, it is very advisable an intelligence-driven approach, according to which decisions are based on real-time knowledge about cyber adversaries and their methods of attack (Ye *et al.*, 2006; Hughes & Love, 2004), although it is also essential to have a defensive and preventive policy.

Tools / software are insufficient to properly address organizational security and do not address failure or flaws in human decision making. Organizations have to better understand and improve their internal decision making processes and security consciousness, and avoid common pitfalls which allow for unaddressed risk. Sometimes, the rapid growth of an organization leaves many security holes and threats to the enterprise to which many major stake holders have voiced concerns. This problem inhibits the company's goal of becoming a global partner in businesses. It is necessary to define adequate methods to secure the ICT services (Benson & Rahman, 2011).

There is some perception that cyberspace can be an area of threats, particularly when it comes to vulnerability of critical infrastructure-based information systems, since if they fail in their functionality, it is even possible to create harmful consequences for organizations and also for countries nationally and internationally. Cyber threats represent an escalating risk to business innovation; they are dynamic and increasing in sophistication, requiring a fresh and more comprehensive approach to defense in order to permit secure decisions. The four theoretical approaches to international relations -- realism, the English School, Neoliberalism and the Copenhagen School -- indicate cyberspace as a source of international insecurity (Eriksson & Giacomello, 2006). In the field of information, security threats can be interpreted as possibilities for occurrence of minor incidents or dramatic disasters that can cause damage to information systems. These incidents and disasters can be deliberate or unintentional, physical or logical in nature and their number is directly related to navigations through cyberspace.

Threats may also have their origin inside. The group of insiders may include users with authorized access to an organization's information technology systems, such as employees, consultants, or customers, and even authorized competitors. Insider attacks against information technology infrastructure are among the security breaches most feared by security professionals. Moreover, insiders' extensive knowledge gives them the capacity to significantly disrupt or destroy the organization' resources or to contaminate the data contained within information systems. If there is the possibility of internal threats, it is necessary to take into account the need for a set of predictive indicators (deliberate markers of threat preparation, verbal behavior and personality traits). Moreover, it should be taken into account the threats made by e-mail which can be an obvious indication that an attack is imminent (Schultz, 2002).

The emergence of the Internet has brought great benefits to humans, but with this evolution, virtual and real threats emerged in the new environment created by man, the cyberspace. The issue of cyber threat created new and complex threats to the sovereignty of nation states and the varied types of organizations in the global economy. Considering that potential threats poses a substantial challenge to existing governance structures, governments and private actors should develop the ability to respond to cyber threats (Pawlak & Wendling, 2013). Some governments are already formulating specific policies in the field of international security information, highlighting the role of internet technologies as cyber weapon used and the potential of social networks to coordinate antigovernment actions.

It is already possible to speak of information warfare as a set of actions that are aimed at getting some superiority on information field in order to be able to affect the opponent's communication networks and the specific information that supports their decision-making processes; at the same time, this superiority can provide important information to allied countries. The concept of cyber warfare can be understood as a set of procedures for offensive and defensive use of information and information systems, aiming to deny, exploit, corrupt or destroy the opponent's values based on information, information systems and computer networks. These procedures can be performed to obtain advantages both in military and in civilian areas. Some authors have devoted their attention to the issue of cyber warfare, presenting this concept focusing on threats:

*Cyber warfare is the unauthorized penetration by, on behalf of, or in support of, a government into another nation's computer or network, or any other activity affecting a computer system, in which the purpose is to add, alter, or falsify data, or cause the disruption of or damage to a computer, or network device, or the objects a computer system controls (Clarke & Knake, 2010, p. 228).*

Maybe one day the acts of computer sabotage can be considered as similar to traditional military actions, creating the right of nations to react with military means.

According to a recent report on the situation of cybercrime, small businesses are vulnerable targets of cyber attacks, because they are the path of least resistance to the agents of cybercrime and also because many small businesses are usually less careful in their cyber defenses (Symantec, 2013). With the purpose of stealing money, hackers can attack small businesses to obtain customer data (e.g. credit card numbers), intellectual property and data relating to bank accounts. Hackers can install malicious software (malware) in small business websites. Through this procedure, customers inadvertently provide some information that is useful to hackers. The use of spyware and malware to disrupt critical infrastructure call into question the ability of governments and private actors to respond to cyber threats (Pawlak & Wendling, 2013). In addition, there may also be attacks on various levels of an organization. Knowledge workers (functions such as research and development) and sellers are the most targeted.

## DEFENSIVE CYBERSECURITY

Some organizations still view insider threats as the most difficult to defend against. However, external threats as a potent force cannot be forgotten, and companies need to be aware of the most effective ways to defend their assets. A defensive policy has the main purpose of avoiding a reliance on any external entity, that is, if one performs a given action unexpectedly, the system that is functioning can remain in operation.

If an organization decides to maintain a prominent position in the search for security in cyberspace, a proactive policy should be implemented to defend their most critical infrastructure and develop security technologies. With a cyber security policy in focus at all times, most organizations can expect to reach a greater chance of success in present global economy within current cyberspace.

The need for a company to become more efficient and integrated with their business partners, as well as the development of personal computing have led to the emergence of a new type of criminal, the "cyber-criminal," and it is important to know when he acts and attacks a given company. This knowledge should be adapted so that companies have capabilities to identify and prevent cyber-crooks to affect the security of their critical assets.

The efforts that should be made require a collective consciousness on the part of all players: governments, official organisms, private companies and citizens. Moreover, it is becoming increasingly desirable to have international cooperation agreements in the light of which these players can share information and experiences about threats, and risks.

Systems of communication and information constitute a kind of nervous system of modern societies and our social life and economic development depend upon them. Due to this so comprehensive dimension, security policies and defensive actions within cyberspace are a priority.

## Living with the Unknown

Organizations must be aware of the opportunities, but also of the risks and the threats that may come from contacts with unknown entities. If organizations are unable to live with the unknown within some situations, there may be a sense of insecurity and an inability to tackle new markets and new business opportunities. The internet makes it possible to meet various forms of unknown entities. But even before there were these computer technologies, many transactions were only possible as an initial phase of a relationship in which one would seek loyalty. Thus, it is easily understood that dealing with the unknown is characteristic of social life and is also one of the bases of socio-economic development and even of scientific innovation.

The internet and the cyberspace enable to move forward in unknown universes and also to look for places that allow companies to evolve and to achieve their objectives. Thus, the proposal must be as follows: we face the unknown but information security and situation awareness requires a cautious approach (Tyworth *et al.*, 2012).

It can be said that what is known limits the organization in different ways. In a sense, it limits and / or conditions the evolving relationship with the entities with which the organization transacts. And when there is no evolution, the organization is limited in a static manner that impedes its adaptation to environments and external entities. However, uncertainty is a very interesting and rich area to make possible some creativity exercises. Often, uncertainty contributes positively to the entry of the organizations into new phases of their evolution.

The unknown is the domain of many possibilities to lead to the creation of new proposals for transactional relationships. Without the ability to live with uncertainty and the unknown, the existence of the organization would only be a repetition of processes and procedures affected by various disabilities to adapt to new ways of relating to markets and business partners.

## The Unknown and the Need for Greater Security

Considering the global society, we must take measures at international level to include organizations, states, and private companies to be able to share information and its treatment according to criteria established and accepted by all. Security-oriented discussions should continue and stronger efforts will help to identify different categories and types of threats and develop a clear and well-defined mapping of the different clusters of issues regarding security of the Internet and on the Internet.

From the beginning it was the unknown and possible threats that marked their presence. In the 70s, the USA initiated a project ("Arpanet" - Advanced Research Projects Agency Network) designed to protect internal communications, and so very necessary in case of war. Later, it was created the Transmission Control Protocol (Transfer Control Protocol / Internet Protocol), making it possible, therefore, that different information systems could communicate. At that time, Internet use was restricted but shortly after, in 1987, the access to their potential for commercial use was extended. Since then, the Internet was no longer restricted to large USA research centers, it started to be a tool for socio-economic relations, and its use would have to conform to a national and international regulation.

In fact, without this regulatory effort, the unknown could prevail and could take forms very negative and even assuming a criminal nature. Recognizing the importance of responding to the challenge of cybercrime that in most cases has a cross-border nature, the Council of Europe has made efforts in order to harmonize internationally laws and practices of defense. Consequently, a document named "Computer-related crime: Recommendation No. R (89) 9" (COE, 1990), was adopted by the Committee of Ministers of the Council of Europe and it included a minimum list of computer fraud, computer forgery, damage to computer data or computer programs, computer sabotage, unauthorized access, unauthorized interception, unauthorized reproduction of a protected computer program.

Also the Organization for Economic Cooperation and Development (OECD), which in 1992 had established guidelines for the security of information systems, due to the development of these systems suffered, began a reanalysis in 1997. For this purpose, a working group was tasked to study the new situation in the increasing number of threats, including the tragedy of September 11, and in July 25, 2002, the OECD Council adopted this document "Guidelines for the Security of Information Systems and Networks: Towards a Culture of Security" (OECD, 2002).

Within the European Union, the European Agency for Networks and Information Security was established in 2004 with the primary objective of strengthening the capacity of member states in the area of prevention, treatment and response to problems of information and of networks in order to reach greater security levels. In turn, also the International Standardization Organization (ISO) revealed concern in setting standards for the security categorization of information systems, highlighting the ISO 17799:2000 which treats aspects such as security policy, security organization, personnel security, physical and environmental, access control and systems development and maintenance, and ISO 15443 more focused on computer security. The educational philosophy of a "world day" was not forgotten: the United Nations established on 17 May as World Day of the Information Society, and in 2006 it has been dedicated to promoting cybersecurity.

## Attacks and Cybercrimes

Since there was a rapid adaptation of commercial transactions to electronic media, companies started to have access to previously restricted markets. Specifically, developing and emerging countries' access to this global and electronic space has been a source of economic value-added. The resulting shift to affordable networked computers has made the cyberspace available to the masses. Given the growth of cyber activities, the absence of a coordinated, comprehensive control framework has added to the spread of various types of cybercrime.

Whether it is cyber-crime, cyber-espionage or a possible militarization of cyberspace, the number of attacks tends to increase in correlation with the increase in the number of computer terminals. The attacks come in many forms: theft of information from the database, inactivate the company's website, financial fraud and irregular transactions, change the authenticity of information or even its theft. Even without considering image problems, the costs for a company can reach hundreds of millions of Euros.

With the purpose of causing more damage in some organizations, cyber criminals and hackers use increasingly sophisticated processes of Denial-of-Service and new methods of distributed attack in order to stay ahead of corporate security protection efforts. Widely accessible DIY (Do-It-Yourself) malware kits, such as Dirt Jumper, can be used to customize botnets capable of performing DDoS attacks. As the total number of DDoS attacks continues to increase, the development of resources DDoS botnet to avoid DDoS mitigation methods will likely feed the already growing fire of DDoS attacks upon companies.

Many threats become sophisticated cyber attacks and cybercrimes. Those situations have to force companies to strengthen their ability to

cyber-security considering the following four objectives:

- Improve operational capacities for faster defensive interventions;
- Increase the level of security of information systems of government organisms;
- Promote cyber-security in higher education and research;
- Improve the security of critical infrastructure.

Modern society depends on computer systems so that any illicit intervention may put lives in danger. The development of information technology has undeniable advantages for society, but also has a dark side of new forms of activity, including computer crime. Although there is unanimity on the existence of the phenomenon of computer crime, it has not been yet possible to reach an agreed definition about what is computer crime. Computer systems allow sophisticated ways to carry out crimes. It is well known that there is an increase in number of computer crimes (Dearne, 2002) and security policies should revise the attitudes to electronic commerce crimes. Cyber-crime is a serious threat for most modern societies as it hinders the necessary adoption of ICT. Some users are concerned with financial fraud schemes and phenomena of cyber bullying and cyber-extortions (Vlachos *et al.*, 2011). There are cybercrimes methodically executed over a period of time against a specific organization ("advanced persistent threats"). The criminals behind these advanced threats use many different tools and mechanisms to accomplish their goal.

In what concerns to cybercrime, law and regulations require a collective response to an international scale, since the Internet is global. Computer-related crimes do not end at the conventional borders of states. Activities that are illegal offline (outside cyberspace) will remain illegal online (in cyberspace). A considerable number of actions to combat cybercrime are already underway in international organizations. The

Council of Europe is dealing with the first world convention on cybercrime. The European Commission presented a legislative proposal on child pornography on the Internet, in accordance with the provisions of the Convention of the Council on Crime in Cyberspace.

The ability to predict the locations of future crimes can be used as an invaluable source of knowledge to the forces and security services, particularly in strategic and tactical perspectives (Groff & La Vigne, 2001). In parallel with the traditional tactics of reducing crime, there must be formulated a strategy for new types of crimes. Today most of the crimes committed in cyberspace can already be considered in our legislation, because the crimes remain the same. There is only a change in the means by which they were made, such as crimes against honor (slander and libel), unfair competition and child pornography.

Organizations and individuals should have a conscious perception of risk coming from hackers and crackers (Smith & Rupp, 2002) and the strong need of secure control procedures (Cardenas *et al.*, 2008). Maybe just a small percentage of people are aware that the presence of computer applications on smart phones and tablets is a risk factor. Furthermore, it is believed that very few companies also perform a calculation of the financial impact of cyber attacks and cybercrimes.

## What is Being Defensive?

It is essential that organizations have a perspective of defensive management which should support the formulation of security policies that consider the global threats existing in cyberspace. It is impossible to analyze the ICT security of an organization by looking only to the computers and network.

It must be examined in its totality considering a global view of company personnel policies, building infrastructure, software, hardware and threats and risks coming from partners and cyberspace. A security analysis includes a comprehensive study of the enterprise, its business function, its environment, purpose, assets, and financial data and then must shift focus to a micro analysis of the symbiotic parts (Whitman & Mattord, 2010).

Cybersecurity can be viewed by different perspectives: some authors examine the legal issues of procedures, others address the international legal regime against terrorism, seemingly covering all the major issues. However, it is increasingly necessary to emphasize the value of an approach that is both defensive and proactive.

The time has come when successful defense requires evolving past conventional approaches in information security to developing competencies in data fusion, knowledge management, and analytics. International collaboration is the key needed to develop, standardize and deploy these updates that have a critical nature. No country can do it alone. The reorganization of internal network security is not able to solve the problem of cybersecurity. It is necessary to make Internet continuously safer.

It is necessary to develop the field of cyber defense using computer security experts and cybercrime and cyber risks specialists and their own skills. We know that many companies and countries have many weaknesses in what concerns assets' protection and information detection systems. Thus, it is essential to define some ways of organizational commitment and research in the field of cyber defense. It can be stated a few:

- Cyber defense and security of information systems should be a major concern of organizations at the highest level of management;
- To encourage the training of engineers specialized in computer security and in particular in the protection of computerized information systems;
- At all levels of management (strategic, intermediate, and operational), to increase awareness of the need for protection of information systems in all functional areas of the organization;

- To develop better analytical systems to enable the detection of attacks and promote the formation of centers of common detection;
- To create more difficult and sophisticated tests to confirm and validate security levels.

When an organization adopts a defensive policy, measures and preventive procedures have to be undertaken to prepare for the possibility of a strong and sustained hostile offensive coming from the insecure cyberspace. Moreover, as long as an organization adopts a defensive policy, management of information security will gain the validity and legitimacy to protect organizational interests and information assets.

## Defensive Security of Informational Networks

International security cooperation can take one of two forms: a) a classical collective security organization promotes security through regulating the behavior of its member states; b) a defensive security organization is designed to protect these members from external threats.

Both forms of security cooperation connect some members to act in concert with respect to threats presented by other members. The emergence of non-state actors, such as terrorist or extremist organizations, challenges traditional forms of collective security (Gleason & Shaihutdinov, 2005), and the goals of a defensive security remain adequate.

Defensive security is a set of two words which individually have a great strength, but together seems to be smoother. In fact, the concept of Defensive Security has a broad spectrum and can sometimes be seen as "non-offensive-defense" or "non-provocative defense", which refers more to the existence of strategic forces, but with no capabilities for a prompt response to a possible mass attack.

We cannot think that the basic defensive software would be sufficient to ensure the protection of critical data and infrastructure. In fact, in order

for government and businesses organizations to maintain good levels of protection from increasingly advanced cyber threats, comprehensive defensive security is needed. And even with advanced and comprehensive solutions, there is still the possibility of unexpected risks.

It is imperative that cybersecurity policies of governments and large corporations insist on raising awareness of all users of computer networks in respect of risks to which they are subjected. Also higher education must carry out its mission of educating every computer engineer about cyber infrastructure and systems, inherent cyber vulnerabilities and threats, and appropriate defensive security procedures. Thus, computer engineers should be trained in universities and companies to enable them to acquire and build skills in the following areas:

- In-depth knowledge and understanding of the basic physical and virtual architecture of cyberspace, including: the individual computer and program, organizational networks and protocols of a network in the cyberspace, and the distributed client-server system that is the world wide web;
- Basic components of the physical and virtual architecture of cyberspace;
- Good and adequate understanding of the model of five pillars of Information Assurance (availability, integrity, authentication, confidentiality, and non-repudiation);
- Full knowledge of the inherent vulnerabilities of information systems that endanger these properties;
- Defensive measures to ensure that information systems retain these properties, and offensive measures that can be used to violate these pillars.

With comprehensive security approaches, it is possible to block a high percentage of the threats, but there is always a margin of error. It is required a continuous proactive approach to ensure that the majority of offensive moves can be rejected. If not, it is essential to implement a mitigation plan with procedures to minimize damage on the level of performance of the organization.

## IN SEARCH OF BETTER SOLUTIONS

It is important that each country can build the foundations for an international understanding of cyber security, especially regarding cyber-crime. To achieve this, there must be a greater participation of companies, government agencies, especially agencies responsible for national security. It is understood by many countries that currently the Budapest Convention (COE, 2001) does not meet the requirements of cybercrimes, taking into account the technological advances that have occurred and it is not even sufficient in terms of international cooperation.

According to the International Telecommunication Union (ITU, 2007), the best areas to focus on promoting cyber security in member countries of OECD are:

- Areas of high attention (priority):
  - Combating cybercrime;
  - Creation of national CERTs / CSIRTs (Computer Emergency Response Teams/Computer Security Incident Response Teams);
  - Increased culture of cybersecurity and its activities;
  - Promoting education.
- Areas that deserve further enhancement (relevant):
  - Research and development;
  - Risk assessment and monitoring;
  - Meeting the demands of small and medium enterprises (SMEs).

It is necessary to formalize the existence of structures that ensure the cybersecurity of each country. These structures, i.e., specialized orga-

nizations, are aimed at enabling the formulation of policies, rules and regulations, research and development of methodologies and technologies focused on cyber security. Considering the need for strong international cooperation, it should be carried out the implementation of a macro-coordination program that fosters processes' integration, in order to ensure availability, integrity, confidentiality and authenticity of the information on behalf of the interests of states and organizations, as well as the resilience of their critical infrastructures.

In order to achieve greater security for the user (taxpayer, consumer, public or private sector), it is essential that the use of information technologies in a cyber environment meets high standards of a very secure operating way. A tendency for the solution of network security is cloud computing. This technique means the use of an evolution of technologies and processes used by professionals in the field of information security and computer forensics. The "cloud" is aimed at storing information in the cloud in order to generate a strong isolation of applications and information. This aims to avoid the proliferation of cybercrime and increases the security level in the context of institutional relations between organizations.

It is urgent to build up better solutions that span from the risk analysis of critical processes to the implementation of security software with distributed nature, which should lead research projects to become more demanding and being a source of new solutions. Organizations should continue to look for better solutions from risk analysis of critical processes to implementation of software in order to enable distributed security in cyberspace. Those efforts should lead research projects to become more demanding and selective in their security criteria.

In the medium term, based on an analysis of technological change in recent years (TSB, 2010), it is possible to suggest some trends:

- **Infrastructure Revolution:** the increasing penetration of high-speed broadband and wireless networks; centralization of computing resources and great adoption of cloud computing; and the proliferation of IP (internet protocol) and connected devices; growth of user interfaces, with emergence of new technologies potentially disruptive;
- **Data Explosion:** Greater sharing of confidential data between organizations and individuals; many people connected globally; multiplication of devices and applications generating data traffic; greater need for classification of information;
- **The World Always Connected:** Greater connectivity between people driven by social networks and other platforms of information connectivity; increase in data mining; increase in national critical infrastructure and connectivity of public services;
- **Future of Finance:** Increased use of electronic commerce and online banking, development of new management models, growth of new payment models;
- **Regulation and Stricter Rules:** Increased regulation on privacy; increased standards of Information Security and Cyber Security; globalization and neutralization of the networks that persist in being forces opposed to regulations and standards;
- **Multiple Internets:** Censorship, new and safer internets, "closed" social networking;
- **New Identity and Trust Model:** Identity becomes increasingly important in the movement of the scope of information security and cybersecurity; new trust models to develop relationships between people.

These trends are evolutionary forces that include greater safety precautions or express the need of a stronger set of efforts to achieve greater levels of protection of organizational assets, information systems and the operation of private communication networks.

To build the best solutions is indispensable to work with great dedication and commitment to create a global culture of cybersecurity that enables the protection of critical information infrastructures from both organizations and countries. The creation of this culture of cyber security requires that organizations and governments of various countries consider very carefully and with a firm commitment their needs in order to protect their assets.

## WHAT CAN BE CONCLUDED

The reflection notes that this chapter offers to computer security experts and researchers sought to emphasize that, in the vast and complex field of cybersecurity, some aspects require enhanced attention and resolute pursuit of lines of scientific research.

It is surely necessary to make the cyber defense and protection of information systems a national priority, taken at the highest level, namely in the context of education and economic competitiveness. User education is a key step toward better defense. By educating users on the dangers of cyberspace and increasing the level of awareness of the threats could reduce the number of infected computers and attacks.

It is essential to increase the number of engineers specialized in the protection of information systems, developing research and consulting activities, and enhance public awareness, for example through communication campaigns inspired by prevention.

Moreover, it is also advisable to make it mandatory for companies and operators of high importance to declare all attacks or attempted violation of security policies, security procedures, or acceptable use policies of informational networks and encourage protective measures.

Navigating in the cyberspace with some security depends on technical education of the users, but also on the scientific and technological development and the capacity of organizations and countries to establish defensive partnerships. In order to achieve better solutions it is essential to formulate cyber security strategies based on even more careful risk management. Cybersecurity certainly require a permanent development based on security policies of governments, companies and scientific research.

# REFERENCES

Amin, A.A., & Sastry, S. (2008). Secure control: Towards survivable cyber-physical systems. In *Proceedings of 28th International Conference on Distributed Computing Systems Workshops, 2008* (pp. 495-500). Academic Press.

Azuwa, M., Ahmad, R., Sahib, S., & Shamsuddin, S. (2012). Technical security metrics model in compliance with ISO/IEC 27001 standard. *International Journal of Cyber-Security and Digital Forensics, 1*(4), 280–288.

Benson, K., & Rahman, S. M. (2011). Security risks in mechanical engineering industries. *International Journal of Computer Science & Engineering Survey, 2*(3), 75–92. doi:10.5121/ijcses.2011.2306

Carlsson, S. & Sawy, O. (2008). Managing the five tensions of IT-enabled decision support in turbulent and high-velocity environments. *Information Systems and e-Business Management, 6*(3), 225-237

Carneiro, A. (2002). *Introdução à Segurança dos Sistemas de Informação (Introduction to Information Systems Security)*. Lisboa: FCA-Editora de Informática.

Carneiro, A. (2007). What is required for growth? *Business Strategy Series, 8*(1), 51–57. doi:10.1108/17515630710686888

Carneiro, A. (2008). When Leadership means more Innovation and Development. *Business Strategy Series, 9*(4), 176–184. doi:10.1108/17515630810891843

Clarke, R. A., & Knake, R. K. (2010). *Cyber War: The next threat to national security and what to do about it*. New York: HarperCollins.

COE. (1990). *Computer-related crime - Recommendation No. R(89) 9 on computer-related crime and final report of the European Committee on Crime Problems*. Strasbourg: Council of Europe.

COE. (2001). Convention on Cybercrime (STE no. 181). Budapest: Council of Europe.

Dearne, K. (2002). Cyber-crime boom. *Information Management & Computer Security, 10*(5), 262–266.

Eriksson, J., & Giacomello, G. (2006). The Information Revolution, Security, and International Relations: (IR)relevant Theory? *International Political Science Review, 27*(3), 221–244. doi:10.1177/0192512106064462

Gleason, G., & Shaihutdinov, M. E. (2005). Collective Security and Non-State Actors in Eurasia. *International Studies Perspectives, 6*(2), 274–284. doi:10.1111/j.1528-3577.2005.00206.x

Goldman, E. H. (2012). The effect of acquisition decision making on security posture. *Information Management & Computer Security, 20*(5), 350–363. doi:10.1108/09685221211286520

Gordon, L. A., Loeb, M. P., & Lucyshyn, W. (2003). Sharing information on computer systems security. *Economic Analysis, 22*(6), 461–485. Journal of Accounting and Public Policy

Gotved, S. (2006). Time and space in cyber social reality. *New Media & Society, 8*(3), 467–486. doi:10.1177/1461444806064484

Groff, E., & La Vigne, N. G. (2001). Mapping an Opportunity Surface of Residential Burglary. *Journal of Research in Crime and Delinquency*, *38*(3), 257–278. doi:10.1177/0022427801038003003

Haimes, Y.Y. (2009). On the Definition of Resilience in Systems. *Risk Analysis*, *29*(4), 498–501. doi:10.1111/j.1539-6924.2009.01216.x PMID:19335545

Hansen, L., & Nissenbaum, H. (2009). Digital Disaster, Cybersecurity, and the Copenhagen School. *International Studies Quarterly*, *53*(4), 1155–1175. doi:10.1111/j.1468-2478.2009.00572.x

Hughes, V., & Love, P. (2004). Toward cyber-centric management of policing: back to the future with information and communication technology. *Industrial Management & Data Systems*, *104*(7), 604–612. doi:10.1108/02635570410550269

International Telecommunication Union (ITU). (2007). *Global cybersecurity agenda (GCA): Framework for international cooperation*. Switzerland: ITU.

Kshetri, N. (2005). Pattern of global cyber war and crime: A conceptual framework. *Journal of International Management*, *11*(4), 541–562. doi:10.1016/j.intman.2005.09.009

NIST. (2002). *Risk management guide for information technology systems*. Special Publication 800-30 of the National Institute of Standards and Technology. CODEN: NSPUE2.

OECD. (2002). *Guidelines for the security of information systems and networks: Towards a culture of security*. Paris: OECD.

Pawlak, P., & Wendling, C. (2013). Trends in cyberspace: Can governments keep up? *Environment Systems and Decisions*, *33*(4), 536–543. doi:10.1007/s10669-013-9470-5

Pfleeger, C. P., & Pfleeger, S. (2006). *Security in computing* (4th ed.). Upper Saddle River, NJ: Prentice Hall.

Saydjari, O. S. (2004). Cyber defense: art to science. *Communications of the ACM - Homeland Security*, *47*(3), 52-57.

Schultz, E. (2002). A framework for understanding and predicting insider attacks. *Computers & Security*, *21*, 526–531. doi:10.1016/S0167-4048(02)01009-X

Smith, A. D., & Rupp, W. T. (2002). Issues in cybersecurity - Understanding the potential risks associated with hackers/crackers. *Information Management & Computer Security*, *10*(4), 178–183. doi:10.1108/09685220210436976

Symantec. (2013). *Internet Security Threat Report 2013, Volume 18*. Available at http://www.symantec.com/security_response/publications/threatreport.jsp

TSB. (2010). Revolution or evolution? Information Security 2020. Technology Strategy Board - TSB, PriceWaterHouseCoopers LLP. UK: TSB: Pricewathercoopers.

Tyworth, M., Giacobe, N.A., Mancuso, V., & Dancy, C. (2012). The distributed nature of cyber situation awareness. *Proceedings of 2012 IEEE International Multi-Disciplinary Conference on Cognitive Methods in Situation Awareness and Decision Support (CogSIMA)*, (pp. 174-178). IEEE.

United Nations Office on Drugs and Crime (UNODC). (2012). *The use of the Internet for terrorist purposes*. United Nations.

United Nations (UN). (1994). *The United Nations manual on the prevention and control of computer related crime*. United Nations Publications.

Utin, D., Utin, M. & Utin, J. (2008). General misconceptions about information security lead to an insecure world. *Information Security Journal: A Global Perspective, 17*(4), 164-169.

Vlachos, V., Minou, M., Assimakopouos, V., & Toska, A. (2011). The landscape of cybercrime in Greece. *Information Management & Computer Security*, *19*(2), 113–123. doi:10.1108/09685221111143051

Wells, W. D., & Chen, Q. (2000). The dimensions of commercial cyberspace. *Journal of Interactive Advertising*, *1*(1), 23–40. doi:10.1080/15252019.2000.10722042

Whitman, M., & Mattord, H. (2010). *Management of Information Security* (3rd ed.). Boca Raton, FL: Delmar, Cengage Learning.

Ye, N., Harish, B., & Farley, T. (2006). Attack profiles to derive data observations, features, and characteristics of cyber attacks. Information, Knowledge, *Systems Management*, *5*(1), 23–47.

## ADDITIONAL READING

(2009). A Survey of Botnet and Botnet Detection. In *Proceedings of Third International Conference on Emerging Security Information, Systems and Technologies, 2009, SECURWARE 09)*, pp. 268-273Feily, M.Shahrestani, A.Ramadass, S.

Bargh, M. S., Choenni, S., Mulder, I., & Pastoor, R. (2012). Exploring a Warrior Paradigm to Design Out Cybercrime. Proceedings of European Intelligence and Security Informatics Conference (EISIC), pp. 84-90

Buzan, B., & Waever, O. (2009). Macrosecuritisation and Security Constellations: Reconsidering Scale in Securitisation Theory. *Review of International Studies*, *35*(2), 253–276. doi:10.1017/S0260210509008511

Carol, H., Jae-Nam, L., & Straub, D. W. (2012). Institutional Influences on Information Systems Security Innovations. *Information Systems Research*, *23*(3), 918–939.

Caruson, K., MacManus, S. A., & McPhee, B. D. (2012). Cybersecurity Policy-Making at the Local Government Level: An Analysis of Threats, Preparedness, and Bureaucratic Roadblocks to Success. *Journal of Homeland Security and Emergency Management*, *9*(2), 1–22. doi:10.1515/jhsem-2012-0003

Choo, K.-K. R. (2011). The cyber threat landscape: Challenges and future research directions. *Computers & Security*, *30*(8), 719–731. doi:10.1016/j.cose.2011.08.004

Dagon, D., Gu, G., Lee, C., & Lee, W. (2007). A taxonomy of botnet structures. In Proceedings of the 23rd Annual Computer Security Applications Conference (ACSAC'07), pp. 325-339

Edelbacher, M., Kratcoski, P., & Theil, M. (2012). *Financial Crimes – A Threat to Global Security*. Boca Raton: CRC Press, Taylor & Francis Group. doi:10.1201/b12158

Gercke, M. (2008). National, Regional and International Legal Approaches in the Fight Against Cybercrime. *Computer Law Review International*, *1*, 7–13.

Gu, G., Perdisci, R., Zhang, J., & Lee, W. (2008). BotMiner: Clustering Analysis of Network Traffic for Protocol- and Structure-Independent Botnet Detection. In *Proceedings of 17th USENIX Security Symposium*, pp. 139-154

Hart, C. (2011). Mobilizing the Cyberspace Race: the Securitization of the Internet and its Implications for Civil Liberties. Cyber-Surveillance in Everyday Life: An International Workshop. Retrieved July 20, 2013 from http://www.digitallymediatedsurveillance.ca/wp-content/uploads/2011/04/Hart-Mobilizing-the-Cyberspace-race.pdf

Hentea, M. (2008). Improving Security for SCADA Control Systems. *Interdisciplinary Journal of Information, Knowledge, and Management*, *3*, 73–86.

Janczewski, L., & Colarik, A. (Eds.). (2008). *Cyber Warfare and Cyber Terrorism*. Hershey: Information Science Reference.

Javaid, M. A. (2012). Cybercrime: Threats and Solutions (October 24, 2012). Retrieved September 22, 2013, from SSRN: http://ssrn.com/abstract=2342400 or http://dx.doi.org/10.2139/ssrn.2342400

Jones, R. A., & Horowitz, B. (2012). A System-Aware Cyber Security architecture. *Systems Engineering*, *15*(2), 225–240. doi:10.1002/sys.21206

McCusker, R. (2007). Transnational organised cyber crime: distinguishing threat from reality. *Crime, Law, and Social Change*, *46*(4-5), 257–273. doi:10.1007/s10611-007-9059-3

McQuade, S. C., III. (2006). We Must Educate Young People About Cybercrime Before They Start College. *The Chronicle of Higher Education*, *53*(14), page B29. Retrieved October 13, 2012, from http://www.rit.edu/news/utilities/pdf/2007/2007-01-05_chronicle_cybercrime.pdf

Neghina, D.-E., & Scarlat, E. (2013). Managing Information Technology Security in the Context of Cyber Crime Trends. *International Journal of Computers, Communications & Control*, *8*(1), 97–104.

Nissenbaum, H. (2005). Where Computer Security Meets National Security. *Ethics and Information Technology*, *7*, 61–73. doi:10.1007/s10676-005-4582-3

Nye, J. S. Jr. (2011). Nuclear lessons for cyber security? *Strategic Studies Quarterly*, *5*(4), 18–37.

Petkac, M. & Badger, L. (2000) Security agility in response to intrusion detection. *Computer Security Applications, 2000. ACSAC '00. 16th Annual Conference*, pp 11-20

Phillips, R., & Sianjina, R. R. (2013). *Cyber Security for Educational Leaders: A Guide to Understanding and Implementing Technology Policies*. New York: Routledge.

Rajab, M. A., Zarfoss, J., Monrose, F., & Terzis, A. (2006). A multifaceted approach to understanding the botnet phenomenon. *Proceedings of the 6th ACM SIGCOMM conference on Internet measurement*, pp. 41-52

Ransbotham, S., & Mitra, S. (2009). Choice and Chance: A Conceptual Model of Paths to Information Security Compromise. *Information Systems Research*, *20*(1), 121–139. doi:10.1287/isre.1080.0174

Schneier, B. (2004). *Secrets and Lies: Digital Security in a Networked World*. Indianapolis, IN: Wiley Publications, Inc.

Stohl, M. (2007). Cyber terrorism: a clear and present danger, the sum of all fears, breaking point or patriot games? *Crime, Law, and Social Change*, *46*(4-5), 223–238. doi:10.1007/s10611-007-9061-9

Wall, D. S. (2004). Digital Realism and the Governance of Spam as Cybercrime. *European Journal on Criminal Policy and Research*, *10*(4), 309–335. doi:10.1007/s10610-005-0554-8

Wall, D. S. (2007). Policing Cybercrimes: Situating the Public Police in Networks of Security within Cyberspace. *Police Practice and Research: An International Journal*, *8*(2), 183–205. doi:10.1080/15614260701377729

Wilshusen, G. C. (2012). *Information Security: Cyber Threats Facilitate Ability to Commit Economic Espionage*, Pub. L. No. GAO-12-876T (2012). Washington, DC: US Government Accountability Office. Retrieved July 15, 2013, from http://www.gao.gov/assets/600/592008.pdf

Yannakogeorgos, P., & Lowther, A. (2013). *Conflict and Cooperation in Cyberspace: The Challenge to National Security*. Boca Raton: Taylor & Francis. doi:10.1201/b15253

## KEY TERMS AND DEFINITIONS

**Botnet:** a) A ro*bot net*work (ro**BOT NET**work) or a network of compromised computer systems linked together for a common purpose. Criminals distribute malicious software (also known as malware) that can turn a given computer into a bot (also known as a zombie) and typically use bots to infect large numbers of computers which form a network, or a *botnet*. Further, they use botnets to send out spam email messages, spread viruses, attack computers and servers, and commit other kinds of crime and fraud. If a computer becomes part of a botnet, it might slow down and the owner might inadvertently be helping criminals; b) Also called a "zombie army," a botnet is a large number of compromised computers that are used to generate spam, relay viruses or flood a network or Web server with excessive requests to cause it to fail (see denial of service attack). The computer is compromised via a Trojan that often works by opening an Internet Relay Chat (IRC) channel that waits for commands from the person in control of the botnet. There is a thriving botnet business selling lists of compromised computers to hackers and spammers.

**Cybercrime:** a) Also referred to as computer crime, or computer-based criminal activity done using computers and the Internet. This includes anything from downloading illegal music files to stealing money from online bank accounts. Cybercrime also includes non-monetary offenses, such as creating and distributing viruses on other computers or posting confidential business information on the Internet; b) Crimes perpetrated over the Internet, typically having to do with online fraud.

**Cyberspace:** a) The electronic system of interlinked networks of computers, bulletin boards, etc. that is thought of as being a boundless environment providing access to information, interactive communication, and, in science fiction, a form of virtual reality; b) The global computer networks that facilitate communications among individuals and organizations; c) The electronic medium of computer networks, in which online communication takes place.

**Defense in-Depth:** The security approach whereby each system on the network is secured to the greatest possible degree. May be used in conjunction with firewalls. Using multiple systems to resist attackers. For example, if an external firewall is breached, an internal intrusion detection system can sound an alarm. If systems are breached and data can be stolen, keeping all vital records encrypted on disk and encrypted during transmission prevents attackers from using it even if they get it.

**Defensive Security:** a) Security policies intended to withstand or deter aggression or attack; b) Security performed so as to avoid risk, danger, or cybercrime threats like espionage, sabotage, or attack.

**Distributed Denial of Service Attack (DDoS):** An attack, often orchestrated by a botnet, which targets websites or computer servers with floods of requests, in order to overwhelm the targeted system and drive it offline; Denial of service (DoS) attacks may be initiated from a single machine, but they typically use many computers to carry out an attack. Since most servers have firewalls and other security software installed, it is easy to lock out individual systems. Therefore, distributed denial of service (DDoS) attacks are often used to coordinate multiple systems in a simultaneous attack. A distributed denial of service attack tells all coordinated systems to send a stream of requests to a specific server at the same time. These requests may be a simple ping or a more complex series of packets. If the server cannot respond to the large number of simultaneous requests, incoming requests will eventually become queued. This backlog of requests may result in a slow response time or a no response at all. When the server is unable to respond to legitimate requests, the denial of service attack has succeeded. DoS attacks are a common method hackers use to attack websites. Since flooding a server with requests does not require any authentication, even a highly secured server is vulnerable. However, a single system is typically not capable of carrying out a successful DoS attack. Therefore, a hacker may create a botnet to control multiple computers at once. A botnet can be used to carry out a DDoS attack, which is far more effective than an attack from a single computer.

**Hackers:** a) This term originally referred to a computer enthusiast, or computerphile, who enjoys computer technology and programming to the point of examining the code of operating systems to figure out how they work. A hacker can "hack" his or her way through the security levels of a computer system or network. This can be as simple as figuring out somebody else's password or as complex as writing a custom program to break another computer's security software; b) Synonymous with *cracker*. A person who gains or attempts to gain unauthorized access to computers or computer networks and tamper with operating systems, application programs, and databases. Crackers are the reason software manufacturers release periodic "security updates" to their programs.

**Malvertisement:** A malicious advertisement, placed by cyber criminals, which redirects visitors to malware. These advertisements are often placed into legitimate online advertising networks and may be displayed on unwitting third-party websites. (MALicious adVERTISING) Placing malicious ads on Web sites that lead users to harmful sites. Malvertisements are not only found on suspicious Web sites, but wind up on reputable, highly trafficked sites.

**Malware:** Also referred to as malicious software, or software which is installed without authorization upon a victim computer that has a malicious or criminal purpose; it comes in many forms and can be any program or source code producing output that the computer owner does not need, want, or expect. For example, malware can be a remote access Trojan horse that can not only open a back door to a remote computer but also control someone's computer or network from a remote location. Malware includes viruses, worms, Trojan horses (that can, for example, spy on the system and display ads when the user least expects it), and malicious active content arriving through email or Web pages visited. These forms of malware normally run without the knowledge and permission of the user.

**Threats:** a) The danger or the possibility of an attack or an incident on a computer system; b) An object, person, or other entity that represents a constant danger to an asset; c) A potential for violation of security, which exists when there is a circumstance, capability, action, or event that could breach security and cause harm; d) A possible danger that might exploit a vulnerability.

**Virus:** a) A type of malware, which spreads in an automated fashion between vulnerable computers, much like a biological virus does with living creatures; b) Computer viruses are small programs or scripts that can negatively affect the health of your computer. These malicious little programs can create files, move files, erase files, consume your computer's memory, and cause your computer not to function correctly. Some viruses can duplicate themselves, attach themselves to programs, and travel across networks. In fact opening an infected e-mail attachment is the most common way to get a virus.

# Chapter 21

# Network Situational Awareness:
## Sonification and Visualization in the Cyber Battlespace

**Tom Fairfax**
*Security Risk Management, UK*

**Christopher Laing**
*Northumbria University, UK*

**Paul Vickers**
*Northumbria University, UK*

## ABSTRACT

*This chapter treats computer networks as a cyber warfighting domain in which the maintenance of situational awareness is impaired by increasing traffic volumes and the lack of immediate sensory perception. Sonification (the use of non-speech audio for communicating information) is proposed as a viable means of monitoring a network in real time and a research agenda employing the sonification of a network's self-organized criticality within a context-aware affective computing scenario is given. The chapter views a computer network as a cyber battlespace with a particular operations spectrum and dynamics. Increasing network traffic volumes are interfering with the ability to present real-time intelligence about a network and so suggestions are made for how the context of a network might be used to help construct intelligent information infrastructures. Such a system would use affective computing principles to sonify emergent properties (such as self-organized criticality) of network traffic and behaviour to provide effective real-time situational awareness.*

## INTRODUCTION

This chapter explores some of the issues surrounding the problem of maintaining cyber situational awareness. Situational awareness is a term with its origins in military doctrine but has found its way into the mainstream and is especially applicable in the context of maintaining cyber security in computer networks. Networks are susceptible to a number of threats to their well-being from traffic congestion to deliberate attacks. In this chapter we show how the concept of cyber as a warfighting domain has traction and how applying a military understanding of the domain and situational awareness within it might help in finding new ways to maintain healthy networks. After

DOI: 10.4018/978-1-4666-6324-4.ch021

explaining the underlying concepts of the cyber operations spectrum and the dynamics underpinning it we show where situational awareness fits into this understanding. Next we explore how the projected growth network traffic volumes may make maintaining situational awareness increasingly challenging, especially as the cyber domain is intrinsically inaccessible to sensory perception which is traditionally needed for situational awareness. The limitations of current approaches to network visualization are touched upon and the possible role of using sonification for situational awareness activities is explored. Following this contextualization we then offer suggestions for potentially fruitful avenues of investigation that may yield big benefits in maintaining network situational awareness.

The principal objectives of this chapter are:

1. A presentation of computer networks as a cyber battlespace.
2. The role of situational awareness in this battlespace.
3. A critique of visualization approaches and the need to consider other modalities for the sensory perception of network behavior.
4. An agenda for future research based on sonification, self organized criticality, network context, and affective computing.

## CYBERSPACE: THE NEW BATTLE SPACE?

There is significant debate in military circles about whether cyber has become the fifth warfighting domain. Traditional doctrine was directed towards operations on land and sea, and a combination of the two. History is well populated with examples of strategic operations combining operations on land supported by sea and vice versa. In the early 20th century, air was added as a third warfighting domain with increasing effect as a range of technologies have rapidly increased capability.

In the second half of the 20th century, space became the fourth warfighting domain and there is vigorous debate amongst practitioners and theorists about whether the cyber environment constitutes the fifth. There are a number of parallel lines of debate, however the central theme is focused on whether the cyber environment (sometimes known as cyberspace) is a discrete area of operations or whether it is a more pervasive concept that runs through all of the other domains.

Part of the principal challenge lies in the fact that whilst land, sea, air and space are physically distinct and are defined by similar criteria, cyberspace is defined in a different way, existing on an electronic plane rather than a physical and chemical one. Some would argue that cyber space is a vein which runs through the other four warfighting domains and exists as a common component rather than as a discrete domain. One can easily see how cyber operations can easily play a significant role in land, sea, air or space warfare, due to the technology employed in each of these domains.

On the other hand, this distinction is dependent on the way that we define the various domains. If our definitions are underpinned by a purely physical paradigm, then it is arguable that cyberspace is a very different type of context to the traditional warfighting domains. If, however, our definitions are based on an operational paradigm, then the distinction is less clear. It is possible to conduct entire operations in the cyber environment, made possible by the interconnected nature of the Internet and associated infrastructures. In the same way, it is common to have joint operations operating across multiple domains, including the cyber environment, and the cyber environment isn't restricted to military warfighting scenarios.

A good example of a comprehensive cyber campaign occurred in April 2007, when Estonia was subjected to a wide range of concerted cyber attacks across a broad spectrum of government, commercial, industrial and media organizations. This sophisticated campaign effectively crippled a significant proportion of the Estonian National infrastructure whilst the attack was taking place. It is interesting that in the wake of the attack, Estonia has developed one of the most significant cyber defence infrastructures in existence.

Another example occurred a year later, in 2008 during the South Ossetia conflict where kinetic operations were preceded by a widespread cyber campaign which effectively blinded the defenders in advance of a rapid Russian advance. In this case cyber was used as part of a blended strategy which achieved strategic disruption of Georgian Public Service infrastructure thus enabling surprise. There are a range of other examples of the use of cyber as either a tool to achieve dislocation or disruption at a strategic level. The list grows steadily as more varied compromises are discovered across a range of government and industrial targets in a range of countries.

## Cyber Operations Spectrum

Though operations in cyberspace are complex, they can be simplified, to some extent, by the cyber operations spectrum. This divides cyber operations into 3 areas:

- **Defense:** Defensive operations take up approximately 80% of cyber activity. This constitutes the work that is (or should be) undertaken by all individuals or organizations. It ranges from simple protection of individual personal equipment to complex security management architectures.
- **Exploitation:** Exploitation is covert activity conducted within an adversaries area of operations. This is generally invisible to the defender (unless compromised by the defender). Exploitation operations range from preparatory activity conducted to enable future activity to protracted information farming operations which are designed to generate intelligence over a protracted period of time.

- **Attack:** The overt phase when effect is brought to bear on a target. There are a wide range of exploits and strategies associated with this phase. It should be noted that a visible attack may well have been preceded by invisible exploitation operations.

A knowledge of where current operations lie within the cyber spectrum is critical to a clear understanding of the cyber environment. It is also helpful to view the actions of adversaries in this context in order to try to understand the adversarial plan and predict their likely future actions.

Traditional protective strategies were often based on the defence of boundaries and perimeters. Whether defended by technology or, in some cases, complete air gaps, boundary based defence was initially effective until attackers found ways to achieve a breach, whether by compromising vulnerable technology or bridging air gaps, as could be seen, for example, in the Stuxnet attack on the Iranian nuclear processing facility (Kerr *et al.* 2010). This boundary-based model is increasingly seen as flawed due to the enormous complexity and granularity of the cyber environment. Increasingly, defensive architectures are seen to be resilient matrices of multiple defensive components. It is no longer credible for organizations to assume that they are completely safe. The sensible security strategy now focuses on raising the bar to reduce the likelihood of a successful attack, but to assume that a proportion of attacks will be successful, but to have the mechanisms in place to identify and manage these events when they occur. Organizations must also ensure that operational architectures are sufficiently resilient to enable them to continue to operate whilst 'under fire'. This has resulted in a subtle but tangible shift from purely protective postures to proactive intelligence management within organizations.

In many cases, the compromise of technology is achieved indirectly. This often involves the compromise of people. A wide and often sophisticated range of social engineering attacks are employed in order to compromise technology using traditional human weaknesses, including greed, curiosity, insecurity and ignorance. The dependence of cyberspace on people also extends the scope of compromise from direct attacks on target systems, to indirect targeting of social, economic, commercial and financial architectures. The traditional 'high threat club' (those organizations who are known to represent high value targets to attackers) are no longer the only organizations with a requirement for active and dynamic information security infrastructures. Information security is now a critical aspect of corporate governance across the organizational spectrum.

## Dynamics of the Cyber Environment

If we assume that warfare is generally a strategic approach by which one or more parties seek to impose their will on another by force, then the cyber environment provides a range of opportunities for attackers and defenders alike. At an operational and tactical level, disruption or dislocation operations can be mounted against a range of kinetic and information based targets. Objectives can range from the destruction of targets to rendering them unusable to an adversary (often through information attacks on the integrity of particular assets), through intelligence gathering, deception and other information operations. At a strategic level, cyber operations provide opportunities to compromise national infrastructures and populations at a systemic level, through attacks on critical national infrastructure targets and services such as financial services, utilities (water, power, waste, etc), telecommunications and emergency response frameworks.

An important driver for the cyber environment is that it effectively becomes an asymmetric enabler. Cyber operations provide a viable attack vector for small nations or influence groups that enables them to directly engage even the largest

power bases (military or otherwise) worldwide. One of the effects of the advent of the cyber environment has been to remove much of what Clausewitz (1873) termed the friction of war. This is exacerbated by the fact that tempo changes are possible, where operations can move rapidly from slow, covert activity to high intensity attack activity with little physical impact.

History has shown that an ability to switch tempo in battle has enormous value in its ability to unhinge adversaries and to compromise their will and ability to fight. This is one of the characteristics that lies at the heart of the 'manoeuverist' doctrine that underpins much of the 20th century warfighting doctrine. Manoeuver warfare is a potentially complex doctrine which is built on simple principles which shape the chosen battlefield through knowledge, understanding and agility. The British Army describes the manoeuverist approach as follows:

*This is an indirect approach which emphasizes understanding and targeting the conceptual and moral components of an adversary's fighting power as well as attacking the physical component. Influencing perceptions and breaking or protecting cohesion and will are essential. The approach involves using and threatening to use force in combinations of violent and non-violent means. It concentrates on seizing the initiative and applying strength against weakness and vulnerability, while protecting the same on our own side. The contemporary Manoeuvrist Approach requires a certain attitude of mind, practical knowledge and a philosophy of command that promotes initiative (Ministry of Defence, 2010, Chapter 5).*

The cyber environment provides an additional dimension within which agility can be achieved, and initiative seized. It is, perhaps, instructive that the practical application of the manoeuverist approach is broken down into the following components:

- **Understanding the Situation:** Using information, intelligence and intuition coupled with a sound understanding of objectives and desired outcomes.

- **Influencing Perceptions:** Planning, gaining and maintaining influence, and the management of key stakeholders.

- **Seizing and Holding the Initiative:** Ensuring that we hold the ability to dictate the course of events, through competitive advantage, awareness and anticipation.

- **Breaking Cohesion and Will in Our Adversaries:** Preventing our adversaries from being able to co-ordinate actions effectively, and compromise their determination to persist.

- **Protecting Cohesion and Will in Ourselves and Our Allies:** Enabling our own freedom of action and ability to co-ordinate our resources, ensuring that we retain the will and coherence to operate.

- **Enhancing and Evolving the Approach through Innovation:** The approach is enhanced through simplicity, flexibility, tempo, momentum and simultaneity.

All of these components are areas where cyber operations can play a significant part both for the attacker and the defender. In military terms, cyber may be seen as a force multiplier, increasing the effect of existing operational capability. There is, however, another side, in that these principles and components can be applied to operations in the cyber environment and, if applied with flexibility, can provide structure to planning.

To return to the initial question — has cyber become the new battlespace? — whilst the role of the cyber environment as a fully-fledged warfighting domain is open to sustained debate, it is very clear that the cyber environment is one in which it is possible to conduct a range of targeted operations. It is also clear that these operations

may be conducted in isolation, or in conjunction with operations in the kinetic sphere (in any of the four principal warfighting domains.)

However we eventually decide to classify this area, we must ensure that we are able to operate within it, at least as effectively as our adversaries are able to. As such, it would be prudent to consider it to be a battlespace, and a high tempo battlespace in which our native situational awareness is limited. It is also a battlespace in which our ability to maintain an agile, proactive posture is critical to our ability to gain and maintain the initiative.

## Situational Awareness and the Information Infrastructure Battlespace

In this section, the authors will attempt to elaborate on the association between the battlespace and situational awareness. As outlined above, terms such as battlespace and attack have become common parlance when discussing the protection of information infrastructures from a wide range of cyber-based information operations, as has another term, situational awareness. What do we mean by situational awareness? Well, Endsley's (1995, p.36) definition "the perception of elements in the environment within a volume of time and space, the comprehension of their meaning, and the projection of their status in the near future", will serve as a useful introduction. However, what does that mean?

The study of situational awareness has its roots in military theory, and has the goal of understanding the state of a particular scope and using that understanding to make decisions about how to proceed and respond to events. There are different models and frameworks for situational awareness in the computer networks field, but there is general agreement that its core consists of three levels (Endsley, 1995):

1. **Perception:** Becoming aware of situational events;

2. **Comprehension:** Interpreting what is happening to form a situational understanding of the events;

3. **Projection (i.e., Prediction):** Using the understanding to inform what actions (if any) should be taken to control the network.

So in essence situational awareness is a process, consisting of (i) becoming conscious of the immediate environment, (ii) and understanding how temporal/spatial events (which you may or may not control) will impact on that environment. It is generally understood that inadequate situational awareness is an element of poor decision-making, especially in those situations that are composed of high information flow, with any disastrous consequences resulting from that poor decision-making being attributed to 'human error', e.g., fighting in a combat zone (MOD, 2010, chapter 5), piloting an airplane (John Boyd, see Angerman, 2004).

However, there are situations where having a good awareness of the current environment, and making the correct decision within a strict time frame is critical; air traffic controllers, network administrators for example. In these examples, monitoring systems providing multiple information sources and formats will assist the decision-making team, all of which will require the team to decipher, analyse and understand. In such time-critical situations, the situational awareness requirement will not remain stable. It could be argued that with an unforeseen event such as an air traffic incident, or malicious infrastructure activity, the successful response to those non-standard events would require a more detailed and informed situational awareness (Smith, 2013).

Unfortunately, cyberspace is characterized, amongst many things, by a lack of natural visibility and tangibility. Humans have sense-based defensive postures. Sight, smell, feel and sound underpin our innate defensive posture. The challenge of cyberspace is that none of these senses, the core of our sensory toolkits, are effective in the cyber environment without technology and tools. Network administrators are therefore depend upon these tools, and the way in which they have been developed and configured to provide them with necessary situational awareness in order to make sense of the network's behaviour.

However, it is not unreasonable to expect that such unforeseen events would cause increased cognitive workload, thereby impacting on the situational awareness and consequently the decision-making time. During this decision-making process, the perceived situational awareness being used during that process will be influenced by the cognitive effort needed to acquire and comprehend that situational awareness (Smith, 2013). The authors in trying to overcome this cognitive effort have proposed a novel way of making data perceptible (for more discussion, see Visualization: Making Data Perceptible).

It should be noted that while SA as a concept is well defined and understood, SA depends on cognitive processes, and unfortunately while the SA concept makes general references to cognitive processing, very little detail on what cognitive processes are involved, or indeed how they function is available (Banbury & Tremblay, 2004). However, it still remains an extremely useful metaphor for describing the perceived understand an individual has of their immediate environment, and in an information-rich, time-constrained environment, a clear understanding of the current state of the battlespace, i.e., situational awareness, becomes a battle-winning factor. In securing cyberspace, situational awareness represents a way of perceiving threat activity to an information infrastructure, such that network administrators can actively defend the network.

When discussing the manoeuverist approach above, we noted that in order to gain and maintain the initiative in a particular area of operations, the first step or component was to achieve an understanding of the area and activity within it. This clearly echoes Endsley's model noting a perception and comprehension of information in order to enable projection; actions to seize the initiative in a particular situation.

Noting that the manoeuverist perspective on situational awareness developed within a kinetic warfighting context (MoD, 2010, chapter 5), it looks in even more detail at information operations, intelligence collection and collation as part of the process to convert perception to comprehension and projection. This is directly relevant to the information space and implies a degree of planning and direction through the acquisition, analysis and dissemination of intelligence. In many contexts, analysis is intuitive and organic, especially in the high tempo information space, however, we must acknowledge its role as an active part of the practical process. It is this transition from information to intelligence which takes us from Endsley's Understanding Phase to the Projection Phase.

Another practical perspective comes from John Boyd. Whilst Endsley's model is useful for understanding the levels of situational awareness, an example from the kinetic sphere readily illustrates how it adds value in a practical context. If we take a brief step into kinetic military doctrine, and view the computer incident response process in the context of Boyd's OODA loop theory (see Angerman, 2004), we find a useful model to review the practical relevance of situational awareness in a combat situation.

John Boyd was commissioned by the US Department of Defense in 1976 to analyze why US pilots in Korea were so successful despite the fact that the opposing Chinese MiG15 aircraft were technically superior in many respects. His simple theory, which postulated that certain aspects of the US aircraft design enabled the pilots to react more quickly to the changing battle, has gained much traction since.

Boyd theorized that combat pilots made decisions using a cycle comprising four steps: observe, orient, decide, and act (OODA). In a contest between two opposing pilots the individual who could complete this cycle the quickest would have the advantage. Boyd suggested that the increased speed at which the US pilots could react and reorient themselves outweighed the technical superiority of the MiG15.

Refinements have since been made to Boyd's OODA model and it is particularly pertinent in the context of cyber security and the defence of information networks. The information network environment is characterized by high tempo and granularity, coupled with low visibilty and tangibility. Administrators are therefore dependent on complex and granular data feeds for data about what is happening, and must often further translate this view into language that can be understood by decision makers. The use of tools can simplify this complex data picture, but each analysis layer introduces margin for error and adds Clausewitzian friction (Clausewitz, 1873). Added to this are the practical limitations of our physical and intellectual physiology; it is practically impossible for most people to sit watching complex visual data feeds concurrently with other activity without quickly losing effectiveness.

We have discussed the role of cyber as a battlespace, and noted that one of the principal challenges associated with this area is that of maintaining situational awareness in an environment which is essentially intangible and invisible. In order to increase our visibility in this area, we need to identify indicators that may warn of attacks or inappropriate activity. The next chapter will discuss one such area that may support this visibility; network traffic analysis.

## NETWORK TRAFFIC VOLUMES

Cisco has reported that global mobile date traffic grew 70% in 2012, with "traffic volumes reaching 885 petabytes per month, up from 520 petabytes per month in 2011" (Cisco, 2013a). The report goes on to make the following prediction for 2017.

*Global mobile data traffic will increase 13-fold between 2012 and 2017. Mobile data traffic will grow at a compound annual growth rate (CAGR) of 66 percent from 2012 to 2017, reaching 11.2 exabytes per month by 2017 (Cisco, 2013a).*

While in a report on data centre IP traffic, Cisco (2013b) present the following estimates of global data centre traffic growth.

*Annual global data centre traffic will reach 7.7 zettabytes by the end of 2017. By 2017, global data centre IP traffic will reach 644 exabytes per month (up from 214 exabytes per month in 2012) (Cisco, 2013b).*

*Global data centre IP traffic will nearly triple over the next 5 years. Overall, data centre IP traffic will grow at a compound annual growth rate (CAGR) of 25 percent from 2012 to 2017 (Cisco, 2013b).*

These estimates are, of course, provided by an organization with a vested interest in seeing an increase in both mobile and data centre traffic volumes, but some corroboration of Cisco's estimates can be found in various reports by Gartner. For example, in their forecast for worldwide mobile data traffic and revenue Ekholm and Fabre (2011) suggest that global mobile data traffic will grow 26-fold between 2010 and 2015. Another Gartner report on the worldwide consumer broadband market estimates that "the number of consumer broadband connections will reach nearly 1.3 billion connections worldwide by 2015" (Elizalde *et al.* 2012). Ekholm *et al.* (2011) expect that "mobile broadband connections to grow five-fold, and to reach 588 million connections by 2015".

Naturally, estimates must be treated with caution, but even a conservative view shows data traffic volumes will double within the next five years. Even so, current network traffic volumes are already huge, with mobile data traffic at over

520 petabytes per month, while data centre IP traffic volumes run at 217 exabytes per month (Cisco, 2013a).

## IMPLICATIONS OF INCREASING DATA VOLUMES: FROM DATA TO INTELLIGENCE

The implications of increasing data volumes are significant. There is much work in the data mining industry to understand and harness the power of what has become known as Big Data. As technology becomes increasingly complex, with 5th, 6th and 7th generation systems being (largely) created by other systems, often generating large quantities of data, industry has both an opportunity and a challenge.

The challenge lies in the conversion of data to information, and ultimately to understanding (intelligence). This process, aligned with Endsley's perception, understanding and projection phases, enables us to understand the environment and, in manoeuverist terms, to do something about it. The challenge is not, however, a straightforward one. In the same way that data mining projects struggle to make sense of big data we must find ways of identifying what we can achieve from data and what is required to turn it into meaningful information and intelligence that enables us to take action. The challenge is so large that it becomes necessary to implement a planned procedure to manage this process, especially as this process is governed by the Intelligence Cycle (FBI, 2013).

### Visualization: Making Data Perceptible

One of the challenges faced when analyzing data is perceptualization, that is, making the data and its properties apprehensible. This thread runs through a number of components in the intelligence cycle. Visualization of data is the process by which intangible and invisible (or possibly merely incomprehensible) data is put in a form in which it can be apprehended and understood by those seeking to convert it to intelligence, or communicate it to those whose duty is to make the decisions required to hold the initiative. This process must be completed in a consistent and timely manner, if it is to produce intelligence that is reliable and useful.

When incidents occur in the computer information space, experience shows that speed and accuracy of initial response is a critical factor in the subsequent successful resolution of the situation. The OODA loop kicks in with operators observing the indicators, orienting themselves and their sensors to understand the problem, deciding on the action, and acting in a timely and decisive way. Traditional monitoring approaches often make this difficult by obfuscating the initial indication and the context and requiring an extensive orientation stage. Ineffectiveness of initial response is consistently seen to be one of the hardest things for people to get right in practice.

One approach that has been taken to presenting administrators with the information they need is the use of information visualization techniques for representing traffic data. A goal of visualization is to use representational techniques that allow the user to more easily interpret complex data than would be achievable by looking at the raw data or using text-based summaries. D'Amico (in McNeese, 2012) stated the design challenge this way:

*... visualization designers must focus on the specific role of the target user, and the stage of situational awareness the visualizations are intended to support: perception, comprehension, or projection.*

## Sonification for Network Monitoring

Much work has been done in applying information visualization techniques to network data for facilitating situational awareness (e.g., see Jajodia

*et al.* 2010) for a recent overview). However, a particularly striking feature of the three-level model is that the first two levels — perception and comprehension — correspond directly with Pierre Schaeffer's two basic modes of musical listening, ´ecouter (hearing, the auditory equivalent of perception) and entendre (literally 'understanding', the equivalent of comprehension). Schaeffer was writing within a musical arts context but Vickers (2012) demonstrated how these modes are applicable to sonification, the auditory equivalent of visualization.

Sonification is a branch of auditory display, a family of representational techniques in which non-speech audio is used to convey information. Here, data relations are mapped to features of an acoustic signal which is then used by the listener to interpret the data. Sonification has been used for many different types of data analysis (see Hermann, Hunt, and Neuhoff (2011) for a broad and recent treatment of the field) but one for which it seems particularly well suited is live monitoring, as would be required in situational awareness applications. The approach described in this chapter provides one way of addressing the challenges outlined above by enabling operators to monitor infrastructures concurrently with other tasks using additional senses. This increases the available bandwidth of operators without overloading individual cognitive functions, and provides a fast and elegant route to practical situational awareness using multiple senses and an increased range of cognitive ability.

Situational awareness requires intelligence to be provided in real time. A major challenge with live real-time network monitoring is that, with the exception of alarms for discrete events, the administrator needs to attend to the console screen to see what is happening. Spotting changing or emerging patterns in traffic flow would need long-term attention to be focused on the display. Therefore, sonification has been proposed as a means of providing situational awareness.

Monitoring tasks can be categorized as direct, peripheral, or serendipitous-peripheral (Vickers, 2011):

*In a direct monitoring task we are directly engaged with the system being monitored and our attention is focused on the system as we take note of its state. In a peripheral monitoring task, our primary focus is elsewhere, our attention being diverted to the monitored system either on our own volition at intervals by scanning the system… or through being interrupted by an exceptional event signalled by the system itself (Vickers, 2011, p. 455).*

A system to sonify network traffic thus allows us to monitor the network in a peripheral mode. In a peripheral monitoring task,

*Our primary focus is elsewhere, our attention being diverted to the monitored system either on our own volition at intervals by scanning the system …or through being interrupted by an exceptional event signalled by the system itself (Vickers, 2011, p. 455).*

Hence, the monitoring becomes a secondary task for the operator who can carry on with some other primary activity. Serendipitous-peripheral is like peripheral monitoring except that the information gained "is useful and appreciated but not strictly required or vital either to the task in hand or the overall goal" (Vickers, 2011, p. 456). Thus, a system to sonify network traffic may allow us to monitor the network in a peripheral mode, the monitoring becoming a secondary task for the operator who can carry on with some other primary activity. Network traffic is a prime candidate for sonification as it comprises series of temporally-related data which may be mapped naturally to sound, a temporal medium (Vickers, 2011).

Gilfix and Crouch's (2000) PEEP system is an early network sonification example but Ballora *et al.* (2010; 2011; 2012) developed the idea to address situational awareness. Using an auditory model of the network packet space they produced a "nuanced soundscape in which unexpected patterns can emerge for experienced listeners". Their approach used the five-level JDL fusion model which is concerned with integrating multiple data streams such that situational awareness is enhanced (see Blasch and Plano, 2002). However, Ballora *et al.* (2010) noted that the high data speeds and volumes associated with computer networks can lead to unmanageable cognitive loads. They concluded:

*The combination of the text-based format commonly used in cyber security systems coupled with the high false alert rates can lead to analysts being overwhelmed and unable to ferret out real intrusions and attacks from the deluge of information. The Level 5 fusion process indicates that the HCI interface should provide access to and human control at each level of the fusion process, but the question is how to do so without overwhelming the analyst with the details.*

## FUTURE RESEARCH DIRECTIONS: TOWARDS AN INTELLIGENT INFORMATION INFRASTRUCTURE

As outlined above, when considering computer networks, there is a general agreement over the core elements of situational awareness. Firstly, the human operator must become aware of events (i.e., they must be able to recognize what is relevant). Then, they must develop an understanding (i.e., they must be able to interpret and comprehend the relevance of those events). Lastly, they must use that understanding to develop appropriate actions to control the network (i.e., they must be to predict the implications of those actions). The question thus arises of what to present to an operator so that situational awareness may be achieved.

Unfortunately, that isn't the only issue. Any derived situational awareness of the current state of the network will require information about the network to be coupled, spatially and temporally (Cooke in McNeese, 2012). In addition, given that current network traffic volumes are huge and will continue to increase, any interpretation and comprehension that results from becoming aware will require that information to be aggregated and presented in an easy-to-understand way.

The predominant approach taken in previous network sonification efforts is to focus on the auditory representation of network traffic primitives, notably the number of bytes and packets crossing the network gateway in a given time period. This would allow for certain levels of analysis with the possibility of profiling traffic to identify certain types of network event.

However, a more fruitful avenue to explore is the identification and analysis of more holistic or emergent network and network traffic properties. In this section we will consider approaching the development of new techniques for situational awareness from two complementary angles; self organized criticality and affective computing (discussed below), which can be used together in a sonification framework. The combination of these two areas within a sonification system, it is suggested, will enable the development of an *intelligent information infrastructure* in which a network is able to monitor its own status and health and, using the real-time monitoring opportunities afforded by sonification, communicate its confidence or its anxieties about its state to a human operator. The components of such an intelligent information infrastructure are now discussed.

## The Self-Organized Criticality of a Network

Complex *natural* systems appear to exhibit an emergent property known as self-organized criticality (SOC), by which the system responds to critical events in order to restore equilibrium (Bak *et al.* 1987). Complex information structures also appear to manifest self-organized criticality (Yang, 2006; Crovella, 1997; Leland, 1993).

Modern networks demonstrate periods of very high activity alternating with periods of relative calm, a characteristic known as 'burstiness' (Leland, 1993). It was commonly thought that ethernet traffic conformed to Poisson or Markovian distribution profiles. This would mean that the traffic would possess a characteristic burst length which, when averaged over a long time scale, would be smooth (Crovella & Bestavros, 1997). However, it has been demonstrated that network traffic shows significant burstiness across a broad range of time scales. When traffic is bursty across different time scales it can be described using the statistical concept of self-similarity and it has been established that ethernet traffic exhibits such self-similarity (Crovella & Bestavros, 1997).

Yang *et al.* (2006) carried out a wavelet analysis of the burstiness of self-similar computer network traffic and showed that the avalanche volume, duration time, and the inter-event time of traffic flow fluctuations obey power law distributions. Bak *et al.* (1987) suggested that such power law distributions in complex systems are evidence of self-organized criticality. Self-organized criticality is a function of an external driving force and an internal relaxation process such that there exists a "separation of time scales" between them. An example that is often used to illustrate this is an earthquake. Stresses within the tectonic plates (the external driving force) take many years to develop, while the earthquake (the internal relaxation process) takes only seconds; so we see a separation of time scales between years and seconds.

Since the length of time required by the external driving force to initiate an internal relaxation process is non-determinable, then the threshold at which the internal relaxation process acts is also non-determinable. Consequently there can exist many differing states, each of which will be 'barely stable', a condition called metastability (Bak *et al.* 1987). Recall that complex systems (such as communication net- works) consist of many internal interactive components. Bak *et al.* (1987) hypothesized that when these complex systems are externally driven then the system's internal components will begin to form random networks. Jensen adds that as the external driver continues these networks will be modified by the "actions of the internal dynamics induced by the external drive" (Jensen, 1998). For the purposes of this chapter we will assume that the external driver of a communication network will be any traffic passing through a network and the internal dynamic is the response of the network to the traffic.

In a study of self-organized criticality in network traffic Guo *et al.* (2008) observed that "from the perspective of traffic engineering, understanding the network traffic pattern is essential" for the analysis of network survivability. However, self-organized criticality is not a discrete variable that can be identified and monitored directly. Instead, its presence is inferred through the analysis of a system's behaviour. Yang *et al.* (2006) measured time-dependent characteristics of a network (in their case, numbers of packets and bytes), after which they constructed a power spectrum. If the spectrum displayed a power law correlation they concluded self-organized criticality was present. We may observe the self-organized criticality, then, by measuring some time-dependent characteristics of the system and comparing changes in successive samples. It is suggested that a repeated series of large changes may well give an indication of network instability, and the possibility of some form of network 'reset'. In this situation, a reset would not mean the catastrophic failure of the network, but may mean the existence of a rapidly increasing level of service traffic restrictions.

## Affective Computing

In a physical battlespace one gains situational awareness through the perception and comprehension of events. One may start to feel a sense of unease or disquiet if a situation seems to be taking a turn for the worse. Given the inherent intangibility of system network events it is worth considering whether the network (or some com-

putational engine working inside it) could itself gather intelligence about events and draw its own conclusions about the relative benignity or malignancy of developing situations. Affective computing is the study of computational systems than can recognize or simulation human emotions and affective states. Therefore, it is theoretically possible to design a monitoring agent that would simulate affective states related to the current state of a network and communicate these to a human operator. This would, potentially, enable the operator to know when the network itself is starting to 'feel' uncomfortable.

Sonification, because of its temporal rather than spatial representational nature offers the scope for creating a real-time affective system that keeps human operators continually in touch with the state of the network. Winters and Wanderley (2013) showed how sonification can communicate affective states in the traditional arousal—valence space. Taking this concept further, Kirke & Miranda's (2013) *pulsed melodic affective processing* (PMAP) technique provides a mechanism for creating an affective sonification system in which the objects of interest being monitored constantly communicate their state using a sonification-based communications protocol. According to Kirke and Miranda PMAP "is a method for the processing of artificial emotions in affective computing." Because the communications protocol is, essentially, a language whose syntax maps to auditory events, the system becomes self sonifying. Effectively, one can choose to listen to any component within a PMAP'ed environment and understand that component's affective state.

## An Intelligent Information Infrastructure

In the above we outlined how an infrastructure could communicate risk or security concerns to its operators, with the operators then taking some ameliorating action. Now, we propose a way by which an infrastructure could use its awareness of its current context to adapt and change (for instance, by altering its 'risky' behaviour, or enhancing its security posture). This would extend the above to include an adaptive network using the methodology outlined in (Bentley, 2005), and (as discussed previously) an emergent property of complex systems known as self-organized criticality. As noted previously a system undergoing self-organized criticality will have many differing states, and at the transition point (from instability to stability) spatial self-similarity occurs (Bak *et al.* 1987). We hypothesize that this spatial self-similarity represents a fractal like geometry, with a 'fractal dimensionality'. Consequently, this fractal structure and dimensionality could drive an adaptive self-organized criticality regulatory network that would act as the infrastructure's operating system, controlling all aspects of the infrastructure, from observing, orientating, deciding, and acting.

The main characteristics of a self-organized critical system are power law fluctuations. We suggest that these power law fluctuations could be used to enable a system to monitor its own internal state (i.e., its current context). The pulsed melodic affective processing technique will communicate that current context (i.e., its affective state, which may consist of anomalies and discontinuities) to the human operator thereby potentially enhancing situation awareness and speed of response to critical incidents.

As well as providing for the adaptation of information infrastructures, additional outcomes could be the verification of the work by Kuehn (2012). Kuehn (2012), while investigating self-organized critical adaptive networks, concluded that information processing in complex systems exhibiting steady-state criticality could reach optimal noise values. If this is the case then self-organized criticality will be a better explanation of network behaviour than either Poisson or Markovian distribution profiles, and as such may result in more robust and resilient information infrastructures.

## CONCLUSION

In this chapter the authors have explored the notion of information infrastructures as a cyber battlespace. In looking at this battlespace, we have also considered the role of situational awareness, in particular how the application of a military approach and the use of situational awareness within that warfighting domain will help to maintain healthy networks. However, given that cyber domain is by its very nature inaccessible to any form of sensory perception (which is an essential aspect of situational awareness), then the predicted increasing levels of network traffic will adversely impact on the development of any situational awareness. In considering this required sensory perception, the authors reviewed current visualization approaches, and concluded that there is a need to consider other modalities for the sensory perception of network behaviour. The discussion then focused on the use of sonification for visualization, and the authors concluded that sonification for situational awareness would offer potential benefits to human operators trying to perceive, comprehend and make decision about the network's behaviour. Following on from this, the authors proposed an agenda for future research. This agenda involved the collaboration of a number of dissimilar activities, namely, sonification, self-organized criticality, network context, and affective computing, which the authors believe will yield benefits for the field of network situation awareness. The authors are currently working on developing a system that sonifies in real time an information infrastructure's self-organized criticality, which is then able to inform operators of both normal and abnormal network traffic and behaviour; details of which will be published later in the year.

# REFERENCES

Angerman, W. S. (2004). *Coming full circle with Boyd's OODA loop ideas: An analysis of innovation diffusion and evolution.* (Unpublished master's thesis). Airforce Institute of Technology, Wright-Patterson AFB, OH.

Bak, P., Tang, C., & Wiesenfeld, K. (1987). Self-organized criticality: An explanation of the 1/f noise. *Physical Review Letters, 59*(4), 381–384. doi:10.1103/PhysRevLett.59.381 PMID:10035754

Ballora, M., Giacobe, N. A., McNeese, M., & Hall, D. L. (2012). Information data fusion and computer network defense. In C. Onwubiko & T. Owens (Ed.), Situational Awareness in Computer Network Defense: Principles, Methods and Applications. IGI Global.

Ballora, M., Giacobe, N. A., & Hall, D. L. (2011). Songs of cyberspace: an update on sonifications of network traffic to support situational awareness. In Proceedings of SPIE Defense, Security, and Sensing. SPIE.

Ballora, M., Panulla, B., Gourley, M., & Hall, D. L. (2010). Preliminary steps in sonifying web log data. In E. Brazil (Ed.), *16th International Conference on Auditory Display* (pp. 83-87). Washington, DC: ICAD.

Banbury, S., & Tremblay, S. (2004). Preface. In S. Banbury, & S. Tremblay (Eds.), *A cognitive approach to situation awareness: Theory and application.* Aldershot, UK: Ashgate Publishing.

Bentley, P. J. (2005). Controlling robots with fractal gene regulatory networks. In L. De Castro, & F. von Zuben (Eds.), *Recent Developments in Biologically Inspired Computing* (pp. 320–339). London: Idea Group Publishing.

Blasch, E. P., & Plano, S. (2002). JDL level 5 fusion model: User refinement issues and applications in group tracking. *Proceedings of the Society for Photo-Instrumentation Engineers, 4729,* 270–279. doi:10.1117/12.477612

Cisco Global Cloud Index. (2013b). Forecast and Methodology, 2012-2017, October 2013, ID: FLGD 11289 10/13. Author.

Cisco Visual Networking Index. (2013a). Global Mobile Data Traffic Forecast Update, 2012-2017, February 2013, ID: FLGD 10855 02/13. Author.

Clausewitz, C. (1874). On War. London: Academic Press.

Crovella, M. E., & Bestavros, A. (1997). Self-similarity in world wide web traffic: Evidence and possible causes. *IEEE/ACM Transactions on Networking, 5*(6), 835–846. doi:10.1109/90.650143

Ekholm, J., De La Vergne, H. J., & Baghdassarian, S. (2011). *Gartner Forecast: Mobile Broadband Connections, Worldwide, 2009-2015.* Gartner.

Ekholm, J., & Fabre, S. (2011). *Gartner forecast: Mobile data traffic and revenue, worldwide, 2010-2015.* Gartner.

Elizalde, F., Ekholm, J., & Sabia, A. (2012). *Gartner Forecast: Consumer Broadband Market, Worldwide, 2009-2015.* Gartner.

Endsley, M. (1995). Toward a theory of situation awareness in dynamic systems. *Human Factors, 37*(1), 32–64. doi:10.1518/001872095779049543

FBI (2013). *The Intelligence Cycle.* Retrieved October 16, 2013, from http://www.fbi.gov/about-us/intelligence/intelligence-cycle

Gilfix, M., & Couch, A. L. (2000). Peep (the network auralizer): Monitoring your network with sound. In *Proceedings of 14th System Administration Conference (LISA 2000),* (pp. 109-117). New Orleans, LA: The USENIX Association.

Guo, C., Wang, L., Huang, L., & Zhao, L. (2008). Study on the internet behavior's activity oriented to network survivability. In *Proceedings of International Conference on Computational Intelligence and Security,* (vol. 1, pp. 432-435). IEEE.

Hermann, T., Hunt, A. D., & Neuhoff, J. (Eds.). (2011). *The sonification handbook.* Berlin: Logos Verlag.

Hyacinthe, B. (2009). *Cyber warriors at war, U.S. national security secrets and fears revealed.* XLibris Corp.

Jensen, H. J. (1998). *Self-organized criticality.* Cambridge, UK: Cambridge University Press. doi:10.1017/CBO9780511622717

Kerr, P., Rollins, J., & Theohary, C. (2010). *The stuxnet computer worm: Harbinger of an emerging warfare capability.* Congressional Research Service.

Kirke, A., & Miranda, E. (2013). Pulsed melodic processing — the Use of melodies in affective computations for increased processing transparency. In S. Holland, K. Wilkie, P. Mulholland, & A. Seago (Eds.), Music and human-computer interaction (pp. 171-188). Springer.

Krekel, B. (2009). *Capability of the People's Republic of China to conduct Cyber Warfare.* US-China Economic and Security Review Commission.

Kuehn, C. (2012). Time-scale and noise optimality in self-organized critical adaptive networks. *Physical Review E: Statistical, Nonlinear, and Soft Matter Physics,* (85), 2.

Leland, W. E., Taqqu, M. S., Willinger, W., & Wilson, D. V. (1993). On the self-similar nature of Ethernet traffic. *SIGCOMM Comput. Commun. Rev.,* 23(4), 183–193. doi:10.1145/167954.166255

Libicki, M. (2012). Cyberspace is not a warfighting domain. *A Journal of Law and Policy for the Information Society,* 8 (2), 325-340.

McNeese, M. (2012). Perspectives on the role of cognition in cyber security. In *Proceedings of the Human Factors and Ergonomics Society 56th Annual Meeting, 2012* (pp. 268-271). Academic Press.

Ministry of Defence (MoD). (2010). *Army doctrine publication – Operations. UK Ministry of Defence, 2010.* Retrieved February 5, 2014, from https://www.gov.uk/government/uploads/system/uploads/attachment_data/file/33695/ADPOperationsDec10.pdf

Rosenzweig, P. (2013). *Cyber Warfare (The changing face of war).* Praeger.

Smith, K. T. (2013). Building a human capability decision engine. *Human Factors,* 2013, 395–402.

Vickers, P. (2011). Sonification for process monitoring. In T. Hermann, A. D. Hunt, & J. Neuhoff (Eds.), *The Sonification Handbook* (pp. 455–492). Berlin: Logos Verlag.

Vickers, P. (2012). Ways of listening and modes of being: Electroacoustic auditory display. *Journal of Sonic Studies,* 2 (1). Retrieved February 5, 2014, from http://journal.sonicstudies.org/vol02/nr01/a04

Winters, R. M., & Wanderley, M. M. (2013). Sonification of emotion: Strategies for continuous display of arousal and valence. In G. Luck, & O. Brabant (Eds.), *Proceedings of the 3rd International Conference on Music and Emotion (ICME3).* ICME3.

Yang, C.-X., Jiang, S.-M., Zhou, T., Wang, B.-H., & Zhou, P.-L. (2006). Self-organized criticality of computer network traffic. In *Communications, Circuits and Systems Proceedings,* (vol. 3, pp. 1740-1743). IEEE.

## KEY TERMS AND DEFINITIONS

**Battlespace:** A military strategy consisting of the integration and combination of the separate elements of nation's armed forces into a unified military theatre of operations.

**Current Context:** A description of events that make up the environment within which something takes place.

**Intelligent Information Infrastructure:** A network able to communicate its current context (risk or security concerns) to its operators, with the operators then taking some ameliorating action.

**PMAP:** Pulsed melodic affective processing. A technique for using affective computing principles to allow a system to sonify itself and communicate information about its state or health to a human listener.

**Self-Organized Criticality:** A property of dynamic systems involving power laws in which macroscopic behaviours are time and scale invariant.

**Situational Awareness:** Perceiving elements in a particular environment in order to understand what is happening and be able to take appropriate actions in response.

**Sonification:** The use of non-speech audio to communicate data and information.

**Visualization:** The mapping of data to visual representations to allow inferences to be drawn about the data.

# Chapter 22
# Can Total Quality Management Exist in Cyber Security:
## Is It Present? Are We Safe?

**Mahesh S. Raisinghani**
*Texas Woman's University, USA*

## ABSTRACT

*This chapter examines the threats in cyber security. It identifies the risk of cyber attacks and argues the inability to defend against those threats in a cyber security program. The introduction provides a brief history of cyber security and how the information highway arrived at this point in cyber security. The first analysis examines the threats in cyber security in personal, private, and government computer systems. The second analysis examines the approaches to attacking those systems. The third analysis examines threats against private companies and government agencies. The final analysis examines major threats to cyber security.*

## INTRODUCTION

During the early years of the information highway, individual users were the major prey for viruses and Trojan attacks. Today, the favorite targets of interest are no longer personal computer users anymore but large organizations and even government agencies. The ease of access to the internet has increased the popularity and vulnerability of internet users. Increasingly skillful users are preying on unskillful users for personal and monetary gain. As personal and government agencies depend more and more on technology to successfully manage day to day activities, they are becoming

more vulnerable to cyber threats and attacks. The types of threats can range from personal attacks from hackers, major environmental disasters, organized crime groups, foreign countries, and/or cyber terrorism groups.

With the increase in global terrorism in global markets, public agencies are becoming increasingly more vulnerable to cyber threats and attacks than any other time in history. The majority of these agencies have experienced some kind of virus, Trojan, or worm affecting the agency computer infrastructure. These events are burdensome and sometimes tragic to the infrastructure of the agency. When developing a cyber program in

DOI: 10.4018/978-1-4666-6324-4.ch022

any organization, one of the major tasks are to identify unknown threats in cyberspace. These agencies must take specific practical measures to prevent these types of risk from affecting the agency information sensitive and Personal Identifiable Information (PII). On October 3rd, 2011, President Obama declared October as "National Cyber security Awareness Month". This proclamation recognized the importance of the threat of cyber security and it is a reminder to us to remain vigilant in our abilities to fight cyber security with events and training to protect our personal and public information in cyberspace.

## TOTAL QUALITY MANAGEMENT

Total Quality Management is an amalgamation of the philosophies of mainly 3 proponents namely W.Edwards Deming, Joseph Juran and Kaoru Ishikawa. The core philosophy of TQM believes that quality implementation was a process that involved all aspect of the organization, TQM also believed that implementing quality from the onset was cheaper than the alternative, believed that if employees wanted to give their best efforts and would do so if they were given the tools, that both senior management and rank and file employees needed to be involved in the quality implementation process.

Total Quality Management came into prominence in the 1980s as that era's term for the description of quality management programs and has become something of a social movement (Hackman & Wageman, 1995), and is currently prevalent in Information Technology, Education, Healthcare and Manufacturing Industries because these organizations realize the need for high quality production in order to compete favorable in their fields, Construction had yet to come to this realization and definitely need to if innovation and development are to be encouraged (Haupt & Whiteman, 2004) .

## WHAT IS CYBER SECURITY?

Cyber Security is defined as the measures taken to protect a computer or computer system (as on the Internet) against unauthorized access or attacks (Webster Dictionary).

## A Brief History of Cyber Security

We as humans have always wanted to process information quickly from merchants in a Chinese market in 1000 B.C. to economist today. The Chinese developed a way to account for large amounts of livestock at the local market during cramped spaces and time. The vendors needed quick and accurate tools to account for the livestock. "This led to the invention of the Abacus, the device many believe was the mother of the digital computer as we know it today, between 1000 B.C. and 500 B.C." (Kizza, 2003, p.2) During the 1800s and early 1900s numerous advancements were made in the design of the computer system. From early days of the Chinese to today, we have witness a rapid emergence of technology and a huge growth in computer systems. During the 1940s, 50s, and 60s companies such as IBM, Honeywell, and Control Data Corporation (CDC) were developing large mainframe computers to process large bits of information. In the sixties the development of the minicomputer, begin the age of the personal computer. The later part of sixties led to the development of large computers sharing more and more information. Later with the development of smaller computers engineers began developing less expensive and smaller computers designed for the individual users. The computers were still fairly expensive for the average household therefore only a select few could afford these computers. At the time companies that build computers did not begin to focus on individual use. It was not until the early seventies that the microprocessor was born. "A microprocessor is an integrated circuit with many transistors on a single board. Before the birth of the microprocessor, computer technology had developed to a point that vacuum tubes and diodes were no longer used." (Kizza, 2003, p.6)

In the 1970s Intel developed the 8008 microprocessor which doubled the improvement of the proceeding speed from 4004 to 8008 from four-bit speed to eight-bit speed. For the first time, a microprocessor could handle both uppercase and lowercase letters, all 10 numerals, punctuation marks, and a host of other symbols (http://www. computerhistory.org/timeline/?year=1972).

Up until this point in history most computers were large and very expensive and their major role was to store and process large amounts of data for large organizations. The 8008 used 3,300 transistors and was the first microprocessor to use a compiler, a system program that interprets user inputs into machine code and machine code to system outputs understandable by the user (Kizza, 2003, p. 6). This revolutionized the computer world with the rate of speed and caused several new companies to manufacture the new minicomputers.

## The Development of Computer Software

With the development of Apple Corporation and their micro computers "Apple I and Apple II" separated the monopoly of large companies and software. Normally the large corporations that employed the computers also standardized the software. This also developed a need for individual computer operating system (OS). In 1976 Gary Kildall developed CP/M, an operating system for personal computers. Widely adopted, CP/M made it possible for one version of a program to run on a variety of computers built around eight-bit microprocessors (http://www.computerhistory. org/timeline/?category=sl). This was the first operating system which led to IBM soliciting Gary Kildall to develop the computer on the Intel 8088 microprocessor. Gary Kildall could not be reached at the time and IBM contacted a young programmer by the name of Bill Gates who had developed the disk operating system (DOS). This led to a partnership with IBM which started the legacy of the Microsoft Corporation. In 1981, the Microsoft Disk Operating System (MS-DOS), the basic software for the newly released IBM PC, established a long partnership between IBM and Microsoft, which Bill Gates and Paul Allen had founded only six years earlier http://www. computerhistory.org/timeline/?category=sl).

## A LOOK AT THREATS IN CYBER SECURITY

### The Threats to Cyber Security

There are over 30 different types of threats that range from individual hackers, natural disasters, foreign government agencies, viruses that can destroy memory, large "worms" that can be exploded in your system, and/or major terrorist attacks that can attack electrical grids and cause devastating system failures. The majority of us are use to worms, viruses, and Trojans that can attack our computer systems. The list below is a list of less known threats that are becoming very dangerous threats to cyber system:

1.  **Bot:** The widely used technique is the use of CAPTCHA, was designed to distinguish between a human user and a less-sophisticated bot by means of a character recognition task. According to a report compiled by Panda Labs, in 2Q 2008, 10 million bot computers were used to distribute spam and malware across the Internet each day http://www.darkreading.com/document. asp?doc_id=161524.

2.  **Adware:** Adware is a form of software design to display legitimate advertisements in your browser in the form of banners and pop ups. A total of 28940 different malicious and potentially unwanted programs were detected on users' computers in August. That is an increase of more than 8,000 on July's

figures and points to a significant increase in the number of in-the-wild threats. http://www.kaspersky.com/news?id=207575678.

3. **Bluesnarfing:** Is a form of theft of personal data from a Bluetooth device such as cell phones or laptops.

4. **Bluejacking:** Is a form of Bluetooth software used to send unwanted or anonymous messages to your Bluetooth device (i.e. cell phones, tablets, and/or Laptops). Bluejacking is not as harmful as Bluesnarfing.

5. **Denial of Service Attack (DoS):** Is a form of computer overload to the company website. The can be harmless until the company starts to lose money from customers who can not visit their website to purchase products.

6. **Mousetrapping:** Is a form of hacking that stops the users from leaving a website. Normally this just a ploy to keep you on the website but can become very time consuming and potentially a dangerous threat to cyber security.

7. **Pharming:** Hackers use pharming to direct you from private legitimate sites to fake lookalike websites in order to steal your personal information.

8. **Phishing:** Is more popular and normally comes in a form of sending emails from reputable company to you in order to retrieve personal identifiable information.

## The Approaches to Attacking Cyber Security

The question to users is "How" and "Why" are our computers being attacked by outsiders. There are three forms or approaches to attacking computers:

1. **Inadvertent disclosure:** Recognize as one of the largest means of internal computer attack issues in the cyber community. Normal users expose their information inadvertently by visiting social media sites such as peer-to-peer sites, lost or stolen computer equipment.

2. **Penetration:** Is an attempt to bypass the security controls of a system or organization for the purpose of gaining access to the computer system by attack on a subject and target.

3. **Subversion:** Subversion has become over pass history as the best means by attackers. Subversion can be summed up in three categories: Insertion of trap doors, Trojan horses and exercising of them, retrieval unauthorized information. Throughout the life cycle of the system insertion can occur.

## A LOOK AT THREATS TO PRIVATE COMPANIES

With the staggering cost of implementing a proper cyber program most major companies are not placing the cyber program as their priority. The Security Exchange commission (SEC) most recently sent out letters to six major companies to report any breaches in their computer systems in the company quarterly finance report. The idea of the SEC is to report the findings for the investors to make their own decision on buying stocks in the company. Cyber-attacks on U.S. computer networks rose 17-fold from 2009 to 2011, according to data cited by General Keith Alexander, head of the National Security Agency and U.S. Cyber Command (Sandler, 2012). In a recent research by Ponemon Institute report the cost of data breaches in overall organizational cost has continue to rise over the past five years as illustrated in figure 1.

For the individual users the threat are increasing access to steal passwords and banking information. New users are most vulnerable when they first purchased their computer and connect to the internet. Due to improper installation of most Anti-viruses software most users unknowingly give hackers opportunity to attack their computers. The next generation of information highway will rely heavily on information in cyberspace. So how serious is the problem with cyber security in the

*Figure 1. Cost to organizations of data breaches*

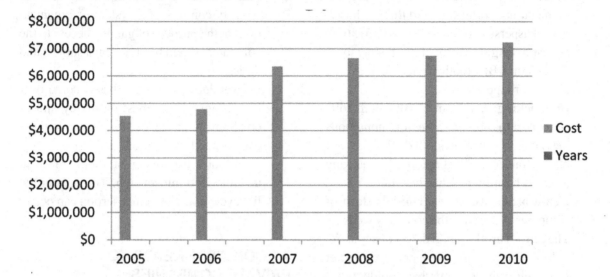

**Source: Ponemon Institute L.L.C., U.S. Cost of a Data Breach, sponsored by Symantec Corp.**

United States and how do we know what state of emergency we need are in. Since computers are a major part of life, it is very important to protect ourselves from attacks.

Most energy producing companies have increased their programs under the programs mandated by the Federal Energy Regulatory Commission and administered by the National Electric Reliability Commission (NERC) (http://www.pbs.org/newshour/rundown/2012/08/are-american-companies-ignoring-significant-cyber-threats-joel-brenner-answers-your-questions.html).

Most experts predict U.S. companies will become the best targets for cyber attacks. Most companies are rushing to protect their IT infrastructure after September 11 and numerous reports of large companies being attacked in the news. In the past companies ranked IT security low on the priority of company cost. Now executives are prioritizing company IT security and waging a war on cyber crimes. In the past most companies planned for natural disasters but today cyber attacks can cause just as much damage. The effects

of a cyber attack can crash complete networks and breach secret company information. Due to cyber attacks, companies have been forced to change the IT security program and rethink the security of the IT intrusion systems. Executives now have to perform risk analysis of the company IT system for cyber attacks from hackers. With increased profits in Personal Identifiable Information (PII) from organized crime and terrorist groups, more and more members are recruiting these hackers to gather and/or steal company information.

## A LOOK AT THREATS TO A GOVERNMENT AGENCY

In the summer of 2005 the Government Accountability Agency (GAO) reported on the Department of Veteran Affairs. The GAO recognized numerous weaknesses in the department's information security policy. The system practices were outdated and showed alarming control weaknesses which put the department operations in jeopardy. These

*Figure 2. Government Accountability Agency's report on information security Weaknesses*
*Source: GAO-06-866T report, Attachment 2. Chronology of Information Security Weaknesses identified by GAO*

| Year | GAO report | VA location or agency | Information security control areas | | | | | |
|---|---|---|---|---|---|---|---|---|
| | | | Access control | Physical security | Segregation of duties | Change control | Service continuity | Security program |
| 1998 | GAO/AIMD-98-175 | Austin | ● | ● | ● | ● | ● | ● |
| | | Dallas | ● | ● | | | ● | ● |
| | | Albuquerque | ● | ● | ● | | ● | ● |
| | | Hines | ● | ▓ | ▓ | ▓ | ▓ | ● |
| | | Philadelphia | ● | ▓ | ▓ | ▓ | ▓ | ● |
| 1999 | GAO/AIMD-99-161 | Austin | ● | | | ● | | ● |
| 2000 | GAO/AIMD-00-232 | Maryland | ● | ● | ● | ● | ● | ● |
| | | New Mexico | ● | ● | ● | ● | ● | ● |
| | | North Texas/Dallas | ● | ● | ● | | ● | ● |
| 2000 | GAO/AIMD-00-5 | VA | ● | | ● | | | ● |
| 2002 | GAO-02-703 | VA | ▓ | ▓ | ▓ | ▓ | ▓ | ● |
| 2005 | GAO-05-552 | VA | ● | ▓ | ● | ● | ● | ● |

● Weakness found in this area

▓ Control area not included in scope of audit

Source: GAO reports.

weaknesses existed primarily because agencies had not yet fully implemented strong information security programs, as required by the Federal Information Security Management Act (FISMA) (GAO-06-866T report). Figure 2 illustrates the key findings in the GAO report.

This type of effect is called a "Breach", and the breach can be from the Internet or storage drives placed in the system by unknown users. The findings from the GAO report led to the conclusion that the security of the VA personal information could be lost or even stolen easily by online hackers/crackers. Also included in the report was that important defense operations could be disrupted by loss of this vital information. Most government agencies create comprehensive computer networks to defend against outside threats. These networks are governed by several authorities one notable is the IEEE (Institute of Electrical and Electronics Engineers). The notion is to develop a standard across agencies to provide protection from outside sources.

The Department of Defense internet is operated by the Department of Information Security Agency (DISA). Today, information is virtual, on demand, and global. Products of the Internet and Web 2.0 have made possible worldwide connections and sharing more convenient. Information traditionally used or generated in either the strategic or operational environment are also used and generated in other environments. The effect of these technologies has empowered users throughout the enterprise to work and share information. This means that the capabilities and services we provide have no known boundaries (http://www.disa.mil/About/Our-Work).

## MAJOR THREATS TO CYBER SECURITY

The major threats to cyber security that continue to cause the private and government sector problems and their root causes are as follows:

1. **Denial of Access/Service:** Due to the ease of implementation and lucrative ways to launch attacks on systems, hackers prefer this method first to attack your systems.

2. **Theft of Important or Personal Identifiable Information (PII):** Due to the lucrative profits in the black markets for personal information PII will continue to be one of the major reasons for criminal hackers.

3. **Manipulation and Destruction of Networks to Gain Access to Sensitive Information:** Due to the major payoff of government secrets foreign countries will continue to attempt to hack into the United States government systems to obtain this information for military gains. Figure 3 illustrates the cost of weighted cyber attacks can put a large dent in any company revenues.

## Implications for Theory and Practice

Shammas-Toma et al., (1998) list a 6 step approach concerned with the process of implementing TQM, the features listed form the body of the conclusion of this study. A conscientious application of these steps should reorganize the construction company for TQM and help bridge the gap in the perspectives of quality between the customer and the construction company. The steps towards a successful implementation are as follows:

1. **Customer/Supplier Relationships:** At each stage in the delivery process the customers and suppliers need to state what their requirements are and they must also help ensure that the requirements are met at each stage and not left over.

2. **Prevention Rather than Detection:** Issues in construction should be forecasted and planned for in advance rather than waiting for them to manifest and then resolving them, following this format will encourage construction companies to develop a more proactive approach toward construction and develop innovations that will address forecasted problems at inception.

3. **Leadership:** The top level management needs to commit to the ideals of TQM and understand that the long term future of the company will be more secure with the benefits that TQM will bring to the company.

4. **Change in Organizational Culture:** The typical work process and attitudes should change in line with the TQM philosophy.

5. **Emphasis on Teamwork:** Problem solving requires cross hierarchical interaction and communication, this should be encouraged.

6. **Use of Statistical Tools:** To adequately measure the effect of a change to TQM has

*Figure 3. Average annualized cybercrime cost weighted by attack frequency*
*Source: Ponemon Institute L.L.C., Second Annual Cost of Cyber Crime Study*

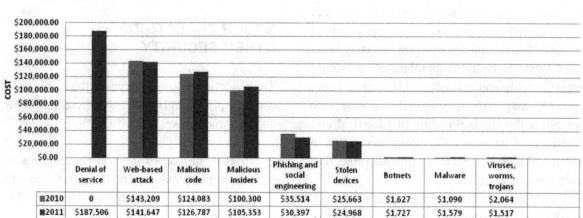

| | Denial of service | Web-based attack | Malicious code | Malicious insiders | Phishing and social engineering | Stolen devices | Botnets | Malware | Viruses, worms, trojans | |
|---|---|---|---|---|---|---|---|---|---|---|
| ■2010 | 0 | $143,209 | $124,083 | $100,300 | $35,514 | $25,663 | $1,627 | $1,090 | $2,064 | |
| ■2011 | $187,506 | $141,647 | $126,787 | $105,353 | $30,397 | $24,968 | $1,727 | $1,579 | $1,517 | |

on the company Statistical tools should be used to measure the performance before and after the change and also to show where improvement in the process is needed.

Another model that an organization can look towards is W. E. Deming's 14 points for management illustrated in Table 1 (Foster, 2007, p. 38). His concept of poor quality stemmed from his belief that poor quality resulted from poor management. The strongest point that this chart makes is creating consistency of purpose within an organization. The goals and focus of cyber security has changed so many times due to the new technology developments in the field such as cloud computing, mobile media, social media, and so forth, that many employees feel lost and do not understand their role in the company. A recommendation for an organization would be to create a strong and clear sense of purpose and company goal for all to understand their role in the company and how the work they do affects our customers and their satisfaction.

A few other key takeaways from Deming that would create a strong impact on customer service quality would be to constantly improve the system, improve leadership, breakdown the barriers between departments and institute education and self-improvement. These items would help employees feel valued, and give them the tools to be more effective in their roles to helping provide an excellent customer experience.

Another model that an organization could consider could be Deming's Deadly diseases illustrated in Table 2. These are behaviors that W.E. Deming described that would keep the competitiveness of a company from achieving top quality. While not all of these "deadly diseases" apply to an organization, a few certainly do have harrowing qualities that need to be examined. The lack of constancy of purpose is echoed here, signaling that this is a huge issues that companies face. Emphasis on short-term profits and running a company on visible figures are items that the company is certainly guilty of – evidence seen in

*Table 1: Deming's 14 points*

| |
|---|
| 1. Create constancy of purpose. |
| 2. Adopt a new philosophy. |
| 3. Cease mas inspection. |
| 4. End awarding business on the basis of price tag. |
| 5. Constantly improve the system. |
| 6. Institute training on the job. |
| 7. Improve leadership. |
| 8. Drive out fear. |
| 9. Break down barriers between departments. |
| 10. Eliminate slogans. |
| 11. 1. Eliminate work standards. |
| 12. Remove barriers to pride. |
| 13. Institute education and self-improvement. |
| 14. Put everybody to work. |

Source: Adapted from W.E. Deming, Out of Crisis (Boston: MIT/CAES, 1986), pp. 18-96.

*Table 2. Deming's deadly diseases*

| |
|---|
| 1. Lack of constancy of purpose. |
| 2. Emphasis on short-term profits. |
| 3. Evaluation of performance, merit rating, or annual review. |
| 4. Mobility of management. |
| 5. Running a company on visible figures alone. |
| 6. Excessive medical costs for employee health care. |
| 7. Excessive costs of warrantees. |

Source: Adapted from W. E. Deming, *Out of the Crisis* (Boston: MIT/CAES, 1986), pp. 97-148

their past performance. The recommendation here would be to again, clearly define company goals and purpose and then continually improve each process internally so that our customer satisfaction externally improves.

A positive change in customer service is a process that takes time and strong leadership as well as the input and work from all levels of the company staff. With process improvement and training customer service satisfaction on the part of buyers and sellers will improve. The company needs to proactive in its dealings and communications with customers and should take each and every feedback and customer behavior as a study to be conducted and see what lessons can be learned from every situation and in turn, apply those lessons learned.

## CONCLUSION

Today more and more arrests for cyber-crimes are being conducted than any other time in history. The question is do we have the right protection against threats in cyberspace. The government and the public sector must work together to identify vulnerabilities to protect vital information. This information affects our economy and military defense systems. We are faced with a problem of who should take the lead in developing the protection of the internet. One of the major issues between private and public sector is "Who protects the information or who owns the information?" The United States must identify the risks to the nation infrastructure and what targets our enemy might take. The major threat to the American system is the crimes against innocent Americans and espionage against the Unites States government. The first defense against threats is an updated Antivirus protection software and/or firewall protection software. The criminal act against innocent civilians has cost millions of dollars and is projected to cost even more. As you can see in the above charts the cost in crime is continuing to clam. But the most important risk to the United States is the risk of espionage which has far more greater consequences of the cost of lives. Because foreign countries and terrorist groups are using this information and tactics aimed at securing military information (i.e. missile data, UAV feeds, and/or aircraft blueprints) the information can cause military conflicts. The U.S. is spearheading the fight against cyber warfare and terrorism in cyberspace. Our attempt to continue to patch our systems is only creating more holes. It's just a matter of time until we cannot protect any vital information and a major cyber attack against our nation.

## ACKNOWLEDGMENT

The author would like to acknowledge Scottie L. Jarrett's (University of Maryland University College) contribution to the research and composition of this chapter.

## REFERENCES

Computer History Museum. (2013). *Timeline of Computer History*. Retrieved on March 10, 2013 from http://www.computerhistory.org/timeline/?year=1972

Defense Information Systems Agency. (2013). *Our Work/DISA 101*. Retrieved on March 10, 2013 from http://www.disa.mil/About/Our-Work

Dillon, G. (2001). *Information Security Management: Global Challenges in the New Millennium*. Idea Group Publishing.

Foster, S. T. (2010). *Managing quality: Integrating the supply chain*. Upper Saddle River, NJ: Prentice Hall.

Geers, K. (2011). *Strategic Cyber Security*. Tallinn, Estonia: CCD COE Publication.

Ghosh, S., Malek-Zavarei, M., & Stohr, E. A. (Eds.). (2004). *Guarding Your Business: A Management Approach to Security*. Kluwer Academic/Plenum. doi:10.1007/b105306

Hackman, J. R., & Wageman, R. (1995). Total quality management: Empirical, conceptual, and practical issues. *Administrative Science Quarterly*, *40*(2), 309–342. doi:10.2307/2393640

Haupt, T. C., & Whiteman, D. E. (2004). Inhibiting factors of implementing total quality management on construction sites. *The TQM Magazine*, *16*(3), 166–173. doi:10.1108/09544780410532891

Hines, A. (2002). *Planning for Survivable Networks: Ensuring Business Continuity*. Wiley Publishing.

Kasbersky Lab. (2008). *Monthly Malware Statistics for August 2008*. Retrieved on March 15, 2013 from http://www.kaspersky.com/news?id=207575678

Kizza, J. (2003). *Ethical and Social Issues in the Information Age*. Springer-Verlag.

Merriam-Webster Dictionary. (2013). *Definition of cybersecurity*. Retrieved on March 10, 2013 from http://www.merriam-webster.com/dictionary/cybersecurity

PBS News Hours. (2012). *Are American companies ignoring significant cyber threats?*. Retrieved on March 15, 2013 from http://www.pbs.org/newshour/rundown/2012/08/are-american-companies-ignoring-significant cyber-threats-joel-brenner-answers-your-questions.html

PMI. (2008). *A guide to the Project Management Body of Knowledge* (4th ed.). Newtown Square.

Sandler, L. (2012). SEC Guidance on Cyber-Disclosure Becomes Rule for Google. *Bloomberg Businessweek*. Retrieved online from http://www.businessweek.com/news/2012-08-29/sec-guidance-on-cyber-disclosure-becomes-rule-for-google

*Security Dark Reading*. (2013). Retrieved on March 10, 2013 from http://www.darkreading.com/document.asp?doc_id=161524

Shammas-Toma, M., Seymour, D., & Clark, L. (1998). Obstacles to implementing total quality management in the UK construction industry. *Construction Management and Economics*, *16*, 177–192. doi:10.1080/014461998372475

Tipton, H. F., & Krause, M. (2005). *Information Security Management Handbook*. Taylor & Francis e-Library.

## KEY TERMS AND DEFINITIONS

**Antivirus Protection Software:** An application software deployed at multiple points in an IT architecture. It is designed to detect and potentially eliminate virus code before damage is done, and repair or quarantine files that have already been infected.

**Denial-of-Service (DoS) Attack:** An assault on a service from a single source that floods it with so many requests that it becomes overwhelmed and is either stopped completely or operates at a significantly reduced rate.

**Information Security Policy:** Ensures that only authorized users (confidentiality) have access to accurate and complete information (integrity) when required (availability).

**Phishing:** This is a type of electronic mail attack that attempts to convince the user that the originator is genuine, but with the intention of obtaining information for use in social engineering.

**Risk Assessment:** A process used to identify and evaluate risk and potential effects. It includes assessing the critical functions necessary for an organization to continue business operations, defining the controls in place to reduce organization exposure and calculate the cost of such controls.

**Security Metrics:** A standard of measurement used in management of security-related activities.

**Wi-Fi Protected Access 2 (WPA2):** This replacement security method for WPA for wireless networks that provides stronger data protection and network access control. It provides enterprise and consumer Wi-Fi users with a high level of assurance that only authorized users can access their wireless networks. Based on the ratified IEEE 802.11i standard, WPA2 provides government-grade security by implementing the National Institute of Standarss and technology (NIST) FIPS 140-2 compliant advanced encryption standard (AES) encryption algorithm and 802.1X-based authentication.

# Section 3
# Legal Aspects and ICT Law

# Chapter 23
# The Gatekeepers of Cyberspace:
## Surveillance, Control, and Internet Regulation in Brazil

**Elisianne Campos de Melo Soares**

*Media and Journalism Investigation Centre, Portugal & Brazilian Association of Cyberculture Researchers, Brazil*

## ABSTRACT

*Cyberspace, like the territories grounded in the physical world, is an environment subject to border control and surveillance for various purposes: governmental, economic, security, among others. As in the physical sphere, governance can serve to enforce rules to avoid abuses and to allow users and institutions to build effective relationships, transparent and harmonious. The purpose of this chapter is to discuss the Civil Rights Framework for the Internet in Brazil ("Marco Civil da Internet"), a project created in 2009 that aims to establish rights and obligations for the operation of the network in this Latin American nation. Before that, however, it is critical to address the issue of control and surveillance on the Internet, revealing their motivations, goals, and work tools.*

## INTRODUCTION

The rapid development of digital technologies has made life in the modern age easier than ever before while allowing people to overcome the geographic barriers, hitherto impossible to surmount. The types of communication made possible by the Internet have brought individuals from the most distant corners of the planet in contact with one another and greatly reduced the costs of goods and services worldwide, as well as facilitating interactivity and accelerating economic, political and social progress.

These accessible, cheaper, and highly efficient methods of communication, however, do not only

herald improvements. With the popularization of digital communication, cybercrimes and surveillance activities have also found new ways of acting more effectively. Whether undertaken by governments or applied by private organizations, surveillance is being used to develop a more subtle form of control. In the context of the so-called "free culture", which has emerged with the inception of the Internet and the growing use of Information Technology (IT) in society, laws regulating intellectual property, for example, are confronted with the need to adapt to changes imposed by the new methods of production, broadcasting and circulation of creative information, brought about by these new technologies.

DOI: 10.4018/978-1-4666-6324-4.ch023

Implementation of cyberspace regulations which is essential for the proper functioning of the web and exercising of the freedom of expression in this new sphere of communication are the fundamental questions related to control and surveillance. Regulation plays a crucial role in enforcing and monitoring limits on the activities developed by companies providing Internet access, preventing indiscriminate use of network users' data for commercial purposes, as well as combatting practices such as traffic shaping. However, the difference between safe navigation and controlled and monitored Internet traffic is very delicate. It is necessary to create regulatory models that respect privacy and allow free navigation for the user, without barriers to full use of digital means with all the benefits they may provide.

The objective of our study is to identify the ways that led us to the digital public sphere that we have today, with its corresponding benefits and dangers. We will discuss the existing regulation model in Brazil, our research case. First, however, is necessary to have in mind the definitions of cyber culture and cyberspace, among other concepts that were born with new technologies (like gatekeeping, net neutrality, etc.). It is necessary to consider the profound metamorphosis that the emergence and the development of the network implied in the roles of the various social actors, and to identify possible paths of these already indispensable tools for interaction, creation and distribution of information.

## TYPES OF SURVEILLANCE AND CONTROL TECHNOLOGIES: WHO ARE THE GATEKEEPERS AND WHAT ROLE DO THEY PLAY IN CYBERSPACE

In the 1950s, David Manning White proposed the concept that became known in the theory of communication as gatekeeping (Sousa, 2002,

p. 39). White had to identify the criteria that would be used to determine what would be selected for publication by news organizations. By observing the operation of the newsrooms of various newspapers in the United States, White concluded that the selection of material for publication depended on arbitrary and subjective factors, beyond merit judgments, experiences, attitudes and expectations of the gatekeepers – the editors of the publications.

The gatekeeper is therefore the one who determines what goes through the gateway on to the finished paper, which will be seen by the reader. This editor is an individual of power in the media universe, because he controls the flows of information and decides whether content should be emphasized or removed altogether. We decided to use the concept of gatekeeper to discuss the individuals able to control what circulates on the Internet through the use of surveillance tools. These gatekeepers of cyberspace were transplanted from traditional media, primarily large enterprises, public organizations and NGOs, to Internet observation. It is to them that we now turn.

Lyon (2004) provides three major categories of surveillance of cyberspace: work-related, security and policing, and marketing. At work, surveillance is characterized by directors and supervisors monitoring sites accessed and email sent by employees to ensure that employees are not viewing inappropriate content (such as pornography, for example) or wasting time at work with activities not relevant to the company. In the United States, a public study conducted in April 2000 indicated that 73.5% of American companies regularly perform some type of surveillance of Internet use by their employees (Castells, 2007, p. 206).

In relation to security and policing, we can include the surveillance proposed by bodies such as the High Authority for the Transmission of Creative Works and Copyright Protection on the Internet (in french: Haute Autorité pour la diffusion des œuvres et la protection des droits sur Internet, HADOPI) in France, which battles against Peer-to-Peer (P2P) networks and the free download of copyrighted music, movies, and books in the virtual world by monitoring user activities. HADOPI proposes that the access servers to the Internet monitor the activity of their users and identify those who violate copyright laws within each Network. After a first warning, if copyright violations persist, the user will lose their right to access the Internet from the point where the infractions were committed, all while being obligated to continue service payments to their contracted Internet provider.

There is also the surveillance conducted by police, such as the American FBI, which in 1995 carried out an operation named "Operation Innocent", an undercover sting operation based in America On-Line (AOL) involving the interception of mail from people suspected of exchanging pornographic depictions of children on the Internet (Zuidwijk & Steeves as cited in Lyon, 2004, p. 115). The federal agency also maintains the Carnivore program, which works in collaboration (voluntary or not) with suppliers of Internet access, first by logging all traffic via email then later cataloging the information based on a template and automated processing of keywords.

Terceiro (1996) maintains that the collection of data on the Internet has enabled the emergence of a new source value: the personal information of Internet users.

*The use of computer networks facilitates the collection of data on their users, what you get with an automatically susceptible sub-product ready for exploitation and marketing purposes. The attack on the privacy of people who assume that data collection has serious concerns regarding their protection, have sought the aid of encryption techniques that until recently belonged solely to the clandestine world of espionage and which today are invaluable in the digital world. (Terceiro, 1996, p. 185)*

The information obtained by marketing surveillance is used on a massive scale, often indiscriminately, and for commercial purposes. Unsurprisingly, companies incessantly seek access to private information relating to users of the Internet: many technologies have been developed for the sole purpose of collecting data used to profile Internet users. Cookies (Client-Side Persistent Information), a kind of digital marker that takes an automatic note of accessed sites on the hard drives of the user's computer itself, are one such technology. Once the cookie has been introduced on a computer, the site server that placed it automatically records all online activity occurring from that device. With the aid of such technologies, marketing and Internet communication firms sell the personal data of its users to its customers to use for commercial purposes or simply to better profile them. Therefore, we see that data-collection technologies have a direct association with the economics of electronic commerce. Most often, these programs gather user activity automatically. As Samarajiva (as cited in Lyon, 2004) notes:

*The so-called "mass clientele" creates incentives for collecting personal data for production and marketing use. Manufacturers or retailers, wishing to establish types of services in their relationship with the customer, collect, store and manipulate information about them to influence their behavior. (Samarajiva as cited in Lyon, 2004, p. 113)*

The technologies that make it possible to download books, magazines, music and movies in digital format to the hard drive of a computer, also enable publishers and leisure companies to record and track the browsing habits of users in order to send customized advertising to every one of their customers.

In the European Union, the largest government initiative in favor of consumer protection resulted in the Privacy Act, under which companies are not permitted to use the personal data of its customers without their explicit approval (Castells, 2007, p. 209). The problem is that many sites include, in their extensive terms of agreement, clauses that state that personal data collected online becomes the legal property of Internet companies and their clients. Few users read these terms of use in their entirety, blindly accepting the conditions – while many of these sites only allow users access after they have agreed to their terms.

Manuel Castells (2007) divides control technologies into three categories: identification technologies, surveillance, and research. Identification technologies include the use of passwords, cookies and authentication processes – the latter using digital signatures that allow other computers to check the origin and characteristics of the device that is connecting to the Internet; a security procedure that has been widely adopted by e-commerce companies and credit card issuers.

Surveillance technologies intercept messages and place markers that follow the flow of communication from a particular computer and monitor the activity of the device. They can identify a specific server as the origin of a given message. Taking advantage of this, and through persuasion or coercion, governments, companies and courts can obtain the personal information of a suspected user from Internet access servers. The above-mentioned HADOPI uses this very process. Research technologies, in turn, flesh out databases through the accumulation of continuously recorded surveillance results and information (Garfinkel as cited in Castells, 2007, p. 205). This is how a profile is built up from various bits of data collected on an individual in digital format, which is not at all dissimilar to how market research is done.

Beniger (1989) warns that, rather than the control in itself, society should fear those who manage and put into place these monitoring instruments – is in the hands of these agents that the true power is concentrated. Being that digital communications are the new tool for control, it is through them that a path to power

leads. Digital media has been used by various agents of interest to exercise and maintain this power. As was stated by Lyon (2004):

*Employers try to reduce the risk of workers who waste time or use company equipment for personal purposes [...] during working hours. The police, in conjunction with other institutions work to prevent the risk of crimes or, more generally, of threatening behavior. And businessmen do everything [...] to avoid the risk of losing opportunities, niche markets and, ultimately, profit (Lyon, 2004, p. 118).*

All establish procedures for collecting data to try to point out risks (or opportunities) and predict results. Therefore, the monitoring spreads, constantly becoming more routine, more intensive (profiles) and pervasive (populations), guided by economic, bureaucratic, and now technological forces.

Surveillance in the virtual world has been primarily the result of the commercialization of the Internet. With the creation of these user identification systems, there is a significant potential for profit by digital verification, and access control companies. The commercial implication of this control involves copyrights on the Internet as well. The implementation of surveillance systems is of great interest for governments, who want to find some way to introduce monitoring tools similar to those in the physical realm into the virtual environment.

*The need to secure and identify communication on the Internet in order to turn a profit, and the need to protect intellectual property rights therein, has resulted in the development of new software architecture (what Lawrence Lessig calls "Code ") that enables the control of this digital communication. Governments around the world support these surveillance technologies and are quick to adopt them to get recover any power they have run the risk of losing (Castells, 2007, p. 203).*

Monitoring by the police, companies and other bodies vested with the authorization granted by the powers that be would be, as Lemos (2007) points out, "[...] a form 'invasion' in the informational sphere, just as breaking into a home would be an invasion of the residential area. The 'digital borders' delineate the informational realm, a continuum between the physical world and the space of electronic information" (p. 225). Surveillance directly affects some important pillars of social life, and can weaken them if used for commercial purposes, for example: "Surveillance practices have implications for privacy and many other cherished values: justice, human dignity, self-determination, social inclusion, security, and so on. Some of these values can be protected if privacy is safeguarded" (Raab, 2008, p. 256).

The collection and storage of arbitrary digital data has become the norm in the virtual world. Herein, then, can be seen the harmful effects of this technological progress (Heuer, 2011, p. 85). The cost of data storage in digital format has become so inexpensive that it is already measured in terabytes (the storage capacity of a current laptop is just over half a terabyte). There are increasingly more databases to record our movements on the Internet – the Library of Congress of the United States, in Washington D.C., recently announced plans to archive all messages posted on Twitter since its inception in 2006.

In fact, our lives have always been under some kind of control – since the creation of notary records for identification in databases of various public services. What has changed as a result of the computerization of society and the advent of the Internet has been the placement of these records in cyberspace. Information is no longer housed in tangible media, minute books and archived documents. It is now only a few clicks away, available across the globe, subject to cross-reference, and more vulnerable than ever to official and unauthorized access. The new modes of surveillance that have emerged via digital technologies are ever more subtle, and ubiquitously pervasive. They are fading more and more from view though have never been watching so closely. Its flexibility can be attributed to its invisibility and mobility on the Internet.

Frois (2008) stresses the change brought about by the omnipresence of digital surveillance:

*[...] In contemporary society, the existence of large computer databases that centralize detailed information of citizens, which is then cross-referenced with information in other surveillance databases, threatens to undermine the right to privacy, our physical and moral integrity, and even – ultimately – the right to choose. [...] What we see is a convergence of profile recognition software covering almost all walks of life, from our bureaucratic and administrative identity, our personal history and genetic biometric features, all the way to the places we visit and people we spend time with. [...] It seems not enough to know who an individual is, the goal (of both State and commercial actors) is to know what that individual wants and will do. We might say that contemporary society, by identifying an individual, we can learn who they are; and by watching them, we can predict what they will do (Frois, 2008, p. 130).*

For Deleuze (1992), the society of control well within our near future, which in practical terms means that surveillance technologies are no longer visible and stationary, but ubiquitous, pervasive, "things," not requiring the individual to be confined and isolated, but rather the opposite: mobile, which allows dynamic control. After all, we must not forget that these technologies have an origin in the military. Every device, which combines mobility and location tracking, by its very nature, can be used to monitor movements and individuals while controlling actions on a day-to-day basis.

Castells (2007) and many other theorists in computer and digital technology have stated that the presence of so many digital records and databases has created the very real fear of a heavily-monitored society, not unlike that predicted in George Orwell's 1984, which might use this tireless monitoring as a form of repression of freedom. It is not Big Brother who watches us, but a multitude of little sisters – surveillance and information processing agencies surrounding us our entire lives – which will record every move we make. In democratic societies where civil rights are traditionally upheld, the transparency of our lives will shape our attitudes significantly. It is not possible to live in a completely transparent society. If this system of surveillance and control of the Internet to develop fully, we could not do what we want. We would have no freedom, or place to hide (Castells, 2007, p. 215).

This brings us to a topic that is heavily discussed in several European countries: the right to oblivion. An example of this right can be found in the French law of 6 January 1978 relating to computers, files and freedoms, which provides in its fortieth article:

*Every individual, looking to protect their identity, may demand that those responsible for data processing rectify, amend, update or delete [...] personal information concerning them [....] soon as it becomes inaccurate, incomplete, misleading, outdated or whose collection, use, disclosure or storage is prohibited. (Commission Nationale de l' Informatique et des Libertés, 1978)*

The European Commission responsible for Justice, Fundamental Rights and Citizenship examines the possibility of revising the policy on data protection to include the right to be forgotten, as was announced in November 2010 by Vice-president Viviane Reding (Heuer, 2011, p. 85).

In Brussels, January 24, 2012, Reding presented a plan that would enable citizens to exercise their right to full protection of personal data. The current European legislation concerning this issue dates from 1995, a time when the Internet did not have the reach and influence it does today. Moreover, recent surveys indicate that 72% of Europeans are concerned about the ends for which companies and businesses are using their personal data (Rituerto, 2012). The plan proposed by Reding enshrines the right to oblivion. In an interview with the Spanish newspaper El País, the Commissioner remarked: "whoever puts personal information on the Internet should have the right to remove it, because it is his" (Rituerto, 2012). His plan includes strengthening national data protection agencies and regulation of policy enforcement at the community level – measures to be implemented by 2015.

In Germany, government and parliament debated over projects aimed at allowing citizens to more effectively manage their digital life. In France, for example a non-binding letter, initiated of the Secretary of State of Technology at the time, Nathalie Kosciusko-Morizet, was adopted in October 2010. Many of the major figures in the French Internet signed the document – with the notable exception of companies like Facebook and Google.

## THE CIVIL RIGHTS FRAMEWORK FOR THE INTERNET IN BRAZIL ("MARCO CIVIL DA INTERNET")

Discussions on the bill to combat cybercrime, named after its author, Senator Eduardo Azeredo, infuriated many Brazilian Internet users. The pressure created by virtual mobilizing caused the then President Luiz Inácio Lula da Silva to request that the Ministry of Justice to draw up "a code relating to the Internet that would be civil rather than penal" (Chaves, 2012). On October 29, 2009 the Secretary of Legislative Affairs of the Ministry of Justice (SAL/MJ), in partnership with the Getúlio Vargas School of Law Foundation in Rio de Janeiro (FGV DIREITO RIO), launched the project to build a collaborative Civil Rights Framework for the Brazilian Internet.

The primary objectives of the regulatory framework is the establishment of principles, guarantees, rights, and duties for the use of the Internet in Brazil, and the determination of guidelines for operation of the Federal, State, and Municipal entities regarding the matter. The regulations on Internet usage in Brazil are founded on human rights and citizenship in digital media, plurality and diversity, openness and collaboration, and finally free enterprise, free competition and consumer protection. Included in its principles are:

1.   Guarantee of freedom of expression, communication and manifestation of thought, as established under the Constitution;
2.   Protection of privacy;
3.   Protection of personal data, as provided by law;
4.   Preservation and guarantee of net neutrality according to regulation;
5.   Preservation of stability, security and functionality of the Internet through technical measures consistent with international standards and by encouraging the use of best practices;
6.   Accountability of agents according to their activities under the law; and
7.   Preservation of the participatory nature of the Internet (Congresso Nacional do Brasil, 2011, pp. 01-02).

The idea of creating a civil regulatory framework diverges significantly from the tendency to establish restrictions, convictions or bans on the use of the Internet. And there is a considerable difference between the Azeredo Bill and the proposed framework above. The latter aims to determine, unequivocally, the rights and responsibilities regarding the use of digital media. The

goal, therefore, is the creation of legislation guaranteeing rights, not rules restricting freedom.

Since digital technology is ever evolving, the text should highlight key civil concepts. The characteristic freedom and openness of the Internet could be threatened if the implemented legislation were too restrictive. "Any initiative in Internet regulation must therefore observe principles such as freedom of expression, individual privacy, respect for human rights and the preservation of the dynamics of the Internet as a space for collaboration" (Ministério da Justiça do Brasil & Fundação Getúlio Vargas, 2009).

Among the topics covered by the text of this civil code, are the responsibilities of providers and users vis-à-vis the content available on the network and measures to regulate and safeguard the fundamental rights of Internet users (such as privacy and freedom of expression). In addition, it many of the guidelines to ensure the proper functioning of the Internet, such as net neutrality. The writers of the civil code decided not to address issues such as cybercrime, telecommunications regulation and copyright in great depth, as they consider these to be issues that are sufficiently large enough to be discussed further individually. But, in some form or other, the principles of this milestone text touch all of these issues, even if not explicitly. Such as is the case of the relationship between copyright and the preservation of Internet-user privacy.

Let us consider, then, the four principal items discussed by this civil code: the storage of data, net neutrality, privacy and responsibility. When a crime is committed by way of the Internet, the only way to identify the criminal is to have access to connection logs. Currently, in Brazil, no law or regulation exists determining if sites or web providers must store this data, or for how long. The text of this legislation states that providers must keep the connection records of their customers, but prohibits them from harvesting information from Web-access records. That is, providers would be required to store the information needed to determine when and which computer individuals connected to the network, but not which sites they visited. The sites themselves are allowed to record this information, but after receiving consent from the user. But, here is the rub. Many lawyers clamor that these access records access have the potential to be criminal evidence – which would require this matter to be covered under criminal, not civil law.

The issue of net neutrality is a central concern of this initiative, and is enveloped by controversy of planetary dimensions. The principle of net neutrality requires that all data packets sent across the Internet must be treated equally, without discrimination of origin, destination or type. Here, maintaining neutrality requires the prevention of practices known as traffic shaping, which allows providers hamper connection to certain pages. As is the case with Internet providers that intentionally disrupt access to Peer-to-Peer (P2P) sharing sites and Voice over Internet Protocol (VoIP) services. In Brazil, Brasil Telecom and three other domestic operators epitomize this behavior, a fact that has placed them among 108 Internet providers cited by Vuze software for the practice of controlling the exchange of data (Vuze, 2008). However, the legislation makes it clear that the only controls that may impair traffic flow information are those "technical requirements necessary for adequate performance of services" (Congresso Nacional do Brasil, 2011, p. 03), acting to improve the functioning of the Internet.

To ensure user privacy, the legislation decrees that personal information may only be accessed with the consent of the user. Critics of the measure often decry this protection, saying it has the potential to hinder police investigations. However, it should be noted that the text grants the authorities access to the personal data of a suspected criminal under investigation, waiving the need paperwork, and preventing these files from being deleted by the server.

Responsibility has to do with the allocation of content published on websites, social networks, etc. Here, the legislation is in line with previous court rulings: the burden falls upon the users themselves, only punishing providers when they do not remove content from their sites within the period prescribed by law to do so.

The entirely collaborative character of the development process of this legislation is unprecedented and in itself embodies its greatest asset. The way in which the law is written frames the Internet as a means: the purpose, to encourage active participation and direct the various social actors involved in the dialogue created there (civil society, researchers, government officials, academics, representatives of the private sector, and the like.). Everyone could register on a website specially made for the purpose of receiving proposals, contributions and opinions.

The process has been divided into two phases. The first, lasting about 45 days (started in October 2009 and ended on December 17, 2009), featured a discussion of ideas on topics proposed for regulation, drawn from the basic text produced by the Ministry of Justice. This basic text contextualizes the pressing issues surrounding the regulation established by the bill to be drafted collectively, and suggests possible ways forward.

Each paragraph of the text was open to debate among registered users of the site. The each user's posted reviews were required to be brief in order to ensure a wide spectrum of input. To avoid restricting the debate, the coordination team hosted several sub-discussion forums aimed at deliberating specific issues with the community. Within these sub-forums, participants could debate extensively on a given topic of interest. Each participant could also vote, for or against, the input of others. These votes served to guide the writing team on the preferences, opinions and interests of the participants, which contributed greatly to the framing of the proposal. At the end of this initial phase, all the debate considerations were synthesized into a single work, and were used to produce a draft bill of law. During this first phase, the discussion site received an average of 1,300 visits daily.

In the second phase the discussion followed the same format, but had as parameter the draft bill done before. Each article, paragraph and clause was open to submit comments by any interested party. The duration of this phase was approximately 50 days (from 08 April to 30 May 2010). During the period, the site received 45,500 visits were made and about 900 comments on the draft (Agência Brasil, 2010). With the completion of the second phase was constructed text currently available.

The public consultation process which was relied on the landmark building has been praised by many jurists and activists of the Internet to be open and democratic, and is a model whose effectiveness has been internationally recognized (Committee to Protect Journalists, 2010; Internet sans frontières, 2010).

## COPYRIGHT AND INTERNET REGULATION: A NEBULOUS RELATIONSHIP

The issue of copyright does not have a clear cut and easily defined relationship with Internet regulation: it, however, does exist, and with the relentless advance of digital technology, a debate on this becomes ever more relevant and necessary.

If we consider the defense of intellectual property (which involves copyright as well as other tools, such as patents and trademarks, for example) as an instrument to prevent Internet users from accessing certain content, we stumble upon a sensitive debate which may lead to unfortunate results. Put simply, the idea is that information and communications technology have the unparalleled capacity to increase ac-

cess to information and knowledge, so that the lack of access to technologies themselves would be detrimental to the development of this very technology.

So in this case, to speak of Internet governance (or control) is not simply limited to a discussion on the technical aspects of the structure and operation of individual networks themselves. According to the Geneva Declaration of Principles, drawn up during the World Summit on the Information Society (WSIS), organized by the United Nations (UN), the management of the Internet encompasses not only largely technical concerns, but also the discussion of any public policy relevant to the management of the Internet as a globally-available resource (United Nations, 2004).

For Mizukami and Souza (2008), as the information and communications technologies increase the possibility of access to content, as well as access to tools for content production, systems of exceptions and limitations to copyright protection emerge as one of key governance concerns.

*If, on one hand, it ensures exclusive rights to authors (and those to whom such rights are transferred), as a way of encouraging the creation and dissemination of intellectual works, it ignores the other interests concerned with access to and use of content, which must be weighed in relation to the incentives that the copyright rules, theoretically, provide (Mizukami & Souza, 2008, p. 06).*

When we associate the idea of regulating copyright protections in cyberspace, our principal concern is the delicate balance between the various interests of different actors involved. The challenge is to preserve an environment of harmony between authors, publishers and users of content without placing barriers to new possibilities the Internet can foster, whether it be in relation to new business models, or in relation to a democratized access to the tools of production and information distribution. The task at hand is balancing these interests in cyberspace, without sacrificing the potential for innovation and access to knowledge that it possesses.

Limitations and exceptions to copyright are often overlooked when discussing Internet regulation. Too few people argue about, for example, the negative effects of overly rigid and inflexible social protection of intellectual property on education, or about the content production the principle of exclusive rights seeks to incentivize. The Internet boom and the accelerated development of technology brought questions, such as those concerning access to knowledge, out of the shadows, but it also gave body - or even the spark of life - to a number of other questions on rights that previously had limited presence in the critical evaluation of the traditional framework.

For Mizukami and Souza (2008), the obstacles to the discussion of the limitations and exceptions to copyright is most prominent in countries of Roman-Germanic legal tradition, characterized by a strong juris naturalist reasoning influence in their discourse (p. 07). They assert that this discourse eliminates the variety of views found in legal literature. This is because it considers that copyright is necessary for the protection of the property and personality of the author (sometimes as the protection of personality through property protection), but does not bring into play the interests of the community, individual rights, and other interests that find themselves affected by this type of exclusive copyright.

Internet users are not the ones who compete with these authors for financial gain, it is the "cultural entrepreneurs" who do that (Ascensão, 2003, p. 17). They already find equal footing with authors in the eyes of the law, considering the fundamental need to protect the investment. Moral rights are increasingly absent in the texts of these new international codes.

For Ascensão (2003), the argument in favor of the entrepreneur is somewhat odd. As a lawyer, he points out, that is not clear why such highly protectionist laws are being implemented for the nominal defense of intellectual creation, while, in reality, they serve only as a protection of investments (p. 18). Investments can and should be protected, but that protection ought to be appropriate and proportional to the task at hand. It is rather odd that copyrights, which serve a different function altogether, are even employed to begin with. If the priority of protectionist copyright laws is defense of investment, then it will be this rather than the quality of the creation itself that will drive copyright industries.

Serra (2012) believes that the problem is in the supply chain of the capitalist system, which imprisons the author in a cycle of dependence on publishers and intermediaries. "The SPA (Portuguese Society of Authors) is aware that the current market models are not as beneficial to the authors, but also know it's hard to leave these models behind. And it is not only up to the authors" (Serra, 2012).

What we see emerging is an entrepreneurial hyper-protectionism in Copyright industries, which has serious consequences. Industries defend this practice and claim that they are able to foster the culture, but the effects indicate the opposite. This hyper-protectionism creates an environment in which access to culture becomes more and more difficult by virtue of the high costs imposed on it. In addition, there are also serious implications in terms of competition: hyper-protectionism only serves to strengthen the most prominent firms in Copyright-exporting countries at home and across the globe. The concentration of "cultural content" businesses protected by the law crowd out and prevent any newcomers from attaining the same level of success. Hyper-protectionism through its rampant use of exclusive rights eliminates competition, and establishes an oligopoly of a grotesque magnitude.

Projects laws like SOPA and ACTA point to a disproportional war between the aforementioned cultural industries and Internet users. Caught in the middle are the authors who are really pawns in the whole debate – defended by the entrepreneurs who vie to protect the profits of which these artists share little. One case that serves to illustrate this point is the Napster file-sharing program on a P2P network that was involved in the first major battle in the legal fight between the music industry and music sharing networks on the Internet.

The central question in the suit was to determine whether the reproduction of Copyright-protected files represented an act of private use or not. In fact, Napster played no part at all in the reproduction. The program, in itself, simply enabled users to locate replicable desired files on the Internet. Pinpointing the location of the file to the user who would then download it. Regarding audiovisual works, the software was even more groundbreaking. Napster did not even locate the files available on the Internet. It merely provided software to subscribers that would allow them to do so. Then these users would themselves locate the files they desired. After intense legal conflicts, Napster sought to adapt to the new restrictions, dolling out compensation to rights holders, but this was unsuccessful. The site was eventually sold, and the new managers now maintain a business model that respects the copyright on digital music files.

The case of Napster is emblematic of several issues, but here we will highlight only two: if it is already this difficult to hold intermediary companies responsible for such violations, what about the users who only violate these rights privately? Another striking feature to emerge from this process is the use of copyright as a means of reducing technological possibilities of the Internet. The difficult balance between these two interests must be found somewhere in the middle, in which the renunciation of free downloading must be matched by more reasonable terms from enterprise; in any case, it should not involve the curtailing of the technological potential of the Internet.

For Ascensão (2003), battles like this are debate on leading intellectual property to a perverse extreme, copyrighting without authors. This does not mean the disappearance of the author, but their transformation into a marginal and expendable figurehead (p. 21). Creativity gradually loses its space, making it more and more of a requirement for industrial innovations than copyright itself. If protection of investments is what is most precious, creativity (and consequently the act of creation, the very mark of an author) sinks lower, becoming something inferior.

Certain additional protections do nothing but protect business and its interests. This is the case of increased protection periods, which in reality is irrelevant to the authors. For industry, this translates into additional time for monopolistic exploitation. Ascensão (2003) continues by discussing the copyright without creation: if what it protects is business activity, it is irrelevant whether the protected object has any characteristic of created work. The only interest is the intellectual merchandise, whatever it may be (p. 23).

## THE PREROGATIVE OF ACCESS TO INFORMATION AND COMMUNICATION AS A HUMAN RIGHT

Looking at the issue of access to information and communication through the lens of human rights is an obvious decision. We chose this route – abandoning still many others such as trade agreement and technical conventions – because we believe that this issue has the most direct impact on individuals, at various levels of society. Being that electronic communications are a fundamental aspect of modern interconnectivity, it is impossible not to consider access to information and communication on the Internet as essential for individuals to act as agents in the international collective. The future of the information society can be imagined as an environment where individuals work and grow, and cyberspace is part of the way to that future. Therefore, on the premise that information is power, and considering that access to communication is a sine qua non for social inclusion and participation, we will focus our attention on the relationship between information and human rights.

At the heart of the criticism leveled against laws to fight piracy are the obviously concerns over the strict sanctions and surveillance actions, such as those that provide for the monitoring of user activities on the Internet and cutting access to users who download copyrighted material. In addition, traffic shaping and other measures that hinder access to the Internet cause controversy, and call into question the legitimacy of laws that prevent people from using technological tools in fullest. Would such restrictions, if truly just in the name of copyright defense, ever extend so far beyond the much more precious right of access to these channels of communication and interaction which have become indispensable?

A BBC World Service study of 27,000 people from 26 countries found that four out of five adults worldwide consider Internet access a fundamental right of human beings. The same survey also showed that 53% of respondents believe that the Internet should not be regulated by governments (BBC Brasil, 2010).

The right of access to digital communication has gradually become seen as a human right. According Peruzzo (2005),

*[... ] worldwide, digital inclusion is seen as a human right, as fundamental as the right of any citizen to access any other media source or a dig-*

*nified existence. Several organizations, scholars and activists have positioned themselves publicly in favor of the right to communication, taking it as a mechanism to effect the democratization of media (Peruzzo, 2005, p. 275).*

Additionally according Peruzzo (2005), discussions on the right to information and communication in the information society also include the rights of the preservation of the public domain, free software and intellectual property, as well as global access to all information and communication technologies (p. 276).

The CRIS Campaign (Communication Rights in the Information Society) movement launched in 2001, led by NGOs from the fields of communication and human rights in various countries, listed in one of his publications some noteworthy debates concerning the issue of the right of access to information. Among the topics, is the attempt to end the censorship and surveillance network established by governments and businesses. For the CRIS Campaign, "the right to communicate is a universal human right that assumes, and works in service of other human rights" (CRIS as cited in Pasquali, 2005, p. 31).

From the theoretical point of view, the right to communication tends to be taken traditionally as a right to freedom of information and expression. This conception is expressed in the laws dealing with the issue. For example, the Universal Declaration of Human Rights (UDHR) of 1948, in its Article 19 provides that "Everyone has the right to freedom of opinion and expression: this right includes freedom without interference to hold opinions and to seek, receive and impart information and ideas through any media regardless of boarders" (United Nations General Assembly, 1948). The American Specialized Conference on Human Rights (1969) states that "Everyone has the right to freedom of thought and expression. This right includes freedom to seek, receive and impart information and ideas of all kinds, regardless of boarders, either orally or in writing or in print, or art, or through any media of his choice" (American Specialized Conference on Human Rights, 1969). As emphasized by León (2002),

*[....] The right to communication is now presented as logical continuation of the historical progression that began with the recognition of rights of the authors of the media, later this was extended to those who work in close relationships with them, and now finally applies to all people, by virtue of the Declaration of Human Rights [....] which grants the right to information; and freedom of expression and opinion. This is part of a more global movement, [....] which incorporates new rights related to the changing communications scene, and provides a more interactive approach to communication, in which social actors are information producers and not simply passive recipients of information (León, 2002, p. 03).*

The freedom of access to technology is another point that also comes to mind when considering the issue of cyberspace. This right is provided for in point 1 of Article 27 of the Universal Declaration of Human Rights, which states that "Everyone has the right to freely participate in the cultural life of the community, to enjoy the arts and to share in scientific advancement and its benefits" (United Nations General Assembly, 1948). According Peruzzo (2005), this right is inspired by the basic moral principle of fairness and the notion that science and technology belong to the common heritage of humankind (p. 107).

Hamelink views the discussion from the perspective of a new approach, which champions the urgent need to adopt a universal declaration of the right to communicate. This right, currently, does not exist in any international law. In 1969, D'Arcy presented such a right to communicate in writing: "The time will come when the Universal Declaration of Human Rights will have to encompass much more than simply man 's right to information... that is, the right of Man

to communicate" (D' Arcy as cited in Hamelink, 2004, p. 268). According to Hamelink, the motivating force behind this new approach was the observation that the articles of the existing human rights law (such as the Universal Declaration of Human Rights or Compromise on Civil and Political Rights) was inadequate to protect communication as an interactive process.

Among several proposals, Hamelink (2004) suggests that the right to communicate should include information rights such as the freedom of access to information on matters of public interest (held by public or private sources) and the right of access to public means of distributing information, ideas and opinions. For the author, part of the right to communicate would also be composed of cultural rights. Among them, the right to enjoy the arts and the benefits of scientific progress and its applications and the right to creativity and artistic independence, literary and academics (Hamelink, 2004, pp. 268-269).

However, the right to communicate implies, in the world of electronic communications, the need to safeguard the privacy of users. Among the rights listed as "protections" by Hamelink (2004), are: the right of the public to be protected against interference with their privacy by the media or the mass media, or public or private agencies involved in data collection; protection of communications among private persons against the interference of public and private groups (p. 269).

As we have already addressed in the introduction of this chapter, the emergence of the Internet has brought with it the illusion of the movement of information and ideas in total freedom. Today the notion of free flow of information has more complex and subtle implications, and involves the two faces of digital media: on one hand, the expanded personal freedoms of individuals; on the other, the opening of the door to systematic information theft, via electronic communication monitoring. We live in what Pasquali (2005) calls "the freedom globally watched" (p.

35). The author emphasizes the beauty of the concept of the free information flow and the need to defend it, but affirms that there is no chance of this state of free information exchange if, what the Nobel-Prize-winning economist, J. E. Stiglitz, called information asymmetry – caused by economic agents who fraudulently accumulate more information than others – is tolerated. As maintained by Pasquali (2005),

*A freedom that does not free is merely selfishness and privilege. The double standard of having free information as an abstract concept, while the information in the real world is treated as a commodity subject to market principles, allowing for the elimination of alternatives, is relationally and semantically dishonest (Pasquali, 2005, p. 37).*

To Scheer (1997), the right of access to information and communication is closely linked to a new form of democracy yet to be experienced that has emerged in cyberspace. According to the author, this is a democracy of simple expression, of enunciation, by each individual, in which human narrative holds sway, without alteration or approval from the powers at be (Scheer, 1997, p. 121). Depriving the user access to the Internet (or even hindering it) is therefore a threat to this new democracy and an attack on each individual's right to enjoy the benefits that Internet technology can provide personal development training as an individual active in the information society.

## FUTURE RESEARCH DIRECTIONS

Considering digital instrument technologies are constantly evolving, forecasts of and recommendations for the better regulation of the Internet are relentlessly advancing as well and the most up-to-date and relevant ideas and concepts easily outstrip the dogmas of the quiet past. However, there exist at the same time immutable societal prescriptions; among them, the principle that laws should always seek to trace the same route society follows as it continues to evolve and change. If society has evolved to be one were public transparency and freedom of expression are not only ubiquitously celebrated but guaranteed in the constitution, the neutral and balanced governance of the Internet, consistent with the pragmatism experienced by citizens in the real world, will only logically follow.

For Brazil and many other countries, the second half of 2013 has been marked by the NSA (National Security Agency) spying scandal in the United States (U.S.). The story was leaked by the former CIA (Central Intelligence Agency) employee, Edward Snowden, and the reaction of the U.S. government has, on several occasions, been heavily criticized by President Dilma Rousseff. In a speech at the 68th United Nations General Assembly on September 24th of the same year, the President underscored the need to resume discussions of the Civil Framework of the Internet in Brazil, since the text addresses, in its many recommendations, the need for Internet security and contributes to the preservation of national sovereignty as it concerns the confidentiality of electronic communications (G1, 2013). Rousseff also spoke on the creation of a "Civil Rights Framework for the global Internet," a piece of legislation that would govern cyberspace on an international scale.

The cooperation seen in these multinational projects for the defense of privacy on the Internet is indicative of the way for digital rights might be internationally recognized and guaranteed. In October 2013, Brazil and Germany (which was also hit by the spying scandal, with the wire tapping of Chancellor Angela Merkel's mobile phone) presented a draft resolution to the UN General Assembly to repudiate the excesses of electronic espionage and recognize that the right to privacy extends to communications on Internet and otherwise. The authors of the proposal say they are "deeply concerned about the human rights violations and abuses that may result from electronic surveillance," including "extraterritorial surveillance, interception of communications or mass collection of personal data" (Público, 2013).

Economic and political pressures intend to crank out this Civil Rights Framework for the Internet in Brazil, but with dramatic alterations to the text. These include the insertion of some controversial measures (including a proposal that would compel Internet service providers to host their servers in the country of operation) and that favor the interests of Internet and telecommunications companies, masking any abuses and endangering the privacy of Internet users. It is imperative that these distortions to the original law are rooted out and that the full text is adopted without changes.

A possible research direction for future studies might be an observation of the real changes that the adoption of the Civil Rights Framework has brought to the every-day experience of Internet users in Brazil. Researchers who are interested in this subject might possibly attempt identifying unforeseen weaknesses in the practical application of this code and suggest solutions for the problems that arise. Additionally, the concept of a Regulatory Framework for the Internet on a global scale, it's limitations, and possibilities might also be an interesting topic of relevance to future academic research.

## CONCLUSION

The concept of the information society is not neutral. Information is not the same as communication. Information is a source of power and mastery of its means of production, control and dissemination can be a factor in increasing inequality in the distribution of power in an already disparate society. Democracy in its most basic form requires that power be broadly distributed – and since information is a source of power, a more egalitarian society would result from the free access to it.

In the world we live in, power is concentrated in various forms and manners, such as ideological, economic, technological, scientific, and informational. Those supporting human rights position themselves against those who threaten or disrespect the freedoms of society. To include the right of access to information and communication in this struggle is to acknowledge the central role the individual plays as an actor in the upkeep of society. Access to information is a prerequisite for the development of the critical, questioning, and active individual who is able to make use of their mind to set themselves free.

Large corporations have the infrastructure of the global Internet in their hands. Almost all of the Internet depends on multinationals, and most are based in the U.S.. Many governments oversee and control their citizens' access to the Internet. When it is in their best political interest, they may impede Internet connectivity with the outside world, as did the Egyptian government, in early 2011, during the movement that later became known as the Arab Spring, which eventually led to the fall of the dictator, Hosni Mubarak (Sapo Notícias, 2011).

In a landmark decision, the Human Rights Council of the UN, composed of 47 countries, recognized the right to freedom of expression on the Internet for the first time, noting as a guaranteed the free access to cyberspace. The recognition took place two days after the European Parliament's decision to eliminate the ACTA, in July 2012. Despite resistance from countries such as China and Cuba, the text of the agreement was finalized with the agreement that this right should be protected by all countries. This is the first UN resolution to affirm that basic prerogatives should be protected in the digital realm, and promoted to the same extent and with the same commitment as human rights are in the physical world.

Both China and Cuba, however, have reservations about the agreement: Chinese Ambassador Xia Jingge argued, for example, "young people need to be protected" from corrupting sites, like those featuring gambling, pornography, violence, fraud, and piracy. "We believe that the free flow of information on the Internet and the secure flow of information on the Internet are interdependent" (Público, 2012). Already Cuban Ambassador Juan Antonio Quintanilla, in an implicit reference to the U.S., made the caveat that the text does not address the issue of "Internet governance" when "we all know that this tool is controlled by a single country in the world" (Público, 2012).

Freedom on the Internet and the power of information sharing were also the central themes of the Forum for Social Entrepreneurship in the New Economy, an event held in June 2012, parallel to the Rio+20 in Rio de Janeiro. In one of the panels, Silvio Meira, President of the Administrative Council of Digital Harbor and chief scientist at the Center for Advanced Studies and Systems in Recife (Cesar), drew attention to the need for "programs not to be programmed." For him, it is necessary to take control of our lives in cyberspace: "Having personal property of our data is absolutely essential. We are being sold as a commodity on the Internet" (Barrêdo, 2012).

The regulation is essential to curb the practice of indiscriminate use of user data in the Internet. It is also necessary to ensure the smooth technical operation of the system with bandwidth speed at fair prices, good quality service, while banning practices that undermine the neutrality of the network, such as, but not limited to, traffic shaping. The regulation should not only concern the access to technology, but also guarantee pluralism of information in circulation and of rights and duties on the Internet. At the same time, privacy protection is a key concern that arises as fundamental in any kind of applied regulation. The protection of personal user data is a central dimension of regulation that crosses all the interaction types on the Internet.

# REFERENCES

G1 (2013). Dilma diz na ONU que espionagem fere soberania e direito internacional. *G1*. Retrieved November 02, 2013, from http://g1.globo.com/mundo/noticia/2013/09/dilma-diz-na-onu-que-espionagem-fere-soberania-e-direito-internacional.html

American Specialized Conference on Human Rights. (1969). *Convenção Americana de Direitos Humanos*. Retrieved June 07, 2013, from http://www.pge.sp.gov.br/centrodeestudos/biblioteca-virtual/instrumentos/sanjose.htm

Ascensão, J. de O. (2003). *Propriedade intelectual e Internet*. Retrieved March 03, 2013, from http://www.fd.ul.pt/Portals/0/Docs/Institutos/ICJ/LusCommune/AscensaoJoseOliveira1.pdf

Barrêdo, J. R. (2012). Ou aprendemos a programar ou seremos programados, diz cientista. *G1*. Retrieved July 04, 2013, from http://g1.globo.com/natureza/rio20/noticia/2012/06/ou-aprendemos-programar-ou-seremos-programados-diz-cientista.html

Beniger, J. (1989). *The control revolution: The Control Revolution: Technological and Economic Origins of the Information Society*. Cambridge, MA: Harvard University Press.

Agência Brasil. (2010). Justiça prorroga prazo para debate sobre Marco Civil na Internet. *Agência Brasil*. Retrieved March 05, 2013, from http://ultimainstancia.uol.com.br/conteudo/noticias/46764/justica+prorroga+prazo+para+debate+sobre+marco+civil+na+internet.shtml

BBC Brasil. (2010). Para 4 em cada 5 pessoas, Internet é direito fundamental, diz pesquisa. *BBC Brasil*. Retrieved June 07, 2013, from http://www.bbc.co.uk/portuguese/lg/noticias/2010/03/100307_pesquisabbc_internetml.shtml?s

Castells, M. (2007). *A Galáxia Internet: Reflexões sobre Internet, Negócios e Sociedade*. Lisbon: Fundação Calouste Gulbenkian.

Chaves, G. (2012). Para especialistas, projeto brasileiro para regular a web é mais democrático. *Correio Braziliense*. Retrieved February 29, 2013, from http://www.correiobraziliense.com.br/app/noticia/tecnologia/2012/01/30/interna_tecnologia,288096/para-especilistas-projeto-brasileiro-para-regular-a-web-e-mais-democratico.shtml

Commission nationale de l'informatique et des libertés. (1978). *Loi du 6 janvier 1978, relative à l'informatique, aux archives et aux libertés*. Retrieved February 03, 2013, from http://www.cnil.fr/fileadmin/documents/approfondir/textes/CNIL-78-17_definitive-annotee.pdf

Committee to Protect Journalists. (2010). Is Brazil the censorship capital of the Internet? Not yet. *Committee to Protect Journalists*. Retrieved March 07, 2013, from http://cpj.org/blog/2010/04/is-brazil-the-censorship-capital-of-the-internet.php

Deleuze, G. (1992). *Post-scriptum sobre as sociedades de controlo*. Retrieved January 01, 2013, from http://www.portalgens.com.br/filosofia/textos/sociedades_de_controlo_deleuze.pdf

Congresso Nacional do Brasil. (2011). *Projeto de Lei 2126/2011: Estabelece princípios, garantias, direitos e deveres para o uso da Internet no Brasil*. Retrieved April 21, 2013, from http://www.camara.gov.br/proposicoesweb/fichadetramitacao?idProposicao=517255

Frois, C. (Ed.). (2008). *A sociedade vigilante – Ensaios sobre identificação, vigilância e privacidade*. Lisbon: Imprensa de Ciências Sociais.

Hamelink, C. J. (2004). Desafios morais na sociedade da informação. In J. Paquete de Oliveira et al. (Eds.), *Comunicação, cultura e tecnologias da informação* (pp. 261–270). Lisbon: Quimera.

Heuer, S. (2011, April). A Rede lembra-se de tudo? *Courrier Internacional*, pp. 84-88.

Internet sans frontiers. (2010). Brésil: Um cadre de loi exemplaire. *Internet sans frontières*. Retrieved March 07, 2013, from http://www.internetsansfrontieres.com/Bresil-un-cadre-de-loi-exemplaire_a154.html

Lemos, A. (2007). Mídia locativa e territórios informacionais. In P. Arantes, & L. Santaella (Eds.), *Estéticas tecnológicas* (pp. 207–230). São Paulo: Editora PUC.

León, O. (2002). *Democratização das comunicações*. Retrieved June 07, 2013, from http://www.dhnet.org.br/w3/fsmrn/fsm2002/osvaldo1_midia.html

Lyon, D. (2004). A World Wide Web da vigilância: a Internet e os fluxos de poder off-world. In J. Paquete de Oliveira et al. (Eds.), *Comunicação, cultura e tecnologias da informação* (pp. 109–126). Lisbon: Quimera.

Ministério da Justiça do Brasil & Fundação Getúlio Vargas. (2009). *Marco Civil da Internet: Seus direitos e deveres em discussão*. Retrieved March 03, 2013, from http://culturadigital.br/marcocivil/

Mizukami, P., & Souza, C. A. P. (2008). *Propriedade Intelectual e Governança da Internet*. Rio de Janeiro: Fundação Getúlio Vargas.

Pasquali, A. (2005). Um breve glossário descritivo sobre comunicação e informação. In J. Marques de Melo, & L. Sathler (Eds.), *Direitos à Comunicação na Sociedade da Informação* (pp. 15–48). São Bernardo do Campo: Universidade Metodista de São Paulo.

Peruzzo, C. M. K. (2005). Internet e Democracia Comunicacional: entre os entraves, utopias e o direito à comunicação. In J. Marques de Melo, & L. Sathler (Eds.), *Direitos à Comunicação na Sociedade da Informação* (pp. 266–288). São Bernardo do Campo: Universidade Metodista de São Paulo.

Público. (2012). Nações Unidas reconhecem o direito à liberdade de expressão na Internet. *Público*. Retrieved July 06, 2013, from http://www.publico.pt/Tecnologia/nacoes-unidas-reconhecem-o-direito-a-liberdade-de-expressao-na-internet-1553694

Público. (2013). Brasil e Alemanha juntam esforços na ONU contra espionagem. *Público*. Retrieved November 02, 2013, from http://www.publico.pt/mundo/noticia/brasil-e-alemanha-juntam-esforcos-na-onu-contra-a-espionagem-1611145

Raab, C. D. (2008). Vigilância e privacidade: As opções de regulação. In A sociedade vigilante – Ensaios sobre identificação, vigilância e privacidade (pp. 255-292). Lisbon: Imprensa de Ciências Sociais.

Rituerto, R. M. (2012). Quien pone datos personales em la red tiene derecho a recuperarlos [Interview with Viviane Reding, European Commissioner for Justice, Fundamental Rights and Citizenship]. *El País*. Retrieved January 25, 2013, from http://tecnologia.elpais.com/tecnologia/2012/01/24/actualidad/1327435171_045260.html

Sapo Notícias. (2011). Egipto: O dia em que a Internet foi parcialmente desligada. *Sapo Notícias*. Retrieved July 06, 2013, from http://livetv.blogs.sapo.pt/731616.html

Scheer, L. (1997). *A democracia virtual*. Lisbon: Edições Século XXI.

Sousa, J. P. (2002). *Teorias da notícia e do jornalismo*. Argos (Utrecht, Netherlands).

Terceiro, J. B. (1996). *Sociedad digital: Del homo sapiens al homo digitalis*. Madrid: Alianza Editorial.

United Nations. (2004). *World Summit on the Information Society (WSIS)*. Retrieved April 21, 2013, from http://www.itu.int/wsis/documents/doc_multi.asp?lang=en&id=1161|1160

United Nations General Assembly. (1948). *Universal Declaration of Human Rights*. Retrieved June 07, 2013, from http://portal.mj.gov.br/sedh/ct/legis_intern/ddh_bib_inter_universal.htm

Vuze. (2008). *First Results from Vuze Network Monitoring Tool Released April 18th, 2008*. Retrieved March 18, 2013, from http://torrentfreak.com//images/vuze-plug-in-results.pdf

## KEY TERMS AND DEFINITIONS

**Cyberculture:** Set of practices, attitudes, modes of thought and values that develop in cyberspace.

**Cyberspace:** Place where digital life unfolds in its various aspects, through interaction between users and their relationship with the space where they act.

**Gatekeeping:** Term, linked to the field of communication, describing the individual, whether they be publisher or person who selects and categorizes information content, and controls the means for its dissemination.

**Human Rights:** Human rights are rights and freedoms to which all are entitled, no matter who they are or where they live.

**Internet Regulation:** Creation and establishment of principles that promote and enable the various actors involved to use the Internet properly.

**Privacy:** It is the right to keep personal information private and to a private life itself.

**Surveillance:** It is the practice of monitoring, through human resources and/or technical movements, actions and habits of individuals or groups of individuals.

# Chapter 24
# Surveillance, Privacy, and Due Diligence in Cybersecurity:
## An International Law Perspective

**Joanna Kulesza**
*University of Lodz, Poland*

## ABSTRACT

*The chapter covers the international law due diligence principle as applied to the prevention of transboundary cyberthreats. The analysis is based on the work of the International Law Commission referring to state responsibility and international liability as applicable to the challenge of international cybersecurity. The first attempts of this application by European international organizations are discussed. This is done in the light of the current political challenge of engaging all states in the discussion on the appropriate standard of cyberthreats prevention. Reaching to the no harm principle of international law, the author argues that all states need to take all necessary measures in order to prevent significant transboundary damage originated by online activities of individuals within their jurisdiction, power, or control. Should they fail to show due diligence they may be held internationally responsible for an omission contrary to their obligation of preventing harm to other states, foreigners, or shared resources.*

## INTRODUCTION

The chapter covers the due diligence standard for preventing cyberthreats according to international law standards. The author describes details of a cyberspace specific due diligence requirement of online service providers and information infrastructure operators in the light of international customary and contractual legal practice. While international law obligations rest directly upon states, they are being implemented through acts of national law, binding upon information services and infrastructure operators within each state jurisdiction. Unlike with other media, the unique transboundary character of the Internet requires a uniform, international standard of due care in preserving the network's resiliency and stability for both: practical and technical reasons. Such an international cybersecurity due diligence standard allows for simultaneously securing all elements of the network at an equal level and makes it easier for intentional companies, operating in various ju-

DOI: 10.4018/978-1-4666-6324-4.ch024

risdictions, to meet professional security standards required according to national laws. The analysis provided within the chapter is derived from rich international law jurisprudence and includes an up-to-date application of the due diligence principle to the challenges posed by transboundary online interactions, in particular to significant transboundary harm inflicted through online activities. The chapter is based on a thorough analysis of due diligence in public international law as the common element of two accountability regimes: the regime of state responsibility for the breach of an international obligation and international risk-liability for transboundary harm. The presented research devolves from the doctrine of international environmental law with its detailed due diligence standard and principle of prevention for the purpose of applying it to cyber-security. It also includes the crucial human rights perspective, calling for a flexible equilibrium between international online security and individual privacy or freedom of speech.

According to the work of the International Law Commission (ILC) significant transboundary damage may result in so-called risk liability. International liability is bound not to state actions, but to its omissions – failures to prevent or at least minimize the risk of significant transboundary harm by inadequately controlling entities causing risk of such harm within state territory, jurisdiction or control. A mechanism designated to aid states in preventing such harm resolves to state monopoly in authorizing private entities for running risk generating enterprises. In order to assess whether a state met its prevention and risk-assessment obligations, the due diligence standard is revoked on a case-by-case basis.

The non-exhaustive list of state authorized monopolies does not explicitly include IT-based services. Yet with the rise of asymmetric threats to international peace and security, especially so-called "cyberterrorism," a question whether it should, is being raised forever more frequently, in particular with reference to the definition of "criti-

cal infrastructure." The principle of prevention originating from international environmental law may be applied to cyberthreats originating from one state territory causing significant transboundary harm outside it. Should that be the case a state might be held liable for its failure to supervise activities conducted by the IT service providers within its territory. States willing to mitigate liability for such failure create forever more strenuous national laws obliging IT professionals to show due diligence. So far however no international due diligence standard for cybersecurity is being directly named, leaving companies operating in numerous jurisdictions one their own when dealing with varying national regulations.

The idea presented within the chapter covers an international cyberspace-specific due diligence standard and a possible liability mechanism, based on the multistakeholder principle recognized within Internet governance. The author answers the question whether a due diligence standard for cyberspace may and if so - ought to be introduced through particular obligations laid upon Internet service providers and critical infrastructure operators. Recognition of such a standard on the international level would set IT companies free from having to invest in costly legal counseling in each and every jurisdiction they enable their services in.

## BACKGROUND

"Transboundary harm" is a significant term in the 21th century international law doctrine and jurisprudence. It is the focal criteria of the ongoing discussions aimed at tracing the limits of state responsibility and international liability for damage caused by private parties acting within state jurisdiction. Transboundary harm may appear when their activities cause detrimental results within the jurisdiction of other states or shared spaces, like the Open Sea or the Antarctic. State responsibility for transboundary harm grew in significance alongside the rapid technological development of the 20th century. The more there were new industrial applications of natural resources, the more troublesome the accompanying harmful effects to agriculture or everyday life became, including air and soil pollution caused by the developing industry or privacy intrusions caused by the growing media industry and increasing state surveillance. The 15 year long Trail Smelter dispute solved in 1941 by U.S. - Canadian arbitration was the first international law case to directly refer to the obligation of states to prevent transboundary harm originating from their territory (Trail Smelter Arbitral Tribunal, 1939; Trail Smelter Arbitral Tribunal, 1941). The case concerned a claim by U.S. residents to oblige a Canadian company, Consolidated Mining and Smelting Company of Canada in Trail, British Columbia, to limit the amount of harmful emissions from its plant located near U.S.-Canadian border, in a town of Trail. Due to steady northern winds the emissions had caused significant damage to natural environment within the U.S. state of Washington, decreasing the crops of U.S. farmers and the value of real estate in the area. While the company agreed to pay damages to the victims, it renounced any obligation to limit the production or the amount of emissions, not willing to risk a decrease in its high income (Allum 2006). The arbitration court called into life in 1935 was tasked with solving the dispute. The tribunal formulated what is known as the no-harm principle, now lying at the foundations of the international good neighborliness standard. It clearly stated that no state may use or allow the use of its territory in such a way as to cause damage outside its jurisdiction. Such a harmful effect, contrary to international law, brings about international responsibility of that state, even though it was not caused by the direct actions of state organs but by private entities. The court formulated a fundamental international law principle according to which a state is always obliged to protect other states from harmful actions of individuals within

its jurisdiction (Trail Smelter Arbitral Tribunal, 1941). The victim state holds therefore a fair and justified expectation for its natural environment not to be significantly contaminated (Trail Smelter Arbitral Tribunal, 1941). The arbitration tribunal followed to recognize that "under the principles of international law, as well as of the law of the United States, no State has the right to use or permit the use of its territory in such a manner as to cause injury by fumes in or to the territory of another or the properties or persons therein, when the case is of serious consequence and the injury is established by clear and convincing evidence" (Trail Smelter Arbitral Tribunal, 1941).

Even though the tribunal did not apply the contemporary notion of state responsibility for the failure of its organs to prevent significant transboundary harm, nor did it identify the contents of the international obligation Canada failed to comply with, the following scholarly work and jurisprudence allow to indicate at least three grounds for Canada's responsibility in the given case. According to Ellis those could be: risk liability, nuisance or lack of due diligence (Ellis, 2006). Since the court calls upon "serious consequence" and "clear and convincing evidence" as grounds for such responsibility, one might justifiably point to the obligation of providing due diligence in international relations as the one having been broken by Canada in the given case (Ellis, 2006).

Such conclusion seems justified in the light of the 1972 Stockholm Declaration of the United Nations Conference on the Human Environment and its Article 21 stipulating the principle of good neighborliness (United Nations Conference on the Human Environment, 1972). The obligation to refrain from inflicting transboundary damage is also derived by the UN Special Rapporteur on international liability Julio Barboza from the political reality where complete and unconditional state sovereignty is not possible (Barboza, 1986). The significance as well as the complexity of the Trail Smelter case were well reflected in the work of the International Law Commission on international liability, continuing from 1978 and partially summarized by the non-binding yet encapsulating contemporary customary law Draft Articles on Prevention adopted by the Commission in 2001 (International Law Commission, 2001). While the international law obligation of prevention, reflecting the no-harm principle fundamental to international environmental law, originated from rich treaty and soft law background of the 1970s environmental law, it finds universal applicability including all significant transboundary harm, also to activities not considered direct threats to the natural environment.

As discussed in detail below "transboundary harm" may arise from any kind of risk entailing activity. States are obliged to stay alert to any new activity of this kind and introduce appropriate preventive measures to limit the risk of prospective transboundary harm. The limits of this obligation of states are traced by the contents of their obligation to show due diligence. The contents of the due diligence principle may be clearly identified when analyzing the last 40 years of work of the International Law Commission. Such an analysis is presented below. Its aim is to allow for the appropriate application of the international law due diligence principle to transboundary threats brought about by the era of cyberspace. The latter are well represented in the political tension surrounding international cyber-attacks. As formulated by White House national security advisor, Tom Donilion in March 2013 "Increasingly, U.S. businesses are speaking out about their serious concerns about sophisticated, targeted theft of confidential business information and proprietary technologies through cyber intrusions emanating from China on an unprecedented scale" (Donilon, 2013). Donilion notably demands Chinese authorities to express their dedication to fighting cybercrimes committed by their residents and to engage in an international dialogue on a due diligence standard for transnational cybersecurity. Donilion's proposal reflects the recent work of the Council of Europe (CoE) and the

European Union (EU), which both have proposed transnational standards for network security and integrity, strongly rooted in international law. The 2011 CoE Recommendation CM/Rec(2011)8 on the protection and promotion of the universality, integrity and openness of the Internet (Council of Europe, 2013) as well as the 2013 EU Proposal for a Directive concerning measures to ensure a high common level of network and information security across the Union both refer to the risks of significant transboundary harm originated by online activities (European Parliament and the Council, 2013). Those documents cover the up-to-date interpretation of international law due diligence principle recognized in numerous treaty-based and customary regimes, including international environmental law, diplomatic and consular relations or the protection of aliens.

## MAIN FOCUS OF THE CHAPTER

### An International Law Obligation of Due Diligence

When describing the principles in its 2001 Draft Articles on Prevention the ILC introduced numerous definitions helpful in assessing the actions and omissions of states possibly leading to its responsibility for the undiligent conduct of its organs. A phrase crucial to assessing the scope of the obligation of prevention is the "risk of causing significant transboundary harm" since only such risk triggers the obligation to prevent it. The ILC defines the "risk of causing significant transboundary harm" as encompassing "a high probability of causing significant transboundary harm or a low probability of causing disastrous transboundary harm" (International Law Commission, 2001). Such definition clearly draws the line for all activities requiring preventive measures at the point of their "high probability of causing significant transboundary harm". Not only does an action need to bring about the threat of significant transboundary harm – that risk needs to be highly probable. Only then is a state obliged to act according to the measures provided for in the 2001 ILC Draft Articles on Prevention. The ILC understands "significant" as "something more" than "detectable" but not at the level of "serious" or "substantial" (International Law Commission, 2001). The level of possible risk of harm is in practice left to be assessed by experts, helping judges in making their decisions, and therefore will rarely be non-controversial or objectively measurable (Clifford, 1998). The arising "significant" harm will only give ground to the preventive obligation should it lead to "a real detrimental effect on matters such as, for example, human health, industry, property, environment or agriculture in other States", as measured by factual and objective standards (International Law Commission, 2001).

Given the diverse nature of the various endeavors undertaken within state borders, it was impossible to draw up an exhaustive list of activities which carry a risk of transboundary harm. A significant help in defining the scope of the obligation discussed was therefore the open catalogue of risk-originating activities proposed by the ILC in the course of its work. Exercising any of such activities within state territory would require of authorities to introduce and enforce appropriate preventive measures. In defining the concept of "dangerous activities" the ILC emphasized however that some undertakings may prove risky only when carried out jointly with other projects, therefore an exhaustive list of such activities would be not only undesired, but actually not possible to draft (Rao, 1998). According to the ILC the preventive obligation of providing due diligence rests upon the country where the risk originating activity takes place (Rao, 2000). The "country of origin" was defined as the one where the risk-originating activities were conducted or the state which in any other manner controlled or exercised jurisdiction over such activities (Barboza 1996). The Commission defined the victim state as any state within whose territory significant

transboundary harm occurred or one that hold jurisdictional competence or control over the territory where such harm appeared (Barboza, 1996; International Law Commission, 2006). According to the ILC "transboundary harm" means "harm caused in the territory of or in other places under the jurisdiction or control of a State other than the State of origin", regardless whether the states share a common border (Barboza 1996).

While describing the catalogue of duties of states in preventing transboundary harm, the Commission indicated the entities whose actions were to be controlled by the state. Deriving from the 1993 Lugano Convention on civil liability for environmental damage and the Convention on Civil Liability for Damage Resulting from Activities Dangerous to the Environment (Council of Europe, 1993), it defined the „operator" as a person who controls the risk-originating activity (Barboza, 1994). The operator should carry the responsibility for significant transboundary harm originated by those activities regardless of whether he was still in control of the activity at the time the harmful consequences occurred. If more than one operator was responsible for the harmful activity they all share joint and several responsibility, unless one of them can prove, that he was responsible only for partial damage, in which case he would be liable only for that part (Barboza,1994).

## A Territorial Obligation

The duty to provide due diligence by a state vis-à-vis risk originating activities ought to be understood primarily in the territorial respect, although according to the ILC that risk covers also those states which are not in direct, physical proximity to the territory where the operator is located. Potential victims may be recruited from among all those touched directly or indirectly by the activity and whose damage could have been rationally foreseen (Barboza, 1993). A state ought to take all necessary endeavors to avoid actions or omissions which can be rationally foreseen as holding potential harm to victim states, that is those states that can be rationally identified as potentially affected by the foreseeable harmful activity (Rao, 1998).

## Sustainable Development

In this context the obligation of due diligence ought to be recognized as a facet of the principle of sustainable development (Rao, 2000), which requires due diligence in preventing significant transboundary harm while implying a joint, yet differentiated set of obligations resting upon individual states. The differences in the scope of individual obligations of states originate from their varied economic and technological capabilities. As a consequence states ought to take "all necessary steps" to prevent transboundary harm, while the ILC decided not to use the term "due diligence" directly but substitute it with a more precise reference to required individual measures (Rao, 2000). While the ILC aimed at declaring a principle of international law, the obligation to prevent transboundary harm was not an absolute one (Barboza, 1996). As discussed above, it was only to be applied to those activities that brought about the risk of causing significant transboundary harm, rather than to refer to any transboundary harm at all. This reflected the generally recognized principle of international responsibility, according to which states were free from responsibility for acts not contrary to international law, yet conducted in their territory, under their jurisdiction or control. According to the interpretation of the Commission this principle freed states also from the responsibility for "clandestine" activities, that is those intentionally conducted in secrecy, ones that even a diligent state would be unable to identify. Moreover the obligation to provide due diligence would be limited to activities that may be identified as holding a risk of significant transboundary harm according to common knowledge in the field (Barboza, 1996). A state ought

to undertake endeavors to identify the potential sources of harm, yet it could be only held responsible should it fail to "undertake all appropriate measures in order to prevent or minimize" the risk of transboundary harm arising. As a consequence the obligation to prevent transboundary harm was described by the ILC as a state's duty to undertake „all appropriate measures" aimed at preventing significant transboundary harm or to minimize the risk thereof. In the case where prevention is impossible, states are obliged to minimize its harmful effects (Barboza, 1996). An obligation so formulated incorporated the principle of due diligence (Barboza, 1996). The phrase "all appropriate measures" contained the obligation to use best available technology in order to identify and minimize the risk of significant transboundary harm (Barboza, 1993). Moreover the very fact of running a risk-originating activity was covered with obligatory insurance of its operators, one proportionate to the risk generated (Barboza, 1993).

Additionally if the state of origin was offered assistance in neutralizing the damage before it appeared or in minimizing its harmful effects by another state or an international organization and recklessly or negligently declined such help, it was to be deemed to have failed in exercising due diligence. If it had accepted such aid, any future damages ought to be accounted for only the actual infractions, not those that that were repaired or prevented (Barboza, 1996). It can be therefore assumed that the due diligence obligation ought to be assessed according to international rather than local or national standards of conduct (Rao, 1998). The Commission confirms this notion by formulating a recommendation where it states that the kind and scope of preventive measures ought to be assessed jointly by the originating state together with the potential victim states and cover the preventive procedures applicable in a particular situation (Rao, 1998). Primarily the state is obliged to undertake all necessary legislative, administrative and other measures aimed at preventing transboundary damage, intact with obligation of due diligence (International Law Commission, 2001). National regulations ought to be applied primarily to execute the regulations and decision aimed at fulfilling the international obligations of the state within its national policies (Rao, 1998).

Even though the requirement of due diligence does not cover the necessity to obtain complete knowledge of all risk originating activities within state jurisdiction, it does contain the duty to undertake measures aimed at identifying new categories of events generating the risk of transboundary harm. It can be therefore assessed that the obligation to undertake preventive measures and the ensuing obligation of due diligence of continuous character. States are therefore bound to undertake constant unilateral measures aimed at preventing or minimizing the risk of significant transboundary harm by introducing and enforcing appropriate policies (Barboza, 1996). Failure to meet this obligation, that is lack of due diligence, is shown where no reasonable effort to draft and implement such policies is made. The obligation to show due diligence is therefore not an obligation of result, that is of actual prevention of damage, but rather an obligation of conduct aimed at preventing certain undesired results, a "best efforts obligation" (Barboza, 1993). The ILC confirmed such an understanding of the principle of due diligence recalling the Rhine pollution case as well as the classic Alabama case, which constituted the need for state vigilance and its obligation to undertake all appropriate measures in its disposal to prevent damage to other sovereigns (Barboza, 1996). The obligation of prevention, based on the principle of due diligence, is therefore to be recognized as an "obligation of conduct and not of result" (Rao, 1998). Also Julio Barboza identified the obligation of prevention directly as the obligation of due diligence (Barboza, 1996). According to him the obligation of due diligence was to be understood as the necessity to undertake certain unilateral measures, aimed at preventing or

minimizing the risk of significant transboundary harm (Rao, 1998). Due diligence provided by state acting through its organs might serve as grounds for acquitting it of international responsibility, regardless of the actual transboundary damage suffered (Barboza, 1996). It requires therefore certain unilateral acts on behalf of state organs aimed at achieving that goal (Barboza, 1996). Baboza argued for such interpretation of the due diligence principle recalling numerous stipulations of international treaties, containing similar obligations, rich body of international soft law and case law, including the River Rhine incident (Barboza, 1994), where despite due diligence on behalf of the state significant transboundary harm arose. The obligation of due diligence implies therefore the need to undertake all reasonable measures, including administrative and executive procedures and policies, aimed at obtaining information on factual and legal options for introducing preventive procedures and executing them in due time (Barboza, 1996).

## Preventive Measures Recognized in International Law

The question of state responsibility for damage occurred in a situation where appropriate legal measures and procedures were introduced, yet their addressees failed to execute them was not clearly answered by the ILC (Barboza, 1993). Barboza argued that state's obligation to enforce certain procedures upon private parties running risk-originating enterprises endowed states with a particularly high level of due diligence resting upon them. States need to carefully draft and enforce procedures aimed at minimizing transboundary harm, using up-to-date technologies available in a given area. Since the obligation of due diligence is a continuous one, it ought to be understood as the need for continuous verification and possible alterations of existing procedures. Following the 1992 Rio Declaration on Environment and Development ILC identified states' obligation to introduce "effective" legislation for a particular area of activities (United Nations Conference on Environment and Development, 1992). As per Principle 11 of the Rio Declaration, "management objectives and priorities should reflect the environmental and developmental context to which they apply" (United Nations Conference on Environment and Development, 1992). Similar language may be found in Principle 23 of the 1972 Stockholm Declaration, which states that regional or national criteria ought to be applied "without prejudice to such criteria as may be agreed upon by the international community".

## Principle of Non-Discrimination

The due diligence principle includes also the obligation of non-discrimination vis-à-vis all operators running potentially risk-originating activities. Should they be held liable, they must be treated by their state of operation equally to all local enterprises regardless of the state of their incorporation or the nationality of its employees or managers. Also the location of the damage must not be grounds for discrimination. All operators must be equal before the law and have equal access to courts or administrative organs of the state (Barboza, 1996). The obligation of non-discrimination applies also to the victims of damage occurred (Rao, 1998).

## Principle of Proportionality

Due diligence requires states to act in accordance with what was generally considered appropriate and proportional in a given situation, depending on the degree of risk of transboundary harm brought about by a given situation. Activities entailing a greater likelihood of significant transboundary harm require therefore a much higher standard of care when designing and executing policies and a higher level of state activity in enforcing them than ones regarding activities not holding risk of transboundary harm (Barboza, 1994; Barboza,

1996; Rao, 1998). As a consequence the level of required due diligence is directly proportionate to the risk of potential damage, originating from a particular activity (Rao, 1998). When assessing the level of due diligence exercised by the state, the scale of undertaken activities, their localization as well as the materials and tools used for the execution of the preventive activities are to be considered according to indications of rationality and logical causality of the procedures applied (Barboza, 1994, Rao, 1998). Also the significance of the risk-originating activities for the economy and technology of the originating state as well as state resources in relation to those applied in the region and worldwide are of issue for the due diligence assessment (Rao, 1998).

## Continuous Character of the Obligation

The obligation of due diligence is a flexible one, as its contents change with time along with the form and meaning of applicable and adequate procedures, standards and norms (Barboza, 1994). Due diligence requires states to keep updated with "technological changes and scientific developments" as well as with "current specifications and standards" (Barboza, 1994; Rao, 1998). Moreover the implementation of "the due diligence obligation" ought to be "directly proportional to the scientific, technical and economic capacities" of states and necessitates "an expanded exchange of information" as well as broad consultations and risk assessment procedures (Rao, 1998). While the economic capacity of a state is one of the criteria for assessing its diligence, the ILC emphasized on numerous occasions that the shortage of economic resources may not serve as the only effective justification for deficient preventive mechanisms (Barboza, 1994; Barboza, 1996). States aiming at preventing transboundary harm are to minimize the risk thereof that is to reduce the possibility of harm to the "lowest point" (Barboza, 1996).

## International Cooperation

The duty to engage in transboundary harm prevention covers however also the obligation to engage in effective international cooperation. It ought to include the exchange of up-to-date technological information as well as data on possible risk of significant transboundary harm, entailing the obligation to share notices on existing threats and undertaken precautionary measures with potentially effected states (Barboza, 1993). The information obligation covers all data regarding the risk-originating activity, confirming the continuous character of the due diligence obligation (Barboza, 1996). It includes the obligation of undertaking continuous efforts in preventing or minimizing transboundary harm, in particular the obligation to continuously monitor activities authorized within its jurisdiction or control and to share information on potential threats with neighboring states (Barboza, 1994; Barboza, 1996). The information shared ought to include all data considered useful in a given case, that is practical in preventing the damage or minimizing its results, not just those necessary or needed for effective prevention (Barboza, 1994).

## Good Neighborliness

As already mentioned due diligence was also derived by the Commission from the principle of good neighborliness, which includes the obligation of each of each state to undertake appropriate measures and refrain from activities aimed at rationally predicable harm to other subject of international law (Barboza, 1996). Moreover, when identifying the due diligence principle in international law the ILC reaffirms states' right to economic self-determination, particularly significant to developing nations. Followingly every state has the right to decide about its specific economic priorities and the use of its natural resources (Rao, 2000). Due diligence is therefore to be applied with respect of principle of sustainable development (Rao, 2000).

## ISSUES, CONTROVERSIES, PROBLEMS

### War on Terror and Transboundary Cyberthreats

The precisely described standard of due diligence in international law is to be, as already mentioned, applied to all international obligations of conduct with respect of state omissions leading to the risk of significant transboundary harm. This fact allows for its applicability to new challenges facing contemporary international law. It seems particularly important when discussing state responsibility for acts of terrorist nature, committed by individuals or private groups acting from within its jurisdiction or territories under state control. While the definition of terrorism has been ground for controversy since mid-20th century, the popularization of electronic communications brought a new facet to this debate. The notion of terrorism is difficult to define – what is terrorism to one may be viewed as a freedom fight or an expression of the right to self-determination by others. Regardless of whether transboundary cyberattacks are acts of terrorism, significant harm caused by them ought to be prevented by the state within whose jurisdiction or control their originators operate. A good example of the scale of harm caused by cyberthreats may be that of the 2007 series of DDoS cyberattacks, originating from Russian territory upon Estonia. The attacks caused a major shutdown of governmental and companies websites offering services to the public, lasting more than two weeks. Without a doubt this significant infraction to Estonia's public life – the limited access to the majority of public services, ought to be considered significant harm to the victim state and its residents. Using the ILC definition they did cause "a real detrimental effect on (…) industry", as measured by factual and objective standards (International Law Commission, 2001). While the attacks caused a major dysfunction in the operation of key public services, Russian authorities, alarmed of the situation, denied help, claiming no responsibility for the acts of individuals conducting the DDoS attacks from Russian territory, yet through international computer networks.

This and other similar events (Shackleford, 2009) invite the discussion on a cyberspace specific standard of due diligence. With the detailed blueprint of due diligence allowing for its qualification as a principle of international law, it ought to be easy to apply all its elements to online conduct. What is more, resolving to due diligence for assessing state responsibility in case of transboundary harm inflicted as a result of individual online actions seems an attractive alternative to the practically impossible attribution of cyberattacks to state authorities. In order to prove state responsibility for cyberattacks one would need to demonstrate that the originators of cyberattacks acted upon a direct order or authorization of state officials.

Regarding the analysis provided above each state is obliged to prevent significant transboundary harm inflicted through online actions of individuals within state jurisdiction, territory or control. In order to achieve that aim states ought to undertake all appropriate measures, including but not limited to introduction of judicial and administrative measures aimed at identifying and putting on trial perpetrators of such attacks. In order to fulfill its due diligence obligation each state ought to engage in international cooperation aimed at preventing such attacks, which includes sharing information on potential threats and jointly identifying effective prevention strategies. While the economic capabilities of states remain a significant issue in preventing transboundary cyberattacks, as mentioned above lack of sufficient financial resources may not be the only ground for allowing a potentially harmful use of one's territory. The obligation of prevention is of continuous nature, inviting states to sustain a collaboration on the issue once it is engaged. The preventive measures ought to be enacted in good faith and remain proportional to the individual threat. The

latter element of the due diligence obligation allows to argue for a higher due diligence standard for critical state infrastructure, such as power plants, water supplies or public transportation supported by computer operated infrastructure.

## Due Diligence in Preventing Transboundary Cyberthreats

It was the CoE that was the first international forum to engage in the debate on due diligence in cyberspace. In 2011 it described in detail due diligence applicable to the protection of online resources. In its Recommendation it called upon all states to work together with other stakeholders, that is with service providers, users and civil society, referring to „all relevant stakeholders" to undertake all necessary measures "to prevent, manage and respond to significant transboundary disruptions to (…) the infrastructure of the Internet" (Council of Europe, 2011). As further explained by the Committee of Ministers this obligation of states ought to be executed "within the limits of non-involvement in day-to-day technical and operational matters" conducted by private entities acting as service providers. This is a reflection of the multistakeholder principle recognized in international Internet law and Internet governance (Kulesza, 2012).

The obligation in pt. 1.3. of the Recommendation sets a minimal standard of care aimed at limiting "the risk and consequences arising from" any "disruptions" (Council of Europe, 2011). In this context "disruptions" are perceived as negative consequences influencing "the stable and ongoing functioning of the network" as a result of "technical failures" (Council of Europe, 2011). The CoE emphasizes the interconnection between effective networks resilience and international cooperation, when stating that "the stability and resilience of the Internet is intrinsically related to (…) its decentralised and distributed nature" (Council of Europe, 2011). As rightfully noted by the CoE, actions taking "place in one jurisdiction may affect the ability of users to have access to information on the Internet in another" (Council of Europe, 2011). This is why it puts the international law no-harm principle as the starting point of its recommendation. It reaffirms general obligation of states to "ensure, in compliance with (…) the principles of international law, that their actions do not have an adverse transboundary impact", making a direct reference to the possible harmful effect such actions might have on the "access to and use of the Internet" (Council of Europe, 2011). Abbreviating the points made in the previous paragraph of this chapter the CoE identifies states' obligation to "ensure that their actions within their jurisdictions do not illegitimately interfere with access to content outside their territorial boundaries or negatively impact the transboundary flow of Internet traffic" as ground for possible responsibility of an non-diligent state (Council of Europe, 2011).

While exercising due diligence states ought to respect the standards of international law, but also pay attention to the standards identified in international human rights law (Council of Europe, 2011). This obligation means that no violations of privacy, like e.g. a blanket surveillance of individual online communications ought to be enforced as a preventive measure since it is clearly a violation of the human right to privacy, identified within numerous international law treaties, including Article 17 of the International Covenant on Civil and Political Rights (ICCPR) (United Nations, 1996). It is therefore clear that the due diligence obligation of preventing transboundary harm online does not include continuous surveillance of all subjects to state jurisdiction, on the contrary – such surveillance would be a breach of international human rights law. What is more, according to the freedom of speech guarantees also provided in international law, just to mention Article 19 ICCPR, any obligation of preventive censorship of online contents, put on e.g. Internet service providers, ought to also be considered a breach of international law (European Court of

Justice, 2011). The same free speech standard does not require states to introduce obligatory authorization of rendering online services, although that is the case for risk-originating activities known to international law. Reflecting the international law due diligence standard CoE encourages states to engage in multilateral cooperation aimed at preventing transboundary harm to Internet's stability and resilience (Council of Europe, 2011). In order to meet that standard states ought to develop and implement emergency procedures for managing and responding to Internet disruptions applicable to all stakeholders, in particular entities running Internet infrastructure (Council of Europe, 2011). They should take an active part in "the development and implementation of common standards, rules and practices aimed at preserving and strengthening the stability, robustness and resilience of the Internet" (Council of Europe, 2011). Moreover states should with no undue delay notify potential victims of any risk of significant transboundary disruptions to the functioning of the network (Council of Europe, 2011). The required response from the state of origin for the significant transboundary harm ought to comprise of four elements. It ought to include a prompt notification of any such risk for all potentially affected states (Council of Europe, 2011). The obligation of sharing with the potentially affected states all available information that is relevant to responding to such disruptions is the second element of this obligation (Council of Europe, 2011). Once the risk of significant transboundary disruptions arises states ought to promptly engage in multilateral consultations aimed at identifying and applying mutually acceptable measures of response to the identified threats (Council of Europe, 2011). Eventually, the element of mutual assistance, present in international law with regard to the obligation of due diligence ought to be introduced "as appropriate" (Council of Europe, 2011). The scope of activities falling within the due diligence obligation ought to be identified "with due regard" to the capabilities of individual states, while states ought to offer their assistance to other affected states in good faith and with the aim of mitigating the harmful results of transboundary disruptions (Council of Europe, 2011).

The obligation of due diligence so perceived with regard to transboundary online communications ought to be implemented "in consultation with relevant stakeholders" and respecting the principle of non-involvement, obliging states to refrain from interference with the "day-to-day technical and operational matters" (Council of Europe, 2011). States ought to act through the introduction of "reasonable: legislative, administrative or any other appropriate measures" needed for the implementation of their international law due diligence obligations (Council of Europe, 2011). While this broadly sketched duty of due diligence in respect of online communications allows to identify the basic efforts required from states in respect of securing online communications, the CoE encourages states to engage "in dialogue and co-operation for the further development of international standards relating to responsibility and liability" for online disruption (Council of Europe, 2011).

A similar idea to that contained in the CoE Recommendation was expressed in the 2013 EU Proposal for a Directive concerning measures to ensure a high common level of network and information security across the Union. According to its stipulations entities operating infrastructure critical to national and international security, including Internet infrastructure rendering online services critical to the functioning of modern communities have so far not been legally obliged to introduce any risk management rules or the procedures of making information on possible risk of significant harm available to state authorities. What follows is, on one hand, lack of effective incentives for business to introduce mature risk management policies, including risk assessment and procedures in case of a system failure. According to a recent Eurostat study less than 30%

of all European enterprises have introduced information infrastructure safety policy (European Commission, 2013). On the other hand however state authorities are becoming increasingly aware of the growing number of security threats originating from private enterprises running critical state infrastructure.

Presently national regulations rarely require telecommunication companies to introduce risk management procedures and notify authorities of incidents involving their information infrastructure. At the same time almost all industry branches rely upon telecommunications infrastructure in their daily operations, including banking services, stock markets, production, transmission and distribution of energy, air, rail and sea transport, health services, internet services as well as public administration.

The European Union looked closely at this emerging problem within a series of documents on information infrastructure security (High Representative of The European Union for Foreign Affairs and Security Policy Brussels, (2013). They lead up to proposed specific obligations for the IT sector set within the 2013 Proposal. The proposed directive is to introduce detailed obligations rooted in national laws for the entities "managing critical infrastructure or providing services essential to the functioning of societies" regarding the fact that currently they are not "under appropriate obligations to adopt risk management measures and exchange information with relevant authorities" (European Commission, 2013). The Directive lays down detailed measures aimed at ensuring "a high common level of network and information security" ("NIS") throughout the EU. Therefore it covers the obligations of states relating to "the prevention, the handling of and the response to risks and incidents affecting networks and information systems" as well as creates a mechanism of cooperation those states "in order to ensure (…) a coordinated and efficient handling of and response to risks and incidents affecting network and information systems", which includes introducing detailed "security requirements for market operators and public administrations" (European Commission, 2013). According to its Article 14 EU states are ensure "that public administrations and market operators take appropriate technical and organizational measures to manage the risks posed to the security of the networks and information systems which they control and use in their operations" (European Commission, 2013). The "all appropriate measures" standard known to international law relating to transboundary harm is perceived with "regard to the state of the art" while the undertaken measures ought to "guarantee a level of security appropriate to the risk presented." They ought to include, in particular, measures "to prevent and minimize the impact of incidents" affecting networks and systems on the services provided, ensuring "the continuity of the services underpinned by those networks and information systems" (European Commission, 2013). The scope of the entities subject to the particular security obligations is to be limited by the exclusion of "undertakings providing public communication networks or publicly available electronic communication services" as defined within the Framework Directive 2002/21/EC on e-commerce, for whom particular security obligations will be introduced through the amendment of the present Article 13 with Articles 13a and 13b of that Directive (European Commission, 2013). At the same time the "network and information system" focal to the proposed regulation ought to be defined through the notion of "an electronic communications network" within the meaning of Directive 2002/21/EC, raising potential issues when it comes to delimiting the scope of individual companies bound by the prospected national regulation.

The prospected regulation introduces national competent authorities responsible for supervising the introduction of the EU standard into national practice. Responsible for the security of network and information systems they are to be designated by each state and monitor the application

of this Directive at national level, supporting "its consistent application throughout the Union". National legislation will be based on a "national NIS strategy and national NIS cooperation plan", defining "the strategic objectives and concrete policy and regulatory measures" aimed at reaching the goal set by the Directive. The strategy should in particular address the criteria for the "identification of the general measures on preparedness, response and recovery, including cooperation mechanisms between the public and private sectors". States will also be endowed with the task of identifying particular systems that are to be included into the scope of the Directive, which provokes the danger of significant variations in national implementations for the EU principles (European Commission, 2013).

The national strategies ought to be based on "on a coordinated response" model set within the "Union NIS cooperation plan". According to Article 12 of the Proposal the plan, adopted by the Commission will include definitions of the "format and procedures for the collection and sharing of compatible and comparable information on risks and incidents by the competent authorities" and of "the procedures and the criteria for the assessment of the risks and incidents by the cooperation network". The Commission will also draft the "the processes to be followed for coordinated responses", including designing the roles and responsibilities and cooperation procedures. According to Article 17 the possible sanctions to apply for the infringements of the national provisions reflecting those of the Directive fall within the competence of the states. They ought to "take all measures necessary to ensure" the implementation of the principles. The sanctions to be provided in national laws "must be effective, proportionate and dissuasive" (European Commission, 2013).

The European example, depicted above, clearly shows the transposition of the international law due diligence standard onto the transboundary information flow of data and information services. Following the due diligence standard states are to be entrusted with the task of listing services whose operators will need to meet particular security obligations under the pain of sanctions. The scope of the infrastructure covered by this obligations and, consequently, the list of operators as well as the measures to be taken in order to provide network security are to be set by individual states.

While this approach seems highly justified from an international law perspective, the European example seem to be isolated on the international arena. A representative demonstration of the international tension surrounding international cybersecurity standard was the already mentioned early 2013 diplomatic exchange between U.S. and China, when the White House demanded China to introduce and enforce measures to stop the harmful online activity originating from its territory (Donilon, 2013). In response to the White House statement Chinese foreign minister, Yang Jiechi, rejected any evidence of state-sponsored cyberattacks and pointed to the U.S. as main source of cyberattacks aimed at Chinese territory China Daily, 2013). This exchange proves that the international community is not yet ready to engage in serious negotiations on the due diligence standard for cyberspace.

## SOLUTIONS AND RECOMMENDATIONS: TOWARDS A DUE DILIGENCE STANDARD FOR CYBERSPACE

The fight against international terrorism introduces a pressing need for intensified international cooperation on cybersecurity. The principle of due diligence, well established in international law, when applied to the cybersecurity challenge allows to identify particular obligations resting upon states when it comes to ensuring international cybersecurity. States ought to refrain from internationally harmful omissions when it comes to significant transboundary harm caused though an online activity initiated from within their jurisdiction, power or control. This obligation translates

directly onto the introduction of necessary national laws and procedures allowing the identification of potential threats and minimizing the risks. As the EU example shows meeting this obligations comes down to identifying the critical infrastructure vulnerable to attacks and putting onto its operators particular security obligations, making private companies' security policies a matter of national and international safety. The contents of those obligations present in national laws ought to reflect a well-informed international consensus based on solid technical knowledge, while respecting individual economic and technological capabilities of each state. Assessing the standard of care for cybersecurity must reflect the specifics of the network it addresses – one managed by various entities, whose cooperation is essential for its flawless functioning. The international Internet law principle of multistakeholderism requires the cooperation between governments, business and civil society in adopting and enforcing Internet related policies and regulations. Just as rightfully argued in the era of nuclear tests by the UN Special Rapporteur García-Amador, „new categories of objective responsibility must be constructed in order to face the growing number of threats brought by technological developments Garcia-Amador, 1960).

The recommended solution for the presented problem of identifying the details of a due diligence standard for cyberspace refers to the need for involving more states into the debate on its desired scope. The European examples of the EU and the CoE show that identifying the due diligence standard for cyberspace is a considerable option for solving the current cyberterrorism problem. It may be perceived as a noteworthy alternative to the military qualification of cyber-attacks as acts of armed aggression allowing for an armed response. Widening the scope of states involved in the discussion on the desired, future content of the international due diligence obligations applicable to cyberspace is the key recommendation. Other issues that need to be looked into include the rights and obligations of private entities covered by the due diligence duties as set within national laws, the uniformisation of such laws and the possible need and form of financial support for those parties and developing states, in order to avoid the risk of economically weaker regions becoming cyberterrorism hubs.

## FUTURE RESEARCH DIRECTIONS

Future research directions include therefore primarily the verification of the applicability of international liability models for cybersecurity. They require the careful assessment of the scope of activities and consequently private entities covered by particular security obligations.

As is the case with e.g. oil transport or nuclear power production risk-originating activities often require two elements: state authorization and a liability fund. Introducing those two elements for cybersecurity seems particularly challenging, as it directly depends on the catalogue of activities identified as originating the risk of significant transboundary harm caused through online activities. Regarding the growing popularity of online services the majority of information systems may be subject to threats potentially causing significant transboundary harm. As e.g. power plants or public transportation systems are being forever more strongly integrated with computer-based systems when it comes to e.g. the production process or route planning respectively, any such computer-based system affecting large numbers of potential victims when compromised might allow for its qualification as part of critical infrastructure and subjecting it to particular security obligations falling onto its operator. International law so far looked at the risk-originating activities as a particularly narrow category, based on numerous international treaties and a soft law background. It covers three major categories of activity: nuclear power production, space exploration and oil transportation. Their common trait was the need for state authorization of any such activity. As cyberthreats may originate from a large number of activities subjecting all of them to state authorization might be considered excessive and therefore undesired, while probably difficult to enforce. While creating a list of activities covered by the due diligence obligation seems rational, subjecting online risk-originating activities to state authorization is undesired.

Identifying entities running risk-originating activities with respect of cybersecurity and obliging them to introduce particular cybersecurity measures according to national law will probably be accompanied by sanctions for not introducing such measures, as provided for in the EU Directive proposal discussed hereinabove. Identifying such a due diligence obligation for information systems operators subjects them however also to liability for harm caused by their omissions. According to the already mentioned ILC documents operators of risk-originating activities carry the responsibility for significant transboundary harm originated by those activities. The international law practice in areas such as oil transportation or nuclear power production led up to the development of comprehensive insurance services accompanying those business sectors as well as to the introduction of liability funds fueled by private entities running such risk originating enterprises. Regarding the scale of possible damage caused by compromised information systems, such as those operating in public transportation or water supplying services civil liability of their operators might exceed by far their financial capabilities. Introducing obligatory or allowing for the introduction of voluntary insurance services or possibly creating a liability fund fueled by those covered by the due diligence obligation referring to cybersecurity should be covered by future research on the issue.

## PRACTICAL IMPLICATIONS

All of the arguments made above are aimed at three groups of addressees: policy makers, civil society and – last but not least – business representatives.

As clearly presented above, the due diligence obligation, present in international law, translates directly onto individual duties for national companies, bound by national laws but also professional ethics and international contracts. As practice of many international organizations shows, with the WTO being its prime example, laws are forever more frequently amended or supplemented with legally non-binding yet practically significant guidelines or recommendations, for businesses to follow. The analysis presented hereinabove allows ICT business managers to foresee what's behind the corner for future security and privacy regulations and act accordingly, by amending their security and privacy policies.

## CONCLUSION

In the light of contemporary international law states are to be held internationally responsible for their omissions in meeting internationally binding customary or treaty-based obligations of conduct. According to the international law no-harm principle states are obliged to introduce all measures necessary to prevent significant damage originating from their jurisdiction or entities in their control caused to foreign states, individuals or shared spaces. The catalogue of activities covered by this obligations is an open one and may include all consequences of human development and the application of new technologies. Meeting this obligation is to be assessed based on a due diligence standard. Any state within the territory, control or jurisdiction of which harmful events take place is under the obligation to provide due diligence in preventing it. Details of this obligation have been thoroughly identified by the International Law Commission within a series of reports. It includes the need to engage in international cooperation and exchange information, aimed at introducing coherent prevention and risk-assessment mechanism. This obligation clearly means that while states are not under an obligation to effectively prevent

all harm, they may not allow for risk originating or directly harmful activities to be conducted by individuals under their jurisdiction or control to the detriment of other states or foreigners.

Regarding the contemporary state on international relations and the growing significance of cyberthreats originated by individuals acting within state jurisdiction, although not directly authorized by the states this international law obligation of due diligence in preventing harmful individual actions seems a useful resource. Due diligence in cyberspace ought to be perceived as an application of the standard set out but he ILC in its work on international liability and responsibility. It allows to identify the individual activities required of states and the measures needed in national legal regimes for this obligation to be considered fulfilled. A following step might be one on detailing a cybersecurity due diligence standard based on a thorough technical analysis as well as a model for individual liability of private entities running risk-originating yet computer based or enhanced services, such as public transportation, water supplies, emergency services etc. The process of identifying such a due diligence model for cyberspace ought to include all actors participating in Internet governance, with states bound by the international law no-harm principle as guardians of the contemporary international legal order leading business and civil society to the negotiating table.

## REFERENCES

Allum, J. R. (2006). An Outcrop of Hel: History, Environment and the Politics of the Trail Smelter Dispute. In R. M. Bratspies, & R. A. Miller (Eds.), *Transboundary Harm in International Law, Lessons from the Trail Smelter Arbitration* (p. 15). Cambridge: Cambridge University Press.

Barboza, J. (1986). *Second report*. U.N. Doc. A/CN.4/402.

Barboza, J. (1993). *Ninth Report of the Special Rapporteur, Mr. Julio Barboza.* U.N. Doc. A/48/10.

Barboza, J. (1994). *Tenth Report of the Special Rapporteur, Mr. Julio Barboza.* U.N. Doc. A/49/10.

Barboza, J. (1996). *Twelfth Report of the Special Rapporteur, Mr. Julio Barboza.* U.N. Doc. A/51/10.

Clifford, M. (1998). *Environmental Crime: Enforcement, Policy, And Social Responsibility.* Gaithersburg, MD: Jones & Bartlett Learning.

Council of Europe. (1993). *Convention on Civil Liability for Damage Resulting from Activities Dangerous to the Environment.* ETS no. 150. Not yet (2013) in force

Council of Europe. (2011). *Recommendation CM/Rec(2011)8 of the Committee of Ministers to member states on the protection and promotion of the universality, integrity and openness of the Internet.* Retrieved October 13, 2013, from https://wcd.coe.int/ViewDoc.jsp?id=1835707

Daily, C. (2013, March 11). US main source of cyberattacks against China. *China Daily.* Retrieved November 29, 2013 from: http://usa.chinadaily.com.cn/china/2013-03/11/content_16296323.htm

Donilon, T. (2013). *The United States and the Asia-Pacific in 2013.* Retrieved October 13, 2013, from http://www.whitehouse.gov/the-press-office/2013/03/11/remarks-tom-donilon-national-security-advisory-president-united-states-a.

Ellis, J. (2006). Has International Law Outgrown Trail Smelter? In R. M. Bratspies, & R. A. Miller (Eds.), *Transboundary Harm in International Law, Lessons from the Trail Smelter Arbitration* (p. 60). Cambridge: Cambridge University Press.

European Commission. (2013). *Proposal for a Directive of the European Parliament and of the Council Concerning measures to ensure a high level of network and information security across the Union COM(2013) 48 final.* Retrieved October 13, 2013, from http://ec.europa.eu/digital-agenda/en/news/eu-cybersecurity-plan-protect-open-internet-and-online-freedom-and-opportunity-cyber-security

European Court of Justice. (2011). *Judgment of the Court (Third Chamber) of 24 November 2011.* Scarlet Extended SA v Société belge des auteurs, compositeurs et éditeurs SCRL (SABAM); case number C-70/10.

European Parliament, European Council. (2002). Directive 2002/21/EC of the European Parliament and of the Council of 7 March 2002 on a common regulatory framework for electronic communications networks and services (Framework Directive). *Official Journal, L,* 108.

Garcia-Amador, F.V. (1960). *Fifth Report on International Responsibility by Mr. F.V. Garcia-Amador, Special Rapporteur. State responsibility.* U.N. Doc. A/CN.4/125

High Representative of The European Union for Foreign Affairs and Security Policy Brussels. (2013). *Joint Communication to the European Parliament, the Council, the European Economic and Social Committee and the Committee of the Regions Cybersecurity Strategy of the European Union: An Open, Safe And Secure Cyberspace.* Retrieved October 13, 2013, from http://ec.europa.eu/digital-agenda/en/news/eu-cybersecurity-plan-protect-open-internet-and-online-freedom-and-opportunity-cyber-security

International Law Commission. (2001). *Draft Articles on Prevention, U.N. Doc. A/56/10* (referred to as: ILC Draft Articles on Prevention). Author.

International Law Commission. (2006). Draft principles on the allocation of loss in the case of transboundary harm arising out of hazardous activities. *U.N. Doc. A, 61*(10), 120.

Kulesza, J. (2012). International Internet law. *Global Change, Peace & Security, 24*(3), 351–364. doi:10.1080/14781158.2012.716417

Rao, P. (1998). *First Report of the Special Rapporteur, Mr. Pemmaraju Sreenivasa Rao.* U.N. Doc. A/CN.4/487.

Rao, P. (2000). *Third Report of the Special Rapporteur, Mr. Pemmaraju Sreenivasa Rao.* U.N. Doc. A/CN.4/510.

Shackelford, S. J. (2009). From Net War to Nuclear War: Analogizing Cyber Attacks in International Law. *Berkeley Journal of International Law, 27,* 192–211.

Trail, S. A. T. (1939). Trail Smelter Arbitral Tribunal Decision. *The American Journal of International Law, 33,* 182–212.

Trail, S. A. T. (1941). Trail Smelter Arbitral Tribunal Decision. *The American Journal of International Law, 35,* 684–736.

United Nations. (1966). *International Covenant on Civil and Political Rights, G.A. res. 2200A (XXI), U.N. Doc. A/6316 (1966).* Author.

United Nations Conference on Environment and Development. (1992). *Report of the United Nations Conference on Environment and Development, Annex I, U.N. Doc. A/CONF.151/26* (Vol. 1). Author.

*United Nations Conference on the Human Environment, Declaration of the United Nations Conference on the Human Environment, Stockholm.* (1972). Retrieved October 13, 2013, from http://www.unep.org/Documents.Multilingual/Default.asp?documentid=97&articleid=1503

## ADDITIONAL READING

Bidgoli, H. (2006). *Handbook of Information Security: Threats, Vulnerabilities, Prevention, Detection, and Management.* New York: John Wiley & Sons.

Campbell, D. (2006). *The Internet: Laws and Regulatory Regimes.* Salzburg: Yorkhill Law Publishing.

Cornish, P. Livingstone, D. Clemente, D. Yorke, C. (2010). On Cyber Warfare A Chatham House Report, London: Chatham House. Retrieved October 13, 2012, from http://www.chathamhouse.org.uk/publications/papers/view/–/id/967/

Delibasis, D. (2006). State Use of Force in Cyberspace for Self–Defence: A New Challenge for a New Century, Peace Conflict and Development: An Interdisciplinary Journal 8. Retrieved October 13, 2012, from http://www.peacestudiesjournal.org.uk/dl/Feb%2006%20DELIBASIS.pdf

Delibasis, D. (2007). The Right to National Self–defense: In Information Warfare Operations, Suffolk: Arena books.

Gelbstein, E. and Kurbalija, J. (2005). Internet governance: issues, actors and divides, Msida: Diplo Foundation.

Hoffer, S. (1998). *World cyberspace law.* New York: Juris Publishing, Inc.

Jorgensen, R. F. (Ed.). (2006). *Human Rights in the Global Information Society.* Cambridge, London: MIT Press.

Joyner, C. C. (2005). *International law in the 21st century: rules for global governance.* Oxford: Rowman & Littlefield.

Kamal, A. (2005). *The Law of Cyber–Space.* Geneva: United Nations Institute of Training and Research.

Kramer, F. D., Starr, S. H. and Wentz, L. (2009). Cyberpower and National Security, Dulles: Potomac Books Inc.

Kulesza, J. (2012). *International Internet Law*. London: Routledge.

Kulesza, J. (2013). Należyta staranność w prawie międzynarodowym, Ars boni et aequi: Poznań.

Kulesza, J. (2014). Due Diligence in Cyberspace [in:] Organizational, Legal, and Technological Dimensions of Information System Administration, I. M. Portela, F. Almeida (eds), Hershey PA: IGI Global: 76 - 95

Personick, S. D., & Patterson, C. A. (Eds.). (2003). *Critical Information Infrastructure Protection and the Law: An Overview of Key Issues*. Washington: National Research Council, The National Academies Press.

Schmitt, M. N. (2001). Computer Network Attack: The Normative Software. *Yearbook of International Humanitarian Law, 4*, 53–85. doi:10.1017/S1389135900000829

Segura–Serrano, A. (2006). Internet Regulation: A Hard–Law Proposal, The Jean Monnet Working Papers 10. Retrieved October 13, 2012, from http://ideas.repec.org/p/erp/jeanmo/p0183.html

Shapiro, A. L. (1998). The Disappearance of Cyberspace and the Rise of Code. *Seton Hall Const. L.J., 8*, 703–723.

Smith, G. J. H. (2007). *Internet law and regulation*. London: Sweet & Maxwell.

van Schewick, B. (2010). *Internet Architecture and Innovation*. Massachusetts: MIT Press.

Weber, R. H. (2010). New Sovereignty Concepts in the Age of Internet. *Journal of Internet Law, 14*(8), 12–20.

## KEY TERMS AND DEFINITIONS

**Critical Infrastructure:** Interconnected networks of people and devices allowing for the delivery of information society services and fulfillment of governmental obligations, including firefighting, transportation services, supply of water or energy or banking services.

**Critical Internet Resources:** Elements of Internet infrastructure critical for its secure and stable functioning. They include, but are not limited to name root servers, Internet's backbone structures and the domain name system, addresses and Internet transmission protocols. The catalogue of CIRs remains disputable, since CIRs sometimes considered elements of national critical infrastructure, especially if they are used to operate elements of that infrastructure, such as power plants of water supply systems.

**Due Diligence:** An international law standard requiring state authorities to show conduct expected of a reasonable government in certain circumstances. Lack of due diligence, affected through omissions of state organs, may result in international responsibility of that state.

**International Internet Law:** Public international law framework for Internet Governance, aimed at applying existing international law instruments to the cyberspace, with due regard to its transboundary characteristic.

**Internet Governance:** Multistakeholder management of resources of the global electronic network, including, but not limited to the management of the Domain Name System, root-servers and Internet Exchange Points.

**Multistakeholderism:** Key principle of Internet governance, requiring joint management of Internet resources by governments, business and the civil society in their respective roles.

**Transboundary Harm:** Risk of damage occurring outside the state where a risk-originating activity is carried out. By contrast, the term "damage" refers to actually affected economic, social, environmental or other negative consequences to the interests of another state or shared resources.

# Chapter 25
# A Routine Activity Theory–Based Framework for Combating Cybercrime

**Dillon Glasser**
*The Richard Stockton College of New Jersey, USA*

**Aakash Taneja**
*The Richard Stockton College of New Jersey, USA*

## ABSTRACT

*Since the government began tackling the problems of cybercrime, many laws have been enacted. A lack of a comprehensive definition and taxonomy of cybercrime makes it difficult to accurately identify report and monitor cybercrime trends. There is not just a lack of international agreement on what cybercrime is; there are different laws in every state within the United States, reflecting the inconsistency of dealing with cybercrime. There is also concern that many times lawyers and information technology professions are unable to understand each other well. The deficiency of cyber laws is an obvious problem and development of effective laws is emerging as an important issue to deal with cybercrime. This research uses the routine activity theory to develop a unified framework by including the motivation of the offender to use a computer as a tool/target, suitability of the target, and the presence (or absence) of guardian. It could help states that want to update their existing laws and cover areas that were previously uncovered.*

## INTRODUCTION

Originally the Internet was considered the Wild West, but legislators and law enforcement have made significant strides in tackling cybercrime. However, cybercrime has changed in recent years due to the growth of new phenomena in internet environments, such as peer to peer networks, social networks, organized cybercrime groups, and powerful new "smart" viruses (Berg, 2007). Cybercrime has "historically referred to crimes happening specifically over networks, especially the Internet, but that term has gradually become a general synonym for computer crime." (Alkaabi, 2011). Cybercrime is different from other crimes because of the way it changes rapidly along with the technology that it uses or abuses.

Cybercriminals today are becoming more sophisticated and organized. They are now using botnets to accomplish crimes such as spamming and denial of service attacks. Technology and cybercrime are moving targets and there should

DOI: 10.4018/978-1-4666-6324-4.ch025

be concern that the slow nature of our government may not be keeping pace. It is therefore not a surprise that old laws are being applied to new age crime. For example, Indiana has no laws pertaining to fraud or theft using a computer. Unfortunately, Indiana is not the only state that is lacking in cyber laws. It has been hard in the past to come to an agreement on what exactly constitutes cybercrime. As lack of a comprehensive definition and taxonomy of cybercrime makes it difficult to accurately identify report and monitor cybercrime trends. The deficiency of cyber laws is an obvious problem and development of effective laws is emerging as an important issue to deal with and combat cybercrime.

According to the routine activity theory, three specific criteria must exist for a crime to take place. There must be a motivated offender, a suitable target, and the absence of a capable guardian. The objective of this research is to use routine activity theory by including the suitability of target and motivation behind cybercrime for creating a unified framework which can be used to develop capable guardians (appropriate laws and policies) to effectively coordinate cybercrime regulation and legislation.

The rest of the paper is organized as follows. Section 2 of the paper describes the background in the areas of cybercrime, federal and state laws related to cybercrime. Section 3 discusses the routine activity theory followed by the unified framework in section 4. Lastly, we present our conclusions and the work ahead.

## BACKGROUND

### Cybercrime

Cybercrime is a very broad term that has "historically referred to crimes happening specifically over networks, especially the Internet, but that term has gradually become a general synonym for computer crime. Cybercrime is different from other crimes because of the way it changes rapidly along with the technology that it uses or abuses. There is a lack of international agreement on what cybercrime is, which the UN has stated as one of the reasons for the lack of international cooperation on tackling cybercrime (Alkaabi, 2011). That is not to say that there is a complete lack of cooperation. When it comes to spam, there has been a significant amount of international cooperation on creating laws to combat it. The Tripartite Memorandum of Understanding on Spam Enforcement cooperation is one example of this. This is a law internationally agreed upon between the United States, Australia, Canada, and the European Union for the purposes of fighting spam (Kigerl, 2012). However, many other areas of cybercrime legislation do not have the same level of cooperation that spam receives, including such things as intellectual property, identity theft, and fraud. This lack of cooperation is a serious problem when considering the international nature of the internet. It is quickly becoming our most important tool, responsible for many different aspects of our everyday life. Technology is always expanding into more parts of our lives.

Not just internationally, there are different laws in every state within the US, reflecting the inconsistency of dealing with cybercrime. For example, New Jersey, the United States 7th largest state by GDP, does not have laws for Content Violations, Unauthorized alteration of data or software for personal or organization gain, or improper use of communications; Alaska, 46th, lacks laws pertaining to interruption of Services such as the infamous Denial of Service attacks that plague the internet. "By far the greatest number of state cybercrime statutes are concerned with computer intrusions and damage caused by intrusions" (Brenner, 2001). This is an epidemic of cybercrime that cannot simply be solved with an expansion of previous non-cybercrime related laws. Given the nature of the cybercrime, these gaps and legal contradictions can cause many issues.

## Federal Laws Related to Cybercrime

Brenner (2001) suggests it is odd that one of the most advanced countries doesn't have uniform federal laws for cybercrime; instead it has many different state laws. These state laws create a complex web with many gaps in the areas of law that should be covered. It states that if federal jurisdiction to legislate exists, federal legislation is appropriate only when federal intervention is required. That will be very difficult with cybercrime due to the fact that the majority of the crimes will take place out of the state's jurisdiction. The federal government's intervention might be necessary in almost all cases. In addition, although federal legislative authority can pre-empt the states' ability to legislate in a given area, it rarely does, so it is unusual for federal criminal law to overlap with state prohibitions that address essentially the same issues.

There are federal laws in the United States that pertain to internet fraud, online child pornography, child luring and related activities, internet sale of prescription drugs and controlled substances, internet sale of firearms, internet gambling, internet sale of alcohol, online securities fraud, and software piracy and intellectual property theft. It is interesting to note that the majority of federal legislation pertaining to cybercrime has to do with internet gambling.

Online gambling can be considered effectively illegal since November 2002 when the United States Court of Appeals for the Fifth Circuit ruled that the Federal Wire Act prohibits electronic transmission of information for sports betting across telecommunications lines. The ruling was not intended to outlaw all forms of gambling. However, the federal department of justice continues publically to take the position that the wire act covers all forms of gambling. Since then legislation has been passed to directly outlaw online gambling within the United States, for example 18 U.S.C. § 1955 (prohibition of illegal gambling businesses). When it became illegal, online gam-

bling companies based in the United States either closed down or went overseas. Gambling continues to flourish online despite it being illegal. As observed by Grossman (2010), "In many cases, we're trying to apply US federal and state statues that were written at a time when there were still rotary phones". This casts doubt into whether or not the current cyber laws are effective.

## State Laws Related to Cybercrime

The framework of our government is that "There is no formal mechanism—at either the state or federal level—which requires or even prods states to adopt uniform, consistent laws" (Brenner, 2001). This is apparent given the many different legal landscapes of each state, and in many cases this is a good thing. It allows our states to provide a more personalized form of government for each region and experiment with new ideas in government on a state level. In regards to cybercrime this may not be the best way to handle things.

In 2001, "Only sixteen states outlawed online stalking or harassment, and several of them required that an offender transmit a 'credible threat' to injure the victim, the victim's family, or 'any other person'" (Brenner, 2001). This lack of legislation on the part of the rest of the states has been filled in to some extent since then, but in different ways. Some states expanded their "obscene phone call" statutes to encompass using a telephone or an "electronic communication device" to contact someone and threaten to injure that person or his/her family, to use obscene language, or to make repeated contacts in an effort to annoy the person (Brenner, 2001 "By far the greatest number of state cybercrime statutes are concerned with computer intrusions and damage caused by intrusions" (Brenner, 2001). This is an epidemic of cybercrime that cannot simply be solved with an expansion of previous non-cybercrime related laws. For something like stalking or harassment, which existed even before the internet in some form, it is not a huge issue to expand previous laws in this manner, but for newer threats that were never before experienced, simply repurposing old laws is not an option.

## LexisNexis 50 State Comparative Legislation/Regulations

LexisNexis, a corporation that provides computer-assisted legal research, has compiled a list of all 50 states comparative legislation/regulations. This list provides a different set of categories for splitting up cybercrime. They have Intellectual Property (**I**), Theft using a computer (**T**), Destruction of a computer (**D**), trespass on a network (**N**), and the destruction of data with a Harmful Program (**H**). These are comparable to the old categories as shown Table 1.

## Alkaabi's Cybercrime Classification

Alkaabi (2011) has developed a cybercrime classification to help organizations fight such crimes by primarily dividing (and subsequently subdividing) computer crime into two categories: Type I crime where the computer, computer network,

or electronic device is the target of the criminal activity; and Type II crime where the computer, computer network, or electronic device is the tool used to commit or facilitate the crime. Alkaabi's research led to refined cybercrime classifications in an attempt to create a comprehensive taxonomy of cybercrime. According to Alkaabi (2011), Type 1 crimes include crimes where the computer hardware is the target of the criminal activity. This was split into four sub-categories which include unauthorized access, malicious code, interruption of services, and theft or misuse of services. Type 2 crimes occur when the hardware is used as a tool and is split into three sub-categories: content violation offences, unauthorized alteration of data, and improper use of telecommunications. So, the motivation of a cybercriminal is to either use computer as a tool to commit crime, or as a target of crime. While the motivation of the offender to use computer as a tool / target is included in Alkaabi's classification, it is also important to consider the characteristics of the target which are being breached to get a complete view of the crime for developing appropriate laws pertaining to the crime.

*Table 1. LexisNexis categorization and cybercrime categories: a comparison*

| Serial Number | Crime | Description | LexisNexis Classification |
|---|---|---|---|
| 1 | Unauthorized Access | Hacking: Unauthorized copying, modifying, deleting or destroying computer data or programs | N |
| 2 | Malicious Code | Virus, Worm, Trojan Horse, Software bomb | H |
| 3 | Interruption of Services | A successful DoS attack or partially successful attack | D |
| 4 | Theft of services or Misuse of services | Theft or Misuse | T, N |
| 5 | Content violations | Child pornography, Harmful Contents, Copyright crimes, Hate crimes, Military Secrets, Intellectual property, Forgery/counterfeit documents | I |
| 6 | Unauthorized Alteration of data or software for personal or organizational gain | Identity theft, Online Fraud, Privacy, Sabotage, Telemarketing/Internet Fraud, Electronic, manipulation of share markets | T |
| 7 | Improper use of communications | Harassment, Online Money laundering, Cyber stalking, Spamming, Conspiracy, Extortion, Drug trafficking, Social engineering fraud. | T |

## ROUTINE ACTIVITY THEORY

Routine Activity Theory is a widely used criminology theory to predict and aggregate street crime rates but has been applied to cybercrime recently (Kigerl, 2012). According to the routine activity theory, three elements are required for a crime to take place: i) a motivated offender; ii) a suitable target, and iii) the absence of a capable guardian. The presence of these components increases the chance that a crime will take place. For example, the availability of suitable targets such as homes containing easily sellable goods in the absence of capable guardians such as police, homeowners, or friends and the presence of motivated offenders such as large number of unemployed teenagers increases the likelihood that a predatory crime will take place. The routine activity perspective has been a staple of the criminal victimization literature in general for nearly three decades now (Pratt et al. 2010).

In the field of cybercrime, Pratt and colleagues (2010) draw on routine activity theory to understand how online routines increase individuals' chances of being targeted for fraud online. According to Reyns (2013), Online banking, shopping, e-mail, instant messaging and downloading

behaviors are risky online routines that increase victimization and expose users to the threat of identity theft. Reyns (2013) conclude that the routine activity approach is effective in explaining online crimes.

## A UNIFIED FRAMEWORK

For the current research, we are focusing on five states: Alabama, Alaska, California, Louisiana, and New Jersey to show the lack of, and difference in laws related to cybercrime in different states These states were chosen with consideration for geography, economics, population, politics, and to some extent their laws. California has the highest GDP of any state. Alaska is one of two Non-contiguous states. New Jersey is the most densely populated of the states. Louisiana, Alabama, and Alaska were Republican states in the recent 2012 election, while California and New Jersey were Democratic. Louisiana was specially picked due to the fact that it is missing no cyber law classifications and was the first state to outlaw online gambling. Table 2 shows states with their LexisNexis classifications compared with their Alkaabi classifications.

From just this comparison it is apparent that Louisiana has laws that cover more areas of cybercrime than the other four states. Alabama needs laws that touch on malicious code, but has laws in the other areas. California interestingly seems to be lacking laws regarding content violations. Considering the fact that Hollywood, which is located in Los Angeles, California, is a nexus of film (a heavily pirated product) the lack of content violations seems incredibly strange. New Jersey is lacking laws in many areas as there are laws that insufficiently cover content violations, unauthorized alteration of data or software, and improper use of communications.

The variations among the state cybercrime statutes may be confusing to victims, lawyers alike. It is therefore important to offer a simpler

*Figure 1. Routine activity theory*

*Table 2. State laws: LexisNexis classifications and Alkaabi classifications*

| States | LexisNexis Classifications | Alkaabi Classification | |
|---|---|---|---|
| | | **Laws Present** | **Laws Absent** |
| Alabama | I, T, D, N | 1, 2, 3, 4, 5, 6, 7, | None (since August 1, 2012) |
| Alaska | T, N, H | 1, 2, 3, 4, 6, | 5,7 (Content violations, Improper use of communications) |
| California | T, D, N, H | 1, 2, 3, 4, 6, 7 | 5 (Content Violations) |
| Louisiana | I, T, D, N, H | 1, 2, 3, 4, 5, 6, 7 | None |
| New Jersey | D, N, H | 1, 4, 6 | 2, 3, 5, 7 (Malicious Code, Interruption of Services, Interruption of Services, Content violations, Improper use of communications) |

*Table 3. Protection mechanism*

| Protection | Definition |
|---|---|
| Confidentiality | Ensures that only authorized parties can view the information. |
| Integrity | Ensures that the information is correct and no unauthorized person or malicious software has altered the data. |
| Availability | Ensures that data is accessible to authorized users. |
| Authentication | Ensures that the individual is who they claim to be and not an imposter. |
| Authorization | The ability to access. |
| Accounting | Tracking of events such as time, date, or location of access. |
| Authenticity | Provides proof of the genuineness of the user. |
| Non Repudiation | Proves that a user performed an action. |

understanding in the form of a framework that may serve as a guideline for states to consider in developing or amending their statutes and applying them. This study uses routine activity theory to develop such a framework.

## Motivated Offender

It is important to consider the motivation of an offender behind a crime while developing any law pertaining to the crime. For example, a crime where the computer is the target of a criminal activity is different than the crimes where the computer is the tool to commit a crime (Alkaabi, 2011). Ac-

cording to Alkaabi (2001), type 1 crimes included crimes where the computer hardware was the target of the criminal activity. This was split into four sub-categories which include unauthorized access, malicious code, interruption of services, and theft or misuse of services. Type 2 crimes are when the hardware is used as a tool and was split into three sub-categories. These three sub categories are content violation offences, unauthorized alteration of data, and improper use of telecommunications. Of course some of these can overlap; therefore some of these may have multiple types. We use Alkaabi's taxonomy to include various cybercrimes.

## Target Characteristic/Suitability

It is important to protect the devices that store, manipulate, and transmit the information, and finally protecting information that provides value to people and organizations that is stored on those devices. To help accomplish these responsibilities there are protections such as CIA and AAA. CIA is Confidentiality, Integrity, and Availability while AAA is Authentication, Authorization, and Accounting. AAA a set of concepts used to protect property, data, and systems from intentional or even unintentional damage. AAA is used to support the Confidentiality, Integrity, and Availability (CIA) security concept. In addition, there is also a need to protect against Nonrepudiation (Table 3

*Table 4. Combating cybercrime: a unified framework*

| | | | Target Characteristic (Suitability) | | | | | | | |
|---|---|---|---|---|---|---|---|---|---|---|
| | | | Confide-ntiality | Integrity | Availa-bility | Authent-ication | Authori-zation | Accou-nting | Non rep-udiation | Other |
| Motivation — Type I Crime | Unauthorized Access | Hacking | Law / Statute | Law/ Statute | | | | | | |
| | | Other | Law / Statute | Law / Statute | | | | | | |
| | Malicious Code | Virus | | | | | | | | |
| | | Worm | | | | | | | | |
| | | Trojan Horse | | | | | | | | |
| | | Software Bomb | | | | | | | | |
| | | Other | | | | | | | | |
| | Interruption of Services | Disrupting services | | | | | | | | |
| | | Denying services | | | | | | | | |
| | | Other | | | | | | | | |
| | Theft or misuse of services | Theft of services | | | | | | | | |
| | | Misuse of services | | | | Law / Statute | Law / Statute | | | |
| | | Other | | | | Law / Statute | Law / Statute | | | |
| Motivation — Type II Crime | Content Violation | Child Pornography | | | | | | | | : |
| | | Hate crime | : | | | | | | | |
| | | Harmful Content | | | | | | | | |
| | | Military services | | | | | | | | |
| | | Copyright crimes | | | | | | | | |
| | | Intellectual property | | | | | | | | |
| | | Forgery | | | | | | | | |
| | | Other | | | | | | | | |
| | Unauthorized alteration of data / software | Identity Theft | | | | : | | | | |
| | | Online Fraud | | | | | | | | |
| | | Privacy | | | | | | | | |
| | | Sabotage | | | | | | | | |
| | | Internet Fraud | | | | | | | | |
| | | Electronic manipulation of share marketers | | | | | | | | |
| | | Other | | | | | | | | |
| | Improper use of commun-ication | Harassment | | | | | | | | |
| | | Online money laundering | | | | | | | | |
| | | Cyber stalking | | | | | | | | |
| | | Spamming | | | | | | | | |
| | | Conspiracy | | | | | | Law / Statute | Law / Statute | Law/ Statute |
| | | Extortion | | | | | | Law / Statute | Law / Statute | Law/ Statute |
| | | Drug Trafficking | | | | | | Law / Statute | Law / Statute | Law/ Statute |
| | | Social engineering / phishing | | | | | | Law / Statute | Law / Statute | Law/ Statute |
| | | Other | | | | | | Law / Statute | Law / Statute | Law/ Statute |

provides definitions for all these terms). Suitability of the target depends on the characteristics of the target in terms of presence, absence, or chances of breaching these protection mechanisms. A target lacking any of these protection mechanisms is prone to cybercrime Cyber-criminals look for targets without adequate protections or try to breach these protections for achieving their objective of using computer as a target or tool to perform the attack.

We propose a two dimensional unified framework (Table 4) by incorporating the motivation behind a cybercrime (y-axis), suitability of the target (x-axis) and appropriate cyber-laws (each cell value). The existing states and federal laws can be mapped on the framework to determine their scope. This framework can also be used to develop cyber-laws that respond to motivation behind the crime and the target characteristic impacted due to the crime.

## FUTURE RESEARCH DIRECTIONS

Future studies can use this framework to study various existing laws in the states and compare them with each other.

## CONCLUSION

We expect the results of this study to make significant contribution to researchers and legislators who want to shape the future of cybercrime law. We expect that our proposed framework will help to better comprehend the motivation behind a cybercrime, suitability of the target and the presence (or absence) of adequate laws. Such a snapshot will help to develop capable guardians (for example: laws, policies) for effectively coordinating cybercrime regulation and legislation. It could help states that want to update their existing laws and cover areas that were previously uncovered. Eventually it could help consolidate laws internationally.

## REFERENCES

Alkaabi, A., Mohay, G., McCullagh, A., & Chantler, N. (2011). Dealing with the problem of cybercrime. In *Proceedings of 2nd International ICST Conference on Digital Forensics & Cyber Crime*, (vol. 53, pp. 1867-8211). ICST. doi:10.1007/978-3-642-19513-6_1

Berg, T. (2007). The Changing Face of Cybercrime New Internet Threats Create Challenges to Law Enforcement. *Michigan Bar Journal, 86*(6), 18.

Brenner, S. W. (2001). State Cybercrime Legislation in the United States of America: A Survey. *Richmond Journal of Law & Technology, 7*, 28–34.

Grabosky, P. N. (2001). Virtual criminality: old wine in new bottles? *Social & Legal Studies, 10*(2), 243–249.

Grossman, W. M. (2010). The charmed life of cybercrime. *Infosecurity, 7*(1), 19–21. doi:10.1016/S1754-4548(10)70014-0

Guinchard, A. (2007). *Criminal Law in the 21st Century: The Demise of Territoriality?* http://dx.doi.org/10.2139/ssrn.1290049

IC3. (2012). Retrieved from Federal Bureau of Investigation website: http://www.ic3.gov/media/annualreport/2011_IC3Report.pdf

Jewkes, Y., & Yar, M. (2010). *Handbook of Internet Crime*. London: Taylor & Francis.

Kigerl, A. (2012). Routine activity theory and the determinants of high cybercrime countries. *Social Science Computer Review, 30*(4), 470–486. doi:10.1177/0894439311422689

Koops, B. (2010). *The Internet and its Opportunities for Cybercrime* (Vol. 1, pp. 735–754). Transnational Criminology Manual.

*Legal Information Institute.* (2012). Retrieved from http://www.law.cornell.edu/uscode/text

*LexisNexis.* (2011). Retrieved from http://www.lexisnexis.com/en-us/home.page

Pratt, T. C., Holtfreter, K., & Reisig, M. D. (2010). Routine online activity and internet fraud targeting: Extending the generality of routine activity theory. *Journal of Research in Crime and Delinquency*, *47*(3), 267–296. doi:10.1177/0022427810365903

Reyns, B. W. (2013). Online Routines and Identity Theft Victimization Further Expanding Routine Activity Theory beyond Direct-Contact Offenses. *Journal of Research in Crime and Delinquency*, *50*(2), 216–238. doi:10.1177/0022427811425539

## KEY TERMS AND DEFINITIONS

**Cyber-Laws:** Laws as applicable to the use of computers, and activities performed and transactions conducted over internet and other networks.

**Cyber Stalking:** The use of the Internet or other electronic means to stalk or harass an individual, a group of individuals, or an organization.

**Hacking:** Seeking and exploiting vulnerabilities in a computer system or computer network.

**Identity Theft:** A form of stealing someone's identity in order to access resources or other benefits in that person's name.

**Phishing:** An attempt to acquire personal information by impersonating as a trustworthy entity in an electronic communication.

**Privacy:** The ability of an individual or group to seclude information about themselves or selectively reveal their information.

**Social Engineering:** Psychological manipulation of people into performing actions or divulging confidential information.

**Spam:** Use of electronic messaging systems to send unsolicited bulk messages.

**Statutes:** Formal written enactment of a legislative authority that governs a state, city, or country.

**Trojan Horses:** A malware which gains privileged access to the operating system while appearing to perform a desirable function but instead drops a malicious payload.

# Chapter 26
# Internet of Things:
## The Argument for Smart Forensics

**Edewede Oriwoh**
*University of Bedfordshire, UK*

**Geraint Williams**
*IT Governance Limited, UK*

## ABSTRACT

*The Internet of Things (IoT), a metaphor for smart, functional Cyberphysical Environments (CPE), is finding some usefulness in various sectors including healthcare, security, transportation, and the Smart Home (SH). Within the IoT, objects potentially operate autonomously to provide specified services and complete assigned tasks. However, the introduction of new technologies and/or the novel application of existing ones usually herald the discovery of unfamiliar security vulnerabilities, which lead to exploits and sometimes to security breaches. There is existing research that identifies IoT-related security concerns and breaches. This chapter discusses existing Digital Forensics (DF) models and methodologies for their applicability (or not) within the IoT domain using the SH as a case in point. The chapter also makes the argument for smart forensics, the use of a smart autonomous system (tagged the Forensics Edge Management System [FEMS]) to provide forensic services within the self-managed CPE of the SH.*

## INTRODUCTION: THE INTERNET OF THINGS

The Internet of Things (IoT) (Lu Tan & Neng Wang, 2010; Uckelmann, 2011) is also referred to variously as the Internet of Objects (Xia, Yang, Wang, & Vinel, 2012), Future Internet (FI) (Hernández-Muñoz et al., 2011), Machine to Machine (M2M) communications (Y. Chen, 2012; Igarashi, Ueno, & Fujisaki, 2012), and the Internet of Everything (IoE) (Castro, Jara, & Skarmeta, 2012; Lin, Leu, Li, & Wu, 2012; Ning & Hu, 2011). It is an extension of traditional networks such as the Internet and social networks. It is the true Network of networks because it describes the potential for the interconnection of every (feasible) object to every other (feasible) object and all the underlying processes and protocols that enable and support these interconnections (Figure 1).

Ericsson estimates that more than 50 billion devices will be connected by 2020 (Ericsson White paper, 2011) while Morgan Stanley suggests that by the same date there will be 75 billion devices connected to the IoT (Proffitt, 2013). These connected items will be of a variety of types and shapes and will vary from traditional

DOI: 10.4018/978-1-4666-6324-4.ch026

*Figure 1. Key interconnected elements that make up the IoT*

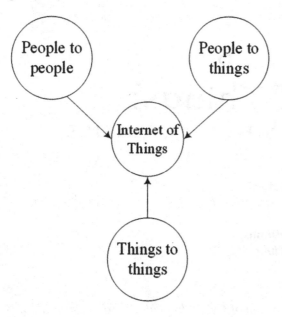

computing devices to ordinary everyday objects. For instance within the Smart Home (SH), Things (also known as *Blogjects* (Nova & Bleecker, 2006), *Spimes* (McFedries, 2010) or *IoT-ware* (Oriwoh, Jazani, Epiphaniou, & Sant, 2013)) may include kettles, cars, fridges, Personal Computers, smart phones and washing machines. Various sectors and industries currently benefit from having these interconnections including the transportation, communication, healthcare, smart houses and leisure industries (Fleisch, 2010; Juels, 2006; Kozlov, Veijalainen, & Ali, 2012; Laranjo, Macedo, & Santos, 2012). In the SH, these objects will be interconnected for the purpose of improving people's lives and making things more convenient for them (Alam, Reaz, & Ali, 2012; Hyungkyu Lee, Jooyoung Lee, & Jongwook Han, 2007). The IoT is enabled by technologies including sensors, Machine to Machine communications (M2M), Radio Frequency Identification (RFID) and so on. See Figure 2 for a summary of some cardinal elements of the IoT including the enabling technologies.

However, although the application domains and benefits of the IoT are numerous, a growing number of security concerns have been recognised in relation to the IoT (Juels, 2006). These concerns include *logical* threats (e.g. Denial of Service or DoS) and *physical* threats (e.g. tampering and theft). The discussion in this chapter is particularly focused on one of the many manifestations of the IoT - the SH, which is described by Ding et al. as "a residence equipped with technology that observes the residents and provides proactive services" (Ding, Cooper, Pasquina, & Fici-Pasquina, 2011). Some example SH projects are described in (Chan, Estève, Escriba, & Campo, 2008).

SH environments are susceptible to both traditional attacks such as burglary, theft, DoS as well as tailored attacks e.g. a fridge used as part of a botnet to propagate malware. There is already research that discusses providing security in home-based IoT applications (Chan et al., 2008; D. Chen et al., 2011; Ding et al., 2011; Ning & Liu, 2012; Seigneur, Jensen, Farrell, Gray, & Chen, 2003). However, there is no guarantee that every single logical and physical security measures will be completely attack-proof. Any breaches within SH environments will therefore have to be investigated both from the physical and the digital perspectives. In this light, some DF models and methodologies have been developed that propose to be applicable to CPE (Ademu, Imafidon, & Preston, 2011; Vlachopoulos, Magkos, & Chrissikopoulos, 2013).

This chapter, for its own part, proposes that as part of addressing security issues within SH environments, DF should become *smart* - i.e. through the use of automated smart devices to provide DF services within homes without the requirement for commercial (human) investigators except when absolutely necessary. As part of this contribution, the Forensics Edge Management System (FEMS) is introduced. Prior to this, a methodology for approaching IoT-based crime scenes is proposed. The aim of the methodology

*Figure 2. The Internet of things' cardinal elements*

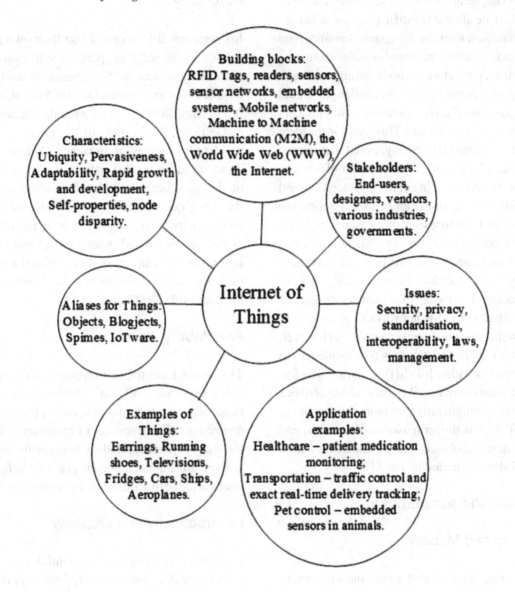

is to answer the following question: what is the best way to approach DF within the IoT context to ensure effective and maximum evidence acquisition and avoid time wastage?

## BACKGROUND

De Silva et al. suggest that future homes will evolve in a similar way to phones (i.e. in their function). They also suggest that homes will play a role in

*protecting* owners and occupants from unforeseen and unavoidable dangers. They describe a SH as having capabilities that allow it to provide home owners with "various facilities" (De Silva, Morikawa, & Petra, 2012). These facilities currently include comfort, location, energy-savings, and security services, among others. Unfortunately, security concerns have been identified as a factor that threaten the adoption of SH solutions by end users (Brush et al., 2011).

This chapter argues that these security concerns should not be allowed to stifle progress in IoT research and development. It suggests that since total freedom from even *attempted* breaches cannot be guaranteed, pro-active methods and approaches to dealing with potential security challenges should be the position taken by academia, policy-makers and other IoT stakeholders. This can be in the form of well-structured DF investigations the results of which, can lead to the identification of sources of security breaches. In addition, lessons learned from DF investigations can be useful during the development of future security measures and tools.

As a contribution towards this solution this chapter recommends a two-pronged approach: a triage-based Incident Response (IR) and DF methodology and the use of a smart device that can be installed within SH networks to provide real-time monitoring and forensics services. However, certain IoT characteristics may pose challenges to DF processes within IoT (SH) scenarios. The following discussion describes these characteristics and how they might influence future approaches to DF. IoT-ware is the term used to describe all end nodes, devices, objects, things, and so on within the IoT domain including the SH.

## The IoT Characteristics

### Ubiquity and Mobility

Atzori et al. contend that within the IoT current security risks have the potential to be more widely distributed (Atzori, Iera, & Morabito, 2010). Part of the reason for this is that within the IoT, IoT-ware such as sensor-tagged vehicles are as distributed as the homes of citizens (static vehicles) and other locations such as roads (moving vehicles) therefore the impact of any propagated attack is more widely spread. As a result, from the perspective of forensics Incident Response Teams (IRT), locating and gaining access to such widely dispersed potential Objects of Forensic Interest (OOFI) (Oriwoh et al., 2013) may be a challenge.

### Autonomy

IoT-ware are able to operate on their own as described by the self-* properties - self-awareness, self-configuration, self-maintenance and self-destruction among others (Dobson, Sterritt, Nixon, & Hinchey, 2010; Gurgen, Gunalp, Benazzouz, & Gallissot, 2013). One of the goals of DF is to identify sources of breaches. Autonomy as encouraged by the IoT affects the achievement of this goal because with autonomous systems there is a question of *control* (who/what did it) and *responsibility* (who/what is at fault?). The subject of responsibility assignment and modelling in *socio-technical systems* - which arguably includes the IoT - is discussed extensively in (Sommerville, 2007).

### Adaptability

This stems from the self-management property. Since IoT-ware can learn and adjust/adapt independently as situations call for it, they can be deemed unreliable sources of forensics evidence since any evidence stored on them can be changed without any human input and possibly before DF teams are able to acquire any evidence from them.

### Heterogeneity and Disparity

From the SH perspective potential sources of evidence will be even more (physically) diverse than in traditional networks. This diversity presents challenges to investigators (Turnbull, 2008). There is a possibility that during investigations, some non-traditional OOFI e.g. fridges might unwittingly be missed simply because they do not fall under the group of items that *digital* IRT are used to accessing or querying for evidence. Another factor is the logical disparity between evidence sources such as sensor (tag) manufacturer ID conventions, timestamp formats and packet headers. In this light, captured sensor logs may rather than assist DF investigations, lead to confusion unless they are effectively sanitized and unified in order to achieve some form of correlation and therefore some usefulness.

## Dual Presence

Within the IoT domain, IoT-ware may have both physical and virtual manifestations. There is ongoing research into the development of methods of establishing these manifestations (Kindberg et al., 2002). This dual presence means that they can be accessed, queried and controlled by their owners both locally and via the World Wide Web (WWW). However, from a DF perspective, it means that sources of evidence will be distributed between these two domains posing interesting questions about how best to access both and obtain best evidence bearing in mind the dual access that users have to them. The use of timestamps will be very useful as one way of countering this challenge since all evidence obtained can be correlated based on their timestamps however this will only be helpful if the evidence needed is acquired before it is tampered with.

## Size

With respect to DF, the size of end devices is not so much a problem as it is a challenge. Accessing certain IoT-ware may prove difficult. Moore's Law still holds true and processors and storage components will be progressively physically smaller (Mattern, 2003). The access to these devices may therefore be a challenge and DF will require a method of acquiring evidence from them without damaging them physically. An alternative may be for courts to be prepared in certain identified circumstances to always accept evidence from alternative sources, a concept discussed in (Oriwoh et al., 2013) where the Next Best Thing (NBT) serves as the source of *best* evidence. However, within the IoT, the miniturisation of objects is not the singular challenge presented to DF and IRTs.

During investigations there is sometimes a need to contain, seize and remove physical evidence from crime scenes. Removing IoT-ware (e.g. fridges) may pose challenge to DF as it currently operates - although probably not so much for physical forensics which already deals with the removal of large objects from crime scenes. This can be resolved by cooperation between the physical and digital forensics teams - which in some instances may be even be one and the same. Alternatively, to counter this IRT may have to increasingly rely on data from central home control servers, external service providers, other end user portable devices and network logs for relevant evidence. Essentially, the best way to approach crime scenes with such irregular evidence sources will have to be agreed during the planning stage.

## Invisibility

The nature of IoT-ware as technology that is enmeshed into our lives (Weiser, 1991) and is hence 'invisible' makes any and all potential IoT security challenges pose even greater risks than more familiar, well-known attacks. This embedded and sometimes non-apparent nature of IoT-ware may, in some instances, lead to loss of useful evidence. A potential solution to this would be the assignment of experienced investigators to these kinds of cases as well as diligence during the investigations. In addition, during IoT-ware deployment - in preparation for possible future DF investigations - *potential* OOFI can be identification. This effective and detailed pre-attack triage should be encouraged even in SH environments.

## Jurisdiction

The wide distribution of OOFI within IoT domains can be across networks in different jurisdictions with different laws and policies. This is already the case with traditional networks such as the Internet however, within the IoT environment, the added dimension of networks such as Personal Area Networks (PAN) (Franklin & Rajan, 2010) and Body Area Networks (BAN) (Khan & Yuce, 2010) and the on-going discussion about user privacy concerns may lead to even more challenging legal wrangling. In addition, *moral* questions and decisions may have to be made. If gaining access to a device may endanger a patient, the moral decision may be to avoid doing so; this means that an alternative way to proceed with the investigation will have to be taken. Again, this can be achieved by identifying and locating alternative sources (i.e. NBT).

## Dynamism

Wireless Sensor Networks (another manifestation of the IoT), as part of their self-management capability, can be configured to continually 'adjust and change' their form. This can be due to various factors such as device migration or even retirement (i.e. self-destruction). Also, there is existing research (Islam, Schmidt, Kolbe, & Andersson, 2012) to support random connection of (trusted) end user devices to Home Area Networks (HAN) (Bouhafs, Mackay, & Merabti, 2012) thereby continually changing the network topologies and router or home server configurations. This potential for networks to be created and broken up without any human input or involvement may pose an interesting challenge when it comes to the basic DF procedure of *locating* OOFI. This becomes even more of a challenge where there is a potential for the break-up (or self-destruction) to be triggered deliberately. This can be used by IoT botnet creators so that the botnets are broken up as soon as there is a chance they are being observed.

## Standards (or the Present Lack There-of)

As the IoT develops, different vendors from small start-ups to large companies, industrial bodies, to governments develop their own 'solutions' to enable communication and interaction between IoT-ware. The absence of industry-wide standards for data protocols, platforms, connectors, etc. may become an issue for DF.

Based on the identified characteristics of the IoT there is a need to consider the applicability of the available tools and approaches to DF. The requirement for new tools is identified by Mohay in (Mohay, 2005). He explains that the possibility that data of evidentiary value may exist in new consumer products which have embedded logic creates a need for investigators to be able to access that data hence the requirement for new tools. The need for new methodologies is also acknowledged in research. Selamat at al. explain that the change in technology being encountered during investigations means a need for new methodologies to approach DF investigations (Selamat, Yusof, & Sahib, 2008). Lempereur et al., explain that "traditional and live forensic analysis techniques are maturing, but as the technologies subject to analysis change, research needs to keep pace and preempt emerging trends" (Lempereur, Merabti, & Shi, 2009).

## Current Digital Forensics (DF) Approaches

This section discusses selected approaches to DF investigations and their applicability or otherwise within the IoT context.

## The Digital Forensics Investigation Model (DFIM)

The DFIM (Ademu et al., 2011) is a four-tier model with an emphasis on iteration of its phases. The phases are Inception phase (this occurs iteratively throughout the entire forensics process), Interaction, Reconstruction and Protection phases. Their work recognises the diversity of devices that are encountered in digital forensics investigations (this is something that the 3-stage framework in (M. Kohn, Eloff, & Olivier, 2006) fails to do when it focusses on only the 'computer' as the source of evidence). However, although according to the authors, the aim of developing the DFIM is as a tool to bring about an improvement of the entire investigation process, their work focuses on digital evidence, describing its characteristics, and defining it as evidence that is "hidden". The DFIM model is limited in its focus in that it does not consider evidence sources that are physically present but which are not *obvious* as sources of digital evidence i.e. cyberphysical evidence.

## The Hybrid Model (Vlachopoulos et al., 2013)

This model introduces the term Hybrid evidence to describe evidence which is not purely physical or digital but having a dual nature. This is similar to the view taken in this chapter although the preferred term is cyberphysical evidence. The hybrid model consists of the preparation, crime scene investigation, and laboratory examination and conclusion phases. The model is proposed for the investigation of crime scenes with either physical-only evidence, digital-only evidence or hybrid evidence. Its developer expounds it as one that "examines the whole process of crime investigations, starting from the notification that a crime has been committed, ending to the findings of the research". This model, although clearly recognising that the focus of DF investigations is becoming more varied and the scope is widening, does not appear to recognise that within the IoT there is a need for very quick responses to attacks else evidence can easily be lost or that a pre-attack triage may be useful to ensure that OOFI are identified quicker during IR. Under certain circumstances in the IoT the Hybrid model will be too slow however it can be applied during investigations *after* the initial response to the crime.

## The Common Process Model for Incident Response (IR) and Computer Forensics

Freiling and Schwittway propose the Common Process Model for Incident Response and Computer Forensics (Freiling & Schwittay, 2007), an amalgamation of the concepts of IR and Computer Forensics (CF). The model is composed of the pre-analysis, analysis and post-analysis phases. The pre-analysis phase comprises detection of the incident(s) as well as all the steps that take place before actual analysis of available evidence. This step is carried out to identify available evidence that may need to be acquired for further analysis. The step can almost be described as a full IR model on its own. The model encapsulates what this chapter proposes - a need to prepare for incidents before they occur so that forensics processes are efficient and so yield relevant results. However, the authors discuss *Computer Forensics* thereby limiting the scope of the model.

## The Abstract Digital Forensics Model (ADFM) (Reith, Carr, & Gunsch, 2002)

According to its proponents, the ADFM model is designed to be applicable to both currently known and future digital crime. The authors argue that some currently available models are too technology-specific and that the ADFM, though drawn from pre-existing models, is proposed to improve upon them and avoid their "shortfalls". Their work recognises a need to develop a more applicable framework and supports the argument made in that this chapter.

## Generic Process Model for Network Forensics (GPMNF) (Pilli, Joshi, & Niyogi, 2010)

This model correctly states that as part of the preparation phase for forensics investigations, it is essential to have sensors deployed on the network to detect intrusions and monitor the network. This research meets this requirement through the use of the FEMS system.

## Integrated Digital Forensics Process Model (IDFPM) (M. D. Kohn, Eloff, & Eloff)

The IDFPM is described by Kohn et al. as a "standardized" model for forensics investigations. Just as with the Hybrid and Integrated Digital Investigation model, the IDFPM recognises the need for the physical forensics and digital forensics to occur simultaneously. It also has as part of the Preparation Phase, an "Infrastructure Readiness" stage. These two points make the IDFPM more suitable to CPE than some of the other existing models and methodologies.

## Automated Forensics

Cohen contends that automation on a large-scale leads to long-term cost reduction. He argues that for some crimes, automation that handles evidence collection and analysis with possibility of presentation of the case outcome for human players is a future vision of forensics (Cohen, 2012). Automated forensics also has the potential to save investigators' time as well as provide repeatable processes which are valuable to forensic investigations. Garfinkel argues that with the increasing complexity of networks and the increasing amounts of data being generated, effective DF automated tools are a necessity (Garfinkel, 2010). Other research (Cantrell, Dampier, Dandass, Niu, & Bogen, 2012; Case, Cristina, Marziale, Richard, & Roussev, 2008; Chen Lin, Li Zhitang, & Gao Cuixia, 2009) shows the inclination towards automating various parts of - or the entire – forensic process with special emphasis on obtaining cogent, relevant information quickly and efficiently without compromising the reliability of the evidence obtained. With the introduction of autonomous,

pervasive, and ubiquitous interconnectivity to the home, users who live in smart houses will do so because they expect to be able to rely on the available technology for various tasks such as remembering when to switch their home heating on and off leaving them free to take care of other preferred duties. The FEMS is a contribution towards realizing this vision of the SH. In addition, the FEMS eliminates the requirement for a skilled examiner to turn up continually at users' homes. This in turn leaves examiners free and available to apply their skills to more specialist crimes.

## Shortcomings of Examined Models

Extensive research has not yet uncovered a forensics model which takes into account the properties of the SH as a dynamic, largely automated and self-managed CPE. None of the models discussed in this chapter consider the benefits of registration of smart devices in a SH as part of the forensics preparation process. In addition, some of the models claim to be applicable to 'future' environments such as the SH however they fail to discuss their plan for approaching such environments in any appreciable detail. There is no real evidence to suggest they have been tested or validated within an IoT-based environment with its peculiar characteristics. Some existing frameworks (Baryamureeba & Tushabe, 2004) appear to assume that there will be luxury of time during investigations and that in these highly dynamic environments OOFI will be readily accessible during and, throughout investigations. The reality is that because of the autonomy of CPE, when a crime is committed the delay between its detection, reporting, arrival of the IRT, and commencement of the investigation, may prove too lengthy for any investigation to find any useful evidence or at the very least, it may mean that vital evidence is lost.

## DF Triage

According to Roussev et al. "DF triage is a partial forensic examination conducted under (significant) time and resource constraints" (Roussev, Quates, & Martell, 2013). This practice is going to be essential for responses to crimes within the IoT, taking the CPE of the SH as an example. As noted before, some of the existing DF models erroneously assume that sources of evidence in crime scenes will be persistent. However, since there is no guarantee of this, it is essential that a form of triage is carried out as soon as a crime scene is approached in order to identify and secure potential sources of evidence. If a pre-preparedness/readiness list that identifies potential OOFIs is readily available this can be used to assist the triage process. In addition, if the FEMS (described later) has identified the sources of suspicious activity - even if not the actual source of the crime - the FEMS output could be useful by helping assisting investigators focus their investigation.

## Digital Forensics Readiness

Evidence from DF investigations can be crucial to decision-making in legal or disciplinary proceedings. A key practice for ensuring that when DF investigations are carried out, investigators can find relevant results in timely manner is the practice of forensics *preparedness*. An extensive discussion of the topic of DF preparedness has been carried out (Rowlingson, 2004) where it is described by the author as "the ability of an organisation to maximize its potential to use digital evidence when required". Effective DF preparedness involves planning for any unanticipated or unwanted activity within digitized environments and this practice will be crucial to investigations in the IoT. Within the SH the need for forensics readiness is essential especially since some SH may be required to be able to self-manage. SH owners might therefore also expect to be able to rely on their homes to manage any (physical, logical and hybrid) security breaches that may arise without

the continual requirement for a human involvement. One way to assist with this process can be through the use of a dedicated device that continually monitors network traffic, acquires logs, responds to and investigates detected anomalies and attacks as they happen.

## THE PROPOSED INCIDENT RESPONSE AND DIGITAL FORENSICS APPROACH

DF would play an important role within the IoT however, in order for DF to remain an effective service it would have to evolve and become *smart* in its methods and tools whilst maintaining forensics principles so that any evidence produced is legally acceptable. Smart forensics encompasses the approaches to forensics that fit into the lifestyle of users in smart CPE - which in the near future would probably be a considerable proportion of the human population. The SANS 2013 *Survey of Forensics and Incident Response* (Henry, Williams, & Wright, 2013) of 450 DF-related companies indicated that some of the respondents consider the "lack of skills, training and/or certification on *proper methodology*" to be a main challenge when it comes to approaching DF in situations that involve 'atypical' evidence sources. It is hoped that the approach introduced in this chapter can provide a solution to this dilemma.

The approach to DF introduced in this chapter has the following aims:

- Ensure that relevant evidence is not lost due to delays and unnecessary activities by IRTs;
- Ensure that relevant evidence is acquired that can be used to support a court case;
- Encourage a minimum standard of forensics preparedness within smart CPE.

The flowchart of the proposed model is shown in Figure 3.

*Figure 3. The SH incident response model*

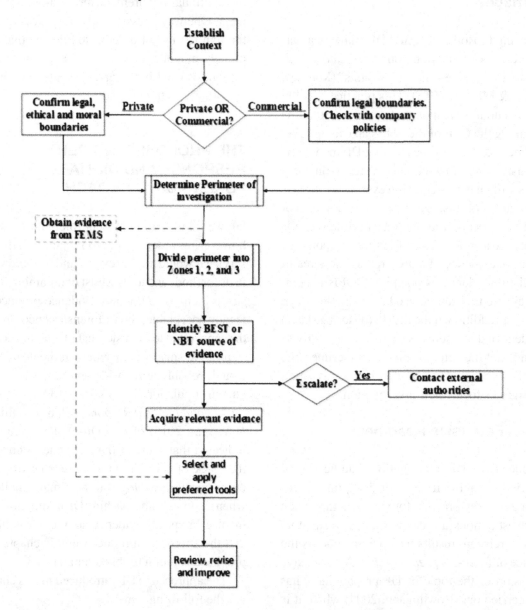

## Establish Context (Commercial or Private)

Due to the scale (amount of data), location of OOFI, as well as privacy and moral concerns, IRTs should begin their approach to investigations by establishing the context of their investigation and identifying any legal or privacy issues and access constraints that may apply.

## Determine Perimeter

The next point of focus for investigators should be to determine the perimeter of the network(s) that they are approaching, its potential size and type. The terms that can be used to illustrate the breadth of a network include Home Area Network (HAN) made up of several Body Area Networks (BAN), while the type can be mobile, fixed, wired, wireless (Wi-Fi, Bluetooth, etc.) and so on.

## Split into Deterministic Sectors Using the 1-2-3 Zones Approach (Oriwoh et al., 2013)

The next step would be to split the crime scene as much as possible into deterministic zones. This can be done by labelling them as internal network, middle zone and external zone (Figure 4). This will aid investigators in gaining an overall picture of the situation that they are faced with.

## Identify 'Best' Sources of Evidence

Applying the Next Best Thing (NBT) approach, any OOFI that cannot be accessed directly for evidence (e.g. a patient's pacemaker) can be listed as relevant whilst a closely related item that may hold relevant evidence (e.g. a hospital server) may be accessed for evidence instead. This way, no matter how remote or inaccessible OOFI are, some evidence can still be extracted and analysed.

## Escalate

Investigators will have to make decisions about what investigations to escalate. For example in a situation where a human subject is refusing to grant investigators access to their property, there has to be a well-defined alternative course of action to be taken so that the investigation can proceed both from a physical investigation perspective as well as a digital one.

*Figure 4. The 1-2-3 zones in a SH*

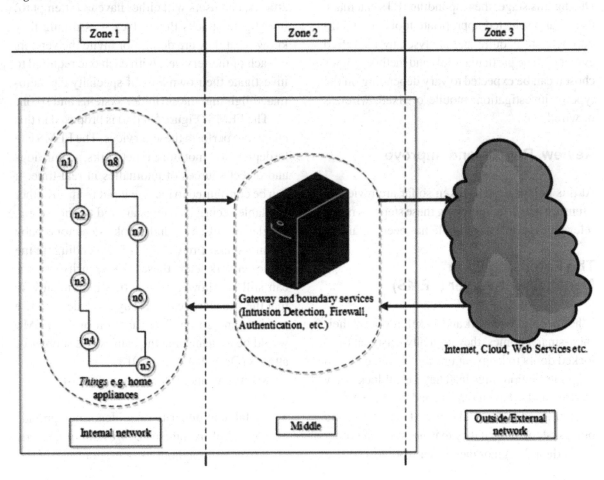

## Acquire Relevant Evidence

Forensic readiness involves the steps taken in preparation for anticipated incidents and it is key to successful forensics investigations. In the SH scenario, one way to ensure that relevant evidence is secured and collected in preparation for an investigation will be to employ the services of the FEMS because as part of its setup, devices in the SH are registered with it after which it monitors, acquires and periodically stores network logs. Alternatively, evidence can be acquired using available forensics tools. As part of hardware evidence acquisition, the best procedure to follow has to be made at this point e.g. to seize evidence or operate in situ, to image wholly or selectively.

## Select and Apply Preferred Tools

During this stage, the responding IRTs can make use of any selected appropriate tools and methodologies to acquire and analyse any identified evidence. The particular tools and methodologies chosen can be expected to vary depending on the type of investigation: mobile or fixed, wireless or wired, etc.

## Review, Revise, and Improve

At this point the steps taken so far are reviewed to ensure that after following these steps, as much relevant evidence as possible has been obtained.

## The Forensics Edge Management Server (FEMS)

When people go to work and lock the doors of their (non-smart) homes, they typically trust that their locked doors to keep out unwanted elements and keep their belongings in. They install locks they can trust and so have an understandable expectation of security and privacy. They trust these locks and other systems even if they may not know anything about their design or their inner workings. When

homes become self-managing - and more susceptible to cyber-style attacks - end users can neither be expected to understand nor have the capability to investigate cyber security attacks such as DoS attacks on their fridges or man-in-the-middle attacks on their X-box consoles.

According to Sang-Hyun et al., the SH can and should be configurable to provide convenience and comfort, entertainment, communication, information and security systems (Sang-Hyun, Lee, & Kyung-Il, 2013). This chapter contends that the SH should be designed to support DF services as well. It should be equipped to withstand cyber-attacks, to investigate them if they are successful and to escalate issues where necessary (e.g. to the police or to external forensics response teams) all without disruption to the user. A forensics device can be deployed to perform these functions in the home. Without such a system to detect and investigate attacks, end users will either have to (attempt to) investigate attacks themselves – assuming they know what they are doing - or invite the vendors of each of the services, with each one required to investigate their own area of specialty e.g. automated lighting, the sprinkler systems and so on.

The FEMS (Figure 5 and 6) is proposed in this chapter to perform these services. The FEMS can be deployed to monitor SH networks, acquire logs and detect sources of anomalies in real-time. It can be configured to receive input from any other available security systems around the house e.g. burglar alarms, fire and smoke detectors, baby monitors, and firewalls. Also, depending on the home network setup, these other security systems can still be allowed to function individually so that the fire alarm can directly send alerts to fire services and so on. The function of the FEMS would be to determine the causes and sources of attacks (Oriwoh & Sant, 2013)

Requirements for the FEMS. It must:

- Maintain integrity of evidence and provide proof of maintenance of Chain of Custody (CoC) throughout its operation;

- Not expose private data or information during its operation;
- Be fast and efficient and not cause (significant) delays on networks;
- Have a user friendly interface;
- Be vendor independent;
- Must make a backup copy of the original evidence.

Once installed on the home network, the FEMS will continually monitor network traffic and capture network logs (the logs are stored for a specified time period with a minimum storage period of 28 days or one month). Whilst setting up the FEMS, the user can specify acceptable

thresholds ranges for certain parameters. Example parameters are minimum living room temperature/time of day, hour to lock front gate, volume of central Bluetooth speaker, week of month and day of week to send grocery shopping list to remote store, among others.

The FEMS forensics operation is triggered when an *event* is detected. An event occurs when a set threshold is exceeded e.g. the lights are switched on too early or too late in the day. All logs captured just before and after the incident was detected are labelled and stored as possibly relevant. Whilst the network monitoring and log acquisition continues online, the decision-making (indicated by the red-coloured rhombus in Figure

*Figure 5. The forensics edge management system: a high-level overview*

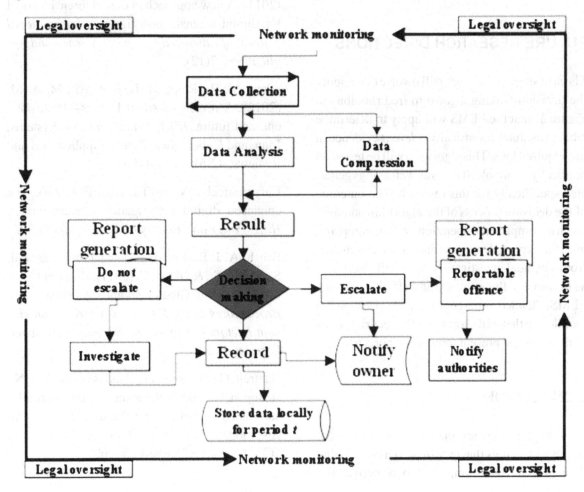

5.), investigation and report preparation phases take place offline. The investigation to find out the cause of the light scheduling problem (i.e. the attack) begins with a parse of the logs to identify and extract forensically relevant information such as source and destination IP addresses and (e.g. device IDs, source of control commands. If successful in identifying the source of the 'attack' the FEMS then prepares a report and notifies the user of the outcome. It also makes suggestions to the user about what they might wish to do next. If the investigation is unsuccessful, it escalates the issue to a designated external party.

Some tools that can be used to realize the FEMS include monitoring tools like *Microsoft Network Monitor* or the Linux *Top* program; *gzip* can be used to compress captured logs; *postfix* can be used to send notifications using email messages.

## FUTURE RESEARCH DIRECTIONS

The next stage of this work will involve developing the decision-making algorithm (red rhombus in Figure 5) that the FEMS will apply to determine what constitutes forensically *relevant* evidence in the acquired logs. This algorithm will be tested on publically-available SH logs as well as logs generated specifically for this research. The outcome of the decision process of the algorithm and time taken to complete the operations will be compared with the expected outcome and time taken during from a manual investigation. This will be done so as to measure the accuracy and efficiency of the FEMS. Planned as part of the FEMS package is a mobile app that will show users the security status of their SH and present forensics reports to them.

## CONCLUSION

This chapter discussed the characteristics of the Internet of Things that may make it a challenging domain to navigate from a DF perspective. The chapter provided an analysis of some current DF approaches and models and highlighted the deficiencies of these approaches with respect to the IoT. Considering the IoT characteristics identified, the chapter introduced an Internet of Things Incident Response and Forensics Methodology that should ensure that during IoT-related investigations, IRT and DF investigations can still be carried with as much relevant evidence as possible acquired and in a timely fashion. The chapter also introduced the Forensics Edge Management System as part of the holistic approach to DF in CPE with particular focus on the SH.

## REFERENCES

Ademu, I. O., Imafidon, C. O., & Preston, D. S. (2011). A new approach of digital forensic model for digital forensic investigation. *International Journal of Advanced Computer Science and Applications, 2*(12).

Alam, M. R., Reaz, M. B. I., & Ali, M. A. M. (2012). A review of smart Homes—Past, present, and future. *IEEE Transactions on* Systems, Man, and Cybernetics, Part C: Applications and Reviews, *42*(6), 1190–1203.

Baryamureeba, V., & Tushabe, F. (2004). The enhanced digital investigation process model. *IEEE Power and Energy Magazine, 10*, 24-32.

Brush, A. J. B., Lee, B., Mahajan, R., Agarwal, S., Saroiu, S., & Dixon, C. (2011). Home automation in the wild: Challenges and opportunities. In *Proceedings of the SIGCHI Conference on Human Factors in Computing Systems.* Vancouver, Canada: ACM.

Cantrell, G., Dampier, D., Dandass, Y. S., Niu, N., & Bogen, C. (2012). Research toward a partially-automated, and crime specific digital triage process model. *Computer and Information Science, 5*(2), 29. doi:10.5539/cis.v5n2p29

Case, A., Cristina, A., Marziale, L., Richard, G. G., & Roussev, V. (2008). FACE: Automated digital evidence discovery and correlation. *Digital Investigation, 5, Supplement*(0), S65-S75.

Castro, M., Jara, A. J., & Skarmeta, A. F. (2012). An analysis of M2M platforms: Challenges and opportunities for the internet of things. In *Proceedings of Innovative Mobile and Internet Services in Ubiquitous Computing (IMIS)*, (pp. 757-762). IMIS.

Chan, M., Estève, D., Escriba, C., & Campo, E. (2008). A review of smart homes—Present state and future challenges. *Computer Methods and Programs in Biomedicine, 91*(1), 55–81. doi:10.1016/j.cmpb.2008.02.001 PMID:18367286

Chen, D., Chang, G., Sun, D., Li, J., Jia, J., & Wang, X. (2011). TRM-IoT: A trust management model based on fuzzy reputation for internet of things. *Computer Science and Information Systems, 8*(4), 1207–1228. doi:10.2298/CSIS110303056C

Chen, Y. (2012). Challenges and opportunities of internet of things. In *Proceedings of Design Automation Conference (ASP-DAC)*, (pp. 383-388). ASP-DAC.

Cohen, F. (2012). *The future of digital forensics.* Unpublished manuscript. Retrieved 21st June 2013, from http://www.all.net/Talks/2012-09-21-Beijing-Keynote.pdf

De Silva, L. C., Morikawa, C., & Petra, I. M. (2012). State of the art of smart homes. *Engineering Applications of Artificial Intelligence, 25*(7), 1313–1321. doi:10.1016/j.engappai.2012.05.002

Ding, D., Cooper, R. A., Pasquina, P. F., & Fici-Pasquina, L. (2011). Sensor technology for smart homes. *Maturitas, 69*(2), 131–136. doi:10.1016/j.maturitas.2011.03.016 PMID:21531517

Dobson, S., Sterritt, R., Nixon, P., & Hinchey, M. (2010). Fulfilling the vision of autonomic computing. *Computer (New York), 43*(1), 35–41.

Ericsson White paper. (2011). *More than 50 billion connected devices.* Unpublished manuscript. Retrieved from http://www.ericsson.com/res/docs/whitepapers/wp-50-billions.pdf

Fleisch, E. (2010). What is the internet of things? An economic perspective. *Economics, Management, and Financial Markets,* (2), 125-157.

Franklin, S. W., & Rajan, S. E. (2010). Personal area network for biomedical monitoring systems using human body as a transmission medium. *International Journal of Bio-Science & Bio-Technology, 2*(2).

Freiling, F. C., & Schwittay, B. (2007). A common process model for incident response and computer forensics. *IMF, 7,* 19–40.

Garfinkel, S. (2010). *Automated computer forensics: Current research areas.* Retrieved June/26, 2013, from http://simson.net/page/Automated_Computer_Forensics

Gurgen, L., Gunalp, O., Benazzouz, Y., & Gallissot, M. (2013). Self-aware cyber-physical systems and applications in smart buildings and cities. In *Proceedings of the Conference on Design, Automation and Test in Europe*, (pp. 1149-1154). Academic Press.

Henry, P., Williams, J., & Wright, B. (2013). *The SANS survey of digital forensics and incident response: A SANS whitepaper* Retrieved from https://blogs.sans.org/computer-forensics/files/2013/07/sans_dfir_survey_2013.pdf

Hernández-Muñoz, J. M., Vercher, J. B., Muñoz, L., Galache, J. A., Presser, M., & Gómez, L. A. H. et al. (2011). *Smart cities at the forefront of the future internet. In The future internet* (pp. 447–462). Springer.

Igarashi, Y., Ueno, M., & Fujisaki, T. (2012). Proposed node and network models for an M2M internet. In *Proceedings of World Telecommunications Congress (WTC)*, (pp. 1-6). WTC.

Islam, R. U., Schmidt, M., Kolbe, H., & Andersson, K. (2012). Nomadic mobility between smart homes. In *Proceedings of Globecom Workshops (GC Wkshps),* (pp. 1062-1067). IEEE.

Juels, A. (2006). RFID security and privacy: A research survey. *IEEE Journal on* Selected Areas in Communications, *24*(2), 381–394.

Khan, J. Y., & Yuce, M. R. (2010). Wireless body area network (WBAN) for medical applications. *Mobile Networks and Applications, 7*(5), 365-376.

Kohn, M., Eloff, J., & Olivier, M. (2006). Framework for a digital forensic investigation. In *Proceedings of the ISSA 2006 from Insight to Foresight Conference, Sandton, South Africa.* ISSA.

Kozlov, D., Veijalainen, J., & Ali, Y. (2012). Security and privacy threats in IoT architectures. In *Proceedings of the 7th International Conference on Body Area Networks,* (pp. 256-262). Academic Press.

Laranjo, I., Macedo, J., & Santos, A. (2012). Internet of things for medication control: Service implementation and testing. *Procedia Technology, 5*(0), 777–786. doi:10.1016/j.protcy.2012.09.086

Lee, H., Lee, J., & Han, J. (2007). The efficient security architecture for authentication and authorization in the home network. In *Proceedings of Natural Computation,* (vol. 5, pp. 713-717). Academic Press.

Lempereur, B., Merabti, M., & Shi, Q. (2009). *Automating evidence extraction and analysis for digital forensics.* Academic Press.

Lin, C., Zhitang, L., & Cuixia, G. (2009). Automated analysis of multi-source logs for network forensics. In *Proceedings of Education Technology and Computer Science,* (pp. 660-664). Academic Press.

Lin, M., Leu, J., Li, K., & Wu, J. C. (2012). Zigbee-based internet of things in 3D terrains. In *Proceedings of Advanced Computer Theory and Engineering (ICACTE),* (vol. 5, pp. 376-380). ICACTE.

Mattern, F. (2003). From smart devices to smart everyday objects. *IEEE Spectrum, 47*(10), 25.

Mohay, G. (2005). Technical challenges and directions for digital forensics. In *Proceedings of Systematic Approaches to Digital Forensic Engineering,* (pp. 155-161). Academic Press.

Ning, H., & Hu, S. (2011). Internet of things: An emerging industrial or a new major? In *Proceedings of Internet of Things (iThings/CPSCom),* (pp. 178-183). iThings.

Ning, H., & Liu, H. (2012). Cyber-physical-social based security architecture for future internet of things. *Advanced in Internet of Things, 2*(1), 1–7. doi:10.4236/ait.2012.21001

Nova, N., & Bleecker, J. (2006). Blogjects and the new ecology of things. In *Proceedings of Lift06 Workshop.* Lift.

Oriwoh, E., & Sant, P. (2013). The forensics edge management system: A concept and design. In *Proceedings of Ubiquitous Intelligence and Computing, (UIC/ATC),* (pp. 544-550). UIC/ATC.

Oriwoh, E., Jazani, D., Epiphaniou, G., & Sant, P. (2013). Internet of things forensics: Challenges and approaches. In *Proceedings of Collaborative Computing: Networking, Applications and Worksharing* (Collaboratecom), (pp. 608-615). Collaboratecom.

Pilli, E. S., Joshi, R. C., & Niyogi, R. (2010). Network forensic frameworks: Survey and research challenges. *Digital Investigation, 7*(1–2), 14–27. doi:10.1016/j.diin.2010.02.003

Proffitt, B. (2013). *How big the internet of things could become: The potential size of the internet things sector could be a multi-trillion dollar market by the end of the decade.* Retrieved November/20, 2013, from http://readwrite.com/2013/09/30/how-big-the-internet-of-things-could-become#feed=/infrastructure&awesm=~oj3jHsZI8rJE6c

Reith, M., Carr, C., & Gunsch, G. (2002). An examination of digital forensic models. *International Journal of Digital Evidence, 1*(3), 1–12.

Rowlingson, R. (2004). A ten step process for forensic readiness. *International Journal of Digital Evidence, 2*(3), 1–28.

Sang-Hyun, L., Lee, J., & Kyung-Il, M. (2013). Smart home security system using multiple ANFIS. *International Journal of Smart Home, 7*(3), 121.

Seigneur, J., Jensen, C. D., Farrell, S., Gray, E., & Chen, Y. (2003). Towards security auto-configuration for smart appliances. In *Proceedings of the Smart Objects Conference.* Academic Press.

Selamat, S. R., Yusof, R., & Sahib, S. (2008). Mapping process of digital forensic investigation framework. *International Journal of Computer Science and Network Security, 8*(10), 163–169.

Sommerville, I. (2007). *Models for responsibility assignment. In Responsibility and dependable systems* (pp. 165–186). Springer. doi:10.1007/978-1-84628-626-1_8

Turnbull, B. (2008). The adaptability of electronic evidence acquisition guides for new technologies. In *Proceedings of the 1st International Conference on Forensic Applications and Techniques in Telecommunications, Information, and Multimedia and Workshop,* (pp. 1:1-1:6). Academic Press.

Uckelmann, D. (Ed.). (2011). *Architecting the internet of things.* Springerverlag. doi:10.1007/978-3-642-19157-2

Vlachopoulos, K., Magkos, E., & Chrissikopoulos, V. (2013). A model for hybrid evidence investigation. *Emerging Digital Forensics Applications for Crime Detection, Prevention, and Security,* 150.

Weiser, M. (1991). The computer for the 21st century. *Scientific American, 265*(3), 94–104. doi:10.1038/scientificamerican0991-94

Xia, F., Yang, L. T., Wang, L., & Vinel, A. (2012). Internet of things. *International Journal of Communication Systems, 25*(9), 1101–1102. doi:10.1002/dac.2417

## KEY TERMS AND DEFINITIONS

**Blogjects:** These are objects with the capability to blog their status and activities.

**Cyberphysical Environments (CPE):** The combination of cyber and physical environments where cyber environments are the non-tangible and tangible technology-based aspects of our existence. Physical environments on the other hand are the natural and non-technology-based aspects of our existence.

**IoT-Ware:** This describes all the objects that are part of a home network including those with embedded intelligence e.g. smart meters and those with attached intelligence e.g. by RFID tagging.

**Objects of Forensics Interest (OOFI):** This refers to all IoT-ware within the IoT landscape with *digital* evidentiary value.

**Smart Forensics:** The use of smart devices and methods that apply scientific techniques to automatically and autonomously perform digital forensics investigations within Smart Home and similar environments in order to produce forensically relevant and acceptable evidence which can be used to aid private/corporate legal, disciplinary or other such proceedings.

**Spimes:** A combination of the words *space* and *time*, it describes products that have identifiable and retrievable lifecycles that describe them from their production to retirement and/or destruction.

# Chapter 27
# Sticks and Stones Will Break My Euros:
## The Role of EU Law in Dealing with Cyber-Bullying through Sysop-Prerogative

**Jonathan Bishop**
*Centre for Research into Online Communities and E-Learning Systems, Wales, UK*

## ABSTRACT

*"Sticks and Stones" is a well-known adage that means that whatever nasty things people say, they will not physically harm one. This is not often the case, as bullying, especially via the Internet, can be quite harmful. There are few anti-bullying laws emanating from the European Union, which is a trading block of 28 member states that have pooled their sovereignty in order to have common laws and practices to boost trade and peace. However, the common legal rules that exist in the EU have implications for those who run websites, including relating to cyber-bullying. These people, known as systems operators, or sysops, can be limited in the powers they have and rules they make through "sysop prerogative." Sysop prerogative means that a systems operator can do anything which has been permitted or not taken away by statute, or which they have not given away by contract. This chapter reviews how the different legal systems in Europe impact on sysops and change the way in which sysop prerogative can be exercised. This includes not just from the EU legal structure, but equally the European Convention on Human Rights (ECHR), which also has implications for sysops in the way they conduct their activities.*

## INTRODUCTION

The famous European philosopher, Socrates, claims a wise person knows what they do not know, according to (Bazelon, 1977). Bazelon quoted this adage at the dawn of the microcomputer revolution. Bazelon also admitted that they knew little about science and technology, and said most judges are the same. The English idiom of 'Sticks and Stones' existed in the 1970s and has

long been associated with human rights, including by authors such as Emilie Hafner-Burton, who thinks 'naming and shaming' is a way to enforce human rights (Hafner-Burton, 2008). The extent that cyber-bullying would evolve from microcomputers was probably not foreseen by Bazelon, yet Hafner-Burton's view of naming and shaming seems appropriate for dealing with cyber-bullies and Internet trolls. The European Union, which has grown in significance since the 1970s, now

DOI: 10.4018/978-1-4666-6324-4.ch027

consists of a block of 28 sovereign states that have pooled their sovereignty for economic advantage. To achieve this advantage often requires 'approximation of law', which is where laws are created that are the same in every country in order to break down the barriers to trade between those countries. Even so, the European Union, analogously to the USA, experiences difficulties even when the laws are adopted in each member state (Jutla, Bodorik, & Dhaliwal, 2002). Something that is clear from the European Union (EU), also called 'The Common Market' from when it was originally created, is that its vastness is exceeded only by that of the Internet. As a legal jurisdiction, the EU has a number of implications for sysops, and the extent of their ability to provide services on a cross-border basis. The adage, 'Sticks and Stones,' is an appropriate one to discuss in relation to EU Law. The full version of this, 'sticks and stones will break my bones but words will never harm me.' is translated into French as, '*la bave du crapaud n'atteint pas la blanche colombe*' (A slime toad does not reach a white dove). As one can see the two idioms are not literal translations of one another, even if the meanings are both the same. That is why in the European Union the concept of 'proportionality' exists. This is where legislation and other law is interpreted on the basis of what it means and what was intended, rather than what is literally written. So under EU law, the French idiom on toads and white doves would be treated exactly the same as the 'sticks and stones' equivalent in English. This is generally the case regardless of whether law is being interpreted in the European Court of Human Rights, or the Court of Justice of the European Union.

The relationship between the European Convention of Human Rights (ECHR) and EU law has been somewhat fragmented. According to (Guild, 2004) no reference was made in the original EU treaty to the ECHR, as it was not expected that both would overlap as the European integration project grew. Emily Reid and others have argued that the European Union has not been ideally set up to take account of human and civil rights, even with its own Charter of Fundamental Rights (Caracciolo di Torella & Reid, 2002). Indeed, it was not until The Maastricht Treaty that scholars began to see the EU as having any implications at all for civil liberties, human rights, or even the implications of the ECHR on domestic law of European countries (Gearty, 1997). The EU and ECHR have never had more relevance than in the age of the Internet. The plans of European countries to intercept e-mail and Internet calls, let alone to covertly tamper with private citizens' computers, contravene the ECHR, and many argue it should be enforced (Caloyannides, 2004). The European Commission claims that e-commerce in the European Union is hampered by lack of consumer trust, and clearly this does nothing to help (Jutla et al., 2002).

## BACKGROUND

The European Union as it is today is founded on the Treaty of Rome, which has been amended a number of times since the Single European Act in the 1980s. Since this re-negotiation of powers of the EU by Margaret Thatcher, there have been several re-negotiations of power, including one under John Major, three under Tony Blair and two under Gordon Brown. Further such re-negotiations have been promised by David Cameron. The common progression among all four leaders prior to David Cameron was a movement to a single legal identity for the European Union rather than the existence of various 'pillars.' This creation of a legal person subsequently led to the EU being awarded the Nobel Peace Prize under David Cameron.

The European Union consists of a number of institutions for the creation and enforcement of legislation and policy. The process under which legislation is usually created involves a proposal from the European Commission. Under the ordinary procedure this is considered by the Council of the European Union, made up of the Ministers of member states, and the European Parliament at the same time. Under the special procedure the Council of Ministers need only ask the Opinion of the European Parliament, but it must consider that opinion.

It is thought that the European Union is not always set up to effectively produce technology law, often due to the lack of elected representatives who are from a technology background. Directives on concepts like cookies, which require consent upfront, often lack an appreciation of the way technology works. Many of the decisions of the EU in relation to technology and technology firms are made in the Courts of Justice of the European Union (CJEU). Notable cases have been Commission v Microsoft, where the European Commission regarded Microsoft's proprietary operating system Windows to be a platform, and that their intellectual property had to be made available to their competitors as a result of this to avoid 'tying.' The CJEU is not to be confused with the European Court of Human Rights (ECtHR). The former exists as an institution of the amended Treaty of Rome, and the latter under the European Convention on Human Rights. These two treaties can be considered 'primary legislation,' whereas the laws made under former, including in the CJEU are called 'secondary legislation.' Even though the two treaties are separate, on the relatively rare occasions when the CJEU deals with fundamental rights, it tends to agree with the ECHR in applying the Treaty of Rome (Goldhaber, 2009).

## SYSOP PREROGATIVE IN A EUROPEAN CONTEXT

The founding freedoms of the European Union include freedom of movement for workers, freedom of establishment, freedom to provide services, free movement of goods and free movement of capital. It might not be expected at first that this would have relevance from a webmaster operating a website in one country for mainly users in that country, but there are significant obligations for sysops operating within the European Union. The most significant piece of secondary legislation affecting sysops is the Electronic Commerce Directive 2000/31/EC on 'certain legal aspects of information society services, in particular electronic commerce, in the Internal Market'. This Directive makes sysops liable for any illegal activity that occurs on their websites of which they are aware of and do nothing about. It also provides a basis for which those affected by what might be seen as unlawful activity by sysops a route to use national court and out-of-court mechanisms to enforce their rights against a sysop.

The main provisions of the European Convention on Human Rights (ECHR) that have relevance to sysops are freedom of thought and expression, right to privacy and also to associate with others. These will be explored throughout this chapter. In the case of the Treaty on the Functioning of the European Union (TFEU), which is an update of the Treaty of Rome, the main provisions are free movement of goods, services, people and capital.

Sysop prerogative has been applied in relation to common law legal systems to mean that a sysop can make any rule they please so long as it hasn't been given away by them through contract or taken from them through legislation. At a European level this concept becomes more complex as there are many different legal systems within the EU, which are not based on common law, where a sysop would only have a right to do something where that was provided for by law. This chapter attempts to identify the areas of European Union, and European Human Rights Law from the Council of Europe, which exist in all EU countries so that the extent of sysop prerogative is clear. However, the role of proportionality, as discussed earlier in relating to treating the English 'Sticks and Stones' idiom the same as the French 'Slime Toad and White Dove' idioms, helps navigate this, including in relation to bullying.

Also important in the running of online communities by sysops is for them to distinguish kudos trolling, which is done to entertaining others, from flame trolling, which is done to harm others for the poster's entertainment only. Again this can cause problems for sysops who have to deal with people from the many diverse legislative frameworks in the European Union. Therefore this chapter will try to find the common ground between these countries by looking at the implications of the European Laws emanating from the European Union and Council of Europe.

The extent that EU law applies to sysop prerogative to all intents and purpose is restricted to cross-border issues and those falling within 'the internal market.' One such restriction are the Distance Selling Directives, which require that websites that charge a fee that discourages EU Citizens from a State other than where a website is based in taking part in posting kudos, including kudos trolling could be considered unlawful as per *Commission v Spain* (C45-93), as it infringes Article 18 TFEU. Much talk in recent years has been the ability of sysops to balance the right of free speech from the rights of protection of one's reputation and their user's privacy. Bazelon as far back as 1976 said that privacy is a liberty that should be championed with special rigor, yet it is very difficult to think how this can be made possible on the Internet, where people are easily bullied by simply having a presence on Twitter or Facebook (Bazelon, 1976). The case of *Bishop v Powell (2006)* showed right to privacy even had to give way with local media figures, and that free speech was an important part of the democratic process. This debate could probably be put to rest if sysops were given the status of 'human rights defenders'. This is presently defined by Resolution 2009/2199 (INI) of the European Parliament on 'human rights defenders'. The European Union's approach to dealing with flame trolling has been very weak. Article 14 of this resolution says the EP, "Emphasises the importance of freedom of speech and the role of the media, both online and offline, as an enabler for human rights defenders."

Article 15 saying it "Considers that the development of new technologies and their impact on human rights defenders needs to be assessed and the results integrated in existing EU programmes on human rights and human rights defenders."

## EUROPEAN CONTRACT LAW AND SYSOP PREROGATIVE

Despite the lofty heights it now seems to have reached, European Union contract law had rather tentative beginnings, contrasting starkly with the central role of contract law (Miller, 2011). Contract law in the European Union evolved differently in each Member State. Most of the European Union as it now is followed the Roman approach to contract law, with the notable exception being Great Britain (Twigg-Flesner, 2008). While Great Britain developed its common law system as distinct from systems based on civil codes it has been argued that the differences are not as great as is claimed by some legal scholars (Zimmermann, 2004). If one were to develop definitions of sysop prerogative distinct in common law and civil code legal systems they might look as follows. In a common law system, the definition could be, "The right a systems operator has to make a rule on something which hasn't been taken from them by statute, or given away by them through contract." And in civil code systems the definition of sysop prerogative could be, "The right a systems operator has to make a rule of something which has been granted to them by law and not given away by them through contract." The distinction, which might be obvious, is that under common law systems, the making of any rule is legal unless statute says otherwise, and that in civil code systems this right is limited by the fact there needs to be an explicit provision enabling them to make a particular rule.

Sysops have much protection in contract law in the United Kingdom, due to its limits in providing third party rights. It is for instance unlikely to be possible for a private individual to enforce a contract with a sysops such as terms and conditions where those terms and conditions are being broken by users other than them. The exception to this might be if such acts by other users are unlawful and have the knowledge of the sysop, as this would mean the Electronic Commerce Directive could be used to remedy the situation.

Much European Union law is contrary to the British way of doing things, as it is equally enforceable against governments and the state (vertical effect) as individuals (horizontal effect). For instance; Article 101(1) TFEU, which prohibits non-competition agreements between firms, was intended to protect third parties, whether competitors or consumers, and not parties to an agreement which was in breach of that provision (Miller, 2011).

## HUMAN AND FUNDAMENTAL RIGHTS IN EUROPE

The European Convention on Human Rights (ECHR) is a treaty formed by the members of the European Union and independent nation states in Europe under the auspices of the Council of Europe, which is distinct from the Council of Ministers. Many of the rights are similar to those in the Charter of Fundamental Rights (CFR) contained within the EU Treaty, but unlike these they apply in all European Countries signed up to it. The CFR on the other hand is not enforceable in the United Kingdom or Poland. Many of the rights conveyed in the ECHR can be found in religious and other codes, practices and conventions, making it as near universal as possible.

### Freedom of Association, Movement of People, and Establishment

Article 11 of the ECHR creates a right for people to associate with one another, including through websites on the Internet. Such platforms have

to take account of, among others, the judgment in *Associated Society of Locomotive Engineers & Firemen v United Kingdom* (ECtHR, App no 11002/05). The case shows that while not being interpreted as imposing an obligation on associations or organisations to admit everyone wishing to join, it is the case that people have a right to apply to join them in order to further the expression of their views. Whilst Article 11 makes it clear that people have the right to associate with others, such as through a public communications network, such others equally have the right not to associate with them. It does not stop trolling for others benefit on a bulletin board from being a right, just because the sysops can withdraw someone's membership on grounds which are non-discriminatory using sysop prerogative. There are some commonalities between these ECHR rights and those under EU law. Freedom of association is inherent in the freedom of establishment, as guaranteed by Article 49 TFEU and expressly extended to setting up companies or firms in Article 54 TFEU (Reich, 2014). There appears to be some conflict between the rights of EU citizens to freedom of association under Article 11 ECHR and the right for EU business to provide services under Article 56 TFEU. This occurs where an undertaking wishes to post their workers overseas, where they are considered to be regulated by the laws of their home country rather than the Member State in which they are being forced to operate (Syrpis, 2012). Whilst one might not expect this to apply to small online communities, the fact that it is possible to have volunteers from all over the EU working on a website based in one locality suggests that EU law does apply. With the bigger social networking service providers such as Facebook, it is very likely they will draw workers from many European Union jurisdictions. On this basis, Facebook may not only have their sysop prerogative limited in the case of the main users of their website, but it may also be limited with regards to any employees they take on in the EU.

## Freedom of Expression

Article 10 ECHR provides that "everyone has the right to freedom of expression (including) to hold opinions and to receive and impart information and ideas without interference by public authority and regardless of frontiers. [...] The exercise of these freedoms, since it carries with it duties and responsibilities, [...] for the prevention of disorder or crime, for the protection of health or morals, for the protection of the reputation or the rights of others, for preventing the disclosure of information received in confidence." Article 11 of the Charter of Fundamental Rights of the European Union states that "(1) Everyone has the right to freedom of expression. This right shall include freedom to hold opinions and to receive and impart information and ideas without interference by public authority and regardless of frontiers. (2) The freedom and pluralism of the media shall be respected."

In Society for the Protection of the Unborn Child (Ireland) v Grogan [1991] ECR 4685 it was found that the distribution of information promoting a service unlawful under national law can be restricted in the case of individuals if they were not the providers of that service in another State where it was lawful. This goes beyond the judgment in Handyside v United Kingdom (1976) 1 EHRR 737, hereinafter referred to as Handyside, meaning the State could describe the promotion of anything unlawful in their country as 'flame trolling'.

The Handyside case established that the State can restrict freedom of expression where it is in accordance with the limitations of Article 10. Law enforcement bodies within the UK are also concerned about the existence of commercial websites featuring sexually explicit content created and maintained by UK citizens, which may be deemed as obscene under the Obscene Publications Act (Akdeniz, 2001). In this case the Obscene Publications Acts were found to be lawful as it aimed to protect "morals in a democratic soci-

ety". Equally, Fatullayev v Azerbaijan (App. No. 40984/07) established that where it is possible to ascertain the identity of a flame troller, and that it is apparent their messages are false or unverified, it is necessary for claimants or prosecutors to provide sufficient and relevant reasons for finding that those statements damaged the reputation of the alleged victims. In re St Peter and St Paul's Church, Chingford - [2007] Fam 67 found that blocking of lawful adult material is an interference with the freedom of expression granted by Article 10 ECHR. The case confirmed the findings in Belfast City Council v Miss Behavin' Ltd [2007] 1 WLR 1420 that access to explicit content in a locality via the Internet is distinguishable from physical manifestations such as a sex shop. The right to enjoy the freedom of expression of others, such as trolling, is not limited by the geographical location of the participant.

## Privacy and the "Right to Be Forgotten"

Article 8 ECHR provides that 'Everyone has the right to respect for his private and family life, his home and his correspondence. [...] There shall be no interference by a public authority with the exercise of this right except such as is in accordance with the law and is necessary in a democratic society'. The Charter of Fundamental Rights of the European Union provides for protection of a person's privacy and protection of their personal data in Articles 7 and 8 respectively. Finally Article 26 TFEU provides the basis on which personal information and other data is protected via Directive 95/46/EC on 'the protection of individuals with regard to the processing of personal data and on the free movement of such data.'

R v Bowden [2000] 2 WLR 1083 and R v Smethurst [2002] 1 Cr App R 6 established that it was necessary in a democratic society to restrict the rights of others to a private life where it affected the legitimate rights of children to exercise their Convention Rights. This can include the right to form friendships online to peacefully interact with others and provide personal information without fear of reprisals. DPP v Collins established that there needs to be a balance between the Article 8 ECHR right to privacy and the Article 10 ECHR right to freedom of expression. Applying DPP v Collins it is apparent that it is the message, not its content, which is the basic ingredient of the meeting a statutory offence relating to flame trolling. It is kudos trolling however, and not a flame, for a scriptwriter to email his or her director about dialogue for a new film, and not open them to prosecution. That is because however intrinsically menacing or offensive the text they are discussing that in its context, such a message threatens nobody and should offend nobody.

European Union law sets some limitations on EU member states' ability to apply their data privacy laws extra-territorially to protect EEA-based companies (Determann, 2012). Whilst the European Convention on Cybercrime was supposed to protect such rights of consumers across Europe and beyond the European Union, some argue that the Convention expands the surveillance powers of government without adequately protecting privacy (Levinson, 2002). The advantage of this however is that it could give European countries an easier means to enforce Internet trolling laws as they could use algorithms to monitor Internet content for signs of abuse, as has been considered for schools using the Classroom 2.0 approach (Bishop, 2012).

It has been argued for many years that the legal system has an obligation to protect people from the psychological abuses that come from technology, such as racism, and greater use of the knowledge of psychiatrists and the law could protect vulnerable persons (Bazelon, 1975). Where such abuses have a long-term effect on someone they are called 'bleasures.' Without such advances proposed by Bazelon, virtual 'sticks and stones' will continue to harm people and those who do it will remain unaccountable. The European Union

has been reviewing its data protection laws in order to take account of the tremendous amount of personal information on social media. Education establishments, such as Swansea University, are already urging their studies to take with regards to being connected to social media when they are intoxicated, and have devised a dedicated policy for the purpose of regulating Internet trolling where alcohol is involved. This might be considered a knee-jerk reaction to the conviction of Liam Stacey, a student at Swansea University who posted racist remarks on Twitter when he was confronted by trolls while drinking in a bar using his mobile phone. A Freedom of Information Request established that Liam Stacey was not, however, disciplined for racism, but for bringing Swansea University into disrepute, which appears more of a concern to Swansea University. This appeared the case in a statement made by registrar Raymond Ciborowski and student council president Tom Upton following the case of Liam Stacey. "We have received complaints from students and alumni about the potential damage this page could do to their own employability, as a result of damage to the university's reputation," they said. "Companies are increasingly searching for information on job applicants and the organisations they are connected to - already 30% of UK HR directors use social media to recruit candidates, and 22% check candidates' online activity." Such problems may not be as drastic if the European Union's reforms take the shape of the judgment in Google Spain v AEPD and Mario Costeja Gonzalez (C-131/12). In this case, Spanish medic Mario Costeja Gonzalez brought legal action against Google after they discovered that Google, as a mere conduit of Internet content, was making available information about them that they wanted kept private. The Court of Justice of the European Union ruled that Mario Costeja Gonzalez was entitled to the "right to be forgotten" under Article 26 TFEU through Directive 95/46/EC (discussed earlier) and that Google had a responsibility to not be a carrier of such personal information. Google's response to this was to put a form on its website for persons to ask for information to be removed from their search engine, which received 12,000 requests on its first day. It might be that US-based operations in order to protect free speech would have to develop means to ensure that those in the EU have the right to privacy and protection of their personal data, while also ensuring that those in the US do not have their rights to freedom of expression impinged up on.

## Free Movement of Capital and E-Money

As discussed earlier, one of the four founding freedoms of the European Union is the free movement of capital (Karmel, 1999). With the increasing importance of cross-border transactions and international companies, including banks and other financial institutions, the unobstructed functioning of the free movement of capital is argued to be at the core of European financial law (Andenas, Gutt, & Pannier, 2005). But the EU's powers over capital is not limited to these areas. Since the beginning of the 21st century the European Union has introduced two e-money directives, with the second repealing the first. The first was introduced with Directive 2000/46/EC on 'the taking up, pursuit and prudential supervision of e-money', when Internet money services like Beenz.com existed as the primary forms of non-State currencies on the Internet (Edmonds & Gray, 2002; Hartmann, 2006). Since then the European Union has introduced Directive 2009/110/EC on 'the taking up, pursuit and prudential supervision of the business of electronic money institutions' (Halpin & Moore, 2009), which has come in the wake of crypto-currencies like Dodgecoin and Bitcoin which are a new type of asset that have been rapidly growing in popularity and are in effect, a form of digital bearer bond with no underlying asset (Silverman, 2013).

## SYSOP PREROGATIVE AND INTERNET TROLLING IN EUROPE

The European Union, presently consisting of 28 member states, is regarded as the most successful peace treaty in history, resulting in it being awarded the Nobel Peace Prize in 2012. The Treaty of Rome initially created the European Economic Community, which with subsequent amendments became the European Community and then the European Union. The ethos of building an economic union was on the basis that if all the member states in Europe were trading with one another, they would be so interdependent it would be counterproductive to engage in war. One might argue that in our post-war environment, it is now essential that the next step be to using the infrastructure of the European Union to promote peace among EU Citizens, particularly in the areas of race and nationality. Understanding the way in which the European Union can discourage flame trolling and increase kudos trolling is therefore essential to achieving European integration.

## Flame Trolling and Cyber-Bullying in an European Context

It is a common view in the EU that online talk is far from the ideals of what political conversation should be, which the fluidity of expression is known to both increase the willingness to speak on political subjects, but also increase the chances for anti-social behavior, such as flame trolling (Stromer-Galley & Wichowski, 2010). The European Convention on Human Rights has been used in many incidents to test the extent to which flames count as free speech over being considered bullying. Handyside (i.e. Handyside v United Kingdom (1976) 1 EHRR 737) gave the State the right to restrict the publication of content to protect "morals" on the basis of "margins of appreciation". This case has been seen as a means for achieving pluralism, tolerance and broadmindedness as the hallmarks of a society, with freedom of expression as one of the essential foundations of a democracy (Murdoch, 2013). This should be particularly helpful to sysops in being flexible with sysop prerogative so that they can adjust to the needs of their members with minimal state intervention.

Pivotal to the Handyside case was the notion of protecting the vulnerable, such as youths, by allowing the state to restrict freedom of expression where it is in the interests of morals one might expect in a democratic society. For many youths, the 'Sticks and Stones' (or 'toads and doves') idioms are an adage and not an emotional reality. The right to freedom of expression similarly exists in the case of cross-border publications in the EU under the "rules of reason" of Article 34 TFEU. The State has the right to restrict the importation of any website or other electronic content from another EU country it considers 'flame trolling' or 'cyber-bullying,' providing this is not based on the quantity of the goods as per R v Henn and Darby [1979] ECR as this would make it a "quantitative restriction". In this case the restriction of pornography by the State was found to be lawful. This is because the ECJ considered the regulation of pornographic material in the UK to be so restrictive that it could be presumed that there was no lawful trade of such goods within the UK for overseas goods (Fairhurst, 1999). This means that a government is free to restrict sysop prerogative through legislation where the content they are restricting does not place sysops in another country at a substantial disadvantage compared to those in the country administering the legislation.

## Kudos Trolling in an European Context

The policy texts of the European Union abound with phrases such as "an information society for all" and "e-inclusion" (Van Dijk, 2009), but the

reality in the case of online communities especially is somewhat different. European Union law often regulates in way not natural to most of its citizens. For instance, considering the cases of Commission v Ireland [1982] ECR 6005 and Apple and Pear Council v Lewis (Case 222/82) there are a number of instances in which the posting of kudos about national products with the authority of the State are restricted or instead lawful. Commission v Ireland found that where a measure (in the case the labelling of products as "Buy Irish") is capable of restricting imports it is illegal under Article 34 TFEU. This could mean that UK Government schemes to accredit websites, such as that carried out by the dissolved Quango, Becta, could be seen to have the same effect of 'flame trolling' non-British websites as not up to standard. Apple and Pear Council v Lewis (Case 222/82) on the other hand found the promotion by the State of a product, even it made reference to 'national qualities' is lawful, providing there are no restrictions on its export or the import of competing products. This means the State could highlight a website as being effective at reducing flame trolling and encouraging kudos trolling, providing it did not discourage the use of similar websites in other EU States.

## IMPLICATIONS AND FUTURE RESEARCH DIRECTIONS

One might conclude that the European legal systems can have a huge impact on systems operators to the extent that sysop prerogative is highly restricted under the laws of the European Union and through the European Union Convention on Human Rights. It might be necessary for sysops to develop some common understanding to ensure they are not restricting the rights of people within Europe to enjoy the Internet freely.

## DISCUSSION

The European Union has been called one of the most successful peace treaties in history. Its accompanying piece of law, the European Convention on Human Rights, while separate has many crossovers. This chapter explored some of these in relation to posting to online communities, especially where this could be considered flame trolling or kudos trolling. An important concept to understand in relation to the rights and responsibilities of online communities is 'sysop prerogative'. Sysop prerogative means that the owner of an online community, known as a systems operator, or sysop, can set any terms and conditions they wish for such a website, where it does not conflict with the law or infringe on an existing contract with a user. This chapter has found that a number of aspects of EU and ECHR law impact on the extent of sysop prerogative. In the context of flame trolling, which is the abusive kind of Internet posts, sysops are restricted in the content they are allowed to publish, which in many cases is based on the terms set by their own member state. However, the rights of member states of the European Union to restrict sysop prerogative in this way is required to not have any effect on the ability of other nations to trade with that state.

In the context of kudos trolling, the European legal systems give people a right to associate freely with one another and express themselves freely also. In some cases this may include expressing content some find objectionable, but this is in many cases can only be prohibited if it could be seen to affect morals or decency. This is reflected directly in Article 11 ECHR, and the right to associate also includes the right to establishment under Articles 45, 54, and 56 TFEU. Equally, in one case the United Kingdom was found to have such strict laws against pornography that a ban on imports of such materials was not unlawful because the market was already restricted so as not to create a genuine disadvantage.

## REFERENCES

Akdeniz, Y. (2001). Controlling illegal and harmful content on the internet. In D. S. Wall (Ed.), *Crime and the internet* (p. 113). London: Brunner-Routledge. doi:10.4324/9780203164501_chapter_8

Andenas, M., Gutt, T., & Pannier, M. (2005). Free movement of capital and national company law. *European Business Law Review*, *16*(4), 757.

Bazelon, D. L. (1975). A jurist's view of psychiatry. *The Journal of Psychiatry & Law*, *3*, 175.

Bazelon, D. L. (1976). Probing privacy. *Gonzaga Law Review*, *12*, 587.

Bazelon, D. L. (1977). Coping with technology through the legal process. *Jurimetrics Journal*, *18*, 241.

Bishop, J. (2012). Co-operative e-learning in the multilingual and multicultural school: The role of 'Classroom 2.0' for increasing participation in education. In P. M. Pumilia-Gnarini, E. Favaron, E. Pacetti, J. Bishop, & L. Guerra (Eds.), *Didactic strategies and technologies for education: Incorporating advancements* (pp. 137–150). Hershey, PA: IGI Global. doi:10.4018/978-1-4666-2122-0.ch013

Caloyannides, M. A. (2004). *Privacy protection and computer forensics*. Norwood, MA: Artech House Publishers.

Caracciolo di Torella, E., & Reid, E. (2002). The changing shape of the" european family" and fundamental rights. *European Law Review*, *27*(1), 80–90.

Determann, L. (2012). *Determann's field guide to international data privacy law compliance*. Cheltenham, UK: Edward Elgar Publishing Ltd.

Edmonds, G., & Gray, D. (2002). Internet dictionary. London: Dorling Kindersley Limited.

Fairhurst, J. O. (1999). The working time directive: A spanish inquisition. *Web Journal of Current Legal Issues, 1999*(3)

Gearty, C. A. (1997). *European civil liberties and the european convention on human rights: A comparative study*. Leiden, The Netherlands: Martinus Nijhoff Publishers.

Goldhaber, M. D. (2009). *A people's history of the european court of human rights*. New Brunswick, NJ: Rutgers University Press.

Guild, E. (2004). *The legal elements of european identity: EU citizenship and migration law*. London: Kluwer Law International.

Hafner-Burton, E. M. (2008). Sticks and stones: Naming and shaming the human rights enforcement problem. *International Organization, 62*, 689–716. doi:10.1017/S0020818308080247

Halpin, R., & Moore, R. (2009). Developments in electronic money regulation–the electronic money directive: A better deal for e-money issuers? *Computer Law & Security Report, 25*(6), 563–568. doi:10.1016/j.clsr.2009.09.010

Hartmann, M. E. (2006). *E-payments evolution. Handbuch E-money, E-payment & M-payment* (pp. 7–18). Springer. doi:10.1007/3-7908-1652-3_2

Jutla, D., Bodorik, P., & Dhaliwal, J. (2002). Supporting the e-business readiness of small and medium-sized enterprises: Approaches and metrics. *Internet Research, 12*(2), 139–164. doi:10.1108/10662240210422512

Karmel, R. S. (1999). Case for a european securities commission, the. *Colum. J. Transnat'L L., 38*, 9.

Levinson, D. (2002). *Encyclopedia of crime and punishment*. London: Sage Publications Ltd.

Miller, L. (2011). *The emergence of EU contract law: Exploring europeanization*. Oxford, UK: Oxford University Press. doi:10.1093/acprof:o so/9780199606627.003.0002

Murdoch, J. (2013). The binding effect of the ECHR in the united Kingdom–Views from scotland. In R. Arnold (Ed.), *The universalism of human rights* (pp. 209–221). Berlin: Springer. doi:10.1007/978-94-007-4510-0_12

Reich, N. (2014). Understanding EU law: Objectives, principles and methods of community law (3rd ed.). Cambridge, UK: Intersentia.

Silverman, N. (2013). The E-Penny opera. *Wilmott, 2013*(67), 22-27.

Stromer-Galley, J., & Wichowski, A. (2010). Political discussion online. The Handbook of Internet Studies, 168-187.

Syrpis, P. (Ed.). (2012). *The judiciary, the legislature and the EU internal market*. Rio de Janeiro: Cambridge University Press. doi:10.1017/CBO9780511845680

Twigg-Flesner, C. (2008). The europeanisation of contract law. London: Routledge Cavendish.

Van Dijk, J. A. G. M. (2009). *One europe, digitally divided. Routledge handbook of internet politics* (pp. 288–305). London: Taylor & Francis.

Zimmermann, R. (2004). Roman law and the harmonisation of private law in europe. In A. S. Hartkamp, M. W. Hesselink, E. Hondius, C. Mak, & E. Du Perron (Eds.), *Towards a european civil code* (pp. 22–23). Deventer, The Netherlands: Kluwer Law International.

## KEY TERMS AND DEFINITIONS

**Charter of Fundamental Rights of the European Union:** A treaty agreed by members of the European Union to apply and go beyond the principles of the European Convention on Human Rights in relation to EU members.

**European Convention on Human Rights:** An international treaty that confers duties on its signatories to protect the rights of their citizens according to the provisions of that treaty.

**European Court of Human Rights:** The European Court of Human Rights (ECtHR) makes decision arising out of claimed breaches of the European Convention on Human Rights.

**European Union:** A trading block of 28 independent countries who pool their sovereignty in order to cooperate for mutual benefit.

**Flame Trolling:** Trolling for the entertainment of oneself to the detriment of others is called flame trolling.

**Kudos Trolling:** Trolling for the mutual entertainment of others is called kudos trolling.

**Sysop:** A person who runs a website or online community is called a systems operator (i.e. sysop for short).

**Sysop Prerogative:** In common law systems, the right a systems operator has to make a rule on something which hasn't been taken from them by statute, or given away by them through contract. In civil code systems the right a systems operator has to make a rule of something which has been granted to them by law and not given away by them through contract.

# Chapter 28
# Trolling Is Not Just a Art. It Is an Science:
## The Role of Automated Affective Content Screening in Regulating Digital Media and Reducing Risk of Trauma

**Jonathan Bishop**

*Centre for Research into Online Communities and E-Learning Systems, Wales, UK*

## ABSTRACT

*This chapter seeks to explore the role media content ratings play in the age of "Internet trolling" and other electronic media issues like "sexting." Using ANOVA to validate a four-factor approach to media ratings based on maturity, the chapter finds the ability of a person to withstand various media content, measured in "knol," which is the brain's capacity to process information, can be used to calculate media ratings. The study concludes it is feasible to have brain-computer interfaces for PCs and kiosks to test the maturity of vulnerable persons and recommend to parents/guardians or cinema managers whether or not to allow someone access to the content they wish to consume. This could mean that computer software could be programmed to automatically censor content that person is likely to be distressed or grossly offended by. Public policy issues relating to these supply-side interventions are discussed.*

## INTRODUCTION

The convergence of media content is posing challenges in terms of protecting the vulnerable while also protecting free speech. Regulating abusive online media content, such as Internet trolling, is not suited to 'before-the-fact' model of current film rating agencies even if the objective rules and judgements used by those agencies are. Basing rating on age appropriateness is also ineffective for the online world, as people will have different

maturity for different content at different ages with some being more prone to offense than others.

Internet trolling as a concept has transformed in definition in recent years from classical trolling, which was the posting of messages in a friendly way, to Anonymous Trolling, which is posted to harm others (Bishop, 2014b; Phillips, 2011). Internet trolling messages posted to entertain others can be seen as 'kudos trolling' and those designed to harm others can be seen as 'flame trolling' (Bishop, 2012b). But this does

DOI: 10.4018/978-1-4666-6324-4.ch028

not mean all flame trolling is 'bad' and should be punished, nor does it mean all kudos trolling is 'good' and should be allowed. In some forums on the Internet, flame trolling is encouraged, such as the criticism of politicians, bankers, or other people who may be part of a group with dislikeable qualities. The consensual nature of these forums it could be argued should not mean their abusive comments should be prosecutable (Starmer, 2013). Equally not all kudos trolling is designed to be in the interests of people. For instance, a type of online community user called a chatroom bob, will often post friendly comments in order to seduce others. They may be a pervert looking to coax naked pictures out of the person, or a sex predator trying to groom a child or other young person (Bishop, 2012c; Jansen & James, 1995; Jansen & James, 2002). A recent example of this was the case of Daniel Perry. Daniel Perry was a 17-year-old man who was tormented into killing himself as part of an online plot to extort money from him. Perry was a popular teenager from Dunfermline, Fife, who took his own life after being targeted by a group of Internet trollers who exploited him for their own gain. Perry took his own life after a Skype conversation with a person he was led to believe was a girl the same age as him, where he shared sexualized videos of himself online known as 'sexting' or 'getting naked on cam' (GNOC). Suddenly a gang then hijacked the chat and threatened to show the video to his family and friends, unless he paid them menaces (i.e. money). Known as 'Nigerian Chatroom Bobs,' due to an urban myth that it is mostly people in Nigeria who extort money from people online, these trollers will use all means to gain the confidence of someone and then extort money from them, which in Daniel Perry's case was attempted through blackmail.

It is therefore necessary to have a more technical way of looking at Internet trolling and other online misdemeanours, such as through linguistic or other forms of studying media (Bishop, 2014b; Hardaker, 2013; Hardaker, 2010). This could in-

volve making it easier to regulate online content, so that mature users know what to expect, and Internet security software providers can better produce software with parental controls to avoid the corruption of the minds of those lacking in maturity (Haravuori, Suomalainen, Berg, Kiviruusu, & Marttunen, 2011; Roche, 2012). Such people may not have been exposed to severe or traumatic content in the past and as a result be less able to cope with it (Dutta-Bergman, 2006). It may therefore be appropriate to refer to those Internet trolling messages which are prosecutable as electronic message faults (EMFls) and those which are not prosecutable as electronic message freedoms (EMFrs).

There appears in the UK to be a cycle of youth justice where young people are at one point seen unfavourably and at another there is increased concern for them (Bernard, 1992; Weijers, 1999). Some have said that whilst there is a developing international literature exploring youth participation in community arts activities, to date relatively little attention has been paid to issues surrounding young people's decision-making within participatory arts projects (Rimmer, 2012). A recent study in Wales has shown how the significant involvement of young people in deciding the outcome of community arts projects rather than simply being led by controlling adults who have their own outdated ideas has seen positive outcomes for communities (Bishop, 2012a). Understanding the effect of the arts and other cultural pursuits on the engagement of persons within society in general is proving to be a particular challenge for such a complex range of activities, sites and settings for arts participation (Gilmore, 2012). Online film reviews and accompanying film ratings have been shown to be significant predictors of both aggregate and weekly box office revenues (Huang & Yen, 2013). It is also the case that consumer generated film ratings have a direct effect on sales (Lee, 2012). This would suggest there is significant merit in basing media ratings on the individual needs and capabilities of consumers.

Young people are usually always presented as up-to-date with the latest technology. Whether they are boffins in the 1980s (Morrow, 2001), the hackers in the 1990s, the millennials in the 2000s or the digital teens in the 2010s (Bishop, 2014a; Cavagnero, 2012), they will at one point need protecting from abusers of the technology and at another be the cause of all the abuse with that technology. It has become clear that whether or not media sources cause crime or behavioural problems that the presence of a stimulus that activates traumatised parts of the brain can affect the sensory perceptions of the persons exposed to them (Bishop, 2012c; Dutta-Bergman, 2006).

## BACKGROUND

The rating of media content has a different regime in most jurisdictions in the world. According to (Smartt, 2011), in the United Kingdom it is the British Board of Film Classification (BBFC) that is responsible for the rating of media content, such as TV, DVD, video games, etc. They say that each year the BBFC rates over 10,000 media sources and in 2010 alone, of 407 films censored there were five that were cut (1.2 per cent), which compared to 1983 where 123 out of the 514 (24 per cent) were cut. (Smartt, 2011) also indicated that the BBFC have the competence to rate a piece of audio-visual media content where it falls into a number of categories. These include where the content is; criminal behaviour, illegal drugs, violent behaviour or incidents, horrific behaviour or incidents, human sexual activity, regardless of whether it is a film or video game (Wilcox, 2011). The difficulty with some online content, such as that arising out of cyberbullying, its that it is not possible to pre-screen it like one can with traditional media, but it can be equally as shocking (Katz, 2012). One notable example of discrepancies between the regulation of film and Internet content is the case of DPP v Collins [2006] 1 WLR 2223. In the Collins case the defendant was found to be guilty of sending grossly offensive messages via a public communications network through persistent phone calls to their local Member of Parliament's staff referring to "foreigners" whom Collins said should "go back to their own country." One should ask therefore, what is the reason why racism exposed in an imaginary world through film, which causes offence to the same magnitude as that by public communications networks, is any more acceptable? Why is hearing something reposted on Twitter for instance more prosecutable than equally bigoted representations of the same vile language shown in films? On this basis, one might argue that the BBFC, considered by (Smartt, 2011) to be one of the most highly regarded and trusted non-governmental organizations in the world, should be given the remit to rate Internet-based media content.

It is likely that BBFC, who have a lot of experience balancing what is simply offensive and what is a GOIOM in the case of film, could add a lot to regulating online media content, but the stronghold of basing ratings on age, are totally unsuited to the digital age we are in. Today, young people, or digital teens as they are sometimes called, are able to mature in their use of media content a lot faster than some of their ancestors were able to. There therefore needs to be a new rating system that goes beyond age, as it should perhaps be considered unacceptable to expose vulnerable people to certain content, just because they happen to be of an arbitrary age where most people have greater maturity. Indeed, the case of DPP v Connolly [2008] 1 W.L.R. 276 found that even among adult professionals, some are likely to find certain images (in this case aborted foetuses) to be GOIOM (in this case by pharmacists), whereas others, such as abortion surgeons, would be unlikely to see it as a GOIOM message. The regulation of media content therefore needs to adapt to go beyond age and provide greater information to the public on the actual content of the file or other media content they are accessing, and not simply assume if they are at the age of majority that it is unlikely they will find it to not be of a GOIOM nature.

## THE EFFECT OF MEDIA AND THE ARTS ON CRIME AND VICE VERSA

The causal linkages between media and crime have long been spoken about. In the 1970s the alleged dangers were from television (Holland, 1972; Levi, 1979), and in the 1990s it was from 'video nasties' (Petley, 1994). Today the social-ill in our societies, so it is said, are caused by online social networking services. Every twenty years – a generational gap – there seems to be a moral panic around the affect the media has on crime and behaviour in general (Bishop, 2014b; Halloran, 1970; Schroeder, 1996). One can see that in the 1970s the television reached saturation point, by the 1990s video games had, and in the 2010s, it seems that the Internet of Things has reached that state. People now have access to the Internet and online media content from a range of devices (Pearce & Rice, 2013). This includes tablet PCs, netbooks, smartphones as well as the traditional PC and specific television and video games devices (Bishop & Mannay, 2014).

In the 1990s politicians lined up to attack the video game manufacturer, Sega, for one of its innovative full-motion-video games, 'Night Trap,' which was criticized for its brutality (Schroeder, 1996). The Conservative Member of Parliament for Birmingham Edgbaston at the time was Jill Knight, known for banning discussing homosexuality in schools and her views on wanting to outlaw Irish Republicans, "This is a new generation of videos, nastier than ever before," she said of Night Trap, "I am extremely concerned to hear of this extraordinary new direction computer games are taking. We should consider legislation against such games because they encourage people to maim, mutilate and murder." The then Member of Parliament for St Helens North and former Labour Party official, John Evans, even called for the Home Office to investigate the game: "The concept is absolutely horrifying," he said.

"How can we allow such a dreadful thing to be freely available to youngsters?" In the 2010s, the Member of Parliament for Liverpool Walton, Steve Rotheram, was vociferously calling for action against Internet trollers in the same way, "Laws of the land need to be constantly updated to reflect social and technological advancements", he said. "My intention is to see a greater conviction rate for those guilty of this vile practice."

## MEASURING THE EFFECTS OF MEDIA CONTENT ON A PERSON'S BRAIN

The extent to which someone can withstand or effectively use media sources can be measured in 'knol.' In the context of the human mind, knol technically refers to the amount of pressure on parts of the brain that acts as a restriction to synaptic flow and thus the plasticity of the mind to efficiently process the requests made of it consciously by the actor, or forced on them by the environment. Those pressures, or 'impressions,' imposed on the actor may include traumatic event such as abuse of violent videos on television, which have the effect of reducing their ability to process information, measured as a 'knol.' The most researched part of the brain in relation to the calculation of knol is the prefrontal cortex (Bishop, 2011b; Bishop, 2012c; Bishop & Goode, 2014). This part of the brain is believed is responsible for many of the social interactions humans have with one another (Baarendse, Counotte, O'Donnell, & Vanderschuren, 2013; Beadle, 2009; Blair, 2007; Dickey et al., 2001; Maiza et al., 2008; Mushiake et al., 2009; Sala et al., 2011; Tanji & Hoshi, 2008). It is hypothesized that if the prefrontal cortex has a high or optimal knol of 0.81 then the flow of information, or neuro-response plasticity, is likely to be greater than the level of involvement required to utilize that part of the brain (Bishop, 2011b).

## Equation 1 Calculating a Phantasy

Equation 1 presents the means by which a phantasy is calculated. A phantasy can be defined most easily as a memory that has an effect on how quickly the brain can perform certain tasks. It can have an inhibiting effect, such as if it is a traumatic memory, or an enabling effect, such as if it is the memory of a loved one. A phantasy is made up of two 'cognitions,' which are essentially the meanings we have attached to those phantasies, which are both linked together in some way by us.

$$p_i = \left( \frac{\left( \left( x + x_1 \right) \right) * \left( y + y_1 \right) - \overline{z} \right) j)}{c} \right)$$

An example that will be used through this section is someone with a social orientation impairment such as autism drawn from (Bishop, 2011b). An SOI who suffered a traumatic assault as an infant might hold a belief that they were harmed by someone (y=3) and then every time someone holding characteristics resembling that person a detachment of 6 is attached to them creating a Flustered phantasy roughly measured in Equation 1.

Using Equation 1 gives a phantasy ($p_i$) of -5, which on its own creates a Pression (P) of 47, which when the Baseline (B) for hours to receive tax credits is added (48-16) to the maximum recommended force (F) of 48.

## Equation 2 Calculating a Pression

The next stage is to compute the 'Pression' for each participant using Equation 2. The Pression (P) is the extent to which a number of phantasies inhibit or enhance performance at a particular point in time.

$$P = \left( \left( \sum_{i+1}^{n} p_i \right) / 5 \right) + F$$

## Equation 3 Calculating a Knol

Equation 3 below shows that the final stage is to calculate the knol, which is the level of possible brain productivity for each person in performing a particular task where certain phantasies become activated as a result of the process represented in Equation 2. Essential to this is the baseline (B) figure.

$$k = \frac{P}{\left( F + B \right)}$$

The B figure reflects the number of hours a person is working or is comfortable working (e.g. often 16 for a person with a disability) and the F figure the maximum they should be expected to work (i.e. 48 according to working time rules in the European Union). Keeping with the example of the SOI, dividing the Pression calculated in Equation 2 by the value of B and F combined gives a knol (k) of 0.5, which below the recommended of 0.81 and the maximum prefrontal cortex potential. This shows that the person with the SOI is not at the optimum capacity that is safely possible.

## AN INVESTIGATION INTO THE EFFECT OF MEDIA CONSUMPTION ON EMFT PROPENSITY: CALCULATING 'KNOL' FROM ATTITUDES TO MEDIA CONTENT

To understand how attitude to media content, in this case the arts, have an impact on knol, this section will apply neuroeconomic equations to demonstrate the variation in knol and how it is calculated. The purpose of this study therefore will be to test out these theories relating to knol using empirical data.

## Methodology

This project made use of secondary data from an ICM Research study (Couldry, Markham, & Livingstone, 2005) and freedom of information requests into the number of incidents of trolling recorded by the police in the UK between 2009 and 2011. Phase One of the ICM research project comprised of detailed qualitative work across six regions of England. The diaries of 37 participants' media consumption were analysed, initial and subsequent interviews were conducted with those respondents, and focus group interviews were conducted with diarists. Phase Two involved a telephone survey of 1,017 people, conducted by ICM Research across the United Kingdom that aimed to produce conclusions on the detailed issues about consumption and citizenship raised in Phase One.

## Preliminary Data Coding and Analysis

The variables in the secondary dataset needed to be re-computed to match those in the equations. One of these was the trolling magnitude scale (Bishop, 2013a; Bishop, 2013b), which is for measuring the gravity of an act of trolling. The computation made the TM values relative to the number of hours spent on the Internet. This was because it was assumed that the longer one is on the Internet the more likely one would be abusive towards others, even if unintentionally (Cassidy, Jackson, & Brown, 2009). On that basis, a trolling magnitude (TM) of 1, which is Playtime, where people are more likely to act in the heat of the moment, was assigned to all the participants who used the Internet 0 to 1 hours. A TM of 2 (i.e. Tactical) was assigned to people who used the Internet for 1 to 3 hours. A TM of 3 (i.e. Strategic) was assigned to people who used the Internet for 3 to 5 hours, and finally, a TM of 4 was assigned to people who used the Internet for between 5 and 7 hours, or greater than 7 hours. This study is important

because it will allow for not only the automated pre-screening of Internet content but by liking knol to trolling magnitude will make it easier to prove injury towards someone by someone else in relation to the offences linked with trolling magnitude (Bishop, 2013a; Bishop, 2013b). In this case it would be when engaging with media in general or art in particular. In Equation 1 the variable F reflects the normal force a human can handle in an average week, measured in hours, which is taken to be 48, based on the European Union's Working Time Directive [2003/88/EC]. In the case of this study, phantasies were computed through the use of a type of cognition called a detachment (rated from 0 to 6) and a plan (rated from -2 to +2). A detachment is an attitude towards a person that makes one anxious and which the mind tries to suppress. A plan is a willingness, or lack of, to perform a particular action.

The detachments were calculated through linking six regions in the UK where data on reports of electronic message faults between 2009 and 2011 were known. This was done by the region with the lowest number of EMF incidents being 0 and the highest number of incidents of flame trolling being 6. This resulted in Yorkshire and the Humber being ranked 0, with 42 incidents and the East of England being ranked 1, with 114 incidents. Wales was ranked 2 with 135 incidents, Scotland 3 with 174 incidents, and South West England 4 with 578 incidents. Northern Ireland was ranked 5 with 1485 incidents and South East England 6 with 1903 incidents.

The three plans used in the study were, 'People like me don't get involved in the arts and culture,' 'There are other things besides arts and culture that I prefer to do in my leisure time,' and 'It's expensive to get involved in arts and culture.' Using the lookup table in Bishop (2011b) for the $x_1$ and $y_1$ variables, Equation 1 was used to produce three phantasies from combining the detachment with the associated plan for each participant.

Participants were asked to state whether they worked full-time, part-time, were a homemaker, registered unemployed, a full-time student, or not working at all. The number of hours worked were harmonized based on official government figures to reflect the 'potential' as opposed to 'actual'. Those working full-time were assigned to 30 hours and those working part-time were assigned to 24 hours. These are the hours required for the respective rates on the UK's Tax Credits system. A homeworker was assigned 35 hours, which is the number of hours required to claim Carers Allowance and a person who was not working or seeking work was assigned 0 hours. Someone registered unemployed and seeking work was assigned 15 hours, which is the maximum one can work and still receive out-of-work benefits, and a full-time student was assigned 21 hours, which is the number of hours one needs to be studying to qualify as a full-time student to receive a reduction in council tax.

The baseline figure, which is a person's individual production possibility in terms of workable hours is then added to the maximum a person can work in an healthy environment, which is 48 hours as signified by F. Adding the baseline and the force together and dividing them by the Pression calculated by Equation 2 then produces a persons speed and performing in a particular setting. In terms of phantasies containing detachments, 0.81 is an ideal figure for someone achieve as they are likely to be able to withstand most abusive content due to media content of a GOIOM nature being suppressed. A knol based on a detachment phantasy score of 0.98 or over is not ideal as this could put a lot of pressure on the prefrontal cortex of the brain which is quite vulnerable. And a knol of below 0.5 is below also not ideal as the phantasy in question is likely to be affecting the person's mental wellbeing and participation in society. Where this reaches around 0.6 then there is an increasing chance the person would not be as productive as they would be at either 0.81 or 0.50.

## Results

Using a One-Way ANOVA, the data was then analysed to see whether there was a significant difference between the knol of those assigned to the 4 groups, to make it worthwhile proceeding with further analysis of difference between the groups.

The ANOVA was successful. The degree of freedom numerator for the dataset of 975 participants was 3 and the degrees of freedom denominator was 971. This gave a CV of 2.08380. As the F for the dataset was 1.145 (0.9388) this was not an ideal outcome, but further inspection of the dataset showed it was the best outcome possible. An eight-factor model gave an F of 0.568 and CV of 1.71672 (a difference of 1.14872) and a five-factor model, as currently used by the police gave an F of 0.891 and CV of 1.94486 (a difference of 1.05386). This shows the four-factor model to be most appropriate for determining media ratings based on knol and number of hours spent on the Internet.

Table 1 shows the number of persons assigned to each trolling magnitude, the Mean knol (k) for each group and the upper and lower knol for those groups using the means from the ANOVA. As can be seen, there is a negative relationship between trolling magnitude and knol. That is, as trolling magnitude increases then knol decreases. This can be interpreted as meaning that in order to troll at a higher magnitude that more effort is needed in the brain to do so. It could also mean that those who have been traumatized to the extent their knol is very low, may be at more risk of trolling at a higher magnitude. The upper and lower bounds of knol in Table 1 could be used to develop models, such as based on neural networks, to understand the breaking points for different people in terms of stimulus and response to develop the automated affective content screening discussed in the next section.

*Table 1. Relationship between trolling magnitude (TM) and knol (k)*

| TM | N | Mean k | L Bound k | U Bound k | Description |
|---|---|---|---|---|---|
| 1 | 90 | 0.7265 | 0.6926 | 0.7604 | The prefrontal cortex is operating nearing its most optimal (0.81) means a person is likely to act in the heat of the moment when their knol is at is greatest. |
| 2 | 285 | 0.7061 | 0.6884 | 0.7239 | The prefrontal cortex has decreased from its optimal state by 0.2 points, meaning a decrease in the value of knol increases self-sanctioned trolling activity. |
| 3 | 519 | 0.7094 | 0.6960 | 0.7228 | The prefrontal cortex becomes further sub-optimal as the magnitude of a trolling offence increases, which might explain why the most determined of trolls have social orientation impairments. |
| 4 | 81 | 0.6843 | 0.6527 | 0.7160 | The prefrontal cortex is at its most sub-optimal when the person has to put a lot of effort into their trolling. |

## AUTOMATED AFFECTIVE CONTENT SCREENING: TOWARDS THE DISTRESS IN THE MIND TEST

Now that this study has shown that there is a link between length of time on the Internet – exposure to the media – and also someone's brain processing capacity (i.e. knol) and the trolling magnitude scale, this makes it possible to suggest intervention and methods for assessing someone's risk of being harmed by certain media content. Using the model from (Bishop & Goode, 2014), which is in Figure 1, the data derived in the earlier section will be used to develop a generalizable framework for determining the risk of content, such as trolling, to people perceiving that stimuli.

In terms of legislation and case law in Great Britain, there is support for varying media content ratings based on the individual who wishes to use them. The case of DPP v Connolly [2008] 1 W.L.R. 276 identified that whether something is of a GOIOM nature is dependent on how much the person being exposed to the media content can withstand it. In this case a number of pharmacists were found to have been 'grossly offended' when sent a picture of an aborted foetus. The court said however that if the communication had been sent to an abortion surgeon, who would not be distressed by the images, then it would be no different from any other political message. On this basis, it is essential ratings systems be changed from being based on age, to being based on something around maturity. Table 2 presents a matrix of various means for assessing media content to determine the maturity needed to consume it. It suggests that maturity is a factor of the strategic thinking required to maximize use of the information in the media content in question without being influenced in such a way that it causes harm to oneself or others. This applies equally to someone who might be extremely vulnerable, such as an infant or a person with an intellectual disability, as well as someone of moderate maturity, who might not find explicit content comforting to watch. Using Table 2, it is possible to easily distinguish between that which could be grossly offensive, indecent, obscene or menacing (GOIOM) at a TM of 1 and that of a TM of 4. Equally it shows which content could cause harassment, alarm or distress, and how this differs with a TM of 2 compared to a TM of 4.

Table 2 incorporates much of the data analysed in the study, including the upper and lower bound knol scores from the study participants shown in Table 1. It can be seen that the higher the average knol the lower the magnitude of trolling. This is because it takes a lot of effort (i.e. involvement) to conduct the higher magnitude forms of trolling, which brings knol down. Table 2 also shows how

*Figure 1. A model for measuring the flow of information through the human brain and body*

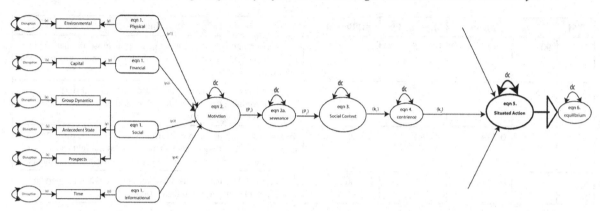

measuring someone's knol – such as in response to a flame or other stressing stimuli – can make it possible to determine the risk to someone of being exposed to such a stimulus.

## AN APPLICATION OF THE DISTRESS IN THE MIND TEST

Consider a child that has been told by their parent that they will see them at their school play. There is nothing explicit in what their parent said. However, if that parent did not turn up at that play the child may be grossly offended. This could be quite traumatic for them if they feel their parent has betrayed them. If the parent keeps missing school plays or similar events where the child wants to make them proud, their phantasy from the original 'betrayal' will strengthen and their knol will increase, which will make them not only less able to be grossly offended over 'minor' upsets, but also less able to notice the positives in situations where they may be at risk of being upset in a similar way.

The level of strategic thinking ability also relates to Trolling Magnitude. Table 2 shows the lower and upper bounds of knol and how they relate to the maturity of different audiences to consume and otherwise use content without suffering HAD or perceiving it as GOIOM. Someone who is at the Playtime level of strategic thinking will be like an infant, who could be easily led astray even though they think they are being clever. It also includes people who would get caught up in the moment, such as people who were intellectually challenged, or regularly victimized. The Tactical level of strategic thinking applies to those who are able to understand concepts like intertextuality and be able to be humoured while also understanding when something humorous could be offensive in the wrong context. The Strategic category of strategic thinking relates to content where the person would have to be able to differentiate those practices and behaviours that harm others and should not be adopted from those which others might get gratification from whilst in other situations other people might be discomforted. Finally, the domination form of strategic thinking requires an advanced level of understanding so that it is possible to know what could severely harm others and also cause harm to oneself. Someone of this maturity in strategic thinking should be able to understand murder plots in media, or be able to see graphic scenes of sexual and other violence, without in any way being corrupted by them. People with a low knol, who are made anxious by this content, should know in advance whether they would be at risk. This content is most suited to people who have a high knol in all situations, including violence, so that it in effect 'goes in one

*Table 2. Proposed media content classification matrix for determining maturity using strategic thinking level and potential gravity*

| TM | Rating (Mean k) | Strategy L Bound k (U Bound k) | Potential Gravity (DSS) | Description / Examples |
|---|---|---|---|---|
| 1 | Exempt (0.7265) | Playtime 0.6926 (0.7604) | Grossly Offensive, Indecent, Obscene or Menacing (Low Flow, High Involvement) | Apply DPP v Connolly [2008] 1 W.L.R. 276. Some people with a high knol who have not been subject to much trauma might find educational or informational content GOIOM whereas others wouldn't. For instance, pornographic or sexual content may disturb or corrupt the mind of a child, but not a teenager. |
| 2 | Universal (0.7061) | Tactical 0.6884 (0.7239) | Harassment, Alarm or Distress (Med Flow, High Involvement) | Apply Chambers v DPP. A person with a lower knol than required for Exempt should not be considered to cause HAD if the content does not make them feel apprehension. For instance, a victim of traumatic abuse should be made to re-live that abuse by being exposed to similar content from a source of information expected to be suitable for vulnerable persons. |
| 3 | Parental Advisory (0.6960) | Strategic 0.6960 (0.7228) | Harassment, Alarm or Distress (Med Flow, Low Involvement) | Apply DPP v Collins [2006] 1 WLR 2223. Some people might find something causes HAD if they are the group the content is referring to. Therefore content should be made in such a way an independent third-party could assess whether something offensive, which may not offend everyone, would cause HAD to a minority audience they are responsible for who might have a moderately low knol in some cases, but much lower in others. |
| 4 | Explicit (0.6843) | Domination 0.6527 (0.7160) | Grossly Offensive, Indecent, Obscene or Menacing (High Flow, Low Involvement) | Apply DPP v Connolly [2008] 1 W.L.R. 276. A person with a low knol, should be able to expect and tolerate explicit material which they might find GOIOM if they are using a dedicated source containing explicit content which others may find to be GOIOM. One should expect to be grossly offended on a 'hard-core porn' website, but not a 'soft porn' website, for instance. However, a person with one of the lowest knol might be GOIOM if the explicit content relates to the traumatic event that may be lowering their knol. |

ear and out the other.' Such people have a clear value system and are unlikely to have suffered any serious abuse. While it is more likely such people will be over the age of 18, where most people will be at less risk of corruption form a high knol, it may not always be the case. Those people at 18 years-old, who may not have had any form of personal, social or health education, or citizenship education, may not be aware of the risks and dangers of the society in which we live. Developing a system of regulating media based on these levels of maturity is essential.

In Bishop (2011a), a system is described that is able to read affective information in a person and recommend a particular course of action to another person. Using the rating system below with this technology, it could be possible for cinemas to be installed with kiosks that assess the risk of viewing a particular film by a particular individual. This could be done through assessing the emotion in their eyes and face, or through a brain-computer interface, which the person wears while watching those clips from the film that trigger distressing emotions. In terms of Internet trolling, a web-cam or brain-computer device could be used by a parent or guardian to calibrate the Internet security software to only display websites which are suited to the maturity of their child. It could also be used as a permanent Internet of Things device, which can be like an audio-video baby monitor that warns parents or guardians when their children are viewing distressing content. The brain-computer device could even act as a 'chastity band' to ensure that sex predators are unable to access content that could give them inappropriate thoughts or encourage them to perform undesirable acts.

## IMPLICATIONS AND FUTURE RESEARCH DIRECTIONS

The data used in this study on Internet trolling was from police records for 2009 to 2011 where they recorded harassment and related offences concerning the Internet. Since 2011 there has been a huge explosion in the reporting of Internet trolling offences, with high profile cases where the public have demanded action be taken and those law enforcement authorities have bowed to that pressure. A future study may be needed to confirm that the findings are still valid using post-2011 data. The study made a link between length of time on the Internet, geography and attitudes towards the arts to derive the figures for determining media ratings and risk to consumers of accessing specific media. Future research may want to perform a regression analysis to confirm the validity of this. The modelling devised in this study need not only apply to the regulating of media content through its analysis, but could actually be used to annotate other environments where distressing material could exist (such as chatrooms and social media) as well as the abstraction of information from computer systems (e.g. for forensic linguistic use) so that it is possible to test the effect of a set of stimuli on a particular person – such as to test whether a suspect recalls a crime they deny committing. This can be done with EEG or MRI scans being analysed to derive the variable values for the equations, such as in terms of flow and involvement.

## DISCUSSION

Media content is regulated in different ways in different legal jurisdictions, although in general they tend to follow an out-of-date age-related system, which may mean someone who is at the age of majority is unlikely to know whether a particular film will contain content they would find grossly offensive, indecent, obscene or menacing (GOIOM). Few democratized jurisdictions have applied the same strict regulatory regime for video and broadcasting as they do for the Internet. The notable exception is Great Britain, where there has been higher reported convictions for the sending of media content that is seen to be GOIOM via a public communications network like the Internet than with regards to commercial communications networks like film, television or video games.

The United Kingdom's media classifications authority – The British Board of Film Classification (BBFC) – has the power to request that any media falling within its remit be cut or censored in other ways in order to meet a certain single rating. The BBFC is a highly respected organisation because it uses objective criteria, unlike organisations like the Advertising Standards Authority which are more reliant on the subjective judgements of officials, even if these in no way reflect reality. It would therefore make sense for the BBFC to cover the regulation of all media content, regardless of frontier. With technology as advanced as it is, it may be possible for film broadcasters, or video on demand websites, to show different versions of the media content to different audiences, depending what is most appropriate for people based on their projected knol in relation to the file or other media content. An organisation like the BBFC would we well placed to devise criteria for what content should be censored by an algorithm and which should not.

Most practicably, using a simple webcam and software kit it could be possible for parents or guardian to be able to assess from using a recommender system that is based on emotion recognition which particular rating for media they believe is appropriate for their child or a vulnerable adult. They could also have more detailed recommendations for specific films. The algorithm could also warn parents when their children are 'getting naked on cam' (GNOC) or taking part in other forms of sexting.

It has long been argued that there is a causal link between media consumption and criminal activity. By presenting a media ratings system which is based on the magnitude of Internet trolling offences, this chapter has shown how these can be used to assess whether there are any such links. By linking severity of an Internet trolling offence to the extent to which a person can withstand being subjected to that intensive of GOIOM media content, then it should be easier to show whether someone reacted in a particular way as a result of being exposed to that stimulus in an overpowering way.

## ACKNOWLEDGMENT

The author would like to acknowledge all those reviewers who provided comments and suggestions on earlier drafts of this chapter. Special thanks are due to Stephanie Lee and Niren Basu of Swansea University's Institute for Life Science for providing the motivation to prepare this chapter as a basis for a future research collaboration. This research was in part funded by a Economic and Social Research Council research grant (# RES-143-25-0011). The data use in the study was collected by ICM Research (Couldry et al., 2005) and various police forces in the United Kingdom.

## REFERENCES

Baarendse, P. J., Counotte, D. S., O'Donnell, P., & Vanderschuren, L. J. (2013). Early social experience is critical for the development of cognitive control and dopamine modulation of prefrontal cortex function. *Neuropsychopharmacology: Official Publication of the American College of Neuropsychopharmacology, 38*(8), 1485-1494. doi:10.1038/npp.2013.47

Beadle, J. N. (2009). *The neuroanatomical basis of empathy: Is empathy impaired following damage to the ventromedial prefrontal cortex?* ProQuest.

Bernard, T. (1992). *The cycle of juvenile justice.* Oxford, UK: Oxford University Press.

Bishop, J. (2011a). Assisting human interaction (AU/GB2011/2011266844 ed.). GB: PCT/GB2011/050814.

Bishop, J. (2011b). *The role of the prefrontal cortex in social orientation construction: A pilot study.* Paper presented to the British Psychological Society's Sustainable Well-being Conference. London, UK.

Bishop, J. (2012b). Scope and limitations in the government of wales act 2006 for tackling internet abuses in the form of 'Flame trolling'. *Statute Law Review, 33*(2), 207–216. doi:10.1093/slr/hms016

Bishop, J. (2012c). Taming the chatroom bob: The role of brain-computer interfaces that manipulate prefrontal cortex optimization for increasing participation of victims of traumatic sex and other abuse online. In *Proceedings of the 13th International Conference on Bioinformatics and Computational Biology (BIOCOMP'12)*. BIOCOMP.

Bishop, J. (2013a). The art of trolling law enforcement: A review and model for implementing 'flame trolling' legislation enacted in great britain (1981–2012). *International Review of Law Computers & Technology, 27*(3), 301–318. doi:10.1080/13600869.2013.796706

Bishop, J. (2013b). The effect of deindividuation of the internet troller on criminal procedure implementation: An interview with a hater. *International Journal of Cyber Criminology, 7*(1), 28–48.

Bishop, J. (2014a). Digital teens and the 'Antisocial Network': Prevalence of troublesome online youth groups and internet trolling in great Britain. *International Journal of E-Politics*.

Bishop, J. (2014b). Representations of 'trolls' in mass media communication: A review of media-texts and moral panics relating to 'internet trolling'. *International Journal of Web Based Communities, 10*(1), 7–24. doi: doi:10.1504/IJWBC.2014.058384

Bishop, J., & Goode, M. M. H. (2014). Towards a subjectively devised parametric user model for analysing and influencing behaviour online using gamification: A review and model. In J. Bishop (Ed.), *Gamification for human factors integration: Social, educational, and psychological issues.* Hershey, PA: IGI Global. doi:10.4018/978-1-4666-5071-8.ch005

Bishop, J., & Mannay, L. (2014). Using the internet to make local music more available to the south wales community. In J. Bishop (Ed.), *Transforming politics and policy in the digital age.* Hershey, PA: IGI Global. doi:10.4018/978-1-4666-6038-0.ch005

Bishop, J. (2012a). Lessons from the emotivate project for increasing take-up of big society and responsible capitalism initiatives. In P. M. Pumilia-Gnarini, E. Favaron, E. Pacetti, J. Bishop & L. Guerra (Eds.), *Didactic strategies and technologies for education: Incorporating advancements* (pp. 208-217). Hershey, PA: IGI Global.

Blair, R. J. R. (2007). The amygdala and ventromedial prefrontal cortex in morality and psychopathy. *Trends in Cognitive Sciences, 11*(9), 387–392. doi:10.1016/j.tics.2007.07.003 PMID:17707682

Cassidy, W., Jackson, M., & Brown, K. N. (2009). Sticks and stones can break my bones, but how can pixels hurt me? students' experiences with cyber-bullying. *School Psychology International, 30*(4), 383–402. doi:10.1177/0143034309106948

Cavagnero, S. M. (2012). Digital teens: An investigation into the use of the web by adolescents. In P. M. Pumilia-Gnarini, E. Favaron, E. Pacetti, J. Bishop, & L. Guerra (Eds.), *Didactic strategies and technologies for education: Incorporating advancements* (pp. 129–136). Hershey, PA: IGI Global. doi:10.4018/978-1-4666-2122-0.ch012

Couldry, N., Markham, T., & Livingstone, S. (2005). *Media consumption and the future of public connection.* London, UK: London School of Economics and Political Science.

Dickey, C., Shenton, M., Voglmaier, M., Niznikiewicz, M., Seidman, L., & Frumin, M. et al. (2001). Prefrontal cortex in schizotypal personality disorder males and females. *Biological Psychiatry, 49*, 336S.

Dutta-Bergman, M. J. (2006). Community participation and internet use after september 11: Complementarity in channel consumption. *Journal of Computer-Mediated Communication, 11*(2), 469–484. doi:10.1111/j.1083-6101.2006.00022.x

Gilmore, A. (2012). Counting eyeballs, soundbites and 'plings': Arts participation, strategic instrumentalism and the london 2012 cultural olympiad. *International Journal of Cultural Policy, 18*(2), 151–167. doi:10.1080/10286632.2011.577283

Halloran, J. D. (1970). Television and delinquency.

Haravuori, H., Suomalainen, L., Berg, N., Kiviruusu, O., & Marttunen, M. (2011). Effects of media exposure on adolescents traumatized in a school shooting. *Journal of Traumatic Stress, 24*(1), 70–77. doi:10.1002/jts.20605 PMID:21268117

Hardaker, C. (2010). Trolling in asynchronous computer-mediated communication: From user discussions to academic definitions. *Journal of Politeness Research.Language, Behaviour. Culture (Canadian Ethnology Society), 6*(2), 215–242.

Hardaker, C. (2013). Uh.... not to be nitpicky, but... the past tense of drag is dragged, not drug.": An overview of trolling strategies. *Journal of Language Aggression and Conflict, 1*(1), 58–86. doi:10.1075/jlac.1.1.04har

Holland, D. (1972). Television and crime-a causal link. *Auckland UL Rev., 2*, 53.

Huang, A. H., & Yen, D. C. (2013). Predicting the helpfulness of online Reviews—A replication. *International Journal of Human-Computer Interaction, 29*(2), 129–138. doi:10.1080/10447 318.2012.694791

Jansen, E., & James, V. (1995). *NetLingo: The internet dictionary.* Oxnard, CA: Netlingo Inc.

Jansen, E., & James, V. (2002). *NetLingo: The internet dictionary.* Oxnard, CA: Netlingo Inc.

Katz, A. (2012). *Cyberbullying and E-safety: What educators and other professionals need to know.* Jessica Kingsley Publishers.

Lee, Y. J. (2012). Exploring the economic values of online user ratings with advertising spending on box office sales. In *Proceedings of the 11th International Workshop on E-Business.* Academic Press.

Levi, R. P. (1979). Violence on television: An old problem with a new picture. *North Carolina Law Review, 58*, 97.

Maiza, O., Razafimandimby, A., Delamillieure, P., Brazo, P., Beaucousin, V., & Lecardeur, L. et al. (2008). Functional deficit in medial prefrontal cortex: A common neural basis for impaired communication in chronic schizophrenia, first episode of schizophrenia and bipolar disorders? *Schizophrenia Research, 98*, 39–39. doi:10.1016/j.schres.2007.12.083

Morrow, V. (2001). Young people's explanations and experiences of social exclusion: Retrieving bourdieu's concept of social capital. *International Journal of Sociology and Social Policy, 21*(4/5/6), 37-63.

Mushiake, H., Sakamoto, K., Saito, N., Inui, T., Aihara, K., & Tanji, J. (2009). Involvement of the prefrontal cortex in problem solving. *International Review of Neurobiology, 85*, 1–11. doi:10.1016/S0074-7742(09)85001-0 PMID:19607957

Pearce, K. E., & Rice, R. E. (2013). Digital divides from access to activities: Comparing mobile and personal computer internet users. *The Journal of Communication, 63*(4), 721–744. doi:10.1111/jcom.12045

Petley, J. (1994). In defence of video nasties'. *British Journalism Review, 5*(3), 52–57.

Phillips, W. (2011, December). LOLing at tragedy: Facebook trolls, memorial pages and resistance to grief online. *First Monday, 16*(12), 11. doi:10.5210/fm.v16i12.3168

Rimmer, M. (2012). The participation and decision making of 'at risk' youth in community music projects: An exploration of three case studies. *Journal of Youth Studies, 15*(3), 329–350. doi:10.1080/13676261.2011.643232

Roche, S. W. (2012). *Internet and technology dangers.* Dragonwood.

Sala, M., Caverzasi, E., Lazzaretti, M., Morandotti, N., De Vidovich, G., & Marraffini, E. et al. (2011). Dorsolateral prefrontal cortex and hippocampus sustain impulsivity and aggressiveness in borderline personality disorder. *Journal of Affective Disorders,* Schroeder, R. (1996). Playspace invaders: Huizinga, baudrillard and video game violence. *Journal of Popular Culture, 30*(3), 143–153.

Smartt, U. (2011). *Media & entertainment law.* London: Routledge.

Starmer, K. (2013). *Guidelines on prosecuting cases involving communications sent via social media.* London: Crown Prosecution Service.

Tanji, J., & Hoshi, E. (2008). Role of the lateral prefrontal cortex in executive behavioral control. *Physiological Reviews, 88*(1), 37. doi:10.1152/physrev.00014.2007 PMID:18195082

Weijers, I. (1999). The double paradox of juvenile justice. *European Journal on Criminal Policy and Research, 7*(3), 329–351. doi:10.1023/A:1008732820029

Wilcox, A. (2011). Regulating violence in video games: Virtually everything. *J.Nat'L Ass'N Admin.L. Judiciary*, *31*, 253.

## KEY TERMS AND DEFINITIONS

**Electronic Message Fault:** A message posted on the Internet or via electronic means that is either unfair or wrongful to a person who is offended by it.

**Grossly Offensive:** A word to describe an electronic message fault that leaves a person feeling apprehension because the message was targeted at them or a group of which they are part.

**Internet Trolling:** The posting of provocative or offensive messages on the Interent.

**Knol:** A knol is a unit of measurement for the easy to which neurological information can pass between the synapses of the brain to access specific functions.

**Phantasy:** A persistent memory that effects the ability of the brain to access functions located where that memory was formed to protect acess to that functioning following an overflow of information to that part of the brain.

**Pression:** The accumulative pressure put on the brain to process information following a person's mind bringing a lot of variables into play at once.

**Trolling Magnitude Scale:** The Trolling magnitude Scale (TMS) is a measurement of the severity of Internet trolling in a given situation.

# Chapter 129

# Section 4
# Case Studies

# Chapter 29
# Honeypots and Honeynets:
## Analysis and Case Study

**José Manuel Fernández Marín**
*University of Almería, Spain*

**Juan Álvaro Muñoz Naranjo**
*University of Almería, Spain*

**Leocadio González Casado**
*University of Almería, Spain*

## ABSTRACT

*This chapter presents a review and a case of study of honeypots and honeynets. First, some of the most important and widely used honeypots in the current market are selected for comparative analysis, evaluating their interaction capacity with an attacker. Second, a self-contained honeynet architecture is implemented with virtual machines. An intrusion test is performed against the honeynet to observe the quality and quantity of the information collected during the attack. The final goal of this analysis is to assess the capacity of monitoring and threat detection of the honeynets and honeypots.*

## INTRODUCTION

Honeypots are network resources, machines or servers that offer easily exploitable services in order to attract possible attackers (Spitzner, 2002; Mokube & Adams, 2007; Mairh, Barik, Verma & Jena, 2011). A honeynet is a network architecture composed of honeypots network, network devices and security tools. The use of honeypots and honeynets allows network and system managers to improve their technological infrastructure security thanks to information collection (The Honeynet Project [THP], 2002; Sadasivam, Samudrala & Yang, 2005). Furthermore, these systems are

essential in research environments oriented to network security since they give the chance to capture, analyze and learn about new threats (Jones & Rommney, 2004; Mairh et al., 2011).

The first section of this chapter classifies honeypots according to their characteristics and interaction levels (Spitzner, 2002). Different locations where a honeypot can be placed within the network infrastructure of an organization will be analyzed, as well as the advantages and drawbacks of using honeypots when they are compared with other current technologies such as IDS, NIDS (Tiware & Jain, 2012), sandboxes and darknets (Mairh et al., 2011; ENISA, 2012). Some of the

DOI: 10.4018/978-1-4666-6324-4.ch029

most important and widely used honeypots in the current market will be selected for comparative analysis (Song et al., 2011). The analysis will be based on the interaction capacity, the realism of the emulated services, and the configuration and administration flexibility of each honeypot (ENISA, 2012).

In the second section, existing classifications and requirements of honeynets will be described (Spitzner, 2002; THP, 2002). Distributed honeynets, widely used in research work, will be introduced in addition to deployed architectures in local environments (Sadasivam et al., 2005; Tiware & Jain, 2012).

Next, a case study which implements a virtual honeynet using virtual machines is proposed (Asrigo, Litty & Lie, 2006). The scheme of this honeynet is based on The Honeynet Project and the Linux Honeywall Roo distribution (THP, 2002; Curran et al., 2005). An intrusion test, simulating a computer attack, will be carried out. Using available tools (THP, 2002), an analysis of the information will be performed before, during and after the attack. The intention of this analysis is to assess the capacity of monitoring and threats detection of the honeynets.

Finally, we will provide the main conclusions of the chapter, discussing the actual value of honeypots and honeynets within an organization (Levine, 2003; Song et al., 2011; ENISA, 2012; Tiware & Jain, 2012).

## CYBERCRIME

Cybercrime has become a primary concern for users, governments and companies due due to the scarcity of security professionals in organizations, poor management practices of private and confidential information by employees and misinformation of society. The scope of professional cybercrime is broadening and keeps covering new fields and technologies to commit crimes. The first cybercriminals acting alone or in small groups, but

today have evolved to a modular organizational model comprising a large number of skilled people that communicate over the network.

Today, there exist different roles within fraudulent organizations like victim recruiters (through phishing or other social engineering techniques), malware coders, money launders (through mules and movements between bank accounts), and more. With this infrastructure, profits increase and the chances of identification and arrest of the organizational components decrease.

Honeypots allow to detect new malware infection vectors, zero-day attacks, intrusion detections, etc. The honeypots are resources used in the detection of those activities related to cybercrime, increasing responsiveness to a malignant activity. They are also widely used for the study of new attack vectors conducted by criminal organizations in the network. The most famous case of the role of honeypots in crime prosecution to the date is known as *United States vs. Ivanov* (United States vs. Ivanov, 2005).

## HONEYPOTS

A honeypot is an intentionally exposed computational resource with the aim of being tested, attacked, compromised, used or accessed in anyway unauthorized. The resource can be a system service, an application user or server, a complete system or just a piece of information as records in a database or office documents (ENISA, 2012).

In a production environment, any attempt to access or interact with the honeypot is a suspicious activity. All activities between a supposed attacker and the honeypot are monitored and analyzed in order to detect and confirm an unauthorized use. In this way, it is possible to take prevention measures or contingency.

There is a large variety of honeypots. Some general purpose honeypots are Honeyd, Specter or Dionaea, capable of simulating several services, even the type of operating system.

## Honeypots Taxonomy

The most important honeypot classifications in the literature are based on the type of exploitable resources, on their level of interaction and their purpose: part of a production or research environment (ENISA, 2012).

## Classification According to Type of Exploitable Resources

This classification distinguishes whether resources of the honeypot are exploited in client or server mode. Additionally, a special type of resource based on accessible information can be included, honeytokens (ENISA, 2012).

In client mode, the honeypot becomes an active system that expects to be attacked, for example, using a vulnerable web browser to visit servers containing malware affecting visitors (Riden, 2008a).

In server mode, exploitable resources are services and applications listening for new connections on given ports on a server. As an example, they may appear as a vulnerable web server or a FTP server (Riden, 2008b).

Honeytokens are resources stored in an information system. A honeytoken can be a text document, an email address, or a record from a database. An alert is triggered when any of these honeytokens have been processed or accessed (ENISA, 2012).

## Classification According to the Level of Interaction

Honeypots can also be classified depending on the capacity of interaction in response to a suspicious connection resulting in an intrusion and compromise a system. There are three levels of interaction.

A low-interaction honeypot simulates services or applications that cannot be exploited to get a total system control. The simulation is limited, because not all commands or requests are recognized and implemented by low-interaction honeypots. The most common or susceptible commands to exploitation are emulated (Almutairi, Parish & Phan, 2012).

High-interaction honeypots are characterized by being real operating systems and services. They allow an attacker to perform a complete intrusion. In this case, the amount of information collected by the honeypot is much higher (Almutairi, 2012).

Finally, hybrid honeypots combine the benefits of high and low interaction honeypots. They are able to detect and analyze malicious traffic and redirect it to a low-interaction honeypot if necessary (ENISA, 2012).

## Classification According to the Purpose

Honeypots are mainly used in two scenarios: i) as part of an organization to monitor the network and as a defense mechanism, and ii) as a research tool to study hacker attacks by computer security professionals (Gibbens & Harsha, 2012).

In a research environment, security analysts attempt to study new hacker's methodologies and most current infection systems or malware. Through their study, one can attempt to create new security measures that allow to face new threats.

In a production environment, honeypots allow to alert administrators of attacks in real time. Usually, honeypots in these environments are reactive, that is, they can execute contingency actions if configured to do so. Once an attack has been identified, managers can take precautionary measures in production resources, updating versions, modifying firewalls, etc. Figure 1 show the honeypots classification.

## Honeypot Locations

A honeypot can be placed at different locations on the network of an organization, each one providing advantages and drawbacks. It is responsibility of the managers to decide the appropriate location of the honeypot (Tiware & Jain, 2012).

*Figure 1. Honeypots classification*

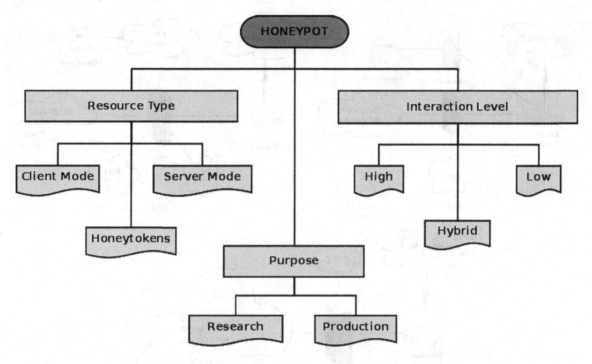

## At the External Network

Placing a honeypot in the public address space of an organization, for example before a BGP (Border Gateway Protocol) router, allows to obtain a lot of information targeted from Internet. This is the most deployed solution in research environments since it allows to collect large amount of malware samples and to detect attacks and zero-day vulnerabilities. Locating the honeypot at this location reduces the risk on the internal network in case it was compromised and used as a jumping machine to access or infect other computers in the network (Joshi & Sardana, 2011).

## At the Demilitarized Zone (DMZ)

This architecture is the most difficult to implement because the honeypots are exposed to Internet services and the internal network. Therefore, the security level applied must be critical. A honeypot in the DMZ can collect information and alert about external attacks to those services allowed by the firewall of the DMZ. The honeypot can detect unauthorized actions from the internal network as well (Joshi & Sardana, 2011).

## At the Internal Network

In the internal network there are PCs and backend servers. Within the internal network there will exist separate subnetworks according to different purpose, geographic location or ownership. Therefore, a network segment without a previously assigned address can be used to deploy one or more honeypots. This separation facilitates network administration, but also allows honeypots to identify internal attacks because the traffic from other internal networks should not interact with the honeypots. Such an activity would be therefore considered as suspicious (Joshi & Sardana, 2011). Figure 2 shows the locations where a honeypot can be placed.

*Figure 2. Honeypot locations: (a) at the external network; (b) at the DMZ; (c) at the internal network*

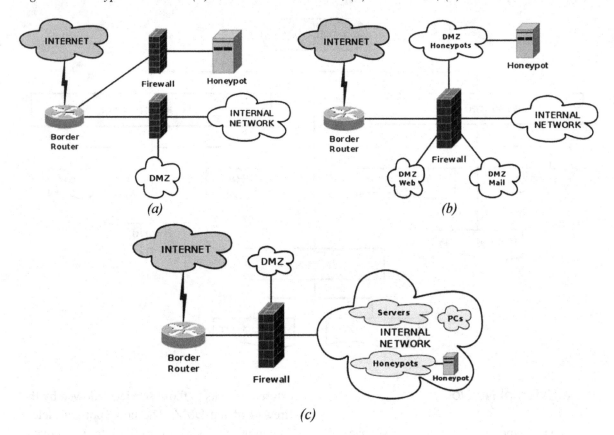

(a)

(b)

(c)

## Honeypots vs. Other Technologies

There are several technologies and tools oriented to malware analysis and intrusion detection (Joshi & Sardana, 2011). The one we choose will depend on our needs. The following paragraphs describe the most important ones.

Sandboxes are security mechanisms that allow files or programs to run in isolated environments and get information from actions they take. This technology is used in malware analysis. Generally, they perform a dynamic and real-time analysis of programs or files executed in a virtual operating system. Sandboxes are used to study malware samples once they have been captured by another tool, for example, through honeypots. Some examples of sandboxes are Cuckoo and Anubis (Egele et al., 2011; Oktavianto & Muhardianto, 2013).

IDS/IPS are technologies based on the detection and mitigation of network attacks. They inspect network packets looking for suspicious patterns. These tools do not capture malware but may block some activities. Generally, IDS/IPS are used in conjunction with other security tools (firewalls, honeypots, honeynets, etc.). Examples of this technology are Snort and Suricata (Team, 2013).

Antiviruses are another tool for analysis and detection of malware. They are a security measure implemented on local computers. The continuously analyze the file system of a computer looking for binaries containing code patterns classified as malignant. Online antivirus engines have become a very useful tool for static analysis of files. As an example, the most popular are VirusTotal, Jotti and Metascan (Ligh, 2010).

## Comparative Analysis of Some Honeypots

This section aims to analyze a series of honeypots through evaluation criteria and tools that show their strong and weak points.

### Laboratory Tests

A properly configured environment allowing a connection between an attacker and the honeypot is needed. This environment has been implemented using VMware, thus providing a virtual test domain (VMware, 2013).

Different honeypots are installed on virtual machines with the recommended operating system for each one. Static addresses were assigned to the honeypot as well as to the attacking machine, both belonging to the same network segment. We chose to use Kali to carry out the batteries of tests on honeypots. Kali is a Linux distribution designed to perform penetration tests (Pritchett & De Smet, 2013). The test batteries were:

- Ports scanning.
- Services identification.
- Interaction by console.
- Checking service objective.
- Service exploitation.

Evaluation criteria analyzed in each honeypot are:

- Offered services.
- Emulated services realism.
- Extensibility.
- Quality of data collected.

### Dionaea Honeypot

Dionaea is a low interaction, general purpose honeypot that offers a variety of network services. It was developed in order to collect malware to be analyzed later. It is written in C language,

but uses embedded Python as script language to develop modular services (The Honeynet Project [THP], n.d.).

### Offered Services

Nmap is used to perform a port scan of the honeypot to check what services are in listen mode. In addition, an attempt is made to obtain the type of applications and versions by Nmap fingerprinting capacity (Pale, 2012). Table 1 shows the results of the scan.

Nmap is able to identify some services, associating them with Dionaea. This capacity detection can lead to a low probability of honeypot success, because the results of the scan would alert the attacker.

### Emulated Services Realism

An important aspect in any honeypot is to provide services that resemble as much as possible to their real analogues. Some of the tested services are:

- **HTTP:** The simulation and the level of interaction of the HTTP service through console and web browser is well accomplished: the emulated service is able to manage

*Table 1. Dionaea services analysis by Nmap*

| Service | Port | Product | Version |
|---------|------|---------|---------|
| HTTP | 80 tcp | Unknown | Unknown |
| HTTPS | 443 tcp | Unknown | Unknown |
| TFTP | 69 up | Unknown | Unknown |
| FTP | 21 tcp | Dionaea honeypot ftpd | Unknown |
| SMB | 445 tcp | Dionaea honeypot smbd | Unknown |
| SIP | 5060 tcp/ udp | Unknown | Unknown |
| SIP | 5061 tcp | Unknown | Unknown |
| MSSQL | 1433 tcp | Dionaea honeypot MS-SQL server | Unknown |
| MYSQL | 3306 tcp | MySQL | 5.0.54 |

most of the requests successfully and also implement all the state codes of the HTTP protocol (Fielding, 1999). Dionaea provides a very efficient HTTP service which, in addition, can be customized to resemble a commercial one, as Apache or IIS.

- **FTP:** The FTP service provides a fine emulation. However enabling this service can be dangerous given that anyone might use it to store files and no useful information would be collected from those activities. Therefore, it should be enabled only in controlled environments.
- **SMB:** Dionaea SMB service is very comprehensive, providing a good collection of information about the attack for analysis. This service provides most of the malware information collected by Dionaea due to the large number of vulnerabilities SMB presents and its ease of exploitation.

## Extensibility

Dionaea has the ability to increase their potential through some tools and plugins listed next.

- **Services:** Additional programs and services may be programmed in Python. Dionaea organizes available services in modules.
- **Logging:** The information obtained is stored in the logs and the SQLite database, facilitating the task of obtaining statistics and information extraction.
- **LogXMPP:** Dionaea implements a version of XMPP (Extensible Messaging and Presence Protocol), service that provides real-time notification. This module has been enhanced to allow the sending of captured binaries to other XMPP servers or to channel members in an IRC chat (XMPP, 2013).
- **SurfIDS:** This module allows you to integrate the honeypot as a component in a distributed intrusion detection system to

analyze malware and attacks (SURFcert IDS, 2013).

- **P0f:** Its function is to detect the operating system versions that attack the honeypot. Performs passive fingerprinting, listening and watching the contents of the packets flowing in the network (Zalewski, 2012).
- **GnuplotSQL:** A module programmed in Python, allowing graphical output of the information stored in the Dionaea database (Dionaea, 2010).
- **DionaeaFR:** A web frontend for Dionaea (RootingPuntoEs, 2013).
- **Binaries Analysis:** This module automatically sends the collected binaries and/or their hashes to different websites for analysis and identification.

## Quality of Collected Data

Dionaea collects almost all data about an attack. Checking the logs, we can see information about:

- IP source and destination.
- TCP/IP ports.
- Users and passwords.
- Vulnerabilities exploited by exploits.
- Binaries captured.
- Commands introduced to interact with services.
- Shellcodes and system calls.
- URLs for downloading malware.
- Timestamps.

The information collected by the honeypot is stored in several files, namely dionaea.log, dionaea-error.log and logsql.sqlite. Dionaea does not provide a warning system, but rather, log files must be inspected in order to detect suspicious activity.

To conclude, Dionaea is one of the most widely used honeypot, especially for catching malware. In addition, Dionaea allows to identify shellcodes contained in exploits and to identify the vulnerabilities exploited by them.

## Honeyd Honeypot

Honeyd is a general purpose honeypot (Provos, 2008). It can emulate many operating systems simultaneously, each with its own services, associate an IP address to each of them through a single network interface and perform spoofing with the Farpd tool (Kirkland, 2010).

## Offered Services

The basic structure of an emulated system and its resources are based on configuration blocks similar to a template for each type of system (Spitzner, 2002; Provos, 2003). The ports are configured to perform a specified action or execute a script when receiving a connection, for instance, simulating a telnet server. Some of these scripts simulating network services are:

- Apache.sh.
- Ssh.sh.
- Telnetd.sh.
- Rpc.sh.
- Ftp.sh.
- Iis.sh.
- Msftp.sh.
- Vnc.sh.
- Web.sh.

Honeyd can act as a proxy, thus allowing (hidden) redirections to a given local port on another server, which usually is a real server or another honeypot with more interaction or specialization.

## Emulated Services Realism

In order to evaluate the honeypot, a template is configured to simulate an operating system "Microsoft Windows Server 2003 Standard Edition" (Valli, 2003). In addition, the following services are configured with scripts: ftp server, vnc, IIS, Exchange and DNS. Also, some typical ports of Windows systems have been configured as opened

to facilitate operating system fingerprinting: 135 tcp, 137 tcp/udp, 139 tcp.

The summary of port scan with Nmap is shown in Table 2.

Services http, ftp, dns and proxying have been tested. Results of this test are shown below.

- **HTTP:** The provided script creates a virtual HTTP server with a customizable website. Requests with the most common options of HTTP have been made, that is, OPTIONS, GET, HEAD, DELETE, and TRACE (Fielding, 1999). The web service is very basic and easy to identify because of a very simple behavior and a small set of implemented error codes. It might be enough for a first impression, though.
- **FTP:** The FTP service provides very little interaction with the attacker as it has a rather poor implementation, only allowing the establishment of the connection and login. Other commands tested (STOR, LIST, SIZE, MDTM) do not allow any action.
- **Proxying and DNS:** Using the proxying option redirects traffic destined to port 53 (dns) to a real server. This is a very useful feature since it greatly increases the capacity of interaction and simulation of the honeypot.

*Table 2. Honeyd services analysis by Nmap*

| Service | Port | Product | Version |
|---|---|---|---|
| FTP | 21 tcp | Microsoft ftpd | 5.0 |
| HTTP | 80 tcp | Unknown | Unknown |
| POP3 | 110 tcp | Microsoft Exchange 2000 pop3d | 6.0.6249.0 |
| MSRPC | 135 tcp | Unknown | Unknown |
| NETBIOS-NS | 137 tcp/udp | Unknown | Unknown |
| NETBIOS-SSN | 139 tcp | Unknown | Unknown |
| IMAP | 143 tcp | Unknown | Unknown |
| VNC | 5901 tcp | Unknown | Unknown |
| DNS | 53 udp | ISC BIND | 9.2.4 |

The capacity of interaction and realism of the offered services by the honeypot depends much of the use of existing scripts and the programming of new ones.

## Extensibility

- **Scripts:** Third-party implementation of simulation scripts for services (Provos, 2008).
- **Honeydsum:** A log analyzer for Honeyd which provides summaries of the honeypot logs and provides outputs in text, HTML and graphics modes (Henrique, 2004).
- **HoneyView:** Another tool to analyze logs with a web interface (Hable, 2003).
- **Honeycomb:** A system with automatic signatures generation for intrusion detection systems. It applies a protocol analysis and pattern detection techniques in the traffic captured on honeypots (Kreibich, 2009).

## Quality of Data Collected

Honeyd only collects information relating to connection attempts:

- IP source and destination.
- TCP/IP ports.
- Timestamps.
- Connection status.
- The identification of the client operating system or the tool used for scanning (if possible).

Honeyd stores the information collected in the following files: syslog, honeyd.log and logs of the service scripts. The honeypot does not have any alert system when it detects an intrusion attempt or interaction with it. To generate reports and to obtain information from the logs, you need to use some of the plugins and tools discussed above.

## Honeyd Conclusion

Honeyd is a very versatile honeypot due to the wide variety of operating systems and services that can simulate. Additionally, it can present complex networks to an attacker by simulating routers.

Its level of interaction is low, but can it be improved by programming scripts services.

## Kippo Honeypot

Kippo is a honeypot for specific use (Secure Shell) (Proyect OpenBSD, 2004). It has become the most important and widespread honeypot dedicated to SSH (Tamminen, 2013).

## Offered Services

We scanned port 22 (ssh) with Nmap, obtaining the following result.

Nmap detected OpenSSH as server application. This identification was possible due to a custom banner included in the data field of a TCP/IP packet of the SSH protocol on the connection establishment.

## Emulated Services Realism

Kippo simulates a customizable file system that interacts with the attacker. For instance, valid users and passwords are stored in a file at the honeypot, which is susceptible to brute force or dictionary attacks.

*Table 3. Kippo service analysis by Nmap*

| Service | Port | Product | Version |
|---------|------|---------|---------|
| SSH | 22 tcp | OpenSSH 5.1p1 Debian 5 (protocol 2.0) | 5.1p1 |

The virtual file system can be emulated from a real one, that is, the file tree structure is stored in a text file. The results of commands as *pwd* or *ls* are read from that file, and if the attacker tries to read, write or execute any of the files, an error is displayed.

Files with content can be included, allowing an intruder to list them. There is a problem, though: some files store static content, for example, *ifconfig*. It the latter is listed, it will always return the same information. Some files or commands with static content already incorporated are: *group, hosts, dmesg, meminfo, issue, passwd, shadow, cpuinfo, ifconfig*, etc.

Also, commands can be included for the attacker to interact with. These commands are programmed in Python and some are lacking some realism as they output static information.

Kippo provides a quite acceptable, very customizable and easy to use and configure simulated environment for SSH connections, making it unique in this type of service.

## Extensibility

- **Commands and Files:** Generation of files with content and scripts.
- **CreateFS:** A script to make a copy of the file system on which the honeypot is running and use it to simulate a virtual environment to the intruder.
- **FSEdit:** Third-party script allowing modifications in the file that stores the virtual tree of directories and files to customize it a bit more (Hubbard, 2013).
- **Kippo-Stats:** An application that displays statistics and graphs of the honeypot logs through web interface (Fontani, 2011).
- **Kippo-Graph:** Another tool that provides information about intrusion attempts on the honeypot. It is more complete than Kippo-stats (Koniaris, 2013).

## Quality of Data Collected

Information collected in logs is:

- IP source.
- TCP/IP ports involved.
- Logs of users and passwords.
- Binary captured.
- Commands entered by the attacker on the console.
- Timestamps.
- Honeypot debugging information, such as establishing and closing connection, key exchange, etc.

Kippo has several logging systems, these are: text logs, MySQL, XMPP (Extensible Messaging and Presence Protocol), but neither has an alert system.

Reports can be generated by extracting information of systems logs or through any of the above tools, as Kippo-Graph.

In conclusion, Kippo has a high degree of simulation and is able to capture the binaries downloaded by an attacker. Its use is recommended for those who want to capture new malware samples and keep track of the activities of the intruder in the virtual system.

Table 4 compares some characteristics of studied honeypots.

*Table 4. Characteristics of studied honeypots*

|  | **Dionaea** | **Honeyd** | **Kippo** |
|---|---|---|---|
| Type | General | General | SSH specific |
| Binary capture | Yes | No | Yes |
| Exploits detection | Yes | No | No |
| Alert system | No | No | No |
| Customization | High | High | Medium |
| Quality of data | High | Medium | High |

## HONEYNETS

A honeynet is a network architecture composed of honeypots, network devices and security tools. Honeypots in a honeynet are real operating systems, that is, are high-interaction honeypots.

When the systems of a honeynet are attacked, the honeynet logs all information about the activities taking place (Spitzner, 2002). For that purpose there are a number of common components to every honeynet:

- **Router:** Routes the traffic to the different devices in the honeynet.
- **Firewall:** Restricts incoming and outgoing traffic to/from the honeynet.
- **IDS/IPS:** Intrusion Detection and Prevention System allowing to analyze in more detail the traffic and content of network packets.
- **Server Logs:** The information collected by honeypots and the rest of devices are sent to a centralized logs server.

### Honeynets Classification and Architectures

Three main types of architectures can be distinguished. These are classified into first (GenI), second (GenII) and third (GenIII) generation (Spitzner, 2002).

### First Generation Honeynets (GenI)

This architecture was created in order to provide a solution to the problems of isolating the actions of attackers and capturing the associated information within a network. The firewall must be configured to allow any incoming traffic addressing the honeypots from outside the honeynet in order to protect administrative network computers (server logs and IDS). It must also restrict outgoing traffic from the honeynet in order to prevent compromised systems from attacking other systems outside the honeynet.

The router only allows to forward outgoing packets from the honeynet with a source IP address belonging to the honeynet. This mechanism helps protecting the network from DoS and spoofing attacks as well SYN Flooding and Smurf.

The IDS searches anomalies in packets or information contained in these that suggest malicious activity, alerting the administrator if it finds evidence of an attack (Team, 2013).

Currently GenI honeynets are effective against automated attacks and the basic techniques of newbies. This model is barely implemented nowadays since it has evolved into a more complete honeynet architecture, which is able to collect more information about advanced attacks (GenII).

### Second Generation Honeynets (GenII)

GenII honeynets provide greater control of the intruder's actions, better tools for information gathering and the ability to integrate into production corporate networks with lower risks.

The main difference in this architecture with respect to GenI is the incorporation of a new component that acts as a gateway of the honeynet. That component is the honeywall, a device that incorporates the functions of firewall and IDS/IPS on the same device (Haile, n.d.).

The honeywall has 3 network interfaces. One of them is connected to the management network. The other two are configured in bridge mode and have no IP addresses, as they only perform actions in layer 2 of the OSI model. The bridge mode configuration does not decrease the TTL field of packets nor performs any routing that would modify packets content. Thanks to that, it is more difficult to detect a honeywall than a Layer 3 router, a typical problem in GenI honeynets.

### Third Generation Honeynets (GenIII)

This generation does not modify the architecture of GenII honeynets, it rather provides improvements in management (Abbasi & Harris, 2009; Rammidi, 2008). Remote administration tools have

*Figure 3. GenI honeynet architecture*

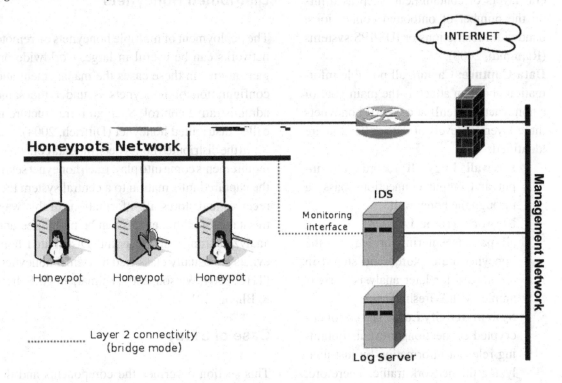

been included and collection and centralization of information are improved, thus facilitating data analysis. For example, a web interface to manage the honeywall, Walleye, is able to correlate events in the honeynet to display the collected information and to manage the honeynet configuration from a single point (The Honeynet Project [THC], 2005).

## Virtual and Physical Honeynets

In a physical honeynet, honeypots and other systems are running on separate physical machines.

A virtual honeynet deploys honeypots and other systems on virtual machines which run on the same physical machine (Rammidi, 2008).

Two types of virtual honeynets exist:

- **Self-Contained Honeynet:** All components (honeypots, honeywall, IDS, router, etc.) are implemented on the same physical machine by using virtualization.

- **Hybrid Honeynet:** Honeypots run on virtual machines within the same physical machine, but the basic devices (honeywall, IDS, router, etc.) are deployed on another physical machine. Hybrid honeynets imply a security enhancement, decreasing the likelihood of having the full honeynet compromised by an attacker.

## Honeynets Requirements

The honeynets require the implementation of methods that allow analyzing all activity that occurs in the honeynet, these methods are (The Honeynet Project [THC], 2004):

- **Data Control:** It allows an attacker or malware to carry out malicious activities within the honeynet, maintaining a balance between freedom and containment of his actions. Data control implements several layers of containment, such as limits on the number of outbound connections, bandwidth restrictions or IDS/IPS systems (Rammidi, 2008).

- **Data Capture:** Capture all possible information about an attack is the main goal of a honeynet. In GenII and GenIII honeynets three layers or levels of data collection are identified:
  - **Firewall Logs:** It records the input and output connections passing through the honeywall.
  - **Network Traffic Logs:** At this level all packets entering or leaving the honeynet are captured and stored in a database for later analysis, for example, with Wireshark.
  - **System Activity Logs:** The use of encrypted connections prevents obtaining relevant information by just analyzing the network traffic. Therefore, it is necessary to capture the information in honeypots. A tool used in GenII and GenIII honeynets is Sebek (Sebek Project, 2008).
- **Data Analysis:** Any piece of information collected by the honeynet is worthless if it is not correctly interpreted. A number of tools facilitate the work of representation and understanding of information. Some of them are (THC, 2004):
  - Frontends for low level data capture: tools such as Snort, Sebek, Wireshark, Snorby and log viewers.
  - Forensic analysis tools: for example, WinInterrogate, Sleuthkit suite or Tripwire.
- **Data Collection:** When administering several honeynets, it is necessary to centralize in a single point all the information captured at each honeynet, so it can be analyzed jointly (Spitzner, 2002). We will show more about this feature in the next section.

## Distributed Honeynets

The deployment of multiple honeynets on remote networks can be useful in large, worldwide organizations: in these cases the management and configuration of honeynets is under the same administrative control. Such an infrastructure is called distributed honeynet (Dittrich, 2004).

In the distributed honeynets, the data collection requirements come into play. Each honeynet sends the captured information to a central system that receives and stores all information. In this way, the status of all honeynets can be monitored and analyzed from a single point. Distributed honeynets are usually classified as GenIII honeynets (THC, 2004; Watson, 2007; Kumar, Singh, Sehgal & Bhatia, 2012).

## Case of Study

This section describes the components and the architecture of a self-contained virtual honeynet implemented by the authors for didactic purposes. We will focus on the practical use and the benefits that a GenIII honeynet brings in detection and analysis of intrusion in the honeynet.

Once the honeynet is deployed, an attack will be launched from an external machine. Its main purpose is to get privileged access to the honeypot. Subsequently, we will analyze the information gathered by the honeynet in order to obtain a full trace of the attack, evaluating in this way the practicality and usefulness of the honeynet.

The honeynet of this case of study is composed of a honeywall or gateway, a high-interaction honeypot and the attacking machine. Figure 6 shows the self-contained virtual honeynet.

The Honeywall Roo Linux distribution was chosen to implement the honeywall: it is a distribution specifically tailored by The Honeynet Project that provides the tools needed for controlling, capturing and analyzing data from a honeynet (THC, 2005).

*Figure 4. GenII and GenII honeynet architecture*

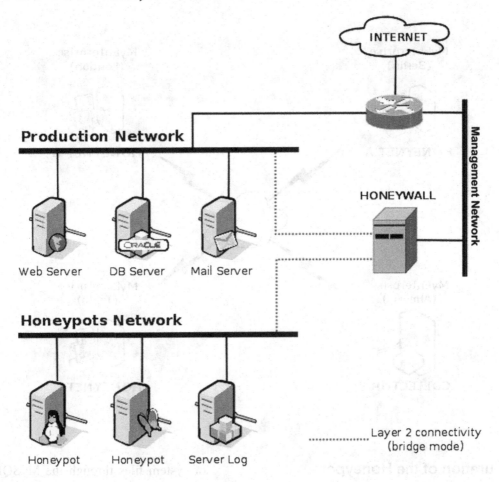

For the honeypot we have chosen the CentOS 5.9 Linux distribution, which is based on Red Hat Enterprise Linux, easy to configure and with enough support by the free community. We have installed a set of applications to generate a vulnerable distribution that would engage any attacker that might analyze the network. In addition, other tools have been installed to monitor the honeypot and integrity thereof.

## Configuration of the Honeynet Connectivity

The external and internal networks of the honeynet are placed in segments with different IP addressing. This configuration is not ideal since the honeywall should act as a bridge between two segments with the same addressing. The decision to implement networks with different addressing for internal and external segments of the honeynet is due to hardware limitations and the characteristics of VMware. Given the entire honeynet (including the honeypot) and the machine attacker are implemented on the same physical computer, connectivity through the VMware virtual switch does not permit to configure the desired routing. One possible solution to the problem would be to include a physical network device between the honeywall and the attacker machine. Figure 7 shows the problematic situation.

Table 5 shows the honeynet networks configured to use the virtual switch of VMware [26].

*Figure 5. Distributed honeynet architecture*

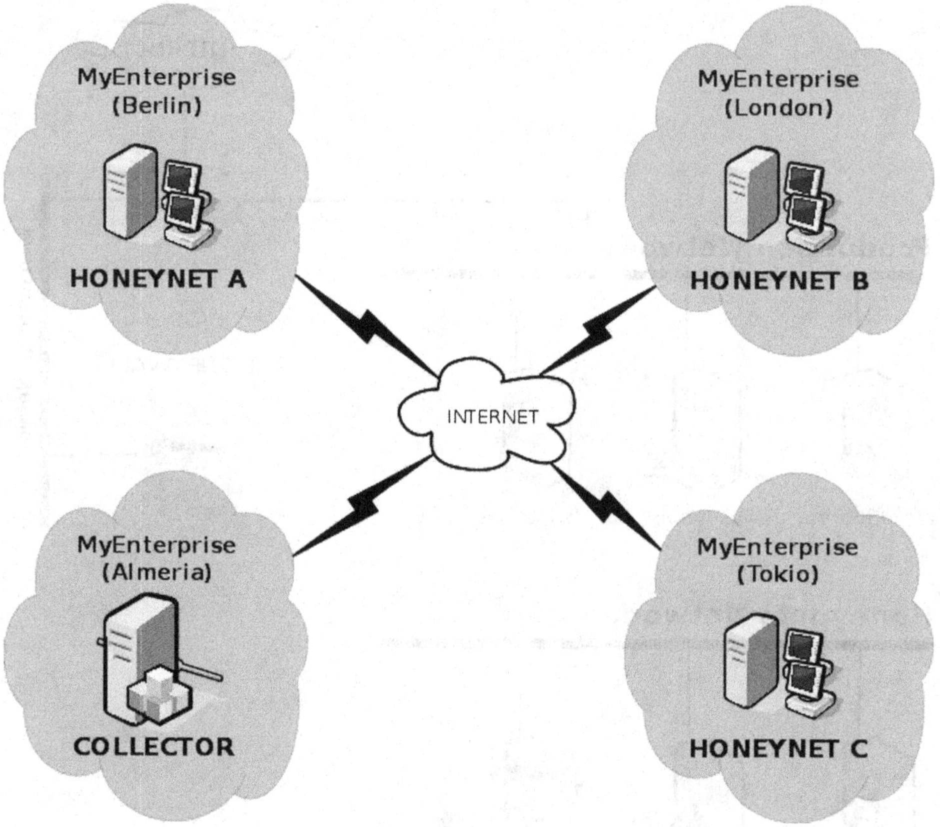

## Configuration of the Honeypot

Configuration details are specified below:

- **Operating System:** CentOS 5.9.
- **Network Configuration:**
  - ○ IP:192.168.30.100/24.
  - ○ Interface: eth0.
  - ○ VMware switch: Host-Only (vmnet3).
- **NTP (Network Time Protocol):** All honeynet devices are synchronized with a NTP server (Mills, 1992).
- **Users without privileges:**
  - ○ Login: mag023.
  - ○ Password: letmein.
- **MySQL v.5.0.51a:** This version presents a code injection vulnerability allowing an unprivileged attacker to obtain the contents of system files through the MySQL console (CVE Details, 2012; MikiSoft, 2011).
  - ○ MySQL remote access to the root user is enabled.
    - ▪ **Login:** root.
    - ▪ **Password:** testing.
- **SystemTap v.1.3:** A monitoring tool that allows you to have control any system event, not application level only, but also at kernel level (SystemTap, n.d.). It contains vulnerability where an attacker can gain root privileges by running a local exploit (CVE-2010-4170) (CVE, 2010).
- **Tripwire:** A security tool oriented file system monitoring. It monitors and alerts about file changes by comparing the hash of each file with its corresponding entry from a database of hashes previously calculated (Tripwire, 2013).

*Figure 6. Self-contained virtual honeynet of the case study*

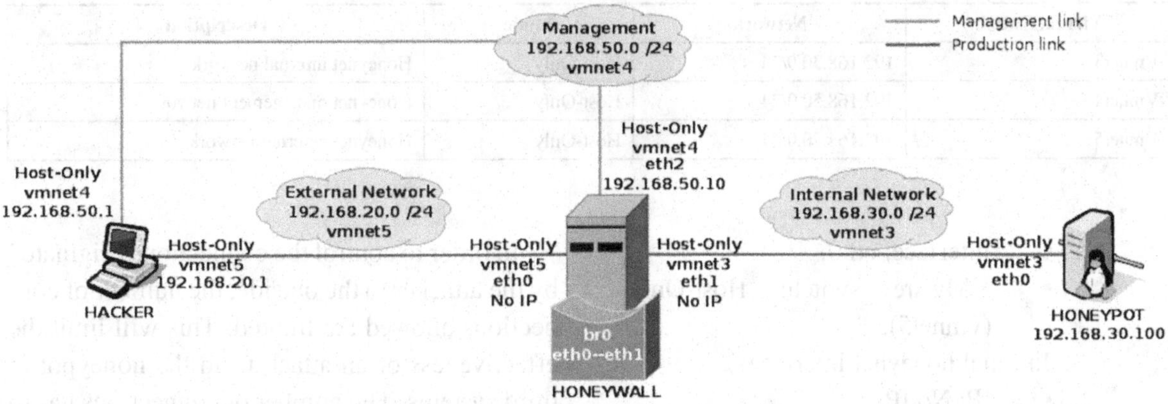

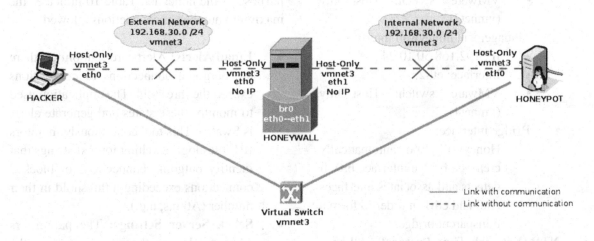

*Figure 7. Connection problem using virtual switch of VMware*

- **Sebek Client:** Sebek is installed on the system as a kernel module, intercepting and recording the information of the attacker when invoked system calls, such as read and write (Sebek Project, 2008). The configuration of Sebek client is listed below:
  - **Interface:** eth0.
  - **Destination IP:** 192.168.50.10 (any IP).
  - **Destination MAC:** 00:0C:29:7E:33:2D (honeywall bridge interface).
  - **Source Port:** 64000.
  - **Destination Port:** 65000.
  - **Magic Value:** 1111.

- **IPTables:** IPTables rules are configured to allow all traffic, that is, the firewall will not block any package. Traffic filtering is performed in the IPTables of the honeywall.

## Configuration of the Honeywall

Honeywall Roo is installed on a virtual machine that will act as the honeywall with the following settings:

- **Operating System:** Honeywall Roo (CentOS 5.0 based Linux) (THC, 2005)
- Network configuration:
  - External honeynet interface:
    - IP: No IP.

*Table 5. Honeynet networks configured to the virtual switch of VMware*

| Virtual Switch | Network | Mode | Description |
|---|---|---|---|
| Vmnet3 | 192.168.30.0/24 | Host-Only | Honeynet internal network |
| Vmnet4 | 192.168.50.0/24 | Host-Only | Honeynet management network |
| Vmnet5 | 192.168.20.0/24 | Host-Only | Honeynet external network |

- Interface: eth0.
- VMware switch: Host-Only (vmnet5).
  ○ Internal honeynet interface:
    - IP: No IP.
    - Interface: eth1.
    - VMware switch: Host-Only (vmnet3).
  ○ Management honeywall interface:
    - IP: 192.168.50.10/24.
    - Interface: eth2.
    - VMware switch: Host-Only (vmnet4).
  ○ Bridge interface:
    - Honeywall Roo automatically creates a bridge interface br0. It detects and associates interfaces eth0 and eth1 in order to form a transparent bridge.
- **NTP (Network Time Protocol):** All honeynet devices are synchronized with a NTP server (Mills, 1992).
- **Users and Remote Access**: There are three management users listed in Table 6. Remote access and a web interface have been enabled for system management purposes.

- **Settings Rules and Connections Limit in IPTables:** The rules for filtering traffic that passes through the honeywall can be represented schematically as shown in Tables 7, 8 and 9.

In order to control the connections originated by the attacker to the outside, the number of connections allowed are limited. This will limit the effectiveness of an attack from the honeypot to third systems. The number of connections has to be adjusted depending on the environment and purpose of the honeynet. Table 10 indicates the maximum number of connections allowed.

- **Email Alerts:** Alerts are sent only if there are outgoing connections or connections exceed the threshold. The application used to monitor these states and generate alerts is Swatch. This tool continuously monitors IPTables log, searching for text strings that identify outgoing connections or blocked connections exceeding a threshold in their number (Atkins, n.d.).
- **Sebek Server Settings:** The parameters must match with those configured on the client installed in the honeypot.

Honeywall Roo uses Hflow2 as a tool for collection and correlation of events. Due to a bug not solved between Sebek and Hflow2, the only way to see the Sebek packets in the Walleye web interface is analyzing related connections flows with the origin and destination ports, 6400 and 65000 respectively (The Honeynet Project, 2007). As an alternative, a script has been developed to display the recorded commands without having to analyze the UDP packets sent by the Sebek client. The content script is as follows:

*Table 6. Management users*

| Application | User | Password |
|---|---|---|
| System | roo | honey |
| System | root | honey |
| Walleye | roo | L3tmein- |

*Table 7. INPUT chain rules*

| Action | Protocol | Interface In | Source | Destination | Ports |
|---|---|---|---|---|---|
| Accept | any | loopback | any | any | any |
| Accept | tcp | eth2 | 192.168.50.0/24 | any | 22, 443 |
| Drop | any | any | any | any | any |

*Table 8. OUTPUT chain rules*

| Action | Protocol | Interface Out | Source | Destination | Ports |
|---|---|---|---|---|---|
| Accept | any | loopback | any | any | any |
| Accept | tcp | eth2 | any | any | 20, 21, 22, 25, 80, 443 |
| Accept | udp | eth2 | any | any | 53, 123, 69 |
| Drop | any | any | any | any | any |

sbk_extract -i eth1 - p65000 >> /var/log/sebek_commands &

The sbk_extract command above listens in the specified interface, eth1, and analyzes packets where the destination port matches 65000. It stores the information in the log sebek_commands with a timestamp.

- **Snort and Snort_Inline:** Snort is running in IDS (Intrusion Detection System) mode and captures all traffic that will be used later for the generation of statistics and packages analysis (Team, 2013). Snort_inline runs as IPS (Intrusion Prevention System). Snort_inline reads all packets assigned to the action QUEUE of a string in IPTables (Haile, n.d.).
- **Walleye Interface:** The web interface concentrates all the information gathered by the honeynet thus making data analysis.

Walleye relates the obtained information by the tools described, Snort, Snort_inline, Sebek, IPTables, etc.

- **P0f:** A passive fingerprinting tool that listens to network traffic in order to identify devices and operating systems in the network (Zalewski, 2012). The identification is possible thanks to the different implementations of the TCP / IP performed by different devices.
- **Argus:** A tool used to interpret the headers of network packets and display them as conversations or sessions. It receives as input a Snort log and after analyzing it, shows a summary thereof.

## Intrusion Test

An intrusion test has been performed consisting of the following:

*Table 9. Forward chain rules*

| Action | Protocol | Interface In | Interface Out | Source | Destination | Ports |
|--------|----------|--------------|---------------|--------|-------------|-------|
| Accept | any | any | any | any | 192.168.30.255 | any |
| Accept | any | any | any | any | 255.255.255.255 | any |
| Accept | any | eth0 | any | any | any | any |
| Accept | udp | eth1 | any | any | 192.168.50.10 | 65000 |
| Accept | udp | eth1 | any | any | 255.255.255.255 | Source:68 Destination:67 |
| Accept | tcp/udp | eth1 | any | 192.168 30.100 | any | 53 |
| Accept | any | eth1 | eth1 | any | any | any |
| Accept | tcp | eth1 | any | 192.168.30.100 | any | any-200 connections/hour |
| Accept | udp | eth1 | any | 192.168.30.100 | any | any-200 connections/hour |
| Accept | icmp | eth1 | any | 192.168.30.100 | any | any-300 connections/hour |
| Accept | any | eth1 | any | 192.168.30.100 | any | any-100 connections/hour |

*Table 10. Connections limits*

| Protocol | Max. Connections | Scale |
|----------|------------------|-------|
| TCP | 200 | hour |
| UDP | 200 | hour |
| ICMP | 300 | hour |
| OTHERS | 100 | hour |

*Table 11. Sebek server settings*

| Parameter | Value |
|-----------|-------|
| IP | 192.168.50.10 |
| UDP port | 65000 |
| Magic value | 1111 |

1. Scanning and identifying honeypot services. Nmap has been used to perform a port scan of the honeypot. A MySQL server database has been detected.

2. The attacker attempts to obtain valid credentials to connect to MySQL. For this, Metasploit Framework, a tool for developing and executing security exploits against a remote machine is used (Rapid7, 2013). Mysql_login Metasploit module is used. This module performs an attack by dictionary against the database and gets a username and password with which to connect to MySQL. Once the credentials have been achieved, the attacker connects directly to the database system using mysql client utility.

3. The attacker reads the content of the files */etc/passwd* and */etc/shadow* after exploiting the aforementioned code injection vulnerability in this version of MySQL. This vulnerability allows extracting the contents of any file on the operating system through the function load_file ('file') of MySQL. The files obtained store information about system user accounts and password hashes of users.

4. With John The Ripper tool, credentials of some users of the honeypot have been obtained from */etc/passwd* and */etc/shadow*. John The Ripper is a cryptographic software that applying brute force for password cracking (Peslyak, 2013).

5. After obtaining the credentials of a user without root privileges (mag023 user), the attacker connects to the honeypot through a SSH connection.

6. The next objective is to gain root privileges. A vulnerable version of Systemtap is detected in the system. The attacker uploads a privilege-elevation exploit to the honeypot for exploiting the Systemtap vulnerability

(CVE-2010-4170). After running the exploit, the attacker gets a shell with root privileges.

7. After running the exploit, the attacker gets a shell with root privileges. With root privileges, the SHV5 rootkit is installed in the honeypot. This rootkit provides backdoor access to the honeypot at any time.

## Analysis of Information of the Honeynet

This section analyzes the information related to the intrusion test, which has been registered by the different components of the honeynet. The infor-

mation collected helps reconstructing the attack and generating timeline, which we show below:

## 10-October-2013 16:38:08

**Description:** Port scanning from IP address 192.168.20.1.

**Evidences:** The connections can be seen in Walleye, as shown in Figure 8. This is possibly a port scanning operation.

In the honeywall IPTables log, has also been registered the port scanning. Below is shown one of the records that evidence the scan.

*Figure 8. Port scanning connections flow*

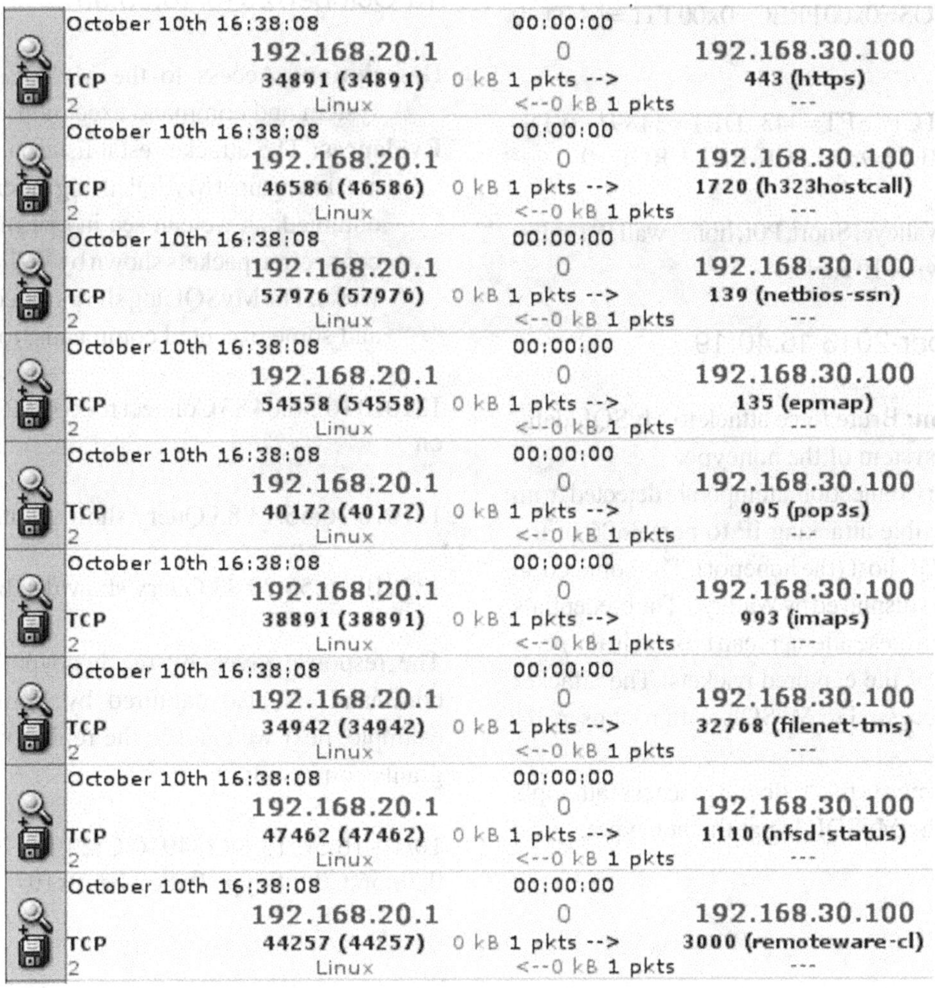

Oct 10 16:38:08 honeywall kernel: INBOUND TCP: IN=br0 OUT=br0 PHYSIN=eth0 PHYSOUT=eth1

SRC=192.168.20.1 DST=192.168.30.100 LEN=60 TOS=0x00 PREC=0x00 TTL=64 ID=45735 DF PROTO=TCP

SPT=34891 DPT=443 WINDOW=14600 RES=0x00 SYN URGP=0

The IPTables honeypot log has also recorded these connection attempts.

Oct 10 16:38:08 centossrv kernel: iptables accept IN= OUT=eth0

SRC=192.168.30.100 DST=192.168.20.1 LEN=40 TOS=0x00 PREC=0x00 TTL=64 ID=0 DF

PROTO=TCP SPT=443 DPT=34891 WINDOW=0 RES=0x00 ACK RST URGP=0

**Sources:** Walleye, Snort, P0f, honeywall IPTables, honeypot IPTables.

## 10-October-2013 16:40:19

**Description:** Brute force attack to MySQL database system of the honeypot.

**Evidences:** Connection attempts are detected from a possible attacking IP to port 3306 of the MySQL host (the honepot). The connection flow is displayed by Walleye. The credentials used in these attempts can be seen in the *pcap* view of the captured packets. The attacker has accessed to MySQL with root user.

Furthermore, the following access attempts appear in the MySQL log at the honeypot.

*Time Command Argument*

131010 16:40:29 Connect Access denied for user 'roosters'@'192.168.20.1'(using password:YES)

131010 16:40:39 Connect Access denied for user 'roosters'@'192.168.20.1'(using password:YES)

131010 16:53:22 Connect Access denied for user 'root'@'192.168.20.1'(using password:YES)

131010 16:53:32 Connect root@192.168.20.1 on

**Sources:** Walleye, Snort, honeywall IPTables, honeypot IPTables, honeypot MySQL log.

## 10-October-2013 16:55:55

**Description:** Access to the MySQL database system and command execution.

**Evidences:** The attacker establishes a new connection against MySQL using the credentials obtained, as we can see in one of the flow connection packets shown by Walleye (*pcap* view). The MySQL log shows the connection and some executed commands, too.

131010 16:56:04 83 Connect root@192.168.20.1 on

131010 16:56:13 83 Query show grants

131010 16:56:20 83 Query show databases

The response given by the honeypot to those commands is also captured by Walleye. For example, next we can see the reply to the show grants command:

10/10-16:56:13.842249 0:C:29:B3:7D:1F -> 0:50:56:C0:0:5 type:0x800 len:0x107

192.168.30.100:3306 -> 192.168.20.1:38089
TCP TTL:64 TOS:0x8 ID:43962 IpLen:20 Dgm-
Len:249 DF

***AP*** Seq: 0x4F16D40F Ack: 0x73FFF44F
Win: 0x16A TcpLen:

TCP Options (3) => NOP NOP TS: 2015674
3150463

01 00 00 01 01 27 00 00 02 03 64 65 66 00 00 00
.....'....def...

11 47 72 61 6E 74 73 20 66 6F 72 20 72 6F 6F
74 .Grants for root

40 25 00 0C 21 00 00 0C 00 00 FD 01 00 1F 00
00 @%..!...........

05 00 00 03 FE 00 00 02 00 7F 00 00 04 7E 47
52 .............~GR

41 4E 54 20 41 4C 4C 20 50 52 49 56 49 4C 45
47 ANT ALL PRIVILEG

45 53 20 4F 4E 20 2A 2E 2A 20 54 4F 20 27 72
6F ES ON *.* TO 'ro

6F 74 27 40 27 25 27 20 49 44 45 4E 54 49 46
49 ot'@'%' IDENTIFI

45 44 20 42 59 20 50 41 53 53 57 4F 52 44 20 27
ED BY PASSWORD '

2A 41 43 35 37 37 35 34 34 36 32 42 36 44 34
43 *AC57754462B6D4C

33 37 33 32 36 33 30 36 32 44 36 30 45 44 43 36
373263062D60EDC6

45 34 35 32 45 35 37 34 44 27 20 57 49 54 48 20
E452E574D' WITH

47 52 41 4E 54 20 4F 50 54 49 4F 4E 05 00 00
05 GRANT OPTION....

FE 00 00 02 00 .....

Finally, the *show databases* command generated an alert at the IDS Snort in Walleye. The
Figure 9 shows this alert.

**Sources:** Walleye, Snort, honeywall IPTables,
honeypot IPTables, honeypot MySQL log.

## 10-October-2013 16:56:35

**Description:** Extraction of unauthorized information through a MySQL vulnerability.

**Evidences:** In the next step, which is a continuation of the previous communication, we can
observe how the *load_file()* function from
MySQL is executed. The attacker successfully extracted the contents of the files /
*etc/passwd* and */etc/shadow*. The collected
information is registered in the MySQL log
and by Walleye. Below is the corresponding
MySQL log entry.

131010 16:56:35 83 Query select load_file ('/etc/
passwd')

*Figure 9. MySQL Snort alert*

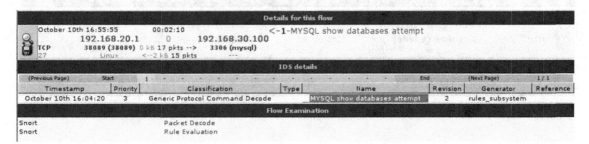

**Sources:** Walleye, Snort, honeywall IPTables, honeypot IPTables, honeypot MySQL log.

## 10-October-2013 17:05:36

**Description:** SSH access to the honeypot.

**Evidences:** A SSH connection is established against the honeypot using the account mag023. Walleye has intercepted the entire communication flow. At the honeypot, the log /var/log/secure has registered the event.

Oct 10 17:05:50 centossrv sshd[3674]: Accepted password for mag023 from 192.168.20.1 port \ 38021 ssh2

Oct 10 17:05:50 centossrv sshd[3674]: pam_unix(sshd:session): session opened for user mag023 \ by (uid=0)

The mag023 account has restricted privileges, probably stolen as a result of the MySQL vulnerability (we know for sure this was the case).

**Sources:** Walleye, Snort, honeywall IPTables, honeypot IPTables, honeypot MySQL log, honeypot /var/log/secure.

## 10-October-2013 17:05:37

**Description:** Execution of commands at the honeypot.

**Evidences:** SSH provides an encrypted connection, therefore, communication cannot be seen in clear text. For this we use Sebek. Figure 10 shows a summary of the flow of Sebek UDP packets in Walleye.

In the log generated by the script of Sebek, /var/log/sebek_commands, the connection and the executed commands can be seen.

[2013-10-10 17:05:37 Host:192.168.30.100 UID:0 PID:3674 COM:sshd ]#SSH-2.0-OpenSSH_6.1

[2013-10-10 17:05:37 Host:192.168.30.100 UID:0 PID:3674 COM:sshd ]#

[2013-10-10 17:05:59 Host:192.168.30.100 UID:500 PID:3677 COM:bash ]#id

[2013-10-10 17:06:05 Host:192.168.30.100 UID:500 PID:3677 COM:bash ]#uname -na

[2013-10-10 17:06:10 Host:192.168.30.100 UID:500 PID:3677 COM:bash ]#w

[2013-10-10 17:06:21 Host:192.168.30.100 UID:500 PID:3677 COM:bash ]#stap -V

**Sources:** Walleye, Snort, honeywall IPTables, honeypot IPTables, honeywall /var/log/sebek_commands.

*Figure 10. Sebek connections flow*

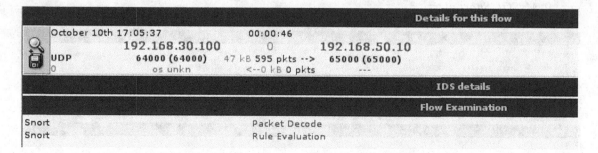

## 10-October-2013 17:08:59

**Description:** Systemtap_exploit.sh file upload to the honeypot.

**Evidences:** The attacker has uploaded the file *systemtap_exploit.sh* to the honeypot using SCP (Secure Copy Protocol).

The connection packets involved in the file transfer and the packets sent by Sebek are registered by Walleye. By analyzing the Sebek packets we can identify the use of SCP and the target path of the file transferred.

00 00 00 03 00 17 80 0A 73 63 70 00 00 00 00 00 ........scp.....

00 00 00 00 00 00 00 21 2F 68 6F 6D 65 2F 6D 61 61 .......!/home/ma

67 30 32 33 2F 73 79 73 74 65 6D 74 61 70 5F 65 g023/systemtap_e

78 70 6C 6F 69 74 2E 73 68 xploit.sh

The log */var/log/secure* at the honeypot side also identifies this transfer. Similarly, the log */var/log/sebek_commands* at the honeywall has also registered the event.

**Sources:** Walleye, Snort, honeywall IPTables, honeypot IPTables, honeywall /var/log/ sebek_commands, honeypot /var/log/secure.

## 10-October-2013 17:09:09

**Description:** Execution of *systemtap_exploit.sh* at the honeypot.

**Evidences:** The execution of systemtap_exploit. sh can be seen in the Sebek log.

[2013-10-10 17:10:48 Host:192.168.30.100 UID:500 PID:3677 COM:bash ]#sh systemtap_exploit.sh

[2013-10-10 17:11:28 Host:192.168.30.100 UID:0 PID:3737 COM:sh ]#id

Note that the command id, executed after the exploit, is invoked with root privileges (see the UID value equal to 0). Therefore, the attacker has achieved an elevation of privileges after exploiting the Systemtap vulnerability.

**Sources:** Walleye, Snort, honeywall IPTables, honeypot IPTables, honeywall /var/log/ sebek_commands.

## 10-October-2013 17:13:46

**Description:** Upload of the file *shv5.tar.gz* to the honeypot.

**Evidences:** The attacker has uploaded the file shv5.tar.gz to the honeypot using SCP again.

Walleye registers the connection corresponding to the file transfer and the packets sent by Sebek.

Upon analysis of the Sebek packets we can easily identify the use of SCP and the target path of the transferred file, just like in the transfer of *systemtap_exploit.sh*.

The logs */var/log/secure* at the honeypot and */var/log/sebek_commands* at the honeywall also warn about this transfer.

The file was not located in the file system of the honeypot, so it was probably deleted by the attacker in order to avoid leaving tracks. Even so, the file could be the rootkit known as SHV5.

**Sources:** Walleye, Snort, honeywall IPTables, honeypot IPTables, honeywall /var/log/ sebek_commands, honeypot /var/log/secure.

## 10-October-2013 17:16:05

**Description:** Configuration and execution of the rootkit.

**Evidences:** In Sebek log can be viewed the commands executed by the attacker on the console with root privileges.

[2013-10-10 17:16:05 Host:192.168.30.100 UID:0 PID:3737 COM:sh ]#pwd

[2013-10-10 17:16:07 Host:192.168.30.100 UID:0 PID:3737 COM:sh ]#ls

[2013-10-10 17:16:24 Host:192.168.30.100 UID:0 PID:3737 COM:sh ]#tar xvzf shv5.tar.gz

[2013-10-10 17:16:30 Host:192.168.30.100 UID:0 PID:3737 COM:sh ]#ls

[2013-10-10 17:16:34 Host:192.168.30.100 UID:0 PID:3737 COM:sh ]#cd shv

[2013-10-10 17:16:35 Host:192.168.30.100 UID:0 PID:3737 COM:sh ]#ls

[2013-10-10 17:16:37 Host:192.168.30.100 UID:0 PID:3737 COM:sh ]#ls -al

[2013-10-10 17:16:53 Host:192.168.30.100 UID:0 PID:3737 COM:sh ]#chmod 777 setup

[2013-10-10 17:16:56 Host:192.168.30.100 UID:0 PID:3737 COM:sh ]#ls -al

[2013-10-10 17:17:50 Host:192.168.30.100 UID:0 PID:3737 COM:sh ]#./setup knocktoopen

[2013-10-10 17:18:32 Host:192.168.30.100 UID:0 PID:3781 COM:setup ]#

[2013-10-10 17:21:10 Host:192.168.30.100 UID:0 PID:4025 COM:3 ]#

[2013-10-10 17:23:16 Host:192.168.30.100 UID:0 PID:3737 COM:sh ]#

An external analysis reveals an SHV5 rootkit directory structure and execution of the *setup* command, wherein the first parameter, *knocktoopen*, indicates the access password and the second one, 1313, is the port where the backdoor listens on the honeypot. By analyzing the flow of Sebek packets in Walleye, we can see how the execution of the rootkit makes changes in the file system of the honeypot. For example, the Tripwire configuration is modified and some system binaries are replaced by modified versions.

**Sources:** Walleye, Snort, honeywall IPTables, honeypot IPTables, honeywall */var/log/ sebek_commands*.

## 10-October-2013 17:26:22

**Description:** The attacker connects to the honeypot backdoor.

**Evidences:** The attacker establishes a connection against the honeypot through the backdoor. The connection flow in Walleye, shown in Figure 11, proves it.

The Sebek log also identifies this new connection along with the commands executed.

[2013-10-10 17:26:31 Host:192.168.30.100 UID:0 PID:4042 COM:3 ]#SSH-1.5-OpenSSH_6.1

[2013-10-10 17:27:00 Host:192.168.30.100 UID:0 PID:4045 COM:bash ]#id

[2013-10-10 17:27:05 Host:192.168.30.100 UID:0 PID:4045 COM:bash ]#pwd

[2013-10-10 17:28:23 Host:192.168.30.100 UID:0 PID:4045 COM:bash ]#ls /

[2013-10-10 17:30:53 Host:192.168.30.100 UID:0 PID:4045 COM:bash ]#ll

*Figure 11. Connection through the backdoor*

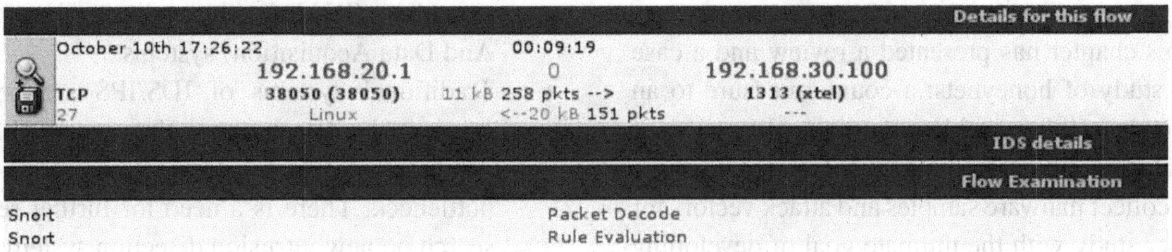

[2013-10-10  17:32:15  Host:192.168.30.100
UID:0 PID:4045 COM:bash ]#ls

[2013-10-10  17:32:18  Host:192.168.30.100
UID:0 PID:4045 COM:bash ]#ps

[2013-10-10  17:32:28  Host:192.168.30.100
UID:0 PID:4045 COM:bash ]#netstat

[2013-10-10  17:33:01  Host:192.168.30.100
UID:0 PID:4045 COM:bash ]#ifconfig

[2013-10-10  17:35:41  Host:192.168.30.100
UID:0 PID:4045 COM:bash ]#exit

**Sources:** Walleye, Snort, honeywall IPTables, honeypot IPTables, honeywall */var/log/ sebek_commands*.

## 10-October-2013 17:31:08

**Description:** Disconnection of the attacker.

**Evidences:** The attacker disconnects from all sessions. The Sebek log identifies those operations.

[2013-10-10  17:31:08  Host:192.168.30.100
UID:0 PID:3737 COM:sh ]#exit

[2013-10-10  17:31:13  Host:192.168.30.100
UID:500 PID:3677 COM:bash ]#exit

[2013-10-10  17:35:41  Host:192.168.30.100
UID:0 PID:4045 COM:bash ]#exit

The log */var/log/secure* at the honeypot also shows these events, except for the connection to the backdoor.

**Sources:** Walleye, Snort, honeywall IPTables, honeypot IPTables, honeywall */var/log/ sebek_commands*, honeypot */var/log/secure*.

## Other Evidences

After the attack on the honeypot, some files have been found modified. The Tripwire file database that stores the snapshot of the filesystem has been corrupted, probably by the action of rootkit. At this point, you cannot make the comparison of the filesystem before the attack. Therefore, Tripwire functionality has not been useful in the analysis of the honeypot in this case.

## Conclusions of the Analysis

The use of appropriate tools has allowed us to reconstruct the intrusion with a high degree of certainty.

Honeywall Roo has shown the large amount of information it is able to gather from the network in an almost transparent way. A honeypot forensic analysis would provide even more information to that already obtained.

## CONCLUSION

This chapter has presented a review and a case of study of honeynets: a countermeasure to an ever increasing problem as the proliferation of malware and network attacks. Honeynets allow to collect malware samples and attack vectors for later study with the ultimate goal of developing protection techniques.

We have analyzed some of the most relevant available honeypots, putting them through a series of tests that expose both the weaknesses and strengths of each one. It was shown that honeypots are very powerful tools that allow us to study and analyze the types of malware and attacks and, what's more, they also serve as early warning systems against security incidents and first line of defense against attacks.

For the case of study, we have implemented a self-contained virtual honeynet along with a high interaction honeypot. An intrusion test was performed, emulating the behavior of a malicious attacker. Later on, the data collected by our honeynet allowed us to perform an analysis of the attack and thus a reconstruction of it. We would like to add that the honeynet allows to obtain information that would not have been possible otherwise.

On the other hand, the same experiment showed that there is still a long way to go in developing realistic honeypots and honeynets.

## FUTURE RESEARCH DIRECTIONS

The area of application of honeypots and honeynets must evolve to adapt to the latest technology if attackers are to be deceived. Some improvements and proposals are listed below.

- Creation of honeypots oriented to mobile telephone systems and tablets, giving special attention on the most popular operating systems: Android, iOS and Windows Phone.

- Improvements and new honeypots designed to SCADA (Supervisory Control And Data Acquisition) systems.
- Traditional systems of IDS/IPS are becoming obsolete because they work with databases of signatures, which represent a bottleneck. There is a need for further research on new intrusion detection systems.
- The most advanced malware verifies whether the attacked system is running on a virtualized environment. If that is the case, it suspends its activities. Virtualization tools should be improved in that direction for use in honeypots.
- The development of a honeypot, mirror of a production system, that were able to make decisions and propose changes in production systems based in the detected intrusions.
- The development of a new honeywall distribution is a pending issue, since the current version is not updated or maintained.
- The development of a self-contained appliance that contains the tools needed to act as a honeywall.

## ACKNOWLEDGMENT

This work was partially funded by the Spanish Ministry of Economy and Competitiveness (TIN2012-37843).

## REFERENCES

Abbasi, F. H., & Harris, R. J. (2009, November). Experiences with a Generation III virtual Honeynet. In *Proceedings of Telecommunication Networks and Applications Conference (ATNAC), 2009 Australasian* (pp. 1-6). IEEE.

Almutairi, A., Parish, D., & Phan, R. (2012). Survey of high interaction honeypot tools: Merits and shortcomings. In *Proceedings of the 13th Annual PostGraduate Symposium on The Convergence of Telecommunications, Networking and Broadcasting, PGNet2012*. PGNet.

Asrigo, K., Litty, L., & Lie, D. (2006). Using VMM-based sensors to monitor honeypots. In *Proceedings of the 2nd International Conference on Virtual Execution Environments (VEE'06)* (pp. 13-23). New York: ACM. doi:10.1145/1134760.1134765

Atkins, T. (n.d.). *Swatch: Simple watcher man page*. Retrieved 2013, from http://linux.die.net/man/1/swatch

Curran, K., Morrissey, C., Fagan, C., Murphy, C., O'Donnell, B., Fitzpatrick, G., & Condit, S. (2005, March). Monitoring hacker activity with a Honeynet. *International Journal of Network Management, 15*(2), 123-134. doi: 10.1002/nem.549.

CVE. (2010). *SystemTap CVE-2010-4170*. Retrieved 2013, from http://cve.mitre.org/cgi-bin/cvename.cgi?name=CVE-2010-4170

CVE Details. (2012). *MySQL 5.0.51a Security Vulnerabilities*. Retrieves 2013, from http://www.cvedetails.com/

Dionaea. (2010). *GnuplotSQL*. Retrieved 2013, from http://carnivore.it/2010/09/19/gnuplotsql

Dittrich, D. (2004). *Creating and managing distributed honeynets using honeywalls. Draft*. University of Washington.

Egele, M., Scholte, T., Kirda, E., & Kruegel, C. (2012). *A survey on automated dynamic malware-analysis techniques and tools. ACM Computing Surveys, 44(2), 6*.

ENISA. (2012, November). *Proactive detection of security incidents: Honeypots study*. Report. CERT Polska (NASK) & ENISA.

Fielding, R. (1999). *RFC2616 Hypertext Transfer Protocol*. Retrieved 2013, from http://tools.ietf.org/html/rfc2616

Fontani, M. (2011). *Kippo-stats*. Retrieved 2013, from https://github.com/mfontani/kippo-stats

Gibbens, M., & Harsha, R. (2012). Honeypots. In *Proceedings of the CSc 466-566 Computer Security 2012*. University of Arizona. Retrieved from http://www.cs.arizona.edu/~collberg/Teaching/466-566/2012/Resources/

Hable, K. (2003). *HoneyView*. Retrieved 2013, from http://honeyview.sourceforge.net/

Haile, J. (n.d.). *Snort-Inline*. Retrieved 2013, from http://snort-inline.sourceforge.net/oldhome.html

Henrique, L. (2004). Honeydsum. Honeyd Tools. Retrieved 2013, from http://www.honeyd.org/tools.php

Hubbard, D. (2013). *FSEdit*. Retrieved 2013, from http://pastebin.com/SwhvR8xM

Jones, J., & Rommney, G. (2004). Honeynets: An educational resource for IT security. In *Proceedings of the 5th Conference on Information Technology Education (CITC5 '04)* (pp. 24-28). New York: ACM. Doi: doi:10.1145/1029533.1029540

Joshi, R. C., & Sardana, A. (2011). *Honeypots: A new paradigm to information security*. Science Publishers.

Kirkland. (2010). Farpd - ARP reply daemon. *Ubuntu Manuals*. Retrieved 2013, from http://manpages.ubuntu.com/manpages/dapper/man8/farpd.8.html

Koniaris, I. (2013). *Kippo-Graph*. Retrieved 2013, from http://sourceforge.net/projects/kippo-graph/

Kreibich, C. (2009). *Honeycomb - Automated signature creation using honeypots*. Retrieved 2013, from http://www.icir.org/christian/honeycomb/

Kumar, S., Singh, P., Sehgal, R., & Bhatia, J. S. (2012). Distributed Honeynet System Using Gen III Virtual Honeynet. *International Journal of Computer Theory & Engineering, 4*(4), 537. doi: 10.7763/IJCTE.2012.V4.527

Levine, J., LaBella, R., Owen, H., Contis, D., & Culver, B. (2003). The use of Honeynets to detect exploited systems across large enterprise networks. In Proceedings of the Systems Information Assurance Workshop. In *Proceedings of IEEE Systems, Man and Cybernetics Society 2003* (pp. 92-99). IEEE. Doi: doi:10.1109/SMCSIA.2003.1232406

Ligh, M., Adair, S., Hartstein, B., & Richard, M. (2010). *Malware Analyst's Cookbook and DVD: Tools and Techniques for Fighting Malicious Code*. Wiley Publishing.

Mairh, A., Barik, D., Verma, K., & Jena, D. (2011). Honeypot in network security: A survey. In *Proceedings of the 2011 International Conference on Communication, Computing & Security (ICCCS '11)* (pp. 600-605). New York: ACM. Doi: doi:10.1145/1947940.1948065

MikiSoft. (2011). *MySQL Injection - Simple Load File and Into OutFile*. Retrieved 2013, from http://www.exploit-db.com/papers/14635/

Mills, D. (1992). *RFC 5905 network time protocol*. Retrieved 2013, from http://tools.ietf.org/html/rfc5905

Mokube, I., & Adams, M. (2007). Honeypots: Concepts, approaches, and challenges. In *Proceedings of the 45th Annual Southeast Regional Conference (ACM-SE 45)* (pp. 321-326). New York: ACM. Doi: doi:10.1145/1233341.1233399

Oktavianto, D., & Muhardianto, I. (2013). *Cuckoo Malware Analysis*. Packt Publishing Ltd.

Pale, P. C. (2012). *Nmap 6: Network Exploration and Security Auditing Cookbook*. Packt Publishing.

Peslyak, A. (2013). *John The Ripper*. Retrieved 2013, from http://www.openwall.com/john/

Pritchett, W. L., & De Smet, D. (2013). *Kali Linux Cookbook*. Packt Publishing Ltd.

Provos, N. (2003). *Honeyd Sample Configurations*. Retrieved 2013, from http://www.honeyd.org/configuration.php

Provos, N. (2008). *Developments of the Honeyd Virtual Honeypot*. Retrieved 2013, from http://www.honeyd.org/

Proyect OpenBSD. (2004). *OpenSSH*. Retrieved 2013, from http://www.openssh.com

Rammidi, G. (2008). *Survey on Current Honeynet Research*. Retrieved 2013, from http://honeynet-project.ca/files/survey.pdf

Rapid7. (2013). *Metasploit Penetration Testing Software*. Retrieved 2013, from http://www.metasploit.com/

Riden, J. (2008a). Client-Side Attack. The Honeynet Project. Retrieved from http://www.honeynet.org/node/157

Riden, J. (2008b). Server Honeypots vs Client Honeypots. The Honeynet Project. Retrieved from http://www.honeynet.org/node/157

RootingPuntoEs. (2013). *DionaeaFR*. Retrieved 2013, from https://github.com/RootingPuntoEs/DionaeaFR

Sadasivam, K., Samudrala, B., & Yang, T. (2005, April). Design of network security projects using honeypots. *Journal of Computing in Small Colleges, 20*(4), 282–293.

Sebek Project. (2008). *Sebek*. Retrieved 2013, from https://projects.honeynet.org/sebek

Song, J., Takakura, H., Okabe, Y., Eto, M., In-oue, D., & Nakao, K. (2011). Statistical analysis of honeypot data and building of Kyoto 2006+ dataset for NIDS evaluation. In *Proceedings of the First Workshop on Building Analysis Datasets and Gathering Experience Returns for Security (BADGERS '11)* (pp. 29-36). New York: ACM. Doi: doi:10.1145/1978672.1978676

Spitzner, L. (2002). *Honeypots: Tracking Hackers*. Addison-Wesley Longman Publishing Co., Inc.

SURFcert IDS. (2013). *SURFcert IDS*. Retrieved 2013, from http://ids.surfnet.nl/

SystemTap. (n.d.). *SystemTap*. Retrieved 2013, from https://sourceware.org/systemtap/index.html

Tamminen, U. (2013). *Kippo SSH Honeypot*. Retrieved 2013, from https://code.google.com/p/kippo/

Team, S. (2013). *Snort Users Manual*. Retrieved from http://www.snort.org/docs

The Honeynet Project. (2002). *Know Your Enemy*. Boston: Addison-Wesley.

The Honeynet Project. (2004). Know Your Enemy, Second Edition: Learning about Security Threats. Addison Wesley.

The Honeynet Project. (2005). *Honeywall Roo*. Retrieved 2013, from https://projects.honeynet.org/honeywall/

The Honeynet Project. (2007). *Sebek Issue*. Retrieved 2013, from http://old.honeynet.org/tools/cdrom/roo/manual/12-knownissues.html

The Honeynet Project. (n.d.). *Dionaea - Catches bugs*. Retrieved 2013, from http://dionaea.carnivore.it/

Tiwari, R., & Jain, A. (2012). Improving network security and design using honeypots. In *Proceedings of the CUBE International Information Technology Conference (CUBE '12)* (pp. 847-852). New York: ACM. Doi: doi:10.1145/2381716.2381875

Tripwire, Inc. (2013). *Tripwire*. Retrieved 2013, from http://sourceforge.net/projects/tripwire/

*United States vs. Ivanov*. (2005). Retrieved from http://www.crime-research.org/articles/hacker0405/

Valli, C. (2003). *Honeyd-A OS Fingerprinting Artifice*. Retrieved 2013, from http://ro.ecu.edu.au/ecuworks/3485/

VMware, Inc. (2013). *Configuring a Virtual Network*. Retrieved 2013, from http://www.vmware.com/support/ws55/doc/ws_net.html

VMware, Inc. (2013). *VMware Virtualization for Desktop & Server, Application, Public & Hybrid Clouds*. Retrieved 2013, from http://www.vmware.com/

Watson, D. (2007). GDH – Global Distributed Honeynet. In *Proceeding of the PacSec 2007 Conference*. Retrieved 2013, from http://www.ukhoneynet.org/PacSec07_David_Watson_Global_Distributed_Honeynet.pdf

XMPP Standards Foundation. (2013). *XMPP*. Retrieved 2013, from http://xmpp.org/

Zalewski, M. (2012). *P0fv3*. Retrieved 2013, from http://lcamtuf.coredump.cx/p0f3/

## KEY TERMS AND DEFINITIONS

**Botnet:** Network composed of infected hosts remotely controlled by an attacker.

**Exploit:** Piece of software that takes advantage of a security vulnerability with the intention of obtaining a behaviour undesired by the legitimate user. Exploits are not malicious code themselves: they are usually used as a first step for other purposes like non-authorized access or malware propagation.

**Intrusion Detection System (IDS):** Piece of software used for non-authorized access detection on computers or networks. These systems usually have virtual sensors (such as network sniffers) that help obtaining external data (normally about network traffic) and thus detecting anomalies arising from attacks.

**Malware:** Kind of software intended for host intrusion and/or damage. The term covers hostile, intrusive and rogue software such as viruses, worms, trojans, most rootkits, scareware, spyware, crimeware and other malicious software.

**Phishing:** Kind of cybercrime committed through social engineering with the intention of obtaining confidential information like passwords or PINs.

**Spam:** Unsolicited or unwanted emails, from an unknown sender, usually of a commercial kind and massively sent.

**Zombie:** Infected computers that can be used by a third party in order to carry out hostile actions against a victim. This use of the computer is made without the knowledge or authorization of the computer's real owner. Once infected, the computer becomes part of a botnet.

# Chapter 30
# Analysis of the Cybercrime with Spatial Econometrics in the European Union Countries

Vítor João Pereira Domingues Martinho
*Polytechnic Institute of Viseu, Portugal*

## ABSTRACT

*The main objective of this chapter is to analyze the crimes related to the new information technologies in the European Union using the data provided by the European Commission and the spatial econometrics approaches. The data were analyzed with several tests, namely the Moran´s I, to verify the existence of global (for all countries of the European Union) and local spatial autocorrelation. The presence of spatial autocorrelation in the data means that the variable analyzed in a determined country is auto correlated with the same variable in the neighboring countries. The data analysis was complemented with some cross-section estimations, considering namely the Lagrange Multiplier tests, to examine the spatial lag and the spatial error autocorrelation. The spatial autocorrelation is a statistical infraction, so the consideration of these subjects prevents result bias and on the other hand allows some conclusions important to help in the definition of adjusted policies.*

## INTRODUCTION

In our days the use of the electronic equipments and of the new technologies of information and communication increased enormously. These technologic improvements was good for our daily life, with new opportunities for economic advances and better development, as well social interactions, cultural exchanges, political evolution and others dynamics in another fields. In this context the internet appearance created a new world of challenges for everybody in every

country. But, unfortunately, not everyone uses the new opportunities in the right way and today we have a lot of problems in the internet world, with some practices that cause many intentional damages for some people and/or organizations and in this framework we talk about the cybercrime.

The cybercrime appear associated namely with the emails fraudulent, racist message in the internet (blogs, online personal homepages, etc), online personal identity theft, critical information theft and/or destruction and financial transactions interference. This is a big problem because many

DOI: 10.4018/978-1-4666-6324-4.ch030

times and many people see their personal or organizational daily live affected with great prejudice and damage costs in their image and budget. In this way is urgent to develop a rigorous system of rules and laws, with adjusted number of institutions associated, to punish adequately the offenders.

Many countries, namely the United States of America and the European Union, developed a significant framework of rules and laws, as well new institutions to work in net, to prevent and avoid the cybercrime in the related countries. The preoccupation of the European Union, for example, is to create a network of cooperation among the different member states, try overcoming the problems that can emerge from the national boundaries and the related problems of the national jurisdiction. The European Union in the last decade defined a relevant number of rules with heavy prison sentences, namely for the offenders of the critical information system.

In this line this work presented here is an innovative research because analyze the cybercrime in an economic perspective and using spatial econometric techniques. There are not, of our knowledge, works that analyze the cybercrime with spatial econometric tools. These techniques, in the present study, allow us to determinate if there are spatial autocorrelation, or in other words, possibilities to investigate if the cybercrime in each European Union country is auto correlated with the cybercrime in the neighbors countries. If there are spatial autocorrelation, this statistical infraction must be taken into account in the data analysis and in the econometric estimations, if not the conclusions are bias. On other hand the analysis of the spatial autocorrelation give us important information helpful, namely to the definition of new policies.

Considering the context defined before, in this work we present, beyond this introduction, a literature revision, a data analyze, some spatial econometric results, some recommendations and finally the conclusions. The universe of analyze was the formerly 27 European Union countries

through data of the year 2012, obtained in the Special Eurobarometer 390, because there are not many information about cybercrime, namely statistical information from official institutions.

## BACKGROUND

The cybercrime analyze needs a multidisciplinary approach, considering that involve many problematic from many subjects. For example, considering the Routine Activity Theory (RAT), Kigerl (2012), in 132 countries, found that the richer countries with more internet users have a tendency to develop more cybercrime actions. On other hand, the countries with more unemployment usually have more internet users and more illicit internet activities. Holt and Bossler (2008) considered also the Routine Activity Theory to analyze the cybercrime occurrences, using a model where the dependent variable is the incidence of on-line cybercrime and the independent variables are the type of computer, the computer utilization, the type of protection and demographic factors (age, gender, employment, etc). Some of the findings support the predicted by the theory. The unemployment among the young people is seen by Kraemer-Mbula et al. (2013), in the actual crisis context as a favorable environment to increase the financial cybercrime, namely in the emergent economies like the BRICS. The national context of each country, namely at security, social, economic, cultural and politic, appear to be determinant for the application of international policies, specifically those related with the legal frameworks (Calderoni, 2010). For developing countries, Kshetri (2013) identified some determinants for the cybercrime, namely those related with the political and economic institutions (corruption, government poorly equipped and weak law adjustment), culture or informal institutions (nationalism and more condescending about the cyber-attack), human capital (less skills and education) and technology (less appropriated technology and less R&D).

In the European Union, specifically, the cybercrime has been analyzed by authors as Mendez (2005), which comparing cybercrime policies between United States, Switzerland and European Union and Stephens and Induruwa (2007), that focusing in the questions related with the training and education needed to prevent and attack the cybercrime.

Recently, the European Union through the Directive 2013/40/EU tried to approach the criminal law of the different European Union countries in the context of the fight to prevent and attack the cybercrime, defining some regulations about the definition of the offenses and the respective punishments and promote the cooperation between the law enforcement institutions. This taking into account that a large cyber-attack in the institutions of the European Union can origins relevant consequences, namely at economic level, not only because the destruction of the information system, but also because the access at confidential information. This Directive predicts that the countries of the European Union define national laws which punish the offenses related with illegal system interference and with illegal data interference in a maximum of prison sentence of at least five years, when these crimes are promoted within a criminal organization context, cause significant damages and are against a fundamental information system.

The cybercrime is related with the old forms of crime (financial crimes, etc) developed through information networks and electronic communication systems (COM, 2007), with illegal practices using the electronic equipments (sexual abuses or racial attacks) and crimes against electronic information networks. The number of cyber crimes increase in the last years and more sophisticated. In fact, in the last two decades the internet had an enormous influence in the everyday life of the people (JOIN, 2013). Today the internet has impact in the social relations, in the business and in our main rights. The internet broken frontiers and promote the democracy in some situations.

Finishing the digital market the Europe could increase its gross domestic product in about 500 billions of euros per year and about 1000 euros per person. It is crucial that the citizens have confidence in the internet in order that the persons use the electronic equipments in their daily tasks.

Almost 80% of the young people have social interactions with the electronic equipments and about 8 trillions of dollars are changed every year in the internet (COM, 2012). In this context about 1 million of persons are everyday victim of the cybercrime and 388 billions of dollars are lost by the offended. Some reports consider these crimes more lucrative than some drugs trade.

The collection of information about the cybercrime in the European Union and change these data among the Member States is fundamental to combat this kind of crime. The definition of forms of cooperation, define new laws and policies and find new technologies to implement in the attack against the cybercrime is urgent (Council of the European Union, 2010).

Some statistics as the World Economic Forum indicate in 2008 which the probability of the crucial information systems collapse in the next years is about 20% and the associated costs about 250 billions of dollars (COM, 2009). Countries as the Estonia Lithuania and Georgia are example of recent severe cyber-attacks. Is important to define a strategy of prevention of the cybercrime in the European Union, adjusted mechanism of detection and response, improve the instruments to protect the crucial information systems, disseminate internationally the intention of the European Union and implementation of the European rules and the different laws defined and related with the cybercrime. The main actions against the cybercrime are prevention and patience.

The costs associated with the crash cars in the United States, in 2010, was estimated in about 99 to 168 billions of dollars, the maritime piracy, in 2005, represents around 0.02% of the total trade, the theft in the retail business is about 1,5% and

2% of the sales per year and the costs with the cybercrime can represent about 70 to 280 billions of dollars, but is not easy to estimate the real costs of the cybercrime, because the companies usually do not a real perception of the situation created with cyber-attacks (Mcafee, 2013). These costs with the cyber-offenses can represent about 508.000 jobs vanished.

Considering the Special Eurobarometer 390 (2012) 53% of the people in the European Union countries use the internet at least one time per day and only 29% say that never use the internet. It is a significant part of the population that utilizes daily the new technologies. The majority utilizes the internet from home, 39% from the work, 16% when are moving and 11% in the education institutions. This is an interesting finding, because in home the peoples maybe are more vulnerable, namely because often the persons do not have secure servers and antiviral systems, as in some institutions, specifically the medium and big organizations. About 53% buy products online, 52% use social interaction online sites, 48% do banking transactions and 20% sell products online. These statistics reflect a significant degree of confidence in the internet system from the European Union citizens. About 48% of the European people do financial transaction is a relevant indicator of trust in the electronic systems. This conclusion is confirmed when 69% of the persons say that are very confident in the internet. The main concerns when do banking payments are about the theft of the personal information and the weak security of the payments in the internet. A big majority say that have listened something about the cybercrime in the last year and hear this from the television. Most of the people think that they are not well informed about the cybercrime. A significant part of the population refers that receives spam e-mails and says that avoid transmit personal information online and that the risks of cybercrime increased in the last year. The great preoccupation of the citizens relatively the cybercrime is associated with the risk of viewing their personal identity theft. Between the European Union countries, the Sweden, Denmark and the Netherlands are more frequent internet users and are, also, well informed about the risks of the internet. In Portugal and Bulgaria the number of frequenters of the internet is lower and the persons consider that are little informed about the cybercrimes. In Portugal the main factors are related with cultural, social and economic causes, namely those related with the level of scholarship between the old people that are a significant part of the Portuguese society. This view about the citizen perceptions around the internet use and the cybercrime in the European Union countries is important to understand the European context and show that there are many to do in this field. The level of thrust in the electronic networks is not so bad, but reflects yet some fears about the internet use.

There are many forms of cyber-attack as the following: child sex criminals, romance scam offenders and persuasion of young people by radical groups (Rashid et al., 2013). Guarnieri and Przyswa (2013), in another perspective focused in the incidence of the cybercrime in the e-consumption.

There are, between others, four problems that avoid having realistic reports about the cybercrime: not interested to report (some firms think that to report can be bad to the business), past experiences (the firms that were victims of cybercrime are not so available to answer to surveys), insufficient mechanism for accounting and unobserved loses (Hyman, 2013).

The cybercrime investigation needs multi professional interactions and law enforcement agencies cooperation (Hunton, 2011 and 2012). Again, the international cooperation, between countries, law enforcement agencies and institutions related with the law definition and implementation, to fight and prevent the cybercrime is, also, argued by Cerezo et al. (2007).

The Online Policy Station is an Italian example in the combat of the cybercrime. Neri et al. (2009) concluded that this initiative, since the beginning, allowed the following results: more efficacies in the crime attack, more interaction of the citizens with the police and more cybercrime related.

The cybercrime was, also, a motive to reflection for Hancock (2000a, 2000b and 2000c), Schultz (2004a, 2004b, 2005a and 2005b), Anonymous (2006), Hilley (2005, 2006 and 2007), Furnell (2008) and Poier (2008). In reality, the cybercrime has increased in the last decade with the increase in the number of computer users and with the proliferation of the internet in many countries, for many purposes and in many types of equipment, not only in the computers, but also, in the mobile phones and in the tablets. Because this the cybercrime appear today in the bank transactions, in the social relationships and in the exchange of information. There are many actions developed by the different institutions to preserve the security of their customers. For example the banks develop more sophisticated software to preserve the financial transitions and other institutions develop more adjusted computer server.

The international jurisdictional conflicts among some countries can be a problem in the cybercrime prevention and attack and sometimes the cyber offenders can explore these contexts (Brenner, 2006).

The cybercrime attack many times exceed the national frontiers and this can be a problem, namely at the different laws existents in each country, because the cybercrime investigation frequently involve different countries (Brenner and Schwerha IV, 2004).

The news technologies enable new social dynamics and new crimes. These contexts, indeed, become necessary new instruments, new laws and adjusted and legal forms of punishment (Drucker and Gumpert, 2000). Sometimes the laws in each country are not adjusted to the cybercrime, or are adjusted to prosecute but not to criminalize the offenders. Brenner (2004) wrote that the federal laws in the United States are adjusted to prosecute the cybercrimes but the criminalization of the virtual infantile pornography is still difficult. These difficulties sometimes are because some questions of semantics like "real" and "virtual" crimes.

The collection of digital proofs is vital in the cybercrime investigation. Many problems in these contexts are related with the inadequate collection of digital evidences (Schwerha IV, 2004).

Some authors, as Hinde (2003), defend that the organizations must have a cybercrime risk supervision board, promote a culture and policies to manage the risks of the cyber-attacks and have a backup plan to deal with the cyber-offenders. This author argues that every organization should have a system to protect the information and confirms if the information protection systems are in accordance with the law. Sometimes the enterprises forgot the following aspects: have good firewalls, have good internet servers, not so good operating system and weak account management (Hinde, 2003). These questions are real for the organizations, but also, for the families and for the persons individually. It is, sometimes, easier for the organizations buy good protection systems than for some persons and families. Anyway, the protection against the cybercrime is not easy, because everyday appear news forms of offenses.

It is important to be alert in the internet and do not expect become rich in few time. On other hand, do not transitions or change information in the internet if you do not know sufficiently well the other person or organization (Philippsohn, 2001). Frequently the persons know some risks in the internet, but decide take those risks, because many factors, namely psychological, physical, cultural and others.

Often the public institutions only look for the cybercrime problems when there is a serious attack to the government internet servers. This reveals that many times the public institutions ignore the real threat of the cybercrime (Speer, 2000).

## MAIN FOCUS OF THE CHAPTER

This chapter focuses on an economic cybercrime research for the first 27 European Union analyzing information obtained, for 2012, from the Special Eurobarometer 390 and doing some spatial econometric estimations with the GeoDa software. This software analyzes and regress cross-sectional spatial statistical data, searching for spatial autocorrelation between the spatial unities, as countries, regions, etc (Anselin, 1988, 1995, 2001, 2002a, 2002b, 2002c, 2002d, 2003a, 2003b and 2004).

The GeoDa software is an important tool for the spatial analysis because is very simple to use is possible to do a free download from the GeoDa center. We cannot forget that the GeoDa analyzes spatial data, so considers data geo referenced, namely though the distances. Because this the GeoDa only read files geo referenced as the shape files that can be built with the ArcGis.

In terms of spatial data investigation the GeoDa allow studies for the global (for the all spatial unities considered, in our case for the all 27 European countries) and the local spatial autocorrelation (for each one spatial unities or in this work for each country) finding the value of Moran I statistics test, for the variable considered, namely the dependent variable. In the global analyze, if the Moran I is positive we have positive spatial autocorrelation, if is negative signify negative spatial autocorrelation and zero reflect no autocorrelation. For the local investigation, the Moran I can have statistical significance or not. If is significant we can find, also, spatial autocorrelation positive or negative It is positive if we find high-high (autocorrelation for high values, in other words there is spatial autocorrelation between values countries with high values for the variable considered) or low-low values. High-low or low-high values signify negative local spatial autocorrelation.

At the regression level are used, namely, the Lagrange Multiplier tests to investigate the spatial lag (when this component is confirmed by the respective Lagrange Multiplier test, this means that the spatial autocorrelation come from the depend variable of the neighbor countries lagged and weight with a matrix of distances built in our case with the GeoDa) and the spatial error components of the model (in this case the spatial autocorrelation come from the error term and the means that the influence from the neighbor countries is random and not identified).

## ISSUES, CONTROVERSIES, PROBLEMS

The cybercrime is indeed a real problem in nowadays that must be researched and analyzed. In this way in the present work were analyzed the answers to five questions carried out in a survey and published in the Special Eurobarometer 390. The questions considered are related with the following: identity theft (Q1); received emails fraudulently asking for money or personal details (Q2); online fraud where goods purchased were not delivered (Q3); accidentally encountering material which promotes racial or religious extremism (Q4); and not being able to access online services (Q5).

From the Table 1 and Figures 1 and 2 is possible to conclude that relatively to the questions Q1 the percentages of persons that answered affirmatively are biggest in the Romania, followed by the Hungary and the United Kingdom. The problems with the cybercrime in some countries are recurrent, despite the effort made by the law enforcement authorities.

The percentage of people relatively to the total (often more occasionally) that answered often is largest in the Bulgaria and in the Austria. The question 2 (Q2, received emails fraudulently asking for money or personal details) is where more people in the 27 European Union countries answered positively (38% often and occasionally). In this case the countries more affected are the Denmark and the Netherlands with 54% for both countries of positive answers. The weight of the often in

*Table 1. Percentage of persons, in the total often and occasionally, who in gave the answer "often"*

| | Identity Theft[1] | Received Emails Fraudulently Asking for Money or Personal Details[2] | Online Fraud Where Goods Purchased Were Not Delivered[3] | Accidentally Encountering Material which Promotes Racial or Religious Offense[4] | Not Being Able to Access Online Services[5] |
|---|---|---|---|---|---|
| | Weight of the Often in the Total (Often More Occasionally) | Weight of the Often in the Total (Often More Occasionally) | Weight of the Often in the Total (Often More Occasionally) | Weight of the Often in the Total (Often More Occasionally) | Weight of the Often in the Total (Often More Occasionally) |
| European Union (27) | 13 | 26 | 8 | 13 | 8 |
| Austria | 36 | 21 | 20 | 22 | 31 |
| Belgium | 10 | 31 | 8 | 15 | 8 |
| Bulgaria | 38 | 33 | 22 | 19 | 38 |
| Republic of Cyprus | 13 | 33 | 13 | 12 | 0 |
| Czech Republic | 20 | 11 | 8 | 5 | 17 |
| Germany | 0 | 17 | 8 | 8 | 9 |
| Denmark | 0 | 30 | 0 | 14 | 0 |
| Estonia | 14 | 20 | 9 | 14 | 8 |
| Greece | 33 | 22 | 0 | 22 | 25 |
| Spain | 13 | 19 | 14 | 21 | 10 |
| Finland | 0 | 19 | 13 | 9 | 6 |
| France | 0 | 28 | 9 | 13 | 0 |
| Hungary | 8 | 12 | 12 | 10 | 7 |
| Ireland | 10 | 30 | 8 | 17 | 15 |
| Italy | 20 | 27 | 15 | 13 | 13 |
| Lithuania | 0 | 18 | 10 | 13 | 9 |
| Luxembourg | 13 | 39 | 8 | 7 | 10 |
| Latvia | 0 | 25 | 0 | 21 | 0 |
| Malta | 0 | 30 | 13 | 17 | 17 |
| The Netherlands | 14 | 33 | 0 | 9 | 0 |
| Poland | 25 | 32 | 17 | 20 | 17 |
| Portugal | 20 | 25 | 20 | 22 | 15 |
| Romania | 31 | 26 | 29 | 15 | 17 |
| Sweden | 0 | 26 | 13 | 10 | 0 |
| Slovenia | 0 | 16 | 0 | 17 | 0 |
| Slovakia | 20 | 11 | 7 | 8 | 11 |
| United Kingdom | 8 | 40 | 6 | 17 | 7 |

Note: 1, 2, 3, 4 and 5 are the order of the five questions considered in this work.

the total is greatest in the United Kingdom. For the question Q3 is the Poland that presents the biggest percentages and is the Greece that shows the lowest values. The weight of the people that answer often is biggest for the Romania. For the Q4 is the Hungary and for the Q5 is the Finland,

*Figure 1. Percentage of persons who answered affirmatively, often and occasionally, to the five considered*

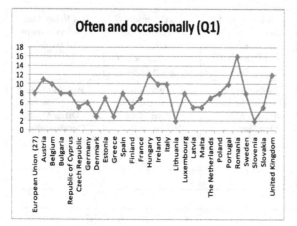

*Percentage of persons who answered affirmatively, often and occasionally, to the question 1 considered (Identity theft)*

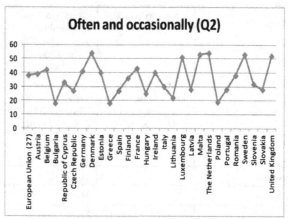

*Percentage of persons who answered affirmatively, often and occasionally, to the question 2 considered (Received emails fraudulently asking for money or personal details)*

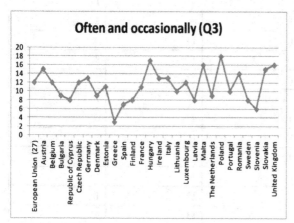

*Percentage of persons who answered affirmatively, often and occasionally, to the question 3 considered (Online fraud where goods purchased were not delivered)*

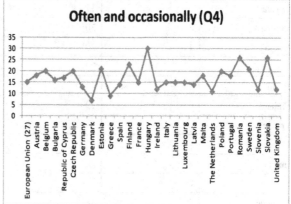

*Percentage of persons who answered affirmatively, often and occasionally, to the question 4 considered (Accidentally encountering material which promotes racial or religious offense)*

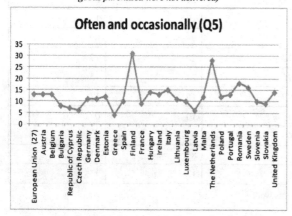

*Percentage of persons who answered affirmatively, often and occasionally, to the question 5 considered (Not being able to access online services)*

*Figure 2. Extreme values of the percentage of persons who answered affirmatively to each one of the five questions considered (often and occasionally)*

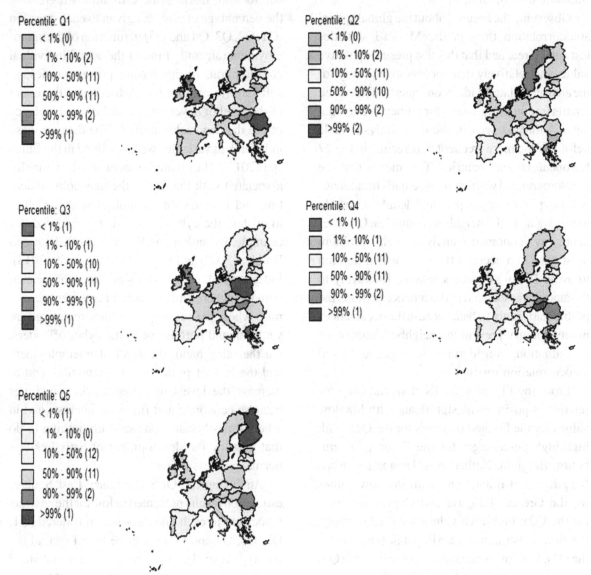

where the percentages for the answers often and occasionally are largest. From this data analysis is possible to conclude that the cybercrime is a problem that affects all the European Union countries, in different forms considering the differences in the answers for the several questions, but there are some countries with more problems than others. On the other hand there are some countries, as the Greece, where the cyber problems are relatively lower.

From here is important to understand that the reality of the cybercrime is not equal in all the countries of the European Union what imply policy to fight the cybercrime and the cyber-offenders adjusted to any situation and any context. This context cannot be forgot when it is tried to define standard general policies for every countries in a certain universe. Sometimes can to have the tentative to standardize the reality and the respective policies, rules and law, when the situation is not standard and not uniform.

Observing the Figure 3 about the global spatial autocorrelation through the Moran´I statistics test can be reached that this test presents positive value, and relatively more or less strong, only for the answers related with second question (received emails fraudulently asking for money or personal details) that, as seen in the data analysis made before, is the more frequent cybercrime in the 27 European Union countries. This means that the problems related with receiving emails fraudulently asking for money or personal details can easily to propagate to the neighbors countries. On other hand, any econometric analysis of this problem must take into account the statistical infraction to avoid finding bias conclusions. Relatively to the answers associated to the others questions the problematic is not so bad, because the occurrences in any country prevent the neighbor country for the situation, considering the negative spatial autocorrelation verified.

From the Figure 4 the local spatial autocorrelation is positive and significant with low-low values for the Finland (answers for the Q1), with high-high percentages for the France, Luxembourg, Belgium, Netherlands, Denmark, United Kingdom and Ireland and with low-low values for the Greece, Bulgaria and Cyprus (answers for the Q2), high-high values for the Germany, Belgium, Austria and Czech Republic (answers for the Q3), low-low percentages for the Ireland (Q4) and low-low for the Bulgaria (Q5). This analyze made for the local spatial autocorrelation confirms the problems of spatial propagation of the issues related with the second question, namely in the middle of the European Union. The good news is that the recent countries from the periphery of the European Union do not present significant local spatial autocorrelation, in a general term, what can be an interesting finding in terms of policies definition to prevent and combat the cybercrime dissemination in the Europe.

Considering the literature review presented before were made some estimations regressing the percentage of answers given to each question (Q1, Q2, Q3, Q4 and Q5) in function of the unemployment rate and of the of the actual individual consumption, in purchasing power parities, in software (to capture for each country the effect of the level of development and of the incidence of use the new technologies). The data for these independent variables were obtained in the Eurostat (2013). The unemployment and the variables associated with the use of the new communication and information technologies, as variables to explain the cybercrime, were considered, for example, by authors as Kigerl (2012), Holt and Bossler (2008) and Kraemer-Mbula et al. (2013). Indeed, the level of development is associated with the cybercrime, namely in emergent economies where the rules against the cybercrime are yet weak and permissive to the cyber-offenders. On the other hand, the level of unemployment and the lack of professional occupation tend to increase the levels of cyber-attack, sometimes because economic and financial interests and in others times because phases with nothing to do that potency the development of activities less normal and less correct.

Analyzing the OLS (Ordinary Last Square) estimation results presented below for the answers associated to each one question considered (Q1, Q2, Q3, Q4 and Q5) it can be found that all the coefficient of the constant term have statistical significance, sign of lack other variables. On the other hand, the coefficient related with the unemployment rate only presents statistical significance for answers of the second question and the coefficient associated with the actual individual consumption, in purchasing power parities, in software only for the answers of the question 4, precisely the models with R square adjusted with highest values (0.391 and 0.201, respectively). This means that receiving emails fraudulently asking for money or personal details is negatively

*Figure 3. Global spatial autocorrelation of the percentage of persons who answered affirmatively to each one of the five questions considered (often and occasionally)*

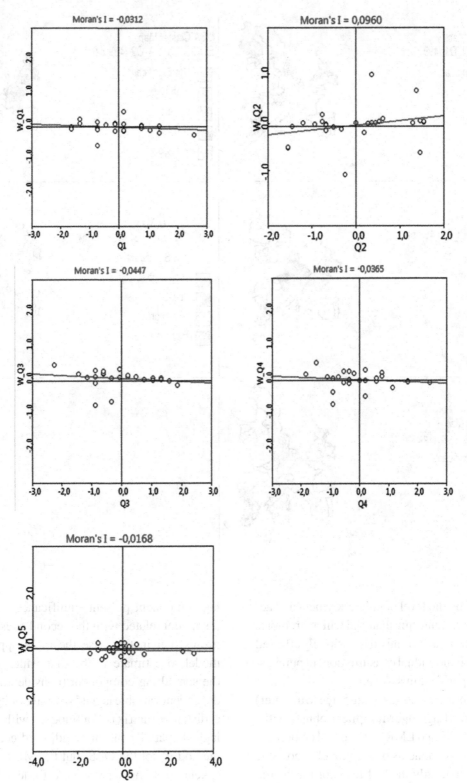

*Figure 4. Local spatial autocorrelation of the percentage of persons who answered affirmatively to each one of the five questions considered (often and occasionally)*

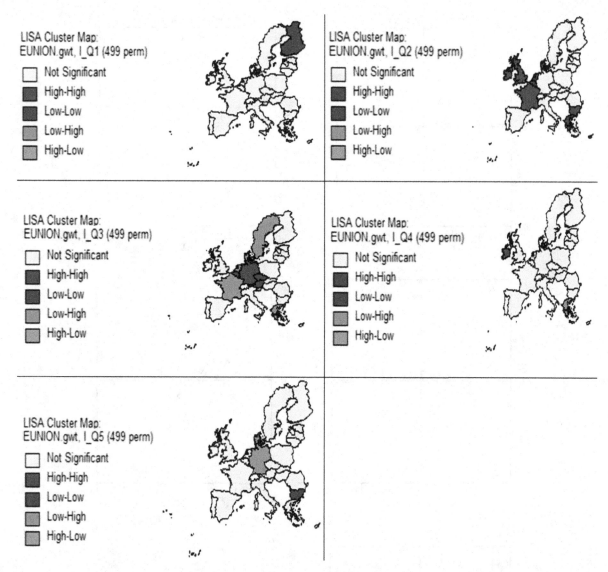

influenced by the level of unemployment and accidentally encountering material which promotes racial or religious extremism is positively affected by the actual individual consumption, in purchasing power parities, in software.

Observing the tests LM (Lagrange Multiplier) and the LMR (Lagrange Multiplier Robust) for the spatial lag ($LM_l$ and $LMR_l$) and spatial error ($LM_e$ and $LMR_e$) components of the model is possible to observe that only the LM tests for the spatial lag component present significance statistics in the model related with the second question. This means that in this case the more appropriated model to estimate is the that which considers the spatial lag component (consideration of the dependent variable lagged spatially weighted with a distance matrix). For models with variables lagged spatially the more adjusted econometric method is not the OLS, but the ML (Maximum Likehood) as presented in the Table 3. So, in the

*Table 2. OLS estimation results for the model considered*

| | Con. | Coef.1 | Coef.2 | JB | BP | KB | M'I | LM$_l$ | LMR$_l$ | LM$_e$ | LMR$_e$ | $\bar{R}^2$ |
|---|---|---|---|---|---|---|---|---|---|---|---|---|
| Q1 | 9,079* (4,807) | -0,210 (-1,044) | 0,017 (1,229) | 0,423 | 1,726 | 1,527 | 0,278 | 0,101 | 0,175 | 0,060 | 0,135 | 0,030 |
| Q2 | 56,925* (10,834) | -2,317* (-4,133) | -0,060 (-1,549) | 2,552 | 1,193 | 3,702 | 2,786* | 7,132* | 6,625* | 2,549 | 2,043 | 0,391 |
| Q3 | 10,892* (5,247) | 0,004 (0,017) | 0,025 (1,633) | 0,301 | 1,917 | 2,277 | -0,173 | 0,319 | 0,004 | 0,333 | 0,018 | 0,025 |
| Q4 | 14,411* (5,180) | 0,212 (0,713) | 0,059* (2,876) | 0,486 | 0,610 | 0,752 | -0,310 | 0,258 | 0,447 | 0,459 | 0,648 | 0,201 |
| Q5 | 16,238* (4,743) | -0,437 (-1,195) | 0,002 (0,074) | 23,185* | 1,978 | 0,699 | 0,576 | 0,008 | 0,150 | 0,001 | 0,143 | 0,022 |

Note: Con., coefficient of the constant; Coef.1, coefficient of the unemployment rate; Coef.2, coefficient of the actual individual consumption, in purchasing power parities, in software; Q1, Q2, Q3, Q4 and Q5, are the five questions considered; JB, test Jarque-Bera; BP, test Breusch-Pagan; KB, test Koenker-Bassett: M'I, Moran's I; LMl, test LM for the component spatial lag; LMRl, robust test LM for the component spatial lag; LMe, test LM for the component spatial error; LMRe, robust test LM for the component spatial error; *, statistically significant for 5%; **, statistically significant for 10%.

*Table 3. ML estimation results for the model considered with spatial effects*

| | Con. | Coef.1 | Coef.2 | Spatial coefficient | Breusch-Pagan | $\bar{R}^2$ |
|---|---|---|---|---|---|---|
| Q2 | 32,977* (4,289) | -2,478* (-5,329) | -0,062* (-1,940) | 0,701* (3,749) | 1,544 | 0,568 |

Note: *, statistically significant for 5%; **, statistically significant for 10%; ***, spatial coefficient for the spatial lag model.

table 3 is showed a new estimation results for the model related with the question 2, but in this case with the spatial effects (the spatial effects must be considered to avoid bias results). The results obtained demonstrate an improvement in the values found, because the coefficient of the constant term diminish, the value of the coefficient associated with the unemployment rate improve slightly, the value related with the software consumption presents now significance statistics and the R square adjusted improve significantly. Indeed, receiving emails fraudulently asking for money or personal details is the more problematic form of cybercrime in the European Union countries, considering the perceptions of the European citizens in survey carried out in 2012.

Relatively the tests to analyze the normality of the sample (Jarque-Bera) and the heteroscedasticity (Breusch-Pagan and Koenker-Bassett) show values that proof the stability of the models.

# SOLUTIONS AND RECOMMENDATIONS

Considering the perceptions of the European Union citizen, the more problematic cybercrime form, in 2012, is receiving emails fraudulently asking for money or personal details. On other hand, is in this form of cybercrime where the empirical analyze made before, with the people perceptions, found more spatial autocorrelation (global, local and spatial lag). This means that the potentiality of this kind of cyber-attack disseminate in the European Union countries cyber problems in its original form or in new variants is real and can be easy and fast.

In this perspective is important and urgent to define a new form of attack this form of cybercrime, developing new technologies in this field and define new policies and laws efficient that can prevent and punish effectively the respective offenders.

## FUTURE RESEARCH DIRECTIONS

To find statistical information for the cybercrime in the European Union countries is not easy and this conditions the studies about this form of crime. In future research is determinant find more statistical data for other variables and for more years. This will allow analyze others dimensions of this kind of offense and will enable analysis about the evolution of the perceptions of the European citizens over different periods and different economic and social frameworks. The internet coming to stay, but not everything is good, so will be important to do more research about these subjects to try understand better some constraints and design more adjusted policies taking into account the new realities that appear in these new contexts, sometimes not well expected by everybody.

## CONCLUSION

The cybercrime is a problematic issue in many countries and namely in the European Union. In fact, the new communication and information technologies improve the quality of life of the people, considering that allow new economic dynamics, new social interactions and other improvements, but created also new problems and conflicts. The several forms of cyber-attacks referred before can origin many perturbations in the daily life of the citizens, with real damages at personal and professional levels, and serious problems related with security of countries when critical information is used by the cyber-offenders. The combat to the cyber-offenses is not easy and appeal many times to international cooperation among countries, because problems of national jurisdictions, and law enforcement agencies. This international cooperation request, also, to some standardization in the definition of the rules and laws against the cybercrime and in the forms of punishment.

In the European Union the more problematic kind of cyber-attack is related with receiving emails fraudulently asking for money or personal details, this considering the answers of the European to a survey carried out by a request of the European Union institutions. On the other, considering the empirical analysis made before, this kind of cybercrime is associated with some real autocorrelation effects between some countries of the European Union. This is a problem and can become a more serious problem in the future, because the cyber-attacks can develop new variants and new forms of this form of cybercrime and disseminate quickly these offenses across the several European countries. In this way, these context request to new equipments and new technologies to prevent and fight the kind of offenses and on the other hand is crucial and urgent find new rules and laws to dissuade efficiently this attacks.

With more information, namely statistical information, will be important to do other analysis, namely with more variables, for other years and with another econometric techniques, for example with panel data that allow captures dynamic effect with growth rate variables.

In conclusion, this is more one original contribution to the study of the problematic cybercrime and is an innovative research, because, in our knowledge, there is not any works about these issues, using the spatial econometric techniques.

## REFERENCES

Anonymous, . (2006). Security views. *Computers & Security*, 25, 238–246.

Anselin, L. (1988). *Spatial Econometrics: Methods and Models*. Dordrecht, Netherlands: Kluwer Academic Publishers. doi:10.1007/978-94-015-7799-1

Anselin, L. (1995). Local Indicators of Spatial Association-LISA. *Geographical Analysis*, *27*, 93–115. doi:10.1111/j.1538-4632.1995. tb00338.x

Anselin, L. (2001). Spatial Econometrics. In A Companion to Theoretical Econometrics. Oxford, UK: Basil Blackwell.

Anselin, L. (2002a). *Spatial Externalities* (Working Paper). Sal, Agecon, Uiuc.

Anselin, L. (2002b). *Properties of tests for spatial error components* (Working Paper). Sal, Agecon, Uiuc.

Anselin, L. (2002c). *Spatial externalities, spatial multipliers and spatial econometrics* (Working Paper). Sal, Agecon, Uiuc.

Anselin, L. (2002d). *Under the hood: Issues in the specification and interpretation of spatial regression models* (Working Paper). Sal, Agecon, Uiuc.

Anselin, L. (2003a). *An introduction to spatial autocorrelation analysis with GeoDa*. Sal, Agecon, Uiuc.

Anselin, L. (2003b). *GeoDa™ 0.9 User's Guide*. Sal, Agecon, Uiuc.

Anselin, L. (2004). *GeoDa™ 0.9.5-i Release Notes*. Sal, Agecon, Uiuc.

Brenner, S. W. (2004). U.S. cybercrime law: Defining offenses. *Information Systems Frontiers*, *6*(2), 115–132. doi:10.1023/ B:ISFI.0000025780.94350.79

Brenner, S. W. (2007). Cybercrime jurisdiction. *Crime, Law, and Social Change*, *46*, 189–206. doi:10.1007/s10611-007-9063-7

Brenner, S. W., & Schwerha, J. J. IV. (2004). Introduction—Cybercrime: A note on international issues. *Information Systems Frontiers*, *6*(2), 111–114. doi:10.1023/B:ISFI.0000025779.42497.30

Calderoni, F. (2010). The European legal framework on cybercrime: striving for an effective implementation. *Crime, Law, and Social Change*, *54*, 339–357. doi:10.1007/s10611-010-9261-6

Cerezo, A. I., Lopez, J., & Patel, A. (2007). International cooperation to fight transnational cybercrime. In *Proceedings of Second International Workshop on Digital Forensics and Incident Analysis* (WDFIA 2007). IEEE Computer Society.

COM. (2007). *Communication from the commission to the European Parliament, the council and the committee of the regions: Towards a general policy on the fight against cyber crime*. Brussels: Commission of the European Communities.

COM. (2009). *Communication from the commission to the European Parliament, the council, the European economic and social committee and the committee of the regions: On critical information infrastructure protection: Protecting Europe from large scale cyber-attacks and disruptions: enhancing preparedness, security and resilience*. Brussels: Commission of the European Communities.

COM. (2012). Communication from the commission to the council and the European Parliament: Tackling crime in our digital age: Establishing a European cybercrime centre. Brussels: European Commission.

Council of the European Union. (2010). *Council conclusions concerning an Action Plan to implement the concerted strategy to combat cybercrime*. Paper presented at the 3010th General Affairs Council Meeting. Luxembourg.

Drucker, S. J., & Gumpert, G. (2000). Cybercrime and punishment. *Critical Studies in Media Communication*, *17*(2), 133–158. doi:10.1080/15295030009388387

Eurostat. (2013). *Several statistics*. Statistics of the European Union.

Furnell, S. (2008). Book reviews: Cybercrime: The transformation of crime in the information age – by D.S. Wall. *The British Journal of Sociology*, 177–179.http://onlinelibrary.wiley.com/doi/10.1111/bjos.2007.59.issue-1/issuetoc doi:10.1111/j.1468-4446.2007.00187_8.x

GeoDa. (2013). Spatial econometric software. GeoDa Center for Geospatial Analysis and Computation.

Guarnieri, F., & Przyswa, E. (2013). Counterfeiting and Cybercrime: Stakes and Challenges. *The Information Society: An International Journal*, *29*(4), 219–226. doi:10.1080/01972243.2013.792303

Hancock, B. (2000a). US and Europe Cybercrime Agreement Problems. *Computers & Security*, *19*(4), 306–307. doi:10.1016/S0167-4048(00)04012-8

Hancock, B. (2000b). G8 Thinks About Cybercrime (It's About Time, Too). *Computers & Security*, *19*(5), 405–407. doi:10.1016/S0167-4048(00)05026-4

Hancock, B. (2000c). Canadian Teen Mafiaboy Pleads Guilty. *Computers & Security*, *19*(8), 669.

Hilley, S. (2005). News. *Digital Investigation*, 2, 171–174.

Hilley, S. (2006). News. *Digital Investigation*, *3*, 187–189. doi:10.1016/j.diin.2006.10.011

Hilley, S. (2007). US cybercrime statistics: FBI hotline gets more than 200,000 complaints. *Digital Investigation*, *4*, 54–55. doi:10.1016/j.diin.2007.04.003

Hinde, S. (2003). The law, cybercrime, risk assessment and cyber protection. *Computers & Security*, *22*(2), 90–95. doi:10.1016/S0167-4048(03)00203-7

Holt, T. J., & Bossler, A. M. (2008). Examining the Applicability of Lifestyle-Routine Activities Theory for Cybercrime Victimization. *Deviant Behavior*, *30*(1), 1–25. doi:10.1080/01639620701876577

Hunton, P. (2011). A rigorous approach to formalising the technical investigation stages of cybercrime and criminality within a UK law enforcement environment. *Digital Investigation*, *7*, 105–113. doi:10.1016/j.diin.2011.01.002

Hunton, P. (2012). Managing the technical resource capability of cybercrime investigation: a UK law enforcement perspective. *Public Money & Management*, *32*(3), 225–232. doi:10.1080/09540962.2012.676281

Hyman, P. (2013). Cybercrime: It's Serious, But Exactly How Serious? *Communications of the ACM*, *56*(3), 18–20. doi:10.1145/2428556.2428563

JOIN. (2013). *Joint communication to the European parliament, the council, the European economic and social committee and the committee of the regions: Cybersecurity strategy of the European Union: An open, safe and secure cyberspace.* Brussels: High Representative of the European Union for Foreign Affairs and Security Policy.

Kigerl, A. (2012). Routine Activity Theory and the Determinants of High Cybercrime Countries. *Social Science Computer Review*, *30*(4), 470–486. doi:10.1177/0894439311422689

Kraemer-Mbula, E., Tang, P., & Rush, H. (2013). The cybercrime ecosystem: Online innovation in the shadows? *Technological Forecasting and Social Change*, *80*, 541–555. doi:10.1016/j.techfore.2012.07.002

Kshetri, N. (2013). Cybercrime and cyber-security issues associated with China: some economic and institutional considerations. *Electronic Commerce Research*, *13*, 41–69. doi:10.1007/s10660-013-9105-4

Mcafee. (2013). *Report: The ECONOMIC impact of cybercrime and cyber espionage*. Center for Strategic and International Studies.

Mendez, F. (2005). The European Union and cybercrime: Insights from comparative federalism. *Journal of European Public Policy, 12*(3), 509–527. doi:10.1080/13501760500091737

Neri, F., Geraci, P., Sanna, G., & Lotti, L. (2009). Online police station, a state-of-the-art Italian semantic technology against cybercrime. *In Proceedings of International Conference on Advances in Social Network Analysis and Mining*. IEEE Computer Society.

Philippsohn, S. (2001). Trends in cybercrime - An overview of current financial crimes on the internet. *Computers & Security, 20*, 53–69. doi:10.1016/S0167-4048(01)01021-5

Poier, S. (2008). Questioning the "Crime" in Cybercrime. *The Information Society: An International Journal, 24*(4), 270–272. doi:10.1080/01972240802191670

Rashid, A., Baron, A., Rayson, P., May-Chahal, C., Greenwood, P., & Walkerdine, J. (2013). Who Am I? Analyzing Digital Personas in Cybercrime Investigations. *Computer, 46*(4), 54–61. doi:10.1109/MC.2013.68

Schultz, E. (2004a). Security views. *Computers & Security, 23*, 533–541. doi:10.1016/j.cose.2004.09.003

Schultz, E. (2004b). Security views. *Computers & Security, 23*, 267–274. doi:10.1016/j.cose.2004.05.001

Schultz, E. (2005a). Security views. *Computers & Security, 24*, 349–358. doi:10.1016/j.cose.2005.06.003

Schultz, E. (2005b). Security views. *Computers & Security, 24*, 427–436. doi:10.1016/j.cose.2005.07.007

Schwerha, J. J. IV. (2004). Cybercrime: Legal Standards Governing the Collection of Digital Evidence. *Information Systems Frontiers, 6*(2), 133–151. doi:10.1023/B:ISFI.0000025782.13582.87

Special Eurobarometer 390. (2012). *Report: Cyber Security*. Conducted by TNS Opinion & Social at the request of the European Commission, Directorate-General Home Affairs. Survey co-ordinated by the European Commission, Directorate-General for Communication (DG COMM "Research and Speechwriting" Unit).

Speer, D. L. (2000). Redefining borders: The challenges of cybercrime. *Crime, Law, and Social Change, 34*, 259–273. doi:10.1023/A:1008332132218

Stephens, P., & Induruwa, A. (2007). Cybercrime investigation training and specialist education for the European Union. In *Proceedings of Second International Workshop on Digital Forensics and Incident Analysis* (WDFIA 2007). IEEE Computer Society.

## KEY TERMS AND DEFINITIONS

**Cybercrime:** Kind of crime developed with the new technologies of communication and information.

**Econometric Techniques:** Application of the statistics rules to the social sciences theory.

**European Union:** Form of monetary integration between countries of the European Continent.

**GeoDa:** Software for geo referenced files.

**Shape Files:** Files geo referenced built for example with the ArcGis software.

**Spatial Autocorrelation:** Correlation in some variables between different spatial unities (countries, regions, etc.).

**Special Eurobarometer 390:** Survey carried out to understand the perceptions of the European Union citizens about the cybercrime.

# Chapter 31
# Cyber Security Model of Artificial Social System Man–Machine

**Calin Ciufudean**
*Stefan cel Mare University, Romania*

## ABSTRACT

*Cyber Security Model of Artificial Social System Man-Machine takes advantage of an important chapter of artificial intelligence, discrete event systems applied for modelling and simulation of control, logistic supply, chart positioning, and optimum trajectory planning of artificial social systems. "An artificial social system is a set of restrictions on agents` behaviours in a multi-agent environment. Its role is to allow agents to coexist in a shared environment and pursue their respective goals in the presence of other agents" (Moses & Tennenholtz, n.d.). Despite conventional approaches, Cyber Security Model of Artificial Social System Man-Machine is not guided by rigid control algorithms but by flexible, event-adaptable ones that makes them more lively and available. All these allow a new design of artificial social systems dotted with intelligence, autonomous decision-making capabilities, and self-diagnosing properties. Heuristics techniques, data mining planning activities, scheduling algorithms, automatic data identification, processing, and control represent as many trumps for these new systems analyzing formalism. The authors challenge these frameworks to model and simulate the interaction of man-machine in order to have a better look at the human, social, and organizational privacy and information protection.*

## INTRODUCTION

We introduce an interdisciplinary framework for investigation technologies and cyber security development stage of the social networks and to anticipate theirs future evolution in respect to technological and environmental changes by proposing a new model for Artificial Social System

(ASoS) behavior. ASoS exist in practically every multi-agent system, and play a major role in the performance and effectiveness of the agents. This is the reason why we introduce a more suggestive model for ASoS. To model these systems, a class of Petri nets is adopted and briefly introduced in the paper. This class allows representing the flow of physical resources and control information data

DOI: 10.4018/978-1-4666-6324-4.ch031

of the ASoS's components. Functional abstractions of the Petri net model also verify the interconnections of interfaces primary components.

In order to model clearly the synchronization involved in these systems, a Petri net model is used. We focus on the performance evaluation of a strongly connected event graph with random firing times. We have an upper bound and a lower bound for the average cycle time of event graphs knowing the initial marking. We propose an algorithm to evaluate the bounds used to calculate an average cycle time and one algorithm to evaluate the performance of the ASoS models.

An Artificial Social System (ASoS) is a set of restrictions on agent's behaviour in a multi-agent environment (Zakarian & Kusiak, 1997). ASoS allows agents to coexist in a shared environment and pursue their respective goals in the presence of other agents. A multi-agent system consists of several agents, where at given point, each agent is in one of several states. In each of its states, an agent can perform several actions. The actions an agent performs at a given point may affect the way the state of this agent and the state of other agents will change. A system of dependent automata consists of two or more agents, each of which may be in one of a finite number of different local states. We denote the set of local states of an agent $i$ by $P_i$. The set $(P_1, P_2, ..., P_n)$ of states of the different agents is called system's configuration. The set of possible actions an agent $i$ can perform is a function of the local state. For every state $p \in P_i$ there is a set $A_i(p)$ of actions that $i$ can perform when in local state p. The row actions $(a_1, ..., a_n)$ denote the actions the different agents perform at a given point and is called their joint action there. An agent's next state is a function of the system's current configuration and the joint action performed by the agents. A goal for an agent is identified with one of its states. That is the reason why an agent has plans how to attain its goal. A plan for agent $i$ in a dependent automata is a function U(p) that associates with every state p of agent i a particular action $a \in$ $A_i(p)$. A plan (Molloy, 1992), (Schultz et al., 2006) is said to guarantee the attainment of a particular goal starting from a particular initial state. A dependent automata system is said to be social if, for every initial state $p_0$ and goal state $p_g$, it is computationally feasible for an agent to devise, on-line, an efficient plan that guarantees to attain the goal $p_g$ state when starting in the initial state $p_0$. For a proper behavior, a dependent automata system is modelled with a social law. Formally, a social law Q for a given dependent automata system consists of functions ($A_1'$, $A_2'$, ..., $A_n'$), satisfying $A_i'(p) \subset A_i(p)$ for every agent i and state $p \in P_i$. Intuitively, a social law will restrict the set of actions an agent is "allowed" to perform at any given state. Given a dependent automata system S and a social law Q for S, if we replace the functions $A_i$ of S by the restricted function $A_i'$, we obtain new dependent automata system. We denote this new system by $S^Q$. In $S^Q$ the agents can behave only in a manner compatible with the social law T. In controlling the actions, or strategies, available to an agent, the social law plays a dual role. By reducing the set of strategies available to a given agent, the social system may limit the number of goals the agent is able to attain. By restricting the behaviors of the other agents, however, the social system may make it possible for the agent to attain more goals and in some cases these goals will be attainable using more efficient plans than in the absence of the social system.

A semantic definition of artificial social systems gives us the ability to reason about such systems. For example, the manufacturer of the agents (e.g., robots) that are to function in the social system will need to reason about whether its creation will indeed be equipped with the hardware and the software necessary to follow the rules. As in these processes are involved many variables and one hardly finds a universal pattern to all possible situations, data basis (even huge ones) will provide only partial solutions. In this work we address a new approach based on artificial social systems modelled with timed Petri nets. In order to reason properly, we need a mathematical model and a description language. We chose the Petri nets model and a prepositional language.

Flexible systems include a set of manual operations and a set of automatic operations. A major consideration in designing a flexible system is its performance. When a machine or other component of the system fails, the system reconfiguration is often less than perfect. The notion of imperfection is called imperfect coverage, and it is defined as probability c that the system successfully reconfigures, when components break down (Schultz et al., 2006). We assume that when the repair of the fail component is completed, its performance isn't the same as of a new one. In this chapter a dependability model for evaluating the performance of a flexible system is presented. The meaning of dependability is:

- System availability;
- Dependence of the performance of flexible system on the performance of its subsystems and components;
- Dependence of designing the stochastic Petri nets model, Markov chains, and special automata over the (max, +) semi ring, which compute the height of heaps of pieces (respectively the throughput of the system).

Stochastic Petri nets (SPN) were developed by associating transitions/places with exponentially distributed random time delays (Guo et al., 1996). These methods are based on results obtained from the underlying Markov chain for such systems. Extended SPN were developed to allow generally distributed transitions delays in the case of non-concurrent transitions. For concurrent transitions, exponential distribution is required for exact solutions. The underlying models of these PN are semi-Markov processes. Heaps of pieces: Viennot observed that trace monoids are isomorphic to heap

monoids, that is monoids in which the generators are pieces (solid rectangular shaped blocks), and where the concatenation consists of piling up one heap above another (Viennot, 1986). This yields a very intuitive graphical representation of trace monoids. For us, a useful interpretation of a heap model consists of viewing pieces as tasks and slots as resources, where by slots we use the model given in (Gaubert & Mairese, 1999). This paper is organized as follows: section 2 presents the discrete event model we used in our work for an flexible manufacturing system (FMS), section 3 deals with the availability calculus of an FMS, including the interaction man-machine, section 4 illustrates the approach given in section 3, section 5 concludes the present work and establishes some future research directions.

## THE STOCHASTIC PETRI NET MODEL OF A FLEXIBLE MANUFACTURING SYSTEM

A SPN is a six-tuple (P, T, I, O, m, F), where:

$P = \{p_1, p2, ..., p_n\}$, n>0, is a finite set of places;

$T = \{t_1, t_2, ..., t_s\}$, s>0, is a finite set of transitions with $P \cup T \neq 0, P \cap T \neq \varnothing$;

I: P×T→N is an input function, where N = {0, 1, 2 ...}; O:P×T→N is an output function;

m: P→N is a marking whose $i^{th}$ component is the number of tokens in the $i^{th}$ place.

An initial marking is denoted by $m_0$; F: T→ R is a vector whose component is a firing time delay with an extended distribution function.

By extended distribution functions we mean that exponential distribution functions are allowed for concurrent transitions. Two transitions are said to be concurrent at marking m if and only if firing either does not disable the other. The firing rule for an SPN provides that when two or more transitions are enabled, the transitions whose associated time delays is statistically the minimum, fires. According to the transition-firing rule in PN, when a transition $t_k$ has only one input place $p_i$, and $p_i$ is marked with at least one token, $t_k$ is enabled. The enabled transition can fire. The firing of $t_k$ removes one token from the $p_i$ and then deposits one token into each output place $p_j$. Let $P(i,k)$ be a probability that transition $t_k$ can fire. The process from the enabling to the firing of $t_k$ requires a time delay, $\tau_k$. This delay $\tau_k$ of a transition can be either a constant or an extended random variable in SPN. $P(i,k)$ and $M(s)$ depend on $\tau_k$ as well as the current marking and the time delays of other enabled transitions at that marking. $M(s)$ denote the moment generating function, and is defined as follows (Gaubert & Mairese, 1999):

$$M\left(s\right) = \int_{-\infty}^{+\infty} e^{st} \cdot f\left(t\right) \cdot dt. \tag{1}$$

where s is an extended parameter, and f(t) is a probability density function of random variable t. Of course, we have:

$$M\left(0\right) = \int_{-\infty}^{+\infty} f\left(t\right) \cdot dt = 1. \tag{2}$$

A transfer function of a stochastic Petri net is defined as the product $P(i,k) \cdot M(s)$, and is:

$$W_k\left(s\right) = P\left(i,k\right) \cdot M\left(s\right). \tag{3}$$

Transition $t_k$ characterized by $P(i,k)$ and $\tau_k$ is expressed by a transition characterized by $W_k(s)$. Three fundamental structures can be reduced into a single transition. The reduction rules can be used to simplify some classes of PN. With these reduction rules we transform PN into finite state machines (in a finite state machine each transition has only one input and one output place, and there is one token in such a net). Figure 1 depicts these reduction rules (Ciufudean & Filote, 2009).

The moment generating functions for the state machine PN which models the flexible systems represent the availability of the cells (subsystems) which form the PN, and are computed with Markov chains models of the subsystems as shown in the following chapter.

## AVAILABILITY OF FLEXIBLE MANUFACTURING SYSTEMS

We defined above the notion of imperfect coverage, c. We will show the impact of imperfect coverage on the performance of the flexible system. We will demonstrate that system availability will be seriously diminished even if this imperfect coverage constitutes a small percentage of the multiple possible flaws of the system. This aspect is generally ignored or overlooked in the current managerial practice. The availability of a system is one probability that should be operational when needed. This availability can be calculated as the sum of all probabilities of operational states of the system. To calculate the availability of a system we need to determine the acceptable levels of functioning degree of the system's states. The availability of the system is considered acceptable when the production capacity of the system can be assured. Considering the big dimensions of a flexible system, the multiple interactions among its elements as well as between the system and the environment, in order to simplify the graphs and reduce the amount of calculus we will divide the system into two subsystems. These two subsystems are the following: equipment subsystem (the machine factor) and the human subsystem (the human factor in flexible activities). In its turn the equipment system is divided into cells. The Markov chain is built for each cell i, where i = 1, 2,..., n (n represents the number of cells

*Figure 1. Equivalent transfer functions for three basic structures of PN*

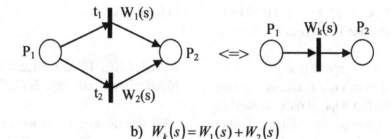

$$a) \quad W_k(s) = W_1(s) \cdot W_2(s)$$

$$b) \quad W_k(s) = W_1(s) + W_2(s)$$

$$c) \quad W_k(s) = \frac{W_1(s) \cdot W_3(s)}{1 - W_2(s)}$$

into which the equipment and human systems are divided) to determine the probability for at least $k_i$ equipment to be operational at a certain moment t, where $k_i$ represents the minimum of well-functioning equipment which preserves the cell i operational (for the equipment subsystem), respectively to determine the maximum allowed number of wrong actions of the workers (human subsystem). The availability of the system is given by the probability of the operator doing his duty between $k_i$ operational equipment in cell i and $k_i + 1$ operational equipment in cell i+1, at moment t. Supposing the levels of the subsystems are statistically independent, the availability of the system is (Jalcin & Boucher, 1999):

$$A(t) = \prod_{i=1}^{n} \left( A_{im}(t) \cdot A_{ih}(t) \right), \qquad (4)$$

where: A(t) is the availability of the flexible system (man-machine system); $A_{im}(t)$ is the availability of the i cell in the equipment system at moment t and $A_{ih}(t)$ is the availability of the cell i in the human subsystem at moment t.

## The Equipment Subsystem

The expectation of an i cell of the equipment system which includes $N_i$ equipment of the type $n_i$ is to ensure the functioning of at least $k_i$ of the equipment for the system to be operational. To determine the availability of the system including imperfect coverage and faulty repairs for each cell there has been introduced a state of malfunctioning caused either by imperfect coverage or by technical failure. To explain the effect of imperfect coverage of the system we will consider that operation $O_1$ can be made with one of the equipment $M_1$, respectively $M_2$.

If the coverage of the subsystem in Figure 2 is perfect, that is c=1, then operation $O_1$ is fulfilled as long as at least one of the equipment is functional. If the coverage is imperfect operation $O_1$ fails with the probability 1-c if one of the equipment $M_1$ or $M_2$ breaks down. In other words, if operation $O_1$ has programmed on equipment $M_1$ which broke down then the system in Figure 2 fails with the probability 1-c. The Markov chain made for cell i in the equipment subsystem is given in Figure 3. The coverage factor is $c_m$, the rate of breaking down of a piece of equipment is $\lambda_m$ (and is exponential), the repairing rate of the equipment is $\mu_m$ (which is also exponential), and the factor of successful repairing of a piece of equipment is $r_m$. In state $k_i$ cell i only has $k_i$ operational equipment. The state of cell i changes from working state $k_i$ into break down state $F_{ki}$ due to imperfect coverage (1-$c_m$), or due to faulty repairing (1-$r_m$). The solution of the Markov chain in Figure 3 is the probability that at least $k_i$ equipment should function in cell i at moment t.

*Figure 2. Subsystem consisting of one operation performed on two machines*

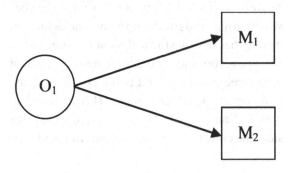

We can calculate this probability according to the following formula (David & Alla, 1992), (Hopkins, 2002):

$$A_i(t) = \sum_{k=k_i}^{N_i} P_{ki}(t), i = 1, 2, ..., n, \tag{5}$$

where: $A_i(t)$ is the availability of the cell i at moment t; $P_{ki}(t)$ is the probability that, at moment t, the cell i should contain $k_i$ operational equipment; $N_i$ is the number of $M_i$ equipment in cell i; $k_i$ is the minimum number of operational equipment in cell i.

## The Human Factor Subsystem

The expectation from the human factor subsystem is that it should ensure the exploitation of equipment with maximum efficiency and safety. To determine the availability of the operator to be capable of performing his duty at moment t, we build this Markov chain (Figure 4) which models the behavior of the cell i of the human subsystem.

In Figure 4, we have: $\lambda_h$ is the rate of wrong actions of the operator; $\mu_h$ is the rate of correct actions of the operator in case of break down; $c_h$ is the covering factor of problems caused by wrong actions or by unexpected events occurred in the system; $r_h$ is the factor of correcting wrong actions of the operators.

In Figure 4 the human operator can be in one of the following states of performing his job: state $N_i$ is the normal working state in which actions are performed by all $N_i$ operators of cell i; state $k_i$ is the working state where actions are performed by $k_i$ operators ($k_i < N_i$); state $F_{ki+u}$ is the working state allowing incorrect actions which can cause technological malfunctioning with no serious consequences on the safety of traffic, where u = 0, ..., $N_i$-$k_i$; state $F_k$ is the state of working incapacity due to wrong actions with serious consequences on traffic safety.

*Figure 3. Markov model for cell i in the equipment subsystem*

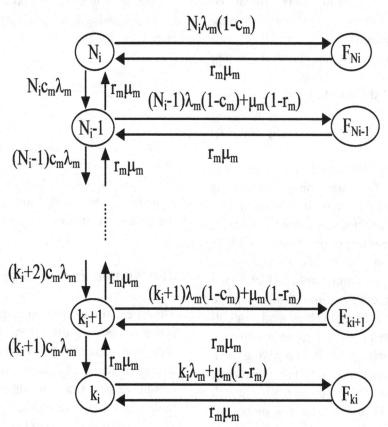

The availability of the human factor performing his duties under normal circumstances is:

$$A_{ih}\left(t\right) = \sum_{x=j}^{m} P_{xi}(t), i = 1, 2, ..., n,\qquad(6)$$

where: $P_{xi}(t)$ is the probability that the operator is in working state x at moment t, in cell i; m is the total number of working states allowed in the system; j is the minimum allowed number of working states.

Attributing supplementary working states to the human factor considerably increases the complexity of the calculus, and furthermore, although the entire system continues to work, certain technological norms are disregarded which leads to low throughput in the flexible system.

## ILLUSTRATIVE EXAMPLE

In order to illustrate the above-mentioned method, we shall consider a building site equipped with electronic and mechanic equipment consisting of three robot arms for load/unload operations and five conveyors. Two robots (e.g. robot arms) and three conveyors are necessary for the daily traffic of FMS's activity. That means that the electronic and mechanic equipment for two robots and three conveyors should be functional, so that the construction materials traffic is fluent. The technician on duty has to make the technical revision for the five conveyors and for the three robots, so that at least three conveyors and two robot arms of the building site work permanently (Liu & Towsleg, 1994), (Nananukul & Gong, 1999). On the other side, the construction engineer has to coordinate

*Figure 4. Markov model for cell i corresponding to the human factor subsystem*

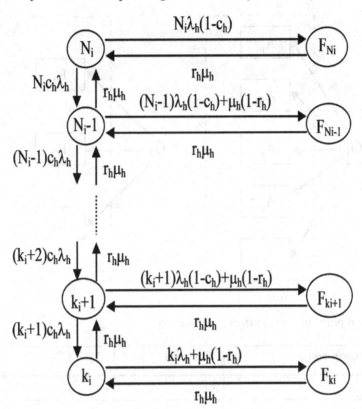

the traffic and the manoeuvres in such manner to keep free at least three conveyors and two robot arms, while the maintenance activities take place on the other two conveyors and one robot. In this example the subsystem of the human factor consists of the decisional factors: the designer (i.e. architect), the construction engineer and the equipment technician (electro-mechanic). The subsystem of the equipment consists of the three robots and five conveyors (including the necessary devices). This subsystem is divided into two cells, depending on the necessary devices (e.g. electro-mechanisms and the electronic equipment for the conveyors, and respectively the electronic and mechanic equipment for the robots), (Ciufudean & Filote, 2009).

All the necessary equipment for the conveyors section are grouped together in the cell $A_1$, are denoted by $Ap_{1...5}$ and serve for the operation $O_1$ (the transport of building materials). The rest

of the equipment denoted by $E_{1...3}$ are grouped together in the cell $A_2$ and serve for the operation $O_2$ (the load/unload operations of building materials by conveyors), according to the Figure 5. The failing/repairing rates of the components are given in Table 1.

For the equipment subsystem there are two Markov chains, one with six states (cell $A_1$) and one with four states (cell $A_2$); the matrix in the Figure 6 corresponds to the first one and the matrix in the Figure 7 corresponds to the second one. The following Markov chains correspond to the human subsystem: 1) with six states (the decisions are made by three factors: the designer, the construction engineer and the electro-mechanic); 2) with four states (the decisions are made only by two of the above-mentioned factors); 3) with two states (the decisions are made by only one human factor). A matrix of the state probabilities corresponds to each Markov chain, and the equations

*Figure 5. The cell structure of the equipment subsystem*

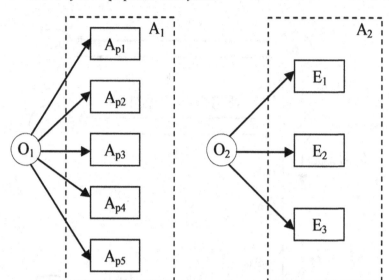

*Table 1. Failing and repair rates for system components*

| System Components | C | $\mu$ | $\lambda$ | r | $K_i$ | $N_i$ |
|---|---|---|---|---|---|---|
| $A_{pi}$ | 0.8 | 1.0 | 0.03 | 0.8 | 3 | 5 |
| $E_i$ | 0.8 | 0.5 | 0.025 | 0.8 | 2 | 3 |
| Human subsystem components | 0.8 | 0.2 | 0.01 | 0.8 | 1 | 1, 2, 3 |

given by the matrix of the state probabilities are functions of time and by solving them we obtain: the expressions of the availabilities for cell $A_1$, respectively $A_2$, from the equipment subsystem calculated with the relation (5); the expression of the availability of the human subsystem calculated with the relation (6); the expression of the availability of the whole system calculated with the relation (4), (Ciufudean & Garcia, 2013).

The equations given by the matrix of the state probabilities are functions of time and by solving them we obtain:

- The expressions of the availabilities for the cell $A_1$, and respectively $A_2$ from the equipment subsystem calculated with the relation (5);

- The expression of the availability of the human subsystem calculated with the relation (6);

- The expression of the availability of the whole system calculated with the relation (4).

The values of these availabilities depending on time are given in the Table 2.

An advantage of the above-mentioned calculus method is the easy calculation of the availability of the whole system and of the elements of the system. The availabilities of the exemplified system are drawn in Figure 14, depending on time and on the number of decision factors. In Figure 14, the numbers x=1, 2, 3 show the availability of the systems corresponding to the Markov chains in Figure 8,

*Figure 6. The matrix of the state probabilities for the cell A1 from the equipment subsystem*

$$
\begin{array}{c}
\quad\quad 3 \quad\quad\quad 4 \quad\quad\quad 5 \quad\quad\quad F_3 \quad\quad\quad F_4 \quad\quad\quad F_5 \\
\begin{array}{c} 3 \\ 4 \\ 5 \\ F_3 \\ F_4 \\ F_5 \end{array}
\begin{bmatrix}
-3\lambda+\mu & 0.8\mu & 0 & 3\lambda+0.2\mu & 0 & 0 \\
3.2\lambda & -(4\lambda+\mu) & 0.8\mu & 0 & 0.8\lambda+0.2\mu & 0 \\
0 & 4\lambda & -(5\lambda) & 0 & 0 & \lambda \\
0.8\mu & 0 & 0 & -(0.8\lambda) & 0 & 0 \\
0 & 0.8\mu & 0 & 0 & -(0.8\lambda) & 0 \\
0 & 0 & 0.8\mu & 0 & 0 & -(0.8\lambda)
\end{bmatrix}
\end{array}
$$

*Figure 7. The matrix of the state probabilities for the cell A2 from the equipment subsystem*

$$
\begin{array}{c}
\quad\quad 2 \quad\quad\quad 3 \quad\quad\quad F_2 \quad\quad\quad F_3 \\
\begin{array}{c} 2 \\ 3 \\ F_2 \\ F_3 \end{array}
\begin{bmatrix}
-(2\lambda+\mu) & 0.8\mu & 2\lambda+0.2\mu & 0 \\
2.4\lambda & -(3\lambda) & 0 & 0.6\lambda \\
0.8\mu & 0 & -(0.8\mu) & 0 \\
0 & 0.8\mu & 0 & -(0.8\mu)
\end{bmatrix}
\end{array}
$$

*Figure 8. The Markov chain corresponding to three of the decisional factors*

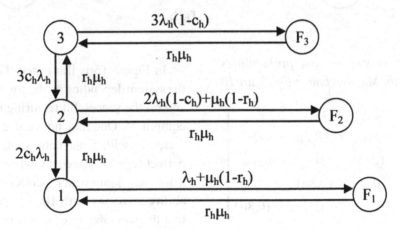

Figure 10 and Figure 12 respectively. The Figure 14 shows that the best functioning of the system can be obtained by using two decisional factors: while the availability of the system in figure 12 is 65% after 12 hours of functioning, the availability of the system in figure 10 is 82%. The availability of the system decreases when the third decisional factor appears, because the diminution due to the risk of imperfect coverage or due to an incorrect decision is greater than the increase due to the excess of information (Bravuso, 1987).

*Figure 9. The matrix of the state probabilities corresponding to the Markov chain in the Figure 8*

$$
\begin{bmatrix}
 & 1 & 2 & 3 & F_1 & F_2 & F_3 \\
 & -(\lambda+\mu) & 0,8\mu & 0 & \lambda+2\mu & 0 & 0 \\
 & 1,6\lambda & -(2\lambda+\mu) & 0,8\mu & 0 & 0,4\lambda+0,2\mu & 0 \\
 & 0 & 2,4\lambda & -(3\lambda) & 0 & 0 & 0,6\lambda \\
 & 0,8\mu & 0 & 0 & -(0,8\mu) & 0 & 0 \\
 & 0 & 0,8\mu & 0 & 0 & -(0,8\mu) & 0 \\
 & 0 & 0 & 0,8 & 0 & 0 & -(0,8\mu)
\end{bmatrix}
$$

*Figure 10. The Markov chain corresponding to two decisional factors*

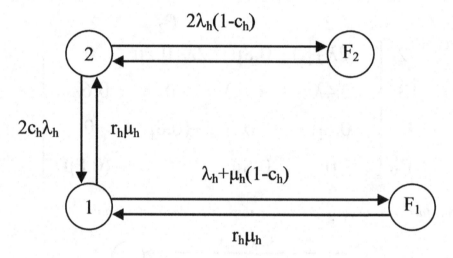

*Figure 11. The matrix of the state probabilities corresponding to the Markov chain in the Figure 10*

$$
\begin{array}{c}
1 \\ 2 \\ F_1 \\ F_2
\end{array}
\begin{bmatrix}
1 & 2 & F_1 & F_2 \\
-(\lambda+\mu) & 0,8\mu & \lambda+0,2\mu & 0 \\
1,6\lambda & -(2\lambda) & 0 & 0,4\lambda \\
0,8\mu & 0 & -(0,8\mu) & 0 \\
0 & 0,8\mu & 0 & -(0,8\mu)
\end{bmatrix}
$$

*Figure 12. The Markov chain corresponding to one decisional factor*

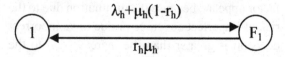

In Figure 15 is illustrated the availability of the system depending on the coverage factors ($c_m$) and on the successful repairing ($r_m$) of deficient equipment. One may notice that the availability increases with 5 percents when the coverage is perfect ($c_m=1$). Moreover, when the repairing of a deficient equipment is perfect ($r_m=1$), the availability increases with 10 percents (we mention that the increases refer to a concrete case where $c_m=0.8$ and $r_m=0.8$). An important conclusion that we can draw is that the presumption of perfect coverage and repairing affects the accuracy of the final result. This presumption is made in the literature in the majority of the analysis models of the system availability (Filote & Ciufudean, 2010).

*Table 2. Availability of the system elements*

| Time [Hours] | Cell $A_1$ | Cell $A_2$ | The Human Subsystem $A_h$ | The Availability of the Railway System A |
|---|---|---|---|---|
| 0 | 1.000000 | 1.000000 | 1.0000000 | 1.00000000 |
| 1 | 0.980013 | 0.985010 | 0.9548293 | 0.92171802 |
| 4 | 0.947011 | 0.951341 | 0.8645392 | 0.77888946 |
| 8 | 0.933510 | 0.933468 | 0.8061449 | 0.70247605 |
| 12 | 0.933010 | 0.927481 | 0.7809707 | 0.67581225 |
| 16 | 0.933129 | 0.926133 | 0.7701171 | 0.66553631 |
| 20 | 0.933060 | 0.925951 | 0.7654364 | 0.66131243 |
| 24 | 0.932891 | 0.925600 | 0.7647893 | 0.65970171 |
| 28 | 0,932762 | 0,925012 | 0,7635876 | 0.65876005 |
| 32 | 0.932132 | 0.924910 | 0.7631243 | 0.65781145 |
| 36 | 0.931902 | 0.924830 | 0.7625786 | 0.65716133 |
| 40 | 0.931819 | 0.924690 | 0.7621289 | 0.65640272 |
| 44 | 0.931791 | 0.924600 | 0.7619786 | 0.65640272 |
| 48 | 0.931499 | 0.924582 | 0.7619456 | 0.65618425 |

*Figure 13. The matrix of the state probabilities corresponding to the Markov chain in the Figure 12*

$$
\begin{array}{cc}
\phantom{F_1}1 & \phantom{-(\lambda}F_1 \\
\begin{matrix}1\\[2.5em]F_1\end{matrix}
\begin{bmatrix}
-(\lambda+0.2\mu) & \lambda+0.2\mu \\[1.5em]
0.8\mu & -(0.8\mu)
\end{bmatrix}
\end{array}
$$

The analysis of the availabilities of the operations $O_1$ and $O_2$ done by the cell $A_1$ and respectively by the cell $A_2$ from the equipment subsystem shows that an increase of the number of the conveyors (from $N_i=5$ and $k_i=3$ to $N_i=5$ and $k_i=4$) in the cell $A_1$ would lead to a decrease of the availability of the operator $O_1$ with 4% (as shown in Figure 16). In the case of the cell $A_2$, a decrease of the total number of robots (from $N_i=3$, $k_i=2$ to $N_i=2$, $k_i=2$) would lead to a decrease of the availability of the operator $O_2$ with 20% (as shown in Figure 17). The conclusion is that an extra robot is critical for the system, because it improves considerably the availability of $O_2$ and, hence, the availability of the system.

The analysis of the availability allows us to establish the lapse of time when changes must be made in the structure of the system (major overhaul, the rotation of the personnel in shifts etc). For example, from Figure 14, if the availability is 70%, the human decisional factor must be replaced every 12 hours (for the system in Figure 12 that is rotating the personnel every 12 hours).

## CONCLUSION

Our work develops heuristics and performance bounds for scheduling, based on heap and automata representation. The performance of a flexible system is evaluated, in many scenarios, with a SPN in which a transition can be associated with either a constant or random firing time delay with an exponential distribution, computed with a Markov model which incorporates the notion of imperfect coverage and imperfect repair factors. An advantage of our model is that the use of large Markov chains is not required. Another advantage is that it allows performing sensitivity analysis of an entire flexible system, as well as of

*Figure 14. The availability of the railway system depending on the number of decisional factors*

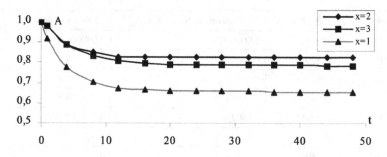

*Figure 15. The variation of the system availability depending on $c_m$ and $r_m$*

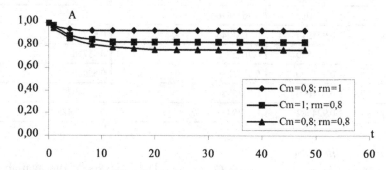

*Figure 16. The analysis of the availability of the cell $A_1$*

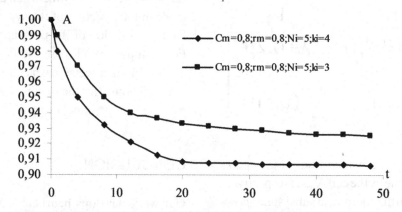

*Figure 17. The analysis of the availability of the cell $A_2$*

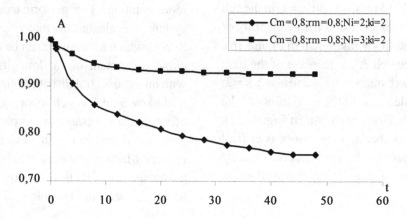

its components. The novelty of this approach is that it incorporates the availability of the human factor. We can generalize the proposed approach, when instead of decomposing the global system in two major subsystems, one can decompose the system into three, four or more subsystems, according to the specific application. We may notice that a large number of subsystems determine an embarrassing growth of the calculus complexity. In this paper we assumed that the failure and repair times were exponential random variables. In real flexible systems, the time distributions are arbitrary, which can be handled by the use of semi-Markov processes. A state transition may not occur at any time, and the failure/repair time can follow an arbitrary distribution. When a failure/repair event occurs, the Markov process representation applies, and the probability of burning a transition to a new state depends only on the current value of state.

## REFERENCES

Bavuso, S.J. (1987). Analysis of typical fault-tolerant architecture using HARP. *IEEE Transactions on Reliability*, R-*36*, 176–185. doi:10.1109/TR.1987.5222335

Ciufudean, C., & Filote, C. (2009a). Safety discrete event models for holonic cyclic manufacturing systems. In *Proceedings of 4th Industrial Conference on Industrial Applications of Holonic and Multi-agent Systems, HoloMAS 2009* (LNCS) (vol. 5696, pp. 225-233). Berlin: Springer Verlag.

Ciufudean, C., & Filote, C. (2009b). Holonic models for traffic control systems. In *Proceedings of 4th Industrial Conference on Industrial Applications of Holonic and Multi-agent Systems, HoloMAS 2009* (LNCS) (vol. 5696, pp. 276-284). Berlin: Springer Verlag.

Ciufudean, C., & Garcia, L. (2013). *Advances in robotics: Modeling, control and applications*. Iconcept Press Ltd.

David, R., & Alla, H. (1992). *Petri nets and Grafcet*. Englewood Cliffs, NJ: Prentice-Hall.

Filote, C., & Ciufudean, C. (2010). Future manufacturing systems - Cap. 2: Discrete event models for flexible manufacturing cells. In T. Aized (Ed.), Tech (pp. 17–39). Academic Press.

Gaubert, St., & Mairese, J. (1999). Modeling and Analysis of Timed Petri Nets Using Heap of Pieces. *IEEE Trans. on Autom. Robot. Contr.*, *44*(4), 683–697.

Guo, D. L., DiCesare, F., & Zhou, M. Ch. (1993). A moment Generating Function Based Approach for Evaluating Extended Stochastic Petri Nets. *IEEE Transactions on Automatic Control*, *38*(2), 321–327. doi:10.1109/9.250484

Hopkins, M. (2002a). *Strategies for determining causes of events* (Technical Report R-306). UCLA Cognitive Systems Laboratory.

Hopkins, M. (2002b). *A proof of the conjunctive in causes and explanations* (Technical Report R-306). UCLA Cognitive Systems Laboratory.

Liu, Z., & Towsleg, D. (1994). Stochastic scheduling in tree-networks. *Advances in Applied Probability*, *26*, 222–241. doi:10.2307/1427588

Molloy, M. K. (1992). Performance analysis using stochastic Petri nets. *IEEE Transactions on Computers*, *31*(9), 913–917.

Moses, Y., & Tennenholtz, M. (n.d.). *Artificial social systems*. Retrieved from www.home.cs.utwente.nl

Nananukul, S., & Gong, W. B. (1999). Rational Interpolation for Stochastic DES's: Convergence Issues. *IEEE Trans. On Autom. Control*, *44*(5), 1070–1073. doi:10.1109/9.763231

Sahmer, R. A., & Trivedi, K. S. (1987). Reliability Modelling Using SHARPE. *IEEE Transactions on Reliability*, R-*36*, 186–193. doi:10.1109/TR.1987.5222336

Schultz, C.P.L., Guesgen, H.W., & Amor, R. (2006). Computer-human interaction issues when integrating qualitative spatial reasoning into geographic information systems. In *Proceedings of ACM International Conference* (pp. 43–51). Christchurch, New Zealand: ACM.

Viennot, G. X. (1986). *Heaps of Pieces, I: Basic definitions and combinatorial lemmas, Combinatoire Enumerative, Labelle and Leroux, Lect. Notes in Math* (pp. 321–350). New York: Springer.

Yalcin, A., & Boucher, T. O. (1999). An Architecture for Flexible Manufacturing Cells with Alternate Machining and Alternate Sequencing. *IEEE Transactions on Robotics and Automation*, *15*(6), 1126–1130. doi:10.1109/70.817676

Zakarian, A., & Kusiak, A. (1997). Modeling Manufacturing Dependability. *IEEE Transactions on Robotics and Automation*, *13*(2), 161–168. doi:10.1109/70.563639

Zuo, M. J., Liu, B., & Murthy, D. N. P. (2000). Replacement-repair policy for multi-state deteriorating products under warranty. *European Journal of Operational Research*, (3), 519–530. doi:10.1016/S0377-2217(99)00107-1

## KEY TERMS AND DEFINITIONS

**Availability:** Is the degree to which a system, subsystem or equipment is in a specified operable and committable state at the start of a mission, when the mission is called for at an unknown, *i.e.* a random, time.

**Coverage:** Is the proportion of the resources that the production system contains the true value of throughput.

**Diagnosis:** Is the identification of the nature and cause of anything.

**Discrete Event System:** Is a discrete-state which contains solely discrete state spaces and event-driven state transition mechanisms.

**Markov Chain:** Is a mathematical system that undergoes transitions from one state to another, among a finite or countable number of possible states.

**Petri Net:** Is a mathematical modeling language for the description of discrete event systems.

**Subsequence:** Is a sequence (set of elements) that can be derived from another sequence by deleting some elements without changing the order of the remaining elements.

# Chapter 32
# Information Disclosure on Social Networking Sites:
## An Exploratory Survey of Factors Impacting User Behaviour on Facebook

**Clare Doherty**
*National University of Ireland Galway, Ireland*

**James Deane**
*Cora Systems, Ireland*

**Michael Lang**
*National University of Ireland Galway, Ireland*

**Regina Connor**
*Allied Irish Bank, Ireland*

## ABSTRACT

*This chapter explores how six constructs—control, trust, perceived risk, risk propensity, perceived legal protection, and privacy disposition—affect information disclosure on the Social Networking Site (SNS) Facebook. Building upon previous related work, an extended causal model of disclosure behaviour is proposed. The hypothesised relationships in this model were tested using survey data collected from 278 social networking site users in Ireland. The results of the analysis provide strong support for the proposed model.*

## INTRODUCTION

Social Networking Sites (SNS) such as Facebook, Twitter and LinkedIn offer a convenient way to maintain existing personal and professional relationships while also developing new ones. With millions of people interacting and communicating online, coupled with the amount of personal information disclosed, this can lead to personal information ending up in the wrong hands and users may unsuspectingly leave themselves susceptible to privacy and security risks in cyberspace

(Harden et al. 2012). SNS are web-based services which allow people to build a public or private profile in a particular system, join users with whom they may or may not share a connection, and view other people's connections within this system (Boyd and Elison 2007). These websites have become particularly popular tools for social experimentation; many users use Facebook for either "social searching" or "social browsing" to interact with people they already know and to meet new people.

DOI: 10.4018/978-1-4666-6324-4.ch032

Disclosing personal information is an important aspect of building relationships with others (Christofides, 2009; Nguyen et al, 2012). Privacy and trust are central concerns as regards on-line behavioural intentions (Liu et al 2005). A person's trusting belief can impact their loyalty of using Facebook, ultimately affecting how active they are and how much information they disclose (Wang, 2013). A trade-off is undertaken when using SNSs between the perceived benefits of using SNS on one hand and the potential risks of personal information disclosure on the other. The perceived benefits of using SNS are not discounts or free services, but social capital or the development of attachment through relationships (Xu et al 2013). A previous study has shown that there is a complimentary relationship between trust and information disclosure online (Henderson and Gilding 2004). When looking at privacy in relation to Facebook it has been said that Facebook should go beyond and try and increase the protection of users from corporate surveillance by protecting users' privacy (Fuchs 2011).

This chapter reports the findings of an exploratory opinion survey conducted in Ireland of 278 SNS users. Because the various SNS providers (e.g. Facebook, LinkedIn, Twitter, Google+, MySpace, FourSquare, Bebo, etc.) have different features, we chose in our questionnaire to specifically concentrate on the most popular SNS, Facebook, as we felt it might have led to confusion and measurement error if participants were instructed to answer questions but not given a clear context. Facebook has enjoyed a rapid increase of its users since it opened up its registration to not only college-based students in 2006 (Joinson, 2008). At the start of 2013, Facebook had 1.11 billion users using the site each month (Associated Press, 2013). Facebook has undergone radical change over the past 24 months by introducing a new "timeline" profile and updating its news feed aspect. However, it has not only changed its profile layout and its profile of users, but more importantly the potential motivations of users.

In this chapter we look at how six constructs affect information disclosure on Facebook: (1) perceived control; (2) trust; (3) perceived risk; (4) perceived legal protection; (5) risk propensity; and (6) privacy disposition. Our research model builds upon aspects of the Privacy Calculus model (Dinev and Hart 2006) and also the previous work of Krasnova et al. (2010), but is different in a number of regards. Whereas those earlier models include perceived control and perceived trust as single constructs, our factor analysis revealed that these two factors each have two distinct components, relating to (a) trust in / perceived control over individuals, and (b) trust in / perceived control over Facebook/on-line companies. Additionally, our model explores a number of factors which have received very little attention in previous studies, being the latter three of those aforementioned.

The chapter is organised as follows: Section 2 provides an overview of previous literature and sets forth the hypotheses to be explored. Section 3 outlines the research approach. A discussion of the findings of our study in presented in Section 4. A number of possible areas for future research are proposed in Section 5. We then present our conclusions in Section 6.

## BACKGROUND

### Perceived Control

Table 1 shows the results of our factor analysis, revealing two separate underlying components: perceived control over individuals, and perceived control over companies.

### Perceived Control over Companies

Previous research reveals that internet users possess a lack of trust in using online companies such as Facebook as they feel that have little control over what these companies do with their personal information. Users do not want their personal in-

*Table 1. Perceived control factor analysis*

| | Factor 1: Perceived Control over Individuals | Factor 2: Perceived Control over Companies |
|---|---|---|
| Your ability to control who can view your information (LEVCON_1) | .784 | .015 |
| Your ability to control the actions of other users (e.g. tagging you in photos, writing on your Wall) (LEVCON_2) | .776 | .269 |
| Your ability to correct inaccurate or untruthful information about yourself (LEVCON_3) | .706 | .377 |
| Your ability to remove embarrassing or damaging information about yourself (LEVCON_4) | .707 | .385 |
| Your ability to prevent your data and actions from being used/analysed by Facebook in ways that you did not intend (LEVCON_5) | .248 | .930 |
| Your ability to prevent your data and actions from being used/analysed by other parties in ways that you did not intend (LEVCON_6) | .219 | .931 |

formation to be sold to other companies. In relation to e-commerce sales through online companies, users concerns are related to their control over information privacy and their level of trust in these companies (Hoffman et al., 1999). The greater the level of control users perceive to have, the more trust they will have in the company and the less concerns they will have in relation to information disclosure. Therefore, we hypothesize that:

**Hypothesis H1a:** Users perceived control over companies is positively related to trust in companies.

## Perceived Control over Individuals

Although trust is an important construct in risk reduction, it does not give users the power to control the behaviour of others (Grabner-Krauter

& Kaluscha, 2003). The ultimate question is whether users can maintain control over personal information once it is disclosed online? A survey conducted into the introduction of Facebook's new interface (news feed and mini feed) resulted in users feeling this interface provides other users with easier access to their information, thus perceiving to provide users with less privacy (increasing privacy concerns) and less control over their personal information (Hoadley et al 2010). As Netchitailova (2012, p.687) puts it, "connecting with people always means giving up some control over your personal details: 'Social' and 'secret' don't work together". It has been claimed that if users perceive they have control, this may in fact be nothing more than an illusion (Langer, 1975). However, as one of our own survey respondents commented, "if you know how to control your privacy on the settings, you are more in control of what people see on your page ... Some people do not know how to sort out their privacy setting to their own choice". Therefore, users will gain trust in other users when they are made aware of and know how to use the privacy tools made available to them on Facebook (Krasnova et al 2010). Therefore, we hypothesize that:

**Hypothesis H1b:** Users perceived control over individuals is positively related to trust in individuals.

## Trust

### Trust in Companies

Trust is important in SNS such as Facebook as the absence of workable rules places a reliance on the socially acceptable behaviour of others (Ridings, 2002). There are several purposes for which one intends to use Facebook and this in turn will affect peoples' trust in Facebook the service provider. While we may privatise our profiles and remain selective about our 'friend-ing' choices, we have little control over the company's use of our information and therefore are placing our ultimate trust in Facebook the company. Thus we are taking a risk when disclosing personal information. A person's beliefs about internet privacy may be a deciding factor of his/her intention to share their personal information. Individuals who use SNS such as Facebook are the trustors, while Facebook providers are the trustees and the site itself is the object of this trust. That is to say, when individuals use SNS such as Facebook they are automatically placing trust in their service provider, and judging by the fact that there are currently 1.1 billion users of the site, it is quite evident that the purpose for which Facebook may use their personal information does not have much impact on their trust in it. If a SNS provider is perceived as being honest and reliable in its handling of users' personal information, users will perceive little risk in disclosing personal information online (Krasnova et al., 2010). Therefore, we hypothesize that:

**Hypothesis H2a:** Users level of trust in companies is negatively related to perceived risk.

## Trust in Individuals

There are several purposes for which one intends to use Facebook and this in turn will affect peoples' trust in other Facebook users (including "friends"). A user's list of Facebook friends/connections can derive from different social relationships, ranging from friendships (e.g. school/childhood companions) to casual connections (e.g. a friend of a friend or someone you met on at a social gathering) arising from different social contexts (Jensen & Sorensen, 2013). The term "friends" can be misleading on Facebook and users should be wary that these "friends" may not be who they say they are, thus not placing a high level of trust when disclosing personal information. We have seen in news bulletins with respect to social influence that some users (teenagers in particular) display greater trust in Facebook; they befriend strangers and then partake in potentially

endangering behaviour in their quest for a sense of belonging. Others use SNS for the purpose of discussing common interests (Ridings, 2002). The more information users disclose, the more other individuals will trust them, thus resulting in the more personal information other users will in turn share (Posey et al., 2010). However, there are also those who use SNS such as Facebook for the purposes of hacking, personal abuse, cyberbullying and other anti-social activities.

Privacy policies should be there to reassure individual's beliefs in Facebook and increase their trust in the SNS and other users. The greater the level of trust users possess in other users on Facebook (including friends), the less risky they feel it is to disclose personal information. Since users are unable to observe what other users do on SNS, they have to implicitly trust them not to use their personal information in unwanted ways (Krasnova et al 2010). Therefore, we hypothesize that:

**Hypothesis H2b:** Users level of trust in individuals is negatively related to perceived risk.

## Perceived Risk

With technology constantly evolving, online users are becoming more aware of the risks to their privacy through the amount of personal information they disclose online, the steps they can take to combat these risks and the level of trust they need to display to ensure they can partake safely. Privacy risk beliefs are defined as the anticipation of a large potential for loss that is related with the release of personal information to others online (Posey et al., 2010). The greater privacy risk individuals perceive themselves at online, the less information they disclose. Therefore, we hypothesize that:

**Hypothesis H3:** Users perceived risk is negatively related to information disclosure.

## Perceived Legal Protection

Not a lot of research has been done to date on a SNS user's perceived legal protection once they disclose personal information online. If a legal framework appears to protect users' privacy, it increases their level of perceived legal protection and increases their overall confidence in the SNS (Veltri et al 2011). The higher an individual's regard for privacy, the lower the trust level and the less information they disclose. This may be increased by an individual's internet literacy or by the enforcement of laws against privacy breaches. As the current EU data protection legislation debate continues, the outcome may prove vital for SNS users disclosure behaviour. The greater the legal protections users perceive themselves to have, the less risky they regard it to disclose personal information online. Therefore, we hypothesize that:

**Hypothesis H4:** Users perceived level of legal protection is negatively related to perceived risk.

## Risk Propensity

Little research has been done on risk propensity in relation to SNS use. When we share information online, the risk to our privacy and security increases and control over this information may fall out of our hands. Disclosure and control on Facebook are not as closely related as people may think but they can be jointly affected by a user's personality traits such as how trusting the user is, if the user is a risk-taker etc. (Christofides 2009). In some regards SNS such as Facebook can be viewed as unsafe platforms for socialising and may pose a risk to vulnerable users such as children and teenagers (Dwyer et al 2007). Risk propensity online refers to the chance that users will take online in relation to the possibility of a privacy breach against their personal information. Those persons with a higher risk propensity are

more willing to knowingly engage in behaviour that may place them at risk of some kind of loss or harm. Therefore, we hypothesize that:

**Hypothesis H5:** Users risk propensity is positively related to information disclosure.

## Privacy Disposition

Table 2 shows the results of a factor analysis based on five privacy concern questions, out of which two components were identified. One of these we have named "privacy disposition", which relates to how a person feels about their privacy in general, whereas the other we have named "Facebook privacy", which is conflated with the previously described factor of trust in companies.

The privacy settings provided by SNS such as Facebook are not flexible enough to protect user data and users do not have control over what others reveal about them. If people followed the same instinct and common sense that they had use when walking to school as children, they would be safe. However, a lot of Facebook users do not exercise the same common sense because they think of themselves as interacting in a safe and protected environment. SNS users reveal personal information in a trade-off in exchange for what the SNS provider has to offer e.g. building an online persona and carving out relationships. However this does not mean that they want to fully sacrifice their privacy for such trade-offs (Netchitailova, 2012). The intrusion of privacy by SNS providers tends to remain invisible to the average user or it is only after the fact that the user becomes aware e.g. once personal information has been used in unintended ways (Debatin et al., 2009).

A previous study found that while respondents claimed to be concerned about their online privacy, they revealed a significant amount of personal, potentially damaging information (Utz & Kramer, 2011). They also found that individuals' concerns did however lead them to exercise more restrictions on their profiles. SNS providers have improved

*Table 2. Privacy disposition factor analysis*

| Variable | Factor 1: Privacy Disposition | Factor 2: Facebook Privacy |
|---|---|---|
| I am generally a private person in my normal everyday life (LAGREE_1) | .819 | 0.10 |
| I tend to reveal minimal personal information about myself online because I value my rights to privacy (LAGREE_2) | .868 | -.094 |
| I feel uncomfortable about my personal information being in the hands of others (LAGREE_3) | .773 | -.197 |
| I believe there is no need to be concerned about disclosing personal information on Facebook (LAGREE_4) | -.144 | .844 |
| It does not bother me that a history of my activities and movements are held by Facebook (LAGREE_5) | -.040 | .865 |

the way people communicate worldwide and how we build relationships. However, is this trade-off we agree to with SNS provider worth the cost of intrusion into our private lives? Therefore, we hypothesize that:

**Hypothesis H6:** Users privacy disposition is negatively related to information disclosure.

## Information Disclosure

Acquisti & Gross (2006, p.2) remark that "one cannot help but marvel at the nature, amount, and detail of the personal information some users provide". Information self-disclosure refers to information about oneself that is revealed to others (Collins & Miller, 1994). Information disclosure is viewed as being necessary for building relationships (Christofides et al., 2009). SNS can be seen as partially to blame for instances of low regard for privacy by users, be it in the form of setting profile visibility low by default, not encouraging strong passwords or not informing users of the risks associated with disclosing personal information. In contrast, there is the belief that when users disclose personal information online they know what they are letting themselves in for; therefore they are partially to blame (Hill, 2011). A user is more likely to fall victim to a security breach due to their lack of awareness of risks, their high level of trust and perceived control of

their disclosed personal information. Therefore, it is vital for users to be aware and educated of the countermeasures that can be put in place on SNS (Lang et al., 2009). Despite the benefits of cyberspace interaction, SNS usage still poses a serious threat to individuals' security. A notable example of this occurred in November 2011, when one of the worst spam/phishing attacks in Facebook's history resulted in images of violence and pornography being posted on many users' profiles after users copied and pasted spam into their browser bars. This incident highlights the serious impact of privacy breaches on Facebook. There are many potential threats to privacy and security in cyberspace with SNS usage such as identity theft due to the disclosure of sensitive personal information (Krasnova et al., 2009). The availability of personal information through online self-disclosure occurs as users believe there are perceived benefits (social capital e.g. the prospect of developing new relationships) of doing so. The possibility of these perceived benefits will not only affect the information disclosure practices of users but also users self disclosure behaviours in the way they communicate with others (Trepte & Reinecke, 2013). Some users reveal a lot of personal information online which leads one to think would users be concerned for their privacy if they thought it fully through that this information may end up in the wrong hands?

## RESEARCH METHOD

### Survey Design and Administration

We chose a single method research design, collecting data through a web-based survey. The target population of our survey comprised of students and professionals in the age bracket 20-30 years old, all of whom use Facebook and live in Ireland. While this sample is not representative of the general public, it nevertheless is a reasonable reflection of the opinions of Facebook users. Prior to the distribution of our survey, we conducted a "soft launch" with a few colleagues to pre-test it. After this feedback minor revisions were made to our survey before it was launched. A survey link was distributed via email to various student class groups. To further expand the research sample, we used the "snowballing" technique of personal contacts to pass on details of the link to the on-line survey. Personal email was also used in order to gain more respondents. The questionnaire comprised 24 questions, mostly being Likert scale items, with a number of check box items and open-ended textboxes. We analysed our data in statistical analysis program SPSS, using descriptive tests, cross tabulations, correlations, tests for differences, and factor analysis.

### Exploratory Factor Analysis

In order to identify patterns of attitude, we carried out principal components factor analysis with a Varimax rotation to finalise the constructs structure resulting in the development of the hypothesised relationships stated below. All indicators loaded strongly (all exceeding 0.6 level) on the variables they were measuring. The Kaiser-Meyer-Oklin values exceeded the recommended value of 0.6 and the Bartlett Test of Sphericity reached statistical significance. Reliability analysis was conducted with the constructs returning a Cronbach's Alpha value in and around the recommended threshold

of 0.7. Table 3 shows the factor loading that was returned for each variable along with Cronbach's alpha value for each construct.

## DISCUSSION OF FINDINGS

A total of 278 survey responses were received, 103 of those respondents were females (37%) and 175 were males (63%). The age population is youth orientated, 70% of the respondents are between the ages 18-23. 61% of respondents were students while 33% were employees. In terms of education, 27% of users had Masters or higher level qualification and 43% had a Bachelor level degree. 31% of users have been on Facebook for 3 years, while 49% of users have been on Facebook for more than 3 years. 41% of users only post updates occasionally while at the opposite ends of the scale, 4% of users post updates every 8 hours. 17% of respondents had 201-300 connections ("Friends"), while 14% of users had 600+ connections. Interestingly 10.5% of users didn't know how many connections they have. 72% of users have their profile visible to all friends while 4% have their profile visible to the public.

The respondents of this survey reveal a large amount of information about themselves on Facebook. Only 21 respondents informed us that they do not reveal their real name on Facebook. More than 90% share photographs of themselves while 85% reveal their birthday online. 78% or respondents reveal their hometown, while 68% reveal their educational history. With 14 different items of personal information asked, the majority of respondents checked 7 or more items. We presented participants with seven different statements to test their level of awareness of Facebook's privacy and data usage policy. This revealed that users' knowledge of what Facebook does with their personal data is very limited. Alarmingly, 48% of users did not know if Facebook sold their personal information to advertisers. 51% did not

*Table 3. Factor analysis*

| Constructs | Item | Standardized Factor Loading | Cronbach's Alpha |
|---|---|---|---|
| Trust in individuals and companies | CONCERN_1 | .644 | |
| | CONCERN_2 | .734 | |
| | CONCERN_3 | .826 | |
| | CONCERN_4 | .844 | |
| | CONCERN_5 | .804 | |
| | CONCERN_6 | .794 | .867 |
| Trust in individuals and companies | LTRUST_1 | .669 | |
| | LTRUST_2 | .875 | |
| | LTRUST_3 | .815 | |
| | LTRUST_4 | .583 | .714 |
| Trust in individuals and companies | ACCEFR_1 | .836 | |
| | ACCEFR_2 | .756 | |
| | ACCEFR_3 | .832 | |
| | ACCEFR_4 | .649 | |
| | ACCEFR_5 | .854 | |
| | ACCEFR_6 | .817 | .687 |
| Perceived legal protection | LAWS_1 | .869 | |
| | LAWS_2 | .898 | |
| | LAWS_3 | .871 | |
| | LAWS_4 | .842 | .802 |
| Privacy disposition | LAGREE_1 | .819 | |
| | LAGREE_2 | .868 | |
| | LAGREE_3 | .773 | |
| | LAGREE_4 | .844 | |
| | LAGREE_5 | .865 | .662 |
| Privacy disposition | EVENTS_1 | .767 | |
| | EVENTS_2 | .741 | |
| | EVENTS_3 | .802 | |
| | EVENTS_4 | .760 | |
| | EVENTS_5 | .811 | .831 |
| Perceived control over Individuals and Companies | LEVCON_1 | .784 | |
| | LEVCON_2 | .776 | |
| | LEVCON_3 | .706 | |
| | LEVCON_4 | .707 | |
| | LEVCON_5 | .930 | |
| | LEVCON_6 | .931 | .844 |
| Perceived Risk | DAMINF_1 | .747 | |
| | DAMINF_2 | .922 | |
| | DAMINF_3 | .872 | |
| | DAMINF_4 | .874 | .877 |
| Perceived Risk | LEVAG_1 | .752 | |
| | LEVAG_2 | .665 | |
| | LEVAG_3 | .707 | |
| | LEVAG_4 | .665 | |
| | LEVAG_5 | .537 | .682 |
| Risk Propensity | LEOFAG_1 | .504 | |
| | LEOFAG_2 | .770 | |
| | LEOFAG_3 | .824 | .503 |
| Information Disclosure | AGREE_1 | .735 | |
| | AGREE_2 | .869 | |
| | AGREE_3 | .847 | |
| | AGREE_4 | .884 | .854 |

know if Facebook gives their personal information to other service providers. A lot of this worry was reflected by respondents in a comment box at the end of the survey. As revealed from the table below, a lot of the respondents *don't know* what Facebook does with their personal information once it is disclosed online. Table 4 highlights user's awareness of Facebook's policies, showing users answers and the correct answer.

## Perceived Control

### Perceived Control over Companies

We asked users to state how much control they feel they have in relation to particular issues on Facebook. As trust and risk-taking are intertwined, control is an important factor. SNS providers such as Facebook can authorise control to users through limited privacy settings but as shown through our analysis, users feel Facebook can also use their information in ways unintended by the owner, no matter how much control they perceive to have (Krasnova, 2010). However, 80% of users feel that they have little or no control over what Facebook can do with their personal information once it is disclosed online. The less trust they possess in Facebook, the less control they feel they have in preventing Facebook use their data

in unintended ways ($r_s$=-.293, p<.01). A user's perceived control over their user options is where SNS providers cannot push privacy into the background (Krasnova, 2010). Our results show that half of our sample has had their Facebook profile maliciously accessed, their privacy violated, or had an unpleasant experience.

### Perceived Control over Individuals

When users feel they have little or no control over their personal information online, they may exercise less caution as regards their privacy. We found that Facebook users believe they have the most control over their ability to control who can view their information and also their ability to control the actions of others. 34% of users feel they have at least some control to correct untruthful information about themselves, but 56% feel they have little or no control over their ability to remove damaging information about them. In contrast with females, a substantial cohort (44%) of male users feel they have more control over who can view their personal information (U=6454, z= -2.06, p<.05). Surprisingly, the more concerned users are that people they know online are not who they say they are, the greater ability they perceive to have over controlling the actions of others ($r_s$ = +.144, p<.05). 56% of users feel they have at

*Table 4. Users awareness of Facebook's policies*

| Policy Awareness Question | True | False | Don't Know | Correct Answer* |
|---|---|---|---|---|
| Your name, profile picture, and Friends list are always publicly available on Facebook | 55.8% | 36% | 8.3% | True |
| Facebook apps have access to your Friends list by default | 42.6% | 19.1% | 38.3% | True |
| Facebook sells your personal information to advertisers | 30.2% | 21.6% | 48.2% | False |
| Facebook gives your personal information to other providers | 30.2% | 18.3% | 51.4% | True |
| Facebook provides a facility to import contact lists from email, address books and mobile phones | 58.8% | 10.5% | 30.7% | True |
| Facebook identifies people that you may know by searching for your details in other user's contact lists | 78.2% | 2.2% | 19.6% | True |
| Facebook does not permit you to delete your account | 29.3% | 46.4% | 24.3% | False |

* Correct as per Facebook's stated policy at the time the survey was undertaken

least some control over their ability to control the actions of other Facebook users. A previous study of Facebook users in Morocco revealed a concern about "preserving face" whereby users avoided disclosing personal information where possible, even if they had a high perceived level of control (Veltri et al 2010). In our survey the more concerned users are that Facebook might use their information for purposes other than explicitly stated in their privacy policy, the less control they feel they have over their ability to prevent their data from being used by Facebook in unintended ways ($r_s = -.252$, $p< .01$). This finding is in contrast with the findings of Veltri et al. (2010), where it was reported that Moroccan Facebook users are confident in their control over their privacy settings. It should be borne in mind that when one discloses personal information online, one never has full control over what can be done with their information. However, by not accepting friend requests from people they do not know, SNS users are taking a precautionary step to prevent personal information ending up in the wrong hands and increasing their regard for privacy. In a previous study, most respondents stated that they would not accept a friend request from someone they do not know, but when then actually issued with a request from an alluring stranger, they did actually accept it (Lang et al 2009). The less control users feel they have over the actions of other Facebook users, the more likely they are to accept a friend request from a person they have never met with whom they have a few mutual friends ($r_s = -.160$, $p< .05$). Female users are more likely to accept a friend request from a person they have never met, with whom they have no mutual friends (U=6710, z= -2.16, p<.05).

## Trust

### Trust in Companies

As expected, the more concerned that users are that Facebook might use their personal for purposes other than explicitly stated in their privacy

policy, the more worried they are about disclosing personal information on Facebook, thus making them less trusting of Facebook ($r_s = -.332$, p<.01). However, lower levels of trust in Facebook does not necessarily mean this results in the disclosure of less personal information disclosed online. When one puts their trust in something, this means they are usually dependent on it (Nikander & Karvonen, 2001). The typical reason for deciding to trust something or somebody is the desire to make decisions simpler reducing complexity. The greater the level of trust you have in Facebook the company, the more control you feel you have over your ability to prevent your data and actions from being used/analysed by online companies in ways you did not intend ($r_s = +.343$, p<.01). However, gaining trust from online users can be slow and if it is lost, it can be difficult and sometimes impossible to regain. Male users have a greater level of trust in Facebook the company (U=7709.5, z= -1.98, p<.05) as 92% of males have some level of trust in Facebook in comparison with 77% of females.

### Trust in Individuals

Our results show that users possess a high level of trust in their own friends on Facebook. However, they still have a fear that something unpleasant might happen to them due to their presence on Facebook ($r_s = -.264$, p<.05). 45% of users feel there is a threat to their privacy due to their presence on Facebook. This result is not surprising as users may have a high level of trust in their own friends; however, there are millions of other users online some of which may set out with malicious intent. Therefore, it doesn't matter how much trust users place in their friends, unpleasant experiences can still happen if personal information gets in the wrong hands.

A significant relationship was found in a previous study between the perceived privacy concerns of the SNS users and trust in an SNS as well as trust between other SNS users and the trust in a SNS (Harden et al., 2012). Users stated their level of trust in their own friends increases, as they feel it is unlikely that somebody could succeed in gaining unauthorised access to their Facebook account ($r_s$=-.176, p<.01). These results are in agreement with a previous study where it was stated that control is important in relation to information privacy as users have been known to take risks in the disclosure of personal information online (Malhorta, 2004). 24% of users feel it is safe to disclose their personal information on Facebook. Although users feel that something unpleasant might happen to them on Facebook, we nevertheless found that as their level of trust in Facebook the company increases, they tend to feel safer in publishing their personal information on the SNS ($r_s$=-.293, p< .01).

## Perceived Level of Risk

Previously we looked at risk propensity, now we will look at users' perceived levels of risk and how this affects their information disclosure on Facebook. Regardless of the amount of trust users place in other Facebook users or Facebook itself, this may still result in taking risks when partaking online. Risk involves active trust in other users and companies (Henderson & Gilding, 2004). Interestingly, the less of a threat users perceive there to be due to their presence on Facebook, the greater the trust they have in other Facebook users ($r_s$=-.317, p<.01). A particular mentality which may have developed is "it will never happen to me!", although as previously reported, many uses already have had unpleasant experiences.

Users find it risky that information they share with friends may be inappropriately disclosed by them to others as they fear it may be then used against them ($r_s$=+.287, p< .01). 46% of users feel their Facebook information could be accessed by someone they don't want and also used against them. Many respondents fear the information they reveal on Facebook may be made available to third parties without their knowledge, making them less trusting of Facebook as they might use the information for purposes other than what is stated in their privacy policy ($r_s$=-.348, p< .01). Users find it a risk to their privacy and security that other Facebook users might abuse their personal information, making it accessible to people they don't want viewing it ($r_s$=+.199, p< .01). Overall, our survey results show that half of the respondents find it risky to post their personal information on Facebook yet they still continue to do so.

## Information Disclosure

A user revealing personal information online is fundamental to the success of SNS as it opens the door for target marketing and social interaction (Chen, 2012). From our sample surveyed, users slightly disagree that they keep their friends regularly updated about what is going on in their private life on Facebook, but males moreso than females have a tendency to keep friends more regularly updated in this way. As earlier analysis showed, females have a tendency to be more risky, yet males tend to disclose more about themselves, both of which are initially determined by the user's level of online trust. Some interesting results were found when analysing the relationship between disclosure and trust. As users keep their friends updated about what is going on in their private life on Facebook, their level of trust in Facebook the company increases ($r_s$=+.150, p<.05). This informs us that the more trust a user has in the Facebook the company, the more risky behaviour they will engage in as they are going to continue updating their friends on Facebook about their private life. Our results show that 58% of users keep a comprehensive profile of themselves on Facebook. When users have something to say, many of them choose to share it on Facebook, which increases their level of concern that other Facebook users might abuse their personal information ($r_s$=.137, p<.05). Regardless of this finding, users still disclose personal information on Facebook. Users level of concern that Facebook might use their information for unintended purposes increases as their trust in Facebook the company decreases

($r_s$= -.383, p<.01). Therefore, users that post less do so because they have concern about how Facebook may use their personal information for other purposes. In a previous study, it was found that users' perceived privacy risk is negatively related to their self-disclosure behaviour on SNS (Krasnova et al., 2010), and again our findings hold up this hypothesis. Our results show that 80% of users fear that information they share with friends may be inappropriately disclosed by these friends to others. Users that keep their friends updated about what is going on in their private life by disclosing personal information are knowingly taking risks in life and on the internet ($r_s$=+.267, p<.01). 53% of respondents fear that people they know online actually may not be who they say they are. 60% stated that they don't reveal a lot of information about themselves on Facebook, yet when asked what personal information they do reveal, on average users disclose more than seven personal information items, which is evidence of Barnes' (2006) "privacy paradox" theory. The top three pieces of information that a user discloses are: real name (91%), photographs of themselves (90%) and birthday (85%). The unlikeliest piece of information that people disclose about themselves is their postal address (5%). Male users have a greater tendency to keep their friends regularly updated about what is going on in their private life through Facebook (U=6426, z=-2.05, p<.05) with 30% of males with more of a tendency than 19% of females. In relation to controls the user has set in relation to who can see their personal information, our results show that 72% of all respondents allow all friends to see what is posted on their Facebook profile. 4% of users allow the public to see what is posted on their Facebook profile. One user expressed a concern over people (e.g. potential employer) they don't want gaining access to view their personal information that is disclosed on Facebook: "I think the new timeline is bad in terms of privacy, it feels with the old layout we had more control over privacy but now it seems that you have to go through every single thing posted to make sure it isn't public. I have more worries about my Facebook use in terms of potential employers seeing anything which isn't favourable or could jeopardise the chance of a new job."

## Perceived Levels of Legal Protection

The perceived legal protection construct allows users to determine if they feel protected by current laws, and how this affects their level of trust when disclosing information online. Across all four law statements, we found positive relationships between these statements and the user's level of trust in their "friends" on Facebook. The more users feel protected by current laws against violation of their privacy on Facebook, their level of trust in their own "Friends" on Facebook also increases ($r_s$=+.209, p<.01). However, 35% of users don't know how well their privacy is protected online. As expected, as users feel they are protected by current laws against damages to their reputation caused by Facebook, their level of trust in "friends of friends" on Facebook increases ($r_s$=+.211, p<.01). Users also feel protected against threats of cybercrime and online fraud ($r_s$=+.178, p<.05) as user's trust in other Facebook users increases. Users feel they have the rights to freely express their personal views on Facebook as trust in Facebook the company increases ($r_s$=+.150, p<.05). A question resulting from these findings is: the more a user trusts their own "friends" on Facebook the more they feel current laws protect them, but is this just because they feel confident in the friends they trust, rather than their knowledge of laws? Further analysis shows that as users level of concern that information shared with friends may be inappropriately disclosed by them to others increases, their feeling of protection by current laws against violation of privacy on Facebook also increases ($r_s$=+.142, p<.05). So the more concern users possess, the greater they feel protected legally, which may result in them taking more steps to safeguard their privacy thus being less trusting.

60% of users feel their rights to freely express their personal views online is protected while 54% feel they are not legally protected against damages to their reputation by Facebook. The users level of concern that information shared with friends may be inappropriately disclosed to others increases as their feeling of protection by current laws against threats of cybercrime and on-line fraud increases ($r_s$=+.136, p<.05). This may be because the greater their knowledge of laws is, the more concerned they are that something untoward might happen to their personal information, therefore they are less trusting and possess a high regard for privacy.

## Risk Propensity

We looked earlier in this chapter at the perceived risk involved in using Facebook and how it affects users information disclosure. Now, we will look at the risk propensity (behaving in a particular way) of users on Facebook and how it affects users information disclosure. To determine risk propensity we asked users for their level of agreement with risk propensity statements. Female users have a greater tendency to knowingly take risks in life and on the internet (U=5731.5, z= -3.18, p<.05) with 31% of females more likely to take risks in general, in comparison with 18% of males. Females are also more likely to visit somewhat "untrustworthy" web pages (U=5426, z=-3.59, p<.05) with 39% of females more likely in comparison with 25% of males. We found a number of relationships between users' level of agreement with the risk propensity questions in relation to users accepting friend requests. Correlations were found between on-line security conscientiousness and the likelihood to accept a "friend" request from a person they have met but are not well acquainted with ($r_s$=-.129, p<.05); a person they have never met, with whom they have a few mutual friends ($r_s$=-.191, p<.01); a person they have never met, with whom they have no mutual friends ($r_s$=-.151, p<.05).

15% of users are conscientious about protecting their online security and privacy. These results confirm what we would expect: the more a user is conscientious about maintaining computer/online security and privacy, the less likely they will accept a friend request from the categories stated above. However we have found users who reveal a lot about themselves on the internet are less conscientious about maintaining their computer's security and online privacy ($r_s$=-.140, p<.05). Results show that a user who accepts a friend request from a person they have never met and they have no mutual friends corresponds with their general tendency to knowingly take risks on the internet ($r_s$=+.149, p<.05) and in life. These results confirm the more risks the users take in life and behaving similarly on the internet, the more users reveal about themselves on Facebook ($r_s$=+.311, p<.01). Engagement in risky and careless online activities with lack of concern for personal online privacy is a factor in security and privacy issues related to online behaviour of Internet users (Bubas et al., 2008).

## Privacy Disposition

A user's privacy can be viewed as being under threat if they reveal too much personal information about themselves online (Fuchs, 2011). The users surveyed agreed that they tend to reveal minimal information about themselves as they feel uncomfortable about personal information being in the hands of others to prevent being the victim of deceit or fraud ($r_s$ =+.215, p<.01). 74% of users agreed that they reveal minimal personal information on Facebook as they value their rights to privacy. However, these results can be debated as further analysis of the results show when asked to choose which personal information items they reveal online, most respondents in fact reveal seven or more item types. The more concerned users were that Facebook might reveal their personal information to other parties without their explicit consent, the more concerned they are that a history of their activities are held by Facebook ($r_s = -.434$, p<.01). 20% of users have had their reputation damaged as a result of information posted on Facebook. This concern that Facebook as a company might divulge their information to other parties without their consent makes them feel uncomfortable about disclosing personal information on the SNS as the users are unsure whose hands their information may end up in. 66% of users believe there is a need to be concerned about disclosing personal information on Facebook. Perceived privacy risks are said to prevent information disclosure by users (Krasnova et al., 2010). When asked whether a particular list of events happened to them on Facebook, female users have had on more occasions their account being maliciously accessed by an unauthorised person (U=6583, z= -2.27, p<.05) with 28% of females in comparison with 17% of males. Females have also been the victim of online fraud, either in Facebook or elsewhere more often than males (U=6979.5, z= -1.99, p<.05), with 9% of females being the victim in comparison with 3% of males.

There is a greater chance the users surveyed would be embarrassed if false information is posted about them on Facebook thus violating their privacy ($r_s = +.125$, p<.05). The results also show that users felt their reputation would be damaged if false information is posted about them ($r_s$=+.257, p=.01). With this potential for false information being posted about users, the users possess a level of trust in relation to other Facebook users which may result in them increasing their regard for privacy in the future. Users reveal information about their lives but it does not mean that they do not care about privacy (Netchitailova, 2012). Surprisingly, users are less likely to be embarrassed by false information posted about them by others if they never had an unpleasant experience as a result of information disclosed by them on Facebook previously (rs=+.188, p<.01). One would think they would in fact be embarrassed especially if it is the first time occurring. The solution to user privacy concerns on Facebook is to use the principle of the lowest common denominator: "only publish things that all connections ought to see" (Jensen and Sorensen 2013, p.60). One user's comment urged Facebook to make their privacy policies easier to understand: "It would be nice if FB made it easier to understand their privacy policies."

## FUTURE RESEARCH DIRECTIONS

Possible areas for future study arising from this study include:

- The reasons why people might accept a "friend" request from somebody they do not know?
- The majority of respondents were not aware that Facebook can use your personal information for ways you did not intend. This could provide the basis for further education that is needed around the area of privacy and SNS (policy awareness education).
- Why do females tend to reveal more information about themselves and take more risks online than males?
- On a larger scale, are females more likely than males to have their accounts maliciously accessed?
- Why do users consider it not risky to disclose their personal information online?
- Does the greater the level of trust users have in their friends affect how protected they feel by current laws?

## CONCLUSION

Since their arrival, Social Networking Sites (SNS) such as Facebook have drawn millions of users and become a place to maintain already existing relationships while also creating new ones. Due to the large amount of users on Facebook, there is a large amount of personal information circulating the SNS. The major concern is that the huge amount of personal information such as birth dates, photographs, home addresses and telephone numbers is being made available by users and this information may end up in the hands of people we do not want it to (for example potential employers, strangers etc.). This leads to risks to individual privacy and security in cyberspace due to the use of SNS's such as Facebook. However, to maintain the success of SNS providers, it is important for users to continue to access and engage on the site to preserve its existence and popularity (Chen, 2013).

In the research reported in this chapter, we conducted a survey to study into the factors that affect information disclosure on Facebook. This study has demonstrated that in general, users feel they have a small amount of control, a small amount of legal protection, some users partake in risky behaviour online, the level of trust depends on the circumstance, and users have a high regard for privacy. For example, this study demonstrated how a loss of control was prompted by changes in privacy settings by Facebook, which triggered user's perceptions of higher privacy concerns and a lower level of trust when disclosing information.

From this research, it appears that the more details that are provided by users, the more active they are on Facebook and the greater number of friends they have. Our results indicate that although Facebook users state they have a high regard for privacy, they are posting a considerable amount of personal information, even though perhaps they may not realise this (Utz & Kramer, 2011; Youn, 2005). Overall, this makes the users trusting of other Facebook users and Facebook the service provider. There is a balance involved between privacy and disclosure (Christofides et al., 2009), while one can reveal only a certain amount of personal information and still have a high regard for privacy. We found that more females have had their account maliciously accessed and they also take more risks online and offline.

This survey confirms the existence of a number of privacy problems, such as users not being fully educated and aware of the policies and privacy issues of Facebook. The more users are educated about SNS and their privacy risks, the greater the chance they will take the correct actions if they develop an understanding of the implications of their behaviour.

This study makes a contribution to policy awareness of SNS use for SNS service providers. SNS usage by users adds vital support to the existence and viability of these SNS's, however service providers need to improve the privacy (awareness, policies, risks) of the site, for example through the implementation of Privacy by Design, whereby privacy is embedded into the design specification and always the default setting, alleviating perceived risks as this can affect site use.

## REFERENCES

Acquisti, A., & Gross, R. (2006). Imagined communities: Awareness, information sharing, and privacy on the Facebook. In G. Danezis & P. Golle, P. (Eds.), *Privacy Enhancing Technologies: 6th International Workshop, PET 2006* (pp. 36–58). Berlin: Springer.

Associated Press. (2013). *Number of active Facebook users over the years*. Retrieved from http://news.yahoo.com/number-active-users-facebook-over-230449748.html

Barnes, S. B. (2007). A privacy paradox: Social networking in the United States. *First Monday*, *11*(9). Retrieved from http://firstmonday.org/ojs/index.php/fm/article/view/1394/1312 doi:10.5210/fm.v11i9.1394

boyd, D. M., & Ellison, N. B. (2007). Social network sites: Definition, history, and scholarship. *Journal of Computer-Mediated Communication*, *13*(1), 210–230. doi:10.1111/j.1083-6101.2007.00393.x

Bubas, G., Orehovacki, T., & Konecki, M. (2008). Factors and Predictors of Online Security and Privacy Behaviour. *Journal of Information and Organizational Sciences*, 32(2), 9–98.

Chen, R. (2013). Living a Private Life in Public Social Networks: An Exploration of Member Self-Disclosure. *Decision Support Systems*, 55(3), 661–668. doi:10.1016/j.dss.2012.12.003

Chen, R. (2013). Member use of social networking sites: an empirical examination. *Decision Support Systems*, 54(3), 1219–1227. doi:10.1016/j.dss.2012.10.028

Christofides, E., Muise, A., & Desmarais, S. (2009). Information disclosure and control on Facebook: are they two sides of the same coin or two different processes? *Cyberpsychology & Behavior*, 12(3), 341–345. doi:10.1089/cpb.2008.0226 PMID:19250020

Collins, N. L., & Miller, L. C. (1994). Self-disclosure and liking: a meta-analytic review. *Psychological Bulletin*, 116(3), 457–475. doi:10.1037/0033-2909.116.3.457 PMID:7809308

Debatin, B., Lovejoy, J. P., Horn, A. K., & Hughes, B. N. (2009). Facebook and online privacy: Attitudes, behaviors, and unintended consequences. *Journal of Computer-Mediated Communication*, 15(1), 83–108. doi:10.1111/j.1083-6101.2009.01494.x

Dinev, T., & Hart, P. (2006). An extended privacy calculus model for e-commerce transactions. *Information Systems Research*, 17(1), 61–80. doi:10.1287/isre.1060.0080

Dwyer, C., Hiltz, S., & Passerini, K. (2007). Trust and Privacy Concern Within Social Networking Sites. A Comparison of Facebook and MySpace. In *Proceedings of the 13th Americas Conference on Information Systems*. Retrieved from http://aisel.aisnet.org/amcis2007/339

Fuchs, C. (2011). An alternative view of privacy on Facebook. *Information*, 2(4), 140–165. doi:10.3390/info2010140

Grabner-Kräuter, S., & Kaluscha, E. A. (2003). Empirical research in on-line trust: a review and critical assessment. *International Journal of Human-Computer Studies*, 58(6), 783–812. doi:10.1016/S1071-5819(03)00043-0

Harden, G., Al Beayeyz, A., & Visinescu, L. (2012). Concerning SNS Use: How do Issues of Privacy and Trust Concern Users? In *Proceedings of the 18th Americas Conference on Information Systems*. Retrieved from http://aisel.aisnet.org/amcis2012/proceedings/SocialIssues/4

Henderson, S., & Gilding, M. (2004). 'I've never clicked this much with anyone in my life': trust and hyperpersonal communication in online friendships. *New Media & Society*, 6(4), 487–506. doi:10.1177/146144804044331

Hill, K. (2010). Where Steve Jobs Stood on Location Privacy in. Retrieved from http://www.forbes.com/sites/kashmirhill/2011/04/25/where-steve-jobs-stood-on-location-privacy-in-2010/

Hoadley, C. M., Xu, H., Lee, J. J., & Rosson, M. B. (2010). Privacy as information access and illusory control: The case of the Facebook News Feed privacy outcry. *Electronic Commerce Research and Applications*, 9(1), 50–60. doi:10.1016/j.elerap.2009.05.001

Hoffman, D. L., Novak, T. P., & Peralta, M. (1999). Building consumer trust online. *Communications of the ACM*, 42(4), 80–85. doi:10.1145/299157.299175

Jensen, J. L., & Sørensen, A. S. (2013). Nobody has 257 Friends. *Nordicom Review*, 34(1), 49–62.

Joinson, N. A. (2008). 'Looking at', 'Looking up' or 'keeping up with people'? Motives and Uses of Facebook. In *Proceedings of the SIGCHI Conference on Human Factors in Computing Systems* (pp. 1027-1036). New York: ACM.

Malhotra, K. NKim, S. S., & Agarwal, J. (2004). Internet Users' Information Privacy Concerns (IUIPC): The Construct, the Scale, and a Casual Model. *Information Systems Research*, *15*(4), 336–355. doi:10.1287/isre.1040.0032

Krasnova, H., Kolesnikova, E., & Guenther, O. (2009). "It Won't Happen To Me!": Self-Disclosure in Online Social Networks. In *Proceedings of the 15th Americas Conference on Information Systems*. Retrieved from http://aisel.aisnet.org/amcis2009/343

Krasnova, H., Spiekermann, S., Koroleva, K., & Hildebrand, T. (2010). Online social networks: why we disclose. *Journal of Information Technology*, *25*(2), 109–125. doi:10.1057/jit.2010.6

Lang, M., Devitt, J., Kelly, S., Kinneen, A., O'Malley, J., & Prunty, D. (2009). Social Networking and Personal Data Security: A Study of Attitudes and Public Awareness in Ireland. In *Proceedings of the 2009 International Conference on Management of e-Commerce and e-Government* (pp. 486-489). Washington, DC: IEEE Computer Society.

Langer, E. J. (1975). The illusion of control. *Journal of Personality and Social Psychology*, *32*(2), 311–328. doi:10.1037/0022-3514.32.2.311

Liu, C., Marchewka, T. J., Lu, J., & Yu, S. C. (2005). Beyond Concern: A Privacy-Trust-Behavioural Intention Model of Electronic Commerce. *Information & Management*, *42*(2), 289–304. doi:10.1016/j.im.2004.01.003

Netchitailova, E. P. (2012). Facebook as a Surveillance Tool: From the Perspective of the User. *tripleC: Communication, Capitalism & Critique. Open Access Journal for a Global Sustainable Information Society*, *10*(2), 683–691.

Nguyen, M., Bin, Y. S., & Campbell, A. (2012). Comparing online and offline self-disclosure: A systematic review. *Cyberpsychology, Behavior and Social Networking*, *15*(2), 103–111. doi:10.1089/cyber.2011.0277 PMID:22032794

Nikander, P., & Karvonen, K. (2001). Users and Trust in Cyberspace. In *Security Protocols: 8th International Workshop* (pp. 1-22). Berlin: Springer.

Posey, C., Lowry, B. P., Roberts, L. T., & Ellis, S. T. (2010). Proposing the online community self-disclosure model: the case of working professionals in France and the U.K. who use online Communities. *European Journal of Information Systems*, *19*(2), 181–195. doi:10.1057/ejis.2010.15

Ridings, C., Gefen, D., & Arinze, B. (2002). Some antecedents and effects of trust in virtual communities. *The Journal of Strategic Information Systems*, *11*(3-4), 271–295. doi:10.1016/S0963-8687(02)00021-5

Trepte, S., & Reinecke, L. (2013). The reciprocal effects of social network site use and the disposition for self-disclosure: A longitudinal study. *Computers in Human Behavior*, *29*(3), 1102–1112. doi:10.1016/j.chb.2012.10.002

Utz, S., & Kramer, C. N. (2009). The privacy paradox on social network sites revisited: The role of individual characteristics and group norms. *Cyberpsychology*, *3*(2). Retrieved from http://cyberpsychology.eu/view.php?cisloclanku=2009111001&article=2

Veltri, F. N., Krasnova, H., & Elgarah, W. (2011). Online disclosure and privacy concerns: A study of Moroccan and American Facebook users. In *Proceedings of the 17th Americas Conference on Information Systems*. Retrieved from http://aisel.aisnet.org/amcis2011_submissions/300

Wang, J. (2013). Factors affecting Social Networking Website Loyalty. *Information Technology Journal, 12*(3), 545–547. doi:10.3923/itj.2013.545.547

Xu, F., Michael, K., & Chen, X. (2013). Factors affectng privacy disclosure on social network sites: an integrated model. *Electronic Commerce Research, 13*(2), 151–168. doi:10.1007/s10660-013-9111-6

Youn, S. (2005). Teenagers' perceptions of online privacy and coping behaviours: a risk-benefit appraisal approach. *Journal of Broadcasting & Electronic Media, 49*(1), 86–110. doi:10.1207/s15506878jobem4901_6

## KEY TERMS AND DEFINITIONS

**Social Networking Sites:** On-line communication channels (e.g. Facebook, LinkedIn, Twitter) which are used to build and maintain relationships between users.

**Privacy:** The state of being secluded from unwarranted intrusion into one's private affairs and not disturbed by other parties.

**Perceived Control:** The extent to which a person believes they can exercise control over the actions of another party.

**Perceived Risk:** The judgement a person makes surrounding the attributes and severity of a risk.

**Risk Propensity:** The extent to which a person is willing to take a chance with respect to possible loss. Persons who are "risk averse" have a low risk propensity; those who are "risk takers" have a high risk propensity.

**Disclosure:** The act of revealing information about oneself.

**Trust:** Confidence that another party will act in good faith and behave in accordance with shared agreements.

# Compilation of References

AACAP. (2008). *Facts for families, the American Academy of Child Adolescent Psychiatry*. Retrieved December 5, 2011, from http://www.aacap.org/galleries/FactsFor-Families/80_bullying.pdf

Aaron, D. B. (2011, November 17). Google android passes 50% of Smartphone Sales. *Bloomberg Businessweek*. Retrieved August 21, 2013, from http://www.businessweek.com/news/2011-11-17/google2android-passes-50-of-smartphone-sales-gartner-says.html

Abbasi, F. H., & Harris, R. J. (2009, November). Experiences with a Generation III virtual Honeynet. In *Proceedings of Telecommunication Networks and Applications Conference (ATNAC), 2009 Australasian* (pp. 1-6). IEEE.

Abbott, J., Bell, J., Clark, A., De Vel, O., & Mohay, G. (2006). Automated recognition of event scenarios for digital forensics. In *Proceedings of the 2006 ACM Symposium on Applied Computing*, (pp. 293-300). ACM.

ABC News. (2010). *Immigrant teen taunted by cyberbullies hangs herself*. Available at http://abcnews.go.com/Health/cyberbullying-factor-suicidemassachusetts-teen-irishimmigrant/story?id=9660938

Ackers, M. J. (2012). Cyberbullying: through the eyes of children and young people. *Educational Psychology in Practice*, *28*(2), 141–157. doi:10.1080/02667363.2012.665356

Acórdão Nº 0546541. (2006). *Tribunal da Relação do Porto* (p. 7). Retrieved from http://www.dgsi.pt/jtrp.nsf/c3fb530030ea1c61802568d9005cd5bb/c4d2a9d88f8d235780257172003d20f2

Acquisti, A., & Gross, R. (2006). Imagined communities: Awareness, information sharing, and privacy on the Facebook. In G. Danezis & P. Golle, P. (Eds.), *Privacy Enhancing Technologies: 6th International Workshop, PET 2006* (pp. 36–58). Berlin: Springer.

Acquisti, A., et al. (2011). *Cyber-bullying and online grooming: Helping to protect against the risks. A scenario on data mining / profiling of data available on the Internet*. Greece, Athens: European Network and Information Security (ENISA). Retrieved January 30, 2014 from https://www.enisa.europa.eu/activities/risk-management/emerging-and-future-risk/deliverables/Cyber-Bullying%20and%20Online%20Grooming

Ademu, I. O., Imafidon, C. O., & Preston, D. S. (2011). A new approach of digital forensic model for digital forensic investigation. *International Journal of Advanced Computer Science and Applications*, *2*(12).

AEPD. (2011). *El derecho fundamental a la protección de datos - Guía para el Ciudadano*. Madri: Agencia Española de Protección de Datos. Retrieved from https://www.agpd.es/portalwebAGPD/CanalDelCiudadano/guias_recomendaciones/index-ides-idphp.php

Agatston, P., Kowalski, R., & Limber, S. (2012). Youth views on cyber bullying. In J. W. Patchin, & S. Hinduja (Eds.), *Cyber bullying prevention and response: Expert perspectives* (pp. 57–71). New York, NY: Routledge.

Agatston, P.W., Kowalski, R., & Limber, S. (2007). Students' Perspectives on Cyber Bullying. *The Journal of Adolescent Health*, *41*(6), S59–S60. doi:10.1016/j.jadohealth.2007.09.003 PMID:18047946

Agência Brasil. (2010). Justiça prorroga prazo para debate sobre Marco Civil na Internet. *Agência Brasil*. Retrieved March 05, 2013, from http://ultimainstancia.uol.com.br/conteudo/noticias/46764/justica+prorroga+prazo+para+debate+sobre+marco+civil+na+internet.shtml

Aharonovsky, G. (2008). *Malicious camera spying using ClickJacking*. Retrieved from http://blog.guya.net/2008/10/07/malicious-camera-spying-using-click-jacking, 2008

Ahmad, M., Wasay, E., & Malik, S. (2012). Impact of employee motivation on customer satisfaction: Study of airline industry in Pakistan. *Interdisciplinary Journal of Contemporary Research in Business*, 4(6), 531–539.

Akdeniz, Y. (2001). Controlling illegal and harmful content on the internet. In D. S. Wall (Ed.), *Crime and the internet* (p. 113). London: Brunner-Routledge. doi:10.4324/9780203164501_chapter_8

Al Mutawa, N., Baggili, I., & Marrington, A. (2012). Forensic analysis of social networking applications on mobile devices. *Digital Investigation*, 9, S24–S33. doi:10.1016/j.diin.2012.05.007

Alam, M. R., Reaz, M. B. I., & Ali, M. A. M. (2012). A review of smart Homes—Past, present, and future. *IEEE Transactions on* Systems, Man, and Cybernetics, Part C: Applications and Reviews, 42(6), 1190–1203.

Alazab, M., Venkatraman, S., Watters, P., Alazab, M., & Alazab, A. (2012). Cybercrime: The case of obfuscated malware. In Global Security, Safety and Sustainability & e-Democracy (pp. 204–211). Springer.

Alexy, E., Burgess, A., Baker, T., & Smoyak, S. (2005). Perceptions of cyberstalking among college students. *Brief Treatment and Crisis Intervention*, 5(3), 279–289. doi:10.1093/brief-treatment/mhi020

Alhaqbani, B., Adams, M., Fidge, C. J., & ter Hofstede, A. H. M. (2013). Privacy-Aware Workflow Management. In M. Glykas (Ed.), *Business Process Management: Theory and Applications* (pp. 111–128). Berlin, Germany: Springer. doi:10.1007/978-3-642-28409-0_5

Alkaabi, A., Mohay, G., McCullagh, A., & Chantler, N. (2011). Dealing with the problem of cybercrime. In *Proceedings of 2nd International ICST Conference on Digital Forensics & Cyber Crime*, (vol. 53, pp. 1867-8211). ICST. doi: 10.1007/978-3-642-19513-6_1

Allen, J. (1983). Maintaining knowledge about temporal intervals. *Communications of the ACM*, 26(11), 832–843. doi:10.1145/182.358434

Allen, J. F. (1984). Towards a general theory of action and time. *Artificial Intelligence*, 23(2), 123–154. doi:10.1016/0004-3702(84)90008-0

Allum, J. R. (2006). An Outcrop of Hel: History, Environment and the Politics of the Trail Smelter Dispute. In R. M. Bratspies, & R. A. Miller (Eds.), *Transboundary Harm in International Law, Lessons from the Trail Smelter Arbitration* (p. 15). Cambridge: Cambridge University Press.

Almeida, A. N., Delicado, A., & Alves, N. A. (2008). *Crianças e internet: Usos e respresentações, a família e a escola*. Unpublished doctoral dissertation, Instituto de Ciências Sociais da Universidade de Lisboa, Lisbon.

Almutairi, A., Parish, D., & Phan, R. (2012). Survey of high interaction honeypot tools: Merits and shortcomings. In *Proceedings of the 13th Annual PostGraduate Symposium on The Convergence of Telecommunications, Networking and Broadcasting, PGNet2012*. PGNet.

Alonso de Escamilla, A., & Nuñez Fernandez, J. (2010). Fundamentos de derecho penal. Colección Praxis, Ed. Universitas.

Alonso de Escamilla, A. (2013). Torturas y otros delitos contra la integridad moral. In *Delitos y faltas* (2nd ed.). Ed. Colex.

Alvarez, G., & Petrovic, S. (2003). A new taxonomy of web attacks suitable for efficient encoding. *Computers & Security*, 22(5), 435–449. doi:10.1016/S0167-4048(03)00512-1

American Specialized Conference on Human Rights. (1969). *Convenção Americana de Direitos Humanos*. Retrieved June 07, 2013, from http://www.pge.sp.gov.br/centrodeestudos/bibliotecavirtual/instrumentos/sanjose.htm

Amin, A.A., & Sastry, S. (2008). Secure control: Towards survivable cyber-physical systems. In *Proceedings of 28th International Conference on Distributed Computing Systems Workshops, 2008* (pp. 495-500). Academic Press.

Ancona, D. G., & Caldwell, D. F. (1992). Demography and design: predictors of new product team performance. *Organization Science, 3*(3), 321–341. doi:10.1287/orsc.3.3.321

Andenas, M., Gutt, T., & Pannier, M. (2005). Free movement of capital and national company law. *European Business Law Review, 16*(4), 757.

Anderson, J. (2012). *The department of defense needs an enterprise-wide approach to cloud.* Retrieved from http://safegov.org/2012/5/17/the-department-of-defense-needs-an-enterprise-wide-approach-to-cloud

Anderson, R., Barton, C., Böhme, R., Clayton, R., van Eeten, M., Levi, M., . . . Savage, S. (2012). Measuring the cost of cybercrime. In *Proceedings of 11th Workshop on the Economics of Information Security*. Academic Press.

Anderson, T., & Sturm, B. (2007, Winter). Cyber bullying from playground to computer. *Young Adult Library Services*, 24-27.

Anderson, P. (2001). Children as researchers - The effects of participation rights on research methodology. In P. Christensen, & A. James (Eds.), *Research with children - Perspectives and practices* (pp. 241–275). London: Routledge Falmer.

Anderson, W. L. (2010). Cyber stalking (cyber bullying)-proof and punishment. *Insights to a Changing World Journal, 4*, 18–23.

*Android Design*. (*2013*). Retrieved August 21, 2013, from http://developer.android.com/design/index.html

*Android IDL Example with Code Description – IPC*. (2013, July 20). Retrieved August 21, 2013, from http://techblogon.com/android-aidl-example-with-code-description-ipc

Angerman, W. S. (2004). *Coming full circle with Boyd's OODA loop ideas: An analysis of innovation diffusion and evolution*. (Unpublished master's thesis). Airforce Institute of Technology, Wright-Patterson AFB, OH.

Ang, R. P., & Goh, D. H. (2010). Cyber bullying among adolescents: The role of affective and cognitive empathy, and gender. *Child Psychiatry and Human Development, 41*(4), 387–397. doi:10.1007/s10578-010-0176-3 PMID:20238160

Anonymous, . (2006). Security views. *Computers & Security, 25*, 238–246.

Anselin, L. (2001). Spatial Econometrics. In A Companion to Theoretical Econometrics. Oxford, UK: Basil Blackwell.

Anselin, L. (2002a). *Spatial Externalities* (Working Paper). Sal, Agecon, Uiuc.

Anselin, L. (2002b). *Properties of tests for spatial error components* (Working Paper). Sal, Agecon, Uiuc.

Anselin, L. (2002c). *Spatial externalities, spatial multipliers and spatial econometrics* (Working Paper). Sal, Agecon, Uiuc.

Anselin, L. (2002d). *Under the hood: Issues in the specification and interpretation of spatial regression models* (Working Paper). Sal, Agecon, Uiuc.

Anselin, L. (1988). *Spatial Econometrics: Methods and Models*. Dordrecht, Netherlands: Kluwer Academic Publishers. doi:10.1007/978-94-015-7799-1

Anselin, L. (1995). Local Indicators of Spatial Association-LISA. *Geographical Analysis, 27*, 93–115. doi:10.1111/j.1538-4632.1995.tb00338.x

Anselin, L. (2003a). *An introduction to spatial autocorrelation analysis with GeoDa*. Sal, Agecon, Uiuc.

Anselin, L. (2003b). *GeoDa™ 0.9 User's Guide*. Sal, Agecon, Uiuc.

Anselin, L. (2004). *GeoDa™ 0.9.5-i Release Notes*. Sal, Agecon, Uiuc.

Antonakopoulou, A., Lioudakis, G. V., Gogoulos, F., Kaklamani, D. I., & Venieris, I. S. (2012). Leveraging Access Control for Privacy Protection: A Survey. In G. Yee (Ed.), *Privacy protection measures and technologies in business organizations: aspects and standards* (pp. 65–94). Hershey, PA: IGI Global.

ArcSight. (2011). *Second annual cost of cybercrime study*. Retrieved from http://www.hpenterprisesecurity.com/collateral/report

Arimatsu, L. (2012). A treaty for governing cyber-weapons: Potential benefits and practical limitations. In *Proceedings of Cyber Conflict (CYCON),* (pp. 1–19). CYCON.

Arthur, C. (2011, February 7). Anonymous attacks US security company. *The Guardian Magazine.* Retrieved from http://www.theguardian.com

Article 29 Data Protection Working Party. (2003). *Working Document on E-Government.* Retrieved November 30, 2013, from http://ec.europa.eu/justice/policies/privacy/docs/wpdocs/2003/e-government_en.pdf

Article 29 Data Protection Working Party. (2007). *Working Document on the processing of personal data relating to health in electronic health records (EHR).* Retrieved November 30, 2013, from http://ec.europa.eu/justice/policies/privacy/docs/wpdocs/2007/wp131_en.pdf

Ascensão, J. de O. (2003). *Propriedade intelectual e Internet.* Retrieved March 03, 2013, from http://www.fd.ul.pt/Portals/0/Docs/Institutos/ICJ/LusCommune/AscensaoJoseOliveira1.pdf

Ascensão, J. O. (1995). Teoria geral do direito civil. (Associação de Estudantes, Ed.) (Faculdade., p. 121). Lisboa: Faculdade de Direito.

Asrigo, K., Litty, L., & Lie, D. (2006). Using VMM-based sensors to monitor honeypots. In *Proceedings of the 2nd International Conference on Virtual Execution Environments (VEE'06)* (pp. 13-23). New York: ACM. doi:10.1145/1134760.1134765

Associated Press. (2013). *Number of active Facebook users over the years.* Retrieved from http://news.yahoo.com/number-active-users-facebook-over-230449748.html

Aston, M., McCombie, S., Reardon, B., & Watters, P. (2009). A preliminary profiling of internet money mules: An Australian perspective. In Proceedings of Ubiquitous, Autonomic and Trusted Computing, (pp. 482–487). UIC-ATC.

Athanasopoulos, E., Pappas, V., & Markatos, E. (2009). Code-Injection Attacks in Browsers Supporting Policies. In *Proceedings of the 2nd Workshop on Web 2.0 Security & Privacy* (W2SP). W2SP.

Atkins, T. (n.d.). *Swatch: Simple watcher man page.* Retrieved 2013, from http://linux.die.net/man/1/swatch

*ATL.* (2009). Retrieved December 4, 2011, from http://www.atl.org.uk/Images/Joint%20ATL%20TSN%20cyberbullying%20survey%202009.pdf

Awad, A., Weidlich, M., & Weske, M. (2011). Visually Specifying Compliance Rules and Explaining their Violations for Business Processes. *Journal of Visual Languages and Computing, 22*(1), 30–55. doi:10.1016/j.jvlc.2010.11.002

Ayed, A., Cuppens-Boulahia, N., & Cuppens, F. (2009). Deploying security policy in intra and inter workflow management systems. In *Proceedings of the 2009 International Conference on Availability, Reliability and Security (ARES 2009)* (pp. 58–65). Washington, DC: IEEE Computer Society.

Azuwa, M., Ahmad, R., Sahib, S., & Shamsuddin, S. (2012). Technical security metrics model in compliance with ISO/IEC 27001 standard. *International Journal of Cyber-Security and Digital Forensics, 1*(4), 280–288.

Baarendse, P. J., Counotte, D. S., O'Donnell, P., & Vanderschuren, L. J. (2013). Early social experience is critical for the development of cognitive control and dopamine modulation of prefrontal cortex function. *Neuropsychopharmacology: Official Publication of the American College of Neuropsychopharmacology, 38*(8), 1485-1494. doi:10.1038/npp.2013.47

Backhouse, J., &, & Dhillon, G. (1996). Structures of Responsibility and Security of Information Systems. *European Journal of Information Systems, 5,* 2–9. doi:10.1057/ejis.1996.7

Backhouse, J., Hsu, C., & Silva, L. (2006). Circuits of Power in Creating De Jure Standards: Shaping an International Information Systems Security Standard. *Management Information Systems Quarterly, 30*(Special issue), 413–438.

*BAE Systems Detica*. (2012). Retrieved from http://www.baesystemsdetica.com/uploads/resources/ORGAN-ISED_CRIME_IN_THE_DIGITAL_AGE_EXECU-TIVE_SUMMARY_FINAL_MARCH_2012.pdf

Baesens, B., Setiono, R., Mues, C., & Vanthienen, J. (2003). Using neural network rule extraction and decision tables for credit-risk evaluation. *Management Science*, *49*(3), 312–329. doi:10.1287/mnsc.49.3.312.12739

Bagchi, K., & Udo, G. (2003). An analysis of the growth of computer and internet security breaches. *Communications of the Association for Information Systems*, *12*, 684–700.

Bak, P., Tang, C., & Wiesenfeld, K. (1987). Self-organized criticality: An explanation of the 1/$f$ noise. *Physical Review Letters*, *59*(4), 381–384. doi:10.1103/PhysRevLett.59.381 PMID:10035754

Balduzzi, M., Egele, M., Kirda, E., Balzarotti, D., & Kruegel, C. (2010). A solution for the automated detection of clickjacking attacks. In *Proceedings of the 5th ACM Symposium on Information, Computer and Communications Security* (pp. 135-144). Beijing, China: ACM.

Baldwin, C. (2012, September 17). Android devices vulnerable to security breaches. *ComputerWeekly.com*. Retrieved August 21, 2013, from http://www.computerweekly.com/news/2240163351/Android-devices-vulnerable-to-security-breaches

Ballora, M., Giacobe, N. A., & Hall, D. L. (2011). Songs of cyberspace: an update on sonifications of network traffic to support situational awareness. In Proceedings of SPIE Defense, Security, and Sensing. SPIE.

Ballora, M., Giacobe, N. A., McNeese, M., & Hall, D. L. (2012). Information data fusion and computer network defense. In C. Onwubiko & T. Owens (Ed.), Situational Awareness in Computer Network Defense: Principles, Methods and Applications. IGI Global.

Ballora, M., Panulla, B., Gourley, M., & Hall, D. L. (2010). Preliminary steps in sonifying web log data. In E. Brazil (Ed.), *16th International Conference on Auditory Display* (pp. 83-87). Washington, DC: ICAD.

Banbury, S., & Tremblay, S. (2004). Preface. In S. Banbury, & S. Tremblay (Eds.), *A cognitive approach to situation awareness: Theory and application*. Aldershot, UK: Ashgate Publishing.

Bandhakavi, S., King, S. T., Madhusudan, P., & Winslett, M. (2010, August). VEX: Vetting browser extensions for security vulnerabilities. In *Proceedings of USENIX Security Symposium* (Vol. 10, pp. 339-354). USENIX.

Bantel, K. A., & Jackson, S. E. (1989). Top management and innovations in banking: Does the composition of the top team make a difference? *Strategic Management Journal*, *10*, 107–124. doi:10.1002/smj.4250100709

Barboza, J. (1986). *Second report*. U.N. Doc. A/CN.4/402.

Barboza, J. (1993). *Ninth Report of the Special Rapporteur, Mr. Julio Barboza*. U.N. Doc. A/48/10.

Barboza, J. (1994). *Tenth Report of the Special Rapporteur, Mr. Julio Barboza*. U.N. Doc. A/49/10.

Barboza, J. (1996). *Twelfth Report of the Special Rapporteur, Mr. Julio Barboza*. U.N. Doc. A/51/10.

Barnes, S. B. (2007). A privacy paradox: Social networking in the United States. *First Monday*, *11*(9). Retrieved from http://firstmonday.org/ojs/index.php/fm/article/view/1394/1312 doi:10.5210/fm.v11i9.1394

Barrêdo, J. R. (2012). Ou aprendemos a programar ou seremos programados, diz cientista. *G1*. Retrieved July 04, 2013, from http://g1.globo.com/natureza/rio20/noticia/2012/06/ou-aprendemos-programar-ou-seremos-programados-diz-cientista.html

Barth, A. (2007). *Adopt "descendant" frame navigation policy to prevent frame hijacking*. Academic Press.

Barth, A., Jackson, C., Reis, C., & Team, T. G. C. (2008). *The security architecture of the Chromium browser*. Academic Press.

Barth, A., Jackson, C., & Mitchell, J. C. (2009). Securing frame communication in browsers. *Communications of the ACM*, *52*(6), 83–91. doi:10.1145/1516046.1516066

Baryamureeba, V., & Tushabe, F. (2004). The enhanced digital investigation process model. In *Proceedings of the Fourth Digital Forensic Research Workshop*. Academic Press.

Bavuso, S.J. (1987). Analysis of typical fault-tolerant architecture using HARP. *IEEE Transactions on Reliability*, R-*36*, 176–185. doi:10.1109/TR.1987.5222335

Bayzick, J., Kontostathis, A., & Edwards, L. (2011). Detecting the Presence of Cyberbullying Using Computer Software. In *Proceedings of WebSci '11*. Retrieved December 4, 2011, from http://www.websci11.org/fileadmin/websci/Posters/63_paper.pdf

Bazelon, D. L. (1975). A jurist's view of psychiatry. *The Journal of Psychiatry & Law, 3*, 175.

Bazelon, D. L. (1976). Probing privacy. *Gonzaga Law Review, 12*, 587.

Bazelon, D. L. (1977). Coping with technology through the legal process. *Jurimetrics Journal, 18*, 241.

BBC Brasil. (2010). Para 4 em cada 5 pessoas, Internet é direito fundamental, diz pesquisa. *BBC Brasil*. Retrieved June 07, 2013, from http://www.bbc.co.uk/portuguese/lg/noticias/2010/03/100307_pesquisabbc_internetml.shtml?s

BBC News US & Canada. (2013). *US cyber command in 'fivefold' staff expansion*. Retrieved from http://www.bbc.co.uk/news/world-us-canada-21235256

BBC News. (2009). *UK has cyber attack capability*. Retrieved from http://news.bbc.co.uk/1/hi/uk_politics/8118729.stm

Beadle, J. N. (2009). *The neuroanatomical basis of empathy: Is empathy impaired following damage to the ventromedial prefrontal cortex?* ProQuest.

Beasley, M. S. (1996). An empirical analysis of the relation between the board of director composition and financial statement fraud. *Accounting Review, 71*(4), 443–465.

Beaucamps, P., Reynaud, D., & Loria-Nancy, F. (2008, June). Malicious firefox extensions. In Proceedings of Symp. Sur La Securite Des Technologies De L'Information Et Des Communications. Academic Press.

Bechtsoudis, A., & Sklavos, N. (2012). Aiming at higher network security through extensive penetration tests. *IEEE Latin America Transactions, 10*(3), 1752–1756. doi:10.1109/TLA.2012.6222581

Beckman, L., Hagquist, C., & Hellström, L. (2013). Discrepant gender patterns for cyber bullyiyng and traditional bullying – An analysis of Swedish adolescent data. *Computers in Human Behavior, 29*(5), 1896–1903. doi:10.1016/j.chb.2013.03.010

Bedeian, A. G., & Mossholder, K. W. (2000). On the use of the coefficient of variation as a measure of diversity. *Organizational Research Methods, 3*(3), 285–297. doi:10.1177/109442810033005

Beniger, J. (1989). *The control revolution: The Control Revolution: Technological and Economic Origins of the Information Society*. Cambridge, MA: Harvard University Press.

Benson, K., & Rahman, S. M. (2011). Security risks in mechanical engineering industries. *International Journal of Computer Science & Engineering Survey, 2*(3), 75–92. doi:10.5121/ijcses.2011.2306

Bentley, P. J. (2005). Controlling robots with fractal gene regulatory networks. In L. De Castro, & F. von Zuben (Eds.), *Recent Developments in Biologically Inspired Computing* (pp. 320–339). London: Idea Group Publishing.

Beran, T. N., & Li, Q. (2005). Cyber-harassment: A study of a new method for an old behavior. *Journal of Educational Computing Research, 32*(3), 265–277. doi:10.2190/8YQM-B04H-PG4D-BLLH

Beresford, D. (2011). *Exploiting Siemens simatic S7 PLCs*. Black Hat.

Berg, T. (2007). The Changing Face of Cybercrime New Internet Threats Create Challenges to Law Enforcement. *Michigan Bar Journal, 86*(6), 18.

Berguer, M. T., & Guidorz, K. (2009). Intersectional approach. Chapel Hill, NC: The University of North Carolina Press.

Bernard, T. (1992). *The cycle of juvenile justice*. Oxford, UK: Oxford University Press.

Berson, M. (2000). The Computer can't see you blush. *Kappa Delta Pi Record*, 158–162. doi:10.1080/00228958.2000.10518777

Bertino, E., Crampton, J., & Paci, F. (2006). Access Control and Authorization Constraints for WS-BPEL. In *Proceedings of the 2006 International Conference on Web Services (ICWS 2006)* (pp. 275–284). Washington, DC: IEEE Computer Society.

Bhat, C. S. (2008). Cyber bullying: Overview and strategies for school counsellors, guidance officers, and all school personnel. *Australian Journal of Guidance & Counselling*, *18*(1), 53–66. doi:10.1375/ajgc.18.1.53

Bilic, V. (2013). Violence among peers in the real and virtual world. *Paediatrics Today*, *9*(1), 78–90. doi:10.5457/p2005-114.65

Birnhack, M. D. (2008). The EU Data Protection Directive: An engine of a global regime. *Computer Law & Security Report*, *24*(6), 508–520. doi:10.1016/j.clsr.2008.09.001

Bishop, J. (2011a). Assisting human interaction (AU/GB2011/2011266844 ed.). GB: PCT/GB2011/050814.

Bishop, J. (2011b). *The role of the prefrontal cortex in social orientation construction: A pilot study*. Paper presented to the British Psychological Society's Sustainable Well-being Conference. London, UK.

Bishop, J. (2012a). Lessons from the emotivate project for increasing take-up of big society and responsible capitalism initiatives. In P. M. Pumilia-Gnarini, E. Favaron, E. Pacetti, J. Bishop & L. Guerra (Eds.), *Didactic strategies and technologies for education: Incorporating advancements* (pp. 208-217). Hershey, PA: IGI Global.

Bishop, J. (2012c). Taming the chatroom bob: The role of brain-computer interfaces that manipulate prefrontal cortex optimization for increasing participation of victims of traumatic sex and other abuse online. In *Proceedings of the 13th International Conference on Bioinformatics and Computational Biology (BIOCOMP'12)*. BIOCOMP.

Bishop, M. (1995). *A taxonomy of unix system and network vulnerabilities* (Technical Report CSE-95-10). Department of Computer Science, University of California at Davis.

Bishop, J. (2012). Co-operative e-learning in the multilingual and multicultural school: The role of 'Classroom 2.0' for increasing participation in education. In P. M. Pumilia-Gnarini, E. Favaron, E. Pacetti, J. Bishop, & L. Guerra (Eds.), *Didactic strategies and technologies for education: Incorporating advancements* (pp. 137–150). Hershey, PA: IGI Global. doi:10.4018/978-1-4666-2122-0.ch013

Bishop, J. (2012b). Scope and limitations in the government of wales act 2006 for tackling internet abuses in the form of 'Flame trolling'. *Statute Law Review*, *33*(2), 207–216. doi:10.1093/slr/hms016

Bishop, J. (2013a). The art of trolling law enforcement: A review and model for implementing 'flame trolling' legislation enacted in great britain (1981–2012). *International Review of Law Computers & Technology*, *27*(3), 301–318. doi:10.1080/13600869.2013.796706

Bishop, J. (2013b). The effect of deindividuation of the internet troller on criminal procedure implementation: An interview with a hater. *International Journal of Cyber Criminology*, *7*(1), 28–48.

Bishop, J. (2014a). Digital teens and the 'Antisocial Network': Prevalence of troublesome online youth groups and internet trolling in great Britain. *International Journal of E-Politics*.

Bishop, J. (2014b). Representations of 'trolls' in mass media communication: A review of media-texts and moral panics relating to 'internet trolling'. *International Journal of Web Based Communities*, *10*(1), 7–24. doi: 10.1504/IJWBC.2014.058384

Bishop, J., & Goode, M. M. H. (2014). Towards a subjectively devised parametric user model for analysing and influencing behaviour online using gamification: A review and model. In J. Bishop (Ed.), *Gamification for human factors integration: Social, educational, and psychological issues*. Hershey, PA: IGI Global. doi:10.4018/978-1-4666-5071-8.ch005

Bishop, J., & Mannay, L. (2014). Using the internet to make local music more available to the south wales community. In J. Bishop (Ed.), *Transforming politics and policy in the digital age*. Hershey, PA: IGI Global. doi:10.4018/978-1-4666-6038-0.ch005

Blair, R. J. R. (2007). The amygdala and ventromedial prefrontal cortex in morality and psychopathy. *Trends in Cognitive Sciences*, *11*(9), 387–392. doi:10.1016/j.tics.2007.07.003 PMID:17707682

Blais, J. (2008). *Chatting, befriending, and bullying. Adolescents' Internet experiences and associated psychosocial outcomes*. Queen's University.

Blais, J., Craig, W., Pepler, D., & Connolly, J. (2008). Adolescents online: The importance of internet activity choices to salient relationships. *Journal of Youth and Adolescence*, *37*(5), 522–536. doi:10.1007/s10964-007-9262-7

Blasch, E. P., & Plano, S. (2002). JDL level 5 fusion model: User refinement issues and applications in group tracking. *Proceedings of the Society for Photo-Instrumentation Engineers*, *4729*, 270–279. doi:10.1117/12.477612

Blasing, T., Batyuk, L., Schmidt, A., Camtepe, S., & Albayrak, S. (2010). An Android Application Sandbox System for Suspicious Software Detection. In *Proceedings of the Proceedings of the 5th International Conference on IEEE Malicious and Unwanted Software*, (pp. 55-62). IEEE.

Blatz, J. (2007). *CSRF: Attack and Defense*. Academic Press.

Blau, J. (2004). The battle against cyber terror. *Computer World*. Retrieved from http://www.computerworld.com/s/article/97953/The_battle_against_cyberterror

Bocij, P. (2004). *Cyberstalking: Harassment in the internet age and how to protect your family*. Westport, CT: Praeger.

Bossler, A. M., & Holt, T. J. (2009). On-line activities, guardianship, and malware infection: An examination of routine activities theory. *International Journal of Cyber Criminology*, *3*(1), 400–420.

Bossler, A. M., & Holt, T. J. (2010). The effect of self-control on victimization in the cyberworld. *Journal of Criminal Justice*, *38*(3), 227–236. doi:10.1016/j.jcrimjus.2010.03.001

Bossler, A. M., Holt, T. J., & May, D. C. (2012). Predicting online harassment victimization among a juvenile population. *Youth & Society*, *44*(4), 500–523. doi:10.1177/0044118X11407525

Botha, R. A., & Eloff, J. H. P. (2001). Separation of duties for access control enforcement in workflow environments. *IBM Systems Journal*, *40*(3), 666–682. doi:10.1147/sj.403.0666

Bovill, M., & Livingstone, S. (2001). *Bedroom culture and the privatization of media use*. Retrieved from http://eprints.lse.ac.uk/archive/00000672

Boyd, D. (2007). *Why Youth (Heart) Social Network Sites: The Role of Networked Publics in Teenage Social Life*. MIT Press.

boyd, D. M., & Ellison, N. B. (2007). Social network sites: Definition, history, and scholarship. *Journal of Computer-Mediated Communication*, *13*(1), 210–230. doi:10.1111/j.1083-6101.2007.00393.x

Brazil Constitution. (n.d.). *Article V*. Retrieved from http://english.tse.jus.br/arquivos/federal-constitution

Brennan, M., Afroz, S., & Greenstadt, R. (2012). Adversarial stylometry: Circumventing authorship recognition to preserve privacy and anonymity.[TISSEC]. *ACM Transactions on Information and System Security*, *15*(3), 1. doi:10.1145/2382448.2382450

Brenner, M. (2009). *Clickjacking and GuardedID*. Retrieved from http://ha.ckers.org/blog/20090204/clickjacking-and-guardedid

Brenner, S. W. (2001). State Cybercrime Legislation in the United States of America: A Survey. *Richmond Journal of Law & Technology*, *7*, 28–34.

Brenner, S. W. (2004). U.S. cybercrime law: Defining offenses. *Information Systems Frontiers*, *6*(2), 115–132. doi:10.1023/B:ISFI.0000025780.94350.79

Brenner, S. W. (2007). Cybercrime jurisdiction. *Crime, Law, and Social Change*, *46*, 189–206. doi:10.1007/s10611-007-9063-7

Brenner, S. W., & Rehberg, M. (2009). Kiddie crime-The utility of criminal law in controlling cyber bullying. *First Amend. L. Rev.*, *8*, 1.

Brenner, S. W., & Schwerha, J. J. IV. (2004). Introduction—Cybercrime: A note on international issues. *Information Systems Frontiers*, *6*(2), 111–114. doi:10.1023/B:ISFI.0000025779.42497.30

Brinkmann, M. (2012, October 13). *Encrypt all data in Android phone*. Retrieved August 21, 2013, from http://www.ghacks.net/2012/10/13/encrypt-all-data-on-your-android-phone

Brown, K., Jackson, M., & Cassidy, W. (2006). Cyberbullying: Developing Policy to direct responses that are equitable and effective in addressing this special form of bullying. *Canadian Journal of Educational Administration and Policy*, *57*, 1–36.

Brunstein Klomek, A., Sourander, A., & Gould, M. (2010). The association of suicide and bullying in childhood to young adulthood: a review of cross-sectional and longitudinal research findings. *Canadian Journal of Psychiatry*, *55*(5), 282–288. PMID:20482954

Brush, A. J. B., Lee, B., Mahajan, R., Agarwal, S., Saroiu, S., & Dixon, C. (2011). Home automation in the wild: Challenges and opportunities. In *Proceedings of the SIGCHI Conference on Human Factors in Computing Systems*. Vancouver, Canada: ACM.

Bubas, G., Orehovacki, T., & Konecki, M. (2008). Factors and Predictors of Online Security and Privacy Behaviour. *Journal of Information and Organizational Sciences*, *32*(2), 9–98.

Buchholz, F., & Falk, C. (2005). Design and implementation of Zeitline: A forensic timeline editor. In *Proceedings of Digital Forensic Research Workshop*. Academic Press.

Burns, A. E. (2013). Corporate e-discovery success starts with information governance. *eForensics Magazine, Database, 2*(8). Retrieved August 5, 2013 from http://eforensicsmag.com/ediscovery-compendium/

Buzzell, T., Foss, D., & Middleton, Z. (2006). Explaining use of online pornography: A test of self-control theory and opportunities for deviance. *Journal of Criminal Justice and Popular Culture*, *13*(2), 96–116.

Byres, E., & Eng, P. (2004). The myths and facts behind cyber security risks for industrial control systems the BCIT industrial security incident database (ISID). *Security*, *116*(6), 1–6.

Byron, T. (2008). *Safer Children in a Digital World - The Report of the Byron Review*. Byron Review – Children and New Technology.

Calderoni, F. (2010). The European legal framework on cybercrime: striving for an effective implementation. *Crime, Law, and Social Change*, *54*, 339–357. doi:10.1007/s10611-010-9261-6

Caloyannides, M. A. (2004). *Privacy protection and computer forensics*. Norwood, MA: Artech House Publishers.

Calvete, E., Orue, I., Estévez, A., Villardón, L., & Padilla, P. (2010). cyber bullying in adolescents: Modalities and aggressors' profile. *Computers in Human Behavior*, *26*(5), 1128–1135. doi:10.1016/j.chb.2010.03.017

Campbell, K., Gordon, L. A., Loeb, M. P., & Zhou, L. (2003). The economic cost of publicly announced information security breaches: empirical evidence from the stock market. *Journal of Computer Security*, *11*, 431–448.

Cantrell, G., Dampier, D., Dandass, Y. S., Niu, N., & Bogen, C. (2012). Research toward a partially-automated, and crime specific digital triage process model. *Computer and Information Science*, *5*(2), 29. doi:10.5539/cis.v5n2p29

Caracciolo di Torella, E., & Reid, E. (2002). The changing shape of the" european family" and fundamental rights. *European Law Review*, *27*(1), 80–90.

Cárdenas, A. A., Amin, S., & Lin, Z.-S. (2011). Attacks against process control systems: Risk assessment, detection, and response categories and subject descriptors. *Security*, 355-366. Retrieved from http://portal.acm.org/citation.cfm?id=1966959

Carletta, J. (1996). Assessing agreement on classification tasks: The kappa statistic. *Computational Linguistics*, *22*(2), 249–254.

Carlsson, S. & Sawy, O. (2008). Managing the five tensions of IT-enabled decision support in turbulent and high-velocity environments. *Information Systems and e-Business Management, 6*(3), 225-237

Carlsson, R., & Karlsson, K. (1970). Age, cohorts, and the generation of generations. *American Sociological Review*, *35*, 710–718. doi: 10.2307/2093946

Carneiro, A. (2002). *Introdução à Segurança dos Sistemas de Informação (Introduction to Information Systems Security)*. Lisboa: FCA-Editora de Informática.

Carneiro, A. (2007). What is required for growth? *Business Strategy Series*, *8*(1), 51–57. doi:10.1108/17515630710686888

Carneiro, A. (2008). When Leadership means more Innovation and Development. *Business Strategy Series*, *9*(4), 176–184. doi:10.1108/17515630810891843

Carrier, B.D., & Spafford, E. (2004). Defining event reconstruction of digital crime scenes. *Journal of Forensic Sciences*, *49*(6), 1291. doi:10.1520/JFS2004127 PMID:15568702

Carrier, B., & Spafford, E. et al. (2003). Getting physical with the digital investigation process. *International Journal of Digital Evidence*, 2(2), 1–20.

Carr, N. (2003). Does IT matter? *Harvard Business Review*, 81(5), 5–12.

Case, A., Cristina, A., Marziale, L., Richard, G., & Roussev, V. (2008). FACE: Automated digital evidence discovery and correlation. *Digital Investigation*, 5, S65-S75.

Cassidy, W., & Bates, A. (2005). 'Drop-outs' and 'pushouts': Finding hope at a school that actualizes the ethic of care. *American Journal of Education*, 112, 66–102. doi:10.1086/444524

Cassidy, W., Brown, K., & Jackson, M. (2011). Moving from cyber -bullying to cyber -kindness: What do students, educators and parents say? In E. Dunkels, G.-M. Franberg, & C. Hallgren (Eds.), *Youth culture and net culture: Online social practices* (pp. 256–277). Hershey, NY: Information Science Reference.

Cassidy, W., Brown, K., & Jackson, M. (2012a). Making Kind Cool": Parents' Suggestions for Preventing Cyber Bullying and Fostering Cyber Kindness. *Journal of Educational Computing Research*, 46(4), 415–436. doi:10.2190/EC.46.4.f

Cassidy, W., Brown, K., & Jackson, M. (2012b). 'Under the radar': Educators and cyber bullying in schools. *School Psychology International*, 33, 520–532. doi:10.1177/0143034312445245

Cassidy, W., Faucher, C., & Jackson, M. (2013). cyber bullying among youth: A comprehensive review of current international research and its implications and application to policy and practice. *School Psychology International*. doi:10.1177/0143034313479697

Cassidy, W., Jackson, M., & Brown, K. (2009). Sticks and stones can break my bones, but how can pixels hurt me? Students' experiences with cyber -bullying. *School Psychology International*, 30(4), 383–402. doi:10.1177/0143034309106948

Castells, M. (2007). *A Galáxia Internet: Reflexões sobre Internet, Negócios e Sociedade*. Lisbon: Fundação Calouste Gulbenkian.

Castro, M., Jara, A. J., & Skarmeta, A. F. (2012). An analysis of M2M platforms: Challenges and opportunities for the internet of things. In *Proceedings of Innovative Mobile and Internet Services in Ubiquitous Computing (IMIS)*, (pp. 757-762). IMIS.

Cavagnero, S. M. (2012). Digital teens: An investigation into the use of the web by adolescents. In P. M. Pumilia-Gnarini, E. Favaron, E. Pacetti, J. Bishop, & L. Guerra (Eds.), *Didactic strategies and technologies for education: Incorporating advancements* (pp. 129–136). Hershey, PA: IGI Global. doi:10.4018/978-1-4666-2122-0.ch012

Cavoukian, A. (2012). Privacy by Design: Origins, Meaning, and Prospects for Assuring Privacy and Trust in the Information Era. In G. Yee (Ed.), *Privacy Protection Measures and Technologies in Business Organizations: Aspects and Standards* (pp. 170–208). New York: IGI Global Pubs.

Cavusoglu, H., Mishra, B., & Raghunathan, S. (2004). A model for evaluating IT security investments. *Communications of the ACM*, 47(7), 87–92. doi:10.1145/1005817.1005828

Cerezo, A. I., Lopez, J., & Patel, A. (2007). International cooperation to fight transnational cybercrime. In *Proceedings of Second International Workshop on Digital Forensics and Incident Analysis* (WDFIA 2007). IEEE Computer Society.

Chandrawanshi, R., & Gupta, H. (2013). Implementation Of An Automated Server Timeline Analysis Tool For Web Forensics. *International Journal of Engineering*, 2(4).

Chan, M., Estève, D., Escriba, C., & Campo, E. (2008). A review of smart homes—Present state and future challenges. *Computer Methods and Programs in Biomedicine*, 91(1), 55–81. doi:10.1016/j.cmpb.2008.02.001 PMID:18367286

Chaves, G. (2012). Para especialistas, projeto brasileiro para regular a web é mais democrático. *Correio Braziliense*. Retrieved February 29, 2013, from http://www.correio-braziliense.com.br/app/noticia/tecnologia/2012/01/30/interna_tecnologia,288096/para-especilistas-projeto-brasileiro-para-regular-a-web-e-mais-democratico.shtml

Chen, K., Clark, A., De Vel, O., & Mohay, G. (2003, November). ECF-event correlation for forensics. In *Proceedings of First Australian Computer Network and Information Forensics Conference* (pp. 1-10). Perth, Australia: Edith Cowan University.

Chen, Y. (2012). Challenges and opportunities of internet of things. In *Proceedings of Design Automation Conference (ASP-DAC),* (pp. 383-388). ASP-DAC.

Chen, D., Chang, G., Sun, D., Li, J., Jia, J., & Wang, X. (2011). TRM-IoT: A trust management model based on fuzzy reputation for internet of things. *Computer Science and Information Systems, 8*(4), 1207–1228. doi:10.2298/CSIS110303056C

Cheng, L., & Liu, H. (2008). Three-factor authentication mode of network payment. *Journal of Computer Applications, 7,* 58.

Chen, R. (2013). Living a Private Life in Public Social Networks: An Exploration of Member Self-Disclosure. *Decision Support Systems, 55*(3), 661–668. doi:10.1016/j.dss.2012.12.003

Chen, R. (2013). Member use of social networking sites: an empirical examination. *Decision Support Systems, 54*(3), 1219–1227. doi:10.1016/j.dss.2012.10.028

Cheung, S., Dutertre, B., Fong, M., Lindqvist, U., Skinner, K., & Valdes, A. (2007, January). Using model-based intrusion detection for SCADA networks. In *Proceedings of the SCADA Security Scientific Symposium* (pp. 1-12). SCADA.

Chickowski, E. (2013). *10 Web-Based Attacks Targeting Your End Users, whitepaper, dark reading.* Retrieved from http://www.darkreading.com/applications/10-web-based-attacks-targeting-your-end/240159280

Child Exploitation and Online Protection Centre (CEOP). (2013). Threat assessment of child sexual exploitation and abuse 2013. London, UK: Child Exploitation and Online Protection Centre.

Childress, S. (2012). Electronic discovery: Where the law and technology collide. *E-Discovery – Legal Issues Guidebook.* Retrieved August 5, 2013 from http://eforensicsmag.com/e-discovery-legal-issues-guidebook-2/

Choi, K. C. (2008). Computer crime victimization and integrated theory: An empirical assessment. *International Journal of Cyber Criminology, 2*(1), 308–333. Retrieved September 1, 2010, from http://cyber.kic.re.kr/data/Kyungchoiijccjan2008.pdf

Christofides, E., Muise, A., & Desmarais, S. (2009). Information disclosure and control on Facebook: are they two sides of the same coin or two different processes? *Cyberpsychology & Behavior, 12*(3), 341–345. doi:10.1089/cpb.2008.0226 PMID:19250020

Chunlei, W., Lan, F., & Yiqi, D. (2010, March). A simulation environment for SCADA security analysis and assessment. In *Proceedings of Measuring Technology and Mechatronics Automation (ICMTMA),* (Vol. 1, pp. 342-347). IEEE.

Churches, D., Gombas, G., Harrison, A., Maassen, J., Robinson, C., & Shields, M. et al. (2006). Programming scientific and distributed workflow with Triana services. *Concurrency and Computation, 18*(10), 1021–1037. doi:10.1002/cpe.992

Cisco Global Cloud Index. (2013b). Forecast and Methodology, 2012-2017, October 2013, ID: FLGD 11289 10/13. Author.

Cisco Visual Networking Index. (2013a). Global Mobile Data Traffic Forecast Update, 2012-2017, February 2013, ID: FLGD 10855 02/13. Author.

Ciufudean, C., & Filote, C. (2009a). Safety discrete event models for holonic cyclic manufacturing systems. In *Proceedings of 4th Industrial Conference on Industrial Applications of Holonic and Multi-agent Systems, HoloMAS 2009* (LNCS) (vol. 5696, pp. 225-233). Berlin: Springer Verlag.

Ciufudean, C., & Filote, C. (2009b). Holonic models for traffic control systems. In *Proceedings of 4th Industrial Conference on Industrial Applications of Holonic and Multi-agent Systems, HoloMAS 2009* (LNCS) (vol. 5696, pp. 276-284). Berlin: Springer Verlag.

Ciufudean, C., & Garcia, L. (2013). *Advances in robotics: Modeling, control and applications.* Iconcept Press Ltd.

Clarke, R. (2010). *Cyber war: The next threat to national security and what to do about it.* New York: Ecco.

Clarke, R. A., & Knake, R. K. (2010). *Cyber War: The next threat to national security and what to do about it.* New York: HarperCollins.

Clarke, R. V. (2004). Technology, criminology and crime science. *European Journal on Criminal Policy and Research, 10*(1), 55–63. doi:10.1023/B:CRIM.0000037557.42894.f7

Clarke, R. V. G. (1997). *Situational crime prevention.* Criminal Justice Press.

Clausewitz, C. (1874). On War. London: Academic Press.

*Clickjacking Defense Cheat Sheet.* (2014). Retrieved from https://www.owasp.org/index.php/Clickjacking_Defense_Cheat_Sheet

Clickjacking. (2012). *Clicjakcing.* Retreived from https://www.owasp.org/index.php/Clickjacking

Clifford, M. (1998). *Environmental Crime: Enforcement, Policy, And Social Responsibility.* Gaithersburg, MD: Jones & Bartlett Learning.

Cloppert, M. (2008). *Ex-tip: an extensible timeline analysis framework in perl.* Bethesda, MD: SANS Institute.

Clough, J. (2012). *Principeles of cybercrime.* Academic Press.

CNECV. C. N. de É. para as C. da V. (2007). *Parecer nº 52/CNECV/07.* Lisboa. Retrieved from http://www.cnecv.pt/admin/files/data/docs/1273054082_Parecer_052_CNECV_2007_BasesdadosADN.pdf

CNPD. (2007a). *Parecer Nº 18/2007D.* Retrieved from http://www.cnpd.pt/bin/decisoes/par/40_18_2007.pdf

CNPD. C. N. de P. de D. (2007b). *Deliberação Nº 227/2007* (p. 15). Retrieved from http://www.estsp.ipp.pt/fileManager/editor/Documentos_Publicos/Comissao de Etica/Acervo C.E./Privacidade_e_Confidencialidade_dos_Dados_Pessoais/7.pdf

Cody, B., Madigan, J., MacDonald, S., & Hsu, K. W. (2007). High speed SOC design for blowfish cryptographic algorithm. *Very Large Scale Integration,* 284-287.

COE. (1990). *Computer-related crime - Recommendation No. R (89) 9 on computer-related crime and final report of the European Committee on Crime Problems.* Strasbourg: Council of Europe.

COE. (2001). Convention on Cybercrime (STE no. 181). Budapest: Council of Europe.

Cohen, F. (2012). *The future of digital forensics.* Unpublished manuscript. Retrieved 21st June 2013, from http://www.all.net/Talks/2012-09-21-Beijing-Keynote.pdf

Cohen, W. W., & Singer, Y. (1999). A simple, fast, and effective rule learner. In *Proceedings of the Sixteenth National Conference on Artificial Intelligence.* Academic Press.

Cohen, L. E., & Felson, M. (1979). Social change and crime rate trends: A routine activity approach. *American Sociological Review, 52*(August), 170–183.

Collins, C. J., & Clark, K. D. (2003). Strategic human resource practices, top management team social networks, and firm performance: The role of human resource practices in creating organizational competitive advantage. *Academy of Management Journal, 46*(6), 740–751. doi:10.2307/30040665

Collins, N. L., & Miller, L. C. (1994). Self-disclosure and liking: a meta-analytic review. *Psychological Bulletin, 116*(3), 457–475. doi:10.1037/0033-2909.116.3.457 PMID:7809308

COM. (2007). *Communication from the commission to the European Parliament, the council and the committee of the regions: Towards a general policy on the fight against cyber crime.* Brussels: Commission of the European Communities.

COM. (2009). *Communication from the commission to the European Parliament, the council, the European economic and social committee and the committee of the regions: On critical information infrastructure protection: Protecting Europe from large scale cyber-attacks and disruptions: enhancing preparedness, security and resilience.* Brussels: Commission of the European Communities.

COM. (2012). Communication from the commission to the council and the European Parliament: Tackling crime in our digital age: Establishing a European cybercrime centre. Brussels: European Commission.

Commission nationale de l'informatique et des libertés. (1978). *Loi du 6 janvier 1978, relative à l'informatique, aux archives et aux libertés.* Retrieved February 03, 2013, from http://www.cnil.fr/fileadmin/documents/approfondir/textes/CNIL-78-17_definitive-annotee.pdf

Committee to Protect Journalists. (2010). Is Brazil the censorship capital of the Internet? Not yet. *Committee to Protect Journalists*. Retrieved March 07, 2013, from http://cpj.org/blog/2010/04/is-brazil-the-censorship-capital-of-the-internet.php

Computer History Museum. (2013). *Timeline of Computer History*. Retrieved on March 10, 2013 from http://www.computerhistory.org/timeline/?year=1972

Congress, . (2002). Homeland security act of 2002. *Public Law*, 107.

Congresso Nacional do Brasil. (2011). *Projeto de Lei 2126/2011: Estabelece princípios, garantias, direitos e deveres para o uso da Internet no Brasil*. Retrieved April 21, 2013, from http://www.camara.gov.br/proposicoesweb/fi chadetramitacao?idProposicao=517255

Cornish, D. B., & Clarke, R. V. (2003). Opportunities precipitators and criminal dispositions: A reply to wortley's critique of situational crime prevention. In M. J. Smith, & D. B. Cornish (Eds.), *Theory and practice in situational crime prevention* (pp. 41–96). New York, USA: Criminal Justice Press.

Cortes, C., & Vapnik, V. (1995). Support-vector networks. *Machine Learning, 20*. Retrieved December 23, 2011, from http://www.springerlink.com/content/k238jx04h-m87j80g/

Costa, S. (2001, October). *A Justica em Laboratorio*. Retrieved from http://www.ces.uc.pt/publicacoes/rccs/artigos/60/SusanaCosta-AJusticaemLaboratorio.pdf

Costa, S., Machado, H., & Nunes, J. A. (2002). *O ADN e a justiça : A biologia forense e o direito como mediadores entre a ciência e os cidadãos*. Publicações Dom Quixote. Retrieved from http://repositorium.sdum.uminho.pt/handle/1822/5320

Couldry, N., Markham, T., & Livingstone, S. (2005). *Media consumption and the future of public connection*. London, UK: London School of Economics and Political Science.

Council of Europe. (1993). *Convention on Civil Liability for Damage Resulting from Activities Dangerous to the Environment*. ETS no. 150. Not yet (2013) in force

Council of Europe. (2011). *Recommendation CM/Rec(2011)8 of the Committee of Ministers to member states on the protection and promotion of the universality, integrity and openness of the Internet*. Retrieved October 13, 2013, from https://wcd.coe.int/ViewDoc.jsp?id=1835707

Council of the European Union. (2010). *Council conclusions concerning an Action Plan to implement the concerted strategy to combat cybercrime*. Paper presented at the 3010th General Affairs Council Meeting. Luxembourg.

Cova, M., Kruegel, C., & Vigna, G. (2010, April). Detection and analysis of drive-by-download attacks and malicious JavaScript code. In *Proceedings of the 19th international conference on World Wide Web* (pp. 281-290). ACM.

CRASH. (2013). *Clean-slate design of resilient, adaptive, secure hosts (CRASH) program*. Retrieved from http://www.darpa.mil/Our_Work/I2O/Programs/Clean-slate_design_of_Resilient_Adaptive_Secure_Hosts_(CRASH).aspx

Cross, D., Shaw, T., Hearn, L., Epstein, M., Monks, H., Lester, L., & Thomas L. (2009). *Australian covert bullying prevalence study (ACBPS)*. Available at http://www.deewr.gov.au/Schooling/NationalSafeSchools/Pages/research.aspx

Crovella, M. E., & Bestavros, A. (1997). Self-similarity in world wide web traffic: Evidence and possible causes. *IEEE/ACM Transactions on Networking, 5*(6), 835–846. doi:10.1109/90.650143

Cullerton-Sen, C., & Crick, N. (2005). Understanding the effects of physical and relational victimization: The utility of multiple perspectives in predicting social-emotional adjustment. *School Psychology Review, 34*, 147–160.

Cuppens, F., & Cuppens-Boulahia, N. (2008). Modeling contextual security policies.[Berlin, Germany: Springer.]. *International Journal of Information Security, 7*(4), 285–305. doi:10.1007/s10207-007-0051-9

Curado, H., & Gomes, P. V. (2011). Os Sistemas de Inteligência num Contexto de Homeland Defence e a Tutela da Privacidade Parte I, 32–37.

Curado, H., & Gomes, P. V. (2012). Os Sistemas de Inteligência num Contexto de Homeland Defence e a Tutela da Privacidade Parte II.

Curran, K., Morrissey, C., Fagan, C., Murphy, C., O'Donnell, B., Fitzpatrick, G., & Condit, S. (2005, March). Monitoring hacker activity with a Honeynet. *International Journal of Network Management, 15*(2), 123-134. Doi: 10.1002/nem.549.

*Cursor Jacking Again.* (2012). Retrieved from http://blog.kotowicz.net/2012/01/cursorjacking-again.html

Curtis, L. (2012). *Virtual vs. reality: An examination of the nature of stalking and cyberstalking.* (Unpublished doctoral dissertation). San Diego State University, San Diego, CA.

CVE Details. (2012). *MySQL 5.0.51a Security Vulnerabilities.* Retrieves 2013, from http://www.cvedetails.com/

CVE. (2010). *SystemTap CVE-2010-4170.* Retrieved 2013, from http://cve.mitre.org/cgi-bin/cvename.cgi?name=CVE-2010-4170

CVE. (2013). *Common vulnerabilities and exposures.* Retrieved from http://cve.mitre.org

Cyber Friendly Schools Project. (2011). *Year 9 curriculum.* Available at http://www.cyber friendly.com.au/images/uploads/school_pdf/teacher-curriculum-cyber 9.pdf

Daily, C. (2013, March 11). US main source of cyberattacks against China. *China Daily.* Retrieved November 29, 2013 from: http://usa.chinadaily.com.cn/china/2013-03/11/content_16296323.htm

Daniela, T. (2011, June). Communication security in SCADA pipeline monitoring systems. In *Proceedings of Roedunet International Conference (RoEduNet),* (pp. 1-5). IEEE.

DARPA. (2013). *Defense science office.* Retrieved from http://www.darpa.mil/Our_Work/DSO/Focus_Areas/Mathematics.aspx

David-Ferdon, C., & Hertz, M. F. (2007). Electronic media, violence, and adolescents: an emerging public health problem. *The Journal of Adolescent Health, 41*(6Suppl 1), S1–S5. doi:10.1016/j.jadohealth.2007.08.020 PMID:18047940

David-Ferdon, C., & Hertz, M. F. (2009). *Electronic media and youth violence: A CDC issue brief for researchers.* Atlanta, GA: Centers for Disease Control.

David, R., & Alla, H. (1992). *Petri nets and Grafcet.* Englewood Cliffs, NJ: Prentice-Hall.

Davies, C. (2011). Digitally strategic: How young people respond to parental views about the use of technology for learning in the home. *Journal of Computer Assisted Learning, 27,* 324–335. doi:10.1111/j.1365-2729.2011.00427.x

Davis, S., & Nixon, C. (2012). Empowering bystanders. In J. W. Patchin, & S. Hinduja (Eds.), *Cyber bullying prevention and response: Expert perspectives* (pp. 93–109). New York, NY: Routledge.

de la Cuesta Arzamendi, J.L., & Mayordomo Rodrigo, V. (2011). Acoso y derecho penal. *Cuadernos del Instituto Vasco de Criminología,* (25).

De Silva, L. C., Morikawa, C., & Petra, I. M. (2012). State of the art of smart homes. *Engineering Applications of Artificial Intelligence, 25*(7), 1313–1321. doi:10.1016/j.engappai.2012.05.002

Dearne, K. (2002). Cyber-crime boom. *Information Management & Computer Security, 10*(5), 262–266.

Debatin, B., Lovejoy, J. P., Horn, A. K., & Hughes, B. N. (2009). Facebook and online privacy: Attitudes, behaviors, and unintended consequences. *Journal of Computer-Mediated Communication, 15*(1), 83–108. doi:10.1111/j.1083-6101.2009.01494.x

Defense Information Systems Agency. (2013). *Our Work/DISA 101.* Retrieved on March 10, 2013 from http://www.disa.mil/About/Our-Work

Deleuze, G. (1992). *Post-scriptum sobre as sociedades de controlo.* Retrieved January 01, 2013, from http://www.portalgens.com.br/filosofia/textos/sociedades_de_controlo_deleuze.pdf

Dempsey, A., Sulkowski, M., Dempsey, J., & Storch, E. (2011). Has cyber technology produced a new group of peer aggressor. *Cyberpsychology, Behavior, and Social Networking, 14*(5), 297-302.

Dempsey, A. G., Sulkowski, M. L., Dempsey, J., & Storch, E. A. (2011). Has cyber technology produced a new group of peer aggressors? *Cyberpsychology, Behavior and Social Networking, 14*(5), 297–302. doi:10.1089/cyber.2010.0108

Denning, D. E. (2000). Cyberterrorism: The logic bomb versus the truck bomb - Centre for world dialogue. *Global Dialogue, 2*, 4.

Design Council. (2002). *Evidence Pack. DAC case studies*. London, UK: Design Council.

Design Council. (2003). *Think thief: A designer's guide to designing out crime*. London, UK: Design Council.

Determann, L. (2012). *Determann's field guide to international data privacy law compliance*. Cheltenham, UK: Edward Elgar Publishing Ltd.

Dickey, C., Shenton, M., Voglmaier, M., Niznikiewicz, M., Seidman, L., & Frumin, M. et al. (2001). Prefrontal cortex in schizotypal personality disorder males and females. *Biological Psychiatry, 49*, 336S.

*Difference between Adware and Spyware*. (2005, July 17). Retrieved August 21, 2013, from http://www.techiwarehouse.com/engine/41cc4355/Difference%20Between%20Adware%20&%20Spyware

Dillon, G. (2001). *Information Security Management: Global Challenges in the New Millennium*. Idea Group Publishing.

Dilmac, B. (2009). Psychological needs as a predictor of cyber bullying: A preliminary report on college students. *Educational Sciences: Theory and Practice, 9*(3), 1307–1325.

Dilmac, B., & Aydoğan, D. (2010). Values as a predictor of cyber -bullying among secondary school students. *International Journal of Human and Social Sciences, 5*(3), 185–188.

Dinakar, K., Reichart, R., & Lieberman, H. (2011). In International AAAI Conference on Weblogs and Social Media. *Artificial Intelligence*, 11-17.

Dinev, T., & Hart, P. (2006). An extended privacy calculus model for e-commerce transactions. *Information Systems Research, 17*(1), 61–80. doi:10.1287/isre.1060.0080

Ding, D., Cooper, R. A., Pasquina, P. F., & Fici-Pasquina, L. (2011). Sensor technology for smart homes. *Maturitas, 69*(2), 131–136. doi:10.1016/j.maturitas.2011.03.016 PMID:21531517

Dionaea. (2010). *GnuplotSQL*. Retrieved 2013, from http://carnivore.it/2010/09/19/gnuplotsql

Dittrich, D. (2004). *Creating and managing distributed honeynets using honeywalls. Draft*. University of Washington.

Dobson, S., Sterritt, R., Nixon, P., & Hinchey, M. (2010). Fulfilling the vision of autonomic computing. *Computer (New York), 43*(1), 35–41.

Doneda, D. C. M. (2000). *Considerações iniciais sobre os bancos de dados informatizados e o direito à privacidade*. Retrieved from http://www.estig.ipbeja.pt/~ac_direito/Consideracoes.pdf

Donilon, T. (2013). *The United States and the Asia-Pacific in 2013*. Retrieved October 13, 2013, from http://www.whitehouse.gov/the-press-office/2013/03/11/remarks-tom-donilon-national-security-advisory-president-united-states-a.

Donlin, M. (2012). You mean we gotta teach that, too? In J. W. Patchin, & S. Hinduja (Eds.), *cyber bullying prevention and response: Expert perspectives* (pp. 110–127). New York, NY: Routledge.

Donnerstein, E. (2012). Internet bullying. *Pediatric Clinics of North America, 59*(3), 623-633, viii. doi: 10.1016/j.pcl.2012.03.019

Dooley, J. J., Pyżalski, J., & Cross, D. (2009). Cyber bullying versus face-to-face bullying. *The Journal of Psychology, 217*(4), 182–188.

Dormann, W., & Rafail, J. (2006). *Securing your web browser*. CERT.

Douligeris, C., & Mitrokotsa, A. (2004). DDoS attacks and defense mechanisms: classification and state-of-the-art. *Computer Networks, 44*(5), 643–666. doi:10.1016/j.comnet.2003.10.003

Dracic, S. (2009). Bullying and peer victimization. Rev. Materia SocioMédica, 21(4), 216-219.

Drucker, S. J., & Gumpert, G. (2000). Cybercrime and punishment. *Critical Studies in Media Communication*, *17*(2), 133–158. doi:10.1080/15295030009388387

Duerager, A., & Livingstone, S. (2012). How can parents support children's internet safety? EU Kids'Online.

Dutta-Bergman, M. J. (2006). Community participation and internet use after september 11: Complementarity in channel consumption. *Journal of Computer-Mediated Communication*, *11*(2), 469–484. doi:10.1111/j.1083-6101.2006.00022.x

Dwyer, C., Hiltz, S., & Passerini, K. (2007). Trust and Privacy Concern Within Social Networking Sites. A Comparison of Facebook and MySpace. In *Proceedings of the 13th Americas Conference on Information Systems*. Retrieved from http://aisel.aisnet.org/amcis2007/339

Eastin, M. S., Greenberg, B. S., & Hofschire, L. (2006). Parenting the Internet. *The Journal of Communication*, *56*(3), 486–504. doi:10.1111/j.1460-2466.2006.00297.x

Eck, J. E., & Clarke, R. V. (2003). Classifying common police problems: A routine activity approach. *Crime Prevention Studies*, *16*, 7–39.

Edmonds, G., & Gray, D. (2002). Internet dictionary. London: Dorling Kindersley Limited.

EDRM LLC. (2010). *Production guide*. Retrieved November 8, 2013 from http://www.edrm.net/resources/guides/edrm-framework-guides/production

Edwards, J. (2011). *DARPA to help shield cloud networks from cyberattack: Mission-oriented resilient clouds program would boost security and reliability*. Retrieved from http://defensesystems.com/articles/2011/08/08/tech-watch-darpa-cloud-security.aspx

Egele, M., Scholte, T., Kirda, E., & Kruegel, C. (2012). *A survey on automated dynamic malware-analysis techniques and tools. ACM Computing Surveys, 44(2), 6.*

Ekblom, P. (1997). Gearing up against crime: A dynamic framework to help designers keep up with the adaptive criminal in a changing world. *International Journal of Risk. Security and Crime Prevention*, *2*(4), 249–265.

Ekblom, P., & Tilley, N. (2000). Going equipped. *The British Journal of Criminology*, *40*(3), 376–398. doi:10.1093/bjc/40.3.376

Ekholm, J., & Fabre, S. (2011). *Gartner forecast: Mobile data traffic and revenue, worldwide, 2010-2015*. Gartner.

Ekholm, J., De La Vergne, H. J., & Baghdassarian, S. (2011). *Gartner Forecast: Mobile Broadband Connections, Worldwide, 2009-2015*. Gartner.

Elixmann. (2003). *Next generation networks and challenges for future competition policy and regulation*. WIK-Diskussionsbeitrag: WIK Wissenschaftliches Institute for Kommunikations dienste GmbH

Elizalde, F., Ekholm, J., & Sabia, A. (2012). *Gartner Forecast: Consumer Broadband Market, Worldwide, 2009-2015*. Gartner.

Ellis, J. (2006). Has International Law Outgrown Trail Smelter? In R. M. Bratspies, & R. A. Miller (Eds.), *Transboundary Harm in International Law, Lessons from the Trail Smelter Arbitration* (p. 60). Cambridge: Cambridge University Press.

Enck, W., Octeau, D., McDaniel, P., & Chaudhuri, S. (2011). A study of android application security. In *Proceedings of the 20th USENIX Conference on Security (SEC 2011)*. USENIX Association.

Endsley, M. (1995). Toward a theory of situation awareness in dynamic systems. *Human Factors*, *37*(1), 32–64. doi:10.1518/001872095779049543

ENISA. (2012, November). *Proactive detection of security incidents: Honeypots study*. Report. CERT Polska (NASK) & ENISA.

Epstein, M., Hars, L., Kransinski, R., Rosner, M., & Zheng, H. (2003). Design and Implementation of a true random number generator based on digital circuits artificats. *Springer Heidelberg*, *2779*, 152–165.

Erdur-Baker, Ö. (2010). Cyberbullying and its correlation to traditional bullying, gender and frequent and risky usage of Internet-mediated communication tools. *New Media & Society*, *12*(1), 109–125. doi:10.1177/1461444809341260

Ericsson White paper. (2011). *More than 50 billion connected devices*. Unpublished manuscript. Retrieved from http://www.ericsson.com/res/docs/whitepapers/wp-50-billions.pdf

Eriksen-Jensen, M. (2013). Holding back the tidal wave of cybercrime. *Computer Fraud & Security*, (3), 10–16

Eriksson, J., & Giacomello, G. (2006). The Information Revolution, Security, and International Relations: (IR) relevant Theory? *International Political Science Review*, *27*(3), 221–244. doi:10.1177/0192512106064462

European Commission. (1995). *Directive 95/46/EC of the European Parliament and of the Council on the protection of individuals with regard to the processing of personal data and on the free movement of such data*. Retrieved from http://ec.europa.eu/justice/policies/privacy/docs/95-46-ce/dir1995-46_part1_en.pdf

European Commission. (2000). Commission Decision of 26 July 2000 pursuant to Directive 95/46/EC of the European Parliament and of the Council on the adequacy of the protection provided by the safe harbour privacy principles and related frequently asked questions issued by the US Department of Commerce. *Official Journal of the European Communities, L 215*, 7–47.

European Commission. (2002). *Directive 2002/58/EC of the European Parliament and of the Council of 12 July 2002 concerning the processing of personal data and the protection of privacy in the electronic communications sector*. Retrieved from http://eur-lex.europa.eu/LexUriServ/LexUriServ.do?uri=OJ:L:2002:201:0037:0037:EN:PDF

European Commission. (2008). Council directive 2008/114/EC of 8 December 2008 on the identification and designation of European critical infrastructures and the assessment of the need to improve their protection. *Official Journal L, 345*(23), 12.

European Commission. (2012). *Proposal for a Regulation of the European Parliament and of the Council on the protection of individuals with regard to the processing of personal data and on the free movement of such data (General Data Protection Regulation)*. Retrieved November 30, 2013, from http://eur-lex.europa.eu/LexUriServ/LexUriServ.do?uri=COM:2012:0011:FIN:EN:PDF

European Commission. (2013). *Europe 2020 initiative*. Retrieved from http://ec.europa.eu/digital-agenda/en

European Commission. (2013). *Proposal for a Directive of the European Parliament and of the Council Concerning measures to ensure a high level of network and information security across the Union COM(2013) 48 final*. Retrieved October 13, 2013, from http://ec.europa.eu/digital-agenda/en/news/eu-cybersecurity-plan-protect-open-internet-and-online-freedom-and-opportunity-cyber-security

European Court of Justice. (2011). *Judgment of the Court (Third Chamber) of 24 November 2011*. Scarlet Extended SA v Société belge des auteurs, compositeurs et éditeurs SCRL (SABAM); case number C-70/10.

European Parliament and Council. (1995). Directive 95/46/EC of the European Parliament and of the Council on the protection of individuals with regard to the processing of personal data and on the free movement of such data. *Official Journal of the European Communities, L 281*, 31–50.

European Parliament and Council. (2002). Directive 2002/58/EC of the European Parliament and of the Council concerning the processing of personal data and the protection of privacy in the electronic communications sector (Directive on privacy and electronic communications). *Official Journal of the European Communities, L 201*, 37–47.

European Parliament and Council. (2006). Directive 2006/24/EC of the European Parliament and of the Council of 15 March 2006 on the retention of data generated or processed in connection with the provision of publicly available electronic communications services or of public communications networks and amending Directive 2002/58/EC. *Official Journal of the European Communities, L 105*, 54–63.

European Parliament, Council, & Commission. (2000). Charter of Fundamental Rights of the European Union. *Official Journal of the European Communities, C 364*, 1–22.

European Parliament, European Council. (2002). Directive 2002/21/EC of the European Parliament and of the Council of 7 March 2002 on a common regulatory framework for electronic communications networks and services (Framework Directive). *Official Journal, L*, 108.

Eurostat. (2013). *Several statistics*. Statistics of the European Union.

Fairhurst, J. O. (1999). The working time directive: A spanish inquisition. *Web Journal of Current Legal Issues, 1999*(3)

Falliere, N., Murchu, L. O., & Chien, E. (2011). *W32: Stuxnet dossier*. Symantec Corp., Security Response.

Fanti, K. A., Demetriou, A. G., & Hawa, V. V. (2012). A longitudinal study of cyber bullying: Examining risk and protective factors. *European Journal of Developmental Psychology, 9*(2), 168–181. doi:10.1080/17405629.2011.643169

Farahmand, F., Navathe, S. B., Sharp, G. P., & Enslow, P. H. (2005). A Management Perspective on Risk of Security Threats to Information Systems. *Information Technology Management, 6*(2-3), 203–225. doi:10.1007/s10799-005-5880-5

FBI (2013). *The Intelligence Cycle.* Retrieved October 16, 2013, from http://www.fbi.gov/about-us/intelligence/intelligence-cycle

Feldman, R., & Dagan, I. (1995). Knowledge discovery in texts. In *Proc. of the First Int. Conf. on Knowledge Discovery (KDD),* (pp. 112–117). KDD.

Felt, A. P., Finifter, M., Chin, E., Hanna, S., & Wagner, D. (2011. A survey of mobile malware in the wild. In *Proceedings of the 1st ACM workshop on Security and privacy in smartphones and mobile devices* (SPSM 2011). ACM.

Fielding, R. (1999). *RFC2616 Hypertext Transfer Protocol.* Retrieved 2013, from http://tools.ietf.org/html/rfc2616

Filote, C., & Ciufudean, C. (2010). Future manufacturing systems - Cap. 2: Discrete event models for flexible manufacturing cells. In T. Aized (Ed.), Tech (pp. 17–39). Academic Press.

Finkelhor, D., Mitchell, K., & Wolak, J. (2000). *Online victimization: A report on the nation's youth (6-00-020).* Alexandria, VA: National Center for Missing & Exploited Children. Retrieved May 10, 2011, from http://www.unh.edu/ccrc/pdf/jvq/CV38.pdf

Finkelhor, D., Mitchell, K., & Wolack, J. (2000). *Online Victimization: A Report on the Nation's Youth.* National Center for Missing & Exploited Children.

Finkelhor, D., Ormrod, R. K., & Turner, H. A. (2007). Poly-victimization: A neglected component in child victimization. *Child Abuse & Neglect, 31,* 7–2. doi:10.1016/j.chiabu.2006.06.008 PMID:17224181

Finkelstein, S., & Hambrick, D. C. (1990). Top-management-team tenure and organizational outcomes: The moderating role of managerial discretion. *Administrative Science Quarterly, 35,* 484–503. doi:10.2307/2393314

Finn, J. (2004). A survey of online harassment at a university campus. *Journal of Interpersonal Violence, 19*(4), 468–483. doi:10.1177/0886260503262083 PMID:15038885

Fischer, V., & Drutarovsky, M. (2003). True Random Number Generator Embedded in Reconfigurable Hardware. *Springer Heidelberg, 2523,* 415–430.

Fisher, B. S., Cullen, F. T., & Turner, M. G. (2002). Being pursued: Stalking victimization in a national study of college woman. *Criminology & Public Policy, 1*(2), 257–308. doi:10.1111/j.1745-9133.2002.tb00091.x

Fleisch, E. (2010). What is the internet of things? An economic perspective. *Economics, Management, and Financial Markets, (2),* 125-157.

FMUP. F. de M. da U. do P. (2004). *Noções gerais sobre outras ciências forenses* (Medicina legal). Retrieved from http://medicina.med.up.pt/legal/NocoesGeraisCF.pdf

Fogie, S., Grossman, J., Hansen, R., Rager, A., & Petkov, P. D. (2011). *XSS Attacks: Cross Site Scripting Exploits and Defense.* Syngress.

Fontani, M. (2011). *Kippo-stats.* Retrieved 2013, from https://github.com/mfontani/kippo-stats

Forde, L. W., & Kennedy, D. R. (1997). Risky lifestyles, routine activities, and the general theory of crime. *Justice Quarterly, 14*(2), 265–294. doi:10.1080/07418829700093331

Forensics Wiki. (2007). *File formats.* Retrieved from http://www.forensicswiki.org/wiki/Category:File_Formats

Fortes, P. A. de C., & Spinetti, S. R. (2004). O agente comunitário de saúde e a privacidade das informações dos usuários. *Cadernos de Saúde Pública, 1328–1333.* Rio de Janeiro. Retrieved from http://www.scielo.br/pdf/csp/v20n5/27.pdf

Fossi, M., Egan, G., Haley, K., Johnson, E., Mack, T., Adams, T., ... & Wood, P. (2010). *Symantec internet security threat report trends for 2010.* Academic Press.

Foster, S. T. (2010). *Managing quality: Integrating the supply chain.* Upper Saddle River, NJ: Prentice Hall.

Fowler, A., & Cronau, P. (2013, May 29). *HACKED! Four Corners.* Australian Broadcasting Corporation. Retrieved from http://www.abc.net.au/4corners/stories/2013/05/27/3766576.htm

Fox, K. A., Nobles, M. R., & Akers, R. L. (2011). Is stalking a learned phenomenon? An empirical test of social learning theory. *Journal of Criminal Justice, 39*(1), 39–47. doi:10.1016/j.jcrimjus.2010.10.002

France, A., Bendelow, G., & Williams, S. (2000). A 'risky' bussiness: researching the health beliefs of children and young people. In A. Lewis & G. Lindsay (Eds.), Researching Children's Perspectives (pp. 150-162). Open University Press.

Franklin, S. W., & Rajan, S. E. (2010). Personal area network for biomedical monitoring systems using human body as a transmission medium. *International Journal of Bio-Science & Bio-Technology, 2*(2).

Frei, S. (2013). Vulnerability threat trends, NSS labs. Retrieved from https://www.nsslabs.com/reports/vulnerability-threat-trends

Freiling, F. C., & Schwittay, B. (2007). A common process model for incident response and computer forensics. *IMF, 7,* 19–40.

Frei, S., Duebendorfer, T., Ollmann, G., & May, M. (2008). *Understanding the web browser threat. TIK.* ETH Zurich.

Frois, C. (Ed.). (2008). *A sociedade vigilante – Ensaios sobre identificação, vigilância e privacidade.* Lisbon: Imprensa de Ciências Sociais.

Fuchs, C. (2011). An alternative view of privacy on Facebook. *Information, 2*(4), 140–165. doi:10.3390/info2010140

Furnell, S. (2008). Book reviews: Cybercrime: The transformation of crime in the information age – by D.S. Wall. *The British Journal of Sociology,* 177–179.http://onlinelibrary.wiley.com/doi/10.1111/bjos.2007.59.issue-1/issuetoc doi:10.1111/j.1468-4446.2007.00187_8.x

G1 (2013). Dilma diz na ONU que espionagem fere soberania e direito internacional. *G1.* Retrieved November 02, 2013, from http://g1.globo.com/mundo/noticia/2013/09/dilma-diz-na-onu-que-espionagem-fere-soberania-e-direito-internacional.html

GAO. (2004). United State government accountability office report: GAO-04-354. Retrived from http://www.gao.gov/new.items/d04354.pdf

GAO. (2007). *Critical infrastructure protection: Multiple efforts to secure control systems are under way, but challenges remain* (Technical Report GAO-07-1036). Report to Congressional Requesters.

Garcia-Amador, F.V. (1960). *Fifth Report on International Responsibility by Mr. F.V. Garcia-Amador, Special Rapporteur. State responsibility.* U.N. Doc. A/CN.4/125

Garfinkel, S. (2010). *Automated computer forensics: Current research areas.* Retrieved June/26, 2013, from http://simson.net/page/Automated_Computer_Forensics

Garfinkel, S. (2001). In D. Russel (Ed.), *Database Nation: The Death of Privacy in the 21st Century.* O'Reilly Media, Inc.

Garg, A., Curtis, J., & Halper, H. (2003). Quantifying the financial impact of IT security breaches. *Information Management & Computer Security, 11*(2), 74–83. doi:10.1108/09685220310468646

Garland, D. (2001). *The culture of control. Crime and social order in comtemporary society.* Chicago, IL: University of Chicago Press.

Gascon, H., Orfila, A., & Blasco, J. (2011). Analysis of update delays in signature-based network intrusion detection systems. *Computers & Security, 30*(8), 613–624. doi:10.1016/j.cose.2011.08.010

Gaubert, St., & Mairese, J. (1999). Modeling and Analysis of Timed Petri Nets Using Heap of Pieces. *IEEE Trans. on Autom. Robot. Contr., 44*(4), 683–697.

Gearty, C. A. (1997). *European civil liberties and the european convention on human rights: A comparative study.* Leiden, The Netherlands: Martinus Nijhoff Publishers.

Geers, K. (2011). *Strategic Cyber Security.* Tallinn, Estonia: CCD COE Publication.

GeoDa. (2013). Spatial econometric software. GeoDa Center for Geospatial Analysis and Computation.

*Get Social Updates of your contact list using Ice cream sandwich.* (2012). Retrieved August 21, 2013, from http://creativeandroidapps.blogspot.com/2012/07/get-social-updates-of-your-contact-list.html

Ghosh, S., Malek-Zavarei, M., & Stohr, E. A. (Eds.). (2004). *Guarding Your Business: A Management Approach to Security.* Kluwer Academic/Plenum. doi:10.1007/b105306

Giani, A., Karsai, G., Roosta, T., Shah, A., Sinopoli, B., & Wiley, J. (2008). A testbed for secure and robust SCADA systems. *SIGBED Review*, *5*(2), 1. doi:10.1145/1399583.1399587

Gibbens, M., & Harsha, R. (2012). Honeypots. In *Proceedings of the CSc 466-566 Computer Security 2012*. University of Arizona. Retrieved from http://www.cs.arizona.edu/~collberg/Teaching/466-566/2012/Resources/

Giedd, J. N. (2012). The Digital Revolution and Adolescent Brain Evolution. *The Journal of Adolescent Health*, *51*, 101–105. doi:10.1016/j.jadohealth.2012.06.002 PMID:22824439

Gilfix, M., & Couch, A. L. (2000). Peep (the network auralizer): Monitoring your network with sound. In *Proceedings of 14th System Administration Conference (LISA 2000)*, (pp. 109-117). New Orleans, LA: The USENIX Association.

Gilmore, A. (2012). Counting eyeballs, soundbites and 'plings': Arts participation, strategic instrumentalism and the london 2012 cultural olympiad. *International Journal of Cultural Policy*, *18*(2), 151–167. doi:10.1080/10286632.2011.577283

Gladyshev, P., & Patel, A. (2004). Finite state machine approach to digital event reconstruction. *Digital Investigation*, *1*(2), 130–149. doi:10.1016/j.diin.2004.03.001

Gleason, G., & Shaihutdinov, M. E. (2005). Collective Security and Non-State Actors in Eurasia. *International Studies Perspectives*, *6*(2), 274–284. doi:10.1111/j.1528-3577.2005.00206.x

Glossary. (2008). *Glossary of cyberbullying terms.* Retrieved November, 21, 2011, from http://www.adl.org/education/curriculum_connections/cyberbullying/glossary.pdf

Goedertier, S., & Vanthienen, J. (2006). Designing Compliant Business Processes with Obligations and Permissions. In J. Eder, & S. Dustdar (Eds.), *Business Process Management Workshops, LNCS 4103* (pp. 5–14). Berlin, Germany: Springer. doi:10.1007/11837862_2

Goldhaber, M. D. (2009). *A people's history of the european court of human rights.* New Brunswick, NJ: Rutgers University Press.

Goldman, E. H. (2012). The effect of acquisition decision making on security posture. *Information Management & Computer Security*, *20*(5), 350–363. doi:10.1108/09685221211286520

Goodin, D. (2007). Electrical supe charged with damaging California canal system. *The Register*. Retrieved from http://www.theregister.co.uk/2007/11/30/canal_system_hack/

Goodin, D. (2008). Gas refineries at defcon 1 as scada exploit goes wild. The Register. Retrieved from http://www.theregister.co.uk/2008/09/08/scada_exploit_released/

Google Play. (2013). *Google play store.* Retrieved August 21, 2013, from https://play.google.com/store?hl=en

Gordon, L. A., Loeb, M. P., & Lucyshyn, W. (2003). Sharing information on computer systems security. *Economic Analysis*, *22*(6), 461–485. Journal of Accounting and Public Policy

Gordon, L., & Loeb, M. (2002). The economics of information security investment. *ACM Transactions on Information and System Security*, *5*(4), 438–457. doi:10.1145/581271.581274

Gordon, L., & Loeb, M. (2006). Budgeting process for information security expenditures. *Communications of the ACM*, *49*(1), 121–125. doi:10.1145/1107458.1107465

Gordon, L., Loeb, M. P., & Sohail, T. (2010). Market value of voluntary disclosures concerning information security. *Management Information Systems Quarterly*, *34*(3), 567–594.

Gorman, S. (2009). Electricity grid in U.S. penetrated by spies. *The Wall Street Journal*. Retrieved from: http://online.wsj.com/article/SB123914805204099085.html

Gottfredson, M. R., & Hirschi, T. (1990). *A general theory of crime*. Standford, UK: Standford University Press.

Gotved, S. (2006). Time and space in cyber social reality. *New Media & Society*, 8(3), 467–486. doi:10.1177/1461444806064484

Governatori, G., Hoffmann, J., Sadiq, S. W., & Weber, I. (2009). Detecting Regulatory Compliance for Business Process Models through Semantic Annotations. In D. Ardagna, M. Mecella, & J. Yang (Eds.), *Business Process Management Workshops 2008, LNBIP 17* (pp. 5–17). Berlin, Germany: Springer. doi:10.1007/978-3-642-00328-8_2

Grabner-Kräuter, S., & Kaluscha, E. A. (2003). Empirical research in on-line trust: a review and critical assessment. *International Journal of Human-Computer Studies*, 58(6), 783–812. doi:10.1016/S1071-5819(03)00043-0

Grabosky, P. N. (2001). Virtual criminality: old wine in new bottles? *Social & Legal Studies*, 10(2), 243–249.

Greco, R., & Braga, R. R. P. (2012, January 23). Da principiologia penal ao direito à intimidade como garantia constitucional. *Direito E Desenvolvimento*. Retrieved from http://unipe.br/periodicos/index.php/direitoedesenvolvimento/article/view/119

Greenleaf, G. (in press). Sheherezade and the 101 Data Privacy Laws: Origins, Significance and Global Trajectories. *Journal of Law & Information Science*.

Grier, C., Tang, S., & King, S. T. (2008, May). Secure web browsing with the OP web browser. In *Proceedings of Security and Privacy, 2008*. IEEE.

Grigg, D. W. (2010). Cyber-aggression: Definition and concept of cyberbullying. *Australian Journal of Guidance & Counselling*, 20, 143–156. doi:10.1375/ajgc.20.2.143

Groff, E., & La Vigne, N. G. (2001). Mapping an Opportunity Surface of Residential Burglary. *Journal of Research in Crime and Delinquency*, 38(3), 257–278. doi:10.1177/0022427801038003003

Gross, E. F. (2004). Adolescent Internet use: What we expect, what teens report. *Journal of Applied Developmental Psychology*, 25(6), 633–649. doi:10.1016/j.appdev.2004.09.005

Grosskurth, A., & Godfrey, M. W. (2005, September). A reference architecture for web browsers. In *Proceedings of Software Maintenance,* (pp. 661-664). IEEE.

Grossman, W. M. (2010). The charmed life of cybercrime. *Infosecurity*, 7(1), 19–21. doi:10.1016/S1754-4548(10)70014-0

Guarnieri, F., & Przyswa, E. (2013). Counterfeiting and Cybercrime: Stakes and Challenges. *The Information Society: An International Journal*, 29(4), 219–226. doi:10.1080/01972243.2013.792303

Gudhjonsson, K. (2010). *Mastering the super timeline with log2timeline*. SANS Reading Room.

Guhring, P. (2006). *Concepts against Man-in-the-Browser Attacks*. Academic Press.

Guild, E. (2004). *The legal elements of european identity: EU citizenship and migration law*. London: Kluwer Law International.

Guinchard, A. (2007). *Criminal Law in the 21st Century: The Demise of Territoriality?* http://dx.doi.org/10.2139/ssrn.1290049

Guitton, C. (2013). Modelling Attribution. In *Proceedings of the 12th European Conference on Information Warfare and Security* (Vol. 1, pp. 91–97). ACPI.

Guitton, C., & Korzak, E. (2013). The Sophistication Criterion for Attribution: Identifying the Perpetrators of Cyber-Attacks. *The RUSI Journal*, 158(4), 62–68. doi:10.1080/03071847.2013.826509

Guo, C., Wang, L., Huang, L., & Zhao, L. (2008). Study on the internet behavior's activity oriented to network survivability. In *Proceedings of International Conference on Computational Intelligence and Security,* (vol. 1, pp. 432-435). IEEE.

Guo, D. L., DiCesare, F., & Zhou, M. Ch. (1993). A moment Generating Function Based Approach for Evaluating Extended Stochastic Petri Nets. *IEEE Transactions on Automatic Control*, 38(2), 321–327. doi:10.1109/9.250484

Gurgen, L., Gunalp, O., Benazzouz, Y., & Gallissot, M. (2013). Self-aware cyber-physical systems and applications in smart buildings and cities. In *Proceedings of the Conference on Design, Automation and Test in Europe,* (pp. 1149-1154). Academic Press.

Guridi, E. (2008). La LO 10/2007, de 8 de octubre, reguladora de la base de datos policial sobre identificadores obtenidos a partir del ADN. *DIARIO LA LEY, Nº 6901*(Año XXIX, Ref. D-78, Editorial LA LEY 6603/2008). Retrieved from http://www.larioja.org/upload/documents/679894_DLL_N_6901-2008.La_LO_102007_reguladora.pdf

Guseong-Dong, Yuseong-Gu, & Daejeon. (2005). *High-performance variable-length packet scheduling algorithm for IP traffic.* CNR Lab. Dept. of EECS, KAIST.

Gutwirth, S., Leenes, R., De Hert, P., & Poullet, Y. (Eds.). (2013). *European Data Protection: Coming of Age.* Berlin, Germany: Springer. doi:10.1007/978-94-007-5170-5

Hable, K. (2003). *HoneyView.* Retrieved 2013, from http://honeyview.sourceforge.net/

Hachman, M. (2014). *Chameleon Clickjacking Botnet Stealing $6 Million a Month.* Retrieved from http://slashdot.org/topic/datacenter/chameleon-clickjacking-botnet-stealing-6-million-a-month/

Hackman, J. R., & Wageman, R. (1995). Total quality management: Empirical, conceptual, and practical issues. *Administrative Science Quarterly, 40*(2), 309–342. doi:10.2307/2393640

Haddon, L., Livingstone, S., & EU Kids Online network. (2012). *EU Kids Online: National perspectives.* London, UK: EU Kids Online.

Haenens, L. d., Vandoninck, S., & Donoso, V. (2013). How to cope and build online resilience? EU Kids Online.

Hafner-Burton, E. M. (2008). Sticks and stones: Naming and shaming the human rights enforcement problem. *International Organization, 62,* 689–716. doi:10.1017/S0020818308080247

Haile, J. (n.d.). *Snort-Inline.* Retrieved 2013, from http://snort-inline.sourceforge.net/oldhome.html

Haimes, Y.Y. (2009). On the Definition of Resilience in Systems. *Risk Analysis, 29*(4), 498–501. doi:10.1111/j.1539-6924.2009.01216.x PMID:19335545

Halloran, J. D. (1970). Television and delinquency.

Halpin, R., & Moore, R. (2009). Developments in electronic money regulation–the electronic money directive: A better deal for e-money issuers? *Computer Law & Security Report, 25*(6), 563–568. doi:10.1016/j.clsr.2009.09.010

Hambrick, D. C., Cho, T. S., & Chen, M.-J. (1996). The Influence of Top Management Team Heterogeneity on Firms' Competitive Moves. *Administrative Science Quarterly, 41,* 659–684. doi:10.2307/2393871

Hamdan, O., Alanazi, B.B., Zaidan, A.A., Zaidan, H.A., Jalab, M., Shabbir, Y., & Al-Nabhani. (2010). New comparative study between DES, 3DES and AES within nine factors. *Journal of Computing, 2*(3).

Hamelink, C. J. (2004). Desafios morais na sociedade da informação. In J. Paquete de Oliveira et al. (Eds.), *Comunicação, cultura e tecnologias da informação* (pp. 261–270). Lisbon: Quimera.

Hancock, B. (2000a). US and Europe Cybercrime Agreement Problems. *Computers & Security, 19*(4), 306–307. doi:10.1016/S0167-4048(00)04012-8

Hancock, B. (2000b). G8 Thinks About Cybercrime (It's About Time, Too). *Computers & Security, 19*(5), 405–407. doi:10.1016/S0167-4048(00)05026-4

Hancock, B. (2000c). Canadian Teen Mafiaboy Pleads Guilty. *Computers & Security, 19*(8), 669.

Hansen, R., & Grossman, J. (2008). Clickjacking. *SecTheory: Internet Security.* Retrieved from http://www.sectheory.com/clickjacking.htm

Hansen, L., & Nissenbaum, H. (2009). Digital Disaster, Cybersecurity, and the Copenhagen School. *International Studies Quarterly, 53*(4), 1155–1175. doi:10.1111/j.1468-2478.2009.00572.x

Hansman, S., & Hunt, R. (2005). A taxonomy of network and computer attacks. *Computers & Security, 24*(1), 31–43. doi:10.1016/j.cose.2004.06.011

Haravuori, H., Suomalainen, L., Berg, N., Kiviruusu, O., & Marttunen, M. (2011). Effects of media exposure on adolescents traumatized in a school shooting. *Journal of Traumatic Stress*, *24*(1), 70–77. doi:10.1002/jts.20605 PMID:21268117

Hardaker, C. (2010). Trolling in asynchronous computer-mediated communication: From user discussions to academic definitions. *Journal of Politeness Research. Language, Behaviour. Culture (Canadian Ethnology Society)*, *6*(2), 215–242.

Hardaker, C. (2013). Uh.... not to be nitpicky, but... the past tense of drag is dragged, not drug.": An overview of trolling strategies. *Journal of Language Aggression and Conflict*, *1*(1), 58–86. doi:10.1075/jlac.1.1.04har

Harden, G., Al Beayeyz, A., & Visinescu, L. (2012). Concerning SNS Use: How do Issues of Privacy and Trust Concern Users? In *Proceedings of the 18th Americas Conference on Information Systems*. Retrieved from http://aisel.aisnet.org/amcis2012/proceedings/SocialIssues/4

Hargreaves, C., & Patterson, J. (2012). An automated timeline reconstruction approach for digital forensic investigations. *Digital Investigation*, *9*, S69–79. doi:10.1016/j.diin.2012.05.006

Hartmann, M. E. (2006). *E-payments evolution. Handbuch E-money, E-payment & M-payment* (pp. 7–18). Springer. doi:10.1007/3-7908-1652-3_2

Haupt, T. C., & Whiteman, D. E. (2004). Inhibiting factors of implementing total quality management on construction sites. *The TQM Magazine*, *16*(3), 166–173. doi:10.1108/09544780410532891

Hearst, M. (1999). Untangling text data mining. In *Proc. of ACL'99 the 37th Annual Meeting of the Association for Computational Linguistics*, (pp. 3-10). ACL.

Helsper, E. J., Kalmus, V., Hasebrink, U., Sagvari, B., & Haan, J. (2013). *Country classification: Opportunities, risks, harm and parental mediation*. London, UK: EU Kids Online, London School of Economics & Political Science.

Helweg-Larsen, K., Schütt, N., & Larsen, H. B. (2012). Predictors and protective factors for adolescent internet victimization: Results from a 2008 nationwide Danish youth survey. *Acta Paediatrica (Oslo, Norway)*, *101*(5), 533–539. doi:10.1111/j.1651-2227.2011.02587.x PMID:22211947

Henderson, S., & Gilding, M. (2004). 'I've never clicked this much with anyone in my life': trust and hyperpersonal communication in online friendships. *New Media & Society*, *6*(4), 487–506. doi:10.1177/146144804044331

Henrique, L. (2004). Honeydsum. Honeyd Tools. Retrieved 2013, from http://www.honeyd.org/tools.php

Henry, P., Williams, J., & Wright, B. (2013). *The SANS survey of digital forensics and incident response: A SANS whitepaper* Retrieved from https://blogs.sans.org/computer-forensics/files/2013/07/sans_dfir_survey_2013.pdf

Hentea, M. (2008). Improving security for SCADA control systems. *Interdisciplinary Journal of Information, Knowledge, and Management*, *3*(12), 4.

Hermann, T., Hunt, A. D., & Neuhoff, J. (Eds.). (2011). *The sonification handbook*. Berlin: Logos Verlag.

Hernández-Muñoz, J. M., Vercher, J. B., Muñoz, L., Galache, J. A., Presser, M., & Gómez, L. A. H. et al. (2011). *Smart cities at the forefront of the future internet*. In *The future internet* (pp. 447–462). Springer.

Hertz, M. F., & David-Ferdon, C. (2008). *Electronic Media and Youth Violence: A CDC Issue Brief for Educators and Caregivers*. Atlanta, GA: Centers for Disease Control.

Hertz, M. F., & David-Ferdon, C. (2011). Online aggression: a reflection of in-person victimization or a unique phenomenon? *The Journal of Adolescent Health*, *48*(2), 119–120. doi:10.1016/j.jadohealth.2010.11.255 PMID:21257108

Heuer, S. (2011, April). A Rede lembra-se de tudo? *Courrier Internacional*, pp. 84-88.

Hickson, I., & Hyatt, D. (2011). *Html5*. W3C Working Draft WD-html5-20110525, May.

Higgins, G. E. (2005). Can low self-control help with the understanding of the software piracy problem? *Deviant Behavior*, *26*(1), 1–24. doi:10.1080/01639620490497947

Higgins, G. E., Fell, B. D., & Wilson, A. L. (2006). Digital piracy: Assessing the contributions of an integrated self-control theory and social learning theory using structural equation modeling. *Criminal Justice Studies*, *19*(1), 3–22. doi:10.1080/14786010600615934

Higgins, G. E., & Makin, D. A. (2004). Self-control, deviant peers, and software piracy. *Psychological Reports*, *95*(3), 921–931. doi:10.2466/pr0.95.3.921-931 PMID:15666930

High Representative of The European Union for Foreign Affairs and Security Policy Brussels. (2013). *Joint Communication to the European Parliament, the Council, the European Economic and Social Committee and the Committee of the Regions Cybersecurity Strategy of the European Union: An Open, Safe And Secure Cyberspace.* Retrieved October 13, 2013, from http://ec.europa.eu/digital-agenda/en/news/eu-cybersecurity-plan-protect-open-internet-and-online-freedom-and-opportunity-cyber-security

Hill, K. (2010). Where Steve Jobs Stood on Location Privacy in. Retrieved from http://www.forbes.com/sites/kashmirhill/2011/04/25/where-steve-jobs-stood-on-location-privacy-in-2010/

Hilley, S. (2005). News. *Digital Investigation*, *2*, 171–174.

Hilley, S. (2007). US cybercrime statistics: FBI hotline gets more than 200,000 complaints. *Digital Investigation*, *4*, 54–55. doi:10.1016/j.diin.2007.04.003

Hinde, S. (2003). The law, cybercrime, risk assessment and cyber protection. *Computers & Security*, *22*(2), 90–95. doi:10.1016/S0167-4048(03)00203-7

Hinduja, S., & Patchin, J. W. (2011). High-tech cruelty. *Educational Leadership, 68*(5), 48-52.

Hinduja, S., & Patchin, J. (2009). *Bullying beyond the schoolyard: Preventing and responding to cyberbullying.* Corwin Press.

Hinduja, S., & Patchin, J. W. (2007). Offline consequences of online victimization. *Journal of School Violence*, *6*(3), 89–112. doi:10.1300/J202v06n03_06

Hinduja, S., & Patchin, J. W. (2008). Cyberbullying: An exploratory analysis of factors related to offending and victimization. *Deviant Behavior*, *29*(2), 129–156. doi:10.1080/01639620701457816

Hinduja, S., & Patchin, J. W. (2010). Bullying, cyber bullying, and suicide. *Archives of Suicide Research*, *14*(3), 206–221. doi:10.1080/13811118.2010.494133 PMID:20658375

Hinduja, S., & Patchin, J. W. (2012a). cyber bullying: Neither an epidemic nor a rarity. *European Journal of Developmental Psychology*, *9*, 539–543. doi:10.1080/17405629.2012.706448

Hinduja, S., & Patchin, J. W. (2012b). *School climate 2.0: Preventing cyber bullying and sexting one classroom at a time.* Thousand Oaks, CA: Corwin.

Hines, A. (2002). *Planning for Survivable Networks: Ensuring Business Continuity.* Wiley Publishing.

Hoadley, C. M., Xu, H., Lee, J. J., & Rosson, M. B. (2010). Privacy as information access and illusory control: The case of the Facebook News Feed privacy outcry. *Electronic Commerce Research and Applications*, *9*(1), 50–60. doi:10.1016/j.elerap.2009.05.001

Hoffman, D. L., Novak, T. P., & Peralta, M. (1999). Building consumer trust online. *Communications of the ACM*, *42*(4), 80–85. doi:10.1145/299157.299175

Holland, D. (1972). Television and crime-a causal link. *Auckland UL Rev.*, *2*, 53.

Holt, T. J. (2007). Subcultural evolution? Examining the influence of on- and off-line experiences on deviant subcultures. *Deviant Behavior*, *28*(2), 171–198. doi:10.1080/01639620601131065

Holt, T. J., & Bossler, A. M. (2008). Examining the Applicability of Lifestyle-Routine Activities Theory for Cybercrime Victimization. *Deviant Behavior*, *30*(1), 1–25. doi:10.1080/01639620701876577

Holzammer, A. (2008). *Security Issues about Web Browser Add-ons.* Seminar Internet Sicherheit, Technisc-he Universit at Berlin.

Hopkins, M. (2002a). *Strategies for determining causes of events* (Technical Report R-306). UCLA Cognitive Systems Laboratory.

Hopkins, M. (2002b). *A proof of the conjunctive in causes and explanations* (Technical Report R-306). UCLA Cognitive Systems Laboratory.

Hoque, N., Bhuyan, M. H., Baishya, R. C., Bhattacharyya, D. K., & Kalita, J. K. (2013). Network attacks: Taxonomy, tools and systems. *Journal of Network and Computer Applications.*

Hossain, S., & Mohammad, Z. (2012). Mitigating program security vulnerabilities: Approaches and challenges. *ACM Computing Surveys, 44*(3), 11:1–11:46.

Hotho, A., Nürnberger, A., & Paaß, G. (2005). A Brief Survey of Text Mining. *Forum American Bar Association, 20*(1), 19–62.

Hovav, A., & D'Arcy, J. (2003). The impact of denial-of-service attack announcements on the market value of firms. *Risk Management & Insurance Review, 6*(2), 97–121. doi:10.1046/J.1098-1616.2003.026.x

Hovav, A., & D'Arcy, J. (2004). The impact of virus attack announcements on the market value of firms. *Information Systems Security, 13*(3), 32–40. doi:10.1201/1086/4453 0.13.3.20040701/83067.5

*How to get the Android device's Primary Email Address.* (2010). Retrieved August 21, 2013, from http://stackoverflow.com/questions/2112965/how-to-get-the-android-devices-primary-e-mail-address

*How to make a phone pall in Android and come back to my when activity call is done.* (2011). Retrieved August 21, 2013, from http://stackoverflow.com/questions/1556987/how-to-make-a-phone-call-in-android-and-come-back-to-my-activity-when-the-call-i

*How to make android phone silent in java.* (2012). Retrieved August 21, 2013, from://stackoverflow.com/questions/10360815/how-to-make-android-phone-silent-in-java

Howard, J. D., & Longstaff, T. A. (1998). *A common language for computer security incidents* (Sandia Report: SAND98-8667). Sandia National Laboratories. Retrieved from http://www.cert.org/research/taxonomy_988667.pdf

Howes, E. L. (2004). *The Anatomy of a 'Drive-by-Download'.* Academic Press.

Hsu, C. (2009). Frame misalignment:interpreting the implementation of information systems certification in an organization. *European Journal of Information Systems, 18*(2), 140–150. doi:10.1057/ejis.2009.7

Huang, L., & Jackson, C. (2011). *Clickjacking attacks unresolved.* Retrieved from http://mayscript.com/blog/david/clickjacking-attacks-unresolved

Huang, L., Moshchuk, A., Wang, Schechter, S., & Jackson, C. (2012). Clickjacking: Attacks and Defenses. In *Proceedings of USENIX Security.* Bellevue, WA: USENIX.

Huang, A. H., & Yen, D. C. (2013). Predicting the helpfulness of online Reviews—A replication. *International Journal of Human-Computer Interaction, 29*(2), 129–138. doi:10.1080/10447318.2012.694791

Hubbard, D. (2013). *FSEdit.* Retrieved 2013, from http://pastebin.com/SwhvR8xM

Huesmann, L.R. (2007). The Impact of Electronic Media Violence: Scientific Theory and Research. *The Journal of Adolescent Health, 41*(6), S6–S13. doi:10.1016/j.jadohealth.2007.09.005 PMID:18047947

Hughes, A. (2013). Ediscovery: Criminal process in a corporate world - How to ensure investigations do not fall short. *eForensics Magazine, 2*(8). Retrieved August 5, 2013 from http://eforensicsmag.com/ediscovery-compendium/

Hughes, V., & Love, P. (2004). Toward cyber-centric management of policing: back to the future with information and communication technology. *Industrial Management & Data Systems, 104*(7), 604–612. doi:10.1108/02635570410550269

Hunton, P. (2011). A rigorous approach to formalising the technical investigation stages of cybercrime and criminality within a UK law enforcement environment. *Digital Investigation, 7,* 105–113. doi:10.1016/j.diin.2011.01.002

Hunton, P. (2012). Data attack of the cybercriminal: Investigating the digital currency of cybercrime. *Computer Law & Security Report, 28*(2), doi:10.1016/j.clsr.2012.01.007

Hunton, P. (2012). Managing the technical resource capability of cybercrime investigation: a UK law enforcement perspective. *Public Money & Management, 32*(3), 225–232. doi:10.1080/09540962.2012.676281

Hu, Q., Hart, P., & Cooke, D. (2007). The role of external and internal influences on information systems security - a neo-institutional perspective. *The Journal of Strategic Information Systems, 16*(2), 153–172. doi:10.1016/j.jsis.2007.05.004

Hyacinthe, B. (2009). *Cyber warriors at war, U.S. national security secrets and fears revealed.* XLibris Corp.

Hyatt, E. C. (2013). *Custom Android Phone*. Retrieved August 21, 2013, from http://sites.google.com/site/edwardcraighyatt/projects/custom-android-phone

Hyman, P. (2013). Cybercrime: It's Serious, But Exactly How Serious? *Communications of the ACM, 56*(3), 18–20. doi:10.1145/2428556.2428563

*IC3*. (2012). Retrieved from Federal Bureau of Investigation website: http://www.ic3.gov/media/annualreport/2011_IC3Report.pdf

ICS-CERT. (2013). ICS-CERT Monthly Monitor Oct-Dec 2012. Retrieved from http://ics-cert.us-cert.gov/monitors/ICS-MM201210

Igarashi, Y., Ueno, M., & Fujisaki, T. (2012). Proposed node and network models for an M2M internet. In *Proceedings of World Telecommunications Congress (WTC)*, (pp. 1-6). WTC.

Igure, V., Laughter, S., & Williams, R. (2006). Security issues in SCADA networks. *Computers & Security, 25*(7), 498–506. doi:10.1016/j.cose.2006.03.001

Igure, V., & Williams, R. (2008). Taxonomies of attacks and vulnerabilities in computer systems. *IEEE Communications Surveys & Tutorials, 10*(1), 6–19. doi:10.1109/COMST.2008.4483667

InDret2009*La introducción del delito de "atti persecutori" en el Código penal italiano*. InDret. Available on line in http://www.indret.com

*INFOSEC Institute*. (2013). Retrieved from http://resources.infosecinstitute.com/botnets-and-cybercrime-introduction/

Inglot, B., Liu, L., & Antonopoulos, N. (2012). A Framework for Enhanced Timeline Analysis in Digital Forensics. In *Proceedings of Green Computing and Communications (GreenCom)*, (pp. 253-256). IEEE.

INL. (2008). *Idaho national laboratory*. National SCADA Test Bed Program. Retrieved from http://www.inl.gov/scada

Intelligence and National Security Alliance (INSA). (2011). *Cyber Intelligence*. Retrieved from http://issuu.com/insalliance/docs/insa_cyber_intelligence/1

International Law Commission. (2001). *Draft Articles on Prevention, U.N. Doc. A/56/10* (referred to as: ILC Draft Articles on Prevention). Author.

International Law Commission. (2006). Draft principles on the allocation of loss in the case of transboundary harm arising out of hazardous activities. *U.N. Doc. A, 61*(10), 120.

International Telecommunication Union (ITU). (2007). *Global cybersecurity agenda (GCA): Framework for international cooperation*. Switzerland: ITU.

Internet sans frontiers. (2010). Brésil: Um cadre de loi exemplaire. *Internet sans frontières*. Retrieved March 07, 2013, from http://www.internetsansfrontieres.com/Bresil-un-cadre-de-loi-exemplaire_a154.html

*Internet Users*. (2012). Retrieved from http://www.internetworldstats.com/stats.htm

Islam, R. U., Schmidt, M., Kolbe, H., & Andersson, K. (2012). Nomadic mobility between smart homes. In *Proceedings of Globecom Workshops (GC Wkshps)*, (pp. 1062-1067). IEEE.

Jablonski, S., & Bussler, C. (1996). *Workflow management — modeling concepts, architecture and implementation*. London, UK: International Thomson Computer Press.

Jackson, M., Cassidy, W., & Brown, K. (2009). Out of the mouth of babes: Students' voice their opinions on cyber-bullying. *Long Island Education Review, 8*(2), 24–30.

Jansen, E., & James, V. (1995). *NetLingo: The internet dictionary*. Oxnard, CA: Netlingo Inc.

Jennings, W. G., Piquero, A. R., & Reingle, J. M. (2012). On the overlap between victimization and offending: A review of the literature. *Aggression and Violent Behavior, 17*(1), 16–26. doi:10.1016/j.avb.2011.09.003

Jensen, H. J. (1998). *Self-organized criticality*. Cambridge, UK: Cambridge University Press. doi:10.1017/CBO9780511622717

Jensen, J. L., & Sørensen, A. S. (2013). Nobody has 257 Friends. *Nordicom Review, 34*(1), 49–62.

Jewkes, Y., & Yar, M. (2010). *Handbook of Internet Crime*. London: Taylor & Francis.

Jeyaraman, S., & Atallah, M. (2006). An empirical study of automatic event reconstruction systems. *Digital Investigation, 3*, 108-115.

John, A., & Sivakumar, T. (2009). Ddos: Survey of traceback methods. *International Journal of Recent Trends in Engineering, 1*(2), 241–245.

Johnson, M. E., & Goetz, E. (2007). Embedding information security into the organization. *IEEE Security and Privacy, May/June*, 16-24.

JOIN. (2013). *Joint communication to the European parliament, the council, the European economic and social committee and the committee of the regions: Cybersecurity strategy of the European Union: An open, safe and secure cyberspace.* Brussels: High Representative of the European Union for Foreign Affairs and Security Policy.

Joinson, N. A. (2008). 'Looking at', 'Looking up' or 'keeping up with people'? Motives and Uses of Facebook. In *Proceedings of the SIGCHI Conference on Human Factors in Computing Systems* (pp. 1027-1036). New York: ACM.

Jones, J., & Rommney, G. (2004). Honeynets: An educational resource for IT security. In *Proceedings of the 5th Conference on Information Technology Education (CITC5 '04)* (pp. 24-28). New York: ACM. Doi: doi:10.1145/1029533.1029540

Jorge, A. (2012). Em risço na internet? Resultados do inquérito EU KIDS ONLINE. In C. Ponte, A. Jorge, J. A. Simões, & D. S. Cardoso (Eds.), *Crianças e Internet em Portugal - Acessos, usos, riscos, mediações: resultados do inquérito europeu EU KIDS ONLINE* (pp. 93–104). MinervaCoimbra.

Joshi, R. C., & Sardana, A. (2011). *Honeypots: A new paradigm to information security.* Science Publishers.

Juels, A. (2006). RFID security and privacy: A research survey. *IEEE Journal on Selected Areas in Communications, 24*(2), 381–394.

Juola, P. (2006). Authorship attribution. *Foundations and Trends in Information Retrieval, 1*(3), 233–334.

Jutla, D., Bodorik, P., & Dhaliwal, J. (2002). Supporting the e-business readiness of small and medium-sized enterprises: Approaches and metrics. *Internet Research, 12*(2), 139–164. doi:10.1108/10662240210422512

Juvonen, J., & Gross, E. F. (2008). Extending the school grounds? Bullying experiences in cyber space. *The Journal of School Health, 78*(9), 496–505. doi:10.1111/j.1746-1561.2008.00335.x PMID:18786042

K&L Gates (n.d.). *Electronic discovery case database.* Retrieved November 10, 2013 from http://ediscovery.klgates.com/search.aspx

Kamphuis, J.H., & Emmelkamp, P.M.G. (2000). Stalking-A contemporary challenger for forensic and clinical psychiatry. *The British Journal of Psychiatry, 176*.

Kane, J., & Portin, P. (2008). *Violência e tecnologia. Bélgica: Comissão Europeia.* DG Justiça, Liberdade e Segurança. Programa Daphne.

Kankanhalli, A., Teo, H. H., & Wei, K. K. (2003). An integrative study of information systems security effectiveness. *International Journal of Information Management, 23*(2), 139–154. doi:10.1016/S0268-4012(02)00105-6

Kantor, I. (2011). *The Clickjacking Attack.* Retrieved from http://javascript.info/tutorial/clickjacking

Kappler, S. Á. de N. (2008). La prueba de ADN en el proceso penal. (S. L. Comares, Ed.). Granada.

Karmel, R. S. (1999). Case for a european securities commission, the. *Colum. J.Transnat'L L., 38*, 9.

Kasbersky Lab. (2008). *Monthly Malware Statistics for August 2008.* Retrieved on March 15, 2013 from http://www.kaspersky.com/news?id=207575678

Kaspersky (2010). *Kaspersky security bulletin. Malware evolution 2010.* Retrieved October 21, 2013, from http://www.securelist.com/en/analysis/204792161/

Kassner, M. (2011). Digital forensics: The science behind 'who done it'. *TechRepublic Blog.* Retrieved November 3, 2013 from http://www.techrepublic.com/blog/it-security/digital-forensics-the-science-behind-who-done-it/6660/

Katz, A. (2012). *Cyberbullying and E-safety: What educators and other professionals need to know.* Jessica Kingsley Publishers.

Katzer, C., Fetchenhauer, D., & Belschak, F. (2009). cyber bullying: Who are the victims? A comparison of victimization in Internet chatrooms and victimization in school. *Journal of Media Psychology, 21*(1), 25–36. doi:10.1027/1864-1105.21.1.25

Kenyon, H. (2013). *Cloud of iron: DARPA hardens cloud computing against cyber attack*. Retrieved from http://breakingdefense.com/2013/01/10/cloud-of-iron-darpa-hardens-cloud-computing-against-cyber-attac/

Kerr, P., Rollins, J., & Theohary, C. (2010). *The stuxnet computer worm: Harbinger of an emerging warfare capability*. Congressional Research Service.

Kešelj, V., Peng, F., Cercone, N., & Thomas, C. (2003). N-gram-based author profiles for authorship attribution. In *Proceedings of the Conference Pacific Association for Computational Linguistics, PACLING* (Vol. 3, pp. 255–264). PACLING.

Khan, M., Chatwin, C., & Young, R. (2007). A framework for post-event timeline reconstruction using neural networks. *Digital Investigation, 4*(3), 146-157.

Khan, J. Y., & Yuce, M. R. (2010). Wireless body area network (WBAN) for medical applications. *Mobile Networks and Applications, 7*(5), 365-376.

Kharif, O. (2012). *'Likejacking': Spammers Hit Social Media*. Retrieved from http://www.businessweek.com/articles/2012-05-24/likejacking-spammers-hit-social-media

Kigerl, A. (2012). Routine activity theory and the determinants of high cybercrime countries. *Social Science Computer Review, 30*(4), 470–486. doi:10.1177/0894439311422689

Kilduff, M., Angelmar, R., & Mehra, A. (2000). Top management-team diversity and firm performance: examining the role of cognitions. *Organization Science, 11*(1), 21–34. doi:10.1287/orsc.11.1.21.12569

Kim, W., Jeong, O.-R., Kim, C., & So, J. (2011). The dark side of the internet: Attacks, costs and responses. *Information Systems, 36*(3), 675–705. doi:10.1016/j.is.2010.11.003

King, J.E., Walpole, C., & Lamon, K. (2007). Surf and Turf Wars Online—Growing Implications of Internet Gang Violence. *The Journal of Adolescent Health, 41*(6), S66–S68. doi:10.1016/j.jadohealth.2007.09.001 PMID:18047950

Kirke, A., & Miranda, E. (2013). Pulsed melodic processing — the Use of melodies in affective computations for increased processing transparency. In S. Holland, K. Wilkie, P. Mulholland, & A. Seago (Eds.), Music and human-computer interaction (pp. 171-188). Springer.

Kirkland. (2010). Farpd - ARP reply daemon. *Ubuntu Manuals*. Retrieved 2013, from http://manpages.ubuntu.com/manpages/dapper/man8/farpd.8.html

Kizza, J. (2003). *Ethical and Social Issues in the Information Age*. Springer-Verlag.

Kjaerland, M. (2006). A taxonomy and comparison of computer security incidents from the commercial and government sectors. *Computers & Security, 25*(7), 522–538. doi:10.1016/j.cose.2006.08.004

Kohn, M., Eloff, J., & Olivier, M. (2006). Framework for a digital forensic investigation. In *Proceedings of the ISSA 2006 from Insight to Foresight Conference, Sandton, South Africa*. ISSA.

Kolari, P., Java, A., Finin, T., Oates, T., & Joshi, A. (2006). Detecting spam blogs: A machine learning approach. In *Proceedings of the 21st National Conference on Artificial Intelligence (AAAI)*. AAAI.

Koniaris, I. (2013). *Kippo-Graph*. Retrieved 2013, from http://sourceforge.net/projects/kippo-graph/

Koops, B. (2010). *The Internet and its Opportunities for Cybercrime* (Vol. 1, pp. 735–754). Transnational Criminology Manual.

Kotulic, A. G., & Clark, J. G. (2004). Why there aren't more information security research studies. *Information & Management, 41*(5), 597–607. doi:10.1016/j.im.2003.08.001

Koukovini, M. N., Papagiannakopoulou, E. I., Lioudakis, G. V., Dellas, N. L., Kaklamani, D. I., & Venieris, I. S. (in press). An ontology-based approach towards comprehensive workflow modelling. *IET Software*.

Kowalski, R. M., Limber, S. P., & Agatston, P. W. (2012). Cyber bullying: Bullying in the digital age (2nd ed.). Malden, MA: Wiley-Blackwell.

Kowalski, R.M., & Limber, S. (2007). Electronic Bullying Among Middle School Students. *The Journal of Adolescent Health, 41*(6), S22–S30. doi:10.1016/j.jadohealth.2007.08.017 PMID:18047942

Kozlov, D., Veijalainen, J., & Ali, Y. (2012). Security and privacy threats in IoT architectures. In *Proceedings of the 7th International Conference on Body Area Networks,* (pp. 256-262). Academic Press.

Kraemer-Mbula, E., Tang, P., & Rush, H. (2013). The cybercrime ecosystem: Online innovation in the shadows. *Technological Forecasting and Social Change, 80*(3), 541–555. doi:10.1016/j.techfore.2012.07.002

Kraft, E. M., & Wang, J. (2009). Effectiveness of cyber bullying prevention strategies: A study on students' perspectives. *International Journal of Cyber Criminology, 3*(2).

Krasnova, H., Kolesnikova, E., & Guenther, O. (2009). "It Won't Happen To Me!": Self-Disclosure in Online Social Networks. In *Proceedings of the 15th Americas Conference on Information Systems.* Retrieved from http://aisel.aisnet.org/amcis2009/343

Krasnova, H., Spiekermann, S., Koroleva, K., & Hildebrand, T. (2010). Online social networks: why we disclose. *Journal of Information Technology, 25*(2), 109–125. doi:10.1057/jit.2010.6

Kreibich, C. (2009). *Honeycomb - Automated signature creation using honeypots.* Retrieved 2013, from http://www.icir.org/christian/honeycomb/

Krekel, B. (2009). *Capability of the People's Republic of China to conduct Cyber Warfare.* US-China Economic and Security Review Commission.

Kruegel, C., & Vigna, G. (2003, October). Anomaly detection of web-based attacks. In *Proceedings of the 10th ACM conference on Computer and communications security* (pp. 251-261). ACM.

Kshetri, N. (2005). Pattern of global cyber war and crime: A conceptual framework. *Journal of International Management, 11*(4), 541–562. doi:10.1016/j.intman.2005.09.009

Kshetri, N. (2013a). Cybercrime and cyber-security issues associated with China: some economic and institutional considerations. *Electronic Commerce Research, 13*(1), 41–69. doi:10.1007/s10660-013-9105-4

Kshetri, N. (2013b). Cybercrimes in the Former Soviet Union and Central and Eastern Europe: current status and key drivers. *Crime, Law, and Social Change, 60*(1), 39–65. doi:10.1007/s10611-013-9431-4

Kuehn, C. (2012). Time-scale and noise optimality in self-organized critical adaptive networks. *Physical Review E: Statistical, Nonlinear, and Soft Matter Physics,* (85), 2.

Kulesza, J. (2012). International Internet law. *Global Change, Peace & Security, 24*(3), 351–364. doi:10.1080/14781158.2012.716417

Kumar, S., Singh, P., Sehgal, R., & Bhatia, J. S. (2012). Distributed Honeynet System Using Gen III Virtual Honeynet. *International Journal of Computer Theory & Engineering, 4*(4), 537. doi: 10.7763/IJCTE.2012.V4.527

Kumar, S., & Gade, R. (2012). Experimental evaluation of Cisco ASA-5510 intrusion prevention system against denial of service attacks. *Journal of Information Security, 3*(2), 122–137. doi:10.4236/jis.2012.32015

Lai, J. Y., Wu, J. S., Chen, S. J., Wu, C. H., & Yang, C. H. (2008, August). Designing a taxonomy of web attacks. In *Proceedings of Convergence and Hybrid Information Technology,* (pp. 278-282). IEEE.

Lan, F., Akylidiz, W.-Y., Lee, M. C., & Vuran, S. M. (2006). Next generation dynamic spectrum access cognitive radio wireless networks: Survey, . *Computer Networks, 50,* 2127–2159.

Lang, M., Devitt, J., Kelly, S., Kinneen, A., O'Malley, J., & Prunty, D. (2009). Social Networking and Personal Data Security: A Study of Attitudes and Public Awareness in Ireland. In *Proceedings of the 2009 International Conference on Management of e-Commerce and e-Government* (pp. 486-489). Washington, DC: IEEE Computer Society.

Langer, E. J. (1975). The illusion of control. *Journal of Personality and Social Psychology, 32*(2), 311–328. doi:10.1037/0022-3514.32.2.311

Laranjo, I., Macedo, J., & Santos, A. (2012). Internet of things for medication control: Service implementation and testing. *Procedia Technology, 5*(0), 777–786. doi:10.1016/j.protcy.2012.09.086

Law, D. M., Shapka, J. D., Hymel, S., Olson, B. F., & Waterhouse, T. (2012). The changing face of bullying: An empirical comparison between traditional and internet bullying and victimization. *Computers in Human Behavior*, *28*(1), 226–232. doi:10.1016/j.chb.2011.09.004

Lawrence, B. S. (1997). The Black Box of Organizational Demography. *Organization Science*, *8*(1), 1–22. doi:10.1287/orsc.8.1.1

Layton, R., Watters, P., & Dazeley, R. (2012). Unsupervised authorship analysis of phishing webpages. In *Proceedings of 2012 International Symposium on Communications and Information Technologies (ISCIT)* (pp. 1104–1109). ISCIT. doi: 10.1109/ISCIT.2012.6380857

Layton, R., Perez, C., Birregah, B., Watters, P., & Lemercier, M. (2013a). Indirect Information Linkage for OSINT through Authorship Analysis of Aliases. In *Trends and Applications in Knowledge Discovery and Data Mining* (pp. 36–46). Springer. doi:10.1007/978-3-642-40319-4_4

Layton, R., Watters, P., & Dazeley, R. (2013b). Automated unsupervised authorship analysis using evidence accumulation clustering. *Natural Language Engineering*, *19*(01), 95–120. doi:10.1017/S1351324911000313

Lee, H., Lee, J., & Han, J. (2007). The efficient security architecture for authentication and authorization in the home network. In *Proceedings of Natural Computation*, (vol. 5, pp. 713-717). Academic Press.

Lee, Y. J. (2012). Exploring the economic values of online user ratings with advertising spending on box office sales. In *Proceedings of the 11th International Workshop on E-Business*. Academic Press.

*Legal Information Institute*. (2012). Retrieved from http://www.law.cornell.edu/uscode/text

*Lei Nº 5/2008*. (2008). Assembleia da República Portuguesa.

*Lei Nº 67/98*. (1998). Assembleia da República Portuguesa.

Leland, W. E., Taqqu, M. S., Willinger, W., & Wilson, D. V. (1993). On the self-similar nature of Ethernet traffic. *SIGCOMM Comput. Commun. Rev.*, *23*(4), 183–193. doi:10.1145/167954.166255

Lemos, A. (2007). Mídia locativa e territórios informacionais. In P. Arantes, & L. Santaella (Eds.), *Estéticas tecnológicas* (pp. 207–230). São Paulo: Editora PUC.

Lempereur, B., Merabti, M., & Shi, Q. (2009). *Automating evidence extraction and analysis for digital forensics*. Academic Press.

León, O. (2002). *Democratização das comunicações*. Retrieved June 07, 2013, from http://www.dhnet.org.br/w3/fsmrn/fsm2002/osvaldo1_midia.html

Levine, J., LaBella, R., Owen, H., Contis, D., & Culver, B. (2003). The use of Honeynets to detect exploited systems across large enterprise networks. In Proceedings of the Systems Information Assurance Workshop. In *Proceedings of IEEE Systems, Man and Cybernetics Society 2003* (pp. 92-99). IEEE. Doi: doi:10.1109/SMCSIA.2003.1232406

Levinson, D. (2002). *Encyclopedia of crime and punishment*. London: Sage Publications Ltd.

Levi, R. P. (1979). Violence on television: An old problem with a new picture. *North Carolina Law Review*, *58*, 97.

*LexisNexis*. (2011). Retrieved from http://www.lexisnexis.com/en-us/home.page

Leyla, N., Mashiyat, A. S., Wang, H., & MacCaull, W. (2010). Towards workflow verification. In H. A. Müller, A. G. Ryman, & A. W. Kark (Eds.), *Proceedings of the 2010 Conference of the Center for Advanced Studies on Collaborative Research (CASCON 2010)* (pp. 253–267). Riverton, NJ: IBM.

Liau, A., Khoo, A., & Ang, P. (2008). Parental awareness and monitoring of adolescent Internet use. *Current Psychology (New Brunswick, N.J.)*, *27*, 217–233. doi:10.1007/s12144-008-9038-6

Libicki, M. (2012). Cyberspace is not a warfighting domain. *A Journal of Law and Policy for the Information Society*, *8* (2), 325-340.

Lieberman, J. (2012). Senator Lieberman's speech on cybersecurity act. *Washington Post*. Retrieved from http://www.washingtonpost.com/blogs/2chambers/post/cybersecurity-bill-fails-in-the-senate/2012/08/02/gJQA-BofxRX_blog.html

Lieberman, H., Dinakar, K., & Jones, B. (2011). Let's gang up on cyber bullying. *Computer*, *44*(9), 93–96. doi:10.1109/MC.2011.286

Liebig, C., Cilia, M., & Buchmann, A. (1999). Event composition in time-dependent distributed systems. In *Proceedings of the Fourth IECIS International Conference on Cooperative Information Systems* (pp. 70-78). Washington, DC: IEEE Computer Society.

Ligh, M., Adair, S., Hartstein, B., & Richard, M. (2010). *Malware Analyst's Cookbook and DVD: Tools and Techniques for Fighting Malicious Code*. Wiley Publishing.

Lin, C., Zhitang, L., & Cuixia, G. (2009). Automated analysis of multi-source logs for network forensics. In *Proceedings of Education Technology and Computer Science*, (pp. 660-664). Academic Press.

Lin, M., Leu, J., Li, K., & Wu, J. C. (2012). Zigbee-based internet of things in 3D terrains. In *Proceedings of Advanced Computer Theory and Engineering (ICACTE)*, (vol. 5, pp. 376-380). ICACTE.

Lin, Y. R., Sundaram, H., Chi, Y., Tatemura, J., & Tseng, B. L. (2008). Detecting splogs via temporal dynamics using self-similarity analysis. *ACM Trans. Web*, *2*(1), 1–35. doi:10.1145/1326561.1326565

Lioudakis, G. V., Gaudino, F., Boschi, E., Bianchi, G., Kaklamani, D. I., & Venieris, I. S. (2010). Legislation-Aware Privacy Protection in Passive Network Monitoring. In I. M. Portela, & M. M. Cruz-Cunha (Eds.), *Information Communication Technology Law, Protection and Access Rights: Global Approaches and Issues* (pp. 363–383). New York: IGI Global Pubs. doi:10.4018/978-1-61520-975-0.ch022

Li, Q. (2006). Cyber bullying in schools a research of gender differences. *School Psychology International*, *27*(2), 157–170. doi:10.1177/0143034306064547

Li, Q. (2007). New Bottle but Old Wine: A Research of Cyberbullying in Schools. *Computers in Human Behavior*, *23*(4), 1777–1791. doi:10.1016/j.chb.2005.10.005

Liu, C., Duarte, R., Granados, O., Tang, J., Liu, S., & Andrian, J. (2012). Critical path based hardware acceleration for cryptosystems. *Journal of Information Processing Systems*, *8*(1), 133–144. doi:10.3745/JIPS.2012.8.1.133

Liu, C., Marchewka, T. J., Lu, J., & Yu, S. C. (2005). Beyond Concern: A Privacy-Trust-Behavioural Intention Model of Electronic Commerce. *Information & Management*, *42*(2), 289–304. doi:10.1016/j.im.2004.01.003

Liu, Z., & Towsleg, D. (1994). Stochastic scheduling in tree-networks. *Advances in Applied Probability*, *26*, 222–241. doi:10.2307/1427588

Liverani, R. S., & Freeman, N. (2009). *Abusing Firefox Extensions*. Defcon17.

Livingstone, & Bober, M. (2003). *UK children go online: Listening to young people's experiences*. Retrieved from http://eprints.lse.ac.uk/archive/0000388

Livingstone, & Bulger, M. (2013). *A global agenda for children's rights in the digital age - Recommendations for developing UNICEF's Research Strategy*. Unicef.

Livingstone, S., & Haddon, L. (2009). *EU Kids Online: Final report*. London, UK: EU Kids Online, London School of Economics & Political Science. Retrieved August 10, 2012, from http://www.lse.ac.uk/media@lse/research/EUKidsOnline/EU%20Kids%20I%20(2006-9)/EU%20Kids%20Online%20I%20Reports/EUKidsOnlineFinalReport.pdf

Livingstone, S., Haddon, L., Gorzig, A., & Olafsson, K. (2011). *EU kids online final report*. Available at http://www2.lse.ac.uk/media@lse/research/EUKidsOnline/EU20Kids20II20(2009-11)/EUKidsOnlineIIReports/Final%20report.pdf

Livingstone, S., Kirwil, L., Ponte, C., & Staksrud, E. (2013). *In their own words: what bothers children online? with the EU Kids Online Network*. London, UK: EU Kids Online, London School of Economics & Political Science. Retrieved August 10, 2012, from http://www.lse.ac.uk/media@lse/research/EUKidsOnline/EU%20Kids%20III/Reports/Intheirownwords020213.pdf

Livingstone, S., & Helsper, E. J. (2007). Taking risks when communicating on the internet: The role of offline social–psychological factors in young people's vulnerability to online risks. *Information Communication and Society*, *10*(5), 619–644. doi:10.1080/13691180701657998

*Lock and Android phone*. (2012). Retrieved August 21, 2013, from http://stackoverflow.com/questions/4793339/lock-an-android-phone

Ludäscher, B., Altintas, I., Berkley, C., Higgins, D., Jaeger, E., & Jones, M. et al. (2006). Scientific workflow management and the Kepler system. *Concurrency and Computation*, *18*(10), 1039–1065. doi:10.1002/cpe.994

Ludäscher, B., Altintas, I., Bowers, S., Cummings, J., Critchlow, T., & Deelman, E. et al. (2009a). Scientific Process Automation and Workflow Management. In A. Shoshani, & D. Rotem (Eds.), *Scientific Data Management: Challenges, Technologies and Deployment* (pp. 467–508). Chapman & Hall/CRC. doi:10.1201/9781420069815-c13

Ludäscher, B., Weske, M., McPhillips, T., & Bowers, S. (2009b). Scientific Workflows: Business as Usual? In U. Dayal, J. Eder, J. Koehler, & H. Reijers (Eds.), *Business Process Management, LNCS 5701* (pp. 31–47). Berlin, Germany: Springer. doi:10.1007/978-3-642-03848-8_4

Lüders, S. (2005). *Control systems under attack?* (No. CERN-OPEN-2005-025). Academic Press.

Lüders, M. H., Brandtzæg, P. B., & Dunkels, E. (2009). Risky contacts. In S. Livingstone, & L. Haddon (Eds.), *Kids Online: Opportunities and risks for children* (pp. 123–134). The Policy Press.

Lu, R., Sadiq, S., & Governatori, G. (2007). Modeling of Task-Based Authorization Constraints in BPMN. In A. H. M. ter Hofstede, B. Benatallah, & H.-Y. Paik (Eds.), *Business Process Management Workshops, LNCS 4928* (pp. 120–131). Berlin, Germany: Springer.

Lu, R., Sadiq, S., & Governatori, G. (2008). Measurement of Compliance Distance in Business Processes. *Information Systems Management*, *25*(4), 344–355. doi:10.1080/10580530802384613

Luyckx, K., & Daelemans, W. (2011). The effect of author set size and data size in authorship attribution. *Literary and Linguistic Computing*, *26*(1), 35–55. doi:10.1093/llc/fqq013

LWG Consulting. (2009). *An introduction to the ediscovery process*. Retrieved November 6, 2013 from http://www.lwgconsulting.com/news/default.aspx?ArticleId=55

Lyon, D. (2004). A World Wide Web da vigilância: a Internet e os fluxos de poder off-world. In J. Paquete de Oliveira et al. (Eds.), *Comunicação, cultura e tecnologias da informação* (pp. 109–126). Lisbon: Quimera.

Mac Sithigh, D. (2013). App law within: Rights and regulation in the smartphone age. *Int. J Law Info Tech*, *21*(2), 154–186. doi: 10.1093/ijlit/eat002

Machado, H. (2011). Construtores da bio(in)segurança na base de dados de perfis de ADN. *Etnográfica (on Line)*. Centro de Estudos de Antropologia Social (CEAS). Retrieved from http://www.scielo.gpeari.mctes.pt/scielo.php?script=sci_arttext&pid=S0873-65612011000100008&lng=pt&nrm=iso&tlng=pt

Machado, H., Silva, S., & Santos, F. (2008). Justiça tecnológica: Promessas e desafios. (E. Ecopy, Ed.) (DS/CICS., p. 176). Porto: Ecopy.

MacKay, W. (2012). *Respectful and responsible relationships: There's no app for that (the report of the nova scotia task force on bullying and cyber bullying)*. Nova Scotia Task Force on Bullying and Cyber Bullying.

Madden, M., Lenhart, A., Cortesi, S., Gasser, U., Duggan, M., Smith, A., & Beaton, M. (2013). *Teens, Social Media, and Privacy*. Washington, DC: Pew Research Center's Internet & American Life Project. Retrieved September 10, 2013, from http://www.pewinternet.org/Reports/2013/Teens-Social-Media-And-Privacy.aspx

Maher, D. (2008). Cyberbullying: An ethnographic case study of one Australian upper primary school class. *Youth Studies Australia*, *27*(4), 50–57.

Mairh, A., Barik, D., Verma, K., & Jena, D. (2011). Honeypot in network security: A survey. In *Proceedings of the 2011 International Conference on Communication, Computing & Security (ICCCS '11)* (pp. 600-605). New York: ACM. doi:10.1145/1947940.1948065

Maiza, O., Razafimandimby, A., Delamillieure, P., Brazo, P., Beaucousin, V., & Lecardeur, L. et al. (2008). Functional deficit in medial prefrontal cortex: A common neural basis for impaired communication in chronic schizophrenia, first episode of schizophrenia and bipolar disorders? *Schizophrenia Research*, *98*, 39–39. doi:10.1016/j.schres.2007.12.083

Malhotra, K. NKim, S. S., & Agarwal, J. (2004). Internet Users' Information Privacy Concerns (IUIPC): The Construct, the Scale, and a Casual Model. *Information Systems Research*, *15*(4), 336–355. doi:10.1287/isre.1040.0032

Marcum, C. D. (2008). Identifying potencial factors of adolescent online victimization for high school seniors. *International Journal of Cyber Criminology, 2*(2), 346–367.

Marczak, M., & Coyne, I. (2010). Cyberbullying at school: Good practice and legal aspects in the United Kingdom. *Australian Journal of Guidance & Counselling, 20*(2), 182–193. doi:10.1375/ajgc.20.2.182

Marinos, L. (2013). *ENISA Threat Landscape 2013. Overview of current and emerging cyber-threats.* Greece, Athens: European Union Agency for Network and Information Security. Retrieved January 30, 2014, from http://www.enisa.europa.eu/activities/risk-management/evolving-threat-environment/enisa-threat-landscape-2013-overview-of-current-and-emerging-cyber-threats

Martin, N., & Rice, J. (2011). Cybercrime: Understanding and addressing the concerns of stakeholders. *Computers & Security, 30*(8), 803–814. doi:10.1016/j.cose.2011.07.003

Mattern, F. (2003). From smart devices to smart everyday objects. *IEEE Spectrum, 47*(10), 25.

Mavrommatis, N. P. P., & Monrose, M. A. R. F. (2008). All your iframes point to us. In *Proceedings of USENIX Security Symposium.* USENIX.

Mayer-Schonberger, V., & Cukier, K. (2013). *Big data: A revolution that will transform how we live, work, and think.* Academic Press.

Mcafee. (2013). *Report: The ECONOMIC impact of cybercrime and cyber espionage.* Center for Strategic and International Studies.

McCombie, S., Watters, P. A., Ng, A., & Watson, B. (2008). Forensic Characteristics of Phishing-Petty Theft or Organized Crime? In Proceedings of WEBIST (pp. 149-157). WEBIST.

McDonagh, M. (2002). E-Government in Australia: the Challenge to privacy of Personal Information. *Int. J Law Info Tech, 10*(3), 327–343. doi:10.1093/ijlit/10.3.327

McGrath, M., & Casey, E. (2002). Forensic psychiatry and the internet: Practical perspectives on sexual predators and obsessional harassers in cyberspace. *Journal of the American Academy of Psychiatry and the Law Online, 30*(1), 81–94. PMID:11931372

McGraw, G. (2013). Cyber war is inevitable (unless we build security in). *The Journal of Strategic Studies, 36*(1), 109–119. doi:10.1080/01402390.2012.742013

McNeese, M. (2012). Perspectives on the role of cognition in cyber security. In *Proceedings of the Human Factors and Ergonomics Society 56th Annual Meeting, 2012* (pp. 268-271). Academic Press.

MDN. (2014). *X-Frame-Options.* Retrieved from https://developer.mozilla.org/en-US/docs/HTTP/X-Frame-Options

Melman, M. (2010). Computer virus in Iran actually targeted larger nuclear facility, 28 September 2010. Retrieved from http://www.haaretz.com/print-edition/news/computer-virus-in-iran-actually-targeted-larger-nuclear-facility-1.316052

Meloy, R., & Gothard, S. (1995). Demographic and clinical comparison of obsessional followers and offenders with mental disorders. *The American Journal of Psychiatry, 152*, 2.

*Memory Management in Android.* (2010, July 5). Retrieved August 21, 2013, from http://mobworld.wordpress.com/2010/07/05/memory-management-in-android/

Mendez, F. (2005). The European Union and cybercrime: Insights from comparative federalism. *Journal of European Public Policy, 12*(3), 509–527. doi:10.1080/13501760500091737

Menesini, E. (2012). Cyber bullying: The right value of the phenomenon. Comments on the paper 'cyber bullying: An overrated phenomenon?'. *European Journal of Developmental Psychology, 9*, 544–552. doi:10.1080/17405629.2012.706449

Menesini, E., & Nocentini, A. (2012). Peer education intervention: Face-to-face versus online. In A. Costabile, & B. A. Spears (Eds.), *The impact of technology on relationships in educational settings* (pp. 139–150). New York, NY: Routledge.

Merriam-Webster Dictionary. (2013). *Definition of cybersecurity.* Retrieved on March 10, 2013 from http://www.merriam-webster.com/dictionary/cybersecurity

Michel, J., & Hambrick, D. (1992). Diversificatio posture and top management team characteristics. *Academy of Management Journal, 35*, 9–37. doi:10.2307/256471

MikiSoft. (2011). *MySQL Injection - Simple Load File and Into OutFile*. Retrieved 2013, from http://www.exploit-db.com/papers/14635/

Miller, B., & Rowe, D. (2012, October). A survey SCADA of and critical infrastructure incidents. In *Proceedings of the 1st Annual conference on Research in information technology* (pp. 51-56). ACM.

Miller, L. (2011). *The emergence of EU contract law: Exploring europeanization*. Oxford, UK: Oxford University Press. doi:10.1093/acprof:oso/9780199606627.003.0002

Mills, D. (1992). *RFC 5905 network time protocol*. Retrieved 2013, from http://tools.ietf.org/html/rfc5905

Ministério da Justiça do Brasil & Fundação Getúlio Vargas. (2009). *Marco Civil da Internet: Seus direitos e deveres em discussão*. Retrieved March 03, 2013, from http://culturadigital.br/marcocivil/

Ministry of Defence (MoD). (2010). *Army doctrine publication – Operations. UK Ministry of Defence, 2010*. Retrieved February 5, 2014, from https://www.gov.uk/government/uploads/system/uploads/attachment_data/file/33695/ADPOperationsDec10.pdf

Mirkovic, J., & Reiher, P. (2004). A taxonomy of DDoS attack and DDoS defense mechanisms. *ACM SIGCOMM Computer Communication Review*, *34*(2), 39–53. doi:10.1145/997150.997156

Mishna, F., Cook, C., Gadalla, T., Daciuk, J., & Solomon, S. (2010). Cyber bullying behaviors among middle and high school students. *The American Journal of Orthopsychiatry*, *80*(3), 362–374. doi:10.1111/j.1939-0025.2010.01040.x PMID:20636942

Mishne, G., Carmel, D., & Lempel, R. (2005). Blocking blog spam with language model disagreement. In *Proceedings of the First International Workshop on Adversarial Information Retrieval on the Web (AIRWeb)*. AIRWeb.

Mitchell, K. J., Finkelhor, D., Jones, L. M., & Wolak, J. (2010). Use of social networking sites in online sex crimes against minors: An examination of national incidence and means of utilization. *The Journal of Adolescent Health*, *47*(2), 183–190. doi:10.1016/j.jadohealth.2010.01.007 PMID:20638011

Mitchell, K., Finkelhor, D., & Wolak, J. (2003). The exposure of youth to unwanted sexual material on the internet: A national survey of risk, impact and prevention. *Youth & Society*, *34*(3), 3300–3358. doi:10.1177/0044118X02250123

Mitchell, K., Finkelhor, D., & Wolak, J. (2007). Youth internet users at risk for the more serious online sexual solicitations. *American Journal of Preventive Medicine*, *32*(6), 532–537. doi:10.1016/j.amepre.2007.02.001 PMID:17533070

Mitre. (2006). *Exposures, C. V. MITRE Corporation. Mitre.* CVE-2006-7228.

Mitre. (2007). *Exposures, C. V. MITRE Corporation.* CVE-2007-3743.

Mitre. (2008). *Exposures, C. V. MITRE Corporation. Mitre.* CVE-2008-3360.

Mizukami, P., & Souza, C. A. P. (2008). *Propriedade Intelectual e Governança da Internet*. Rio de Janeiro: Fundação Getúlio Vargas.

Mlynski, M. (2012). *Mozilla Foundation Security Advisory 2012*. Retrieved from http://www.mozilla.org/security/ann-ounce/2012/mfsa2012-60.html

Mlynski, M. (2013). *Mozilla Foundation Security Advisory 2013*. Retrieved from http://www.mozilla.org/security/ann-ounce/2013/ mfsa2013-15.html

Mohay, G. (2005). Technical challenges and directions for digital forensics. In *Proceedings of Systematic Approaches to Digital Forensic Engineering*, (pp. 155-161). Academic Press.

Mokube, I., & Adams, M. (2007). Honeypots: Concepts, approaches, and challenges. In *Proceedings of the 45th Annual Southeast Regional Conference (ACM-SE 45)* (pp. 321-326). New York: ACM. doi:10.1145/1233341.1233399

Molloy, M. K. (1992). Performance analysis using stochastic Petri nets. *IEEE Transactions on Computers*, *31*(9), 913–917.

Monks, C. P., Robinson, S., & Worlidge, P. (2012). The emergence of cyber bullying: A survey of primary school pupil's perceptions and experiences. *School Psychology International*, *33*, 477–491. doi:10.1177/0143034312445242

Moore, R. (2011). *Cybercrime: Investigating high-technology computer crime.* Academic Press.

Morrissey, S. (2010). *iOS forensic analysis: For iPhone, iPad, and iPod touch.* Apress.

Morrow, V. (2001). Young people's explanations and experiences of social exclusion: Retrieving bourdieu's concept of social capital. *International Journal of Sociology and Social Policy, 21*(4/5/6), 37-63.

Moses, Y., & Tennenholtz, M. (n.d.). *Artificial social systems.* Retrieved from www.home.cs.utwente.nl

MRC. (2013). *Mission-oriented resilient clouds initiative.* Retrieved from http://www.darpa.mil/Our_Work/I2O/Programs/Mission-oriented_Resilient_Clouds_(MRC).aspx

Muir, D. (2005). *Violence against Children in Cyberspace. ECPAT International.* End Child Prostitution, Child Pornography and Trafficking of Children for Sexual Purposes.

Muñoz Conde, F. (2011). Diversas modalidades de acoso punible en el Código Penal. In T. lo Blanch (Ed.), El acoso: Tratamiento penal y procesal. Academic Press.

Muñoz, M. M. (1996). *El debate sobre las implicaciones científicas, éticas, sociales y legales del Proyecto Genoma Humano. Aportaciones epistemológicas.* Universidad de Granada.

Mura, G., Topcu, C., Erdur-Baker, O., & Diamantini, D. (2011). An international study of cyber bullying perception and diffusion among adolescents. *Procedia - Social and Behavioral Sciences, 15*, 3805-3809. doi: 10.1016/j.sbspro.2011.04.377

Murdoch, J. (2013). The binding effect of the ECHR in the united Kingdom–Views from scotland. In R. Arnold (Ed.), *The universalism of human rights* (pp. 209–221). Berlin: Springer. doi:10.1007/978-94-007-4510-0_12

Musa, W. (2013). *Improving cybersecurity audit processes in the U.S. government.* (Unpublished doctoral dissertation). National Graduate School, Falmouth, MA.

Mushiake, H., Sakamoto, K., Saito, N., Inui, T., Aihara, K., & Tanji, J. (2009). Involvement of the prefrontal cortex in problem solving. *International Review of Neurobiology, 85*, 1–11. doi:10.1016/S0074-7742(09)85001-0 PMID:19607957

Myers, C., Powers, S., & Faissol, D. (2009). Taxonomies of cyber adversaries and attacks: A survey of incidents and approaches. Lawrence Livermore National Laboratory.

Nachreiner, C. (2013). *Profiling Modern Hackers: Hacktivists, Criminals, and Cyber Spies. Oh My!* Retrieved from http://watchguardsecuritycenter.com/2013/05/30/hacker-profiles/

Nakamura, A. (1993). *Kanjo hyogen jiten* [Dictionary of Emotive Expressions]. Tokyo: Tokyodo Publishing. (in Japanese)

Nananukul, S., & Gong, W. B. (1999). Rational Interpolation for Stochastic DES's: Convergence Issues. *IEEE Trans. On Autom. Control, 44*(5), 1070–1073. doi:10.1109/9.763231

Nathan, E. (2009). *Reputational orientations and aggression: Extending reputation enhancement theory to upper primary school aged bullies.* (Doctoral thesis). The University of Western Australia, Perth, Australia. Retrieved from https://repository.uwa.edu.au/R/-?func¼dbin-jump-ull&object_id¼12681&local_base¼GEN01-INS01

National Conference of State Legislatures. (2012). *State cyberstalking and cyberharassment laws.* Available at http://www.ncsl.org/IssuesResearch/TelecommunicationsInformationTechnolgy/CyberstalkingLaws/tabid/13495/Default.aspx

NCPC. (2006). *Cyberbullying.* Retrieved December 4, 2011, from http://www.ncpc.org/cyberbullying

NERC-CIP. (2008). *Critical infrastructure protection.* North American Electric Reliability Corporation. Retrieved from http://www.nerc.com/cip.html

Neri, F., Geraci, P., Sanna, G., & Lotti, L. (2009). Online police station, a state-of-the-art Italian semantic technology against cybercrime. *In Proceedings of International Conference on Advances in Social Network Analysis and Mining.* IEEE Computer Society.

Netchitailova, E. P. (2012). Facebook as a Surveillance Tool: From the Perspective of the User. *tripleC: Communication, Capitalism & Critique. Open Access Journal for a Global Sustainable Information Society, 10*(2), 683–691.

Neto, J. B. de A. (2003). *Banco de dados genéticos para fins criminais: considerações iniciais.* Porto Alegre. Retrieved from http://www3.pucrs.br/pucrs/files/uni/poa/direito/graduacao/tcc/tcc2/trabalhos2008_2/joao_beccon.pdf

New York Times. (2007). *A hoax turned fatal draws anger but no charges.* Available at http://www.nytimes.com/2007/11/28/us/28hoax.html?ref=meganmeier&_r=0

Nguyen, M., Bin, Y. S., & Campbell, A. (2012). Comparing online and offline self-disclosure: A systematic review. *Cyberpsychology, Behavior and Social Networking, 15*(2), 103–111. doi:10.1089/cyber.2011.0277 PMID:22032794

Nicholson, A., Webber, S., Dyer, S., Patel, T., & Janicke, H. (2012). SCADA security in the light of cyber-warfare. *Computers & Security, 31*(4), 418–436. doi:10.1016/j.cose.2012.02.009

Nicol, G., Wood, L., Champion, M., & Byrne, S. (2001). *Document object model (DOM) level 3 core specification.* Academic Press.

Nidhi Singhal, J.P.S, & Raina. (2002). Comparative analysis of AES and RC4 algorithms for better utilization. *International Journal of Computer Trends and Technology, 11*, 177.

Nikander, P., & Karvonen, K. (2001). Users and Trust in Cyberspace. In *Security Protocols: 8th International Workshop* (pp. 1-22). Berlin: Springer.

Niland, M. (2003) Computer virus brings down train signals. *InformationWeek.* Retrieved from http://www.informationweek.com/news/security/vulnerabilities/showArticle.jhtml?articleID1/413100807

Ning, H., & Hu, S. (2011). Internet of things: An emerging industrial or a new major? In *Proceedings of Internet of Things (iThings/CPSCom),* (pp. 178-183). iThings.

Ning, H., & Liu, H. (2012). Cyber-physical-social based security architecture for future internet of things. *Advanced in Internet of Things, 2*(1), 1–7. doi:10.4236/ait.2012.21001

NIST. (2002). *Risk management guide for information technology systems.* Special Publication 800-30 of the National Institute of Standards and Technology. CODEN: NSPUE2.

Nocentini, A., Calmaestra, J., Schultze-Krumboltz, A., Scheithauer, H., Ortega, R., & Menesini, E. (2010). cyber bullying: Labels, behaviours and definition in three European countries. *Australian Journal of Guidance & Counselling, 20*, 129–142. doi:10.1375/ajgc.20.2.129

Noscript. (2014). *Noscript Firefox Extension.* Retrieved from http://noscript.net

Nova, N., & Bleecker, J. (2006). Blogjects and the new ecology of things. In *Proceedings of Lift06 Workshop.* Lift.

Nuclear Regulatory Commission. (2007). *NRC information notice: 2007e15: effects of ethernet-based, non-safety related controls on the safe and continued operation of nuclear power stations.* Retrieved from http://www.nrc.gov/reading-rm/doc-collections/gen-comm/info-notices/2007/in200715.pdf

Nunes (Relat.), R. (2006). *Estudo Nº E/07/APB06 sobre a perspectíva ética das bases de dados genéticos* (Vol. 1997, pp. 1–18). Porto: APB - Associação Portuguesa de Bioética. doi:ESTUDO N.° E/07/APB/06

Nunes, R. (2013). GeneÉtica. (Almedina, Ed.). Coimbra.

Nuñez Fernandez, J. (2011). Las medidas de seguridad y reinserción social in Curso de Derecho penal. Parte General. Ed. Dykinson.

*NY Times.* (2013). Retrieved from http://www.nytimes.com/2013/02/25/world/asia/us-confronts-cyber-cold-war-with-china.html?pagewanted=all

Obama, B. (2012). *President Obama's comments on cyber security.* Retrieved from http://www.whitehouse.gov/cybersecurity

Oberheide, J., Cooke, E., & Jahanian, F. (2008). Cloudav: Nversion antivirus in the network cloud. In *Proceedings of the 17th USENIX Security Symposium* (Security'08). San Jose, CA: USENIX.

Obied, A., & Alhajj, R. (2009). Fraudulent and malicious sites on the web. *Applied Intelligence, 30*(2), 112–120. doi:10.1007/s10489-007-0102-y

Object Management Group (OMG). (2011). *Business Process Modeling Notation (BPMN) Version 2.0.* Retrieved November 30, 2013, from http://www.omg.org/spec/BPMN/2.0/

OECD. (2002). *Guidelines for the security of information systems and networks: Towards a culture of security.* Paris: OECD.

Oktavianto, D., & Muhardianto, I. (2013). *Cuckoo Malware Analysis.* Packt Publishing Ltd.

Olson, L. N., Daggs, J. L., Ellevold, B. L., & Rogers, T. K. (2007). Entrapping the innocent: Toward a theory of child sexual predators' luring communication. *Communication Theory, 17*(3), 231–251. doi:10.1111/j.1468-2885.2007.00294.x

Olsson, J., & Boldt, M. (2009, September). Computer forensic timeline visualization tool. *Digital Investigation, 6*, S78–87. doi:10.1016/j.diin.2009.06.008

Olweus, D. (2012a). Cyber bullying: An overrated phenomenon? *European Journal of Developmental Psychology, 9*, 520–538. doi:10.1080/17405629.2012.682358

Olweus, D. (2012b). Comments on cyber bullying article: A rejoinder. *European Journal of Developmental Psychology, 9*, 559–568. doi:10.1080/17405629.2012.705086

Oman, P., & Phillips, M. (2007). *Intrusion detection and event monitoring in SCADA networks.* Springer. doi:10.1007/978-0-387-75462-8_12

Orgánica, L. (1999). *15/1999. Cortes Generales de España.* Madrid: España.

Orgánica, L. (2007). *10/2007. Cortes Generales de España.* Madrid: España.

Oriwoh, E., & Sant, P. (2013). The forensics edge management system: A concept and design. In *Proceedings of Ubiquitous Intelligence and Computing, (UIC/ATC),* (pp. 544-550). UIC/ATC.

Oriwoh, E., Jazani, D., Epiphaniou, G., & Sant, P. (2013). Internet of things forensics: Challenges and approaches. In *Proceedings of Collaborative Computing: Networking, Applications and Worksharing* (Collaboratecom), (pp. 608-615). Collaboratecom.

Ortony, A., Clore, G., & Foss, M. (1987). The referential structure of the affective lexicon. *Cognitive Science, 11*(3), 341–364. doi:10.1207/s15516709cog1103_4

OSVDB. (2013). *Open source vulnerability database.* Retrieved from http://osvdb.org

Oswall, M. (2013). Joining the dots – Intelligence and proportionality. *PDP, 13*(6).

OWASP. (2013). *Data Validation.* Retrieved from https://www.owasp.org/index.php/Data_Validation

Palanisamy, R., & Mukerji, B. (2012). Security and Privacy Issues in E-Government. In M. A. Shareef, N. Archer, & S. Dutta (Eds.), *E-Government Service Maturity and Development: Cultural, Organizational and Technological Perspectives* (pp. 236–248). New York: IGI Global Pubs.

Pale, P. C. (2012). *Nmap 6: Network Exploration and Security Auditing Cookbook.* Packt Publishing.

Palfrey, J., & Gasser, U. (2008). *Digital born. Understanding the first generation of digital natives.* New York, NY: Basic Books.

Palmer, G. (2001). A road map for digital forensic research. In *Proceedings of First Digital Forensic Research Workshop,* (pp. 27-30). Academic Press.

Pao, D., Or, N., & Cheung, R. C. (2013). A memory-based NFA regular expression match engine for signature-based intrusion detection. *Computer Communications, 36*(10-11), 1255–1267. doi:10.1016/j.comcom.2013.03.002

Papagiannakopoulou, E. I., Koukovini, M. N., Lioudakis, G. V., Garcia-Alfaro, J., Kaklamani, D. I., & Venieris, I. S. et al. (2013). A Privacy-Aware Access Control Model for Distributed Network Monitoring. *Computers & Electrical Engineering, 39*(7), 2263–2281. doi:10.1016/j.compeleceng.2012.08.003

Papazoglou, M. P., & van den Heuvel, W.-J. (2007). Service Oriented Architectures: Approaches, Technologies and Research Issues. *The VLDB Journal, 16*(3), 389–415. doi:10.1007/s00778-007-0044-3

Parker, T. (2011). *Stuxnet redux: Malware attribution & lessons learned.* Black Hat DC 2011. Retrieved from www. blackhat. com/html/bh-dc-11/bh-dc-11-archives. html# Parker

Pasquali, A. (2005). Um breve glossário descritivo sobre comunicação e informação. In J. Marques de Melo, & L. Sathler (Eds.), *Direitos à Comunicação na Sociedade da Informação* (pp. 15–48). São Bernardo do Campo: Universidade Metodista de São Paulo.

Patchin, J. W., & Hinduja, S. (2012). Cyber bullying: An update and synthesis of the research. In J. W. Patchin, & S. Hinduja (Eds.), Cyber bullying prevention and response: Expert perspectives (pp. 13–35). New York, NY: Routledge.

Patchin, J. W., & Hinduja, S. (2006). Bullies move beyond the schoolyard; a preliminary look at cyberbullying. *Youth Violence and Juvenile Justice, 4*(2), 148–169. doi:10.1177/1541204006286288

Patchin, J. W., & Hinduja, S. (2011). Traditional and non-traditional bullying among youth: A test of General Strain Theory. *Youth & Society, 43*, 727–751. doi:10.1177/0044118X10366951

Patel, Ramzan, Ganapathy, & Sundaram. (2005). Efficient constructions of variable-input-length block ciphers. *LNCS, 3357*, 326–340.

Pathe, M., & Mullen, P.E. (1997). The impact o f stalkers in their victims. *The British Journal of Psychiatry, 174.*

Paul, S., Smith, P. K., & Blumberg, H. H. (2012). Comparing student perceptions of coping strategies and school interventions in managing bullying and cyberbullying incidents. *Pastoral Care in Education, 30*(2), 127–146. doi:10.1080/02643944.2012.679957

Pawlak, P., & Wendling, C. (2013). Trends in cyberspace: Can governments keep up? *Environment Systems and Decisions, 33*(4), 536–543. doi:10.1007/s10669-013-9470-5

PBS News Hours. (2012). *Are American companies ignoring significant cyber threats?*. Retrieved on March 15, 2013 from http://www.pbs.org/newshour/rundown/2012/08/are-american-companies-ignoring-significant cyber-threats-joel-brenner-answers-your-questions.html

Pearce, K. E., & Rice, R. E. (2013). Digital divides from access to activities: Comparing mobile and personal computer internet users. *The Journal of Communication, 63*(4), 721–744. doi:10.1111/jcom.12045

Pease, K. (2001). *Cracking crime through design.* London, UK: Design Council.

Perren, S., Corcoran, L., Cowie, H., Dehue, F., Garcia, D., Mc Guckin, C., Sevcikova, A., Tsatsou, P., & Vollink, T. (2012). *Coping with cyber bullying: A systematic literature review.* Final Report of the COST IS 0801 Working Group 5 (published online).

Peruzzo, C. M. K. (2005). Internet e Democracia Comunicacional: entre os entraves, utopias e o direito à comunicação. In J. Marques de Melo, & L. Sathler (Eds.), *Direitos à Comunicação na Sociedade da Informação* (pp. 266–288). São Bernardo do Campo: Universidade Metodista de São Paulo.

Peslyak, A. (2013). *John The Ripper.* Retrieved 2013, from http://www.openwall.com/john/

Pessoa, T., Matos, A., Amado, J., & Jäger, T. (2011). Cyberbullying – do diagnóstico de necessidades à construção de um manual de formação. *SIPS - Pedagogía Social: Revista Interuniversitária,* 57-70.

Petersen, M. A. (2008). Estimating standard errors in finance panel data sets: Comparing approaches. *Review of Financial Studies, 22*(1), 435–480. doi:10.1093/rfs/hhn053

Petley, J. (1994). In defence of video nasties'. *British Journalism Review, 5*(3), 52–57.

Petri, C. A. (1962). *Kommunikation mit Automaten.* (Ph. D. Thesis). University of Bonn, Bonn, Germany.

Pfeffer, A., Call, C., Chamberlain, J., Kellogg, L., Ouellette, J., Patten, T., et al. (2012, October). Malware analysis and attribution using genetic information. In *Proceedings of Malicious and Unwanted Software* (MALWARE), (pp. 39-45). IEEE.

Pfeffer, J. (1983). *Organizational Demography.* Greenwich: JAI Press.

Pfleeger, C. P., & Pfleeger, S. (2006). *Security in computing* (4th ed.). Upper Saddle River, NJ: Prentice Hall.

Philippsohn, S. (2001). Trends in cybercrime - An overview of current financial crimes on the internet. *Computers & Security, 20*, 53–69. doi:10.1016/S0167-4048(01)01021-5

Phillips, W. (2011, December). LOLing at tragedy: Facebook trolls, memorial pages and resistance to grief online. *First Monday, 16*(12), 11. doi:10.5210/fm.v16i12.3168

PhonePay Plus. (2013). *Phonepayplus.org.uk.* Retrieved August 21, 2013, from http://www.phonepayplus.org.uk

Pieschl, S., Porsch, T., Kahl, T., & Klockenbusch, R. (2013). Relevant dimensions of cyber bullying — Results from two experimental studies. *Journal of Applied Developmental Psychology*. doi:10.1016/j.appdev.2013.04.002

Pilli, E. S., Joshi, R. C., & Niyogi, R. (2010). Network forensic frameworks: Survey and research challenges. *Digital Investigation*, *7*(1-2), 14–27. doi:10.1016/j.diin.2010.02.003

Pletscher, T. (2005). *Companies and the Regulatory Jungle*. Paper presented at the 27th International Conference of Data Protection and Privacy Commissioners. Monteux, Switzerland.

PMI. (2008). *A guide to the Project Management Body of Knowledge* (4th ed.). Newtown Square.

Poier, S. (2008). Questioning the "Crime" in Cybercrime. *The Information Society: An International Journal*, *24*(4), 270–272. doi:10.1080/01972240802191670

Poolsappasit, N. (2010). *Towards an efficient vulnerability analysis methodology for better security risk management* (Doctoral dissertation). Retrieved from ProQuest dissertations and theses database. (Document ID 3419113).

Portela, I. M., & Cruz-Cunha, M. M. (Eds.). (2010). *Information Communication Technology Law, Protection and Access Rights: Global Approaches and Issues*. New York: IGI Global Pubs. doi:10.4018/978-1-61520-975-0

Posey, C., Lowry, B. P., Roberts, L. T., & Ellis, S. T. (2010). Proposing the online community self-disclosure model: the case of working professionals in France and the U.K. who use online Communities. *European Journal of Information Systems*, *19*(2), 181–195. doi:10.1057/ejis.2010.15

Postmes, T., & Spears, R. (1998). Deindividuation and anti-normative behavior: A meta-analysis. *Psychological Bulletin*, *123*, 238–259. doi:10.1037/0033-2909.123.3.238

Postmes, T., Spears, R., & Lea, M. (1998). Breaching or building social boundaries? SIDE-effects of computer-mediated communication. *Communication Research*, *25*, 689–715. doi:10.1177/009365098025006006

Poullet, Y. (2006). The Directive 95/46/EC: Ten Years After. *Computer Law & Security Report*, *22*(3), 206–217. doi:10.1016/j.clsr.2006.03.004

Poulsen, K. (2003). Slammer worm crashed Ohio nuke plant net. *The Register*. Retrieved from http://www.theregister.co.uk/2003/08/20/slammer_worm_crashed_ohio_nuke/

Pratt, T. C., Holtfreter, K., & Reisig, M. D. (2010). Routine online activity and internet fraud targeting: Extending the generality of routine activity theory. *Journal of Research in Crime and Delinquency*, *47*(3), 267–296. doi:10.1177/0022427810365903

Press, R., & Cooper, M. (2003). *The design experience*. Chichester, UK: John Wilet and Sons.

Preuß, J., Furnell, S. M., & Papadaki, M. (2007). Considering the potential of criminal profiling to combat hacking. *Journal in Computer Virology*, *3*(2), 135–141. doi:10.1007/s11416-007-0042-4

Prichard, J., Watters, P. A., & Spiranovic, C. (2011). Internet subcultures and pathways to the use of child pornography. *Computer Law & Security Report*, *27*(6), 585–600. doi:10.1016/j.clsr.2011.09.009

Pritchett, W. L., & De Smet, D. (2013). *Kali Linux Cookbook*. Packt Publishing Ltd.

Privacy Act of 1974 § 102, 42 U.S.C. § 4332 (1974).

Privitera, C., & Campbell, M. (2009). Cyberbullying: The new face of workplace bullying? *Cyberpsychology & Behavior*, *12*(4), 395–400. doi:10.1089/cpb.2009.0025 PMID:19594381

Proffitt, B. (2013). *How big the internet of things could become: The potential size of the internet things sector could be a multi-trillion dollar market by the end of the decade*. Retrieved November/20, 2013, from http://readwrite.com/2013/09/30/how-big-the-internet-of-things-could-become#feed=/infrastructure&awesm=~oj3jHsZI8rJE6c

Provos, N. (2003). *Honeyd Sample Configurations*. Retrieved 2013, from http://www.honeyd.org/configuration.php

Provos, N. (2008). *Developments of the Honeyd Virtual Honeypot*. Retrieved 2013, from http://www.honeyd.org/

Provos, N., Friedl, M., & Honeyman, P. (2003, August). Preventing privilege escalation. In *Proceedings of the 12th USENIX Security Symposium* (Vol. 12, pp. 231-242). USENIX.

Provos, N., McNamee, D., Mavrommatis, P., Wang, K., & Modadugu, N. (2007, April). The ghost in the browser analysis of web-based malware. In *Proceedings of the first conference on First Workshop on Hot Topics in Understanding Botnets* (pp. 4-4). Academic Press.

Proyect OpenBSD. (2004). *OpenSSH*. Retrieved 2013, from http://www.openssh.com

Ptaszynski, M., Dybala, P., Matsuba, T., Masui, F., Rzepka, R., & Araki, K. (2010). Machine learning and affect analysis against cyberbullying. In *Proceedings of the Linguistic And Cognitive Approaches To Dialog Agents Symposium*. De Montfort University.

Ptaszynski, M., Dybala, P., Rzepka, R., & Araki, K. (2009). Affecting corpora: Experiments with automatic affect annotation system - A case study of the 2channel forum. In *Proceedings of The Conference of the Pacific Association for Computational Linguistics 2009* (PACLING-09), (pp. 223-228). PACLING.

Público. (2012). Nações Unidas reconhecem o direito à liberdade de expressão na Internet. *Público*. Retrieved July 06, 2013, from http://www.publico.pt/Tecnologia/nacoes-unidas-reconhecem-o-direito-a-liberdade-de-expressao-na-internet-1553694

Público. (2013). Brasil e Alemanha juntam esforços na ONU contra espionagem. *Público*. Retrieved November 02, 2013, from http://www.publico.pt/mundo/noticia/brasil-e-alemanha-juntam-esforcos-na-onu-contra-a-espionagem-1611145

Queiroz, C., Mahmood, A., Hu, J., Tari, Z., & Yu, X. (2009, October). Building a SCADA security testbed. In *Proceedings of Network and System Security*, (pp. 357-364). IEEE.

Quinlan, R. (1993). *C4.5: Programs for Machine Learning*. San Mateo, CA: Morgan Kaufmann Publishers.

Raab, C. D. (2008). Vigilância e privacidade: As opções de regulação. In A sociedade vigilante – Ensaios sobre identificação, vigilância e privacidade (pp. 255-292). Lisbon: Imprensa de Ciências Sociais.

Raines, S. (2013). *Conflict management for managers: resolving workplace, client, and policy disputes*. San Francisco, CA: Jossey-Bass.

Rammidi, G. (2008). *Survey on Current Honeynet Research*. Retrieved 2013, from http://honeynetproject.ca/files/survey.pdf

Rao, P. (1998). *First Report of the Special Rapporteur, Mr. Pemmaraju Sreenivasa Rao*. U.N. Doc. A/CN.4/487.

Rao, P. (2000). *Third Report of the Special Rapporteur, Mr. Pemmaraju Sreenivasa Rao*. U.N. Doc. A/CN.4/510.

Rapid7. (2013). *Metasploit Penetration Testing Software*. Retrieved 2013, from http://www.metasploit.com/

Rashid, A., Baron, A., Rayson, P., May-Chahal, C., Greenwood, P., & Walkerdine, J. (2013). Who Am I? Analyzing Digital Personas in Cybercrime Investigations. *Computer*, *46*(4), 54–61. doi:10.1109/MC.2013.68

Raskauskas, J., & Stotlz, A. (2007). Involvement in traditional and electronic bullying among adolescents. *Developmental Psychology*, *43*, 564–575. doi:10.1037/0012-1649.43.3.564 PMID:17484571

Recommind, Inc. (2013). *Predictive coding*. Retrieved November 11, 2013 from http://www.recommind.com/predictive-coding

ReCrim2010 *La respuesta juridico-penal frente al stalking en España: presente y future*. ReCrim. Available on line in http://www.uv.es/recrim

Rehm, L. (2012, October 25). *A Guide to Android OS*. Retrieved August 21, 2013, from http://connect.dpreview.com/post/8437301608/guide-to-android-os

Reich, N. (2014). Understanding EU law: Objectives, principles and methods of community law (3rd ed.). Cambridge, UK: Intersentia.

Reis, C., & Adviser-Levy, H. M. (2009). *Web browsers as operating systems: supporting robust and secure web programs*. University of Washington.

Reith, M., Carr, C., & Gunsch, G. (2002). An examination of digital forensic models. *International Journal of Digital Evidence*, *1*(3), 1–12.

Reyns, B. W. (2013). Online routines and identity theft victimization: Futher expanding routine activity theory beyond direct-contact offenses. *Journal of Research in Crime and Delinquency, 50*(2), 216–238. doi:10.1177/0022427811425539

Reyns, B. W., Henson, B., & Fisher, B. S. (2011). Being pursued online: Apllying cyberlifestyle-routine activities theory to cyberstalking victimization. *Criminal Justice and Behavior, 38*(11), 1149–1169. doi:10.1177/0093854811421448

Reza, H., & Mazumder, N. (2012). A secure software architecture for mobile computing. In *Proceedings of the 9th International Conference on Information Technology-New Generations* (ITNG 2012). Las Vegas, NVL ITNG.

Ribaux, O. (2013). *Science forensique.* Academic Press.

Richard, G., III, & Roussev, V. (2006). Digital forensics tools: the next generation. In Digital Crime and Forensic Science in Cyberspace (pp. 75-90). Idea Group Publishing.

Riden, J. (2008a). Client-Side Attack. The Honeynet Project. Retrieved from http://www.honeynet.org/node/157

Riden, J. (2008b). Server Honeypots vs Client Honeypots. The Honeynet Project. Retrieved from http://www.honeynet.org/node/157

Ridings, C., Gefen, D., & Arinze, B. (2002). Some antecedents and effects of trust in virtual communities. *The Journal of Strategic Information Systems, 11*(3-4), 271–295. doi:10.1016/S0963-8687(02)00021-5

Rimmer, M. (2012). The participation and decision making of 'at risk'youth in community music projects: An exploration of three case studies. *Journal of Youth Studies, 15*(3), 329–350. doi:10.1080/13676261.2011.643232

Rinaldi, S. M., Peerenboom, J. P., & Kelly, T. K. (2001). Identifying, understanding, and analyzing critical infrastructure interdependencies. *Control Systems IEEE.* Retrieved from http://ieeexplore.ieee.org/lpdocs/epic03/wrapper.htm?arnumber=969131

Ringrose, J., Gill, R., Livingstone, S., & Harvey, L. (2012). *A qualitative study of children, young people and 'sexting'.* NSPCC.

Rituerto, R. M. (2012). Quien pone datos personales em la red tiene derecho a recuperarlos [Interview with Viviane Reding, European Commissioner for Justice, Fundamental Rights and Citizenship]. *El País.* Retrieved January 25, 2013, from http://tecnologia.elpais.com/tecnologia/2012/01/24/actualidad/1327435171_045260.html

Rivers, I., & Noret, N. (2010). 'I h8 u': Findings from a five-year study of text and email bullying. *British Educational Research Journal, 36,* 643–671. doi:10.1080/01411920903071918

Roche, S. W. (2012). *Internet and technology dangers.* Dragonwood.

Rogers, M. (2003). The role of criminal profiling in the computer forensics process. *Computers & Security, 22*(4), 292–298. doi:10.1016/S0167-4048(03)00405-X

RootingPuntoEs. (2013). *DionaeaFR.* Retrieved 2013, from https://github.com/RootingPuntoEs/DionaeaFR

Rosenzweig, P. (2013). *Cyber Warfare (The changing face of war).* Praeger.

Roulo, C. (2013). *DOD information technology evolves toward cloud computing.* Retrieved from http://www.defense.gov/news/newsarticle.aspx?id=118999

Rouse, M. (2010). *Electronic discovery (e-discovery or discovery).* Retrieved November 5, 2013 from http://searchfinancialsecurity.techtarget.com/definition/electronic-discovery

Rouse, M. (2012). *Predictive coding.* Retrieved November 11, 2013 from http://searchcompliance.techtarget.com/definition/predictive-coding

Rouskas, G. N., & Baldine, I. (1997). Multicast Routing with End-to-End Delay and Delay Variation Constraints. *IEEE Journal on Selected Areas in Communications, 15,* 346–356. doi:10.1109/49.564133

Rowlingson, R. (2004). A ten step process for forensic readiness. *International Journal of Digital Evidence, 2*(3). Retrieved February 16, 2013 from 3, http://www.utica.edu/academic/institutes/ecii/publications/articles/A0B13342-B4E0-1F6A-156F501C49CF5F51.pdf

Rowlingson, R. (2004). A ten step process for forensic readiness. *International Journal of Digital Evidence, 2*(3), 1–28.

Russell, N., & ter Hofstede, A. H. M. (2009). new YAWL: towards workflow 2.0. In L. K. Jensen, & W. M. P. van der Aalst (Eds.), Transactions on Petri Nets and Other Models of Concurrency II, (LNCS) (vol. 5460, pp. 79–97). Berlin, Germany: Springer.

Russell, N., ter Hofstede, A. H. M., Edmond, D., & van der Aalst, W. M. P. (2005a). Workflow data patterns: identification, representation and tool support. In L. Delcambre, C. Kop, H. C. Mayr, J. Mylopoulos, & O. Pastor (Eds.), *Proceedings of the 24th International Conference on Conceptual Modeling (ER 2005)*, (LNCS) (vol. 3716, pp. 353–368). Berlin, Germany: Springer.

Russell, N., ter Hofstede, A. H. M., van der Aalst, W. M. P., & Edmond, D. (2005b). Workflow resource patterns: identification, representation and tool support. In O. Pastor, & J. Falcão e Cunha (Eds.), *Proceedings of the 17th International Conference on Advanced Information Systems Engineering (CAiSE 2005)*, (LNCS) (vol. 3520, pp. 216–232). Berlin, Germany: Springer.

Russell, N., ter Hofstede, A. H. M., van der Aalst, W. M. P., & Mulyar, N. (2006). *Workflow Control-Flow Patterns: A Revised View.* Technical Report BPM-06-22. BPM Center.

Rydstedt, G., Bursztein, E., Boneh, D., & Jackson, C. (2010). Busting frame busting: A study of clickjacking vulnerabilities at popular sites. In *Proceedings of the Web 2.0 Security and Privacy.* Oakland, CA: Academic Press.

Sabella, R. (2012). How school counselors can help. In J. W. Patchin, & S. Hinduja (Eds.), *cyber bullying prevention and response: Expert perspectives* (pp. 72–92). New York, NY: Routledge.

Sadasivam, K., Samudrala, B., & Yang, T. (2005, April). Design of network security projects using honeypots. *Journal of Computing in Small Colleges, 20*(4), 282–293.

Sahin, M., Aydin, B., & Sari, S. V. (2012). Cyber Bullying Cyber Victimization and Psychological Symptoms: A Study in Adolescent. *Cukurova University Faculty of Education Journal, 41*(1), 53–59.

Sahmer, R. A., & Trivedi, K. S. (1987). Reliability Modelling Using SHARPE. *IEEE Transactions on Reliability, R-36*, 186–193. doi:10.1109/TR.1987.5222336

Sala, M., Caverzasi, E., Lazzaretti, M., Morandotti, N., De Vidovich, G., & Marraffini, E. et al. (2011). Dorsolateral prefrontal cortex and hippocampus sustain impulsivity and aggressiveness in borderline personality disorder. *Journal of Affective Disorders,* Schroeder, R. (1996). Playspace invaders: Huizinga, baudrillard and video game violence. *Journal of Popular Culture, 30*(3), 143–153.

Salton, G., Wong, A., & Yang, C. S. (1975). A vector space model for automatic indexing. *Communications of the ACM, 18*(11), 613–620. doi:10.1145/361219.361220

Sanchez, H., Kumar, S. (2011). *Twitter Bullying Detection.* Retrieved December 34, 2011, from http://users.soe.ucsc.edu/~shreyask/ism245-rpt.pdf

Sandler, L. (2012). SEC Guidance on Cyber-Disclosure Becomes Rule for Google. *Bloomberg Businessweek.* Retrieved online from http://www.businessweek.com/news/2012-08-29/sec-guidance-on-cyber-disclosure-becomes-rule-for-google

Sanger, D. (2012, June 1). Obama order sped up wave of cyberattacks against Iran. *The New York Times.* Retrieved from http://www.nytimes.com/2012/06/01/world/middleeast/obama-ordered-wave-of-cyberattacks-against-iran.html

Sang-Hyun, L., Lee, J., & Kyung-Il, M. (2013). Smart home security system using multiple ANFIS. *International Journal of Smart Home, 7*(3), 121.

Sapo Notícias. (2011). Egipto: O dia em que a Internet foi parcialmente desligada. *Sapo Notícias.* Retrieved July 06, 2013, from http://livetv.blogs.sapo.pt/731616.html

Saydjari, O. S. (2004). Cyber defense: art to science. *Communications of the ACM - Homeland Security, 47*(3), 52-57.

Schatz, B., Mohay, G., & Clark, A. (2004). Rich event representation for computer forensics. In *Proceedings of the Fifth Asia-Pacific Industrial Engineering and Management Systems Conference (APIEMS 2004).* APIEMS.

Scheer, L. (1997). *A democracia virtual.* Lisbon: Edições Século XXI.

Schneier. (1993). Description of a new variable-length key, 64-bit block cipher (blowfish). In *Proceedings of Fast Software Encryption, Cambridge Security Workshop,* (pp. 191-204). Academic Press.

Scholte, T., Balzarotti, D., & Kirda, E. (2012). Quo vadis? a study of the evolution of input validation vulnerabilities in web applications. In *Financial Cryptography and Data Security* (pp. 284–298). Springer. doi:10.1007/978-3-642-27576-0_24

Schreck, C. J. (1999). Criminal victimization and self-control: An extension and test of a general theory of crime. *Justice Quarterly*, *16*(3), 633–654. doi:10.1080/07418829900094291

Schultz, C.P.L., Guesgen, H.W., & Amor, R. (2006). Computer-human interaction issues when integrating qualitative spatial reasoning into geographic information systems. In *Proceedings of ACM International Conference* (pp. 43–51). Christchurch, New Zealand: ACM.

Schultz, E. (2002). A framework for understanding and predicting insider attacks. *Computers & Security*, *21*, 526–531. doi:10.1016/S0167-4048(02)01009-X

Schwerha, J. J. IV. (2004). Cybercrime: Legal Standards Governing the Collection of Digital Evidence. *Information Systems Frontiers*, *6*(2), 133–151. doi:10.1023/B:ISFI.0000025782.13582.87

Sclafani, S. (2009). *Clickjacking & OAuth*. Retrieved from http://stephensclafani.com/2009/05/04/clickjacking-oauth

Sebek Project. (2008). *Sebek*. Retrieved 2013, from https://projects.honeynet.org/sebek

*Security Dark Reading*. (2013). Retrieved on March 10, 2013 from http://www.darkreading.com/document.asp?doc_id=161524

*Security Tips* . (2013). Retrieved August 21, 2013, from http://developer.android.com/training/articles/security-tips.html

Seigle-Morris, A. (2013). *Electronic disclosure (eDisclosure): Myths and reality*. Retrieved July 9, 2013 from http://www.portcullis-security.com/edisclosure-myths-and-reality

Seigneur, J., Jensen, C. D., Farrell, S., Gray, E., & Chen, Y. (2003). Towards security auto-configuration for smart appliances. In *Proceedings of the Smart Objects Conference*. Academic Press.

Selamat, S. R., Yusof, R., & Sahib, S. (2008). Mapping process of digital forensic investigation framework. *International Journal of Computer Science and Network Security*, *8*(10), 163–169.

*Send S. M. S. in Android*. (2013). Retrieved August 21, 2013, from http://stackoverflow.com/questions/4967448/send-sms-in-android

Sengupta, A., & Chaudhuri, A. (2011). Are social networking sites a source of online harassment for teens? Evidence from survey data. *Children and Youth Services Review*, *33*, 284–290. doi:10.1016/j.childyouth.2010.09.011

Sesé, M. O. (2007). *La nueva ley del ADN en España*. Retrieved from http://librosgratis.net/book/espana-material-de-derecho-procesal-civil-basado-en-la-ley-de-enjuiciamiento-civil_79459.html

*Set Wallpaper using WallpaperManager*. (2011, March 28). Retrieved August 21, 2013, from http://android-er.blogspot.com/2011/03/set-wallpaper-using-wallpaper-manager.html

Shabtai, A., Fledel, Y., & Elovici, Y. (2010). Automated static code analysis for classifying android applications using machine learning. In *Proceedings of the 2010 International Conference on Computational Intelligence and Security* (CIS 2010) (pp. 329-333). CIS.

Shabtai, A., Fledel, Y., Kanonov, U., Elovici, Y., Dolev, S., & Glezer, C. (2010, March). Google Android: A Comprehensive Security Assessment. *IEEE Security & Privacy*, 35-44.

Shackelford, S. J. (2009). From Net War to Nuclear War: Analogizing Cyber Attacks in International Law. *Berkeley Journal of International Law*, *27*, 192–211.

Shahriar, H., Devendran, V., & Haddad, H. (2013). ProClick: A Framework for Testing Clickjacking Attacks in Web Applications. In *Proceedings of 6th ACM/SIGSAC International Conference on Security of Information and Networks*, (pp. 144-151). Aksaray, Turkey: ACM.

Shammas-Toma, M., Seymour, D., & Clark, L. (1998). Obstacles to implementing total quality management in the UK construction industry. *Construction Management and Economics*, *16*, 177–192. doi:10.1080/014461998372475

Shankland, S., & Skillings, J. (2009). *Intel to pay AMD $1.25 billion in antitrust settlement.* Retrieved November 8, 2013 from http://news.cnet.com/8301-1001_3-10396188-92.html

Sharma, P., Xu, Z., Banerjee, S., & Lee, S.-J. (2006). Estimating network proximity and latency. *ACM SIGCOMM Computer Communication Review, 36*(3), 39–50. doi:10.1145/1140086.1140092

Short, S., & Kaluvuri, S. P. (2011). A Data-Centric Approach for Privacy-Aware Business Process Enablement. In M. van Sinderen & P. Johnson (Eds.), *Proceedings of the 3rd International IFIP Working Conference on Enterprise Interoperability (IWIT 2011), LNBIP 76* (pp. 191–203). Berlin, Germany: Springer.

Sigholm, J., & Bang, M. (2013). Towards offensive cyber counterintelligence. In *Proceedings of the 2013 European Intelligence and Security Informatics Conference*, (pp. 166–171). Uppsala, Sweden: IEEE Computer Society.

Silic, M., Krolo, J., & Delac, G. (2010, May). Security vulnerabilities in modern web browser architecture. In *Proceedings of the 33rd International Convention* (pp. 1240-1245). IEEE.

Silverman, N. (2013). The E-Penny opera. *Wilmott, 2013*(67), 22-27.

Simmons, C., Shiva, S., Dasgupta, D., & Wu, Q. (2009). *AVOIDIT: A cyber attack taxonomy* (Technical Report CS-09-003). University of Memphis.

Siponen, M., & Iivari, J. (2006). Six design theories for IS security policies and guidelines. *Journal of the Association for Information Systems, 7*(7), 445–472.

Skinner, W. F., & Fream, A. M. (1997). A social learning theory analysis of computer crime among college students. *Journal of Research in Crime and Delinquency, 34*(4), 495–518. doi:10.1177/0022427897034004005

Slonje, R., & Smith, P. K. (2008). cyber bullying: Another main type of bullying. *Scandinavian Journal of Psychology, 49*(2), 147–154. doi:10.1111/j.1467-9450.2007.00611.x PMID:18352984

Smahel, D., Helsper, E., Green, L., Kalmus, V., Blinka, L., & Ólafsson, K. (2012). *Excessive internet use among European children.* London, UK: EU Kids Online, London School of Economics & Political Science. Retrieved December 11, 2012, from http://www.lse.ac.uk/media@lse/research/EUKidsOnline/EU%20Kids%20III/Reports/ExcessiveUse.pdf

Smartt, U. (2011). *Media & entertainment law.* London: Routledge.

Smith, P. K. (2012b). Cyber bullying and cyber aggression. In S. R. Jimerson, A. B. Nickerson, M. J. Mayer, & M. J. Furlong (Eds.), Handbook of school violence and school safety: International research and practice (2nd ed.) (pp. 93–103). New York, NY: Routledge.

Smith, P. K., & Slonje, R. (2010). Cyber bullying: The nature and extent of a new kind of bullying, in and out of school. In S. R. Jimerson, S. M. Swearer, & D. L. Espelage (Eds.), Handbook of bullying in schools: An international perspective (pp. 249–262). New York, NY: Routledge.

Smith, P. K., Mahdavi, J., Carvalho, M., & Tippett, N. (2006). *An investigation into cyber bullying, its forms, awareness and impact, and the relationship between age and gender in cyber bullying.* Research Brief No. RBX03-06. London: DfES.

Smith, T. (2001). Hacker jailed for revenge sewage attacks. *The Register.* Retrieved from http://www.theregister.co.uk/2001/10/31/hacker_jailed_for_revenge_sewage/

Smith, A. D., & Rupp, W. T. (2002). Issues in cybersecurity - Understanding the potential risks associated with hackers/crackers. *Information Management & Computer Security, 10*(4), 178–183. doi:10.1108/09685220210436976

Smith, K. G., Smith, K. A., Sims, H. P. Jr, O'Bannon, D. P., Scully, J. A., & Olian, J. D. (1994). Top management team demography and process: The role of social integration and communication. *Administrative Science Quarterly, 39*(3), 412–438. doi:10.2307/2393297

Smith, K. T. (2013). Building a human capability decision engine. *Human Factors, 2013*, 395–402.

Smith, P. K. (2012a). cyber bullying: Challenges and opportunities for a research program—a response to Olweus (2012). *European Journal of Developmental Psychology, 9*, 553–558. doi:10.1080/17405629.2012.689821

Smith, P. K., Madsen, K. C., & Moody, J. C. (1999). What causes the age decline in reports of being bullied at school? Towards a developmental analysis of risks of being bullied. *Educational Research*, *41*(3), 267–285. doi:10.1080/0013188990410303

Smith, P. K., Mahdavi, J., Carvalho, M., Fisher, S., Russell, S., & Tippett, N. (2008). cyber bullying: Its nature and impact in secondary school pupils. *Journal of Child Psychology and Psychiatry, and Allied Disciplines*, *49*(4), 376–385. doi:10.1111/j.1469-7610.2007.01846.x PMID:18363945

Soares, N. F. (2006). A Investigação Participativa no Grupo Social da Infância: Currículo sem Fronteiras. *Currículo sem Fronteiras*, *6*, 25-40.

Solove, D. J. (2006). A Brief History of Information Privacy Law. In C. Wolf (Ed.), *Proskauer on Privacy: A Guide to Privacy and Data Security Law in the Information Age* (pp. 1–46). New York: Practising Law Institute.

Sommer, P. (2012). Digital evidence, digital investigations and e-disclosure: A guide to forensic readiness for organisations, security advisers and lawyers (3rd ed.). Information Assurance and Advisory Council.

Sommerville, I. (2007). *Models for responsibility assignment. In Responsibility and dependable systems* (pp. 165–186). Springer. doi:10.1007/978-1-84628-626-1_8

Song, J., Takakura, H., Okabe, Y., Eto, M., Inoue, D., & Nakao, K. (2011). Statistical analysis of honeypot data and building of Kyoto 2006+ dataset for NIDS evaluation. In *Proceedings of the First Workshop on Building Analysis Datasets and Gathering Experience Returns for Security (BADGERS '11)* (pp. 29-36). New York: ACM. doi:10.1145/1978672.1978676

Sontag, L. M., Clemans, K. H., Graber, J. A., & Lyndon, S. (2011). Traditional and cyber aggressors and victims: A comparison of psychosocial characteristics. *Journal of Youth and Adolescence*, *40*(4), 392–404. doi:10.1007/s10964-010-9575-9 PMID:20680425

Sood, A. K., & Enbody, R. J. (2013). Crimeware-as-a-service—A survey of commoditized crimeware in the underground market. *International Journal of Critical Infrastructure Protection*.

Sood, A. K., & Enbody, R. J. (2011). Malvertising—exploiting web advertising. *Computer Fraud & Security*, (4), 11–16.

Sood, A. K., Enbody, R. J., & Bansal, R. (2013). Dissecting SpyEye: Understanding the design of third generation botners. *Computer Networks*, *57*, 436–450. doi:10.1016/j.comnet.2012.06.021

Sousa, J. P. (2002). *Teorias da notícia e do jornalismo. Argos (Utrecht, Netherlands)*.

Special Eurobarometer 390. (2012). *Report: Cyber Security*. Conducted by TNS Opinion & Social at the request of the European Commission,Directorate-General Home Affairs. Survey co-ordinated by the European Commission, Directorate-General for Communication (DG COMM "Research and Speechwriting" Unit).

Speer, D. L. (2000). Redefining borders: The challenges of cybercrime. *Crime, Law, and Social Change*, *34*, 259–273. doi:10.1023/A:1008332132218

Spitzner, L. (2002). *Honeypots: Tracking Hackers*. Addison-Wesley Longman Publishing Co., Inc.

Stanciu, N. (2013). Technologies, methodologies and challenges in network intrusion detection and prevention systems. *Informatica Economica*, *17*(1), 144–156. doi:10.12948/issn14531305/17.1.2013.12

Starmer, K. (2013). *Guidelines on prosecuting cases involving communications sent via social media*. London: Crown Prosecution Service.

Stephens, P., & Induruwa, A. (2007). Cybercrime investigation training and specialist education for the European Union. In *Proceedings of Second International Workshop on Digital Forensics and Incident Analysis* (WDFIA 2007). IEEE Computer Society.

Stevens, J. M., Beyer, J. M., & Trice, H. M. (1978). Assessing personal, role, and organizational predictors of managerial commitment. *Academy of Management Journal*, *21*(3), 380–396. doi:10.2307/255721 PMID:10246524

Stouffer, K., Falco, J., & Scarfone, K. (2007). *Guide to industrial control systems (ICS) security special publication 800-82 second public draft*. National Institute of Standards and Technology.

Stout, T. (2006). *Improving the decision making process for information security through a pre-implementation impact review of security countermeasures* (Doctoral dissertation). Retrieved from ProQuest dissertations and theses database (Document ID 3215299)

Stover, D. (2006). Treating cyber bullying as a school violence issue. *Education Digest, 72*(4), 40–42.

Straub, D. W. (1990). Effective IS security: An empirical study. *Information Systems Research, 1*(3), 255–276. doi:10.1287/isre.1.3.255

Straub, D. W., & Nance, W. (1990). Discovering and discipline computer abuse in organizations: A field study. *Management Information Systems Quarterly, 14*(1), 45–60. doi:10.2307/249307

Straub, D. W., & Welke, R. J. (1998). Coping with systems risk: Security planning models for management decision making. *Management Information Systems Quarterly, 22*(4), 441–469. doi:10.2307/249551

Stromer-Galley, J., & Wichowski, A. (2010). Political discussion online. The Handbook of Internet Studies, 168-187.

Subrahmanyam, K., Greenfield, P. M., & Tynes, B. (2004). Constructing sexuality and identity in an internet teen chat room. *Journal of Applied Developmental Psychology, 25*(6), 651–666. doi:10.1016/j.appdev.2004.09.007

Sule, D. (2013). Digital forensics 101: Case study using FTK imager. *eForensics Magazine, 2*(2). Retrieved February 27, 2013 from http://eforensicsmag.com/forensics-analysis-with-ftk/

SURFcert IDS. (2013). *SURFcert IDS*. Retrieved 2013, from http://ids.surfnet.nl/

Suto, L. (2008). *Clickjacking Details*. Retrieved from http://ha.ckers.org/blog/20081007/clickjacking-details

Symantec Corporation. (2011). *2011 Norton cybercrime report*. Retrieved October 15, 2013, from http://now-static.norton.com/now/en/pu/images/Promotions/2012/cybercrime/assets/downloads/en-us/NCR-DataSheet.pdf

Symantec Corporation. (2012). *2012 Annual Security Report*. Retrieved from http://www.symantec.com/annualreport

Symantec Corporation. (2012). *2012 Norton cybercrime report*. Retrieved October 15, 2013, from http://now-static.norton.com/now/en/pu/images/Promotions/2012/cybercrimeReport/2012_Norton_Cybercrime_Report_Master_FINAL_050912.pdf

Symantec. (2010). *Symantec intelligence quarterly report: October - December, 2010, targeted attacks on critical infrastructures*. Author.

Symantec. (2013). *Internet Security Threat Report 2013, Volume 18*. Available at http://www.symantec.com/security_response/publications/threatreport.jsp

Syrpis, P. (Ed.). (2012). *The judiciary, the legislature and the EU internal market*. Rio de Janeiro: Cambridge University Press. doi:10.1017/CBO9780511845680

SystemTap. (n.d.). *SystemTap*. Retrieved 2013, from https://sourceware.org/systemtap/index.html

Tamminen, U. (2013). *Kippo SSH Honeypot*. Retrieved 2013, from https://code.google.com/p/kippo/

Tangen, D., & Campbell, M. (2010). cyber bullying prevention: One primary school's approach. *Australian Journal of Guidance & Counselling, 20*, 225–234. doi:10.1375/ajgc.20.2.225

Tanji, J., & Hoshi, E. (2008). Role of the lateral prefrontal cortex in executive behavioral control. *Physiological Reviews, 88*(1), 37. doi:10.1152/physrev.00014.2007 PMID:18195082

Team, S. (2013). *Snort Users Manual*. Retrieved from http://www.snort.org/docs

Ter Louw, M., Lim, J. S., & Venkatakrishnan, V. N. (2008). Enhancing web browser security against malware extensions. *Journal in Computer Virology, 4*(3), 179–195. doi:10.1007/s11416-007-0078-5

Terceiro, J. B. (1996). *Sociedad digital: Del homo sapiens al homo digitalis*. Madrid: Alianza Editorial.

Tester, D. (2013). Is the TJ Hooper case relevant for today's information security environment? *ISACA Journal, 2*. Retrieved November 14, 2013 from m.isaca.org/Jounal/Past-Issues/2013/Volume-2/Pages/default.aspx

The Honeynet Project. (2002). *Know Your Enemy*. Boston: Addison-Wesley.

The Honeynet Project. (2004). Know Your Enemy, Second Edition: Learning about Security Threats. Addison Wesley.

The Honeynet Project. (2005). *Honeywall Roo*. Retrieved 2013, from https://projects.honeynet.org/honeywall/

The Honeynet Project. (2007). *Sebek Issue*. Retrieved 2013, from http://old.honeynet.org/tools/cdrom/roo/manual/12-knownissues.html

The Honeynet Project. (n.d.). *Dionaea - Catches bugs*. Retrieved 2013, from http://dionaea.carnivore.it/

The National Archives. (2011). *Digital Continuity to Support Forensic Readiness*. Retrieved March 23, 2013 from http://www.utica.edu/academic/institutes/ecii/publications/articles/A0B13342-B4E0-1F6A-156F501C-49CF5F51.pdf

Tipton, H. F., & Krause, M. (2005). *Information Security Management Handbook*. Taylor & Francis e-Library.

Tiwari, R., & Jain, A. (2012). Improving network security and design using honeypots. In *Proceedings of the CUBE International Information Technology Conference (CUBE '12)* (pp. 847-852). New York: ACM. doi:10.1145/2381716.2381875

Tokunaga, R. S. (2010). Following you home from school: A critical review and synthesis of research on cyber bullying victimization. *Computers in Human Behavior, 26*, 277–287. doi:10.1016/j.chb.2009.11.014

Torney, R., Vamplew, P., & And Yearwood, J. (2012). Using Psycholinguistic Features For Profiling First Language Of Authors. *Journal of the American Society for Information Science American Society for Information Science, 63*, 1256–1269. doi:10.1002/asi.22627

Trail, S. A. T. (1939). Trail Smelter Arbitral Tribunal Decision. *The American Journal of International Law, 33*, 182–212.

Treacy, B., & Bapat, A. (2013). Purpose limitation – Clarity at last?. *PDP, 13*(11).

Trepte, S., & Reinecke, L. (2013). The reciprocal effects of social network site use and the disposition for self-disclosure: A longitudinal study. *Computers in Human Behavior, 29*(3), 1102–1112. doi:10.1016/j.chb.2012.10.002

Trevathan, J., & Myers, T. (2012). Anti-social networking? *World Academy of Science. Engineering and Technology, 72*, 127–135.

Tripwire, Inc. (2013). *Tripwire*. Retrieved 2013, from http://sourceforge.net/projects/tripwire/

TSB. (2010). Revolution or evolution? Information Security 2020. Technology Strategy Board - TSB, PriceWaterHouseCoopers LLP. UK: TSB: Pricewathercoopers.

Turk, R. (2005) *Cyber incidents involving control systems* (Technical Report INL/EXT-05-00671). Idaho National Laboratory.

Turnbull, B. (2008). The adaptability of electronic evidence acquisition guides for new technologies. In *Proceedings of the 1st International Conference on Forensic Applications and Techniques in Telecommunications, Information, and Multimedia and Workshop*, (pp. 1:1-1:6). Academic Press.

Turner, D., & Oeschger, I. (2003). *Creating XPCOM Components*. Open Source.

Twigg-Flesner, C. (2008). The europeanisation of contract law. London: Routledge Cavendish.

Tyworth, M., Giacobe, N.A., Mancuso, V., & Dancy, C. (2012). The distributed nature of cyber situation awareness. *Proceedings of 2012 IEEE International Multi-Disciplinary Conference on Cognitive Methods in Situation Awareness and Decision Support (CogSIMA)*, (pp. 174-178). IEEE.

U.S. Congress. (1996). Health Insurance Portability and Accountability Act. *Public Law*, 104–191.

Uckelmann, D. (Ed.). (2011). *Architecting the internet of things*. Springerverlag. doi:10.1007/978-3-642-19157-2

Udassin, E. (2008). Control system attack vectors and examples: Field site and corporate network. In *Proc. S4 SCADA security conference*. SCADA.

UNICEF. (2011). *Child Safety online: Global challenges and strategies*. UNICEF.

United Nations (UN). (1994). *The United Nations manual on the prevention and control of computer related crime*. United Nations Publications.

United Nations Conference on Environment and Development. (1992). *Report of the United Nations Conference on Environment and Development, Annex I, U.N. Doc. A/CONF.151/26* (Vol. 1). Author.

*United Nations Conference on the Human Environment, Declaration of the United Nations Conference on the Human Environment, Stockholm.* (1972). Retrieved October 13, 2013, from http://www.unep.org/Documents.Multilingual/Default.asp?documentid=97&articleid=1503

United Nations General Assembly. (1948). *Universal Declaration of Human Rights*. Retrieved June 07, 2013, from http://portal.mj.gov.br/sedh/ct/legis_intern/ddh_bib_inter_universal.htm

United Nations Office on Drugs and Crime (UNODC). (2012). *The use of the Internet for terrorist purposes.* United Nations.

United Nations. (1948). *Universal Declaration of Human Rights*. Retrieved November 30, 2013, from http://www.ohchr.org/EN/UDHR/Documents/60UDHR/bookleten.pdf

United Nations. (1966). *International Covenant on Civil and Political Rights, G.A. res. 2200A (XXI), U.N. Doc. A/6316 (1966)*. Author.

United Nations. (2004). *World Summit on the Information Society (WSIS)*. Retrieved April 21, 2013, from http://www.itu.int/wsis/documents/doc_multi.asp?lang=en&id=1161|1160

United States Computer Emergency Readiness Team (US-CERT). (2013). *Malicious Code*. Retrieved from http://www.us-cert.gov/government-users/reporting-requirements

United States National Institute of Standards and Technology (NIST). (2013). *Cyber Framework*. Retrieved from http://www.nist.gov/itl/cyberframework.cfm

United States Office of Management and Budget (OMB). (2012). *FY2011 Report to congress on implementation the federal information security management act of 2002.* Retrieved from http://www.whitehouse.gov/sites/default/files/omb/assets/egov_docs/fy12_fisma.pdf

*United States vs. Ivanov.* (2005). Retrieved from http://www.crime-research.org/articles/hacker0405/

UNODC. (2013). *Comprehensive study on cybercrime.* UNODC.

USA-PA. (2001). *U.S.A. Patriot Act, 2001*. Retrieved from http://www.epic.org/privacy/terrorism/hr3162.html

US-CERT. (2008). *Control systems security program.* Retrieved from http://www.us-cert.gov/control_systems/index.html

Utin, D., Utin, M. & Utin, J. (2008). General misconceptions about information security lead to an insecure world. *Information Security Journal: A Global Perspective, 17*(4), 164-169.

Utz, S., & Kramer, C. N. (2009). The privacy paradox on social network sites revisited: The role of individual characteristics and group norms. *Cyberpsychology, 3*(2). Retrieved from http://cyberpsychology.eu/view.php?cisloclanku=2009111001&article=2

Uzun, H., Szewczyk, S. H., & Varma, R. (2004). Board composition and corporate fraud. *Financial Analysts Journal, 60*(3), 33–43. doi:10.2469/faj.v60.n3.2619

Valentini, G., & Lassonde, W. et al. (2011). An overview of energy efficiency techniques in cluster computing systems. *Cluster Computing*, 1–13.

Valkenburg, P. M., & Buijzen, M. (2003). Children, computer games, and the Internet. *Netherlands Journal of Social Sciences, 39*(1), 24–34.

Valli, C. (2003). *Honeyd-A OS Fingerprinting Artifice.* Retrieved 2013, from http://ro.ecu.edu.au/ecuworks/3485/

van der Aalst, W. M. P., & ter Hofstede, A. H. M. (2005). YAWL: yet another workflow language. *Information Systems, 30*(4), 245–275. doi:10.1016/j.is.2004.02.002

van der Aalst, W. M. P., ter Hofstede, A. H. M., Kiepuszewski, B., & Barros, A. P. (2003). Workflow Patterns. *Distributed and Parallel Databases, 14*(1), 5–51. doi:10.1023/A:1022883727209

Van Dijk, J. A. G. M. (2009). *One europe, digitally divided. Routledge handbook of internet politics* (pp. 288–305). London: Taylor & Francis.

Van Kesteren, A., & Jackson, D. (2007). *The xmlhttprequest object* (Working Draft WD-XMLHttpRequest-20070618). World Wide Web Consortium.

Vandoninck, S., d'Haenens, L., & Roe, K. (2013). Online risks: Coping strategies of less resilient children and teenagers across Europe. *Journal of Children and Media, 7*(1), 60–78. doi:10.1080/17482798.2012.739780

Veltri, F. N., Krasnova, H., & Elgarah, W. (2011). Online disclosure and privacy concerns: A study of Moroccan and American Facebook users. In *Proceedings of the 17th Americas Conference on Information Systems*. Retrieved from http://aisel.aisnet.org/amcis2011_submissions/300

Verizon. (2013). *2011 data breach investigations report*. Retrieved from http://www.verizonenterprise.com/resources/reports/rp_data-breach-investigations-report-2011_en_xg.pdf

Verma, M., Hussain, S., & Kushwah, S. (2012). Cyber law: Approach to prevent cybercrime. *International Journal of Research in Engineering Science and Technology, 1*(3), 123–129.

Vickers, P. (2012). Ways of listening and modes of being: Electroacoustic auditory display. *Journal of Sonic Studies, 2* (1). Retrieved February 5, 2014, from http://journal.sonicstudies.org/vol02/nr01/a04

Vickers, P. (2011). Sonification for process monitoring. In T. Hermann, A. D. Hunt, & J. Neuhoff (Eds.), *The Sonification Handbook* (pp. 455–492). Berlin: Logos Verlag.

Viennot, G. X. (1986). *Heaps of Pieces, I: Basic definitions and combinatorial lemmas, Combinatoire Enumerative, Labelle and Leroux, Lect. Notes in Math* (pp. 321–350). New York: Springer.

Villacampa Estiarte, C. (2013). Delito de acecho/stalking: Art. 172 ter in Estudio crítico sobre el Anteproyecto de reforma penal de 2012. Ed. Tirant lo Blanch Reformas.

Vlachopoulos, K., Magkos, E., & Chrissikopoulos, V. (2013). A model for hybrid evidence investigation. *Emerging Digital Forensics Applications for Crime Detection, Prevention, and Security, 150.*

Vlachos, V., Minou, M., Assimakopouos, V., & Toska, A. (2011). The landscape of cybercrime in Greece. *Information Management & Computer Security, 19*(2), 113–123. doi:10.1108/09685221111143051

VMware, Inc. (2013). *Configuring a Virtual Network.* Retrieved 2013, from http://www.vmware.com/support/ws55/doc/ws_net.html

VMware, Inc. (2013). *VMware Virtualization for Desktop & Server, Application, Public & Hybrid Clouds*. Retrieved 2013, from http://www.vmware.com/

Volonino, L., & Redpath, I. (2010). e-Discovery for dummies. Wiley Publishing, Inc.

von Marées, N., & Petermann, F. (2012). cyber bullying: An increasing challenge for schools. *School Psychology International, 33*(5), 467–476. doi:10.1177/0143034312445241

Vroom, V., & Pahl, B. (1971). Relationship between age and risk-taking among managers. *The Journal of Applied Psychology, 55*, 399–405. doi:10.1037/h0031776

Vulnerabilities, C. (2001). *Exposures (CVE)*. Retrieved from http://cve.mitre.org/

Vuze. (2008). *First Results from Vuze Network Monitoring Tool Released April 18th, 2008*. Retrieved March 18, 2013, from http://torrentfreak.com//images/vuze-plug-in-results.pdf

Wade, A., & Beran, T. (2011). Cyberbullying: The New Era of Bullying. *Canadian Journal of School Psychology, 26*(1), 44–61. doi:10.1177/0829573510396318

Wales, N. S., & Smith, S. (2012). *Building a Taxonomy for Cybercrimes*. Academic Press.

Walker, M. (2012). *Certified Ethical Hacker: Exam guide: All-in-one.* New York: McGraw-Hill.

Waller, M. J., Huber, G. P., & Glick, W. H. (1995). Functional Background as a determinnant of executives' selective perception. *Academy of Management Journal, 38*, 943–974. doi:10.2307/256616

Walrave, M., & Heirman, W. (2011). cyber bullying: Predicting victimization and perpetration. *Children & Society, 25*(1), 59–72. doi:10.1111/j.1099-0860.2009.00260.x

Walsh, S. (2009). *Dallas security guard facing charges for installing malware on hospital computers*. Retrieved from http://www.technologytell.com/gadgets/48623/dallas-security-guard-facing-charges-for-installing-malware-on-hospital-com/

Wang, J. (2013). Factors affecting Social Networking Website Loyalty. *Information Technology Journal, 12*(3), 545–547. doi:10.3923/itj.2013.545.547

Wang, J., Iannotti, R. J., & Nansel, T. R. (2009). School bullying among adolescents in the United States: Physical, verbal, relational, and cyber. *The Journal of Adolescent Health*, *45*(4), 368–375. doi:10.1016/j.jadohealth.2009.03.021 PMID:19766941

Wang, T., Kannan, K. N., & Rees, J. (2013). The association between the disclosure and the realization of information security risk factors. *Information Systems Research*, *24*(2), 201–218. doi:10.1287/isre.1120.0437

Wang, T., Rees, J., & Kannan, K. (2013). The Textual Contents of Media Reports of Information Security Breaches and Profitable Short-Term Investment Opportunities. *Journal of Organizational Computing and Electronic Commerce*, *23*(3), 200–223. doi:10.1080/10919392.2013.807712

Watson, D. (2007). GDH – Global Distributed Honeynet. In *Proceeding of the PacSec 2007 Conference*. Retrieved 2013, from http://www.ukhoneynet.org/PacSec07_David_Watson_Global_Distributed_Honeynet.pdf

Watters, P. A., McCombie, S., Layton, R., & Pieprzyk, J. (2012). Characterising and predicting cyber attacks using the Cyber Attacker Model Profile (CAMP). *Journal of Money Laundering Control*, *15*(4), 430–441. doi:10.1108/13685201211266015

WEF. (2013). *Global risk 2013*. WEF.

Weijers, I. (1999). The double paradox of juvenile justice. *European Journal on Criminal Policy and Research*, *7*(3), 329–351. doi:10.1023/A:1008732820029

Weiser, M. (1991). The computer for the 21st century. *Scientific American*, *265*(3), 94–104. doi:10.1038/scientificamerican0991-94

Wells, W. D., & Chen, Q. (2000). The dimensions of commercial cyberspace. *Journal of Interactive Advertising*, *1*(1), 23–40. doi:10.1080/15252019.2000.10722042

Werner, N. E., Bumpus, M. F., & Rock, D. (2010). Involvement in internet aggression during early adolescence. *Journal of Youth and Adolescence*, *39*(6), 607–619. doi:10.1007/s10964-009-9419-7 PMID:20422350

Westrup, D. (1998). Applying functional analysis to stalking. In The psychology of stalking: Clinical and forensic perspectives. New York: Academic Press.

*What is Malware ?* (2013). Retrieved August 21, 2013, from http://www.microsoft.com/security/resources/malware-whatis.aspx

Whitby, P. (2011). *Is your child safe online? A parents guide to the internet, Facebook, mobile phones & other new media*. White Ladder.

Whitcroft, O. (2013). Social media – Challenges in control of information. *PDP*, *13*(7).

White House. (2013). *Executive order on improving critical infrastructure cybersecurity*. Retrieved from http://www.whitehouse.gov/the-press-office/2013/02/12/executive-order-improving-critical-infrastructure-cybersecurity

White, B. (2013, March 12). *Lessons of AMD v. Intel* [Video file]. Retrieved from http://www.youtube.com/watch?v=jQ_9uLkw_Uo

Whitman, M. (2011). *Principles of information security*. Boston, MA: Course Technology.

Whitman, M., & Mattord, H. (2010). *Management of Information Security* (3rd ed.). Boca Raton, FL: Delmar, Cengage Learning.

Whittle, H., Hamilton-Giachritsis, C., Beech, A., & Collings, G. (2013). A review of online grooming: Characteristics and concerns. *Aggression and Violent Behavior*, *18*(1), 62–70. doi:10.1016/j.avb.2012.09.003

Wiersema, M. F., & Bantel, K. A. (1992). Top management team demography and corporate strategic change. *Academy of Management Journal*, *35*(1), 91–121. doi:10.2307/256474

Wilard, N. (2008). *Educator's Guide to Cyberbullying and Cyberthreats*. Retrieved December 24, 2011, from http://csriu.org/cyberbully/docs/cbcteducator.pdf

Wilard, N. (2007). *Cyberbullying and Cyberthreats: Responding to the Challenge of Online Social Aggression, Threats, and Distress* (2nd ed.). Research Press.

Wilcox, A. (2011). Regulating violence in video games: Virtually everything. *J.Nat'L Ass'N Admin.L. Judiciary*, *31*, 253.

Willard, N. (2007). *Educator's guide to cyber bullying and cyber threats 2007*. Available at http://www.cyberbully.org/cyber bully/docs/cbcteducator

Williams, K. R., & Guerra, N. G. (2007). Prevalence and predictors of Internet bullying. *The Journal of Adolescent Health, 41*(6), S14–S21. doi:10.1016/j.jadohealth.2007.08.018 PMID:18047941

Williams, K. Y., & O'Reilly, C. A. (1998). *Demography and diversity in organizations*. Greenwich: JAI Press.

Winters, R. M., & Wanderley, M. M. (2013). Sonification of emotion: Strategies for continuous display of arousal and valence. In G. Luck, & O. Brabant (Eds.), *Proceedings of the 3rd International Conference on Music and Emotion (ICME3)*. ICME3.

Witt, S., Feja, S., Speck, A., & Prietz, C. (2012). Integrated privacy modeling and validation for business process models, In *EDBT/ICDT Workshops (EDBT-ICDT '12)* (pp. 196–205). New York, NY, USA: ACM.

Wolak, J., Mitchell, K., & Finkelhor, D. (2004). Internet-initiated sex crimes against minors: Implications for prevention based on findings from a national study. *The Journal of Adolescent Health, 35*, 11–20. doi:10.1016/j.jadohealth.2004.05.006 PMID:15488437

Wolak, J., Mitchell, K., & Finkelhor, D. (2006). *Online victimization of children: Five years later*. Washington, DC: National Center for Missing and Exploited Children.

Wolak, J., Mitchell, K., & Finkelhor, D. (2007). Does Online Harassment Constitute Bullying? An Exploration of Online Harassment by Known Peers and Online-Only Contacts. *The Journal of Adolescent Health, 41*(6), S51–S58. doi:10.1016/j.jadohealth.2007.08.019 PMID:18047945

Wolak, J., Mitchell, K., & Finkelhor, D. (2007). Unwanted and wanted exposure to online pornography in a national sample of youth internet users. *Pediatrics, 119*, 247–257. doi:10.1542/peds.2006-1891 PMID:17272613

Wolter, C., Schaad, A., & Meinel, C. (2008). Task-Based Entailment Constraints for Basic Workflow Patterns. In I. Ray, & N. Li (Eds.), *Proceedings of the 13th ACM Symposium on Access Control Models (SACMAT 2008)* (pp. 51–60). New York, NY: ACM.

Wolter, C., Menzel, M., Schaad, A., Miseldine, P., & Meinel, C. (2009). Model-driven business process security requirement specification. *Journal of Systems Architecture, 55*(4), 211–223. doi:10.1016/j.sysarc.2008.10.002

Wolter, C., & Schaad, A. (2007). Modeling of Task-Based Authorization Constraints in BPMN. In G. Alonso, P. Dadam, & M. Rosemann (Eds.), *Business Process Management, LNCS 4714* (pp. 64–79). Berlin, Germany: Springer. doi:10.1007/978-3-540-75183-0_5

Wootton, A. B., Davey, C., Cooper, R., & Press, M. (2003). *The crime lifecycle: Generating design against crime ideas*. Salford, UK: The University of Salford.

Workflow Management Coalition (WfMC). (1995). *The Workflow Reference Model — Issue 1.1*. Retrieved November 30, 2013, from http://www.wfmc.org/reference-model.html

Working Party Opinion 03/2013 (WP203) on the purpose limitation principle in the Data Protection Directive (95/46/EC)

Worthen, M.R. (2007). Education Policy Implications from the Expert Panel on Electronic Media and Youth Violence. *The Journal of Adolescent Health, 41*(6), S61–S63. doi:10.1016/j.jadohealth.2007.09.009 PMID:18047948

Xia, F., Yang, L. T., Wang, L., & Vinel, A. (2012). Internet of things. *International Journal of Communication Systems, 25*(9), 1101–1102. doi:10.1002/dac.2417

XMPP Standards Foundation. (2013). *XMPP*. Retrieved 2013, from http://xmpp.org/

Xu, F., Michael, K., & Chen, X. (2013). Factors affectng privacy disclosure on social network sites: an integrated model. *Electronic Commerce Research, 13*(2), 151–168. doi:10.1007/s10660-013-9111-6

Yalcin, A., & Boucher, T. O. (1999). An Architecture for Flexible Manufacturing Cells with Alternate Machining and Alternate Sequencing. *IEEE Transactions on Robotics and Automation, 15*(6), 1126–1130. doi:10.1109/70.817676

Yang, C.-X., Jiang, S.-M., Zhou, T., Wang, B.-H., & Zhou, P.-L. (2006). Self-organized criticality of computer network traffic. In *Communications, Circuits and Systems Proceedings,* (vol. 3, pp. 1740-1743). IEEE.

Yar, M. (2005). The novelty of "cyber-crime": An assessment in light of routine activity theory. *European Journal of Criminology*, 2(4), 407–427. doi:10.1177/147737080556056

Ybarra, M. L., D, P., Diener-west, M., Leaf, P. J. (2007). Examining the Overlap in Internet Harassment and School Bullying: Implications for School Intervention. *The Journal of Adolescent Health*, 41(1), S42–50. doi:10.1016/j.jadohealth.2007.09.004 PMID:17577533

Ybarra, M. L., Mitchell, K. J., Wolak, J., & Finkelhor, D. (2006). Examining characteristics and associated distress related to Internet harassment: findings from the Second Youth Internet Safety Survey. *Pediatrics*, 118(4), e1169–1177. doi:10.1542/peds.2006-0815 PMID:17015505

Ybarra, M.L. (2004). Youth engaging in online harassment: associations with caregiver?child relationships, Internet use, and personal characteristics*1. *Journal of Adolescence*, 27(3), 319–336. doi:10.1016/j.adolescence.2004.03.007 PMID:15159091

Ybarra, M.L., & Mitchell, K. (2004). Online aggressor/targets, aggressors, and targets: a comparison of associated youth characteristics. *Journal of Child Psychology and Psychiatry, and Allied Disciplines*, 45(7), 1308–1316. doi:10.1111/j.1469-7610.2004.00328.x PMID:15335350

Ybarra, M., Mitchell, K., Finkelhor, D., & Wolak, J. (2007). Internet prevention messages: Targeting the right online behaviors. *Archives of Pediatrics & Adolescent Medicine*, 161(2), 138–145. PMID:17283298

Ye, N., Harish, B., & Farley, T. (2006). Attack profiles to derive data observations, features, and characteristics of cyber attacks. Information, Knowledge, *Systems Management*, 5(1), 23–47.

Yilmaz, H. (2011). Cyber bullying in Turkish middle schools: An exploratory study. *School Psychology International*, 32, 645–654. doi:10.1177/0143034311410262

Yin, D., Xue, Z., Hong, L., Davison, B., Kontostathis, A., & Edwards, L. (2009). Detection of Harassment on Web 2.0. In *Proceedings of the 1st Content Analysis in Web 2.0 Workshop*. Madrid, Spain: CAW.

Youl, T. (2004). *Phishing Scams: Understanding the latest trends*. The Confidence Group Pty Ltd.

Youn, S. (2005). Teenagers' perceptions of online privacy and coping behaviours: a risk-benefit appraisal approach. *Journal of Broadcasting & Electronic Media*, 49(1), 86–110. doi:10.1207/s15506878jobem4901_6

Yuan, E., & Tong, J. (2005). Attributed Based Access Control (ABAC) for Web Services. In *Proceedings of IEEE International Conference on Web Services (ICWS '05)* (pp. 561–569). Washington, DC: IEEE Computer Society.

Zakarian, A., & Kusiak, A. (1997). Modeling Manufacturing Dependability. *IEEE Transactions on Robotics and Automation*, 13(2), 161–168. doi:10.1109/70.563639

Zalewski, M. (2012). *P0f v3*. Retrieved 2013, from http://lcamtuf.coredump.cx/p0f3/

Zalewski, M. (2010). *Browser security handbook*. Google Code.

Zeigler, A. (2008). IE8 and Loosely-Coupled IE (LCIE). *The Windows Internet Explorer Weblog (MSDN IEBlog)*, 11.

Zetter, K. (2010). Blockbuster worm aimed for infrastructure, but no proof Iran nukes were target. Wired. Retrieved from http://www.wired.com/threatlevel/2010/09/stuxnet/

Zetter, K. (2011). *How digital detectives deciphered stuxnet, the most menacing malware in history*. Retrieved from http://www.wired.com/threatlevel/2011/07/how-digital-detectives-decipheredstuxnet/all/1

Zhu, B., & Sastry, S. (2010, April). SCADA-specific intrusion detection/prevention systems: A survey and taxonomy. In *Proceedings of the 1st Workshop on Secure Control Systems (SCS)*. SCS.

Zimmermann, R. (2004). Roman law and the harmonisation of private law in europe. In A. S. Hartkamp, M. W. Hesselink, E. Hondius, C. Mak, & E. Du Perron (Eds.), *Towards a european civil code* (pp. 22–23). Deventer, The Netherlands: Kluwer Law International.

Zuo, M.J., Liu, B., & Murthy, D. N. P. (2000). Replacement-repair policy for multi-state deteriorating products under warranty. *European Journal of Operational Research*, (3), 519–530. doi:10.1016/S0377-2217(99)00107-1

# About the Contributors

**Maria Manuela Cruz-Cunha** is currently an Associate Professor in the School of Technology at the Polytechnic Institute of Cavado and Ave, Portugal. She holds a Dipl. Eng. in the field of Systems and Informatics Engineering, an MSci in the field of Information Society, and a DrSci in the field of Virtual Enterprises all from the University of Minho (Portugal). She teaches subjects related to Information Systems, Information Technologies, and Organizational Models in undergraduate and post-graduate studies. She supervises several PhD projects in the domain of Virtual Enterprises and Information Systems and Technologies. She regularly publishes in international peer-reviewed journals and participates in international scientific conferences. She serves as a member of the Editorial Board and Associate Editor for several International Journals and for several Scientific Committees of International Conferences. She has authored and edited several books and her work appears in more than 120 papers published in journals, book chapters and conference proceedings. She is the co-founder and co-chair of several international conferences: *CENTERIS – Conference on ENTERprise Information Systems* and *ViNOrg - International Conference on Virtual and Networked Organizations: Emergent Technologies and Tools*. She is the editor in-chief of the *International Journal of Web Portals* and of *ICT'ae – Information and Communication Technologies for the advanced enterprise: an international journal*.

**Irene Maria Portela** is currently an Assistant Professor in the School of Management at the Polytechnic Institute of Cavado and Ave, Portugal. She is graduated in Law, holds has a Master in Public Administration and holds a PhD in Law, in the field of Anti-Terrorism Law from Universy of Santiago de Compostela (Spain). She teaches subjects related with Constitutional Law to undergraduated and post-graduated studies. She regularly publishes in international peer-reviewed journals and participates on international scientific conferences. Her work appears in several papers published in journals, book chapters, and conference proceedings.

* * *

**Aurélie Bertaux** defended a PhD thesis in 2010 to obtain the title of Doctor of Computer Science. In 2013, she became associate professor at the university of Burgundy in France, in LE2I UMR CNRS 6306 (Laboratory of Electronics, Informatics and Image). Her research stands in Data Mining, especially in Formal Concept Analysis (developed during her PhD) and in Graph Mining (developed during a post doc in Grenoble Informatics Laboratory, France). Now working in the CheckSem research team, she starts to develop skills in the field of the team: Ontologies, and to build bridges between those three domains.

**R. C. Biradar** is working as Professor and HOD in the Information Science and Engineering Department at the Reva Institute of Technology and Management, Bangalore, India. He obtained his PhD from Visvesvaraya Technological University, Belgaum, India. He has many publications in reputed national/international journals and conferences. Some of the journals where his research articles published are Elsevier, IET and Springer publications having very good impact factors. His research interests include multicast routing in mobile ad hoc networks, wireless Internet, group communication in MANETs, software agent technology, network security, multimedia communication, wireless sensor networks, mesh networks, etc. He is a reviewer of various reputed journals and conferences and chaired many conferences. He is a member IETE, India, member IE, India, member of ISTE, India, Senior member of IEEE, USA, member of IACSIT. He has been listed in Marqui's Who's Who in the World (2012Ed).

**Jonathan Bishop** is an information technology executive, researcher, and writer. He is probably the most published author in the area of Internet trolling law, holding a Masters of Law degree in European Union Law. Jonathan has been involved in the bringing of civil claims for cases related to Internet trolling and of defending in criminal cases. Jonathan founded the Scientific, Economic and Legal Issues affecting Virtual Communities and Electronic Learning (Selivcel) Project in 2007 and has published in learned journals in the area of cyber-space law since 2010, including in international law. In his spare time, Jonathan enjoys swimming, chess, and listening to music.

**Alberto Carneiro** is a Professor of Management and Information Systems. He has been Head of the Sciences and Technologies Department at the Autonomous University of Lisbon. He received a PhD in Engineering and Industrial Management from the Technical University of Lisbon and an MSc in Business Administration with a specialization in Strategic Management and Planning from the same University. Dr. Alberto Carneiro focuses on management of information systems (security and control) at industrial strategic management, and the adoption of innovation and new services development. He is the author of some textbooks on auditing and security of information systems. Moreover, he has written and presented more than twenty-seven articles and communications in international and national conferences and workshops. He is a member of Editorial Advisory Board of the Business Strategy Series, the Iberian Association of Information Systems and Technologies (http://www.aisti.eu), the Portuguese Association of Marketing, and the Portuguese Association for Higher Education. His professional activities include executive training programs and consultancy to firms of several industries.

**Leocadio González Casado** is a computer engineer from Granada University and obtained his degree in 1992 and a PhD in Computer Science from Málaga University in 1999. He is an associate professor in the University of Almería from 2002. His teaching activities are focused on Computer Networks. He is a researcher of TIC146: High Performance Computing - Applications research group. During 2010-2012 he was the main researcher of that group. He has participated in more than twenty national and international research projects. His main research areas are: i) Global Optimization, to find the global maxima/minima of an usually nonlinear objective function using an exhaustive search by branch-and-bound algorithms i i) Parallel computing, mainly on solving irregular problems that need dynamic load balancing strategies; iii) Computer security, in secure P2P computation, access control in wireless sensors with energy and resources limitations, and pay per view multimedia streaming. His publications are shown in http://www.hpca.ual.es/~leo/curr.html.

**Yoan Chabot** is a PhD student involved in a joint cotutelle between the University College Dublin, School of Computer Science and Informatics and Le2i Laboratory, University of Burgundy. His research interests are in the area of Semantic Web and Digital Forensics. His current work is focusing on the use of ontologies to improve the efficiency of forensic tools.

**Calin Ciufude** graduated from the Romanian Technical University of Cluj Napoca in 1986, and received a PhD degree in control systems from Ploiesti "Petroleum - Gas" University in 2000. His employment experience includes the Romanian Railway Company as head of the Remote Control Railway Laboratory Suceava (1990-2001). In 2001, he joined the "Stefan cel Mare" University of Suceava, Computers and Control Systems Department, where he currently is an Associate Professor. He is a member of several scientific organization: honour member of the Romanian Society of Electrical and Control Engineering, the RomanianTechnical Experts Corp, and the Research Board of Advisors of the American Biographical Institute. In 2005, he received The Excellence Diploma of the Installations Faculty of Technical University of Constructions Bucharest, Romania. His special fields of interest include discrete event systems and diagnosis of control systems.

**Regina Connor** holds a Bachelors of Commerce International degree and a Masters degree in Electronic Commerce from the National University of Ireland, Galway. She has worked with Dunnes Stores, Micros Fidelio, SuperValu, and is currently employed as a Bank Official with AIB.

**Vanessa N. Cooper** holds a BS degree in Computer Science from Kennesaw State University, Kennesaw, Georgia. Currently, she is a graduate student and research assistant in the Department of Computer Science at Kennesaw State University, Georgia, USA. At Kennesaw State University, Vanessa has worked closely with her professors as a teaching assistant and a research assistant in the Department of Computer Science. Her research interests are cyber security, data analytics, machine learning, and mobile development. Vanessa has several years of experience as a software developer for mobile applications, and she is a member of the Association for Computing Machinery and the IEEE – Computer Society.

**Henrique Curado** is a Professor at the School of Allied Health Sciences – Polytechnic Institute of Porto, Portugal, where he's Vice-president of the Scientific Council, Director of the Department of Management and Administration in Health and Member of the Ethics Committee. Since 2013, he's been a member of the Portuguese Tax Court of Arbitration. From 2007-2009, he was a Legal Adviser to the Government and to the National Parliament of East Timor as well as a Visiting-Professor at the National University, and he's one of the authors of the Annotated Constitution of the Democratic Republic of East Timor (2011). He's a Direction member, former Vice-president, and Treasurer of the Portuguese Union of Superior Education. With a Degree in Law (1992) and an MSc in European Economics (1996), both at the University of Coimbra, he's now drafting his PhD thesis in law on the subject of body interventions.

**James Deane** holds a Bachelors of Commerce degree and a Masters degree in Electronic Commerce from the National University of Ireland, Galway. He is currently employed as a Business Consultant with Cora Systems.

**Teresa Sofia Pereira Dias de Castro**, PhD student, is a Scholarship Researcher at the University of Minho (Portugal). She has a Masters Degree in Child Studies – Information and Communication Technology and a first degree in Philosophy and Humanities. She has been involved in a European Research Project on Internet Safety. Her research interests are related to the use of internet by children and young people.

**Avelina Alonso de Escamilla** graduated in 1979 at the University Complutense of Madrid and obtained her PhD in Law (1983) with Honors from the University of Alcalá de Henares. She practicedlaw in Madrid from 1979 to 1994. She was a member of the Legal Council in the Metropolitan Company in Madrid from 1979 to 1988. She joined the Faculty of Law at the University of Alcalá de Henares as an Associate Professor of Criminal Law in 1985, and then as a Professor since 1991. In 1994, she joined as an Assistant Professor of Criminal Law at the Universidad San Pablo-CEU of where she is a Professor since 1998. From 1995 to 1999, she served as Academic Secretary of the Faculty of Law. Since 2004, she has been a member of the Editorial Board of the Criminal Law and Criminal Procedure journal, *Criminal Law*. At present, she is a member of the following Masters: Police Science Masters at the University of Alcalá de Henares, Corporate insolvency Masters at the University CEU San Pablo, Gender-based violence Masters at the University of Valencia, Criminal Law and Criminal Procedure Masters at the Madrid Bar Association, She is the author of several monographs, including "El Juez de Vigilancia Penitenciaria" (1985) and "Responsabilidad Penal de directivos y órganos de empresas y sociedades" (1996), and numerous opinion articles that cover both the General and the Special Criminal Law and particularly, Prison Law. Is coauthor of the Handbook *Derecho Penal. Parte Especial* (6th edition 2011) and *Delitos y faltas* (2nd edition 2013).

**Nikolaos Dellas** was born in Preveza, Greece, in 1980. He received his Diploma Degree and his PhD degree from the Electrical and Computer Engineering School of National Technical University of Athens (NTUA), Greece, in 2003 and 2010, respectively. During the last 10 years, he worked in several EU and national commercial and research projects. His research interests include security and privacy in communication networks, middleware, mobile and distributed systems, as well as peer-to-peer technologies and performance evaluation. He has several publications in international journals and international conferences related to these fields. He is also a member of the Technical Chamber of Greece.

**Elisianne Campos de Melo Soares** obtained her Bachelors degree in Journalism from the University of Fortaleza (Fortaleza, Ceará, Brazil). She received her Masters degree in Culture and Communication from the University of Lisbon (Lisboa, Portugal). She is a law student at the Federal University of Rio Grande do Norte (Natal, Rio Grande do Norte, Brazil). During the Journalism graduation, she completed an exchange programme at the University of Nice – Sophia Antipolis (Nice, France). It was on a course taken during this period that the interest in studying Law and Communication came up. She is affiliated with the Media and Journalism Investigation Centre (CIMJ – New University of Lisbon) and to the Brazilian Association of Cyberculture Researchers (ABCiber). Her research studies are dedicated to themes related to cyberculture, democracy, copyrights, human rights, internet, new technologies, privacy and online surveillance.

**Vamshee Krishna Devendran** is currently pursuing a Masters of Science in Computer Science degree from Kennesaw State University, Georgia, USA. He completed his undergraduate course in Electronics and Communication Engineering from RMD Engineering College, Chennai, India. He worked for HCL Technologies as a software developer for more than 2 years. His primary research interests include web application security vulnerabilities and their mitigation techniques. His research project includes distributed file systems and computation algorithms. He is a reviewer of ACMSE and is serving as a PC member of PC member of Big Data, Data Mining, HPC, and Computational Science.

**Clare Doherty** is a PhD candidate at National University of Ireland Galway. Her research area is Information Systems Privacy and Security. She holds a Bachelors of Commerce degree and a Masters degree in Electronic Commerce from the National University of Ireland, Galway. She previously worked for Storm Technology.

**Tom Fairfax** is Managing Director of Security Risk Management, an information security consultancy assisting a wide range of clients to implement effective information and payment card security, respond to incidents, and enable their organizations to operate safely (or as safely as possible). He has been working in information security since the early 1990s, following service with the British Army in an Armoured Reconnaissance Regiment. Since 2000, he has served as a member of the Land Information Assurance Group, (LIAG) which has provided the British Army with its principal cyber security capability over the past decade. In his time with both regular and reserves, he has seen service across the globe in a number of operational and peacetime theatres. In uniform and out, Tom and his teams have been lucky enough to be involved in a range of tasks and assignments worldwide, delivering Cyber and Information Security Support to a range of clients (including HM Forces) throughout UK and overseas.

**M.S. Gaur** is a Professor of Computer Engg at MNIT in Jaipur India. He earned a PhD from the University of Southampton, UK and is working in the area of Information and Network Security. He has supervised 6 PhD candidates in the areas of Information and Network Security and Malware analysis. His current research interests are Static and Dynamic Malware analysis, Simulation and emulation of network attacks, Networks on Chip, and Reliable systems design.

**Dillon Glasser** graduated from the Richard Stockton College of New Jersey with a degree in Computer Science and Information Systems. He also competed on the Cross Country and Track team while at Stockton and held four school records. Dillon has worked as an intern at the Federal Aviation Administration as a college tutor and teacher in both Israel and South Korea. He is preparing for a career in cyber law, where he can use his experience and knowledge of computer science together with law.

**Slawomir Grzonkowski** is a Principal Research Engineer at Symantec Security Technology and Response (STAR), malware operations, Ireland. In the past, he was a post-doctoral researcher at the Digital Enterprise Research Institute (DERI), at NUI Galway, where he was also the leader of the Security Privacy and Trust Unit (USPT). His PhD research was conducted in the area of security and privacy aspects of the Internet and Semantic Web technologies, covering many distinct domains such as cryptography, trust, access control, and system usability. His post-doctoral studies were funded by

Cisco Inc. and let him continue his work on the same topics in the context of industry. He published more than 25 articles in journals, books, and refereed conferences. Dr. Grzonkowski is a frequent reviewer and a PC member of security-related conferences and journals. He also serves as Associate Editor of the IEEE Transactions on CE.

**Hisham Haddad** holds a PhD degree in Computer Science from Oklahoma State University, Stillwater, Oklahoma. Currently, he is a Professor of Computer Science at Kennesaw State University, Georgia, USA. At Kennesaw State University, he served as undergraduate CS Program Coordinator and Assistant Chair, and he teaches both undergraduate and graduate courses. He has been involved in the development of computer-based instructional tools for classroom teaching and he is active participant in ongoing curriculum development efforts. His research interests include Software Engineering, Object-Oriented Technologies, Software Reuse, Software Security, and CS education. His work is published in professional journals and refereed International and National conferences. Dr. Haddad is active member of the professional community, regular participant in professional activities, and a member of several professional organizations. He is an active participant in conference organizations and a regular technical reviewer for many conferences and journals.

**Carol Hsu** is a Professor in the Department of Information Management at National Taiwan University. She holds a PhD in information systems from the London School of Economics and Political Science. Her current research interests focus on the organizational and cultural issues related to information IT diffusion in the financial industry and information security management. Her work has been published in the *MIS Quarterly, Information Systems Research, European Journal of Information Systems* and *Communications of the ACM*. She also serves as Associate Editor for *Information Systems Journal* and *Information & Management*.

**Dimitra I. Kaklamani** is a Professor in the School of Electrical and Computer Engineering (ECE), National Technical University of Athens (NTUA). She received her PhD degree in Electrical and Computer Engineering from the School of ECE, NTUA in 1992. In April 1995, April 2000, October 2004, and February 2009, she was elected as Lecturer, Assistant Professor, Associate Professor, and Professor, respectively, with the School of ECE, NTUA. She has published around 300 journal and conference papers and has participated in several EU and national research projects. Her research interests span across various fields and include the use of object-oriented methodologies and middleware technologies for the development of distributed systems and privacy-aware infrastructures, and the development of visualisation and real-time simulation techniques for solving complex, large scale modelling problems of microwave engineering and information transmission systems. She is an Editor of an international book by Springer-Verlag (2000) in applied computational electromagnetics and reviewer for several IEEE journals.

**Tahar Kechadi** is currently Professor of Computer Science at CSI, UCD. His research interests span the areas of Data Mining, distributed data mining heterogeneous distributed systems, Grid and Cloud Computing, and digital forensics and cyber-crime investigations. Prof Kechadi has published over 210 research articles in refereed journals and conferences. He serves on the scientific committees for a number of international conferences and he organised and hosted some of the leading conferences in his area. He is currently an editorial board member of the Journal of Future Generation of Computer Systems and of IST Transactions of Applied Mathematics-Modelling and Simulation. He is a member of the communication of the ACM journal and IEEE computer society. He is regularly invited as a keynote speaker in international conferences or to give a seminar series in some Universities worldwide.

**Maria N. Koukovini** received her Diploma in Electrical and Computer Engineering from the School of Electrical and Computer Engineering, National Technical University of Athens, in 2007. Since 2008, she is a research associate of the National Technical University and the Research Institute of Communication and Computer Systems (ICCS) and has participated in various research and development projects, both national and European. In 2014, she received her Dr.-Ing. degree, focusing primarily on the injection of inherent privacy awareness in dynamic and distributed environments. Her research interests include workflow management systems, semantic web technologies, software engineering, security and privacy protection, and communication technologies. She has several publications in these areas, while also contributing to standardization activities (e.g., ETSI ISG MOI).

**Adamantios Koumpis** is since, December 2012, a Research Fellow at the Digital Enterprise Research Institute of the National University of Ireland, Galway, Republic of Ireland with responsibilities for fundraising, research strategy design, and development of synergies with European industry for new projects design. Before this, Adamantios headed the Research Programmes Division of ALTEC Software S.A., which he founded in 1996 (an independent division of Unisoft S.A.) where he was responsible for the design, planning, and implementation of research and development projects for funding by the European Commission. Adamantios has successfully led more than 50 commercial and research projects for new technology development, technology adoption, and user uptake, both at the European and the national level in several areas such as E-Commerce, public sector, and business enterprise re-organisation and information logistics, involving the linking of data/information repositories with knowledge management and business engineering models.

**Ana Kovacevic** is an assistant professor at the University of Belgrade, Faculty of Security Studies. She received her BS, MS degrees from School of Electrical Engineering, University of Belgrade, and PhD degree in Informatics and Software Engineering from the Department of Information Systems and Technologies, FON - School of Business administration, University of Belgrade. She has been working in all phases in software development in numerous projects in Electric power industry of Serbia. Also she participated in multidisciplinary projects, where her area was information retrieval, database systems, or upgrading systems to better information security. Her research interests are in the areas of information security, data mining, text mining, databases and visualization information.

**Joanna Kulesza** is an assistant professor at the Department of International Law and International Relations, Faculty of Law and Administration, University of Lodz, Poland. She has been a visiting lecturer with the Oxford Internet Institute, Norwegian Research Center for Computers and Law, Westfälische Wilhelms Universität Münster and Justus-Liebig-Universität Gießen. She was a post-doctoral researcher at the University of Cambridge and Ludwig Maximilians University Munich. She worked for the European Parliament, Polish Ministry of Foreign Affairs, and the Council of Europe. She is the author of four monographs on international and Internet law and over 30 peer-reviewed papers. Kulesza just concluded her work on a monograph on due diligence principle in international law.

**Christopher Laing** is a University Fellow at Northumbria University, Project Director of the nuWARP, and Consultant: Information Security Risk Management for the European Network and Information Security Agency. His research focuses on emergent complex behaviour in information infrastructures. He holds a PhD in Secure Decision Making from the University of Bristol and is a Fellow of the IET, and a Senior Fellow of the Higher Education Academy.

**Michael Lang** has been a lecturer in information systems at NUI Galway since 1996, having previously worked for a number of years in industry. His research and teaching areas are information systems development, business systems analysis and design, information systems security and ethics, and information systems education. Dr. Lang's work has been featured in a number of leading international journals including *IEEE Multimedia, IEEE Software, Information & Software Technology, Requirements Engineering, Information Systems Management, Communications of the AIS, Journal of Information Systems Education*, and *Scandinavian Journal of Information Systems*. He has also presented at numerous international workshops and conferences. He is currently serving on the editorial board of three international journals and the executive steering committee of the *International Conference on Information Systems Development* and has acted as a reviewer or associate editor for all the principal international journals and conferences within the discipline of information systems.

**Vijay Laxmi** is an Associate Professor of Computer Engg at MNIT Jaipur India. She received her PhD from the University of Southampton, UK and is working in the area of Information and Network Security. She has supervised 7 PhD candidates in the areas of Information and Network Security and Malware analysis. Her current research interests are Image processing, Algorithms, Malware analysis, Simulation and emulation of network attacks, Networks on Chip, and Reliable systems design.

**Robert Layton** is a Research Fellow at the Internet Commerce Security Laboratory (www.icsl.com. au) and Deputy Director of the Centre for Informatics and Applied Optimisation (CIAO) at the Federation University Australia. His research looks at attribution methods for cyberattacks, most notably using authorship analysis for indirect attribution, whereby attacks can be linked even without directly linking evidence. His research has been successfully applied to many areas including phishing, spam, social media, online scams, and even historical works. Dr Layton's work links industry to academia, with direct industry partnerships. Dr Layton's research is funded through the ICSL, a joint partnership between Westpac, the Australian Federal Police, and Federation University Australia.

**Georgios V. Lioudakis** received his Dr.-Ing. degree in Electrical and Computer Engineering from the National Technical University of Athens (NTUA) in 2008. He has participated in several European and national research projects. His research interests include security and privacy protection, software engineering, workflow management, middleware and distributed systems, as well as the application of ontologies in these fields. He has several publications in these areas, while being active in standardisation (e.g., ETSI ISG MOI). During the period 2008—2011, he has been an Adjunct Lecturer in the Department of Telecommunications Science and Technology at the University of Peloponnese, Greece.

**José Manuel Fernández Marín** obtained his Computer Engineer degree (2013) and his Expert in Management and Security of Computer System certification (2007) from the University of Almería. He currently works as a security consultant in S2 Group S.L. and is specialized in network management and security systems.

**Vítor João Pereira Domingues Martinho** is a Coordinator Professor at the Polytechnic Institute of Viseu, Portugal. He has been pursuing his PhD, since 2007, in Economics from the University of Coimbra, Portugal. He was President of the Scientific Council, President of the Directive Council, and President of the Agricultural Polytechnic School of Viseu, Portugal, since 2006 to 2012. He also, had functions as Vice-President of the Scientific Council and the Assembly of Representatives in this school and political functions at the local level and supra municipal level. Currently, he is the President of the Direction of the Association of Forest Producers of Viseu, Portugal. He was an Erasmus student in the Faculty of Economics from the University of Verona, Italy, participated in various technical and scientific events nationally and internationally, has published several technical and scientific papers, is referee of some scientific and technical journals, and participates in the evaluation of national and international projects.

**Marlene Matos** is a Psychologist, with a Masters (MA) and PhD in Justice Psychology at the University of Minho. She has been an Assistant Professor at the University of Minho, since 2006, teaching courses in several areas of Psychology including Assessment and Intervention on Social, Community and Organizational contexts and Forensic Psychology, to undergraduate and post-graduate studies. Principal research interests and publications are in criminal victimization. She is a postgraduate (Masters and PhD) students' supervisor in several areas of Psychology. She is a scientific supervisor of Justice and Community Unit, Psychology Service at the University of Minho, and coordinator of the Advanced Course with Short Duration: Training of Experts in Forensic Psychological Assessment. He is the main researcher in many research funded, such as "Stalking in Portugal: Prevalence, impact and intervention," "GAM - victims support group groups," and "Multiple victimization of socially excluded women".

**WeSam Musa** currently serves as an adjunct cyber security professor at the University of Maryland University College. Professor Musa also serves as a cyber security expert for the United States Federal Government. He is also a peer reviewer for the *International Journal of Computer and Information Technology*. Professor Musa is a member of the Institute of Electrical and Electronics Engineers and the Armed Forces Communications and Electronics Association's Washington, D.C. chapter. Professor Musa earned his degree from George Mason University. He also holds many of the leading vendors' certifications, such as Certified Ethical Hacker, Certified Security Analyst, Security+, Network+, A+, Project+, ITIL V3, and Microsoft Certified System Administrator.

**Juan Álvaro Muñoz Naranjo** received his BS in Computer Science (2007) and his masters degree (2008) from the University of Almería, Spain. In the same institution and as part of the Supercomputation-Algorithms research group he obtained the PhD degree in 2013. His research work and publications are focused on information and communications security, including secure multicast and secure peer-to-peer multimedia streaming. His personal web page is http://www.hpca.ual.es/~jalvaro.

**Raja Jitendra Nayaka** is working as Senior Engineer at Core R&D, ITI Ltd, Bangalore, under the Ministry of Communications, Govt. of India. He has over 18 years of experience in design and development of telecom products. He obtained his MTech in VLSI Design and Embedded Systems from Reva Institute of Technology and Management, Bangalore, India. Presently, he is perusing his PhD from VTU Belgaum, India. He has vast experience in cryptography, network security, switching and transmission, Internet, SDH, and Optical Communication. He has many publications in reputed national and international journals and conferences. His research articles were published in Elsevier and IEEEXplore. His field of interest includes telecommunications, wireless sensor networks, FPGA based embedded system and IP core designs.

**Christophe Nicolle** defended a PhD thesis in 1996 at the Université de Bourgogne (France) to obtain the title of Doctor in Computer Science. The subject of his PhD thesis was multi-model translation in cooperative information systems. In 1996, he integrated the Computer Science Department of the Institut Universitaire de Technologies (IUT Dijon, France) where he became responsible for several courses (databases, networks, information systems modeling...). In 1996, he also integrated the laboratoire d'Electronique, Informatique et Image (LE2I, UMR CNRS 6306) where he developed research activities addressing semantic interoperability of information systems. From his research results, he created in 2001 the Active3D company which developed a collaborative ontology-based web platform for building facility management. Since 2009, he has been Deputy Director of the LE2I and manager of the Checksem research team.

**Dragana Nikolić** holds a BSc degree in Nuclear Engineering from the Electrical Engineering Faculty, University of Belgrade, Serbia, and a PhD degree in Physical Science from the Imperial College of Science, Technology and Medicine, University of London, UK. She is with the Centre of Nuclear Technology and Research NTI, Vinča Institute, since 1983. As an expert in nuclear safety and security, she has developed and managed multidisciplinary projects of specific technical complexity with the aim to implement/upgrade systems and measures for capacity building in nuclear security, support for non-proliferation of weapons of mass destruction and counterterrorism, including the mechanisms for nuclear security related information analysis, data processing and secure information distribution. She was the coordinator of the international technical cooperation projects, and has been involved in the organization of a number of international conferences, workshops and training courses. Her research interests include risk assessment, protection of nuclear critical infrastructure, monitoring systems for illicit trafficking of nuclear and other radioactive materials and nuclear forensics.

**Edewede Oriwoh** is a current PhD student of the Computer Science and Technology (CST) Department at the University of Bedfordshire (UoB), United Kingdom. Her PhD research centres on developing Forensics solutions for the Internet of Things' (IoT) landscape. She graduated from Lagos State University (LASU) Nigeria in 2005 with a BSc in Electronic and Computer Engineering and from UoB in 2010, with a MSc (Distinction) in Computer Security and Forensics. Her other research interests include computer networking, security, and IoT stakeholders' rights and responsibilities. She has published several peer-reviewed papers with International Conferences and related events. She is a member of the Internet Society (ISOC) and a Student Member of the IEEE. She has held certifications as a Certified Hacking

Forensic Investigator (CHFI), a Certified Ethical Hacker (CEH), and a Cisco Certified Network Associate (CCNA). She is a singer/songwriter with a keen interest in philosophy - her over twenty quotes and sayings are available online.

**António José Osório** has a PhD in Education. He has experience on Initial and in-Service Teacher Training, as well as Master and PhD courses in the field of ICT. He has very good research experience in using e-learning environments, collaborative learning environments in the internet, and good expertise in research with LOGO. He is responsible for the co-ordination of several national projects concerning the implementation of ICT and specially "Internet in Schools" in the Braga region.

**Eugenia I. Papagiannakopoulou** received her Dipl.-Ing and PhD degree in Electrical and Computer Engineering from the School of Electrical and Computer Engineering, National Technical University of Athens, in 2007 and 2014, respectively. Since 2008, she has been a research associate of the National Technical University and the Research Institute of Communication and Computer Systems (ICCS) and has participated in various research and development projects, both national and European. Her research interests include security and privacy protection in dynamic and distributed systems, semantic web technologies and software engineering, and she has several publications related to these fields. She has been a member of the Technical Chamber of Greece since 2008.

**Filipa Pereira** is a Psychologist, with a Masters (MA) in Justice Psychology, and she is a current PhD student in Justice Psychology at the Research Center of Psychology, University of Minho, Portugal. She is developing a PhD project in the domain of cyberstalking victimization among adolescents. Her PhD project is being funded by a grant from the Foundation for Science and Technology (SFRH/BD/78004/2011). Her main research interests and publications are in criminal victimization. Her major concern is in interpersonal violence and the role of information and communication technologies as a creators, facilitators, and moderators of aggressive interactions among adolescents. In 2010, she developed her Masters thesis on the stalking topic, specifically on "Perceptions and personal experiences of unwanted attention among Portuguese male students".

**Mahesh S. Raisinghani**, is an associate professor in the Executive MBA program at the TWU School of Management. Dr. Raisinghani was awarded the 2008 Excellence in Research and Scholarship award and the 2007 G. Ann Uhlir Endowed Fellowship in Higher Education Administration. His research has been published in several academic journals such as *IEEE Transactions on Engineering Management, Information & Management,Information Resources Management Journal, International Journal of Innovation and Learning, Journal of E-Commerce Research, International Journal of Distance Education Technologies, Journal of IT Review, Journal of Global IT Management*, and *Journal of IT Cases and Applications Research* among others, and international/national conferences. Dr. Raisinghani serves as the Editor in Chief of the International Journal of Web based Learning and Teaching Technologies. He is on the board of the Global IT Management Association and an advisory board member of the World Affairs Council. He is included in the millennium edition of *Who's Who in the World, Who's Who among Professionals, Who's Who among America's Teachers,* and *Who's Who in Information Technology.*

**Iris Reychav** holds a MsC in Industrial Engineering and has 10 years of experience at Motorola in the field of information systems. She earned her PhD from Bar-Ilan University's Graduate School of Business Administration and did her post- doctoral work at the Faculty of Management of Tel Aviv University. Today, she is a Senior lecturer at Ariel University. Her current research interests include information systems planning, knowledge management, social aspects of system development, and e-learning technologies HCI (technology collaboration aspects).

**Anil Saini** is a Research Scholar at Malaviya National Institute of Technology, Jaipur, India. He received his Bachelors of Engineering Degree in Electronics and Communications from M.B.M Engineering College, Jodhpur, India and Masters of Engineering Degree in Software Systems from B.I.T.S, Pilani, India. He is currently a PhD student in the Department of Computer Engineering at the Malaviya National Institute of Technology, Jaipur, India. His research interests include Browser Attacks, Security Model, Network Security, and Cyber Forensics.

**Alvaro M. Sampaio** is an Industrial Designer, with a Masters (MSc) in Design, Materials, and Product Management, and a PhD in Polymer Engineering. He is devoted to the activities of product design and development, more specifically, in the field of socially responsible design in a user-centered design methodology. He is motivated by the relationship between people and objects, mainly the needs and wants and the problems and difficulties that arise in the scope of that relationship. He essentially sees people as a source of inspiration and as the main focus of Design and the designer as a creator/facilitator/moderator of interactions. He is an Assistant Professor at the Polytechnic Institute of Cávado and Ave, Portugal, teaching courses in several areas of Industrial Design including Product design and development, Design management and Design methodologies, at the graduate and undergraduate level.

**Hossain Shahriar** is currently an Assistant Professor of Computer Science at Kennesaw State University, Georgia, USA. His research interests include software and application level security vulnerabilities and their mitigation techniques and digital forensics. Dr. Shahriar has published over 35 peer reviewed research articles in international journals and conferences. His research has attracted a number of awards including the *Best Paper Award* in IEEE DASC, an *Outstanding Research Achievement Award* from Queen's University, Canada, and an *IEEE Kingston Section Research Excellence Award*. He has been a reviewer of many international journals and served as a PC member of international conferences on software, computer, and application security. Currently, he is serving as an associate editor of *International Journal of Secure Software Engineering*. Dr. Shahriar is a member of the ACM, ACM SIGAPP, and IEEE. More information about his research and background can be found at http://cs.kennesaw.edu/hshahria/.

**Shraga Sukenik** was born in the United States and moved to Israel in the mid 90's. After service in the Israeli Army, he studied at Bar Ilan University and received a BA in psychology with a minor in criminology. He is currently studying for a Masters Degree in Industrial and Occupational Psychology at Ariel University and working as an intern at the Tnufa Industrial Consulting Company. His current research is focused on the issue of disingenuously positive performance evaluations and their impact on the workplace. Other areas of interest include evaluating alternative approaches to cyber crime prevention and the integration of general philosophy into Jewish law.

**Dauda Sule**, CISA. He is currently the Marketing Manager of Audit Associates Limited which is a consultancy firm that specializes in designing and organizing training programs pertaining to auditing, fraud detection and prevention, information security and assurance, and anti-money laundering. He is a CISA and has an MSc in Computer Security from the University of Liverpool. He has previous experience of over five years in the Nigerian Banking industry, and also did some time in Gtech Computers (a computer and allied services company) as a systems security and assurance supervisor. He has written of articles for eForensics Magazine and ISACA Journal.

**Aakash Taneja** is an Associate Professor of Computer Science and Information Systems at the Richard Stockton College of New Jersey. He received his PhD in Information Systems from the University of Texas at Arlington. His current research interests include IS identity, information security and privacy, IS adoption, organizational behavior, and issues in online environment. He has published in *Communications of the ACM, IEEE Transactions on Professional Communication, Journal of Organizational Behavior, Journal of Accounting Education, Journal of Computing Sciences in Colleges, Journal of Information Systems Education,* and various conference proceedings.

**Javier Valls-Prieto** is a Professor of criminal law at the University of Granada. He did his doctoral research at the Institute of Criminology and Economical Criminal Law at Freiburg University, Germany. After that in 2005 he was awarded a Postdoctoral Research Fullbright Fellowship by the Ministry of Education to work at the *Forschungsstelle für Europäisches Straf- und Strafprozessrecht* (Research Center for European Criminal and Criminal Procedural Law). His main papers are about the European criminal law and the problems around the Harmonization of European Directives and Framework Decisions. He is currently collaborating in a FP7 European Research Program as an expert in European Privacy Law and the criminological aspects related to organized crime. The "ePoolice" project is an early warning scanner designed to detect organized crime linked to human and drug trafficking, cybercrime, money laundering, etc.

**Laurentiu Vasiliu** is CEO of Peracton founded in 2010 to provide cutting-edge R&D and software analytics solutions for trading and investment. He has extensive IT research and project execution experience having worked previously as group leader and post-doctoral researcher at DERI Institute. There he managed several EU and Irish funded projects in the area of semantic web and applied IT research. Laurentiu holds a PhD Degree in IT/Industrial Engineering (National University of Ireland, Galway, 2004) and an Engineering Degree in Industrial Robotics (Bucharest Polytechnic University, 1997).

**Iakovos S. Venieris** is a Professor in the School of Electrical and Computer Engineering, National Technical University of Athens (NTUA) since 1994 and director of Intelligent Communications and Broadband Networks Laboratory (ICBNet). He received a Dipl.-Ing. degree from the University of Patras in 1988, and a PhD degree from the NTUA in 1990, all in Electrical and Computer Engineering. His research interests are in the fields of distributed systems, security and privacy, software and service engineering, multimedia, mobile communications and intelligent networks. He has over 350 publications in the above areas and has received several national and international awards for academic achievement. He has served as associate editor of *IEEE Communications Letters, Computer Communications*

(Elsevier), and *IEEE Communications Magazine*. He is co-editor of the books *Enhancing the Internet with the CONVERGENCE System* (Springer, 2014), *Object Oriented Software Technologies in Telecommunications* (Wiley, 2000), and *Intelligent Broadband Networks* (Wiley, 1998).

**Paul Vickers** is a UK Chartered Engineer, holds a BSc degree in Computer Studies from Liverpool Polytechnic, and a PhD in Software Engineering and HCI from Loughborough University. He is currently a Reader in Computer Science and Computational Perceptualization at Northumbria University where he conducts research into visualization and auditory display and in their intersection with creative digital media.

**Tawei Wang** is currently an Assistant Professor of Accounting and Accuity LLP Accounting Faculty Fellow at the University of Hawaii at Manoa. He received his PhD from Krannert Graduate School of Management at Purdue University. His current research interests are disclosures as well as financial reporting, risk management, and IT management. His papers have appeared in several leading journals including *Information Systems Research, Journal of Banking and Finance, Decision Support Systems, Journal of Organizational Computing and Electronic Commerce, Journal of Accounting and Public Policy,* and the *Journal of Information Systems* among others. His papers have also been accepted by leading conferences including *AAA Annual Meeting, Annual Meeting of the Academy of Management, INFORMS, Workshop on the Economics of Information Security, Workshop on the Information Systems and Economics, Americas Conference on Information Systems,* and the *Pacific Asia Conference on Information Systems*.

**Paul A. Watters** is Professor of Information Technology at Massey University. His research interests include cyber security, computer forensics, open source intelligence analysis, anti-phishing, privacy, data sharing, and strategies to reduce demand for child exploitation material. He previously worked at the University of Ballarat, the Medical Research Council (UK) and Macquarie University. His work has been cited 1,302 times (h-index=15, i-10 index=33). Professor Watters has worked closely with the government and the industry on many projects including Westpac, IBM, the Australian Federal Police (AFP), and the Attorney General's Department.

**Geraint Williams** is a lead information security consultant and PCI QSA. He has performed penetration testing and vulnerability assessments for various clients. Geraint leads the IT Governance CISSP Accelerated Training Programme along with the PCI Foundation and Implementer training courses. He has broad technical knowledge of security and IT infrastructure, including high performance computing and cloud computing. His certifications include CISSP, PCI QSA, CREST Registered Tester, CEH, and CHFI. Geraint has also been appointed as an honorary visiting Fellow at the University of Bedfordshire and is a subject matter expert for the digital forensics and cyber security courses within the Dept of Computer and Information Systems. Geraint has published a number of papers in journals and presented at information security conferences, as well as being a co-author on a book on the PCI DSS.

# Index